SOURCEBOOK ON
CONTRACT LAW

Second Edition

Cavendish
Publishing
Limited

London • Sydney

SOURCEBOOK ON CONTRACT LAW

Second Edition

David Oughton
Professor of Commercial Law
De Montfort University, Leicester

Martin Davis
Principal Lecturer in Law
De Montfort University, Leicester

Cavendish
Publishing
Limited

London • Sydney

Second edition first published in Great Britain 2000 by Cavendish Publishing Limited, The Glass House, Wharton Street, London WC1X 9PX, United Kingdom
Telephone: +44 (0)20 7278 8000   Facsimile: +44 (0)20 7278 8080
Email: info@cavendishpublishing.com
Website: www.cavendishpublishing.com

© Oughton, D and Davis, M   2000
First edition   1996
Second edition   2000

British Library Cataloguing in Publication Data

Oughton, DW
Sourcebook on contract law – 2nd ed – (Sourcebook series)
1 Contracts – England 2 Contracts – Wales
I Title II Davis, Martin, 1949–
346.4'2'02

ISBN 1 85941 584 9

Printed and bound in Great Britain by
Biddles Ltd, Guildford and King's Lynn

ACKNOWLEDGMENTS

The publishers and authors wish to thank the following publishers, authors and copyright holders for their permission to reprint materials from the books and periodicals listed:

Basil Blackwell Publishers Ltd for extracts from Beale, H (with Dugdale, A), 'Contracts between businessmen: planning and the use of contractual remedies' (1975) 2 British Journal of Law and Society 45.

Butterworths/Tolley Publishers Ltd for extracts from: the All England Law Reports; Cooke, PJ and Oughton, D, *The Common Law of Obligations*, 3rd edn, 2000; Collins, H, *The Law of Contract*, 3rd edn, 1997.

Cambridge Law Journal and MP Thompson for extracts from: Thompson, MP, 'From representation to expectation – estoppel as a cause of action' [1983] CLJ 257, pp 275–77.

Columbia Law Review for extracts from Fuller, L, 'Consideration and form' (1941) 31 Columbia Law Review 799, pp 800–03.

Crown copyright material is reproduced with the permission of the Controller of Her Majesty's Stationery Office.

Fontana Press and HarperCollins Publishers for extracts from Brownsword, JN and Adams, JN, *Understanding Contract Law*, 2nd edn, 1994.

Foundation Press Ltd for extracts from Macneil, I, *Contract: Exchange Transactions and Relations*, 2nd edn, 1978, pp 11–12.

The Incorporated Council of Law Reporting for England and Wales for extracts from the Law Reports and the Weekly Law Reports.

Lloyd's of London Press Ltd for extracts from Lloyd's Law Reports.

Northwestern University Press for extracts from Macneil, I, 'Contracts adjustment of long term economic relations under classical, neo-classical and relational contract law' (1978) 72 NWULR 854.

Oxford University Press for extracts from Atiyah, PS, *Essays on Contract*, revised edn, 1990; *Promises, Morals and the Law*, 1981.

Sweet & Maxwell Ltd for extracts from: Hamson, C, 'The reform of consideration' (1938) 54 LQR 233, p 234; (1939) 55 LQR 518 (Winfield); Atiyah, PS, 'Contracts, promises and the law of obligations' (1978) 94 LQR 193, p 203; Harris, D, Ogus, A and Phillips, J, 'Contact remedies and the consumer surplus' (1979) 95 LQR 581, pp 582–83, 586–89, 596–97; Treitel, GH, 'Mistake in contract' (1988) 104 LQR 504, pp 504–07; Adams, JN, 'The battle of forms' [1983] JBL 297, p 298; Phang, A, 'Implied terms in English law – some recent developments' [1993] JBL 242, pp 243–46; Treitel, GH, *The Law of Contract*, 10th edn, 1999, pp 1–6 (with omissions) and pp 853–54; *Frustration and Force Majeure*, 1994, pp 490–93.

Every effort has been made to trace all the copyright holders, but if any have been inadvertently overlooked, the publishers will be pleased to make the necessary arrangements at the first opportunity.

PREFACE

In this book, the authors have attempted to compile a selection of materials on the law of contract consisting of case law, statutory material and academic commentary which will assist students in this subject at both degree level and higher non-degree level. It is hoped that the selection of materials and accompanying text will permit an appreciation of the key issues relevant to the study of this branch of the law.

By selecting academic commentary, as well as case law and statutory materials, the authors hope that students will be able to glean an understanding of the wider context in which the law of contract operates. The materials selected are also augmented by a brief analysis of the relevant issues in text form, thereby providing readers with the opportunity to engage in wide reading by reference to footnoted material.

The book is based on an issues approach, being subdivided into four parts, namely: (I) Introduction; (II) Contract Formation and Negotiation; (III) Obligations and Risks; and (IV) Performance, Breach and Remedies for Breach of Contract. The first of these parts examines briefly the purposes served by the various rules gathered together under the banner of contract law and pays some attention to policies and ideologies underlying many of the case extracts which follow in later chapters of the book. Part II, on contract formation and negotiation, critically examines the so called classical rules of contract formation and questions whether agreement supported by bargain based consideration is really the basis for contract formation. This part also includes a chapter on the notion of good faith in contract negotiation and the modern expectation that a contracting party will not seek to gain an unfair advantage over others. Part III deals with the issues of obligations and risks arising from the contract and the role of the court as an allocator of risks arising from the contracting process. This part also considers the rules on contractual fairness and generally examines the legal concepts which allow a court to police the contract in the interests of justice. The final part is the longest and concentrates on what is, in practical terms, the most important aspect of contract law, namely, the rules applicable to performance of the contract and the remedies for breach of contract.

Throughout the book, the authors have attempted to relate rules of the law of contract to other aspects of the law of civil obligations. As a result, there is reference to relevant rules of tort law and the law of restitution, which should enable students to place this subject in its wider context. The part on remedies in particular makes a number of comparisons between 'contractual' rules and 'tortious' rules, especially in relation to the issues of remoteness of loss, quantification of damages and factual causation.

Readers should note the changes to terminology since the coming into force of the Civil Procedure Rules 1999. We have used the new term 'claimant' when discussing general principles of law and the decided cases post-CPR, but have kept the old style 'plaintiff' in extracts from and discussion of pre-CPR cases.

In this edition, there have been changes in the responsibilities of the authors. While the first edition of this book was written substantially by the first named author, Martin Davis has taken a much bigger responsibility for updating work in this edition. For taking this additional responsibility, David Oughton is very appreciative.

The authors would like to express their thanks and appreciation to all the staff at Cavendish Publishing, especially Cara Annett for her unfailing patience in waiting for the arrival of the manuscript. Furthermore, we both very much appreciate the considerable help afforded by Veronica Matthew at De Montfort University, particularly for her unstinting help in reviewing the first edition and helping at proof stage. Authors invariably need support from those closest to them. David Oughton would like to thank Sue, Gareth and Karen for putting up with a sometimes grumpy husband and father as he sat staring at a computer screen awaiting inspiration. Their support is much appreciated. Martin Davis would similarly like to thank Jennie.

As far as possible, we have attempted to state the law as it stood at the end of September 2000.

David Oughton
Martin Davis
October 2000

CONTENTS

PART III: OBLIGATIONS AND RISKS

PART IV: PERFORMANCE, BREACH AND
REMEDIES FOR BREACH OF CONTRACT

TABLE OF CASES

TABLE OF STATUTES

TABLE OF STATUTORY INSTRUMENTS

PART I

INTRODUCTION

CHAPTER 1

WHAT IS CONTRACT LAW ALL ABOUT?

LAW OF CONTRACT, LAW OF CONTRACTS
OR THE LAW RELATING TO CONTRACTS?

The phrase 'the law of contract' might suggest that there is a single model of contract law applicable to all types of contract. Indeed, the assumption that there is a single model of contract law underlies the 19th century 'classical model' of contract law. This 19th century model, which has so influenced the development of modern contract, was underpinned by the values of sanctity of bargain, freedom of dealing and emphasises the advantage of the market over government intervention. The typical classical contract has been described in the following fashion:

> A bilateral executory agreement. It consists of an exchange of promises; the exchange is deliberately carried through by a process of offer and acceptance, with the intention of creating a binding deal. When the offer is accepted, the agreement is consummated, and a contract comes into existence before anything is actually done by the parties. No performance is required ... The contract is binding because the parties intend to be bound ... When the contract is made, it binds each party to performance, or in default to a liability to pay damages in lieu. *Prima facie*, these damages represent the value of the innocent party's disappointed expectations.[1]

It is true that some contracts do conform to this image, but it must also be appreciated that there are many which do not. In the chapters which follow, case extracts are taken from a number of different types of contract, some of which may be seen as exceptions to a general rule established at the time of the development of the classical theory of contractual obligations. Where these so called exceptional cases emerge, there may be a pattern based on the type of contract concerned. For example, much of what might have been called contract law some years ago may have become part of a new subject area. Typical examples of this sort of movement can be found in employment law cases or consumer law cases. The employment relationship is such that very often, classical rules of contract law simply do not adequately serve the needs of the parties, because of the long term nature of the contract entered into by the parties.[2] In order to deal with the problems of the workplace, Parliament has had to intervene in many areas, so much so that although classical

---

1   See Atiyah, 1986 (reprinted 1990), pp 11–12.
2   See Chapter 10.

contract law principles may state a general rule, very often, the law for the purposes of employment contracts may differ.

The classical model of contractual relations outlined above works on the basis of freedom of contract. It assumes the contract arena is a level playing field on which all participants are equal in terms of bargaining power. But this is patently not the case. Many of the rules developed in the 20th century recognise that individual consumers do not have the same bargaining strength as a multinational company. The consumer requires protection, especially in the light of the widespread use by business of the 'standard form' contract.[3] Some rules towards this end have been developed at common law but, to a large extent, common law development has been hindered by the conflict between the needs of consumers and the principle of freedom of contract espoused in the classical theory.

Even in the field of purely commercial contracts, where the classical theory appears to have its strongest hold, there are exceptions. What must be appreciated is that traders operate on an international level and the ancient law merchant had started to develop before the 19th century classical theory took hold. In order to cater for the needs of the trading community, some of the classical rules were modified to take account of established trading practice. Thus, a number of the rules gathered together under the doctrine of consideration[4] are modified to take account of practices established many years earlier by the trading community. For example, the rule that consideration must not be past has no application in relation to bills of exchange, for the simple reason that to insist on this classical principle would go against centuries of established trading practice.

In the light of these observations, it is probably better to regard English contract law as a law of contracts, rather than a law of contract, despite the existence of a generalised framework of rules which govern most contracts and with which this book is concerned.

A problem which will be encountered in a number of the following chapters is that, for one reason or another, a contract may fail. This may be due to a formation problem[5] or there may be present some vitiating element such as a mistake,[6] a misrepresentation[7] or an element of actual or presumed coercion.[8] Alternatively, the contract might terminate due to some external event beyond the control of the parties or due to a breach of contract by one of the parties. If the contract fails, the terms of the contract may not be available

---

3   See Chapter 8.
4   See Chapter 3.
5   See Chapters 2 and 3.
6   See Chapters 2 and 6.
7   See Chapters 4, 13 and 14.
8   See Chapters 7 and 14.

to govern the relationship between the parties. Instead, some other aspect of the law may have to be invoked in order to resolve the issue. What this serves to illustrate is that the law of contract is not just about making contracts and that there are overlaps with other areas of law concerned with private law rights and obligations. Thus, where a contract fails, it may be the case that there has been a partial performance by one party which has conferred a benefit on the other. If the contract itself is unable to determine how this is to be paid for, it may be necessary to have recourse to restitutionary principles instead.[9]

Furthermore, other aspects of a wider law of civil obligations may impinge on the parties to a contract. For example, although the doctrine of privity of contract states that only the parties to a contract may sue and be sued on that contract,[10] there is nothing to prevent the application of rules from another branch of the law of obligations, where appropriate. Thus, the parties to a contract may find that they are subject to principles established by the law of tort, such as the duty to take reasonable care when dealing with others whom you can foresee as likely to be affected by your acts or omissions. Accordingly, rules of the law of contract must not be taken in isolation, since there may be other relevant rules which affect the rights and obligations of the parties.

PROMISES AND RELIANCE

A primary concern of contract law is the enforcement of promises and it is this concern which dominates the classical theory. The parties make an agreement by the process of offer and acceptance, under which a number of promises are exchanged. This model of the contractual relationship naturally emphasises the voluntary nature of the transaction. Each party to the contract freely undertakes an obligation or a series of obligations in return for something given by the other. However, this idea of the voluntary exchange of promises does not always match reality. A number of instances will be encountered in which it is difficult to say that there has been an exchange in the classical sense of that word. In these circumstances, the replacement for the agreed exchange basis for liability may be an element of reliance.[11] For example, unilateral contracts, under which there is a promise in return for an act are particularly difficult to explain in terms of the classical model. But a reliance based analysis seems to provide a more satisfactory explanation. Thus, if I offer a reward to anyone who finds my missing dog, the reason for the enforcement of my promise to pay is that the finder of the dog has acted in reliance upon

---

9   See Chapter 14.
10 See Chapter 15.
11 See Chapter 3.

my promise. Other examples of reliance liability can be found where there is an attempt to vary the terms of a long term contractual arrangement.[12] One of the problems which may arise in this context is that one of the parties promises to vary the existing terms of the contract, for example, by agreeing to pay more than that which was originally contracted. However, applying classical rules, the other party must give consideration for that promise. Unfortunately, what may be given in return for the promise is little more than continued performance of the existing terms of the contract which, in classical terminology, does not involve a true exchange. However, through the application of rules on promissory estoppel, if the promisee relies upon the promise of the other party, that promise may become enforceable to the extent that is necessary in order to achieve a fair result.

IDEOLOGIES OF CONTRACT LAW

Some of the extracted materials in later chapters reveal differences in approach between members of the judiciary. One of the possible reasons for these conflicts is that judges may approach a given set of facts from differing ideological positions. In the extract which follows, the authors identify four different ideologies, which to a greater or lesser extent may colour the way in which a particular set of case facts is analysed. On the one hand, there is the formalist approach, which draws on a step by step analysis of existing case law. The formalist judge is heavily influenced by the doctrine of precedent and his approach to a particular case will involve an application of the rules developed in earlier cases. A difficulty with this approach is that, unless the formalist judge is careful, he might find himself laying down very conservative decisions, with the result that there is unlikely to be any sharp change of direction in the law to take account of changing conditions. Adams and Brownsword comment as follows:

> The formalist view gravitates around the rule-book. Its influence can be characterised in the following ways.
>
> First, and foremost, the rule-book governs. Lawton LJ's observations on the problem of the 'battle of the forms' (in *Butler Machine Tool*) reflect this attitude:
>
>> 'The problem is how should that battle be conducted? The view taken by the judge was that the battle should extend over a wide area and the court should do its best to look into the minds of the parties and make certain assumptions. In my judgment, the battle has to be conducted in accordance with set rules ... The rules relating to a battle of this kind have been known for the past 130-odd years.'

---

12 See Chapter 10.

The new problem presented by the 'battle of the forms' was to be resolved according to the traditional rules. The world may change, but the traditional rules of contract, like Ol' Man River, 'jus' keep rollin' along'.

Secondly, the rule-book is viewed as a closed logical system. Rule-book exercises are exercises in the logic of the concepts of contract. Just as one plus one must equal two, formalists view contractual concepts as having a logic of their own. The traditional schematic approach to formation, particularly, reflects this aspect of formalism.

Thirdly, the conceptual purity and integrity of the rule book is to be maintained. Formalists are uncomfortable when they encounter ill-fitting or otherwise deviant doctrines. The attempt to clean up the doctrine of fundamental breach, from *Suisse Atlantique* onwards, is a good example of a formalist purifying operation.

Fourthly, formalism tends towards doctrinal conservatism. Thus, formalists tend to confine innovations, such as the *High Trees* principle and collateral contracts. If such 'dangerous' ideas are to be used, they must be used with caution. In the same way, formalism encourages judges to base themselves on well established, rather than less well established, ground (see, for example, the preference for the construction approach towards exemption clauses, the preference for an intention-based approach to implied terms, the reluctance to employ the concept of good faith, etc).

Fifthly, as Geoffrey Lane LJ said in *Gibson v Manchester City Council*, 'sympathy and politics' are not material considerations (that is, for formalist judges – unless, of course, the rule-book makes such considerations material). Judges may sympathise with a litigant, but if the rule-book is against that party, then that is conclusive. Hard cases make bad law (that is, introduce *ad hoc* distinctions into the rule book). In the same way, politics, interpreted broadly as judicial values and commitments, must not influence a formalist judge. A judge may regard a particular rule as unfair or inconvenient, but this must not act as an excuse for deviation from the rule-book.

Sixthly, formalism implies an uncritical acceptance, and a mechanical application, of the rule-book doctrines. Shibboleths such as 'freedom of contract' and 'sanctity of contract' are cited without critical reflection on their doctrinal purpose, or the social context in which they are to be applied. Formalism takes the idea that 'justice is blind' quite literally: the rule-book is to be applied blind to any consideration of the merits of the case, the purpose or point of the rules, or the context of the dispute.

Seventhly, because formalism favours the routine application of the rule-book, it works best with clear general rules which do not involve the exercise of judicial discretion. Of course, the facts have to be found, but once found, general rules promise more or less mechanical application. Accordingly, formalists prefer a rule which either straightforwardly allows or disallows exemption clauses to one which allows exemption clauses if they satisfy a requirement of reasonableness. It simply is not possible to apply a reasonableness requirement in a routine mechanical fashion, although formalists will no doubt strive to structure the discretion along the lines of certain general rules of thumb.

Finally, it is also possible to view as corollaries of a formalist outlook the tendency both to eschew responsibility for major law reform ('This is best left to Parliament') and to interpret appeal court jurisdiction narrowly ('Provided that the trial court asked the right legal question and provided that the answer acted upon was not totally unreasonable, then the ruling must stand'). The former tendency can be seen as a byproduct of formalist caution coupled with the formalist belief that the function of judges is to apply, not to make, the rules. The latter tendency is assisted by the formalist detachment from the results of cases. Consequently, when a case comes up on appeal, the question for the appeal court is not whether the trial judge got the right result, but whether the right rules were applied.[13]

Secondly, there are realist judges, who seek to achieve the correct result in a given set of circumstances. Achieving the right result may sometimes involve a bit of 'rule bending', but it is the result that matters. A consequence of a realist approach is that judges who are wedded to this ideology may appear to be highly innovative. However, to the realist, necessity is the mother of invention – if a way out of a tight corner has to be found, then it will be found. Adams and Brownsword continue as follows:

Realism is the antithesis of formalism. It follows that each of the formalist tendencies is matched by a realist tendency which pushes in the opposite direction.

First, the rule book is not decisive. The most important aspects of a dispute are the facts and the decision; rules are a secondary consideration. If formalism is rule-orientated, realism is result-orientated. In many ways, Lord Devlin's observation that 'The true spirit of the common law is to override theoretical distinctions when they stand in the way of doing practical justice' (*Ingram v Little* (1961)) enshrines the realist articles of faith.

Secondly, the logic of the rule-book concepts is by no means the be-all and end-all. Immediately, one thinks here of Lord Denning's criticisms of traditional offer and acceptance analysis, and of his cavalier exploits with regard to consideration. But Lord Denning is not alone in such a realist disregard for the logic of the concepts. For example, the logic of the concepts did not prevent the majority finding the required contractual connection in *The Eurymedon*, nor did it stop the House of Lords finding a remedy for Mrs Beswick.

Thirdly, realists do not regard blotting the rule-book as the ultimate sin. If practical justice demands some running repairs, then the elegance or conceptual neatness of the solution hardly matters. What matters is that the repair job works. Formalists may pour scorn on such realist patch-up jobs as the device of the collateral contract or the doctrine of the fundamental term, but realists can take such criticisms without flinching. Realists know a spatchcock solution when they see one, but a solution is at least a solution.

Fourthly, realism tends towards doctrinal and conceptual innovation. Judges are not to be discouraged from sowing new doctrinal seeds (for example,

---

13 Adams and Brownsword, 2000, pp 168–70.

promissory estoppel, unconscionability, economic duress, the doctrine of the innominate term) simply because it is not clear how the doctrinal plant will grow. Nor are judges to be discouraged from cultivating newly born ideas. If a recent innovation supports a particular decision, then there is no reason to eschew such support in favour of a traditional ground for the same decision.

Fifthly, for realist judges, 'sympathy and politics' *do* matter. It is all very well complaining that hard cases make bad law; but if judges ignore the obvious merits of a case, practical justice goes by the board and the law is rightly accused of being an ass. Likewise, politics, broadly interpreted, *do* count. Where a judge considers a particular rule or its application unfair, or inconvenient, he should recognise the force of these considerations. On the realist view, judges must act as custodians of practical justice and convenience, not simply as the keepers of the code.

Sixthly, for realists, the mechanical and uncritical adoption and application of the rule book will not do. Rules are laid down for a purpose, to defend some principle or to support some policy. When rules no longer serve their intended purpose, when they become detached from their point, slavish adherence to the rule book undermines the spirit of their enactment. The drive towards consumer protection is the outstanding example of a realist recognition that the world changes and that, in a changing social context, the original intent of the rules may become perverted by their continued uncritical application. (To avoid misunderstanding, we should emphasise that realists are not tied to the purposes underpinning the rule book. In the final analysis, the rule-book, whether read literally or purposively, is marginal to realism.)

Seventhly, realism is not necessarily inconvenienced by a rule-book which is riddled with discretions. At least, for realists of a consumer-welfarist persuasion, if the rules enjoin judges to decide according to the canons of reasonableness, fairness, conscionability, and the like, this is no problem, for it is precisely how such realist judges will want to decide anyway.

Finally, because realists have a passion for results rather than rules, they will tend to take a broad view of appeal court jurisdiction. For realists, the point of an appeal is not to test out whether the trial court applied the right rules, but primarily to assess the result handed down. Accordingly, appeal courts should feel free to overturn trial court rulings where they are judged to have arrived at the wrong result. Similarly, where the rule-book is in obvious and urgent need of reform, realists do not see the sense of simply exhorting the legislature to come to their rescue. If the legislature duly reforms the law, all well and good, but, in the meantime, realist judges will think that they have a responsibility to get on with the reforming work themselves: ('There is a bill now before Parliament which gives effect to the test of reasonableness (that is, the bill which led to UCTA). This is a gratifying piece of law reform: but I do not think we need wait for that bill to be passed into law. You never know what may happen to a bill. Meanwhile the common law has its own principles ready to hand' (*per* Lord Denning MR in *Levison v Patent Steam Carpet Cleaning Co Ltd* 1978).)

Not only do realist judges put results before rules, they put pragmatism ahead of conceptual purity.[14]

Thirdly, there are judges who will approach a case from a market-individualist angle. On the one hand, they take the view that the market is there to facilitate exchange – it is the law which must serve business, not vice versa. Competitive exchange must be encouraged as far as possible and promises must be kept. In many respects, this view is very much in line with the ideologies underlying the classical model of contractual relations. Of paramount importance in this regard is the matter of certainty and predictability. At all costs, businessmen and their lawyers need to know where they stand so far as the law is concerned, with the result that the market-individualist judge will frown on new developments which leave the parties to a contract guessing as to what the end result will be.

The individualist approach also tends to militate against interventionism. The market, as far as possible, should be left to regulate itself. Adams and Brownsword offer the following distinction:

(a) The Market Ideology

According to market-individualism, the marketplace is a site for competitive exchange. The function of contract is not simply to facilitate exchange, it is to facilitate *competitive* exchange. Contract establishes the ground rules within which competitive commerce can be conducted. Thus, subject to fraud, mistake, coercion and the like, bargains made in the market must be kept. In many ways, the line drawn between (actionable) misrepresentation and mere non-disclosure epitomises this view. There are minimal restraints on contractors: the law of the market is not the law of the jungle, and this rules out misrepresentations. However, non-disclosure of some informational advantage is simply prudent bargaining – contractors are involved in a competitive situation and cannot be expected to disclose their hands or otherwise negotiate in good faith (see Lord Ackner's remarks in *Walford v Miles*). In line with these assumptions, market-individualists attach importance to the following considerations.

First, the security of transactions is to be promoted. This means that where a party, having entered the market, reasonably assumes that he has concluded a bargain, then the courts will defend that assumption. The courts' acceptance of an objective approach to contractual intention, their caution with respect to subjective mistake, and their vigorous defence of third party purchasers (see the mistake of identity cases) reflect the concern for security of contract. Ideally, of course, security of transactions means that a party gets the performance he has bargained for, but, as the market reveals an increasing number of transactions where performance is delayed, the opportunities for non-performance increase. To protect the innocent party, contract espouses the expectation measure of damages (it is the next best thing to actual performance) and, in the principle of sanctity of contract (which we will

---

14   Adams and Brownsword, 2000, pp 170–72.

consider under the individualistic side), it takes a hard line against excuses for non-performance.

Secondly, it is important for those who enter into the market to know where they stand. This means that the ground rules of contract should be clear. Hence, the restrictions on contracting must not only be minimal (in line with the competitive nature of the market), but also must be clearly defined (in line with the market demand for predictability, calculability, etc). The postal acceptance rule is a model for the market-individualist: clear, simple and not hedged around with qualifications which leave contractors constantly unsure of their position. Similarly, the traditional classification approach to withdrawal encapsulates all the virtues of certainty, which are dear to the market-individualist. Conversely, the uncertainty inherent in the consequential approach weakens its appeal to market-individualists, even though they may be unavoidably drawn to it where particular terms cannot be dealt with under the classification test.

Thirdly, since contract is concerned essentially with the facilitation of market operations, the law should accommodate commercial practice, rather than the other way round. Therefore, market-individualists sound the alarm bells as soon as the rules of contract fall out of line with and impede commercial practice. The majority judgment of the Privy Council in *The Eurymedon* is an outstanding example of market-individualist re-alignment of the law; and *Williams v Roffey* and *Hillas v Arcos* testify to an evolving market-individualist recognition that technical formation requirements should be relaxed to facilitate agreed adjustments to commercial contracts. In the same way, deference to commercial practice accounts for the relatively smooth acceptance of incorporation of terms by reasonable notice, and stamps the pronouncements of the House of Lords in *Photo Production* as thoroughly market-individualist.

Finally, we should notice the import of the commonplace that many of the rules concerning formation (for example, the rules determining whether a display of goods is an offer or an invitation to treat) simply hinge on convenience. This may well be a statement of the obvious, but the obvious should never be neglected. Contract is concerned to avoid market inconvenience, precisely because its market-individualism commits it to a policy of facilitating market dealing.

(b) The Individualistic Ideology

A persistent theme in market-individualism is that judges should play a non-interventionist role with respect to contracts. This distinctive non-interventionism derives from the individualistic side of the ideology. The essential idea is that parties should enter the market, choose their fellow contractors, set their own terms, strike their bargains and stick to them. The linchpins of this individualistic philosophy are the doctrines of 'freedom of contract' and 'sanctity of contract'.

The emphasis of freedom of contract is on the parties' freedom of choice. First, the parties should be free to choose one another as contractual partners (that is, partner-freedom). Like the tango, contract takes two. And, ideally, the two should consensually choose one another. Secondly, the parties should be free to choose their own terms (that is, term-freedom). Contract is competitive, but the exchange should be consensual. Accordingly, if Jack refuses to deal with the butcher because his mother has warned him about talking to strangers, this is his prerogative; he is exercising his right of partner-freedom. Equally, if Jack agrees to trade the family's last cow for the butcher's magic beans, this too is his prerogative; he is exercising his right of term-freedom (even though we may think he exercises it stupidly). Contract is about unforced choice.

In practice, of course, freedom of contract has been considerably eroded. Anti-discrimination statutes restrict partner-freedom; and term-freedom has been restricted by both the common law (for example, in its restrictions on illegal contracts) and by statute (for example, UCTA). Moreover, the development of monopolistic enterprises, in the public and private sector alike, has made it impossible for the weaker party actually to *exercise* the freedoms in many cases. For example, if one wants a British family car, a railway ride, etc, the other contractual partner is virtually self-selecting (the British corporatist tradition, though much eroded in recent years, must in part account for our tolerance for monopolies). Similarly, where the other side is a standard form or a standard price contractor, the consumer has no say in setting the terms. Nevertheless, none of this should obscure the thrust of the principle of freedom of contract, which is that one should have the freedoms and that the law should restrict them as little as possible – indeed, it is consistent with the principle (in a widely held view) that the law should facilitate the freedoms by striking down monopolies.

Although the principle of partner-freedom still has some life in it (for example, in defending the shopkeeper's choice of customer), it is the principle of term-freedom which is the more vital. Term-freedom can be seen as having two limbs:

(i)   the free area within which the parties are permitted, in principle, to set their own terms should be maximised; and

(ii) parties should be held to their bargains, that is, to their agreed terms (provided that the terms fall within the free area).

Some of the fundamental issues in *Suisse Atlantique* can be related to these two limbs as follows: the House of Lords' support for freedom of contract in *Suisse Atlantique* was primarily support for the first limb. Their Lordships were not prepared to prohibit certain sorts of exemption clauses in the way that, for example, penalty clauses are banned. The effect of exemption clauses remained a matter of the meaning of particular clauses in the light of the parties' intentions (as determined by the rules of construction). However, the preferred construction approach did not prevent later courts from violating the second limb of the principle of term-freedom. Of course, this meant that lip service only was being paid to freedom of contract. To give term-freedom a real bite, both limbs of the principle must be acted upon.

The second limb of term-freedom is none other than the principle of sanctity of contract. By providing that parties should be held to their bargains, the principle of sanctity of contract has a double emphasis. First, if parties must be held to their bargains, they should be treated as masters of their own bargains, and the courts should not indulge in *ad hoc* adjustment of terms which strike them as unreasonable or imprudent. Secondly, if parties must be *held* to their bargains, then the courts should not lightly relieve contractors from performance of their agreements. It will be appreciated that, while freedom of contract is the broader of the two principles, it is sanctity of contract which accounts for the distinctive market-individualistic stand against paternalistic intervention in particular cases.

A glance back over the chapters in this part of the book will reveal that the modern law is littered with examples of the principle of sanctity of contract in operation. We first encountered its non-interventionist philosophy in Lord Wilberforce's powerful dissent in *Schuler v Wickman* and, not surprisingly, the same philosophy underpins his speech (and those of the other members of the House) in *Photo Production*. However, the principle goes beyond particular judgments. It is the foundation for such landmarks, as the doctrine that the courts will not review the adequacy of consideration; the principle that the basis of implied terms is necessity, not reasonableness (see *Liverpool City Council v Irwin*); the hard line towards unilateral collateral mistake (see, for example, *Smith v Hughes*); common mistake (see *Bell v Lever Brothers Ltd*) and frustration (see *Davis v Fareham*); the cautious reception of economic duress; the anxiety to limit the doctrine of inequality of bargaining power; the resistance to the citation of relatively unimportant uncertainty as a ground for release from a contract (see, for example, *Foley v Classique Coaches Ltd*); and the reluctance to succumb to arguments of economic waste or unreasonableness as a basis for release from a bargain (see, for example, *White & Carter*). The principle of sanctity of contract is a thread which runs through contract from beginning to end, enjoining the courts to be ever-vigilant in ensuring that established or new doctrines do not become an easy exit from bad bargains. (Of course, we are not suggesting that such bargains are necessarily products in the first place of free bargaining in the literal sense. Especially in those cases where standard forms are involved they are a product of some rather artificial rules of incorporation (see, especially, *L'Estrange v Graucob*). But courts in this century have tended to regard the contracts resulting from the application of such rules as exercises in term-freedom.[15]

Finally, there is a consumer-welfarist approach which adopts an interventionist stance, particularly with a view to the protection of weaker parties and the promotion of justice and fairness in contractual dealings. Consumer-welfarists are likely to be attracted by notions of good faith and fair dealing and, if a particular rule does not fit with this ideology, a way round it must be found. Adams and Brownsword conclude as follows:

If the 19th century is usually viewed as the classical period for the doctrines associated with market-individualism, so the 20th century is for consumer-welfarism (particularly from 1945 onwards). The recent burgeoning of consumer-welfarism is, of course, hardly surprising. A policy of consumer

---

15 Adams and Brownsword, 2000, pp 172–77.

protection would have to await the development of a consumer society and a policy of welfarism could be expected to grow as it became accepted that government had a responsibility to maintain a welfare programme.

Although the consumer-welfarist ideology clearly stands for a policy of consumer protection and for principles of fairness and reasonableness in contract, it lacks the unity and coherence of market-individualism. It does not start with the market-individualist premise that all contracts should be minimally regulated. Rather, it presupposes that consumer contracts are to be closely regulated and that commercial contracts, although still ordinarily to be viewed as competitive transactions, are to be subject to rather more regulation than market-individualists would allow. The difficulties with consumer-welfarism appear as soon as one attempts to identify its particular guiding principles (that is, its operative principles and conceptions of fairness and reasonableness).

Without attempting to draw up an exhaustive list of the particular principles of consumer-welfarism, we suggest that the following number amongst its leading ideas:

(1) The principle of reasonable reliance: contractors should not 'blow hot and cold' in their dealings with one another. A person should not encourage another to act in a particular way or to form a particular expectation (or acquiesce in another's so acting or forming an expectation), only then to act inconsistently with that encouragement (or acquiescence). This principle is relevant to the Court of Appeal's support for the council-house purchasers in the *Manchester City Council* cases (that is, *Storer* and *Gibson*) and (with rather different facts) for the unilateral contract offerees in *Errington v Errington*; and, of course, it is central to *High Trees* and the equitable estoppel cases. The most important application of the principle is to offer some protection to those who reasonably rely in precontractual situations (in anticipation of a contract) and in situations where contractual terms have been adjusted (as in *High Trees*). Potentially, the principle could operate beyond the shadow of exchange-based agreement to become the modern paradigm for contract.

(2) The principle of proportionality: an innocent party's remedies for breach should be proportionate to the seriousness of the consequences of the breach. This underwrites the *Hong Kong* consequential approach to withdrawal and it explains the attitude of the majority of their Lordships in *Schuler v Wickman*. We can also see this principle at work in regulating contractual provisions dealing with the amount of damages. Thus, penalty clauses are to be rejected, because they bear no relationship to the innocent party's real loss (they are disproportionately excessive), and exemption clauses are unreasonable because they err in the opposite direction.

(3) The principle of bad faith (and good faith): a party who cites a good legal principle in bad faith should not be allowed to rely on that principle. Hence, in *The Hansa Nord*, the buyer was not allowed to rely (in bad faith) on the breach as a legitimate ground for withdrawal; and, in *Nicolene Ltd v Simmonds*, the seller was not allowed to rely (in bad faith) on the alleged uncertainty of the contract. In both cases, we can sense that the courts were

aware of the danger of one party planting traps in the contract in order to facilitate release if so desired. The general principle of bad faith may also explain the rejection of the nephew's reliance on privity in *Beswick v Beswick* and Rees' reliance on promissory estoppel in *D & C Builders v Rees*, and it fits with the regulation of economic duress in *Atlas Express v Kafco*. In all these cases, it would have been an abuse of legal doctrine to allow (bad faith) reliance, and this would be inconsistent with the general requirement of good faith.

(4) The principle that no man should profit from his own wrong: this was a principle of which Lord Atkin was certainly conscious in *Bell v Lever Bros Ltd*, but, of course, it had to give way to his market-individualist thinking. However, the equitable mistake cases, such as *Solle v Butcher* and *Magee v Pennine*, act on this principle and the decisions in *Beswick* and *D & C Builders* derive support from it.

(5) The principle of unjust enrichment: no party, even though innocent, should be allowed unjustly to enrich himself at the expense of another. Accordingly, it is unreasonable for an innocent party to use another's breach as an opportunity for unfair enrichment: hence, again, the prohibition on penalty clauses, the anxiety about the use made of cost of performance damages, and perhaps the argument in *White & Carter*, which (unsuccessfully) pleaded the unreasonableness of continued performance. Equally, frustration should not entail unfair financial advantage (see, for example, the Law Reform (Frustrated Contracts) Act 1943 and *Krell v Henry*).

(6) The better loss-bearer principle: where a loss has to be allocated to one of two innocent parties, it is reasonable to allocate it to the party who is better able to carry the loss. As a rule of thumb, commercial parties are deemed to be better loss-bearers than consumers. The decisions in *Ingram v Little* and *Oscar Chess* exemplify this principle.

(7) The principle of exploitation: a stronger party should not be allowed to exploit the weakness of another's bargaining situation, but parties of equal bargaining strength should be assumed to have a non-exploitative relationship. The first part of this principle, its positive interventionist aspect, pushes for a general principle of unconscionability (see *Lloyds Bank Ltd v Bundy*) and justifies the policy of consumer protection. The latter (qualifying) aspect of the principle, however, is equally important, for it invites a non-interventionist approach to commercial contracts (see, for example, Lord Denning's views in *Howard Marine* and in *British Crane Hire v Ipswich Plant Hire*).

(8) The principle of a fair deal for consumers: consumers should be afforded protection against sharp advertising practice (see *Carlill v Carbolic Smoke Ball Co Ltd*), against misleading statements (see, for example, *Curtis v Chemical Cleaning and Dyeing Co*), against false representations (see *Dick Bentley*) and against restrictions on their ordinary rights (see, for example, *Thornton v Shoe Lane Parking Ltd* and *Karsales (Harrow) Ltd v Wallis*). Moreover, consumer disappointment should be properly compensated (see, for example, *Jarvis v Swans Tours Ltd*).

(9) The principle of informational advantage: representors who have special informational advantage must stand by their representations; but representees who have equal informational opportunity present no special case for protection. The positive aspect of the principle of informational advantage is protective (see, for example, *Esso Petroleum Co Ltd v Mardon*), but its negative aspect offers no succour to representees who are judged able to check out statements for themselves (see, for example, Lord Denning's views in *Howard Marine*).

(10) The principle of responsibility for fault: contractors who are at fault should not be able to avoid responsibility for their fault. This principle threatens both exemption clauses which deal with negligence (see, for example, the decision in *George Mitchell*, the thinking of the minority in *The Eurymedon* and of the majority in *Howard Marine*) and indemnity clauses which purport to pass on the risk of negligence liability (see, for example, *Phillips v Hyland*).

(11) The paternalistic principle: contractors who enter into imprudent agreements may be relieved from their bargains where justice so requires. The case for paternalistic relief is at its most compelling where the party is weak or naive (see, for example, *Cresswell v Potter, Lloyds Bank Ltd v Bundy, Schroeder v Macaulay*, etc). Although the consumer-welfarist line on common mistake and frustration suggests a general concern to cushion the effects of harsh bargains, it is an open question to what extent consumer-welfarists would push the paternalistic principle for the benefit of commercial contractors.

As we have seen, some of these ideas can generate novel doctrines such as equitable estoppel and unconscionability. However, consumer-welfarism also attempts to feed reasonableness into existing contractual categories. Thus, consumer-welfarists would like to see categories such as implied terms, mistake, and frustration grounded in reasonableness, in order to open the door to the employment of the particular principles of the ideology. Lord Denning's attempts to make such a move in respect of implied terms and frustration have failed, but the equitable doctrine of common mistake continues to enjoy support. The most spectacular success has been with exemption clauses which are generally regulated under a regime of reasonableness by UCTA. Now that consumer-welfarists have a secure base, the question is how they will operationalise their discretion.

We have suggested that consumer-welfarists will not always agree about the application of the reasonableness requirement. We can assume that they will uniformly continue with the principle of a fair deal for consumers, but we can expect a division of opinion with regard to commercial contracts. Some consumer-welfarists will observe the limitations built into the principle of exploitation. This means that, because commercial contractors are assumed to be roughly equal in terms of bargaining strength, the courts will refrain from interfering with their arrangements. Such thinking parallels the market-individualist inspired approach in *Photo Production*. Against this, however, some consumer-welfarists will give priority to the principle of responsibility for fault. This means that, even though commercial contracts are not seen as exploitative, it is thought to be unreasonable to use contractual provisions to avoid liability for fault.

Consumer-welfarism suffers from its pluralistic scheme of principles. Where a dispute clearly falls under just one of its principles, there is no difficulty, but as soon as more than one principle is relevant, there is potentially a conflict. Without a rigid hierarchy of principles, the outcome of such conflicts will be unpredictable, as different judges will attach different weights to particular principles. It follows that consumer-welfarism is unlikely ever to attain the consistency of its market-individualist rival.[16]

It should not be assumed that a particular judge necessarily falls wholly within one camp. Often, it will be the case that a particular decision is influenced by more than one of these ideologies but, as a starting point for understanding many of the decisions extracted in later chapters, these categories provide useful food for thought.

VOLUNTARILY ASSUMED AND LEGALLY IMPOSED OBLIGATIONS

It is important not to think of contract law in isolation. In many areas, rules of the law of contract overlap and complement rules which emanate from another branch of the law of civil obligations. The three main branches of the law of obligations are those of contract, tort and restitution, but there are differences in the way in which each branch operates. One point of distinction is said to be that contractual liabilities are voluntarily assumed, whereas tortious and restitutionary duties are imposed by law. This distinction should not be applied too rigidly, as there are exceptions to it.

It is true that many contractual obligations are based upon the free choice of the parties following an agreement, but there are other contractual obligations which have nothing to do with voluntary assumption of responsibility. In particular, terms implied by statute such as those contained in ss 12–15 of the Sale of Goods Act 1979 are imposed by operation of law. So also are those terms implied by the courts as a necessary incident of the type of contract entered into by the parties.[17] Thus, terms implied by law in contracts of employment and tenancy agreements are not voluntarily assumed obligations.

At the same time, it is not true that voluntarily assumed duties are the exclusive preserve of the law of contract. In particular, there are a number of tortious duties which also turn on this issue. For example, the rule in *Hedley Byrne & Co Ltd v Heller & Partners Ltd*[18] in relation to liability for a negligent mis-statement is said to turn in part upon whether the defendant has

---

16   Adams and Brownsword, 2000, pp 177–82.
17   See Chapter 5.
18   [1964] AC 465.

voluntarily entered a relationship so that it is reasonable to impose liability for failing to take care when preparing and delivering advice to another.[19]

PROTECTED INTERESTS

A further method of distinguishing contractual obligations from those which exist in other branches of obligations law is to consider what interests are protected by a particular set of rules. Generally, it is said that the law of contract is primarily concerned with the claimant's expectation interest. Accordingly, the normal measure of damages for a breach of contract is concerned with protecting the claimant's expectation that the defendant will carry out his undertakings. Accordingly, the claimant should be put in the position he would have been in had the contract been performed according to his expectations.[20] This contrasts with the so called tortious measure of damages, which is concerned with restoring the status quo or putting the claimant in the position he was in before any wrong was committed by the defendant. It also differs from restitutionary remedies which are concerned with disgorging from the defendant the benefit he has derived at the claimant's expense.[21]

Whether contractual remedies do truly protect the claimant's expectations of performance is a moot point when one considers the limitations on an award of damages for breach of contract.[22] In particular, the effect of the rules on mitigation of loss and remoteness of damage are such that, in practice, the claimant will recover little more than his out of pocket loss, which, in practical terms, means that the remedy has restored the status quo. If this is the case, the contractual measure of damages is effectively the same as the tortious measure of damages.

While the law of contract is seen as the primary protector of the expectation interest, it is not the exclusive protector of that interest. For example, there are limited instances in which the tort of negligence has been used to compensate the claimant for harm to his legitimate expectations. For example, in *White v Jones*,[23] negligence on the part of the defendants, a firm of solicitors, caused the plaintiff to lose her entitlement to a pecuniary legacy under the will of a client of the defendants. Despite the fact that there was no contractual relationship between the defendants and the plaintiff, the

---

19 See, also, *Henderson and Others v Merrett Syndicates Ltd* [1994] 3 All ER 506; *White v Jones* [1995] 1 All ER 691.

20 *Robinson v Harman* (1848) 1 Ex D 850, p 855 and see Chapter 13.

21 See Chapter 14.

22 See Chapter 12.

23 [1995] 1 All ER 691.

defendant was nonetheless liable in damages for the loss suffered by the plaintiff. This could not be said to represent status quo loss, since, before the wrong was done, the plaintiff had no interest in the testator's property. Accordingly, there was no status quo to restore. Instead, what the plaintiff was awarded was a sum which put her into the position she would have been in had the defendants done what they were required to do on behalf of the testator, their client.

CONCURRENT CONTRACTUAL AND TORTIOUS LIABILITY

It is sometimes the case that the conduct of the defendant amounts to the commission of a tort and a breach of contract at the same time. In these circumstances, there is said to be concurrent liability.[24] Thus, where there is a contract for the supply of services, there is both a tortious duty on the supplier to exercise reasonable care and skill and an identical contractual duty,[25] although it is possible for the contractual supplier of a service to undertake to guarantee the fitness of the service he provides for a particular purpose.[26]

A particular problem which can arise in this context is whether a tortious duty exceeds any duty owed under the contract. To put this another way, does contract trump tort or does tort trump contract? The case referred to in the following extract has, to a certain extent, muddied the waters in this particular area:

Tai Hing Cotton Mill v Liu Chong Hing Bank Ltd [1985] 2 All ER 947, pp 957–58, PC

Lord Scarman: Their Lordships do not believe that there is anything to the advantage of the law's development in searching for a liability in tort where the parties are in a contractual relationship. This is particularly so in a commercial relationship. Though it is possible, as a matter of legal semantics, to conduct an analysis of the rights and duties inherent in some contractual relationships, including that of banker and customer either as a matter of contract law when the question will be what, if any, terms are to be implied or as a matter of tort law when the task will be to identify a duty arising from the proximity and character of the relationship between the parties, their Lordships believe it to be correct in principle and necessary for the avoidance of confusion in the law to adhere to the contractual analysis: on principle, because it is a relationship in which the parties have, subject to a few

---

24 See *Midland Bank Ltd v Hett, Stubbs, Kemp & Co (A Firm)* [1979] Ch 384; *Forsikringsaktieselskapet Vesta v Butcher* [1988] 2 All ER 43; *Spring v Guardian Assurance plc* [1994] 3 All ER 129.

25 Supply of Goods and Service Act 1982, s 13.

26 *Greaves & Co (Contractors) Ltd v Baynham Meikle & Partners* [1975] 3 All ER 99.

exceptions, the right to determine their obligations to each other, and for the avoidance of confusion because different consequences do follow according to whether liability arises from contract or tort, for example, in the limitation of action. Their Lordships respectfully agree with some wise words of Lord Radcliffe in his dissenting speech in *Lister v Romford Ice and Cold Storage Co Ltd* [1957] 1 All ER 125, p 139; [1957] AC 555, p 587. After indicating that there are cases in which a duty arising out of the relationship between employer and employee could be analysed as contractual or tortious, Lord Radcliffe said:

> Since, in any event, the duty in question is one which exists by imputation or implication of law and not by virtue of any express negotiation between the parties, I should be inclined to say that there is not real distinction between the two possible sources of obligation. But it is certainly, I think, as much contractual as tortious. Since, in modern times, the relationship between master and servant, between employer and employed, is inherently one of contract, it seems to me entirely correct to attribute the duties which arise from that relationship to implied contract.

> Their Lordships do not, therefore, embark on an investigation whether, in the relationship of banker and customer, it is possible to identify tort as well as contract as a source of the obligations owed by the one to the other. Their Lordships do not, however, accept that the parties' mutual obligations in tort can be any greater than those to be found expressly or by necessary implication in their contract. If, therefore, as their Lordships have concluded, no duty wider than that recognised in *Macmillan* and *Greenwood* can be implied into the banking contract in the absence of express terms to that effect, the respondent banks cannot rely on the law of tort to provide them with greater protection than that for which they have contracted.

Taken literally, this *dictum* suggests that an action for negligence will be ruled out where there is a contractual relationship between the parties. Certainly, one effect of this view is that if the claimant has brought an action for breach of contract and has failed, he cannot circumvent his failure in contract by suing in tort instead.[27]

However, in later cases, Lord Scarman's views have been tempered and explained. It now appears that an action in tort will not be ruled out where a contractual relationship exists, so long as the tortious duty does not undermine the voluntarily assumed obligations of the parties under the contract:

Johnstone v Bloomsbury Health Authority [1991] 2 All ER 293, CA

Sir Nicholas Browne-Wilkinson VC: In my judgment, the approach adopted in the *Tai Hing* case shows that where there is a contractual relationship between the parties, their respective rights and duties have to be analysed wholly in contractual terms and not as a mixture of duties in tort and contract. It necessarily follows that the scope of the duties owed by one party to the

---

27 *National Bank of Greece v Pinios, The Maira (No 1)* [1990] 1 AC 637.

other will be defined by the terms of the contract between them. Therefore, if there is a term of the contract which is in general terms (for example, a duty to take reasonable care not to injure the employee's health) and another term which is precise and detailed (for example, an obligation to work on particular tasks notwithstanding that they involve an obvious health risk expressly referred to in the contract), the ambit of the employer's duty of care for the employee's health will be narrower than it would be were there no such express terms. In the absence of such express term, an employer would be in breach of the normal obligation not knowingly to put the employee's health at risk. But the express term postulated would demonstrate that, in that particular contract, the duty was restricted to taking such care of the employee's health as was consistent with the employee working on the specified high risk tasks. The express and the implied terms of the contract have to be capable of coexistence without conflict. (I am, of course, ignoring the effect of the Unfair Contract Terms Act 1977 or any statutory duties overriding the contract.)

Therefore, I agree with Leggatt LJ and disagree with Stuart-Smith LJ that, in the present case, the scope of the duty of care for the plaintiff's health owed by the authority falls to be determined taking into account the express terms of para 4(b) of the contract. If the contract, on its true construction, were to impose an absolute obligation to work 48 hours' overtime per week on average, it would, in my judgment, preclude an argument by the employee that the employer, in requiring 48 hours per week overtime, was in breach of his implied duty of care for the employee's health.

But this case is not the same as the example I have used above. Although para 4(b) imposes an absolute duty on the plaintiff to work for 40 hours and, in addition, an obligation 'to be available' for a further 48 hours per week on average, the authority has a discretion as to the number of hours it calls on the plaintiff to work 'overtime'. There is no incompatibility between the plaintiff being under a duty to be available for 48 hours' overtime and the authority having the right, *subject to its ordinary duty not to injure the plaintiff*, to call on him to work up to 48 hours' overtime on average. There is, in the present contract, no incompatibility between the plaintiff's duty on the one hand and the authority's right, subject to the implied duty as to health, on the other. The implied term does not contradict the express term of the contract.

In my judgment, there must be some restriction on the authority's rights. In any sphere of employment other than that of junior hospital doctors, an obligation to work up to 88 hours in any one week would be rightly regarded as oppressive and intolerable. But even that is not the limit of what the authority claims. Since the plaintiff's obligation is to be available 'on average' for 48 hours per week, the authority claims to be entitled to require him to work more than 88 hours in some weeks, regardless of possible injury to his health. Thus, the plaintiff alleges that he was required to work for 100 hours during one week in February 1989 and 105 hours during another week in March 1989. How far can this go? Could the authority demand of the plaintiff that he worked 130 hours (out of the total of 168 hours available) in any one week, even if this would manifestly involve injury to his health? In my judgment, the authority's right to call for overtime under para 4(b) is not an absolute right, but must be limited in some way. There is no technical legal reason why the authority's discretion to call for overtime should not be exercised in conformity with the normal implied duty to take reasonable care not to injure their employee's health.

In my judgment, *Ottoman Bank v Chakarian* [1930] AC 277 provides substantial support for this view. In that case, the employee was, under his contract of employment, bound to serve the bank in Turkey or elsewhere. The employee was ordered to work at a branch in Turkey where his personal safety was at risk, as the employers well knew. The employee disobeyed the order and left the branch in Turkey. He was thereupon dismissed for failure to obey the order. The Privy Council held that 'the risk to [the employee] was such that he was not bound to obey the order, which was therefore not a lawful one' (see [1930] AC 277, p 285). There, as in the present case, there was a provision under which the employer had the right to require the employee to work in Turkey and the employee, under the terms of the contract, was bound to serve there if so required. Even so, it was held that the employer did not have the right to select Turkey, knowing that this involved risk to the employee's physical well being: see, also, *Turner v Mason* (1845) 14 M & W 112, pp 117–18; 153 ER 411, pp 413–14.

Mr Beloff QC submitted that *Chakarian*'s case and the principle there applied depended on the fact that, in that case, the risk to the employee from being in Turkey depended upon circumstances which only arose after the date of the contract. He relied on the passage in *Chitty on Contracts* (26th edn, 1989, Vol 2, para 3977), which states that an employee is not bound to obey 'an order which places him in danger not reasonably contemplated at the time he entered the employment'. Neither *Chakarian*'s case, nor the *dicta* in *Turner v Mason* make any reference to the need for the risk of danger to have arisen subsequently to the date of contract. In my judgment, the principle does not depend on that factor: it depends on the employer's implied obligation to safeguard his employee's health, subject to which obligation the employer is bound to exercise optional rights conferred on him by the contract.

In my judgment, therefore, notwithstanding para 4(b) of the contract, the authority could not lawfully require the plaintiff to work so much overtime in any week as it was reasonably foreseeable would damage his health. Whether or not the authority did in fact require such unlawful overtime will depend on the facts as they emerge at trial. The relief claimed should not be struck out at this stage.

Accordingly, the authority's appeal will be dismissed and the plaintiff's appeal will be allowed so as to permit the plea in para 4(i) of the reply to stand, but para 4(ii) will be struck out.

PART II

CONTRACT FORMATION AND NEGOTIATION

CHAPTER 2

AGREEMENT

Conventional wisdom dictates that at the core of the notion of contract lies the idea of agreement. For example, Treitel writes:

> The first requisite of a contract is that the parties should have reached agreement.[1]

In similar vein, the current edition of Cheshire, Fifoot and Furmston states:

> A contracting party, unlike a tortfeasor, is bound because he has agreed to be bound.[2]

Finally, in *Chitty*, it is observed that:

> There may be said to be three basic essentials to the creation of a contract: agreement, contractual intention and consideration.[3]

This chapter is, correspondingly, concerned with examining the notion of agreement in English contract law, including such matters as 'agreement', mistake and the communication rules concerning the incorporation of terms into unsigned contracts. However, conventional wisdom has not gone unchallenged.

AGREEMENT: MYTH OR REALITY?

Atiyah comments as follows:

> Let me turn now to a more challenging question. To what extent is it true to say that contractual liabilities arise from agreement or promises or depend on the voluntary assumption of obligation? I want to begin by suggesting that the power of the classical model here derives largely from its stress on the executory contract. If two parties do exchange promises to carry out some performance at a future date and if, immediately on the exchange of promises, a binding legal obligation comes at once into existence, then it seems inexorably to follow that the obligation is created by the agreement, by the intention of the parties. If they have done nothing to implement the agreement, if no actions have followed the exchange of promises, then, manifestly, the legal obligation cannot arise from anything except the exchange of promises. Thus far, the classical model appears to be impregnable. But closer examination suggests that the area of impregnability is really rather small.

---

1 Treitel, 1999, p 8.
2 Cheshire, Fifoot and Furmston, 1996, p 29.
3 Chitty, 1994, p 89.

The first point to note is that wholly executory contracts are rarer, more ephemeral in practice and somewhat less binding than the classical model of contract would suggest. In the classical model, as I have suggested, the executory transaction lies at the very heart of contract. It is precisely because the classical model largely defines contract in terms of executory transactions that it necessarily locates the source of contractual liability in what the parties intend, rather than in what they do. But large numbers of contracts are regularly made in which the making and the performance, or at least part performance, are simultaneous or practically simultaneous events. Consider such simple transactions as the boarding of a bus, or the purchase of goods in a supermarket or a loan of money. Is it really sensible to characterise these transactions as agreements or exchanges of promises? Is it meaningful or useful to claim that a person who boards a bus is promising to pay his fare? If so, would it not be just as meaningful to say that when he descends from the bus and crosses the road, he promises to cross with all due care for the safety of other road users? I do not, of course, deny that all these transactions involve some element of voluntary conduct. People do not generally board buses, buy goods in a supermarket or borrow money in their sleep. But they involve much else besides voluntary conduct. They usually involve the rendering of some benefit, of actions of detrimental reliance or both. A person who is carried by a bus from point A to point B after voluntarily boarding the bus can normally be presumed to have derived some benefit from the arrangements. Does his liability to pay his fare have nothing to do with this element of benefit? A person who borrows money and actually receives the loan is, according to the classical model of contract, liable to repay the money merely because he promised to repay it. The fact that he received the money appears to be largely irrelevant.[4]

Even the most convinced advocates of the standard approach concede that, on occasions, the 'agreement' model is hard to sustain in any wholly convincing way, but here the admitted exemptions are not seen as bringing the whole notion into question. Treitel states:

A contract is an agreement giving rise to obligations which are enforced or recognised by law. The factor which distinguishes contractual from other legal obligations is that they are based on the agreement of the contracting parties. This proposition remains generally true, in spite of the fact that it is subject to a number of important qualifications.

The first such qualification is that the law is often concerned with the objective appearance, rather than with the actual fact, of agreement.

'If, whatever a man's real intention may be, he so conducts himself that a reasonable man would believe that he was assenting to the terms proposed by the other party, and that other party upon that belief enters into a contract with him, the man thus conducting himself would be equally bound as if he had intended to agree to the other party's terms.'[5]

---

4   Atiyah, 1986 (reprinted 1990), pp 19–20
5   Blackburn J in *Smith v Hughes* [1871] LR 6 QB 597.

This objective principle is based on the needs of commercial convenience. Considerable uncertainty would result if A, after inducing B reasonably to believe that he (A) had agreed to certain terms, could then escape liability merely by showing he had no 'real intention' to enter into that agreement ...

The idea that contractual obligations are based on agreement must, secondly, be qualified, because contracting parties are normally expected to observe certain standards of behaviour. These are the result of terms implied by law. For example, a person who sells goods or enters into a contract of employment is bound by many such implied terms. The parties may be able to vary or exclude some such terms by contrary agreement but, unless they do so, they are bound by many duties to which they have not expressly agreed and of which they may have never thought ...

The idea that contractual obligations are based on agreement must, thirdly, be qualified in relation to the scope of the principle of freedom of contract. In the 19th century, judges took the view that persons of full capacity should, in general, be allowed to make what contracts they liked: the law only interfered on fairly specific grounds such as misrepresentation, undue influence or illegality. It did not interfere merely because one party was economically more powerful than the other and so able to drive a hard bargain. This attitude became particularly important when the courts recognised the validity of standard form contracts by which one party excluded or limited his common law liabilities. In the present century, this practice of contracting on standard terms has become very common and it is arguable that a customer who contracts on such standard terms has them imposed on him and does not really 'agree' to them at all. This argument is particularly strong where the supplier has a monopoly or where all suppliers in a particular field use the same standard terms. The customer may then only be able to accept those terms or do without the goods or services in question and, in many cases, he cannot in practice do without it ...

In the cases so far considered, the parties are free to decide whether or not to enter into the relationship (though the law may fix some or all of its incidents), but there are other cases in which the law, to some extent, restricts even this freedom. For example, at common law, a common innkeeper may be liable criminally or in tort for refusing, without sufficient excuse, to accommodate a guest. By statute, injunctions may be granted, and damages awarded, against persons who withhold supplies from retailers on the ground of price-cutting, and against persons whose refusal to make certain contracts amounts to unlawful discrimination on grounds of race or sex; and it is unlawful to refuse a person employment because he is, or is not, a member of a trade union.

In Treitel's opinion, however, despite the above qualifications, it remains broadly true that the law of contract is concerned with the circumstances in which agreements are legally binding. Thus, it deals mainly with the two questions of agreement and legal effects or enforceability.

The tension between the conventional view of contract as being agreement or promise based and the pragmatism often exhibited by the courts in practice will feature at many points during this chapter.[6]

However, on the assumption that contract is, in some sense, based on agreement, it is necessary to examine how such agreements are formed.

OFFER AND ACCEPTANCE

Agreements in the above sense are usually thought to arise via a process of offer and acceptance; a proposal by one party which is, eventually, assented to in broadly the same terms by the other party. It might be thought that the law would require an actual subjective intent to be bound (on either side) by the proposed contract, for there to be in the well known (if misleading) phrase, a *consensus ad idem* (or meeting of minds) However, the overwhelming weight of opinion, both academic and judicial, is that an objective approach is preferred, and a party's intentions are to be judged by the way a reasonable person in the other party's position would have understood them. In the words of Blackburn J:

> If, whatever a man's real intention may be, he so conducts himself that a reasonable man would believe that he was assenting to the terms proposed by the other party, and that other party upon that belief enters into the contract with him, the man thus conducting himself would be equally bound as if he had intended to agree to the other party's terms.[7]

There is some dispute as to whether the objective position to be adopted is that of a reasonable person in the promisee position (broadly, the approach adopted by Blackburn J in the above passage) or the detached objectivity or 'fly on the wall' perspective of the (supposedly) disinterested third party observer (most typically, the court).[8] However, the general approach, both academic and judicial, is in line with the views of Blackburn J.[9]

The process of negotiation or interaction by which agreement conventionally arises (the process of offer and acceptance) does not neatly encompass all contracting situations, particularly where standard forms are utilised or where the execution of a contract is virtually contemporaneous

---

6   Equally 'tense' is the often fierce debate between those writers adopting a broadly Atiyah influenced approach, and those (like Treitel) propounding the continued vitality of the classical model. A recent example is the response by Atiyah himself (1986, p 363) to an observation by Beatson, 1986, p 19 that recent judicial decisions indicated that the 'classical law of contract' was far from dead.

7   Blackburn J in *Smith v Hughes* [1871] LR 6 QB 597.

8   Contrast the views of Howarth, 1984, p 265 with those of Vorster, 1987, p 274.

9   See Treitel, above.

with its completion. On a number of occasions, Lord Denning expressed the view that the 'offer and acceptance' perspective was often artificial. For example, in *Gibson v Manchester City Council*,[10] a dispute arose over whether a binding contract to sell a council house had been formed, despite apparently incomplete 'accord' via the offer and acceptance process. Lord Denning stated that, instead, one ought to 'look at the correspondence as a whole and at the conduct of the parties, and see therefrom whether the parties have come to an agreement on everything that was material'.

In general, Lord Denning's views have not been received sympathetically, as the following passage from Lord Diplock's judgment in the House of Lords in the same case makes only too clear:

Gibson v Manchester City Council [1979] 1 WLR 294, HL, p 297

Lord Diplock: My Lords, there may be certain types of contract, though I think they are exceptional, which do not fit easily into the normal analysis of a contract as being constituted by offer and acceptance; but a contract alleged to have been made by an exchange of correspondence between the parties in which the successive communications other than the first are in reply to one another, is not one of these. I can see no reason in the instant case for departing from the conventional approach of looking at the handful of documents relied upon as constituting the contract sued upon and seeing whether upon their true construction there is to be found in them a contractual offer by the corporation to sell the house to Mr Gibson and an acceptance of that offer by Mr Gibson. I venture to think that it was by departing from this conventional approach that the majority of the Court of Appeal was led into error.[11]

In his judgment in *Trentham v Archital Luxfer*,[12] Steyn LJ appears to position himself between these two views:

Trentham v Archital Luxfer [1993] 1 Lloyd's Rep 25, CA, p 27

Steyn LJ: Before I turn to the facts, it is important to consider briefly the approach to be adopted to the issue of contract formation in this case. It seems to me that four matters are of importance. The first is the fact that English law generally adopts an objective theory of contract formation. That means that, in practice, our law generally ignores the subjective expectations and the unexpressed mental reservations of the parties. Instead, the governing criterion is the reasonable expectations of honest men. And, in the present case, that means that the yardstick is the reasonable expectations of sensible businessmen. Secondly, it is true that the coincidence of offer and acceptance will, in the vast majority of cases, represent the mechanism of contract formation. It is so in the case of a contract alleged to have been made by an exchange of correspondence. But it is not necessarily so in the case of a contract

---

10 [1978] 1 WLR 520, CA, p 523H.
11 [1979] 1 WLR 294, HL, p 297D.
12 [1993] 1 Lloyd's Rep 25, CA, p 27.

alleged to have come into existence during and as a result of performance. See *Brogden v Metropolitan Railway* (1877) 2 App Cas 666; *New Zealand Shipping Co Ltd v AM Satterthwaite & Co Ltd* [1974] 1 Lloyd's Rep 534, p 539, col 1; [1975] AC 154, p 167 D–E; *Gibson v Manchester City Council* [1979] 1 WLR 294. The third matter is the impact of the fact that the transaction is executed, rather than executory. It is a consideration of the first importance on a number of levels. See *British Bank for Foreign Trade Ltd v Novinex* [1949] 1 KB 628, p 630. The fact that the transaction was performed on both sides will often make it unrealistic to argue that there was no intention to enter into legal relations. It will often make it difficult to submit that the contract is void for vagueness or uncertainty. Specifically, the fact that the transaction is executed makes it easier to imply a term resolving any uncertainty or, alternatively, it may make it possible to treat a matter not finalised in negotiations as inessential. In this case, fully executed transactions are under consideration. Clearly, similar considerations may sometimes be relevant in partly executed transactions. Fourthly, if a contract only comes into existence during and as a result of performance of the transaction it will frequently be possible to hold that the contract impliedly and retrospectively covers precontractual performance. See *Trollope & Colls Ltd v Atomic Power Construction Ltd* [1963] 1 WLR 333.

This issue is explored further in relation to the topic of acceptance by conduct later in this chapter.

OFFER

An offer is a legal commitment, a proposal which invites, indeed presupposes, eventual acceptance. At its simplest, an offer is a proposal of such a kind that it can be converted into a binding contract by the simple response 'I accept'. From this, it follows that offers should be unconditional and unqualified, not requiring further discussion or negotiation to establish what degree of commitment is being given. Equally, the proposal must be made with (objectively determined) legal intent. In *Carlill v Carbolic Smoke Ball Co*,[13] during November 1891, the manufacturers of a medicinal preparation called the 'Carbolic Smoke Ball' placed a number of advertisements in magazines and newspapers to the effect that the product would be highly effective in warding off the effects of, and indeed would 'positively cure', a range of ailments, including influenza. Moreover, they stated that if used as specified (three times a day for two weeks), they would guarantee the prophylactic effect of the smoke ball and would pay £100 to anyone who, despite using it as specified, still contracted influenza 'or any disease caused by taking cold'. Mrs Carlill bought a smoke ball from a chemist and used it as directed, but still contracted influenza. She sued the company for the £100 promised. Amongst

---

13   [1893] 1 QB 256, CA.

the many defences they put forward, the company claimed that the advertisement had not been intended to constitute a legally binding offer. Hawkins J in the Queen's Bench Division disagreed,[14] as did, unanimously, the Court of Appeal:[15]

Carlill v Carbolic Smoke Ball Co [1893] 1 QB 256, CA, p 266

Bowen LJ: ... the defendants contend next, that it is an offer the terms of which are too vague to be treated as a definite offer, inasmuch as there is no limit of time fixed for the catching of the influenza and it cannot be supposed that the advertisers seriously meant to promise to pay money to every person who catches the influenza at any time after the inhaling of the smoke ball. It was urged also that if you look at this document you will find much vagueness as to the persons with whom the contract was intended to be made – that, in the first place, its terms are wide enough to include persons who may have used the smoke ball before the advertisement was issued; at all events, that it is an offer to the world in general and, also, that it is unreasonable to suppose it to be a definite offer, because nobody in their senses would contract themselves out of the opportunity of checking the experiment which was going to be made at their own expense. It is also contended that the advertisement is rather in the nature of a puff or a proclamation than a promise or offer intended to mature into a contract when accepted. But the main point seems to be that the vagueness of the document shews that no contract whatever was intended. It seems to me that, in order to arrive at a right conclusion, we must read this advertisement in its plain meaning, as the public would understand it. It was intended to be issued to the public and to be read by the public. How would an ordinary person reading this document construe it? It was intended unquestionably to have some effect and I think the effect which it was intended to have was to make people use the smoke ball, because the suggestions and allegations which it contains are directed immediately to the use of the smoke ball, as distinct from the purchase of it. It did not follow that the smoke ball was to be purchased from the defendants directly or even from agents of theirs directly. The intention was that the circulation of the smoke ball should be promoted and that the use of it should be increased. The advertisement begins by saying that a reward will be paid by the Carbolic Smoke Ball Co to any person who contracts the increasing epidemic after using the ball. It has been said that the words do not apply only to persons who contract the epidemic after the publication of the advertisement, but include persons who had previously contracted the influenza. I cannot so read the advertisement. It is written in colloquial and popular language, and I think that it is equivalent to this: '£100 will be paid to any person who shall contract the increasing epidemic after having used the carbolic smoke ball three times daily for two weeks.' And it seems to me that the way in which the public would read it would be this, that if anybody, after the advertisement was

---

14   [1892] 2 QB 484.
15   [1893] 1 QB 256, CA.

published, used three times daily for two weeks the carbolic smoke ball and then caught cold, he would be entitled to the reward. Then again, it was said: 'How long is this protection to endure? Is it to go on for ever or for what limit of time?' I think that there are two constructions of this document, each of which is good sense and each of which seems to me to satisfy the exigencies of the present action. It may mean that the protection is warranted to last during the epidemic and it was during the epidemic that the plaintiff contracted the disease. I think, more probably, it means that the smoke ball will be a protection while it is in use. That seems to me the way in which an ordinary person would understand an advertisement about medicine and about a specific against influenza. It could not be supposed that after you have left off using it you are still to be protected for ever, as if there was to be a stamp set upon your forehead that you were never to catch influenza because you had once used the carbolic smoke ball. I think the immunity is to last during the use of the ball. That is the way in which I should naturally read it, and it seems to me that the subsequent language of the advertisement supports that construction. It says: 'During the last epidemic of influenza, many thousand carbolic smoke balls were sold, and in no ascertained case was the disease contracted by those using [not "who had used"] the carbolic smoke ball,' and it concludes with saying that one smoke ball will last a family several months (which imports that it is to be efficacious while it is being used), and that the ball can be refilled at a cost of 5s. I, therefore, have myself no hesitation in saying that I think, on the construction of this advertisement, the protection was to enure during the time that the carbolic smoke ball was being used. My brother, the Lord Justice who preceded me, thinks that the contract would be sufficiently definite if you were to read it in the sense that the protection was to be warranted during a reasonable period after use. I have some difficulty myself on that point, but it is not necessary for me to consider it further, because the disease here was contracted during the use of the carbolic smoke ball.

Was it intended that the £100 should, if the conditions were fulfilled, be paid? The advertisement says that £1,000 is lodged at the bank for the purpose. Therefore, it cannot be said that the statement that £100 would be paid was intended to be a mere puff. I think it was intended to be understood by the public as an offer which was to be acted upon.

But it was said there was no check on the part of the persons who issued the advertisement, and that it would be an insensate thing to promise £100 to a person who used the smoke ball unless you could check or superintend his manner of using it. The answer to that argument seems to me to be that if a person chooses to make extravagant promises of this kind he probably does so because it pays him to make them, and, if he has made them, the extravagance of the promises is no reason in law why he should not be bound by them.

There are clearly many statements or undertakings which, although presupposing an eventual contractual 'tie', fall short of the necessary requirement of legal intent and unconditionality to constitute an offer in the above sense. One party may simply respond to a request for information (for example, by stating the price at which they might be prepared to sell a house)[16] or, more obviously still, may request such information (for example, as to whether goods or services are available).[17] The common practice of giving estimates or quotations clearly raises these issues.

In a number of stock situations, the courts appear to have adopted *prima facie* presumptions which, although capable of being displaced by clear contrary intention, lay down the general approach of the law. The contrast here is usually said to be between 'offers' and 'invitations to treat' (invitations to offers to negotiate or make offers in their turn and so incapable of acceptance in themselves). The four most widely accepted examples of this are: displays of goods in stores; advertisements; auction sales; and invitations to tender.

Displays of goods

The classic authority is that of *Pharmaceutical Society of Great Britain v Boots Cash Chemists (Southern) Ltd*.[18]

The defendant carried on a business comprising the retail sale of drugs at premises at Edgware, which were entered in the register of premises kept pursuant to s 12 of the Pharmacy and Poisons Act 1933, and from which they regularly sold drugs by retail. The premises comprised a single room, so adapted that customers could serve themselves, and the business there was described by a printed notice at the entrance as 'Boot's Self-Service'. On entry, each customer passed a barrier where a wire basket was obtained. Beyond the barrier, the principal part of the room contained shelves on which articles were displayed. On the shelves in the chemist's department, drugs, including proprietary medicines, were displayed in individual packages or containers with a conspicuous indication of the retail price of each. One section of the shelves in the chemist's department was devoted exclusively to drugs which were included in, or which contained substances included in, Pt I of the Poisons List referred to in s 17(1) of the Pharmacy and Poisons Act 1933; no such drugs were displayed on any shelves outside the section.

The staff employed by the defendant at the premises comprised a manager, a registered pharmacist, three assistants and two cashiers, and, during the time when the premises were open for the sale of drugs, the manager, the registered pharmacist and one or more of the assistants were present in the room. Each customer selected from the shelves the article which he wished to buy and placed it in the wire basket. In order to leave the

---

16 *Harvey v Facey* [1893] AC 552.
17 *Interfoto v Stiletto* [1989] QB 433, p 436.
18 [1953] 1 QB 401, CA.

premises, the customer had to pass by one of the two exits, at each of which was a cash desk where a cashier was stationed who scrutinised the articles selected by the customer, assessed the value and accepted payment. The chemist's department was under the personal control of the registered pharmacist.

The pharmacist was stationed near the poisons section and was in view of the cash desks. In every case involving the sale of a drug, the pharmacist supervised that part of the transaction which took place at the cash desk and was authorised by the defendants to prevent at that stage of the transaction, if he thought fit, any customer from removing any drug from the premises. No steps were taken by the defendant to inform the customers of the pharmacist's authorisation before they selected any article which they wished to purchase.

On 13 April 1951, at the defendant's premises, two customers, following the procedure outlined above, respectively purchased a bottle containing a medicine known as compound syrup of hypophophites, containing 0.01% w/v strychnine, and a bottle containing medicine known as famel syrup, containing 0.23% w/v codeine, both of which substances were poisons included in Pt I of the Poisons List.

The question for the opinion of the court was whether the sales instanced on 13 April 1951 were effected by or under the supervision of a registered pharmacist, in accordance with the provisions of s 18(1)(a)(iii) of the Pharmacy and Poisons Act 1933.

The Lord Chief Justice answered the question in the affirmative.

The Pharmaceutical Society appealed:

Pharmaceutical Society of Great Britain v Boots Cash Chemists (Southern) Ltd [1953] 1 QB 401, CA, p 404

Somervell LJ: This is an appeal from a decision of the Lord Chief Justice on an agreed statement of facts, raising a question under s 18(1)(a)(iii) of the Pharmacy and Poisons Act 1933. The plaintiffs are the Pharmaceutical Society, incorporated by Royal Charter. One of their duties is to take all reasonable steps to enforce the provisions of the Act. The provision in question is contained in s 18. [His Lordship read the section and stated the facts, and continued:] It is not disputed that in a chemist's shop where this self-service system does not prevail, a customer may go in and ask a young woman assistant, who will not herself be a registered pharmacist, for one of these articles on the list, and the transaction may be completed and the article paid for, although the registered pharmacist, who will no doubt be on the premises, will not know anything himself of the transaction, unless the assistant serving the customer or the customer requires to put a question to him. It is right that I should emphasise, as did the Lord Chief Justice, that these are not dangerous drugs. They are substances which contain very small proportions of poison and I imagine that many of them are the type of drug which has a warning as to what doses are to be taken. They are drugs which can be obtained under the law, without a doctor's prescription.

The point taken by the plaintiff is this: it is said that the purchase is complete if and when a customer going round the shelves takes an article and puts it in the receptacle which he or she is carrying, and that therefore, if that is right, when the customer comes to the pay desk, having completed the tour of the premises, the registered pharmacist, if so minded, has no power to say: 'This drug ought not to be sold to this customer.' Whether and in what circumstances he would have that power we need not inquire, but one can, of course, see that there is a difference if supervision can only be exercised at a time when the contract is completed.

I agree with the Lord Chief Justice in everything that he said, but I will put the matter shortly in my own words. Whether the view contended for by the plaintiff is a right view depends on what are the legal implications of this layout – the invitation to the customer. Is a contract to be regarded as being completed when the article is put into the receptacle, or is this to be regarded as a more organised way of doing what is done already in many types of shops – and a bookseller is perhaps the best example – namely, enabling customers to have free access to what is in the shop, to look at the different articles, and then, ultimately, having got the ones which they wish to buy, to come up to the assistant saying 'I want this'? The assistant in 999 times out of 1,000 says 'That is all right' and the money passes and the transaction is completed. I agree with what the Lord Chief Justice has said and with the reasons which he has given for his conclusion, that, in the case of an ordinary shop, although goods are displayed and it is intended that customers should go and choose what they want, the contract is not completed until the customer having indicated the articles which he needs, the shopkeeper, or someone on his behalf, accepts that offer. Then the contract is completed. I can see no reason at all, that being clearly the normal position, for drawing any different implication as a result of this layout.

The Lord Chief Justice, I think, expressed one of the most formidable difficulties in the way of the plaintiffs' contention when he pointed out that, if the plaintiffs are right, once an article has been placed in the receptacle, the customer himself is bound and would have no right, without paying for the first article, to substitute an article which he saw later of a similar kind and which he perhaps preferred. I can see no reason for implying from this self-service arrangement any implication other than that which the Lord Chief Justice found in it, namely, that it is a convenient method of enabling customers to see what there is and choose, and possibly put back and substitute, articles which they wish to have, and then to go up to the cashier and offer to buy what they have so far chosen. On that conclusion, the case fails, because it is admitted that there was supervision in the sense required by the Act and at the appropriate moment of time. For these reasons, in my opinion, the appeal should be dismissed.

Birkett LJ and Romer LJ delivered concurring judgments.[19]

It is hard to resist the conclusion that, here, the courts were swayed by the undesirable consequences which they felt would follow from upholding the Pharmaceutical Society's arguments. Nevertheless, despite its particular context, the case confirms what had generally been taken to be the law concerning retail displays. In response to the lay question 'If the shopkeeper doesn't want to sell, why is he putting the goods on display?', the courts, if required to rationalise, might well have expressed themselves in similar (if less pungent!) terms to the following passage from Winfield:[20]

> One illustration is worth discussion here. What is the effect of display in a shop window of goods with a price marked upon them? Our own law reports are silent upon the point, but the better view seems to be that this is no more than an invitation to do business ... surely a natural interpretation of the display of goods in a shop with a marked price upon them would be that the shopkeeper impliedly reserves to himself a right of selecting his customer. A shop is a place for bargaining, not for compulsory sales. Presumptively, the importance of the personality of the customer cannot be eliminated. If the display of such goods were an offer, then the shopkeeper might be forced to contract with his worst enemy, his greatest trade rival, a reeling drunkard or a ragged and verminous tramp. That would be a result scarcely likely to be countenanced by the law. Even in a business like that of the innkeeper or the common carrier, where there is by law a duty to render services to such persons as may apply for them, the personal element is never entirely excluded. An innkeeper is not bound to accommodate a common prostitute, a railway company in not bound to find transport for one who is not in a fit condition to travel. Of course, a tradesman may frame his proposal in such a way as to abrogate any choice in his selection of a customer. But it is not easy to imagine a case in which he would be likely to do so, and some instances, which might at first sight appear to amount to such abrogation, are more likely to be construed as retaining it. Thus, even if the ticket on a clock in a jeweller's window were 'For sale for £1, cash down, to first comer', we still think that it is only an invitation to do business and that the first comer must be one of whom the jeweller approves.[21]

---

19 To hold that the display of goods is not normally an offer to sell them does not of course solve the overall problem of how contracts are concluded in such a situation. The likeliest analysis is that by presenting the goods at the checkout, the customer is offering to buy them and that this offer is accepted by the ringing up of the goods by the shop assistant. However, this is not without its own difficulties, particularly if it subsequently becomes clear that the customer has insufficient money to pay for all the goods rung up. Problems generally in this area are explored by Unger, 1953, p 369.

20 (1939) 55 LQR 518.

21 Winfield's final remarks are particularly contentious and the *Boots* case should not be seen as precluding retailers from being held to have made offers where they clearly indicate that goods *will* be sold. See Unger, 1953, for further discussion of this.

Advertisements

The legal position here mirrors that of retail displays (to which it is closely related). Indeed, in *Partridge v Crittenden*,[22] Lord Parker CJ stated that he came to this conclusion 'with less reluctance' than in retail display cases, since 'when one is dealing with advertisements and circulars, unless they indeed come from manufacturers, there is business sense in their being construed as invitations to treat, and not offers for sale ...'[23] It should, of course, be noted that, even here there are exceptions, as the *Carlill* case and other 'offer of reward' cases demonstrate. Lord Parker also indicates another possibility with his rather cryptic references to manufacturers' advertisements (is it clear why the position of manufacturers should be different?).

Auctions

The general rule is that the advertisement of an auction and, indeed, the announcement of the lots for sale by the auctioneer are merely invitations to treat. The bidders successively make offers to buy the goods, until, finally, acceptance is signified by the auctioneer bringing down the hammer.[24] Again, the undesirable consequences of a contrary rule figure heavily in the courts' thinking, as is demonstrated in the judgment of Blackburn J in the case of *Harris v Nickerson*:[25]

Harris v Nickerson (1873) LR 8 QB 286, p 287

Blackburn J: I am of opinion that the judge was wrong.

The facts were that the defendant advertised *bona fide* that certain things would be sold by auction on the days named and, on the third day, a certain class of things, viz, office furniture, without any previous notice of their withdrawal, were not put up. The plaintiff says, in as much as I confided in the defendant's advertisement, and came down to the auction to buy the furniture (which it is found as a fact he was commissioned to buy) and have had no opportunity of buying, I am entitled to recover damages from the defendant, on the ground that the advertisement amounted to a contract by the defendant with anybody that should act upon it, that all the things advertised would be actually put up for sale and that he would have an opportunity of bidding for them and buying. This is certainly a startling proposition and would be excessively inconvenient if carried out. It amounts to saying that any one who advertises a sale by publishing an advertisement becomes responsible to everybody who

---

22 [1968] 1 WLR 1204, p 1209.

23 The same principle was held to apply in *Grainger v Gough* [1896] AC 325, by the House of Lords, with regard to a circular to the regular customers of a wine merchant announcing (with prices) the availability of the new season's wines.

24 See *Payne v Cave* (1789) 3 Term Rep 148 and the Sale of Goods Act 1979, s 57(2).

25 (1873) LR 8 QB 286, p 287.

attends the sale for his cab hire or travelling expenses. As to the cases cited: in the case of *Warlow v Harrison*, the opinion of the majority of the judges in the Exchequer Chamber appears to have been that an action would lie for not knocking down the lot to the highest *bona fide* bidder when the sale was advertised as without reserve; in such a case, it may be that there is a contract to sell to the highest bidder and that if the owner bids, there is a breach of the contract; there is very plausible ground at all events for saying, as the minority of the Court thought, that the auctioneer warrants that he has power to sell without reserve. In the present case, unless every declaration of intention to do a thing creates a binding contract with those who act upon it and, in all cases, after advertising a sale, the auctioneer must give notice of any articles that are withdrawn, or be liable to an action, we cannot hold the defendant liable.

The difficulties caused by a strict application of the above rules to a case where an auction is advertised as being 'without reserve' (that is, there is no reserve price on the lots) are noted by Blackburn J in his reference to the earlier case of *Warlow v Harrison*.[26] The pragmatic solution appears to be to view the auctioneer in such a case as making a personal offer at the auction that the sale is 'without reserve', such an offer being accepted by the highest bid. A similar dilemma and, in some respects, a similar solution, is seen in the discussion of tenders below.

Invitations to tender

A statement that goods are to be sold by tender is not normally an offer, so that the person making the statement is not bound to sell to the person making the highest tender (*Spencer v Harding*).[27] Similarly, a statement inviting tenders for the supply of goods or for the execution of work is not normally an offer. The tenders themselves are the offers and there is no contract until one of them is accepted.

However, what of the situation where the invitation contains an express statement that the highest or, as the case may be, lowest tender will be accepted? Here again, the normal rule applied inflexibly could cause injustice and could cause the law to be out of line with legitimate business expectations. Again, the solution appears to lie in viewing the person inviting tenders as specifically undertaking or offering to accept the highest or lowest tender, this personal undertaking being accepted by the appropriate tenderer. The point was dealt with in the case of *Harvela Investments Ltd v Royal Trust Co of Canada*.[28] The case is not without its complications. However, in essence, it concerned an invitation by the Royal Trust Co to two rivals for shares in the company to submit sealed bids by a fixed date. It was stated that the highest

---

26 (1859) 1 E & E 309.

27 (1870) LR 5 CP 561.

28 [1986] AC 207, HL.

bid would be accepted. One of the rivals (Harvela Investments Ltd) made a bid of $2,175,000; the other (Sir Leonard Outerbridge) made a bid of $2,100,000 'or $101,000 in excess of any other offer ...'.

The first question for the courts was the legal result of the 'referential' element of Sir Leonard's bid. The House of Lords unanimously held that this could and should be discounted as being incompatible with the spirit of fixed and sealed bidding and, in practice, unworkable if adopted generally. The second question was the result of the Royal Trust Co having committed themselves to accept the highest bid (now Harvela's). Again, the House unanimously held that it did involve binding legal obligations of a distinct, personal nature.[29]

Unilateral offers

From time to time in the cases and elsewhere in these materials, the concept of the 'unilateral contract' is discussed. If taken literally, this would indicate a 'one sided' contract, an idea which fits very uneasily with the idea of contract as being based on agreement. In truth, what is really being discussed is a 'uni-promise' contract – the key distinction between a 'unilateral' and a 'bilateral' contract lies in the fact that, in the former, there is no exchange of promises – a promise is given in return for an act. For example, all advertisements of rewards are seen as not presupposing any counter-promise or undertaking, but merely envisaging that interested parties will seek to perform the task(s) in question to win the prize. Unilateral contracts are traditionally seen as exceptions, indeed, as exceptions which cause difficulties, to the normal process of offer and acceptance (further examples are seen below). For those critical of the classical model, however, the emphasis they give to the fact of performance and the reality of reliance on others is highly instructive.

The classic exposition of the basic nature of unilateral offers and unilateral contracts comes in the judgment of Bowen LJ in the case of *Carlill v Carbolic Smoke Ball Co.* (The facts and other aspects of this case are considered above.) In this extract, the passage begins at p 268:

Carlill v Carbolic Smoke Ball Co [1893] 1 QB 256, CA, p 268

Bowen LJ: It was also said that the contract is made with all the world – that is, with everybody, and that you cannot contract with everybody. It is not a contract made with all the world. There is the fallacy of the argument. It is an offer made to all the world, and why should not an offer be made to all the

---

29 Perhaps the clearest analysis of the way in which such a binding obligation could come about is to be found in the judgment of Peter Gibson J in *Harvela* [1985] Ch 103, p 119. (For a further variation of this theme, see *Blackpool and Fylde Aeroclub Ltd v Blackpool Borough Council* [1990] 1 WLR 1195.)

world which is to ripen into a contract with anybody who comes forward and performs the condition? It is an offer to become liable to anyone who, before it is retracted, performs the condition and, although the offer is made to the world, the contract is made with that limited portion of the public who come forward and perform the condition on the faith of the advertisement. It is not like cases in which you offer to negotiate, or you issue advertisements that you have got a stock of books to sell, or houses to let, in which case, there is no offer to be bound by any contract. Such advertisements are offers to negotiate – offers to receive offers – offers to chaffer, as, I think, some learned judge in one of the cases has said. If this is an offer to be bound, then it is a contract the moment the person fulfils the condition.

That seems to me to be sense and it is also the ground on which all these advertisement cases have been decided during the century; and it cannot be put better than in Willes J's judgment in *Spencer v Harding*:

> 'In the advertisement cases,' he says, 'there never was any doubt that the advertisement amounted to a promise to pay the money to the person who first gave information. The difficulty suggested was that it was a contract with all the world. But that, of course, was soon overruled. It was an offer to become liable to any person who before the offer should be retracted should happen to be the person to fulfil the contract, of which the advertisement was an offer or tender. That is not the sort of difficulty which presents itself here. If the circular had gone on, 'and we undertake to sell to the highest bidder,' the reward cases would have applied, and there would have been a good contract in respect of the persons.'

As soon as the highest bidder presented himself, says Willes J, the person who was to hold the *vinculum juris* on the other side of the contract was ascertained, and it became settled.

Then it was said that there was no notification of the acceptance of the contract. One cannot doubt that, as an ordinary rule of law, an acceptance of an offer made ought to be notified to the person who makes the offer, in order that the two minds may come together. Unless this is done, the two minds may be apart, and there is not that consensus which is necessary according to the English law – I say nothing about the laws of other countries – to make a contract. But there is this clear gloss to be made upon that doctrine, that, as notification of acceptance is required for the benefit of the person who makes the offer, the person who makes the offer may dispense with notice to himself if he thinks it desirable to do so, and I suppose there can be no doubt that where a person in an offer made by him to another person, expressly or impliedly intimates a particular mode of acceptance as sufficient to make the bargain binding, it is only necessary for the other person to whom such offer is made to follow the indicated method of acceptance; and if the person making the offer, expressly or impliedly intimates in his offer that it will be sufficient to act on the proposal without communicating acceptance of it to himself, performance of the condition is a sufficient acceptance without notification.

That seems to me to be the principle which lies at the bottom of the acceptance cases, of which two instances are the well known judgment of Mellish LJ, in *Harris*'s case, and the very instructive judgment of Lord Blackburn in *Brogden v Metropolitan Railway Co*, in which he appears to me to take exactly the line I have indicated.

Now, if that is the law, how are we to find out whether the person who makes the offer does intimate that notification of acceptance will not be necessary in order to constitute a binding bargain? In many cases, you look to the offer itself. In many cases, you extract from the character of the transaction that notification is not required and, in the advertisement cases, it seems to me to follow as an inference to be drawn from the transaction itself that a person is not to notify his acceptance of the offer before he performs the condition, but that if he performs the condition notification is dispensed with. It seems to me that from the point of view of common sense no other idea could be entertained. If I advertise to the world that my dog is lost and that anybody who brings the dog to a particular place will be paid some money, are all the police or other persons whose business it is to find lost dogs to be expected to sit down and write me a note, saying that they have accepted my proposal? Why, of course, they at once look after the dog and, as soon as they find the dog, they have performed the condition. The essence of the transaction is that the dog should be found and it is not necessary under such circumstances, as it seems to me, that, in order to make the contract binding, there should be any notification of acceptance. It follows from the nature of the thing that the performance of the condition is sufficient acceptance without the notification of it, and a person who makes an offer in an advertisement of that kind makes an offer which must be read by the light of that common sense reflection. He does, therefore, in his offer, impliedly indicate that he does not require notification of the acceptance of the offer.

The possibility of invoking a unilateral contract has often proved helpful to courts who wish to give rights to someone relying on another's promise (often to their detriment) without wishing to impose contractual burdens on them. Good examples of this can be seen regarding auctions 'without reserve' (in favour of the highest *bona fide* bidder) and invitations to tender combined with promises to take the highest or lowest tender submitted (in favour of the tenderer). A very clear example of this comes in the following passage from Peter Gibson J in the High Court in *Harvela Investments Ltd v Royal Trust Co of Canada* (see above, fn 29):

I accept the submission of counsel for Harvela that the present case is an example of a unilateral contract, in the sense of a contract brought into existence by the act of one party in response to a conditional promise by another. Royal Jersey by the invitation telex promised to accept Harvela's bid if that were the highest offer in accordance with the terms of the invitation telex, and Harvela, by responding thereto by making the highest bid brought the contract into existence.

ACCEPTANCE

At its simplest, an acceptance is an unconditional assent to the terms proposed in the offer. Much of the relevant law is reasonably straightforward and capable of being reduced to a series of propositions. In essence, a valid acceptance comprises the following elements:

- the offer must still be in force and open to acceptance;
- the acceptance must be unconditional and must not introduce any fresh terms of a significant or material nature;
- the acceptance is only valid, in general, when received by the offeror.

There are, however, cases which are (according to taste) either exceptions or illustrative of the deficiencies in the basic rules – for example, acceptance in unilateral contracts and the special situation of acceptance by post. Certainly, in this area, the classical model often strains to fit with commercial and social realities, a problem perhaps most apparent in the so called 'battle of the forms'.

The offer must still be in force

Therefore, it must not have lapsed, nor have been revoked or withdrawn by the offeror, nor (earlier) rejected by the offeree.

Lapse

This issue causes few real difficulties. Offers will lapse after a 'reasonable time' has passed (depending on the nature of the commodity or transaction); after the expiry of a stated time period and, in most situations, on the death of the offeror or offeree.[30] In a practical sense, lapse happens 'automatically' without the offeror or the offeree needing to do anything specific. Theoretically, it can be viewed as based on either a perception that the offeror has impliedly revoked the offer or (probably better) that it has been impliedly rejected by the offeree.[31]

Revocation

An offer can be revoked at any time before it is validly accepted. For a revocation to be effective, it should have reached the offeree (or at least be in

---

30   Mellish LJ in *Dickinson v Dodds* [1876] 2 Ch D 463, CA.
31   Buckley J in *Manchester Diocesan Council v Commercial and General Investments* [1969] 3 All ER 1593, p 1599.

the hands of an agent). Here, the objective nature of agreement as discussed earlier comes into sharp focus. It is, conventionally, seen as insufficient to simply change one's mind about the offer, or even to take steps to contract with a third party (for example, by disposing of goods elsewhere). Instead, the change of mind must in some way be communicated to the offeree – at least sufficiently to have made a reasonable person in the offeree's position aware of the new reality. The classic authority for this is usually seen to be the case of *Dickinson v Dodds*.[32]

On Wednesday 10 June, Dodds offered in writing to sell houses to Dickinson. He stated that his offer would remain open until Friday 12 June at 9 am. On Thursday afternoon, Dickinson discovered from Berry (his agent) that Dodds had been negotiating with a third party, Allan, to sell the houses. Despite this, Dickinson purported to accept the offer via a letter communicated through Berry to Dodds by Friday 12 June at around 7 am. It transpired that, on Thursday, Dodds had agreed to sell the houses to Allan. The judge at first instance found in favour of Dickinson. The Court of Appeal reversed this decision:

Dickinson v Dodds [1876] 2 Ch D 463, CA, p 471

James LJ (after referring to the document of the 10th of June, 1874, continued): The document, though beginning 'I hereby agree to sell' was nothing but an offer and was only intended to be an offer, for the plaintiff himself tells us that he required time to consider whether he would enter into an agreement or not. Unless both parties had then agreed, there was no concluded agreement then made; it was, in effect and substance only, an offer to sell. The plaintiff, being minded not to complete the bargain at that time, added this memorandum: 'This offer to be left over until Friday, 9 o'clock am, 12th June, 1874.' That shews it was only an offer. There was no consideration given for the undertaking or promise, to whatever extent it may be considered binding, to keep the property unsold until 9 o'clock on Friday morning; but, apparently, Dickinson was of opinion, and probably Dodds was of the same opinion, that he (Dodds) was bound by that promise and could not in any way withdraw from it or retract it until 9 o'clock on Friday morning, and this probably explains a good deal of what afterwards took place. But it is clear settled law, on one of the clearest principles of law, that this promise, being a mere *nudum pactum* was not binding, and that at any moment before a complete acceptance by Dickinson of the offer, Dodds was as free as Dickinson himself. Well, that being the state of things, it is said that the only mode in which Dodds could assert that freedom was by actually and distinctly saying to Dickinson, 'Now I withdraw my offer'. It appears to me that there is neither principle nor authority for the proposition that there must be an express and actual withdrawal of the offer, or what is called a retractation. It must, to constitute a contract, appear that the two minds were at one at the same moment of time, that is, that there was an offer continuing up to the time of the acceptance. If

---

32 [1876] 2 Ch D 463, CA.

there was not such a continuing offer, then the acceptance comes to nothing. Of course, it may well be that the one man is bound in some way or other to let the other man know that his mind with regard to the offer has been changed; but, in this case, beyond all question, the plaintiff knew that Dodds was no longer minded to sell the property to him as plainly and clearly as if Dodds had told him in so many words, 'I withdraw the offer'. This is evident from the plaintiff's own statements in the bill.

The plaintiff says in effect that, having heard and knowing that Dodds was no longer minded to sell to him, and that he was selling or had sold to some one else, thinking that he could not in point of law withdraw his offer, meaning to fix him to it, and endeavouring to bind him, 'I went to the house where he was lodging, and saw his mother-in-law, and left with her an acceptance of the offer, knowing all the while that he had entirely changed his mind. I got an agent to watch for him at 7 o'clock the next morning, and I went to the train just before 9 o'clock, in order that I might catch him and give him my notice of acceptance just before 9 o'clock, and when that occurred, he told my agent, and he told me, 'you are too late', and he then threw back the paper'. It is to my mind quite clear that before there was any attempt at acceptance by the plaintiff, he was perfectly well aware that Dodds had changed his mind and that he had, in fact, agreed to sell the property to Allan. It is impossible, therefore, to say there was ever that existence of the same mind between the two parties which is essential in point of law to the making of an agreement. I am of opinion, therefore, that the plaintiff has failed to prove that there was any binding contract between Dodds and himself.

Mellish LJ: I am of the same opinion. The first question is whether this document of the 10th of June 1874, which was signed by Dodds, was an agreement to sell, or only an offer to sell, the property therein mentioned to Dickinson; and I am clearly of opinion that it was only an offer, although it is in the first part of it, independently of the postscript, worded as an agreement. I apprehend that, until acceptance, so that both parties are bound, even though an instrument is so worded as to express that both parties agree, it is in point of law only an offer and, until both parties are bound, neither party is bound. It is not necessary that both parties should be bound within the Statute of Frauds, for if one party makes an offer in writing and the other accepts it verbally, that will be sufficient to bind the person who has signed the written document. But, if there be no agreement, either verbally or in writing, then, until acceptance, it is in point of law an offer only, although worded as if it were an agreement. But it is hardly necessary to resort to that doctrine in the present case, because the postscript calls it an offer, and says, 'This offer to be left over until Friday, 9 o'clock am.' Well, then, this being only an offer, the law says – and it is a perfectly clear rule of law – that, although it is said that the offer is to be left open until Friday morning at 9 o'clock, that did not bind Dodds. He was not in point of law bound to hold the offer over until 9 o'clock on Friday morning. He was not so bound either in law or in equity. Well, that being so, when on the next day he made an agreement with Allan to sell the property to him, I am not aware of any ground on which it can be said that that contract with Allan was not as good and binding a contract as ever was made. Assuming Allan to have known (there is some dispute about it, and Allan does not admit that he knew of it, but I will assume that he did) that Dodds had made the offer to Dickinson and had given him till Friday morning at 9 o'clock to accept it, still, in point of law, that could not prevent Allan from making a more favourable offer than Dickinson and entering at once into a binding agreement with Dodds.

Then Dickinson is informed by Berry that the property has been sold by Dodds to Allan. Berry does not tell us from whom he heard it, but he says that he did hear it, that he knew it and that he informed Dickinson of it. Now, stopping there, the question which arises is this – if an offer has been made for the sale of property and, before that offer is accepted, the person who has made the offer enters into a binding agreement to sell the property to somebody else, and the person to whom the offer was first made receives notice in some way that the property has been sold to another person, can he after that make a binding contract by the acceptance of the offer? I am of opinion that he cannot. The law may be right or wrong in saying that a person who has given to another a certain time within which to accept an offer is not bound by his promise to give that time; but, if he is not bound by that promise and may still sell the property to someone else, and if it be the law that, in order to make a contract, the two minds must be in agreement at some one time, that is, at the time of the acceptance, how is it possible that when the person to whom the offer has been made knows that the person who has made the offer has sold the property to someone else, and that, in fact, he has not remained in the same mind to sell it to him, he can be at liberty to accept the offer and thereby make a binding contract? It seems to me that would be simply absurd. If a man makes an offer to sell a particular horse in his stable, and says, 'I will give you until the day after tomorrow to accept the offer' and, the next day, goes and sells the horse to somebody else and receives the purchase-money from him, can the person to whom the offer was originally made then come and say, 'I accept', so as to make a binding contract and so as to be entitled to recover damages for the non-delivery of the horse? If the rule of law is that a mere offer to sell property, which can be withdrawn at any time and which is made dependant on the acceptance of the person to whom it is made, is a mere *nudum pactum*, how is it possible that the person to whom the offer has been made can by acceptance make a binding contract after he knows that the person who has made the offer has sold the property to someone else? It is admitted law that, if a man who makes an offer dies, the offer cannot be accepted after he is dead, and parting with the property has very much the same effect as the death of the owner, for it makes the performance of the offer impossible. I am clearly of opinion that, just as when a man who has made an offer dies before it is accepted, it is impossible that it can then be accepted, so when once the person to whom the offer was made knows that the property has been sold to someone else, it is too late for him to accept the offer and, on that ground, I am clearly of opinion that there was no binding contract for the sale of this property by Dodds to Dickinson, and even if there had been, it seems to me that the sale of the property to Allan was first in point of time. However, it is not necessary to consider if there had been two binding contracts, which of them would be entitled to priority in equity, because there is no binding contract between Dodds and Dickinson.

The case is interesting for a number of reasons. First, it indicates that a promise to hold an offer open is not binding, unless contained in a deed or given for some consideration in return (see Chapter 3).[33] Secondly, it clearly indicates that the offeror need not communicate his/her revocation personally, nor even attempt to, so long as objectively clear information reaches the offeree (it is not clear whether any source of such information will suffice).[34, 35] Thirdly, in the judgments there is an undoubted tension – in part, they echo the 'objective principle' with their references to 'knowing' that the property has been sold, but, elsewhere, there is a strong subjective flavour. Are we witnessing here the 'birth pangs' of the classical model?

Rejection

An outright refusal of an offer brings the offer to an end, so that it is not open for subsequent acceptance. Likewise, a counter-proposal (counter-offer) is seen as functioning as a rejection of the original offer. The basic approach of the courts is demonstrated clearly in *Hyde v Wrench*,[36] where Wrench (on 6 June) offered to sell his farm to Hyde for £1,000. Hyde offered £950 in return. On 27 June, Wrench rejected this counter-offer. On 29 June, Hyde agreed to pay £1,000, but, by this time, Wrench was not interested. It was held that there was not a binding contract:

Hyde v Wrench (1840) 49 ER 132 RC

Lord Langdale MR: Under the circumstances stated in this bill, I think there exists no valid binding contract between the parties for the purchase of the property. The defendant offered to sell it for £1,000 and, if that had been at once unconditionally accepted, there would have been a perfect binding contract; instead of that, the plaintiff made an offer of his own, to purchase the property for £950 and he thereby rejected the offer previously made by the defendant. I think that it was not afterwards competent for him to revive the proposal of the defendant, by tendering an acceptance of it; and that, therefore, there exists no obligation of any sort between the parties; the demurrer must be allowed.

---

33 By giving consideration (even to a very small degree), the offeree would acquire distinct 'option' rights over the offer – see *Mountford v Scott* [1975] 1 All ER 198.

34 Some commentators have suggested that the third party should be a 'reliable source' of such information, but this qualification does not appear in the judgments.

35 The Law Commission's 1975 (Working Paper No 60) recommendation that such 'firm offers' should be binding in a business context irrespective of the presence or absence of consideration was never taken further.

36 (1840) 49 ER 132, RC. Even a purported acceptance which contains different terms and conditions than those contained in the offer is likely to be viewed as a counter-offer and so, a rejection of the original offer. See *Northland Airliners v Dennis Ferranti Meters* [1970] 114 SJ 845. This point is explained further below, p 61.

The approach adopted here appears to be reasonable at first glance. However, quite apart from the specific difficulties it causes in relation to contracts made via standard forms, there are, on closer examination, some difficulties with the basic approach. It appears to envisage that all contractual negotiations are 'cut and dried', so that each party in turn stakes out their position and (normally) wholly rejects the position of the other (if they do not unconditionally accept it).

The reality of most negotiations is, of course, very different – an offeree may wish to accept the basic proposal of another whilst introducing modifications, say, as to time of delivery, or payment by instalments. The rigidity of the basic model adopted by English law does not readily allow for this, in that any significant modification contained in a proposed acceptance will be seen as a counter-offer (to be valid, an acceptance must be unconditional) and as a rejection of the original offer. The law does not seem to provide for 'in principle' acceptances or commitments.

One slight qualification to the above is that a mere enquiry will not be viewed as a counter-offer – an offeree can request information about the offer without rejecting it (although without some subsequent unconditional acceptance, there will equally be no contract and the offer may eventually lapse or be revoked). The point is demonstrated well in the case of *Stevenson, Jacques and Co v McLean*.[37] The defendant, being possessed of warrants for iron, wrote from London to the plaintiff at Middlesborough, asking whether they could get him an offer for the warrants. Further correspondence ensued and, ultimately, the defendant wrote to the plaintiff fixing 40 s per ton net cash as the lowest price at which he could sell, stating that he would hold the offer open till the following Monday. The plaintiff, on Monday morning at 9.42 am, telegraphed to the defendant: 'Please wire whether you would accept 40 for delivery over two months or, if not, longest limit you could give.' The defendant sent no answer to this telegram and, after its receipt on the same day, he sold the warrants and, at 1.25 pm, telegraphed to plaintiff that he had done so. Before the arrival of his telegram to that effect, the plaintiff, having at 1 pm found a purchaser for the iron, sent a telegram at 1.34 pm to the defendant, stating that they had secured his price. The defendant refused to deliver the iron and the plaintiff brought an action against him for non-delivery.

Lush J, at first instance, found that a binding contract had come into being at 1.34 pm:

Stevenson, Jacques and Co v McLean (1880) 5 QB 346, p 349

Lush J: Two objections were relied on by the defendant: first, it was contended that the telegram sent by the plaintiff on the Monday morning was a rejection

37 (1880) 5 QB 346.

of the defendant's offer and a new proposal on the plaintiffs' part, and that the defendant had therefore a right to regard it as putting an end to the original negotiation.

Looking at the form of the telegram, the time when it was sent and the state of the iron market, I cannot think this is its fair meaning. The plaintiff Stevenson said he meant it only as an inquiry, expecting an answer for his guidance, and this, I think, is the sense in which the defendant ought to have regarded it.

It is apparent throughout the correspondence that the plaintiff did not contemplate buying the iron on speculation, but that their acceptance of the defendant's offer depended on their finding someone to take the warrants off their hands. All parties knew that the market was in an unsettled state and that no one could predict, at the early hour when the telegram was sent, how the prices would range during the day. It was reasonable that, under these circumstances, they should desire to know before business began whether they were to be at liberty in case of need to make any and what concession as to the time or times of delivery, which would be the time or time of payment, or whether the defendant was determined to adhere to the terms of his letter; and it was highly unreasonable that the plaintiff should have intended to close the negotiation while it was uncertain whether they could find a buyer or not, having the whole of the business hours of the day to look for one. Then again, the form of the telegram is one of inquiry. It is not 'I offer 40 for delivery over two months', which would have likened the case to *Hyde v Wrench*, where one party offered his estate for £1,000 and the other answered by offering £950. Lord Langdale, in that case, held that after the £950 had been refused, the party offering it could not, by then agreeing to the original proposal, claim the estate, for the negotiation was at an end by the refusal of his counter-proposal. Here there is no counter-proposal. The words are, 'Please wire whether you would accept 40 for delivery over two months or, if not, the longest limit you would give'. There is nothing specific by way of offer or rejection, but a mere inquiry, which should have been answered and not treated as a rejection of the offer. This ground of objection therefore fails.[38]

Exceptional cases

As stated above, the apparent simplicity of the conventional model of acceptance is complicated in a number of cases. At the very least, these cases illustrate limitations to the normal model. However, they also (yet again) indicate a tension between conventional theory and the desire of the courts to take account of commercial realities and produce 'workable' law. The four exceptional cases discussed here are: acceptance by conduct; acceptance in unilateral contracts; postal acceptances; and the 'battle of the forms'.

---

38 The decision on the facts of any given case as to whether a response is a counter-offer or a request for information is not always an easy one. Eg, contrast the different views expressed on this point in *Gibson v Manchester City Council* by Lane LJ in the Court of Appeal ([1978] 1 WLR 531) and Lord Edmund Davies in the House of Lords ([1979] 1 WLR 302).

Acceptance by conduct

The core idea in acceptance is that it is an unconditional assent to an offer. The concept of assent might suggest that there must always be a written or verbal response by the offeree to the offer to conclude a contract. A moment's reflection, however, indicates that there are a large number of situations which are contractual on any rational analysis, and yet in which the establishing of a response by the offeree in the above sense would be difficult and artificial, or simply impossible. An offer to buy goods is followed by their despatch in return; an offer concerning the performance of some service is followed by the commencement of the work, and so on. There is ample authority for establishing that, in such situations, an offer can be accepted by the conduct of the offeree, so long as such conduct can be seen as indicating an intention to accept the offer. A clear illustration is provided by the case of *Taylor v Allon*.[39]

Allon's motor insurance expired on 5 April 1964. From 16 April, he was insured under a temporary cover note for 30 days from another insurance company. He was also in possession of a temporary cover note from his old insurance company, purporting to cover him from 6 April onwards. Allon used his car on a public road on 15 April. His conviction for driving without insurance (contrary to s 201 of the Road Traffic Act 1960) was confirmed by the Divisional Court. The court was prepared to treat the extension of insurance cover (from 6 April) by the first company as an offer to Allon to renew his policy. Equally, it was prepared in principle to countenance the possibility of his use of the car as an acceptance of such an offer, despite the lack of any direct communication by him to the company. However, on the facts his own admission, he indicated that he had not intended to accept the offer:

Taylor v Allon [1966] 1 QB 304, p 311

Lord Parker CJ: Bearing in mind that a valid insurance for the purposes of the section must arise from an enforceable contract, it seems to me that the contract, if any, contained in the temporary covering note must arise by offer and acceptance. It is conceded that the policy that expired had no provisions for extended cover and, accordingly, this document sending this temporary cover note must, in my judgment, be treated as an offer to insure for the future. It may be, although I find it unnecessary to decide in this case, that there can be an acceptance of such an offer by conduct and without communication with the insurance company. It may well be, as it seems to me, that if a man took his motor car out on the road in reliance on this temporary cover, albeit that there had been no communication of that fact to the insurance company, there would be an acceptance, and that the contract so created would contain an implied promise by the insured to pay, either in the renewal premium when that was paid, or if it was not paid, for the period for which the temporary cover note had, as it were, been accepted.

---

39 [1966] 1 QB 304.

I find it unnecessary in the present case to decide that matter and, for this reason, that it seems to me that the defendant must at any rate go to the length of saying that he knew of the temporary cover and that he took out his motor car in reliance on it. In fact, as I have already said, the defendant never gave any evidence at all. Further, from the justices' clerk's notes which, again, we have been allowed to refer to, it appears that when he was stopped by the police and asked to produce his insurance certificate, he produced the old insurance certificate which expired on 5 April and he also produced the cover note from the new insurance company which commenced on 16 April. When the police pointed out that, therefore, on 15 April, he was not covered, he not only did not refer to the temporary cover note, but he said then that he had been negotiating a change of insurance companies and did not realise that it, presumably the original certificate, had run out. It was only at the hearing and, I think, at the second hearing, that this temporary cover note, this extended cover, was produced by the defendant's solicitor.

In those circumstances, it seems to me that the defendant has never gone to the length of showing that he knew of the temporary cover, that he acted in reliance on it and, thereby, had accepted the offer contained in it. I think that the justices came to a correct decision in law and I would dismiss this appeal.

In their own terms, judgments such as that of Lord Parker do not depart from conventional ideas of offer and acceptance. Instead, they import into the standard approach the notion of implied offers and acceptances, typically based on the conduct of the parties. The nature of the actions performed in the context in which they occur are such as implying promises to be bound, implying agreement. However, if reference is made to Atiyah, it can readily be argued that the key is the parties' performance – with consequential benefits and (detrimental) reliance.

The crucial authority in this area is undoubtedly the House of Lords decision in *Brogden v Directors of the Metropolitan Railway Co*.[40] Since 1870, Brogden had supplied the Metropolitan Railway Co with coal. In November 1871, Brogden proposed entering into a contract. After preliminary discussion, the railway company sent a draft form of the agreement to Brogden. Brogden filled in certain parts which had been left blank (including the name of the person to act as arbitrator in case of dispute), wrote 'approved' on the draft, signed it and sent it back to the railway company. The latter, without comment, retained the draft. No further formal execution of the contract took place. Subsequently, further supplies of coal were ordered and delivered and, from time to time (usually in case of dispute), reference was made to 'the contract'. Finally, disagreements arose between the parties, and Brogden denied that a binding contract existed.

The most instructive judgment in the House of Lords is that of Lord Blackburn:

---

40   (1877) 2 App Cas 666, HL.

Brogden v Directors of the Metropolitan Railway Co (1877) 2 App Cas 666, HL, p 690

Lord Blackburn: My Lords, in this case, the question which has now to be decided is, I believe, quite a question of fact, but part of what was said in the Court of Common Pleas would raise an important question of law if it were to be taken in a way in which it was not necessary for either Lord Coleridge or Mr Justice Brett to hold it, and in which, therefore, they both said, looking to the facts which had been found, they did not hold it. I wish to say upon that point that I cannot agree with what seems to be their view. Mr Justice Brett, referring to the case of *Ex p Harris* before the Lords Justices and other cases, says that, looking to all this, he has come 'to a strong opinion that the moment one party has made a proposition of terms to another and it can be shewn by sufficient evidence that that other has accepted those terms in his own mind, then the contract is made, before that acceptance is intimated to the proposer'. And he goes on to say, applying that to the present case, that, to his mind, as soon as Burnett put the letter into his drawer, a contract was made, although none was formally entered into.

My Lords, I must say that that is contrary to what my impression is, and that I cannot agree in it. If the law was as intimated by Mr Justice Brett, there would be nothing to discuss in the present case. But I have always believed the law to be this, that when an offer is made to another party and, in that offer, there is a request express or implied that he must signify his acceptance by doing some particular thing, then as soon as he does that thing, he is bound. If a man sent an offer abroad saying 'I wish to know whether you will supply me with goods at such and such a price and, if you agree to that, you must ship the first cargo as soon as you get this letter', there can be no doubt that, as soon as the cargo was shipped, the contract would be complete, and if the cargo went to the bottom of the sea, it would go to the bottom of the sea at the risk of the orderer. So, again, where, as in the case of *Ex p Harris,* a person writes a letter and says, 'I offer to take an allotment of shares' and he expressly or impliedly says, 'If you agree with me, send an answer by the post', there, as soon as he has sent that answer by the post, and put it out of his control, and done an extraneous act which clenches the matter, and shews beyond all doubt that each side is bound, I agree the contract is perfectly plain and clear.

But when you come to the general proposition which Mr Justice Brett seems to have laid down, that a simple acceptance in your own mind, without any intimation to the other party, and expressed by a mere private act, such as putting a letter into a drawer, completes a contract, I must say I differ from that. It appears from the Year Books that as long ago as the time of Edward IV, Chief Justice Brian decided this very point. The plea of the defendant in that case justified the seizing of some growing crops, because he said the plaintiff had offered him to go and look at them, and if he liked them, and would give 2s 6d for them, he might take them; that was the justification. That case is referred to in a book which I published a good many years ago, *Blackburn on Contracts of Sale,* and is there translated. Brian gives a very elaborate judgment, explaining the law of the unpaid vendor's lien, as early as that time, exactly as the law now stands, and he consequently says: 'This plea is clearly bad, as you have not shewn the payment or the tender of the money'; but he goes farther, and says (I am quoting from memory, but I think I am quoting correctly), 'moreover, your plea is utterly naught, for it does not shew that when you had made up your mind to take them you signified it to the plaintiff, and your having it in your own mind is nothing, for it is trite law that the thought of man is not triable, for even the devil does not know what the thought of man is; but I grant you this, that if in his offer to you he had said, "Go and look at them, and if you are pleased with them signify it to such and such a man", and if you had signified it to such and such a man, your plea would have been good, because that was a matter of fact.'

I take it, my Lords, that that which was said 300 years ago and more is the law to this day, and it is quite what Lord Justice Mellish in *Ex p Harris* accurately says that, where it is expressly or impliedly stated in the offer that you may accept the offer by posting a letter, the moment you post the letter, the offer is accepted. You are bound from the moment you post the letter, not, as it is put here, from the moment you make up your mind on the subject.

But my Lords, while, as I say, this is so upon the question of law, it is still necessary to consider this case farther upon the question of fact. I agree, and I think every judge who has considered the case does agree, certainly Lord Chief Justice Cockburn does, that though the parties may have gone no farther than an offer on the one side, saying, 'Here is the draft' (for that I think is really what this case comes to) and the draft so offered by the one side is approved by the other, everything being agreed to except the name of the arbitrator, which the one side has filled in and the other has not yet assented to, if both parties have acted upon that draft and treated it as binding, they will be bound by it. When they had come so near as I have said, still it remained to execute formal agreements, and the parties evidently contemplated that they were to exchange agreements, so that each side should be perfectly safe and secure, knowing that the other side was bound. But, although that was what each party contemplated, still I agree (I think the Lord Chief Justice Cockburn states it clearly enough), 'that, if a draft having been prepared and agreed upon as the basis of a deed or contract to be executed between two parties, the parties, without waiting for the execution of the more formal instrument, proceed to act upon the draft, and treat it as binding upon them, both parties will be bound by it. But it must be clear that the parties have both waived the execution of the formal instrument and have agreed expressly, or as shewn by their conduct, to act on the informal one'.

I think that is quite right and I agree with the way in which Mr Herschell in his argument stated it, very truly and fairly. If the parties have, by their conduct, said, that they act upon the draft which has been approved of by Mr Brogden, and which if not quite approved of by the railway company, has been exceedingly near it, if they indicate by their conduct that they accept it, the contract is binding.

(Lord Blackburn went on to express some reservations about whether contractual intent had been made out on the facts, but finally concurred in the unanimous decision of the House that a binding contract did exist.)

The case has continued to generate controversy; at the very least it is proof positive that a contract can be discovered despite incomplete execution of a formalised contract, the court placing primary reliance on parties' conduct. However, does it illustrate, perhaps even prove, the Atiyah thesis, or is it an unusual (if not wholly exceptional) case to be confined largely to its own facts? Certainly, it can be made to fit the conventional offer and acceptance model; Metropolitan's sending of the draft amounting to an offer, Brogden's 'variations' and return of the draft equalling a counter-offer and the placing of orders by Metropolitan (on the implicit basis of the varied draft) amounting to an acceptance of the counter-offer.[41] On the other hand, in *Trentham v Archital Luxfer*,[42] Steyn LJ firmly places the emphasis on the fact of performance and the (consequential) legitimate expectations of the parties, rather than any implication of assent:

> In a case where the transaction was fully performed, the argument that there was no evidence upon which the judge could find that a contract was proved is implausible. A contract can be concluded by conduct. Thus, in *Brogden v Metropolitan Railway* ... decided in 1877, the House of Lords concluded in a case in which the parties had asked in accordance with an unsigned draft agreement for the delivery of coal that there was a contract on the basis of the draft. That inference was drawn from the performance in accordance with the terms of the draft agreement ...

What is clear from Lord Blackburn's judgment is that some conduct or performance is required to conclude a contract, a merely passive assent will not suffice. As it is often put, silence is not acceptance. This is illustrated in *Felthouse v Bindley*.[43] A and B, verbally agreed for the purchase of a horse by A from B. A few days afterwards, B wrote to A, saying that he had been informed that there was a misunderstanding as to the price, A having imagined that he had bought the horse for £30, B that he had sold it for 30 guineas. A thereupon wrote to B proposing to split the difference, adding 'If I hear no more about him, I consider the horse is mine at £30 15 s'. To this, no reply was sent. No money was paid and the horse remained in B's possession. Six weeks afterwards, the defendant, an auctioneer who was employed by B to sell his farming stock and who had been directed by B to reserve the horse in question as it had already been sold, mistakenly put it up with the rest of the livestock and sold it. After the sale, B wrote to A a letter which substantially amounted to an acknowledgment that the horse had been sold to him.

At both first instance and on appeal, it was held that the plaintiff could not succeed against the defendant auctioneer in the tort of conversion, because ownership in the horse had not resided in the plaintiff at the relevant time,

---

41 Alternative constructions are possible, for example, that the placing of orders by Metropolitan amounted to a further counter-offer, accepted by Brogden in delivering the coal.

42 [1993] 1 Lloyd's Rep 25, CA, p 29.

43 (1863) 142 ER 1037.

there being no binding contract between the plaintiff and B concerning the sale of the horse. The case is complicated by the fact that, at that time, s 4 of the Statute of Frauds 1677 specified that a contract for the sale of goods for £10 or more needed to be either accompanied by a memorandum in writing or some form of delivery or part payment. It was the failure to satisfy s 4 which largely led to the Exchequer Chamber to uphold the first instance decision. However, at first instance, the point concerning the need for some manifestation of acceptance does emerge clearly. For example, *per* Willes J:

Felthouse v Bindley (1863) 142 ER 1037, p 1039

Willes J: I am of opinion that the rule to enter a nonsuit should be made absolute. The horse in question had belonged to the plaintiffs' nephew, John Felthouse. In December 1860, a conversation took place between the plaintiff and his nephew relative to the purchase of the horse by the former. The uncle seems to have thought that he had on that occasion bought the horse for £30, the nephew that he had sold it for 30 guineas: but there was clearly no complete bargain at that time. On the 1 January 1861, the nephew writes, – 'I saw my father on Saturday. He told me that you considered that you had bought the horse for £30. If so, you are labouring under a mistake, for 30 guineas was the price I put upon him, and you never heard me say less. When you said you would have him, I considered you were aware of the price.' To this the uncle replies on the following day, 'Your price, I admit, was 30 guineas. I offered £30; never offered more: and you said the horse was mine. However, as there may be a mistake about him, I will split the difference. If I hear no more about him, I consider the horse mine at £30 15s'. It is clear that there was no complete bargain on the 2 January: and it is also clear that the uncle had no right to impose upon the nephew a sale of his horse for £30 15s unless he chose to comply with the condition of writing to repudiate the offer. The nephew might, no doubt, have bound his uncle to the bargain by writing to him: the uncle might also have retracted his offer at any time before acceptance. It stood an open offer, and so, things remained until 25 February, when the nephew was about to sell his farming stock by auction. The horse in question being catalogued with the rest of the stock, the auctioneer (the defendant) was told that it was already sold. It is clear, therefore, that the nephew in his own mind intended his uncle to have the horse at the price which he (the uncle) had named – £30 15s, but he had not communicated such his intention to his uncle or done anything to bind himself. Nothing, therefore, had been done to vest the property in the horse in the plaintiff down to the 25 February, when the horse was sold by the defendant. It appears to me that, independently of the subsequent letters, there had been no bargain to pass the property in the horse to the plaintiff and, therefore, that he had no right to complain of the sale.

This passage is, clearly, open to serious criticism – to talk of the uncle 'imposing' a sale on his nephew is surely a misuse of language. Of course, offerees need protection from less than scrupulous offerors – it would clearly be wrong to infer assent from silence or activity, unless the evidence is very clear that the offeree did intend to enter into a contract[44] However, where it is clear that the offeree does have such an intention (as was surely the case in *Felthouse*), an inflexible rule that silence is not acceptance is hard to justify. In the US, the *Restatement of Contracts*[45] takes the approach that:

> ... where an offeree fails to reply to an offer his silence and inaction operate as an acceptance ... where the offeror has stated or given the offeree reason to understand that assent may be manifested by silence or inaction and the offeree in remaining silent or inactive intends to accept the offer.

It must be said, however, that the conventional view that silence alone will not suffice continues, in this country, to be reflected in judicial decisions.[46]

Acceptance in unilateral contracts

In this area, at least, there is not even the pretence of promise-based agreement (at least not on the part of the offeree). As Bowen LJ in *Carlill v Carbolic Smoke Ball Co* illustrates very clearly, the essence of the acceptance required by the offeree lies in performance of the task(s) specified by the offeror. The willingness of the courts to countenance the unilateral contract exception has provided opportunities to avoid difficulties that would be caused by a more conventional form of contract, but has also caused problems – particularly in integrating unilateral contracts within the normal rules.

A good example of the opportunities opened up by unilateral contracts came in *Daulia Ltd v Four Millbank Nominees Ltd*.[47] The plaintiff wished to buy certain properties which the first defendants were in a position to sell as mortgagees. The plaintiff claimed that there was an oral agreement that the first defendants would exchange contracts for the sale of the properties if the plaintiff attended at the first defendants' offices with a draft contract in the terms already agreed and a banker's draft for the amount of the deposit. The plaintiff duly attended at the first defendants' offices but the first defendants refused to exchange contracts. The plaintiff claimed damages for breach of the oral agreement.

In the event, the plaintiff's action failed in that there was no 'note or memorandum' in writing as (then) required by s 40(1) of the Law of Property Act 1925, nor was there a sufficient act of part performance. However, the Court of Appeal thought that, but for this, the claim would have succeeded.

---

44 As, eg, where goods are sent to someone unsolicited (often termed inertia selling) it would be quite wrong to infer a willingness to purchase them by the offeree, merely from the latter's failure to respond. The unwilling customer's position in this respect is now strengthened further by the Unsolicited Goods and Services Act 1971.

45 See para 72.

46 Eg, the Court of Appeal decision in *Palmer v Metropolitan Borough of Sandwell* [1987] 20 HLR 74.

47 [1978] 2 WLR 623, CA.

The point appears most clearly in the judgment of Goff LJ:

Daulia Ltd v Four Millbank Nominees Ltd [1978] 2 WLR 623, CA, p 624

Goff LJ: I therefore turn to the first question. Was there a concluded unilateral contract by the first defendants to enter into a contract for sale on the agreed terms? The concept of a unilateral or 'if contract' is somewhat anomalous, because it is clear that, at all events until the offeree starts to perform the condition, there is no contract at all, but merely an offer which the offeror is free to revoke.

Doubts have been expressed whether the offeror becomes bound so soon as the offeree starts to perform or satisfy the condition, or only when he has fully done so.

In my judgment, however, we are not concerned in this case with any such problem, because, in my view, the plaintiff had fully performed or satisfied the condition when they presented themselves at the time and place appointed with a banker's draft for the deposit, and their part of the written contract for sale duly engrossed and signed and there tendered the same, which I understand to mean proffered it for exchange. Actual exchange, which never took place, would not in my view have been part of the satisfaction of the condition but something additional which was inherently necessary to be done by the plaintiffs to enable, not to bind, the first defendants to perform the unilateral contract.

Accordingly, in my judgment, the answer to the first question must be in the affirmative.

Even if my reasoning so far be wrong, the conclusion in my view is still the same for the following reasons. Whilst I think the true view of a unilateral contract must, in general, be that the offeror is entitled to require full performance of the condition which he has imposed and short of that he is not bound, that must be subject to one important qualification, which stems from the fact that there must be an implied obligation on the part of the offeror not to prevent the condition becoming satisfied, which obligation it seems to me must arise as soon as the offeree starts to perform. Until then, the offeror can revoke the whole thing but, once the offeree has embarked on performance, it is too late for the offeror to revoke his offer.

It was clearly far more appropriate to view the plaintiff as having acquired a right (subject to s 40) to conclude final contracts for the properties, rather than viewing them as having already concluded such a contract by attending. The concept of the unilateral contract fulfils this obvious need.

However, the case also illustrates one potential difficulty with acceptance in such situations. Conventionally, any offer can be revoked before it is unconditionally accepted. At what point does an offer of a unilateral contract become irrevocable? Strict logic might suggest that this will only be when the conditions are fulfilled – after all, until then, neither side is conclusively bound, the offeror's promise(s) being conditional on all his conditions being met. However, by this point, the offeree may well have legitimate expectations that the offer will not be revoked – not least because of the substantial degree of detrimental reliance he may have incurred (particularly so when the offer is of a reward for performing potentially time consuming and expensive tasks). Goff LJ (above) indicates that the courts are likely to regard the offer as irrevocable[48] once performance has commenced (whether on the basis of a secondary implied contract or otherwise). This would also seem to follow from the case of *Errington v Errington and Woods*.[49] A father, wishing to provide a home for his son, who had recently married, purchased a dwelling-house through a building society, paying a lump sum and leaving the balance on mortgage to be paid by weekly instalments. He retained the conveyance in his own name and paid the rates, but promised that if the son and daughter-in-law continued in occupation and duly paid the instalments until the last one was paid, he would then transfer the property to them. When the father died, he, by his will, left all his property, including the house in question, to his widow. Up to that time, the son and the son's wife had together occupied the dwelling-house and paid the instalments, but the son then left his wife and went to live with his widowed mother. The wife continued to occupy the dwelling-house and to pay the instalments.

The mother brought an action for possession against the daughter-in-law. At first instance, and on appeal, the action was dismissed. Amongst other points, the Court of Appeal held that the father had made the offer of a unilateral contract to his son and daughter-in-law which was irrevocable by him once payment of the mortgage instalments had commence:

Errington v Errington and Woods [1952] 1 KB 290, CA, p 295

Denning LJ: It is to be noted that the couple never bound themselves to pay the instalments to the building society; and I see no reason why such obligation should be implied. It is clear law that the court is not to imply a term unless it is necessary; and I do not see that it is necessary here. Ample content is given to the whole arrangement by holding that the father promised that the house should belong to the couple as soon as they paid off the mortgage. The parties did not discuss what was to happen if the couple failed to pay the instalments to the building society, but I should have thought it clear that, if they did fail to pay the instalments, the father would not be bound to transfer the house to them. The father's promise was a unilateral contract – a promise of the house in return for their act of paying the instalments. It could not be revoked by him once the couple entered on performance of the act, but it would cease to bind if they left it incomplete and unperformed, which they

---

48 It is normally assumed that such offers can be revoked by the offeror giving her change of heart equivalent publicity to that given to the original offer. English authority on the point is scarce, but see the US Supreme Court case of *Shuey v US* (1875) 92 US 73.

49 [1952] 1 KB 290, CA.

have not done. If that was the position during the father's lifetime, so it must be after his death. If the daughter-in-law continues to pay all the building society instalments, the couple will be entitled to have the property transferred to them as soon as the mortgage is paid off; but if she does not do so, then the building society will claim the instalments from the father's estate and the estate will have to pay them. I cannot think that, in those circumstances, the estate would be bound to transfer the house to them any more than the father himself would have been.

Acceptance by the post

At the beginning of this, it was stated that one of the normal criteria for a valid acceptance is that it must have been communicated to and received by the offeror. The fact that this criterion is not is not applied universally is seen again in relation to contracts which take place via the medium of the post. At its simplest, since *Adams v Lindsell*,[50] English law has adopted a rule that an acceptance via the post is valid from the moment of posting, not merely from when the letter is received by the offeror. In *Household Fire Insurance Co v Grant*,[51] this was said to still be the case, even though the letter of acceptance never arrives at all.[52]

The standard 'post rule' is subject to a number of qualifications. For example, to take advantage of the special 'dispensation' which the rule confers, the offeree must at least make sure that the letter is posted (for example, into an appropriate post box, through a mailroom, into the hands of a post office employee authorised to receive mail and so on).[53] Also, it must be inherently reasonable to use the post as a mode of acceptance, which would appear to eliminate the application of the rule from situations when the offer indicates (expressly or impliedly) that time is 'of the essence' or when (to the knowledge of the offeree) there is likely to be significant delay in the post.[54]

In essence, the post rule appears to rest more on commercial convenience than on logic – the offeree should be entitled to assume that a deal is closed once a letter is placed into the post and an offeror can always debar the use of the post if the risk element involved appears too great.[55]

---

50 (1818) 1 B & Ald 681

51 (1879) 4 Ex D 216

52 For an examination of the post rule in an international context, see Winfield, 1939, pp 505–15; and Evans, 1966.

53 For a good illustration of the need for effective posting, see *Re London and Northern Bank ex p Jones* [1900] 1 Ch 220.

54 The issue of 'reasonableness' is demonstrated clearly in the case of *Henthorn v Fraser* [1892] 2 Ch 27.

55 In Gardner, 1992, Simon Gardner places the origins of the rule in mid-Victorian confidence at the efficiency of the postal services – in effect as soon as a letter was posted it was as good as delivered!

Thesiger J appears to reach this conclusion in *Household Fire Insurance Co v Grant*:[56]

Household Fire Insurance Co v Grant (1879) 4 Ex D 216, pp 223–24

Thesiger J: There is no doubt that the implication of a complete, final and absolutely binding contract being formed as soon as the acceptance of an offer is posted may, in some cases, lead to inconvenience and hardship. But such there must be at times in every view of the law. It is impossible in transactions which pass between parties at a distance and have to be carried on through the medium of correspondence to adjust conflicting rights between innocent parties, so as to make the consequences of mistake on the part of a mutual agent fall equally upon the shoulders of both. At the same time, I am not prepared to admit that the implication in question will lead to any great or general inconvenience or hardship. An offerer, if he chooses, may always make the formation of the contract which he proposes dependant upon the actual communication to himself of the acceptance. If he trusts to the post, he trusts to a means of communication which, as a rule, does not fail, and if no answer to his offer is received by him, and the matter is of importance to him, he can make inquiries of the person to whom the offer was addressed. On the other hand, if the contract is not finally concluded, except in the event of the acceptance actually reaching the offerer, the door would be opened to the perpetration of much fraud, and, putting aside this consideration, considerable delay in commercial transactions, in which despatch is, as a rule, of the greatest consequence, would be occasioned; for the acceptor would never be entirely safe in acting upon his acceptance until he had received notice that his letter of acceptance had reached its destination.

If this is true, it follows that a rule based on implicit convenience must give way to the express intentions and desires of the parties. In effect, it should be possible to exclude the post rule whilst still retaining the post as a means of communication. This view received some support from the case of *Holwell Securities v Hughes*.[57] Here, Holwell was granted an option by Hughes over his house in north London. The option stated that it should be 'exercisable by notice in writing' to Hughes 'at any time within six months' (the time limit to expire on 19 April). In error, Holwell's solicitor sent the letter taking up the option to Hughes' solicitor, rather than Hughes personally. A copy was prepared for despatch to Hughes. This would (by the 'back door') have been a valid exercise of the option. However, despite evidence of it being typed and sent to the mail room it was never received by Hughes. Holwell claimed that the post rule could be invoked, so as to establish a binding contract despite the failure of the letter to reach its destination. The Court of Appeal rejected this, holding that, even if the copy letter had been posted (which was not clear), the

---

56 (1879) 4 Ex D 216, pp 223–24.
57 [1974] 1 WLR 155, CA.

requirement that the option be 'exercisable by notice in writing' was fatal to the invocation of the post rule. The court's thinking emerged clearly from the following passage from the judgment of Russell LJ:

Holwell Securities v Hughes [1974] 1 WLR 155, CA, p 157

Russell LJ: It is the law in the first place that *prima facie* acceptance of an offer must be communicated to the offeror. On this principle, the law has engrafted a doctrine that if, in any given case, the true view is that the parties contemplated that the postal service might be used for the purpose of forwarding an acceptance of the offer, committal of the acceptance in a regular manner to the postal service will be acceptance of the offer so as to constitute a contract, even if the letter goes astray and is lost. Nor, as was once suggested, are such cases limited to cases in which the offer has been made by post. It suffices, I think, at this stage to refer to *Henthorn v Fraser*. In the present case, as I read a passage in the judgment below, Templeman J concluded that the parties here contemplated that the postal service might be used to communicate acceptances of the offer (by exercise of the option); and I agree with that.

But that is not and cannot be the end of the matter. In any case, before one can find that the basic principle of the need for communication of acceptance to the offeror is displaced by this artificial concept of communication by the act of posting, it is necessary that the offer is, in its terms, consistent with such displacement and not one which, by its terms, points rather in the direction of actual communication.

The relevant language here is, 'The said option shall be exercisable by a notice in writing to the Intending Vendor ...', a very common phrase in an option agreement. There is, of course, nothing in that phrase to suggest that the notification to the defendant could not be made by post. But the requirement of the 'notice ... to', in my judgment, is language which should be taken expressly to assert the ordinary situation in law that acceptance requires to be communicated or notified to the offeror, and is inconsistent with the theory that acceptance can be constituted by the act of posting, referred to by Anson as 'acceptance without notification'.

It is, of course, true that the instrument could have been differently worded. An option to purchase within a period given for value has the characteristic of an offer that cannot be withdrawn. The instrument might have said 'The offer constituted by this option may be accepted in writing within six months': in which case, no doubt the posting would have sufficed to form the contract. But that language was not used and, as indicated, in my judgment, the language used prevents that legal outcome. Under this head of the case, the hypothetical problems were canvassed to suggest difficulties in the way of that conclusion. What if the letter had been delivered through the letter box of the house in due time, but the defendant had either deliberately or fortuitously not been there to receive it before the option period expired? This does not persuade me that the artificial posting rule is here applicable. The answer might well be that in the circumstances the defendant had impliedly invited communication by use of an orifice in his front door designed to receive communications ...

Accordingly, I would dismiss the appeal and Buckley LJ authorises me to say that he agrees with the judgment I have delivered.

It is not hard to detect a degree of hostility to (or at least scepticism about) the functioning of the post rule in the above passage. Moreover, although the post rule was initially extended to telegrams (a now largely defunct point), whenever the courts have been asked to extend the rule to more modern forms of communication, they have refused. The cases largely turn on the use of the telex, but it is highly likely that the same approach would be adopted as regards such media as the fax and electronic mail. The logic of the refusal to extend the rule has normally been seen as resting on the relative immediacy of the telex and the consequent reduction in problems caused by delay, but it can be argued that there is an inherent judicial unwillingness to extend the post rule beyond its 19th century boundaries. In 1955, the Court of Appeal held that a telexed acceptance was only valid when received (the case involved a dispute over whether a contract was made in London, from where the telex was sent, or in Amsterdam where it was received. The court held the latter):

Entores Ltd v Miles Far East Corpn [1955] 2 QB 327, CA, p 332

Denning LJ: The question for our determination is: Where was the contract made?

When a contract is made by post, it is clear law throughout the common law countries that acceptance is complete as soon as the letter of acceptance is put into the post box, and that is the place where the contract is made. But there is no clear rule about contracts made by telephone or by telex. Communications by these means are virtually instantaneous and stand on a different footing.

The problem can only be solved by going in stages. Let me first consider a case where two people make a contract by word of mouth in the presence of one another. Suppose, for instance, that I shout an offer to a man across a river or a courtyard but I do not hear his reply because it is drowned by an aircraft flying overhead. There is no contract at that moment. If he wishes to make a contract, he must wait till the aircraft is gone and then shout back his acceptance so that I can hear what he says. Not until I have his answer am I bound. I do not agree with the observations of Hill J in *Newcomb v De Roos* (2 E & E, p 275).

Now I take a case where two people make a contract by telephone. Suppose, for instance, that I make an offer to a man by telephone and, in the middle of his reply, the line goes dead so that I do not hear his words of acceptance. There is no contract at that moment. The other man may not know the precise moment when the line failed. But he will know that the telephone conversation was abruptly broken off, because people usually say something to signify the end of the conversation. If he wishes to make a contract, he must therefore get through again as to make sure that I heard. Suppose next that the line does not go dead, but it is nevertheless so indistinct that I do not catch what he says and I ask him to repeat it. He then repeats it and I hear his acceptance. The contract is made, not on the first time when I do not hear, but only the second time when I do hear. If he does not repeat it, there is no contract. The contract is only complete when I have his answer accepting the offer.

Lastly, take the telex. Suppose a clerk in a London office taps out on the teleprinter an offer which is immediately recorded on a teleprinter in a Manchester office, and clerk at that end taps out an acceptance. If the line goes dead in the middle of the sentence of acceptance, the teleprinter motor will stop. There is then obviously no contract. The clerk, at Manchester must get through again and send his complete sentence. But it may happen that the line does not go dead, yet the message does not get through to London. Thus the clerk at Manchester may tap out his message of acceptance and it will not be recorded in London because the ink at the London end fails or something of that kind. In that case the Manchester clerk will not know of the failure but the London clerk will know of it and will immediately send back a message 'not receiving'. Then, when the fault is rectified, the Manchester clerk will repeat his message. Only then is there a contract. If he does not repeat it, there is not contract. It is not until his message is received that the contract is complete.

In all the instances I have taken so far, the man who sends the message of acceptance knows that it has not been received or he has reason to know it. So, he must repeat it. But suppose that he does not know that his message did not get home. He thinks it has. This may happen if the listener on the telephone does catch the words of acceptance, but nevertheless does not trouble to ask for them to be repeated: or if the ink on the teleprinter fails at the receiving end, but the clerk does not ask for the message to be repeated: so that the man who sends an acceptance reasonably believes that his message has been received. The offeror in such circumstances is clearly bound, because he will be estopped from saying that he did not receive the message of acceptance. It is his own fault that he did not get it. But if there should be a case where the offeror without any fault on his part does not receive the message of acceptance – yet the sender of it reasonably believes it has got home when it has not – then I think there is no contract.

My conclusion is that the rule about instantaneous communications between the parties is different from the rule about the post. The contract is only complete when the acceptance is received by the offeror: and the contract is made at the place where the acceptance is received.

Applying the principles which I have stated, I think that the contract in this case was made in London where the acceptance was received. It was therefore a proper case for service out of the jurisdiction.

In a broadly similar dispute (save that the parties were this time in London and Vienna), the House of Lords in 1982 approved and applied *Entores*. *Brinkibon Ltd v Stahag Stahl*[58] illustrates the thinking of the House of Lords and include (in the passage from Lord Wilberforce's judgment) some cautionary remarks:

Brinkibon Ltd v Stahag Stahl [1983] 2 AC 34, p 41

Lord Wilberforce: The first of these alternatives raises the question whether an acceptance by telex sent from London but received in Vienna causes a contract

---

58 [1983] 2 AC 34, p 41.

to be made in London, or in Vienna. If the acceptance had been sent by post, or by telegram, then, on existing authorities, it would have been complete when put into the hands of the post office – in London. If, on the other hand, it had been telephoned, it would have been complete when heard by the offeror – in Vienna. So, in which category is a telex communication to be placed? Existing authority of the Court of Appeal decides in favour of the latter category, that is, a telex is to be assimilated to other methods of instantaneous communication: see *Entores Ltd v Miles Far East Corpn* [1955] 2 QB 327. The appellants ask that this case, which has stood for 30 years, should now be reviewed.

Now such review as is necessary must be made against the background of the law as to the making of contracts. The general rule, it is hardly necessary to state, is that a contract is formed when acceptance of an offer is communicated by the offeree to the offeror. And if it is necessary to determine where a contract is formed (as to which I have already commented) it appears logical that this should be at the place where acceptance is communicated to the offeror. In the common case of contracts, where oral or in writing *inter praesentes*, there is no difficulty; and again logic demands that even where there is not mutual presence at the same place and at the same time, if communication is instantaneous, for example, by telephone or radio communication, the same result should follow.

Then there is the case – very common – of communication at a distance, to meet which the so called 'postal rule' has developed. I need not trace its history: it has firmly been in the law at least since *Adams v Lindsell* (1818) 1 B & Ald 681. The rationale for it, if left somewhat obscure by Lord Ellenborough CJ, has since been well explained. Mellish LJ in *In re Imperial Land Co of Marseilles (Harris' Case)* (1872) LR 7 Ch App 587, p 594 ascribed it to the extraordinary and mischievous consequences which would follow if it were held that an offer might be revoked at any time until the letter accepting it had been actually received: and its foundation in convenience was restated by Thesiger LJ in *Household Fire and Carriage Accident Insurance Co Ltd v Grant* (1879) 4 ExD 216, 223. In these cases too it seems logical to say that the place, as well as the time, of acceptance should be where (as when) the acceptance is put into the charge of the post office.

In this situation, with a general rule covering instantaneous communication *inter praesentes*, or at a distance, with an exception applying to non-instantaneous communication at a distance, how should communications by telex be categorised? In *Entores Ltd v Miles Far East Corpn* [1955] 2 QB 327, the Court of Appeal classified them with instantaneous communications. Their ruling, which has passed into the textbooks, including *Williston on Contracts*, 3rd edn (1957), appears not to have caused either adverse comment, or any difficulty to business men. I would accept it as a general rule. Where the condition of simultaneity is met, and where it appears to be within the mutual intention of the parties that the contractual exchanges should take place in this way, I think it a sound, but not necessarily a universal rule.

Since 1955, the use of telex communication has been greatly expanded and there are many variations on it. The senders and recipients may not be the principals to the contemplated contract. They may be servants or agents with limited authority. The message may not reach, or be intended to reach, the designated recipient immediately: messages may be sent out of office hours, or at night, with the intention, or upon the assumption, that they will be read at a later time. There may be some error or default at the recipient's end which prevents receipt at the time contemplated and believed in by the sender. The message may have been sent and/or received through machines operated by third persons. And many other variations may occur. No universal rule can cover all such cases: they must be resolved by reference to the intentions of the parties, by sound business practice and in some cases by a judgment where the risks should lie: see *Household Fire and Carriage Accident Insurance Co Ltd v Grant*, 4 ExD 216, p 227 *per* Baggallay LJ and *Henthorn v Fraser* [1892] 2 Ch 27 *per* Lord Herschell.

The present case is, as *Entores Ltd v Miles Far East Corpn* [1955] 2 QB 327 itself, the simple case of instantaneous communication between principals, and, in accordance with the general rule, involves that the contract (if any) was made when and where the acceptance was received. This was on 4 May 1979, in Vienna.

Lord Fraser: My Lords, I am in full agreement with the reasoning of my noble and learned friends, Lord Wilberforce and Lord Bradon of Oakbrook. I wish only to add a comment on the subject of where a contract is made, when it is made by an offer accepted by telex between parties in different countries. The question is whether acceptance by telex falls within the general rule that it requires to be notified to the offeror in order to be binding, or within the exception of the postal rule whereby it becomes binding when (and where) it is handed over to the post office. The posting rule is based on considerations of practical convenience, arising from the delay that is inevitable in delivering a letter. But it has been extended to apply to telegrams sent through the post office, and in strict logic there is much to be said for applying it also to telex messages sent by one business firm to another. There is very little, if any, difference in the mechanisms of transmission between a private telex from one business office to another, and a telegram sent through the post office – especially one sent from one large city to another. Even the element of delay will not be greatly different in the typical case where the operator of the recipient's telex is a clerk with no authority to conclude contracts, who has to hand it to his principal. In such a case a telex message is not in fact received instantaneously by the responsible principal. I assume that the present case is not of that sort.

Nevertheless I have reached the opinion that, on balance, an acceptance sent by telex directly from the acceptor's office to the offeror's office should be treated as if it were an instantaneous communication between principals, like a telephone conversation. One reason is that the decision to that effect in *Entores Ltd v Miles Far East Corpn* [1955] 2 QB 327 seems to have worked without leading to serious difficulty or complaint from the business community. Secondly, once the message has been received on the offeror's telex machine, it is not unreasonable to treat it as delivered to the principal offeror, because it is his responsibility to arrange for prompt handling of messages within his own office. Thirdly, a party (the acceptor) who tries to send a message by telex can generally tell is his message has not been received on the other party's (the offeror's) machine, whereas the offeror, of course, will not know if an unsuccessful attempt has been made to send an acceptance to him. It is therefore convenient that the acceptor, being in the better position, should have the responsibility of ensuring that his message is received. For these reasons, I think it is right that in the ordinary simple case, such as I take this to be, the general rule and not the postal rule should apply.

If it is assumed that the post rule has no direct application to the telex (and so on), the question remains as to when such a communication is received. The point is dealt with somewhat obliquely in *Brinkibon*[59] and, more directly, in *The Brimnes*,[60] albeit in the context of the effectiveness of a purported repudiation of a contract. The *prima facie* rule appears to be that such a message is valid when received on their machine (even if not seen until some time later). This is, however, subject to the condition that the message is sent during what the offeror can reasonably assume to be the normal business hours of the offeror. If sent outside these hours, it will only be received, at the earliest, at the start of the next business day.

The 'battle of the forms'

The standard model of acceptance and contract negotiation referred to throughout this section works best when a contract under scrutiny is individually negotiated. In such a situation (particularly if the parties negotiate on an approximately equal footing and have some knowledge of each other's typical business practices), it is relatively realistic to conceptualise the process in terms of offers, counter-offers, rejections and so on (although even here, the model is open to criticism for want of flexibility). However, where, as is increasingly common, the negotiations consist largely of the automatic exchange of *pro-formas* concerning (for example) orders and the acceptance of orders, with the parties standard terms printed on the back, does it make sense to adopt the standard model? The issue came to a head interestingly, if ultimately inconclusively, in the 1979 Court of Appeal case of *Butler Machine Tool Co Ltd v Ex-Cell-O Corpn (England) Ltd*.[61] On 23 May 1969, the plaintiff sellers offered to deliver a machine tool for the price of £75,535. Delivery was to be in 10 months and it was a condition that orders were accepted only on the terms set out in the quotation which were to prevail over any terms in the buyers' order. The sellers' terms included a price variation

---

59   See, eg, in the passage from Lord Wilberforce's judgment, p 158, above.
60   [1975] 1 QB 929.
61   [1979] 1 WLR 401, CA

clause whereby it was a condition of acceptance that goods would be charged at prices ruling at the date of delivery. The defendant buyers replied on 27 May 1969, giving an order with differences from the sellers' quotation and with their own terms and conditions, which had no price variation clause. The order had a tear-off acknowledgment for signature and return which accepted the order 'on the terms and conditions thereon'. On 5 June 1969, the sellers, after acknowledging receipt of the order on 4 June, returned the acknowledgment form duly completed with a covering letter stating that delivery was to be 'in accordance with our revised quotation of 23 May for delivery in ... March/April 1970'.

The machine was ready by about September 1970, but the buyers could not accept delivery until November 1970. The sellers invoked the price increase clause and claimed £2,892 for the increase due to the rise in costs between 27 May 1969 and 1 April 1970, when the machine should have been delivered. Thesiger J gave judgment for the sellers for £2,892 and interest. The buyers appealed.

The Court of Appeal unanimously reversed the first instance decision, all three judges feeling that the conclusive act was the sellers' return of the tear-off acknowledgment slip. However, the reasons given by the judges for arriving at their decision differed. Bridge LJ and Lawton LJ broadly applied the standard model of 'offer – counter-offer – acceptance' to this 'battle of the forms', although both of them were clearly aware of the difficulties that this would cause. Lord Denning's approach, not untypically, ranged much more widely. Unlike the other two judges, who can be seen to adopt a broadly 'last shot' theory (that is, that the 'battle' is won by the person who submits their terms last), Lord Denning was prepared to countenance a number of other possibilities. The following passages serve to indicate these divergences in approach:

Butler Machine Tool Co Ltd v Ex-Cell-O Corpn (England) Ltd [1979] 1 WLR 401, CA, p 402

Lawton LJ: The modern commercial practice of making quotations and placing orders with conditions attached, usually in small print, is indeed likely, as in this case to produce a 'battle of the forms'. The problem is how should that battle be conducted? The view taken by Thesiger J was that the battle should extend over a wide area and the court should do its best to look into the minds of the parties and make certain assumptions. In my judgment, the battle has to be conducted in accordance with set rules. It is a battle more on classical 18th century lines, when convention decided who had the right to open fire first rather than in accordance with the modern concept of attrition.

The rules relating to a battle of this kind have been known for the past 130 odd years. They were set out by Lord Langdale MR in *Hyde v Wrench* (1840) 3 Beav 334, p 337, to which Lord Denning MR has already referred; and, if anyone should have thought they were obsolescent, Megaw J in *Trollope & Colls Ltd v Atomic Power Constructions Ltd* [1963] 1 WLR 333, p 337 called attention to the fact that those rules are still in force.

When those rules are applied to this case, in my judgment, the answer is obvious. The sellers started by making an offer. That was in their quotation. The small print was headed by the following words 'General. All orders are accepted only upon and subject to the terms set out in our quotation and the following conditions. These terms and conditions shall prevail over any terms and conditions in the buyer's order'.

That offer was not accepted. The buyers were only prepared to have one of these very expensive machines on their own terms. Their terms had very material differences in them from the terms put forward by the sellers. They could not be reconciled in any way. In the language of Art 7 of the Uniform Law on the Formation of Contracts for the International Sale of Goods (see Sched 2 of the Uniform Laws on International Sales Act 1967), they did 'materially alter the terms' set out in the offer made by the plaintiff.

As I understand *Hyde v Wrench* (1840) 3 Beav 334, and the cases which have followed, the consequence of placing the order in that way, if I may adopt Megaw J's words [1963] 1 WLR 333, p 337, was 'to kill the original offer'. It follows that the court has to look at what happened after the buyers made their counter-offer. By letter dated 4 June 1969, the plaintiff acknowledged receipt of the counter-offer, and they went on in this way: 'Details of this order have been passed to our Halifax works for attention and a formal acknowledgment of order will follow in due course.'

That is clearly a reference to the printed tear-off slip which was at the bottom of the buyer's counter-offer. By letter dated 5 June 1969, the sales office manager at the plaintiffs' Halifax factory completed that tear-off slip and sent it back to the buyers.

It is true, as Mr Scott had reminded us, that the return of that printed slip was accompanied by a letter which had this sentence in it: 'This is being entered in accordance with our revised quotation of 23 May for delivery in 10/11 months.' I agree with Lord Denning MR that, in a business sense, that refers to the quotation as to the price and to the identity of the machine, and it does not bring into the contract the small print conditions on the back of the quotation. Those small print conditions had disappeared from the story. That was when the contract was made. At that date, it was a fixed price contract without a price escalation clause.

As I pointed out in the course of argument to Mr Scott, if the letter of 5 June accompanied the form acknowledging the terms which the buyers had specified had amounted to a counter-offer then, in my judgment, the parties never were ad idem. It cannot be said that the buyers accepted the counter-offer by reason of the fact that ultimately they took physical delivery of the machine, they had made it clear by correspondence that they were not accepting that there was any price escalation clause in any contract which they had made with the plaintiff.

I agree with Lord Denning MR that this appeal should be allowed.

Bridge LJ: The first offer between the parties here was the plaintiff sellers' quotation dated 23 May 1969. The conditions of sale in the small print on the back of that document, as well as embodying the price variation clause, to which reference has been made in the judgments already delivered, embodied a number of other important conditions. There was a condition providing that orders should in no circumstances be cancelled without the written consent of the sellers and should only be cancelled on terms which indemnified the sellers against loss. There was a condition that the sellers should not be liable for any loss or damage from delay however caused. There was a condition purporting to limit the sellers' liability for damage due to defective workmanship or materials in the goods sold. And there was a condition providing that the buyers should be responsible for the cost of delivery.

When one turns from that document to the buyers' order of 27 May 1969, it is perfectly clear not only that that order was a counter-offer but that it did not purport in any way to be an acceptance of the terms of the sellers' offer dated 23 May. In addition, when one compares the terms and conditions of the buyers' offer, it is clear that they are in fact contrary in a number of vitally important respects to the conditions of sale in the sellers' offer. Amongst the buyers' proposed conditions are conditions that the price of the goods shall include the cost of delivery to the buyers' premises; that the buyers shall be entitled to cancel for any delay in delivery; and a condition giving the buyers a right to reject if on inspection the goods are found to be faulty in any respect.

The position then was, when the sellers received the buyers' offer of 27 May, that that was an offer open to them to accept or reject. They replied in two letters dated 4 and 5 June respectively. The letter of 4 June was an informal acknowledgment of the order, and the letter of 5 June enclosed the formal acknowledgment, as Lord Denning MR and Lawton LJ have said, embodied in the printed tear-off slip included in the order itself and including the perfectly clear and unambiguous sentence 'We accept your offer on the terms and conditions stated thereon'. On the face of it, at that moment of time, there was a complete contract in existence, and the parties were ad idem as to the terms of the contract embodied in the buyers' order.

Mr Scott has struggled manfully to say that the contract concluded on those terms and conditions was in some way overruled or varied by the references in the two letters dated 4 and 5 June to the quotation of 23 May 1969. The first refers to the machinery being as quoted on 23 May. The second letter says that the order has been entered in accordance with the quotation of 23 May. I agree with Lord Denning MR and Lawton LJ that that language has no other effect than to identify the machinery and to refer to the prices quoted on 23 May. But on any view, at its highest, the language is equivocal and wholly ineffective to override the plain and unequivocal terms of the printed acknowledgment of order which was enclosed with the letter of 5 June. Even if that were not so and if Mr Scott could show that the sellers' acknowledgment of the order was itself a further counter-offer, I suspect that he would be in considerable difficulties in showing that any later circumstance amounted to an acceptance of that counter-offer in the terms of the original quotation of 23 May by the buyers. But I do not consider that question further because I am content to rest upon the view that there is nothing in the letter of 5 June which overrides the plain effect of the acceptance of the order on the terms and conditions stated thereon.

I too would allow the appeal and enter judgment for the defendants.

Lord Denning MR: This case is a 'battle of the forms'. The plaintiff, the Butler Machine Tool Co Ltd, suppliers of a machine, on 23 May 1969, quoted a price for a machine tool of £75,535. Delivery was to be given in 10 months. On the back of the quotation, there were terms and conditions. One of them was a price variation clause. It provided for an increase in the price if there was an increase in the costs and so forth. The machine tool was not delivered until November 1970. By that time costs had increased so much that the sellers claimed an additional sum of £2,892 as due to them under the price variation clause.

The defendant buyers, Ex-Cell-O Corpn (England) Ltd, rejected the excess charge. They relied on their own terms and conditions. They said: 'We did not accept the sellers' quotation as it was. We gave an order for the self-same machine at the self-same price, but on the back of our order, we had our own terms and conditions. Our terms and conditions did not contain any price variation clause.'

The judge held that the price variation clause in the sellers' form continued through the whole dealing and so the sellers were entitled to rely upon it. He was clearly influenced by a passage in *Anson's Law of Contract*, 24th edn (1975), pp 37 and 38, of which the editor is Professor Guest: and also by Treitel, *The Law of Contract*, 4th edn (1975), p 15. The judge said that the sellers did all that was necessary and reasonable to bring the price variation clause to the notice of the buyers. He thought that the buyer would not 'browse over the conditions' of the sellers: and then, by printed words in their (the buyers') document, trap the sellers into a fixed price contract.

I am afraid that I cannot agree with the suggestion that the buyers 'trapped' the sellers in any way. Neither party called any oral evidence before the judge. The case was decided on the documents alone. I propose therefore to go through them.

On 23 May 1969, the sellers offered to deliver one 'Butler' double column plane-miller for the total price of £75,535. Delivery 10 months (subject to confirmation at time of ordering), other terms and conditions are on the reverse of this quotation. On the back, there were 16 conditions in small print, starting with this general condition: 'All orders are accepted only upon and subject to the terms set out in our quotation and the following conditions. These terms and conditions shall prevail over any terms and conditions in the buyer's order.'

Clause 3 was the price variation clause. It said: 'Prices are based on present day costs of manufacture and design and having regard to the delivery quoted and uncertainty as to the cost of labour, materials, etc, during the period of manufacture, we regret that we have no alternative but to make it a condition of acceptance of order that goods will be charged at prices ruling upon date of delivery.'

The buyers replied on 27 May 1969, giving an order in these words: 'Please supply on terms and conditions as below and overleaf.' Below there was a list of the goods ordered, but there were differences from the quotation of the sellers in these respects: (i) there was an additional item for the cost of installation, £3,100; and (ii) there was a different delivery date – instead of 10 months, it was 10–11 months.

Overleaf, there were different terms as to the cost of carriage: in that it was to be paid to the delivery address of the buyers: whereas the sellers' terms were ex-warehouse. There were different terms as to the right to cancel for late delivery. The buyers in their conditions reserved the right to cancel if delivery was not made by the agreed date: whereas the sellers in their conditions said that cancellation of order due to late delivery would not be accepted.

On the foot of the buyers' order there was a tear-off slip headed: 'Acknowledgment: Please sign and return to Ex-Cell-O. We accept your order on the terms and conditions stated thereon – and undertake to deliver by – Date – signed.' In that slip the delivery date and signature were left blank ready to be filled in by the sellers.

On 5 June 1969, the sellers wrote this letter to the buyers: 'We have pleasure in acknowledging receipt of your official order dated 27 May covering the supply of one Butler Double Column Plane-Miller. This being delivered in accordance with our revised quotation of 23 May for delivery in 10/11 months, that is, March/April 1970. We return herewith duly completed your acknowledgment of order form.'

They enclosed the acknowledgment form duly filled in with the delivery date March/April 1970 and signed by the Butler Machine Tool Co.

No doubt, a contract was then concluded. But on what terms? The sellers rely on their general conditions and on their last letter which said 'in accordance with our revised quotation of 23 May' (which had on the back the price variation clause). The buyers rely on the acknowledgment signed by the sellers which accepted the buyers' order 'on the terms and conditions stated thereon' (which did not include a price variation clause).

If those documents are analysed in our traditional method, the result would seem to me to be this: the quotation of 23 May 1969, was an offer by the sellers to the buyers containing the terms and conditions on the back. The order of 27 May 1969, purported to be an acceptance of that offer in that it was for the same machine at the same price, but it contained such additions as to cost of installation, date of delivery and so forth that it was in law a rejection of the offer and constituted a counter-offer. That is clear from *Hyde v Wrench* (1840) 3 Beav 334. As Megaw J said in *Trollope & Colls Ltd v Atomic Power Constructions Ltd* [1963] 1 WLR 333, p 337: '... the counter-offer kills the original offer.' The letter of the sellers of 5 June 1969 was an acceptance of that counter-offer, as is shown by the acknowledgment which the sellers signed and returned to the buyers. The reference to the quotation of 23 May referred only to the price and identity of the machine.

To go on with the facts of the case. The important thing is that the sellers did not keep the contractual date of delivery which was March/April 1970. The machine was ready about September 1970 but by that time the buyers' production schedule had to be rearranged as they could not accept delivery until November 1970. Meanwhile the sellers had invoked the price increase clause. They sought to charge the buyers an increase due to the rise in costs between 27 May 1969 (when the order was given), and 1 April 1970 (when the machine ought to have been delivered). It came to £2,892. The buyers rejected the claim. The judge held that the sellers were entitled to the sum of £2,892 under the price variation clause. He did not apply the traditional method of analysis by way of offer and counter-offer. He said that in the quotation of 23 May 1969, 'one finds the price variation clause appearing under a most emphatic heading stating that it is a term or condition that is to prevail'. So he held that it did prevail.

I have much sympathy with the judge's approach to this case. In many of these cases our traditional analysis of offer, counter-offer, rejection, acceptance and so forth is out of date. This was observed by Lord Wilberforce in *New Zealand Shipping Co Ltd v AM Satterthwaite & Co Ltd* [1975] AC 154, p 167. The better way is to look at all the documents passing between the parties – and glean from them, or from the conduct of the parties, whether they have reached agreement on all material points – even though there may be differences between the forms and conditions printed on the back of them.

As Lord Cairns said in *Brogden v Metropolitan Railway Co* (1877) 2 App Cas 666, p 672: '... there may be a consensus between the parties far short of a complete mode of expressing it, and that consensus may be discovered from letters or from other documents of an imperfect and incomplete description.'

Applying this guide, it will be found that in most cases when there is a 'battle of forms', there is a contract as soon as the last of the forms is sent and received without objection being taken to it. That is well observed in *Benjamin's Sale of Goods*, 9th edn (1974), p 84. The difficulty is to decide which form, or which part of which form, is a term or condition of the contract. In some cases the battle is won by the man who fires the last shot.

He is the man who puts forward the latest terms and conditions: and if they are not objected to by the other party, he may be taken to have agreed to them. Such was *British Road Services Ltd v Arthur V Crutchley & Co Ltd* [1968] 1 Lloyd's Rep 271, pp 281–82, *per* Lord Pearson; and the illustration given by Professor Guest in *Anson's Law of Contract*, 24th edn, pp 37 and 38, when he says that: '... the terms of the contract consist of the terms of the offer subject to the modifications contained in the acceptance. In some cases, the battle is won by the man who gets the blow in first. If he offers to sell at a named price on the terms and conditions stated on the back and the buyer orders the goods purporting to accept the offer – on an order form with his own different terms and conditions on the back – then if the difference is so material that it would affect the price, the buyer ought not to be allowed to take advantage of the difference unless he draws it specifically to the attention of the seller. There are yet other cases where the battle depends on the shots fired on both sides. There is a concluded contract but the forms vary. The terms and conditions of both parties are to be construed together. If they can be reconciled so as to give a harmonious result, all well and good. If differences are irreconcilable – so that they are mutually contradictory – then the conflicting terms may have to be scrapped and replaced by a reasonable implication.'

In the present case, the judge thought that the sellers in their original quotation got their blow in first: especially by the provision that 'these terms and conditions shall prevail over any terms and conditions in the buyer's order'. It was so emphatic that the price variation clause continued through all the subsequent dealings and that the buyers must be taken to have agreed to it. I can understand that point of view. But I think that the documents have to be considered as a whole. And, as a matter of construction, I think the acknowledgment of 5 June 1969 is the decisive document. It makes it clear that the contract was on the buyers' terms and not on the sellers' terms and the buyers' terms did not include a price variation clause.

I would therefore allow the appeal and enter judgment for the defendants.

As stated above, in some key respects, the case is inconclusive. However, it can be argued that there is, at least, a majority in favour of the last shot model as the general approach, and of the broad applicability of the standard 'offer – counter-offer – acceptance' criteria to the typical battle. Is this satisfactory? Are Lord Denning's alternative suggestions any more helpful? There has been extensive academic debate on the point.[62]

The problem is also one which is commonly found in other jurisdictions.[63] Indeed, the solution (or attempted solution) adopted by Sched 2 of the Uniform Law on International Sales Act 1967 featured in argument in Butler. The universality of the problems caused by these 'production line' contracts indicates that no solution is likely which would meet all objections. Nevertheless, academic objections to the standard approach (as exemplified by the majority judgments in the Court of Appeal in *Butler*) can be summarised as follows:

- it may encourage parties to exchange standardised documentation *ad infinitum* in the hope of firing the last shot;

- it is artificial in concentrating on implied counter-offers and acceptances rather than the reality of the extent to which performance under an assumed contract has already taken place;

- it can lead to arbitrary results – depending on how the last shot is construed. For example, in *Butler*, is it clear why the tear-off slip was uniformly seen as carrying more weight than the sellers' accompanying letter, which could be seen as contradicting it?

Numerous alternative suggestions have been made, ranging from a first shot approach (which would require the offeree to expressly bring any variations on the terms initially laid down by the offeror expressly to the offeror's attention) to Lord Denning's 'compromise contract' solution (which has the

---

62 Eg, Jacobs, 1985; McKendrick, 1988; Rawlings, 1979; Adams, 1979; and Adams (1980) JBL 298.

63 *Ibid*, Jacobs.

obvious weakness of separating out agreement 'in principle' from the detailed terms on which any such agreement will rest). It seems clear that the courts could fruitfully explore restitutionary principles[64] in this area when considerable work has been carried out under an assumed contract rather than struggle to find the last shot when the terms of the parties are diametrically opposed.[65] However, it may be that any model has flaws, but the standard model at least has the merits of relative simplicity. The issues are clearly summarised by John Adams:[66]

> The criticism of the traditional approach is that it encourages businessmen to fire salvoes at each other in the hope of firing the last shot, that it may put a party in an invidious position of either not performing or performing and by implication accepting the other's standard terms, and that it allows one party to withdraw even though the other might then have substantially performed. The main criticism of Lord Denning's approach is said to be that it will not discourage the firing of salvoes, that virtually any term can affect the price, and that terms are difficult to categorise. In practice, however, it is improbable that any rule will have much effect on the way businessmen operate. Fundamentally what is wrong with Lord Denning's approach is that, like ss 2–207 of the Uniform Commercial Code, it conflates the problem as to whether an 'acceptance' differing from the terms of the offer should amount to a rejection, with the problem as to whether there is a contact at all. In many cases it is reasonable to suppose that a differing 'acceptance' is not a rejection. Going on to the next step and recognising that there is a binding contract is quite something else, however. As Professor Waddams points out, there is a basic contradiction in holding that a definite expression of acceptance is an acceptance, even though it states terms additional to or different from those offered.
>
> It is also, however, implicit in Lord Denning's approach that each case is to be considered on its own merits: that there is no production line solution to the problems of these production line transactions. A detailed analysis of the facts of any given case will frequently, if not usually, point to a solution. It may, for example, be apparent in a 'one shot' deal that the parties had in fact contracted with one another before any standard forms came on the scene, that is, from an identifiable time both parties had started to behave as though they were in a contractual relationship with one another, suggesting that from their point of view the outlines of a deal were sufficiently filled out from that time. In this case it would be reasonable to conclude that a legally binding contract had come into existence, and the standard forms could thus be ignored. In other areas there may have been a course of dealing between the parties which may point to the basis on which it is reasonable to suppose they were contracting in

---

64 See McKendrick, 1988.

65 One interesting question related to this is the extent to which businessmen do read the small print and the degree to which they are likely to be aware of the variations in each other's standard terms (and possibly take advantage of this fact). Generally on this, see Beale and Dugdale, 1975, particularly at pp 48–51.

66 [1983] JBL 298.

the case in hand. On a more legalistic level, the counter-terms may be meaningless or trivially different. In such cases they may be ignored, especially where the problem is that a party is apparently attempting to seize on a breach of such a term as a way of escaping from the contract ...

Where parties are not agreed on the essential terms the only solution is to hold that no contract exists. Any recovery thereafter has to be based on restitution as in the unreported case of *British Steel Corpn v Cleveland Bridge Engineering Co Ltd*, or more controversially detrimental reliance ...

Any attempt to formulate a tidy set of answers to the problems raised by these production line contracts is likely to be futile. Each case needs to be looked at carefully on its own facts. Often the fairest result, as in the *Cleveland Bridge* case, will be achieved by holding that neither party's terms apply, and by dealing with the apportionment of compensation under the principles of restitution and reliance. In other cases, however, the course of dealings between the parties may indicate that in fact they are operating under a particular set of conditions. By contrast, in 'one shot' transactions, it may be obvious that the parties had entered into a contractual relationship before any question of a 'battle of the forms' arose. There are also, as noted above, other possibilities which may point to the solution in a given case.[67]

THE CONTENT OF AGREEMENTS

On the assumption that the process described above does broadly represent the true picture in English law as to how contracts come into being, the question remains what exactly are the parties agreeing to and to what terms and conditions they are binding themselves. It is normally assumed that in a conventional bilateral contract the exchange of promises which produces the contract also contains the reciprocal undertakings of the parties. On that basis, it might be thought that the law in this section would be relatively straightforward and uncontentious – largely a mechanical 'following through' of the basic rules of offer and acceptance. The reality is rather difficult; first, there is the usual tension between generalised theory and the need to produce workable law; secondly, there is the need for the courts to be wary that one party (perhaps via the small print of a written proposal) does not take advantage of the other. Unsurprisingly, even though the rules here are of general application, most of the key decisions are in the area of exemption changes where the potential for such abuse is particularly great.[68]

---

67   For further case law on the 'battle of the forms', see *British Road Services v Arthur V Crutchley* [1968] 1 All ER 811 (particularly at pp 816–17); *Transmotors Ltd v Robertson Buckley & Co* [1970] 1 Lloyd's Rep 224; and *OTM Ltd v Hydrancutics* [1981] 2 Lloyd's Rep 211.

68   A notable exception is *Interfoto v Stiletto* [1989] QB 433 (see below, p 78).

As regards written and signed contracts, the usual view is that the Divisional Court's decision in *L'Estrange v Graucob Ltd*[69] is conclusive. If so, the rule is that a person is bound by any contract to which they have appended their signature. The effect of signature (in the absence of fraud, duress, misrepresentation or a possible plea of *non est factum*) is seen as indicating assent to the terms proposed in the contract. In this case, the buyer of cigarette vending machine for use in a seaside café had signed a sales agreement (printed on brown paper!) in the presence of the representative of the seller. The machine did not work satisfactorily, and the buyer (Mrs L'Estrange) claimed damages for (*inter alia*) breach of an implied warranty that the machine was not fit for the purpose for which it was sold. The principal defence of the seller was that the sales agreement contained a clause expressly providing for the exclusion of all implied warranties. The buyer agreed that she had not read the agreement, and knew nothing of its content. Moreover, the clause excluding warranties could not easily be read, owing to the smallness of the print. The Divisional Court (Scrutton and Maugham LJJ) found in favour of the seller. In the words of Scrutton LJ (at p 404): 'In this case, the plaintiff has signed a document headed "Sales Agreement", which she admits had to do with an intended purchase and which contained a clause excluding all conditions and warranties. That being so, the plaintiff, having put her signature to the document and not having been induced to do so by any fraud or misrepresentation, cannot be heard to say that she is not bound by the terms of the document because she has not read them.'

The decision is often cited as an extreme instance of the courts' refusal to countenance any solution which limits parties' freedom to contract, however unjust the results.[70] It has been argued[71] that the decision flies in the face of a more general legal requirement that a person needs to consent to a disputed term to be bound by it. However, the normal view is that it does represent good (if somewhat debatable) law and that the required consent is to be inferred from the fact of signature if freely given. All this, of course, assumes that the writing is, at least, legible!

If the contract under scrutiny is not signed, the rules are more involved. In brief, a person is only bound by a term if she has been given reasonable notice of it (via a document which must be viewed as contractual) before or at the time of the formation of the contract, or if she has effective notice of it because of a previous consistent course of dealings.

---

69   [1934] 2 KB 394.

70   In *George Mitchell v Finney Lock Seeds Ltd* [1983] 1 QB 284, p 297, Lord Denning MR talked of it being part of a 'bleak winter for our law of contract'. Even at the time, it was described as 'a menace to the community' (CPA London 51 LQR 272).

71   Spencer, 1973.

As regards 'reasonable notice', the decision from which most of the law ultimately derives is *Parker v South Eastern Railway*.[72] The plaintiff deposited his bag in the cloakroom at the defendant's station. He paid 2 d and was given a ticket, on the face of which was printed the times at which the cloakroom was open and the words 'see back'. On the back was a clause stating that the company would not be responsible for any package exceeding the value of £10, and a placard to the same effect was hung in the cloakroom. The bag, which was worth more than £10, was lost or stolen, and the plaintiff claimed its value. The trial judge left two questions to the jury: (1) did the plaintiff read, or was he aware of, the special condition upon which the article was deposited?; (2) was the plaintiff, under the circumstances, under any obligation, in the exercise of reasonable and proper caution, to read or make himself aware of the condition? The jury answered both questions in the negative, and the judgment was directed for the plaintiff:

Parker v South Eastern Railway (1877) 2 CPD 416, CA, p 422

Mellish LJ: The question then is whether the plaintiff was bound by the conditions contained in the ticket. In an ordinary case, where an action is brought on a written agreement which is signed by the defendant, the agreement is proved by proving his signature, and, in the absence of fraud, it is wholly immaterial that he has not read the material and does not know its contents. The parties may, however, reduce their agreement into writing, so that the writing constitutes the sole evidence of the agreement, without signing it; but in that case there must be evidence independently of the agreement itself to prove that the defendant has assented to it. In that case, also, if it is proved that the defendant has assented to the writing constituting the agreement between the parties, it is, in the absence of fraud, immaterial that the defendant had not read the agreement and did not know its contents. Now if in the course of making a contract one party delivers to another a paper containing writing, and the party receiving the paper knows that the paper contains conditions that the party delivering intends to constitute the contract, I have no doubt that the party receiving the paper does, by receiving and keeping it, assent to the conditions contained in it, although he does not read them, and does not know what they are ... If the person receiving the ticket does not know that there is any writing upon the back of the ticket, he is not bound by a condition printed on the back ... the plaintiffs admitted that they knew there was writing on the back of the ticket, [but] they swore not only that they did not read it, but that they did not know or believe that the writing contained conditions ...

Now, I am of opinion that we cannot lay down, as a matter of law, either that the plaintiff was bound or that he was not bound by the conditions printed on the ticket, from the mere fact that he knew there was writing on the ticket, but did not know that the writing contained conditions. I think there may be cases

---

72   [1877] 2 CPD 416, CA.

in which a paper containing writing is delivered by one party to another in the course of a business transaction, where it would be quite reasonable that the party receiving it should assume that the writing contained in it no condition, and should put it in his pocket unread. For instance, if a person driving through a turnpike-gate received a ticket upon paying the toll, he might reasonably assume that the object of the ticket was that by producing it he might be free from paying toll at some other turnpike-gate, and might put it in his pocket unread. On the other hand, if a person who ships goods to be carried on a voyage by sea receives a bill of lading signed by the master, he would plainly be bound by it, although afterwards in an action against the shipowner for the loss of the goods, he might swear that he had never read the bill of lading, and that he did not know that it contained the terms of the contract of carriage, and that the shipowner was protected by the exceptions contained in it. Now the reason why the person receiving the bill of lading would be bound seems to me to be that in the great majority of cases persons shipping goods do know that the bill of lading contains the terms of the contract of carriage; and the shipowner, or the master delivering the bill of lading, is entitled to assume that the person shipping goods has that knowledge. It is, however, quite possible to suppose that a person who neither a man of business nor a lawyer might on some particular occasion ship goods without the least knowledge of what a bill of lading was, but, in my opinion, such a person must bear the consequences of his own exceptional ignorance, it being plainly impossible that business could be carried on if every person who delivers a bill of lading had to stop to explain what a bill of lading was.

Now the question we have to consider is whether the railway company were entitled to assume that a person depositing luggage and receiving a ticket in such a way that he could see that some writing was printed on it, would understand that the writing contained the conditions of contract, and this seems to me to depend upon whether people in general would in fact, and naturally, draw that inference. The railway company, as it seems to me, must be entitled to make some assumptions respecting the person who deposits luggage with them: I think they are entitled to assume that he can read, and that he undertakes the English language, and that he pays such attention to what he is about as may be reasonably expected from a person in such a transaction as that of depositing luggage in a cloak-room. The railway company must, however, take mankind as they find them, and if what they do is sufficient to inform people in general that the ticket contains conditions, I think that a particular plaintiff ought not to be in a better position than other persons on account of his exceptional ignorance or stupidity or carelessness. But if what the railway company do is not sufficient to convey to the minds of people in general that the ticket contains conditions, then they have received goods on deposit without obtaining the consent of the persons depositing them to the conditions limiting their liability. I am of opinion, therefore, that the proper direction to leave the jury in these cases is, that if the person receiving the ticket did not see or know that there was any writing on the ticket, he is not bound by the conditions; that if he knew there was writing, and knew or believed that the writing contained conditions, then he is bound by the conditions; that if he knew there was writing on the ticket, but did not know or believe that the writing contained conditions, nevertheless, he would be bound, if the delivering of the ticket to him in such a manner that he could see there was writing upon it, was, in the opinion of the jury, reasonable notice that the writing contained conditions.

(Baggallay LJ substantially agreed with Mellish LJ.)

Bramwell LJ: The plaintiffs have sworn that they did not know that the printing was the contract, and we must act as though that was true and we believed it, at least as far as entering the verdict for the defendants is concerned. Does this make any difference? The plaintiffs knew of the printed matter. Both admit they knew it concerned them in some way, though they said they did not know what it was; yet neither pretends that he knew or believed it was not the contract. Neither pretends he thought it had nothing to do with the business in hand; that he thought it was an advertisement or other matter unconnected with his deposit of a parcel at the defendants' cloak-room. They admit that, for anything they knew or believed, it might be, only they did not know or believe it was, the contract. Their evidence is very much that they did not think, or, thinking, did not care about it. Now they claim to charge the company, and to have the benefit of their own indifference. Is this just? Is it reasonable? Is it the way in which any other business is allowed to be conducted? Is it even allowed to a man to 'think', 'judge', 'guess', 'chance' a matter, without informing himself when he can, and then when his 'thought', 'judgment', 'guess' or 'chance' turns out wrong or unsuccessful, claim to impose a burden or duty on another which he could not have done had he informed himself as he might?

... Has not the giver of the paper a right to suppose that the receiver is content to deal on the terms in the paper? What more can be done? Must he say, 'Read that'? As I have said, he does so in effect when he puts it into the other's hands. The truth is, people are content to take these things on trust. They know that there is a form which is always used – they are satisfied it is not unreasonable, because people do not usually put unreasonable terms into their contracts. If they did, then dealing would soon be stopped. Besides, unreasonable practices would be known. The very fact of not looking at the paper shews that this confidence exists. It is asked: What if there was some unreasonable condition, as for instance to forfeit £1,000 if the goods were not removed in forty-eight hours? Would the depositor be bound? I might content myself by asking: Would he be, if he were told 'our conditions are on this ticket', and he did not read them? In my judgment, he would not be in either case. I think there is an implied understanding that there is no condition unreasonable to the knowledge or the party tendering the document and not insisting on it being read – no condition not relevant to the matter in hand. I am of opinion, therefore, that the plaintiffs, having notice of the printing, were in the same situation as though the porter had said, 'Read that, it concerns the matter in hand' that if the plaintiffs did not read it, they were as much bound as if they had read it and had not objected.

An order was made for a new trial.

The difficulty with the case is that although the court was unanimous in its decision (in effect, because the judge had misdirected the jury), there is clear divergence in opinion as to what the law should be; between Mellish LJ and Baggallay LJ on the one hand and Bramwell LJ on the other. The latter's robust views on the need for parties to look after their own interests would seem to leave little scope for judicial intervention.[73] In general, the law has developed more along the lines indicated by Mellish LJ. For example, the latter's point that some tickets might reasonably be regarded as mere receipts was applied in *Chapleton v Barry Urban District Council*,[74] in relation to the hire of a seaside deckchair.[75] The linked question of reasonableness of notice has featured in numerous decisions, the courts taking a particularly hard line on any attempt to introduce into the equation subjective matters such as illiteracy or lack of experience (the 'reasonable man' in this context appears to be akin to a rather cautious lawyer!). Moreover, where standard terms are perceived by the courts to be in the public domain – their existence being a matter (supposedly) of common knowledge and experience, it may be very hard to argue that unawareness of the terms was reasonable. These points are illustrated in the notorious case of *Thompson v London, Midland and Scottish Railway Co.*[76]

The plaintiff (who could not read) acquired, through her niece, a day excursion ticket from Darwen to Manchester. On her return to Darwen, she suffered injuries through the defendant's negligence. The basis of the defence was a standard condition contained in the company's timetable which excluded liability for any injury, however caused.[77] The front and back of the excursion ticket had, in combination, stated that tickets were issued subject to the conditions to be found in the timetable. The Court of Appeal found that reasonable notice had been given despite Mrs Thompson's illiteracy.[78] The following passage from the judgment of Lord Hanworth MR indicates the court's thinking:

---

73 Atiyah notes (in 1979, pp 374–80) that Bramwell was acknowledged even amongst his contemporaries for having strong views on self reliance.

74 [1940] 1 KB 532

75 The line between a 'mere receipt' and a 'contractual document' is notoriously difficult to draw. Which side of the line would, for example, a cloakroom ticket lie? Perhaps more fundamentally, it can be argued that rather than being a wholly independent principle the 'voucher or receipt' argument is merely a facet of the 'reasonable notice' requirement.

76 [1930] 1 KB 41, CA.

77 Of course such a clause would now be void, in any event, under the Unfair Contract Terms Act 1977, s 2(1).

78 Another part of the 'bleak winter' – *per* Lord Denning MR in *George Mitchell v Finney Lock Seeds Ltd* [1983] 1 QB 284. Arguably, the situation would be different if the person reliant on the clause knew, or ought to have known, that the person he was dealing with was illiterate, or did not understand English, see *Geier v Kujawa West and Warne Bros (Transport)* [1970] Lloyd's Rep 364.

Thompson v London, Midland and Scottish Railway Co [1930] 1 KB 41, CA, p 46

Lord Hanworth MR: Dealing with the condition, I must just say a word or two more as to its nature. The ticket issued to the plaintiff had in plain and unmistakable terms in type as large as the other words upon the face of the ticket: 'Excursion, For conditions see back'. There is no difficulty in reading those words any more than there is a difficulty in reading the words 'Third Class' or 'Manchester' down below. Then on the back of the ticket is printed also in type, which if small is easily legible: 'Issued subject to the conditions and regulations of the company's timetables and notices and excursion and other bills. Return as per bill.' In the timetable at p 552, there is this condition, which is relied upon and which I have read. The condition on the back makes the first reference to the company's timetables, but it also refers to notices and excursion and other bills. In the excursion bills, which contain some notes as to the tickets to be issued and the charges to be made and the dates on which passengers can travel at a single fare for a double journey, there is a reference to the conditions and the inquirer is directed to the timetable. Ultimately, therefore, the timetable is the place where this particular condition is found. Any person who took the trouble to follow out the plain and legible words on the ticket 'See Conditions' would be directed without difficulty to the source of the conditions and would be able to find it. Obviously, persons who are minded to go for a day journey of this sort do not take the trouble to make an examination of all the conditions, but two things are plain, first, that any person who takes this ticket is conscious that there are some conditions on which it is issued and, also, secondly, that it is priced at a figure far below the ordinary price charged by the railway company, and from that it is a mere sequence of thought that one does not get from the railway company the ticket which they provide at the higher figure of 5s 4d.

The plaintiff in this case cannot read; but, having regard to the authorities, and the condition of education in this country, I do not think that avails her in any degree. The ticket was taken for her by her agent. The time of the train was ascertained for her by Miss Aldcroft's father and he had made the specific inquiry in order to see at what time and under what circumstances there was an excursion train available for the intending travellers. He ascertained, therefore, and he had the notice put before him before ever the ticket was taken, that there were conditions on the issue of excursion and other reduced-fare tickets ...

It appears to me important to bear in mind that we are dealing with a special contract made for a special transit by an excursion train. We are not dealing with the ordinary schedule of trains available to everyone at the usual rate. We are dealing with a particular transit, in respect of which the father of Miss Aldcroft went down to the station to know if and when such transit was available, and ascertained both the time and the price; and he could have learned all the conditions if he had been so minded.

What was certainly clear from all these cases was that a set of conditions was to be treated as one entity, in respect of which reasonable notice was (or was not) given. In general, the courts resisted any notion that certain terms (perhaps because of their harsh or one-sided nature) might have to have special attention drawn to them (perhaps by being in large print or being printed in red).[79] Not for the first time, Lord Denning was the first judge to question this seriously, initially in *J Spurling Ltd v Bradshaw*,[80] where he stated 'Some clauses I have seen would need to be printed in red ink on the face of the document with a red hand pointing to it before the notice could be held to be sufficient'. He reiterated these views on numerous occasions, perhaps most graphically in *Thornton v Shoe Lane Parking*.[81] However, wider judicial support for his view was lacking until the decision of the Court of Appeal in *Interfoto Picture Library Ltd v Stiletto Visual Programmes Ltd*.[82]

The plaintiffs ran a photographic transparency lending library. Following a telephone inquiry by the defendants, the plaintiffs delivered to them 47 transparencies, together with a delivery note containing nine printed conditions. Condition 2 stipulated that all the transparencies had to be returned within 14 days of delivery; otherwise a holding fee of £5 a day and value added tax would be charged for each transparency retained thereafter. The defendants, who had not used the plaintiffs' services before, did not read the conditions and returned the transparencies four weeks later whereupon the plaintiffs invoiced the defendants for £3,783.50. The defendants refused to pay and the plaintiffs brought an action to recover that sum. The judge gave judgment in favour of the plaintiffs for the amount claimed.

This decision was overturned by the Court of Appeal who held, *inter alia*, that the unusual and one-sided nature of the clause in question had made it incumbent on the plaintiff to do more than they had done to bring it to the defendants' attention. Instead, they could only recover on a *quantum meruit* for the retention of the transparencies – a sum equivalent to that generally charged in the trade:[83]

---

79 Although Lawrence LJ in *Thompson* [1930] 1 KB 41, CA, p 53 did refer to the condition as 'a reasonable condition, which need not have special attention directed to it' – perhaps implying that an 'unreasonable condition' might require such attention. Sankey LJ (at p 56) even suggested that a wholly unreasonable condition might be void.

80 [1956] 1 WLR 461.

81 [1971] 2 QB 163.

82 [1989] QB 433.

83 Bingham LJ ranges even more widely – in somewhat Denning-like fashion! – [1989] QB 433, p 439 – seeing the courts' stringent notice requirement for unexpected or onerous terms as in a pragmatic common law equivalent of the widespread civil law requirement of good faith in contracting. Of course the common law has never felt able to take the further step of simply declaring an 'unreasonable' term to be void, although this may well be the position on occasions under Unfair Contract Terms Act 1977, ss 2(1), 6(2) and 7(2). For further discussion of this, see Chapters 7 and 8.

Interfoto Picture Library Ltd v Stiletto Visual Programmes Ltd [1989] QB 433, p 434

Dillon LJ: There was never any oral discussion of terms between the parties before the contract was made. In particular, there was no discussion whatever of terms in the original telephone conversation when Mr Beeching made his preliminary inquiry. The question is therefore whether Condition 2 was sufficiently brought to the defendants' attention to make it a term of the contract which was only concluded after the defendants had received, and must have known that they had received the transparencies and the delivery note.

This sort of question was posed, in relation to printed conditions in the ticket cases, such as *Parker v South Eastern Railway Co* (1877) 2 CPD 416 in the last century. At that stage, the printed conditions were looked at as a whole and the question considered by the courts was whether the printed conditions as a whole had been sufficiently drawn to the to a customer's attention to make the whole set of conditions part of the contract; if so the customer was bound by the printed conditions even though he had never read them.

More recently the question has been discussed whether it is enough to look at a set of printed conditions as a whole. When for instance one condition in a set is particularly onerous does something special need to be done to draw customers' attention to that particular condition? In an *obiter dictum* in *J Spurling Ltd v Bradshaw* [1956] 1 WLR 461, p 466 (cited in *Chitty on Contracts*, 25th edn, 1983, Vol 1, p 408), Denning LJ stated: 'Some clauses which I have seen would need to be printed in red ink on the face of the document with a red hand pointing to it before the notice could be held to be sufficient.'

Then in *Thornton v Shoe Lane Parking Ltd* [1971] 2 QB 163, both Lord Denning MR and Megaw LJ held as one of their grounds of decision, as I read their judgments, that where a condition is particularly onerous or unusual, the party seeking to enforce it must show that condition, or an unusual condition of that particular nature, was fairly brought to the notice of the other party. Lord Denning MR, at pp 169H–70D, restated and applied what he had said in the *Spurling* case, and held that the court should not hold any man bound by such a condition unless it was drawn to his attention in the most explicit way. Megaw LJ deals with the point, at pp 172–73, where he said: 'I agree with Lord Denning MR that the question here is of the particular condition on which the defendants seek to rely, and not of the conditions in general. When the conditions sought to be attached all constitute, in Lord Dunedin's words [in *Hood v Anchor Line (Henderson Brothers) Ltd*] [1918] AC 846, p 847, "the sort of restriction ... that is usual", it may not be necessary for a defendant to prove more than that the intention to attach some conditions has been fairly brought to the notice of the other party. But at least where the particular condition relied on involves a sort of restriction that is not shown to be usual in that class of contract, a defendant must show that his intention to attach an unusual condition of that particular nature was fairly brought to the notice of the other party. How much is required as being, in the words of Mellish LJ [in *Parker v South Eastern Railway Co*] 2 CPD 416, p 424, "reasonably sufficient to give the plaintiff notice of the condition" depends upon the nature of the restrictive condition.

In the present case, what has to be sought in answer to the third question is whether the defendant company did what was reasonable fairly to bring to the notice of the plaintiff, at or before the time when the contract was made, the existence of this particular condition. This condition is that part of the clause – a few words embedded in a lengthy clause – which Lord Denning MR has read, by which, in the midst of provisions as to damage to property, the defendants sought to exempt themselves from liability for any personal injury suffered by the customer while he was on their premises. Be it noted that such a condition is one which involves the abrogation of the right given to a person such as the plaintiff by statute, the Occupiers' Liability Act 1957. True, it is open under that statute for the occupier of property by a contractual term to exclude that liability. In my view, however, before it can be said that a condition of that sort, restrictive of statutory rights, has been fairly brought to the notice of a party to a contract there must be some clear indication which would lead an ordinary sensible person to realise that, at or before the time of making the contract, that a term of that sort, relating to personal injury, was sought to be included. I certainly would not accept that the position has been reached today in which it is to be assumed as a matter of general knowledge, custom, practice, or whatever is the phrase that is chosen to describe it, that when one is invited to go upon the property of another for such purposes as garaging a car, a contractual term is normally included that if one suffers any injury on those premises as a result of negligence on the part of the occupiers of the premises they shall not be liable.'

Counsel for the plaintiffs submits that *Thornton v Shoe Lane Parking Ltd* [1971] 2 QB 613 was a case of an exemption clause and that what their Lordships said must be read as limited to exemption clauses and in particular exemption clauses which would deprive the party on whom they are imposed of statutory rights. But what their Lordships said was said by way of interpretation and application of the general statement of the law by Mellish LJ in *Parker v South Eastern Railway Co*, 2 CPD 416, pp 423–24 and the logic of it is applicable to any particular onerous clause in a printed set of conditions of the one contracting party which would not be generally known to the other party.

Condition 2 of these plaintiffs' conditions is in my judgment a very onerous clause. The defendants could not conceivably have known, if their attention was not drawn to the clause, that the plaintiffs were proposing to charge a 'holding fee' for the retention of the transparencies at such a very high and exorbitant rate.

At the time of the ticket cases in the last century, it was notorious that people hardly ever troubled to read printed conditions on a ticket or delivery note or similar document. That remains the case now. In the intervening years, the printed conditions have tended to become more and more complicated and more and more one sided in favour of the party who is imposing them, but the other parties, if they notice that there are printed conditions at all, generally still tend to assume that such conditions are only concerned with ancillary matters of form and are not of importance. In the ticket cases, the courts held that the common law required that reasonable steps be taken to draw the other party's attention to the printed conditions or they would not be part of the contract. It is, in my judgment, a logical development of the common law into modern conditions that it should be held, as it was in *Thornton v Shoe Lane Parking Ltd* [1971] 2 QB 163, that, if one condition in a set of printed conditions is particularly onerous or unusual, the party seeking to enforce it must show that the particular condition was fairly brought to the attention of the other party.

In the present case, nothing whatsoever was done by the plaintiffs to draw the defendants' attention particularly to Condition 2; it was merely one of the four columns' width of conditions printed across the foot of the delivery note. Consequently Condition 2 never, in my judgment, became part of the contract between the parties.

I would therefore allow this appeal and reduce the amount of the judgment which the judge awarded against the defendants to the amount which he would have awarded on a quantum meruit on his alternative findings, that is, the reasonable charge of £3.50 per transparency per week for the retention of the transparencies beyond a reasonable period, which he fixed at 14 days from the date of their receipt by the defendants.

Of course, in all this discussion of 'reasonableness' of notice, it must never be forgotten that the notice must be given in time. A notice which is given only after the contract has been concluded is of no effect. This point is central to many of the decisions mentioned above – in *Thornton*, the contract was seen as complete the moment the barrier lifted,[84] so that, quite apart from the question of reasonableness the ticket came too late to have legal effect, whereas in *Thompson*, the contract was viewed as still incomplete at the moment of the issue of the ticket.[85] The point is graphically illustrated in *Olley v Marlborough Court Ltd*,[86] where the plaintiff was not bound by a disclaiming notice in her hotel bedroom when she made the contract earlier at the reception desk.

As stated above, a final alternative method of incorporation of terms and conditions is via a course of dealings. The idea underlying this is that, although on the occasion in question no notice may have been given, previous dealings between the parties on the same conditions should have put the other party on notice that the conditions in question were the normal basis for

---

84 See, eg, Lord Denning MR [1971] 1 WLR 589: '... the offer was accepted when Mr Thornton drove up to the entrance and, by the movement of his car, turned the light from red to green, and the ticket was thrust at him. The contract was then concluded and it could not be altered by any words printed on the ticket itself ...'

85 This is particularly controversial but consistent with the other, 'ticket' cases, eg, *Alexander v Railway Executive* [1951] 2 KB 882; *Hood v Anchor Line* [1918] AC 837; *Henderson v Stevenson* (1875) LR 2 SC & Div 470; and *Sugar v London Midland Scottish* [1941] 1 All ER 172. The offer is clearly seen as being made by the railway company leaving matters open for final acceptance or rejection by the customer. Would this apply even if the advertising did not refer to the restriction?

86 [1949] 1 KB 532.

contracting. It appears that for this principle to operate, the course of dealings needs to be long, continuous and consistent.[87] It also seems implicit in the cases that it is considerably easier to advance this argument in a commercial context rather than a consumer one (where it is far less reasonable to assume that information in the small print would put someone on guard).[88]

MISTAKE AND MISUNDERSTANDING
IN AGREEMENT FORMATION

It was indicated at the beginning of this chapter that (whatever the precise meaning of contract) the common law adopts a broadly objective test as to contract formation. It follows from this that merely because one party mistakenly believes some fact of the contract (for example, the precise nature of the subject matter) to be other than it is, this will not invalidate the existence of a contract, unless (at the very least) this mistake was so obvious as to be objectively apparent. A classic illustration of this is the well known case of *Smith v Hughes*,[89] which concerned the sale of oats believed by the buyer to be old – but which the seller knew to be new. Cockburn LJ sums up the general judicial approach:

Smith v Hughes (1871) LR 6 QB 597, p 606

Cockburn LJ: It only remains to deal with an argument which was pressed upon us, that the defendant in the present case intended to buy old oats and the plaintiff to sell new, so the two minds were not *ad idem*; and that, consequently, there was no contract. This argument proceeds on the fallacy of confounding what was merely a motive operating on the buyer to induce him to buy with one of the essential conditions of the contract. Both parties were agreed as to the sale and purchase of this particular parcel of oats. The defendant believed the oats to be old, and was thus induced to agree to buy them, but he omitted to make their age a condition of the contract. All that can be said is that the two minds were not *ad idem* as to the age of the oats; they certainly were *ad idem* as to the sale and purchase of them. Suppose a person were to buy a horse without a warranty, believing him to be sound, and the horse turns out unsound, could it be contended that it would be open to him to say that, as he had intended to buy a sound horse and the seller to sell an

---

87 The lack of sufficient length, or consistency appears to be the basis of the decisions in *Hollier v Rambler Motors Ltd* [1972] 2 QB 71 (three or four transactions in five years not sufficient) and *McCutcheon v David Macbrayne Ltd* [1964] 1 WLR 125 (the parties contracted sometimes on one set of terms, and sometimes on another). On the other side of the line, see *Hardwick Game Farm v Suffolk Agricultural Poultry Producers Association* [1969] 2 AC 31 (three or four contracts a month for three years was held to be sufficient).

88 This seems implicit, at least, in the *McCutcheon* and *Hollier* decisions, above.

89 (1871) LR 6 QB 597.

unsound one, the contract was void, because the seller must have known from the price the buyer was willing to give, or from his general habits as a buyer of horses, that he thought the horse was sound? The cases are exactly parallel.

A case normally seen as illustrating a mistake which would have been apparent to a reasonable person is *Raffles v Wichelhaus*.[90, 91] The parties agreed on the sale and purchase of 125 bales of cotton, to arrive '*ex Peerless* from Bombay'. In fact, there were two ships named Peerless sailing from Bombay that autumn, one in October and one in December. The defendant argued that he had intended only to purchase deliveries from the October *Peerless*, whereas the plaintiff argued that he had only had the December ship in mind. The Court of Exchequer found in favour of the defendant:

Raffles v Wichelhaus (1864) 159 ER 375

Milward (in support of the demurer): The contract was for sale of a number of bales of cotton of a particular description, which the plaintiff was ready to deliver. It is immaterial by what ship the cotton was to arrive, so that it was a ship called the *Peerless*. The words 'to arrive *ex Peerless*', only mean that if the vessel is lost on the voyage, the contract is to be at an end. [Pollock CB. It would be a question for the jury whether both parties meant the same ship called the *Peerless*.] That would be so if the contract was for the sale of a ship called the *Peerless*; but it is for the sale of cotton on board a ship of that name. [Pollock CB. The defendant only bought that cotton which was to arrive by a particular ship. It may as well be said, that if there is a contract for the purchase of certain goods in a warehouse A, that is satisfied by the delivery of goods of the same description in warehouse B.] In that case there would be goods in both warehouses; here it does not appear that the plaintiff had any goods on board the other *Peerless*. [Martin B: It is imposing on the defendant a contract different from that which he entered into.] [Pollock CB: It is like a contract for the purchase of wine coming from a particular estate in France or Spain, where there are two estates of that name.] The defendant has no right to contradict by parol evidence a written contract good upon the face of it. He does not impute misrepresentation or fraud, but only says that he fancied the ship was a different one. Intention is of no avail, unless stated at the time of the contract. [Pollock CB: One vessel sailed in October and the other in December. The time of sailing is no part of the contract.]

Mellish: There is nothing on the face of the contract to show that any particular ship called the *Peerless* was meant; but the moment it appears that two ships called the *Peerless* were about to sail from Bombay there is a latent ambiguity, and parol evidence may be given for the purpose of showing that the defendant meant one *Peerless* and the plaintiff another. That being so, there

---

90   (1864) 159 ER 375.

91   For further discussion of 'mutual' agreement mistake, see *Frederick E Rose Ltd v William Pim Ltd* [1953] 2 QB 450 and for a good modern illustration of the principles in action, see *Centrovincial Estate plc v Merchant Investors Assurance Co Ltd* [1983] Com LR 158, CA.

was no *consensus ad idem,* and therefore no binding contract. He was then stopped by the court.

Per curiam. There must be judgment for the defendants.[92]

The likelihood of such a finding (based on what is often termed a 'mutual' mistake) is greater when the mistake of one party has been 'triggered' by some conduct of the other (even if there is no finding that the other intended or was even aware of the error). A good illustration of this is *Scriven Bros & Co v Hindley & Co.*[93]

The plaintiff instructed an auctioneer to sell by auction a number of bales of hemp and of tow. The goods were described in the auctioneer's catalogue as so many bales in different lots with the same shipping marks and without disclosing the difference in the commodities. Before the sale, samples of the hemp and tow were on view in a showroom on the floor of which the catalogue numbers of the lots of hemp and tow were marked in chalk opposite the respective samples, and the defendants' manager examined the hemp but not the tow, as he was not intending to bid for tow. When the lots representing the tow were put up for sale in the auction room, the defendants' buyer made a bid which was an extravagant price for tow, and the lots were at once knocked down to him.

In an action against the defendants for the price of the tow, the jury found that the auctioneer intended to sell tow; that the defendants' buyer intended to bid for hemp; that the auctioneer believed that the bid was made under a mistake, but that he had reasonable grounds for believing that the mistake was merely as to value; that the form of the catalogue and the negligence of the defendants' manager in not more closely examining the samples at the showroom and identifying them with the lots in the catalogue contributed to cause the mistake.

On this basis, Lawrence J found that a binding contract for the tow had not come into being:

Scriven Bros & Co v Hindley & Co [1913] 3 KB 564, p 568

Lawrence J: In this case the plaintiff brought an action for £476 12s 7d, the price of 560 cwt 2 qrs 27 lbs of Russian tow, as being due for goods bargained and sold. The defendants by their defence denied that they agreed to buy this Russian tow, and alleged that they bid for Russian hemp and that the tow was knocked down to them under a mistake of fact as to the subject-matter of the supposed contract. The circumstances were these. [The learned judge stated the facts and the findings of the jury as set out above, and continued:] Upon

---

92 The conventional view of *Raffles* has been challenged by Simpson, 1975, p 268 – particularly in the light of the rather muddled reporting of the case, mixing submission by counsel and judicial 'intervention'.

93 [1913] 2 KB 564.

these findings both plaintiff and defendants claimed to be entitled to judgment. A number of cases were cited upon either side. I do not propose to examine them in detail because I think that the findings of the jury determine what my judgment should be in this case ... Once it was admitted that Russian hemp was never before known to be consigned or sold with the same shipping marks as Russian tow from the same cargo, it was natural for the person inspecting the 'SL' goods and being shown the hemp to suppose that the 'SL' bales represented the commodity hemp ... To rely upon a purchaser's discovering chalk marks upon the floor of the showrooms seems to me unreasonable as demanding an amount of care upon the buyers which the vendor had no right to exact.

Where the parties are not at cross-purposes, but one is aware of the other's mistake (a situation commonly referred to as unilateral mistake), and indeed may even have induced such a result, the law is somewhat different. Clearly, in many cases, that contract will be, at least, voidable for fraudulent misrepresentation (see Chapter 4). However, many, perhaps a majority, of the cases have involved a distinct sequence of events, turning on a mistake by one party as to the other's identity and leading to difficulties with third party rights. Typically, a would-be seller of goods is tricked by a con-man into believing that the con-man is someone else and, on the basis of that, the seller allows the con-man to buy the goods and take them away on credit, or against a cheque. Before the seller discovers the fraud, the con-man resells the goods to an innocent third party (for cash) and then disappears.[94] In an attempt to recover the goods from the third party, the original seller brings an action of conversion against him, claiming that no 'title' in the goods passed. Whether this argument succeeds depends largely on whether an initially binding (if voidable) contract existed between the seller and the con-man. In principle, the issue is a simple one: with whom did the original seller intend to contract – the con-man or the person he was pretending to be? In practice, the resolution of this question has caused the courts some difficulty and the cases are not all easy to reconcile.[95] Many of the older decisions (perhaps influenced by an earlier theory of subjective contract formation, based on a *consensus ad idem*) come down in favour of the original seller, although most of the later ones go the other way (but see *Ingram v Little*). Conventionally, two principles are at work: first, that the identity of the other was seen as crucial to the seller in deciding whether to contract or not (rather than merely that person's perceived creditworthiness); secondly, that in a face to face contract (often termed *inter praesentes*), it is difficult to rebut the *prima facie* presumption that there is a contract with the person physically present. In practice, however, the

---

94 It may, of course, be possible for the seller to avoid the problem if he takes action to 'avoid' or rescind the contract in time for fraudulent misrepresentation – see *Car and Universal Finance Co Ltd v Caldwell* [1965] 1 QB 525 and Chapter 4.

95 See, further, *King's Norton Metal v Edridge, Merrett & Co* (1897) 14 TLR 98, in which *Cundy v Lindsay* was distinguished; *Phillips v Brooks* [1919] 2 KB 243; and *Boulton v Jones* (1857) 2 LJ Ex 117.

desire to achieve a just result seems to explain the results in the cases. An early House of Lords decision was *Cundy v Lindsay*,[96] where the con-man was named Blenkarn, and had an address at 37 Wood Street. A well respected firm called Blenkiron & Co carried on business at 123 Wood Street. Blenkarn, in ordering handkerchiefs from Lindsay, signed his name so as to look like Blenkiron. The goods were sent on credit and some were resold to Cundy before the fraud was discovered. It was held in both the Court of Appeal and House of Lords that no contract had come into being between Lindsay and Blenkarn. Lord Cairns LC stated:

> How is it possible to imagine that in that state of things any contract could have arisen between the respondents and Blenkarn the dishonest man? Of him, they knew nothing, and of him, they never thought. With him, they never intended to deal. Their minds never even for an instant of time rested on him, and as between him and them there was no consensus of mind which could lead to any agreement or any contract whatsoever.

A particularly controversial decision is *Ingram v Little*.[97] The plaintiffs were joint owners of a car which they advertised for sale. A con-man called, and agreed to buy the car. However, the plaintiffs were unwilling to take a cheque in payment. The con-man then claimed to be a PGM Hutchinson of Stanstead House, Stanstead Road, Caterham. After verifying this name and address in the telephone directory, the plaintiffs agreed to let the con-man buy the car and pay by cheque. The cheque was dishonoured and the con-man then sold the car to Little and disappeared. The Court of Appeal by a majority (Sellers and Pearce LJJ) found that no contract had come into being between the plaintiffs and the con-man, thereby upholding the decision of the judge at first instance:

Ingram v Little [1960] 3 WLR 504, CA

Pearce LJ: An apparent contract made orally *inter praesentes* raises particular difficulties. The offer is apparently addressed to the physical person present. *Prima facie*, he, by whatever name he is called, is the person to whom the offer is made. His physical presence identified by sight and hearing preponderates over vagaries of nomenclature. '*Praesentia corporis tollit errorem nominis*' said Lord Bacon. Yet clearly, though difficult, it is not impossible to rebut the *prima facie* presumption that the offer can be accepted by the person to whom it is physically addressed. To take two extreme instances. If a man orally commissions a portrait from some unknown artist who had deliberately passed himself off, whether by disguise or merely by verbal cosmetics, as a famous painter, the impostor could not accept the offer. For, though the offer is made to him physically, it is obviously, as he knows, addressed to the famous painter. The mistake in identity on such facts is clear and the nature of the contract makes it obvious that identity was of vital importance to the offeror.

96 (1878) 3 App Cas 459.
97 [1960] 3 WLR 504, CA

At the other end of the scale, if a shopkeeper sells goods in a normal cash transaction to a man who misrepresents himself as being some well known figure, the transaction will normally be valid, for the shopkeeper was ready to sell the goods for cash to the world at large and the particular identity of the purchaser in such a contract was not of sufficient importance to override the physical presence identified by sight and hearing. Thus, the nature of the proposed contract must have a strong bearing on the question whether the intention of the offeror (as understood by his offeree) was to make his offer to some other particular identity, rather than to the physical person to whom it was orally offered.

In our case, the facts lie in the debatable area between two extremes ... I should hesitate long before interfering with [the learned judge's] finding of fact and I would only do so if compelled by the evidence or by the view that the judge drew some erroneous inference ... I am not persuaded that on the evidence he should have found otherwise.

Devlin LJ dissented strongly:[98]

In my judgment, the court cannot arrive at a satisfactory solution in the present case except by formulating a presumption and taking it at least as a starting point. The presumption that a person is intending to contract with the person to whom he is actually addressing the words of the contract seems to me to be a simple and sensible one and supported by some good authority. It is adopted in *Benjamin on Sale*, 8th edn, 1950, p 102, where two decisions in the United States are referred to, *Edmunds v Merchants Despatch Co* and *Phelps v McQuade*. The reasoning in the former case was adopted by Horridge J in *Phillips v Brooks Ltd*, the latter case is a decision of the New York Court of Appeals. All these three cases still stand as the law in their respective jurisdictions. *Corbin on Contract*, 1951, Vol 3, s 602, p 385, cites them and a number of others, and states the general principle in the US as follows: 'The courts hold that if A appeared in person before B, impersonating C, an innocent purchaser from A gets the property in the goods against B.' ...

What seems plain to me is that the presumption cannot in the present case be rebutted by piling up the evidence to show that Miss Ingram would never have contracted with H unless she had thought him to be PGM Hutchinson. That fact is conceded and, whether it is proved *simpliciter* or proved to the hilt, it does not go any further than to show that she was the victim of fraud ...

The fact that Miss Ingram refused to contract with H until his supposed name and address had been 'verified' goes to show that she regarded his identity as fundamental. In this, she was misguided. She should have concerned herself with creditworthiness, rather than identity. The fact that H gave PGM Hutchinson's address in the directory was no proof that he was PGM

---

98 Devlin LJ was scathing of the illogicalities of much of the pre-existing 'learning' on this topic throughout his judgment. His own view can best be summed up in his comment that 'the true spirit of the common law is to override theoretical distinctions when they stand in the way of doing practical justice'. Devlin's own view of 'practical justice' would have been (if the law had permitted him to do so) to apportion loss between the parties, depending on the degree of culpability each bore. In this, he is behaving in a classic 'judicial realist' fashion: see Chapter 1.

Hutchinson; and, if he had been, that fact alone was no proof that his cheque would be met. Identity, therefore, did not really matter ...

It is for the court to determine what, in the light of all the circumstances, is to be deemed essential. In my judgment, in the present case, H's identity was immaterial. His creditworthiness was not, but creditworthiness in relation to contract is not a basic fact; it is only a way of expressing the belief that each party normally holds that the other will honour his promise.

It is hard to escape the conclusion that sympathy for the plaintiffs (two elderly sisters – Elsie and Hilda – and their friend Mrs Badger!) must have had some bearing on the court's decision.[99] A more reliable guide to the usual approach of the courts is to be found in the later case of *Lewis v Averay*[100] (in which *Ingram* was distinguished).

Lewis owned a car which he wanted to sell. He advertised it in a newspaper. A con-man made an arrangement to view the car. After doing so, he stated that he was Richard Greene (an actor well known at the time for his portrayal of Robin Hood in the television series of the same name) and produced a pass for Pinewood Studios (where the television series was filmed). The con-man then wrote out a cheque in the name of 'R Green' and took the vehicle and its documents away. The cheque was later dishonoured, but meanwhile, the con-man had sold the car to Averay, an innocent third party.

It might be thought that, if anything, the plaintiff's case here would be stronger that in *Ingram* – the accompanying proof of identity was more substantial. There was (presumably) some facial resemblance to Richard Greene (who, arguably, would have been recognisable to most people at the time), whereas selling to PGM Hutchinson was largely a matter of the apparent creditworthiness of living at a good address, selling to Richard Greene might, just, be a matter of pride. Instead, it was held by the Court of Appeal that the contract with the con-man was valid and the car could not be recovered from Averay.

The basic approach of the courts appears in the judgment of Megaw LJ. As ever, Lord Denning MR goes further!

Lewis v Averay [1971] 3 WLR 603, CA, p 608

Megaw LJ: For myself, with very great respect, I find it difficult to understand the basis, either in logic or in practical considerations, of the test laid down by the majority of the court in *Ingram v Little*. That test is I think accurately recorded in the headnote: '... where a person physically present and negotiating to buy a chattel fraudulently assumed the identity of an existing third person, the test to determine to whom the offer was addressed was how

---

99 Or (perhaps) the fact that the innocent third party was, nevertheless, a car dealer (in *Lewis v Averay*, he was a private buyer (a student)).

100 [1971] 3 WLR 603, CA.

ought the promisee to have interpreted the promise ... therefore, the passing of property, and therefore the right of third parties, if the test is correct, is made to depend on the view which some rogue should have formed, presumably knowing that he is a rogue, as to the state of mind of the opposite party, to the negotiation, who does not know that he is dealing with a rogue.'

However that may be, and assuming that the test as so stated is indeed valid, in my view this appeal can be decided on a short and simple point. It is the point which was put at the outset of his argument by counsel for the defendant. The well known textbook on the *Law of Contract*, Cheshire and Fifoot, deals with the question of invalidity of a contract by virtue of unilateral mistake and, in particular, unilateral mistake relating to mistaken identity. The learned editors describe what in their submission are certain facts that must be established in order to enable one to avoid contract on the basis of unilateral mistake by him as to the identity of the opposite party. The first of those facts is that at the time when he made the offer he regarded the identity of the offeree as a matter of vital importance. To translate that into the facts of the present case, it must be established that at the time of offering to sell his car to the rogue, Mr Lewis regarded the identity of the rogue as a matter of vital importance. In my view, counsel for the defendant is abundantly justified, on the notes of the evidence and on the findings of the learned judge, in his submission that the mistake of Mr Lewis went no further than a mistake as to the attributes of the rogue. It was simply a mistake as to the creditworthiness of the man who was there present and who described himself as Mr Green ...

Lord Denning MR: This case therefore raises the question: what is the effect of a mistake by one party as to the identity of the other? It has sometimes been said that, if a party makes a mistake as to the identity of the persons with whom he is contracting, there is no contract, or, if there is a contract, it is a nullity and void, so that no property can pass under it. This has been supported by a reference to the French jurist Pothier but I have said before, and I repeat now, his statement is no part of English law. I know that it was quoted by Viscount Haldane in *Lake v Simmons* and, as such, misled Tucker J in *Sowler v Potter* into holding that a lease was void whereas it was really voidable. But the statement by Pothier has given rise to such refinements that is time it was dead and buried altogether.

For instance, in *Ingram v Little,* the majority of the court suggested that the difference between *Phillips v Brooks* and *Ingram v Little* was that in *Phillips v Brooks,* the contract of sale was concluded (so as to pass the property to the rogue) before the rogue made the fraudulent misrepresentation, whereas in *Ingram v Little,* the rogue made the fraudulent misrepresentation before the contract was concluded. My own view is that, in each case, the property in the goods did not pass until the seller let the rogue have the goods.

Again it has been suggested that a mistake as to the identity of a person is one thing: and a mistake as to his attributes is another. A mistake as to identity, it is said, avoids a contract; whereas a mistake as to attributes does not. But this is a distinction without a difference. A man's very name is one of his attributes. It is also a key to his identity. If, then, he gives a false name, is it a mistake as to his identity or a mistake as to his attributes? These fine distinctions do no good to the law.

As I listened to the argument in this case, I felt it wrong that an innocent purchaser (who knew nothing of what had passed between the seller and the rogue) should have his title depend on such refinements. After all, he has acted with complete circumspection and in entire good faith; whereas it was the seller who let the rogue have the goods and thus enabled him to commit the fraud, I do not, therefore, accept the theory that a mistake as to identity renders a contract void.

I think the true principle is that which underlies the decision of this court in *King's Norton Metal Co Ltd v Edridge, Merrett & Co Ltd* and of Horridge J in *Phillips v Brooks Ltd*, which has stood for these last 50 years. It is this: when two parties have come to a contract – or rather what appears, on the face of it, to be a contract – the fact that one party is mistaken as to the identity of the other does not mean that there is no contract, or that the contract is a nullity and void from the beginning. It only means that the contract is voidable, that is, liable to be set aside at the instance of the mistaken person, so long as he does not do so before third parties have in good faith acquired rights under it.

Applied to the cases such as the present, this principle is in full accord with the presumption stated by Pearce LJ and also by Devlin in *Ingram v Little*. When a dealing is had between a seller like Mr Lewis and a person who is actually there present before him, then the presumption in law is that there is a contract, even though there is a fraudulent impersonation by the buyer representing himself as a different man than he is. There is a contract made with the very person there, who is present in person. It is liable no doubt to be avoided for fraud but it is still a good contract under which title will pass unless and until it is avoided ...

CHAPTER 3

THE ENFORCEMENT OF PROMISE

On the assumption that the law of contract is primarily concerned with either the enforcement of promises or giving a remedy where there has been a breach of a promise, it is necessary to determine which promises will be given legal recognition in the form of an available remedy and which will not.

REASONS FOR ENFORCING PROMISES

Cooke and Oughton comment as follows:

There are both moral and economic reasons for the protection of expectations. Morally, it is right that promises should be kept, but it is not the case that all promises are legally enforceable. Moreover it has been argued that promises will usually be made in order to get something and that they tend to encourage acts of reliance. If the promisor gets what he seeks or if there is an act of reliance by the promisee, this enhances the case for enforcing the promise. Moreover, if the promisee's expectation interest is protected, this serves as an encouragement to the promisor to fulfil his promise, thereby upholding the operation of the market economy. In this way, the protection of the expectation interest encourages the efficient movement of resources to the person who values them most. If only the status quo or reliance interest were to be protected, there would be no incentive to contracting parties to perform. But if the expectation interest is protected, such an incentive does then arise. A further economic justification for protecting the expectation interest is that an exchange of promises may act as a deliberate risk allocation device which allows a business to shift the risk of a particular loss to someone who is better able to take the risk or avoid it in some way. However, such risks may not always be capable of being absorbed by the person to whom they are transferred. In such a case, judicial or parliamentary intervention in favour of the weaker party may be justified. Sometimes a promise may be kept for reasons other than legal compulsion. For example, it has been shown by empirical research that promises may be kept by businessmen because they deal frequently with a particular business and do not wish to lose that business relationship for the future.[1]

Atiyah suggests that:

If promises are binding – as the utilitarian would have it – because of the expectations they generate, and the acts of reliance to which they lead, then how is one to distinguish between a promise and ... a firm resolve or

---

1   Cooke and Oughton, 2000, p 63.

declaration that one intends to act in a certain way? ... A person who states that he intends to act in a particular manner may, quite rationally, provoke the response, 'But do you promise?', and that question would be meaningless if the statement of intent could itself amount to a promise.

Again, if it is reliance and expectations which make promises binding, it would have to be admitted that the question whether a particular utterance was a binding promise would often be incapable of a precise answer. As a lawyer would say, it would become a question of degree ...

Whether a person whose utterances lead another to have expectations, or to act on them, is under a moral obligation as a result, is often a complex and difficult question. Nobody is likely to dispute that in most circumstances it ... will be relevant ... to know whether the expectations or reliance were reasonable or justified. And any attempt to answer that question must surely pay some regard to the terms of an explicit promise.[2]

These passages suggest a number of reasons why promises are enforced – they may create reasonable expectations in the mind of the promisee; they may be reasonably relied on by the promisee and there may be some moral obligation to keep a promise once having made it. However, the fact that there are disputes in which it is alleged that there has been a breach of contract shows that people do not always keep the promises they make. It should be asked why this is the case.

Atiyah offers the following explanation:

One common reason why people break promises is that a return promise has been, or is likely to be, broken by the promisee. And this itself is some indication of the fact that people who make promises very often – perhaps usually – do so because they want to get something from the promisee which they can only get by doing so ... Promises of this kind do not confer an uncovenanted benefit on the promisee. On the contrary, it is the promisor who often benefits from such a promise, for it is the means of deferring a liability, rather than that of creating an obligation. To take a simple illustration, a person wishes to buy goods, but has not the cash to pay the price; he asks the seller to give him credit, that is to say to accept a promise of payment in lieu of actual payment. In a case of this nature, the buyer's obligation to pay the price surely derives from his purchase of the goods, rather than from his promise ... Of course, it must be clear that the transaction is not a gift (and that no doubt depends on the intentions and relationship of the parties), but once this possibility is ruled out, the voluntary acceptance or receipt of the goods is the necessary and sufficient condition for his liability.[3]

At its simplest, Atiyah's argument is that it is the actions of the parties and not their promises which justify the imposition of contractual liability. But he also points out that it is necessary to distinguish between a gift based on a purely gratuitous promise and one which does give rise to liability.

---

2   Atiyah, 1981, pp 50–51.
3   Cooke and Oughton, 2000, pp 143–44.

What may serve to distinguish a gratuitous promise from a promise enforceable in law is the fact of an express or implied request. Thus, if there is a promise to pay money or to do some act or to forbear from doing a particular thing in circumstances in which there has been no request to make the payment or do the act etc, the promise is likely to be regarded as gratuitous and unenforceable, unless there is evidence of reasonable reliance on the promise (see below, p 136).

A further important factor in determining whether a promise is enforceable is whether or not it has been acted upon. A key feature of much of Atiyah's work is that the paradigm 19th century model of promissory liability is premised on the belief that a set of purely executory promises is just as enforceable as a promise in return for an executed act. Atiyah, however, points to the fact that, in the 20th century, there are numerous examples of promises which have not been acted upon which do not give rise to contractual liability. This is especially so in the consumer sector where there is some evidence that purely executory promises will not always be enforceable:

Consumer Credit Act 1974

67 Cancellable agreements

A regulated agreement may be cancelled by the debtor or hirer in accordance with this Part if the antecedent negotiations included oral representations made when in the presence of the debtor or hirer by an individual acting as, or on behalf of, the negotiator, unless:

(a) the agreement is secured on land, or is a restricted use credit agreement to finance the purchase of land or is an agreement for a bridging loan in connection with the purchase of land, or

(b) the unexecuted agreement is signed by the debtor or hirer at premises at which any of the following is carrying on any business (whether on a permanent or temporary basis) –

(i) the creditor or owner;

(ii) any party to a linked transaction (other than the debtor or hirer or relative of his);

(iii) the negotiator in any antecedent negotiations.

68 Cooling-off period

The debtor or hirer may serve notice of cancellation of a cancellable agreement between his signing of the unexecuted agreement and:

(a) the end of the fifth day following the day on which he received a copy under s 63(2) or a notice under s 64(1)(b);[4] or

(b) if ... s 64(1)(b) does not apply, the end of the 14th day following the day on which he signed the unexecuted agreement.

---

4   Consumer Credit Act 1974, s 63(2) requires the creditor to supply a copy of the executed credit agreement and s 64(1)(b) requires the creditor to send the debtor notice of his cancellation rights.

Other similar provisions allowing for cancellation of concluded, executory contracts can be found in ss 5 and 6 of the Timeshare Act 1992 and the Consumer Protection (Cancellation of Contracts Concluded Away From Business Premises) Regulations 1987.[5]

In the commercial sector, there are probably stronger reasons for enforcing mutual promises, especially since there is generally an expectation that a person who makes a promise expects to have to keep it and he can assume that the same goes for any other business contracting party.

The idea that promises give rise to expectations is an integral part of the bargain theory which is considered in more detail below, but there is also a school of thought which emphasises the moral nature of the practice of promise keeping rather than the economic nature of promises as part of the process of bargaining. This alternative approach can be described as the 'will theory' which turns on the internalisation of the enforcement of promises – the reason for enforcement is moral compulsion of having promised something in the first place.[6]

It is clear that not all promises have legal consequences and a number of different rules of the law of contract impinge on this issue. These include rules which stipulate the form which certain types of contract are to take, the doctrine of consideration and rules on intention to create legal relations.

FORMALITIES

The common law has never embraced the view that, in general, contracts have to take any particular form, and there are relatively few types of contract today to which specific rules as to form exist. On one argument, a legal system which adopts rigid requirements as to the form of contracts may be regarded as primitive and less well developed.[7] However, this is not necessarily true since there are many major legal systems, in the developed world, in which a strict requirement of form can be found. For example, in Scotland, where there is no doctrine of consideration, there is a marked emphasis on formal requirements and in many parts of the common law world, an equivalent of the Statute of Frauds 1677 still survives.

For the purposes of English law, the Statute of Frauds 1677 required certain types of contract to be evidenced in writing, but most of the listed varieties of contract subject to this requirement may now be entered into in any form. Despite the reversal of the requirement of written evidence, there

---

5   SI 1987/2117; SI 1988/958.
6   See Fried, 1981, pp 35–38. Fried admits that his theory is not an explanation of what the law is, but what, in his opinion, it should be.
7   Atiyah, 1979, p 172.

are certain residual categories of contract to which formal requirements still attach.[8] Moreover, a requirement that a particular type of contract must take some specified form is sometimes of value as a means of consumer protection. For example, regulated consumer credit agreements are required to comply with a specified form designed to ensure that the debtor is aware of the nature and consequences of the credit agreement he has entered into.[9] Apart from the 'cautionary function', legal formalities may also serve other purposes.

Fuller offers the following view:

The functions performed by legal formalities

The evidentiary function

The most obvious function of a legal formality is, to use Austin's words, that of providing 'evidence of the existence and purport of the contract, in case of controversy.' The need for evidentiary security may be satisfied in a variety of ways: by requiring a writing, or attestation, or the certification of a notary. It may even be satisfied, to some extent, by such a device as the Roman *stipulatio*, which compelled an oral spelling out of the promise in a manner sufficiently ceremonious to impress its terms on participants and possible bystanders.

The cautionary function

A formality may also perform a cautionary or deterrent function by acting as a check against inconsiderate action. The seal in it original form fulfilled this purpose remarkably well. The affixing and impressing of a wax wafer – symbol in the popular mind of legalism and weightiness – was an excellent device for inducing the circumspective frame of mind appropriate in one pledging his future. To a less extent any requirement of a writing, of course, serves the same purpose, as do requirements of attestation, notarisation, etc.

The channeling function

Though most discussions of the purposes served by formalities go no further than the analysis just presented, this analysis stops short of recognising one of the most important functions of form. That a legal formality may perform a function not yet described can be shown by the seal. The seal not only insures a

---

8 Contracts for the sale or other disposition of an interest in land entered into after 27 September 1989 must be made in writing; Law of Property (Miscellaneous Provisions) Act 1989, s 2; similar contracts entered into before 27 September 1989 must have been evidenced in writing; Law of Property Act 1925, s 40; a lease of land for a period of more than three years must be made under seal; Law of Property Act 1925, ss 52 and 54(2); bills of exchange and bills of sale must be made in writing: respectively, Bills of Exchange Act 1882, s 3(1) and Bills of Sale Act 1878 (Amendment) Act 1882, s 9; contracts of guarantee must be evidenced in writing: Statute of Frauds 1677, s 4.

9 Consumer Credit Act 1974, s 60, given effect by the Consumer Credit (Agreements) Regulations 1983 SI 1983/1553 as amended. Failure to adhere to the prescribed form renders the regulated agreement not properly executed (Consumer Credit Act 1974, s 61) with the result that it may only be enforced against the debtor by way of court order (Consumer Credit Act 1974, s 65).

satisfactory memorial of the promise and induces deliberation in the making of it. It serves also to mark or signalise the enforceable promise; it furnishes a simple and external test of enforceability. This function of form Ihering described as 'the facilitation of judicial diagnosis' and he employed the analogy of coinage in explaining it:

> Form is for a legal transaction what the stamp is for a coin. Just as the stamp of the coin relieves us from the necessity of testing the metallic content and weight – in short, the value of the coin (a test which we could not avoid if uncoined metal were offered to us in payment), in the same way legal formalities relieve the judge of an inquiry whether a legal transaction was intended, and – in case different forms are fixed for different legal transactions – which was intended.

In this passage, it is apparent that Ihering has placed an undue emphasis on the utility of form for the judge, to the neglect of its significance for those transacting business out of court.

The thing which characterises the law of contracts and conveyances is that in this field forms are deliberately used, and are intended to be so used, by the parties whose acts are to be judged by the law. To the businessman who wishes to make his own or another's promise binding, the seal was at common law available as a device for the accomplishment of his objective. In this aspect form offers a legal framework into which the party may fit his actions, or, to change the figure, it offers channels for the legally effective expression of intention. It is with this aspect of form in mind that I have described the third function of legal formalities as the 'channeling function'.

Interrelations of the three functions

Though I have stated the three functions of legal form separately, it is obvious that there is an intimate connection between them. Generally speaking, whatever tends to accomplish one of these purposes will also tend to accomplish the other two. He who is compelled to do something which will furnish a satisfactory memorial of his intention will be induced to deliberate. Conversely, devices which induce deliberation will usually have an evidentiary value. Devices which insure evidence or prevent inconsiderateness will normally advance the desideratum of channeling, in two different ways. In the first place, he who is compelled to formulate his intention carefully will tend to fit it into legal and business categories. In this way the party is induced to canalise his own intention. In the second place, wherever the requirement of a formality is backed by the sanction of the invalidity of the informal transaction (and this is the means by which requirements of form are normally made effective), a degree of channeling results automatically. Whatever may be its legislative motive, the formality in such a case tends to effect a categorisation of transactions into legal and non-legal.[10]

Conversely, formal requirements are generally regarded as cumbersome, impracticable and unnecessarily time consuming. Moreover, it is difficult to

---

10 Fuller, 1941, pp 800–03.

decide what contracts should be subject to formal requirements. This can cause particular difficulties where contracts of different varieties with similar characteristics are subject to different rules as to form. For example, contracts of guarantee are very similar to contracts of indemnity, yet the latter may be made orally, whereas the former must be evidenced in writing. Accordingly, a number of very fine distinctions have grown up between the two types of contract in order to avoid the problem of unenforceability.

CONSIDERATION

Since, for the most part, contracts do not have to take any particular form, some other means of distinguishing enforceable promises from the unenforceable has to be employed. For the purposes of English law, this mechanism is provided partly by the rules on consideration.[11] The rule is that for a promise to be enforceable, consideration must be furnished by the promisee. Thus, if X promises to paint Y's house and Y gives something or promises to refrain from doing something in return, there is consideration for X's promise so that he is contractually bound to paint Y's house.

Definitions of consideration

In *Currie v Misa*,[12] it was stated that 'a valuable consideration, in the sense of the law, may consist either in some right, interest, profit or benefit accruing to the one party, or some forbearance, detriment, loss or responsibility given, suffered or undertaken by the other'.

What this definition reveals is an element of reciprocity. Something must be given by the promisee in return for the promise of the other party. That is, the promisee must confer some benefit on the promisor or the promisee must suffer some detriment in return for the promise of the other party. However, this definition is defective in one important respect. It suggests that the consideration for the promise must be executed in the sense that the detriment *must have been suffered* or the benefit *must have been conferred*. However, other definitions also take account of the notion of executory consideration.

Pollock,[13] in an approach adopted by Lord Dunedin in *Dunlop Pneumatic Tyre Co Ltd v Selfridge and Co Ltd*,[14] states that 'An act or forbearance of the one

---

11 The rules on consideration may now be little more than a mere formality. See *Vantage Navigation Corpn v Suhail, The Alev* [1989] 1 Lloyd's Rep 138, p 147, *per* Hobhouse J.

12 (1875) LR 10 Ex 153.

13 Pollock, 1950, p 133.

14 [1915] AC 847, HL.

party, or the promise thereof, is the price for which the promise of the other is bought, and the promise thus, given for value is enforceable':

The *United States Restatement* states that:

(1) To constitute consideration, a performance or a return promise must be bargained for.

(2) A performance or return promise is bargained for if it is sought by the promisor in exchange for his promise and is given by the promisee in exchange for that promise.

(3) The performance may consist of:

(a) an act other than a promise; or

(b) a forbearance; or

(c) the creation, modification or destruction of a legal relation.[15]

As in the case of the *Currie v Misa* definition, the Pollock definition and that given in the *United States Restatement*, both emphasise the element of reciprocity or bargain, but this is by no means universally accepted. Not all promises are necessarily bargained for. For example, it will be seen below that a promise may be enforced because it has been relied upon by the person to whom it was addressed. Moreover, a promise may be made with a view to obtaining some benefit or avoiding some disbenefit.

It is suggested that a number of key features have to be considered in determining whether there is a good consideration for a given promise, these being:

- the voluntariness of the promisor's actions;

- whether that which has been promised has been requested by the promisee;

- whether there is any legal value in that which is given in return for the promise of the other party;

- whether there is any reciprocal arrangement between the promisor and the promisee which involves either the conferment of a benefit on the promisor or results in some detriment to the promisee;

- whether it is contrary to public policy to enforce the promise.

Voluntariness

Since contractual obligations are generally said to be enforceable only if voluntarily undertaken, it follows that a promise which has been given under illegitimate pressure will not be enforceable. Whilst this issue is of some importance in determining whether there is a good consideration for a promise, the matter of voluntariness is pertinent to the application of rules on

---

15 *United States Restatement, Contracts* (2nd), para 71.

duress which are to be considered in a later chapter.[16] Moreover, whether or not a promise has been voluntarily given also raises issues of public policy which will be considered in more detail in this chapter.

In *North Ocean Shipping Co v Hyundai Construction Co*,[17] a shipbuilding company entered into a contract for the construction of an oil tanker under which the price was fixed and payable in five instalments of US $1,547,000. In order to facilitate payment, the company agreed to open a letter of credit in favour of the purchasers. After the owners had paid the first instalment, the US dollar was devalued, so that performance of the contract by the shipbuilders became uneconomic. The shipbuilders then asked the owners to pay 10% more than was originally agreed. The owners asserted that there was no legal ground on which they could be required to pay this additional amount and continued to pay the second and third instalments in accordance with the terms of the contract. However, the shipbuilders returned these payments and asked for a final reply from the owners as to whether they would agree to a 10% increase in the contract price. Moreover, the shipbuilders also indicated that, unless there was agreement on this matter, they would have to terminate the contract. In order to avert the possibility that they might lose a lucrative charter of the tanker on completion, the owners reluctantly agreed to pay the extra 10%, stating that they were under no obligation to do so. In order to effect this increase in price, the shipbuilders arranged for changes to be made to the letter of credit they had opened. Subsequently, the oil tanker was completed and, some eight months later, the owners commenced proceedings, in which they claimed the return of the additional payment of 10%. It was held that there was consideration for the promise to pay the extra 10% in the form of an additional undertaking by the shipbuilders to increase the amounts specified in the letter of credit. However, there was also evidence of duress in the form of illegitimate economic pressure in the threat to break the contract without any legal justification. This had the effect of rendering the contract voidable so that the owners had the option of avoiding or affirming the new arrangement. However, the court held that by delaying so long in instituting proceedings, the owners had affirmed:

North Ocean Shipping Co v Hyundai Construction Co [1979] QB 705, p 716

Mocatta J: It is unnecessary for me to deal with a number of the additional points which Mr Hamilton advanced against the argument that there was no consideration. I shall have to deal with some of them on ... the argument that the increased price agreement and the additional payments made in consequence thereof resulted from a form of duress ... There has been considerable discussion in the books whether, if an agreement is made under

16 See Chapter 7.
17 [1979] QB 705.

duress of goods to pay a sum of money and there is some consideration for the agreement, the excess sum can be recovered. The authority for this suggested distinction is *Skeate v Beale* (1841) 11 Ad and El 983. It was there said by Lord Denman CJ, that an agreement was not void because made under duress of goods, the distinction between that case and the cases of money paid to recover goods wrongfully seized being said to be obvious in that the agreement was not compulsorily but voluntarily entered into. Kerr J in *Occidental Worldwide Investment Corpn v Skibs A/S Avanti (The Siboen and The Sibotre)* [1976] 1 Lloyd's Rep 293, p 335, gave strong expression to the view that the suggested distinction based on *Skeate v Beale* would not be observed today. He said, though *obiter*, that *Skeate v Beale* would not justify a decision: 'For instance, if I should be compelled to sign a lease or some other contract for a nominal but legally sufficient consideration under an imminent threat of having my house burnt down or a valuable picture slashed, though without any threat of physical violence to anyone, I do not think that the law would uphold the agreement.'

I think the facts found in this case do establish that the agreement to increase the price by 10% reached at the end of June 1973 was caused by what may be called 'economic duress'. The Yard were adamant in insisting on the increased price without having any legal justification for so doing and the owners realised that the Yard would not accept anything other than an unqualified agreement to the increase. The owners might have claimed damages in arbitration against the Yard with all the inherent unavoidable uncertainties of litigation, but in view of the position of the Yard vis à vis their relations with Shell it would be unreasonable to hold that this is the course they should have taken: see *Astley v Reynolds* (1731) 2 Str 915. The owners made a very reasonable offer of arbitration coupled with security for any award in the Yard's favour that might be made, but this was refused. They then made their agreement, which can truly I think be said to have been made under compulsion, by the telex of June 28 without prejudice to their rights. I do not consider the Yard's ignorance of the Shell charter material. It may well be that had they known of it they would have been even more exigent.

If I am right in the conclusion reached with some doubt earlier that there was consideration for the 10% increase agreement reached at the end of June 1973, and it be right to regard this as having been reached under a kind of duress in the form of economic pressure, then what is said in *Chitty on Contracts*, 24th edn, 1977, Vol 1, para 442, p 207, to which both counsel referred me, is relevant, namely, that a contract entered into under duress is voidable and not void:

On the other hand, the findings of fact in the special case present difficulties whether one is proceeding on the basis of a voidable agreement reached at the end of June 1973, or whether such agreement was void for want of consideration, and it were necessary in consequence to establish that the payments were made involuntarily and not with the intention of closing the transaction.

I have already stated that no protest of any kind was made by the owners after their telex of June 28 1973, before their claim in this arbitration on 30 July 1975, shortly after in July of that year, the *Atlantic Baroness*, a sister ship of the

Atlantic Baron, had been tendered, though, as I understand it, she was not accepted and arbitration proceedings in regard to her are in consequence taking place. There was therefore a delay between 27 November 1974, when the *Atlantic Baron* was delivered and 30 July 1975, before the owners put forward their claim.

The owners were, therefore, free from the duress on 27 November 1974, and took no action by way of protest or otherwise between their important telex of 28 June 1973, and their formal claim for the return of the excess 10% paid of 30 July 1975, when they nominated their arbitrator. One cannot dismiss this delay as of no significance, though I would not consider it conclusive by itself.

Requests

One view of the rules on consideration dealt with below is that their primary function is to distinguish between gratuitous and legally enforceable promises. If a promise is not solicited through the request of the promisee, there is a fair chance that it will be regarded as simply the promise of a gift for which there is no consideration and which consequently is legally unenforceable, unless there is a formal reason for the validity of the promise by virtue of its being contained in a deed.

In *Re Hudson, Creed v Henderson*,[18] Hudson orally promised to pay £20,000 to the Jubilee Fund of the Congregational Union. In addition, he also completed and signed a blank form repeating the promise, the form being headed, 'Congregational Union of England and Wales – Jubilee Fund'. Some £12,000 had been paid when Hudson died, but his estate declined to make any further payments. It was held that there was no enforceable contract, because no consideration had been given for the promise to pay. Moreover, the requirement of s 4 of the Statute of Frauds 1677, which said that there should be a sufficient written memorandum of agreement was also not satisfied:

Re Hudson, Creed v Henderson (1885) 54 LJ Ch 811, p 814

Pearson J: I believe this is the first time in the annals of the Court of Chancery, or of the court which has succeeded to it, in which an attempt has been made, and made against a dead man's estate, to make it liable for a promise given by him during his lifetime to make a charitable contribution to any object.

The first question is whether or not there is any contract at all to pay – I mean a contract in the legal sense of the word 'contract'; was there any consideration of any sort or description for Mr Hudson's promise to pay £20,000 – anything that could be considered a consideration either in this court or elsewhere? I am utterly at a loss to ascertain that there was any consideration. The parties

---

18   (1885) 54 LJ Ch 811. See, also, *Re Cory* (1912) TLR 18 and the Canadian case *Dalhousie College v Boutilier Estate* [1934] 3 DLR 593. Of course, most charitable bequests are contained in a will or deed of gift (in the latter case for tax purposes), so that, in practice, the legal enforceability of such promises is rarely problematic.

expressed their intention to contribute, and I have no doubt that, if Mr Hudson had lived and had been able to pay his two remaining instalments of £4,000 each, he would have paid them; but then he would have paid them in the same manner in which he paid the previous instalments – not as being bound by a legal contract to pay or as paying a debt, but as making, from time to time, a charitable gift which he had expressed his intention to make and which he continued minded to make. Now here the only promise was this, that at the meeting he said that he would give – that is to say, that he intended to give – £20,000 What is the consideration for the promise which was to make it a contract? There was no consideration at all. Mr Cookson says that there really was a consideration, because the consideration was the risks and liabilities which the parties were to undertake who composed themselves into a committee and became the distributors of the fund. In the first place, there was no duty between themselves and Mr Hudson which they undertook at that time – there was no binding obligation between themselves and Mr Hudson; and I put it to Mr Cookson just now when he was pressing this point: Supposing that at the end of the year, before any more instalments than one had been paid, this committee had chosen to dissolve itself and to relinquish any trouble whatever in the distribution of the fund whether it was gathered in or not, was there any obligation between Mr Hudson and the committee which would have given Mr Hudson any control over the committee, or have made the committee liable to him for not discharging its duty in distributing the fund which is said to be the consideration for the contract? Of course, there was none. It was voluntary on the part of both parties – voluntary on the part of Mr Hudson and voluntary on the part of the committee. The whole thing from beginning to end was nothing more than this: an intention of this gentleman to contribute to the fund, and an intention of the committee, so long as the different members of it remained members of that committee, to dispose of that fund according to the purposes for which it was contributed.

If a specific request is made by the promisor and he derives some benefit from what is given in return for his request, there are strong reasons for enforcing his promise. This remains the case even where the only thing requested is a promise in return. Thus, a simple exchange of promises will often be sufficient to render the promisee on each side legally enforceable. Where a person makes a promise and there is objective evidence that he has derived some material benefit through a specific request there are even stronger reasons for wishing to enforce his promise. This benefit might be indirect only, but provided the beneficial action on the part of the promisee has been specifically requested, there may be a sufficient reason for enforcing the promisor's promise.

In *Chappell and Co Ltd v Nestlé Co Ltd*,[19] Hardy, a record manufacturing company, sold to Nestlé a number of recordings of the popular song 'Rockin' Shoes', a musical work, the copyright of which was vested in Chappell and Co. These records were incorporated by Nestlé into cardboard discs which

---

19 [1960] AC 87, HL.

bore advertising material for their chocolate and were made available to the public at a price of 1 s 6 d plus three wrappers from Nestlé chocolate bars. The wrappers, when received, were thrown away. It was held that there had been a sale by retail, but that a sale by retail, for the purposes of s 8 of the Copyright Act 1956, required a consideration which consisted only of money. In this case, part of the consideration was to be found in the acquisition and delivery of the chocolate bar wrappers. Accordingly, Nestlé's operations were not covered by s 8, with the result that there was a breach of copyright:

Chappell and Co Ltd v Nestlé Co Ltd [1960] AC 87, HL, p 108

Lord Reid: To determine the nature of the contract one must find the intention of the parties as shown by what they said and did. The Nestlé Co's intention can hardly be in doubt. They were not setting out to trade in gramophone records. They were using these records to increase their sales of chocolate. Their offer was addressed to everyone. It might be accepted by a person who was already a regular buyer of their chocolate; but, much more important to them, it might be accepted by people who might become regular buyers of their chocolate if they could be induced to try it and found they liked it. The inducement was something calculated to look like a bargain, a record at a very cheap price. It is in evidence that the ordinary price for a dance record is 6s 6d. It is true that the ordinary record gives much longer playing time than the Nestlé records and it may have other advantages. But the reader of the Nestlé offer was not in a position to know that.

It seems to me clear that the main intention of the offer was to induce people interested in this kind of music to buy (or perhaps get others to buy) chocolate which otherwise would not have been bought. It is, of course, true that some wrappers might come from the chocolate which had already been bought or from chocolate which would have been bought without the offer, but that does not seem to me to alter the case. Where there is a large number of transactions – the notice mentions 30,000 records – I do not think we should simply consider an isolated case where it would be impossible to say whether there had been a direct benefit from the acquisition of the wrappers or not. The requirement that wrappers should be sent was of great importance to the Nestlé Co; there would have been no point in their simply offering records for 1s 6d each. It seems to me quite unrealistic to divorce the buying of the chocolate from the supplying of the records. It is a perfectly good contract if a person accepts an offer to supply goods if he: (a) does something of value to the supplier; and (b) pays money: the consideration is both (a) and (b). There may have been cases where the acquisition of the wrappers conferred no direct benefit on the Nestlé Co, but there must have been many cases where it did. I do not see why the possibility that in some cases the acquisition of the wrappers did not directly benefit the Nestlé Co should require us to exclude from consideration the cases where it did. And even where there was no direct benefit from the acquisition of the wrappers there may have been an indirect benefit by way of advertisement.

I do not think that it matters greatly whether this kind of contract is called a sale or not. The appellants did not take the point that this transaction was not a sale. But I am bound to say that I have some doubts. If a contract under which a person is bound to do something as well as to pay money is a sale, then either the price includes the obligation as well as the money, or the consideration is the price plus the obligation. And I do not see why it should be different if he has to show that he has done something of value to the seller. It is to my mind illegitimate to argue – this is a sale, the consideration for a sale is the price, price can only include money or something which can be readily converted into an ascertainable sum of money, therefore anything like wrappers which have no money value when delivered cannot be part of the consideration.

The respondents avoid this difficulty by submitting that acquiring and delivering the wrappers was merely a condition which gave a qualification to buy and was not part of the consideration for sale. Of course, a person may limit his offer to persons qualified in a particular way, for example, members of a club.

But where the qualification is the doing of something of value to the seller, and where the qualification only suffices for one sale and must be re-acquired before another sale, I find it hard to regard the repeated acquisitions of the qualification as anything other than parts of the consideration for the sales. The purchaser of records had to send three wrappers for each record, so he had first to acquire them. The acquisition of wrappers by him was, at least in many cases, of direct benefit to the Nestlé Co and required expenditure by the acquirer which he might not otherwise have incurred. To my mind, the acquiring and delivering of the wrappers was certainly part of the consideration in these cases and I see no good reason for drawing a distinction between these and other cases.

Was receipt of the chocolate bar wrappers merely the motive for making the promise to supply a gramophone record?[20] What actual benefit was derived from making the promise? Is the reason for enforcing the promise anything other than the fact that there was a specific request and that the promisor got what he/she asked for?

On the issue of motive, the dissenting judgment of Viscount Simonds is instructive:

Viscount Simonds (p 102): The problem, therefore, and the only problem, is whether there is a retail sale with a retail selling price within the meaning of the section. The contention that it is not is stated in various ways. Upjohn J, in a passage cited with approval by Romer LJ, said: 'The vital part of this transaction is to get in three wrappers and that represents a great deal of value to Nestlé's, because it is evidence of an advertising campaign pushing up their sales. That is the value to them. This bears no resemblance at all to the transaction to which, in my judgment, the section is pointing, that is, an

---

20 Cf *Thomas v Thomas* (1842) 2 QB 851, where it was held that consideration and motive are distinct.

ordinary retail sale with an ordinary retail selling price. I think it is quite wrong to suppose that the retail selling price here is 1s 6d. The purchaser has to purchase three bars of chocolate and that is the real value of this transaction to Nestlé's ... Under Nestlé's method of selling them, the copyright owner gets a royalty assessed upon the cash part only of each sale, and he gets nothing in respect of the consideration which, although indirect, passes from the customers and is received by the company.'

There are here two somewhat different conceptions. First, the transaction is not such an ordinary retail sale as contemplated by the section, because the vendor gets something of value, viz, the evidence of an advertising campaign pushing up the sales: secondly, it is not within the section, because the vendor gets from the purchaser a consideration for the sale of the record which the copyright owner does not share, for it is not included in the retail selling price upon which the royalty is based. In the latter case, the wrappers are treated as part of the consideration moving from the purchaser, in the former as evidence of a collateral advantage which has already accrued to the vendor. It is necessary to distinguish these two aspects of the matter. In the contention that the sale is not an ordinary retail sale and therefore not within the section because the vendor gets not only the cash price but also evidence of an advantage already accrued, I see no merit. It is irrelevant what is the vendor's motive for selling a record for 1s 6d if that is the selling price. It may be part of an advertising campaign for the sale of other goods: but there is nothing in the Act which impels me to read into the section a qualification that the selling price is to be disregarded and the article denied protection if the vendor's motive in fixing it is anything but to obtain the maximum amount commercially possible. The alternative view is that the production of three chocolate wrappers is part of the price of the record and that, as it is incapable of valuation, the necessary particulars cannot be given and the statutory requirements satisfied.

In my opinion, my Lords, the wrappers are not part of the selling price. They are admittedly themselves valueless and are thrown away and it was for that reason, no doubt, that Upjohn J was constrained to say that their value lay in the evidence they afforded of success in an advertising campaign. That is what they are. But what, after all, does that mean? Nothing more than that someone, by no means necessarily the purchaser of the record, has in the past bought not from Nestlé's but from a retail shop three bars of chocolate and that the purchaser has thus, directly or indirectly, acquired the wrappers. How often he acquires them for himself, how often through another, is pure speculation. The only thing that is certain is that, if he buys bars of chocolate from a retail shop or acquires the wrappers from another who has bought them, that purchase is not, or at the lowest is not necessarily, part of the same transaction as his subsequent purchase of a record from the manufacturers.

I conclude, therefore, that the objection fails, whether it is contended that (in the words of Upjohn J) the sale 'bears no resemblance at all to the transaction to which the section ... is pointing' or that the three wrappers form part of the selling price and are incapable of valuation. Nor is there any need to take what, with respect, I think is a somewhat artificial view of a simple transaction. What can be easier than for a manufacturer to limit his sales to those members of the public who fulfil the qualification of being this or doing that? It may be assumed that the manufacturer's motive is his own advantage. It is possible that he achieves his object. But that does not mean that the sale is not a retail sale to which the section applies or that the ordinary retail selling price is not the price at which the record is ordinarily sold, in this case 1s 6d.

More recent authorities seem to work on the basis that if there is a specific request and the promisor has got what he has asked for then, in the absence of policy factors, there is no reason why the promise should not be enforced, especially if the promisor receives some benefit or avoids some detriment.

In *Williams v Roffey Bros and Nicholls (Contractors) Ltd*,[21] the plaintiff entered into a sub-contract with the defendants, whereby he agreed to complete carpentry work in a block of flats on which the defendants, as main contractors, were working. The agreed price for the work was £20,000, but it later became apparent that this was insufficient to allow him to work at a profit. The main contract into which the defendants had entered contained penalty clauses should the work not be completed on time. With the prospect of these penalties in mind, the defendants initiated negotiations which led to him offering to pay the plaintiff an additional amount of £10,300 should the carpentry work be completed on time. The defendants made only one additional payment of £1,500, whereupon the plaintiff stopped work and sued for the additional payments which had been promised. The Court of Appeal held that there was consideration for the promise to pay the additional amounts in that the request to complete the work on time, if complied with, secured for the promisor a benefit or avoided some detriment. Furthermore, provided the promise to pay the extra amount was not secured by economic duress or fraud, there was no overriding public policy reason for denying the validity of the defendants' promise:

Williams v Roffey Bros and Nicholls (Contractors) Ltd [1991] 1 QB, CA, p 15

Glidewell LJ: Accordingly, following the view of the majority in *Ward v Byham* [1956] 1 WLR 496 and of the whole court in *Williams v Williams* [1957] 1 WLR 148 and that of the Privy Council in *Pao On* [1980] AC 614, the present state of the law on this subject can be expressed in the following proposition: (i) if A has entered into a contract with B to do work for, or to supply goods or services to, B in return for payment by B; and (ii) at some stage before A has completely performed his obligations under the contract B has reason to doubt whether A will, or will be able to, complete his side of the bargain; and (iii) B thereupon promises A an additional payment in return for A's promise to perform his contractual obligations on time; and (iv) as a result of giving his promise, B obtains in practice a benefit or obviates a disbenefit; and (v) B's promise is not given as a result of economic duress or fraud on the part of A; then (vi) the benefit to B is capable of being consideration for B's promise, so that the promise will be legally binding.

---

21   [1991] 1 QB 1, CA.

As I have said, Mr Evans accepts that in the present case by promising to pay the extra £10,300 his client secured benefits. There is no finding, and no suggestion that, in this case, the promise was given as a result of fraud or duress. If it be objected that the propositions above contravene the principle in *Stilk v Myrick* (1809) 2 Camp 317, I answer that, in my view, they do not; they refine, and limit the application of that principle, but they leave the principle unscathed, for example, where B secures no benefit by his promise. It is not in my view surprising that a principle enunciated in relation to the rigours of seafaring life during the Napoleonic wars should be subjected during the succeeding 180 years to a process of refinement and limitation in its application in the present day. It is therefore my opinion that on his findings of fact in the present case, the judge was entitled to hold, as he did, that the defendants' promise to pay the extra £10,300 was supported by valuable consideration, and thus constituted an enforceable agreement.

The cases so far considered have all involved a specific request, but the request principle may also come into play in circumstances in which the court is prepared to imply a request that certain work be done and to imply a promise at that time that the work will be paid for. This device has proved to be useful in avoiding the harsher effects of one of the classical rules that consideration may be executory or executed but it may not be past. Past consideration may consist in an act or promise to perform an act which precedes the promise to pay.[22] This principle has never commanded complete support in the commercial world and there are commercial practices which flatly contradict it.[23] Moreover, where there is an implied request that certain work be done, there is a willingness to ignore the rule on past consideration:

Pao On v Lau Yiu Long [1980] AC 614, p 629

Lord Scarman: The Board agrees with Mr Neill's submission that the consideration expressly stated in the written guarantee is sufficient in law to support the defendants' promise of indemnity. An act done before the giving of a promise to make a payment or to confer some other benefit can sometimes be consideration for the promise. The act must have been done at the promisor's request: the parties must have understood that the act was to be remunerated either by a payment or the conferment of some other benefit: and payment, or the conferment of a benefit, must have been legally enforceable had it been promised in advance. All three features are present in this case. The promise given to Fu Chip under the main agreement not to sell the shares for a year was at the first defendant's request. The parties understood at the time of the main agreement that the restriction on selling must be compensated for by the benefit of a guarantee against a drop in price: and such a guarantee would be legally enforceable. The agreed cancellation of the subsidiary agreement left,

---

22 See, eg, *Roscorla v Thomas* (1842) 3 QB 234; and *Re McArdle* [1951] Ch 669.

23 Bills of Exchange Act 1882, s 27(1) permits past consideration to support an action on a bill of exchange. Limitation Act 1980, s 27(5) allows an acknowledgment of a statute barred debt to be supported by a past consideration.

as the parties knew, the plaintiffs unprotected in a respect in which at the time of the main agreement all were agreed they should be protected.

Mr Neill's submission is based on *Lampleigh v Brathwait* (1615) Hobart 105. In that case the judges said, at p 106: 'First ... a meer voluntary courtesie will not have a consideration to uphold an assumpsit. But if that courtesie were moved by a suit or request of the party that gives the assumpsit, it will bind, for the promise, though it follows, yet it is not naked, but couples it self with the suit before, and the merits of the party procured by that suit, which is the difference.'

The modern statement of the law is in the judgment of Bowen LJ in *Re Casey's Patents* [1892] 1 Ch 104, pp 115–16; Bowen LJ said: 'Even if it were true, as some scientific students of law believe, that a past service cannot support a future promise, you must look at the document and see if the promise cannot receive a proper effect in some other way. Now, the fact of a past service raises an implication that at the time it was rendered it was to be paid for, and, if it was a service which was to be paid for, when you get in the subsequent document a promise to pay, that promise may be treated either as an admission which evidences or as a positive bargain which fixes the amount of that reasonable remuneration on the faith of which the service was originally rendered. So that here, for past services, there is ample justification for the promise to give the third share.'

(The facts of this case are considered in more detail in relation to the issue of duress in Chapter 7.)

Of course, it will not always prove possible to either imply a request that work be done or that a service be carried out. Further, even where a request can be implied, it may not be in circumstances where it would be realistic to anticipate a reward for carrying out the service. There is a world of difference between requesting a patent agent to introduce a patent to the commercial world (as in *Re Casey's Patents*) and (say) asking a friend to help with some DIY. In the latter type of case, or where there is no request (express or implied) the rules on past consideration can still 'bite'.

Most of the principal rules of the doctrine of consideration, as it is now stated, were developed in the 19th century, during which period the dominant view was that only bargain promises were enforceable. The bargain theory[24] presumed a requirement of request in the sense that the promisee would give something of value in return for the promise of the other party. The bargain theory also spawned a number of other rules, some of which have given rise to controversy in more recent years (below).

It should be noted, however, that the rules on what is a good consideration for a promise tend to reflect the values of the day and that what was not a good consideration in the 19th century may be recognised as a sufficient consideration to justify the enforcement of a promise in a different age. For

---

24 For support for this theory, see Hamson, 1938.

example, it should become clear that some non-bargain promises are now enforceable with the result that reliance by the promisee on the fulfilment of the promisor's promise or the receipt of a valuable benefit by the promisor may now be sufficient reasons for the enforcement of a promise, despite the fact that there is no obvious bargain between the parties.

Bargain promises

Hamson states that 'Consideration, offer and acceptance are an indivisible trinity, facets of one identical notion which is that of bargain. Indeed consideration may be explained as merely the acceptance viewed from the offeror's side. Acceptance is defined to be the doing of an act (which may be the giving of a promise or the rendering of a performance) which is requested by the offeror in exchange for his promise; it is the response to an offer. An act done at the request of the offeror in response to his promise is consideration; and consideration in its essence is nothing else but response to such a request'.[25]

A bargain presupposes an element of reciprocity – the promise, in order to be enforceable, must be given in return for something regarded as being of value in the eyes of the law. From this base premise, a number of rules have developed, namely:

- consideration need not be adequate;
- consideration must be sufficient;
- consideration must not be past;
- consideration must move from the promisee.

Consideration need not be adequate

The rule on adequacy is a manifestation of the classical theory of contractual obligations. On the assumption that each contracting party is left to his own devices to secure for himself the best bargain possible, it is understandable that the 19th century rule on adequacy of consideration should develop. The rule dictates that a court will never ask whether the contracting parties have obtained value for their money, since in a world of free enterprise, contracting parties should be left to decide on the value of the thing sold and it is not for the court to free a man from a bad bargain. Accordingly, if a man so chooses, he may pay 25 p for a Rolls Royce motor car, provided the seller is prepared to accept that price. In a number of instances, the courts have not been prepared

---

25   Hamson, 1938, p 234.

to interfere with the arrangements made by the parties, even where the contract might appear to have been made at an undervalue.[26]

Generally, the refusal of the courts to take account of the apparent inadequacy of consideration has been applauded by economists[27] on the basis that the courts are not in the best position to assess value. This is something best left to the contracting parties themselves so as to most efficiently move resources to the person who values them the most. However, in some instances, the presumption that a contractual exchange does increase value may be rebutted, in which case, the courts may have regard to the adequacy of consideration. For example, it will be seen that a key issue in deciding whether a court may grant equitable relief on the basis of undue influence is whether the consideration is grossly unfair.[28] Moreover, there may be other instances in which the court finds itself in a position where it must have regard to the question whether one of the contracting parties has received value for money. For example, in deciding whether goods sold are of satisfactory quality, the court must have regard, *inter alia*, to the price paid.[29] Thus, if a person pays a high price, he can expect a correspondingly high standard of quality.[30]

Consideration must be sufficient

The rule that consideration must be sufficient, but need not be adequate appears at first to be contradictory. The extent to which there is more than a verbal contradiction depends on the meaning to be ascribed to 'sufficiency'. Broadly 'insufficiency' in this context means that what is given in return for the promise must have *some* value, in the eyes of the law. Does this mean that anything will do, so long as there is *something* there? It has been seen above that literal value for money is not generally insisted upon by the courts since it is left to the contracting parties to value what has been contracted for – an essentially subjective approach. However, it is clear from the rules on sufficiency that value in its sufficiency sense is not approached on a completely subjective basis. If it were, then any promise would be enforceable, because the promisor, as a presumed rational being, must have seen some value in the thing(s) requested in return for their promise.

The rules outlined below are based on a structure created in the 19th century, which emphasises bargain as a key element in the definition of a

---

26 See, eg, *Chappell and Co Ltd v Nestlé and Co Ltd* [1960] AC 87 considered above. See, also, *Mountford v Scott* [1975] Ch 258.

27 See Posner, 1992, pp 70–71.

28 See Chapter 7.

29 Sale of Goods Act 1979, s 14(2A).

30 *Rogers v Parish (Scarborough) Ltd* [1987] 2 All ER 232.

good consideration. However, the bargain theory does not cover all cases in which there has been held to be a good consideration.

Economic value

The approach taken by the courts has been that the consideration for a promise must have some value in the eyes of the law. This might be taken to mean that in order to amount to a good consideration, what is given must have some economic value. Thus, it has been held that natural love and affection cannot constitute a good consideration.[31] The justification for this approach seems to be that the provision of natural love and affection may be merely the motive for the making of a promise and that consideration differs from motive.[32] Thus, purely intangible returns, such as an undertaking to refrain from complaining about a proposed distribution of property, have been held not to amount to a good consideration for a promise to discharge a debtor from responsibility for his debt.[33] Likewise, it has been observed that to promise to compromise a claim which is known to be unenforceable involves neither benefit to the person who agrees not to pursue his claim nor detriment to the other party with the result that there is no consideration.[34]

Conversely, there appear to be a number of decisions of more recent origin which seem to demonstrate that the motive for making a promise may be artificially regarded as a sufficient consideration, thereby justifying the enforcement of the promise. For example, the extract from *Chappell and Co Ltd v Nestlé Co Ltd* (above) appears to be such a case, since the chocolate bar wrappers were thrown away, which may indicate that they were of no value to the promisor, with the result that their receipt was probably no more than a motive for the making of the promise. Similarly, *Hamer v Sidway*[35] (an American case, which probably also represents the true position in English law) may also fall within the same category.

---

31 *Brett v JS* (1600) Cro Eliz 756. Similarly, a promise to refrain from boring a relative with complaints about lack of equal treatment has been held not to amount to a good consideration for a promise to discharge the debts of the promisor: *White v Bluett* (1853) 23 LJ Ex 36.

32 *Thomas v Thomas* (1842) 2 QB 851. Historically, consideration was almost synonymous with motive: see Simpson, 1975, Chapter VII. Accordingly, the 19th century approach to the law of contract was responsible for something verging on a sea change.

33 *White v Bluett* (1853) 23 LJ Ex 36.

34 *Wade v Simeon* (1846) 2 CB 548. Conversely, forbearance to sue was regarded as a good consideration where the success of the claim was in doubt: *Horton v Horton (No 2)* [1961] 1 QB 215. Similarly, but with what justification is not clear, a compromise arrangement was held to be valid where the claim was bad but was believed by the promisee to be good: *Cook v Wright* (1861) 1 B & S 559.

35 (1891) 124 NY 538, Court of Appeals, New York.

In this case, William Storey Senior agreed to pay his nephew $5,000 if the nephew would agree to refrain from drinking liquor, using tobacco, swearing, and playing cards or billiards for money until he should reach the age of 21. The question arose as to the validity of this promise, it being alleged by the promisor that there was no consideration to support it. The nephew won the case:

Hamer v Sidway (1891) 124 NY 538, Court of Appeals, New York

Parker J: The defendant ... asserts that the promisee by refraining from the use of liquor and tobacco was not harmed, but benefited; that that which he did was best for him to do, independently of his uncle's promise – and insists that it follows that, unless the promisor was benefited, the contract was without consideration ... The promisee used tobacco, occasionally drank liquor and he had a legal right to do so. That right he abandoned for a period of years on the strength of the promise of the testator that, for such forbearance, he would give him $5,000. We need not speculate on the effort which may have been required to give up those stimulants. It is sufficient that he restricted his lawful freedom of action within certain prescribed limits upon the faith of his uncle's agreement, and now, having fully performed the conditions imposed, it is of no moment whether such performance actually proved a benefit to the promisor, and the court will not inquire into it; but, were it a proper subject of inquiry, we see nothing in this record that would permit a determination that the uncle was not benefited in a legal sense.

Would the court's response have differed if the nephew had promised to refrain from smoking cannabis or driving his sports car in excess of the national speed limit? If so, why?

What would have been the position if the nephew was a member of a religious cult, the rules of which were that no member was allowed to smoke, swear or gamble and that the nephew always intended to honour his religious beliefs? See *Arrale v Costain Civil Engineering Ltd*,[36] where it was observed that it is not consideration to refrain from a course of conduct which it was never intended to pursue.[37]

Is it important that the agreement was between family members – would Hamer have been approached on a different footing in English law had the court had the benefit of the decision in *Balfour v Balfour*,[38] considered below?

To insist that consideration must always have a literal economic value is undoubtedly wrong. If applied literally it would seem to undermine the idea that incurring a detriment alone is sufficient consideration for another's promise, and would cast doubt on many of the 'reward' cases. It has never seriously been suggested that 'walking to York', returning a lost dog to its

---

36 [1976] 1 Lloyd's Rep 98.
37 *Ibid*, p 106, *per* Geoffrey Lane LJ.
38 [1919] 2 KB 571.

owner or sniffing a smoke ball have to be proved to be of economic value to the person promising the reward. Indeed, in *Carlill v Carbolic Smoke Ball Co Ltd* [1893] 1 QB 256, p 271, Bowen LJ stated 'Inconvenience sustained by one party at the request of the other is enough to create a consideration'. (Of course, on the facts, he also felt the company received a benefit at least indirectly, because the use of the smoke balls would help promote their sale. This would have some ascertainable economic value.)

Performance of existing duties owed by law

A number of 19th century decisions suggest that if the promisee simply performs that which he is legally bound to perform, he will provide an insufficient consideration for the promise of the other party. Thus, if a witness agrees, for reward, to attend court in order to give evidence on behalf of the promisor, the promise of the latter will be unenforceable because it is given in return for something which has no value in the eyes of the law.[39]

If one adheres to the bargain theory, the problem of performance of an existing legal duty can be side-stepped by saying that the promisee has done more than he is legally bound to do.

In *Glasbrook Bros Ltd v Glamorgan County Council*,[40] the county council, as a police authority, had a responsibility in law to provide sufficient protection to life and property without payment. The appellants, during an industrial dispute at their colliery, requested police protection, insisting that the colliery could only be adequately protected if a body of police officers was stationed at the colliery. In the opinion of the police authority, an itinerant force was sufficient, but it was indicated that police officers could be billeted at the colliery if the appellants were to agree to pay for the additional protection. A majority of the House of Lords held that there was nothing illegal in this agreement and that by doing more than they were legally obliged to do, the police authority had provided consideration for the promise to pay:

Glasbrook Bros Ltd v Glamorgan County Council [1925] AC 270, HL, p 277

Viscount Cave LC: No doubt, there is an absolute and unconditional obligation binding the police authorities to take all steps which appear to them to be necessary for keeping the peace, for preventing crime, or for protecting property from criminal injury; and the public, who pay for this protection through the rates and taxes, cannot lawfully be called upon to make a further payment for that which is their right. This was laid down by Pickford LJ in the case of *Glamorganshire Coal Co v Glamorganshire Standing Joint Committee* [1916] 2 KB 206 in the following terms: 'If one party to a dispute is threatened with

39 *Collins v Godefroy* (1831) 1 B & Ad 950.
40 [1925] AC 270, HL.

violence by the other party, he is entitled to protection from such violence, whether his contention in the dispute be right or wrong, and to allow the police authority to deny him protection from that violence, unless he pays all the expense in addition to the contribution which with other ratepayers he makes to the support of the police is only one degree less dangerous than to allow that authority to decide which party is right in the dispute and grant or withhold protection accordingly. There is a moral duty on each party to the dispute to do nothing to aggravate it and to take reasonable means of self-protection, but the discharge of this duty by them is not a condition precedent to the discharge by the police authority of their own duty.'

With this statement of the law, I entirely agree, and I think that any attempt by a police authority to extract payment for services which fall within the plain obligations of the police force, should be firmly discountenanced by the courts. But it has always been recognised that, where individuals desire that services of a special kind which, though not within the obligations of a police authority, can most effectively be rendered by them, should be performed by members of the police force, the police authorities may (to use an expression which is found in the Police Pensions Act 1890) 'lend' the services of constables for that purpose in consideration of payment. Instances are the lending of constables on the occasions of large gatherings in and outside private premises, as on the occasions of weddings, athletic or boxing contests or race meetings, and the provision of constables at large railway stations. Of course, no such lending could possibly take place if the constables were required elsewhere for the preservation of order; but (as Bankes LJ pointed out) an effective police force requires a margin of reserve strength in order to deal with emergencies, and to employ that margin of reserve, when not otherwise required, on special police service for payment is to the advantage both of the persons utilising their services and of the public who are thereby relieved from some part of the police charges.

Atkin LJ put the contrary view in the form of a dilemma when he said: 'Either they were performing this public duty in giving the protection asked for, in which case I think they cannot charge, or, which no one suggests, they were at the request of an individual doing something which it was not their duty to do, in which case it seems to me both public policy and s 10 of the County Police Act 1839, make the contract illegal and void.'

With great respect to the learned Lord Justice, I am disposed to think that this reasoning rests on an ambiguous use of the word 'duty'. There may be services rendered by the police which, although not within the scope of their absolute obligations to the public, may yet fall within their powers, and in such cases public policy does not forbid their performance. I do not understand the reference in the above passage to s 10 of the Act of 1839 ...

I conclude, therefore, that the practice of lending constables for special duty in consideration of payment is not illegal or against public policy; and I pass to the second question – namely, whether in this particular case the lending of the 70 constables to be billeted in the appellants' colliery was a legitimate application of the principle. In this connection, I think it important to bear in mind exactly what it was that the learned trial judge had to decide. It was no part of his duty to say – nor did he purport to say – whether, in his judgment, the billeting of the 70 men at the colliery was necessary for the prevention of violence or the protection of the mines from criminal injury. The duty of determining such questions is cast by law, not upon the courts after the event, but upon the police authorities at the time when the decision has to be taken ...

Similarly, in *Ward v Byham*,[41] it was held that, if the mother of an illegitimate child agrees to keep the child well looked after and happy, she provides good consideration for the promise of the child's father to pay maintenance. The majority of the Court of Appeal felt able to base their decision on the conventional ground that the mother had agreed to do more than her public duty to maintain the child[42] by treating the undertaking to keep the child happy as an additional performance amounting to consideration for the father's promise.[43]

Performance of an existing contractual duty owed to the promisor

The bargain theory of consideration also generated the immensely inconvenient rule that the performance of an existing contractual duty owed by the promisee to the promisor could not constitute a good consideration. It followed that in the case of an attempted variation of an existing contractual arrangement, there was often no consideration for the promise to vary if all the promisee did was to continue to work towards the original objective of the contract. Thus, it has been held that a promise by a ship's master to pay extra remuneration to crew members who remained loyal in the face of a small scale desertion by others was not supported by continued performance of the existing contractual obligations of the loyal crew members.[44] In *Stilk v Myrick*,[45] the plaintiff was entitled to payment at the rate of £5 per month for working a ship from London to the Baltic and back. In the course of the voyage, two members of the crew deserted, but no replacements could be found by the ship's master. The master subsequently promised the remaining nine members of the crew that if they were to work the ship back to London, the wages of the deserters would be shared equally between the nine loyal members:

Stilk v Myrick (1809) 170 ER 1168, p 1169

Lord Ellenborough: ... The agreement is void for want of consideration. There was no consideration for the ulterior pay promised to the mariners who

---

41   [1956] 1 WLR 496.
42   As required by the National Assistance Act 1948, s 42.
43   [1956] 1 WLR 496, p 501, *per* Morris LJ.
44   *Stilk v Myrick* (1809) 170 ER 1168.
45   *Ibid.*

remained with the ship. Before they sailed from London, they had undertaken to do all they could under all the emergencies of the voyage. They had sold all their services till the voyage should be completed. If they had been at liberty to quit the ship at Cronstadt, the case would have been quite different; or if the captain had capriciously discharged the two men who were wanting, the others might not have been compellable to take the whole duty on themselves, and their agreeing to do so might have been a sufficient consideration for the promise of an advance of wages. But the desertion of part of the crew is to be considered an emergency of the voyage as much as their death; and those who remain are bound by the terms of their original contract to exert themselves to the utmost to bring the ship in safety to her destined port.

If it is possible to find in the performance of the promisee something over and above the requirements of the contract prior to the promise to vary, then there may be a good consideration for the promisor's promise. For example, in another desertion case, a promise by the ship's master to pay additional remuneration to loyal crew members was held to be enforceable where the return voyage was considered to be a venture different in kind from that originally envisaged by the parties because of the increased danger involved in sailing a ship substantially short-handed and in potentially dangerous and relatively unchartered waters.[46] However, it will be seen below that the actual performance of an existing contractual duty may be regarded as a bird in the hand, thereby constituting an indirect benefit to the promisor sufficient to render his promise enforceable.[47]

Performance of an existing contractual duty owed to a third party

Where the promisee is already under a contractual duty to a third party, the question has arisen whether his performance of that duty can amount to consideration for a new promise made by the promisor. A strict application of the bargain theory might suggest that if the promisee is already bound to perform, then nothing of legal value has been given in return for the promise of the other party.[48] However, the courts have been readily prepared to regard the performance of the existing duty under the contract with the third party as something of value to the promisor. One particular context in which this problem has arisen is where the promisor, the promisee and the third party are all participants in a 'network' contract,[49] under which all parties are working towards some common objective. For example, in international contracts for the sale of goods, there are frequently a number of distinct

---

46   *Hartley v Ponsonby* (1857) 7 E & B 872.

47   See the section on public policy below and the extract from *Williams v Roffey Bros and Nicholls (Contractors) Ltd* [1990] 1 All ER 512, considered above.

48   For a rough example of reasoning of this kind, see *Jones v Waite* (1839) 5 Bing NC 341.

49   See Adams and Brownsword, 1990, and see, also, Chapter 10.

parties working towards the fulfilment of the common objective of securing the sale and delivery of the goods from the seller to the buyer. In a typical contract of this kind, the seller will arrange for shipment of the goods through the medium of a carrier, the carrier may have arranged for the goods to be unloaded at their destination by a firm of stevedores. Moreover, the transaction may have been financed under the terms of a commercial credit, which will involve the participation of banks acting on behalf of the buyer and the seller. In this network of contractual arrangements, it is always possible that one party may perform a duty he already owes to another party in the network and it is quite possible that this performance may be regarded as consideration for a promise made by one of the other parties to the network. In *New Zealand Shipping Co Ltd v AM Satterthwaite & Co Ltd*,[50] the terms of a bill of lading stated that the carrier was not responsible for loss or damage to the cargo unless the action was brought within one year of the date on which loss or damage occurred. The bill further provided that the same immunity should extend to the carrier's servants, agents and independent contractors. The carrier was a wholly owned subsidiary of the stevedores who unloaded the ship in New Zealand. In the course of unloading a drill owned by the consignee, damage was caused by the stevedores who were then sued for their negligence more than a year from the date on which damage was caused. The principal issue was whether the stevedores were entitled to the protection of the immunity from suit provided for in the bill of lading. Standard commercial practice in this type of contract indicated that the consignee should be insured against transit risks, including damage resulting from the process of unloading the cargo. However, a literal application of the doctrine of privity of contract suggested that the stevedores were not parties to the bill of lading with the result that they might still be liable for the damage to the cargo caused by their negligence. In a supreme example of judicial pragmatism expounding market-realist considerations, Lord Wilberforce, expressing the majority view of the panel, was able to construct a contract between the stevedores and the consignee, based on a promise by the consignee to exempt the stevedores from liability if they were to fulfil their contractual obligation to the carrier to unload the ship on its arrival in New Zealand.

On the issue of consideration, Lord Wilberforce observed:

New Zealand Shipping Co Ltd v AM Satterthwaite & Co Ltd, The Eurymedon [1975] AC 154, PC, p 167

Lord Wilberforce: If the choice, and the antithesis, is between a gratuitous promise, and a promise for consideration, as it must be in the absence of a

---

50   *The Eurymedon* [1975] AC 154.

tertium quid, there can be little doubt which, in commercial reality, this is. The whole contract is of a commercial character, involving service on one side, rates of payment on the other and qualifying stipulations as to both. The relations of all parties to each other are commercial relations entered into for business reasons of ultimate profit. To describe one set of promises, in this context, as gratuitous, or *nudum pactum*, seems paradoxical and is *prima facie* implausible. It is only the precise analysis of this complex of relations into the classical offer and acceptance, with identifiable consideration, that seems to present difficulty, but this same difficulty exists in many situations of daily life, for example: sales at auction; supermarket purchases; boarding an omnibus; purchasing a train ticket; tenders for the supply of goods; offers of rewards; acceptance by post; warranties of authority by agents; manufacturers' guarantees; gratuitous bailments; bankers' commercial credits. These are all examples which show that English law, having committed itself to a rather technical and schematic doctrine of contract, in application takes a practical approach, often at the cost of forcing the facts to fit uneasily into the marked slots of offer, acceptance and consideration.

In their Lordships' opinion, the present contract presents much less difficulty than many of those above referred to. It is one of carriage from Liverpool to Wellington. The carrier assumes an obligation to transport the goods and to discharge at the port of arrival. The goods are to be carried and discharged, so the transaction is inherently contractual. It is contemplated that a part of this contract, viz discharge, may be performed by independent contractors – viz the appellant. By cl 1 of the bill of lading, the shipper agrees to exempt from liability the carrier, his servants and independent contractors in respect of the performance of this contract of carriage. Thus, if the carriage, including the discharge, is wholly carried out by the carrier, he is exempt. If part is carried out by him, and part by his servants, he and they are exempt. If part is carried out by him and part by an independent contractor, he and the independent contractor are exempt. The exemption is designed to cover the whole carriage from loading to discharge, by whomsoever it is performed: the performance attracts the exemption or immunity in favour of whoever the performer turns out to be. There is possibly more than one way of analysing this business transaction into the necessary components: that which their Lordships would accept is to say that the bill of lading brought into existence a bargain initially unilateral but capable of becoming mutual between the shipper and the appellant made through the carrier as agent. This became a full contract when the appellant performed services by discharging the goods. The performance of these services for the benefit of the shipper was the consideration for the agreement by the shipper that the appellant should have the benefit of the exemptions and limitations contained in the bill of lading.

The following points require mention: in their Lordships' opinion, consideration may quite well be provided by the appellant, as suggested, even though (or if) it was already under an obligation to discharge to the carrier. (There is no direct evidence of the existence or nature of this obligation, but their Lordships are prepared to assume it.) An agreement to do an act which the promisor is under an existing obligation to a third party to do, may quite well amount to valid consideration and does so in the present case: the promisee obtains the benefit of a direct obligation which he can enforce. This proposition is illustrated and supported by *Scotson v Pegg* (1861) 6 H and N 295, which their Lordships consider to be good law.

In this particular case, what seems to have been the guiding factor in holding that there was a good consideration for the promise to exempt the stevedores from liability was that there was some indirect benefit to the buyer in securing the delivery of the goods to their destination, subject to the terms of the bill of lading which formed the basis of the whole network of contracts between the various parties. Accordingly, the decision is overtly benefit based. However, other cases involving the performance of an existing contractual duty owed to a third party raise issues of reasonable reliance[51] and will be considered in more detail below.

Consideration must not be past

The so called rule against past consideration is another product of the bargain theory. If the act alleged to be consideration for a promise is executed before the date on which the promise was made, there is a past consideration which is generally said not to provide a good reason for enforcing the promise. Thus, in *Re McArdle*,[52] the plaintiff and her husband moved into a house which had been left to him and other members of his family under the terms of their deceased father's will. Without any request from the other family members, the plaintiff arranged for the property to be improved and decorated at a cost of £488. Subsequently, the other members of the family promised to pay the plaintiff £488 for the work she had done, but the promise was held to be unenforceable for want of consideration.

This result is understandable to the bargain theorist since there was no request for the work to be done and there was no discernible bargain between the parties. When the plaintiff arranged for the work to be done, she had no expectation that she would be paid by the other members of her family. She had not bargained for payment.

Of course, as already indicated in many cases there will be an express or implied request for the work to be done in circumstances where there is a 'reasonable expectation' of eventual payment for the work. If this is so then the inconvenience of the past consideration doctrine can be avoided without doing violence to bargain theory.[53]

---

51 See, eg, *Shadwell v Shadwell* (1860) 9 CB (NS) 159; 142 ER 62; *Scotson v Pegg* (1861) 6 H & N 295; and *Chichester v Cobb* (1866) 14 LT 433.

52 [1951] Ch 669.

53 *Re Casey's Patents, Stewart v Casey* [1892] 1 Ch 104; *Lampleigh v Brathwait* (1605) Hobart 105. See, also, the extract from *Pao On v Lau Yiu Long* [1980] AC 614, above.

Consideration must move from the promisee

The most overtly bargain-based rule of the doctrine of consideration is that consideration must move from the promisee,[54] that is, the reason for enforcing the promise must be found in the acts, omissions or words of the promisee. This, of course, envisages a bilateral relationship between the contracting parties and is very closely related to the doctrine of privity of contract, since if a person cannot show he is a party to the consideration, it is said to follow that he cannot be a party to the alleged bargain.[55] As will be demonstrated in Chapter 15, there are many exceptions to the rule, both common law and (in particular) statutory.

Critique: consideration, public policy and modern values

The real issue in many of the cases concerned with consideration is often one of public policy. It must be asked whether it is in the public interest for the promise to be enforced. Generally, if a person makes a specific request and he gets what he has asked for, there should be no policy reason for denying the enforceability of the promise he makes. In *Ward v Byham*,[56] the unmarried parents of an illegitimate child separated, with the result that the mother of the child was under a legal duty imposed by s 42 of the National Assistance Act 1948 to maintain the child. On separation, the father of the child wrote to the mother of the child stating, 'I am prepared to let you have the child and pay you up to £1 a week allowance for her, providing you can prove that she will be well looked after and happy and also that she is allowed to decide for herself whether or not she wishes to come and live with you'.

Some time later, the mother of the child remarried and the father stopped making his payments. In an action brought by the mother for the £1 per week promised by the father, it was held that the mother had provided consideration for the father's promise, although the reasoning of the members of the Court of Appeal differs somewhat:

Ward v Byham [1956] 1 WLR 496, CA, p 497

Denning LJ: The father agrees to let the mother have the child, provided the child herself wishes to come and provided also the mother satisfies the father that she will be well looked after and happy. The other thing is the future maintenance of the child. The father promises to pay the mother up to £1 per week so long as the mother looks after the child.

The mother now brings this action, claiming that the father should pay her £1 per week, even though she herself has married. The only point taken before us

---

54 See *Price v Easton* (1833) 4 B & Ad 433.
55 See *Tweddle v Atkinson* (1861) 1 B & S 363.
56 [1956] 1 WLR 496, CA.

in answer to the claim is that it is said that there was no consideration for the promise by the father to pay £1 a week, because, when she looked after the child, the mother was only doing that which she was legally bound to do, and that is no consideration in law. In support of this proposition, reliance was placed on a statement by Parke B, in the course of argument in *Crowhurst v Laverack* ((1852) 8 Exch 208, p 213).

By statute, the mother of an illegitimate child is bound to maintain it, whereas the father is under no such obligation (see s 42 of the National Assistance Act 1948). If she is a single woman, the mother can apply to the magistrates for an affiliation order against the father and it might be thought that consideration could be found in this case by holding that the mother must be taken to have agreed not to bring affiliation proceedings against the father. In her evidence, the mother said, however, that she never at any time had any intention of bringing affiliation proceedings. It is now too late for her to bring them, because she has married and is no longer a single woman.

I approach the case, therefore, on the footing that, in looking after the child, the mother is only doing what she is legally bound to do. Even so, I think that there was sufficient consideration to support the promise. I have always thought that a promise to perform an existing duty or the performance of it should be regarded as good consideration, because it is a benefit to the person to whom it is given. Take this very case. It is as much a benefit for the father to have the child looked after by the mother as by a neighbour. If he gets the benefit for which he stipulated, he ought to honour his promise, and he ought not to avoid it by saying that the mother was herself under a duty to maintain the child.

I regard the father's promise in this case as what is sometimes called a unilateral contract, a promise in return for an act, a promise by the father to pay £1 a week in return for the mother's looking after the child. Once the mother embarked on the task of looking after the child, there was a binding contract. So long as she looked after the child, she would be entitled to £1 a week.

Contrast the approach adopted by Morris LJ, with whom Parker LJ agreed:

Morris LJ (p 498): I think that the letter of 27 July 1954, shows that there was consideration for the agreement and promise of the father. After the mother was made to leave the home in May 1954, the child in fact stayed with the father until July. The terms of the father's letter of 27 July suggest that he was animated by a concern for the well being of the child. The phrases that he uses are evidence of that. When the mother asked for the child, the answer was in the terms of the letter. Counsel for the father submits that there was a duty on the mother to support the child, that no affiliation proceedings were in prospect or were contemplated, and that the effect of the arrangement that followed the letter was that the father was merely agreeing to pay a bounty to the mother.

It seems to me that the terms of the letter negative those submissions, for the father says: 'Providing you can prove that [the child] will be well looked after and happy and also that she is allowed to decide for herself whether or not she wishes to come and live with you.'

The father goes on to say that the child is then well and happy and looking much stronger than ever before. 'If you decide what to do, let me know as soon as possible.' It seems to me, therefore, that the father was saying, in effect: irrespective of what may be the strict legal position, what I am asking is that you shall prove that the child will be well looked after and happy, and also that you must agree that the child is to be allowed to decide for herself whether or not she wishes to come and live with you. If those conditions were fulfilled the father was agreeable to pay. On those terms, which, in fact, became operative, the father agreed to pay £1 a week. In my judgment, there was ample consideration there to be found for his promise, which I think was binding.

If the mother was doing what she was legally bound to do, where was the consideration for the promise to pay? Denning LJ suggested it lay in the fact that the father derives a benefit from having the child looked after. The unstated rationale of Denning LJ's judgment is that there is no public policy reason for denying the validity of the father's promise. This issue is taken further by Lord Denning in *Williams v Williams* considered below.

What had the promisor asked for in *Ward v Byham*? Was it unreasonable to expect the mother of the child to do what he was asking? Did the father of the child, in practice, gain a benefit from the mother's performance of a duty which, legally, she was obliged to perform? Had the mother extorted the father's promise to pay for the upkeep of the child?

The reasoning of the majority in *Ward v Byham* suggests that in terms of the conventional 'contract rule-book' there was consideration for the father's promise to pay. Does this smack of judicial 'formalism', that is, an attempt to keep new cases within the bounds of existing legal principle regardless of the extreme difficulty in doing so?

Adams and Brownsword offer the following analysis:

The rival approaches in *Ward v Byham* reflect the general distinction between a formalist and a realist approach to the question of sufficiency of consideration. For formalists, the enforcement of promises must be consistent with traditional consideration theory, and thus engenders some elaborate conceptual gymnastics. In the existing legal duty cases, like *Ward v Byham*, the record is kept pure by conjuring up 'extra' detriment on the part of the person who already has a legal duty. Similarly in the past consideration cases ... the circle is squared by implying a prior promise to pay for the service. For realists, however, sufficiency of consideration is to be determined less by 'consideration considerations' than by 'public policy considerations' whether market-individualist or consumer-welfarist. Accordingly, formalist gymnastics are both unnecessary and irrelevant.[57]

In the following case, Lord Denning was more explicit in his reference to the relevance of policy considerations:

---

57 Adams and Brownsword, 2000, p 77.

Williams v Williams [1957] 1 WLR 149, CA

Denning LJ: In this case, a wife claims sums due to her under a maintenance agreement. No evidence was called in the court below because the facts are agreed. The parties were married on 25 April 1945: they have no children. On 24 January 1952, the wife deserted the husband. On 26 March 1952, they signed the agreement now sued upon, which has three clauses: '(1) the husband will pay to the wife for her support and maintenance a weekly sum of One Pound 10 Shillings to be paid every four weeks during the joint lives of the parties so long as the wife shall lead a chaste life the first payment hereunder to be made on the 15th day of April 1952; (2) the wife will out of the said weekly sum or otherwise support and maintain herself and will indemnify the husband against all debts to be incurred by her and will not in any way at any time hereafter pledge the husband's credit; (3) the wife shall not, so long as the husband shall punctually make the payments hereby agreed to be made, commence or prosecute against the husband any matrimonial proceedings other than proceedings for dissolution of marriage but, upon the failure of the husband to make the said weekly payments as and when the same become due, the wife shall be at full liberty on her election to pursue all and every remedy in this regard either by enforcement of the provisions hereof or as if this agreement had not been made.'

So far as we know, the parties have remained apart ever since. On 1 June 1955, the husband petitioned for divorce, on the ground of his wife's desertion and, on 12 October 1955, a *decree nisi* was made against her. On 2 December 1955, the decree was made absolute. In this action the wife claims maintenance at the rate of £1 10s a week under the agreement for a period from October 1954, to October 1955. The sum claimed is £30 5s 9d, which is the appropriate sum after deduction of tax.

The husband disputes the claim, on the ground that there was no consideration for his promise. Clause 2, he says, is worthless and cl 3 is unenforceable.

Let me first deal with cl 3. It is settled law that a wife, despite such a clause as cl 3 can make application to the magistrates or to the High Court for maintenance. If this wife made such an application, the husband could set up the fact of desertion as an answer to the claim, but he could not set up cl 3 as a bar to the proceedings. The clause is void, and as such is no consideration to support the agreement: see *Bennett v Bennett* [1952] 1 KB 249.

But, in the present case, the husband says that, as the wife deserted him, he was under no obligation to maintain her and she was not entitled to pledge his credit in any way. Clause 2 therefore gives him nothing and is valueless to him. The husband says that *Goodinson v Goodinson* [1954] 2 QB 118 is distinguishable, because there was no finding in that case that the wife was in desertion and, moreover, the wife promised to maintain the child as well as herself.

Now I agree that, in promising to maintain herself whilst she was in desertion, the wife was only promising to do that which she was already bound to do. Nevertheless, a promise to perform an existing duty is, I think, sufficient consideration to support a promise, so long as there is nothing in the transaction which is contrary to the public interest. Suppose that this agreement had never been made and the wife had made no promise to maintain herself and did not do so. She might then have sought and received public assistance or have pledged her husband's credit with tradesmen: in which case, the National Assistance Board might have summoned him before the magistrates or the tradesmen might have sued him in the county court. It is true that he would have an answer to those claims because she was in desertion, but nevertheless he would be put to all the trouble, worry and expense of defending himself against them. By paying her 30s a week and taking this promise from her that she will maintain herself and will not pledge his credit, he has an added safeguard to protect himself from all this worry, trouble and expense. That is a benefit to him which is good consideration for his promise to pay maintenance. That was the view which appealed to the county court judge: and I must say that it appeals to me also.

There is another ground on which good consideration can be found. Although the wife was in desertion, nevertheless, it must be remembered that desertion is never irrevocable. It was open to her to come back at any time. Her right to maintenance was not lost by the desertion. It was only suspended. If she made a genuine offer to return which he rejected, she would have been entitled to maintenance from him. She could apply to the magistrates or the High Court for an order in her favour. If she did so, however, whilst this agreement was in force, the 30s would be regarded as *prima facie* the correct figure. It is a benefit to the husband for it to be so regarded, and that is sufficient consideration to support his promise.

I construe this agreement as a promise by the husband to pay his wife 30s a week in consideration of her promise to maintain herself during the time she is living separate from him, whether due to her own fault or not.

The wife cannot throw over the agreement and seek more maintenance from him unless new circumstances arise making it reasonable to allow her to depart from it. The husband cannot throw it over unless they resume married life together (in which case it will by inference be rescinded) or they are divorced (in which case it is a post-nuptial settlement and can be varied accordingly), or perhaps other circumstances arise not envisaged at the time of the agreement. Nothing of that kind has, however, occurred here. The husband must honour his promise.

I would dismiss the appeal accordingly.

However, the following extract shows that the spirit of Lord Denning's views on the role of policy may be instrumental in the decision of a court whilst some regard is still notionally made to formal requirements. In *Williams v Roffey Bros and Nicholls (Contractors) Ltd*,[58] Glidewell LJ states as follows:

---

58 [1991] 1 QB 1, CA.

Williams v Roffey Bros & Nicholls (Contractors) Ltd [1991] 1 QB, CA, p 11

Glidewell LJ: In *North Ocean Shipping Co Ltd v Hyundai Construction Ltd* [1979] QB 705, Mocatta J regarded the general principle of the decision in *Stilk v Myrick* as still being good law. He referred to two earlier decisions of this court, dealing with wholly different subjects, in which Denning LJ sought to escape from the confines of the rule, but was not accompanied in his attempt by the other members of the court ...

Glidewell LJ then discussed the decision in *Ward v Byham* considered above and continued:

As I read the decision of Morris LJ [in *Ward v Byham*] he and Parker LJ held that, though in maintaining the child, the plaintiff was doing no more than she was obliged to do by law, nevertheless, her promise that the child was well looked after and happy was a practical benefit to the father, which amounted to consideration for his promise.

Glidewell LJ then considered the reasoning employed by Denning LJ in the Court of Appeal in *Williams v Williams* and continued:

However, the other members of the court (Hodson and Morris LJJ) declined to agree with this expression of view, although agreeing with Denning LJ in finding that there was consideration because the wife's desertion might not have been permanent, and thus there was a benefit to the husband.

Accordingly, following the view of the majority in *Ward v Byham* and of the whole court in *Williams v Williams* and that of the Privy Council in *Pao On v Lau Yiu Long* [1980] AC 614 ...

Glidewell LJ then stated the six part proposition detailed above.

The problem with the view expressed by Glidewell LJ is that it is far from clear if the authorities on which he relies do support the propositions which he puts forward. The reasoning of the majority in *Ward v Byham* and the proposition said to represent the decision of the whole court in *Williams v Williams* is supposedly based on the promisee having done more than she was obliged to do. In itself, this is a questionable analysis in that as already indicated Denning's views on public policy in *Williams v Williams* are, if anything, clearer than the views he expressed in *Ward v Byham*. Moreover, Glidewell LJ appears to have been able to derive from these cases the view that in each case there was something of benefit conferred on the promisor. In reality, the views expressed by Denning LJ in both of these cases would appear to provide stronger support for the result in *Williams v Roffey*, particularly in the absence of anything in the negotiations proved to be indicative of fraud or duress (and so against public policy).

Fairness of exchange

Classical contract law can be said to be based on the values of individualism and freedom of contract, which leaves a contracting party the antagonistic defender of his or her own position. In a climate based on such values, the role of the court is minimal. However, it can be suggested that modern values may be more based on co-operation and that courts may be more concerned with fairness in the exchange process. In *Williams v Williams*, *Ward v Byham* and *Williams v Roffey*, the promisor had made a specific request and got what he/she asked for. But it is not difficult to change the facts of these cases in a manner which might disclose difficult policy issues. Suppose, in *Williams v Roffey*, it was not the promisor, but the promisee who had instigated the negotiations and there was a veiled threat to the effect, 'unless you pay me an inflated price for completing the work, I will not go ahead, and I know I have you over a barrel, because I am aware that unless the building work is completed on time, you will have to pay a heavy penalty'. In these circumstances, the court is likely to refuse to allow a contracting party to take unfair advantage of his stronger bargaining position and may promote the value of social co-operation.

In *D & C Builders Ltd v Rees*,[59] the plaintiffs were a firm of builders who had carried out work on the defendant's shop to the value of almost £747. Two hundred and fifty pounds had been paid on account and the plaintiffs had given the defendant a £14 allowance, so that the outstanding debt was one of almost £483. The defendant did not pay when asked to do so and refrained from replying to requests for payment until some four months later, when the defendant's wife offered to pay £300 in full and final settlement. The plaintiffs were in desperate financial circumstances and, if they did not accept payment of the £300, they faced the possibility of bankruptcy – a fact of which the defendant was aware. The defendant's wife consistently refused to pay any more than the £300 offered and the question arose whether the plaintiffs could sue for the balance of the debt due. At first instance, it was held that there was no binding settlement, so that there was no bar to the plaintiffs recovering the balance of the debt. On appeal by the defendant, the Court of Appeal unanimously found in favour of the plaintiffs on the basis that under the rule in *Foakes v Beer*,[60] payment of a lesser sum does not satisfy a greater debt. Lord Denning MR also thought that the doctrine of promissory estoppel would not assist the defendant since he and his wife had sought to take unfair advantage of the plaintiffs' position:

D & C Builders Ltd v Rees [1966] 2 QB 617, CA, p 624

Danckwerts LJ: ... *Foakes v Beer*, applying the decision in *Pinnel's Case* (1602) 5 Co Rep 117a settled definitely the rule of law that the payment of a lesser sum than the amount of a debt due cannot be a satisfaction of the debt, unless there is some benefit to the creditor added so that there is an accord and satisfaction ... I also agree that, in the circumstances of the present case, there was no true

---

59 [1966] 2 QB 617, CA.

60 (1884) 9 App Cas 605.

accord. The Reeses really behaved very badly. They knew of the plaintiffs' financial difficulties and used their awkward situation to intimidate them. The plaintiffs did not wish to accept the sum of £300 in discharge of the debt of £482, but were desperate to get some money. It would appear also that the defendant and his wife misled the plaintiffs as to their own financial position. Rees, in his evidence, said: 'In June I could have paid £700 odd. I could have settled the whole bill.' There is no evidence that by August, or even November, their financial situation had deteriorated so that they could not pay the £482.

Lord Denning MR (p 626) [In relation to the possible application of 'promissory estoppel',[61] Lord Denning stated the principle enunciated in *Hughes v Metropolitan Railway* and continued]: This principle has been applied to cases where the creditor agrees to accept a lesser sum in discharge of a greater. So much so that we can now say that, when a creditor and a debtor enter on a course of negotiation, which leads the debtor to suppose that on payment of the lesser sum, the creditor will not enforce payment of the balance, and on the faith thereof the debtor pays the lesser sum and the creditor accepts it in satisfaction: then the creditor will not be allowed to enforce payment of the balance when it would be inequitable to do so ...

In applying this principle, however, we must note the qualification. The creditor is barred from his legal rights only when it would be inequitable for him to insist on them. Where there has been a true accord, under which the creditor voluntarily agrees to accept a lesser sum in satisfaction, and the debtor acts on that accord by paying the lesser sum and the creditor accepts it, then it is inequitable for the creditor afterwards to insist on the balance. But he is not bound unless there has been truly an accord between them.

In the present case ... it seems to me that there was no true accord. The debtor's wife held the creditor to ransom. The creditor was in need of money to meet his commitments, and she knew it ... She could properly have said: 'We cannot pay you more than £300. Please accept it on account.' But she had no right to insist on his taking it in settlement. When she said, 'We will pay you nothing unless you accept £300 in settlement', she was putting undue pressure on the creditor. She was making a threat to break the contract (by paying nothing) and she was doing it so as to compel the creditor to do what he was unwilling to do and she succeeded ... There is also no equity in the defendant to warrant any departure from the due course of law. No person can insist on a settlement procured by intimidation.

See, also, *North Ocean Shipping Co Ltd v Hyundai Construction Ltd*,[62] cited above. Determining whether a person has crossed the line between extortion and legitimate commercial pressure is often a difficult decision to make. Relevant factors seem to include whether the promisor has taken his decision to make the promise with his eyes open. Thus, if he has first obtained legal advice, the promisor may find that his promise is enforceable.

---

61 Considered in more detail below.
62 *The Atlantic Baron* [1979] QB 705.

In *Pao On v Lau Yiu Long*,[63] the plaintiffs owned shares in a private company which had one principal asset (a building under construction) which the defendants wished to acquire. The proposed method of acquisition was that a public company in which the defendants were the majority shareholder should buy from the plaintiffs their shares in the private company, the price to be paid by the issue of shares by the plaintiffs to the public company. In order not to depress the market for shares in the public company, the plaintiffs agreed, at the defendants' request, to retain 60% of the shares until after April 1974. A subsidiary agreement was made between the plaintiffs and the defendants whereby the plaintiffs were protected against a fall in value of the shares pending the handover date in April, but this also had the effect of denying the plaintiffs any advantage should the price of those shares rise during the same period. As a result, the plaintiffs refused to complete the main agreement, unless the defendants agreed to cancel the subsidiary agreement and replace it with a guarantee by way of indemnity should the value of the shares fall. The defendants, fearing the delays of litigation and the possible adverse effects on the public company, agreed to issue the guarantee, but only after having taken legal advice. Subsequently, the value of the shares in the private company did fall and the plaintiffs sought to enforce the guarantee. The Privy Council held that although the defendants had been subject to commercial pressure, they had not been coerced into giving the guarantee with the result that the contract was not voidable on the ground of duress:

Pao On v Lau Yiu Long [1980] AC 614, p 635

Lord Scarman: Duress, whatever form it takes, is a coercion of the will so as to vitiate consent. Their Lordships agree with the observation of Kerr J in *Occidental Worldwide Investment Corpn v Skibs A/S Avanti* [1976] 1 Lloyd's Rep 293, p 336 that in a contractual situation commercial pressure is not enough. There must be present some factor 'which could in law be regarded as a coercion of his will so as to vitiate his consent'. This conception is in line with what was said in this Board's decision in *Barton v Armstrong* [1976] AC 104, p 121 by Lord Wilberforce and Lord Simon of Glaisdale – observations with which the majority judgment appears to be in agreement. In determining whether there was a coercion of will such that there was no true consent, it is material to inquire whether the person alleged to have been coerced did or did not protest; whether, at the time he was allegedly coerced into making the contract, he did or did not have an alternative course open to him such as an adequate legal remedy; whether he was independently advised; and whether after entering the contract he took steps to avoid it. All these matters are, as was recognised in *Maskell v Horner* [1915] 3 KB 106, relevant in determining whether he acted voluntarily or not.

---

63 [1980] AC 614.

In the present case, there is unanimity amongst the judges below that there was no coercion of the first defendant's will. In the Court of Appeal, the trial judge's finding (already quoted) that the first defendant considered the matter thoroughly, chose to avoid litigation, and formed the opinion that the risk in giving the guarantee was more apparent than real was upheld. In short, there was commercial pressure, but no coercion. Even if this Board was disposed, which it is not, to take a different view, it would not substitute its opinion for that of the judges below on this question of fact.

It is, therefore, unnecessary for the Board to embark upon an inquiry into the question whether English law recognises a category of duress known as 'economic duress'.

It is also clear that *Williams v Roffey* does not apply in all circumstances. In particular, it appears that English law now makes an unsustainable distinction between the performance of an existing duty to provide a service or supply goods and the performance of a duty to pay money. Following *Williams v Roffey*, the performance of an existing duty to provide a service appears to be capable of amounting to consideration for a promise to pay extra reward, provided there is no reason of policy to suggest otherwise, but the same cannot be said of a promise to pay money. In *Foakes v Beer*,[64] Julia Beer had a High Court judgment debt against John Foakes for the sum of £2,090 19s. She came to an agreement with him that if he paid off the debt via a £500 down payment and subsequent six monthly instalments of £150 (effectively, payment over five years) she would 'not take any proceedings whatever on the said judgment'. John Foakes paid off the judgment debt in full, but was then sued by Julia Beer for interest which had accrued under the judgment. The agreement of 21 December 1876 had made no express mention of interest and the promise 'not to take any proceedings' was ambiguous; it could either have meant not suing on the judgment at all (even for interest) or merely not issuing proceedings for enforcement of the judgment whilst John Foakes was paying off the original sum. The House of Lords was prepared, for the sake of argument, to assume the former construction, but even so felt that Julia Beer's promise was not binding on her, because of a lack of consideration. She could, therefore, legitimately claim interest:

Foakes v Beer (1884) 9 App Cas 605, p 611

Earl of Selborne LC: But the question remains whether the agreement is capable of being legally enforced. Not being under seal, it cannot be legally enforced against the respondent, unless she received consideration for it from the appellant, or unless, though without consideration, it operates by way of accord and satisfaction, so as to extinguish the claim for interest. What is the consideration? On the face of the agreement, none is expressed, except a

---

64   (1884) 9 App Cas 605.

present payment of £500, on account and in part of the larger debt then due and payable by law under the judgment. The appellant did not contract to pay the future instalments of £150 each, at the times therein mentioned; much less did he give any new security, in the shape of negotiable paper, or in any other form. The promise *de futuro* was only that of the respondent that if the half-yearly payments of £150 each were regularly paid, she would 'take no proceedings whatever on the judgment'. No doubt, if the appellant had been under no antecedent obligation to pay the whole debt, his fulfilment of the condition might have imported some consideration on his part for that promise. But he was under that antecedent obligation; and payment at those deferred dates, by the forbearance and indulgence of the creditor, of the residue of the principal debt and costs, could not (in my opinion) be a consideration for the relinquishment of interest and discharge of the judgment, unless the payment of the £500, at the time of signing the agreement, was such a consideration. As to accord and satisfaction, in point of fact, there could be no complete satisfaction, so long as any future instalment remained payable; and I do not see how any mere payments on account could operate in law as a satisfaction ad interim, conditionally upon other payments being afterwards duly made, unless there was a consideration sufficient to support the agreement while still unexecuted. Nor was anything, in fact, done by the respondent in this case, on the receipt of the last payment, which could be tantamount to an acquittance, if the agreement did not previously bind her.

The question, therefore, is nakedly raised by this appeal, whether your Lordships are now prepared, not only to overrule, as contrary to law, the doctrine stated by Sir Edward Coke to have been laid down by all the judges of the Common Pleas in *Pinnel's Case* in 1602, and repeated in his note to Littleton, s 344(2) but to treat a prospective agreement, not under seal, for satisfaction of a debt, by a series of payments on account to a total amount less than the whole debt, as binding in law, provided those payments are regularly made; the case not being one of a composition with a common debtor, agreed to, *inter se*, by several creditors. I prefer so to state the question instead of treating it (as it was put at the Bar) as depending on the authority of the case of *Cumber v Wane*, decided in 1718. It may well be that distinctions, which in later cases have been held sufficient to exclude the application of that doctrine, existed and were improperly disregarded in *Cumber v Wane*; and yet that the doctrine itself may be law, rightly recognised in *Cumber v Wane*, and not really contradicted by any later authorities. And this appears to me to be the true state of the case. The doctrine itself, as laid down by Sir Edward Coke, may have been criticised, as questionable in principle, by some persons whose opinions are entitled to respect, but it has never been judicially overruled; on the contrary I think it has always, since the sixteenth century, been accepted ads law. If so, I cannot think that your Lordships would do right, if you were now to reverse, as erroneous, a judgment of the Court of Appeal, proceeding upon a doctrine which has been accepted as part of the law of England for 280 years.

The doctrine, as stated in *Pinnel's Case*, is 'that payment of a lesser sum on the day' (it would of course be the same after the day), 'in satisfaction of a greater, cannot be any satisfaction for the whole, because it appears to the Judges, that by no possibility a lesser sum can be a satisfaction to the plaintiff for a greater sum'. As stated in Coke Littleton, 212(b), it is, 'where the condition is for payment of £20, the obligor or feoffor cannot at the time appointed pay a lesser sum in satisfaction of the whole, because it is apparent that a lesser sum of money cannot be a satisfaction of a greater;' adding (what is beyond controversy), that an acquittance under seal, in full, satisfaction of the whole, would (under like circumstances) be valid and binding.

The distinction between the effect of a deed under seal and that of an agreement by parol, or by writing not under seal, may seem arbitrary, but it is established in our law; nor is it really unreasonable or practically inconvenient that the law should require particular solemnities to give to a gratuitous contract the force of a binding obligation. If the question be (as in the actual state of the law, I think it is), whether consideration is, or is not, given in a case of this kind, by the debtor who pays down part of the debt presently due from him, for a promise by the creditor to relinquish, after certain further payments on account, the residue of the debt, I cannot say that I think consideration is given, in the sense in which I have always understood that word as used in our law. It might be (and, indeed, I think it would be) an improvement in our law if a release or acquittance of the whole debt, on payment of any sum which the creditor might be content to receive by way of accord and satisfaction (though less than the whole), were held to be, generally, binding, though not under seal; nor should I be unwilling to see equal force given to a prospective agreement, like the present, in writing though not under seal; but I think it impossible, without refinements which practically alter the sense of the word, to treat such a release or acquittance as supported by any new consideration proceeding from the debtor. All the authorities subsequent to *Cumber v Wane*, which were relied upon by the appellant at your Lordships' Bar (such as *Sibree v Tripp*, *Curlewis v Clark*, and *Goddard v O'Brien*) have proceeded upon the distinction, that, by giving negotiable paper or otherwise, there had been some new consideration for a new agreement, distinct from mere money payments in or towards discharge of the original liability. I think it unnecessary to go through those cases, or to examine the particular grounds on which each of them was decided. There are no such facts in the case now before your Lordships. What is called "any benefit, or even any legal possibility of benefit", in Mr Smith's notes to *Cumber v Wane*, is not (as I conceive), that sort of benefit which a creditor may derive from getting payment of part of the money due to him from a debtor who might otherwise keep him at arm's length, or possibly become insolvent, but is some independent benefit, actual or contingent, of a kind which might in law be a good and valuable consideration for any other sort of agreement not under seal.

Foakes v Beer is, in every respect, an unsatisfactory decision, a triumph of formal reasoning despite the serious 'market oriented' and 'realist' concerns of the judges as to the inconvenience of the rule they were espousing. The Earl of

Selborne, in the passage extracted above, feels that the opposite rule would be an improvement in the law, and Lord Blackburn stated that (at p 622) 'all men of business ... every day recognise and act on the ground that prompt payment of part of their demand may be more beneficial to them than it would be to insist on their rights and enforce payment of the whole'. Nevertheless it still appears to represent the general position at common law (albeit with a number of important exceptions). It has recently been stated to be unaffected by the decision in *Williams v Roffey*.

In *Re Selectmove Ltd*,[65] the company owed substantial amounts of tax (PAYE) to the Inland Revenue. A director of the company met a Mr Polland, a collector of taxes, to explain the company's trading position. It was proposed to Polland that the company should pay off amounts of past tax due in instalments of £1,000 per month and should make prompt payment of all future amounts due. Polland was prepared to recommend the proposal to his superiors given the continuing support offered to the company by its bankers. In the event the company heard nothing from the Revenue. More than likely the rules on (non) acceptance by silence (see Chapter 2) and the lack of any obvious authority by Polland to give any formal undertaking binding the Revenue were enough to decide the case. However, one of the other issues raised was whether there was in any event consideration for the promise to accept payment of the arrears by instalments. The Court of Appeal found itself bound by the decision in *Foakes v Beer* and was unable to apply the decision in *Williams v Roffey* in favour of the company:

Re Selectmove Ltd [1995] 1 WLR 474 CA, p 479

Peter Gibson LJ: There are two elements to the consideration which the company claims was provided by it to the Revenue. One is the promise to pay off its existing liability by instalments ... The other is the promise to pay future PAYE and NIC as they fell due. Mr Nugee suggested that implicit in the latter was the promise to continue trading. But that cannot be spelt out of Mr Ffook's evidence as to what was agreed with Polland. Accordingly, the second element is no more than a promise to pay that which it was bound to pay under the fiscal legislation at the date when it was bound to make such payment ...

Mr Nugee, however, submitted that an additional benefit to the Revenue was conferred by the agreement in that the Revenue stood to derive practical benefits therefrom: it was likely to recover more from not enforcing its debt against the company, which was known to be in financial difficulties, than from putting the company into liquidation ... He relied on the decision of this court in *Williams v Roffey Bros and Nicholls (Contractors) Ltd* [1991] 1 QB 1 ... for the proposition that a promise to perform an existing obligation can amount to good consideration provided there are practical benefits to the promisee ...

Mr Nugee submitted that although Glidewell LJ in terms confined his remarks to a case where B is to do the work for or supply goods or services to A, the

---

65 [1995] 1 WLR 474.

same principle must apply where B's obligation is to pay A ... I see the force of the argument, but the difficulty that I feel with it is that, if the principle of the *Williams* case is to be extended to an obligation to make payment, it would in effect leave the principle in *Foakes v Beer* 9 App Cas 605 without any application. When a creditor and a debtor who are at arm's length reach an agreement on the payment of the debt by instalments to accommodate the debtor, the creditor will no doubt always see a practical benefit to himself in so doing. In the absence of authority there would be much to be said for the enforceability of such a contract. But that was a matter expressly considered in *Foakes v Beer,* yet held not to constitute good consideration in law. *Foakes v Beer* was not even referred to in *Williams v Roffey Bros & Nicholls (Contractors) Ltd* [1991] 1 QB 1 and it is in my judgment impossible, consistently with the doctrine of precedent, for this court to extend the principle of the *Williams* case to any circumstances governed by the principle of *Foakes v Beer* 9 App Cas 605. If that extension is to be made, it must be by the House of Lords or, perhaps even more appropriately, by Parliament after consideration by the Law Commission.

Is this an example of formalism at work? Is there sufficient in the House of Lords' decision in *Foakes v Beer* to allow it to be distinguished? Does *Foakes v Beer* apply to cases where the debtor pays the amount he is required to pay, but at a later stage than was originally agreed or does it apply only where the debtor pays less than the amount he owes to the creditor?[66]

One of the important policies at work is that the courts will not countenance the possibility of extortion. The same policy also raises its head in some of the cases in which a forbearance to sue has failed to disclose a good consideration on the ground that there is a public interest not to allow someone to pursue a claim when he knows he does not have a good cause of action. To adopt a different rule might encourage the exertion of improper pressure.

If a person agrees to compromise a valid claim for an uncertain amount, or even a genuinely doubtful claim, a promise to forego the claim will be regarded as consideration for a promise to pay a sum of money in settlement of the claim. However, in the case of *Wade v Simeon*, the claim was demonstrably bound to fail. Because of this additional factor, there was held to be no consideration for the promise to settle:

Wade v Simeon (1846) 2 CB 548, p 564

Tindal CJ: The fourth plea states that the plaintiff never had any cause of action against the defendant in respect of the subject matter of the action in the Court of Exchequer, which he, the plaintiff, at the time of the commencement of the said action, and thence until the time of the making of the promise in the first count mentioned, well knew. By demurring to that plea, the plaintiff

---

66 See *Vanbergen v St Edmunds Properties Ltd* [1933] 2 KB 223.

admits that he had no cause of action against the defendant in the action therein mentioned, and that he knew it. It appears to me, therefore, that he is estopped from saying that there was any valid consideration for the defendant's promise. It is almost *contra bonos mores*, and certainly contrary to all the principles of natural justice, that a man should institute proceedings against another, when he is conscious that he has no good cause of action. In order to constitute a binding promise, the plaintiff must shew a good consideration, something beneficial to the defendant, or detrimental to the plaintiff. Detrimental to the plaintiff it cannot be, if he has no cause of action: and beneficial to the defendant it cannot be; for, in contemplation of law, the defence upon such an admitted state of facts must be successful, and the defendant will recover costs, which must be assumed to be a full compensation for all the legal damage he may sustain. The consideration, therefore, altogether fails.

Social co-operation

Many contractual relationships fail to typify the paradigm bilateral relationship which seems to dominate the 19th century rule-book. Instead, many modern relationships work on the basis of co-operation and inter-dependence. In such a climate, the law should encourage the acceptance of responsibility towards others and should foster trust in and respect for others. This is especially so in long term business relationships which may involve complex inter-relationships in which it is essential for the parties to co-operate with each other in order to ensure satisfactory completion of the long-term objective for the benefit of all concerned. In such relationships, there may be gaps in the planning process and the whole arrangement may be geared towards flexibility rather than certainty.[67] Moreover, it may be that insistence on fine detail in long term business relationships is bad for continuing business relations.[68]

THE PROPER ADMINISTRATION OF JUSTICE

If there is a suspicion that a witness is demanding payment for his attendance at court, this would seem to undermine the proper administration of justice. Similarly, a demand by a police authority for payment prior to their intervention to restore law and order would almost certainly offend public policy. On the other hand, if the police do more than is necessary to maintain

---

67 See Macneil, 1978a, p 865.
68 See Beale and Dugdale, 1975.

law and order by providing additional services requested by the promisor, there would appear to be no public policy argument against enforcing the promise of reward.[69] Moreover, similar considerations also appear to play a part when determining whether there is an intention to create legal relations. In particular, in deciding whether or not to allow a particular claim to be heard in a commercial court an important consideration is whether to do so might adversely affect the proper administration of justice.

In *Balfour v Balfour*,[70] the plaintiff sued her husband, the defendant, for money owed to her under an alleged verbal maintenance agreement entered into prior to the defendant's departure to Ceylon (Sri Lanka) to take up a government posting. In addition to the amounts claimed under this alleged agreement, the plaintiff had also obtained an order for restitution of conjugal rights (which included the right to pledge her husband's credit) and an order for alimony. The court held that there was no intention to create legal relations with the result that the verbal agreement as to maintenance was unenforceable. However the reasoning of Atkin LJ also reveals that other policy considerations were at work:

Balfour v Balfour [1919] 2 KB 571, CA, p 578

Atkin LJ: The defence to this action on the alleged contract is that the defendant, the husband, entered into no contract with his wife, and for the determination of that it is necessary to remember that there are agreements between parties which do not result in contracts within the meaning of that term in our law. The ordinary example is where two parties agree to take a walk together, or where there is an offer and an acceptance of hospitality. Nobody would suggest in ordinary circumstances that those agreements result in what we know as a contract, and one of the most usual forms of agreement which does not constitute a contract appears to me to be the arrangements which are made between husband and wife.

To my mind those agreements, or many of them, do not result in contracts at all, and they do not result in contracts even though there may be what as between other parties would constitute consideration for the agreement. The consideration, as we know, may consist either in some right, interest, profit or benefit accruing to one party, or some forbearance, detriment, loss or responsibility given, suffered or undertaken by the other. That is a well known definition, and it constantly happens, I think, that such arrangements made between husband and wife are arrangements in which there are mutual promises, or in which there is consideration in form within the definition that I have mentioned. Nevertheless, they are not contracts, and they are not contracts because the parties did not intend that they should be attended by legal consequences. To my mind, it would be of the worst possible example to

---

69 See the discussion of *Glasbrook Bros v Glamorgan County Council* [1925] AC 270, considered above.

70 [1919] 2 KB 571, CA.

hold that agreements such as this resulted in legal obligations which could be enforced in the Courts. It would mean this – that when the husband makes his wife a promise to give her an allowance of 30s or £2 a week, whatever he can afford to give her, for the maintenance of the household and children, and she promises so to apply it, not only could she sue him for his failure in any week to supply the allowance, but he could sue her for non-performance of the obligation, express or implied, which she had undertaken upon her part. All I can say is that the small courts of this country would have to be multiplied one hundredfold if these arrangements were held to result in legal obligations. They are not sued upon, not because the parties are reluctant to enforce their legal rights when the agreement is broken, but because the parties, in the inception of the arrangement, never intended that they should be sued upon. Agreements such as these are outside the realm of contracts altogether. The common law does not regulate the form of agreements between spouses. Their promises are not sealed with seals and sealing wax. The consideration that really obtains for them is that natural love and affection which counts for so little in these cold Courts. The terms may be repudiated, varied or renewed as performance proceeds or as disagreements develop, and the principles of the common law as to exoneration and discharge and accord and satisfaction are such as find no place in the domestic code. The parties themselves are advocates, judges, Courts, sheriff's officer and reporter. In respect of these promises each house is a domain into which the King's writ does not seek to run, and to which his officers do not seek to be admitted. The only question in this case is whether or not this promise was of such a class or not. For the reasons given by my brethren it appears to me to be plainly established that the promise here was not intended by either party, to be attended by legal consequences.

PROMISES WHICH INDUCE RELIANCE

The bargain theory considered above operates on the principle that contracting parties voluntarily exchange promises with the result that each promise is enforceable because of the price paid by the other party in the form of an exchanged promise. The notion of request is necessary in this process. However, there are a number of decisions which are difficult to square with this model of enforceability, but which may be better explained on the basis that the promisor's promise has induced some act of reasonable reliance on the part of the promisee:

Consider next the possibility of detrimental reliance by the promisee. Is it not manifest that a person who has actually worsened his position by reliance on a promise has a more powerful case for redress than one who has not acted in reliance on the promise at all? A person who has not relied on a promise (nor paid for it) may suffer disappointment of his expectations, but he does not actually suffer a pecuniary loss. The disappointment of an expectation may of course be treated as a species of loss by definition, as indeed the law generally does treat it, if the expectation derives from Contract. But no definitional jugglery can actually equate the position of the party who suffers a diminution of his assets in reliance on a promise, and a person who suffers no such diminution.[71]

In the extract above, Atiyah argues that what lies at the root of the apparent 'bankruptcy' of the classical model of contract formation is the over-emphasis placed on the importance of the executory contract. If one accepts that there are numerous contracts which do not conform to the classical exchange model of liability, an alternative justification for the enforcement of promises is that of reasonable reliance. In the case of contracts in which there is an executed performance on the part of the promisee which has been induced by the promise of the promisor, it is the promisee's action in reliance that justifies the enforcement of the promise. Reliance-based models of enforcement exist elsewhere, as the following extract illustrates:

Promise reasonably inducing action or forbearance

(1) A promise which the promisor should reasonably expect to induce action or forbearance on the part of the promisee or a third person and which does induce such action or forbearance is binding if injustice can be avoided only by enforcement of the promise. The remedy granted for such breach may be limited as justice requires.

(2) A charitable subscription or a marriage settlement is binding under sub-s (1) without proof that the promise induced action or forbearance.[72]

Statements capable of inducing reliance

In the course of an exchange relationship, a number of statements may be made, all of which are capable of inducing some degree of reliance, but it does not follow that all of these statements will give rise to promissory liability. In the first instance, there are factual statements, which if inaccurate may give rise to an action for rescission of the induced contract or for damages for misrepresentation.[73] Alternatively, the untrue statement of fact may give rise to an estoppel, whereby the maker of the statement is prevented (estopped) from asserting the truth if his misleading statement has induced an act of reasonable, detrimental reliance on the part of the person to whom the statement was addressed. For these purposes, however, it is essential that the statement is factual rather than promissory, so that if the defendant merely states his intention, the principle of estoppel by representation will be inapplicable.

---

71 Atiyah, 1978, p 203.
72 *United States Restatement, Contracts* (2nd), para 90.
73 See Chapters 4, 13 and 14.

In *Jorden v Money*,[74] Money borrowed £1,200 from Jorden's brother for the purposes of an unsuccessful speculation. Subsequently, Jorden became her deceased brother's executrix and was entitled to the benefit of a judgment debt entered in favour of the deceased brother. Money had given a bond to the brother as security for payment of the debt, but Jorden had on various occasions said that she did not intend to enforce the bond, believing that Money had been unfairly treated. These statements led Money to believe that the bond would not be enforced and in reliance on the belief that this was the case, he gave his prospective parents-in-law an assurance that he was free from the debt of £1,200. Money sought a declaration that Jorden had abandoned the bond. Such an order was granted at first instance and supported in the Court of Appeal. However, the House of Lords reversed these earlier decisions:

Jorden v Money (1854) 5 HLC 185; (1854) 10 ER 868, HL, p 880

Lord Cranworth LC: There are two grounds upon which it is said that the parties have lost their right to enforce the bond. The one is that, previously to William Money's marriage, Mrs Jorden, then Miss Marnell, represented that the bond had been abandoned, that she had given up her right upon it, and upon the faith of that representation the marriage was contracted. And then it is said that upon a principle well known in the law, founded upon good faith and equity, a principle equally of law and of equity, if a person makes any false representation to another, and that other acts upon that false representation, the person who has made it shall not afterwards be allowed to set up that what he said was false, and to assert the real truth in place of the falsehood which has so misled the other. That is a principle of universal application and has been particularly applied to cases where representations have been made as to the state of the property of persons about to contract marriage, and where, upon the faith of such representations, marriage has been contracted. There, the person who has made the false representations has, in a great many cases, been held bound to make his representations good.

I am bound to state my view of the case; I think that that doctrine does not apply to a case where the representation is not a representation of a fact, but a statement of something which the party intends or does not intend to do. In the former case it is a contract, in the latter it is not; what is here contended for, is this, that Mrs Jorden, then Miss Marnell, over and over again represented that she abandoned the debt. Clothe that in any words you please, it means no more than this, that she would never enforce the debt; she does not mean, in saying that she had abandoned it, to say that she had executed a release of the debt so as to preclude her legal right to sue. All that she could mean was that she positively promised that she never would enforce it. My opinion is that, if all the evidence had come up to the mark, which, for reasons I shall presently state, I do not think it did, that if upon the very eve of the marriage she had said, 'William Money, I never will enforce the bond against you', that would

---

74   (1854) 5 HLC 185, HL.

not bring it within these cases. It might be, if all statutable requisites, so far as there are statutable requisites, had been complied with, that it would have been a very good contract whereby she might have bound herself not to enforce the payment. That, however, is not the way in which it is put here; in short, it could not have been, because it must have been a contract reduced into writing and signed; but that is not the way in which this case is put; it is put entirely upon the ground of representation.

What is the difference between this case and those considered above under the bargain theory of consideration? It has been argued by Atiyah[75] that this is an example of reliance-based consideration and that, but for the prevailing rule on contract formalities,[76] there would have been an enforceable promise. However, even for the purposes of reliance theory, there ought to be some evidence of an express or implied request that the action in reliance be performed.

In *Shadwell v Shadwell*,[77] an uncle wrote to his nephew, 'I am glad to hear of your intended marriage with Ellen Nicholl; and, as I promised to assist you at starting, I am happy to tell you that I will pay you £150 yearly during my life and until your annual income derived from your profession of a Chancery barrister shall amount to 600 guineas (£630) – your ever affectionate uncle'.

The uncle paid during his lifetime, but his executors ceased to pay the annuity on his death. In an action to recover the amount of the annuity, the court, by a majority held that there was consideration for the promise to pay:

Shadwell v Shadwell (1860) 9 CB (NS) 159; (1860) 142 ER 62, p 68

Erle CJ: Now, do these facts shew that the promise was in consideration either of a loss to be sustained by the plaintiff or a benefit to be derived from the plaintiff to the uncle, at his, the uncle's, request? My answer is in the affirmative.

First, do these facts shew a loss sustained by the plaintiff at his uncle's request? When I answer this in the affirmative, I am aware that a man's marriage with the woman of his choice is in one sense a boon, and in that sense the reverse of a loss: yet, as between the plaintiff and the party promising to supply an income to support the marriage, it may well be also a loss. The plaintiff may have made a most material change in his position, and induced the object of his affection to do the same, and may have incurred pecuniary liabilities resulting in embarrassments which would be in every sense a loss if the income which had been promised should be withheld; and, if the promise was made in order to induce the parties to marry, the promise so made would be in legal effect a request to marry.

---

75 Atiyah, 1986, pp 53–58
76 The Statute of Frauds 1677 required a written memorandum evidencing the existence of a contract of this type. Atiyah argues that the plaintiff was merely trying to circumvent the effect of the statute by pleading an estoppel.
77 (1860) 9 CB (NS) 159.

Secondly, do these facts shew a benefit derived from the plaintiff to the uncle, at his request? In answering again in the affirmative, I am at liberty to consider the relation in which the parties stood and the interest in the settlement of his nephew which the uncle declares. The marriage primarily affects the parties thereto; but in a secondary degree it may be an object of interest to a near relative, and in that sense a benefit to him. This benefit is also derived from the plaintiff at the uncle's request. If the promise of the annuity was intended as an inducement to the marriage, and the averment that the plaintiff, relying on the promise, married, is an averment that the promise was one inducement to the marriage, this is the consideration averred in the declaration; and it appears to me to be expressed in the letter, construed with the surrounding circumstances.

No case showing a strong analogy to the present was cited: but the importance of enforcing promises which have been made to induce parties to marry has been often recognised; and the cases cited, of *Montefiori v Montefiori*, 1 W Bl 363, and *Bold v Hutchinson*, 20 Beavan 250, are examples. I do not feel it necessary to advert to the numerous authorities referred to in the learned arguments addressed to us, because the decision turns upon the question of fact, whether the consideration for the promise is proved as pleaded. I think it is; and therefore my judgment on the first demurrer is for the plaintiff.

Byles J (dissenting) was unable to find any consideration. There is much force in his view that there was no request, in which case the rationale for the decision of the majority appears to be reliance based:

Byles J (p 69): Marriage of the plaintiff at the testator's express request would be, no doubt, an ample consideration. But marriage of the plaintiff without the testator's request is no consideration to the testator. It is true that marriage is or may be a detriment to the plaintiff: but detriment to the plaintiff is not enough, unless it either be a benefit to the testator, or be treated by the testator as such by having been suffered at his request. Suppose a defendant to promise a plaintiff – 'I will give you £500 if you break your leg' – would that detriment to the plaintiff, should it happen, be any consideration? If it be said that such an accident is an involuntary mischief, would it have been a binding promise if the testator had said – 'I will give you £100 a year while you continue in your present chambers?'. I conceive that the promise would not be binding, for want of a previous request by the testator.

Now, the testator in the case before the court derived, so far as appears, no personal benefit from the marriage. The question, therefore, is still further narrowed to this point, – Was the marriage at the testator's request? Express request there was none. Can any request be implied? The only words from which it can be contended that it is to be implied, are the words 'I am glad to hear of your intended marriage with Ellen Nicholl'. But it appears from the fourth plea that the marriage had already been agreed on, and that the testator knew it. These words, therefore, seem to me to import no more than the satisfaction of the testator at the engagement – an accomplished fact. No request can, as it seems to me, be inferred from them. And, further, how does it appear that the testator's implied request, if it could be implied, or his promise, if that promise alone would suffice, or both together, were intended to cause the marriage or did cause it, so that the marriage can be said to have taken place at the testator's request or, in other words, in consequence of that request?

It seems to me not only that this does not appear, but that the contrary appears; for the plaintiff, before the letter had already bound himself to marry, by placing himself not only under a moral, but under a legal objection to marry, and the testator knew it.

Was there a request in *Shadwell*? Is the view of Byles J to be preferred to that of the majority? Is there any strong policy reason for wishing to enforce what amounts to a marriage settlement? Does the difficulty in identifying a request and the possible absence of detrimental reliance explain the provision contained in *The United States Restatement, Contracts* (2nd), para 90?

The principal difficulty with the distinction between promises and statements of fact is that the line between the two is often very difficult to draw. For example, in *Jorden v Money*, did the defendant state that she had released the debt? Did she state her present intention not to enforce the bond or did she promise not to enforce the bond? In either of the first two cases, the statement is one of fact and will not give rise to promissory liability.

In *Kleinwort Benson Ltd v Malaysia Mining Corpn Bhd*,[78] the plaintiffs had made a loan facility available to a subsidiary of the defendants. Initially, the plaintiffs had asked for a guarantee of the subsidiary company's debts, which had been declined by the defendants. Instead, they issued a letter of comfort in which they stated that it was their policy, at all times, to ensure that the subsidiary was in a position to meet its debts (para 3). In return for the acceptance of this letter instead of a guarantee, there was a small increase in the commission payable to the plaintiffs. Subsequently, the subsidiary company went into liquidation and the plaintiffs sought to recover the amount of the loan from the defendants, who refused to pay. The Court of Appeal held that the letter of comfort was not a contractual promise, but was a factual statement of the defendants' present intention, which did not continue into the future:

Kleinwort Benson Ltd v Malaysia Mining Corpn Bhd [1989] 1 WLR 379, CA, p 385

Ralph Gibson LJ: The statement in para 3, however, was not, it was submitted, a contractual promise and was not intended to have legal effect as such. It was nevertheless, in counsel's submission, not devoid of legal significance: it was a representation of fact as to the policy of the defendants at the time that the statement was made; and the plaintiffs were entitled to rely on it as a statement of the current policy of the defendants. If it were shown to have been untrue to

78 [1989] 1 WLR 379, CA.

the knowledge of the defendants at the time when it was made, the plaintiffs would have had a claim in deceit, but there has been no suggestion of that nature.

In addition, the plaintiffs were entitled to rely on the representation as to the current policy of the defendants unless and until they were told that the policy had been changed. If the policy did change, without notice from the defendants so that the representation ceased to be true, and the plaintiffs thereafter relied on it by making further advances to Metals, they would have, it was said, 'a cause of action in misrepresentation', but no cause of action in contract ...

The main attack on the analysis and reasoning of the judge, which counsel for the defendants developed, was directed at the application by Hirst J of the proposition, illustrated by *Edwards v Skyways Ltd* [1964] 1 WLR 349, that a promise, made for consideration in a commercial transaction, will be taken to have been intended to have contractual effect in law, unless the contrary is clearly shown. The proposition was not disputed on behalf of the defendants before Hirst J, or this court. It was, however, submitted that the principle is of no assistance in deciding whether, on the evidence and on their true construction, the words in question are words of promise or not ...

For my part, I am persuaded that the main criticism of the judgment of Hirst J advanced by counsel for the defendants are well founded and I would, for the reasons which follow, allow this appeal. In my judgment the defendants made a statement as to what their policy was, and did not in para 3 of the comfort letter expressly promise that such policy would be continued in future. It is impossible to make up for the lack of express promise by implying such a promise, and indeed, no such implied promise was pleaded. My conclusion rests on what, in my judgment, is the proper effect and meaning which, on the evidence, is to be given to para 3 of the comfort letters ...

In my judgment, counsel for the defendants is right in his submission that the presumption described in *Edwards v Skyways Ltd* had no application to the issues in this case once the plea of a separate agreement or understanding to the effect that the comfort letters should have no legal effect had disappeared from the case for want of evidence to support it. The introduction of that plea into the case appears to have served only to distract attention from what, if I am right, are the clear merits of the defendants' case as to the meaning and effect of para 3 of the comfort letters.

To explain why, in my view, the presumption applied by Hirst J had no application to this case, it is necessary to examine in some detail the issues in *Edwards v Skyways Ltd*.

The central question in this case, in my judgment, is that considered in *Esso Petroleum Co Ltd v Mardon* [1976] QB 801, on which counsel for the plaintiffs relied in this court but which was not cited to Hirst J. That question is whether the words of para 3, considered in their context, are to be treated as a warranty or contractual promise. Paragraph 3 contains no express words of promise. Paragraph 3 is in its terms a statement of present fact and not a promise as to future conduct. I agree with the submission of counsel for the defendants that, in this regard, the words of para 3 are in sharp contrast with the words of para 2 of the letter: 'We confirm that we will not', etc. The force of this point is not limited, as Hirst J stated it, to the absence from para 3 of the words 'We confirm'. The real contrast is between the words of promise, namely 'We will not' in para 2, and the words of statement of fact, 'It is our policy' in para 3. Hirst J held that, by the words of para 3, the defendants gave an undertaking that now and at all times in the future, so long as Metals should be under any liability to the plaintiffs under the facility arrangements, it is and will be the defendants' policy to ensure that Metals is in a position to meet their liabilities. To derive that meaning from the words it is necessary to add the words emphasised, namely 'and will be', which do not appear in para 3. In short, the words of promise as to the future conduct of the defendants were held by Hirst J to be part of the necessary meaning of the words used in para 3. The question is whether that view of the words can be upheld.

The absence of express words of warranty as to present facts or the absence of express words of promise as to future conduct does not conclusively exclude a statement from the status of warranty or promise. According to the well known *dictum* of Holt CJ, 'an affirmation can only be a warranty, provided it appears on evidence to have been so intended': see Ormrod LJ in *Esso Petroleum Co Ltd v Mardon* [1976] QB 801, p 824, citing Viscount Haldane LC in *Heilbut Symons and Co v Buckleton* [1913] AC 30, p 38.

Next, the first draft of the comfort letter was produced by the plaintiffs. Paragraph 1 contained confirmation that the defendants knew of and approved of the granting of the facilities in question by the plaintiffs to Metals, and para 2 contained the express confirmation that the defendants would not reduce their current financial interest in Metals until (in effect) facilities had been paid or the plaintiffs consented. Both are relevant to the present and future moral responsibility of the defendants. If the words of para 3 are to be treated as intended to express a contractual promise by the defendants as to their future policy, which Hirst J held the words to contain, then the recitation of the plaintiffs' approval and the promise not to reduce their current financial interest in Metals, would be of no significance. If the defendants have promised that at all times in the future it will be the defendants' policy to ensure that Metals is in a position to meet its liabilities to the plaintiffs under the facility, it would not matter whether they had approved or disapproved, or whether they had disposed of their shares in Metals. Contracts may, of course, contain statements or promises which are caused to be of no separate commercial importance by the width of a later promise in the same document. Where, however, the court is examining a statement which is by its express words no more than a representation of fact, in order to consider whether it is shown to have been intended to be of the nature of a contractual promise or warranty, it seems to me to be a fact suggesting at least the absence of such intention if, as in this case, to read the statement as a contractual promise is to reduce to no significance two paragraphs included in the plaintiffs' draft, both of which have significance if the statement is read as a representation of fact only. That point can be made more plainly thus: if para 3 in its original or in its final form was intended to contain a binding legal promise by the defendants to ensure the ability of Metals to pay the sums due under the facility, there was no apparent need or purpose for the plaintiffs, as bankers, to waste ink on paras 1 and 2.

Do the words 'at all times' indicate not just a person's present intention, but also his or her future intention? If so, does this sound like a promise? Is there detriment if a person makes a loan facility available in reliance on a letter of comfort? For what reasons are letters of comfort issued?

Contractual promises and other statements of intention

It has been seen above that if a promise is supported by some reciprocal act, forbearance or promise, there is consideration for the promise, with the result that it should be enforceable under the bargain theory. However, the mere presence of consideration does not always mean that the promise is enforceable as there may be an absence of an intention to create legal relations. The problem of intention to create legal relations most often arises in the context of domestic arrangements, for example, between estranged spouses or where there has been some sort of social arrangement between friends. Although decisions in this area are often couched in terms of whether the parties intended to create legal relations, there are strong policy overtones to many of the decisions.[79] In particular, there is a fear that the civil justice system might be overwhelmed if commercial courts had to deal with large numbers of domestic and social disputes.[80] In contrast, it is generally very unlikely that an arrangement between business contracting parties will be held unenforceable for want of an intention to create legal relations except in cases where the parties have very clearly stated an intention not to be bound[81] or in cases where it is clear that further negotiations are to take place with the result that there is no concluded agreement. This last matter is well illustrated in cases where a letter of intent has been issued so that work may commence prior to the parties reaching a concluded agreement. If there are still material aspects of the contractual relationship to be sorted out, the court may find itself in a position where a contractual solution cannot be offered, but this does not prevent the application of restitutionary principles if one party has been enriched by the performance of the other.[82]

The role of reasonable reliance in respect of the issue of intention to create legal relations should not be underestimated, since if one party has acted

---

79 For further discussion of the policy issue, see p 135, above.

80 See *Balfour v Balfour* [1919] 2 KB 571, p 579, *per* Atkin LJ.

81 See *Edwards v Skyways Ltd* [1964] 1 All ER 494, p 500, *per* Megaw J. For a rare example of a business arrangement which was binding in honour only, see *Rose and Frank Co v JR Crompton Bros Ltd* [1925] AC 445.

82 See *British Steel Corpn v Cleveland Bridge and Engineering Co Ltd* [1984] 1 All ER 504.

upon a promise which was initially expressed to be made without an intention to be bound, there are strong reasons for holding the promise which induces reliance to be enforceable. Thus, in domestic arrangements, the fact that the promisee has acted to his or her detriment in the belief that the promise of the other party will be fulfilled will often provide a reason for enforcing the promise of that other.

In *Merritt v Merritt*,[83] a husband and wife married in 1941 and built a house as a matrimonial home. Subsequently, the marriage was dissolved when the husband went to live with another woman. In 1966, the husband agreed to pay the wife £40 per month if she would agree to pay the £180 debt still owed to a building society in respect of the former matrimonial home. The wife agreed to this, provided the husband agreed to sign a document which stated that, in consideration of the wife paying all charges in connection with the house, he would agree to transfer the house into her sole ownership. The wife kept her side of the bargain and subsequently obtained an order that the house belonged to her. This was granted and the husband was ordered to join in the necessary conveyance:

Merritt v Merritt [1970] 1 WLR 1211, CA, p 1213

Lord Denning MR: The first point taken on his behalf by Mr Thompson is that the agreement was not intended to have legal relations. It was, he says, a family arrangement such as was considered by the court in *Balfour v Balfour* [1919] 2 KB 571 and in *Jones v Padavatton* [1969] 1 WLR 328. So, the wife could not sue upon it.

I do not think those cases have any application here. The parties there were living together in amity. In such cases their domestic arrangements are ordinarily not intended to create legal relations. It is altogether different when the parties are not living in amity but are separated, or about to separate. They then bargain keenly. They do not rely on honourable understandings. They want everything cut and dried. It may safely be presumed that they intend to create legal relations.

Mr Thompson then relied on the recent case of *Gould v Gould* [1970] 1 QB 275, when the parties had separated, and the husband agreed to pay the wife £12 a week 'so long as he could manage it'. The majority of the court thought those words introduced such an element of uncertainty that the agreement was not intended to create legal relations. But for that element of uncertainty, I am sure the majority would have held the agreement to be binding. They did not differ from the general proposition which I stated at p 280 that: '... when husband and wife, at arm's length, decide to separate, and the husband promises to pay a sum as maintenance to the wife during the separation, the court does, as a rule, impute to them an intention to create legal relations.'

In all these cases, the court does not try to discover the intention by looking into the minds of the parties. It looks at the situation in which they were placed

---

83   [1970] 1 WLR 1211, CA.

and asks itself: would reasonable people regard the agreement as intended to be binding?

Mr Thompson sought to say that this agreement was uncertain because of the arrangement for £40 a month maintenance. That is obviously untenable. Next, he said that there was no consideration for the agreement. That point is no good. The wife paid the outstanding amount to the building society. That was ample consideration. It is true that the husband paid her £40 a month, which she may have used to pay the building society. But still, her act in paying was good consideration.

Likewise, where a business arrangement is clearly expressed to be made without an intention to create legal relations, as soon as the arrangement is acted upon by the parties, it will give rise to ordinary legal rights.

In *Rose and Frank and Co v JR Crompton Bros Ltd*,[84] arrangements were made between the respondents, an English company and the appellants, an American firm under which the appellants became the sole agents of the respondents in respect of the supply of tissues for carbonising paper. It was agreed that the arrangement should be extended three years at a time subject to six months' notice being given on either side. The 'contract' further stated, 'This arrangement is not entered into, nor is this memorandum written, as a formal legal agreement and shall not be subject to legal jurisdiction in the Law Courts ... but is only a definite expression and record of the purpose and intention of the ... parties to which they each honourably pledge themselves'.

Disputes arose and the respondents terminated the agreement without notice. Before the dispute arose, orders had been placed for the respondents' goods by the appellants which had been accepted by the respondents. Although it was held that the agreement was not binding because of the honourable pledge clause, it was accepted that once an order had been placed and accepted, then on each such occasion there was a binding contract of sale. The House of Lords accepted as correct the reasoning of the Court of Appeal ([1923] 2 KB 261) in the same case:

Rose and Frank and Co v JR Crompton Bros Ltd [1925] AC 445, HL, p 454

Scrutton LJ: Now it is quite possible for parties to come to an agreement by accepting a proposal with the result that the agreement concluded does not give rise to legal relations. The reason for this is that the parties do not intend that their agreement shall give rise to legal relations. This intention may be implied from the subject matter of the agreement, but it may also be expressed by the parties. In social and family relations, such an intention is readily implied, whereas in business matters the opposite result would ordinarily follow. But I can see no reason why, even in business matters, the parties should not intend to rely on each other's good faith and honour, and to exclude all idea of settling disputes by any outside intervention, with the

---

84 [1925] AC 445, HL.

accompanying necessity of expressing themselves so precisely that outsiders may have no difficulty in understanding what they mean ...

Regarding the orders already placed and accepted, the House of Lords preferred the minority view expressed in the Court of Appeal by Atkin LJ:

> **Lord Phillimore**: With regard to the next point – namely, the right of the plaintiffs to recover damages for non-delivery of the goods specified in the particular orders for the year 1919 – it should be stated that the defence under the Sale of Goods Act was abandoned at the trial. On this point I agree with your Lordships in preferring the judgments of Bailhache J and Atkin LJ to that of the majority of the Court of Appeal.
>
> According to the course of business between the parties which is narrated in the unenforceable agreement, goods were ordered from time to time, shipped, received and paid for under an established system; but the agreement being unenforceable, there was no obligation on the American company to order goods or upon the English companies to accept an order. Any actual transaction between the parties, however, gave rise to the ordinary legal rights; for the fact that it was not of obligation to do the transaction did not divest the transaction when done of its ordinary legal significance. This, my Lords, will, I think, be plain if we begin at the latter end of each transaction.
>
> Goods were ordered, shipped, and received. Was there no legal liability to pay for them? One stage further back. Goods were ordered, shipped and invoiced. Was there no legal liability to take delivery? I apprehend that, in each of these cases, the American company would be bound. If the goods were short-shipped or inferior in quality, or if the nature of them was such as to be deleterious to other cargo on board or illegal for the American company to bring into their country, the American company would have its usual legal remedies against the English companies or one of them. Business usually begins in some mutual understanding without a previous bargain.

A particularly important instance in which non-bargain promises may be enforceable where they induce reasonable reliance may arise where a person is estopped from denying the enforceability of his promise. Typically, this issue will arise in the context of an ongoing contractual relationship where one party has promised to vary the terms of the original contract and, in so doing, has induced an act of reasonable reliance on the part of the promisee. In such cases, it is quite possible that the bargain theory of consideration will encounter difficulties. To say that the promisee has given something of legal value in return for the promise of the other party will often be difficult to establish, since, in ongoing relationships of this kind, it is likely that the promisee will do no more than he is already bound to do under the original terms of the contract. However, where the promisor's promise induces reasonable reliance on the part of the promisee, it may be inequitable not to enforce the promise, in which case the court may enforce the promisee's equity by preventing the promisor from taking advantage of the technical absence of consideration.

Such was the conclusion of Denning J in *Central London Property Trust v High Trees House Ltd*.[85] Under the terms of a lease entered into in 1937, the defendant tenant agreed to pay a yearly ground rent of £2,500 for a block of flats for a period of 99 years. In early 1940, due to the wartime conditions then prevailing, only very few of the flats had been leased to tenants and it became apparent that the defendant was not in a position to pay the annual rent. Discussions took place between the defendant and the plaintiff landlord, in which it was agreed that the rent would be halved as from January 1940. By 1945, all the flats were let, but the defendant was still paying only £1,250 per annum and the plaintiff served notice in September 1945 that the rent should be restored to £2,500 per annum and initiated via the instigation of the receiver 'friendly' proceedings to test the legal position. The defendant argued, *inter alia*, that the rent reduction applied to the whole of the term of the lease and that the plaintiff was estopped from demanding rent at the higher rate. Denning J held that the plaintiff was estopped from demanding the full rent while the conditions which gave rise to the agreement to reduce the rent prevailed. But since those conditions had ceased to exist by 1945, the plaintiff was at liberty to serve notice of an intention to charge the full rent:

Central London Property Trust v High Trees House Ltd [1947] KB 130, p 134

Denning J: With regard to estoppel, the representation made in relation to reducing the rent, was not a representation of an existing fact. It was a representation, in effect, as to the future, namely, that payment of the rent would not be enforced at the full rate but only at the reduced rate. Such a representation would not give rise to an estoppel, because, as was said in *Jorden v Money*, a representation as to the future must be embodied as a contract or be nothing.

But what is the position in view of developments in the law in recent years? The law has not been standing still since *Jorden v Money*. There has been a series of decisions over the last 50 years which, although they are said to be cases of estoppel are not really such.

They are cases in which a promise was made which was intended to create legal relations and which, to the knowledge of the person making the promise, was going to be acted on by the person to whom it was made, and which was in fact so acted on. In such cases the courts have said that the promise must be honoured [after considering a number of cases his Lordship continued]...

As I have said, they are not cases of estoppel in the strict sense. They are really promises – promises intended to be binding, intended to be acted on, and in fact acted on. *Jorden v Money* can be distinguished, because there the promisor made it clear that she did not intend to be legally bound, whereas in the cases to which I refer the proper inference was that the promisor did intend to be bound. In each case, the court held the promise to be binding on the party

---

85 [1947] KB 130. In what seems to have been his first reported decision, Denning J started as he intended to continue!

making it, even though under the old common law it might be difficult to find any consideration for it. The courts have not gone so far as to give a cause of action in damages for the breach of such a promise, but they have refused to allow the party making it to act inconsistently with it. It is in that sense, and that sense only, that such a promise gives rise to an estoppel. The decisions are a natural result of the fusion of law and equity ...

In my opinion, the time has now come for the validity of such a promise to be recognised. The logical consequence, no doubt is that a promise to accept a smaller sum in discharge of a larger sum, if acted upon, is binding notwithstanding the absence of consideration: and if the fusion of law and equity leads to this result, so much the better. That aspect was not considered in *Foakes v Beer* [(1884) 9 App Cas 605]. At this time of day however, when law and equity have been joined together for over seventy years, principles must be reconsidered in the light of their combined effect. It is to be noticed that in the Sixth Interim Report of the Law Revision Committee, paras 35 and 40, it is recommended that such a promise as that to which I have referred, should be enforceable in law even though no consideration for it has been given by the promisee. It seems to me that, to the extent I have mentioned, that result has now been achieved by the decisions of the courts.

I am satisfied that a promise such as that to which I have referred is binding and the only question remaining for my consideration is the scope of the promise in the present case. I am satisfied on all the evidence that the promise here was that the ground rent should be reduced to £1,250 a year as a temporary expedient while the block of flats was not fully, or substantially fully let, owing to the conditions prevailing. That means that the reduction in the rent applied throughout the years down to the end of 1944, but early in 1945 it is plain that the flats were fully let, and, indeed the rents received from them (many of them not being affected by the Rent Restrictions Acts), were increased beyond the figure at which it was originally contemplated that they would be let. At all events the rent from them must have been very considerable. I find that the conditions prevailing at the time when the reduction in rent was made, had completely passed away by the early months of 1945. I am satisfied that the promise was understood by all parties only to apply under the conditions prevailing at the time when it was made, namely when the flats were only partially let, and that it did not extend any further than that. When the flats became fully let, early in 1945, the reduction ceased to apply.

In those circumstances, under the law as I hold it, it seems to me that rent is payable at the full rate for the quarters ending 29 September and 25 December 1945.

If the case had been one of estoppel, it might be said that, in any event, the estoppel would cease when the conditions to which the representation applied came to an end, or it also might be said that it would only come to an end on notice. In either case it is only a way of ascertaining what is the scope of the representation. I prefer to apply the principle that a promise intended to be binding, intended to be acted on and in fact acted on, is binding so far as its terms properly apply. Here, it was binding as covering the period down to the early part of 1945 and, as from that time, full rent is payable.

In *High Trees,* was the tenant a debtor? If so how does the principle enunciated by Denning J sit with the rule in *Foakes v Beer* that part payment of a debt does not satisfy the whole debt? The *High Trees* principle is said to be based on the principle in *Hughes v Metropolitan Railway Co,*[86] but are the two cases directly comparable? *Hughes* says that if a landlord tells a tenant that he does not have to perform a duty owed by the tenant to the landlord, the landlord cannot treat non-performance of the duty as an actionable breach of contract if the tenant takes him at his word. Does Denning J's principle in *High Trees* work on the same basis?

A moot point in relation to the enforcement of promises which induce reliance is whether the reliance of the promisee must cause him to suffer some detriment or not. It has been seen from the extract in *Jorden v Money*[87] that, for the purposes of estoppel by representation, there is a definite requirement of detriment. The same also appears to be true of cases of proprietary estoppel, under which the owner of land is estopped from denying the promisee's title where he has allowed the promisee to believe that he has acquired an interest in the promisor's land.[88] However, whether the same is true in cases of promissory estoppel is less clear since there are authorities which go both ways.[89] It is suggested that detriment should not usually be regarded as a requirement since there will be reliance enough if the promisor has generated in the promisee a reasonable expectation that his promise will be fulfilled and that it would be inequitable for the promisor to go back on his word. However, it is clear that any prospect of promissory estoppel being used as a true 'consideration substitute' (as yet a rather distant prospect in English law) would require an element of detriment to be demonstrated. On this see the Australian case of *Waltons Stores (Interstate) Ltd v Maher.*[90] There is no immediate likelihood of Maher being applied in its entirety in this country, but the judgements repay careful examination, particularly those of Mason CJ and Wilson J at pp 520–24 and Brennan J at pp 532–42.

---

86 (1877) 2 App Cas 439.

87 (1854) 5 HLC 185.

88 *AG of Hong Kong v Humphrey's Estate Ltd* [1987] 2 All ER 387, p 392, *per* Lord Templeman; *Lloyd's Bank v Rossett* [1990] 1 All ER 1111, pp 1118–19, *per* Lord Bridge.

89 In support of a requirement of detriment or (at least) of some 'altering of position' which may amount to the same thing are *Tool Metal Manufacturing Co Ltd v Tungsten Electric Co Ltd* [1955] 1 WLR 761, p 764, *per* Viscount Symonds; *Ajayi v RT Briscoe (Nigeria) Ltd* [1964] 1 WLR 1326, p 1331, *per* Lord Hodson. In support of a requirement of simple reliance, without detriment are *Central London Property Trust Ltd v High Trees House Ltd* [1947] KB 130, p 135, *per* Denning J; *WJ Alan and Co Ltd v El Nasr Export and Import Co Ltd* [1972] 2 QB 189, p 213, *per* Lord Denning MR.

90 (1988) 76 ALR 513.

Effects of reliance

It has been seen above that where action in reliance on a promise has been requested, there will usually be a sufficient consideration to justify the enforcement of the promise. But reliance may also justify judicial intervention in favour of the promisee by means other than through the use of the doctrine of consideration. In particular, the different varieties of estoppel have the effect of enforcing promises which induce reasonable reliance, but it is apparent that promises which are not supported by consideration have a much more limited effect than those which are so supported.

An important matter of debate is whether promises which induce reliance can be treated as creating rights in the promisee where none previously existed. It is apparent that where the promisee's reliance is regarded as consideration for the promise of the other party, that enforcement of the promise will create new rights in favour of the promisee. This serves to reinforce the primary function of the law of contract, namely to facilitate the deliberate exchange of resources by the parties to the contract. However, where promises are given effect through the use of rules on estoppel, it is less clear that new rights are created in favour of the promisee. A key question in this regard is whether estoppel-based rules operate by way of a defence only or whether they can be used to create a new cause of action in favour of the promisee.

The traditional view of an estoppel as an evidential device suggests that it may operate only as a defence. This view is normally stated in the terms that an estoppel, especially the variety known as promissory estoppel, may be used as a shield, but not as a sword.[91] This should not be taken to mean that estoppel may only operate in favour of a defendant, rather that any party to legal proceedings may set up as a defence an estoppel where the other party seeks to insist upon his strict legal rights.

In *Combe v Combe*,[92] a wife obtained a *decree nisi* for divorce against her husband. Subsequently, the husband promised to pay the wife an allowance of £100 per year, tax free. The divorce was then made absolute, but the husband did not make any payments. Moreover, the wife made no application to court for a maintenance order, but instead sought to enforce her husband's promise. This action failed on the ground that there was no consideration for the promise, there being no evidence that the wife had declined to seek court maintenance at her husband's request. Moreover, principles of promissory estoppel were of no assistance as the wife was seeking to create a cause of action where none previously existed:

---

91 Cf the position under the *United States Restatement, Contracts* (2nd), para 90, which makes it clear that the American equivalent of estoppel can be used to found a cause of action where justice so requires. This was discussed at length in *Waltons v Maher*.

92 [1951] 1 All ER 767, CA.

Combe v Combe [1951] 1 All ER 767, CA, p 769

Denning LJ: Much as I am inclined to favour the principle of the *High Trees* case, it is important that it should not be stretched too far, lest it should be endangered. It does not create new causes of action where none existed before. It only prevents a party from insisting on his strict legal rights when it would be unjust to allow him to do so, having regard to the dealings which have taken place between the parties. That is the way it was put in the case in the House of Lords which first stated the principle – *Hughes v Metropolitan Railway Co* – and, in the case in the Court of Appeal which enlarged it – *Birmingham and District Land Co v London and North Western Railway Co.* It is also implicit in all the modern cases in which the principle has been developed. Sometimes it is a plaintiff who is not allowed to insist on his strict legal rights. Thus, a creditor is not allowed to enforce a debt which he has deliberately agreed to waive if the debtor has carried on business or in some other way changed his position in reliance on the waiver: Sometimes it is a defendant who is not allowed to insist on his strict legal rights. His conduct may be such as to debar him from relying on some condition, denying some allegation, or taking some other point in answer to the claim. Thus, a government department, who had accepted a disease as due to war service, were not allowed afterwards to say it was not, when the soldier, in reliance on the assurance, had abstained from getting further evidence about it: *Robertson v Minister of Pensions*. A buyer who had waived the contract date for delivery was not allowed afterwards to set up the stipulated time as an answer to the seller: *Charles Rickards Ltd v Oppenheim*. A tenant who had encroached on an adjoining building, asserting that it was comprised in the lease, was not allowed afterwards to say that it was not included in the lease: *JF Perrott & Co Ltd v Cohen*. A tenant who had lived in a house rent free by permission of his landlord, thereby asserting that his original tenancy had ended, was not afterwards allowed to say that his original tenancy continued: *Foster v Robinson*. In none of these cases was the defendant sued on the promise, assurance, or assertion as a cause of action in itself. He was sued for some other cause, for example, a pension or a breach of contract, or possession, and the promise, assurance, or assertion only played a supplementary role, though, no doubt, an important one. That is, I think, its true function. It may be part of a cause of action, but not a cause of action in itself. The principle, as I understand it, is that where one party has, by his words or conduct, made to the other a promise or assurance which was intended to affect the legal relations between them and to be acted on accordingly, then, once the other party has taken him at his word and acted on it, the one who gave the promise or assurance cannot afterwards be allowed to revert to the previous legal relations as if no such promise or assurance had been made by him, but he must accept their legal relations subject to the qualification which he himself has so introduced, even though it is not supported in point of law by any consideration, but only by his word.

Seeing that the principle never stands alone as giving a cause of action in itself, it can never do away with the necessity of consideration when that is an essential part of the cause of action. The doctrine of consideration is too firmly fixed to be overthrown by a side wind. Its ill effects have been largely mitigated of late, but it still remains a cardinal necessity of the formation of a contract, although not of its modification or discharge. I fear that it was my failure to make this clear in *Central London Property Trust Ltd v High Trees House Ltd*, which misled Byrne J in the present case. He held that the wife could sue on the husband's promise as a separate and independent cause of action by itself, although, as he held, there was no consideration for it. That is not correct. The wife can only enforce the promise if there was consideration for it. That is, therefore, the real question in the case: was there sufficient consideration to support the promise?

The effect of the decision in *Combe v Combe* has been the subject of criticism, since its effect is to deny a remedy in many cases where there has been reasonable reliance on a promise not given in a true bargain relationship. In contrast with *Combe v Combe*, it has been observed elsewhere that it is not a bar to raising an estoppel as a defence where the effect of doing so is to enable a party to enforce a cause of action which would not otherwise exist.

In *Amalgamated Investment and Property Co Ltd v Texas Commerce International Bank Ltd*,[93] there was held to be no estoppel (the facts are not relevant for these purposes), but on the issue of the use of principles of estoppel as giving rise to a cause of action, the judgment of Brandon LJ is instructive:

Amalgamated Investment and Property Co Ltd v Texas Commerce International Bank Ltd [1982] 1 QB 84, CA, p 131

Brandon LJ: I turn to the second argument advanced on behalf of the plaintiffs, that the bank is here seeking to use estoppel as a sword rather than a shield, and that that is something which the law of estoppel does not permit. Another way in which the argument is put is that a party cannot found a cause of action on an estoppel.

In my view, much of the language used in connection with these concepts is no more than a matter of semantics ...

What I would regard as the true proposition of law [is] that, while a party cannot in terms found a cause of action on an estoppel, he may, as a result of being able to rely on an estoppel, succeed on a cause of action on which, without being able to rely on that estoppel, he would necessarily have failed.

Moreover, the rule in *Combe v Combe* may only apply to cases of promissory estoppel and may not have the same force in relation to promises which intimate that the promisee has been or will be given an interest in or over the promisor's land, which may be enforced, where equity so demands, through the use of rules on proprietary estoppel. Here, the demands of equity are that the promisor should not act unconscionably where he has actively encouraged

---

93   [1982] 1 QB 84, CA.

another to believe that he has acquired an interest and that other has incurred some expense[94] or has in some other way acted to his detriment.[95]

It should be emphasised that there are substantial differences in the way in which promises are enforced through the medium of rules based on estoppel as compared with the enforcement of promises under the doctrine of consideration. In particular, a promise supported by consideration, subject to other rules on the validity of contractual promises, will be enforceable in full against the promisor. In contrast, the equitable solution provided by rules on promissory and proprietary estoppel will reflect the equities of the case in hand and should not be regarded as a device intended to protect the promisee's expectations of performance of the promise of the other party. However, where the equities so demand, it may be necessary to confer on the promisee rights which did not previously exist before the promisor indicated that the promisee was to acquire an interest in or over the land in question. *Waltons Stores v Maher* indicates the utility of estoppel as a means of enforcing promises where it is equitable to do so, but also makes it abundantly clear that the purpose of such equitable intervention is not to give effect to the promisee's expectation that the promisor's promise will be fulfilled. Developments along these lines in English law, it is suggested, would be desirable.

As has been observed above, where there is a contractual promise supported by consideration, the promise will create fully enforceable rights in favour of the promisee, but the same is not true of promises which induce reliance in the absence of consideration. In some instances, a promise may be made which binds the promisor only temporarily, for example one made for a specific purpose during a finite period, and which temporarily suspends the promisor's right to insist upon his strict legal rights until he has served reasonable notice on the promisee of his intention to revert to a pre-existing set of contractual obligations.

In *Hughes v Metropolitan Railway Co*,[96] a landlord gave his tenant six months' notice to repair the leased premises in October 1874. Under the terms of the lease, failure to comply with such a notice rendered the lease forfeitable. While the period of notice was running, the parties to the lease entered negotiations for the sale of the lease. It was indicated that while these negotiations were continuing, repairs would not be effected. The negotiations commenced but were broken off by the landlord at the end of December 1874. Six months after service of the notice to repair, the landlord sought to treat the lease as forfeited. The tenant sought equitable relief from forfeiture:

---

94 *Dillwyn v Llewelyn* (1862) 4 De GF & J 517; and *Hussey v Palmer* [1972] 1 WLR 1286.
95 *Crabb v Arun DC* [1976] Ch 179.
96 (1877) 2 App Cas 439, HL.

Hughes v Metropolitan Railway Co (1877) 2 App Cas 439, HL, p 448

Lord Cairns LC: It is the first principle upon which all courts of equity proceed, that if parties who have entered into definite and distinct terms involving certain legal results – certain penalties or legal forfeiture – afterwards by their own act or with their own consent enter upon a course of negotiation which has the effect of leading one of the parties to suppose that the strict rights arising under the contract will not be enforced, or will be kept in suspense, or held in abeyance, the person who otherwise might have enforced those rights will not be allowed to enforce them where it would have been inequitable having regard to the dealings which have thus taken place between the parties.

The decision in *Hughes* has led to the view that the doctrine of estoppel may only be used to suspend a promisor's right to return to the original terms of his contract with the promisee and that the promisor's rights are not extinguished for all time. However, it does appear to be the case that in certain circumstances, a non-bargain promise which induces reasonable reliance on the part of the promisee will extinguish the rights of the promisor,[97] for all time, if equity so demands. This is most likely to be the case where it is impossible for the parties to return to the original terms of their contract, for example, where third party rights have arisen and it would be inequitable to interfere with such rights:

Emanuel Ajayi v RT Briscoe (Nigeria) Ltd [1964] 1 WLR 1326, PC, p 1330

Lord Hodson: The principle which has been described as quasi-estoppel and perhaps more aptly as promissory estoppel, is that when one party to a contract in the absence of fresh consideration agrees not to enforce his rights an equity will be raised in favour of the other party. This equity is, however, subject to the qualification: (a) that the other party has altered his position; (b) that the promisor can resile from his promise on giving reasonable notice, which need not be a formal notice, giving the promisee a reasonable opportunity of resuming his position; (c) the promise only becomes final and irrevocable if the promisee cannot resume his position ...

In this case, the promisee was unable to satisfy the requirements established in Lord Hodson's judgment, principally because there was no evidence of detrimental reliance on the promisor's promise which was considered to be a requirement. As earlier noted (see fn 89, above) in other cases, detriment is not said to be a necessary requirement for the operation of the rules on promissory estoppel.

A generally stated feature of the law of contract is that it exists to protect the reasonable expectations of the promisee. Thus, if the promisor promises to confer some benefit on the promisee, but fails to live up to his promise, the

---

97 See *Motor Oil Hellas SA v Shipping Corpn of India, The Kanchenjunga* [1990] 1 Lloyd's Rep 391, p 399, *per* Lord Goff.

remedies which the law provides for breach of contract supposedly serve to place the party not in breach in the position he would have been in had the promise been performed.[98] In contrast, many reliance based obligations arise by operation of law through the medium of tortious duties to exercise reasonable care. Here the basis of any award of damages is to return the injured party to the position he was in before the defendant's wrong was committed. As such, the interest protected is not one of expectation of performance, but instead the status quo interest – the claimant is compensated so as to restore the status quo before the defendant committed his wrong. While many reliance based obligations do involve the protection of the status quo interest, it should not be assumed that this is always the case. In particular, it should not be assumed that expectations of performance are entirely irrelevant where a promisee has reasonably relied upon the promise of the other party. Statements other than purely contractual promises are also capable of engendering expectations in another person. Much of the difficulty associated with identifying the interest protected when promises which induce reliance are enforced arises from the view in *Combe v Combe* that the doctrine of promissory estoppel operates as a shield rather than as a sword. However it has been seen that there may be circumstances in which the courts may allow certain varieties of estoppel to be used as a means of creating new rights where none previously existed, so as to adequately protect the equity raised in favour of the promisee resulting from his reasonable reliance on the promise of the other party.

Thompson identifies the main arguments in support of the view that reliance upon a non-contractual promise may now protect the promisee's expectation interest:

According to the orthodox model of contract, unless a promise is made under seal, it will be unenforceable unless the promisee either does, or promises to do, something in return. This bargain theory of contract has been subjected to searching criticism, however, by Professor Atiyah. He sets out, in full, the orthodox account of the doctrine of consideration which, he then argues, is not borne out by case law. His general thesis is that consideration is merely a reason for enforcing a promise but not the only reason. Instead, he insists, promises are enforced in various circumstances for other reasons, but when consideration in the orthodox sense is absent. As a classic example of this is the following situation: 'The promisor does not state any act which is to be performed by the promisee but the promisee does act in reliance on the promise in a way which was the natural and foreseeable result of the promise.' This, as Atiyah points out, is not regarded by orthodox theory as a contract but, nevertheless, one finds the promise enforced in certain circumstances. Central to this argument is his analysis of *Jorden v Money*. He argues that P's marriage in reliance on the representation that the bond would not be enforced was actually a contract, albeit unenforceable due to the Statute of Frauds. With

---

98 See Chapter 13.

respect, it is submitted that this is not so. It is clear from the speech of Lord Cranworth that the case was argued on the basis of a representation of intention, which the House of Lords held was not actionable unless it was contractual.

This, of course, begs the question as to why a statement of intention which was foreseeably relied upon was not a contract. The answer, it is submitted, is that the plaintiff did not promise he would marry in return for the promise not to enforce the bond. It is the inherent uncertainty as to what is reasonably foreseeable that is one major objection to Atiyah's thesis. Another is the uncertainty as to what the promisor is to be taken to have promised when he is responsible for inducing some expectation in the other party, but quite what that expectation is is unclear.

The reason why certainty must exist in contract but is inessential in equitable estoppel lies in the different nature of the remedies available. In contract, the available remedies are specific performance and damages. To award specific performance, or damages for loss of expectation interest, one must be able to ascertain exactly what it was that was promised. If one party encourages a neighbour to build a house on the former's land, this may well give rights in equity but can hardly do so at law. There has not been an express promise of anything; yet the acts done in reliance are equally consistent with a promise to give a personal licence to occupy the land or a promise to convey it. It is not possible to be sure which.

It is the inflexibility of contractual remedies which militates against foreseeable reliance on a promise operating as a contract. Estoppel is, however, flexible. When an expectation is clearly defined, it can in appropriate circumstances be fulfilled entirely, although this will not always be the case. Conversely, the expectation may not be fulfilled at all but compensation may be awarded for money spent in reliance, rather than the normal contractual position when a party may choose to claim damages either for his reliance interest or his expectation interest. In short, because of the flexibility of equity, one does not need to identify an express promise or representation; one simply ascertains when it would be unconscionable for one party to deny an expectation that the other has acted on. The court then has an unfettered discretion to decide to what extent that expectation should be fulfilled.[99]

Moreover, the dispute as to whether the rules on estoppel serve to extinguish the promisor's right to go back on his word or whether that right is merely suspended pending the service of reasonable notice appears to be a dispute which centres on the interest protected when equity intervenes in favour of the promisee. If the promisor's ability to insist upon his strict legal rights is extinguished altogether, this would seem to suggest that the promisee's expectations of performance of the promise are being protected. However, it should not be assumed that merely because new rights are created in favour of the promisee, this should always be taken as an indication that all promises

---

99 Thompson, 1983.

which induce reasonable reliance result in a remedy which protects the promisee's expectation in full. It should be emphasised that where rules on promissory and proprietary estoppel are concerned, the remedy given is equitable and the justice involved in enforcing a promise will have to be placed in high regard. In some instances, the equities of a particular case may involve the enforcement of the promisor's promise in full, but this will not always be the case. Thus, if the promisor has acted in a ruthless manner in seeking to deny the legitimate expectations of the promisee in circumstances which provide evidence of reasonable and detrimental reliance on the promise, the court may have little option but to enforce the promise in full.[100]

The controversy as to whether simple reliance or detrimental reliance is a requirement for the purposes of the different varieties of estoppel is also a matter which impinges on the question whether the promisee's expectation interest is protected or not. If detrimental reliance is not a requirement in cases of promissory estoppel, as some of the relevant *dicta* suggest, it seems likely that the interest protected is the promisee's expectation of performance of the promise made by the other party. However, if the view expressed by the Australian High Court in *Waltons Stores (Interstate) Ltd v Maher* correctly states the guiding principle, detriment to the promisee is a requirement, but the promisor's promise may be enforced only to the extent necessary to avoid the unconscionable and detrimental effects of a refusal by the promisor to honour his promise. Here, it is arguable that the reason for enforcing the promise is that the promisee is entitled to be protected against the denial of a future right.

---

100 See, eg, *Pascoe v Turner* [1979] 1 WLR 431.

CHAPTER 4

NEGOTIATING IN GOOD FAITH

Subject to some exceptions, English law has never adopted a requirement of good faith in contractual negotiations. Unlike in civilian legal systems, the fundamental principle *pacta sunt servanda*,[1] which forms the basis of an principle of good faith, was never regarded with any great significance by the common law courts. Indeed, it has been observed recently that the repudiation by one of the parties of his moral responsibility is not a matter for the courts.[2]

Nonetheless, greater exposure to European influence in recent years has led to certain legislative developments aimed at limited harmonisation of contract law within the European Union, some of which are heavily influenced by civilian doctrine and the notion of good faith in contractual dealings. Foremost among these developments must be the EC Directive on Unfair Terms in Consumer Contracts,[3] which has led to the laying before Parliament of the Unfair Terms in Consumer Contracts Regulations 1994 and 1999[4] and which now requires terms in consumer contracts which have not been individually negotiated to be in 'plain, intelligible language'. Moreover, terms which are contrary to the requirement of good faith and which cause a significant imbalance in the rights and obligations of the parties to the detriment of the consumer may be regarded as unfair and unenforceable.

European developments apart, there are other aspects of English contract law which can be said to border on a requirement of good faith in contracting, which will be considered in this chapter. In particular, there appears to be a duty on contracting parties to behave decently towards each other, to warn each other of risks and not to take unfair advantage of a stronger position. This seems close to a duty not only not to deceive but also to deal fairly and openly with others:[5, 6]

---

1   Promises will be honoured.

2   *Kleinwort Benson Ltd v Malaysia Mining Corpn Bhd* [1989] 1 WLR 379, p 394.

3   93/13/EEC OJ L 95/29.

4   SI 1994/3159, in force from 1 July 1995, and SI 1999/2083, in force from 1 October 1999. These Regulations are considered in more detail in Chapter 8.

5   *Interfoto Picture Library Ltd v Stiletto Visual Programmes Ltd* [1989] 1 QB 433, pp 439 and 442, *per* Bingham LJ.

6   Inspired both by Bingham LJ's comments in *Interfoto* and the implications of the 1993 Directive there is a growing literature on the implications of good faith in the common law of contract. See, eg, Adams and Brownsword, 1995, Chapter 7; Beatson and Friedman (eds), 1995; Harrison, 1997; and Brownsword, Howells and Wilhelmsson (eds), 1994.

Interfoto Picture Library Ltd v Stiletto Visual Programmes Ltd [1988] 1 All ER 348, CA, p 352

Bingham LJ: In many civil law systems, and perhaps in most legal systems outside the common law world, the law of obligations recognises and enforces an overriding principle that in making and carrying out contracts parties should act in good faith. This does not simply mean that they should not deceive each other, a principle which any legal system must recognise; its effect is perhaps most aptly conveyed by such metaphorical colloquialisms as 'playing fair', 'coming clean' or 'putting one's cards face upwards on the table'. It is, in essence, a principle of fair and open dealing. In such a forum, it might, I think, be held on the facts of this case that the plaintiffs were under a duty in all fairness to draw the defendants' attention specifically to the high price payable if the transparencies were not returned in time and, when the 14 days had expired, to point out to the defendants the high cost of continued failure to return them.

English law has, characteristically, committed itself to no such overriding principle, but has developed piecemeal solutions in response to demonstrated problems of unfairness. Many examples could be given. Thus, equity has intervened to strike down unconscionable bargains. Parliament has stepped in to regulate the imposition of exemption clauses and the form of certain hire-purchase agreements. The common law also has made its contribution, by holding that certain classes of contract require the utmost good faith, by treating as irrecoverable what purport to be agreed estimates of damage but are in truth a disguised penalty for breach and in many other ways.

The well known cases on sufficiency of notice are, in my view, properly to be read in this context. At one level, they are concerned with a question of pure contractual analysis, whether one party has done enough to give the other notice of the incorporation of a term in the contract. At another level, they are concerned with a somewhat different question, whether it would in all the circumstances be fair (or reasonable) to hold a party bound by any conditions or by a particular condition of an unusual and stringent nature.

(The facts and other aspects of this decision are considered in Chapters 2 and 8.)

Bingham LJ refers to the piecemeal development of English law, which appears to be an accurate reflection of the present state of the law. Certain aspects of the rules on contract formation and variation appear to introduce an element of good faith in contractual negotiations. In particular, the manner in which the rules on promissory and proprietary estoppel have developed suggests that the foundation for these rules is that of good faith, fairness and justice.[7] Moreover, in some limited respects, the common law rules on lock-out agreements, under which a contracting party agrees for a limited time to deal only with a particular person, introduce an element which verges on something close to a requirement of good faith. However, the general rule

---

7   See materials in Chapter 3, particularly pp 147–58.

remains substantially intact with the result that, except in a small number of cases, there is no duty to disclose facts peculiarly within the knowledge of one of the parties, due in part to the historical strength of the common law rule of *caveat emptor*. Whilst there is a well established rule that a contracting party must not actively mislead the other by means of an actionable misrepresentation, English law has not gone down the road requiring contracting parties to reveal to the other all facts relevant to the contract which is being negotiated.

DISCLOSURE OF MATERIAL FACTS AND THE REQUIREMENT OF GOOD FAITH

As a general rule, English law does not impose upon the parties to a contract a general duty to disclose information to the other party to the contract. Instead, due to the influence of the principle *caveat emptor*, it is the duty of each party to look after his own interests and exercise his own judgment in deciding whether or not to enter into a particular contract. While this approach can be viewed as consistent with the principle of freedom of contract, which is important in purely business relationships, the same approach to consumer contracts may not be so well founded. Moreover, even in commercial contracts, there is always the danger of sharp practice, which needs to be guarded against (in most other EU countries, a 'good faith' requirement of openness and disclosure applies to business as well as consumer contracts).

However, the fact that English law has failed to develop any coherent duty of disclosure may not always be fatal, since there are alternative avenues which may be pursued. For example, some of the problems which might be dealt with by a duty of disclosure can be covered through the process of implying terms into a contract. Indeed, such an approach may be better in some cases since, *prima facie*, the only remedy for a failure to disclose is rescission of the contract, whereas the breach of an implied term may lead to other possible remedies, such as damages.[8] In certain instances, sharp practice may be dealt with under rules relating to induced mistake, but since the common law only recognises a very limited range of mistakes, it is more likely than not that relief at common law will be refused:

Bell v Lever Bros [1932] AC 161, HL, p 227

> **Lord Atkin**: It now becomes necessary to deal with the second point of the plaintiffs, namely, that the contract of 19 March 1929 could be avoided by them in consequence of the non-disclosure by Bell of his misconduct as to the cocoa

---

8   *Bank of Nova Scotia v Hellenic Mutual War Risks Association, The Good Luck* [1990] 1 QB 818, reversed on other grounds in [1992] 1 AC 233.

dealings. Fraudulent concealment has been negatived by the jury; this claim is based upon the contention that Bell owed a duty to Levers to disclose his misconduct, and that in default of disclosure the contract was voidable. Ordinarily, the failure to disclose a material fact which might influence the mind of a prudent contractor does not give the right to avoid the contract. The principle of *caveat emptor* applies outside contracts of sale. There are certain contracts expressed by the law to be contracts of the utmost good faith, where material facts must be disclosed; if not, the contract is voidable. Apart from special fiduciary relationships, contracts for partnership and contracts of insurance are the leading instances. In such cases the duty does not arise out of contract; the duty of a person proposing an insurance arises before a contract is made, so of an intending partner. Unless this contract can be brought within this limited category of contracts *uberrimae fidei*, it appears to me that this ground of defence must fail. I see nothing to differentiate this agreement from the ordinary contract of service and I am aware of no authority which places contracts of service within the limited category I have mentioned. It seems to me clear that master and man negotiating for an agreement of service are as unfettered as in any other negotiation. Nor can I find anything in the relation of master and servant, when established, that places agreements between them within the protected category. It is said that there is a contractual duty of the servant to disclose his past faults. I agree that the duty in the servant to protect his master's property may involve the duty to report a fellow servant whom he knows to be wrongfully dealing with that property. The servant owes a duty not to steal, but, having stolen, is there superadded a duty to confess that he has stolen? I am satisfied that to imply such a duty would be a departure from the well-established usage of mankind and would be to create obligations entirely outside the normal contemplation of the parties concerned. If a man agrees to raise his butler's wages, must the butler disclose that two years ago he received a secret commission from the wine merchant; and if the master discovers it, can he, without dismissal or after the servant has left, avoid the agreement for the increase in salary and recover back the extra wages paid? If he gives his cook a month's wages in lieu of notice can he, on discovering that the cook has been pilfering the tea and sugar, claim the return of the month's wages? I think not. He takes the risk; if he wishes to protect himself, he can question his servant, and will then be protected by the truth or otherwise of the answers.

I agree with the view expressed by Avory J in *Healey v Société Anonyme Française Rubastic* on this point. It will be noticed that Bell was not a director of Levers, and, with respect, I cannot accept the view of Greer LJ that if he was in fiduciary relationship to the Niger Company he was in a similar fiduciary relationship to the shareholders, or to the particular shareholders (Levers) who held 99% of the shares. Nor do I think that it is alleged or proved that in making the agreement of 19 March 1929, Levers were acting as agents for the Niger Company. In the matter of the release of the service contract and the payment of £30,000 they were acting quite plainly for themselves as principals. It follows that on this ground also the claim fails.

The result is that, in the present case, servants unfaithful in some of their work retain large compensation which some will think they do not deserve.

Nevertheless, it is of greater importance that well established principles of contract should be maintained than that a particular hardship should be redressed and I see no way of giving relief to the plaintiffs in the present circumstances, except by confiding to the courts loose powers of introducing terms into contracts which would only serve to introduce doubt and confusion where certainty is essential.

For the facts of this case and discussion of the issue of common mistake, see Chapter 6.

The general approach advocated in *Bell v Lever Bros* has been consistently applied across a whole range of cases with the result that there are very few instances in which a party will be required to disclose relevant information to the other party. Indeed, in some instances, the attachment of English law to the idea that a contracting party is entitled to stay silent no matter how relevant the information might be to the other party is surprising, especially where it allows that person to act in what can be described as little more than a dishonest fashion. For example, in *Wales v Wadham*,[9] a husband and wife were in the process of negotiating a divorce settlement. In those negotiations, the wife failed to reveal the fact that she intended to marry a very wealthy man as soon as the divorce was finalised. Had this intention been known at the time, it would have had a substantial effect on the final settlement, since the amount the husband agreed to pay was based on an assumption that the wife would be dependant upon the amount he paid her.[10] What makes the decision all the more odd is that this was not a business relationship, with the result that this approach cannot be justified on the basis of market principles.

In general, there is no duty of disclosure, in the sense that a person is not obliged to speak. However, if a person starts to speak, he cannot later remain silent and allow the other party to the contract to draw a false impression from his subsequent silence. Moreover, it has been observed that 'a single word or ... a nod or a wink, or a shake of the head or a smile'[11] may amount to an actionable misrepresentation.

If a person makes a statement which is literally true, but which nonetheless creates a misleading impression, liability may attach. It follows that telling only half the truth can be just as damaging as telling an outright lie. For example, in *Curtis v Chemical Cleaning & Dyeing Co Ltd*,[12] an attendant in a dry cleaning shop presented the plaintiff with a receipt for clothes left for cleaning purposes. The plaintiff noted that the receipt contained small print

---

9   [1977] 1 WLR 199.

10 Such an outcome will no longer prevail since under the presently applicable statutory rules, the court now requires full disclosure so that it may properly exercise its statutory discretions: *Jenkins v Livesey* [1985] AC 424.

11 *Walters v Morgan* (1861) 42 ER 1056, p 1059, *per* Lord Campbell. For an amusing practical illustration, see *R v Barnard* (1837) C & P 784.

12 [1951] 1 KB 805.

and asked the attendant what it meant. She was told that the relevant terms purported to exclude the liability of the proprietors for damage to beads and sequins attached to the garment. However, the truth was that the exemption of liability extended to all damage howsoever caused. It was held that, because only half the truth had been revealed, the defendants were effectively estopped from relying upon the exemption clause with the result that the plaintiff was able to recover damages. Also, in *Dimmock v Hallett*,[13] where an auctioneer had misleadingly stated that two farms on a freehold property were let, whereas in fact the tenant farmers had served notice to quit. As Sir G Turner LJ stated (at p 28), 'The purchaser ... would be led to suppose ... that he was purchasing with continuing tenancies at fixed rents, whereas he would, in fact, have to find tenants immediately after the completion of his purchase'. Intriguingly, his Lordship also noted that 'The Court requires good faith in conditions of sale, and looks strictly at the statements contained in them'.

Moreover, once a person has started to speak, he comes under a duty to keep the other party appraised of any subsequent change in circumstances of which the speaker becomes aware.

In *With v O'Flanagan*,[14] the defendant owned a medical practice which he wished to sell. In the course of negotiations, it was stated that the practice took in £2,000 per annum. At the time of speaking, this statement was true, but because the defendant was in poor health, the receipts from the practice fell off to almost nothing. In the circumstances, it was held that the defendant was duty bound to inform the prospective purchasers of the change and that because this had not been done, the plaintiff was entitled to rescind the contract:

With v O'Flanagan [1936] 1 Ch 575, CA, p 586

Romer LJ: The only principle invoked by the appellants in this case is as follows. If A with a view to inducing B to enter into a contract makes a representation as to a material fact, then if at a later date and before the contract is actually entered into, owing to a change of circumstances, the representation then made would to the knowledge of A be untrue and B subsequently enters into the contract in ignorance of that change of circumstances and relying upon that representation, A cannot hold B to the bargain. There is ample authority for that statement and, indeed, I doubt myself whether any authority is necessary, it being, it seems to me, so obviously consistent with the plainest principles of equity.

Lord Wright MR (p 581): As to the law, which has been challenged, I want to say this. I take the law to be as it was stated by Fry J in *Davies v London and Provincial Marine Insurance Co* where it is perhaps most fully expressed. In that case, certain friends of an agent had agreed to deposit a sum of money for

13   [1866–67] LR Ch App 21.
14   [1936] 1 Ch 575, CA.

what was alleged to have been defaults on his part. The company who had employed him were under the belief and were advised that the default of the agent constituted felony, but they were later advised that these acts did not amount to felony and they withdrew the order for his arrest, and then still later in the day the friends of the agent agreed to deposit a sum of money on the footing of what they had been told earlier in the day before the arrest had been withdrawn – these statements had not been corrected – and on that footing it was held by Fry J 'that the change of circumstances ought to have' been stated to the intending sureties, and that the agreement must be rescinded and the money returned to the sureties. 'I need not read the whole of the passage in the judgment, but I need only refer to one or two points. The learned judge points out: (1) 'Where parties are contracting with one another, each may, unless there be a duty to disclose, observe silence even in regard to facts which he believes would be operative upon the mind of the other; and it rests upon those who say that there was a duty to disclose, to show that the duty existed.' Then the learned judge points out that, in many cases, there is such a duty as between persons in a confidential or a fiduciary relationship where the pre-existing relationship involves the duty of entire disclosure. Then his Lordship says: 'In the next place, there are certain contracts which have been called contracts *uberrimae fidei* where, from their nature, the Court requires disclosure from one of the contracting parties.' The learned judge refers to contracts of partnership and marine insurance. Then he goes on: (2) 'Again, in ordinary contracts the duty may arise from circumstances which occur during the negotiation. Thus, for instance, if one of the negotiating parties has made a statement which is false in fact but which he believes to be true and which is material to the contract, and during the course of the negotiation he discovers the falsity of that statement, he is under an obligation to correct his erroneous statement; although if he had said nothing he very likely might have been entitled to hold his tongue throughout.' Then he adds what was material in that case and what is material in this case: 'So, again, if a statement has been made which is true at the time, but which during the course of the negotiations becomes untrue, then the person who knows that it has become untrue is under an obligation to disclose to the other the change of circumstances.'

Statutory exceptions

In a limited number of cases, English law does recognise a duty of disclosure. Many of these exceptions are statute based and will often be directed towards the protection of the party perceived to be the weaker, such as a consumer-debtor under a consumer credit agreement who is statutorily required to be supplied with information relating to the indebtedness he has taken on.[15] Similarly, there are statutory duties to disclose information relating to the composition of food and medicines under the Food Safety Act 1990 and the Medicines Act 1968 and regulations made thereunder.

15 Consumer Credit Act 1974, s 55.

Insurance

Insurance contracts are said to be contracts *uberrimae fidei* or contracts of utmost good faith. As a result, there is a duty of disclosure on both sides of the contract. But the most important aspect of the duty is that a person proposing insurance must disclose all facts[16] material to the insured risk. The justification for this approach is said to be that the insurer is engaged in a process of speculation and needs to know as much as possible so as to allow him to 'compute the contingent chance'.[17] For these purposes, it is important to emphasise that what must be disclosed are facts relevant to the risk, which might serve to affect the mind of a prudent insurer in deciding whether to accept the risk or what premium to set.[18] Moreover, it seems that for these purposes a fact is material if a prudent insurer would wish to consider it even if it later transpires that the fact has not, in any way, influenced the insurer's decision on whether to accept the risk.[19]

The duty of disclosure in insurance contracts is not confined to the insured, since the insurer is also required to disclose to the insured facts relevant to the insurance contract.

In *Banque Financière de la Cité v Westgate Insurance Co Ltd*,[20] the defendants accepted a proposal for insurance against credit risks, but failed to disclose to the insured bank that the broker through whom the insurance was arranged, had to their knowledge, been guilty of fraud in relation to a previous, similar contract of insurance. This knowledge was of particular importance since the broker is regarded as the agent of the insured. When the bank made a claim under the insurance policy, the insurer sought to avoid the contract on the ground of the broker's fraud, but it was held that the insurer's failure to disclose a material fact was such that the insured could rescind the contract and recover any premiums paid. However, in the circumstances, this was not a particularly valuable remedy since the insured event had occurred with the result that the insured was unable to recover the policy moneys from the insurer. Nor was he able to recover damages in respect of the loss suffered:

---

16 The rule is confined to facts with the result that there is no duty to disclose a matter which can only relate to a person's opinion, such as whether the proposer for life assurance is suffering from an illness of which he could not have been aware because he has not yet consulted a medical expert: *Joel v Law Union & Crown Insurance Co* [1908] 2 KB 863.

17 *Carter v Boehm* (1766) 3 Burr 1905, *per* Lord Mansfield.

18 Marine Insurance Act 1906, s 18(2).

19 *Pan Atlantic Insurance Co Ltd v Pine Top Insurance Co Ltd* [1995] 1 AC 501.

20 [1990] 1 QB 665, CA.

Banque Financière de la Cité v Westgate Insurance Co Ltd [1990] 1 QB 665, CA, p 769

Slade LJ: We begin with a statement of basic principle of the English law of contract: 'Ordinarily, the failure to disclose a material fact which might influence the mind of a prudent contractor does not give the right to avoid the contract. The principle of *caveat emptor* applies outside contracts of sale. There are certain contracts expressed by the law to be contracts of the utmost good faith, where material facts must be disclosed; if not, the contract is voidable. Apart from special fiduciary relationships, contracts for partnership and contracts of insurance are the leading instances. In such cases, the duty does not arise out of contract; the duty of a person proposing an insurance arises before a contract is made, so of an intending partner.' See *Bell v Lever Bros Ltd* [1932] AC 161, p 227, *per* Lord Atkin.

The common features of contracts which are classified by the law as contracts *uberrimae fidei* is that by their very nature one party is likely to have the command of means of knowledge not available to the other. In the leading case of *Carter v Boehm* (1766) 3 Burr 1905, Lord Mansfield CJ described the rationale behind the duty of disclosure falling on the insured in the case of contracts of insurance at p 1909:

> Insurance is a contract upon speculation. The special facts, upon which the contingent chance is to be computed, lie most commonly in the knowledge of the *insured* only: the underwriter trusts to his representation, and proceeds upon confidence that he does not keep back any circumstance in his knowledge, to mislead the underwriter into a belief that the circumstance does not exist and to induce him to estimate the *risque*, as if it did not exist. The keeping back such circumstance is a fraud and therefore the policy is *void*. Although the suppression should happen through *mistake*, without any fraudulent intention; yet still, the underwriter is *deceived* and the policy is *void*; because the *risque* run is really different from the *risque* understood and intended to be run, at the time of the agreement.
>
> ...

In our judgment, with respect to the judge, the test of materiality adumbrated by him is not an entirely satisfactory one. True, it is that all contracts of insurance are (in the words of s 17 of the 1906 Act applicable to contracts of marine insurance) based on the utmost good faith. However, in the case of commercial contracts, broad concepts of honesty and fair dealing, however laudable, are a somewhat uncertain guide when determining the existence or otherwise of an obligation which may arise even in the absence of any dishonest or unfair intent; they are not the tests embodied in s 18 of the 1906 Act. More importantly, in our judgment, it would be too broad a proposition to state that any fact is material if it is 'calculated to influence the decision of the insured to conclude the contract of insurance'. To give one example, it might well be that in a particular case proposed insurers would be aware of another reputable underwriter who would be prepared to underwrite the same risk at a substantially lower premium. In our judgment the mere existence of the relationship of insurers and insured would not place on them the duty to inform the insured of this fact.

In adapting the well established principles relating to the duty of disclosure falling on the insured to the obverse case of the insurer himself, due account must be taken of the rather different reasons for which the insured and the insurer require the protection of full disclosure. In our judgment, the duty falling on the insurer must at least extend to disclosing all facts known to him which are material either to the nature of the risk sought to be covered or the recoverability of a claim under the policy which a prudent insured would take into account in deciding whether or not to place the risk for which he seeks cover with that insurer.

It is common ground that the acquisition by Mr Dungate in June 1980 of knowledge of Mr Lee's dishonesty did not place him under any obligation to make disclosure to the banks by virtue of the already subsisting contract of insurance: see *Lishman v Northern Maritime Insurance Co* (1875) LR 10 CP 179. It is, however, submitted on behalf of Keysers that a duty of disclosure rested on Hodge (through Mr Dungate) during the negotiations for the amendment of the Ultron primary layer policy which preceded the second Ultron loan. These negotiations, as has already appeared, resulted in the conclusion of a further contract of insurance between Hodge and the insured on 24 June 1980. In our judgment, the question whether or not Hodge discharged its duty of full disclosure must be determined by reference to the point of time immediately before the conclusion of that further contract.

It was submitted on behalf of Hodge that there had been no failure to discharge any such duty. Counsel submitted (and we are disposed to accept) that Mr Lee's dishonest conduct could not be said to be material to the additional risk to which Hodge was subjecting itself by the amendment to the Ultron primary layer policy provided for by the further contract of 24 June 1980. He went on to submit that this dishonest conduct was equally not material to the recoverability of a claim under the amended policy, on the grounds that it would not by itself have entitled the insurers either to avoid the policy or to invoke the fraud exclusion clause.

In our judgment, however, this approach to the question of materiality is too narrow. In the section of this judgment headed 'Common ground on this appeal' and, under issue (1), we have set out certain facts which we consider that Mr Dungate knew in June 1980 and onwards. These facts by themselves must have sufficed to make Mr Dungate aware that the broker through whom the banks had been dealing had not only committed acts of serious dishonesty towards all parties concerned over the past few months, but was well capable of committing other acts of deception in the future. We think it clear that such facts were material to the recoverability of a claim under the amended Ultron first layer policy which, if disclosed to him, a prudent insured would have taken into account in deciding whether or not to make the new arrangements for insurance with Hodge in June 1980. The reason is that he would have recognised a possible danger that the policy, either in its original form or in its amended form, might in the future prove to be unenforceable because of the fraud exclusion clause, or voidable, if Mr Lee's dishonesty were found to have extended to the arrangements for the original placing of the insurance policy with Hodge or its amendment.

The facts known by Mr Dungate demonstrating the dishonesty of the broker through whom the banks were negotiating with him were thus material facts which it was his duty to disclose to them before they concluded the contractual arrangements with the insurers which were concluded on 24 June 1980.

It follows that, in our judgment: (a) Hodge, through Mr Dungate, was in breach of this duty of disclosure owed to the banks in June 1980; (b) in the absence of supervening events depriving them of this right, the banks, on discovering the non-disclosure, would have had the right to rescind the further contract of insurance concluded on 24 June 1980 and to demand the return of the further premium paid by them in September 1980.

However, this is not the relief arising out of the non-disclosure which Keysers seek. A claim for the return of the premium raised in its respondent's notice has not been pursued in this court. Instead, Keysers seek damages for breach of the obligation of disclosure. To this claim we now turn.

Other duties of disclosure

Many of the cases concerning undue influence considered below[21] are based upon the existence of a relationship of trust and confidence. The nature of that relationship may be such that the party relied upon should disclose to the weaker party information which is relevant to their relationship. In *Tate v Williamson*,[22] the appellant was a property owning student who had fallen into a state of financial embarrassment. He sought advice on this matter from the respondent, who advised the sale of the land owned by the appellant. The respondent then offered to buy the land without advising the appellant that the land was worth twice the amount paid for it due to the presence of mineral deposits under the land. The respondent's failure to disclose this information was regarded as a ground for rescission of the contract on the ground that there was a relationship which gave rise to the presumption of undue influence.

MISREPRESENTATION

While there is no general rule to the effect that a contracting party must disclose information within his knowledge, English law does impose a relatively strict duty not to make false statements which induce the other

---

21 See Chapter 7.
22 (1866) 2 Ch App 55.

party to enter into a contract with him. In these circumstances, the primary remedy is that of rescission of the contract,[23] but, depending on the nature of the misrepresentation, there is also the possibility of an action for damages, either as of right[24] or at the discretion of the court.[25]

In order to amount to a misrepresentation, the defendant's statement must be a false statement of fact which induces the other party to enter into a contract with him. This raises two principal issues, namely what is a statement of fact and secondly what is to be regarded as an inducement.

Statements of fact, statements of intention, statements of opinion and commendatory puffs

It is said to be an essential requirement of an actionable misrepresentation that it should be a statement of fact. Because of this rule, there are a number of types of statement which will not give rise to a remedy for misrepresentation. In the first place, a promise as to the future or a statement of intention is not a misrepresentation. The reason for this is that a misrepresentation must be a statement which can be categorised as either true or false at the time it was made. Promises, in contrast, may or may not come true. If a promise is not fulfilled, this is a matter which may give rise to an action for breach of contract, provided the promise is supported by consideration and on the assumption that the promise becomes a term of the contract made between the parties.[26] In the absence of consideration, a bare promise is generally unenforceable in English law.

However, simply to say that all statements which relate to the future are not actionable as a misrepresentation is not true. For example, it may be implicit in a statement which appears to be one of future intention that a certain present state of facts exists. In particular, the statement may be construed as a factual statement as to the state of mind of the representor at the time he makes his statement. Thus, if a person makes a promise but the facts, at the time that promise is made, are such that the representor knows the statement cannot come true, that 'promise' can be treated as a statement of fact. For example, if an international airline adopts a policy of over-booking all of its flights, in order to take account of passengers who may not take up seats they have booked, a confirmation of an available seat, although it appears to

---

23   See Chapter 14.

24   Eg, for the tort of deceit in the case of a fraudulent misrepresentation or for negligence at common law or under the Misrepresentation Act 1967, s 2(1), in the case of a negligent misrepresentation. On these matters, see Chapter 13.

25   Misrepresentation Act 1967, s 2(2), which gives a discretion to award damages in lieu of rescission. See Chapters 13 and 14.

26   For materials on the distinction between terms and representations, see Chapter 5.

relate to the future may be regarded as a statement of fact on the basis that the airline must know there will be circumstances in which more passengers may turn up for a flight than there are seats available.[27] In this regard, it has been said that the state of a man's mind is as much a fact as the state of his digestion![28]

In *Edgington v Fitzmaurice*,[29] the directors of a company issued a prospectus inviting investment in the company in return for the issue of secured debentures. The prospectus falsely stated that the money invested would be used to complete alterations to buildings owned by the company and to generally expand the company's business activities. In fact, the money lent by the plaintiff was used to meet debts owed by the company – a purpose the directors had in mind but did not state in the prospectus. The Court of Appeal dismissed an appeal against an order for rescission of the contract on the ground that there had been a fraudulent misrepresentation:

Edgington v Fitzmaurice (1885) 29 Ch D 459, CA, p 481

Bowen LJ: This is an action for deceit, in which the plaintiff complains that he was induced to take certain debentures by the misrepresentations of the defendants and that he sustained damage thereby. The loss which the plaintiff sustained is not disputed. In order to sustain his action, he must first prove that there was a statement as to facts which was false and, secondly, that it was false to the knowledge of the defendants or that they made it not caring whether it was true or false. For it is immaterial whether they made the statement knowing it to be untrue, or recklessly, without caring whether it was true or not, because to make a statement recklessly for the purpose of influencing another person is dishonest. It is also clear that it is wholly immaterial with what object the lie is told. That is laid down in Lord Blackburn's judgment in *Smith v Chadwick*, but it is material that the defendant should intend that it should be relied on by the person to whom he makes it. But, lastly, when you have proved that the statement was false, you must further shew that the plaintiff has acted upon it and has sustained damage by so doing: you must shew that the statement was either the sole cause of the plaintiff's act, or materially contributed to his so acting. So the law is laid down in *Clarke v Dickson*, and that is the law which we have now to apply.

The alleged misrepresentations were three. First, it was said that the prospectus contained an implied allegation that the mortgage for £21,500 could not be called in at once, but was payable by instalments. I think that, upon a fair construction of the prospectus, it does so allege; and, therefore, that the prospectus must be taken to have contained an untrue statement on that point; but it does not appear to me clear that the statement was fraudulently made by

---

27 See, eg, *British Airways Board v Taylor* [1976] 1 All ER 65, a case decided under the provisions of the Trade Descriptions Act 1968, s 14, which imposes criminal liability for false factual statements relating to the provision of a service.

28 *Edgington v Fitzmaurice* (1885) 29 Ch D 459, p 483, *per* Bowen LJ.

29 (1885) 29 Ch D 459, CA.

the defendants. It is therefore immaterial to consider whether the plaintiff was induced to act as he did by that statement.

Secondly, it is said that the prospectus contains an implied allegation that there was no other mortgage affecting the property except the mortgage stated therein. I think there was such an implied allegation, but I think it is not brought home to the defendants that it was made dishonestly; accordingly, although the plaintiff may have been damnified by the weight which he gave to the allegation, he cannot rely on it in this action: for in an action of deceit the plaintiff must prove dishonesty. Therefore, if the case had rested on these two allegations alone, I think it would be too uncertain to entitle the plaintiff to succeed.

But, when we come to the third alleged misstatement, I feel that the plaintiff's case is made out. I mean the statement of the objects for which the money was to be raised. These were stated to be to complete the alterations and additions to the buildings, to purchase horses and vans, and to develop the supply of fish.

A mere suggestion of possible purposes to which a portion of the money might be applied would not have formed a basis for an action of deceit. There must be a misstatement of an existing fact: but the state of a man's mind is as much a fact as the state of his digestion. It is true that it is very difficult to prove what the state of a man's mind at a particular time is, but if it can be ascertained it is as much a fact as anything else. A misrepresentation as to the state of a man's mind is, therefore, a misstatement of fact. Having applied as careful consideration to the evidence as I could, I have reluctantly come to the conclusion that the true objects of the defendants in raising the money were not those stated in the circular. I will not go through the evidence, but looking only to the cross-examination of the defendants, I am satisfied that the objects for which the loan was wanted were misstated by the defendants, I will not say knowingly, but so recklessly as to be fraudulent in the eye of the law.

A statement of opinion, if genuinely believed, is not to be regarded as a factual statement. This stance is also closely related to the attitude adopted in English law towards advertising and mere commendatory 'puffs'. So far as the latter are concerned, many statements made by a manufacturer or trader advertising his/her product or his wares are such that no reasonable person would be influenced by them. Thus, a statement to the effect that a particular brand of beer reaches parts of the body not reached by rival products or that a particular toilet soap would (daily) increase the users 'loveliness' are not statements which would be taken seriously by any reasonable person. Moreover such 'sales talk' or 'type' is incapable of objective verification one way or the other. The argument on similar lines advanced by the defendant company in *Carlill v Carbolic Smoke Ball Co Ltd*[30] failed because their statement that use of the ball would 'positively cure' a list of ailments and diseases was objectively verifiable and would be taken seriously by ordinary consumers.

---

30   [1893] 1 QB 256, CA. The case is discussed extensively in Chapter 2.

As regards opinions, it is not possible for a person to qualify every statement he makes with the words 'I believe' or 'I think'. In some cases, a seeming statement of fact is self evidently nothing more than an (often uninformed) statement of opinion.

In *Bissett v Wilkinson*,[31] the owner of the land which was the subject matter of the contract had stated that the land was capable of holding 2,000 sheep. In fact, the land had never been used for sheep farming for anything longer than a very short period of time. Moreover, when it had been used for sheep farming, only a small part of the land had been applied to that purpose. The respondents argued that the statement was a misrepresentation and refused to proceed with the contract. The Privy Council held that the statement did not amount to an actionable misrepresentation, because it was nothing more than a genuine opinion, and that any reasonable person in the appellant's position would have realised this:

Bissett v Wilkinson [1927] AC 177, PC, p 179

Lord Merrivale: Sheep farming was the purpose for which the respondents purchased the lands of the plaintiff. One of them had no experience of farming. The other had been before the war in charge of sheep on an extensive sheep-farm carried on by his father, who had accompanied and advised him in his negotiation with the appellant and had carefully inspected the lands at Avondale. In the course of coming to his agreement with the respondents, the appellant made statements as to the property which, in their defence and counterclaim, the respondents alleged to be misrepresentations ...

In an action for rescission, as in an action for specific performance of an executory contract, when misrepresentation is the alleged ground of relief of the party who repudiates the contract, it is, of course, essential to ascertain whether that which is relied upon is a representation of a specific fact, or a statement of opinion, since an erroneous opinion stated by the party affirming the contract, though it may have been relied upon and have induced the contract on the part of the party who seeks rescission, gives no title to relief unless fraud is established. The application of this rule, however, is not always easy, as is illustrated in a good many reported cases, as well as in this. A representation of fact may be inherent in a statement of opinion and, at any rate, the existence of the opinion in the person stating it is a question of fact. In *Karberg*'s case, Lindley LJ, in the course of testing a representation which might have been, as it was said to be by interested parties, one of opinion or belief, used this inquiry: 'Was the statement of expectation a statement of things not really expected?' The Court of Appeal applied this test and rescinded the contract which was in question. In *Smith v Land and House Property Corpn,* there came in question a vendor's description of the tenant of the property sold as 'a most desirable tenant' – a statement of his opinion, as was argued on his behalf in an action to enforce the contract of sale. This description was held by the Court of Appeal to be a misrepresentation of fact, which, without proof of

---

31 [1927] AC 177, PC.

fraud, disentitled the vendor to specific performance of the contract of purchase. 'It is often fallaciously assumed' said Bowen LJ, 'that a statement of opinion cannot involve the statement of fact. In a case where the facts are equally well known to both parties, what one of them says to the other is frequently nothing but an expression of opinion. The statement of such opinion is in a sense a statement of fact, about the condition of the man's own mind, but only of an irrelevant fact, for it is of no consequence what the opinion is. But if the facts are not equally well known to both sides, then a statement of opinion by one who knows the facts best involves very often a statement of a material fact, for he impliedly states that he knows facts which justify his opinion.' The kind of distinction which is in question is illustrated again in a well known case of *Smith v Chadwick*. There, the words under consideration involved the inquiry in relation to the sale of an industrial concern whether a statement of 'the present value of the turnover or output' was of necessity a statement of fact that the produce of the works was of the amount mentioned, or might be and was a statement that the productive power of the works was estimated at so much. The words were held to be capable of the second of these meanings. The decisive inquiries came to be: what meaning was actually conveyed to the party complaining; was he deceived, and, as the action was based on a charge of fraud, was the statement in question made fraudulently?

In the present case, as in those cited, the material facts of the transaction, the knowledge of the parties respectively, and their relative positions, the words of representation used and the actual condition of the subject matter spoken of, are relevant to the two inquiries necessary to be made: What was the meaning of the representation? Was it true?

In ascertaining what meaning was conveyed to the minds of the now respondents by the appellant's statement as to the 2,000 sheep, the most material fact to be remembered is that, as both parties were aware, the appellant had not and, so far as appears, no other person had at any time carried on sheep farming upon the unit of land in question. That land as a distinct holding had never constituted a sheep farm. The two blocks comprised in it differed substantially in character. Hogan's block was described by one of the respondents' witnesses as 'better land'. 'It might carry' he said, 'one sheep or perhaps two or even three sheep to the acre. He estimated the carrying capacity of the land generally as little more than half a sheep to the acre. And Hogan's land had been allowed to deteriorate during several years before the respondents purchased. As was said by Sim J: 'In ordinary circumstances, any statement made by an owner who has been occupying his own farm as to its carrying capacity would be regarded as a statement of fact ... This, however, is not such a case. The defendants knew all about Hogan's block and knew also what sheep the farm was carrying when they inspected it. In these circumstances ... the defendants were not justified in regarding anything said by the plaintiff as to the carrying capacity as being anything more than an expression of his opinion on the subject.' In this view of the matter, their Lordships concur.

Whether the appellant honestly and, in fact, held the opinion which he stated remained to be considered. This involved examination of the history and condition of the property. If a reasonable man with the appellant's knowledge could not have come to the conclusion he stated, the description of that conclusion as an opinion would not necessarily protect him against rescission for misrepresentation. But what was actually the capacity in competent hands of the land the respondents purchased had never been, and never was, practically ascertained. The respondents, after two years' trial of sheep-farming, under difficulties caused in part by their inexperience, found themselves confronted by a fall in the values of sheep and wool which would have left them losers if they could have carried 3,000 sheep. As is said in the judgment of Ostler J: 'Owing to sheep becoming practically valueless, they reduced their flock and went in for cropping and dairy farming in order to make a living.'

It does not follow from this that every statement of opinion will be sufficient to allow the speaker to avoid liability. For example, in some instances, the facts may be such that the speaker clearly does not hold the opinion expressed. In others a seeming statement of opinion implies the existence of facts which turn out to be untrue. For example, in *Smith v Land & House Property Corpn*,[32] a landlord stated that a sitting tenant in a hotel which he proposed to sell was 'most desirable'. This would have suggested to a reasonable purchaser that, at the very least, rent was paid on time and without pressure. In fact, the opposite was the case.. In the circumstances, it was held by the Court of Appeal that if the facts are not equally well known to both parties, then a statement of opinion by the party who does know the facts can amount to a statement of fact, since the speaker impliedly states that he knows the facts which justify his expression of opinion. This seems to indicate that a person with greater skill or knowledge may be guilty of a misrepresentation where he expresses an opinion which is not justified in the light of the known facts. By analogy, if a skilled person makes a forecast of future events, he may find that his opinion or forecast gives rise to liability on the basis that he should have exercised greater care before making the statement to the other party. For example, in *Esso Petroleum Ltd v Mardon*,[33] an expert acting on behalf of the appellants forecast that a petrol filling station would have a throughput of 200,000 gallons by the third year of operation. On the face of it, this was no more than an expression of opinion, but because it was a statement made by an avowed expert the defendants' were held liable on the alternative bases that the defendant had been negligent in failing to take reasonable care in preparing the forecast or that there was a collateral warranty that reasonable care would be taken in preparing the advice given. It is important to appreciate that this case was based on facts which arose before the Misrepresentation Act 1967, with the result that, at the time, there was no

---

32   (1884) 28 Ch D 7.
33   [1976] QB 801.

action for damages for misrepresentation, unless the court was able to discover a contractual promise or if the case fell within the tortious rules on negligent misstatement established in *Hedley Byrne & Co Ltd v Heller & Partners Ltd*.[34]

Inducement

The second essential requirement of an actionable misrepresentation raises a causal issue, namely has the misrepresentation induced the other party to enter into the contract? In this respect, the misrepresentee bears the burden of proving that it was the misrepresentation that induced him to enter into the contract. It follows that, if the misrepresentee admits that he took no notice of the statement made by the other party, there will be no inducement and no actionable misrepresentation. In *Smith v Chadwick*,[35] the plaintiff purchased shares in a company, but later sought to rescind the contract on the ground that the company prospectus contained a false statement to the effect that a certain Mr Grieve was a member of the board of directors. In the course of cross-examination, the plaintiff had admitted that he had not been influenced by the statement when he purchased the shares. As a result, the contract stood, since the false statement was not the cause of the plaintiff entering into the contract in respect of which rescission was sought.

Similarly, if the claimant tests the statement for accuracy and he or a third party acting on his behalf discovers the truth, it is likely that the claimant will be considered not to have been induced to enter into the contract by the defendant's misrepresentation. For example, if the defendant makes false statements about the earning capacity of a business and the claimant employs a professional accountant to verify the statements, it would seem to follow that the claimant's reliance is on his third party expert rather than upon the defendant's false statement.[36]

What seems to underlie the requirement of inducement is that it must be reasonable for the misrepresentee to rely upon the false statement in entering into the contract. Is it reasonable to rely upon a representation, when the representee is given the means to check the accuracy of the other party's statement? The other cases suggest that, generally, it is. For example, in *Redgrave v Hurd*,[37] the plaintiff bought a house and solicitor's practice from the defendant, having been informed of the value of the practice and having been given copies of the business accounts. In fact, the plaintiff did not bother

---

34 [1964] AC 465.
35 (1884) 9 App Cas 187.
36 *Attwood v Small* (1838) 7 ER 684.
37 (1881) 20 Ch D 1. For further details on this case, see Chapter 14.

to read the accounts and, had he done so, he would probably have discovered the extent of the defendant's misrepresentation. It was held, nonetheless, that the plaintiff had relied on the false statement and was therefore entitled to rescission of the contract.

If *Redgrave v Hurd* was decided today, it might be necessary to reconsider whether the court was correct in reaching this conclusion. It is clear that the common law counterpart of a misrepresentation, namely the negligent misstatement, requires reasonableness of reliance.[38] At the very least, this issue should be 'centre stage' today. How would it be resolved? Policy dictates that if the misrepresentation is fraudulent an opportunity of inspection (spurned or taken) should not bar reliance on the misrepresentation. To hold otherwise would be a green light for the more effective 'con artist'! If, on the other hand, the misrepresentation is wholly innocent (particularly if greater expertise resides in the representee) reliance may not be reasonable. As regards negligent misrepresentation, the policy to be adopted is not clear; perhaps the answer lies in the respective skill and knowledge of the parties, particularly as it has now been recognised that at least for the purposes of an action under s 2(1) of the Misrepresentation Act 1967, apportionment of damages for contributory negligence is a possibility.[39] It should be noted that, at the time of the decision in *Redgrave*, only two types of misrepresentation were recognised: innocent or fraudulent.

OTHER ASPECTS OF FAIRNESS IN THE NEGOTIATION PROCESS

Generally, the common law is concerned with the issue of procedural as opposed to substantive unfairness in the sense that where a requirement of fairness is imposed, it is generally regarded as a matter which relates to the formation of a valid agreement. However, a feature of many aspects of modern contract law is that of social co-operation which ought to lead to the conclusion that the parties to contract negotiations should deal with each other in good faith. It is perhaps easier for the courts to recognise bad faith and deal with it accordingly rather than to impose a positive duty to act in good faith, particularly given the uncertainties which are bound to be generated by such a positive doctrine. (See the *dictum* from Bingham LJ at fn 5, above and, generally, Chapter 8.)

---

38 See *Hedley Byrne & Co v Heller & Partners Ltd* [1964] AC 465; and *Caparo Industries plc v Dickman* [1990] 2 AC 605.

39 *Gran Gelato Ltd v Richcliff (Group) Ltd* [1992] 1 All ER 865. See, also, *Alliance & Leicester Building Society v Edgestop* [1994] 2 All ER 38, which maintains the conventional view that apportionment is not permitted in an action for the tort of deceit.

There are also indications that a limited form of good faith is a factor in other areas, such as agreements to lock oneself out of negotiations with another person and in relation to invitations to tender.

In *Blackpool and Fylde Aero Club Ltd v Blackpool Borough Council*,[40] the council made invitations to tender for the operation of pleasure flights from Blackpool airport, specifying that tenders should be received by a particular date and time. The plaintiffs submitted a tender entirely in accordance with the specifications laid down, but their tender was not even considered. The Court of Appeal held that there was a duty to ensure that all conforming tenders were considered and that the plaintiffs were entitled to damages for their lost opportunity:

Blackpool and Fylde Aero Club Ltd v Blackpool Borough Council [1990] 1 WLR 1195, CA, p 1200

Bingham LJ: The judge resolved the contractual issue in favour of the club, holding that an express request for a tender might in appropriate circumstances give rise to an implied obligation to perform the service of considering that tender. Here, the council's stipulation that tenders received after the deadline would not be admitted for consideration gave rise to a contractual obligation (on acceptance by submission of a timely tender) that such tenders would be admitted for consideration.

In attacking the judge's conclusion on this issue, Mr Toulson for the council, made four main submissions. First, it was submitted that an invitation to tender in this form was well established to be no more than a proclamation of willingness to receive offers. Even without the first sentence of the council's invitation to tender in this case, the council would not have been bound to accept the highest or any tender. An invitation to tender in this form was an invitation to treat, and no contract of any kind would come into existence unless or until, if ever, the council chose to accept any tender or other offer. For these propositions reliance was placed on *Spencer v Harding* (1870) LR 5 CP 561 and *Harris v Nickerson* (1873) LR 8 QB 286.

Secondly, Mr Toulson submitted that on a reasonable reading of this invitation to tender the council could not be understood to be undertaking to consider all timely tenders submitted. The statement that late tenders would not be considered did not mean that timely tenders would. If the council had meant that it could have said it. There was, although counsel did not put it in these words, *no maxim exclusio unius, expressio alterius*.

Thirdly, the court should be no less rigorous when asked to imply a contract than when asked to imply a term in an existing contract or to find a collateral contract. A term would not be implied simply because it was reasonable to do so: *Liverpool City Council v Irwin* [1977] AC 239, p 253. In order to establish collateral contracts, not only the terms of such contracts, but the existence of an

---

animus contrahendi on the part of all the parties to them must be clearly shewn: see *Heilbut Symons & Co v Buckleton* [1913] AC 30, p 47. No lower standard was applicable here and the standard was not satisfied.

Fourthly, Mr Toulson submitted that the warranty contended for by the club was simply a proposition 'tailor-made to produce the desired result' (to quote Lord Templeman in *CBS Songs Ltd v Amstrad Consumer Electronics plc* [1988] 2 All ER 484, p 497; [1988] AC 1013, p 1059) on the facts of this particular case. There was a vital distinction between expectations, however reasonable, and contractual obligations: see *Lavarack v Woods of Colchester Ltd* [1967] 1 QB 278, p 294, *per* Diplock LJ. The club here expected its tender to be considered. The council fully intended that it should be. It was in both parties' interests that the club's tender should be considered. There was thus no need for them to contract. The court should not subvert well understood contractual principles by adopting a woolly pragmatic solution designed to remedy a perceived injustice on the unique facts of this particular case ...

A tendering procedure of this kind is, in many respects, heavily weighted in favour of the invitor. He can invite tenders from as many or as few parties as he chooses. He need not tell any of them who else, or how many others, he has invited. The invitee may often, although not here, be put to considerable labour and expense in preparing a tender, ordinarily without recompense if he is unsuccessful. The invitation to tender may itself, in a complex case, although again not here, involve time and expense to prepare, but the invitor does not commit himself to proceed with the project, whatever it is; he need not accept the highest tender; he need not accept any tender; he need not give reasons to justify his acceptance or rejection of any tender received. The risk to which the tenderer is exposed does not end with the risk that his tender may not be the highest (or, as the case may be, lowest). But where, as here, tenders are solicited from selected parties all of them known to the invitor, and where a local authority's invitation prescribes a clear, orderly and familiar procedure (draft contract conditions available for inspection and plainly not open to negotiation, a prescribed common form of tender, the supply of envelopes designed to preserve the absolute anonymity of tenderers and clearly to identify the tender in question and an absolute deadline) the invitee is in my judgment protected at least to this extent: if he submits a conforming tender before the deadline he is entitled, not as a matter of mere expectation but of contractual right, to be sure that his tender will after the deadline be opened and considered in conjunction with all other conforming tenders or at least that his tender will be considered if others are. Had the club, before tendering, inquired of the council whether it could rely on any timely and conforming tender being considered along with others, I feel quite sure that the answer would have been 'of course'. The law would, I think, be defective if it did not give effect to that.

It is of course true that the invitation to tender does not explicitly state that the council will consider timely and conforming tenders. That is why one is concerned with implication. But the council does not either say that it does not bind itself to do so and, in the context, a reasonable invitee would understand the invitation to be saying, quite clearly, that if he submitted a timely and conforming tender it would be considered, at least if any other such tender were considered.

I readily accept that contracts are not to be lightly implied. Having examined what the parties said and did, the court must be able to conclude with confidence both that the parties intended to create contractual relations and that the agreement was to the effect contended for. It must also, in most cases, be able to answer the question posed by Mustill LJ in *Hispanica de Petroleos SA v Vencedora Oceanica Navegacion SA, The Kapetan Markos NL (No 2)* [1987] 2 Lloyd's Rep 321, p 331: 'What was the mechanism for offer and acceptance?' In all the circumstances of this case (and I say nothing about any other), I have no doubt that the parties did intend to create contractual relations to the limited extent contended for. Since it has never been the law that a person is only entitled to enforce his contractual rights in a reasonable way (*White & Carter (Councils) Ltd v McGregor* [1962] AC 413, p 430, *per* Lord Reid) counsel for the club was, in my view, right to contend for no more than a contractual duty to consider. I think it plain that the council's invitation to tender was, to this limited extent, an offer, and the club's submission of a timely and conforming tender an acceptance.

Mr Toulson's fourth submission on behalf of the council is a salutary warning, but it is not a free standing argument: if, as I hold, his first three submissions are to be rejected, no subversion of principle is involved. I am, however, pleased that what seems to me the right legal answer also accords with the merits as I see them.

I accordingly agree with the judge's conclusion on the contractual issue, essentially for the reasons which he more briefly gave.

In reaching its decision, the court was clearly heavily influenced by the perceived unfairness of any other result, which would have weighted the tendering procedure even more in favour of the council. It should, of course, be noted that the court was also concurred not to interfere with the procedure too much – the implied contract only obliged them to give full and fair consideration to all tenders; it did not oblige them to accept any particular tender.

Similar considerations also apply to the issue of letters of intent which are capable of inducing acts of reliance on the part of the addressee. Reliance losses such as expenditure incurred in the belief that a contract will be made may be recovered if assurances in the letter of intent can be treated as forming the basis of a collateral contract.[41]

Where negotiations for the sale of a business have commenced, the vendor is bound to be interested in obtaining the best price possible. During this process, he may encounter others, apart from the person with whom he is

---

41 *Turriff Construction Ltd v Regalia Knitting Mills Ltd* (1972) 222 Estates Gazette 169. Generally, for collateral contracts, see Chapter 5.

negotiating, who show an interest in purchasing the business. In these circumstances, assurances may be made by the vendor which encourage one of the potential purchasers to incur expense. Here, it is necessary to consider whether those assurances have contractual force. The classical response to this problem is that if there is no concluded agreement, no contractual obligations will arise.[42] If tenets of good faith are invoked, it is possible to arrive at a different conclusion, although if all that has been said amounts to no more than an agreement to negotiate no binding obligation will exist.

In *Courtney and Fairbairn Ltd v Tolaini Bros (Hotels) Ltd*,[43] the respondents wished to develop a hotel. The appellants were property developers who were able to obtain the necessary finance. In the course of negotiations it was agreed that the appellants would find someone to lend the necessary money for the purposes of development and that the respondent would use the appellants' services once the necessary finance had been obtained. The appellants obtained the necessary finance, but the respondent engaged the services of another property developer, using the finance facilities procured by the appellants. The Court of Appeal held that what had been entered into was nothing more than an agreement to agree with the result that the alleged contract was void for incompleteness:

Courtney and Fairbairn Ltd v Tolaini Bros (Hotels) Ltd [1975] 1 WLR 297, CA, p 299

Lord Denning MR: After the meeting, on 10 April 1969, Mr Courtney wrote to Mr Tolaini this letter: 'Re: Thatched Barn Hotel ... I am now in a position to introduce you to those who: (a) are interested in your proposals; (b) have access to the necessary finance ... I think I should mention, at this point, that my commercial interest in this matter is that of a Building Contractor. I am interested in it due to the fact that Mr Sacks, whom I have known for some years, is aware that I work for a number of large investing and development concerns, and thought it possible that I might be in a position to be of service to you. You will understand, therefore, that in addition to making myself useful to you, my objective is to build the three projects mentioned, namely, the Motel, the Filling Station, and the future Hotel, or other development, on the "Green Belt" area of your site. [Then follow these important words:] Accordingly, I would be very happy to know that, if my discussions and arrangements with interested parties lead to an introductory meeting, which in turn leads to a financial arrangement acceptable to both parties you will be prepared to instruct your Quantity Surveyor to negotiate fair and reasonable contract sums in respect of each of the three projects as they arise. (These would, incidentally be based upon agreed estimates of the net cost of work and general overheads with a margin for profit of 5%) which, I am sure you will agree, is, indeed, reasonable.'

---

42 This is particularly likely if a substantial amount remains unsettled, and subject to future negotiation, see *British Steel Corpn v Cleveland Bridge and Engineering Co Ltd* [1984] 1 All ER 504.

43 [1975] 1 WLR 297, CA.

On 21 April 1969, there was a meeting between the parties at the Thatched Barn Hotel. Mr Courtney said he wanted to have something in writing from Mr Tolaini before he went further. Accordingly, Mr Tolaini did write a letter on 28 April 1969, in the terms: 'In reply to your letter of the 10 April, I agree to the terms specified therein and I look forward to meeting the interested party regarding finance.'

Those are the two letters on which the issue depends. But I will tell the subsequent events quite shortly. Mr Courtney did his best. He found a person interested who provided finance of £200,000 or more for the projects. Mr Tolaini on his side appointed his quantity surveyor with a view to negotiating with Mr Courtney the price for the construction work. But there were differences of opinion about the price. And nothing was agreed. In the end, Mr Tolaini did not employ Mr Courtney or his company to do the construction work. Mr Tolaini instructed other contractors and they completed the motel and other works. But then Mr Tolaini took advantage of the finance which Mr Courtney had made possible, but he did not employ Mr Courtney's company to do the work. Naturally enough, Mr Courtney was very upset. He has brought this action, in which he says that there was a contract by which his company were to be employed as builders for the work, and it was a breach of contract by Mr Tolaini or his company to go elsewhere and employ somebody else. Mr Courtney's company claimed the loss of profits which they would have made if they had been employed as builders for this motel ...

I am afraid that I have come to a different view from the judge. The reason is because I can find no agreement on the price or on any method by which the price was to be calculated. The agreement was only an agreement to 'negotiate' fair and reasonable contract sums. The words of the letter are 'your Quantity Surveyor to negotiate fair and reasonable contract sums in respect of each of the three projects as they arise'. Then there are words which show that estimates had not yet been agreed, but were yet to be agreed. The words are: 'These [the contract sums] would, incidentally be based upon agreed estimates of the net cost of work and general overheads with a margin for profit of 5%.' Those words show that there were no estimates agreed and no contract sums agreed. All was left to be agreed in the future. It was to be agreed between the parties themselves. If they had left the price to be agreed by a third person such as an arbitrator, it would have been different. But, here, it was to be agreed between the parties themselves.

Now, the price in a building contract is of fundamental importance. It is so essential a term that there is no contract unless the price is agreed or there is an agreed method of ascertaining it, not dependant on the negotiations of the two parties themselves. In a building contract, both parties must know at the outset, before the work is started, what the price is to be or, at all events, what agreed estimates are. No builder and no employer would ever dream of entering into a building contract for over £200,000 without there being an estimate of the cost and an agreed means of ascertaining the price.

In the ordinary course of things, the architects and the quantity surveyors get out the specification and the bills of quantities. They are submitted to the contractors. They work out the figures and tender for the work at a named price; and there is a specified means of altering it up or down for extras or omissions and so forth, usually by means of an architect's certificate. In the absence of some such machinery, the only contract which you might find is a contract to do the work for a reasonable sum or for a sum to be fixed by a third party. But here there is no such contract at all. There is no machinery for ascertaining the price, except by negotiation. In other words, the price is still to be agreed. Seeing that there is no agreement on so fundamental a matter as the price, there is no contract.

But then this point was raised. Even if there was not a contract actually to build, was not there a contract to negotiate? In this case, Mr Tolaini did instruct his quantity surveyor to negotiate, but the negotiations broke down. It may be suggested that the quantity surveyor was to blame for the failure of the negotiations. But does that give rise to a cause of action? There is very little guidance in the book about a contract to negotiate. It was touched on by Lord Wright in *Hillas & Co Ltd v Arcos Ltd*, where he said: 'There is then no bargain except to negotiate, and negotiations may be fruitless and end without any contract ensuing.' Then he went on: '... yet even then, in strict theory, there is a contract (if there is good consideration) to negotiate, though in the event of repudiation by one party the damages may be nominal, unless a jury think that the opportunity to negotiate was of some appreciable value to the injured party.'

That tentative opinion by Lord Wright does not seem to me to be well founded. If the law does not recognise a contract to enter into a contract (when there is a fundamental term yet to be agreed) it seems to me it cannot recognise a contract to negotiate. The reason is because it is too uncertain to have any binding force. No court could estimate the damages because no one can tell whether the negotiations would be successful or would fall through; or if successful, what the result would be. It seems to me that a contract to negotiate, like a contract to enter into a contract, is not a contract known to the law. We were referred to the recent decision of Brightman J about an option, *Mountford v Scott*; but that does not seem to me to touch this point. I think we must apply the general principle that when there is a fundamental matter left undecided and to be the subject of negotiation, there is no contract. So I would hold that there was not any enforceable agreement in the letters between the plaintiff and the defendants. I would allow the appeal accordingly.

Courtney and Fairbairn concerned a 'lock-in' agreement. However, it seems that there is a different approach where a negotiating party agrees to lock himself out of dealings with someone else, provided what has been agreed is sufficiently definite.

In *Walford v Miles*,[44] the defendants had been negotiating with X for the sale of a business, but were dissatisfied with the price offered. Subsequently, they entered into negotiations with the plaintiffs who provided a letter from their bankers to the effect that credit of £2 million was available should the

---

44 [1992] 2 AC 128.

plaintiffs decide to purchase the business. In return, the defendants agreed not to give further consideration to any alternative proposal and that they would cease to deal with X. At all times, the defendants kept in contact with X and subsequently sold the business to him after his offer had been raised to £2 million. The House of Lords held that the defendants were liable in damages to the limited extent that they had agreed to lock themselves out of negotiations with others for a specified period of time:

Walford v Miles [1992] 2 AC 128, p 137

Lord Ackner: In the Court of Appeal and before your Lordships, Mr Naughton submitted that the *Courtney and Fairbairn Ltd* and the *Mallozzi* cases were distinguishable from the present case, because that which was referred to negotiation with a view to agreement in those cases was an existing difference between the parties. In the present case, so it was contended, by the end of the telephone conversation on 17 March there was no existing difference. Every point that had been raised for discussion had been agreed. However, this submission overlooked that what had been 'agreed' on the telephone on 17 March was 'subject to contract'. Therefore the parties were still in negotiation even in relation to those matters. Further, there were many other matters which had still to be considered and agreed.

Before your Lordships, it was sought to argue that the decision in the *Courtney & Fairbairn Ltd* case was wrong. Although the cases in the US did not speak with one voice your Lordships' attention was drawn to the decision of the United States Court of Appeals, Third Circuit in *Channel Home Centers Division of Grace Retail Corpn v Grossman* (1986) 795 F 2d 291 as being 'the clearest example' of the American cases in the appellants' favour. That case raised the issue whether an agreement to negotiate in good faith, if supported by consideration, is an enforceable contract. I do not find the decision of any assistance. While accepting that an agreement to agree is not an enforceable contract, the United States Court of Appeals appears to have proceeded on the basis that an agreement to negotiate in good faith is synonymous with an agreement to use best endeavours and, as the latter is enforceable, so is the former. This appears to me, with respect, to be an unsustainable proposition. The reason why an agreement to negotiate, like an agreement to agree, is unenforceable is simply because it lacks the necessary certainty. The same does not apply to an agreement to use best endeavours. This uncertainty is demonstrated in the instant case by the provision which it is said has to be implied in the agreement for the determination of the negotiations. How can a court be expected to decide whether, subjectively, a proper reason existed for the termination of negotiations? The answer suggested depends upon whether the negotiations have been determined 'in good faith'. However, the concept of a duty to carry on negotiations in good faith is inherently repugnant to the adversarial position of the parties when involved in negotiations. Each party to the negotiations is entitled to pursue his (or her) own interest, so long as he avoids making misrepresentations. To advance that interest he must be entitled, if he thinks it appropriate, to threaten to withdraw from further negotiations or to withdraw in fact in the hope that the opposite party may seek to reopen the negotiations by offering him improved terms. Mr Naughton, of course, accepts that the agreement upon which he relies does not contain a duty to complete the negotiations. But that still leaves the vital question: how is a vendor ever to know that he is entitled to withdraw from further negotiations? How is the court to police such an 'agreement'? A duty to negotiate in good faith is as unworkable in practice as it is inherently inconsistent with the position of a negotiating party. It is here that the uncertainty lies. In my judgment, while negotiations are in existence either party is entitled to withdraw from these negotiations, at any time and for any reason. There can be, thus, no obligation to continue to negotiate until there is a 'proper reason' to withdraw. Accordingly, a bare agreement to negotiate has no legal content.

The validity of the agreement as originally pleaded in the statement of claim

Paragraph 5 of the statement of claim, as unamended, followed the terms of the oral agreement as recorded in the penultimate paragraph of the letter of 18 March. It alleged that for good consideration (and this certainly covered the provision by the appellants of the 'comfort letter') Mr Miles on behalf of himself and his wife agreed that they: 'would terminate negotiations with any Third Party or consideration of any alternative with a view to concluding an agreement with the [appellants] and, further, that even if he received a satisfactory proposal from any Third Party prior to the close of business on 20 March 1987, he would not deal with that Third Party or give further consideration to any alternative.'

Despite the insistence by Mr Naughton upon the implied term pleaded in the amendment involving the obligation to negotiate, Bingham LJ, in his dissenting judgment, considered that that obligation could be severed from the agreement. He concluded that the agreement, as originally pleaded, was a valid and enforceable agreement and entitled the appellants to recover whatever damages they could establish resulted in law from its repudiation.

Before considering the basis of Bingham LJ's judgment, I believe it is helpful to make these observations about a so called 'lock-out' agreement. There is clearly no reason in English contract law why A, for good consideration, should not achieve an enforceable agreement whereby B agrees for a specified period of time not to negotiate with anyone except A in relation to the sale of his property. There are often good commercial reasons why A should desire to obtain such an agreement from B. B's property which A contemplates purchasing may be such as to require the expenditure of not inconsiderable time and money before A is in a position to assess what he is prepared to offer for its purchase or whether he wishes to make any offer at all. A may well consider that he is not prepared to run the risk of expending such time and money unless there is a worthwhile prospect, should he desire to make an offer to purchase, of B, not only then still owning the property, but of being prepared to consider his offer. A may wish to guard against the risk that, while he is investigating the wisdom of offering to buy B's property, B may have already disposed of it or, alternatively, may be so advanced in negotiations with a third party as to be unwilling or for all practical purposes unable to negotiate with A. But I stress that this is a negative agreement – B, by agreeing not to negotiate for this fixed period with a third party, locks himself out of such negotiations. He has in no legal sense locked himself into negotiations with A. What A has achieved is an exclusive opportunity, for a fixed period, to try and come to terms with B, an opportunity for which he has, unless he makes his agreement under seal, to give good consideration. I therefore cannot accept Mr Naughton's proposition, which was the essential reason for his amending para 5 of the statement of claim by the addition of the implied term, that without a positive obligation on B to negotiate with A the lock-out agreement would be futile.

The agreement alleged in para 5 of the unamended statement of claim contains the essential characteristics of a basic valid lock-out agreement, save one. It does not specify for how long it is to last. Bingham LJ sought to cure this deficiency by holding that the obligation upon the respondents not to deal with other parties should continue to bind them 'for such time as it reasonable in all the circumstances'. He said: '... the time would end once the parties, acting in good faith, had found themselves unable to come to mutually acceptable terms ... The defendants could not ... bring the reasonable time to an end by procuring a bogus impasse, since that would involve a breach of the duty of reasonable good faith which parties such as these must, I think, be taken to owe to each other.'

However, as Bingham LJ recognised, such a duty, if it existed, would indirectly impose upon the respondents a duty to negotiate in good faith. Such a duty, for the reasons which I have given above, cannot be imposed. That it should have been thought necessary to assert such a duty helps to explain the reason behind the amendment to para 5 and the insistence of Mr Naughton that without the implied term the agreement, as originally pleaded, was unworkable – unworkable because there was no way of determining for how long the respondents were locked out from negotiating with any third party.

Thus, even if, despite the way in which the Walford's case was pleaded and argued, the severance favoured by Bingham LJ was permissible, the resultant agreement suffered from the same defect (although for different reasons) as the agreement contended for in the amended statement of claim, namely that it too lacked the necessary certainty, and was thus unenforceable.

I would accordingly dismiss this appeal with costs.

The problem *Walford v Miles* raises is that, whilst recognising the viability of a 'lock-out' agreement in certain circumstances, it also explicitly states that English law does not recognise a contract to negotiate or an agreement to agree previously because this would (to be workable) require a duty to carry on the negotiations in good faith. Not only was this seen as lacking the degree of certainty required by English law, it was even stated to be 'inherently repugnant to the adversarial position of the parties when involved in negotiations'. This at least focuses on the key issue raised at the beginning of this chapter but its response to this issue is (seemingly) entirely negative reflecting a highly traditional approach to the bargaining process as one of a battle of opposed interests, rather than an attempt to produce a solution which both sides understand and 'own'.

On the other hand (and paradoxically?), Lord Ackner's judgment does go some way down the road of a requirement of good faith, in that he is of the opinion that an undertaking to use best endeavours to negotiate an agreement with the other party could be sufficiently certain to be enforceable. Surely this imports an element of good faith? If someone undertakes to use his best endeavours to reach an agreement, there must be circumstances in which those best endeavours are unsuccessful. If they are unsuccessful this may be because the defendant, in bad faith, has failed to attempt to reach an agreement. In having recognised one variety of duty to negotiate in good faith, the bare assertion that a general duty to negotiate in good faith is unenforceable on the grounds of lack of certainty and general 'policy' seems very unconvincing.

PART III

OBLIGATIONS AND RISKS

CHAPTER 5

THE TERMS OF THE CONTRACT

In this chapter and Chapter 6, it is proposed to consider the issue of judicial construction of contracts with a view to the allocation of risks of loss. A preliminary issue is to identify those statements made in the course of negotiations which are to be classified as terms of the contract. In this regard, it is important to distinguish between terms and representations. Terms are promises which form part of the contract, the breach of which will give rise to an action for damages for breach of contract or, in some cases, repudiation of the contract. In contrast, representations are statements which are capable of inducing a contract and on the facts appear to have done so, but which do not necessarily become part of the contract itself.

A second issue is to determine whether the language used by the parties is of sufficient clarity to allow for a clear interpretation. In some cases, the language used by the parties may be ambiguous, in which case, the ambiguity is likely to be construed against the party who wishes to rely upon a particular term of the contract.[1] Ambiguity apart, it is sometimes the case that the terms of the contract are vague or incomplete to the extent that it is difficult to interpret what the parties intended, in which case, the contract may fail altogether.

In order to ascertain the intentions of the parties, it is necessary to consider the terms of the contract and how they are to be interpreted. Those terms may be expressly agreed between the parties or, alternatively, the court may have to imply terms into the contract, either to give effect to the presumed intentions of the parties or out of necessity so as to make business sense of the dealings between the parties.

If non-fulfilment of a contractual promise arises due to the failure of the other party to do that which he/she promised, the law will usually provide a remedy, subject to the rules on remoteness of damage (which provide that only those losses reasonably contemplated by the parties at the time they made the contract will be recoverable). Due to these rules, there will be some losses which will not be subject to the risk allocation process considered below.

In determining where a particular risk of loss should lie, close regard must be had to the terms of the contract entered into by the parties, since it may be possible to determine from the terms who is intended to bear that risk. For

---

1   The application of the *contra proferentem* rule in relation to exemption clauses is considered in further detail in Chapter 8.

example, in *Clark v Lindsay*,[2] the plaintiff had purchased a ticket giving him access to premises which overlooked the route of King Edward VII's coronation procession. The procession was cancelled and the question arose whether the plaintiff was entitled to recover the £50 he had paid. It was held that, normally, the contract would have been void on the basis of a common mistake of fact that, unknown to the parties, it was inevitable that the procession would be postponed at the time the contract was made (on such mistakes, see, further, Chapter 6). This would have enabled the plaintiff to recover his money. However, on learning that postponement was likely, the parties had varied the contract by inserting a clause entitling the plaintiff to the room whenever the procession took place. This precluded the normal operation of the law on mistake.

TERMS AND REPRESENTATIONS

The history of the distinction between contractual terms and mere representations is important as it serves to explain some of the more extreme interpretations of what is a contractual term. For present purposes, the watershed date is 1967, when the Misrepresentation Act was passed. Prior to that date, unless it could be proved that a non-contractual representation had been made fraudulently[3] or fell within the fault based rule on negligently caused economic loss resulting from a misstatement[4] there was no available action for damages. However, subject to some restrictions, a contract induced by a mere representation could be rescinded.[5] The importance of the distinction between contractual terms and representations is not as great as it used to be since the Misrepresentation Act now allows an action for damages for negligent misrepresentation[6] and gives the court a discretion to award damages in lieu of rescission for a purely innocent misrepresentation.[7]

If a statement made in the course of negotiations is regarded as a contractual term, in theory, breach of that term will give rise to an action for expectation damages for loss of a bargain as opposed to the purely tortious measure of damages applicable under s 2(1) of the Misrepresentation Act 1967, which seeks to restore the parties to the position they were in before the statement was relied upon.

---

2 (1903) 19 TLR 202.
3 *Derry v Peek* (1889) 14 App Cas 337.
4 *Hedley Byrne & Co v Heller & Partners Ltd* [1964] AC 465.
5 See Chapter 14.
6 Misrepresentation Act 1967, s 2(1), discussed in Chapter 13.
7 *Ibid*, s 2(2), discussed in Chapter 13.

In theory, whether a statement is to be regarded as a term of the contract or as a representation depends upon the intention of the parties.[8] However, as a meaningful test, this has its drawbacks. By virtue of the fact that a dispute has arisen, there may be an indication that the parties have differing views on the importance to be attached to a particular statement and that there is therefore no common intention to be found. Nevertheless, the courts have developed a number of guidelines intended to assist in determining whether the parties intended a particular statement to take effect as a contractual promise or as a mere representation.

Often, the parties will reduce their contract to writing, in which case, an obvious port of call is the written instrument. But it does not follow from this that only those statements contained in the contractual document are the terms of the contract. It is perfectly possible for an oral statement of some significance to be treated as a contractual term even though it does not appear in the final written version of the contract. This result may be achieved by the discovery of a collateral contract, namely, a contract the consideration for which is entry into the main contract.

In *Evans (J) & Son (Portsmouth) Ltd v Merzario (Andrea) Ltd*,[9] the plaintiffs were importers of machinery who regularly used the transportation service provided by the defendants, who were forwarding agents. The defendants employed a set of standard terms of contracting, which exempted them from liability for loss or damage to the goods otherwise than when they were in the defendants' custody. The contract further provided that the defendants had complete freedom in respect of the means, route and procedure to be followed in the handling and transportation of goods. The goods which the plaintiffs required to be carried were liable to rust if carried on deck and on several previous occasions the defendants had always carried the plaintiffs' machinery below deck. On the present occasion, the defendants had altered their transportation practice by shifting to the use of containers, some of which were to be stacked on deck. Because of their worries about rusting, the plaintiffs sought an oral assurance that their cargo would be carried below deck which was duly given. Subsequently, a moulding machine belonging to the plaintiffs was inadvertently carried on deck and due to the fact that it had not been properly fastened down, the machine was lost when the container in which it was being carried fell overboard.

The Court of Appeal held that although the oral assurance was not included in the written terms of the contract, it was nonetheless part of the contract:

---

8   *Heilbut Symons & Co Ltd v Buckleton* [1913] AC 30.
9   [1976] 1 WLR 1078, CA.

Evans (J) & Son (Portsmouth) Ltd v Merzario (Andrea) Ltd [1976] 1 WLR 1078, CA, p 1081

Lord Denning MR: So, after these containers fell off the deck into the water, the English importers, through their insurers, claimed damages against the forwarding agents. In reply, the forwarding agent said there was no contractual promise that the goods would be carried under deck. Alternatively, if there was, they relied on the printed terms and conditions. The judge held there was no contractual promise that these containers should be carried under deck. He thought that, in order to be binding, the initial conversation ought to be contemporaneous, and that here it was too remote in point of time from the actual transport; furthermore that, viewed objectively, it should not be considered binding. The judge quoted largely from the well known case of *Heilbut, Symons & Co v Buckleton* in which it was held that a person is not liable in damages for an innocent misrepresentation; and that the courts should be slow to hold that there was a collateral contract. I must say that much of what was said in that case is entirely out of date. We now have the Misrepresentation Act 1967 under which damages can be obtained for innocent misrepresentation of fact. This Act does not apply here because we are concerned with an assurance as to the future. But even in respect of promises as to the future, we have a different approach nowadays to collateral contracts. When a person gives a promise, or an assurance to another, intending that he should act on it by entering into a contract, and he does act on it by entering into the contract, we hold that it is binding: see *Dick Bentley Productions Ltd v Harold Smith (Motors) Ltd*. That case was concerned with a representation of fact, but it applies also to promises as to the future. Following this approach, it seems to me plain that Mr Spano gave an oral promise or assurance that the goods in this new container traffic would be carried under deck. He made the promise in order to induce Mr Leonard to agree to the goods being carried in containers. On the faith of it, Mr Leonard accepted the quotations and gave orders for transport. In those circumstances the promise was binding. There was a breach of that promise and the forwarding agents are liable – unless they can rely on the printed conditions.

Roskill LJ: The real question, as I venture to think, is not whether one calls this an assurance or a guarantee, but whether that which was said amounted to an enforceable contractual promise by the defendants to the plaintiffs that any goods thereafter entrusted by the plaintiffs to the defendants for carriage from Milan to the UK via Rotterdam and thence by sea to England would be shipped under deck. The matter was apparently argued before the learned judge on behalf of the plaintiffs on the basis that the defendants' promise (if any) was what the lawyers sometimes call a collateral oral warranty. That phrase is normally only applicable where the original promise was external to the main contract, the main contract being a contract in writing, so that usually parol evidence cannot be given to contradict the terms of the written contract. But that doctrine, as it seems to me, has little or no application where one is not concerned with a contract in writing (with respect, I cannot accept counsel for the defendants' argument that there was here a contract in writing) but with a contract which, as I think, was partly oral, partly in writing and partly by conduct. In such a case, the court does not require to have recourse to lawyers' devices such as collateral oral warranty in order to seek to adduce evidence which would not otherwise be admissible. The court is entitled to look at and should look at all the evidence from start to finish in order to see what the bargain was that was struck between the parties. That is what we have done in this case and what, with great respect, I think the learned judge did not do in the course of his judgment. I unreservedly accept counsel for the defendants' submission that one must not look at one or two isolated answers given in evidence; one should look at the totality of the evidence. When one does that, one finds first, as I have already mentioned, that these parties had been doing business in transporting goods from Milan to England for some time before; secondly, that transportation of goods from Milan to England was always done on trailers which were always under deck; thirdly, that the defendants wanted a change in the practice – they wanted containers used instead of trailers; fourthly, that the plaintiffs were only willing to agree to that change if they were promised by the defendant that those containers would be shipped under deck, and would not have agreed to the change but for that promise. The defendants gave such a promise which to my mind against this background plainly amounted to an enforceable contractual promise. In those circumstances it seems to me that the contract was this: 'If we continue to give you our business, you will ensure that those goods in containers are shipped under deck'; and the defendants agreed that this would be so.

A key concept in determining whether a statement is to be regarded as a term of the contract or a representation is that of reasonable reliance. If a person can reasonably expect to rely upon the accuracy of what the other party says and that that other party is warranting or guaranteeing the accuracy of their statement, it is likely that their statement will be construed to be a term of the contract. In this regard the skill of the party to whom the statement is made and the skill of the maker of the statement appear to have an important impact. Accordingly, a statement about a motor vehicle made by a consumer owner to a car dealer and a statement made by a car dealer to a consumer purchaser may well be treated differently. In the former case the person to whom the statement is made has the skill to discover the truth or falsity of the assertions of the other and it is unreasonable to expect them to place full 'contractual' reliance on the statements on assertions. In contrast, in the latter case, if the skilled dealer makes a false statement which misleads the consumer, he ought to know better and may be expected to bear the consequences.

In *Dick Bentley Productions Ltd v Harold Smith (Motors) Ltd*,[10] the plaintiff asked the defendant to find him a 'well vetted' Bentley car. The car supplied by the defendant had had some work done to it and the defendant told the plaintiff that the car came supplied with a replacement engine and gearbox and that it had only done 20,000 miles since. The plaintiff subsequently sought

---

10 [1965] 1 WLR 623.

damages for breach of warranty on the ground that the defendant had made a statement about mileage which proved to be false:

Dick Bentley Productions Ltd v Harold Smith (Motors) Ltd [1965] 1 WLR 623, p 627

Lord Denning MR: The first point is whether this representation, namely that the car had done twenty thousand miles only since it had been fitted with a replacement engine and gearbox, was an innocent misrepresentation (which does not give rise to damages), or whether it was a warranty. It was said by Holt CJ and repeated in *Heilbut, Symons & Co v Buckleton*: 'An affirmation at the time of the sale is a warranty, provided it appear on evidence to be so intended.' But that word 'intended' has given rise to difficulties. I endeavoured to explain in *Oscar Chess Ltd v Williams* that the question whether a warranty was intended depends on the conduct of the parties, on their words and behaviour, rather than on their thoughts. If an intelligent bystander would reasonably infer that a warranty was intended, that will suffice. What conduct, then? What words and behaviour, lead to the inference of a warranty?

Looking at the cases once more, as we have done so often, it seems to me that if a representation is made in the course of dealings for a contract for the very purpose of inducing the other party to act on it, and it actually induces him to act on it by entering into the contract, that is *prima facie* ground for inferring that the representation was intended as a warranty. It is not necessary to speak of it as being collateral. Suffice it that the representation was intended to be acted on and was in fact, acted on. But the maker of the representation can rebut this inference if he can show that it really was an innocent misrepresentation, in that he was in fact, innocent of fault in making it, and that it would not be reasonable in the circumstances for him to be bound by it. In the *Oscar Chess* case, the inference was rebutted.

Salmon LJ: I agree. I have no doubt at all that the learned county court judge reached a correct conclusion when he decided that Mr Smith gave a warranty to the second plaintiff, Mr Bentley, and that that warranty was broken. Was what Mr Smith said intended and understood as a legally binding promise? If so, it was a warranty and as such may be part of the contract of sale or collateral to it. In effect, Mr Smith said: 'If you will enter into a contract to buy this motor car from me for £1,850, I undertake that you will be getting a motor car which has done no more than 20,000 miles since it was fitted with a new engine and a new gearbox.' I have no doubt at all that what was said by by Mr Smith was so understood and was intended to be so understood by Mr Bentley.

I accordingly agree that the appeal should be dismissed.

In *Oscar Chess Ltd v Williams*,[11] the plaintiffs were car dealers who took from the defendant a second hand car in part exchange for a new car. The defendant had falsely, but honestly asserted that the trade-in vehicle was a

---

11 [1957] 1 WLR 370.

1948 model when, in fact, it was a 1939 model. This difference was material in that it affected the trade-in value of the car by £115. In the Court of Appeal, it was held that the defendant's statement was no more than an innocent misrepresentation, which, at the time, did not give rise to an action for damages:

Oscar Chess Ltd v Williams [1957] 1 WLR 370, CA, p 373

Denning LJ: I entirely agree with the judge that both parties assumed that the Morris car was a 1948 model and that this assumption was fundamental to the contract. This does not prove, however, that the representation was a term of the contract. The assumption was based by both of them on the date given in the registration book as the date of first registration. They both believed that the car was a 1948 model, whereas it was only a 1939 one. They were both mistaken and their mistake was of fundamental importance.

The effect of such a mistake is this: It does not make the contract a nullity from the beginning, but it does in some circumstances enable the contract to be set aside in equity. If the buyer had come promptly, he might have succeeded in getting the whole transaction set aside in equity on the ground of this mistake (see *Solle v Butcher* [1949] 2 All ER 1107), but he did not do so and it is now too late for him to do it (see *Leaf v International Galleries* [1950] 1 All ER 693). His only remedy is in damages and to recover these he must prove a warranty.

In saying that he must prove a warranty, I use the word 'warranty' in its ordinary English meaning to denote a binding promise. Everyone knows what a man means when he says, 'I guarantee it', or 'I warrant it' or 'I give you my word on it'. He means that he binds himself to it ...

During the last 100 years, however, the lawyers have come to use the word 'warranty' in another sense. They use it to denote a subsidiary term in a contract as distinct from a vital term which they call a 'condition'. In so doing they depart from the ordinary meaning, not only of the word 'warranty', but also of the word 'condition'. There is no harm in their doing this, so long as they confine this technical use to its proper sphere, namely, to distinguish between a vital term, the breach of which gives the right to treat the contract as at an end, and a subsidiary term which does not ...

These different uses of the word seem to have been the source of confusion in the present case. The judge did not ask himself, 'Was the representation (that the car was a 1948 Morris car) intended to be a warranty?' He asked himself, 'Was it fundamental to the contract?'. He answered it by saying that it was fundamental and, therefore, it was a condition and not a warranty. By concentrating on whether it was fundamental, he seems to me to have missed the crucial point in the case, which is whether it was a term of the contract at all. The crucial question is: was it a binding promise or only an innocent misrepresentation? The technical distinction between a 'condition' and a 'warranty' is quite immaterial in this case, because it is far too late for the buyer to reject the car. He can, at best, only claim damages. The material distinction here is between a statement which is a term of the contract and a statement which is only an innocent misrepresentation. This distinction is best expressed by the ruling of Holt CJ 'Was it intended as a warranty or not?', using the word 'warranty' there in its ordinary English meaning: because it gives the exact shade of meaning that is required. It is something to which a man must be taken to bind himself.

In applying this test, however, some misunderstanding has arisen by the use of the word 'intended'. It is sometimes supposed that the tribunal must look into the minds of the parties to see what they themselves intended. That is a mistake. Lord Moulton made it quite clear, in *Heilbut, Symons & Co v Buckleton* ([1913] AC 30, p 51), that 'The intention of the parties can only be deduced from the totality of the evidence ...' The question whether a warranty was intended depends on the conduct of the parties, on their words and behaviour, rather than on their thoughts. If an intelligent bystander would reasonably infer that a warranty was intended, that will suffice. And this, when the facts are not in dispute, is a question of law ...

It is instructive to take some recent instances to show how the courts have approached this question. When the seller states a fact which is or should be within his own knowledge and of which the buyer is ignorant, intending that the buyer should act on it and he does so, it is easy to infer a warranty; see *Couchman v Hill* ([1947] 1 All ER 103), where a farmer stated that a heifer was unserved, and *Harling v Eddy* ([1951] 2 All ER 212), where he stated that there was nothing wrong with her. So also if the seller makes a promise about something which is or should be within his own control; see *Birch v Paramount Estates Ltd* ((1956) 16 Estates Gazette 396), decided on 2 October 1956, in this court, where the seller stated that the house would be as good as the show house. If, however, the seller, when he states a fact, makes it clear that he has no knowledge of his own but has got his information elsewhere, and is merely passing it on, it is not so easy to imply a warranty. Such a case was *Routledge v McKay* ([1954] 1 All ER 855), where the seller stated that a motorcycle combination was a 1942 model, and pointed to the corroboration of that statement to be found in the registration book, and it was held that there was no warranty. Turning now to the present case, much depends on the precise words that were used. If the seller says: 'I believe the car is a 1948 Morris. Here is the registration book to prove it', there is clearly no warranty. It is a statement of belief, not a contractual promise. If, however, the seller says: 'I guarantee that it is a 1948 Morris. This is borne out by the registration book, but you need not rely solely on that. I give you my own guarantee that it is', there is clearly a warranty. The seller is making himself contractually responsible, even though the registration book is wrong ...

What is the proper inference from the known facts? It must have been obvious to both that the seller had himself no personal knowledge of the year when the car was made. He only became owner after a great number of changes. He must have been relying on the registration book. It is unlikely that such a person would warrant the year of manufacture. The most that he would do would be to state his belief, and then produce the registration book in verification of it. In these circumstances the intelligent bystander would, I suggest, say that the seller did not intend to bind himself so as to warrant that the car was a 1948 model. If the seller was asked to pledge himself to it, he would at once have said 'I cannot do that. I have only the log book to go by, the same as you'.

The judge seems to have thought that there was a difference between written contracts and oral contracts. If an oral representation is afterwards recorded in writing, it is good evidence that it was intended as a warranty. If it is not put into writing, it is evidence against a warranty being intended; but it is by no means decisive. There have been many cases, such as *Birch v Paramount Estates Ltd*, where the courts have found an oral warranty collateral to a written contract. When, however, the purchase is not recorded in writing at all, it must not be supposed that every representation made in the course of the dealing is to be treated as a warranty. The question then is still: was it intended as a warranty? In the leading case of *Chandelor v Lopus* in 1603, a man by word of mouth sold a precious stone for £100, affirming it to be a bezoar stone, whereas it was not. The declaration averred that the seller affirmed it to be a bezar stone, but did not aver that he warranted it to be so. The declaration was held to be ill because (Cro Jac at p 4): '... the bare affirmation that it was a bezar stone, without warranting it to be so, is no cause of action ...' That has been the law from that day to this and it was emphatically re-affirmed by the House of Lords in *Heilbut, Symons & Co v Buckleton* ([1913] AC, pp 38 and 50).

One final word. It seems to me clear that the plaintiffs, the motor dealers who bought the car, relied on the year stated in the log-book. If they had wished to make sure of it, they could have checked it then and there, by taking the engine number and chassis number and writing to the makers. They did not do so at the time, but only eight months later. They are experts and, as they did not make that check at the time, I do not think that they should now be allowed to recover against the innocent seller who produced to them all the evidence which he had, namely, the registration book. I agree that it is hard on the plaintiffs to have paid more than the car is worth, but it would be equally hard on the seller to make him pay the difference. He would never have bought the Hillman car unless he had received the allowance of £290 for the Morris car.

Contrast the dissenting judgment of Morris LJ (p 379):

Morris LJ: The only point taken on behalf of the defendant was that the statement which was made did not form a part of the contract. The learned judge rejected this. He held that it was not only a term but an essential term. In my judgment, he was correct. The statement that the car was a 1948 car was not a mere representation in respect of the subject matter of the contract: the statement was adopted as the foundation of the contract which they made. The promise to pay £290 for that particular car (a figure arrived at by reference to the value of 1948 cars) was the counterpart of a term of the contract that that particular car was a 1948 model.

The learned judge held that, if the plaintiffs had discovered after the making of the contract but before property in the car had passed that it was a 1939 car, they could have refused to go on with the transaction: that they could have refused for the reason that it was a condition of the contract that the car was a 1948 model ...

The plaintiffs do not allege that there was any collateral oral warranty. They submit that the statement of the defendant was not something detached from the contract, but was a part of the contract and was in legal terminology a condition. In my judgment, it was a stipulation of the contract which was a condition. But by the time that the plaintiffs ascertained that the car was a 1939 car, it was too late for them to take any other course than to treat the breach of condition as a breach of warranty (see s 11 of the Sale of Goods Act 1893 [now s 11(4) of the Sale of Goods Act 1979]). On this basis the learned judge held that the plaintiffs were relegated to a right to claim damages, which he assessed at £115, being the difference between the value which the car would have had if it had been a 1948 car and its actual true value, which he found was £175 ...

The learned judge in the present case considered *Routledge v McKay* and correctly distinguished it from the present one. In the present case, there was not, as in *Routledge v McKay*, an antecedent statement and then a later written contract which omitted any incorporation of or reference to the statement. *Routledge v McKay* is distinguishable on three grounds. In the present case there was a statement made at the time of the transaction: there was no written contract: and, in so far as there was a document brought into existence, the document consisted of an invoice addressed to the defendant which recorded the complete transaction and which expressly described the car for which an allowance of £290 was being made as a '1948 Morris 10 saloon'. The statement made which described the Morris car was, therefore, an integral part of the contract. It was, I consider, a condition of the contract, on which the plaintiffs contracted: compare *Bannerman v White* ((1861) 10 CBNS 844). In *Couchman v Hill* ([1947] 1 All ER 103), a statement was made that a heifer was 'unserved'. There was, in that case, a discussion whether the description 'unserved' constituted a warranty or a condition. In his judgment, with which the other members of the court concurred, Scott LJ said: '... as a matter of law, I think every item in a description which constitutes a substantial ingredient in the "identity" of the thing sold is a condition, although every such condition can be waived by the purchaser who thereon becomes entitled to treat it as a warranty and recover damages. I think there was, here, an unqualified condition which, on its breach, the plaintiff was entitled to treat as a warranty and recover the damages claimed.'

In the present case, on a consideration of the evidence which he heard, the learned judge came to the conclusion that the statement which he held to have been made by the defendant at the time of the making of the contract was a statement made contractually. It seems to me that the totality of the evidence points to that view. The statement related to a vitally important matter: it described the subject matter of the contract then being made and directed the parties to, and was the basis of, their agreement as to the price to be paid or credited to the defendant. In the language of Scott LJ, it seems to me that the statement made by the defendant was 'an item in [the] description' of what was being sold and that it constituted a substantial ingredient in the identity of the thing sold. It is with diffidence that I arrive at a conclusion differing from that of my Lords, but I cannot see that the learned judge in any way misdirected himself or misapplied any principle of law, and I see no reason for disturbing his conclusion.

If a statement relates to the description of the subject matter of the contract, is this too fundamental a matter to be treated as no more than a representation? If the statement does relate to the identity of the very thing which is the subject of the contract, is it to be regarded as an absolute guarantee that what has been described will be delivered or is there room for the reliance-based approach of the majority? That reliance is a key factor even in relation to descriptive statements is also borne out in the following case:

In *Harlingdon & Leinster Enterprises Ltd v Christopher Hull (Fine Art) Ltd,*[12] the defendant company was asked to dispose of two paintings described in an auction catalogue as being by Gabriele Münter, a German expressionist painter. Hull, the owner of the defendant company had no expertise in this particular area. The paintings were to be sold at Christies. The plaintiffs were known to have an interest in German expressionist art and were contacted by the defendant. Subsequently, the plaintiffs bought the paintings, being aware that Hull had no interest or expertise in this type of art. A price of £6,000 was agreed for one of the paintings, but it was later discovered that it was not a genuine Münter. In an action by the plaintiffs against the defendant company, the Court of Appeal held that the descriptive statement did not give rise to an action for breach of contract. The reason for this was that, in order to give rise to liability, it was necessary for the descriptive statement to have been relied upon by the person to whom it was addressed. In the present case, it was sufficiently clear that the defendants did not profess to have any particular skill in relation to this type of art and that it was, therefore, not reasonable for the plaintiffs to rely on what the defendant had said:

Harlingdon & Leinster Enterprises Ltd v Christopher Hull (Fine Art) Ltd [1990] 3 WLR 13, CA, p 18

Nourse LJ: Section 13(1) of the Sale of Goods Act 1979 is in these terms: 'Where there is a contract for the sale of goods by description, there is an implied condition that the goods will correspond with the description.'

The sales to which the subsection is expressed to apply are sales 'by description'. Authority apart, those words would suggest that the description must be influential in the sale, not necessarily alone, but so as to become an essential term, that is, a condition, of the contract. Without such influence, a description cannot be said to be one by which the contract for the sale of the goods is made.

[In *Varley v Whipp* [1900] 1 QB 513] Channell J said, at p 516: The term 'sale of goods by description' must apply to all cases where the purchaser has not seen the goods, but is relying on the description alone. It applies in a case like the present, where the buyer has never seen the article sold, but has bought by the description. In that case, by s 13 of the Sale of Goods Act 1893, there is an implied condition that the goods shall correspond with the description, which

---

12 [1990] 3 WLR 13, CA.

is a different thing from a warranty. The most usual application of that section no doubt is to the case of unascertained goods, but I think it must also be applied to cases such as this where there is no identification otherwise than by description ...

In *Gill & Duffus SA v Berger & Co Inc* [1984] AC 382, p 394, the facts of which need not be stated, Lord Diplock, with whose speech the other members of the House of Lords agreed, said this of s 13: '... while "description" itself is an ordinary English word, the Act contains no definition of what it means when it speaks in that section of a contract for the sale of goods being a sale "by description". One must look to the contract as a whole to identify the kind of goods that the seller was agreeing to sell and the buyer to buy ... where, as in the instant case, the sale (to use the words of s 13) is "*by* sample as well as *by* description", characteristics of the goods which would be apparent on reasonable examination of the sample are unlikely to have been intended by the parties to form part of the "description" by which the goods were sold, even though such characteristics are mentioned in references in the contract to the goods that are its subject matter.'

These observations, in emphasising the significance to be attached to the word 'by', show that one must look to the contract as a whole in order to identify what stated characteristics of the goods are intended to form part of the description by which they are sold ...

It is suggested that the significance which some of these authorities attribute to the buyer's reliance on the description is misconceived. I think that that criticism is theoretically correct. In theory, it is no doubt possible for a description of goods which is not relied on by the buyer to become an essential term of a contract for their sale. But, in practice, it is very difficult, and perhaps impossible, to think of facts where that would be so. The description must have a sufficient influence in the sale to become an essential term of the contract and the correlative of influence is reliance. Indeed, reliance by the buyer is the natural index of a sale by description. It is true that the question must, as always, be judged objectively and it may be said that previous judicial references have been to subjective or actual reliance. But each of those decisions, including that of Judge Oddie in the present case, can be justified on an objective basis. For all practical purposes, I would say that there cannot be a contract for the sale of goods by description where it is not within the reasonable contemplation of the parties that the buyer is relying on the description. For those purposes. I think that the law is correctly summarised in these words of *Benjamin on sale*, which should be understood to lay down an objective test: 'Specific goods may be sold as such ... where, though the goods are described, the description is not relied upon, as where the buyer buys the goods such as they are.'

In giving his decision on this question, Judge Oddie said: 'There can clearly be a sale by description where the buyer has inspected the goods if the description relates to something not apparent on inspection. Every item in a description which constitutes a substantial ingredient in the identity of the thing sold is a condition.'

Later, having said that he had not been referred to any similar case where a sale in reliance on a statement that a painting was by a particular artist had been held to be a sale by description, the judge continued: 'In my judgment, such a statement could amount to a description and a sale in reliance on it to a sale by description within the meaning of the 1979 Act. However, on the facts of this case, I am satisfied that the description by Mr Hull before the agreement was not relied on by Mr Runkel in making his offer to purchase which was accepted by Mr Hull. I conclude that he bought the painting as it was. In these circumstances, there was not in my judgment a sale by description.'

I agree. On a view of their words and deeds as a whole, the parties could not reasonably have contemplated that the defendants were relying on the plaintiffs' statement that the painting was by Gabriele Münter. On the facts which he found the judge could not, by a correct application of the law, have come to any other decision.

Contrast the dissenting judgment of Stuart-Smith LJ (at p 24):

Stuart-Smith LJ: Every item in a description which constitutes a substantial ingredient in the 'identity' of the thing being sold is a condition: see *per* Scott LJ in *Couchman v Hill* [1947] KB 554, p 559. That the identity of the artist who painted a picture can be a substantial ingredient in the identity of the thing sold seems to be beyond question. And it was so regarded by Denning LJ in *Leaf v International Galleries* [1950] 2 KB 86, p 89, in which he said: 'There was a term in the contract as to the quality of the subject matter, namely, as to the person by whom the picture was painted – that it was by Constable.'

Most of the essential facts are to be found clearly set out in the judge's careful judgment and have been fully set out in the judgment of Nourse LJ; I need not repeat them. The judge's conclusion on the question of sale by description is to be found in the following passage of his judgment:

In my judgment, such a statement [that the painting was by Münter] could amount to a description and a sale in reliance on it to a sale by description within the meaning of the 1979 Act. However, on the facts of this case I am satisfied that the description by Mr Hull before the agreement was not relied on by Mr Runkel in making his offer to purchase, which was accepted by Mr Hull. I conclude that he bought the painting as it was. In these circumstances there was not, in my judgment, a sale by description. It follows that there was no breach of it even though the painting did not correspond with the description. Even if, contrary to my earlier conclusion, the description in the invoice was made prior to the agreement I am satisfied that in those circumstances Mr Runkel did not rely on it and there was still no sale by description or breach of any implied condition under s 13.

I have not found this last sentence easy to follow, since the judge had already expressly held that the invoice gave effect to what had been orally agreed earlier and nothing was added. Be that as it may, the nub of his conclusion is that Mr Runkel did not rely on the description but on his own judgment as to the authorship of the painting. For my part, I have great difficulty in understanding how the concept of reliance fits into a sale by description. If it is a term of the contract that the painting is by Münter, the purchaser does not have to prove that he entered into the contract in reliance on this statement. This distinguishes a contractual term or condition from a mere representation which induces a purchaser to enter into a contract. In the latter case, the person to whom the representation is made must prove that he relied on it as a matter of fact ...

In my judgment, the matter can be tested in this way. If, following the telephone conversation, Mr Runkel had arrived at the defendants' gallery, seen the painting, bargained about the price and agreed to buy it, it seems to me beyond argument that it would have been a sale by description. And, indeed, counsel for the defendants was at one time disposed to concede as much. Had the invoice been a contractual document, as it frequently is, again, it seems to me clear that the sale would have been a sale by description. In fact, the invoice was written out subsequently to the oral contract; but the judge held, rightly as it seems to me, that it gave effect to what had been agreed. It was cogent evidence of the oral contract.

How does it come about that what would otherwise be a sale by description in some way ceased to be one? It can only be as a result of the conversation between Mr Hull and Mr Runkel before the bargain was actually struck. If Mr Hull had told Mr Runkel that he did not know one way or the other whether the painting was by Münter in spite of the fact that he had so described it or that he could only say that the painting was attributed to Münter, and that Mr Runkel must make up his mind for himself on this point, I can well see that the effect of what had previously been said about the identity of the painter might have been cancelled or withdrawn and was no longer effective at the time of the contract. But Mr Hull did not say that, as the judge found. And I cannot see that this is the effect of what was said. Merely to say that he knew nothing of the painter and did not like her paintings does not in any way to my mind necessarily mean that he was cancelling or withdrawing what he had previously said, based as it was on the auction catalogue. Nor does the fact that it was recognised that the plaintiffs were more expert in German expressionist art than Mr Hull advance the matter. It would, in my judgment, be a serious defect in the law if the effect of a condition implied by statute could be excluded by the vendor's saying that he was not an expert in what was being sold or that the purchaser was more expert than the vendor. That is not the law; it has long been held that conditions implied by statute can only be excluded by clear words. There is nothing of that kind in this case.

The skill of the maker of the statement is also a relevant factor where the statement is not one of fact, but one of informed opinion. Accordingly, a forecast made by an expert which relates to the likely profitability of a particular business enterprise may be regarded as a contractual term where it is reasonable for the person to whom the statement was addressed to rely upon it. In these circumstances, however, it is important to recognise that the maker of the statement has merely warranted that he will take reasonable care in preparing his informed opinion – he does not guarantee that the other party can expect to be placed in the position suggested by the expression of opinion so as to allow an award of full expectation damages in the event of breach.

In *Esso Petroleum Ltd v Mardon*,[13] an experienced representative employed by Esso estimated that the likely throughput of petrol on a garage site would reach 200,000 gallons by the third year of operation. As a result of this estimate, the plaintiff was persuaded to enter into a tenancy agreement with Esso for a period of three years. In fact, the throughput never reached more than 78,000 gallons and the plaintiff gave notice to quit. In order to appease the plaintiff, Esso reduced his rent, but the plaintiff continued to lose money. Subsequently, Esso sought possession of the site, but the plaintiff counterclaimed for damages in respect of the representation which had induced him to enter into the contract. Since the facts forming the basis of the dispute occurred before 1967, the Misrepresentation Act did not apply, but it was alleged that there was either a breach of a collateral warranty or that the statement amounted to a negligent misstatement within the meaning of the rule in *Hedley Byrne v Heller*.

Both claims succeeded in the Court of Appeal:

Esso Petroleum Ltd v Mardon [1976] 1 QB 801, CA, p 817

Lord Denning MR:

Collateral warranty

Ever since *Heilbut, Symons & Co v Buckleton* [1913] AC 30, we have had to contend with the law as laid down by the House of Lords that an innocent misrepresentation gives no right to damages. In order to escape from that rule, the pleader used to allege – I often did it myself – that the misrepresentation was fraudulent, or alternatively a collateral warranty. At the trial we nearly always succeeded on collateral warranty. We had to reckon, of course, with the *dictum* of Lord Moulton, at p 47, that 'such collateral contracts must from their very nature be rare'. But more often than not, the court elevated the innocent misrepresentation into a collateral warranty: and thereby did justice – in advance of the Misrepresentation Act 1967. I remember scores of cases of that kind, especially on the sale of a business. A representation as to the profits that had been made in the past was invariably held to be a warranty. Besides that experience, there have been many cases since I have sat in this court where we have readily held a representation – which induces a person to enter into a contract – to be a warranty sounding in damages ...

Mr Ross-Munro, retaliated, however, by citing *Bissett v Wilkinson* [1927] AC 177, where the Privy Council said that a statement by a New Zealand farmer that an area of land 'would carry 2,000 sheep' was only an expression of opinion. He submitted that the forecast here of 200,000 gallons was an expression of opinion and not a statement of fact and that it could not be interpreted as a warranty or promise.

Now, I would quite agree with Mr Ross-Munro that it was not a warranty – in this sense – that it did not guarantee that the throughput would be 200,000

13 [1976] 1 QB 801, CA.

gallons. But, nevertheless, it was a forecast made by a party – Esso – who had special knowledge and skill. It was the yardstick by which they measured the worth of a filling station. They knew the facts. They knew the traffic in the town. They knew the throughput of comparable stations. They had much experience and expertise at their disposal. They were in a much better position than Mr Mardon to make a forecast. It seems to me that if such a person makes a forecast, intending that the other should act upon it – and he does act upon it, it can well be interpreted as a warranty that the forecast is sound and reliable in the sense that they made it with reasonable care and skill. It is just as if Esso said to Mr Mardon: 'Our forecast of throughput is 200,000 gallons. You can rely upon it as being a sound forecast of what the service station should do. The rent is calculated on that footing.' If the forecast turned out to be an unsound forecast such as no person of skill or experience should have made, there is a breach of warranty. Just as there is a breach of warranty when a forecast is made – 'expected to load' by a certain date – if the maker has no reasonable grounds for it: see *Samuel Sanday and Co v Keighley, Maxted and Co* (1922) 27 Com Cas 296; or bunkers 'expected 600/700 tons': see *Efploia Shipping Corpn Ltd v Canadian Transport Co Ltd (The Pantanassa)* [1958] 2 Lloyd's Rep 449, pp 455–57, *per* Diplock J. It is very different from the New Zealand case, where the land had never been used as a sheep farm and both parties were equally able to form an opinion as to its carrying capacity: see, particularly, *Bissett v Wilkinson* [1927] AC 177, pp 183–84.

In the present case, it seems to me that there was a warranty that the forecast was sound, that is, Esso made it with reasonable care and skill. That warranty was broken. Most negligently, Esso made a 'fatal error' in the forecast they stated to Mr Mardon and on which he took the tenancy. For this, they are liable in damages.

Other factors which have been considered relevant in determining whether a statement is a term of the contract or a mere representation include the clarity with which the requirements of one of the parties have been stated. For example, a buyer of goods might have so clearly identified his need for goods of a particular quality or description that if the seller confirms his willingness to supply complying goods the confirmation can be regarded as nothing less than a fundamental term of the contract. Thus, in *Bannerman v White*,[14] the buyer had insisted that he would only purchase hops which had not been cultivated using sulphur, adding that if they had he would not bother even to ask the price. He was given an oral assurance that the seller's hops had not been treated with sulphur, but it subsequently transpired that a significant portion of the hops had. Given the obvious importance of the seller's assertion, it was held that this was a term of the contract, the breach of which entitled the buyer to reject the hops sold to him by the seller.

In other instances, there may be a period of delay between the making of a particular statement and the date on which the contract is finalised. The

---

14   (1861) 142 ER 685.

longer the period of delay, the more likely it is that the statement will lose some of its force, with the result that it is more likely the statement will be regarded as a representation rather than a term of the contract.[15]

CERTAINTY OF TERMS

In any process of interpretation, the raw material with which the courts are to work must sufficiently clearly express the intentions of the parties. It has been seen already that in determining when contractual obligations arise, an important factor is often whether or not an agreement has been reached. One particular problem which may arise in this regard is that the language used by the parties in the process of reaching an agreement is ambiguous, incomplete or vague to the extent that interpretation becomes impossible.

Ambiguity

Where it is alleged that a term is ambiguous, it is important to emphasise that ambiguity is not to be equated with mere difficulty of interpretation.[16] What is necessary is that the term under consideration must be capable of more than one interpretation. This ambiguity may be patent or latent.

Patent ambiguities may arise where the contract is self-contradictory or where it contains provisions which are obviously incompatible with each other. Thus, if an option contract states a specified date for expiry and a definite duration of a specified number of days, which result in a different expiry date, it is likely that the specified date of expiry will prevail.[17] In cases of latent ambiguity, conflicting evidence given by the parties may reveal differences of interpretation, in which case further evidence may be admitted in order to resolve the ambiguity. For example, the phrase 'fair market price' does not immediately reveal an ambiguity, but if there are two different market prices which might apply, a potential ambiguity arises from the circumstances. In such a case, further evidence may need to be called to prove which market price was in contemplation.[18]

It should be appreciated that the courts will not lightly treat a contract as void on the ground of ambiguity. Where possible, employing the objective theory of agreement, they will seek to discover some element of consensus. However, in some cases this will not be possible, in which case, the contract may be regarded as either void for ambiguity or possibly void on the ground

---

15 *Routledge v McKay* [1954] 1 WLR 615.
16 *Scammell & Nephew Ltd v Ouston* [1941] 1 All ER 14, p 25, *per* Lord Wright.
17 *Sawley Agency Ltd v Ginter* (1966) 58 DLR (2d) 757.
18 *Great Western Railway Co v Bristol Corpn* [1918] 87 LJ Ch 414, p 429, *per* Lord Wrenbury.

that there is an operative mistake. For example, in *Raffles v Wichelhaus*,[19] the parties contracted for the sale of goods to be shipped on board a vessel called *Peerless* which was due to sail from Bombay. In fact, there were two ships by the name of *Peerless*, one of which was due to sail in December and the other in October. The parties each had a different ship in mind. On these facts, it was held that there was no contract. It might not, however, take much to alter the facts of the case to reveal a situation in which the court would almost certainly find evidence of agreement on an objective basis. Suppose, for example, the contract had been one for the sale of oil, one of the ships was an oil tanker and the other was a general cargo vessel. In these circumstances, an objective understanding of the agreement would lead the reasonable man to believe that the parties had in mind the use of the oil tanker in performance of the contract.

Although as a general rule, the courts will strive to keep the contract alive by seeking to resolve the ambiguity, it may not be possible to choose between the rival interpretations. In this case, the contract is likely to fail on the ground that there is no finalised agreement. In such a case, the court may be forced to apply restitutionary principles in order to determine how a particular risk of loss is to be allocated. For example, in *Lind (Peter) & Co Ltd v Mersey Docks & Harbour Board*,[20] construction work had commenced under the terms of a letter of intent and was completed before the parties had reached any agreement on a price fixing mechanism. The main difficulty was that Lind & Co Ltd were adamant that any agreement as to price should allow for alterations in raw material costs whereas the Harbour Board insisted upon a fixed price contract. Lind & Co had submitted two tenders, one of which stipulated a fixed price and the other of which allowed for price variation. The Board had accepted 'your tender', but it was not clear which tender had been accepted. In the event, since neither party could agree, the court held that there was no contract on the terms of either tender, but since the construction work was complete, it was necessary to determine Lind's entitlement to payment on the basis of a *quantum meruit*, taking account of the reasonable value of the work completed and the value of that work to the Board.

Uncertainty or vagueness

Where a term in a contract is meaningless or unintelligible or where the court is unable to select between a number of reasonably possible interpretations of it or where the terms of the contract require further agreement between the parties so as to allow implementation of the term, it is said that the term is uncertain. The consequence of uncertainty or vagueness is that either the

---

19   (1864) 159 ER 375.
20   [1984] 1 All ER 504.

contract does not come into existence at all on the basis that there is an incomplete agreement or it may serve to invalidate a particular term, leaving the rest of the contract intact.

In *Scammell & Nephew Ltd v Ouston*,[21] the relevant term in a contract for the supply of a lorry stated that the price was payable 'on hire-purchase terms' over two years. However the words 'on hire-purchase terms' is capable of any number of interpretations, given the wide variety of hire-purchase terms which may be applicable to a given contract. Accordingly, the contract was considered to be so vague as to be unenforceable:

Scammell & Nephew Ltd v Ouston [1941] 1 All ER 14, HL, p 21

Lord Wright: At the oral conversations, the respondents had clearly insisted that a hire-purchase agreement was essential. No terms, however, of such an agreement had been settled, nor, indeed, had it been discussed with whom the agreement would be made. HC Ouston, when asked in cross-examination, 'The hire-purchase agreement, of course, you did not expect, I suppose, to be with Messrs Scammells, did you?' replied: 'I knew very well it would not have been. To the best of my knowledge, anyhow, I thought it would be, as it turned out to be, with United Dominions.'

JG Ouston said in evidence that he always told Cook quite definitely that they wanted to purchase on hire-purchase terms and that there never was any question of an out-and-out purchase. The appellants were obviously content that the deal should be on a hire-purchase basis, and proceeded with the completion of the van ...

There are, in my opinion, two grounds on which the court ought to hold that there never was a contract. The first is that the language used was so obscure and so incapable of any definite or precise meaning that the court is unable to attribute to the parties any particular contractual intention. The object of the court is to do justice between the parties, and the court will do its best, if satisfied that there was an ascertainable and determinate intention to contract, to give effect to that intention, looking at substance, and not mere form. It will not be deterred by mere difficulties of interpretation. Difficulty is not synonymous with ambiguity, so long as any definite meaning can be extracted. The test of intention, however, is to be found in the words used. If these words, considered however broadly and technically, and with due regard to all the just implications, fail to evince any definite meaning on which the court can safely act, the court has no choice but to say that there is no contract. Such a position is not often found, but I think that it is found in this case. My reason for so thinking is not only based on the actual vagueness and unintelligibility of the words used, but is confirmed by the startling diversity of explanations, tendered by those who think there was a bargain, of what the bargain was. I do not think it would be right to hold the appellants to any particular version. It was all left too vague. There are many cases in the books of what are called illusory contracts – that is, where the parties may have thought they were

---

21   [1941] 1 All ER 14, HL.

making a contract, but failed to arrive at a definite bargain. It is a necessary requirement that an agreement, in order to be binding, must be sufficiently definite to enable the court to give it a practical meaning. Its terms must be so definite, or capable of being made definite without further agreement of the parties, that the promises and performances to be rendered by each party are reasonably certain. In my opinion, that requirement was not satisfied in this case.

However, I think that the other reason, which is that the parties never in intention, nor even in appearance, reached an agreement, is a still sounder reason against enforcing the claim. In truth, in my opinion, their agreement was inchoate, and never got beyond negotiations. They did, indeed, accept the position that there should be some form of hire-purchase agreement, but they never went on to complete their agreement by settling between them what the terms of the hire-purchase agreement were to be. The furthest point they reached was an understanding or agreement to agree upon hire-purchase terms. However, as Lord Dunedin said in *May & Butcher Ltd v R* (reported in a note to *Foley v Classique Coaches Ltd*) at p 21: 'To be a good contract, there must be a concluded bargain, and a concluded contract is one which settles everything that is necessary to be settled and leaves nothing to be settled by agreement between the parties. Of course, it may leave something which still has to be determined, but then that determination must be a determination which does not depend upon the agreement between the parties ...'

It is here necessary to remember what a hire-purchase agreement is. It is not a contract of sale, but of bailment. The owner of the chattel lets it out on hire for a periodic rent on the terms that, on completion of the agreed number of payments, and on due compliance with the various terms of the agreement, the hirer is to have the option to buy the chattel on payment of 1 s or some nominal sum. The condition that the hirer is not to become owner automatically on completion of the agreed payments, but merely has an option to purchase, was adopted to avoid difficulties under the Factors Act or the Bills of Sale Act, as explained by this House in *Helby v Matthews* and *McEntire v Crossley Brothers*. While the bailment continues, the property remains in the letter. Such a transaction, though not a contract of sale, is used in practice to carry out a sale transaction, with the advantage to the buyer of credit facilities. Though the property in the chattel does not pass while the agreement is current, the hirer gets the use of it. What would be the price if it were a contract of sale has to be increased by whatever sum is necessary for interest and bank charges until the periodic instalments have been discharged. Terms must accordingly be arranged in respect of the period of the bailment as to user, repairs, insurance, rights of retaking possession on the hirer's default, and various other matters. A hire-purchase agreement is, therefore, in practice a complex arrangement. Thus, when, in the letter of 8 December 1937, the condition of hire-purchase was introduced into what had seemed, on the letters, to be proceeding as a contract of sale, there was a complete change in the character of the transaction, and a complex arrangement had necessarily to be substituted for a simple agreement to sell. It was not even clear who were to be parties to the hire-purchase agreement, or what their respective roles were to be. The respondents, it is clear, were necessary parties. The appellants also were necessary parties, because it was their chattel which was being dealt with. The finance company was also a necessary party. However, there were at least two possible ways of carrying out the deal. The hire-purchase agreement might be in such terms that the appellants were the letters and the respondents the hirers, and the purchase price was to be discharged by periodic instalments in the form of negotiable instruments, payable to the appellants, thus, enabling the appellants to discount the bills with the finance company, who, on the security of the bills drawn by the respondents and indorsed by the appellants, would pay the appellants the purchase price at once, keeping as their eventual profit the extra amount which was added to the price for interest and bank charges. Such an arrangement must obviously involve the making of a special tripartite agreement. Another possible method would be for the appellants to agree with the respondents to sell the van to the finance company on the stipulation that the latter should agree to let the van to the respondents under a hire-purchase agreement. Clearly, in that case also, a special tripartite agreement would be necessary. There was perhaps a third possible mode under which the appellants sold the van for cash (at least as regards the balance, for the transaction was, in part, barter) to the respondents, who, having become purchasers, then transferred the van to the finance company on a hire-purchase agreement in consideration of the company advancing the price. Even in such a case, the appellants would, I think, in practice be a necessary party, because the finance company would require the undertaking of the appellants to transfer the van direct to them and the respondents' concurrence in that undertaking. Otherwise, the finance company would be paying cash without at once obtaining their security in the form of the van. Thus, a tripartite agreement would be necessary. However, I need not consider that case, because it was clearly not contemplated by the parties. The correspondence shows that the terms of the hire-purchase agreement were to be matters of joint concern to the three parties who were to agree upon them. What is clear is that, while a hire-purchase agreement was being demanded, its exact form and its exact terms were left for future agreement ...

The court may import terms on the proof of custom or by implication. However, it is, in my opinion, a very different matter to make an entire contract for the parties, as the court would be doing if the course suggested by MacKinnon LJ, was adopted. That is simply making a contract for the parties. The analogy he cited of a cif contract is, in my opinion, no true analogy. These initial letters have a definite and complete meaning under the law merchant, just as much as the meaning of a bill of exchange, or the general effect of a marine insurance contract, is determined by the law merchant. The law has not defined, and cannot of itself define, what are the normal and reasonable terms of a hire-purchase agreement. Though the general character of such an agreement is familiar, it is necessary for the parties in each case to agree upon the particular terms. It may perhaps be that this might be done in particular circumstances by general words of reference. For instance, if it were stipulated that there should be 'a usual' hire-purchase agreement, the court might be able, if supplied with appropriate evidence, to define what are the terms of such an agreement. However, there was nothing of the sort in this case, and I reserve my opinion on any such hypothetical case. I think this appeal should be allowed.

The appeal was allowed. Contrast the judgment of Viscount Maugham (at p 16):

> **Viscount Maugham**: It is a regrettable fact that there are few, if any, topics on which there seems to be a greater difference of judicial opinion than those which relate to the question whether, as the result of informal letters or like documents, a binding contract has been arrived at. Many well-known instances are to be found in the books, the latest being that of *Hillas & Co Ltd v Arcos Ltd*. The reason for these different conclusions is that laymen, unassisted by persons with a legal training, are not always accustomed to use words or phrases with a precise or definite meaning. In order to constitute a valid contract, the parties must so express themselves that their meaning can be determined with a reasonable degree of certainty. It is plain that, unless this can be done, it would be impossible to hold that the contracting parties had the same intention. In other words, the consensus ad idem would be a matter of mere conjecture. This general rule, however, applies somewhat differently in different cases. In commercial documents connected with dealings in a trade with which the parties are perfectly familiar, the court is very willing, if satisfied that the parties thought that they made a binding contract, to imply terms, and, in particular, terms as to the method of carrying out the contract, which it would be impossible to supply in other kinds of contract: *Hillas & Co Ltd v Arcos Ltd* at pp 511, 512 and 514.
>
> My Lords, it is beyond dispute that, if an alleged contract is partly verbal and partly in writing, it is necessary to take the whole of the negotiations into consideration for the purpose of seeing whether the parties are truly agreed on all material points, for, if they are not, there is no binding contract. Nor is it right to construe a letter or other document forming a part of the negotiations in such a case without regard to the verbal statements which also form a part of them. To construe the language of such a letter, so to speak, *in vacuo* might easily result in giving to the words, as used by the writer, a meaning which, in the circumstances of the case, he did not intend the words to bear, or one which the recipient of the letter did not attribute to them. Accordingly, the words in the letter, 'This order is given on the understanding that the balance of purchase price can be had on hire-purchase terms over a period of two years', must be read together with the parol evidence of JG Ouston in order to give those words their true meaning. So read, I cannot myself doubt, they are not an attempt to impose a new condition, whether precedent or subsequent, but are merely a reminder of the common intention of the parties from the start, though perhaps – and even of that I am not certain – the reference to the period of two years was something which had not previously been agreed.
>
> We come, then, to the question as to the effect of the so-called purchase being on 'hire-purchase terms' and, here, we are confronted with a strange and confusing circumstance. The term 'hire-purchase' for a good many years past has been understood to mean a contract of hire by the owner of a chattel conferring on the hirer an option to purchase on the performance of certain conditions: *Helby v Matthews* ...
>
> What do the words 'hire-purchase terms' mean in the present case? They may indicate that the hire-purchase agreement was to be granted by the appellants,

or, on the other hand, by some finance company acting in collaboration with the appellants. They may contemplate that the appellants were to receive by instalments a sum of £168 spread over a period of two years upon delivering the new van and receiving the old car or, on the other hand, that the appellants were to receive from a third party a lump sum of £168 and that the third party, presumably a finance company, was to receive from the respondents a larger sum than £168, to include interest and profit spread over a period of two years. Moreover, nothing is said (except as to the two years period) as to the terms of the hire-purchase agreement – for instance, as to the interest payable, and as to the rights of the letter, whoever he may be, in the event of default by the respondents in payment of the instalments at the due dates. As regards the last matters, there was no evidence to suggest that there are any well-known 'usual terms' in such a contract, and I think that it is common knowledge that In fact, many letters, though by no means all of them, insist on terms which the legislature regards as so unfair and unconscionable that it was recently found necessary to deal with the matter in the Hire-Purchase Act 1938. These, my Lords, are very serious difficulties, and, when we find, as we do, in this curious case, that the trial judge and the three Lords Justices, and even the two counsel who addressed your Lordships for the respondents, were unable to agree upon the true construction of the alleged agreement, it seems to me that it is impossible to conclude that a binding agreement has been established by the respondents.

The mere fact that the terms of the contract are vague or uncertain should not be taken to mean that in all cases, the contract will fail. Where a term is ambiguous, it has been seen that the courts will apply the *contra proferentem* rule against the person who seeks to rely on the ambiguous language of the contract. Accordingly, the person who uses ambiguous language can expect an unfavourable interpretation. Similarly, in the case of vagueness or uncertainty, the courts are unlikely to receive with sympathy any argument to the effect that the contract should fail where it is raised by the person who is responsible for the presence of the term in the contract:

Nicolene Ltd v Simmonds [1953] 1 All ER 822, CA, p 825

Denning LJ: This case raises a short, but important, point which can be stated quite simply. There was a contract for the sale of three thousand tons of steel reinforcing bars; the seller broke his contract, and when the buyer claimed damages the seller set up the defence that, owing to a sentence in one of the letters which were alleged to constitute the contract, there was no contract at all. The material words are: 'We are in agreement that the usual conditions of acceptance apply.' There were no usual conditions of acceptance and so it is said that those words are meaningless, that there is nothing to which they can apply, and that, therefore, there was never any contract between the parties.

In my opinion, a distinction must be drawn between a clause which is meaningless and a clause which is yet to be agreed. A clause which is meaningless can often be ignored, while still leaving the contract good, whereas a clause which has yet to be agreed may mean that there is no contract at all, because the parties have not agreed on all the essential terms. I take it to be clear law that, if one of the parties to a contract inserts into it an exempting condition in his own favour which the other side agrees and it afterwards appears that that condition is meaningless or is so ambiguous that no ascertainable meaning can be given to it, that does not render the whole contract a nullity. The only result is that the exempting condition is a nullity and must be rejected. It would be strange, indeed, if a party could escape every one of his obligations by inserting a meaningless exemption from some of them. The proposition which I have stated is supported by the numerous cases where it has been held that, if a man signs a contract expressly as agent for a named company and there is no such company in existence, the courts do not hold that there is no contract, but only reject the meaningless words 'as agent for the company' and hold that the individual himself was a party to the contract. So, also, if a person signs 'as agent' and has no principal, the words 'as agent' are rejected and the contract is held to be a good contract between the parties ...

I would just say a word about the recent decision of McNair J, in *British Electrical & Associated Industries (Cardiff) Ltd v Patley Pressings Ltd*, where the contract note contained the clause 'subject to force majeure conditions'. If the true construction of the documents in that case was that an essential term had yet to be agreed, it would fall within the cases to which I have already referred, but, if the true view was that the exempting clause was agreed, but was 'so vague and uncertain as to be incapable of any precise meaning' (which is how McNair J, described it), I should have thought that it could be ignored without impairing the validity of the contract. It was clearly severable from the rest of the contract, whereas the term in *G Scammell & Nephew Ltd v Ouston* was not.

In the case before the court, there was nothing yet to be agreed. There was nothing left to further negotiation. The parties merely agreed that 'the usual conditions of acceptance apply'. That clause was so vague and uncertain as to be incapable of any precise meaning. It is clearly severable from the rest of the contract, and can be rejected without impairing the sense or reasonableness of the contract as a whole, and it should be so rejected. The contract should be held to be good and the clause should be ignored. The parties themselves treated the contract as subsisting, and they regarded it as creating binding obligations between them and it would be most unfortunate if the law should say otherwise.

Incompleteness

It is common for contracting parties in business to leave open certain aspects of their contracts, especially in contracts which are set for performance at some future time. It is understandable that will be so, for there are a number of uncertainties which the parties may wish to resolve at a later date. For example, it may be considered helpful not to agree a fixed price in times of inflation, but instead to reach agreement once raw material costs have been sorted out. Similarly, in consumer contracts for the provision of services, it is often the case that no date of performance is fixed by the contract. Unfortunately, law and business practice do not always converge, since a rigid application of the so called general rule on incompleteness may result in a decision to the effect that there is no binding contract where the parties have failed to cover all aspects of their agreement.

In relation to matters such as the price in a contract for the sale of goods or for the supply of services, the absence of agreement is not fatal since certain statutory provisions allow for the substitution of a reasonable charge for the goods or services provided:

Sale of Goods Act 1979

8 Ascertainment of price

(1) The price in a contract of sale may be fixed by the contract, or may be left to be fixed in a manner agreed by the contract, or may be determined by the course of dealing between the parties.

(2) Where the price is not determined as mentioned in sub-s (1) above, the buyer must pay a reasonable price

(3) What is a reasonable price is a question of fact dependant on the circumstances of each particular case.

9 Agreement to sell at valuation

(1) Where there is an agreement to sell goods on the terms that the price is to be fixed by the valuation of a third party, and he cannot or does not make the valuation, the agreement is avoided; but if the goods or any part of them have been delivered to and appropriated by the buyer he must pay a reasonable price for them.

(2) Where the third party is prevented from making a valuation by the fault of the seller or the buyer, the party not at fault may maintain an action for damages against the party at fault.

Supply of Goods and Services Act 1982

14 Implied term about time for performance

(1) Where, under a contract for the supply of a service by a supplier acting in the course of a business, the time for the service to be carried out is not fixed by the contract, left to be agreed in a manner agreed by the contract or determined by the course of dealing between the parties, there is an implied term that the supplier will carry out the service within a reasonable time.

(2) What is a reasonable time is a question of fact.

15 Implied term about consideration

(1) Where, under a contract for the supply of a service, the consideration for the service is not determined by the contract, left to be determined in a manner agreed by the contract or determined by the course of dealing

between the parties, there is an implied term that the party contracting with the supplier will pay a reasonable charge.

(2) What is a reasonable charge is a question of fact.

These provisions recognise that contracting parties do leave certain matters incomplete and accordingly provide for the payment of a reasonable sum or for performance within a reasonable time. However, it is important to appreciate that in the case of s 8 of the Sale of Goods Act 1979, the implied term that a reasonable amount will be paid has been held to operate only where the contract is silent on a price fixing mechanism.

In *May & Butcher Ltd v R*,[22] it was alleged that there was a valid contract for the sale of tentage on terms which stated, *inter alia*, that 'the price or prices to be paid, and the date or dates on which payment is to be made ... shall be agreed upon from time to time between' the parties:

May & Butcher Ltd v R [1934] 2 KB 17n, HL, p 21

Viscount Dunedin: To be a good contract, there must be a concluded bargain, and a concluded contract is one which settles everything that is necessary to be settled and leaves nothing to be settled by agreement between the parties. Of course, it may leave something which still has to be determined, but then that determination which does not depend upon the agreement between the parties. In the system of law in which I was brought up, that was expressed by one of those *brocards* of which perhaps we have been too fond, but which often express very neatly what is wanted: *Certum est quod certum reddi potest.* Therefore, you may very well agree that a certain part of the contract of sale, such as price, may be settled by someone else. As a matter of the general law of contract all the essentials have to be settled. What are the essentials may vary according to the particular contract under consideration. We are here dealing with sale, and undoubtedly price is one of the essentials of sale, and if it is left still to be agreed between the parties, then there is no contract. It may be left to the determination of a certain person, and if it was so left and that person either would not or could not act, there would be no contract because the price was to be settled in a certain way and it has become impossible to settle it in that way, and therefore there is no settlement. No doubt as to goods, the Sale of Goods Act 1893 says that if the price is not mentioned and settled in the contract it is to be a reasonable price. The simple answer in this case is that the Sale of Goods Act provides for silence on the point and here there is no silence, because there is a provision that the two parties are to agree. As long as you have something certain, it does not matter. For instance, with regard to price it is a perfectly good contract to say that the price is to be settled by the buyer ...

Here, there was clearly no contract. There would have been a perfectly good settlement of price if the contract had said that it was to be settled by arbitration by a certain man, or it might have been quite good if it was said that it was to be settled by arbitration under the Arbitration Act so as to bring in a

---

material plan by which a certain person could be put in action. The question then arises: has anything of that sort been done? I think clearly not. The general arbitration clause is one in very common form as to disputes arising out of the arrangements. In no proper meaning of the word can this be described as a dispute arising between the parties; it is a failure to agree, which is a very different thing from a dispute.

As regards the option point. I do not think it can be more neatly put than it was by Rowlatt J when he said: 'It is an option to offer terms on terms that are not agreed. An option to offer a contract which is not a contract seems to me not to carry the case any further than the first way of putting it.' For these reasons, I agree in the motion.

This decision may be viewed as excessively formalist and is difficult to reconcile with other decisions. In particular, it has been observed that in cases of this kind, the courts must tread a careful path in order not to be seen as 'the destroyer of bargains' while, at the same time, avoiding making a contract for the parties.[23] A further relevant issue in *May and Butcher Ltd v R* is that there was also a provision in the contract to the effect that disputes arising under the contract would be referred to arbitration. In these circumstances, it might be possible for the court to ascertain a reasonable price on the basis that the parties have agreed to submit themselves to an objective valuation of the subject matter of the contract. In this way, the court would be able to avoid being a 'destroyer of bargains'.

In *Foley v Classique Coaches Ltd*,[24] the parties entered a contract for the sale of land adjoining a garage owned by the plaintiff. The contract stipulated that in return for the sale of the land, the defendant would buy all the petrol they needed from the plaintiff 'at a price to be agreed by the parties in writing and from time to time'. As in *May and Butcher Ltd v R*, there was also a provision to the effect that disputes would be referred to arbitration. When a dispute arose over the price payable for petrol, it was alleged that the contract was void for incompleteness. However, the Court of Appeal was prepared to imply a term to the effect that the defendant would pay a reasonable price:

Foley v Classique Coaches Ltd [1934] 2 KB 1, CA, p 9

Scrutton LJ: A good deal of the case turns upon the effect of two decisions of the House of Lords which are not easy to fit in with each other. In the first of these cases, *May and Butcher Ltd v R* known as the tentage case, the plaintiffs were buying surplus stores from a government department. In the Court of Appeal, two members of the court took the view that, in as much as there was a provision that the stocks were to be offered from time to time at prices to be agreed, there was no binding contract because an agreement to make an agreement does not constitute a contract, and that the language of the

---

23   *Hillas & Co v Arcos* [1932] All ER Rep 494, p 499, *per* Lord Tomlin.
24   [1934] 2 KB 1, CA.

arbitration clause that any dispute as to the construction of the agreement should be referred was irrelevant. Then came the Russian timber case of *Hillas & Co Ltd v Arcos Ltd,* in which there was an agreement between Hillas & Co Ltd and the representatives of the Russian government, under which Hillas & Co Ltd, were to purchase over the season 22,000 standards of softwood goods of fair specification, and under a later clause in the same agreement, they had an option to purchase in the next year 100,000 standards, with no particulars as to the sort of wood or as to the terms and ports of shipment or any of the other matters one expects to find dealt with on a sale of a large quantity of Russian timber over a period. The Court of Appeal came to the conclusion that, as the House of Lords in *May and Butcher Ltd v R* considered that where a detail had to be agreed upon there was no agreement until that detail was agreed, they were bound to follow the decision in *May and Butcher Ltd v R* and to hold that there was no effective agreement in respect of the option, because the terms had not been agreed. It turned out that we were wrong in so deciding and that we had misunderstood the decision in *May and Butcher Ltd v R.* The House in *Hillas & Co Ltd v Arcos Ltd* took this line. It is quite true that there seems to be considerable vagueness about the agreement, but the parties managed to perform the contract so far as it related to 22,000 standards, and so the House thought there was an agreement as to the option which the parties would be able to perform in spite of the lack of details. It is true that in the first year the parties got through quite satisfactorily; that was because during that year the majority of English buyers were boycotting the Russian sellers. In the second year the position was different. The English buyers had changed their view and were buying large quantities of Russian timber, so that obviously different conditions were then prevailing. The House of Lords said that in *Hiller v Arcos* they had not laid down universal principles of construction in *May and Butcher Ltd v R* and that each case must be decided on the construction of the particular document, whilst, in *Hillas & Co Ltd v Arcos Ltd*, they found that the parties believed they had a contract.

In the present case, the parties obviously believed they had a contract, and they acted on that belief for three years. They had an arbitration clause which related to the subject matter of the agreement as to the supply of petrol, and it seems to me that this arbitration clause applies to any failure to agree as to the price. As in the case of a tied house, there is to be implied in this contract a term that the petrol shall be supplied at a reasonable price and shall be of reasonable quality. For these reasons, I have come to the conclusion that the Lord Chief Justice was right in holding that there was an effective and enforceable contract, although no definite price had been agreed with regard to the petrol in the future.

Executed and executory contracts

It should be observed that the courts will strain not to treat a term as void for ambiguity, uncertainty or incompleteness, especially in circumstances in which one or other of the parties has already moved towards performance of what he believes to be his obligations under the contract. Where there is part performance on one side, the other party is likely to have received some valuable benefit for which it is reasonable that he should pay. Likewise, the part performer may be seen to have relied to his detriment on the words or actions of the other party.

In *British Bank for Foreign Trade v Novinex*,[25] the defendants had been introduced to clients by the plaintiffs and a contract between those clients and the defendants had followed. The defendants further agreed to pay an unspecified commission to the plaintiffs in respect of any follow-up orders which were attributable to the initial introduction. Such orders were placed, but the defendants denied liability to pay commission on the ground that there was no legally enforceable agreement because of the vagueness of the language used by the parties. The Court of Appeal held that a term could be implied to the effect that the defendants would pay a reasonable commission, the consideration for which was the plaintiffs' rendering of a valuable service which was of benefit to the defendants:

British Bank for Foreign Trade v Novinex [1949] 1 All ER 155, CA, p 158

Cohen LJ: I turn next to the main question. Is this an enforceable agreement? A number of authorities have been cited to us, to which I do not propose to refer in detail, because, in my view, the effect of the authorities is correctly stated in the learned judge's judgment where he says: 'The principle to be deduced from the cases is that, if there is an essential term which has yet to be agreed and there is no express or implied provision for its solution, the result in point of law is that there is no binding contract. In seeing whether there is an implied provision for its solution, however, there is a difference between an arrangement which is wholly executory on both sides, and one which has been executed on one side or the other. In the ordinary way, if there is an arrangement to supply goods at a price "to be agreed", or to perform services on terms "to be agreed", then, although, while the matter is still executory there may be no binding contract, nevertheless, if it is executed on one side, that is, if the one does his part without having come to an agreement as to the price or the terms, then the law will say that there is necessarily implied from the conduct of the parties a contract that, in default of agreement, a reasonable sum is to be paid.'

With that statement of the principle of law I respectfully agree. My difference with the learned judge is only on the question whether he has correctly applied that statement of principle to the facts of this case. The learned judge goes on: 'The difficulty is to apply the distinction in this case. This is not a case of services to be rendered for wages or goods to be supplied for a price. It is an arrangement in regard to repeat transactions or follow-up transactions, in respect of which the person effecting the original introduction has performed

---

25 [1949] 1 All ER 155, CA.

no fresh service whatever apart from his original introduction. He has, however, done his part. He has effected the original introduction.'

If I may pause there for a moment, I can see no difference in principle between a case where the service which is rendered is labour and a case where the service is an introduction. It seems to me here that, whatever the value of the service may be, the plaintiffs have rendered to the defendants the service which was intended to be the consideration for the agreement to pay commission on future orders. I cannot think that there is a difference in principle between such a service and an agreement to serve an employer as a clerk or in any other capacity. The learned judge goes on to say that, in his view, it is impossible to apply the principle to the present case because there is so much left in the air. He says: 'Is commission to be payable until the crack of doom?' In my view, if the defendants go on dealing with Pritchard & Gee until the crack of doom, they will have to go on paying commission to the plaintiffs, if they are in existence, until that doom occurs. As was pointed out in *Levy v Goldhill* by Peterson J, parties having entered into a bargain have it in their power to put an end to it, and so the defendants here need not go on dealing with Messrs Pritchard & Gee. Therefore, I do not feel any difficulty on those points ...

Then the learned judge says: 'Is it confined to oilskins or does it apply to business of an entirely different kind, in different commodities, by different departments and so forth?' Here, again, I can find no ambiguity in the agreement, and I do not, therefore, feel any difficulty in answering the question in favour of the second alternative. The real point comes where the learned judge goes on: 'And what is the amount of the commission to be? If there is no usual or customary commission, how can anyone say what is a reasonable commission for a follow-up transaction or a repeat transaction? That appeared clearly from the evidence which showed that when parties are negotiating for the price they are going to pay, they take account of any commission they have to pay to agents.'

Denning J goes on to say that this shows that the agreement is too vague, but this argument involves the proposition that the agreement had not said in terms: 'We also undertake to cover you with a reasonable commission on any other business transacted with your friends.' Denning J regarded that condition as being too vague to be enforceable. I cannot agree with his view. I think that the court should take the view that a jury properly directed would be able to arrive at a proper conclusion as to what in the circumstances of this case is a reasonable commission.

(His Lordship then considered what would be a reasonable commission in respect of the transactions and concluded that it would not exceed 1/4 d per skin.)

Where the contract remains purely executory and there is no evidence of reliance on either side, there may be less reason to uphold the contract. Thus, in *Bushwall Properties Ltd v Vortex Properties Ltd*,[26] there was an executory

___

26 [1976] 2 All ER 283.

agreement to sell land for £500,000, the price to be paid in three instalments of £250,000, £125,000 and £125,000. It was further agreed that a proportionate part of the land would be released at each payment date. The parties had made no provision for allocation of the proportionate parts, with the result that the contract was held to be void for uncertainty. In these circumstances, no actual benefit, apart from a mere expectation, would have been conferred on either party; therefore, there was no urgent need to look for an implied solution.

EXPRESS TERMS

Where the parties have entered a contract, a number of statements may have been made, some of which form part of the contract, which, in the event of breach, will give rise to a remedy for breach of contract. In contrast, other statements may have a lesser effect if interpreted to amount to no more than a representation which has induced the other party to enter into the contract with the representor. The distinction between contractual terms and representations is pursued in more depth earlier in this chapter.

Even if a statement is regarded as a contractual promise, it is important to consider whether it is a guarantee that a particular result will be achieved or whether it is a promise of some lesser nature. If a person has given a guarantee, then if the guaranteed result is not achieved, it is reasonable to assume that the parties intended liability for the breach of promise to place the promisee in the position he would have been in had the promise been fulfilled. Accordingly, subject to restrictions on an award of damages,[27] the promisee ought to be given damages in respect of his expectation loss. In contrast, if all the promisor has promised is that he will exercise reasonable care and skill in performing a particular task, the promisee cannot expect to recover more than the out of pocket loss he has suffered as a result of relying on the promise of the other party.

In *Esso Petroleum Co Ltd v Mardon* (the facts and extracts from which are considered above), it should be appreciated that Esso's representative did not guarantee that Mardon would be in any particular position by the end of the three year period. Accordingly, the damages recovered by the plaintiff did no more than to place him in the position he was in before the statement was made to him. This required no more than the recoupment of the set-up expenditure incurred by the plaintiff as a result of entering a contract he would not otherwise have entered had he known the truth:

---

27 Considered in more detail in Chapter 12.

Esso Petroleum Co Ltd v Mardon [1976] QB 801, CA, p 820

Lord Denning MR:

The measure of damages

Mr Mardon is not to be compensated here for 'loss of a bargain'. He was given no bargain that the throughput would amount to 200,000 gallons a year. He is only to be compensated for having been induced to enter into a contract which turned out to be disastrous for him. Whether it be called breach of warranty or negligent misrepresentation, its effect was not to warrant the throughput, but only to induce him to enter the contract. So, the damages in either case are to be measured by the loss he suffered. Just as in *Doyle v Olby (Ironmongers) Ltd* [1969] 2 QB 158, 167, he can say: '... I would not have entered into this contract at all but for your representation. Owing to it, I have lost all the capital I put into it. I also incurred a large overdraft. I have spent four years of my life in wasted endeavour without reward: and it will take me some time to re-establish myself.'

For all such loss, he is entitled to recover damages. It is to be measured in a similar way as the loss due to a personal injury. You should look into the future so as to forecast what would have been likely to happen if he had never entered into this contract: and contrast it with his position as it is now as a result of entering into it. The future is necessarily problematical and can only be a rough-and-ready estimate. But it must be done in assessing the loss.

Ormrod LJ (at p 823): The judge's reasons for rejecting Mr Mardon's contention that this was a warranty are summarised in this passage in his judgment [1975] QB 819, p 825: 'I think that the authorities indicate conclusively that, to constitute a warranty, a statement must, first, be intended by the maker to constitute a promise which can be described as a warranty or, putting it into common language, it must be a statement by which the maker says: 'I guarantee that this will happen.' Secondly, to constitute a warranty a statement must be of such nature that it is susceptible in relation to its content of constituting a clear contractual obligation on the part of the maker of the statement.'

With great respect, I think that in formulating the first of these reasons, the judge misled himself. It was no part of Mr Mardon's case that the plaintiffs had warranted that the throughput would reach 200,000 gallons in the third year. His case was that the plaintiffs, through Mr Leitch and Mr Allen, had, by implication, warranted that on a careful assessment they – that is, Esso Petroleum Co Ltd – had estimated the throughput of this service station at 200,000 gallons in the third year ...

If it is necessary in this context (which I doubt) to draw a hard and fast distinction between statements of fact and statements of opinion, the judge, rightly in my view, regarded this as a statement of fact. It was precisely equivalent to saying that Esso rated this service station as one of their 'Grade A' or 'Four Star' sites.

On this basis, no question of a guaranteed throughput arises; had it failed to reach the estimate owing to a cause or causes outside the plaintiffs' control, for example, an unforeseen traffic diversion scheme, greatly reducing the traffic flow in Eastbank Street, or the appearance across the street of a rival filling station, there would have been no breach of warranty on the part of the plaintiffs.

Where there is a dispute between the parties, the first job facing the court will be to interpret the express terms of the contract. In this area, it is difficult to identify any general rules as such and the courts appear to proceed on a case by case basis. At one stage, it could be said that there was a parol evidence rule to the effect that if the parties had reduced their contract to writing, the courts would not permit extrinsic evidence to be adduced in order to show what were the true intentions of the parties. However, the number of exceptions to the rule is so great that the Law Commission has concluded that there is little evidence of the continued existence of the rule as such.[28] The one area where it can be said that there are rules of interpretation is in relation to exemption clauses, but these matters are considered elsewhere in this book.[29]

What is clear is that the courts are not prepared to interpret the terms of a contract literally, if the effect of this would be to produce an absurd result which the parties, as reasonable businessmen, could not possibly have intended.

In *Schuler AG v Wickman Machine Tool Sales Ltd*,[30] it was alleged that there had been a breach amounting to wrongful termination of a distributorship agreement. However, whether the breach was wrongful depended upon the proper construction of the terms of the contract, one of which provided that it was a condition of the contract that Wickman would send its representatives to visit certain motor vehicle manufacturers at least once a week for the purposes of soliciting orders:

Schuler AG v Wickman Machine Tool Sales Ltd [1974] AC 235, p 251

Lord Reid: Schuler maintain that the word 'condition' has now acquired a precise legal meaning; that, particularly since the enactment of the Sale of Goods Act 1893, its recognised meaning in English law is a term of a contract, any breach of which by one party gives to the other party an immediate right to rescind the whole contract. Undoubtedly, the word is frequently used in that sense. There may, indeed, be some presumption that in a formal legal document it has that meaning. But it is frequently used with a less stringent meaning. One is familiar with printed 'conditions of sale' incorporated into a contract, and with the words 'for conditions, see back' printed on a ticket. There it simply means that the 'conditions' are terms of the contract.

---

28 Law Commission, No 154, 1986, para 2.7.

29 See Chapters 2 and 8.

30 [1974] AC 235. The facts of the case are considered in more detail in Chapter 9, as are further technical issues concerning the construction of the agreement.

In the ordinary use of the English language, 'condition' has many meanings, some of which have nothing to do with agreements. In connection with an agreement it may mean a pre-condition: something which must happen or be done before the agreement can take effect. Or it may mean some state of affairs which must continue to exist if the agreement is to remain in force. The legal meaning on which Schuler rely is, I think, one which would not occur to a layman; a condition in that sense is not something which has an automatic effect. It is a term the breach of which by one party gives to the other an option either to terminate the contract or to let the contract proceed and, if he so desires, sue for damages for the breach.

Sometimes a breach of a term gives that option to the aggrieved party because it is of a fundamental character going to the root of the contract, sometimes it gives that option because the parties have chosen to stipulate that it shall have that effect. Blackburn J said in *Bettini v Gye*: 'Parties may think some matter, apparently of very little importance, essential; and if they sufficiently express an intention to make the literal fulfilment of such a thing a condition precedent, it will be one ...'

In the present case, it is not contended that Wickman's failures to make visits amounted in themselves to fundamental breaches. What is contended is that the terms of cl 7 'sufficiently express an intention' to make any breach, however small, of the obligation to make visits a condition so that any such breach shall entitle Schuler to rescind the whole contract if they so desire.

Schuler maintain that the use of the word 'condition' is in itself enough to establish this intention. No doubt, some words used by lawyers do have a rigid, inflexible meaning. But we must remember that we are seeking to discover intention as disclosed by the contract as a whole. Use of the word 'condition' is an indication – even a strong indication – of such an intention, but it is by no means conclusive. The fact that a particular construction leads to a very unreasonable result must be a relevant consideration. The more unreasonable the result the more unlikely it is that the parties can have intended it, and if they do intend it the more necessary it is that they shall make that intention abundantly clear.

Clause 7(b) requires that over a long period each of the six firms shall be visited every week by one or other of two named representatives. It makes no provision for Wickman being entitled to substitute others even on the death or retirement of one of the named representatives. Even if one could imply some right to do this, it makes no provision for both representatives being ill during a particular week. And it makes no provision for the possibility that one or other of the firms may tell Wickman that they cannot receive Wickman's representative during a particular week. So if the parties gave any thought to the matter at all they must have realised the probability that in a few cases out of the 1,400 required visits a visit as stipulated would be impossible. But if Schuler's contention is right, failure to make even one visit entitles them to terminate the contract however blameless Wickman might be. This is so unreasonable that it must make me search for some other possible meaning of the contract. If none can be found then Wickman must suffer the consequences. But only if that is the only possible interpretation.

If I have to construe cl 7 standing by itself then I do find difficulty in reaching any other interpretation. But if cl 7 must be read with cl 11, the difficulty disappears. The word 'condition' would make any breach of cl 7(b), however excusable, a material breach. That would then entitle Schuler to give notice under cl 11(a)(i) requiring the breach to be remedied. There would be no point in giving such a notice if Wickman were clearly not in fault but if it were given Wickman would have no difficulty in shewing that the breach had been remedied. If Wickman were at fault, then, on receiving such a notice, they would have to amend their system so that they could shew that the breach had been remedied. If they did not do that within the period of the notice, then Schuler would be entitled to rescind.

In my view, that is a possible and reasonable construction of the contract and I would therefore adopt it. The contract is so obscure that I can have no confidence that this is its true meaning but for the reasons which I have given I think that it is the preferable construction.

Contrast Lord Wilberforce's dissenting judgment (at p 262):

Lord Wilberforce: The second legal issue which arises I would state in this way: whether it is open to the parties to a contract, not being a contract for the sale of goods, to use the word 'condition' to introduce a term, breach of which ipso facto entitles the other party to treat the contract at an end.

The proposition that this may be done has not been uncriticised. It is said that this is contrary to modern trends which focus interest rather on the nature of the breach, allowing the innocent party to rescind or repudiate whenever the breach is fundamental, whether the clause breached is called a condition or not: that the affixing of the label 'condition' cannot pre-empt the right of the court to estimate for itself the character of the breach. Alternatively it is said that the result contended for can only be achieved if the consequences of a breach of a 'condition' (that the other party may rescind) are spelt out in the contract. In support of this line of argument reliance is placed on the judgment of the Court of Appeal in *Hong Kong Fir Shipping Co Ltd v Kawasaki Kisen Kaisha Ltd.*

My Lords, this approach has something to commend it: it has academic support. The use as a promissory term of 'condition' is artificial, as is that of 'warranty' in some contexts. But in my opinion this use is now too deeply embedded in English law to be uprooted by anything less than a complete revision ...

Does cl 7(b) amount to a 'condition' or a 'term'? (To call it an important or material term adds, with all respect, nothing but some intellectual assuagement.) My Lords, I am clear in my own mind that it is a condition, but your Lordships take the contrary view. On a matter of construction of a particular document, to develop the reasons for a minority opinion serves no purpose. I am all the more happy to refrain from so doing because the judgments of Mocatta J, Stephenson LJ and, indeed, of Edmund Davies LJ on construction, give me complete satisfaction and I could in any case add little of value to their reasons. I would only add that, for my part, to call the clause arbitrary, capricious or fantastic, or to introduce as a test of its validity the ubiquitous reasonable man (I do not know whether he is English or German) is to assume, contrary to the evidence, that both parties to this contract adopted a standard of easygoing tolerance rather than one of aggressive, insistent punctuality and efficiency. That is not an assumption I am prepared to make, nor do I think myself entitled to impose the former standard on the parties if their words indicate, as they plainly do, the latter. I note finally, that the result of treating the clause, so careful and specific in its requirements, as a term is, in effect, to deprive the appellants of any remedy in respect of admitted and by no means minimal breaches. The arbitrator's finding that these breaches were not 'material' was not, in my opinion, justified in law in the face of the parties' own characterisation of them in their document: indeed the fact that he was able to do so, and so leave the appellants without remedy, argues strongly that the legal basis of his finding – that cl 7(b) was merely a term – is unsound.

Did Lord Reid and the majority re-write the contract to give effect to what they thought ought to have been agreed? If so, why did the House of Lords in *Liverpool City Council v Irwin* stamp on Lord Denning's attempt to introduce the notion of a 'reasonable' implied term (see below)?

IMPLIED TERMS[31]

In classical terminology, the role of the court is to act as an umpire and to give effect to what the parties to a contract have agreed. However, the parties to a contract frequently fail to define all their duties, in which case the court may imply terms into the contract. Such terms may fall into one of three categories, namely, terms implied in law, terms implied in fact and terms implied by way of customary usage or business practice whilst the final category has relatively clear boundaries, the line between terms implied by law, and terms implied in fact may not always be so clear cut. Once owing from the sphere of terms implied by statute the use of the terminology 'implied term' conjures up a picture of the court reading into a contract what is logically implied in the language used by the parties. In reality, although the court may read into a contract a term that the parties may have contemplated but did not express, and may imply a term which the parties would have accepted if the matter had been brought to their attention, it is also true that a term can sometimes be implied where the court thinks this is desirable in the interests of justice and fairness. To talk in terms of agreement in all these cases is likely to lead to anomalies. This is particularly so where terms have been implied in the interests of justice and fairness.

---

31 See Phang, 1990.

Terms implied in fact

These are terms implied on a one-off basis so as to give effect to the presumed intention of both parties. For the most part, such terms need to be so obvious that, if an officious bystander suggested the term should be implied, both parties would immediately agree to its implication.[32] It is apparently insufficient that the term sought to be implied is a reasonable one[33] as this might be seen to involve the court in the process of making a contract for the parties.

(The facts of the following case are immaterial.)

Shirlaw v Southern Foundries (1926) Ltd [1939] 2 All ER 113; affd [1940] AC 701

> **Mackinnon LJ (p 124):** I recognise that the right or duty of a court to find the existence of an implied term or implied terms in a written contract is a matter to be exercised with care, and a court is too often invited to do so upon vague and uncertain grounds. Too often, also, such an invitation is backed by the citation of a sentence or two from the judgment of Bowen LJ, in *The Moorcock*. They are sentences from an *extempore* judgment as sound and sensible as are all the utterances of that great judge, but I fancy that he would have been rather surprised if he could have foreseen that these general remarks of his would come to be a favourite citation of a supposed principle of law, and I even think that he might sympathise with the occasional impatience of his successors when *The Moorcock* is so often flashed before them in that guise. For my part, I think that there is a test that may be at least as useful as such generalities. If I may quote from an essay which I wrote some years ago, I then said: '*Prima facie*, that which in any contract is left to be implied and need not be expressed is something so obvious that it goes without saying.'
>
> Thus, if, while the parties were making their bargain, an officious bystander were to suggest some express provision for it in their agreement, they would testily suppress him with a common: 'Oh, of course.' At least it is true, I think, that, if a term were never implied by a judge unless it could pass that test, he could not be held to be wrong.

The requirement seems to be that both parties must readily agree to the term implied. From this it follows that unawareness of relevant facts may prove fatal, since both parties must be capable of assenting to the term. In *KC Sethia (1944) Ltd v Partabmull Rameshwar*,[34] the sellers of a quantity of Indian jute were unable to perform the contract of sale because they had failed to obtain a

---

32 *Shirlaw v Southern Foundries (1926) Ltd* [1939] 2 KB 206; affd [1940] AC 701. See, also, *Marcan Shipping Ltd v Polish SS Co, The Manifest Lipkowy* [1989] 2 Lloyd's Rep 138.

33 *Reigate v Union Manufacturing Co (Ramsbottom) Ltd* [1918] 1 KB 592; *Trollope and Colls Ltd v North Western Metropolitan Regional Hospital Board* [1973] 1 WLR 601; *Liverpool City Council v Irwin* [1977] AC 239.

34 [1950] 1 All ER 51; affd [1951] 2 Lloyd's Rep 89.

quota for sale to Italy. The Italian buyers were unaware of any regulations imposing quotas; therefore, it was held that no term could be implied that the contract was subject to quota.

Moreover, if one of the parties probably would not have agreed to the implication of the term, the court is unlikely to make the implication, even it it appears reasonable to do so.

In *Shell (UK) Ltd v Lostock Garage Ltd*,[35] the defendants had agreed to obtain their supplies of petrol and oil solely from Shell. During a petrol price war, Shell gave subsidies to some of its garages, but not to the defendants, at a time when independent garages were also offering subsidies. The defendants obtained supplies of petrol from another source. In an action by Shell to obtain an injunction, the defendants argued that a term should be implied that Shell would not abnormally discriminate against them. It was held that, as desirable as such a term might seem, one could not be implied, because Shell probably would not have agreed to it had it been suggested by an officious bystander:

Shell (UK) Ltd v Lostock Garage Ltd [1977] 1 All ER 481, CA, p 486

Lord Denning MR:

Implied terms

It was submitted by counsel for Lostock that there was to be implied in the solus agreement a term that Shell, as the supplier, should not abnormally discriminate a against the buyer and/or should supply petrol to the buyer on terms which did not abnormally discriminate against him. He said that Shell had broken that implied term by giving support to the two Shell garages and refusing it to Lostock; that, on that ground, Shell were in breach of the solus agreement; and that Lostock were entitled to terminate it.

This submission makes it necessary once again to consider the law as to implied terms. I ventured with some trepidation to suggest that terms implied by law could be brought within one comprehensive category, in which the courts could imply a term such as was just and reasonable in the circumstances: see *Greaves & Co (Contractors) Ltd v Baynham Meikle & Partners; Liverpool City Council v Irwin*. But, as I feared, the House of Lords have rejected it as quite unacceptable. As I read the speeches, there are two broad categories of implied terms.

(i) The first category

The first category comprehends all those relationships which are of common occurrence, such as the relationship of seller and buyer, owner and hirer, master and servant, landlord and tenant, carrier by land or by sea, contractor for building works, and so forth. In all those relationships the courts have imposed obligations on one party or the other, saying they are implied terms. These obligations are not founded on the intention of the parties, actual or presumed, but on more general considerations, see *Luxor (Eastbourne) Ltd v*

35 [1977] 1 All ER 481, CA.

Cooper per Lord Wright; *Lister v Romford Ice and Cold Storage Co, per* Viscount Simonds and Lord Tucker (both of whom give interesting illustrations); *Liverpool City Council v Irwin, per* Lord Cross of Chelsea and Lord Edmund-Davies. In such relationships, the problem is not solved by asking: 'what did the parties intend?' or 'would they have unhesitatingly agreed to it, if asked?'. It is to be solved by asking: 'Has the law already defined the obligation or the extent of it?' If so, let it be followed. If not, look to see what would be reasonable in the general run of such cases (see *per* Lord Cross of Chelsea) and then say what the obligation shall be. The House in *Liverpool City Council v Irwin* went through that very process. They examined the existing law of landlord and tenant, in particular that relating to easements, to see if it contained the solution to the problem; and, having found that it did not, they imposed an obligation on the landlord to use reasonable care. In these relationships the parties can exclude or modify the obligation by express words, but unless they do so, the obligation is a legal incident of the relationship which is attached by the law itself and not by reason of any implied term.

Likewise, in the general law of contract, the legal effect of frustration does not depend on an implied term. It does not depend on the presumed intention of the parties, nor on what they would have answered, if asked, but simply on what the court itself declares to amount to a frustration: see *Davis Contractors v Fareham Urban District Council per* Lord Radcliffe; *Ocean Tramp Tankers Corpn v V/O Sovfracht, The Eugenia.*

(ii) The second category

The second category comprehends those cases which are not within the first category. These are cases, not of common occurrence, in which from the particular circumstances a term is to be implied. In these cases the implication is based on an intention imputed to the parties from their actual circumstances: see *Luxor (Eastbourne) Ltd v Cooper, per* Lord Wright. Such an imputation is only to be made when it is necessary to imply a term to give efficacy to the contract and make it a workable agreement in such manner as the parties would clearly have done if they had applied their mind to the contingency which has arisen. These are the 'officious bystander' type of case: see *Lister v Romford Ice & Cold Storage Co, per* Lord Tucker. In such cases, a term is not to be implied on the ground that it would be reasonable, but only when it is necessary and can be formulated with a sufficient degree of precision. This was the test applied by the majority of this court in *Liverpool City Council v Irwin*; and they were emphatically upheld by the House on this point; see *per* Lord Cross of Chelsea and Lord Edmund-Davies.

There is this point to be noted about *Liverpool City Council v Irwin*. In this court, the argument was only about an implication in the second category. In the House of Lords that argument was not pursued. It was only the first category.

Into which of the two categories does the present case come? I am tempted to say that a solus agreement between supplier and buyer is of such common occurrence nowadays that it could be put into the first category; so that the law could imply a term based on general considerations. But I do not think this would be found acceptable. Nor do I think the case can be brought within the second category. If Shell had been asked at the beginning, 'Will you agree not to discriminate abnormally against the buyer?', I think they would have declined. It might be a reasonable term, but it is not a necessary term. Nor can it be formulated with sufficient precision. On this point I agree with Kerr J. It should be noticed that in *Esso Petroleum Co Ltd v Harper's Garage (Stourport) Ltd* Mocatta J also refused to make such an implication and there was no appeal from his decision.

In the circumstances, I do not think any term can be implied.

An alternative to the officious bystander test is one to the effect that a term may be implied in order to give business efficacy to the transaction.[36]

In *The Moorcock*,[37] the plaintiffs had entered a contract with the defendants under which it was agreed that the plaintiffs' vessel would discharge and load a cargo at the defendants' wharf. Both parties were aware that there was a danger of grounding at low tide. Because of a failure to take care on the part of the defendants, the plaintiffs' vessel was damaged at low tide due to the unevenness of the river bed. The contract made no express provision for this event, but it was held that a term could be implied to the effect that the defendants would take reasonable care to see that the berth at the jetty was safe to use:

The Moorcock (1889) 14 PD 64, CA, p 68

Bowen LJ: The question which arises here is whether when a contract is made to let the use of this jetty to a ship which can only use it as is known by *both* parties, by taking the ground, there is by implied warranty on the part of the owners of the jetty, and, if so, what is the extent of the warranty. Now, an implied warranty, or as it is called a covenant in law, as distinguished from an express contract or express warranty, really is in every instance founded on the presumed intention of the parties and upon reason. It is the implication which the law draws from what must obviously have been the intention of the parties, an implication which the law draws with the object of giving efficacy to the transaction and preventing such a failure of consideration as cannot have been within the contemplation of either of the parties. I believe that if one were to take all the instances, and they are many, of implied warranties and covenants in law, it will be seen that in all these cases the law is raising an implication from the presumed intention of the parties with the object of giving to the transaction such efficacy as both parties must have intended it should have. In business transactions such as this what the law desires to effect by the implication is to give such business efficacy to the transaction as must have been intended by both parties; not to impose on one side all the perils of the transaction, or to emancipate one side from all the chances of failure, but to

---

36 *The Moorcock* (1889) 14 PD 64, p 68, *per* Bowen LJ; *Luxor (Eastbourne) Ltd v Cooper* [1941] AC 108, p 137, *per* Lord Wright; *Barrett v Lounova (1982) Ltd* [1989] 1 WLR 137, p 141, *per* Kerr LJ.

37 (1889) 14 PD 64.

make each party promise in law as much, at all events, as it must have been in the contemplation of both parties that he should be responsible for, in respect of those perils or chances

Now what did each party in the present case know? Because, if we are examining into their presumed intention, we must examine into their minds as to what the transaction was. Both parties knew that the jetty was let for the purpose of profit and knew that it could only be used by the ship taking the ground and lying on the ground. They must have known that it was by grounding that she would use the jetty. They must have known, both of them, that, unless the ground was safe, the ship would be simply buying an opportunity of danger, and that all consideration would fail unless the ground was safe. In fact, the business of the jetty could not be carried on except on such a basis. The master and crew of the ship could know nothing, whereas the defendants or their servants might, by exercising reasonable care, know everything. The defendants or their servants were on the spot at high and low tide, morning and evening. They must know what had happened to the ships that had used the jetty before, and with the slightest trouble they could satisfy themselves in case of doubt, whether the berth was or not safe. The ship's owner, on the other hand, had not the means of verifying the state of the jetty, because the berth itself might be occupied by another ship at any moment.

Now the question is how much of the peril or the safety of this berth is it necessary to assume that the shipowner and the jetty owner intended respectively to bear – in order that such a minimum of efficacy should be secured for the transaction, as both parties must have intended it to bear. Assume that the berth outside had been actually under the control of the owners of the jetty, that they could, of course, have repaired it and made it fit for the purpose of loading and unloading. If this had been the case, it seems to me that *Mersey Docks Trustees v Gibbs* ((1866) LR 1 HL 93) shows that those who owned the jetty, who take money for its use, and who have under their control the *locus in quo*, are bound to take all reasonable care to prevent danger to those using the jetty, either to make the berth good or else not to invite ships to go to the jetty, that is, either to make it safe or to advise ships not to go there. But there is a distinction in the present instance. The berth here was not under the actual control of the defendants. The berth is in the bed of the river and it may be said that those owning the jetty have no duty cast upon them by statute or common law to repair the bed of the river, and that they have no power to interfere with it except with the licence of the Conservators. Now it does make a difference where the entire control of the *locus in quo*, be it canal, or dock or river, is not under the control of the persons who are taking * for accommodation which involve its user, and, therefore, we must modify, to a certain extent, our view of the necessary implication which the law would make in the present case as to the duties of the parties receiving the remuneration. We must do so for the reason laid down by Holt CJ, in his famous judgment in *Coggs v Bernard* (2 Ld Raym 918) where he says: '... it would be unreasonable to charge persons with a trust further than the nature of the thing puts it in their power to perform.'

Applying that modification, which is a reasonable modification, to this case, it may well be said that the law will not imply that the persons, who had not control of the place, have taken reasonable care to make it good, but it does not follow that they are relieved from all responsibility, a responsibility. They are on the spot. They must know that the jetty cannot be used unless reasonable care is taken, if not to make it safe, at all events to see whether it is safe. No one can tell whether reasonable safety has been secured except themselves, and I think that, if they let out their jetty for use, they at all events imply that they have taken reasonable care to see that the berth, which is the essential part of the use of the jetty, is safe, and, if it is not safe, and if they have not taken such reasonable care, it is their duty to warn persons with whom they have dealings that they have not done so. This is a business transaction as to which the parties may at any moment make any bargain they please, and either side may by the contract throw upon the other the burden of the unseen and existing danger.

The question is what inference is to be drawn where the parties are dealing with each other on the assumption that the negotiations are to have some fruit, and where they say nothing about the burden of this kind of unseen peril, leaving the law to raise such inferences as are reasonable from the very nature of this transaction. So far as I am concerned, I do not wish it to be understood that I at all consider this is a case of a duty on the part of the defendants to see that the access to the jetty is kept clear. The difference between access to the jetty and the use of the jetty seems to me, as Mr Finlay says it is, only a question of degree, but when you are dealing with implications which the law prescribes, you cannot afford to neglect questions of degree, and it is just that difference of degree which brings one case on the line and prevents another from approaching it. I confess that on the broad view of this case I think that business could not be carried on unless there was an implication of, at all events, in a case where a jetty, to the extent I have laid down, is to be used like the present one. Therefore, although this case is a novel one, I feel no difficulty in drawing the inference that this case comes within the line.

Whether there is a difference between the two tests is a moot point. It has been said that the bystander test is broader than the efficacy test in that the former involves an objective, reasonable man approach and that the latter is a more stringent test, operating only in order to make a contract workable.[38] Conversely, the view has been expressed that the two tests are the same, namely that in order to give business efficacy to the contract a term may be implied where the parties, as reasonable men, would have agreed to its implication without hesitation.[39] However, there are differences between the tests, since the efficacy test appears to have little to do with the intentions of the parties.

---

38 *Associated Japanese Bank (International) Ltd v Crédit du Nord SA* [1989] 1 WLR 255, p 263, *per* Steyn J.

39 *Liverpool City Council v Irwin* [1977] AC 239, p 258, *per* Lord Cross; *Bank of Nova Scotia v Hellenic Mutual War Risks Association, The Good Luck* [1989] 3 All ER 628, p 665, *per* May LJ.

It seems that if either test is satisfied, a term may be implied.[40] However, the difficulty here is that the officious bystander test is based on the presumed intention of both parties, whereas to make a contract workable under the efficacy test involves consideration of what the reasonable person considers necessary and involves imposing an obligation, despite the intentions of the parties.[41] What does appear to flow from both tests is that a term cannot be implied simply because it is reasonable to do so. However, the language used by the courts sometimes suggests that reasonable terms may be implied.

When Bowen LJ in *The Moorcock* referred to a covenant in law and to the implication of terms on the grounds of reason, he appeared not to be exclusively concerned with the intention of the parties. In the circumstances, it would be difficult to say that the officious bystander test had been satisfied, since one of the parties might not have agreed to the implication of such a term. From this, it follows that the parties' intentions are not always crucial in deciding what obligations should be implied. Instead, it seems that, in appropriate circumstances, a term can be implied where it is reasonable to do so, for example, to give business efficacy to a transaction. Certainly, the term implied in *The Moorcock* was regarded by Bowen LJ as a reasonable modification to the arrangements made by the parties.[42]

Evidence that a court may sometimes imply a reasonable term in a contract can be found in cases where the parties to a contract cannot agree on the price to be paid for the thing sold. For a long time, there was a rule to the effect that, if a contract provided for a method of ascertaining the price but that method could not be put into effect, the court would not substitute an alternative method even where one of the parties was at fault. However, in *Sudbrook Trading Estate Ltd v Eggleton*,[43] an option to purchase the reversion of a number of leases provided that the price payable should be determined by valuers, one to be nominated by each of the parties. The lessors refused to appoint a valuer. The House of Lords held that, on its true construction, the contract was for a sale at a fair and reasonable price. Provided all other necessary preconditions had been satisfied, the court could substitute its own machinery so as to ascertain a fair and reasonable price. It was considered important that the parties had chosen to have the price assessed by

---

40 *Marcan Shipping Ltd v Polish SS Co, The Manifest Lipkowy* [1989] 2 Lloyd's Rep 138, p 142, *per* May LJ.

41 *Barrett v Lounova (1982) Ltd* [1989] 2 WLR 137. Arguably, this case is more indicative of a term imposed by law, analogising a tenancy falling outside what is now the Landlord and Tenant Act 1985, s 11, with tenancies falling within s 11.

42 (1886) 14 PD 64, p 70. There is significant (perhaps not wholly unintended) ambiguity in Bowen LJ's judgment on this point. Eg, at p 68, he states that the implied term is based on the presumed intention of the parties, whilst, at p 70, he states that 'the law [must] raise such inferences as are reasonable from the very nature of the transaction'.

43 [1983] 1 AC 444.

professional valuers who would apply objective standards in coming to their assessment.[44]

However, it is clear that, were the language used by the parties explicit and clear, it is largely impossible to imply 'reasonable' terms which contradict the clear language of the contract. If a builder agrees to construct the walls of a house using nine inch brick and he complies with the contract specification, a term that the house will be reasonably fit for habitation may not be implied.[45] The reason for this is that the implication of such a term would be inconsistent with the express terms of the contract.[46] However, consistent with what was said in *The Moorcock*, the builder may be under a duty to warn the plaintiff that the design of the house is defective. Furthermore, if there is no express contrary provision in the contract, a court may be willing to imply a term to the effect that a building is fit for habitation.[47]

Terms implied in law

Many contractual obligations arise out of rules of law imposed upon the parties either by statute or by the court acting out of necessity. In these circumstances, any resort to the notion of agreement as an explanation of the source of the obligation is unhelpful, since these obligations are imposed by operation of law.

The clearest examples of legally imposed contractual obligations can be found in statutory provisions. For example, in sale of goods transactions, ss 12–15 of the Sale of Goods Act 1979 imply terms relating to title, description, quality and fitness. If the contract is one for the supply of a service, there are implied terms concerning the exercise of reasonable care and skill, the charge payable and the time taken to render the service under ss 13–15 of the Supply of Goods and Services Act 1982:

Sale of Goods Act 1979

13 Sale by description

(1) Where there is a contract for the sale of goods by description, there is an implied term that the goods will correspond with the description.

(1A) As regards England and Wales and Northern Ireland, the term implied by sub-s (1) above is a condition.

---

44 [1983] 1 AC 444, p 479, *per* Lord Diplock; p 483, *per* Lord Fraser of Tullybelton. See, also, p 486, *per* Lord Russell of Killowen.

45 *Lynch v Thorne* [1956] 1 All ER 744.

46 *Johnstone v Bloomsbury Health Authority* [1991] 2 WLR 1362, p 1372, *per* Leggatt LJ.

47 *Basildon District Council v JE Lesser (Properties) Ltd* [1985] 1 All ER 20.

(2) If the sale is by sample as well as by description, it is not sufficient that the bulk of the goods corresponds with the sample if the goods do not also correspond with the description.

(3) A sale of goods is not prevented from being a sale by description by reason only that, being exposed for sale or hire, they are selected by the buyer.

14 Implied terms about quality or fitness

(1) Except as provided by this section and s 15 below and subject to any other enactment, there is no implied term about the quality or fitness for any particular purpose of goods supplied under a contract of sale.

(2) Where the seller sells goods in the course of a business, there is an implied term that the goods supplied under the contract are of satisfactory quality.

(2A) For the purposes of this Act, goods are of satisfactory quality if they meet the standard that a reasonable person would regard as satisfactory, taking account of any description of the goods, the price (if relevant) and all the other relevant circumstances.

(2B) For the purposes of this Act, the quality of goods includes their state and condition and the following (among others) are in appropriate cases aspects of the quality of goods:

(a) fitness for all the purposes for which goods of the kind in question are commonly supplied;

(b) appearance and finish;

(c) freedom from minor defects;

(d) safety; and

(e) durability.

(2C) The term implied by sub-s (2) above does not extend to any matter making the quality of goods unsatisfactory:

(a) which is specifically drawn to the buyer's attention before the contract is made;

(b) where the buyer examines the goods before the contract is made, which that examination ought to reveal; or

(c) in the case of a contract for sale by sample, which would have been apparent on a reasonable examination of the sample.

(3) Where the seller sells goods in the course of a business and the buyer, expressly or by implication, makes known:

(a) to the seller; or

(b) where the purchase price or part of it is payable by instalments and the goods were previously sold by a credit-broker to the seller, to that credit-broker, any particular purpose for which the goods are being bought, there is an implied term that the goods supplied under the contract are reasonably fit for that purpose, whether or not that is a purpose for which such goods are commonly supplied, except where the circumstances show that the buyer does not rely, or that it is unreasonable for him to rely, on the skill or judgment of the seller or credit-broker.

(4) An implied term about quality or fitness for a particular purpose may be annexed to a contract of sale by usage.

(5) The preceding provisions of this section apply to a sale by a person who in the course of a business is acting as agent for another as they apply to a sale by a principal in the course of a business, except where that other is not selling in the course of a business and either the buyer knows that fact or reasonable steps are taken to bring it to the notice of the buyer before the contract is made.

(6) As regards England and Wales and Northern Ireland, the terms implied by sub-ss (2) and (3) above are conditions.

(7) Paragraph 5 of Sched 1 below applies in relation to a contract made on or after 18 May 1973 and before the appointed day, and para 6 in relation to one made before 18 May 1973.

(8) In sub-s (7) above and para 5 of Sched 1 below, references to the appointed day are to the day appointed for the purposes of those provisions by an order of the Secretary of State made by statutory instrument.

15 Sale by sample

(1) A contract of sale is a contract for sale by sample where there is an express or implied term to that effect in the contract.

(2) In the case of a contract for sale by sample there is an implied [term]:

    (a) that the bulk will correspond with the sample in quality;

    ...

    (c) that the goods will be free from any defect, making their quality unsatisfactory which would not be apparent on reasonable examination of the sample.

(3) As regards England and Wales and Northern Ireland, the term implied by sub-s (2) above is a condition.

15A Modification of remedies for breach of condition in non-consumer cases

(1) Where in the case of a contract of sale:

    (a) the buyer would, apart from this subsection, have the right to reject goods by reason of a breach on the part of the seller of a term implied by s 13, 14 or 15 above, but;

    (b) the breach is so slight that it would be unreasonable for him to reject them, then, if the buyer does not deal as consumer, the breach is not to be treated as a breach of condition but may be treated as a breach of warranty.

(2) This section applies unless a contrary intention appears in, or is to be implied from, the contract.

(3) It is for the seller to show that a breach fell within sub-s (1)(b) above.

(4) This section does not apply to Scotland.

Supply of Goods and Services Act 1982

13 Implied term about care and skill

In a contract for the supply of a service where the supplier is acting in the course of a business, there is an implied term that the supplier will carry out the service with reasonable care and skill.

14 Implied term about time of performance

See above.

15 Implied term about consideration

See above.

In addition to express statutory provisions, terms may be implied where they are necessary consequences of distinct types of legal relationships. As Lord Denning MR put it in *Shell (UK) Ltd v Lostock Garage Ltd* (see fn 50, below) 'relationships of common occurrence'. Thus, there are terms which necessarily arise out of the relationship between the supplier and the consumer of goods and services, an employer and an employee, a landlord and a tenant, and a builder and the person who commissions the building. In cases of this kind, the court examines earlier authorities and the general policy of the law to decide what obligations the law imposes. The main difficulty in this regard is whether the contract entered into is one which is of a defined type. For example, the contract may be one between banker and customer but, at the same time, is so carefully drawn up on a one-off basis that it falls outside the general class.[48] But there appears to be an alternative approach to the problem in that new fact situations may be promoted to the status of a defined type of contract. Thus, a contract for the sale and purchase of travellers' cheques has been described as self-evidently such a contract,[49] although the issue of whether a solus agreement was of a defined class seemed to cause much greater difficulty some 13 years earlier.[50]

In the case of the employer/employee relationship, it is regarded as implicit the contract that the employee is reasonably skilled,[51] that the employee will act in good faith[52] and will faithfully serve his employer,[53] and that he will indemnify his employer against liabilities incurred due to his

---

48 *National Bank of Greece SA v Pinios Shipping Co (No 1), The Maira* [1989] 1 All ER 213, p 219, *per* Lloyd LJ.

49 *El Awadi v Bank of Credit and Commerce International SA* [1989] 1 All ER 242, p 253, *per* Hutchinson J.

50 *Shell (UK) Ltd v Lostock Garage Ltd* [1977] 1 All ER 481. Even Lord Denning felt (at p 488) that, although such a conclusion 'tempted' him, he did 'not think [it] would be found acceptable'.

51 *Harmer v Cornelius* (1858) 5 CB (NS) 236.

52 *Robb v Green* [1895] 2 QB 315.

53 *Hivac Ltd v Park Royal Scientific Instruments Ltd* [1946] Ch 169.

wrongful act.[54] In return, the employer is under a duty, *inter alia*, to provide a safe place of work.[55]

The legal incidents of the landlord and tenant relationship consist of, *inter alia*, a covenant that the tenant will enjoy quiet possession; that a furnished property will be reasonably fit for habitation; that the landlord will not frustrate the use of the land for the purpose for which it was let, and that the landlord will keep any common areas in a reasonable state of repair. The tenant also owes certain obligations which are referred to as implied terms. For example, he must not commit waste by pulling down or altering property and he must keep the premises in a good state of repair.

After an examination of earlier authorities, it may be discovered that there is no guidance on whether a particular term can be implied. Here, the court may imply terms on the basis of necessity, but implying a term simply because it is reasonable to do so, is apparently not permitted.

In *Liverpool City Council v Irwin*,[56] the local authority had let a flat in a tower block to the appellant. The tenancy agreement consisted of a list of tenants' obligations with no corresponding landlord's duties. Due to the actions of vandals, certain common areas, including lifts, stairways and rubbish chutes, became either inoperative or unsafe to use. As a protest against these conditions, the defendant refused to pay his rent and the council sought to regain possession of the flat. The council had sent workmen on a regular basis to repair damage caused to the common areas, but they were unable to keep pace with the damage caused. The appellant asked for the implication of a term that he would have quiet enjoyment of the property. The House of Lords held that the nature of the contract implicitly required the landlord to exercise reasonable care to maintain the common areas. However, nothing more than this was necessary, therefore the council was not under an absolute obligation to maintain the services concerned:

Liverpool City Council v Irwin [1977] AC 239, p 252

Lord Wilberforce: I consider first the appellants' claim insofar as it is based on contract. The first step must be to ascertain what the contract is. This may look elementary, even naive, but it seems to me to be the essential step and to involve, from the start, an approach different, if simpler, from that taken by the members of the Court of Appeal. We look first at documentary material. As is common with council lettings there is no formal demise or lease or tenancy agreement. There is a document headed 'Liverpool Corporation, Liverpool City Housing Department' and described as 'Conditions of Tenancy'. This contains a list of obligations on the tenant – he shall do this, he shall not do that, or he shall not do that without the corporation's consent. This is an

---

54 *Lister v Romford Ice and Cold Storage Ltd* [1957] AC 555.
55 *Matthews v Kuwait Bechtel Corpn* [1959] 2 QB 57.
56 [1977] AC 239.

amalgam of obligations added to from time to time, no doubt, to meet complaints, emerging situations, or problems as they appear to the council's officers. In particular there have been added special provisions relating to multi-storey flats which are supposed to make the conditions suitable to such dwellings. We may note under 'Further special notes' some obligations not to obstruct staircases and passages, and not to permit children under 10 to operate any lifts. I mention these as a recognition of the existence and relevance of these facilities. At the end there is a form for signature by the tenant stating that he accepts the tenancy. On the landlords' side, there is nothing, no signature, no demise, no covenant; the contract takes effect as soon as the tenants sign the form and are let into possession.

We have then a contract which is partly, but not wholly, stated in writing. In order to complete it, in particular to give it a bilateral character, it is necessary to take account of the actions of the parties and the circumstances. As actions of the parties, we must note the granting of possession by the corporation and reservation by it of the 'common parts' – stairs, lifts, chutes, etc As circumstances we must include the nature of the premises, viz a maisonette for family use on the ninth floor of a high block, one which is occupied by a large number of other tenants, all using the common parts and dependant on them, none of them having any expressed obligation to maintain or repair them.

To say that the construction of a complete contract out of these elements involves a process of 'implication' may be correct: it would be so if implication means the supplying of what is not expressed. But there are varieties of implications which the courts think fit to make and they do not necessarily involve the same process. Where there is, on the face of it, a complete, bilateral contract, the courts are sometimes willing to add terms to it, as implied terms: this is very common in mercantile contracts where there is an established usage: in that case the courts are spelling out what both parties know and would, if asked, unhesitatingly agree to be part of the bargain. In other cases, where there is an apparently complete bargain, the courts are willing to add a term on the ground that without it the contract will not work – this is the case, if not of *The Moorcock* itself on its facts, at least of the doctrine of *The Moorcock* as usually applied. This is, as was pointed out by the majority in the Court of Appeal, a strict test – though the degree of strictness seems to vary with the current legal trend, and I think that they were right not to accept it as applicable here. There is a third variety of implication, that which I think Lord Denning MR favours, or at least did favour in this case, and that is the implication of reasonable terms. But though I agree with many of his instances, which In fact, fall under one or other of the preceding heads, I cannot go so far as to endorse his principle; indeed, it seems to me, with respect, to extend a long, and undesirable, way beyond sound authority.

The present case, in my opinion, represents a fourth category or, I would rather say, a fourth shade on a continuous spectrum. The court here is simply concerned to establish what the contract is, the parties not having themselves fully stated the terms. In this sense the court is searching for what must be implied.

What then should this contract be held to be? There must first be implied a letting, that is, a grant of the right of exclusive possession to the tenants. With this there must, I would suppose, be implied a covenant for quiet enjoyment, as a necessary incident of the letting. The difficulty begins when we consider the common parts. We start with the fact that the demise is useless unless access is obtained by the staircase; we can add that, having regard to the height of the block, and the family nature of the dwellings, the demise would be useless without a lift service; we can continue that there being rubbish chutes built in to the structures and no other means of disposing of light rubbish there must be a right to use the chutes. The question to be answered – and it is the only question in this case – is what is to be the legal relationship between landlord and tenant as regards these matters.

There can be no doubt that there must be implied: (i) an easement for the tenants and their licensees to use the stairs; (ii) a right in the nature of an easement to use the lifts; and (iii) an easement to use the rubbish chutes.

But are these easements to be accompanied by any obligation on the landlord, and what obligation? There seem to be two alternatives. The first, for which the corporation contends, is for an easement coupled with no legal obligation, except such as may arise under the Occupiers' Liability Act 1957 as regards the safety of those using the facilities, and possibly such other liability as might exist under the ordinary law of tort. The alternative is for easements coupled with some obligation on the part of the landlords as regards the maintenance of the subject of them, so that they are available for use.

My Lords, in order to be able to choose between these, it is necessary to define what test is to be applied, and I do not find this difficult. In my opinion such obligation should be read into the contract as the nature of the contract itself implicitly requires, no more, no less; a test in other words of necessity. The relationship accepted by the corporation is that of landlord and tenant; the tenant accepts obligations accordingly, in relation, *inter alia*, to the stairs, the lifts and the chutes. All these are not just facilities, or conveniences provided at discretion; they are essentials of the tenancy without which life in the dwellings, as a tenant, is not possible. To leave the landlord free of contractual obligation as regards these matters, and subject only to administrative or political pressure, is, in my opinion, totally inconsistent with the nature of this relationship. The subject matter of the lease (high-rise blocks) and the relationship created by the tenancy demands, of its nature, some contractual obligation on the landlord.

I do not think that this approach involves any innovation as regards the law of contract. The necessity to have regard to the inherent nature of a contract and of the relationship thereby established was stated in this House in *Lister v Romford Ice & Cold Storage Co Ltd*. That was a case between master and servant and of a search for an 'implied term'. Viscount Simonds made a clear distinction between a search for an implied term such as might be necessary to give 'business efficacy' to the particular contract and a search, based on wider consideration, for such a term as the nature of the contract might call for, or as a legal incident of this kind of contract. If the search were for the former, he said: 'I should lose myself in the attempt to formulate it with the necessary precision'. We see an echo of this in the present case, when the majority in the Court of Appeal, considering a 'business efficacy term', that is a *'Moorcock'* term, found themselves faced with five alternative terms and therefore rejected all of them. But that is not, in my opinion, the end, or indeed the object, of the search ...

It remains to define the standard. My Lords, if, as I think, the test of the existence of the term is necessity the standard must surely not exceed what is necessary having regard to the circumstances. To imply an absolute obligation to repair would go beyond what is a necessary legal incident and would indeed be unreasonable. An obligation to take reasonable care to keep in reasonable repair and usability is what fits the requirements of the case. Such a definition involves – and I think rightly – recognition that the tenants themselves have their responsibilities. What it is reasonable to expect of a landlord has a clear relation to what a reasonable set of tenants should do for themselves.

I would hold therefore that the corporation's obligation is as I have described.

Lord Cross (p 257): When it implies a term in a contract the court is sometimes laying down a general rule that in all contracts of a certain type – sale of goods, master and servant, landlord and tenant, and so on – some provision is to be implied unless the parties have expressly excluded it. In deciding whether or not to lay down such a *prima facie* rule the court will naturally ask itself whether in the general run of such cases the term in question would be one which it would be reasonable to insert. Sometimes, however, there is no question of laying down any *prima facie* rule applicable to all cases of a defined type but what the court is being in effect asked to do is to rectify a particular – often a very detailed – contract by inserting in it a term which the parties have not expressed. Here it is not enough for the court to say that the suggested term is a reasonable one the presence of which would make the contract a better or fairer one: it must be able to say that the insertion of the term is necessary to give – as it is put – 'business efficacy' to the contract and that if its absence had been pointed out at the time both parties – assuming them to have been reasonable men – would have agreed without hesitation to its insertion. The distinction between the two types of case was pointed out by Viscount Simonds and Lord Tucker in their speeches in *Lister v Romford Ice and Cold Storage Co Ltd*, but I think that Lord Denning MR in proceeding – albeit with some trepidation – to 'kill off' Mackinnon LJ's 'officious bystander' must have overlooked it. Counsel for the appellants did not In fact, rely on this passage in the speech of Lord Denning MR. His main argument was that when a landlord lets a number of flats or offices to a number of different tenants giving all of them rights to use the staircases, corridors and lifts there is to be implied, in the absence of any provision to the contrary, an obligation on the landlord to keep the 'common parts' in repair and the lifts in working order. But, for good measure, he also submitted that he could succeed on the 'officious bystander' test.

I have no hesitation in rejecting this alternative submission. We are not here dealing with an ordinary commercial contract by which a property company is letting one of its flats for profit. The corporation is a public body charged by law with the duty of providing housing for members of the public selected because of their need for it at rents which are subsidised by the general body of ratepayers. Moreover, the officials in the corporation's housing department would know very well that some of the tenants in any given block might subject the chutes and lifts to rough treatment and that there was an ever-present danger of deliberate damage by young 'vandals' – some of whom might, in fact, be children of the tenants in that or neighbouring blocks. In these circumstances, if at the time when the appellants were granted their tenancy one of them had said to the corporation's representative: 'I suppose that the council will be under a legal liability to us to keep the chutes and the lifts in working order and the staircases properly lighted', the answer might well have been – indeed I think, as Roskill LJ thought, in all probability would have been – 'Certainly not'. The official might have added in explanation: 'Of course, we do not expect our tenants to keep them in repair themselves – though we do expect them to use them with care and to co-operate in combatting vandalism.'

In deciding what terms are necessary, the court will take into account general policy considerations. To this extent, the court does consider what is reasonable in the circumstances. It may be argued that the House of Lords' insistence that a term must be necessary before it will be implied is simply resorting to the pure fiction that courts will not make a contract for the parties. Certainly, there can be no doubt that, in cases where the court enquires what are the general incidents of a particular relationship, it is quite possible that the officious bystander test will not be satisfied.[57] If the court is engaged in a process of taking policy considerations into account, what it is asking is whether a legal duty should be imposed upon one of the parties to a contract. For example, in *Lister v Romford Ice and Cold Storage Co Ltd*,[58] the appellant was employed by the respondents as a lorry driver. In the course of his employment, he negligently injured his father, a fellow employee. The father successfully sued the respondents, who sued the appellant for his breach of contract. The appellant argued that there should be an implied term that the respondents should indemnify him against liability he might incur in the course of his employment if they were insured against the risk concerned. The House of Lords decided in favour of the respondents, holding that, while an employee impliedly undertakes to use reasonable care and skill, no term could be implied on the part of the employer that he would grant an indemnity to the employee. Some of the justifications for this decision were couched in terms of the officious bystander test. For example, it was said that both parties would not have agreed to the term.[59] However, this was not the real issue. An argument which was particularly persuasive was that it would

---

57 [1977] AC 239, p 253, *per* Lord Wilberforce.

58 [1957] AC 555.

59 *Ibid*, p 578, *per* Viscount Simonds.

be undesirable to allow a driver to be indemnified by his employer because he might then drive less carefully. In this respect, the court was not concerned with terms implied in fact, but rather with the question whether a term in law should be implied. But if this is the case, the policy issue is perhaps one which ought to be resolved by Parliament rather than the courts.

The implication arising from the decision in Irwin is that there is a difference between the officious bystander test and that based on necessity. This distinction is also borne out by a later decision in the House of Lords, where it has been observed that there is a difference between 'the search for a term necessary to give business efficacy to a particular contract and the search, based on wider considerations, for a term which the law will imply as a necessary incident of a definable category of contractual relationship'.[60] The problem with this view is that the word 'necessary' is used in the formulation of both tests which would seem to suggest a degree of duplication in the apparently quite different tests for implying a term in a contract.

Phang illustrates the problems which may flow from this apparent confusion:

> In *Scally v Southern Health and Social Services Board*, the plaintiffs sued the defendant health boards for breach of contract, negligence and breach of statutory duty, alleging that the latter had failed to adequately advise and inform them of their statutory and contractual rights to purchase added years at advantageous rates in order to ensure the reception of full benefits under a statutory superannuation scheme which required a total of 40 years' contributory service. The House of Lords held that, whilst there had been no breach of statutory duty, the defendants were nevertheless in breach of an implied term in the respective contracts of employment which placed an obligation on the defendants to take reasonable steps to bring the right of the plaintiffs to purchase added years to the attention of the latter.

> What has not, however, been clarified is the actual practical criterion to be applied. It is clear that the criterion for the narrower category of terms implied in fact, is that of necessity; however, in so far as the broader category of terms implied in law is concerned, the learned Lord of Appeal says, 'I fully appreciate that the criterion to justify an implication of this kind is necessity, not reasonableness'.

> Lord Bridge based his decision on the broader category of terms implied in law. Whilst acknowledging that the invocation of terms implied in fact (premised on the narrower business efficacy test) was a possibility, the learned Lord of Appeal was nevertheless of the view that 'this may be stretching the doctrine of implication for the sake of business efficacy beyond its proper reach'. What is of particular interest is Lord Bridge's formulation of the distinction between terms implied in fact, and terms implied in law which he surprisingly characterised as a 'clear distinction' – in his words, the (respective) distinction was 'between the search for an implied term necessary to give

---

60 *Scally v Southern Health and Social Services Board* [1991] 3 WLR 778, p 787, *per* Lord Bridge.

business efficacy to a particular contract and the search, based on wider considerations, for a term which the law will imply as a necessary incident of a definable category of contractual relationship'. He was of the view that '[i]f any implication is appropriate here, it is, I think, of this latter type'.

This suggests that the touchstone even for terms implied in law is *also* that of 'necessity,' thus, replicating the very same confusion engendered by Lord Wilberforce in the *Liverpool City Council* case. Not surprisingly, Lord Bridge actually cities, *inter alia*, Lord Wilberforce's speech in the *Liverpool City Council* case as drawing a *'clear* distinction' between terms implied in fact, and terms implied in law. Indeed, it might be added that in the *Tai Hing Cotton Mill* case, Lord Scarman, delivering the judgment of the Board, after citing Lord Wilberforce in the *Liverpool City Council* case, utilises the notion of *'necessary* incident' four times in the following two pages of the reported judgment. The confusion, as I pointed out in the earlier article, lies in allocating the criterion of 'necessity' to both categories, for if the criterion is the same, wherein lies the difference? Further, terms implied in law are predicated on broader considerations of public policy, thus, suggesting that the criterion of *reasonableness* would be a more appropriate rubric to adopt. Yet – as we have seen – Lord Bridge clearly rejects the criterion of reasonableness. I ventured to suggest elsewhere that the criterion of necessity operates differently, depending upon which category of implied terms is involved. In other words – and to make that point clearer – the same concept (here, of 'necessity') may have different meanings in different contexts. In the category of terms implied in fact, the criterion of necessity is a truly narrow one, having regard to the specific position of the contracting parties themselves. Where terms implied in law are concerned, however, the criterion of necessity is a much broader one: the presence (or absence) of necessity is ascertained by reference to not only the category of contract concerned but also to broader policy factors. It is, however, submitted that this adherence to the criterion of necessity in this wider category of terms is, whilst explicable on the basis just proffered, undesirable inasmuch as it leads to semantic and terminological confusion. What is, in substance, being referred to is the criterion of reasonableness. It is true that endorsement of the criterion of reasonableness would be to engender possible undesirable psychological effects (premised on the well-worn but no less significant concept of 'floodgates'). However, clarity should be the overriding consideration. If the criterion of reasonableness is thought unsatisfactory (primarily because of Lord Denning MR's earlier endorsement of it), then some other terminology (such as 'public policy considerations') might be more appropriate. It can, of course, be argued that if the distinction is tolerably clear despite the semantic difficulties, the formulation should be left as it is. This argument is, however, a double-edged one, for if possible linguistic confusion may result, why should the distinction not be made clearer? It is thus, respectfully submitted that a clearer distinction (in the context of practical criteria) ought to be made.[61]

---

61   Phang, 1993, pp 243–46.

Terms implied by custom or out of business practice

In addition to implied terms imposed on the parties by operation of law and those apparently representing the intention of the parties, terms may also be implied by virtue of custom or usage. To regard customary practice as being based on the presumed intention of the parties is somewhat unrealistic. If a custom is regarded as reasonable, it will bind the parties, even though they might not have been aware of it.[62] If the express terms of a contract are inconsistent with some customary practice, then the custom will not be binding, and will be regarded as unreasonable.

Trade usage may be referred to in order to ascertain the content of the contract. For example, trade associations may produce standard form documents for use by members. These standard forms may be taken to represent business practice, thereby containing the relevant contract terms in the event of a dispute.[63]

CLASSIFICATION OF TERMS

How a particular term of the contract is to be classified is important because it impinges on the remedial consequences of a breach of that term. At one stage, the remedy available to a party in the event of a breach of contract by the other would depend on how the broken term was classified. In this regard, English law has drawn a distinction between conditions of the contract and warranties. In purely general terms, the distinction between a condition and a warranty is that a condition is a fundamental term which goes to the root of the contract, whereas a warranty is a subsidiary term, breach of which entitles the party not in breach to damages in respect of any loss occasioned by the breach of warranty.

Since one of the consequences of the classification of a term as a condition is that the innocent party is permitted to discharge himself from the performance of his primary obligations under the contract, it should be clear that a breach of condition must be a serious matter. On occasions, certain obligations are classified by statute as conditions of the contract,[64] in which case, unless the statute provides otherwise,[65] the court has no option but to treat breach of the term as giving rise to a right to treat the primary

---

62   *Smith v Reynolds* (1893) 9 TLR 494.

63   See *British Crane Hire Ltd v Ipswich Plant Hire Ltd* [1975] QB 303, p 311, *per* Lord Denning MR.

64   See, eg, Sale of Goods Act 1979, ss 13(1), 14(2) and 14(3). Contrast the implied terms in the Supply of Goods and Services Act 1982, ss 13, 14 and 15, which are called merely 'terms'.

65   As is now the case in relation to insignificant breaches of the implied terms in sale of goods contracts following the enactment of the new Sale of Goods Act 1979, s 15A(1)(b).

performance obligations of the parties as discharged. In other cases, the parties may have agreed in advance that certain obligations are so important that non-fulfilment would be fatal and there may be provision in the contract allowing for withdrawal in such circumstances. However, as a general rule, the right to treat one's performance obligations as being at an end is regarded as an exceptional remedy as the traditional common law approach is that an award of damages should most frequently be regarded as an adequate remedy. But this begs the question when is an award of damages to be regarded as an inadequate remedy?

The range of tests used to distinguish a breach of condition from a breach of warranty is broad. To start with, there is a statutory definition of a warranty for the purposes of sale of goods contracts, but this provides little help, stating no more than the consequences of a term being a condition or a warranty:

Sale of Goods Act 1979

11

(3) Whether a stipulation in a contract is a condition, the breach of which may give rise to a right to treat the contract as repudiated, or a warranty, the breach of which may give rise to a claim for damages but not to a right to reject the goods and treat the contract as repudiated, depends, in each case on the construction of the contract; and a stipulation may be a condition, though called a warranty in the contract.

The traditional tests[66] employed to distinguish a condition from a warranty include asking whether the breach goes to the root of the contract; whether the breach strikes at an essential or fundamental term; whether the consequences of the breach deprive the innocent party of substantially the whole of the benefit he bargained for;[67] whether the consequences of the breach are such that it would be unfair to the innocent party to hold him to the contract and confine him to an action for damages only.[68] All these matters are discussed more fully in Chapter 9.

---

66 See, further, Chapter 9.
67 See *Hong Kong Fir Shipping Co Ltd v Kawasaki Kisen Kaisha Ltd* [1962] 2 QB 26.
68 See *Decro-Wall International SA v Practitioners in Marketing Ltd* [1971] 2 All ER 216.

CHAPTER 6

UNANTICIPATED RISKS

INTRODUCTION

Where the parties enter into a contractual relationship, it will not always be the case that the contract will be performed without mishap. It has been seen in the previous chapter that disputes may arise based on an alleged failure to perform the contract according to its terms, in which case, the court must interpret the express terms of the contract, or imply terms so as to make sense of the agreement the parties have reached.

This chapter is concerned with the position where the parties discover it is either impossible to perform the contract as originally understood or some external event has rendered performance of the contract radically different from what was originally intended.

In all of these cases, the court must play the role of risk allocator. What has happened is that a risk of loss has emerged and it must be decided by the court where that risk should lie. The classical contract theory epitomised by the rules on offer and acceptance, in their purest sense, dealt with these issues by asking what have the parties agreed. Accordingly, if there was no evidence of any agreement as to how a particular risk of loss should be allocated, the classical response was to treat the loss as lying where it fell. A stark illustration of the point can be found in cases involving what would now be called frustrating events prior to the development of the doctrine of frustration. For example, it was once held that if a sailor agreed, for a lump sum, to work a ship for a complete voyage, he would be entitled to no payment at all unless the voyage was completed, even if the reason for not completing the voyage was that the sailor had been killed *en route*.[1]

PRINCIPLES OF RISK ALLOCATION

Contractual behaviour is very much concerned with risk taking in the sense that the parties to a contract will have expectations as to the outcome of the contracting process, some of which may not be fulfilled.

Non-fulfilment of expectations may arise due to some event beyond the parties' control in which case, the court will have to determine where that risk

---

1   *Paradine v Jane* (1647) 82 ER 897.

of loss should lie. In pursuing this task, an obvious starting point will be to consider the parties' own intentions in relation to the risk, which may be ascertained by reference to the terms of the contract. It can be assumed that rational individuals entering an exchange relationship will have made arrangements for events which create a risk of loss. Accordingly, those who are risk-averse may have made arrangements through the use of *force majeure* clauses, exemption clauses, the designation of a term as a condition or a warranty or a cancellation clause. These and other like devices serve to allocate the risk of loss according to the terms of the contract. If the other party is prepared to accept the risk, the reason may be that he believes he is in a better position to cover the risk by insurance or that he is less risk averse than the other party and is prepared to take the consequences if the risk does arise. Thus, it is important to construe the language of the contract, whether the problem is one of frustration or mistake.[2] For example, if the parties make provision for an event which would not otherwise be regarded as a frustrating event, the court must ask whether the relevant provision is worded so as to cover the event in question. Similar issues also arise in relation to mistakes provided for in the contract. Thus, in *William Sindall plc v Cambridgeshire County Council*,[3] it was held that where a seller of land had limited his liability for defects in title known to him, he would not be liable in respect of an easement of which he had no knowledge.

Another important consideration in the risk allocation process is who is the least cost avoider. A relevant factor in this regard is that one of the parties to a contract may have been in a better position than the other to prevent the risk of loss from materialising, in which case, rules of risk allocation may suggest that he is the person who should accept the risk of loss. Accordingly, it is said that a person who brings about a frustrating event through his own actions cannot rely upon the rules on frustration of contracts, on the basis that English law does not give relief in respect of 'self-induced frustration'.[4] Similarly, a person who could have performed his contractual obligations in some other perfectly reasonable manner may be required to accept the risk of loss and will not be able to treat the contract as frustrated when the manner of performance which he had contemplated is no longer possible. This principle is often reflected in the rule that an external event must frustrate the common intention of both parties to the contract.[5]

---

2   See *Hoecheong Products Ltd v Cargill (Hong Kong) Ltd* [1995] 1 Lloyd's Rep 584; *The Kriti Rex* [1996] 2 Lloyd's Rep 171.
3   [1994] 1 WLR 1016.
4   *Maritime National Fish Ltd v Ocean Trawlers Ltd* [1935] AC 524; *Lauritzen AS v Wijsmuller BV, The Super Servant Two* [1990] 1 Lloyd's Rep 1.
5   See *Blackburn Bobbin Co Ltd v Allen* [1918] 2 KB 467.

In this chapter, it is proposed to consider, in relation to the issue of construction of contracts, the issue of unforeseen risks. These may arise either before the parties enter their contract or after performance of the contract has commenced. In either event, it will be necessary for the court to determine how such risks of loss are to be allocated. For the purposes of English law, the devices used to allocate such risks are, in the case of pre-contract risks, rules on mistake and in the case of post-contract risks, the rules encapsulated in the doctrine of frustration.

NON-AGREEMENT MISTAKES

Fundamental mistakes

Where a mistake is operative, it serves to negative, or in some cases to nullify consent.[6] The former type of mistake is concerned with the question of agreement and is not considered in any detail at this stage.[7] Mistakes which nullify consent, on the other hand, do raise important issues of risk allocation. Typically, such mistakes[8] are shared by both parties and will give rise to a common misunderstanding which is fundamental to the decision of both parties to enter into the agreement.

The primary consideration in relation to expectation mistakes is that, in order to be operative, the mistake must be fundamental and must relate to a fact which existed at the time the contract was entered into. In this respect, it is sometimes said that there is a difference between a mistake as to the substance of the contract and a mistake as to motive.[9]

In *Bell v Lever Bros Ltd*,[10] Bell and Snelling were two executive officers of a subsidiary of Lever Bros who had been offered substantial compensation packages in return for their agreement to terminate their contracts with Lever Bros. In fact, the two officers had committed serious breaches[11] of their contracts which would have entitled Lever Bros to dismiss them without compensation. Lever Bros subsequently discovered the earlier breaches of

---

6   *Bell v Lever Bros Ltd* [1932] AC 161, p 217, *per* Lord Atkin.

7   See Chapter 2, above. Relevant mistakes of this kind include those which prevent a valid agreement from arising such as where the parties have contracted at cross-purposes and mistakes as to identity.

8   Often called 'common' mistakes signifying that the mistaken belief is shared or expectation mistakes signifying that the mistake relates to certain assumptions made by the parties prior to entering into the contract and which affect the expectations of the parties as to the outcome of the contract they have entered into.

9   This distinction appears to derive from the Roman law notion of errors *in substantia*.

10 [1932] AC 161, HL.

11 They had made secret profits out of their contracts which was expressly forbidden by a term in each contract of employment.

contract and sought to set aside the compensation packages, alleging fraud and mistake. The allegation of fraud was rejected by the jury, mainly on the basis of a crucial finding of fact that Bell and Snelling had forgotten about their earlier breaches of duty at the time they entered into the compensation contracts with Lever Bros. Two claims were advanced on the basis of mistake. First, it was argued that Lever Bros had made a unilateral mistake as to the terms of the contract, but this was rejected on the ground that Bell and Snelling had no duty to disclose their breaches of contract. Accordingly, the House of Lords was left to decide the case on the basis of the issue of common mistake. In the event, the House of Lords decided by a majority of three to two that the mistake related only to a quality of the service contract and that Lever Bros had therefore got what they had contracted for. Because of the factual complexity of the case, and some of the less believable conclusions reached by the jury, the judgments can be a little difficult to follow. In particular, it should be appreciated that although one of the majority, Lord Blanesburgh, also decided the case partly on the basis that Lever Bros had failed to properly amend their pleadings so as to admit a claim of common mistake. Also some of the judgments refer to a mutual mistake rather than a common mistake, but the case is concerned with the issue of a mistake which is shared by or common to both parties to the contract:

Bell v Lever Bros Ltd [1932] AC 161, HL, p 217

Lord Atkin: My Lords, the rules of law dealing with the effect of mistake on contract appear to be established with reasonable clearness. If mistake operates at all it operates so as to negative or in some cases to nullify consent. The parties may be mistaken in the identity of the contracting parties, or in the existence of the subject matter of the contract at the date of the contract, or in the quality of the subject matter of the contract. These mistakes may be by one party, or by both, and the legal effect may depend upon the class of mistake above mentioned. Thus, a mistaken belief by A that he is contracting with B, whereas in fact, he is contracting with C, will negative consent where it is clear that the intention of A was to contract only with B. [So the agreement of A and B to purchase a specific article is void if in fact, the article had perished before the date of sale.] In this case, though the parties in fact, were agreed about the subject matter, yet a consent to transfer or take delivery of something not existent is deemed useless, the consent is nullified. As codified in the Sale of Goods Act the contract is expressed to be void if the seller was in ignorance of the destruction of the specific chattel. I apprehend that if the seller with knowledge that a chattel was destroyed purported to sell it to a purchaser, the latter might sue for damages for non-delivery though the former could not sue for non-acceptance, but I know of no case where a seller has so committed himself. This is a case where mutual mistake certainly and unilateral mistake by the seller of goods will prevent a contract from arising. Corresponding to mistake as to the existence of the subject matter is mistake as to title in cases where, unknown to the parties, the buyer is already the owner of that which the seller purports to sell to him. The parties intended to effectuate a transfer of ownership: such a transfer is impossible: the stipulation is *naturali ratione inutilis*. This is the case of *Cooper v Phibbs*, where A agreed to take a lease of a fishery from B, though contrary to the belief of both parties at the time A was tenant for life of the fishery and B appears to have had no title at all. To such a case, Lord Westbury applied the principle that if parties contract under a mutual mistake and misapprehension as to their relative and respective rights the result is that the agreement is liable to be set aside as having proceeded upon a common mistake. Applied to the context, the statement is only subject to the criticism that the agreement would appear to be void rather than voidable. Applied to mistake as to rights generally it would appear to be too wide. Even where the vendor has no title, though both parties think he has, the correct view would appear to be that there is a contract: but that the vendor has either committed a breach of a stipulation as to title, or is not able to perform his contract. The contract is unenforceable by him but is not void.

Mistake as to quality of the thing contracted for raises more difficult questions. In such a case, a mistake will not affect assent unless it is the mistake of both parties, and is as to the existence of some quality which makes the thing without the quality essentially different from the thing as it was believed to be. Of course, it may appear that the parties contracted that the article should possess the quality which one or other or both mistakenly believed it to possess. But in such a case there is a contract and the inquiry is a different one, being whether the contract as to quality amounts to a condition or a warranty, a different branch of the law. The principles to be applied are to be found in two cases which, as far as my knowledge goes, have always been treated as authoritative expositions of the law. The first is *Kennedy v Panama Royal Mail Co.*

In that case the plaintiff had applied for shares in the defendant company on the faith of a prospectus which stated falsely but innocently that the company had a binding contract with the government of New Zealand for the carriage of mails. On discovering the true facts the plaintiff brought an action for the recovery of the sums he had paid on calls. The defendants brought a cross action for further calls. Blackburn J, in delivering the judgment of the court (Cockburn CJ, Blackburn, Mellor and Shee JJ), said: 'The only remaining question is one of much greater difficulty. It was contended by Mr Mellish, on behalf of Lord Gilbert Kennedy, that the effect of the prospectus was to warrant to the intended shareholders that there really was such a contract as is there represented, and not merely to represent that the company *bona fide* believed it [and that the difference in substance between shares in a company with such a contract and shares in a company whose supposed contract was not binding, was a difference in substance in the nature of the thing; and that the shareholder was entitled to return the shares as soon as he discovered this, quite independently of fraud, on the ground that he had applied for one thing and got another]. And, if the invalidity of the contract really made the shares he obtained different things in substance from those which he applied for, this would, we think, be good law. The case would then resemble *Gompertz v Bartlett* and *Gurney v Womersley*, where the person who had honestly sold what he thought a bill without recourse to him, was nevertheless held bound to return the price on its turning out that the supposed bill was a forgery in the one case, and void under the stamp laws in the other; in both cases the ground of this decision being that the thing handed over was not the thing paid for. A similar principle was acted on in *Ship's Case*. There is, however, a very important difference between cases where a contract may be rescinded on account of fraud, and those in which it may be rescinded on the ground that there is a difference in substance between the thing bargained for and that obtained. It is enough to show that there was a fraudulent representation as to any part of that which induced the party to enter into the contract which he seeks to rescind; but where there has been an innocent misrepresentation or misapprehension, it does not authorise a rescission unless it is such as to show that there is a complete difference in substance between what was supposed to be and what was taken, so as to constitute a failure of consideration.'

The next case is *Smith v Hughes*, the well-known case as to new and old oats. The action was in the county court, and was for the price of oats sold and delivered and damages for not accepting oats bargained and sold.

The court ordered a new trial. It is not quite clear whether they considered that if the defendant's contention was correct, the parties were not *ad idem* or there was a contractual condition that the oats sold were old oats. In either case the defendant would succeed in defeating the claim.

In these cases, I am inclined to think that the true analysis is that there is a contract, but that the one party is not able to supply the very thing whether goods or services that the other party contracted to take; and therefore the contract is unenforceable by the one if executory, while if executed the other can recover back money paid on the ground of failure of the consideration.

We are now in a position to apply to the facts of this case the law as to mistake so far as it has been stated. It is essential on this part of the discussion to keep in mind the finding of the jury acquitting the defendants of fraudulent misrepresentation or concealment in procuring the agreements in question. Grave injustice may be done to the defendants and confusion introduced into the legal conclusion, unless it is quite clear that in considering mistake in this case no suggestion of fraud is admissible and cannot strictly be regarded by the judge who has to determine the legal issues raised. The agreement which is said to be void is the agreement contained in the letter of 19 March 1929, that Bell would retire from the Board of the Niger Company and its subsidiaries, and that in consideration of his doing so Levers would pay him as compensation for the termination of his agreements and consequent loss of office the sum of £30,000 in full satisfaction and discharge of all claims and demands of any kind against Lever Brothers, the Niger Company or its subsidiaries. The agreement, which as part of the contract was terminated, had been broken so that it could be repudiated. Is an agreement to terminate a broken contract different in kind from an agreement to terminate an unbroken contract, assuming that the breach has given the one party the right to declare the contract at an end? I feel the weight of the plaintiffs' contention that a contract immediately determinable is a different thing from a contract for an unexpired term, and that the difference in kind can be illustrated by the immense price of release from the longer contract as compared with the shorter. And I agree that an agreement to take an assignment of a lease for five years is not the same thing as to take an assignment of a lease for three years, still less a term for a few months. But, on the whole, I have come to the conclusion that it would be wrong to decide that an agreement to terminate a definite specified contract is void if it turns out that the agreement had already been broken and could have been terminated otherwise. The contract released is the identical contract in both cases, and the party paying for release *gets exactly what he bargains for*. It seems immaterial that he could have got the same result in another way, or that if he had known the true facts he would not have entered into the bargain. A buys B's horse; he thinks the horse is sound and he pays the price of a sound horse; he would certainly not have bought the horse if he had known as the fact is that the horse is unsound. If B has made no representation as to soundness and has not contracted that the horse is sound, A is bound and cannot recover back the price. A buys a picture from B; both A and B believe it to be the work of an old master, and a high price is paid. It turns out to be a modern copy. A has no remedy in the absence of representation or warranty. A agrees to take on lease or to buy from B an unfurnished dwelling-house. The house is in fact, uninhabitable. A would never have entered into the bargain if he had known the fact. A has no remedy, and the position is the same whether B knew the facts or not, so long as he made no representation or gave no warranty. A buys a roadside garage business from B abutting on a public thoroughfare: unknown to A, but known to B, it has already been decided to construct a bypass road which will divert substantially the whole of the traffic from passing A's garage. Again, A has no remedy. All these cases involve hardship on A and benefit B, as most people would say, unjustly. They can be supported on the ground that it is of paramount importance that contracts should be observed, and that if parties honestly comply with the essentials of the formation of contracts – that is, agree in the same terms on the same subject matter – they are bound, and must rely on the stipulations of the contract for protection from the effect of facts unknown to them.

This brings the discussion to the alternative mode of expressing the result of a mutual mistake. It is said that in such a case as the present there is to be implied a stipulation in the contract that a condition of its efficacy is that the facts should be as understood by both parties – namely, that the contract could not be terminated till the end of the current term. The question of the existence of conditions, express or implied, is obviously one that affects not the formation of contract, but the investigation of the terms of the contract when made. A condition derives its efficacy from the consent of the parties, express or implied. They have agreed, but on what terms. One term may be that unless the facts are or are not of a particular nature, or unless an event has or has not happened, the contract is not to take effect. With regard to future facts such a condition is obviously contractual. Till the event occurs the parties are bound. Thus, the condition (the exact terms of which need not here be investigated) that is generally accepted as underlying the principle of the frustration cases is contractual, an implied condition. Sir John Simon formulated for the assistance of your Lordships a proposition which should be recorded: 'Whenever it is to be inferred from the terms of a contract or its surrounding circumstances that the consensus has been reached upon the basis of a particular contractual assumption, and that assumption is not true, the contract is avoided: that is, it is void *ab initio* if the assumption is of present fact and it ceases to bind if the assumption is of future fact.'

I think few would demur to this statement, but its value depends upon the meaning of 'a contractual assumption,' and also upon the true meaning to be attached to 'basis,' a metaphor which may mislead. When used expressly in contracts, for instance, in policies of insurance, which state that the truth of the statements in the proposal is to be the basis of the contract of insurance, the meaning is clear. The truth of the statements is made a condition of the contract, which failing, the contract is void unless the condition is waived. The proposition does not amount to more than this, that, if the contract expressly or impliedly contains a term that a particular assumption is a condition of the contract, the contract is avoided if the assumption is not true. But we have not advanced far on the inquiry how to ascertain whether the contract does contain such a condition. Various words are to be found to define the state of things which make a condition. 'In the contemplation of both parties fundamental to the continued validity of the contract', 'foundation essential to its existence', 'a fundamental reason for making it', are phrases found in the important judgment of Scrutton LJ in the present case. The first two phrases appear to me to be unexceptionable. They cover the case of a contract to serve in a particular place, the existence of which is fundamental to the service, or to procure the services of a professional vocalist, whose continued health is essential to performance. But 'a fundamental reason for making a contract' may, with respect, be misleading. The reason of one party only is presumedly not intended, but in the cases I have suggested above, of the sale of a horse or of a picture, it might be said that the fundamental reason for making the contract was the belief of both parties that the horse was sound or the picture an old master, yet in neither case would the condition as I think exist. Nothing is more dangerous than to allow oneself liberty to construct for the parties contracts which they have not in terms made by importing implications which would appear to make the contract more businesslike or more just. The implications to be made are to be no more than are 'necessary' for giving business efficacy to the transaction, and it appears to me that, both as to existing facts and future facts, a condition would not be implied unless the new state of facts makes the contract something different in kind from the contract in the original state of facts. Thus, in *Krell v Henry*, Vaughan Williams LJ finds that the subject of the contract was 'rooms to view the procession': the postponement, therefore, made the rooms not rooms to view the procession. This also is the test finally chosen by Lord Summer in *Bank Line v Arthur Capel & Co*, agreeing with Lord Dunedin in *Metropolitan Water Board v Dick Kerr*, where, dealing with the criterion for determining the effect of interruption in 'frustrating' a contract, he says: 'An interruption may be so long as to destroy the identity of the work or service, when resumed, with the work or service when interrupted.' We therefore get a common standard for mutual mistake and implied conditions whether as to existing or as to future facts. Does the state of the new facts destroy the identity of the subject matter as it was in the original state of facts? To apply the principle to the infinite combinations of facts that arise in actual experience will continue to be difficult, but if this case results in establishing order into what has been a somewhat confused and difficult branch of the law, it will have served a useful purpose.

I have already stated my reasons for deciding that in the present case the identity of the subject matter was not destroyed by the mutual mistake, if any, and need not repeat them.

Lord Thankerton (p 231): In the absence of fraud, which the jury has negatived, I am of opinion that neither a servant nor a director of a company is legally bound forthwith to disclose any breach of the obligations arising out of the relationship, so as to give the master or the company the opportunity of dismissal; on subsequent discovery, the master or company will not be entitled to hold the dismissal as operating from the date of the breach, but will be liable for wages or salary earned by the servant during the intervening period.

Turning next to the question of mutual error or mistake, I think that the respondents' contention may be fairly stated as follows – namely, that in concluding the agreements of March 1929, all parties proceeded on the mistaken assumption that the appellants' service agreements were not liable to immediate termination by Lever Brothers by reason of the appellants' misconduct, and that such common mistake involved the actual subject matter of the agreements, and did not merely relate to a quality of the subject matter.

The cases on this branch of the law are numerous, and in seeking the principle on which they rest I will at first confine my attention to those which relate to innocent mutual mistake on formation of the contract, as it appears to me that the cases relating to facts arising subsequently to the formation of the contract may be found to rest on a somewhat different principle.

But first let me define the exact position as at the date of the agreements of March 1929. The service agreements of both appellants were then existing as binding legal contracts, although it was in the power of Lever Brothers, had they then known of the appellants' breach of contract, to have terminated the contracts but, until the exercise of such power, the contracts remained binding. It is also clear that an essential purpose of the agreements of March 1929, was to secure the termination of these service agreements. The mistake was not as to the existence of agreements which required termination – for such did exist – but as to the possibility of terminating them by other means.

The respondents maintain that the service agreements surrendered to them are not the service agreements paid for, in respect that they were immediately defeasible by them. Blackburn J proceeds: 'There is, however, a very important difference between cases where a contract may be rescinded on account of fraud, and those in which it may be rescinded on the ground that there is a difference in substance between the thing bargained for and that obtained. It is enough to show that there was a fraudulent representation as to *any part* of that which induced the party to enter into the contract which he seeks to rescind; but where there has been an innocent misrepresentation or misapprehension, it does not authorise a rescission unless it is such as to show that there is a complete difference in substance between what was supposed to be and what was taken, so as to constitute a failure of consideration. For example, where a horse is bought under a belief that it is sound, if the purchaser was induced to buy by a fraudulent representation as to the horse's soundness, the contract may be rescinded. If it was induced by an honest misrepresentation as to its soundness, though it may be clear that both vendor and purchaser thought that they were dealing about a sound horse and were in error, yet the purchaser must pay the whole price, unless there was a warranty.'

In the present case, there being no obligation to disclose, the appellants, if they had had their misconduct in mind, would have been entitled to say nothing about it, and the respondents, in the absence of fraud, would have been bound by the contracts, even though, if they had known, they would not have entered into the contracts, but would have terminated the service agreements. I have difficulty in seeing how the fact that the appellants did not remember at the time is to put the respondents in a better position.

The phrase 'underlying assumption by the parties', as applied to the subject matter of a contract, may be too widely interpreted so as so include something which one of the parties had not necessarily in his mind at the time of the contract; in my opinion it can only properly relate to something which both must necessarily have accepted in their minds as an essential and integral element of the subject matter. In the present case, however probable it may be, we are not necessarily forced to that assumption. *Cooper v Phibbs* is a good illustration, for both parties must necessarily have proceeded on the mistaken assumption that the lessor had the right to grant the lease and that the lessee required a lease; Lord Westbury says: 'The respondents believed themselves to be entitled to the property, the petitioner believed that he was a stranger to it, the mistake is discovered, and the agreement cannot stand.'

In *Scott v Coulson,* it was common ground that at the date of the contract for sale of the life policy both parties supposed the assured to be alive, the result being that the plaintiffs were willing to accept as the best price they could get for the policy a sum slightly in advance of its surrender value and very much below the sum due on the death of the assured. As a matter of fact the assured was dead. It was therefore clear that the subject matter of the contract was a policy still current with a surrender value and that accordingly the subject matter did not exist at the date of the contract. *Couturier v Hastie,* where the cargo sold was held not to have existed at the date of sale, and *Strickland v Turner,* where the annuitant was in fact, dead at the date of sale of the annuity, were cases where the subject matter was not in existence at the date of the contract. There are many other cases to the same effect, but I think that it is true to say that in all of them it either appeared on the face of the contract that the matter as to which the mistake existed was an essential and integral element of the subject matter of the contract, or it was an inevitable inference from the nature of the contract that all the parties so regarded it.

In the present case the terms of the contracts throw no light on the question, and, as already indicated, I do not find sufficient material to compel the inference that the appellants, at the time of the contract, regarded the indefeasibility of the service agreements as an essential and integral element in the subject matter of the bargain.

Lord Blanesburgh (p 198): The appellants have not had the opportunity of showing by evidence the extent to which Levers received consideration for the settlement agreements over and above their release from liability for the further payments for which, on the hypothesis, it was by all parties assumed that they remained liable. The mistake must go to the whole consideration. I have already indicated the general nature of the further advantages derived by Levers from the settlement agreements, as these appear on the record, but this aspect of the case has not been developed in evidence, because in the action as fought it was not either relevant or necessary so to do.

But I would add a word on the second ground relied upon by the Lords Justices in support of the learned judge's order – namely, that it could be upheld for the reason that Levers' unilateral mistake, which was certainly pleaded, resulted from a neglect on the part of the appellants of their duty, when negotiating the agreements of settlement, to disclose to Levers their offending transactions – a duty which was certainly not pleaded.

My Lords, I am in entire agreement with the answer given to this suggestion by my two noble friends opposite made on the assumption that Levers were the employers of the appellants and that the 'offence' in their transactions had only temporarily passed from their minds.

But if the true position be, as I have I believe shown, that the appellants were not in any relevant sense the servants of Levers and that the only reason why their transactions were 'offending' was that they involved Niger in a breach of the directors' clause of the pool agreement, of the existence of which the appellants were not merely forgetful but were in complete ignorance, what then, I would ask, remains of any duty on their part to disclose? My Lords, in that view of the situation the duty was I suggest plainly non-existent.

The action therefore, in my judgment, so far as it was contested, entirely fails.

My Lords, I confess that I arrive without reluctance at this conclusion of the whole matter. It appears to me to accord with a sound view both of justice and of fairness. I should have deemed it unfortunate if the appellants had been left in enjoyment of the profit accruing from the offending transactions and if they had not been required to pay the nominal damage which the jury considered these transactions occasioned to Niger. But that result has not followed. For both the profit and the damage they remain accountable, as is wholesome.

Further acceptance, however, by your Lordships' House of the orders appealed from would have meant that, after the complete failure of the grave charges of fraud preferred against officials whose ability and services had brought to Niger advantages of untold value, these officials, the appellants, would have been left exposed to the same consequences as if the charges had all been true. Speaking only for myself I feel relieved to be able to take a view of equity and procedure which shields, the appellants from such a consequence.

Nor is it to my mind unjust that, their profit accounted for, the appellants should be left in possession by way of return for their services of sums which, while they may seem bountiful to minds disciplined in a school of progressive austerity, would doubtless, by those engaged in great business, be regarded as no more than adequate to the occasion.

The various statements made by the majority in *Bell v Lever Bros Ltd* may be taken to mean that the mistake must relate to a fact, the accuracy of which is a condition precedent to liability. If that condition precedent fails and the contract is executory, the contract is unenforceable. If the contract is partly executed in that one of the parties has paid money under the contract, there will be a total failure of consideration, since the contract is void *ab initio*, with the result that the party paying money under the contract will be able to recover what he has paid.

The main difficulty with the tests in *Bell v Lever Bros Ltd* as applied to the facts of the case is that it is difficult to imagine what will be a fundamental mistake sufficient at common law to render the contract void, short of total destruction of the subject matter of the contract without the knowledge of either party.[12] Alternatively, there appear to be circumstances in which a contract may be declared void at common law on the ground that the shared mistake of the parties renders the contract as originally envisaged legally or physically impossible to perform, such as where the parties mistakenly believe that land is capable of producing a certain quantity of a crop in a given season.[13] Similarly, a contract to take a lease of land may be declared void if, unknown to the parties, the 'lessee' is already the legal owner of the land.[14]

In the majority of the cases in which an operative fundamental mistake has been found to exist, the state of affairs over which the parties are mistaken has been a matter directly relevant to the contract into which the parties have entered. However, it is possible for the matter in respect of which the mistake is made to relate to another contract. For example, if A guarantees B's ability to pay for goods sold by C to B under a separate contract, a condition precedent to A's liability under the contract of guarantee is that the goods which are the subject matter of the contract between B and C (an 'accessory' contract) do exist.

In *Associated Japanese Bank v Crédit du Nord SA*,[15] the plaintiff entered into a sale and leaseback agreement in respect of certain machinery with Bennett. In fact, no such machinery existed. In order to protect their interests, the plaintiffs insisted that Bennett's obligations under this contract were guaranteed with the defendant bank. The contract of guarantee was assumed to have been entered into on the understanding that the machinery existed. Did this mean that the contract of guarantee was void for mistake on the ground that there had been the failure of a condition precedent to the liability of the defendant bank to pay under the contract of guarantee?

---

12 Sale of Goods Act 1979, s 6. See, also, *Strickland v Turner* (1852) 7 Ex 208.
13 *Sheikh Bros Ltd v Ochsner* [1957] AC 136.
14 *Cooper v Phibbs* (1867) LR 2 HL 149.
15 [1988] 3 All ER 902.

Associated Japanese Bank v Crédit du Nord SA [1988] 3 All ER 902, p 909

Steyn J: Throughout the law of contract two themes regularly recur: respect for the sanctity of contract and the need to give effect to the reasonable expectations of honest men. Usually, these themes work in the same direction. Occasionally, they point to opposite solutions. The law regarding common mistake going to the root of a contract is a case where tension arises between the two themes. That is illustrated by the circumstances of this extraordinary case.

Mistake

The common law regarding mutual or common mistake

There was a lively debate about the common law rules governing a mutual or common mistake of the parties as to some essential quality of the subject matter of the contract. Counsel for CDN submitted that *Bell v Lever Bros Ltd* [1932] AC 161; [1931] All ER 1 authoritatively established that a mistake by both parties as to the existence of some quality of the subject matter of the contract, which makes the subject matter of the contract without the quality essentially different from the subject matter as it was believed to be, renders the contract void *ab initio*. Counsel for AJB contested this proposition. He submitted that at common law a mistake even as to an essential quality of the subject matter of the contract will not affect the contract, unless it resulted in a total failure of consideration. It was not clear to me that this formulation left any meaningful and independent scope for the application of common law rules in this area of the law. In any event, it is necessary to examine the legal position in some detail.

The landmark decision is undoubtedly *Bell v Lever Bros Ltd*. Normally, a judge of first instance would simply content himself with applying the law stated by the House of Lords. There has, however, been substantial controversy about the rule established in that case. It seems right therefore to examine the effect of that decision against a somewhat wider framework. In the early history of contract law, the common law's preoccupation with consideration made the development of a doctrine of mistake impossible. Following the emergence in the nineteenth century of the theory of *consensus ad idem* it became possible to treat misrepresentation, undue influence and mistake as factors vitiating consent. Given that the will theory in English contract law was cast in objective form, judging matters by the external standard of the reasonable man, both as to contract formation and contractual interpretation, it nevertheless became possible to examine in what circumstances mistake might nullify or negative consent. But even in late Victorian times there was another powerful policy consideration militating against upsetting bargains on the ground of unexpected circumstances which occurred before or after the contract. That was the policy of *caveat emptor* which held sway outside the field of contract law subsequently codified by the Sale of Goods Act in 1893. Nevertheless, principles affecting the circumstances in which consent may be vitiated gradually emerged. The most troublesome areas proved to be two related areas, viz common mistake as to essential quality of the subject matter of the contract and post-contractual frustration.

Bell v Lever Bros Ltd was a vitally important case: The facts of that case are so well known as to require no detailed exposition.

Lord Atkin held [1932] AC 161, p 218; [1931] All ER 1, p 28): '... a mistake will not affect assent unless it is the mistake of both parties, and is as to the existence of some quality which makes the thing without the quality essentially different from the thing as it was believed to be.'

In my view, none of the other passages in Lord Atkin's speech detract from that statement of the law. Lord Thankerton came to a similar conclusion. He held that common mistake 'can only properly relate to something which both must necessarily have accepted in their minds as an essential and integral part of the subject matter' (see [1932] AC 161, p 235; [1931] All ER 1, p 36).

That seems to me exactly the same test as Lord Atkin enunciated.

Lord Blanesburgh's speech proceeded on different lines. It must not be forgotten that the issue of common mistake was only put forward at the eleventh hour. Lord Blanesburgh would have refused the necessary amendment, but he expressed his 'entire accord' with the substantive views of Lord Atkin and Lord Thankerton (see [1932] AC 161, pp 198–99; [1931] All ER 1, p 18–19). The majority were therefore in agreement about the governing principle.

It seems to me that the better view is that the majority in *Bell v Lever Bros Ltd* had in mind only mistake at common law. That appears to be indicated by the shape of the argument, the proposed amendment placed before the House of Lords (see [1932] AC 161, p 191; [1931] All ER 1, p 15) and the speeches of Lord Atkin and Lord Thankerton. But, if I am wrong on this point, it is nevertheless clear that mistake at common law was in the forefront of the analysis in the speeches of the majority.

The law has not stood still in relation to mistake in equity. Today, it is clear that mistake in equity is not circumscribed by common law definitions. A contract affected by mistake in equity is not void, but may be set aside on terms: see *Solle v Butcher* [1949] 2 All ER 1107; [1950] 1 KB 671; *Magee v Pennine Insurance Co Ltd* [1969] 2 All ER 891; [1969] 2 QB 507; *Grist v Bailey* [1966] 2 All ER 875; [1967] Ch 532. It does not follow, however, that *Bell v Lever Bros Ltd* is no longer an authoritative statement of mistake at common law. On the contrary, in my view, the principles enunciated in that case clearly still govern mistake at common law. It is true that in *Solle v Butcher* [1949] 2 All ER 1107, p 1119; [1950] 1 KB 671, p 691, Denning LJ interpreted *Bell v Lever Bros Ltd* differently. He said that a common mistake, even on a most fundamental matter, does not make the contract void at law. That was an individual opinion. Neither Bucknill LJ (who agreed in the result) nor Jenkins LJ (who dissented) even mentioned *Bell v Lever Bros Ltd*. In *Magee v Pennine Insurance Co Ltd* [1969] 2 All ER 891, p 893; [1969] 2 QB 507, p 514, Lord Denning MR returned to the point. About *Bell v Lever Bros Ltd*, he simply said: 'I do not propose ... to go through the speeches in that case. They have given enough trouble to commentators already.' He then repeated his conclusion in *Solle v Butcher*. Winn LJ dissented. Fenton Atkinson LJ agreed in the result, but it is clear from his judgment that he did not agree with Lord Denning MR's interpretation of *Bell v Lever Bros Ltd* (see [1969] 2 All ER 891, p 896; [1969] 2 QB 507, pp 517–18). Again, Lord Denning MR's observation represented only his own view. With the profoundest respect to the former Master of the Rolls, I am constrained to say that, in my view, his interpretation of *Bell v Lever Bros Ltd* does not do justice to the speeches of the majority.

When Lord Denning MR referred in *Magee v Pennine Insurance Co Ltd* to the views of commentators, he may have had in mind comments in Cheshire and Fifoot, *Law of Contract*, 6th edn, 1964, p 196. In substance, the argument was that the actual decision in *Bell v Lever Bros Ltd* contradicts the language of the speeches. If the test was not satisfied there, so the argument runs, it is difficult to see how it could ever be satisfied see the latest edition of this valuable textbook for the same argument (Cheshire, Fifoot and Furmston, *Law of Contract*, 11th edn, 1986, pp 225–26). This is a point worth examining because at first glance it may seem persuasive. *Bell v Lever Bros Ltd* was a quite exceptional case; all their Lordships were agreed that common mistake had not been pleaded and would have required an amendment in the House of Lords if it were to succeed. The speeches do not suggest that the employees were entitled to keep both the gains secretly made and the golden handshakes. The former were clearly recoverable from them. Nevertheless, the golden handshakes were very substantial. But there are indications in the speeches that the so called 'merits' were not all in favour of Lever Bros. The company was most anxious, because of a corporate merger, to terminate the two service agreements.

There was apparently a doubt whether the voidability of the service agreements if revealed to the company *at the time of the severance contract* would have affected the company's decision.

Lord Atkin clearly regarded it as a hard case on the facts, but concluded 'on the whole' that the plea of common mistake must fail (see [1932] AC 161, p 223; [1931] All ER 1, p 30). It is noteworthy that Lord Atkin commented on the scarcity of evidence as to the subsidiaries from the boards of which the two employees resigned (see [1932] AC 161, p 212; [1931] All ER 1, p 25). Lord Blanesburgh's speech was directed to his conclusion that the amendment ought not to be allowed. He did, however, make clear that 'the mistake must go to the whole consideration' and pointed to the advantages (other than the release from the service agreements) which Lever Bros received (see [1932] AC 161, pp 181 and 197; [1931] All ER Rep 1, pp 10 and 18). Lord Blanesburgh emphasised that Lever Bros secured the future co-operation of the two employees for the carrying through of the amalgamation (see [1932] AC 161, pp 181; [1931] All ER Rep 1, p 10). And the burden, of course, rested squarely on Lever Bros. With due deference to the distinguished authors who have argued that the actual decision in *Bell v Lever Bros Ltd* contradicts the principle enunciated in the speeches it seems to me that their analysis is altogether too simplistic, and that the actual decision was rooted in the particular facts of the case. In my judgment, there is no reason to doubt the substantive reasons emerging from the speeches of the majority.

No one could fairly suggest that, in this difficult area of the law, there is only one correct approach or solution. But a narrow doctrine of common law mistake (as enunciated in *Bell v Lever Bros Ltd*), supplemented by the more flexible doctrine of mistake in equity (as developed in *Solle v Butcher* and later cases), seems to me to be an entirely sensible and satisfactory state of the law: see *Sheikh Bros Ltd v Ochsner* [1957] AC 136. And there ought to be no reason to struggle to avoid its application by artificial interpretations of *Bell v Lever Bros Ltd*.

It might be useful if I now summarised what appears to me to be a satisfactory way of approaching this subject. Logically, before one can turn to the rules as to mistake, whether at common law or in equity, one must first determine whether the contract itself, by express or implied condition precedent or otherwise, provides who bears the risk of the relevant mistake. It is at this hurdle that many pleas of mistake will either fail or prove to have been unnecessary. Only if the contract is silent on the point is there scope for invoking mistake. That brings me to the relationship between common law mistake and mistake in equity. Where common law mistake has been pleaded, the court must first consider this plea. If the contract is held to be void, no question of mistake in equity arises. But, if the contract is held to be valid, a plea of mistake in equity may still have to be considered: see *Grist v Bailey* [1966] 2 All ER 875; [1967] Ch 532 and the analysis in *Anson's Law of Contract*, 26th edn, 1984, pp 290–91. Turning now to the approach to common law mistake, it seems to me that the following propositions are valid although not necessarily all entitled to be dignified as propositions of law.

The first imperative must be that the law ought to uphold rather than destroy apparent contracts. Secondly, the common law rules as to a mistake regarding the quality of the subject matter, like the common law rules regarding commercial frustration, are designed to cope with the impact of unexpected and wholly exceptional circumstances on apparent contracts. Thirdly, such a mistake in order to attract legal consequences must substantially be shared by both parties, and must relate to facts as they existed at the time the contract was made. Fourthly, and this is the point established by *Bell v Lever Bros Ltd*, the mistake must render the subject matter of the contract essentially and radically different from the subject matter which the parties believed to exist. While the civilian distinction between the substance and attributes of the subject matter of a contract has played a role in the development of our law (and was cited in the speeches in *Bell v Lever Bros Ltd*), the principle enunciated in *Bell v Lever Bros Ltd* is markedly narrower in scope than the civilian doctrine. It is therefore no longer useful to invoke the civilian distinction. The principles enunciated by Lord Atkin and Lord Thankerton represent the *ratio decidendi* of *Bell v Lever Bros Ltd*. Fifthly, there is a requirement which was not specifically discussed in *Bell v Lever Bros Ltd*. What happens if the party who is seeking to rely on the mistake had no reasonable grounds for his belief? An extreme example is that of the man who makes a contract with minimal knowledge of the facts to which the mistake relates but is content that it is a good speculative risk. In my judgment a party cannot be allowed to rely on a common mistake where the mistake consists of a belief which is entertained by him without any reasonable grounds for such belief: see *McRae v Commonwealth Disposals Commission* (1951) 84 CLR 377, p 408. That is not because principles such as estoppel or negligence require it, but simply because policy and good sense dictate that the positive rules regarding common mistake should be so qualified. Curiously enough this qualification is similar to the civilian concept where the doctrine of error *in substantia* is tempered by the principles governing *culpa in contrahendo*. More importantly, a recognition of this qualification is consistent with the approach in equity where fault on the part of the party adversely affected by the mistake will generally preclude the granting of equitable relief: see *Solle v Butcher* [1949] 2 All ER 1107, p 1120; [1950] 1 KB 671, p 693.

Applying the law to the facts

It is clear, of course, that, in this case, both parties, the creditor and the guarantor, acted on the assumption that the lease related to existing machines. If they had been informed that the machines might not exist, neither AJB nor CDN would for one moment have contemplated entering into the transaction. That, by itself, I accept, is not enough to sustain the plea of common law mistake. I am also satisfied that CDN had reasonable grounds for believing that the machines existed. That belief was based on CDN's discussions with Mr Bennett, information supplied by National Leasing, a respectable firm of lease brokers, and the confidence created by the fact that AJB were the lessors.

The real question is whether the subject matter of the guarantee (as opposed to the sale and lease) was essentially different from what it was reasonably believed to be. The real security of the guarantor was the machines. The existence of the machines, being profit earning chattels, made it more likely that the debtor would be able to service the debt. More importantly, if the debtor defaulted and the creditor repossessed the machines, the creditor had to give credit for $97^1/2\%$ of the value of the machines. If the creditor sued the guarantor first, and the guarantor paid, the guarantor was entitled to be subrogated to the creditor's rights in respect of recovery against the debtor: see Goff and Jones *Law of Restitution*, 3rd edn, 1986, pp 533–36. No doubt the guarantor relied to some extent on the creditworthiness of Mr Bennett. But I find that the prime security to which the guarantor looked was the existence of the four machines as described to both parties. For both parties, the guarantee of obligations under a lease with non-existent machines was essentially different from a guarantee of a lease with four machines which both parties at the time of the contract believed to exist. The guarantee is an accessory contract. The non-existence of the subject matter of the principal contract is therefore of fundamental importance. Indeed the analogy of the classic *res extincta* cases, so much discussed in the authorities, is fairly close. In my judgment, the stringent test of common law mistake is satisfied; the guarantee is void *ab initio*.

Equitable mistake

Having concluded that the guarantee is void *ab initio* at common law, it is strictly unnecessary to examine the question of equitable mistake. Equity will give relief against common mistake in cases where the common law will not, and it provides more flexible remedies, including the power to set aside the contract on terms. It is not necessary to repeat my findings of fact save to record again the fundamental nature of the common mistake, and that CDN was not at fault in any way. If I had not decided in favour of CDN on construction and common law mistake, I would have held that the guarantee must be set aside on equitable principles. Unfortunately, and counsel are not to blame for that, the question of the terms (if any) to be imposed (having regard particularly to sums deposited by Mr Bennett with CDN) were not adequately explored in argument. If it becomes necessary to rule on this aspect, I will require further argument.

In *Associated Japanese Bank v Crédit du Nord*, the need to give effect to the reasonable expectations of honest men was considered to be more important than the principle which underlies *Bell v Lever Bros*, namely that the courts must preserve the sanctity of contracts. In this light, is there any difficulty in reconciling the two decisions?

Treitel comments as follows:

There remains the question just how the *Associated Japanese Bank* case is to be distinguished from *Bell v Lever Bros Ltd*. At first sight, there are obvious similarities between the two cases. In both, the subject matter of the contract alleged to be affected by the mistake was an earlier contract; and in both that earlier contract was liable to be rescinded by one of the parties to the subsequent contract. The grounds for rescission were indeed different: in *Bell v Lever Bros Ltd,* the earlier contract could have been rescinded for breaches of duty by Bell and Snelling, while in the *Associated Japanese Bank* case the ground for rescission of that contract was the fraud of Bennett in inducing the plaintiffs to enter into it. The earlier contract in *Bell v Lever Bros Ltd* was, moreover, between the same parties as the contract alleged to be affected by the mistake, while in the *Associated Japanese Bank* case the earlier contract was not between those same parties but between one of those parties and a third party. But these would not be satisfactory grounds for the different conclusions reached in the two cases; nor are they relied on by Steyn J, who distinguishes *Bell v Lever Bros Ltd* on the ground that it was 'a quite exceptional case' and that the actual decision was 'rooted in the facts of the particular case'. Those facts were that Lever Bros Ltd derived benefits from the contract in dispute: they were 'most anxious, because of a corporate merger, to terminate the two service agreements'; that it was not clear that they would not have entered into the disputed contract if they had known of the voidability of the service agreements (see [1932] AC 161, p 236, *per* Lord Thankerton); and that they were interested in securing the future co-operation of Bell and Snelling in carrying through the proposed merger. One can also, so far as the merits of the case are concerned, make the point that the rule of law entitling Lever Bros Ltd to dismiss Bell and Snelling without notice and without compensation would, if it had been applied in that case, have operated with draconian effect. Bell and Snelling had, through their work for the subsidiary company of which they were officers, substantially increased the profitability and capital value of that company. In comparison with these matters, the benefits which they had derived from their breaches of duty were trivial. There was no question that they were liable to hand these benefits over to Lever Bros Ltd; indeed, they offered to do so when the true facts came to light (see [1932] AC 161, p 183). All this is not to condone their undoubted lapses from strict principles of commercial morality; but a penalty of £50,000 for such lapses would have been unduly severe. It is perhaps not fanciful to suggest that, in *Bell v Lever Bros Ltd*, a narrow doctrine of mistake corrected an injustice that would have flowed from the rule of law under which a relatively trivial breach, which caused the innocent party no loss, nevertheless gave that party a ground for rescinding the contract.

In the *Associated Japanese Bank* case, there were no similar factors which could be said, on the 'merits,' to tip the balance in favour of upholding the contract. There was, moreover, an explicit finding that both parties believed that the machines existed, and that *neither* of them would, if aware of the true facts, have 'for one moment contemplated entering into the transaction'. In *Bell v Lever Bros Ltd,* there was no similar finding: on the contrary, Lord Thankerton said that there was not sufficient evidence to compel the inference that Lever Bros Ltd would not have entered into the contract if they had known the true facts. 'The real question, is whether the subject *matter of the guarantee* (as opposed to the sale and lease) was essentially different from what it was reasonably believed to be'. He concludes that there was such an essential difference, principally because 'the real security of the guarantor was the machines'. Their supposed existence provided 'security' in two ways: first, by enabling the debtor to earn money (by using them) and so to service the debt; and, secondly, by virtue of the terms of the lease which provided for termination on the lessee's default and for the making of certain payments by him; but which also entitled him to a 'refund' of 97.5% of any resale proceeds of the machines, a right to which the guarantor would be entitled to be subrogated.

A more serious problem is that, while the 'security' points just described might make the guarantee 'essentially different' from the defendants' point of view, it is hard to see how they could have had this effect from the point of view of the plaintiffs, who were no doubt concerned for their own security but may be supposed to have been indifferent as to the security of the defendants. No doubt, the plaintiffs also thought that their security lay in part in the existence of the machines, but that security was believed by them to arise under other contracts than that in suit: under the sale and lease back, not under the guarantee. It was presumably because the plaintiffs did not regard that security as adequate that they sought the further security of a bank guarantee. The conclusion that the plaintiffs, no less than the defendants, regarded the subject matter as it was as essentially different from the subject matter as it was believed to be can perhaps be most easily explained by looking at the transaction as a whole and not at the guarantee in isolation. There is a hint of this approach in Steyn J's description of the guarantee as an 'accessory contract' so that the 'non-existence of the subject matter of the principal contract is of fundamental importance. Indeed, the analogy of the classic *res extincta* cases ... is very close'. It is not, of course, exact: the subject matter of the guarantee was not a *res extincta*, but an obligation under a contract which (as another part of the judgment holds) was not itself void but only voidable.

The *Associated Japanese Bank* case can no doubt be distinguished from *Bell v Lever Bros Ltd* by describing the latter case as 'quite exceptional;' but greater difficulty arises from the well-known examples given by Lord Atkin in the latter case of mistakes which would not make a contract void at law, such as the sale of a horse mistakenly believed to be sound, or of a dwelling house mistakenly believed to be inhabitable or of a picture mistakenly believed to be an old master, but in fact, a modern copy (see [1932] AC 161, p 224). These examples seem to show that Lord Atkin, at least, did not confine himself to the special facts before him, but intended to formulate principles of more general application. While there is no direct conflict between the cases, the difference in result illustrates the conflict of policies, described at the beginning of the *Associated Japanese Bank* case: 'respect for the sanctity of contract' prevailed in *Bell v Lever Bros Ltd*, but yielded in the *Associated Japanese Bank* case to 'the need to give effect to the reasonable expectations of honest men'.[16]

The difficulty with the view expressed in *Associated Japanese Bank (International) Ltd v Crédit du Nord SA* is that the non-existent machines were not the subject matter of the contract of guarantee, but if the guarantee and the leaseback are regarded as part of a composite transaction, an analogy can be drawn with those cases in which the subject matter of the void contract is non-existent. What seems to matter is whether the parties think they are dealing with one thing, but discover that they are dealing with something very different. For example in *Grains & Fourrages SA v Huyton*[17] the price for two lots of goods was agreed under the common misapprehension that the correct quality certificates had been exchanged. However, unknown to the parties the certificates had been interchanged and related, respectively, to the wrong lot of goods.

If, as Steyn J in *Associated Japanese Bank v Crédit du Nord* suggests, *Bell v Lever Bros Ltd* is an exceptional case, how has it come to represent the general rule? In one sense, the two cases can be reconciled on the basis of the test employed by Steyn J in *Associated Japanese Bank v Crédit du Nord*, namely that what matters is the key question in the risk allocation process – what are the expectations of reasonable businessmen? In *Associated Japanese Bank v Crédit du Nord*, there is evidence to suggest that neither of the parties, had they known the machines did not exist, would have 'for one moment contemplated entering into the transaction'. In contrast, in *Bell v Lever Bros Ltd*, it is arguable that there was some merit in not treating Bell's and Snelling's breaches of their contract as sufficiently serious to justify the penalty of losing the agreed compensation payment in full.

The more difficult question, in the light of *Bell v Lever Bros Ltd* is whether a mere mistake as to quality is capable of being so fundamental as to render a contract void. Generally, it can be said that in a contract for the sale of goods,

---

16   Treitel, 1989, pp 504–07.
17   [1997] 1 Lloyd's Rep 628

if the parties are mistaken as to the quality of the thing purchased, the mistake will not be fundamental, since the buyer will have got what he contracted for, albeit of a different quality, although much will depend upon the terms of the contract and the description of that which is contracted for. It follows that a contract for the sale of a painting believed by both parties to be by John Constable will not be void if the painting is later discovered not to be a Constable.[18]

In other circumstances the courts may contrive to use alternative doctrines in order to get round the problem of mistake as to quality. For example, in *Gamerco SA v ICM/Fair Warning Ltd*,[19] the court dubiously applied the doctrine of frustration so as to allow the use of the apportionment provisions of the Law Reform (Frustrated Contracts) Act 1943, as opposed to allowing losses to lie where they fell, which is the consequence of an application of common law rules on mistake. In *Gamerco*, the plaintiffs agreed to promote a rock concert to be staged by the defendants in Madrid. Shortly before the date of the performance, but after conclusion of the contract, the venue was discovered to be unsafe due to the use of high alumina cement in its construction. As a result, the Spanish authorities banned the use of the venue and no alternative stadium was available. While the problem could have been dealt with through the use of rules on mistake, the court contrived to treat it as a case of frustration. As a case on mistake, the court would have had to grapple with the category known as mistake as to quality and the difficulty of fitting the facts of the case within the restrictive analysis of this category in *Bell v Lever Bros*.

While the common law rule appears to be primarily concerned with risks of loss which arise from a shared mistake, it is clear that the same principles can be applied just as much to unexpected gains. Thus, if A sells to B a painting, both parties believing that it is a relatively valueless modern copy, can A later seek to set aside the contract if the painting transpires to be an old master on the ground that there is a fundamental, shared mistake? An application of *Bell v Lever Bros* principles, especially the examples given in Lord Atkin's judgment would suggest that such a mistake is not sufficiently fundamental and that the original contract should remain sacrosanct. However, in *Sherwood v Walker*,[20] the plaintiffs agreed to buy a cow called 'Rose 2nd of Aberlone' from the defendant for $80, which was a price appropriate to an animal sold for beef. Both parties believed the cow to be barren, but the plaintiff subsequently discovered that the animal was in calf, with the result that Rose's value was substantially increased to around $750.

---

18 *Leaf v International Galleries Ltd* [1950] 2 KB 86. See, also, *Harlingdon & Leinster Enterprises Ltd v Christopher Hull Fine Art Ltd* [1990] 1 All ER 737.

19 [1995] 1 WLR 1226. See discussion of this case in relation to the rules on frustration, below, p 282 *et seq*.

20 (1887) 66 Mich 568; 33 NW 919 (Supreme Court of Michigan).

Having discovered this fact, the defendant refused to deliver. A majority of the court held that the parties had contracted on the understanding that that the cow was incapable of breeding. Accordingly, there had been a mistake not merely as to quality, but as to the very nature of the thing sold. It was thought that there was as much difference between an ox and a cow as there was between the animal the plaintiff bought and the one which both parties believed to be the subject matter of the contract.

The difficulty with *Sherwood v Walker* when compared with the reasoning employed in *Bell v Lever Bros* is that the former looks suspiciously like a case in which the court has rectified what amounts to little more than a bad bargain.

One way of viewing the difference between *Sherwood* and *Bell* is that the cases reveal a policy conflict in the way different judges approach the issue of risk allocation. On the one hand, there is a market-individualist approach to cases of mistake which seeks to uphold the sanctity of contracts and will therefore result in only the smallest number of cases in which the courts will upset a bargain on the ground of a shared mistake. On the other hand, there are cases in which the courts are more prepared to consider notions of fairness and justice in determining whether a mistake invalidates an agreement. It is not surprising that this alternative approach has developed in equity rather than at common law, as a simple glance at the form of relief granted in each case reveals a substantial difference. The common law answer in cases of shared fundamental mistake is that the contract is void *ab initio* – the contract is treated as if it never existed. In contrast, the equitable solution is to order rescission of the contract, but on terms that attempt to do justice between the parties. Thus, it is possible in equity to order rescission of the contract but then to add a rider to the effect that there should be a renegotiation of the contract on terms which take account of the fact in respect of which the parties were mistaken.

In *Solle v Butcher*,[21] the defendant leased to the plaintiff a flat. Both parties believed that the relevant property was not covered by the provisions of the Rent Restriction Acts, with the result that the defendant could charge a rent of £250 per annum. However, it later transpired that the relevant legislation was applicable with the result that the maximum rent payable was only £140. Such a mistake would not have been operative at common law, but the court held that the contract was voidable in equity, provided there was a fundamental mistake and no fault on the part of the person seeking relief:

Solle v Butcher [1950] 1 KB 671, CA, p 690

Denning LJ: In this plight, the landlord seeks to set aside the lease. He says, with truth, that it is unfair that the tenant should have the benefit of the lease for the outstanding five years of the term at £140 a year, when the proper rent

---

21   [1950] 1 KB 671, CA.

is £250 a year. If he cannot give a notice of increase now, can he not avoid the lease? The only ground on which he can avoid it is on the ground of mistake. It is quite plain that the parties were under a mistake. They thought that the flat was not tied down to a controlled rent, whereas in fact, it was. In order to see whether the lease can be avoided for this mistake it is necessary to remember that mistake is of two kinds: first, mistake which renders the contract void, that is, a nullity from the beginning, which is the kind of mistake which was dealt with by the courts of common law; and, secondly, mistake which renders the contract not void, but voidable, that is, liable to be set aside on such terms as the court thinks fit, which is the kind of mistake which was dealt with by the courts of equity. Much of the difficulty which has attended this subject has arisen because, before the fusion of law and equity, the courts of common law, in order to do justice in the case in hand, extended this doctrine of mistake beyond its proper limits and held contracts to be void which were really only voidable, a process which was capable of being attended with much injustice to third persons who had bought goods or otherwise committed themselves on the faith that there was a contract.

Let me first consider mistakes which render a contract a nullity. All previous decisions on this subject must now be read in the light of *Bell v Lever Bros Ltd*. (The correct interpretation of that case, to my mind, is that, once a contract has been made, that is to say, once the parties, whatever their inmost states of mind, have to all outward appearances agreed with sufficient certainty in the same terms on the same subject matter, then the contract is good unless and until it is set aside for failure of some condition on which the existence of the contract depends, or for fraud, or on some equitable ground. Neither party can rely on his own mistake to say it was a nullity.) From the beginning, no matter that it was a mistake which to his mind was fundamental, and no matter that the other party knew that he was under a mistake. *A fortiori*, if the other party did not know of the mistake, but shared it. The cases where goods have perished at the time of sale, or belong to the buyer, are really contracts which are not void for mistake but are void by reason of an implied condition precedent, because the contract proceeded on the basic assumption that it was possible of performance. So far as cases later than *Bell v Lever Bros Ltd* are concerned, I do not think that *Sowler v Potter* can stand with *King's Norton Metal Co Ltd v Edridge*, which shows that the doctrine of French law as enunciated by Pothier is no part of English law. Nor do I think that the contract in *Nicholson and Venn v Smith-Marriot*, was void from the beginning.

Applying these principles, it is clear that here there was a contract. The parties agreed in the same terms on the same subject matter. It is true that the landlord was under a mistake which was to him fundamental: he would not for one moment have considered letting the flat for seven years if it meant that he could only charge £140 a year for it. He made the fundamental mistake of believing that the rent he could charge was not tied down to a controlled rent; but, whether it was his own mistake or a mistake common to both him and the tenant, it is not a ground for saying that the lease was from the beginning a nullity.

Any other view would lead to remarkable results, for it would mean that, in the many cases where the parties mistakenly think a house is outside the Rent

Restriction Acts when it is really within them, the tenancy would be a nullity, and the tenant would have to go: with the result that the tenants would not dare to seek to have their rents reduced to the permitted amounts lest they should be turned out.

Let me next consider mistakes which render a contract voidable, that is, liable to be set aside on some equitable ground. Whilst presupposing that a contract was good at law, or at any rate not void, the court of equity would often relieve a party from the consequences of his own mistake, so long as it could do so without injustice to third parties. The court, it was said, had power to set aside the contract whenever it was of opinion that it was unconscientious for the other party to avail himself of the legal advantage which he had obtained.

The court had, of course, to define what it considered to be unconscientious, but in this respect equity has shown a progressive development. It is now clear that [a contract will be set aside if the mistake of the one party has been induced by a material misrepresentation of the other, even though it was not fraudulent or fundamental; or if one party, knowing that the other is mistaken about the terms of an offer, or the identity of the person by whom it is made, lets him remain under his delusion and concludes a contract on the mistaken terms instead of pointing out the mistake.] That is, I venture to think, the ground on which the defendant in *Smith v Hughes* would be exempted nowadays, and on which, according to the view by Blackburn J of the facts, the contract in *Lindsay v Cundy*, was voidable and not void; and on which the lease in *Sowler v Potter*, was, in my opinion, voidable and not void.

A contract is also liable in equity to be set aside if the parties were under a common misapprehension either as to facts or as to their relative and respective rights, provided that the misapprehension was fundamental and that the party seeking to set it aside was not himself at fault.

The House of Lords in 1867 in the great case of *Cooper v Phibbs,* affirmed the doctrine there acted on as correct. In that case an uncle had told his nephew, not intending to misrepresent anything, but being in fact, in error that he (the uncle) was entitled to a fishery; and the nephew after the uncle's death, acting in the belief of the truth of what the uncle had told him, entered into an agreement to rent the fishery from the uncle's daughters, whereas it actually belonged to the nephew himself. The mistake there as to the title to the fishery did not render the tenancy agreement a nullity. If it had done, the contract would have been void at law from the beginning and equity would have had to follow the law. There would have been no contract to set aside and no terms to impose. The House of Lords, however, held that the mistake was only such as to make it voidable or, in Lord Westbury's words, 'liable to be set aside' on such terms as the court thought fit to impose; and it was so set aside.

The principle so established by *Cooper v Phibbs* has been repeatedly acted on: see, for instance, *Earl Beauchamp v Winn* and *Huddersfield Banking Co Ltd v Lister*. It is in no way impaired by *Bell v Lever Bros Ltd*, which was treated in the House of Lords as a case at law depending on whether the contract was a nullity or not. If it had been considered on equitable grounds, the result might have been different. In any case, the principle of *Cooper v Phibbs* has been fully restored by *Norwich Union Fire Insurance Society Ltd v William H Price Ltd*.

Applying that principle to this case, the facts are that the plaintiff, the tenant, was a surveyor who was employed by the defendant, the landlord, not only to arrange finance for the purchase of the building and to negotiate with the rating authorities as to the new rateable values, but also to let the flats. He was the agent for letting, and he clearly formed the view that the building was not controlled. He told the valuation officer so. He advised the defendant what were the rents which could be charged. He read to the defendant an opinion of counsel relating to the matter, and told him that in his opinion he could charge £250 and that there was no previous control. He said that the flats came outside the Act and that the defendant was 'clear'. The defendant relied on what the plaintiff told him, and authorised the plaintiff to let at the rentals which he had suggested. The plaintiff not only let the four other flats to other people for a long period of years at the new rentals, but also took one himself for seven years at £250 a year. Now he turns round and says, quite unashamedly, that he wants to take advantage of the mistake to get the flat at £140 a year for seven years instead of the £250 a year, which is not only the rent he agreed to pay, but also the fair and economic rent; and it is also the rent permitted by the Acts on compliance with the necessary formalities. If the rules of equity have become so rigid that they cannot remedy such an injustice, it is time we had a new equity, to make good the omissions of the old. But, in my view, the established rules are amply sufficient for this case.

On the defendant's evidence, which the judge preferred, I should have thought there was a good deal to be said for the view that the lease was induced by an innocent material misrepresentation by the plaintiff. It seems to me that the plaintiff was not merely expressing an opinion on the law: he was making an unambiguous statement as to private rights; and a misrepresentation as to private rights is equivalent to a misrepresentation of fact for this purpose: *MacKenzie v Royal Bank of Canada*. But it is unnecessary to come to a firm conclusion on this point, because, as Bucknill LJ has said, there was clearly a common mistake, or, as I would prefer to describe it, a common misapprehension, which was fundamental and in no way due to any fault of the defendant; and *Cooper v Phibbs* affords ample authority for saying that, by reason of the common misapprehension, this lease can be set aside on such terms as the court thinks fit.

What terms then, should be imposed here? If the lease were set aside without any terms being imposed, it would mean that the plaintiff, the tenant, would have to go out and would have to pay a reasonable sum for his use and occupation. That would, however, not be just to the tenant.

The situation is similar to that of a case where a long lease is made at the full permitted rent in the common belief that notices of increase have previously been served, whereas in fact, they have not. In that case, as in this, when the lease is set aside, terms must be imposed so as to see that the tenant is not unjustly evicted.

If the mistake here had not happened, a proper notice of increase would have been given and the lease would have been executed at the full permitted rent. I think that this court should follow these examples and should impose terms which will enable the tenant to choose either to stay on at the proper rent or to go out.

In my opinion, therefore, the appeal should be allowed. The declaration that the standard rent of the flat is £140 a year should stand. An order should be made on the counterclaim that, on the defendant's giving the undertakings which I have mentioned, the lease be set aside. An account should be had to determine the sum payable for use and occupation. The plaintiff's claim for repayment of rent and for breach of covenant should be dismissed. In respect of his occupation after rescission and during the subsequent licence, the plaintiff will be liable to pay a reasonable sum for use and occupation. That sum should, *prima facie*, be assessed at the full amount permitted by the Acts, not, however, exceeding £250 a year. *Mesne* profits as against a trespasser are assessed at the full amount permitted by the Acts, even though notices of increase have not been served, because that is the amount lost by the landlord. The same assessment should be made here, because the sums payable for use and occupation are not rent, and the statutory provisions about notices of increase do not apply to them. All necessary credits must, of course, be given in respect of past payments, and so forth.

This equitable jurisdiction is far less concerned with market-individualist ideology, but more with justice and fairness, indicating a much greater regard for the reasonable expectations of honest businessmen. But, as the decision in *Associated Japanese Bank v Crédit du Nord* indicates, such considerations cannot now be ignored for the purposes of the common law rule either.

Adams and Brownsword state as follows:[22]

In England, there are two contrasting approaches to common mistake. First, there is the so called 'common law' approach, which tackles the problem along market-individualist lines. Accordingly, relief for common mistake is regarded as exceptional. This is the mews of the 'hawks'. Secondly, there is the so called 'equitable' approach, which applies the very different ideas associated with consumer-welfarism. Relief for common mistake is judged here in the light of principles of fairness: this is the 'dovecote'.

In the leading case on the common law approach, *Bell v Lever Bros Ltd*, Levers' claim for the return of the money rested on common mistake and/or the employees' (non-fraudulent) failure to disclose their illicit cocoa dealings. Levers won at the trial and before the Court of Appeal, but the House of Lords ruled three to two against them, with Lord Atkin's majority speech dominating.

Lord Atkin approached both the common mistake and non-disclosure questions in a textbook market-individualist manner, though presented in a form which derives from Roman law. On the common mistake issue, having noted exceptional cases such as *Couturier v Hastie*, he tackled the thorny area of common mistakes as to quality: 'Mistake as to quality of the thing contracted for raises more difficult questions. In such a case a mistake will not affect assent unless it is the mistake of both parties, and is as to the existence of some quality which makes the thing without the quality essentially different from the thing as it was believed to be.'

---

22 Adams and Brownsword, 2000, pp 125–29.

Applying this principle, Lord Atkin indicated that he would regard a common mistake as inoperative where, for instance, a purchaser bought a horse which, although unsound, was assumed by the parties to be sound, the purchaser paying the price of a sound horse. In the same way, according to Lord Atkin, there would be no operative mistake where a fake painting, assumed by the parties to be an old master, was sold for an old master's price. Such contracts work a hardship on the purchaser, but, in the absence of representation or warranty, common mistake must not be used to undermine sanctity of contract. Thus, whilst conceding the weight of Levers' contention, Lord Atkin did not judge the mistake to be anything more than an expensive inoperative mistake of quality – Levers got what they bargained for, they simply made a bad bargain.

For the dissenting Law Lords in *Bell*, however, the case was relatively straightforward. Following the same sort of legal principle as the majority, the minority held that the mistake was 'as fundamental to the bargain as any error one can imagine' *per* Lord Warrington.

If we assume that the thinking of all judges in *Bell* was market-individualist, then there is evidently some scope for disagreement within the market-individualist camp. Given that relief for common mistake must not jeopardise the security of market transactions, the question is how the minority in *Bell* could defend their softer approach. An attractive argument is that while market-individualists should not allow common mistake to be used to renegotiate the terms of a transaction, it is safe to release a party from a contract which, had the true facts been known, he would not have been prepared to make on any terms (an alternative way of putting it is to say that the mistake went beyond the risks exchanged by formation). With regard to *Bell*, the dissenting Law Lords seem to have good grounds for saying that, had the facts been known, Levers would not have entered into the golden handshake agreements *at all*. Hence, the uncompromising view of the majority was inappropriate. This prompts the mischievous thought that the market-individualists (judged by their own standards) got it wrong in Bell.

Alongside the common law approach to common mistake runs the equitable approach, which is usually traced to the majority decision of the Court of Appeal in *Solle v Butcher*.

The tenant sought to recover the rent he had overpaid. On the face of it, such a mistake, calling merely for an adjustment of rent, could not possibly qualify under the restrictive approach adopted in *Bell v Lever Bros* In *Solle*, however, Denning LJ by-passed *Bell* by saying that the question there had been whether the agreement was void for mistake, not whether it was voidable for mistake under broader equitable principles.

Accordingly, the lease was set aside on the grounds of a common misapprehension as to the application of the Rent Acts, with the plaintiff being given the option of taking a new lease at a reasonable rent (not exceeding £250 per annum).

The *Solle* approach does not start with market-individualist thinking. Rather, it turns on consumer-welfarist ideas of reasonableness and fair play between the parties. In *Solle* itself, Lord Denning was struck by the unreasonableness of the plaintiff first advising the defendant that the rent could lawfully be set at £250 and then turning round 'quite unashamedly' (*per* Denning LJ) and trying to take advantage of the parties' common misapprehension. No court of conscience could stand by and let this happen.

Shared mistakes and principles of risk allocation

It has been seen that both the common law and equity insist that a mistake must be fundamental before a court will grant relief. This insistence on fundamentality is misleading in that all it illustrates is that small risks can normally be allowed to lie where they fall, but greater risks need to be allocated by the court in the absence of any indication in the contract that the parties wish a particular loss to be allocated in a particular way. Moreover, what is fundamental appears to differ according to whether the court applies the common law rule or principles of equity, since it is clear that in equity, relief may be given for a mistake of law,[23] a mistake as to value[24] or for a mistaken inference.[25]

It has been indicated above that a better basis on which to analyse cases on shared mistake is to apply the three cardinal principles of risk allocation, namely, what are the reasonable expectations of the parties; who is the best insurer against the risk and who is the least cost avoider.

Reasonable expectations

The majority of cases in which relief has been given for a shared mistake have involved either physical or legal impossibility of performance. To grant relief in such cases makes sense on the basis that no contracting party can reasonably expect the other to go through with a contract when it has become bereft of value. In such cases, there can be no reasonable expectation of performance and any payment made under the contract can be recovered since there is a total failure of consideration.

Since the reasonable expectations of the parties are best discovered from the contract itself, it follows that if the contract can be construed so as to provide a solution in the event of what might otherwise be regarded as a case of shared mistake, then it is appropriate to give effect to what the parties have agreed. Accordingly, where there is a contract of marine insurance which provides for policy moneys to be paid whether the ship insured is 'lost or not lost', it does not matter that at the time the contract was made, unknown to the parties, that the ship insured had already perished. In this instance, the

---

23 *Allcard v Walker* [1896] 2 Ch 369.
24 *Re Garnett* (1885) 31 Ch D 1. See, also, *Amalgamated Investment & Property Co Ltd v John Walker & Sons Ltd* [1977] 1 WLR 164.
25 *Solle v Butcher* [1950] 1 KB 671; *Grist v Bailey* [1967] Ch 532.

parties have expressly provided that the insurer will be liable to bear the risk of loss.

In *Associated Japanese Bank v Crédit du Nord SA*,[26] the facts and the decision insofar as it relates to the issue of mistake are considered above. However, the ratio in this case is based on the issue of construction of the contract:

Associated Japanese Bank v Crédit du Nord SA [1988] 3 All ER 902, p 908

Steyn J:

The construction point

The first question to be considered is whether the guarantee was expressly made subject to a condition precedent that the four machines existed. The factual matrix, which is relevant to this question of construction, is that both parties, the creditor and the guarantor, were induced to commit themselves by information supplied by the lease brokers employed by Mr Bennett. That information included the statement, which was made expressly or by necessary implication, that the four machines existed. And it matters not that AJB thought that Mr Bennett owned the machines, while CDN thought that AJB owned the machines. The fact is that both parties were informed, and believed, that the machines existed. Against that contextual scene, CDN provided a guarantee to AJB: 'In consideration of your leasing four Textile Compression Packaging machines to British Consolidated Engineering Company ... pursuant to a Leasing Contract dated 29 February 1984 ...'

The only other provision of the guarantee which is relevant to this question of construction is cl 6 of the guarantee. It reads as follows: '*This Guarantee and your rights under it shall not be affected or prejudiced* by your holding or taking any other or further securities or by your varying releasing or omitting or neglecting to enforce any such securities or by your giving time for payment or granting any other indulgence to or making any other arrangements with or accepting any composition from the Lessee or *subject to our prior consent to any such variation by your varying the terms of the Leasing Contract made between yourselves and the Lessee or by the substitution of any other goods comprised in such contract.*' (Emphasis added.)

Clause 6 of the guarantee therefore contemplated the existence of the machines, and made provision for a right of substitution only if the guarantor granted consent. Against that background the question is whether it was expressly agreed that the guarantee would only become effective if there was a lease of four existing machines. The point is not capable of elaborate analysis. It is a matter of first impression. On balance, my conclusion is that, sensibly construed against its objective setting, the guarantee was subject to an express condition precedent that there was a lease in respect of four existing machines. If this conclusion is right, AJB's claim against CDN as guarantor or as sole or principal debtor under cl 11 fails.

---

26   [1988] 3 All ER 902.

If my conclusion about the construction of the guarantee is wrong, it remains to be considered whether there was an implied condition precedent that the lease related to four existing machines. In the present contract such a condition may only be held to be implied if one of two applicable tests is satisfied. The first is that such an implication is necessary to give business efficacy to the relevant contract, that is, the guarantee. In other words, the criterion is whether the implication is necessary to render (the guarantee) workable. That is usually described as *The Moorcock* test (see *The Moorcock* (1889) 14 PD 64; [1886–90] All ER 530). It may well be that this stringent test is not satisfied because the guarantee is workable in the sense that all that is required is that the guarantor who assumed accessory obligations must pay what is due under the lease. But there is another type of implication which seems more appropriate in the present context. It is possible to imply a term if the court is satisfied that reasonable men, faced with the suggested term which was *ex hypothesi* not expressed in the contract, would without hesitation say, 'Yes, of course, that is so obvious that it goes without saying': see *Shirlaw v Southern Foundries (1926) Ltd* [1939] 2 All ER 113, p 124; [1939] 2 KB 206, p 227, *per* MacKinnon LJ. Although broader in scope than *The Moorcock* test, it is nevertheless a stringent test, and it will only be permissible to hold that an implication has been established on this basis in comparatively rare cases, notably when one is dealing with a commercial instrument such as a guarantee for reward. Nevertheless, against the contextual background of the fact that both parties were informed that the machines existed, and the express terms of the guarantee, I have come to the firm conclusion that the guarantee contained an implied condition precedent that the lease related to existing machines. Again, if this conclusion is right, AJB's claim against CDN as guarantor or as sole or principal debtor under cl II fails.

Where the parties have reduced their contract to writing, it may be the case that the written instrument does not include all the terms of the contract. In this case, it may be possible for the written instrument to be rectified in equity so as to give effect to the reasonable expectations of the parties. For these purposes, it is important to emphasise that it is the instrument which is rectified and that there is no principle which allows the court to give the equitable remedy of rectification of a contract.[27]

Since it is the reasonable expectations of both parties which matter, the general rule is that rectification will only be granted where the instrument fails to record the common intention of both parties to the contract.[28] Thus, rectification will not be granted where the expectations of only one of the parties is not recorded in the document,[29] although this is subject to the rule on induced mistake, considered below.

---

27 *McKenzie v Coulson* (1869) LR 8 Eq 368; *Rose v Pim* [1953] 2 QB 450.

28 *Riverlate Properties Ltd v Paul* [1975] Ch 133.

29 *Bates (Thomas) & Son Ltd v Wyndham's (Lingerie) Ltd* [1981] 1 All ER 1077; *A Roberts & Co Ltd v Leicestershire County Council* [1961] Ch 555.

It has been observed above that although rules on mistake are generally concerned with the allocation of losses, they may also be employed to deal with unexpected gains. This too is in line with the principle that regard should be had to the reasonable expectations of both parties, since if a person makes a gain which he did not reasonably expect to make as a result of a mistake made by the other party, it may be reasonable to assume that neither party had any intention that the gain be made. Accordingly, at common law there may be an operative fundamental mistake and in equity relief may also be granted. For example, in *Hartog v Colin & Shields*,[30] there was a trade custom to the effect that hareskins were normally sold at a price per piece, but the defendant had offered to sell the same commodity at a price per pound. Normally, there were three pieces to the pound, with the result that the buyer stood to make a substantial gain. There was also correspondence between the parties which referred to a price per piece, but the buyer purported to accept the offer and sued when the defendant failed to deliver. Because of the relevant trade custom, the buyer was taken to be aware of the defendants' mistake and, applying the common law rule, it was held that he could not expect to benefit from the gain which would otherwise have been made had the contract been valid. Singleton J held[31] that: 'The offer was wrongly expressed, and the defendants by their evidence, and by the correspondence, have satisfied me that the plaintiff could not reasonably have supposed that the offer contained the offeror's real intention. Indeed I am satisfied to the contrary. That means that there must be judgment for the defendants.'

Similar principles also apply where the court is considering the remedy of rectification. The fact that the party seeking rectification is aware of the mistake of the other party is a factor the court will consider in determining whether an alteration of the written instrument should be ordered. The fact that one party is aware of the mistake of the other is a factor which points to the possibility of an unwarranted and unexpected gain. If the defendant is aware of the mistake made by the other party, it is likely that the court will not grant an order or rectification. At one stage, the courts appeared to require actual awareness of the mistake, but more recent authorities suggest that awareness may be implied, especially in circumstances in which the party seeking relief has been guilty of misleading the other. In *Commission for the New Towns v Cooper (Great Britain) Ltd*,[32] the view was expressed that if A intends B to be mistaken and diverts B's attention from discovering the mistake by making false or misleading statements and B makes the mistake which A intends, then even if A does not know of the mistake, but merely suspects that B is mistaken, this will be sufficient to allow rectification. Thus in Cooper A arranged a meeting with B reasonably leading B to believe that the

---

30   [1939] 3 All ER 566.
31   *Ibid*, p 567.
32   [1995] Ch 259

meeting was to discuss an issue different to A's intended motive, namely, to secure the transfer of an option which B enjoyed over commercial property assigned to A. In the course of this meeting, A gave the impression that he was looking to expand the business run from those premises, when, in fact, he wished to close the business down, provided he was able to secure the transfer of B's option to himself. As a result of the meeting, B transferred the option to A, but later sought rectification of the written document when A's real motives were discovered. At first instance, it was held that, since A did not have actual knowledge of B's mistake, rectification was not possible. However, the Court of Appeal reversed this ruling on the ground that the contract should be performed in accordance with B's understanding as to what had been agreed. Accordingly, the contract was rectified in the light of A's unconscionable conduct.

In *Bates (Thomas) & Son Ltd v Wyndham's (Lingerie) Ltd*,[33] the tenants of premises leased from the plaintiffs, on previous occasions, had contracted for an option to renew the lease at a rental to be fixed by arbitration, in the event of a dispute. The new lease which the parties had entered into did not contain any provision for arbitration. The tenants were aware of the omission, but did not draw the fact to the attention of the plaintiffs. In the event, the court declined to order rectification because there was a chance of some inequitable benefit to the person who was aware of the plaintiff's mistake:

Bates (Thomas) & Son Ltd v Wyndham's (Lingerie) Ltd [1981] 1 All ER 1077, CA, p 1085

Buckley LJ: The landlords claim rectification in the present case on the basis of a principle enunciated by Pennicuick J in *A Roberts & Co, Ltd v Leicestershire County Council* [1961] 2 All ER 545, pp 551–52; [1961] Ch 555 at 570: 'The second ground rest on the principle that a party is entitled to rectification of a contract on proof that he believed a particular term to be included in the contract and that the other party concluded the contract with the omission or a variation of that term in the knowledge that the first party believed the term to be included ... The principle is stated in *Snell's Principles of Equity*, 25th edn, 1960, p 569, as follows: "By what appears to be a species of equitable estoppel, if one party to a transaction knows that the instrument contains a mistake in his favour but does nothing to correct it, he (and those claiming under him) will be precluded from resisting rectification on the ground that the mistake is unilateral and not common."'

Of course, if a document is executed in circumstances in which one party realises that in some respect it does not accurately reflect what down to that moment had been the common intention of the parties, it cannot be said that the document is executed under a common mistake, because the party who has realised the mistake is no longer labouring under the mistake. There may be cases in which the principle enunciated by Pennicuick J applies, although there

---

33 [1981] 1 All ER 1077, CA.

is no prior common intention, but we are not, I think, concerned with such a case here, for it seems to me, on the facts that I have travelled through, that it is established that the parties had a common intention down to the time when Mr Avon realised the mistake in the terms of the lease, a common intention that the rent in respect of any period after the first five years should be agreed or, in default of agreement, fixed by an arbitratory.

The principle so enunciated by Pennicuick J was referred to with approval in this court in *Riverlate Properties Ltd v Paul* [1974] 2 All ER 656, p 660; [1975] Ch 133, p 140, where Russell LJ, reading the judgment of the court, said: 'It may be that the original conception of reformation of an instrument by rectification was based solely on common mistake: but certainly in these days rectification may be based on such knowledge on the part of the defendant: see For example, *A Roberts & Co Ltd v Leicestershire County Council.* Whether there was in any particular case knowledge of the intention and mistake of the other party must be a question of fact to be decided on the evidence. Basically it appears to us that it must be such as to involve the lessee in a degree of sharp practice.'

For this doctrine (that is to say the doctrine of *A Roberts v Leicestershire County Council*) to apply I think it must be shown: first, that one party, A, erroneously believed that the document sought to be rectified contained a particular term or provision, or possibly did not contain a particular term or provision which, mistakenly, it did contain; second, that the other party, B, was aware of the omission or the inclusion and that it was due to a mistake on the part of A; third, that B has omitted to draw the mistake to the notice of A. And I think there must be a fourth element involved, namely that the mistake must be one calculated to benefit B If these requirements are satisfied, the court may regard it as inequitable to allow B to resist rectification to give effect to A's intention on the ground that the mistake was not, at the time of execution of the document, a common mistake.

Which decision produced the fairer result – *Hartog v Colin & Shields* or *Thomas Bates & Son Ltd v Wyndham's (Lingerie) Ltd*? What is the difference between holding a contract void and rectifying an existing contractual document so as to give effect to what is almost certainly the presumed intention of the contracting parties? Would it be possible to rectify a contractual document in circumstances in which the offeree does not have actual knowledge of the offeror's mistake, but the circumstances are such that had he thought about it, the offeree ought to have realised that the offeror was mistaken? (See *The Nai Genova* [1984] 1 Lloyd's Rep 353, where it was observed that in all cases in which rectification has been ordered, the offeree has had actual knowledge of the mistake.)

Apart from the equitable remedy of rectification, the court may also order other equitable remedies such as an injunction or specific performance, although in doing so, the court may grant the remedy on terms which do justice to both parties. This line of approach is particularly likely to be followed in cases where the defendant stands to make a gain which, on the facts, it is clear he did not harbour any reasonable expectation of making.

In *Grist v Bailey*,[34] the defendant contracted to sell a freehold house to the plaintiff for £850, subject to the rights of a sitting tenant. In fact, both the sitting tenant and his wife had died. With vacant possession, the property was worth £2,250 and the evidence clearly showed that the plaintiff's agent would not have expected to be able to purchase property of the kind in question for £850 had there been no protected tenancy. Although the mistake was not of a kind which would allow the court to treat the contract as void at common law, it was held, nonetheless, that the court could grant rescission of the contract in equity subject to the imposition of a term to the effect that the plaintiff should have the opportunity to purchase the property at a price which reflected the fact that it was offered with vacant possession:

Grist v Bailey [1967] Ch 532, p 538

Goff J: In *Solle v Butcher*, as it seems to me, Denning LJ clearly drew a distinction between the effect of mistake at law which, where effective at all, makes the contract void, and in equity, where it is a ground for rescission or for refusing specific performance; and, as it further seems to me, he clearly thought that this was wider than the jurisdiction at law.

Mr Baden Fuller has submitted that there is no difference between law and equity and no case which suggests that *Bell v Lever Bros Ltd*, does not cover the whole field, save what he describes as one casual remark of Denning LJ in Solle v Butcher, and he says, moreover, that Denning LJ himself resiled from his earlier view in the later case, *Leaf v International Galleries*. I cannot accept this interpretation of Denning LJ's judgment, or indeed of *Solle v Butcher* as a whole. I think it was a carefully considered view of the relevant law and equity, and I do not think Denning LJ in *Leaf v International Galleries* resiled from it in any way.

I cannot dismiss what Denning LJ said in *Solle v Butcher* as a mere *dictum*. It was in my judgment the basis of the decision and is binding on me; and, as I have said, I think Bucknill LJ took the same view.

Then I have to decide first, was there a common mistake in this case; secondly, was it fundamental; and perhaps thirdly, was the defendant at fault?

It is clearly established that the defendant did not know that either Mr or Mrs Brewer had died. Even if Mr Bailey knew that Mrs Brewer was dead, as to which I have no evidence, I am bound to infer that he did not know that Mr Brewer was also dead. Mr Ginn did not know that either was dead, and Mr Rider said that he first learned that Mr Brewer was dead after the date of the agreement, and that he then learned that Mr Terry Brewer was in occupation. Mr Rider further gave evidence that so far as investment was concerned his mind went no further than that the sort of prices they were discussing were prices relevant to a tenant remaining there, and that he assumed all along there was a protected tenant and that when the purchase was completed they would have a protected tenant, and again that he would never have expected to get

---

34 [1967] Ch 532.

this property for anything like £850 with vacant possession. He said he made his offer on the basis that there was a protected tenant and that he would stay there.

Such being the state of the evidence, in my judgment, there was a common mistake, namely, that there was still subsisting a protected tenancy in favour of Mr or Mrs Brewer; and it is to be remembered that the language of clause 7 of the agreement is 'subject to the existing tenancy thereof'. In my view, this was nonetheless a common mistake, though the parties may have differed in their belief as to who the tenant was, whether Mr or Mrs Brewer, although that may have a bearing on materiality.

Then, was it fundamental? In view of Mr Rider's own evidence to which I have referred, and the evidence of Mr Cooper Hurst, a surveyor called on behalf of the defendant, that in his opinion the vacant possession value as at August 1964, was £2,250, in my judgment it must have been, if Mr Terry Brewer had no rights under the Rent and Mortgage Interest Restrictions Acts 1920 to 1957.

This was the case pleaded in para 3 of the defence and counterclaim, but it depends upon showing that Mrs Brewer was the contractual tenant, since then her husband became statutory tenant, and the effect of s 12(1)(g) of the Increase of Rent and Mortgage Interest (Restrictions) Act 1920 was spent, leaving no protection for Mr Terry Brewer: see *Summers v Donohue*.

The onus of proving the premise upon which that way of presenting her case depends is upon the defendant, and in my opinion she has failed to discharge it.

There remains one other point, and that is the condition laid down by Denning LJ that the party seeking to take advantage of the mistake must not be at fault. Denning LJ did not develop that at all and it is not, I think, with respect, absolutely clear what it comprehends. Clearly, there must be some degree of blame worthiness beyond the mere fault of having made a mistake, but the question is, how much, or in what way? I think each case must depend on its own facts, and I do not consider that the defendant or her agents were at fault so as to disentitle them to relief.

It was argued that the vendor should know who her tenants are, but this was a case of a long standing and informal tenancy, the rent under which was paid simply by attendance in the outer office, where it was received by some junior boy or girl, and Mr Brewer had but recently died.

The result, in my judgment, is that the defendant is entitled to relief in equity, and I do not feel that this is a case for simply refusing specific performance. Accordingly, the action fails, and on the counterclaim I order rescission. It is clear that this, being equitable relief, may be granted unconditionally or on terms, and Mr Godfrey, on behalf of the defendant, has offered to submit to a term that the relief I have ordered should be on condition that the defendant is to enter into a fresh contract at a proper vacant possession price, and, if required by the plaintiff, I will impose that term.

Best insurer and least cost avoider

In the risk allocation process, it is important to consider how best to allocate a particular risk of loss. If one of the parties is actually or constructively aware of the risk of loss and has failed to take precautions to guard himself against that risk, he may be regarded as the most appropriate person to bear that risk. Furthermore, if one of the parties is responsible for bringing about the mistake of the other, the party who induces the mistake may be regarded as the least cost avoider, in the sense that he was in the best position to take steps to avert the risk of loss by not engaging in the activity which leads the other party to form his mistaken belief.

Where one of the parties is assumed to have been aware of the risk, there will often be an element of speculation involved and the court may work on the assumption that the loss was intended by the parties to lie where it falls.

In *Amalgamated Investment and Property Co Ltd v John Walker & Sons Ltd*,[35] a property developer purchased a warehouse with the intention of using the site as part of an extensive property development. Unknown to the parties, the property had been listed as a building of special architectural and historical interest. As a consequence of this listing, the property fell in value from approximately £1,710,000 to £210,000. The court held that neither the common law nor equity could provide relief, since the risk of a fall in value was considered to be one which every owner and purchaser must recognise that he is subject to:

Amalgamated Investment and Property Co Ltd v John Walker & Sons Ltd [1977] 1 WLR 164, CA, p 171

Buckley LJ: It has been contended before us that there was here a common mistake of fact on a matter of fundamental importance, in consequence of which the contract ought to be set aside. Reliance has been placed upon the decision of the Court of Appeal in *Solle v Butcher* [1950] 1 KB 671 and the decision of Goff J in *Grist v Bailey* [1967] Ch 532.

Mr Balcombe, appearing for the purchasers, says that the purchasers bought the property as property which was ripe for development and that the vendors sold upon the same basis, and that by reason of the decision to list the property, the property was not in fact, ripe for development. Therefore he says there was a common mistake as to the nature of the property, and the purchaser is entitled to rescission. So, the alleged common mistake was that the property was property suitable for and capable of being developed.

For the application of the doctrine of mutual mistake as a ground for setting the contract aside, it is of course necessary to show that the mistake existed at the date of the contract; and so Mr Balcombe relies in that respect not upon the signing of the list by the officer who alone was authorised to sign it on behalf

---

35   [1977] 1 WLR 164, CA.

of the Secretary of State, but upon the decision of Miss Price to include the property in the list. That decision, although in fact, it led to the signature of the list in the form in which it was eventually signed, was merely an administrative step in the carrying out of the operations of the branch of the ministry. It was a personal decision on the part of Miss Price that the list should contain the particular property with which we are concerned. But there was still the possibility that something else might arise before the list was signed. Some communication might have been received from some outside body which threw some light upon the qualifications of this building for listing, which might have resulted in its being excluded from the list as it was actually signed. Indeed, the head of the department might himself, had he known of the circumstances, have formed a different opinion from the opinion formed by Miss Price, or Miss Price might, I suppose, herself have changed her mind during the time between preparing the list, sending it to the typing pool and eventually laying it before her superior for signature.

The crucial date, in my judgment, is the date when the list was signed. It was then that the building became a listed building, and it was only then that the expectations of the parties (who no doubt both expected that this property would be capable of being developed, subject always of course to obtaining planning permission, without it being necessary to obtain listed building permission) were disappointed. In my judgment, there was no mutual mistake as to the circumstances surrounding the contract at the time when the contract was entered into. The only mistake that there was, was one which related to the expectation of the parties. They expected that the building would be subject only to ordinary town planning consent procedures and that expectation has been disappointed.

How does this case differ from *Grist v Bailey*? Surely, in the later case, there was also an element of speculation over the price of the property, in which case, should not the risk of loss have rested where it fell, namely on the shoulders of the vendor? A possible reason for the difference lies in the fact that the loss in *Amalgamated Properties v Walker* fell on the shoulders of an experienced businessman, whereas in *Grist v Bailey*, the loss would have fallen on the shoulders of a private vendor. Collins[36] suggests that *Grist v Bailey* evidences a paternalistic approach to the issue of mistake in equity:

> The process of judicial revision is not so simple as to compare the obligation of one party before and after the unexpected event in order to discover whether the event has substantially increased the cost of performance of his obligation.
>
> Where the parties enjoyed comparable resources for devising a complex commercial transaction and exercised those resources in order to create a contract which attempted to allocate all the risks between the parties, then it is unlikely except in calamitous circumstances that the courts will be prepared to accept that unexpected events have created any imbalance in the obligations. If, on the other hand, either one or both parties lack these skills, then the

---

36   Collins, 1997, p 281.

contract is less likely to be regarded as a presumptively fair allocation of the burdens of unforeseen and unprovided for eventualities.

The contrast between *Amalgamated Investment and Property Co Ltd v John Walker & Sons Ltd* and *Grist v Bailey* illustrates this differential treatment. In the former case, the plaintiffs sought to avoid a contract for the purchase of a building intended for redevelopment when, shortly after signing the agreement, it emerged that the government had designated the building one of special architectural or historical interest which immediately reduced the market value of the property. In *Grist v Bailey,* the vendor of a house claimed rescission of the contract on the ground that he had mistakenly believed that it was occupied by a tenant with statutorily protected tenure which reduced the price. Whereas the English Court of Appeal in the former case gave short shrift to the plaintiff's argument that they should be relieved from their calamitous contract on the ground that the government order was just one of those risks which purchasers of property take, the High Court in *Grist v Bailey* bent over backwards to permit the vendor, who was an ordinary houseowner with no special skills, to rescind the contract because of his mistake about vacant possession. These cases may be distinguished on a number of grounds. Most commentators would point out that the mistake in *Grist v Bailey* existed at the time of the contract, whereas in *Amalgamated Investment and Property Co Ltd v John Walker & Sons Ltd,* the administrative order was only finally issued after the contract had been signed. But if this distinction should make a difference, which I doubt, then it should argue in favour of precisely the opposite outcome, for the courts may be justifiably more reluctant to set aside contracts on the grounds of unexpected events when it was possible for the parties to have discovered the truth of the matter before committing themselves. Alternatively, it might be asserted that the mistake in one case was more fundamental than the other, though in monetary terms this is a tough argument to present since the drop in value in *Amalgamated Investment and Property Co Ltd v John Walker & Sons Ltd* was from £1,710,000 to approximately £200,000. It is more realistic, however, to acknowledge that, whereas the parties in one case were commercial enterprises, aware of the risks of property development, the parties in the other were ordinary householders and relatively naive about the risks associated with their transaction. The courts adopt a criterion of fairness which discriminates between types of contractors, forcing commercial enterprises to shoulder more risks of misadventure than ordinary individuals.

FRUSTRATION OF CONTRACTS

A frustrating event is one which occurs after the contract has been entered into and is sufficiently fundamental to destroy the foundation of the contract[37] or which renders performance of the contract radically different from that

---

[37] *Krell v Henry* [1903] 2 KB 740, p 751, *per* Vaughan Williams LJ.

which was originally agreed.[38] Just as in the case of the common law rules on shared mistake, the emphasis is upon the fundamentality of the interruption to the performance of the contract. However, it has been seen already that the test of fundamentality gives very few answers to the question: when is a contract frustrated? Moreover the concentration on the issue of fundamentality also disguises the important risk allocation role played by the rules gathered together under the doctrine of frustration. Like the rules on shared mistake, many of the principles underlying the doctrine of frustration also consider the intentions of the parties, who is the superior risk bearer and who is the least cost avoider.

In historical terms, the doctrine of frustration is a relative newcomer to the battery of rules which regulate the contracting process, being traceable to a mid-19th century case[39] which sought to justify the excuse for non-performance of existing contractual obligations on the ground that there was an implied condition that if a particular thing was expected by the parties to exist and that thing was destroyed without fault on either side, neither party should be expected to perform that which had become impossible. Subsequently, the doctrine was extended to cover cases in which performance was literally possible but in which the external event rendered futile any further performance of the contractual obligations of both parties.[40]

The difficulty with the implied term approach to the doctrine of frustration is that in classical terminology, a term implied by the courts should represent the presumed intention of both of the parties to the contract. However, by its nature, a frustrating event will usually be one which is beyond the contemplation of both parties, thus explaining why no provision was made for it in the contract. In these circumstances, it can be nothing more than pure fiction to say that the parties had a presumed intention that in the event that the frustrating event should occur, both parties have impliedly agreed that the other should be released from the obligation to perform the contract. Moreover, the parties will not necessarily view the contract in the light of the frustrating event in the same way, since if one of the parties is in a stronger position should the loss be treated as lying where it falls, he may be happy to insist on the continuing validity of the contract whereas the party in the weaker position will prefer to treat his performance obligations as being at an end. Instead, the more modern approach to frustration is to ask what would the parties, as fair and reasonable men, have agreed upon had they had the frustrating event in contemplation. Accordingly, the rules on the frustration of contracts involve an attempt by the courts to find a reasonable and just

---

38 *Davis Contractors Ltd v Fareham Urban District Council* [1956] AC 696, pp 728–29, *per* Lord Radcliffe.

39 *Taylor v Caldwell* (1863) 122 ER 309.

40 Commonly referred to as cases of frustration of purpose, typified by voyage charterparties frustrated by the unavailability of the particular ship contracted for: *Jackson v Union Marine Insurance Co Ltd* (1874) LR 10 CP 125.

solution[41] based on a policy of judicial intervention where there is no fault on either side of the contract:[42]

Davis Contractors Ltd v Fareham Urban District Council [1956] AC 696, HL, p 719

Lord Reid: Frustration has often been said to depend on adding a term to the contract by implication: for example, Lord Loreburn in *FA Tamplin SS Co Ltd v Anglo-Mexican Petroleum Products Co Ltd*, after quoting language of Lord Blackburn, said: 'That seems to me another way of saying that from the nature of the contract it cannot be supposed the parties, as reasonable men, intended it to be binding on them under such altered conditions. Were the altered conditions such that, had they thought of them, they would have taken their chance of them, or such that as sensible men they would have said "if that happens, of course, it is all over between us"? What, in fact, was the true meaning of the contract? Since the parties have not provided for the contingency, ought a court to say it is obvious they would have treated the thing as at an end?'

I find great difficulty in accepting this as the correct approach because it seems to me hard to account for certain decisions of this House in this way.

I may be allowed to note an example of the artificiality of the theory of an implied term given by Lord Sands in *James Scott & Sons Ltd v Del Sel*: 'A tiger has escaped from a travelling menagerie. The milkman fails to deliver the milk. Possibly the milkman may be exonerated from any breach of contract; but, even so, it would seem hardly reasonable to base that exoneration on the ground that "tiger days excepted" must be held as if written into the milk contract.'

It appears to me that frustration depends, at least in most cases, not on adding any implied term, but on the true construction of the terms which are in the contract read in light of the nature of the contract and of the relevant surrounding circumstances when the contract was made.

In my view, the proper approach to this case is to take from the arbitrator's award all facts which throw light on the nature of the contract, or which can properly be held to be extrinsic evidence relevant to assist in its construction and then, as a matter of law, to construe the contract and to determine whether the ultimate situation, as disclosed by the award, is or is not within the scope of the contract so construed.

Lord Radcliffe (p 726): I must say briefly what I understand to be the legal principle of frustration. It is not always expressed in the same way, but I think that the points which are relevant to the decision of this case are really beyond dispute. The theory of frustration belongs to the law of contract and it is represented by a rule which the courts will apply in certain limited

---

41 *Joseph Constantine SS Co Ltd v Imperial Smelting Corpn Ltd* [1942] AC 154, pp 186, *per* Lord Wright.

42 *Paal Wilson & Co A/S v Paartenreederei Hannah Blumenthal, The Hannah Blumenthal* [1983] 1 All ER 34, p 44, *per* Lord Brandon.

circumstances for the purpose of deciding that contractual obligations, *ex facie* binding, are no longer enforceable against the parties. The description of the circumstances that justify the application of the rule and, consequently, the decision whether in a particular case those circumstances exist are, I think, necessarily questions of law.

It has often been pointed out that the descriptions vary from one case of high authority to another. Even as long ago as 1918, Lord Summer was able to offer an anthology of different tests directed to the factor of delay alone, and delay, though itself a frequent cause of the principle of frustration being invoked, is only one instance of the kind of circumstance to which the law attends (see *Bank Line Ltd v Arthur Capel & Co*). A full current anthology would need to be longer yet. But the variety of description is not of any importance so long as it is recognised that each is only a description and that all are intended to express the same general idea. I do not think that there has been a better expression of that general idea than the one offered by Lord Loreburn in *FA Tamplin SS Co Ltd v Anglo-Mexican Petroleum Products Co Ltd.* It is shorter to quote than to try to paraphrase it: '... a court can and ought to examine the contract and the circumstances in which it was made, not of course to vary, but only to explain it, in order to see whether or not from the nature of it the parties must have made their bargain on the footing that a particular thing or state of things would continue to exist. And if they must have done so, then a term to that effect will be implied, though it be not expressed in the contract ... no court has an absolving power, but it can infer from the nature of the contract and the surrounding circumstances that a condition which is not expressed was a foundation on which the parties contracted.'

So expressed, the principle of frustration, the origin of which seems to lie in the development of commercial law, is seen to be a branch of a wider principle which forms part of the English law of contract as a whole. But, in my opinion, full weight ought to be given to the requirement that the parties 'must have made' their bargain on the particular footing. Frustration is not to be lightly invoked as the dissolvent of a contract.

Lord Loreburn ascribes the dissolution to an implied term of the contract that was actually made. This approach is in line with the tendency of English courts to refer all the consequences of a contract to the will of those who made it. But there is something of a logical difficulty in seeing how the parties could even impliedly have provided for something which *ex hypothesi* they neither expected nor foresaw; and the ascription of frustration to an implied term of the contract has been criticised as obscuring the true action of the court which consists in applying an objective rule of the law of contract to the contractual obligations that the parties have imposed upon themselves. So long as each theory produces the same result as the other, as normally it does, it matters little which theory is avowed (see *British Movietonews Ltd v London and District Cinemas Ltd*, *per* Viscount Simon). But it may still be of some importance to recall that, if the matter is to be approached by way of implied term, the solution of any particular case is not to be found by inquiring what the parties themselves would have agreed on had they been, as they were not, forewarned. It is not merely that no one can answer that hypothetical question:

it is also that the decision must be given 'irrespective of the individuals concerned, their temperaments and failings, their interest and circumstances' (*Hirji Mulji v Cheong Yue SS Co Ltd*). The legal effect of frustration 'does not depend on their intention or their opinions, or even knowledge, as to the event'. On the contrary, it seems that when the event occurs 'the meaning of the contract must be taken to be, not what the parties did intend (for they had neither thought nor intention regarding it), but that which the parties, as fair and reasonable men, would presumably have agreed upon if, having such possibility in view, they had made express provision as to their several rights and liabilities in the event of its occurrence' (*Dahl v Nelson, per* Lord Watson).

By this time it might seem that the parties themselves have become so far disembodied spirits that their actual persons should be allowed to rest in peace. In their place there rises the figure of the fair and reasonable man. And the spokesman of the fair and reasonable man. And the spokesman of the fair and reasonable man, who represents after all no more than the anthropomorphic conception of justice, is and must be the court itself. So perhaps it would be simpler to say at the outset that frustration occurs whenever the law recognises that without default of either party a contractual obligation has become incapable of being performed because the circumstances in which performance is called for would render it a thing radically different from that which was undertaken by the contract. *Non haec in foedera veni.* It was not this that I promised to do.

There is, however, no uncertainty as to the materials upon which the court must proceed. 'The data for decision are, on the one hand, the terms and construction of the contract, read in the light of the then existing circumstances, and on the other hand the events which have occurred' (*Denny, Mott & Dickson Ltd v James B Fraser & Co Ltd, per* Lord Wright). In the nature of things there is often no room for any elaborate inquiry. The court must act upon a general impression of what its rule requires. It is for that reason that special importance is necessarily attached to the occurrence of any unexpected event that, as it were, changes the face of things. But, even so, it is not hardship or inconvenience or material loss itself which calls the principle of frustration into play. There must be as well such a change in the significance of the obligation that the thing undertaken would, if performed, be a different thing from that contracted for.

Is there any greater objection to applying an implied terms approach to cases of frustration than there is to any other case where a term is implied on the basis of the presumed intention of the parties (discussed in the previous chapter)? Does not Lord Watson in *Dahl v Nelson, Donkin & Co*[43] hit the nail on the head when he observes that what matters is not the intention of the parties, but what they, as reasonable men, would have done had they had the frustrating event in mind?

---

43   (1881) 6 App Cas 38.

Frustration and principles of risk allocation

The intentions of the parties

If the contract expressly allocates the risk of loss arising from a particular event to one party rather than the other, it should follow as a matter of course that the court should heed the intention of the parties. However, the nature of frustrating events is that in the majority of cases, there will be no express provision, but it may still be possible to infer an intention from the nature of the contract. This appears to be particularly the case where the contract involves long-term speculation in which case, it may be reasonable to assume that the party engaged in the speculation must bear the risk that his speculative venture may not work to his advantage.[44] Sometimes, a term of the contract may be capable of interpretation in such a way that it may apply to a particular event, but if the provision is worded very generally, it may be given only a restricted field of application. Thus, in *Metropolitan Water Board v Dick Kerr & Co Ltd*,[45] a construction contract provided that in the event of delays 'however occasioned' the contractor would be given additional time in which to complete the project. However, this was held not to extend to a government order which required the cessation of work and the disposal of all the contractor's equipment during a period of war. The interpretation placed upon the relevant provision by the House of Lords was that it was obviously intended to apply to short term interruptions such as strikes, bad weather or shortage of materials, but not to such a fundamental change of circumstances which had altered the whole basis of the contract as resulted from the emergency order. Accordingly, the contract was held to have been frustrated.

Generally, where performance of a contract becomes illegal, it is assumed that the intention of the parties, as reasonable businessmen, is that further performance of the contract should cease. This is usually justifiable on public policy grounds in cases of trading with the enemy. More difficult are cases in which performance of the contract becomes illegal without the involvement of the public policy considerations that attend cases of trading with the enemy. There may be circumstances in which subsequent legislation strikes at the very root of the agreement between the parties, in which case the contract will be frustrated. Thus, if there is a contract for the sale of pine wood, but subsequent legislation renders it illegal to sell at the price agreed between the parties and to import timber of the kind contracted for, the contract is frustrated.[46] Likewise, if it becomes clear that the venue for a rock concert cannot be used because it is unsafe and will not be licensed by the appropriate

---

44 See, eg, *Larrinaga & Co v Société Franco-Américaine des Phosphates de Médulla* (1923) 92 LJ KB 455.

45 [1918] AC 119.

46 *Denny Mott & Dickson Ltd v James B Fraser & Co Ltd* [1944] AC 265.

authorities as a venue for a public performance, it would appear that the supervening illegality is best regarded as the basis for discharge of the contract.[47]

In some cases, there may appear to be provision for a particular event, but on closer examination, it may be discovered that the parties' intentions have not been fully set out. It is important that the court is able to discover the intention of the parties in relation to the particular risk of loss under consideration. Thus, if a contract provides for what should happen if a chartered ship becomes unavailable, this should not be taken to apply the same result to the non-availability of a cargo.[48] Similarly, if a charterparty allows the charterer to cancel the contract in the event of requisition of the chartered ship, it does not follow from this that a similar right is automatically extended to the ship owner in similar circumstances. In such a case, the express provision will be regarded as incomplete and the court will have to approach the issue of risk allocation on the basis of the doctrine of frustration:

Bank Line Ltd v Arthur Capel & Co Ltd [1919] AC 435, HL, p 439

Lord Finlay LC: The two most important clauses for the purposes of the present appeal are the twenty-sixth and the thirty-first, which run as follows:

26   That the steamer shall be delivered under this charter not before 1 April 1915, and should the steamer not have been delivered latest on the 30th day of April 1915, charterers to have the option of cancelling this charter.

That, should it be proved that the steamer, through unforeseen circumstances, cannot be delivered by the cancelling date, charterers, if required, shall within forty-eight hours after receiving notice thereof declare whether they cancel or will take delivery of the steamer.

31   Charterers to have option of cancelling this charterparty should steamer be commandeered by Government during this charter.

The first question that falls to be determined is whether, as contended by the respondents, the doctrine of frustration of the adventure as terminating the contract is excluded by the terms of the charterparty. The clauses relied on as having this effect are clauses 26 and 31. In my opinion, neither of these clauses can have the effect of preventing the termination of the charterparty by the requisition in the present case and the detention under it.

The twenty-sixth clause provides that if the steamship should not have been delivered by the end of April 1915, the charterers were to have the option of cancelling the charter. This option would apply, if there were any delay beyond April 30, and if the delay was through unforeseen circumstances (in other words, if it was not due to the default of the owners) it was provided by

---

47   See *Gamerco SA v ICM/Fair Warning Ltd* [1995] 1 WLR 1226. To argue that it was the state of the stadium which frustrated the contract would raise questions as to whether the appropriate legal mechanism is the doctrine of frustration or that of mistake, since the defect in the stadium must have been present at the time the contract was made.

48   *Pioneer Shipping Ltd v BTP Tioxide Ltd, The Nema* [1982] AC 724.

the second paragraph that the charterers might be called on to declare within 48 hours whether they cancelled or would take delivery of the steamship. It was urged for the respondents that this clause meant that only the charterers could cancel in case of non-delivery, and that however long the owners might have been prevented from delivering by unforeseen circumstances beyond their control, they were bound to hold the vessel at the disposal of the charterers. I cannot read clause as having any such effect. The charter was to be for 12 months from delivery, which the owners were to make by the end of April, unless prevented by unforeseen circumstances, in which case, the charterers had the option of cancelling, however short the delay. If, owing to unforeseen circumstances, it became impossible for the owners to deliver under the charterparty until many months after the end of April, the whole character of the adventure would be changed. A charter for 12 months from April is clearly very different from a charter for 12 months from September. In such a case, the adventure contemplated by the charter is entirely frustrated, and the owner, when required to enter into a charter so different from that for which he had contracted, is entitled to say *non hæc in foedera veni*. In other words, the owner is entitled to say that the contract is at an end on the doctrine of the frustration of the adventure as explained in *Tamplin SS Co v Anglo-Mexican Petroleum Products Co*. It would be quite unreasonable to construe cl 26 as meaning that the owners are in such a case to hold the vessel at the disposal of the charterers for an unlimited period.

Clause 31 cannot be relied on on behalf of the respondents any more than cl 26. Clause 31 merely means that, in case of the vessel being commandeered, the charterers might cancel at once without having to show that the detention was likely to last so long as to put an end to the contract within the meaning of the authorities.

The difficulty with this case is that if the parties had foreseen the possibility of requisition and its possible effects on the charterer, why did they not also foresee that the ship owner would be affected by requisition? If provision is made in one respect, but not in another, is it not possible to infer an intention that the ship owner is not to be permitted to cancel the contract in the event of requisition? Are there other factors which influenced the court's decision? For example, the contract did not provide a fixed date for the commencement of the 12 month period of charter and, at the time of requisition, the ship had not been placed at the charterer's disposal. If the owner had not been excused from his obligations under the contract, he would have been in possession of a ship he could do nothing with since he could be required by the charterer, at any time, to make the ship available. But whilst it was in government service, the owner would be unable to honour his obligations under the contract. If the ship had been placed at the charterer's disposal before the occurrence of the frustrating event, would the decision have been different?

Impossibility of performance

In cases which involve an application of the doctrine of frustration, it is much more likely that there will be no provision in the contract for the allocation of risks. In these circumstances, it is for the court to determine what the parties, as reasonable businessmen, would have intended in the circumstances. Where performance of the contract has become physically impossible due to, for example, destruction of the subject matter of the contract,[49] destruction of the premises where machinery is to be installed,[50] where a specific vessel has been nominated to carry a cargo and the named ship becomes unavailable[51] or where the intended performer of a contract of personal service becomes seriously ill[52] or dies,[53] it would be reasonable to assume that the parties did not intend each other to be held to the contract.

In *Taylor v Caldwell*,[54] the parties entered into a contract which they inaccurately described as one for the 'letting' of a music hall[55] for the purpose of holding a series of concerts. The proposed dates of use were in June, July and August 1861, but after the date of contracting and before the first of the performance dates, the music hall was destroyed by fire. No evidence pointed to fault on either side and the contract made no provision for the event:

Taylor v Caldwell (1863) 3 B & S 826; 122 ER 573, QB, p 577

Blackburn J: The parties inaccurately call this a 'letting' and the money to be paid a 'rent'; but the whole agreement is such as to shew that the defendants were to retain the possession of the hall and gardens so that there was to be no demise of them, and that the contract was merely to give the plaintiffs the use of them on those days. Nothing however, in our opinion, depends on this. The agreement then proceeds to set out various stipulations between the parties as to what each was to supply for these concerts and entertainments, and as to the manner in which they should be carried on. The effect of the whole is to shew that the existence of the music hall in the Surrey Gardens in a state fit for a concert was essential for the fulfilment of the contract – such entertainments as the parties contemplated in their agreement could not be given without it.

After the making of the agreement, and before the first day on which a concert was to be given, the hall was destroyed by fire. This destruction, we must take it on the evidence, was without the fault of either party, and was so complete that in consequence the concerts could not be given as intended. And the

---

49 *Taylor v Caldwell* (1863) 3 B & S 826.
50 *Appleby v Myers* (1867) LR 2 CP 651.
51 *Nickoll & Knight v Ashton Edridge & Co* [1901] 2 KB 126.
52 *Condor v Baron Knights Ltd* [1966] 1 WLR 87. Long term imprisonment would appear to have the same effect: *Shepherd & Co Ltd v Jerrom* [1986] 3 All ER 589.
53 *Stubbs v Holywell Railway Co* (1867) LR 2 Exch 311.
54 (1863) 3 B & S 826, QB.
55 What was granted was a licence to use the hall on a certain number of occasions.

question we have to decide is whether, under these circumstances, the loss which the plaintiffs have sustained is to fall upon the defendants. The parties when framing their agreement evidently had not present to their minds the possibility of such a disaster, and have made no express stipulation with reference to it, so that the answer to the question must depend upon the general rules of law applicable to such a contract.

There seems no doubt that where there is a positive contract to do a thing, not in itself unlawful, the contractor must perform it or pay damages for not doing it, although in consequence of unforeseen accidents, the performance of his contract has become unexpectedly burdensome or even impossible.

There is a class of contracts in which a person binds himself to do something which requires to be performed by him in person; and such promises, for example, promises to marry, or promises to serve for a certain time, are never in practice qualified by an express exception of the death of the party; and therefore in such cases the contract is in terms broken if the promisor dies before fulfilment. Yet it was very early determined that, if the performance is personal, the executors are not liable; *Hyde v The Dean of Windsor* (Cro Eliz 552, pp 553). See 2 Wms Exors 1560, 5th edn, where a very apt illustration is given. 'Thus', says the learned author, 'if an author undertakes to compose a work, and dies before completing it, his executors are discharged from this contract: for the undertaking is merely personal in its nature, and, by the intervention of the contractor's death, has become impossible to be performed.'

But this rule is only applicable when the contract is positive and absolute, and not subject to any condition either express or implied: and there are authorities which, as we think, establish the principle that where, from the nature of the contract, it appears that the parties must from the beginning have known that it could not be fulfilled unless when the time for the fulfilment of the contract arrived some particular specified thing continued to exist, so that, when entering into the contract, they must have contemplated such continuing existence as the foundation of what was to be done; there, in the absence of any express or implied warranty that the thing shall exist, the contract is not to be construed as a positive contract, but as subject to an implied condition that the parties shall be excused in case, before breach, performance becomes impossible from the perishing of the thing without default of the contractor.

There seems little doubt that this implication tends to further the great object of making the legal construction such as to fulfilment the intention of those who entered into the contract. For in the course of affairs men in making such contracts in general would, if it were brought to their minds, say that there should be such a condition.

These are instances where the implied condition is of the life of a human being, but there are others in which the same implication is made as to the continued existence of a thing. For example, where a contract of sale is made amounting to a bargain and sale, transferring presently the property in specific chattels, which are to be delivered by the vendor at a future day; there, if the chattels, without the fault of the vendor, perish in the interval, the purchaser must pay the price and the vendor is excused from performing his contract to deliver, which has thus, become impossible.

It may, we think, be safely asserted to be now English law that in all contracts of loan of chattels or bailments if the performance of the promise of the borrower or bailee to return the things lent or bailed, becomes impossible because it has perished, this impossibility (if not arising from the fault of the borrower or bailee from some risk which he has taken upon himself) excuses the borrower or bailee from the performance of his promise to redeliver the chattel.

The principle seems to us to be that, in contracts in which the performance depends on the continued existence of a given person or thing, a condition is implied that the impossibility of performance arising from the perishing of the person or thing shall excuse the performance.

In none of these cases is the promise in words other than positive, nor is there any express stipulation that the destruction of the person or thing shall excuse the performance; but that excuse is by law implied, because from the nature of the contract it is apparent that the parties contracted on the basis of the continued existence of the particular person or chattel. In the present case, looking at the whole contract, we find that the parties contracted on the basis of the continued existence of the music hall at the time when the concerts were to be given; that being essential to their performance.

We think, therefore, that the music hall having ceased to exist, without fault of either party, both parties are excused, the plaintiffs from taking the gardens and paying the money, the defendants from performing their promise to give the use of the hall and gardens and other things. Consequently the rule must be absolute to enter the verdict for the defendants.

Had the contract been one to lease the premises for a fixed term of years, it seems much less likely that the contract would have been frustrated for reasons considered in more detail below.[56]

The example above is a fairly simple illustration that if a contract becomes physically incapable of performance, the parties to that contract, as reasonable businessmen cannot expect it to continue. But it should not be assumed that just because something which is important to the performance of the contract has been destroyed, the parties are discharged from the responsibility to perform all of the obligations created by the contract. For example, a contract to manage a ship may create a number of obligations, only some of which are dependant upon the continued existence of the ship, but others of which may survive the loss of the vessel at sea.[57]

---

56 See the discussion of *National Carriers Ltd v Panalpina (Northern) Ltd* [1981] AC 675 in relation to who is the best insurer against certain types of risk.

57 Similar considerations apply to Lord Diplock's distinction between primary and secondary obligations in *Photo Production Ltd v Securicor Transport Ltd* [1980] AC 827, under which secondary obligations such as the duty to pay damages may survive the discharge of a primary obligation such as the duty to pay for the services of the other party after a fundamental breach of contract.

In *Glafki Shipping Co SA v Pinios Shipping Co*,[58] the defendants owned the Maira and entrusted its management to the plaintiffs, who arranged insurance in respect of the vessel. Subsequently, the ship exploded and sank. When the insurers paid the value of the ship under the terms of the insurance, the defendants argued, *inter alia*, that the management contract with the plaintiffs was frustrated:

Glafki Shipping Co SA v Pinios Shipping Co, The Maira (No 2) [1985] 1 Lloyd's Rep 300, p 311

Kerr LJ: After the loss of the vessel on 10 April 1978, the managers continued to draw their monthly remuneration of $4,000 until some date in July. The issue was whether they were entitled to do so or whether the management agreement had been frustrated by the loss of the vessel, with the result that they were only entitled to a *quantum meruit* for the work which they did thereafter.

The latter was the solution which the arbitrator adopted. The management agreement contained no relevant provision for its termination before the discharge of all liabilities under the second mortgage.

As the arbitrator and judge both pointed out, the loss of the vessel would not put an end to all acts of management which required to be performed, such as repatriating and paying off the master and crew and dealing with all outstanding claims. On the other hand, these matters might take a long time to clear up entirely, and it could hardly be suggested that the managers should be entitled to continue to receive their full remuneration until the last detail had been dealt with. This might take many months and involve little work towards the end. Accordingly, if the arbitrator's solution is not correct, then it would no doubt be necessary to imply a term to the effect that the remuneration should gradually be reduced in proportion to whatever work might remain to be done, bearing in mind that the main subject matter of the agreement, the management of the vessel's employment and trade, had disappeared. In the result, therefore, the financial consequences might well turn out to be virtually the same on either solution.

It therefore falls to this court to deal with the question of law – as we accept it is in this case – whether or not the management agreement was frustrated when the vessel was lost. On balance, though not with quite the same confidence as the judge, we agree with him that it was not. In addition to the reasons which he gives, we think that it is important to bear in mind that it could hardly have been the intention of the parties that the managers should be entitled to wash their hands of all duties concerning the vessel as soon as she was lost, as would have been their right if the loss had led to an immediate frustration. We therefore also agree with the judge's conclusion on this point.

---

58 *The Maira (No 2)* [1985] 1 Lloyd's Rep 300.

Impracticability

Impossibility of performance is not the same as impracticability or difficulty of performance. In the latter case, if the court were to treat the contract as frustrated, the impression might be given that the parties were being relieved from the ordinary consequences of an imprudent commercial bargain.[59] Moreover, in many such cases, impracticability of performance is usually a matter which could have been guarded against by one of the parties in which case he may be regarded as the least cost avoider and be required to accept the risk of loss himself.

In *Tsakiroglou & Co Ltd v Noblee Thorl GmbH*,[60] the parties entered into a contract for the sale of goods at a price which included the cost of the goods, insurance and carriage to Hamburg. Performance of the contract became rather more expensive than was originally anticipated due to the closure of the Suez Canal. Both parties had envisaged the use of the canal, but the contract made no provision for renegotiation in the event of closure of this route. It was held that the contract was not frustrated as there was an alternative, but more expensive route via the Cape of Good Hope:

Tsakiroglou & Co Ltd v Noblee Thorl GmbH [1962] AC 93, HL, p 112

Viscount Simonds: I come then to the main issue and, as usual, I find two questions interlocked: (1) what does the contract mean? In other words, is there an implied term that the goods shall be carried by a particular route?; (2) is the contract frustrated?

It is convenient to examine the first question first, though the answer may be inconclusive. For it appears to me that it does not automatically follow that, because one term of a contract, for example, that the goods shall be carried by a particular route, becomes impossible of performance, the whole contract is thereby abrogated. Nor does it follow, because as a matter of construction a term cannot be implied, that the contract may not be frustrated by events. In the instant case, for example, the impossibility of the route via Suez, if that were assumed to be the implied contractual obligation, would not necessarily spell the frustration of the contract.

It is put in the forefront of the appellants' case that the contract was a contract for the shipment of goods via Suez.

A variant of this contention was that there should be read into the contract by implication the words 'by the usual and customary route' and that, as the only usual and customary route at the date of the contract was via Suez, the contractual obligation was to carry the goods via Suez. Though this contention has been viewed somewhat differently, I see as little ground for the implication. In this I agree with Harman LJ, for it seems to me that there are

---

59 *Pioneer Shipping Ltd v BTP Tioxide Ltd, The Nema* [1982] AC 724, p 752, *per* Lord Roskill.
60 [1962] AC 93, HL.

precisely the same grounds for rejecting the one as the other. Both of them assume that sellers and buyers alike intended and would have agreed that, if the route via Suez became impossible, the goods should not be shipped at all. Inasmuch as the buyers presumably wanted the goods and might well have resold them, the assumption appears wholly unjustified. Freight charges may go up or down. If the parties do not specifically protect themselves against change, the loss must lie where it falls.

I turn now to what was the main argument for the appellants: that the contract was frustrated by the closure of the canal.

We are concerned with a cif contract for the sale of goods, not a contract of affreightment, though part of the sellers' obligation will be to procure a contract of affreightment. There is no evidence that the buyers attached any importance to the route. They were content that the nuts should be shipped at any date in November or December. There was no evidence, and I suppose could not be, that the nuts would deteriorate as the result of a longer voyage and a double crossing of the Equator, nor any evidence that the market was seasonable. In a word, there was no evidence that the buyers cared by what route or, within reasonable limits, when the nuts arrived. What, then, of the sellers? I recall the well known passage in the speech of Lord Atkinson in *Johnson v Taylor Bros & Co Ltd*, where he states the obligations of the vendor of goods under a cif contract, and ask which of these obligations is (to use McNair J's word) 'fundamentally' altered by a change of route. Clearly, the contract of affreightment will be different and so may be the terms of insurance. In both these respects the sellers may be put to greater cost: their profit may be reduced or even disappear. But it hardly needs reasserting that an increase of expense is not a ground of frustration: see *Larrinaga & Co Ltd v Société Franco-Américaine des Phosphates de Médulla, Paris*.

Nothing else remains to justify the view that the nature of the contract was 'fundamentally' altered. That is the word used by Viscount Simon in *British Movietonews Ltd v London and District Cinemas Ltd* and by my noble and learned friend Lord Reid in *Davis Contractors Ltd v Fareham Urban District Council*. In the latter case, my noble and learned friend Lord Radcliffe used the expression 'radically different' and I think that the two expressions mean the same thing, as perhaps do other adverbs which have been used in this context. Whatever expression is used, I venture to say what I have said myself before and others more authoritatively have said before me: that the doctrine of frustration must be applied within very narrow limits. In my opinion this case falls far short of satisfying the necessary conditions.

Unavailability

If the parties expect a particular thing to be available in order to allow performance of the contract, the fact that that thing becomes unavailable may serve to defeat the reasonable expectations of both parties. Thus, if a nominated ship becomes unavailable[61] or the cargo intended to be carried does not materialise,[62] and there is no fault on either side, the contract made on the assumption that the ship or cargo will be available may be frustrated. Similarly, the parties to a contract to develop an oil exploration concession reasonably assume that the government of the country in which the concession has been granted will not expropriate mineral exploration rights.[63]

The problem with unavailability is that it may be only temporary, in which case it will be important to consider the wider facts of the case in order to determine whether the unavailability does truly defeat the expectations of the parties as reasonable businessmen. For example, the short-term unavailability of a ship which is the subject matter of a long-term time charter may not have the same effect as the unavailability of a ship which is intended to be used in the performance of a voyage charterparty.

In *Jackson v Union Marine Insurance Co Ltd*,[64] in November 1871, the plaintiff was required by a voyage charterparty to 'proceed with all dispatch' from Liverpool to Newport, where the ship was to pick up a cargo of iron rails to be transported to San Francisco. The contract also provided exemption from liability for the dangers and accidents of navigation. The plaintiff effected insurance on the cargo. Subsequently, before the ship reached Newport, it ran aground in January 1872 and was not released from its position until February 1872. The damage to the ship was such that it would not be repaired until August 1872. In mid-February 1872, the charterers hired another ship. The court held that the contract was frustrated with the result that the plaintiffs could not maintain an action against the charterers for not loading a cargo:

Jackson v Union Marine Insurance Co Ltd (1874) LR 10 CP 125, p 142

Bramwell B: If this charterparty be read as a charter for a definite voyage or adventure, then it follows that there is necessarily an implied condition that the ship shall arrive at Newport in time.

The two stipulations, to use all possible dispatch, and to arrive in time for the voyage, are not repugnant; nor is either superfluous or useless. The shipowner, in the case put, expressly agrees to use all possible dispatch: that is not a condition precedent; the sole remedy for and right consequent on the breach of it is an action. He also impliedly agrees that the ship shall arrive in time for the voyage: that is a condition precedent as well as an agreement; and its non-performance not only gives the charterer a cause of action, but also releases him. Of course, if these stipulations, owing to excepted perils, are not performed, there is no cause of action, but there is the same release of the charterer. The same reasoning would apply if the terms were, to 'use all

---

61 *Bank Line Ltd v Arthur Capel & Co Ltd* [1919] AC 435.
62 *Pioneer Shipping Co Ltd v BTP Tioxide, The Nema* [1982] AC 724.
63 *BP Exploration Co (Libya) Ltd v Hunt (No 2)* [1979] 1 WLR 783.
64 (1874) LR 10 CP 125.

possible dispatch, and further, and as a condition precedent, to be ready at the port of loading on 1 June'. That reasoning also applies to the present case. If the charter be read, as for a voyage or adventure not precisely defined by time or otherwise, but still for a particular voyage, arrival at Newport in time for it is necessarily a condition precedent. It seems to me it must be so read. I should say reason and good sense require it. The difficulty is supposed to be that there is some rule of law to the contrary. This I cannot see; and it seems to me that, in this case, the shipowner undertook to use all possible dispatch to arrive at the port of loading, and also agreed that the ship should arrive there 'at such a time that in a commercial sense the commercial speculation entered into by the shipowner and charterers should not be at an end, but in existence'. That latter agreement is also a condition precedent. Not arriving at such a time puts an end to the contract; though, as it arises from an excepted peril, it gives no cause of action.

Now, what is the effect of the exception of perils of the seas, and of delay being caused thereby? Suppose it was not there, and not implied, the shipowner would be subject to an action for not arriving in a reasonable time, and the charterers would be discharged.

The words are there. What is their effect? I think this: they excuse the shipowner, but give him no right. The charterer has no cause of action, but is released from the charter. When I say *he* is, I think both are. The condition precedent has not been performed, but by default of neither. The exception is an excuse for him who is to do the act, and operates to save him from an action to make his non-performance not a breach of contract, but does not operate to take away the right the other party would have had, if the non-performance had been a breach of contract, to retire from the engagement: and, if one party may, so may the other.

...

There is, then, a condition precedent that the vessel shall arrive in a reasonable time. On failure of this, the contract is at the end and the charterers discharged, though they have no cause of action, as the failure arose from an excepted peril. The same result follows, then, whether the implied condition is treated as one that the vessel shall arrive in time for that adventure, or one that it shall arrive in a reasonable time, that time being, in time for the adventure contemplated. And in either case, as in the express cases supposed, and in the analogous cases put, non-arrival and incapacity by that time ends the contract; the principle being, that, though non-performance of a condition may be excused, it does not take away the right to rescind from him for whose benefit the condition was introduced.

On these grounds, I think that, in reason, in principle, and for the convenience of both parties, it ought to be held in this case that the charterers were, on the finding of the jury, discharged.

A further difficult issue in unavailability cases is that of speculation. If a ship subject to a long term time charter becomes temporarily unavailable due to requisition for the purposes of war service, it will be necessary for the court to speculate as to the likely duration of the period of requisition. Clearly, one possibility is that the ship might be released at a fairly early stage, with the result that it can be returned to the charterer so that the residue of the charter period may be satisfied. Conversely, the war may be longer lasting than was anticipated at the outset, with the result that there is no value to the charterer when the ship is returned to him. Essentially, when a contract is frustrated is a matter of fact, and an appellate court is unlikely to interfere with the trial judge's or arbitrator's decision:

Kodros Shipping Corpn v Empresa Cubana De Flotes, The Evia (No 2) [1983] 1 AC 736, HL, p 767

Lord Roskill: My Lords, finally the date of frustration adopted by Mr Eckersley, namely, 4 October 1980, was attacked. Learned counsel for the appellants conceded that he could not suggest that Mr Eckersley had in any way misdirected himself, or that no reasonable arbitrator could have selected that date. One has only to read Mr Eckersley's reasons to see that he clearly applied his mind to the right tests and reached his conclusion as stated in para 61 after considering all the relevant facts. I find it quite impossible to say that his choice of date was wrong.

My Lords, attempts were made to review this choice of date by reference to dates chosen by other distinguished arbitrators or umpires in other cases said to raise the same issue. Two other arbitrators, or umpires, were said to have chosen 24 November 1980. This date is some seven weeks later than the date chosen by Mr Eckersley. Your Lordships were invited to study the reasons for those other awards which were included with your Lordships' papers and your Lordships declined to do so. My Lords, I am sure that your Lordships were entirely right to adopt that attitude, for it must be wrong in principle to consider other awards arising from different questions of fact. In preparing this speech I have not referred to either of those two awards. Lord Denning MR said that it was desirable for the same result to be reached in similar cases. No doubt in a perfect world that would be right. But in an imperfect world different opinions can be legitimately formed on matters of this kind. The learned Master of the Rolls in his judgment referred to what I had said in *The Nema* [1982] AC 724 with the agreement of all my noble and learned friends then sitting, including my noble and learned friend, Lord Diplock, namely, that where questions of degree are involved opinions may, and often do, legitimately differ. I am not in the least surprised at this difference of opinion. The charterparties in question may well have been of differing characteristics and of different lengths. The discharge of cargo may have been completed on a different date. The several masters, officers and crew may have left their ships on different dates. A host of differing factors may have arisen, and in common with all your Lordships I resolutely decline to investigate the facts found in other cases to see which choice of date is to be preferred. The choice of date in this case, as in the others, was for the umpire or arbitrator concerned and is not a matter for your Lordships' House. I would dismiss this appeal.

In the case of longer term ventures, such as a time charter under which a ship is hired for a number of years, it is often the case that the court is required to speculate as to the likely duration of the period of interruption. In these circumstances, if there is still time to run under the charterparty, it will be difficult to treat the contract as frustrated since the charterer might still obtain some value from the remainder of the period of hire.

In *Tamplin SS Co Ltd v Anglo-Mexican Petroleum Products Co Ltd*,[65] a time charter was entered into for a period of 60 months for the purposes of lawful trade between safe ports. Under the contract, the charterer was permitted to sub-let the vessel on Admiralty service. At a time when the charter had almost three years to run, the ship was requisitioned for war service, the charterer being handsomely compensated for the loss of the ship. The charterer was willing to continue to pay the hire charges, but the owner sought to have the contract discharged for frustration:

Tamplin SS Co Ltd v Anglo-Mexican Petroleum Products Co Ltd [1916] 2 AC 397, HL, p 403

Earl Loreburn: When a lawful contract has been made and there is no default, a court of law has no power to discharge either party from the performance of it unless either the rights of some one else or some Act of Parliament give the necessary jurisdiction. But a court can and ought to examine the contract and the circumstances in which it was made, not of course to vary, but only to explain it, in order to see whether or not from the nature of it the parties must have made their bargain on the footing that a particular thing or state of things would continue to exist. And if they must have done so, then a term to that effect will be implied, though it be not expressed in the contract. In applying this rule it is manifest that such a term can rarely be implied except where the discontinuance is such as to upset altogether the purpose of the contract. Some delay or some change is very common in all human affairs, and it cannot be supposed that any bargain has been made on the tacit condition that such a thing will not happen in any degree.

Sometimes, it is put that performance has become impossible and that the party concerned did not promise to perform an impossibility. Sometimes it is put that the parties contemplated a certain state of things which fell out otherwise. It is in my opinion the true principle, for no court has an absolving power, but it can infer from the nature of the contract and the surrounding circumstances that a condition which is not expressed was a foundation on which the parties contracted.

When this question arises in regard to commercial contracts, as happened in *Dahl v Nelson, Donkin & Co*; *Geiple v Smith* and *Jackson v Union Marine Insurance Co*, the principle is the same, and the language used as to 'frustration of the adventure' merely adapts it to the class of cases in hand. In all these three cases, it was held, to use the language of Lord Blackburn, 'that a delay in carrying out a charterparty, caused by something for which neither party was responsible, if so great and long as to make it unreasonable to require the

---

65 [1916] 2 AC 397, HL.

parties to go on with the adventure, entitled either of them, at least while the contract was executory, to consider it at an end.' That seems to me another way of saying that from the nature of the contract it cannot be supposed the parties, as reasonable men, intended it to be binding on them under such altered conditions. Were the altered conditions such that, had they thought of them, they would have taken their chance of them, or such that as sensible men they would have said 'if that happens, of course, it is all over between us'? What, in fact, was the true meaning of the contract? Since the parties have not provided for the contingency, ought a court to say it is obvious they would have treated the thing as at an end?

Applying the principle to the present case, I find that these contracting parties stipulated for the use of this ship during a period of five years, which would naturally cover the duration of many voyages. Certainly, both sides expected that these years would be years of peace. They also expected, no doubt, that they would be left in joint control of the ship, as agreed, and that they would not be deprived of it by any act of state. But I cannot say that the continuance of peace or freedom from an interruption in their use of the vessel was a tacit condition of this contract. On the contrary, one at all events of the parties might probably have thought, if he thought of it at all, that war would enhance the value of the contract, and both would have been considerably surprised to be told that interruption for a few months was to release them both from a time charter that was to last five years. On the other hand, if the interruption can be pronounced, in the language of Lord Blackburn already cited, 'so great and long as to make it unreasonable to require the parties to go on with the adventure', then it would be different. Both of them must have contracted on the footing that such an interruption as that would not take place, and I should imply a condition to that effect. Taking into account, however, all that has happened, I cannot infer that the interruption either has been or will be in this case such as makes it unreasonable to require the parties to go on. There may be many months during which this ship will be available for commercial purposes before the five years have expired. It might be a valuable right for the charterer during those months to have the use of this ship at the stipulated freight. Why should he be deprived of it? No one can say that he will or that he will not regain the use of the ship, for it depends upon contingencies which are incalculable. The owner will continue to receive the freight he bargained for so long as the contract entitles him to it, and if, during the time for which the charterer is entitled to the use of the ship, the owner received from the government any sums of money for the use of her, he will be accountable to the charterer.

Frustration of purpose

The cases so far considered have all involved events which make it impossible for the intended performer to fulfil his contractual obligations. However, there are other instances in which the doctrine of frustration has been invoked where performance is literally possible, but in which the performance on one side is so bereft of value that it would be unreasonable for one of the parties to expect the other to pay for what he has received.

A series of cases based on the cancellation of the coronation of King Edward VII illustrate the problem. In the belief that there would be certain public celebrations of the King's coronation, many contractual arrangements were made, for example, for the hire of rooms overlooking the route of the intended coronation procession. When the King's illness caused the cancellation of these events, the question arose whether these contracts were frustrated.

In *Krell v Henry*,[66] the parties entered into a contract for the hire of a room in a property in Pall Mall, overlooking the intended route of the coronation procession of King Edward VII. Owing to the illness of the King, the coronation procession was cancelled and the question arose whether the contract to hire the room was frustrated or not. Ostensibly, the decision of the Court of Appeal is based on the view that it was the basis of the contract that there would be an event to observe from the hired room and that accordingly, the common intention of both parties had been frustrated when the relevant festivities were cancelled. That the hire involved something out of the ordinary can be understood from the fact that the hire charge levied was substantially higher than would normally be expected for a room of the kind under consideration:[67]

Krell v Henry [1903] 2 KB 740, CA, p 747

Vaughan Williams LJ: The real question in this case is the extent of the application in English law of the principle of the Roman law which has been adopted and acted on in many English decisions, and notably in the case of *Taylor v Caldwell*. That case at least makes it clear that 'where, from the nature of the contract, it appears that the parties must from the beginning have known that it could not be fulfilled unless, when the time for the fulfilment of the contract arrived, some particular specified thing continued to exist, so that when entering into the contract they must have contemplated such continued existence as the foundation of what was to be done; there, in the absence of any express or implied warranty that the thing shall exist, the contract is not to be considered a positive contract, but as subject to an implied condition that the parties shall be excused in case, before breach, performance becomes impossible from the perishing of the thing without default of the contractor'. The doubt in the present case arises as to how far this principle extends. Whatever may have been the limits of the Roman law, the case of *Nickoll v Ashton* makes it plain that the English law applies the principle not only to cases where the performance of the contract becomes impossible by the cessation of existence of the thing which is the subject matter of the contract,

---

66 [1903] 2 KB 740, CA.

67 The hire charge of £75 for two days' use was more than an average man would earn in several months.

but also to cases where the event which renders the contract incapable of performance is the cessation or non-existence of an express condition or state of things, going to the root of the contract, and essential to its performance.

I think that you first have to ascertain, not necessarily from the terms of the contract, but, if required, from necessary inferences, drawn from surrounding circumstances recognised by both contracting parties, what is the substance of the contract, and then to ask the question whether that substantial contract needs for its foundation the assumption of the existence of a particular state of things. If it does, this will limit the operation of the general words, and in such case, if the contract becomes impossible of performance by reason of the non-existence of the state of things assumed by both contracting parties as the foundation of the contract, there will be no breach of the contract thus limited.

In my judgment the use of the rooms was let and taken for the purpose of seeing the royal procession. It was not a demise of the rooms, or even an agreement to let and take the rooms. It is a licence to use rooms for a particular purpose and none other. And in my judgment the taking place of those processions on the days proclaimed along the proclaimed route, which passed 56A Pall Mall, was regarded by both contracting parties as the foundation of the contract; and I think that it cannot reasonably be supposed to have been in the contemplation of the contracting parties, when the contract was made, that the coronation would not be held on the proclaimed days, or the processions not take place on those days along the proclaimed route; and I think that the words imposing on the defendant the obligation to accept and pay for the use of the rooms for the named days, although general and unconditional, were not used with reference to the possibility of the particular contingency which afterwards occurred. It was suggested in the course of the argument that if the occurrence, on the proclaimed days, of the coronation and the procession in this case were the foundation of the contract, and if the general words are thereby limited or qualified, so that in the event of the non-occurrence of the coronation and procession along the proclaimed route they would discharge both parties from further performance of the contract, it would follow that if a cabman was engaged to take some one to Epsom on Derby Day at a suitable enhanced price for such a journey, say £10, both parties to the contract would be discharged in the contingency of the race at Epsom for some reason becoming impossible; but I do not think this follows, for I do not think that in the cab case the happening of the race would be the foundation of the contract. No doubt the purpose of the engager would be to go to see the Derby, and the price would be proportionately high; but the cab had no special qualifications for the purpose which led to the selection of the cab for this particular occasion. Any other cab would have done as well. Moreover, I think that, under the cab contract, the hirer, even if the race went off, could have said, 'Drive me to Epsom; I will pay you the agreed sum; you have nothing to do with the purpose for which I hired the cab', and that if the cabman refused he would have been guilty of a breach of contract, there being nothing to qualify his promise to drive the hirer to Epsom on a particular day. Whereas in the case of the coronation, there is not merely the purpose of the hirer to see the coronation procession, but it is the coronation procession and the relative position of the rooms which is the basis of the contract as much for the lessor as the hirer; and I think that if the King, before the coronation day and after the contract, had died, the hirer could not have insisted on having the rooms on the days named. It could not in the cab case be reasonably said that seeing the Derby race was the foundation of the contract, as it was of the licence in this case. Whereas in the present case, where the rooms were offered and taken, by reason of their peculiar suitability from the position of the rooms for a view of the coronation procession, surely the view of the coronation procession was the foundation of the contract, which is a very different thing from the purpose of the man who engaged the cab – namely, to see the race – being held to be the foundation of the contract. Each case must be judged by its own circumstances. In each case one must ask oneself, first, what, having regard to all the circumstances, was the foundation of the contract? Secondly, was the performance of the contract prevented? Thirdly, was the event which prevented the performance of the contract of such a character that it cannot reasonably be said to have been in the contemplation of the parties at the date of the contract? If all these questions are answered in the affirmative (as I think they should be in this case), I think both parties are discharged from further performance of the contract. I think that the coronation procession was the foundation of this contract, and that the non-happening of it prevented the performance of the contract; and, secondly, I think that the non-happening of the procession, to use the words of Sir James Hannen in *Baily v De Crespingny,* was an event 'of such a character that it cannot reasonably be supposed to have been in the contemplation of the contracting parties when the contract was made, and that they are not to be held bound by general words which, though large enough to include, were not used with reference to the possibility of the particular contingency which afterwards happened'. The test seems to be whether the event which causes the impossibility was or might have been anticipated and guarded against. It seems difficult to say, in a case where both parties anticipate the happening of an event, which anticipation is the foundation of the contract, that either party must be taken to have anticipated, and ought to have guarded against, the event which prevented the performance of the contract. In both *Jackson v Union Marine Insurance Co* and *Nickoll v Ashton,* the parties might have anticipated as a possibility that perils of the sea might delay the ship and frustrate the commercial venture: in the former case the carriage of the goods to effect which the charterparty was entered into; in the latter case the sale of the goods which were to be shipped on the steamship which was delayed. But the court held in the former case that the basis of the contract was that the ship would arrive in time to carry out the contemplated commercial venture, and in the latter that the steamship would arrive in time for the loading of the goods the subject of the sale. I wish to observe that cases of this sort are very different from cases where a contract or warranty or representation is implied, such as was implied in *The Moorcock,* and refused to be implied in *Hamlyn v Wood.* But *The Moorcock* is of importance in the present case as shewing that whatever is the suggested implication – be it condition, as in this case, or warranty or representation – one must, in judging whether the implication ought to be made, look not only at the words of the contract, but also at the surrounding facts and the knowledge of the parties of those facts. There seems to me to be ample authority for this proposition. Thus, in *Jackson v Union Marine Insurance Co*, in the Common Pleas, the question whether the object of the voyage had been frustrated by the delay of the ship was left as a question of fact to the jury, although there was nothing in the charterparty defining the time within which the charterers were to supply the cargo of iron rails for San Francisco, and nothing on the face of the charterparty to indicate the importance of time in the venture; and that was a case in which, as Bramwell B points out in his judgment, *Taylor v Caldwell* was a strong authority to support the conclusion arrived at in the judgment – that the ship not arriving in time for the voyage contemplated, but at such time as to frustrate the commercial venture, was not only a breach of the contract but discharged the charterer, though he had such an excuse that no action would lie.

I myself am clearly of opinion that in this case, where we have to ask ourselves whether the object of the contract was frustrated by the non-happening of the coronation and its procession on the days proclaimed, parol evidence is admissible to shew that the subject of the contract was rooms to view the coronation procession, and was so to the knowledge of both parties. When once this is established, I see no difficulty whatever in the case. It is not essential to the application of the principle of *Taylor v Caldwell* that the direct subject of the contract should perish or fail to be in existence at the date of performance of the contract. It is sufficient if a state of things or condition expressed in the contract and essential to its performance perishes or fails to be in existence at that time. In the present case the condition which fails and prevents the achievement of that which was, in the contemplation of both parties, the foundation of the contract, is not expressly mentioned either as a condition of the contract or the purpose of it; but I think for the reasons which I have given that the principle of *Taylor v Caldwell* ought to be applied. This disposes of the plaintiff's claim for £50 unpaid balance of the price agreed to be paid for the use of the rooms.

In *Herne Bay Steam Boat Co v Hutton*,[68] the defendant chartered a steamboat from the plaintiffs for a period of two days with the intention of taking a party of people to view the 'naval review and for a day's cruise round the fleet'. The naval review was cancelled, along with the other festivities planned to coincide with King Edward VII's coronation. The defendant did not use the steamboat and the plaintiffs sued for the outstanding balance of the hire charge. Unlike the decision in *Krell v Henry*, it was held that the contract was not frustrated and that the plaintiffs were entitled to judgment:

Herne Bay Steam Boat Co v Hutton [1903] 2 KB 683, CA, p 688

Vaughan Williams LJ: According to my understanding of this contract, this ship was placed at the disposal of Mr Hutton really for those two days. Mr Hansell says this does not constitute a demise of the ship, and with that I agree. It is very rarely that a charterparty does contain a demise of a ship. Generally

---

68 [1903] 2 KB 683, CA.

speaking, the ship is not demised at all, but remains under the management and control of her owner. But, at the same time, this contract does, in my opinion, place the ship at the disposal of Mr Hutton, just as a charterparty places the vessel, the subject of it, at the disposal of the charterers.

That being so, what is there besides in the present case? Only this, that Mr Hutton, in hiring this vessel, had two objects in view: first, of taking people to see the naval review, and, secondly, of taking them round the fleet. Those, no doubt, were the purposes of Mr Hutton, but it does not seem to me that because, as it is said, those purposes became impossible, it would be a very legitimate inference that the happening of the naval review was contemplated by both parties as the basis and foundation of this contract, so as to bring the case within the doctrine of *Taylor v Caldwell*. On the contrary, when the contract is properly regarded, I think the purpose of Mr Hutton, whether of seeing the naval review or of going round the fleet with a party of paying guests, does not lay the foundation of the contract within the authorities.

Having expressed that view, I do not know that there is any advantage to be gained by going on in any way to define what are the circumstances which might or might not constitute the happening of a particular contingency as the foundation of a contract. I will content myself with saying this, that I see nothing that makes this contract differ from a case where, for instance, a person has engaged a brake to take himself and a party to Epsom to see the races there, but for some reason or other, such as the spread of an infectious disease, the races are postponed. In such a case it could not be said that he could be relieved of his bargain. So in the present case it is sufficient to say that the happening to the naval review was not the foundation of the contract.

Romer LJ (p 690): The case cannot, in my opinion, be distinguished in principle from many common cases in which, on the hiring of a ship, you find the objects of the hiring stated. Very often, you find the details of the voyage stated with particularity, and also the nature and details of the cargo to be carried. If the voyage is intended to be one of pleasure, the object in view may also be stated, which is a matter that concerns the passengers. But this statement of the objects of the hirer of the ship would not, in my opinion, justify him in saying that the owner of the ship had those objects just as much in view as the hirer himself.

The view I have expressed with regard to the general effect of the contract before us is borne out by the following considerations. The ship (as a ship) had nothing particular to do with the review or the fleet, except as a convenient carrier of passengers to see it: any other ship suitable for carrying passengers would have done equally as well. Just as in the case of the hire of a cab or other vehicle, although the object of the hirer might be stated, that statement would not make the object any the less a matter for the hirer alone, and would not directly affect the person who was letting out the vehicle for hire. In the present case I may point out that it cannot be said that by reason of the failure to hold the naval review there was a total failure of consideration. That cannot be so. Nor is there anything like a total destruction of the subject matter of the contract. Nor can we, in my opinion, imply in this contract any condition in favour of the defendant which would enable him to escape liability. A condition ought only to be implied in order to carry out the presumed intention of the parties, and I cannot ascertain any such presumed intention here. It follows that, in my opinion, so far as the plaintiffs are concerned, the objects of the passengers on this voyage with regard to sightseeing do not form the subject matter or essence of this contract.

Singleton LJ (p 692): It is said that, by reason of the reference in the contract to the 'naval review', the existence of the review formed the basis of the contract, and that as the review failed to take place the parties became discharged from the further performance of the contract, in accordance with the doctrine of *Taylor v Caldwell*. I am unable to arrive at that conclusion. It seems to me that the reference in the contract to the naval review is easily explained; it was inserted in order to define more exactly the nature of the voyage, and I am unable to treat it as being such a reference as to constitute the naval review the foundation of the contract so as to entitle either party to the benefit of the doctrine in *Taylor v Caldwell*. I come to this conclusion the more readily because the object of the voyage is not limited to the naval review, but also extends to a cruise round the fleet. The fleet was there, and passengers might have been found willing to go round it. It is true that in the event which happened the object of the voyage became limited, but, in my opinion, that was the risk of the defendant whose venture the taking the passengers was.

In terms of risk allocation, is *Krell v Henry* a suspect decision? If the procession had gone ahead in the pouring rain and all participants had worn waterproof clothing, there would have been a spectacle to watch, but it would not have had the expected appeal. But, in such a case, the contract probably would not have been frustrated. Why did it make a difference that the whole event was cancelled? In one sense, this was a speculative venture, in which case it might make sense to allocate the risk of loss to the speculator, namely, the person hiring the room. However, the speculation issue can be reinterpreted when one considers the likelihood of re-staging the event. If one assumes that the coronation procession would be rescheduled using the same route, owners of properties overlooking the route would stand to make a double profit if contracts made in anticipation of the cancelled event were held not to be frustrated. In contrast, on the facts of *Herne Bay SS Co v Hutton*, it seems unlikely that the fleet would remain static off Spithead indefinitely, pending the convalescence of the King. Accordingly, the likelihood of a royal review of the fleet being re-staged was much less than a reorganised coronation procession. On this basis, it appeared to be more reasonable to treat the contract as binding, despite the absence of the King, who was no doubt the major attraction rather than a large number of grey, but apparently impressive, ships.

The least cost avoider

A second feature of cases involving the application of the doctrine of frustration is that the courts will seek to discover which of the parties is in the best position to take reasonable steps to avoid the risk of loss created by the contract. In this regard, it is relevant to consider whether a contract may be frustrated if the risk of loss is foreseeable; whether either of the parties has been at fault, especially where the frustrating event is self-induced and whether there are reasonable steps which could have been taken by one of the parties which might have averted the risk of loss.

Foreseeable risks

If a particular risk of loss has been foreseen, it may be reasonable to assume that the parties will have provided for that eventuality in their contract. Taken to its logical conclusion, this should mean that the risk of loss should lie where it falls.[69] Similarly, even if the event has not been provided for in the contract but ought to have been foreseen by the parties, it will normally be the case that the risk should lie where it falls.[70] However, there appear to be cases in which the fact of foreseeability has not prevented the use of the doctrine of frustration, since the test of foresight appears to be very strict.

In *Tatem Ltd v Gamboa*,[71] a ship was chartered expressly for the purpose of evacuating civilians from Spain during the Spanish Civil War. A term of the contract provided that hire charges continued to be payable until the ship was redelivered. The ship was seized by Nationalist forces, but was eventually released so that the charterer could return it to its owner some six weeks after the expiry of the agreed period of hire. The owners claimed hire charges in respect of the full period, including the six weeks during which time the ship was under the control of the Nationalists. It was held that the contract was frustrated because although detention was probably foreseeable, the duration of the detention was not foreseeable:

Tatem Ltd v Gamboa [1939] 1 KB 132, p 135

Goddard J: Sir Robert Aske, on the other hand, has argued very strongly that the enterprise in this case cannot be said to have been frustrated, because both sides must be taken to have contemplated when they made this contract that the ship might be seized – indeed, that the risk of seizure was plain and obvious to everybody – and that it must be taken that that was one of the risks which the ship was running.

I do not feel that I can hold on the evidence which I have before me that a risk of seizure of the description which took place here, and the detaining of the vessel not only for the period of her charter but for a long period thereafter, was a risk which was contemplated by the parties. It may well be that they

---

69 *Krell v Henry* [1903] 2 KB 740, p 752, *per* Vaughan Williams LJ.
70 *Davis Contractors Ltd v Fareham UDC* [1956] AC 696, p 731, *per* Lord Radcliffe.
71 [1939] 1 KB 132.

thought that the Nationalists might seize the ship and hold it for the chartered period so long as it was under charter to the Republican Government. It may well be that the parties contemplated that the Nationalists would hesitate, after the charter had come to an end, to seize and detain a British ship which had no contraband on board and which, after the period for which it was chartered, would be most unlikely to be engaged in the work, however humanitarian it may have been, of evacuating civil population.

I will assume that the parties contemplated that the ship might be seized and detained as she was. It is difficult to reconcile all the judgments and speeches which have been made on this difficult subject of frustration.

Viscount Finlay said in *Larrinaga & Co Ltd v Société Franco-Américaine des Phosphates de Médulla, Paris*:

> When certain risks are foreseen the contract may contain conditions providing that in certain events the obligation shall cease to exist. But even when there is no express condition in the contract, it may be clear that the parties contracted on the basis of the continued existence of a certain state on facts, and it is with reference to cases alleged to be of this kind that the doctrine of 'frustration' is most frequently invoked. If the contract be one which for its performance depends on the continued existence of certain buildings or other premises, it is an implied condition that the premises should continue to be in existence, and their total destruction by fire without fault on the part of those who have entered into the contract will be a good defence. Such a contract does not as a matter of law imply a warranty that the buildings or other property shall continue to exist.

Sir Robert Aske meets this point by saying there cannot be frustration where the circumstances must have been contemplated by the parties. By 'circumstances', I mean circumstances which are afterwards relied on as frustrating the contract. It is true that in many of the cases there is found the expression 'unforeseen circumstances,' and it is argued that 'unforeseen circumstances' must mean circumstances which could not have been foreseen. But it seems to me, with respect, that, if the true doctrine be that laid down by Lord Haldane, frustration depends on the absolute disappearance of the contract; or, if the true basis be, as Lord Finlay put it, 'the continued existence of a certain state of facts', it makes very little difference whether the circumstances are foreseen or not. *If the foundation of the contract goes, it goes whether or not the parties have made a provision for it.* The parties may make provision about what is to happen in the event of this destruction taking place, but if the true foundation of the doctrine is that once the subject matter of the contract is destroyed, or the existence of a certain state of facts has come to an end, the contract is at an end, that result follows whether or not the event causing it was contemplated by the parties. It seems to me, therefore, that when one uses the expression 'unforeseen circumstances' in relation to the frustration of the performance of a contract one is really dealing with circumstances which are unprovided for, circumstances for which (and in the case of a written contract one only has to look at the document) the contract makes no provision.

To the same effect, I think, are the cases which deal with this doctrine in relation to the requisitioning of ships. When the war had proceeded but a very short time the Admiralty Requisitioning Board was set up. Ships were requisitioned freely, and I suppose it is not putting it too high to say that no shipowner knew when his ship would be requisitioned. Accordingly, one finds, for instance, in *Bank Line Ltd v Arthur Capel & Co* that the charterparty actually provided for requisition. It provided that the charterers were to have the option of cancelling the charterparty should the steamer be commandeered by the government during the charter, and yet for reasons which appear in the speeches in the House of Lords it was held that it did not prevent the doctrine of frustration of performance applying. It seems to me that the parties must have had before them the possibility, or the probability if you will, of requisition every bit as much as the parties had of seizure in this case.

Is it strange that the parties had foreseen and provided for the possibility that the ship might be lost at sea? In this case, the contract provided that the charterer would be under no obligation to continue to pay hire charges. Since detention was probably also a foreseeable eventuality, might it not be reasonable to assume that, as the contract was silent on the matter, the charterer was not to be excused from his obligation to continue to pay? The issue which Goddard J addresses is how long that obligation continued.

Reasonable steps necessary to avert the risk of loss

Where events make performance of the contract as intended more difficult or more expensive, it is often useful to consider which of the parties might have taken steps to mitigate the effects of the event which creates the difficulty in performance. For example, in *Tsakiroglou & Co Ltd v Noblee Thorl GmbH*,[72] it was alleged that a contract to carry a cargo cif from Sudan to Hamburg was frustrated due to the closure of the Suez Canal. Undoubtedly, the parties did contemplate the use of the canal for the purposes of shipment, but it was accepted by the House of Lords that the carrier could have taken the step of arranging shipment by an alternative route. Accordingly, the risk of loss was allocated to the carrier.

The least cost avoider principle also appears to apply to cases in which it is claimed that the frustrating event defeats the expectations of only one of the parties. Here, the guiding rule is that in order for an external event to be properly regarded as a frustrating event, it must defeat the common intention of both parties. Thus, if one of the parties enters a contract to purchase future goods[73] from the other and has not been made aware of the fact that the goods must be obtained from a particular source, if that source dries up due to

---

72 [1962] AC 93. For extracts from this case, see above.
73 Goods which the seller has yet to abstract, grow or manufacture or acquire from another supplier.

some event beyond the control of both parties, it is likely that the seller will bear the risk of loss, as only his expectations have been defeated. The buyer may be able to assume, quite reasonably, that the seller can obtain supplies from elsewhere.

In *Blackburn Bobbin Co Ltd v Allen & Sons Ltd*,[74] the parties entered a contract for the sale of Finnish birch timber. At the time of contracting, the buyer was not aware that the seller would have to import the timber from Finland. It subsequently transpired that owing to the general disorganisation of transport caused by the outbreak of war, it became impossible to obtain deliveries from Finland. The seller sought to have the contract discharged on the ground of frustration. It was held that since the buyer was unaware that the timber had to be imported from Finland, he could have made one of a number of assumptions. For example, he might have believed that the seller had timber stockpiled in the UK or that supplies were readily available from other Scandinavian countries. Accordingly, only the expectations of the seller had been frustrated with the result that the risk of loss fell on the seller. He was the least cost avoider in the sense that he could have taken steps at an earlier stage to secure the timely performance of the contract:

Blackburn Bobbin Co Ltd v Allen & Sons Ltd [1918] 2 KB 467, CA, p 468

Pickford LJ: This is an appeal from a decision of McCardie J, and the point raised is whether an implication is to be read into the contract the performance of which has been interfered with or prevented by matters arising out of the war.

The defendants contend that the contract was at an end because it was in the contemplation of both parties that the defendants should be able to supply the timber according to the ordinary method of supplying it in the trade, and that when that became impossible both parties were discharged from their obligations. In my opinion, McCardie J was right in saying that the principle of these cases did not apply to discharge the defendants in this case. He has found that the plaintiffs were unaware at the time of the contract of the circumstance that the timber from Finland was shipped direct from a Finnish port to Hull, and that they did not know whether the transport was or was not partly by rail across Scandinavia, nor did they know that timber merchants in this country did not hold stocks of Finnish birch. I accept the finding that in fact, the method of dispatching this timber was not known to the plaintiffs. But there remains the question, Must they be deemed to have contracted on the basis of the continuance of that method although they did not in fact, know of it? I see no reason for saying so. Why should a purchaser of goods, not specific goods, be deemed to concern himself with the way in which the seller is going to fulfil his contract by providing the goods he has agreed to sell? The sellers in this case agreed to deliver the timber free on rail at Hull, and it was no concern of the buyers as to how the sellers intended to get the timber there. I can see no

---

74 [1918] 2 KB 467, CA.

reason for saying – and to free the defendants from liability this would have to be said – that the continuance of the normal mode of shipping the timber from Finland was a matter which both parties contemplated as necessary for the fulfilment of the contract. To dissolve the contract the matter relied on must be something which both parties had in their minds when they entered into the contract, such for instance as the existence of the music hall in *Taylor v Caldwell*, or the continuance of the vessel in readiness to perform the contract, as in *Jackson v Union Marine Insurance Co*. Here there is nothing to show that the plaintiffs contemplated, and there is no reason why they should be deemed to have contemplated, that the sellers should continue to have the ordinary facilities for dispatching the timber from Finland. As I have said, that was a matter which to the plaintiffs was wholly immaterial. It was not a matter forming the basis of the contract they entered into.

For the reasons I have given, the defendants have failed on the facts to make out their case that the contract was dissolved. The appeal will be dismissed.

Fault and self-induced frustration

An essential requirement of the doctrine of frustration is that the frustrating event must have occurred without fault on either side of the contract. This also impinges on the least cost avoider principle, since it is relatively easy to see that someone who is at fault is also the person who was in the best position to avert the risk of loss. In deciding what role is to be played by the fault principle, it is important to appreciate that the only fault that matters is that of the person who seeks to treat his obligation to perform as discharged. Thus, if the person required to perform under the contract has brought about the event which it is alleged frustrates the contract, the judicial response is likely to be that the frustrating event was self-induced and that the loss should lie where it falls. However, if the person at fault is happy to keep the contract alive, he will not be permitted to plead his own fault as a reason for denying the other party the chance to treat the contract as frustrated. Thus, in *Shepherd & Co Ltd v Jerrom*,[75] an employee had committed a criminal offence with the result that he was given a custodial sentence. The employee argued that because he was at fault the contract could not be discharged on the ground of frustration. The Court of Appeal disagreed, *inter alia*, on the ground that the only fault that matters is that of the person seeking to treat the contract as frustrated and that since the employer was not at fault, he was entitled to plead the impossibility of performance arising from the fact that his employee would not be available for work for some time.

The main difficulty is to determine what is meant by the word 'fault'. For example, does it include only deliberate actions or breaches of duty or does

---

75   [1986] 3 All ER 589.

fault entail only that the party alleging frustration should have control over the event in question?[76]

It seems that the word fault may have three different meanings. In the first place, it is clear that if the party seeking to have the contract discharged on the ground of frustration has brought about that event through a breach of his own contractual obligations to the other party, he will not be allowed to set up that breach as a reason for discharge of the contract.

In *Ocean Tramp Tankers Corpn v V/O Sovfracht*,[77] the charterer of a ship deliberately diverted the vessel into a known war zone, in the vicinity of the Suez Canal at the time of the Suez Crisis. This action was in direct contravention of an express provision of the contract which provided that the ship should not be taken into such an area without the consent of the owner. Subsequently, the ship was caught up in hostilities and was trapped in the Suez Canal. The owners denied that there was a frustrating event and alleged that the charterers' conduct amounted to a repudiation of the contract:

Ocean Tramp Tankers Corpn v V/O Sovfracht, The Eugenia [1964] 2 QB 226, CA, p 237

Lord Denning MR: The second question is whether the charterparty was frustrated by what took place. The arbitrator has held it was not. The judge has held that it was. Which is right? One thing that is obvious is that the charterers cannot rely on the fact that *The Eugenia* was trapped in the canal; for that was their own fault. They were in breach of the war clause in entering it. They cannot rely on a self-induced frustration, see *Maritime National Fish Ltd v Ocean Trawlers Ltd*. But they seek to rely on the fact that the canal itself was blocked. They assert that even if *The Eugenia* had never gone into the canal, but had stayed outside (in which case she would not have been in breach of the war clause), nevertheless she would still have had to go round by the Cape. And that, they say, brings about a frustration, for it makes the venture fundamentally different from what they contracted for.

A second variety of fault appears to exist where a person has deliberately and freely elected to act in a way which brings about the frustrating event. Such action will not involve a breach of contract on the party alleging frustration, but it would seem to be logical to require the party alleging frustration to have, at least, some choice in the direction he moves. Thus, if the event which it is alleged has frustrated the contract leaves the performing party with a number of options, such as fulfilling some contracts, but not others it would

---

76 See *Wilson (Paal) & Co A/S v Partenreederei Hannah Blumenthal, The Hannah Blumenthal* [1983] 1 AC 854, p 882, *per* Griffiths LJ. An alternative way of putting the matter is to ask if the party seeking to be discharged from his obligation to perform was responsible for the occurrence of the alleged frustrating event: *Lauritzen A/S v Wijsmuller BV, The Super Servant Two* [1990] 1 Lloyd's Rep 1, p 11, *per* Bingham LJ.

77 *The Eugenia* [1964] 2 QB 226, CA.

seem to follow that a conscious choice has been made and that that choice will preclude the operation of the doctrine of frustration of contracts.

In *Maritime National Fish Ltd v Ocean Trawlers Ltd*,[78] the appellants wished to use a type of fishing net known as an 'otter trawl' with five ships; three of which they owned and two of which they had chartered. In order to be able to use this type of net in the waters they wished to fish, it was necessary to obtain a government licence. An application for five such licences was duly made, but only three were granted. In the light of this state of affairs, the appellants decided that they would not apply any of the licences granted to a ship named the *St Cuthbert* which they had on charter from the respondents. In due course, the appellants claimed that the charterparty with the respondents was frustrated due to the decision of the Canadian government department in not granting a sufficient number of licences for the use of otter trawls. However, the Privy Council held that, since the appellants had a free choice in deciding which ships to license, they must have been taken to have elected not to license the *St Cuthbert*. Accordingly, the frustrating event was said to be self-induced.

The decision in *Maritime National Fish* is defensible in the sense that the appellants did have a choice, but the position ought to be different if the performing party is left with no choice but to breach one contract and perform another. In terms of the principles of risk allocation, if the performing party is left with no choice at all, it may make more sense to treat the contract as frustrated, especially since the remedial rules provided for in the Law Reform (Frustrated Contracts) Act 1943, where they apply, allow for a limited degree of loss sharing as between both parties to the contract. However, this does not appear to represent English law, where the view has been taken that even where the performing party is left with Hobson's choice, the doctrine of frustration has no application where he is seen to have made a conscious choice between one contract and another.

In *Lauritzen A/S v Wijsmuller BV*,[79] the defendants contracted to carry the *Dan King*, an oil rig owned by the plaintiffs, to Rotterdam, using a transportation vessel known as 'Super Servant One' or 'Super Servant Two'. In fact, the defendants intended to use the latter as *Super Servant One* had been committed to other contracts. Subsequently, *Super Servant Two* sank and the question arose whether the *Dan King* contract was frustrated. It was held that since the defendants elected not to perform the *Dan King* contract, the frustrating event was self-induced:

---

78 [1935] AC 524.
79 *The Super Servant Two* [1990] 1 Lloyd's Rep 1, CA.

Lauritzen A/S v Wijsmuller BV, The Super Servant Two [1990] 1 Lloyd's Rep 1, CA, p 8

Bingham LJ: The argument in this case raises important issues on the English law of frustration. Before turning to the specific questions, I think it helpful to summarise the established law so far as relevant to this case.

The essence of frustration is that it should not be due to the act or election of the party seeking to rely on it (*Hirji Mulji*, p 510; *Maritime National Fish Ltd*, p 530; *Joseph Constantine SS Ltd*, p 170; *Denny Mott & Dickson Ltd*, p 274; *Davis Contractors Ltd*, p 728. A frustrating event must be some outside event or extraneous change of situation (*Paal Wilson & Co A/S v Partenreederi Hannah Blumenthal (The Hannah Blumenthal)*, [1983] 1 Lloyd's Rep 103, p 112; [1983] 1 AC 854, p 909).

A frustrating event must take place without blame or fault on the side of the party seeking to rely on it (*Bank Line Ltd*, p 452; *Joseph Constantine SS Ltd*, p 171; *Davis Contractors Ltd*, p 729; *The Hannah Blurrienthal*, [1982] 1 Lloyd's Rep 582, p 592; [1983] 1 Lloyd's Rep 103, p 112; [1983] 1 AC 854, pp 882 and 909).

Mr Clarke for Wijsmuller submitted that the extraneous supervening event necessary to found a plea of frustration occurred when *Super Servant Two* sank on 29 January 1981. The *Dan King* contract was not, however, thereupon frustrated but remained alive until Wijsmuller decided a fortnight later that that contract could not be, or would not be, performed. There was, he submitted, factually, no break in the chain of causation between the supervening event and the non-performance of the contract. He acknowledged that *Maritime National Fish Ltd* contained observations on their face inimical to his argument, but distinguished that as a decision on causation confined to its own peculiar facts and laying down no general rule. For authoritative support, Mr Clarke relied on cases dealing with the application of *force majeure* clauses in commodity contracts and, in particular, on an unreported judgment of Mr Justice Robert Goff, as he then was, adopted with approval by the Court of Appeal in *Bremer Handelsgesellschaft MbH v Continental Grain Co* [1983] 1 Lloyd's Rep 269, at p 292: '... the question resolves itself into a question of causation; in my judgment, at least in a case in which a seller can (as in the present case) claim the protection of a clause which protects him where fulfilment is hindered by the excepted peril, subsequent delivery of his available stock to other customers will not be regarded as an independent cause of shortage, provided that in making such delivery, the seller acted reasonably in all the circumstances of the case ...'

A similar approach was reflected in other cases: see, for example, *Intertradex SA v Lesieur – Tourteaux SARL* [1977] 2 Lloyd's Rep 146, p 155, *per* Mr Justice Donaldson as he then was; [1978] 2 Lloyd's Rep 509, p 513, *per* Lord Denning MR. Reliance was also placed on passages in *The Law of Contract* (7th edn) by Professor Treitel, which the judge quoted in his judgment at p 152. Thus, Mr Clarke urged, this was a case in which Wijsmuller could not perform all their contracts once *Super Servant Two* was lost; they acted reasonably (as we must assume) in treating the *Dan King* contract as one they could not perform; so, the sinking had the direct result of making that contract impossible to perform.

Mr Legh-Jones answered that since the contract provided for the carriage to be performed by one or other vessel the loss of one did not render performance radically different, still less impossible. That apart, Wijsmuller's argument fell foul of the principles summarised above, since (among other things) the frustration they sought to establish did not bring the contract to an end forthwith, without more and automatically and was not independent of the act or election of Wijsmuller. The *force majeure* cases were good law so far as they went, but it was one thing to construe and apply a consensual *force majeure* clause, another to determine whether the facts were such that the law should hold the contract to be discharged.

Had the *Dan King* contract provided for carriage by *Super Servant Two* with no alternative, and that vessel had been lost before the time for performance, then assuming no negligence by Wijsmuller (as for purposes of this question we must), I feel sure the contract would have been frustrated. The doctrine must avail a party who contracts to perform a contract of carriage with a vessel which, through no fault of his, no longer exists. But that is not this case. The *Dan King* contract did provide an alternative. When that contract was made one of the contracts eventually performed by *Super Servant One* during the period of contractual carriage of *Dan King* had been made, the other had not, at any rate finally. Wijsmuller have not alleged that when the *Dan King* contract was made either vessel was earmarked for its performance. That, no doubt, is why an option was contracted for. Had it been foreseen when the *Dan King* contract was made that *Super Servant Two* would be unavailable for performance, whether because she had been deliberately sold or accidentally sunk, Lauritzen at least would have thought it no matter, since the carriage could be performed with the other. I accordingly accept Mr Legh-Jones' submission that the present case does not fall within the very limited class of cases in which the law will relieve one party from an absolute promise he has chosen to make.

But I also accept Mr Legh-Jones' submission that Wijsmuller's argument is subject to other fatal flaws. If, as was argued, the contract was frustrated when Wijsmuller made or communicated their decision on 16 February, it deprives language of all meaning to describe the contract as coming to an end automatically. It was, indeed, because the contract did not come to an end automatically on 29 January, that Wijsmuller needed a fortnight to review their schedules and their commercial options. I cannot, furthermore, reconcile Wijsmuller's argument with the reasoning or the decision in *Maritime National Fish Ltd*. In that case, the Privy Council declined to speculate why the charterers selected three of the five vessels to be licensed but, as I understand the case, regarded the interposition of human choice after the allegedly frustrating event as fatal to the plea of frustration. If Wijsmuller are entitled to succeed here, I cannot see why the charterers lost there. The cases on frustrating delay do not, I think, help Wijsmuller since it is actual and prospective delay (whether or not recognised as frustrating by a party at the time) which frustrates the contract, not a party's election or decision to treat the delay as frustrating. I have no doubt that force majeure clauses are, where their terms permit, to be construed and applied as in the commodity cases on which Wijsmuller relied, but it is, in my view, inconsistent with the doctrine of frustration as previously understood on high authority that its application should depend on any decision, however reasonable and commercial, of the party seeking to rely on it.

The issue between the parties was short and fundamental: what is meant by saying that a frustrating event, to be relied on, must occur without the fault or default, or without blame attaching to, the party relying on it?

Mr Clarke's answer was that a party was precluded from relying on an event only when he had acted deliberately or in breach of an actionable duty in causing it. Those conditions were not met here since it was not alleged Wijsmuller sank *Super Servant Two* deliberately and at the material time Wijsmuller owed Lauritzen no duty of care if (as I have held) cl 15 did not apply when the vessel sank. Mr Clarke relied on tentative doubts expressed in *Joseph Constantine SS Ltd*, whether mere negligence would render an event 'self-induced'.

Mr Legh-Jones argued for a less restrictive approach. He relied on what Lord Justice Griffiths, as he then was, said in *The Hannah Blumenthal*, [1982] 1 Lloyd's Rep 582, p 592; [1983] 1 AC 854, p 882:

> *Denmark Productions Ltd v Boscobel Productions Ltd* [1969] 1 QB 699 best illustrates what is meant by default in the context of frustration. The essence of frustration is that it is caused by some unforeseen supervening event over which the parties to the contract have no control and for which they are therefore not responsible. To say that the supervening event occurs without the default or blame or responsibility of the parties is, in the context of the doctrine of frustration, but another way of saying it is a supervening event over which they had no control. The doctrine has no application and cannot be invoked by a contracting party when the frustrating event was at all times within his control; still less can it apply in a situation in which the parties owed a contractual duty to one another to prevent the frustrating event occurring.

Wijsmuller's test would, in my judgment, confine the law in a legalistic strait-jacket and distract attention from the real question, which is whether the frustrating event relied upon is truly an outside event or extraneous change of situation or whether it is an event which the party seeking to rely on it had the means and opportunity to prevent but nevertheless caused or permitted to come about. A fine test of legal duty is inappropriate; what is needed is a pragmatic judgment whether a party seeking to rely on an event as discharging him from a contractual promise was himself responsible for the occurrence of that event.

Lauritzen have pleaded in some detail the grounds on which they say that *Super Servant Two* was lost as a result of the carelessness of Wijsmuller, their servants or agents. If those allegations are made good to any significant extent Wijsmuller would (even if my answer to Question 2(a) is wrong) be precluded from relying on their plea of frustration.

A more coherent rule in these Hobson's choice cases might be that the order in which the various contracts were made should be taken into account. Treitel argues along these lines and concludes that the decision in *The Super Servant Two* may be amenable to such an analysis:

VI Choosing between several contracts

Frustration is sometimes said to be self-induced where it is due to the 'act' or 'election' of the party claiming to be discharged. This way of stating the principle can give rise to difficulty where a party has entered into a number of contracts and is deprived by the supervening event of the power of performing them all, but not of the power of performing one or some of them. Where the subject matter is physically divisible, a possible solution in such cases is to apportion it between the various claimants. But this solution is not available where the subject matter cannot be physically divided on discharge.

The first case is the decision of the Privy Council in *Maritime National Fish Ltd v Ocean Trawlers Ltd*. On the facts, there clearly was such an election, for the defendants could have allocated one of the three licences to the *St Cuthbert* rather than to one of their own trawlers. But suppose that the defendants had operated only the two chartered trawlers, had obtained only one licence, and that the licensing requirement had been introduced after both charterparties were concluded. The question would then have arisen whether their choice to allocate their only licence to one of the trawlers would have been an 'election', so as to exclude the doctrine of frustration in relation to the charter of the other. It is submitted that the doctrine should not have been excluded in such a case. The charterer's capacity to perform both contracts is (in the case put) just as effectively removed as his capacity to perform a single contract would have been removed if he had chartered only one trawler and been refused a licence for that one.

The view that frustration is excluded in such circumstances is, nevertheless, supported by the second of the two cases here to be considered, *The Super Servant Two*.

Three lines of reasoning are given in the judgments, but it is submitted with great respect that none of them is wholly convincing. First, it was said that the *Maritime National Fish* case had established that a party could not rely on frustration where his failure or inability was due to his 'election'; and that the court in *The Super Servant Two* should follow that decision. It is, however, submitted that the two cases are readily distinguishable: in the *Maritime National Fish* case, it was possible for the charterer to perform all the contracts which he had made with the owners of the other trawlers, even though only three licences had been allocated to him; while in *The Super Servant Two*, it was no longer possible, after the loss of the ship, for the carrier to perform all the contracts which he had made to carry drilling rigs during the period in question. Secondly, it was said that, if the carrier were given the choice which of the contracts he would perform, frustration of the other or others could come about only as a result of the exercise of that choice, and such a position would be inconsistent with the rule that frustration occurs automatically, without any election by either party. Again, it is submitted that this line of reasoning is not conclusive since the rule that frustration operates automatically is subject to qualification precisely in cases of allegedly self-induced frustration: we have seen, for example, that the imprisonment of an employee is a circumstance on which the employer, but not the employee, can rely as a ground of discharge, so that discharge cannot in such cases be described as automatic.

It may, from this point of view, be relevant that, in *The Super Servant Two*, some of the contracts which the carrier chose to perform (by the use of his other ship during the relevant period) had not been made 'at any rate finally' until after the contract with the plaintiffs; and that, even after the loss of the *Super Servant Two*, the carrier had continued to negotiate for extra fees to be paid under one of those contracts, 'before finally allocating the *Super Servant One* to the performance of these contracts'. The third reason given for the decision is that 'It is within the promisor's own control how many contracts he enters into and the risk should be his'. But this argument seems to undermine the whole basis of the doctrine of frustration: it has just as much force where the promisor enters into a single contract as it has where he enters into two or more, with different contracting parties. This, indeed, is the fundamental objection to the reasoning of *The Super Servant Two*, and it is submitted that the rationale of the doctrine should lead to discharge of some of the contracts where the supervening event which makes it impossible to perform them all occurs without the fault of the party claiming discharge. Consistency with the reasoning of the *Maritime National Fish* case could be preserved by holding that which contracts were to be discharged should depend, not on the free election of the party who can no longer perform, but on a rule of law. On this view, the actual decision in *The Super Servant Two* could be justified by reference to the order in which the various contracts with the carrier were made.[80]

The final variety of fault comes in the form of simple negligence which results in the incapacity of the performing party to fulfil his obligations under the contract. If the fault on the part of the performer also amounts to the breach of an existing duty owed to the other party, the doctrine of frustration will apply. However, the more difficult question is whether fault not amounting to the breach of a duty owed to the other party but which prevents the performer from completing his contractual obligations will also serve to invoke the doctrine of frustration. It has been suggested that an opera singer who goes out in the rain and catches a cold might be able to hide behind the doctrine of frustration if she is unable to participate in a concert engagement made with the other party, provided there was no deliberation on the part of the singer.[81] Whether or not the personal fault of the performer may frustrate the contract is unclear, but the matter may be resolved through an application of the evidential rules on burden of proof. It is clear that in a civil action the rule is that he who affirms must prove, so that the onus of proving self-induced frustration will lie on the person who alleges it as a reason for keeping the contract intact. Accordingly, it will be for the party not at fault to prove that the other party brought about the event which it is alleged frustrates the

---

80   Treitel, 1994, pp 490–93.

81   *Joseph Constantine SS Line Ltd v Imperial Smelting Corpn Ltd* [1942] AC 154, pp 166–67, *per* Lord Simon.

contract. If it cannot be shown on a balance of probability that the fault of the performer brought about the frustrating event, then the parties will be discharged from their contract on the ground of supervening incapacity:

Joseph Constantine SS Line Ltd v Imperial Smelting Corpn Ltd [1942] AC 154, HL, p 166

> **Lord Simon**: For purposes of clearness and to avoid possible misunderstanding hereafter, I must add (though this is not necessary for the present decision) that I do not think that the ambit of 'default' as an element disabling the plea of frustration to prevail has as yet been precisely and finally determined. 'Self-induced' frustration, involves deliberate choice, and those cases amount to saying that a man cannot ask to be excused by reason of frustration if he has purposely so acted as to bring it about. 'Default' is a much wider term and in many commercial cases dealing with frustration is treated as equivalent to negligence. Yet, in cases of frustration of another class, arising in connection with a contract for personal performance, it has not, I think, been laid down that, if the personal incapacity is due to want of care, the plea fails. Some day it may have to be finally determined whether a prima donna is excused by complete loss of voice from an executory contract to sing if it is proved that her condition was caused by her carelessness in not changing her wet clothes after being out in the rain. The implied term in such a case may turn out to be that the fact of supervening physical incapacity dissolves the contract without inquiring further into its cause, provided, of course, that it has not been deliberately induced in order to get out of the engagement.

The best insurer

While prevention is one way of averting a risk of loss, it is equally possible to insure against such a risk. In this regard, insurance includes both market insurance and self-insurance. For example, in a contract for the sale of goods to be shipped to the buyer's place of business, once property in those goods has passed to the buyer then, in the absence of a contrary intention, the buyer will be on risk and he will be expected to insure those goods against transit risks.

In the course of the negotiating process, it may be expected that the parties will communicate with each other and that risks of loss may be allocated as between the parties according to who is regarded as the best insurer against those risks. It may be the case that one of the parties is in a better position than the other to absorb the risk. For example, in *Tsakiroglou & Co Ltd v Noblee Thorl GmbH*,[82] a voyage charterparty was allegedly frustrated due to the closure of the Suez canal, thereby rendering the voyage longer and more expensive than had been planned. The cargo owner, being a commercial organisation with a

---

82 [1962] AC 93.

wide range of customers, might have been able to raise the price of his end product, thereby spreading the increased cost among a greater number of people.

In some instances, it is arguable that the best insurer principle has been ignored with the result that the judicial allocation of risk may have been subject to criticism. Arguably, such a case was *Tatem Ltd v Gamboa*,[83] in which the ship detained during the Spanish Civil War was considered to be at the risk of the owner, because the contract was held to be frustrated. However, it has been observed already that the contract provided that the charterer would not be responsible for hire charges if the ship was lost, but made no provision for the allocation of responsibility should the ship be detained. Although the parties were silent on the matter, one reason for not making any such provision might have been that the owners would have found it easier to insure against loss rather than detention and that it was the implied intention of the parties that the charterer should obtain insurance in this last respect, if he was able to do so.

In relation to long term contractual arrangements such as a lease of land, there used to be a view to the effect that the doctrine of frustration had no application.[84] It is clear now that this is no longer the case and that there is no contract to which the doctrine applies. However, there is still a considerable reluctance to treat such long-term contracts as frustrated because there is always the possibility that the frustrating event may abate so that further performance in the future becomes possible.[85] In this respect, it is arguable that the tenant is regarded as the best insurer against the risk of interruption of a lease rather than the landlord. One reason for this may be that long term contractual arrangements of this kind can be viewed as a form of speculation and it is generally the case that the speculator is deemed to accept the risks inherent in his speculative venture.[86]

In *National Carriers Ltd v Panalpina (Northern) Ltd*,[87] a warehouse was leased to the defendants for a period of 10 years from 1 January 1974. The terms of the lease provided that the premises were not to be used for any purpose other than warehousing, except with the consent of the plaintiffs. The only means of street access to the premises was closed by the local authority in May 1979 due to the dangerous state of repair of another building. The street remained closed for a period of 20 months. In an action by the plaintiffs for the

---

83 [1939] 1 KB 132.

84 The consequence of the decision in *Paradine v Jane* (1647) 82 ER 897 was that the tenant was regarded as an absolute insurer against disruption to a lease.

85 *Cricklewood Property & Investment Trust Ltd v Leighton's Investment Trust Ltd* [1945] AC 221, p 229, *per* Viscount Simon LC.

86 See, eg, *Amalgamated Investment and Property Co Ltd v Walker & Sons* [1977] 1 WLR 164.

87 [1981] AC 675, HL.

recovery of unpaid rent, it was argued by the defendants that the lease was frustrated. The House of Lords held that, in principle, the doctrine of frustration was applicable to leases, but that in the circumstances, given the likely length of continuance of the lease, there was no triable issue as to the applicability of the doctrine of frustration:

National Carriers Ltd v Panalpina (Northern) Ltd [1981] AC 675, HL, p 688

Lord Hailsham LC: This discussion brings me to the central point at issue in this case which, in my view, is whether or not there is anything in the nature of an executed lease which prevents the doctrine of frustration, however formulated, applying to the subsisting relationship between the parties.

The point, though one of principle, is a narrow one. It is the difference immortalised in *HMS Pinafore* between 'never' and 'hardly ever'.

Is there anything in principle which ought to prevent a lease from ever being frustrated? I think there is not. In favour of the opposite opinion, the difference in principle between real and chattel property was strongly urged. But I find it difficult to accept this, once it has been decided, as has long been the case, that time and demise charters even of the largest ships and of considerable duration can in principle be frustrated. This was sufficiently well established by 1943 to make these charters worthy of an express exception upon an exception in s 2(5) of the Law Reform (Frustrated Contracts) Act 1943 and, since then, the Suez cases have supervened. There would be something anomalous in the light of what has been going on recently in the Shatt al Arab to draw a distinction between a leased oil tank and a demise – chartered oil tanker. Other anomalies would follow if the absolute principle were to be applied to leases. Goff J appears to have found difficulty in applying frustration to an agreement for a lease (which creates an equitable estate in the land capable of being specifically enforced and thereby converted into a legal estate operating as from the beginning of the equitable interest): see *Rom Securities Ltd v Rogers (Holdings) Ltd* (1967) 205 EG 427. Personally, I find the absurdities postulated by Megarry and Wade, *The Law of Real Property*, 4th edn, in the case of the destruction by fire of the upper flat of a tenement building unacceptable if the 'never' doctrine were rigidly applied, and I am attracted by Professor Treitel's argument (at p 669 of the current edition of his work on contracts, *The Law of Contract*, 5th edn) of the inequitable contrast between a contract for the provision of holiday accommodation which amounted to a licence, and was thus, subject to the rule in *Taylor v Caldwell* (1863) 3 B & S 826, and a similar contract amounting to a short lease. Clearly, the contrast would be accentuated if Goff J's view be accepted as to the applicability of the doctrine to agreements for a lease.

I accept of course that systems of developed land law draw a vital distinction between land, which is relatively permanent, and other types of property which are relatively perishable. But one can overdo the contrast. Coastal erosion as well as the 'vast convulsion of nature' postulated by Viscount Simon LC in the *Cricklewood* case [1945] AC 221, p 229 can, even in this island, cause houses, gardens, even villages and their churches to fall into the North Sea, and, although the law of property in Scotland is different, as may be seen from *Tay Salmon Fisheries Co Ltd v Speedie* 1929 SC 593, whole estates can there, as Lord President Clyde points out at p 600, be overblown with sand for centuries and so fall subject to the *rei interitus* doctrine of the civil law.

In the result, I come down on the side of the 'hardly ever' school of thought. No doubt, the circumstances in which the doctrine can apply to leases are, to quote Viscount Simon LC in the *Cricklewood* case at p 231, 'exceedingly rare'. Lord Wright appears to have thought the same, whilst adhering to the view that there are cases in which frustration can apply, at p 241. But, as he said in the same passage: '... the doctrine of frustration is modern and flexible and is not subject to being constricted by an arbitrary formula.' To this school of thought I respectfully adhere. Like Lord Wright, I am struck by the fact that there appears to be no reported English case where a lease has ever been held to have been frustrated. I hope this fact will act as a suitable deterrent to the litigious, eager to make legal history by being first in this field. But I am comforted by the implications of the well known passage in the *Compleat Angler* (Pt i, Chapter 5) on the subject of strawberries: 'Doubtless, God could have made a better berry, but doubtless God never did.' I only append to this observation of nature the comment that it does not follow from these premises that He never will and, if it does not follow, an assumption that He never will becomes exceedingly rash.

In the event, my opinion is that the appeal should be dismissed with costs.

Lord Wilberforce (p 694): Two arguments only by way of principle have been suggested. The first is that a lease is more than a contract: it conveys an estate in land. This must be linked to the fact that the English law of frustration, unlike its continental counterparts, requires, when it applies, not merely adjustment of the contract, but its termination. But this argument, by itself, is incomplete as a justification for denying that frustration is possible. The argument must continue by a proposition that an estate in land once granted cannot be divested – which, as Viscount Simon LC pointed out in the *Cricklewood* case [1945] AC 221, p 229, begs the whole question.

It was pointed out, however, by Atkin LJ in *Matthey v Curling* [1922] 2 AC 180, p 200, in a passage later approved by Viscount Simon [1945] AC 221, p 230, that as a lease can be determined, according to its terms, upon the happening of certain specified events, there is nothing illogical in implying a term that it should be determined on the happening of other events – namely, those which in an ordinary contract work a frustration.

In the second place, if the argument is to have any reality, it must be possible to say that frustration of leases cannot occur because in any event the tenant will have that which he bargained for, namely, the leasehold estate. Certainly this may be so in many cases – let us say most cases. Examples are *London and Northern Estates Co v Schlesinger* [1916] 1 KB 20, where what was frustrated (viz, the right of personal occupation) was not at the root of the contract, and requisitioning cases, for example, *Whitehall Court Ltd v Ettlinger* [1920] 1 KB 680, where, again, the tenant was left with something he could use. But there may also be cases where this is not so. A man may desire possession and use of land or buildings for, and only for, some purpose in view and mutually contemplated. Why is it an answer, when he claims that this purpose is 'frustrated', to say that he has an estate if that estate is unusable and unsaleable? In such a case, the lease, or the conferring of an estate, is a subsidiary means to an end, not an aim or end of itself.

The second argument of principle is that on a lease the risk passes to the lessee, as on a sale it passes to the purchaser (see *per* Lord Goddard in the *Cricklewood* case). But the two situations are not parallel. Whether the risk – or any risk – passes to the lessee depends on the terms of the lease: it is not uncommon, indeed, for some risks – of fire or destruction – to be specifically allocated. So in the case of unspecified risks, which may be thought to have been mutually contemplated, or capable of being contemplated by reasonable men, why should not the court decide on whom the risks are to lie? And if it can do this and find that a particular risk falls upon the lessor, the consequence may follow that upon the risk eventuating the lessee is released from his obligation.

To provide examples, as of a 999 year lease, during which a frustrating event occurs, or of those in decided cases (see above), to show that in such cases frustration will not occur, is insufficient as argument. These examples may be correct: they may cover most, at least most normal, cases. But the proposition is that there can be no case outside them and that I am unable to accept.

The principal difficulty in this regard is that the longer the contract has to run the more difficult it becomes to say whether an alleged frustrating event will have a serious effect on the performance obligations of the parties. The position may be different so far as contracts for the sale of land are concerned even though the contract may have the effect of creating an equitable interest in the land.[88]

Reversal of unjust enrichment

Since the effect of frustration is that the parties are discharged from their performance obligations from the date of the frustrating event and that the contract is terminated automatically,[89] it may be that benefits have been conferred on one party due to the partial performance of the other or that one of the parties has made a payment under the contract prior to the date of frustration. In either case, there is the prospect that one of the parties may be unjustly enriched at the expense of the other party. This eventuality was not dealt with very well at common law, since the rule which developed was that unless there was a total failure of consideration,[90] any sums of money paid or payable before the date of frustration were not recoverable.[91] The problems

88 See *Wong Lai Ying v Chinachem Investment Co Ltd* (1979) 13 Build LR 81 (unforeseen landslip frustrated contract of sale where development would have been delayed for 30 months). See, also, *Johnson & Co (Barbados) Ltd v NSR Ltd* [1997] AC 400 (contract for the sale of land not frustrated by a threat of compulsory purchase)

89 *Hirji Mulji v Cheong Yue SS Co* [1926] AC 497, p 505.

90 *Fibrosa Spolka Akcyjna v Fairbairn, Lawson, Combe, Barbour & Co Ltd* [1943] AC 32.

91 *Chandler v Webster* [1904] 1 KB 493.

created by the common law rule were addressed by Parliament in the Law Reform (Frustrated Contracts) Act 1943, considered below, but the unjust enrichment principle is also relevant in other respects in determining whether a particular event is capable of frustrating a contract.

If the decision to treat a contract as frustrated might give one of the parties an undue advantage this may operate as a justification for refusing to treat the contract as frustrated. For example, in *Tamplin SS Co v Anglo-Mexican Petroleum Products Co Ltd*,[92] an oil tanker was chartered for a period of five years, but was subject to government requisition when the charterparty still had nearly three years to run. In the circumstances, there was no prejudice to the charterers, since the government compensation payable to the charterers exceeded the agreed hire charges. However, the owners of the ship claimed that the contract was frustrated. The House of Lords held, by a narrow majority, that the contract was not frustrated. One explanation for the action of the owners is that they wanted to secure the increased benefit of the government compensation in replacement for the lower hire charges. In this case, it is readily understandable that the majority of the House of Lords preferred not to allow the owners to benefit in this way at the expense of the charterers.

Remedies, unjust enrichment and frustration

Where a contract is frustrated, the common law rule stipulates that the parties are discharged from their respective obligations from the date of the frustrating event. A particular problem with this rule is that prior to the date of frustration, it is quite possible that one of the parties has made an advance payment for the goods or services which are the subject matter of the contract. Alternatively, a party required to produce an end product or provide a service may have incurred expenditure in partial fulfilment of the requirements of the contract. In either event, if losses are left to lie where they fall, there is the prospect that one of the parties stands to gain at the expense of the other. In these circumstances, since the contract is frustrated, the party who has suffered a loss will have no action for damages, since the parties are discharged from their contractual performance obligations, in which case, the settlement of the parties' rights will be dealt with on a restitutionary basis.

Money paid or payable before the date of frustration

At common law, if one of the parties had paid a sum of money or the contract provided for payment prior to the date on which the contract was said to be frustrated, that amount was irrecoverable, unless there was a total failure of

---

92 [1916] 2 AC 397.

consideration. Thus, in *Chandler v Webster*,[93] the plaintiff contracted to hire a room which overlooked the route of the coronation procession of King Edward VII. However, due to the King's illness, the procession was cancelled with the result that the contract was held to be frustrated. The contract provided for payment of the hire charge in advance and some, but not all, of that advance payment had been made. It was held that the plaintiff was not only unable to recover the amount he had paid in advance, but was also obliged to pay those sums provided for in the contract which were due before the date of frustration.

In *Chandler*, it was considered that the contract had to be void *ab initio* before there could be a total failure of consideration, but in this respect the decision must be regarded as incorrect. Subsequently, in *Fibrosa v Fairbairn*,[94] it was held by the House of Lords that it was unnecessary to show that the contract was void *ab initio* in order for there to be a total failure of consideration, provided there was no value in the performance on one side so that the other party, who had made an advance payment, would be entitled to recover the amount he had paid. Despite this decision, problems still remained. For example, the common law rule made no provision for the value of the work done by the party who had received payment. Moreover, the rule was confined to cases of total failure of consideration, so that if the plaintiff received some benefit, however small, he would be unable to recover the amount he had paid to the other party.

In order to meet these criticisms, Parliament responded in the form of the Law Reform (Frustrated Contracts) Act 1943, although it should be observed that the Act does not apply to certain types of contract,[95] such as voyage charterparties, contracts for the carriage of goods by sea, contracts of insurance and contracts for the sale of specific goods under which the goods perish before risk has passed to the buyer:[96]

Law Reform (Frustrated Contracts) Act 1943

1

(2) All sums paid or payable to any party in pursuance of the contract before the time when the parties were so discharged (in this Act referred to as 'the time of discharge') shall, in the case of sums so paid, be recoverable from him as moneys received by him for the use of the party by whom the sums were paid, and, in the case of sums so payable, cease to be so payable:

Provided that, if the party to whom the sums were so paid or payable incurred expenses before the time of discharge in, or for the purpose of, the performance of the contract, the court may, if it considers it just to do so,

---

93   [1904] 1 KB 493.
94   *Fibrosa Spolka Akcyjna v Fairbairn, Lawson, Combe, Barbour & Co Ltd* [1943] AC 32.
95   By virtue of the Law Reform (Frustrated Contracts) Act 1943, s 2(5).
96   Sale of Goods Act 1979, s 7.

having regard to all the circumstances of the case, allow him to retain or, as the case may be, recover the whole or any part of the sums so paid or payable, not being an amount in excess of the expenses so incurred.

Section 1(2) manages to avoid the language of total failure of consideration, treating the action as one for moneys had and received instead. The effect of the opening paragraph of s 1(2) is that, now, sums paid in advance or sums agreed to be paid in advance are respectively, recoverable or not payable in the event of frustration of the contract. However, the proviso to s 1(2) goes on to allow for compensation of the party who has partially performed the contract, since the value of that performance may be set off against the sums paid or payable by the other party. The concluding words of s 1(2) also make it clear that there is a ceiling upon any compensation allowed under the provision, in that no more may be set off than the actual value of the expenditure incurred.

The main problem with this provision is that it is not truly restitutionary in nature, if the proper definition of a restitutionary action requires an unjust enrichment by the defendant *at the plaintiff's expense*. Under s 1(2), the expense incurred by the performing party still appears to be recoverable even where his performance has conferred no benefit on the party having made the advance payment. For example, it would appear that the expenditure incurred by the manufacturer of the machinery in *Fibrosa v Fairbairn* would be recoverable under s 1(2), despite the fact that at the time when the contract was frustrated when war broke out, no machinery had been delivered and no benefit had been conferred on the intended purchaser.

On the wording of the proviso to s 1(2), it would appear that what has been introduced is a statutory recognition of the defence of change of position.[97] But this view is not wholly borne out by the wording of the proviso which specifies that the expenses, to be recoverable, must have been incurred 'in or for the purpose of the performance of the contract'. Accordingly, the change of position must result from something related to the contract itself and must not be extraneous to it. On a wide view of the defence of change of position, if the moneys paid by one party were to be spent by the other on purchasing equipment intended to be used in the performance of another contract, this might be sufficient to support the defence.

In other respects, the proviso to s 1(2) covers issues which fall outside the scope of the judicially developed defence of change of position. For example, the use of the words 'sums so paid ... or payable' indicate that money does not have to be paid to the recipient in order for the 'compensation' provisions to apply. Accordingly, the proviso seems to go beyond restitution simpliciter and operates a system of just and reasonable loss apportionment.[98]

---

97 *BP Exploration Co (Libya) Ltd v Hunt (No 2)* [1979] 1 WLR 783, p 800, *per* Robert Goff J.
98 Burrows, 1993, p 285.

In exercising its discretion under s 1(2), the court may have regard to any expenses incurred by the payor, since this is a relevant factor in determining whether there has been an unjust enrichment.

In *Gamerco SA v ICM/ Fair Warning (Agency) Ltd*,[99] the promoter of a rock concert made an advance payment to the intended performers at the concert. Subsequently, the contract was held to be frustrated on the ground that the permit to hold the concert at the stadium was withdrawn for safety reasons. The claimants (promoters) had paid the group $412,500 prior to the date on which the contract was frustrated, but both the promoters and the group had incurred expenditure in preparing for the concert. It was held that the promoters were entitled to recover the pre-payment and that the group was not entitled to anything under the proviso to s 1(2):

Gamerco SA v ICM/ Fair Warning (Agency) Ltd [1995] 1 WLR 1226, QBD, p 1234

Garland J: The contract, having been discharged by frustration, the plaintiffs were entitled to recover from the second defendants the advance payment of US$412,500 (less the sum returned by the first defendants) by virtue of section 1(2) of the Act of 1943 ...

In addition, the balance net of tax, £362,500, ceases to be payable.

The issue which I have to decide is whether and, if so, to what extent, the defendants can set off against the US$412,500 expenses incurred before the time of discharge in or for the purpose of performance of the contract. It is perhaps surprising that over a period of 50 years there is no reported case on the operation of section 1(2), although it was considered, *obiter*, by Robert Goff J in *BP Exploration Co (Libya) Ltd v Hunt (No 2)* [1979] 1 WLR 783, p 800. The section has, of course, received the attention of textbook writers, most recently that of Professor Treitel in *Frustration and* Force Majeure (1994) ...

I therefore turn to the proviso and sub-s (4).[100]

The approach to the proviso

The following have to be established: (1) that the defendants incurred expenses paid or payable; (2) before the discharge of the contract on 2 July; (3) in performance of the contract (which is not applicable); or (4) for the purposes of the performance of the contract; and (5) that it is just in all the circumstances to allow them to retain the whole or any part of the sums so paid or payable.

The onus of establishing these matters must lie on the defendant. It is, in the broad sense, his case to be made out and I am assisted by the Victorian case of *Lobb v Vasey Housing Auxiliary (War Widows Guild)* [1963] VR 239 under the

---

99 [1995] 1 WLR 1216
100 Law Reform (Frustrated Contracts) Act 1943, s 1(4) provides: 'In estimating, for the purposes of the foregoing provisions of this section, the amount of any expenses incurred by any party to the contract, the court may, without prejudice to the generality of the said provisions, include such sum as appears to be reasonable in respect of overhead expenses and in respect of any work or services performed personally by the said party.'

corresponding Victorian Act of 1959, which is in very similar terms to the Act of 1943.

I have already dealt with (1), (2) and (4) so far as the evidence allows. I turn to (5). I take the following matters into consideration: (a) my assumption that the relevant expenses of US$50,000 was undisputed; (b) it was undisputed that the plaintiffs incurred expenses in excess of 52 m pesetas (approximately £285,000); (c) neither party conferred any benefit on the other or on a third party ...; (d) the plaintiff's expenditure was wholly wasted, as was the defendants'; (e) the plaintiffs were concerned with one contract only. The defendants were concerned with the last of 20 similar engagements, neither party being left with any residual benefit or advantage; (f) as already stated, I entirely ignore any insurance recoveries in accordance with sub-s (5).

Various views have been advanced as to how the court should exercise its discretion and these can be categorised as follows:

(1) *Total retention.* This view was advanced by the Law Revision Committee in 1939 (Cmd 6009) on the questionable ground that 'it is reasonable to assume that in stipulating for pre-payment, the payee intended to protect himself from loss under the contract'. ...

(2) *Equal division*: This was discussed by Professor Treitel in *Frustration and Force Majeure* ... There is some attraction in splitting the loss, but what if the losses are very unequal? Professor Treitel considers statutory provisions in Canada and Australia, but makes the point that equal division is unnecessarily rigid and was rejected by the Law Revision Committee in the 1939 Report to which reference has already been made. The parties may, he suggests, have an unequal means of providing against the loss by insurers, but he appears to overlook sub-s (5). It may well be that one party's expenses are entirely thrown away while the other is left with some realisable or otherwise usable benefit or advantage. Their losses may, as in the present case, be very unequal. Professor Treitel therefore favours the third view.

(3) *Broad discretion*: It is self-evident that any rigid rule is liable to produce injustice. The words 'if it considers it just to do so having regard to all the circumstances of the case' clearly confer a very broad discretion. Obviously, the court must not take into account anything which is not 'circumstance of the case' or fail to take into account anything that is and then exercise its discretion rationally. I see no indication in the Act, the authorities or the relevant literature that the court is obliged to incline towards either total retention or equal division. Its task is to do justice in a situation which the parties had neither contemplated nor provided for, and to mitigate the possible harshness of allowing all loss to lie where it has fallen.

I have not found my task easy. As I have made clear, I would have welcomed assistance on the true measure of the defendants' loss and the proper treatment of overhead and non-specific expenditure. Because the defendants have plainly suffered some loss, I have made a robust assumption. In all the circumstances, and having particular regard to the plaintiffs' loss, I consider that justice is done by making no deduction under the proviso. ...

Benefits in kind conferred under a frustrated contract

Under the common law rule, where a contract became frustrated, losses would lie where they fell. Accordingly, if one of the parties had gone some way towards the completion of his performance obligations on the date when the contract was held to be frustrated, he would be entitled to no payment in respect of his performance, even if this meant that the other party stood to gain as a result of that performance. Parliament enacted s 1(3) of the Law Reform (Frustrated Contracts) Act 1943 to deal with this situation.

Law Reform (Frustrated Contracts) Act 1943

1

(3) Where any party to the contract has, by reason of anything done by any other party thereto in, or for the purpose of, the performance of the contract, obtained a valuable benefit (other than a payment of money to which the last foregoing sub-section applies) before the time of discharge, there shall be recoverable from him by the said other party such sum (if any), not exceeding the value of the said benefit to the party obtaining it, as the court considers just, having regard to all the circumstances of the case and, in particular: (a) the amount of any expenses incurred before the time of discharge by the benefited party in, or for the purpose of, the performance of the contract, including any sums paid or payable by him to any other party in pursuance of the contract and retained or recoverable by that party under the last foregoing sub-section; and (b) the effect, in relation to the said benefit, of the circumstances giving rise to the frustration of the contract.

As in the case of s 1(2), since the contract has come to an end due to the operation of the doctrine of frustration, the solution provided by s 1(3) must be restitutionary rather than contractual. Since s 1(3) is essentially concerned with benefits in kind, such as the value of partly manufactured goods or partially completed services, there is a problem of subjective devaluation, namely that services, and in some cases goods, cannot be restored and in any case there may be the problem that although expensive to provide, partially completed services may confer little or no value on the other party until the service contracted for has been carried out in full. For example, in *Appleby v Myers*,[101] a contract for the installation of machinery in a factory was held to be frustrated when the factory was destroyed by fire. At the time of the frustrating event, the machinery had been partly manufactured, but, as the contract provided for no payment until completion, the manufacturer was entitled to no payment in respect of the work he had done. At the same time, it would also be difficult to say that at the time of frustration, there was any substantial benefit to the factory owner, and in any event, the value of a half

---

101 (1867) LR 2 CP 651.

completed machine would almost certainly be less than half that of a completed machine of the same kind.

How s 1(3) operates has been the subject of a detailed and critical analysis by Robert Goff J[102] in the case of *BP Exploration Co Ltd v Hunt (No 2)*,[103] the defendant was granted a concession to explore for oil in Libya. He did not have the physical resources to carry out the exploration himself, so he sold a half share in the concession to BP, on condition that they would bear the initial cost of exploration. Accordingly, under this arrangement, BP's expenses at the outset were likely to be very substantial, but on the assumption that oil was discovered, that expenditure would be recouped as oil continued to come on stream. The nature of the contract was that should oil not be discovered, the risk would be borne by BP, but, on the assumption that oil was discovered, BP's expenses would be paid for out of the defendant's receipts. Oil was discovered in 1967, but in 1971, the Libyan Government expropriated BP's share of the concession and, in 1973, the defendant's share was also expropriated. Accordingly, BP had received some payment, but this went only so far as to cover two-thirds of their initial expenditure. On the other hand, since the defendant had no expenses, all moneys received by him amounted to profit once the concession had been paid for.

Goff J adopted a two stage approach to s 1(3), stating that it was necessary first to identify and value what benefit had been conferred on the defendant, since on the wording of s 1(3), this set a ceiling on the amount which could be awarded by way of a just sum. Secondly, it was necessary to award a just sum, taking account of the value of the benefit conferred and the cost to the performer of the work he had done prior to the frustrating event. For these purposes, the benefit to the defendant will be assessed by reference to the end product of the service provided by the other party:

BP Exploration Co Ltd v Hunt (No 2) [1979] 1 WLR 783, p 799
Robert Goff J:

The principle of recovery

The principle, which is common to both s 1(2) and (3), and indeed is the fundamental principle underlying the Act itself, is prevention of the unjust enrichment of either party to the contract at the other's expense. It was submitted by Mr Rokison, on behalf of BP, that the principle common to both subsections was one of restitution for net benefits received, the net benefit being the benefit less an appropriate deduction for expenses incurred by the defendant. This is broadly correct so far as s 1(2) is concerned; but, under s 1(3), the net benefit of the defendant simply provides an upper limit to the award – it does not measure the amount of the award to be made to the plaintiff. This is because, in s 1(3), a distinction is drawn between the plaintiff's performance

---

102 Goff J's judgment was subsequently affirmed in the House of Lords [1982] 1 All ER 925.
103 [1979] 1 WLR 783.

under the contract and the benefit which the defendant has obtained by reason of that performance – and the net benefit obtained by the defendant from the plaintiff's performance may be more than a just sum payable in respect of such performance, in which event a sum equal to the defendant's net benefit would not be an appropriate sum to award to the plaintiff.

The Act is not designed to do certain things: (i) it is not designed to apportion the loss between the parties. There is no general power under either s 1(2) or 1(3) to make any allowance for expenses incurred by the plaintiff (except, under the proviso to s 1(2), to enable him to enforce *pro tanto* payment of a sum payable, but unpaid before frustration) and expenses incurred by the defendant are only relevant insofar as they go to reduce the net benefit obtained by him and thereby limit any award to the plaintiff; (ii) it is not concerned to put the parties in the position in which they would have been if the contract had been performed; (iii) it is not concerned to restore the parties to the position they were in before the contract was made.

An award under the Act may have the effect of rescuing the plaintiff from an unprofitable bargain. This may certainly be true under s 1(2), if the plaintiff has paid the price in advance for an expected return which, if furnished, would have proved unprofitable; if the contract is frustrated before any part of that expected return is received, and before any expenditure is incurred by the defendant, the plaintiff is entitled to the return of the price he has paid, irrespective of the consideration he would have recovered had the contract been performed.

Claims under s 1(3)

In contract, where an award is made under s 1(3), the process is more complicated. First, it has to be shown that the defendant has, by reason of something done by the plaintiff in, or for the purpose of, the performance of the contract, obtained a valuable benefit (other than a payment of money) before the time of discharge. That benefit has to be identified, and valued, and such value forms the upper limit of the award. Secondly, the court may award to the plaintiff such sum, not greater than the value of such benefit, as it considers just having regard to all the circumstances of the case, including in particular the matters specified in s 1(3)(a) and (b).

Identification of defendant's benefit

In the course of the argument before me, there was much dispute whether, in the case of services, the benefit should be identified as the services themselves, or as the end product of the services. One example canvassed (because it bore some relationship to the facts of the present case) was the example of prospecting for minerals. If minerals are discovered, should the benefit be regarded (as Mr Alexander [acting for Hunt] contended) simply as the services of prospecting, or (as Mr Rokison [acting for BP] contended) as the minerals themselves being the end product of the successful exercise? Now, I am satisfied that it was the intention of the legislature, to be derived from s 1(3) as a matter of construction, that the benefit should in an appropriate case be identified as the end product of the services. This appears, in my judgment, not only from the fact that s 1(3) distinguishes between the plaintiff's performance and the defendant's benefit, but also from s 1(3)(b), which clearly relates to the product of the plaintiff's performance. Let me take the example of a building contract. Suppose that a contract for work on a building is frustrated by a fire which destroys the building and which, therefore, also destroys a substantial amount of work already done by the plaintiff. Although it might be thought just to award the plaintiff a sum assessed on a *quantum meruit* basis, probably a rateable part of the contract price, in respect of the work he has done, the effect of s 1(3)(b) will be to reduce the award to nil, because of the effect, in relation to the defendant's benefit, of the circumstances giving rise to the frustration of the contract. It is quite plain that, in s 1(3)(b), the word 'benefit' is intended to refer, in the example I have given, to the actual improvement to the building, because that is what will be affected by the frustrating event; the subsection therefore contemplates that, in such a case, the benefit is the end product of the plaintiff's services, not the services themselves. This will not be so in every case, since in some cases the services will have no end product; for example, where the services consist of doing such work as surveying, or transporting goods. In each case, it is necessary to ask the question: what benefit has the defendant obtained by reason of the plaintiff's contractual performance? But it must not be forgotten that, in s 1(3), the relevance of the value of the benefit is to fix a ceiling to the award. If, for example, in a building contract, the building is only partially completed, the value of the partially completed building (ie the product of the services) will fix a ceiling for the award; the stage of the work may be such that the uncompleted building may be worth less than the value of the work and materials that have gone into it, particularly as completion by another builder may cost more than completion by the original builder would have cost. In other cases, however, the actual benefit to the defendant may be considerably more than the appropriate or just sum to be awarded to the plaintiff, in which event the value of the benefit will not, in fact, determine the *quantum* of the award. I should add, however, that, in a case of prospecting, it would usually be wrong to identify the discovered mineral as the benefit. In such a case, there is always (whether the prospecting is successful or not) the benefit of the prospecting itself, that is, of knowing whether or not the land contains any deposit of the relevant minerals; if the prospecting is successful, the benefit may include also the enhanced value of the land by reason of the discovery; if the prospector's contractual task goes beyond discovery and includes development and production, the benefit will include the further enhancement of the land by reason of the installation of the facilities, and also the benefit of in part transforming a valuable mineral deposit into a marketable commodity.

I add by way of footnote that all these difficulties would have been avoided if the legislature had thought it right to treat the services themselves as the benefit. In the opinion of many commentators, it would be more just to do so; after all, the services in question have been requested by the defendant, who normally takes the risk that they may prove worthless, from whatever cause. In the example I have given of the building destroyed by fire, there is much to be said for the view that the builder should be paid for the work he has done, unless he has (for example by agreeing to insure the works) taken upon himself the risk of destruction by fire. But my task is to construe the Act as it stands. On the true construction of the Act, it is, in my judgment, clear that the defendant's benefit must, in an appropriate case, be identified as the end product of the plaintiff's services, despite the difficulties which this construction creates, difficulties which are met again when one comes to value the benefit.

Valuing the benefit

Since the benefit may be identified with the product of the plaintiff's performance, great problems arise in the valuation of the benefit. First, how does one solve the problem which arises from the fact that a small service may confer an enormous benefit, and conversely, a very substantial service may confer only a very small benefit? The answer presumably is that at the stage of valuation of the benefit (as opposed to assessment of the just sum) the task of the court is simply to assess the value of the benefit to the defendant. For example, if a prospector after some very simple prospecting discovers a large and unexpected deposit of a valuable mineral, the benefit to the defendant (namely, the enhancement in the value of the land) may be enormous; it must be valued as such, always bearing in mind that the assessment of a just sum may very well lead to a much smaller amount being awarded to the plaintiff. But conversely, the plaintiff may have undertaken building work for a substantial sum which is, objectively speaking, of little or no value – for example, he may commence the redecoration, to the defendant's execrable taste, of rooms which are in good decorative order. If the contract is frustrated before the work is complete, and the work is unaffected by the frustrating event, it can be argued that the defendant has obtained no benefit, because the defendant's property has been reduced in value by the plaintiff's work; but the partial work must be treated as a benefit to the defendant, since he requested it, and valued as such. Secondly, at what point in time is the benefit to be valued? If there is a lapse of time between the date of the receipt of the benefit, and the date of frustration, there may in the meanwhile be a substantial variation in the value of the benefit. If the benefit had simply been identified as the services rendered, this problem would not arise; the court would simply award a reasonable remuneration for the services rendered at the time when they were rendered, the defendant taking the risk of any subsequent depreciation and the benefit of any subsequent appreciation in value. But that is not what the Act provides: s 1(3)(b) makes it plain that the plaintiff is to take the risk of depreciation or destruction by the frustrating event. If the effect of the frustrating event upon the value of the benefit is to be measured, it must surely be measured upon the benefit as at the date of frustration.

Assessment of the just sum

The principle underlying the Act is prevention of the unjust enrichment of the defendant at the plaintiff's expense. Where, as in cases under s 1(2), the benefit conferred on the defendant consists of payment of a sum of money, the plaintiff's expense and the defendant's enrichment are generally equal; and, subject to other relevant factors, the award of restitution will consist simply of an order for repayment of a like sum of money. But where the benefit does not consist of money, then the defendant's enrichment will rarely be equal to the plaintiff's expense. In such cases, where (as in the case of a benefit conferred under a contract thereafter frustrated) the benefit has been requested by the defendant, the basic measure of recovery in restitution is the reasonable value of the plaintiff's performance – in a case of services, a *quantum meruit* or reasonable remuneration, and in a case of goods, a *quantum valebat* or reasonable price. Such cases are to be contrasted with cases where such a benefit has not been requested by the defendant. In the latter class of case, recovery is rare in restitution; but if the sole basis of recovery was that the defendant had been incontrovertibly benefited, it might be legitimate to limit recovery to the defendant's actual benefit – a limit which has (perhaps inappropriately) been imported by the legislature into s 1(3) of the Act. However, under s 1(3) as it stands, if the defendant's actual benefit is less than the just or reasonable sum which would otherwise be awarded to the plaintiff, the award must be reduced to a sum equal to the amount of the defendant's benefit.

The approach adopted by Robert Goff J can create particular difficulties where the end product is eccentric, where there is no end product and where the end product is destroyed by the frustrating event, since in each of these cases, there may be little or no value to the defendant in what has been provided. Since it is the value of the benefit which dictates what just sum is to be awarded, it follows that the expenditure incurred by the performer may be considerably greater than the benefit to the other party.

Applying these principles to *BP Exploration Co (Libya) Ltd v Hunt*, the benefit to Hunt was substantial since he began to make a profit from an early stage, that benefit being assessed at $85 million. Moreover, since this benefit was well in excess of the expenditure incurred by BP (assessed at $34.5 million), the award under s 1(3) was a relatively simple matter and BP was able to recoup all of its expenditure, while still leaving Hunt with a reasonable profit from his speculative venture.

It has been seen that s 1(2) appears to operate something resembling, but not identical to, the common law defence of change of position. Section 1(3), on the other hand, seems to reflect more exactly restitutionary principles. The common law change of position defence would take account of events occurring before and after the frustrating event so that where, for example, a building is in the process of being constructed but is subsequently destroyed by fire, the owner would be treated as having derived a benefit initially by having received part of what he contracted for before the frustrating event. But once the building is destroyed, this could be regarded as a change of position, thereby justifying a refusal to grant a remedy. The decision of Robert Goff J in *BP Exploration v Hunt* seems to operate more or less along these lines in the sense that, if there is no end value in the service provided, it appears unlikely that a just sum will be awarded. In this sense, this interpretation of s 1(3) does not seem to provide for loss apportionment in the same way as does s 1(2).

Some, including Treitel,[104] would argue that Robert Goff's judgment placed too narrow an interpretation on s 1(3), and that due emphasis ought to be given to the words, 'before the time of discharge' in s 1(3) and, in particular, the wording of s 1(3)(b):

> The machinery of the Act worked satisfactorily in *BP Exploration (Libya) Ltd v Hunt* because the valuable benefit, even when reduced in the light of the frustrating event, exceeded the just sum. But the position would have been different if the expropriation had occurred immediately before oil had begun to flow and if no compensation for expropriation had been paid. On the reasoning of the judgment, there would then have been no valuable benefit (beyond the 'farm-in' oil); for that reasoning has regard to 'the circumstances giving rise to the frustration' within s 1(3)(b) in valuing the benefit rather than in assessing the just sum. The same reasoning is adopted in an example which closely resembles *Appleby v Myers:* 'Suppose that a contract for work on a building is frustrated by a fire which destroys the building and which therefore destroys a substantial amount of the work already done by the plaintiff. Although it might be thought just to award the plaintiff a sum assessed on a *quantum meruit* basis, the effect of s 1(3)(b) will be to reduce the award to nil ...' If this is right, *Appleby v Myers* would not be affected by the Act; but in view of the evident reluctance with which the learned judge reached this conclusion it is submitted that an alternative interpretation of s 1(3) is to be preferred. This would make the destruction of the benefit relevant, not to the identification of the benefit, but to the assessment of the just sum. Two points seem to support such an interpretation. First, s 1(3) applies where a valuable benefit has been obtained before the time of discharge: thus, to identify the benefit in a case like *Appleby v Myers* the court must look at the facts as they were before, and not after, the fire. The partly completed installation would at least *prima facie* be a benefit, in that completion of the installation would be likely to cost less after part of the work had been done. Secondly, there is the structure of the sub-section. This begins by setting out the circumstances in which the court has power to make an award (that is, when a valuable benefit has been obtained) and then provides guidelines for the exercise of that power. The guideline contained in s 1(3)(b) is introduced by the words 'such sum as the court thinks just having regard to ... (b) ...'; and these words seem to link the guideline to the exercise rather than to the existence of the court's discretion. This interpretation cannot cause any injustice, for if the court thinks that very little or nothing should be awarded it can exercise its discretion to that effect; and for this purpose the court can certainly take the destruction of the benefit into account so as to split the loss in such proportions as the court thinks just. But if such destruction necessarily led to the conclusion that no valuable benefit had been obtained before frustration, the court would have no discretion to award anything at all. It would be a pity

---

104 Treitel, 1999, pp 853–54.

if this useful discretion were restricted in a way that is neither clearly required by the words of the sub-section nor necessary to promote justice.

The discretion is in any case restricted to cases in which the defendant has received something of value. It is not enough for the plaintiff to incur trouble and expense. Thus, a person who orders goods from a manufacturer does not receive a valuable benefit merely because the manufacturer has bought the raw materials and started to make the goods. The manufacturer can only recover in respect of these expenses if he has stipulated for an advance payment, so that he can invoke s 1(2).

The power to make an award in respect of a valuable benefit under s 1(3) is, in theory, additional to the power to make an award in respect of expenses under s 1(2). Thus, if a party who has incurred expenses has also both conferred a valuable benefit and received (or stipulated for) a prepayment he can claim under both subsections. But any amount awarded in respect of expenses will be taken into account in deciding how much should be awarded in respect of valuable benefit, and vice versa. If the party who has incurred expenses has received a valuable benefit other than money (for example, a 'prepayment' in kind) he cannot make any claim in respect of expenses under s 1(2) as that subsection only applies where a *sum of money* is paid or payable. But the court can reach much the same result under s 1(3), for it can take the expenses into account in deciding how much the recipient of the valuable benefit should pay for it.

CHAPTER 7

CONTRACTUAL UNFAIRNESS

CONFLICTING VALUES

Two opposing values cause strains within the law of contract. On the one hand, there is a desire to do justice, but at the same time, the courts are keen to promote certainty or predictability. The contract rule book developed in the 19th century is generally said to epitomise the value of certainty. In *Printing and Numerical Registering Co v Sampson*,[1] it was observed that:

> If there is one thing which more than any other public policy requires it is that *men of full age and competent understanding* shall have the utmost liberty of contracting, and that their contracts when entered into *freely and voluntarily* shall be held sacred and shall be enforced by the courts of justice.

This is, of course, almost a eulogy to the economic, even moral, virtues of unfettered free enterprise, but the words italicised show that judicial intervention is permitted on the grounds of justice or fairness where a person has not contracted freely or where one of the parties is disadvantaged.

The instances in which the courts are likely to invoke the value of justice include those which fall broadly under the banner of inequality of bargaining power. Most of the rules designed to operate in this way are equitable in origin, and can be said to be concerned with either procedural fairness or substantive fairness. Procedural fairness requires that a person should not be allowed to keep the benefits of a contract which has been unfairly brought into existence, for example, one extracted by fraud, force or other unfair conduct.[2] Substantive unfairness arises where the terms of a particular contract favour one party over the other. Generally, courts are less likely to intervene in cases of substantive unfairness unless a presumption of procedural unfairness is also raised.[3] Policy considerations underlie the rules concerning unfairness; in particular, a desire to protect the public interest and weaker parties. Protection of the public interest is largely reflected in rules relating to illegal contracts and the desire to protect weaker parties is borne out by many modern consumer protection initiatives and the rules on duress, undue influence, restraint of trade and the control of exclusion clauses.

---

1   (1875) LR 19 Eq 462, p 465, *per* Lord Jessell MR.

2   *Hart v O'Connor* [1985] AC 1000, p 1017.

3   *Ibid*. Of course, as Lord Brightman also noted, procedural unfairness and substantive unfairness (which he termed 'contractual imbalance') may well overlap in practice.

INEQUALITY OF BARGAINING
POWER – A GENERAL PRINCIPLE?

In some jurisdictions, an express attempt has been made to state a generalised principle of unconscionability. For example, in the US, the Uniform Commercial Code, para 2-302, provides:

> If the court as a matter of law finds the contract or any clause of the contract unconscionable at the time it was made, the court may refuse to enforce the contract, or it may enforce the remainder of the contract without the unconscionable clause, or it may so limit the application of any unconscionable clause as to avoid any unconscionable result.

English Law has never committed itself to such a generalised principle, despite some brave attempts:

Lloyds Bank Ltd v Bundy [1975] QB 326, CA, p 339

Lord Denning MR:

General principles

Gathering all together, I would suggest that through all these instances there runs a single thread. They rest on 'inequality of bargaining power.' By virtue of it, the English law gives relief to one who, without independent advice, enters into a contract upon terms which are very unfair or transfers property for a consideration which is grossly inadequate, when his bargaining power is grievously impaired by reason of his own needs or desires, or by his own ignorance or infirmity, coupled with undue influences or pressures brought to bear on him by or for the benefit of the other. When I use the word 'undue', I do not mean to suggest that the principle depends on proof of any wrongdoing. The one who stipulates for an unfair advantage may be moved solely by his own self-interest, unconscious of the distress he is bringing to the other. I have also avoided any reference to the will of the one being 'dominated' or 'overcome' by the other. One who is in extreme need may knowingly consent to a most improvident bargain, solely to relieve the straits in which he finds himself. Again, I do not mean to suggest that every transaction is saved by independent advice. But the absence of it may be fatal. With these explanations, I hope this principle will be found to reconcile the cases. Applying it to the present case, I would notice these points:

(1) The consideration moving from the bank was grossly inadequate. The son's company was in serious difficulty. The overdraft was at its limit of £10,000. The bank considered that its existing security was insufficient. In order to get further security, it asked the father to charge the house – his sole asset – to the uttermost. It was worth £10,000. The charge was for £11,000. That was for the benefit of the bank. But not at all for the benefit of the father, or indeed for the company. The bank did not promise to continue the overdraft or to increase it. On the contrary, it required the overdraft to be reduced. All that the company gained was a short respite from impending doom.

(2) The relationship between the bank and the father was one of trust and confidence. The bank knew that the father relied on it implicitly to advise him about the transaction. The father trusted the bank. This gave the bank much influence on the father. Yet the bank failed in that trust. It allowed the father to charge the house to his ruin.

(3) The relationship between the father and the son was one where the father's natural affection had much influence on him. He would naturally desire to accede to his son's request. He trusted his son.

(4) There was a conflict of interest between the bank and the father. Yet the bank did not realise it. Nor did it suggest that the father should get independent advice. If the father had gone to his solicitor – or to any man of business – there is no doubt that any one of them would say: 'You must not enter into this transaction. You are giving up your house, your sole remaining asset, for no benefit to you. The company is in such a parlous state that you must not do it.'

These considerations seem to me to bring this case within the principles I have stated. But, in case that principle is wrong, I would also say that the case falls within the category of undue influence of the second class stated by Cotton LJ in *Allcard v Skinner* (1887) 36 Ch D 145, p 171. I have no doubt that the assistant bank manager acted in the utmost good faith and was straightforward and genuine. Indeed, the father said so. But beyond doubt he was acting in the interests of the bank – to get further security for a bad debt. There was such a relationship of trust and confidence between them that the bank ought not to have swept up his sole remaining asset into its hands – for nothing – without his having independent advice. I would therefore allow this appeal.

English law gives relief to one who, without independent advice, enters into a contract or transfers property for a consideration which is grossly inadequate, when his bargaining power is grievously impaired by reason of his own needs or desires, or by his own ignorance or infirmity, coupled with undue influences or pressures brought to bear on him by or for the benefit of the other.

Had Lord Denning's approach been developed, such a principle would be broad in its application. It would extend to cover cases falling within the common law and equitable rules on duress and undue influence (considered below), plus contracts in restraint of trade, and onerous exemption clauses. However, it would range more widely (and less predictably) over the general territory of exploitation, victimisation and unfair advantage. In the immediate aftermath of *Bundy*, there was considerable academic speculation about how English law might develop in this area.[4]

---

4   See, eg, Waddams, 1976; and Carr, 1975. The latter author went so far as to suggest 'Lord Denning [attempts] to do for the various species of undue influence and duress what Lord Atkin did for the various categories of negligence in *Donoghue v Stevenson*. We may be witnessing the spawning of a benevolent giant'.

However, despite further valiant efforts by Lord Denning to develop these principles,[5] the 'genie' was put firmly back in the bottle by the House of Lords in:

National Westminster Bank plc v Morgan [1985] AC 686, p 707

Lord Scarman: Lord Denning MR believed that the doctrine of undue influence could be subsumed under a general principle that English courts will grant relief where there has been 'inequality of bargaining power'. He deliberately avoided reference to the will of one party being dominated or overcome by another. The majority of the court did not follow him; they based their decision on the orthodox view of the doctrine as expounded in *Allcard v Skinner* (1887) 36 Ch D 145. The opinion of the Master of the Rolls, therefore, was not the ground of the court's decision, which was to be found in the view of the majority, for whom Sir Eric Sachs delivered the leading judgment.

Nor has counsel for the respondent sought to rely on Lord Denning MR's general principle: and, in my view, he was right not to do so. The doctrine of undue influence has been sufficiently developed not to need the support of a principle which by its formulation in the language of the law of contract is not appropriate to cover transactions of gift where there is no bargain. The fact of an unequal bargain will, of course, be a relevant feature in some cases of undue influence. But it can never become an appropriate basis of principle of an equitable doctrine which is concerned with transactions 'not to be reasonably accounted for on the ground of friendship, relationship, charity, or other ordinary motives on which ordinary men act' (Lindley LJ in *Allcard v Skinner*). And, even in the field of contract, I question whether there is any need in the modern law to erect a general principle of relief against inequality of bargaining power. Parliament has undertaken the task – and it is essentially a legislative task – of enacting such restrictions upon freedom of contract as are in its judgment necessary to relieve against the mischief: for example, the hire-purchase and consumer protection legislation, of which the Supply of Goods (Implied Terms) Act 1973, the Consumer Credit Act 1974, the Consumer Safety Act 1978, the Supply of Goods and Services Act 1982 and the Insurance Companies Act 1982 are examples. I doubt whether the courts should assume the burden of formulating further restrictions.

DURESS

The classical rule book understanding of duress is that it is a variety of procedural unfairness which prevents a valid agreement from being reached, due largely to the 'overborne will' theory, which emerges from some of the case extracts below. But, arguably, where a person is faced with a threat amounting to common law duress, his consent is real, albeit that he had made

---

5   See, eg, *Re Brocklehurst* [1977] 3 WLR 696, p 707.

'Hobson's' choice. More recent authorities appear to have moved away from a literal application of the 'overborne will' theory and, instead, concentrate on the impropriety or otherwise of the words or actions of the person making the threat. Where the courts are more concerned with the actions of the threatener, they would appear to be as much concerned with the substantive fairness of the result as with the procedural improprieties in the process.[6]

Threats sufficient to constitute duress

The traditional rule at common law confined actionable duress to actual or threatened physical violence to the person or unlawful constraint of the person.[7] Thus, threats of lawful imprisonment[8] or threats directed at property[9] at one time, did not amount to common law duress.

There was a wider jurisdiction to intervene in equity and through the application of restitutionary principles. In equity, a threat to expose a person to lawful prosecution was regarded as a sound basis for rendering a contract voidable for undue pressure.[10] Also, a restitutionary action for moneys had and received could be used to reverse an unjust enrichment derived from a threat to damage property belonging to another.[11]

Twentieth century authorities began to recognise that a threat to property could be just as coercive as a threat to the person, and what began to develop was a recognition of the notion of economic duress. Accordingly, it was observed, obiter, that a threat to burn a man's house or to slash a valuable painting would be sufficient to invalidate a contract made as a result of the threat.[12] Subsequently, it came to be recognised that a threat to interfere with a contract might also suffice, with the result that if, in the course of renegotiating a contract, one party improperly threatens not to perform unless the other party makes some concession, that threat may amount to actionable duress. But this, in turn, raises the difficulty of distinguishing between actionable duress and hard bargaining. Factors which may assist in distinguishing these matters seem to include whether the person subject to the threat has raised a protest.[13]

---

6   See Atiyah, 1986 (reprinted 1990), pp 345–46.

7   See, eg, *Barton v Armstrong* [1976] AC 104.

8   *Cumming v Ince* (1847) 11 QB 112.

9   *Skeate v Beale* (1840) 11 Ad & El 983.

10   *Williams v Bayley* (1886) LR 1 HL 200.

11   *Maskell v Horner* [1915] 3 KB 106.

12   *Occidental Worldwide Investment Corpn v Skibs A/S Avanti, The Siboen and The Sibotre* [1976] 1 Lloyd's Rep 293, p 335, *per* Kerr LJ.

13   *Ibid.*

In *North Ocean Shipping Co Ltd v Hyundai Construction Co Ltd*,[14, 15] the defendants threatened not to complete the construction of an oil tanker unless the plaintiffs were prepared to pay 10% on top of the contract price. Unknown to the defendants, the plaintiffs had arranged a profitable charter of the ship on completion. The plaintiffs were advised that the defendants had no legal entitlement to the extra 10%, with the result that they agreed to pay, without prejudice to their legal rights. Eight months after completion of the ship, the plaintiffs sought to recover the excess payment. It was held, in principle, that the threat not to complete did constitute economic duress, but the delay in commencing proceedings and the absence of any protest constituted an affirmation of the contract:

North Ocean Shipping Co Ltd v Hyundai Construction Co Ltd, The Atlantic Baron [1979] QB 705, p 714

Mocatta J: Having reached the conclusion that there was consideration for the agreement made on 28 and 29 June 1973, I must next consider whether even if that agreement, varying the terms of the original shipbuilding contract of 10 April 1972, was made under a threat to break that original contract and the various increased instalments were made consequently under the varied agreement, the increased sums can be recovered as money had and received. Mr Longmore submitted that they could be, provided they were involuntary payments and not made, albeit perhaps with some grumbling, to close the transaction.

Certainly this is the well established position if payments are made, for example, to avoid the wrongful seizure of goods where there is no prior agreement to make such payments. The best known English case to this effect is probably *Maskell v Horner* [1915] 3 KB 106, where the plaintiff had over many years paid illegal tolls on his goods offered for sale in the vicinity of Spitalfields Market. The plaintiff had paid under protest, though the process was so prolonged, that the protests became almost in the nature of jokes, though the plaintiff had in fact suffered seizures of his goods when he had not paid. Lord Reading CJ did not say that express words of protest were always necessary, though they might be useful evidence to negative voluntary payments; the circumstances taken as a whole must indicate that the payments were involuntary. Buckley LJ, at p 124, regarded the making of a protest before paying to avoid the wrongful seizure of one's goods as 'a further factor', which went to show that the payment was not voluntary. Pickford LJ, at p 126, likewise regarded the fact of protest as 'some indication' that the payer intended to resist the claim.

There are a number of well known examples in the books of English cases where the payments made have been involuntary by reason of some wrongful threatened action or inaction in relation to goods and have subsequently been

---

14 *The Atlantic Baron* [1979] QB 705.
15 See Chapter 3.

recovered, but where the issue has not been complicated by the payments having been made under a contract. Some of these cases have concerned threats to seize, seizure or wrongful detention of goods. *Maskell v Horner* being the best known modern example of the former two categories and *Astley v Reynolds* (1731) 2 Str 915 a good example of the latter category, where a pawnbroker refused to release plate when the plaintiff tendered the money lent and, on demand, more than the legal rate of interest, since without this the pawnbroker would not release the plaintiff's plate. The plaintiff recovered the excess, as having paid it under compulsion and it was held no answer that an alternative remedy might lie in trover.

Mr Longmore referred me to other cases decided in this country bordering upon what he called economic duress as distinct from duress to goods. Thus in *Parker v Great Western Railway Co* (1844) 7 Man & G 253, approved in *Great Western Railway Co v Sutton* (1869) LR 4 HL 226, it was held that the railway was not entitled to differentiate adversely between charges on goods made against one carrier or packer using the railway and others. Excess charges payable by such persons were recovered. In advising the House of Lords in the latter case, Willes J said, at p 249: '... I have always understood that when a man pays more than he is bound to do by law for the performance of a duty which the law says is owed to him for nothing, or for less than he has paid, there is a compulsion or concussion in respect of which he is entitled to recover the excess by *condictio indebiti,* or action for money had and received. This is every day's practice as to excess freight.'

I may here usefully cite a further short passage from the valuable remarks of Kerr J in *The Siboen and The Sibotre* [1976] 1 Lloyd's Rep 293, p 336, where he said: 'It is true that in that case, and in all the three Australian cases, it was held that there had been no consideration for the settlement which the courts reopened. But I do not think that it would have made any difference if the defendants in these cases had also insisted on some purely nominal but legally sufficient consideration. If the contract is void the consideration would be recoverable in quasi-contract; if it is voidable equity could rescind the contract and order the return of the consideration.'

It is also interesting at this point to quote a few sentences from an article entitled 'Duress as a vitiating factor in contract' by Mr Beatson, Fellow of Merton College, Oxford, in (1974) 33 CLJ 97, 108: 'It is submitted that there is no reason for making a distinction between actual payments and agreements to pay. If that is so there is nothing to prevent a court from finding that duress of goods is a ground upon which the validity of a contract can be impeached ... The law was accurately stated by the courts of South Carolina as early as 1795, when it was said that "... whenever *assumpsit* will lie for money extorted by duress of goods, a party may defend himself against any claim upon him for money to be paid in consequence of any contract made under similar circumstances".'

Before proceeding further it may be useful to summarise the conclusions I have so far reached. First, I do not take the view that the recovery of money paid under duress other than to the person is necessarily limited to duress to goods falling within one of the categories hitherto established by the English cases. I would respectfully follow and adopt the broad statement of principle laid down by Isaacs J cited earlier and frequently quoted and applied in the Australian cases. Secondly, from this it follows that the compulsion may take the form of 'economic duress' if the necessary facts are proved. A threat to break a contract may amount to such 'economic duress'. Thirdly, if there has been such a form of duress leading to a contract for consideration, I think that contract is a voidable one which can be avoided and the excess money paid under it recovered ...

I do not attach any special importance to the lack of protest made at the time of the assignment, since the documents made no reference to the increased 10%. However, by the time the *Atlantic Baron* was due for delivery in November 1974, market conditions had changed radically, as is found in para 39 of the special case and the owners must have been aware of this. The special case finds in para 40, as stated earlier, that the owners did not believe that if they made any protest in the protocol of delivery and acceptance that the Yard would have refused to deliver the vessel or the *Atlantic Baroness* and had no reason so to believe. Mr Longmore naturally stressed that in the rather carefully expressed findings in paras 39 to 44 of the special case, there is no finding that if at the time of the final payments the owners had withheld payment of the additional 10% the Yard would not have delivered the vessel. However, after careful consideration, I have come to the conclusion that the important points here are that since there was no danger at this time in registering a protest, the final payments were made without any qualification and were followed by a delay until 31 July 1975, before the owners put forward their claim, the correct inference to draw, taking an objective view of the facts, is that the action and inaction of the owners can only be regarded as an affirmation of the variation in June 1973 of the terms of the original contract by the agreement to pay the additional 10%. In reaching this conclusion, I have not, of course, overlooked the findings in para 45 of the special case, but I do not think that an intention on the part of the owners not to affirm the agreement for the extra payments not indicated to the Yard can avail them in the view of their overt acts. As was said in *Deacon v Transport Regulation Board* [1958] VR 458, p 460, in considering whether a payment was made voluntarily or not: 'No secret mental reservation of the doer is material. The question is – what would his conduct indicate to a reasonable man as his mental state.' I think this test is equally applicable to the decision this court has to make whether a voidable contract has been affirmed or not, and I have applied this test in reaching the conclusion I have just expressed.

This should not be taken to mean that every threat of non-performance will amount to economic duress, since, as observed above, there is a distinction between duress and hard bargaining. Moreover, if there is evidence that the party seeking relief has entered the renegotiation with his eyes open, he cannot be heard to complain at a later stage. Often, this will be the case where the party seeking relief has had legal advice before deciding to submit to the pressure brought to bear by the other party.

In *Pao On v Lau Yiu Long*,[16, 17] the plaintiffs agreed to sell a partly constructed building to the defendants. The arrangement involved a transfer of shares in a subsidiary company which owned the building. It was subsequently realised by the plaintiffs that, by agreeing to sell the shares at a fixed price, the defendants might make a considerable profit if the shares were to rise in value. The plaintiffs threatened to pull out of the deal unless the defendants were prepared to abandon the original contract and replace it with a contract of indemnity which would protect the plaintiffs from a fall in value of the shares, but would allow them to benefit from any rise in value prior to the date of the final transfer of ownership of the building. The defendants feared adverse publicity which might affect public confidence in the company if the contract were not performed. Under pressure, they complied with the plaintiffs' demands. Subsequently, the shares fell in value, and the plaintiffs sought to recover their loss under the indemnity contract. It was held that there was no duress, as the defendants had carefully considered their position and, after advice, chose to avoid litigation for commercial reasons. In determining whether a threat constitutes duress, it is necessary to consider whether the victim protested; whether there was any alternative course of action open to the victim such as the pursuit of an adequate legal remedy; whether the victim was independently advised, and whether, after making the contract, the victim took sufficient steps to avoid it:

Pao On v Lau Yiu Long [1980] AC 614, p 634

Lord Scarman: The American Law Institute in its *Restatement of the Law, Contracts*, Chapter 3, s 84(d), has declared that performance (or promise of performance) of a contractual duty owed to a third person is sufficient consideration. This view (which accords with the statement of our law in *New Zealand Shipping Co Ltd v AM Satterthwaite & Co Ltd* [1975] AC 154) appears to be generally accepted, but only in cases where there is no suggestion of unfair economic pressure exerted to induce the making of what *Corbin on Contracts* calls 'the return promise'.

Their Lordships' knowledge of this developing branch of American law is necessarily limited. In their judgment it would be carrying audacity to the point of foolhardiness for them to attempt to extract from the American case law a principle to provide an answer to the question now under consideration. That question, their Lordships repeat is whether, in a case where duress is not established, public policy may nevertheless invalidate the consideration if there has been a threat to repudiate a pre-existing contractual obligation or an unfair use of a dominating bargaining position. Their Lordships' conclusion is that, where businessmen are negotiating at arm's length, it is unnecessary for the achievement of justice and unhelpful in the development of the law, to invoke such a rule of public policy. It would also create unacceptable anomaly.

---

16 [1980] AC 614.

17 See Chapter 3.

It is unnecessary because justice requires that men, who have negotiated at arm's length, be held to their bargains, unless it can be shown that their consent was vitiated by fraud, mistake or duress. If a promise is induced by coercion of a man's will, the doctrine of duress suffices to do justice. The party coerced, if he chooses and acts in time, can avoid the contract. If there is no coercion, there can be no reason for avoiding the contract where there is shown to be a real consideration which is otherwise legal.

Such a rule of public policy as is now being considered would be unhelpful because it would render the law uncertain. It would become a question of fact and degree to determine in each case whether there had been, short of duress, an unfair use of a strong bargaining position. It would create anomaly because, if public policy invalidates the consideration, the effect is to make the contract void. But, unless the facts are such as to support a plea of *non est factum*, which is not suggested in this case, duress does no more than confer upon the victim the opportunity, if taken in time, to avoid the contract. It would be strange if conduct less than duress could render a contract void, whereas duress does no more than render a contract voidable. Indeed, it is the defendants' case in this appeal that such an anomaly is the correct result. Their case is that the plaintiffs, having lost by cancellation the safeguard of the subsidiary agreement, are without the safeguard of the guarantee because its consideration is contrary to public policy, and that they are debarred from restoration to their position under the subsidiary agreement because the guarantee us void, not voidable. The logical consequence of Mr Leggatt's submission is that the safeguard which all were at all times agreed the plaintiffs should have – the safeguard against fall in value of the shares – has been lost by the application of a rule of public policy. The law is not, in their Lordships' judgment, reduced to countenancing such stark injustice: nor is it necessary, when one bears in mind the protection offered otherwise by the law to one who contracts in ignorance of what he is doing or under duress. Accordingly, the submission that the additional consideration established by the extrinsic evidence is invalid on the ground of public policy is rejected.

The effect of duress

It is generally stated that a contract brought about by duress is voidable at the instance of the victim of a threat constituting duress.[18] This is also consistent with the decision in *North Ocean Shipping Co Ltd v Hyundai Construction*,[19] to the effect that a plea of duress can be met by a defence of affirmation of the contract. Such an analysis seems wholly consonant with 'economic' duress, where it is quite realistic to view a (temporarily) valid contract as having

---

18 *Pao On v Lau Yiu Long* [1980] AC 614, p 634, *per* Lord Scarman; *Universe Tankships Inc of Monrovia v International Transport Workers Federation* [1983] AC 366, p 383, *per* Lord Diplock; *Dimskal Shipping Co SA v International Transport Workers Federation, The Evia Luck (No 2)* [1992] 1 Lloyd's Rep 115, p 120, *per* Lord Goff. *Barton v Armstrong* [1976] AC 104, p 120, *per* Lord Cross *contra* – contract void.

19 [1979] QB 705.

arisen, albeit one produced by undue commercial pressure. However, in cases of 'traditional' duress involving the direct threat (or application) of physical force, it seems a little odd to think of any true contract as having ever come into existence.

The classical view of duress was that it should overbear the will of the victim, but this has been described more recently as an unhelpful approach.[20] This is especially so since it over-emphasises the reaction of the person who is threatened, to the exclusion of an examination of the conduct of the person who threatens. Moreover, if the will of the party seeking relief is overborne, the sole reason for entering the contract will have been the duress, but it is clear that the coercive pressure must be a reason for making the contract but need not be *the* reason or even the *predominant* or *clinching* reason.[21] Despite this, recent decisions have paid lip service to the overborne will theory, saying that duress must constitute a coercion of the will so as to vitiate consent.[22]

The fallacy of the overborne will theory has been exposed in *The Universe Sentinel*[23] (considered below), where it was stated that if the victim of a threat of duress is fully aware of the nature and terms of the contract into which he enters, it cannot be said that his will has been overborne. A proper enquiry into the issue of unconscionability does not concentrate upon the mind of the victim, instead it should concentrate on the nature of the threat and the legitimacy of the demand.

The case concerned the 'blacking' of a large oil tanker, the *Universe Sentinel*, at Milford Haven. The action was taken at the instigation of the ITF, a union representing transport workers, including seamen, world wide. The purpose of this action was to compel the owners of ships sailing under 'flags of convenience' (in this case, Liberia) to employ their crews on terms comparable to those contained in collective agreements for ships registered in W Europe. The specific demands, before this ship would be allowed to soil were that the owners would comply with the (above) collective agreement condition and would also pay US$80,000 into a special ITF welfare fund. The majority of the House (Lords Scarman and Brandon dissenting) found that there had been economic duress, and that the (consequential) right of the owners to recover their money was unaffected by the trade union immunity contained in the (then) s 13 of the Trade Union and Labour Relations Act 1974. The dissentients felt that the payments were irrecoverable, because they had arisen out of a trade dispute, and so were a legitimate exercise of pressure and did not constitute duress:

---

20 *Dimskal Shipping Co SA v International Transport Workers Federation, The Evia Luck (No 2)* [1992] 1 Lloyd's Rep 115, p 120, *per* Lord Goff

21 *Barton v Armstrong* [1976] AC 104, p 119, *per* Lord Cross.

22 *Pao On v Lau Yiu Long* [1980] AC 614, p 636 *per* Lord Scarman; *Atlas Express v Kafco (Importers and Distributors) Ltd* [1989] 1 All ER 641, p 645, *per* Tucker J.

23 [1983] AC 366.

The Universe Sentinel sub nom Universe Tankships Inc of Monrovia v International Transport Workers Federation [1982] 2 WLR 803, HL, p 820

Lord Cross: The 'duress' point raises the question whether the demand made by ITF that the appellants should make contributions to the welfare fund was a 'legitimate' demand, in the sense that, although compliance with it was enforced by pressure that amounted to duress, the appellants are, nevertheless, not entitled to recover the contributions as 'money had and received'. The fact that your Lordships do not agree on the answer to be given to this question, shows that it is a difficult one. Up to a point, there was agreement between the parties. In the first place, it was common ground between them that, although none of the provisions of the Trade Union and Labour Relations Act 1974 have any direct application to this case, guidance as to where the line should be drawn in the field of industrial relations between 'legitimate' and 'illegitimate' demands by a trade union can be found in the provisions of the Act giving immunity from liability in tort for certain acts done in contemplation or furtherance of a trade dispute, and that the demand in this case would rank as legitimate if a refusal by the appellants to comply with it would have given rise to a dispute between the appellants and ITF connected with the terms and conditions of employment of the crew of the Universe Sentinel. Secondly, it was common ground that if a trade union were to make two demands one of which was legitimate and the other not, the existence of the legitimate demand would not preclude the employer from recovering money paid under duress in compliance with the illegitimate demand. If, to take an example suggested by Lord Diplock, ITF had coupled its demand that the appellants should increase the wages of the crew with a demand that they should contribute to a fund to assist the guerrillas in El Salvador, and the appellants had complied with both demands under duress, the fact that they could not recover the increase in wage payments would not preclude them from recovering the contributions to the guerrilla fund. I would add, although, on the facts of this case, the point does not arise for decision, that I fully concur with the view expressed by my noble and learned friend in the concluding paragraph of his speech, that in the case supposed, it would have made no difference to the right of the appellants to recover the payments to the guerrilla fund that ITF had insisted, as a condition of lifting the 'blacking' of the vessel, that an undertaking by the appellants to make the payments should be inserted in the contracts of employment of each member of the crew and that the appellants had, under duress entered into such undertakings with each member. A trade union cannot turn a dispute which in reality has no connection with terms and conditions of employment into a dispute connected with terms and conditions of employment by insisting that the employer inserts appropriate terms into the contracts of employment into which he enters ...

It appears from Art 5 of the special agreement that the rates of contribution to the welfare fund are fixed by ITF and may be increased by it from time to time at its discretion. ITF called no evidence to explain the position disclosed by these accounts. The assets of the welfare fund, which at the end of 1978 were worth some £7,870,000 net are – as a matter of law – the property of ITF to use as it likes. No doubt, it would be only in very exceptional circumstances that

ITF would apply any of those assets to purposes other than the purposes of the Seafarers' Section. But even if one assumes that in practice the welfare fund will always be applied for the purposes set out in rule 2, I cannot see how a contribution to the welfare fund differs in principle from a contribution to the general funds of a seamen's union – nor did I understand counsel for the respondents to contend that there was any difference. His reply to the point was to say 'the appellants admit that they cannot recover the crew membership fees; what difference is there between them and the contributions to the welfare fund?'. To my mind, there is a world of difference. By paying his membership fees and getting his membership card, the member secures a right to certain benefits and services from the union. These are analogous to the benefits obtained from a private health insurance scheme or a private pension fund, and the fees paid are presumably calculated with some reference to the expense of providing the benefits and services. If an employer defrays the expense of obtaining such benefits for his employees, his payments are in substance additional wages and the benefits obtained are properly described as 'fringe benefits' of the employment. By contrast, the members of the crew do not obtain any rights to benefit from the welfare fund as a result of the appellants' contributions to it. Their chance of receiving some benefit from the fund is just the same whether or not the appellants contribute to the fund or whether or not they remain in the employment of the appellants. All that one can say is that the contributions add to the resources of the union. It might, I suppose, be argued that any increase in the wealth of a trade union must be beneficial to its members. As a general proposition, that might well be doubted; but even if it were universally true, the fact would not establish any connection between the demand and the terms and conditions of employment of the crew. I cannot bring myself to think that, even in this day and age, a demand that an employer shall make contributions to union funds at rates fixed from time to time by the union – for that, as I see it, is all that this demand amounts to – is a demand which can be legitimately enforced by duress. In fact, of course, the appellants did not enter into any agreements with the members of the crew to make the welfare contributions but, as I have already indicated, I do not think that if they had entered into such agreements under duress that circumstance would have precluded them from recovering the payments.

I agree with my noble and learned friends, Lord Diplock and Lord Russell of Killowen, that the appeal should be allowed.

Lord Scarman (dissenting) (p 828): It is, I think, already established law that economic pressure can in law amount to duress; and that duress, if proved, not only renders voidable a transaction into which a person has entered under its compulsion but is actionable as a tort, if it causes damage or loss: *Barton v Armstrong* [1976] AC 104 and *Pao On v Lau Yiu Long* [1980] AC 614. The authorities upon which these two cases were based reveal two elements in the wrong of duress: (1) pressure amounting to compulsion of the will of the victim; and (2) the illegitimacy of the pressure exerted. There must be pressure, the practical effect of which is compulsion or the absence of choice. Compulsion is variously described in the authorities as coercion or the vitiation of consent. The classic case of duress is, however, not the lack of will to submit but the victim's intentional submission arising from the realisation that there is no other practical choice open to him. This is the thread of principle which links the early law of duress (threat to life or limb) with later developments when the law came also to recognise as duress first the threat to property and now the threat to a man's business or trade. The development is well traced in Goff and Jones, *The Law of Restitution*, 2nd edn, 1978, Chapter 9.

The absence of choice can be proved in various ways, for example, by protest, by the absence of independent advice, or by a declaration of intention to go to law to recover the money paid or the property transferred: see *Maskell v Horner* [1915] 3 KB 106. But none of these evidential matters goes to the essence of duress. The victim's silence will not assist the bully, if the lack of any practicable choice but to submit is proved. The present case is an excellent illustration. There was no protest at the time, but only a determination to do whatever was needed as rapidly as possible to release the ship. Yet nobody challenges the judge's finding that the owner acted under compulsion. He put it thus [1981] ICR 129, p 143: 'It was a matter of the most urgent commercial necessity that the plaintiffs should regain the use of their vessel. They were advised that their prospects of obtaining an injunction were minimal, the vessel would not have been released unless the payment was made, and they sought recovery of the money with sufficient speed once the duress had terminated.'

The real issue in the appeal is, therefore, as to the second element in the wrong duress: was the pressure applied by the ITF in the circumstances of this case one which the law recognises as legitimate? For, as Lord Wilberforce and Lord Simon of Glaisdale said in *Barton v Armstrong* [1976] AC 104, p 121D: '... the pressure must be one of a kind which the law does not regard as legitimate.'

As the two noble and learned Lords remarked at p 121D, in life, including the life of commerce and finance, many acts are done 'under pressure, sometimes overwhelming pressure': but they are not necessarily done under duress. That depends on whether the circumstances are such that the law regards the pressure as legitimate.

In determining what is legitimate, two matters may have to be considered. The first is as to the nature of the pressure. In many cases, this will be decisive, though not in every case. And so, the second question may have to be considered, namely, the nature of the demand which the pressure is applied to support.

The origin of the doctrine of duress in threats to life or limb, or to property, suggests strongly that the law regards the threat of unlawful action as illegitimate, whatever the demand. Duress can, of course, exist even if the threat is one of lawful action: whether it does so depends upon the nature of the demand. Blackmail is often a demand supported by a threat to do what is lawful, for example, to report criminal conduct to the police. In many cases, therefore, 'what [one] has to justify is not the threat, but the demand ...': see *per* Lord Atkin in *Thorne v Motor Trade Association* [1937] AC 797, p 806.

The present is a case in which the nature of the demand determines whether the pressure threatened or applied, that is, the blacking, was lawful or unlawful. If it was unlawful, it is conceded that the owner acted under duress and can recover. If it was lawful, it is conceded that there was no duress and the sum sought by the owner is irrecoverable. The lawfulness or otherwise of the demand depends upon whether it was an act done in contemplation or furtherance of a trade dispute. If it was, it would not be actionable in tort: s 13(1) of the Act. Although no question of tortious liability arises in this case and s 13(1) is not, therefore, directly in point, it is not possible, in my view, to say of acts which are protected by statute from suit in tort that they nevertheless can amount to duress. Parliament having enacted that such acts are not actionable in tort, it would be inconsistent with legislative policy to say that, when the remedy sought is not damages for tort but recovery of money paid, they become unlawful.

For these reasons I conclude that the demand for contributions related to the terms and conditions of employment on the ship, and, if it had been resisted by the owner, would have led to a trade dispute. Blacking the ship in support of the demand was, therefore, not actionable in tort. It was, accordingly, a legitimate exercise of pressure and did not constitute duress. The owner cannot recover the contributions. I would dismiss the appeal.

This extract from Lord Scarman's dissenting judgment appears to reject the overborne will theory altogether, preferring to describe duress as 'involving not the lack of will to submit[24] (sic), but the victim's intentional submission arising from the realisation that there is no practical choice open to him' If so, where does this leave Lord Scarman's own judgment in *Pao On v Lau Yiu Long*?

It follows from this that there are two elements in cases of alleged duress. First, there must be illegitimate pressure and, secondly, there must be an absence of practical choice available to the victim. For these purposes, illegitimate pressure seems to cover more than just wrongful threats such as one to commit a crime, tort or breach of other legal or equitable duty. The judgments in *The Universe Sentinel* also embrace the notion of illegitimate pressure which involves no threat to break a duty owed in law. Thus, a threat to allow a workers' strike to take place has been regarded as sufficient:[25]

> **Lord Diplock (p 812):** My Lords, I turn to the second ground on which repayment of the $6,480 is claimed, which I will call the duress point. It is not disputed that the circumstances in which ITF demanded that the shipowners should enter into the special agreement and the typescript agreement and should pay the moneys of which the latter documents acknowledge receipt, amounted to economic duress upon the shipowners; that is to say, it is conceded that the financial consequences to the shipowners of *The Universe Sentinel* continuing to be rendered off-hire under her time charter to Texaco, while the blacking continued, were so catastrophic as to amount to a coercion

---

24 Submit should read resist: *B & S Contracts & Design Ltd v Victor Green Publications Ltd* [1984] ICR 419, p 428, *per* Kerr LJ.

25 *Ibid*, p 383.

of the shipowners' will which vitiated their consent to those agreements and to the payments made by them to ITF. This concession makes it unnecessary for your Lordships to use the instant appeal as the occasion for a general consideration of the developing law of economic duress as a ground for treating contracts as voidable and obtaining restitution of money paid under economic duress as money had and received to the plaintiffs' use. That economic duress may constitute a ground for such redress was recognised, albeit obiter, by the Privy Council in *Pao On v Lau Yiu Long* [1980] AC 614. The Board in that case referred with approval to two judgments at first instance in the commercial court which recognised that commercial pressure may constitute duress: one by Kerr J in *Occidental Worldwide Investment Corporation v Skibs A/S Avanti* [1976] 1 Lloyd's Rep 293, the other by Mocatta J in *North Ocean Shipping Co Ltd v Hyundai Construction Co Ltd* [1979] QB 705, which traces the development of this branch of the law from its origin in the 18th and early 19th century cases.

It is, however, in my view crucial to the decision of the instant appeal to identify the rationale of this development of the common law. It is not that the party seeking to avoid the contract which he has entered into with another party, or to recover money that he has paid to another party in response to a demand, did not know the nature or the precise terms of the contract at the time when he entered into it or did not understand the purpose for which the payment was demanded. The rationale is that his apparent consent was induced by pressure exercised upon him by that other party which the law does not regard as legitimate, with the consequence that the consent is treated in law as revocable unless approbated either expressly or by implication after the illegitimate pressure has ceased to operate on his mind. It is a rationale similar to that which underlies the avoidability of contracts entered into and the recovery of money exacted under colour of office, or under undue influence or in consequence of threats of physical duress.

Commercial pressure, in some degree, exists wherever one party to a commercial transaction is in a stronger bargaining position than the other party. It is not, however, in my view, necessary, nor would it be appropriate in the instant appeal, to enter into the general question of the kinds of circumstances, if any, in which commercial pressure, even though it amounts to a coercion of the will of a party in the weaker bargaining position, may be treated as legitimate and, accordingly, as not giving rise to any legal right of redress. In the instant appeal the economic duress complained of was exercised in the field of industrial relations to which very special considerations apply ...

The use of economic duress to induce another person to part with property or money is not a tort *per se*; the form that the duress takes may, or may not, be tortious. The remedy to which economic duress gives rise is not an action for damages but an action for restitution of property or money exacted under such duress and the avoidance of any contract that had been induced by it; but where the particular form taken by the economic duress used is itself a tort, the restitutional remedy for money had and received by the defendant to the plaintiff's use is one which the plaintiff is entitled to pursue as an alternative remedy to an action for damages in tort.

In extending into the field of industrial relations, the common law concept of economic duress and the right to a restitutionary remedy for it which is currently in process of development by judicial decisions, this House would not, in my view, be exercising the restraint that is appropriate to such a process if it were so to develop the concept that, by the simple expedient of 'waiving the tort', a restitutionary remedy for money had and received is made enforceable in cases in which Parliament has, over so long a period of years, manifested its preference for a public policy that a particular kind of tortious act should be legitimised in the sense that I am using that expression.

Typically, duress will be relevant where there is an attempted re-negotiation of the terms of an existing contract. If one of the parties is unable to proceed for financial reasons, it may make sense to go to the other party to explain the position. But does telling the truth amount to an implied threat? In the law of tort, there is a distinction between threats, warnings and inducements and a threat requires an intimation that unless the addressee acts in a particular way, something will be done which the addressee will not like.[26] It follows that merely passing on information will not be a threat. If a similar test is applied to cases of duress, it would seem to follow that it should be implicit in what the defendant says that unfortunate consequences might result from a failure to comply with the demand.

It is also relevant to consider the nature of the demand. The more unreasonable the demand, the more likely it is that the threat will be regarded as illegitimate.

The second issue is whether the victim has any practical choice available to him. The presence or absence of practical choice may be established by reference to any protest made by the victim, and the fact that the victim has received legal advice before deciding what to do. The mere fact that the party subject to the threat remains silent, will not necessarily be an indication of affirmation of the contract. It is also relevant to consider whether the victim could reasonably be expected to pursue an alternative remedy. If the practical effect of the pressure is to give the victim no choice, then the pressure is likely to amount to duress. Thus, if the chances of obtaining an injunction to avert the threat are minimal or non-existent[27] or if seeking an alternative remedy is risky or disruptive to business, the threat may still amount to duress.[28]

The way the rule has been formulated in recent authorities suggests that what matters is the illegitimacy rather than the wrongfulness of the threat, which suggests that a threat of lawful action could now be regarded as duress, despite the fact that this departs from the orthodox position at common law.

---

26 *Hodges v Webb* [1920] 2 Ch 70, p 89, *per* Peterson J.

27 *Dimskal Shipping Co SA v International Transport Workers Federation, The Evia Luck (No 2)* [1992] 1 Lloyd's Rep 115.

28 *Vantage Navigation Corpn v Suhail, The Alev* [1989] 1 Lloyd's Rep 138, p 146, *per* Hobhouse J.

Nevertheless there are *dicta* which accept that a threat can be illegitimate where it threatens lawful action.[29] But this does not mean that any threat, lawful or unlawful, will constitute duress, because the nature of the demand must be balanced against what is threatened and it may require a particularly unconscionable threat of lawful action to tip the scales. While, in principle, it may be accepted that a threat of lawful action can amount to duress, it is clear from the following extract that, in the context of arm's length dealings between two commercial enterprises, it is unlikely that such a threat will amount to duress, especially where the party making the threat believes that his demand is perfectly valid.

In *CTN Cash and Carry Ltd v Gallagher Ltd*,[30] the plaintiffs operated a number of cash and carry warehouses from which they supplied cigarettes purchased from the defendants. There was no continuing relationship between the parties with the result that each consignment of cigarettes was delivered separately under the standard terms presented by the defendants (which included credit facilities) and which they had an absolute discretion to withdraw.

On this occasion, an order was placed for £17,000 worth of cigarettes, which the defendants mistakenly delivered to the wrong warehouse. It was agreed that the cigarettes would be transferred to the correct warehouse, but, before this could be done, the consignment was stolen. Believing that the goods were at the plaintiffs' risk, the defendants invoiced them for the price of the stolen goods. This invoice was rejected, whereupon the defendants threatened to withdraw credit facilities. The plaintiffs then paid the invoice but later sought to recover the payment on the ground that the defendants' threat amounted to duress. On the facts, it was held that the defendants were entitled to vary the terms on which they contracted, with the result that the threat to withdraw credit facilities, since made reasonably and in good faith, did not amount to duress. Moreover, it was considered that to introduce the notion of 'lawful act duress' in a commercial context would be to introduce an undesirable element of uncertainty with far-reaching implications:

CTN Cash and Carry Ltd v Gallagher Ltd [1994] 4 All ER 714, CA, p 717

Steyn LJ: On appeal, the plaintiffs accept that, if the case for duress does not succeed, the claim for repayment must fail. It seems to me not to matter whether the correct analysis of the facts is that an agreement was made that the plaintiffs would pay the sum in question or whether payment is to be regarded simply as a unilateral act of the plaintiffs. In either event, the claim must succeed if the case of duress is made out; if that case is not made out, the claim must fail.

---

29 *The Universe Sentinel* [1983] 1 AC 366, p 401, *per* Lord Scarman; *Dimskal Shipping Co SA v International Transport Workers Federation, The Evia Luck (No 2)* [1992] 1 Lloyd's Rep 115, p 121, *per* Lord Goff.

30 [1994] 4 All ER 714, CA.

Miss Heilbron QC, who appeared for the plaintiffs, submitted that the deputy judge erred in rejecting the plea of duress. She submitted that the payment was made under illegitimate pressure. She emphasised that there was objectively no legal basis for demanding the price of the goods, and the threat of withdrawing the credit facilities was made solely in order to obtain the payment. The threat was powerful because the removal of credit would have seriously jeopardised the plaintiffs' business. The clear purpose, she said, was to extort money to which the plaintiffs were in truth not entitled. In the circumstances, the threat was illegitimate and the case of duress was made out.

Miss Heilbron cited a number of authorities which illustrate developments in this branch of the law. While I found the exercise of interest, I was reminded of the famous aphorism of Oliver Wendell Holmes that general propositions do not solve concrete cases. It may only be a half-truth, but, in my view, the true part applies to this case. It is necessary to focus on the distinctive features of this case, and then to ask whether it amounts to a case of duress.

The present dispute does not concern a protected relationship. It also does not arise in the context of dealings between a supplier and a consumer. The dispute arises out of arm's length commercial dealings between two trading companies. It is true that the defendants were the sole distributors of the popular brands of cigarettes. In a sense the defendants were in a monopoly position. The control of monopolies is, however, a matter for Parliament. Moreover, the common law does not recognise the doctrine of inequality of bargaining power in commercial dealings (see *National Westminster Bank plc v Morgan* [1985] 1 All ER 821; [1985] AC 686). The fact that the defendants were in a monopoly position cannot therefore by itself convert what is not otherwise duress into duress.

A second characteristic of the case is that the defendants were in law entitled to refuse to enter into any future contracts with the plaintiffs for any reason whatever or for no reason at all. Such a decision not to deal with the plaintiffs would have been financially damaging to the defendants, but it would have been lawful. *A fortiori*, it was lawful for the defendants, for any reason or for no reason, to insist that they would no longer grant credit to the plaintiffs. The defendants' demand for payment of the invoice, coupled with the threat to withdraw credit, was neither a breach of contract nor a tort.

A third, and critically important, characteristic of the case is the fact that the defendants *bona fide* thought that the goods were at the risk of the plaintiffs and that the plaintiffs owed the defendants the sum in question. The defendants exerted commercial pressure on the plaintiffs in order to obtain payment of a sum which they *bona fide* considered due to them. The defendants' motive in threatening withdrawal of credit facilities was commercial self-interest in obtaining a sum that they considered due to them.

Given the combination of these three features, I take the view that none of the cases cited to us assist the plaintiffs' case. Miss Heilbron accepted that there is no decision which is in material respects on all fours with the present case. It is, therefore, unnecessary to disinter all those cases and to identify the material distinctions between each of those decisions and the present case. But Miss

Heilbron rightly emphasised to us that the law must have a capacity for growth in this field. I entirely agree.

I also readily accept that the fact that the defendants have used lawful means does not by itself remove the case from the scope of the doctrine of economic duress. Professor Birks, in *An Introduction to the Law of Restitution*, 1989, p 177, lucidly explains:

> Can lawful pressures also count? This is a difficult question, because if the answer is that they can, the only viable basis for discriminating between acceptable and unacceptable pressures is not positive law but social morality. In other words, the judges must say what pressures (though lawful outside the restitutionary context) are improper as contrary to prevailing standards. That makes the judges, not the law or the legislature, the arbiters of social evaluation. On the other hand, if the answer is that lawful pressures are always exempt, those who devise outrageous, but technically lawful means of compulsion must always escape restitution until the legislature declares the abuse unlawful. It is tolerably clear that, at least where they can be confident of a general consensus in favour of their evaluation, the courts are willing to apply a standard of impropriety rather than technical unlawfulness.

And there are a number of cases where English courts have accepted that a threat may be illegitimate when coupled with a demand for payment even if the threat is one of lawful action (see *Thorne v Motor Trade Association* [1937] 3 All ER 157, pp 160–61; [1937] AC 797, pp 806–07, *Mutual Finance Ltd v John Wetton & Sons Ltd* [1937] 2 All ER 657; [1937] 2 KB 389 and *Universe Tankships Inc of Monrovia v International Transport Workers' Federation* [1982] 2 All ER 67, pp 76 and 89; [1983] 1 AC 366, pp 384 and 401). On the other hand, Goff and Jones *Law of Restitution*, 3rd edn, 1986, p 240, observed that English courts have wisely not accepted any general principle that a threat not to contract with another, except on certain terms, may amount to duress.

We are being asked to extend the categories of duress of which the law will take cognisance. That is not necessarily objectionable, but it seems to me that an extension capable of covering the present case, involving 'lawful act duress' in a commercial context in pursuit of a *bona fide* claim, would be a radical one with far-reaching implications. It would introduce a substantial and undesirable element of uncertainty in the commercial bargaining process. Moreover, it will often enable *bona fide* settled accounts to be reopened when parties to commercial dealings fall out. The aim of our commercial law ought to be to encourage fair dealing between parties. But it is a mistake for the law to set its sights too highly when the critical inquiry is not whether the conduct is lawful but whether it is morally or socially unacceptable. That is the inquiry in which we are engaged. In my view there are policy considerations which militate against ruling that the defendants obtained payment of the disputed invoice by duress.

Outside the field of protected relationships, and in a purely commercial context, it might be a relatively rare case in which 'lawful act duress' can be established. And it might be particularly difficult to establish duress if the defendant *bona fide* considered that his demand was valid. In this complex and changing branch of the law I deliberately refrain from saying 'never.' But as the law stands, I am satisfied that the defendants' conduct in this case did not amount to duress.

It is an unattractive result, inasmuch as the defendants are allowed to retain a sum which at the trial they became aware was not in truth due to them. But, in my view, the law compels the result.

It should, however, be noted that Sir Donald Nicholls VC in the same case hinted strongly that were a claim to be brought by CTN for restitution of the money on the grounds of unjust enrichment it would stand a good chance of success (on unjust enrichment, see, further, Chapter 14).

UNDUE PRESSURE AND UNDUE INFLUENCE

It has been observed above that the common law rule on duress was originally somewhat more strict than now appears to be the case. In the light of this early strict approach to judicial intervention, the courts of equity developed a set of rules designed to mitigate the hardship which might otherwise have been caused. In particular, a contract or a gift might be set aside in equity on the ground that influence had been expressly exerted by one party on the other for the purpose of securing the benefit of the gift or the contract. Alternatively, there are circumstances in which undue influence may be presumed in the absence of evidence to the contrary:

Allcard v Skinner (1887) 36 Ch D 145, CA, p 171

Cotton LJ: Is the plaintiff entitled to recall the stock now in question and still in hand? There is no decision in point with reference to a case like the present. For, although in the case of *Whyte v Meade*, a deed of gift by a nun was set aside, there were in that case special circumstances which prevent it being treated as an authority in favour of the plaintiff. The question is – does the case fall within the principles laid down by the decisions of the Court of Chancery in setting aside voluntary gifts executed by parties who, at the time, were under such influence as, in the opinion of the court, enabled the donor afterwards to set the gift aside? These decisions may be divided into two classes – first, where the court has been satisfied that the gift was the result of influence expressly used by the donee for the purpose; secondly, where the relations between the donor and donee have at or shortly before the execution of the gift been such as to raise a presumption that the donee had influence over the donor. In such a case, the court sets aside the voluntary gift, unless it is proved that, in fact, the gift was the spontaneous act of the donor acting under circumstances which enabled him to exercise an independent will and which justifies the court in holding that the gift was the result of a free exercise of the donor's will. The first class of cases may be considered as depending on the principle that no one shall be allowed to retain any benefit arising from his own fraud or wrongful act. In the second class of cases the court interferes, not on the ground that any wrongful act has in fact been committed by the donee, but on the ground of public policy, and to prevent the relations which existed between the parties and the influence arising therefrom being abused.

The width of Cotton LJ's remarks, linking the basis of equitable intervention to public policy and abuse of power has been a source of controversy in many subsequent cases, those wishing to take a narrower view of the court's role having often preferred the approach of Lindley LJ in the same case (at p 182):

> What then is the principle? Is it that it is right and expedient to save persons from the consequences of their own folly? Or is that it is right and expedient to save them from being victimised by other people? In my opinion, the doctrine of undue influence is founded upon the second of these two principles.

Actual undue pressure

A person seeking relief in equity in respect of alleged undue pressure is required to show that the other party obtained a dominating influence over him; had the capacity to exert influence; that influence was exercised; that its exercise was undue and that its exercise brought about the transaction.

Equity has been prepared to intervene in cases in which the common law was not prepared to give relief. For example, a threat of lawful imprisonment has been held sufficient to justify setting the contract aside on the ground of unfair and improper conduct.[31] The person alleging undue pressure must prove this to the satisfaction of the court,[32] which will require him to show that the transaction entered into is wrongful in the sense that the person seeking relief has been forced, tricked or misled into parting with property.[33]

At one point, it was also thought that, even in cases of actual undue pressure, the transaction entered into had to be to the manifest disadvantage of the person subject to the pressure, but there is now no longer any such requirement.

In *CIBC Mortgages plc v Pitt*,[34] a husband and wife jointly owned the matrimonial home (worth £270,000 in 1986) which was mortgaged to a building society to the extent of £16,700. Subsequently, the husband told his wife that he would like to borrow money on the security of the property for the purpose of buying shares. The wife was not happy with this, but

31 *Williams v Bayley* (1866) LR 1 HL 200.
32 *Howes v Bishop* [1909] 2 KB 390.
33 *Allcard v Skinner* (1887) 36 Ch D 145, pp 182–83, *per* Lindley LJ.
34 [1994] 1 AC 200.

eventually agreed after the husband had applied pressure. A 20 year mortgage with the plaintiffs was arranged for a sum of £150,000, the stated purpose being to pay off the existing mortgage and to buy a holiday home. Documents relating to the mortgage were prepared, which the wife signed without reading them. At no stage was she advised of the content of the documents, nor was she advised to seek independent advice. Accordingly, she was not aware of the amount of the loan. Once the existing mortgage debt was settled, the husband used the remainder of the loan to speculate on the stock market and, in the 1987 stock market crash, he lost a substantial amount, with the result that he could no longer continue to repay mortgage instalments as they became due. The plaintiffs now sought an order for possession of the matrimonial home, which the wife contested on the ground that she had been induced to sign the relevant documents by misrepresentation, duress and undue influence. The trial judge held that there was actual undue influence, but this decision was reversed in the Court of Appeal on the ground that there was no manifest disadvantage to the wife in entering into the mortgage transaction. This decision, in turn, was reversed by the House of Lords on the ground that, in cases of 'actual undue influence', there is no requirement of manifest disadvantage, thereby finding in favour of the wife:

CIBC Mortgages plc v Pitt [1994] 1 AC 200, p 207

Lord Browne-Wilkinson:

Manifest disadvantage

In the present case, the Court of Appeal, as they were bound to, applied the law laid down in *National Westminster Bank plc v Morgan* [1985] 1 All ER 821; [1985] AC 686, as interpreted by the Court of Appeal in *Bank of Credit and Commerce International SA v Aboody* [1990] 1 QB 923: a claim to set aside a transaction on the grounds of undue influence, whether presumed (*Morgan*) or actual (*Aboody*), cannot succeed unless the claimant proves that the impugned transaction was manifestly disadvantageous to him. Before your Lordships, Mrs Pitt submitted that the Court of Appeal in *Aboody* erred in extending the need to show manifest disadvantage in cases of actual, as opposed to presumed, undue influence. Adopting the classification used in *O'Brien*'s case,* p189 a-g, it is argued that although *Morgan*'s case decides that the claimant must show that the impugned transaction was disadvantageous to him in order to raise the presumption of undue influence within Class 2A or 2B, there is no such requirement where it is proved affirmatively that the claimant's agreement to the transaction was actually obtained by undue influence within Class 1.

In the *Morgan* case, it was alleged that Mrs Morgan had been induced to grant security to the bank by the undue influence of one of the bank's managers. Mrs Morgan did not allege actual undue influence within Class 1, but relied exclusively on a presumption of undue influence within Class 2. It was held that the bank manager had never in fact assumed such a role as to raise any presumption of undue influence. However, in addition, it was held that Mrs Morgan could not succeed, because she had not demonstrated that the transaction was manifestly disadvantageous to her. Lord Scarman (who delivered the leading speech) rejected a submission that the presumption of undue influence was based on any public policy requirements. In reliance on the judgment of Lindley LJ in *Allcard v Skinner* (1887) 36 Ch D 145, and the decision of the Privy Council in *Poosathurai v Kannappa Chettiar* (1919) LR 47 Ind App 1, he laid down the following proposition ([1985] AC 686, p 704): 'Whatever the legal character of the transaction, the authorities show that it must constitute a disadvantage sufficiently serious to require evidence to rebut the presumption that in the circumstances of the relationship between the parties it was procured by the exercise of undue influence. In my judgment, therefore, the Court of Appeal erred in law in holding that the presumption of undue influence can arise from the evidence of the relationship of the parties without also evidence that the transaction itself was wrongful in that it constituted an advantage taken of the person subjected to the influence which, failing proof to the contrary, was explicable only on the basis that undue influence had been exercised to procure it ...'

My Lords, I am unable to agree with the Court of Appeal decision in *Aboody*. I have no doubt that the decision in *Morgan* does not extend to cases of actual undue influence. Despite two references in Lord Scarman's speech to cases of actual undue influence, as I read his speech, he was primarily concerned to establish that disadvantage had to be shown, not as a constituent element of the cause of action for undue influence, but in order to raise a presumption of undue influence within Class 2. That was the only subject matter before the House of Lords in *Morgan* and the passage I have already cited was directed solely to that point. With the exception of a passing reference to *Ormes v Beadel* (1860) 2 Gif 166; 66 ER 70, all the cases referred to by Lord Scarman were cases of presumed undue influence. In the circumstances, I do not think that this House can have been intending to lay down any general principle applicable to all claims of undue influence, whether actual or presumed.

Whatever the merits of requiring a complainant to show manifest disadvantage in order to raise a Class 2 presumption of undue influence, in my judgment there is no logic in imposing such a requirement where actual undue influence has been exercised and proved. Actual undue influence is a species of fraud. Like any other victim of fraud, a person who has been induced by undue influence to carry out a transaction which he did not freely and knowingly enter into is entitled to have that transaction set aside as of right. No case decided before *Morgan* was cited (nor am I aware of any) in which a transaction proved to have been obtained by actual undue influence has been upheld nor is there any case in which a court has even considered whether the transaction was, or was not, advantageous. A man guilty of fraud is no more entitled to argue that the transaction was beneficial to the person defrauded than is a man who has procured a transaction by misrepresentation. The effect of the wrongdoer's conduct is to prevent the wronged party from bringing a free will and properly informed mind to bear on the proposed transaction which accordingly must be set aside in equity as a matter of justice.

I therefore hold that a claimant who proves actual undue influence is not under the further burden of proving that the transaction induced by undue influence was manifestly disadvantageous: he is entitled as of right to have it set aside.

I should add that the exact limits of the decision in *Morgan* may have to be considered in the future. The difficulty is to establish the relationship between the law as laid down in *Morgan* and the long standing principle laid down in the abuse of confidence cases, viz the law requires those in a fiduciary position who enter into transactions with those to whom they owe fiduciary duties to establish affirmatively that the transaction was a fair one: see for example *Demarara Bauxite Co Ltd v Hubbard* [1923] AC 673; *Moodie v Cox* [1917] 2 Ch 71, and the discussion in *BCCI v Aboody* [1990] 1 QB 923, p 962. The abuse of confidence principle is founded on considerations of general public policy, viz that, in order to protect those to whom fiduciaries owe duties as a class from exploitation by fiduciaries as a class, the law imposes a heavy duty on fiduciaries to show the righteousness of the transactions they enter into with those to whom they owe such duties. This principle is in sharp contrast with the view of this House in *Morgan* that ,in cases of presumed undue influence: (a) the law is not based on considerations of public policy; and (b) that it is for the claimant to prove that the transaction was disadvantageous rather than for the fiduciary to prove that it was not disadvantageous. Unfortunately, the attention of this House in *Morgan* was not drawn to the abuse of confidence cases and, therefore, the interaction between the two principles (if indeed they are two separate principles) remains obscure: see, also, David Tipledy, 'The limits of undue influence' (1985) 48 MLR 579; and *Wright v Carter* [1903] 1 Ch 27.

Presumed undue influence

Certain types of relationship may give rise to a presumption of undue influence, based upon the belief that one party has been guilty of the victimisation of the other.[35] In these circumstances, there is a presumption that the unconscionable behaviour of one party has given him an unfair advantage over the other or has acquired some advantage over the other party. The remedy given is rescission of the contract designed to restore the parties to the position they were in before the contract was made.

Relationships to which the presumption applies

After some uncertainty, it appears that there is no transaction to which the presumption of undue influence cannot apply.

---

35   *National Westminster Bank plc v Morgan* [1985] AC 686, pp 705–06, *per* Lord Scarman. Lord Scarman expressly preferred the approach of Lindley LJ in *Allcard v Skinner* (above) and disclaimed any wider powers which might be gleaned from Cotton LJ's judgment in this case. Victimisation was the key, not more generalised public policy considerations.

In *Goldsworthy v Brickell*,[36] the plaintiff, an 85 year old widower, who owned a farm worth about £1 million, had come to trust and rely upon his neighbour, the defendant, for help in running his farm. Despite the fact that there was no evidence of actual undue pressure, the relationship was regarded as one to which the presumption of undue influence could apply, with the result that an agreement under which the defendant rented the farm from the plaintiff at a very low rent, coupled with a favourable option to purchase, could be set aside:

Goldsworthy v Brickell [1987] Ch 378, p 400

Nourse LJ: I now come to the question of undue influence. On this question, the argument of Mr Pryor for the defendant was mainly founded on four propositions. First, since the plaintiff's case has throughout been one of dishonest persuasion, it can only succeed if there is proved to have been some form of dishonesty or conscious abuse of power by the defendant. Secondly, the plaintiff must prove a relationship which can properly be described as one of domination of the plaintiff by the defendant. Thirdly, the judge's findings as to the situation, physical and mental condition, character and disposition of the plaintiff in 1976–77 are wholly inconsistent with the existence of such a relationship. Fourthly, the transaction effected by the tenancy and partnership agreements was not manifestly and unfairly disadvantageous to the plaintiff. The fourth of these propositions stands on its own and can be treated separately. The first three run more or less together and, since they have proceeded on some notable misconceptions as to the circumstances in which courts of equity have set aside transactions on the ground of undue influence, require those circumstances to be restated.

Undue influence is of two kinds: (1) express or, as it is nowadays more usually known, actual undue influence; and (2) that which, in certain circumstances, is presumed from a confidential relationship, by which, in this context, is meant a relationship wherein one party has ceded such a degree of trust and confidence as to require the other, on grounds of public policy, to show that it has not been betrayed or abused. In cases where there is no confidential relationship actual undue influence must be proved. In cases where there is such a relationship it is sometimes alleged, but need not be proved and may never have occurred. Occasionally, even where there is no direct evidence of influence, it is found that there is both a confidential relationship and actual undue influence; *In Re Craig (Decd)*.

At least since the time of Lord Eldon LC, equity has steadfastly and wisely refused to put limits on the relationships to which the presumption can apply. Nor do I believe that it has ever been distinctly held that there is any relationship from which it cannot in any circumstances be dissociated. But there are several well defined relationships, such as parent and child, superior and member of a sisterhood, doctor and patient and solicitor and client, to

---

36 [1987] Ch 378. *In Re Craig (Decd)* [1971] Ch 95 provides another excellent, and highly colourful, example of a relationship of influence, confidentiality and even actual domination.

which the presumption is, as it were, presumed to apply unless the contrary is proved. In such relationships it would seem that you only have to look at the relative status of the parties in order to presume that the requisite degree of trust and confidence is there. But there are many and various other relationships lacking a recognisable status to which the presumption has been held to apply. In all of these relationships, whether of the first kind or the second, the principle is the same. It is that the degree of trust and confidence is such that the party in whom it is reposed, either because he is or has become an adviser of the other or because he has been entrusted with the management of his affairs or everyday needs or for some other reason, is in a position to influence him into effecting the transaction of which complaint is later made. And, with respect to certain arguments which have been advanced in the present case, it is here necessary to state the obvious, which is that, in cases where functions of this sort constitute the substratum of the relationship, there is no need for any identity of subject matter between the advice which is given or the affairs which are managed on the one hand and the transaction of which complaint is made on the other. Nor, as will be shown, is it necessary for the party in whom the trust and confidence is reposed to dominate the other party in any sense in which that word is generally understood.

Because they have occasioned little or no debate on this appeal, three further general observations may be briefly made. First, it is not every relationship of trust and confidence to which the presumption applies. No generalisation is possible beyond the definition already attempted. Secondly, with relationships to which it does apply, the presumption is not perfected and remains inoperative until the party who has ceded the trust and confidence makes a gift so large, or enters into a transaction so improvident, as not to be reasonably accounted for on the ground of friendship, relationship, charity or other ordinary motives on which ordinary men act. Although influence might have been presumed beforehand, it is only then that it is presumed to have been undue. Thirdly, in a case where the presumption has come into operation the gift or transaction will be set aside, unless it proved to have been the spontaneous act of the donor or grantor acting in circumstances which enable him to exercise an independent will and which justify the court in holding that the gift or transaction was the result of a free exercise of his will.

Mr Pryor's first proposition ignores the distinction between actual and presumed undue influence. It is true that no actual influence was found. But, if the judge was correct in holding, first and expressly, that there was a confidential relationship, secondly and impliedly, that the transaction was so improvident as not to be reasonably accounted for by ordinary motives and, thirdly and expressly, that it was not the spontaneous act of the plaintiff acting in the requisite circumstances, no further proof was required. To say that a plaintiff who fails to establish a primary case of actual influence must fail in his attempt to establish a confidential relationship to support the presumption is, with all due respect, a *non sequitur*.

Although the presumption can apply to any relationship, nonetheless, there remains a distinction between two groups of cases. In the first instance, there are relationships to which the presumption will be readily assumed to apply, in the absence of evidence to the contrary. This group appears to include the relationship between a parent and child,[37] religious adviser and disciple,[38] doctor and patient[39] and solicitor and client.[40]

The second group does not immediately give rise to the presumption, but requires specific proof (sometimes more readily found than others; see above) that there was the required degree of 'trust and confidence' between the parties. The relationship between employer and employee, husband and wife and a parent and child outside the household will not be automatically relationships in which undue influence will be presumed. However, the serious risk of 'abuse of power' that could still exist in many such cases is likely to lead the courts to examine them with particular care, to see if there was potential for undue influence on the particular facts. For example in *Barclays Bank v O'Brien*,[41] Lord Browne-Wilkinson states that the law treats married women 'more tenderly' than others and, in *Credit Lyonnais v Burch*,[42] there was said to be significant scope for excessive influence by the owner of a small company over a junior employee.

The relationship is usually one in which one person relies on the advice or guidance of another; the person giving the advice or guidance is aware of that reliance; the person relied upon will usually obtain some benefit or have some interest in the conclusion of the transaction, and the relationship is one of confidence out of which influence naturally grows.

In *Lloyd's Bank Ltd v Bundy*,[43] the defendant was an elderly farmer whose son's business was in financial difficulty. He had already guaranteed his son's debts to the extent of £7,500, securing the guarantee on his own house. A representative of the bank advised the defendant that the bank could only continue to support the son's business if the defendant would increase the charge on his house to £11,000. The defendant's position was not explained to him by the bank, nor did the defendant obtain any independent advice. The Court of Appeal held that the defendant had placed confidence in the bank and that, since it was in the interest of the bank that the guarantee should be executed, the transaction could be set aside:

---

37 *Bullock v Lloyds Bank Ltd* [1955] Ch 317.
38 *Allcard v Skinner* (1887) 36 Ch D 145.
39 *Dent v Bennett* (1839) 4 My & Cr 269.
40 *Wright v Carter* [1903] 1 Ch 27.
41 [1994] 1 AC 180, 190.
42 [1997] 1 All ER 144.
43 [1975] QB 326, CA.

Lloyd's Bank Ltd v Bundy [1975] QB 326, CA, p 341

Sir Eric Sachs: As was pointed out in *Tufton v Sperni* [1952] 2 TLR 516, the relationships which result in such a duty must not be circumscribed by reference to defined limits; it is necessary to 'refute the suggestion that, to create the relationship of confidence, the person owing the duty must be found clothed in the recognisable garb of a guardian, trustee, solicitor, priest, doctor, manager, or the like' (Sir Raymond Evershed MR).

Everything depends on the particular facts, and such a relationship has been held to exist in unusual circumstances as between purchaser and vendor, as between great uncle and adult nephew, and in other widely differing sets of circumstances. Moreover, it is neither feasible nor desirable to attempt closely to define the relationship, or its characteristics, or the demarcation line showing the exact transition point where a relationship that does not entail that duty passes into one that does (see Ungoed-Thomas J in *In Re Craig (Decd)* [1971] Ch 95, 104).

On the other hand, whilst disclaiming any intention of seeking to catalogue the elements of such a special relationship, it is perhaps of a little assistance to note some of those which have, in the past, frequently been found to exist where the court has been led to decide that this relationship existed as between adults of sound mind. Such cases tend to arise where someone relies on the guidance or advice of another, where the other is aware of that reliance and where the person upon whom reliance is placed obtains, or may well obtain, a benefit from the transaction or has some other interest in it being concluded. In addition, there must, of course, be shown to exist a vital element which in this judgment will for convenience be referred to as confidentiality. It is this element which is so impossible to define and which is a matter for the judgment of the court on the facts of any particular case.

Confidentiality, a relatively little used word, is being here adopted, albeit with some hesitation, to avoid the possible confusion that can arise through referring to 'confidence'. Reliance on advice can in many circumstances be said to import that type of confidence which only results in a common law duty to take care – a duty which may co-exist with, but is not co-terminous with, that of fiduciary care. 'Confidentiality' is intended to convey that extra quality in the relevant confidence that is implicit in the phrase 'confidential relationship' (see *per* Lord Chelmsford LC in *Tate v Williamson* (1866) 2 Ch App 55, 62; Lindley LJ in *Allcard v Skinner*, 36 Ch D 145, 181; and Wright J in *Morley v Loughnan* [1893] 1 Ch 736, 751) and may perhaps have something in common with 'confiding' and also 'confidant' when, for instance, referring to someone's 'man of affairs'. It imports some quality beyond that inherent in the confidence that can well exist between trustworthy persons who in business affairs deal with each other at arm's length. It is one of the features of this element that once it exists, influence naturally grows out of it (see Sir Raymond Evershed MR in *Tufton's* case [1952] 2 TLR 516, 523, following Lord Chelmsford LC in *Tate v Williamson* (1866) 2 Ch App 55, 61).

It was inevitably conceded on behalf of the bank that the relevant relationship can arise as between banker and customer. Equally, it was inevitably conceded on behalf of Mr Bundy that, in the normal course of transactions by which a customer guarantees a third party's obligations, the relationship does not arise. The onus of proof lies on the customer who alleges that, in any individual case, the line has been crossed and the relationship has arisen.

Before proceeding to examine the position further, it is as well to dispose of some points on which confusion is apt to arise. Of these, the first is one which plainly led to misapprehension on the part of the county court judge. Undue influence is a phrase which is commonly regarded – even in the eyes of a number of lawyers – as relating solely to occasions when the will of one person has become so dominated by that of another that, to use the county court judge's words, 'the person acts as the mere puppet of the dominator'. Such occasions, of course, fall within what Cotton LJ, in *Allcard v Skinner* (1887) 36 Ch D 145, p 171, described as the first class of cases to which the doctrine on undue influence applies. There is, however, a second class of such cases. This is referred to by Cotton LJ as follows: 'In the second class of cases, the court interferes, not on the ground that any wrongful act has in fact been committed by the donee, but on the ground of public policy, and to prevent the relations which existed between the parties and the influence arising therefrom being abused.'

It is thus to be emphasised that, as regards the second class, the exercise of the court's jurisdiction to set aside the relevant transaction does not depend on proof of one party being 'able to dominate the other as though a puppet' (to use the words again adopted by the county court judge when testing whether the defence was established), nor any wrongful intention on the part of the person who gains a benefit from it; but, on the concept that, once the special relationship has been shown to exist, no benefit can be retained from the transaction, unless it has been positively established that the duty of fiduciary care has been entirely fulfilled. To this second class, however, the judge never adverted and plainly never directed his mind.

It is also to be noted that what constitutes fulfilment of that duty (the second issue in the case now under consideration) depends again on the facts before the court. It may in the particular circumstances entail that the person in whom confidence has been reposed should insist on independent advice being obtained or ensuring in one way or another that the person being asked to execute a document is not insufficiently informed of some factor which could affect his judgment. The duty has been well stated as being one to ensure that the person liable to be influenced has formed 'an independent and *informed* judgment,' or, to use the phraseology of Lord Evershed MR in *Zamet v Hyman* [1961] 1 WLR 1442, p 1446, 'after full, free and *informed* thought'. (The underlining in each case is mine.) As to the difficulties in which a person may be placed and as to what he should do when, there is a conflict of interest between him and the person asked to execute a document: see *Bank of Montreal v Stuart* [1911] AC 120, p 139.

Stress was placed in argument for the bank on the effect of the word 'abused' as it appears in the above cited passage in the judgment of Cotton LJ and in other judgments and textbooks. As regards the second class of undue influence, however, that word in the context means no more than that once the existence of a special relationship has been established, then any possible use of the relevant influence is, irrespective of the intentions of the persons possessing it, regarded in relation to the transaction under consideration as an abuse – unless and until the duty of fiduciary care has been shown to be fulfilled or the transaction is shown to be truly for the benefit of the person influenced. This approach is a matter of public policy.

One further point on which potential confusion emerged in the course of the helpful addresses of counsel stemmed from submissions to the effect that Mr Head, the assistant bank manager, should be cleared of all blame in the matter. When one has to deal with claims of breach of either common law or fiduciary care, it is not unusual to find that counsel for a big corporation tends to try and focus the attention of the court on the responsibility of the employee who deals with the particular matter rather than on that of the corporation as an entity. What we are concerned with in the present case is whether the element of confidentiality has been established as against the bank: Mr Head's part in the affair is but one link in a chain of events. Moreover, when it comes to a question of the relevant knowledge which will have to be discussed later in this judgment, it is the knowledge of the bank and not merely the personal knowledge of Mr Head that has to be examined.

Having discussed the nature of the issues to which the county court judge should have directed his mind, it is now convenient to turn to the evidence relating to the first of them – whether the special relationship has here been shown to exist at the material time ...

The situation was thus one which to any reasonably sensible person, who gave it but a moment's thought, cried aloud Mr Bundy's need for careful independent advice. Over and above the need any man has for counsel when asked to risk his last penny on even an apparently reasonable project, was the need here for informed advice as to whether there was any real chance of the company's affairs becoming viable if the documents were signed. If not, there arose questions such as 'what is the use of taking the risk of becoming penniless without benefiting anyone but the bank? Is it not better both for you and your son that you, at any rate, should still have some money when the crash comes? Should not the bank at least bind itself to hold its hand for some given period?'. The answers to such questions could only be given in the light of a worthwhile appraisement of the company's affairs – without which Mr Bundy could not come to an informed judgment as to the wisdom of what he was doing.

No such advice to get an independent opinion was given; on the contrary, Mr Head chose to give his own views on the company's affairs and to take this course, though he had at trial to admit: 'I did not explain the company's affairs very fully as I had only just taken over.' (Another answer that escaped entry in the judge's original notes.)

On the above recited facts, the breach of the duty to take fiduciary care is manifest. It is not necessary for Mr Bundy to rely on another factor tending to show such a breach. The bank knew full well that Mr Bundy had a well known solicitor of standing, Mr Trethowan, who usually advised him on important matters – including the previous charge signed in May 1969, only seven months earlier. Indeed, on that occasion, the bank seems very properly to have taken steps which either ensured that Mr Trethowan's advice was obtained or at least assumed it was being obtained. It is no answer that Mr Head, relatively a newcomer to the Bundy accounts at the Salisbury branch, may not personally have known these matters – it is the bank's knowledge that is material. Incidentally, Mr Head had discussed the relevant accounts with his manager.

The existence of the duty and its breach having thus been established, there remains the submission urged by Mr Rankin that whatever independent advice had been obtained, Mr Bundy would have been so obstinately determined to help his son that the documents would anyway have been signed. That point fails for more than one reason, of which it is sufficient to mention two. First, on a question of fact, it ignores the point that the independent advice might well have been to the effect that it would benefit the son better in the event of an almost inevitable crash if his father had some money left after it occurred – advice which could have affected the mind of Mr Bundy. Secondly, once the relevant duty is established, it is contrary to public policy that benefit of the transaction he retained by the person under that duty unless he positively shows that the duty of fiduciary care has been fulfilled: there is normally no room for debate on the issue as to what would have happened had the care been taken ...

There remains to mention that Mr Rankin, whilst conceding that the relevant special relationship could arise as between banker and customer, urged in somewhat doom-laden terms that a decision taken against the bank on the facts of this particular case would seriously affect banking practice. With all respect to that submission, it seems necessary to point out that nothing in this judgment affects the duties of a bank in the normal case where it is obtaining a guarantee, and in accordance with standard practice explains to the person about to sign its legal effect and the sums involved. When, however, a bank, as in the present case, goes further and advises on more general matters germane to the wisdom of the transaction, that indicates that it may – not necessarily must – be crossing the line into the area of confidentiality so that the court may then have to examine all the facts including, of course, the history leading up to the transaction, to ascertain whether or not that line has, as here, been crossed. It would indeed be rather odd if a bank which vis à vis a customer attained a special relationship in some ways akin to that of a 'man of affairs' – something which can be a matter of pride and enhance its local reputation – should not, where a conflict of interest has arisen as between itself and the person advised, be under the resulting duty now under discussion. Once, as was inevitably conceded, it is possible for a bank to be under that duty, it is, as in the present case, simply a question for 'meticulous examination' of the particular facts to see whether that duty has arisen. On the special facts here, it did arise and it has been broken.

The decision in *Bundy* should not be taken to mean that the relationship of banker and customer will always be classified as one of confidence and trust. Indeed, *Bundy* has been referred to as a special case which turned on its own facts.[44] It would appear that, normally, the banker and customer relationship

---

44 *National Westminster Bank plc v Morgan* [1985] AC 686, p 698, *per* Lord Scarman.

is not one of confidence, and that the presumption of undue influence does not apply.

In *National Westminster Bank plc v Morgan*,[45] the respondent's husband's business was in deep financial trouble and he was unable to keep up payments due under the mortgage on the family home. The bank agreed to refinance the debt in order to avoid threatened foreclosure by the original mortgagees. The bank took a legal charge on the property. The respondent only agreed to this after having been assured by the bank that the arrangement covered no more than the amount of the original loan. In fact, this assurance was inaccurate, as the mortgage extended to cover all of the husband's liabilities to the bank. When the husband died, the question arose whether the mortgage could be set aside on the ground of undue influence. The House of Lords held that the bank had not crossed the line which distinguished a normal business relationship from one in which the bank was able to exert influence over their customer. In particular, the fact that the arrangement was not to the manifest disadvantage of the respondent was considered to be a key factor in the decision:

National Westminster Bank plc v Morgan [1985] 1 AC 686, p 702

Lord Scarman: As to the facts, I am far from being persuaded that the trial judge fell into error when he concluded that the relationship between the bank and Mrs Morgan never went beyond the normal business relationship of banker and customer. Both Lords Justices saw the relationship between the bank and Mrs Morgan as one of confidence in which she was relying on the bank manager's advice. Each recognised the personal honesty, integrity, and good faith of Mr Barrow. Each took the view that the confidentiality of the relationship was such as to impose upon him a 'fiduciary duty of care'. *It was his duty,* in their view, to ensure that Mrs Morgan had the opportunity to make an independent and informed decision: but he failed to give her any such opportunity. They, therefore, concluded that it was a case for the presumption of undue influence.

My Lords, I believe that the Lords Justices were led into a misinterpretation of the facts by their use, as is all too frequent in this branch of the law, of words and phrases such as 'confidence', 'confidentiality', 'fiduciary duty'. There are plenty of confidential relationships which do not give rise to the presumption of undue influence (a notable example is that of husband and wife, *Bank of Montreal v Stuart* [1911] AC 120); and there are plenty of non-confidential relationships in which one person relies upon the advice of another, for example, many contracts for the sale of goods. Nor am I persuaded that the charge, limited as it was by Mr Barrow's declaration to securing the loan to pay off the Abbey National debt and interest during the bridging period, was disadvantageous to Mrs Morgan. It meant for her the rescue of her home upon

---

45   [1985] 1 AC 686.

the terms sought by her – a short term loan at a commercial rate of interest. The Court of Appeal has not, therefore, persuaded me that the judge's understanding of the facts was incorrect.

But, further, the view of the law expressed by the Court of Appeal was, as I shall endeavour to show, mistaken. Dunn LJ, at p 90, while accepting that in all the reported cases to which the court was referred the transactions were disadvantageous to the person influenced, took the view that, in cases where public policy requires the court to apply the presumption of undue influence, there is no need to prove a disadvantageous transaction. Slade LJ also clearly held that it was not necessary to prove a disadvantageous transaction where the relationship of influence was proved to exist.

Like Dunn LJ, I know of no reported authority where the transaction set aside was not to the manifest disadvantage of the person influenced. It would not always be a gift: it can be a 'hard and inequitable' agreement (*Ormes v Beadel* (1860) 2 Gif 166, p 174); or a transaction 'immoderate and irrational' (*Bank of Montreal v Stuart* [1911] AC 120, p 137) or 'unconscionable', in that it was a sale at an undervalue (*Poosathurai v Kannappa Chettiar* (1919) LR 47 IA 1, pp 3–4). Whatever the legal character of the transaction, the authorities show that it must constitute a disadvantage sufficiently serious to require evidence to rebut the presumption that in the circumstances of the relationship between the parties it was procured by the exercise of undue influence. In my judgment, therefore, the Court of Appeal erred in law in holding that the presumption of undue influence can arise from the evidence of the relationship of the parties without also evidence that the transaction itself was wrongful in that it constituted an advantage taken of the person subjected to the influence which, failing proof to the contrary, was explicable only on the basis that undue influence had been exercised to procure it.

The principle justifying the court in setting aside a transaction for undue influence can now be seen to have been established by Lindley LJ in *Allcard v Skinner* (1887) 36 Ch D 145. It is not a vague 'public policy', but specifically the victimisation of one party by the other. It was stated by Lindley LJ in a famous passage at pp 182–83:

> The principle must be examined. What then is the principle? Is it that it is right and expedient to save persons from the consequences of their own folly or is it that it is right and expedient to save them from being victimised by other people? In my opinion, the doctrine of undue influence is founded upon the second of these two principles. Courts of equity have never set aside gifts on the ground of the folly, imprudence, or want of foresight on the part of donors. The courts have always repudiated any such jurisdiction. *Huguenin v Baseley* (1807) 14 Ves Jun 273 is itself a clear authority to this effect. It would obviously be to encourage folly, recklessness, extravagance and vice if persons could get back property which they foolishly made away with, whether by giving it to charitable institutions or by bestowing it on less worthy objects. On the other hand, to protect people from being forced, tricked or misled in any way by others into parting with their property is one of the most legitimate objects of all laws; and the equitable doctrine of undue influence has grown out of and

been developed by the necessity of grappling with insidious forms of spiritual tyranny and with the infinite varieties of fraud ...

In *Poosathurai v Kannappa Chettiar* (1919) LR 47 Ind App 1, p 3, Lord Shaw of Dunfermline, after indicating that there was no difference upon the subject of undue influence between the Indian Contract Act 1872 and English law quoted s 16(3) of the Indian statutory provision: 'Where a person who is in a position to dominate the will of another enters into a contract with him, and the transaction appears on the face of it, or on the evidence, to be unconscionable, the burden of proving that such contract was not induced by undue influence shall lie upon the person in the position to dominate the will of the other.'

He then proceeded at p 4, to state the principle in a passage of critical importance, which, since, so far as I am aware, the case is reported only in the Indian Reports, I think it helpful to quote in full: 'It must be established that the person in a position of domination has used that position to obtain unfair advantage for himself, and so to cause injury to the person relying upon his authority or aid. Where the relation of influence, as above set forth, has been established, and the second thing is also made clear, namely, that the bargain is with the "influencer", and in itself unconscionable, then the person in a position to use his dominating power has the burden thrown upon him, and it is a heavy burden, of establishing affirmatively that no domination was practised so as to bring about the transaction, but that the grantor of the deed was scrupulously kept separately advised in the independence of a free agent. These general propositions are mentioned because, if laid alongside of the facts of the present case, then it appears that one vital element – perhaps not sufficiently relied on in the court below, and yet essential to the plaintiff's case – is wanting. It is not proved as a fact in the present case that the bargain of sale come to was unconscionable in itself or constituted an advantage unfair to the plaintiff; it is, in short, not established as a matter of fact that the sale was for undervalue.'

The wrongfulness of the transaction must, therefore, be shown: it must be one in which an unfair advantage has been taken of another. The doctrine is not limited to transactions of gift. A commercial relationship can become a relationship in which one party assumes a role of dominating influence over the other. In *Poosathurai's* case, (1919) LR 47 Ind App 1, the Board recognised that a sale at an undervalue could be a transaction which a court could set aside as unconscionable if it was shown or could be presumed to have been procured by the exercise of undue influence. Similarly a relationship of banker and customer may become one in which the banker acquires a dominating influence. If he does and a manifestly disadvantageous transaction is proved, there would then be room for the court to presume that it resulted from the exercise of undue influence.

This brings me to *Lloyds Bank Ltd v Bundy* [1975] QB 326.

Lord Scarman refers to the judgment of Sir Eric Sachs extracted above and continues:

This is good sense and good law, though I would prefer to avoid the term 'confidentiality' as a description of the relationship which has to be proved. In truth, as Sir Eric recognised, the relationships which may develop a dominating influence of one over another are infinitely various. There is no substitute in this branch of the law for a 'meticulous examination of the facts'.

A meticulous examination of the facts of the present case reveals that Mr Barrow never 'crossed the line'. Nor was the transaction unfair to Mrs Morgan. The bank was, therefore, under no duty to ensure that she had independent advice. It was an ordinary banking transaction whereby Mrs Morgan sought to save her home; and she obtained an honest and truthful explanation of the bank's intention which, notwithstanding the terms of the mortgage deed which, in the circumstances, the trial judge was right to dismiss as 'essentially theoretical', was correct: for no one has suggested that Mr Barrow or the bank sought to make Mrs Morgan liable, or to make her home the security, for any debt of her husband other than the loan and interest necessary to save the house from being taken away from them in discharge of their indebtedness to the building society.

For these reasons, I would allow the appeal. In doing so, I would wish to give a warning. There is no precisely defined law setting limits to the equitable jurisdiction of a court to relieve against undue influence. This is the world of doctrine, not of neat and tidy rules. The courts of equity have developed a body of learning enabling relief to be granted where the law has to treat the transaction as unimpeachable unless it can be held to have been procured by undue influence. It is the unimpeachability at law of a disadvantageous transaction which is the starting point from which the court advances to consider whether the transaction is the product merely of one's own folly or of the undue influence exercised by another. A court in the exercise of this equitable jurisdiction is a court of conscience. Definition is a poor instrument when used to determine whether a transaction is or is not unconscionable: this is a question which depends upon the particular facts of the case.

In this case, the main ground for decision was that the transaction entered into was not manifestly disadvantageous to the plaintiff. If anything, the transaction was advantageous to the respondent because it served to save her from losing the matrimonial home. Lord Scarman distinguishes between gifts and commercial transactions because, in the case of a gift, the disadvantage is plain to see and does not have to be proved, since the donor has given away something of his own. However, the extent to which manifest disadvantage is to be regarded as a feature of these cases must now be doubted. In cases of actual undue pressure the requirement has been disposed of following the House of Lords' decision in *CIBC Mortgages plc v Pitt*[46] (considered above), but the extract from that case also reveals that the correctness of the decision in *Morgan* in relation to presumed undue influence may have to be considered at some future stage. Further evidence of this trend is to be found in the recent Court of Appeal decision, *Barclays Bank plc v Coleman*,[47] in which the court

---

46   [1994] 1 AC 200.
47   [2000] 1 All ER 385.

states that if such a requirement existed any disadvantage, provided it was 'clear and obvious and more than *de minimis*' may be small. The message is very clear that *Morgan* is something of an aberration on this point, proceeding from an unwarranted reliance on a single appeal from India (*Poosathurai*) and, at an appropriate point, the House of Lords will override it. As Nourse LJ states (at p 399): 'Although in *CIBC Mortgages plc,* judicial courtesy no doubt prevented Lord Browne-Wilkinson from saying so, my strong impression is that he thought its introduction into cases of presumed undue influence was no more appropriate than into cases of actual undue influence.'

A further uncertainty arising out of the decision in *Morgan* is that Lord Scarman does not make it clear which class of undue influence he was dealing with. Subsequently, the Court of Appeal in *Bank of Credit & Commerce International SA v Aboody,*[48] adopted a threefold classification, namely:

- Class 1   Actual undue influence.
- Class 2A   Presumed undue influence arising out of recognised relationships such as solicitor and client, etc.
- Class 2B   Presumed undue influence not based on a recognised relationship, but in which there is a relationship of trust and confidence.

Lord Scarman at no point indicates which of the relevant categories the respondent in *Morgan* fell into.

Vicarious undue influence

In *Morgan,* as in *Bundy,* the wrongdoer was an employee of the bank, but a far more common problem is that such pressure as is applied comes from a relative of the party seeking relief. Usually, that relative will be a spouse, but there are also cases in which the pressure is applied by, for example, an independent son or daughter on ageing parents.[49]

In these circumstances, the relative who has applied pressure may be seen to be acting on behalf of the lender. Here the question is whether the person for whose benefit the contract is made can be in any better position than the person who exerts influence. At one stage, the judicial approach to this type of case involved asking whether the intermediary could be regarded as an agent on behalf of the lender,[50] but some of the cases applying this approach turned

---

48 [1990] 1 QB 923. This classification was subsequently approved by the House of Lords in *Barclays Bank plc v O'Brien* (below), even though *Aboody* itself was overruled on other grounds (above).

49 See *Avon Finance Co Ltd v Bridger* [1985] 2 All ER 281.

50 *Chaplin v Brammall* [1908] 1 KB 233; *Kings North Trust Ltd v Bell* [1986] 1 WLR 119; *Coldunell Ltd v Gallon* [1986] 2 WLR 466.

the fiction of agency into an artform which was completely divorced from the commercial idea of an agency relationship.

The most important matter now is to consider whether the lender is affected by the wrong-doing of the spouse who has applied pressure. For the purpose, there is no difference between misrepresentation and undue influence, following the leading authority of *Barclays Bank plc v O'Brien*.[51] The House of Lords made it clear that there was no automatic presumption of undue influence in this type of case and the court must examine the relationship between the husband and wife to discover whether the wife has or has not exercised an independent judgment. If there is an absence of independent judgment, there is undue influence, but it must also be established that the lender is affected by that influence. The House of Lords accept that this will be the case either if there is a true agency relationship between the lender and the spouse[52] or other 'close' person applying the pressure or where the lender is taken to have notice of the undue influence.

In *Barclays Bank plc v O'Brien*,[53] Mr and Mrs O'Brien married in 1963. Mr O'Brien was a chartered accountant with his own practice. He also had an interest in a fabrication company of which he was auditor. In 1986 and 1987, he wanted to increase his stake in that company and to do so, he wished to borrow money from the appellants by increasing his overdraft facility from £40,000 to £135,000. The appellants agreed to this provided they were given a guarantee secured by a second charge over the O'Briens' matrimonial home.

Mr O'Brien took the respondent to a sub-branch of the bank, where documents relating to the guarantee, already signed by Mr O'Brien, were produced by a clerk. Mrs O'Brien signed the documents, but she was given no explanation of their significance, nor was she told that she should seek legal advice on the matter of the guarantee. It transpired that what had been signed was a guarantee unlimited in amount of all the liabilities of Mr O'Brien's company, and that Mr O'Brien had misrepresented what he wanted his wife to sign.

The House of Lords, upholding the decision of the Court of Appeal, held that the bank was taken to have notice of the husband's misrepresentation with the result that the guarantee was voidable at Mrs O'Brien's instance:

---

51 1994] 1 AC 180.

52 Although the word spouse is used here, it is clear from Lord Browne-Wilkinson's judgment that the rule in *O'Brien* extends to cohabitees, provided the lender is aware of the facts (p 198).

53 [1994] 1 AC 180.

Barclays Bank plc v O'Brien [1994] 1 AC 180, p 188

Lord Browne-Wilkinson:

Policy considerations

The large number of cases of this type coming before the courts in recent years reflects the rapid changes in social attitudes and the distribution of wealth which have recently occurred. Wealth is now more widely spread. Moreover, a high proportion of privately owned wealth is invested in the matrimonial home. Because of the recognition by society of the equality of the sexes, the majority of matrimonial homes are now in the joint names of both spouses. Therefore in order to raise finance for the business enterprises of one or other of the spouses, the jointly owned home has become a main source of security. The provision of such security requires the consent of both spouses.

In parallel with these financial developments, society's recognition of the equality of the sexes has led to a rejection of the concept that the wife is subservient to the husband in the management of the family's finances. A number of the authorities reflect an unwillingness in the court to perpetuate law based on this outmoded concept. Yet, as Scott LJ in the Court of Appeal rightly points out, although the concept of the ignorant wife leaving all financial decisions to the husband is outmoded, the practice does not yet coincide with the ideal ([1993] QB 109, p 139). In a substantial proportion of marriages, it is still the husband who has the business experience and the wife is willing to follow his advice without bringing a truly independent mind and will to bear on financial decisions. The number of recent cases in this field shows that in practice many wives are still subjected to, and yield to, undue influence by their husbands. Such wives can reasonably look to the law for some protection when their husbands have abused the trust and confidence reposed in them.

On the other hand, it is important to keep a sense of balance in approaching these cases. It is easy to allow sympathy for the wife who is threatened with the loss of her home at the suit of a rich bank to obscure an important public interest, viz the need to ensure that the wealth currently tied up in the matrimonial home does not become economically sterile. If the rights secured to wives by the law renders vulnerable loans granted on the security of matrimonial homes, institutions will be unwilling to accept such security, thereby reducing the flow of loan capital to business enterprises. It is therefore essential that a law designed to protect the vulnerable does not render the matrimonial home unacceptable as security to financial institutions.

With these policy considerations in mind I turn to consider the existing state of the law. The whole of the modern law is derived from the decision of the Privy Council in *Turnbull & Co v Duval* [1902] AC 429 which, as I will seek to demonstrate, provides an uncertain foundation. Before considering that case however, I must consider the law of undue influence which (though not directly applicable in the present case) underlies both *Turnbull v Duval* and most of the later authorities.

Undue influence

A person who has been induced to enter into a transaction by the undue influence of another (the wrongdoer) is entitled to set that transaction aside as against the wrongdoer. Such undue influence is either actual or presumed. In *Bank of Credit and Commerce International SA v Aboody* (1988) [1990] 1 QB 923, p 953, the Court of Appeal helpfully adopted the following classification:

Class 1 *actual undue influence*. In these cases, it is necessary for the claimant to prove affirmatively that the wrongdoer exerted undue influence on the complainant to enter into the particular transaction which is impugned.

Class 2 *presumed undue influence*. In these cases, the complainant only has to show, in the first instance, that there was a relationship of trust and confidence between the complainant and the wrongdoer of such a nature that it is fair to presume that the wrongdoer abused that relationship in procuring the complainant to enter into the impugned transaction. In Class 2 cases, therefore, there is no need to produce evidence that actual undue influence was exerted in relation to the particular transaction impugned: once a confidential relationship has been proved, the burden then shifts to the wrongdoer to prove that the complainant entered into the impugned transaction freely, for example by showing that the complainant had independent advice. Such a confidential relationship can be established in two ways, viz:

Class 2A Certain relationships (for example solicitor and client, medical advisor and patient) as a matter of law raise the presumption that undue influence has been exercised;

Class 2B Even if there is no relationship falling within Class 2A, if the complainant proves the *de facto* existence of a relationship under which the complainant generally reposed trust and confidence in the wrongdoer, the existence of such relationship raises the presumption of undue influence. In a Class 2B case therefore, in the absence of evidence disproving undue influence, the complainant will succeed in setting aside the impugned transaction merely by proof that the complainant reposed trust and confidence in the wrongdoer without having to prove that the wrongdoer exerted actual undue influence or otherwise abused such trust and confidence in relation to the particular transaction impugned.

As to dispositions by a wife in favour of her husband, the law for long remained in an unsettled state. In the 19th century some judges took the view that the relationship was such that it fell into Class 2A, that is, as a matter of law undue influence by the husband over the wife was presumed. It was not until the decisions in *Howes v Bishop* [1909] 2 KB 390 and *Bank of Montreal v Stuart* [1911] AC 120 that it was finally determined that the relationship of husband and wife did not as a matter of law raise a presumption of undue influence within Class 2A. It is to be noted therefore that, when *Turnbull v Duval* was decided in 1902, the question whether there was a Class 2A presumption of undue influence as between husband and wife was still unresolved.

An invalidating tendency?

Although there is no Class 2A presumption of undue influence as between husband and wife, it should be emphasised that in any particular case a wife may well be able to demonstrate that *de facto* she did leave decisions on financial affairs to her husband thereby bringing herself within Class 2B, that is, that the relationship between husband and wife in the particular case was such that the wife reposed confidence and trust in her husband in relation to their financial affairs and therefore undue influence is to be presumed. Thus, in those cases which still occur where the wife relies in all financial matters on her husband and simply does what he suggests, a presumption of undue influence within Class 2B can be established solely from the proof of such trust and confidence without proof of actual undue influence.

In the appeal in *CIBC Mortgages plc v Pitt* (judgment in which is to be given immediately after that in the present appeal), post p 200, Mr Price, for the wife, argued that, in the case of transactions between husband and wife, there was an 'invalidating tendency', that is, although there was no Class 2A presumption of undue influence, the courts were more ready to find that a husband had exercised undue influence over his wife than in other cases. Scott LJ, in the present case, also referred to the law treating married women 'more tenderly' than others. This approach is based on *dicta* in early authorities. In *Grigby v Cox* (1750) 1 Ves Sen 517, Lord Hardwicke, whilst rejecting any presumption of undue influence, said that a court of equity 'will have more jealousy' over dispositions by a wife to a husband. In *Yerkey v Jones* (1939) 63 CLR 649, p 675, Dixon J refers to this 'invalidating tendency'. He also refers to the court recognising 'the opportunities which a wife's confidence in her husband gives him of unfairly or improperly procuring her to become surety' (see p 677).

In my judgment, this special tenderness of treatment afforded to wives by the courts is properly attributable to two factors. First, many cases may well fall into the Class 2B category of undue influence because the wife demonstrates that she placed trust and confidence in her husband in relation to her financial affairs and therefore raises a presumption of undue influence. Second, the sexual and emotional ties between the parties provide a ready weapon for undue influence: a wife's true wishes can easily be overborne because of her fear of destroying or damaging the wider relationship between her and her husband if she opposes his wishes.

For myself, I accept that the risk of undue influence affecting a voluntary disposition by a wife in favour of a husband is greater than in the ordinary run of cases where no sexual or emotional ties affect the free exercise of the individual's will.

Undue influence, misrepresentation and third parties

Up to this point I have been considering the right of a claimant wife to set aside a transaction as against the wrongdoing husband when the transaction has been procured by his undue influence. But, in surety cases, the decisive question is whether the claimant wife can set aside the transaction, not against the wrongdoing husband, but against the creditor bank. Of course, if the wrongdoing husband is acting as agent for the creditor bank in obtaining the surety from the wife, the creditor will be fixed with the wrongdoing of its own agent and the surety contract can be set aside as against the creditor. Apart from this, if the creditor bank has notice, actual or constructive, of the undue influence exercised by the husband (and consequentially of the wife's equity to set aside the transaction) the creditor will take subject to that equity and the wife can set aside the transaction against the creditor (albeit a purchaser for value) as well as against the husband: see *Bainbrigge v Browne* (1881) 18 Ch D 188; and *BCCI v Aboody* [1990] 1 QB 923, p 973. Similarly, in cases such as the present where the wife has been induced to enter into the transaction by the husband's misrepresentation, her equity to set aside the transaction will be enforceable against the creditor if either the husband was acting as the creditor's agent or the creditor had actual or constructive notice.

Turnbull v Duval

This case provides the foundation of the modern law: the basis on which it was decided is, to say the least, obscure ...

The subsequent authorities

The authorities in which the principle derived from *Turnbull v Duval* has been applied are fully analysed in the judgment of Scott LJ and it is unnecessary to review them fully again.

Scott LJ analyses the cases as indicating that, down to 1985, there was no decision which indicated that the agency theory, rather than the special equity theory, was the basis of the decision in *Duval*. I agree. But that is attributable more to the application of the *Duval* principle than to any analysis of its jurisprudential basis. The only attempts to analyse the basis of the decision in *Duval*'s case were the Australian decisions in *Bank of Victoria Ltd v Mueller* [1925] VLR 642 and the judgment of Dixon J in *Yerkey v Jones* 63 CLR 649. The former decision was reached by applying the Romilly heresy which, as I have already said, is bad law. The judgment of Dixon J undoubtedly supports the special equity theory.

From 1985 down to the decision of the Court of Appeal in the present case, the decisions have all been based on the agency theory, that is, that the principal debtor has acted in breach of duty to his wife, the surety, and that, if the principal debtor was acting as the creditor's agent but not otherwise, the creditor cannot be in any better position than its agent, the husband. In all the cases since 1985, the principal debtor has procured the agreement of the surety by a legal wrong (undue influence or misrepresentation). In all the cases, emphasis was placed on the question whether the creditor was infected by the debtor's wrongdoing because the debtor was acting as the agent of the creditor in procuring the wife's agreement to stand as surety. I am unable to agree with Scott LJ that the decision in *Kingsnorth Trust Ltd v Bell* [1986] 1 WLR 119 was not based on the agency theory: Dillon LJ, at p 123F–G, expressly makes it a necessary a condition that the creditor has entrusted to the husband the task of obtaining his wife's signature.

However, in four of the cases since 1985, attention has been drawn to the fact that, even in the absence of agency, if the debtor has been guilty of undue influence or misrepresentation, the creditor may not be able to enforce the surety contract if the creditor had notice, actual or constructive, of the debtor's conduct: see *Avon Finance Co Ltd v Bridger* [1985] 2 All ER 281, *per* Brandon LJ; *Coldunell Ltd v Gallon* [1986] QB 1184, p 1199; *Midland Bank plc v Shephard* [1988] 17, p 23; and *BCCI v Aboody* [1990] 1 QB 923, p 973. As will appear, in my view, it is the proper application of the doctrine of notice which provides the key to finding a principled basis for the law.

Accordingly, the present law is built on the unsure foundations of *Turnbull v Duval*. Like most law founded on obscure and possibly mistaken foundations it has developed in an artificial way, giving rise to artificial distinctions and conflicting decisions. In my judgment your Lordships should seek to restate the law in a form which is principled, reflects the current requirements of society and provides as much certainty as possible.

Conclusions

(a) Wives

My starting point is to clarify the basis of the law. Should wives (and perhaps others) be accorded special rights in relation to surety transactions by the recognition of a special equity applicable only to such persons engaged in such transactions? Or should they enjoy only the same protection as they would enjoy in relation to their other dealings? In my judgment, the special equity theory should be rejected. First, I can find no basis in principle for affording special protection to a limited class in relation to one type of transaction only. Secondly, to require the creditor to prove knowledge and understanding by the wife in all cases is to reintroduce by the back door either a presumption of undue influence of Class 2A (which has been decisively rejected) or the Romilly heresy (which has long been treated as bad law). Thirdly, although Scott LJ found that there were two lines of cases one of which supported the special equity theory, on analysis although many decisions are not inconsistent with that theory the only two cases which support it are *Yerkey v Jones* 63 CLR 649 and the decision of the Court of Appeal in the present case. Finally, it is not necessary to have recourse to a special equity theory for the proper protection of the legitimate interests of wives as I will seek to show.

In my judgment, if the doctrine of notice is properly applied, there is no need for the introduction of a special equity in these types of cases. A wife who has been induced to stand as a surety for her husband's debts by his undue influence, misrepresentation or some other legal wrong has an equity as against him to set aside that transaction. Under the ordinary principles of equity, her right to set aside that transaction will be enforceable against third parties (for example, against a creditor) if either the husband was acting as the third party's agent or the third party had actual or constructive notice of the facts giving rise to her equity. Although there may be cases where, without artificiality, it can properly be held that the husband was acting as the agent of the creditor in procuring the wife to stand as surety, such cases will be of very rare occurrence. The key to the problem is to identify the circumstances in which the creditor will be taken to have had notice of the wife's equity to set aside the transaction.

The doctrine of notice lies at the heart of equity. Given that there are two innocent parties, each enjoying rights, the earlier right prevails against the later right if the acquirer of the later right knows of the earlier right (actual notice) or would have discovered it had he taken proper steps (constructive notice). In particular, if the party asserting that he takes free of the earlier rights of another knows of certain facts which put him on inquiry as to the possible existence of the rights of that other and he fails to make such inquiry or take such other steps as are reasonable to verify whether such earlier right does or does not exist, he will have constructive notice of the earlier right and take subject to it. Therefore where a wife has agreed to stand surety for her husband's debts as a result of undue influence or misrepresentation, the creditor will take subject to the wife's equity to set aside the transaction if the circumstances are such as to put the creditor on inquiry as to the circumstances in which she agreed to stand surety.

It is at this stage that, in my view, the 'invalidating tendency' or the law's 'tender treatment' of married women becomes relevant. As I have said above, in dealing with undue influence, this tenderness of the law towards married women is due to the fact that, even today, many wives repose confidence and trust in their husbands in relation to their financial affairs. This tenderness of the law is reflected by the fact that voluntary dispositions by the wife in favour of her husband are more likely to be set aside than other dispositions by her: a wife is more likely to establish presumed undue influence of Class 2B by her husband than by others because, in practice, many wives do repose in their husbands trust and confidence in relation to their financial affairs. Moreover the informality of business dealings between spouses raises a substantial risk that the husband has not accurately stated to the wife the nature of the liability she is undertaking, that is, he has misrepresented the position, albeit negligently.

Therefore, in my judgment, a creditor is put on inquiry when a wife offers to stand surety for her husband's debts by the combination of two factors: (a) the transaction is on its face not to the financial advantage of the wife; and (b) there is a substantial risk in transactions of that kind that, in procuring the wife to act as surety, the husband has committed a legal or equitable wrong that entitles the wife to set aside the transaction.

It follows that, unless the creditor who is put on inquiry takes reasonable steps to satisfy himself that the wife's agreement to stand surety has been properly obtained, the creditor will have constructive notice of the wife's rights.

What, then are the reasonable steps which the creditor should take to ensure that it does not have constructive notice of the wife's rights, if any? Normally, the reasonable steps necessary to avoid being fixed with constructive notice consist of making inquiry of the person who may have the earlier right (ie the wife) to see if whether such right is asserted. It is plainly impossible to require of banks and other financial institutions that they should inquire of one spouse whether he or she has been unduly influenced or misled by the other. But in my judgment the creditor, in order to avoid being fixed with constructive notice, can reasonably be expected to take steps to bring home to the wife the risk she is running by standing as surety and to advise her to take independent advice. As to past transactions, it will depend on the facts of each case whether the steps taken by the creditor satisfy this test. However, for the future, in my judgment, a creditor will have satisfied these requirements if it insists that the wife attend a private meeting (in the absence of the husband) with a representative of the creditor at which she is told of the extent of her liability as surety, warned of the risk she is running and urged to take independent legal advice. If these steps are taken, in my judgment, the creditor will have taken such reasonable steps as are necessary to preclude a subsequent claim that it had constructive notice of the wife's rights. I should make it clear that I have been considering the ordinary case where the creditor knows only that the wife is to stand surety for her husband's debts. I would not exclude exceptional cases where a creditor has knowledge of further facts which render the presence of undue influence not only possible but probable. In such cases, the creditor to be safe will have to insist that the wife is separately advised.

I am conscious that in treating the creditor as having constructive notice because of the risk of Class 2B undue influence or misrepresentation by the husband I may be extending the law as stated by Fry J in *Bainbrigge v Browne* (1881) 18 Ch D 188, p 197 and the Court of Appeal in *BCCI v Aboody* [1990] 1 QB 923, p 973. Those cases suggest that for a third party to be affected by constructive notice of presumed undue influence the third party must actually know of the circumstances which give rise to a presumption of undue influence. In contrast, my view is that the risk of Class 2B undue influence or misrepresentation is sufficient to put the creditor on inquiry. But my statement accords with the principles of notice: if the known facts are such as to indicate the possibility of an adverse claim that is sufficient to put a third party on inquiry.

If the law is established as I have suggested, it will hold the balance fairly between on the one hand the vulnerability of the wife who relies implicitly on her husband and, on the other hand, the practical problems of financial institutions asked to accept a secured or unsecured surety obligation from the wife for her husband's debts. In the context of suretyship, the wife will not have any right to disown her obligations just because subsequently she proves that she did not fully understand the transaction: she will, as in all other areas of her affairs, be bound by her obligations unless her husband has, by misrepresentation, undue influence or other wrong, committed an actionable wrong against her. In the normal case, a financial institution will be able to lend with confidence in reliance on the wife's surety obligation provided that it warns her (in the absence of the husband) of the amount of her potential liability and of the risk of standing surety and advises her to take independent advice.

Mr Jarvis QC for the bank urged that this is to impose too heavy a burden on financial institutions. I am not impressed by this submission. The report by Professor Jack's Review Committee on *Banking Services: Law and Practice*, 1989, Cmnd 622, recommended that prospective guarantors should be adequately warned of the legal effects and possible consequences of their guarantee and of the importance of receiving independent advice ...

Good banking practice (which applies to all guarantees, not only those given by a wife) largely accords with what I consider the law should require when a wife is offered as surety. The only further substantial step required by law beyond that good practice is that the position should be explained by the bank to the wife in a personal interview. I regard this as being essential because a number of the decided cases show that written warnings are often not read and are sometimes intercepted by the husband. It does not seem to me that the requirement of a personal interview imposes such an additional administrative burden as to render the bank's position unworkable.

(b) Other persons

I have hitherto dealt only with the position where a wife stands surety for her husband's debts. But in my judgment the same principles are applicable to all other cases where there is an emotional relationship between cohabitees. The 'tenderness' shown by the law to married women is not based on the marriage ceremony but reflects the underlying risk of one cohabitee exploiting the emotional involvement and trust of the other. Now that unmarried cohabitation, whether heterosexual or homosexual, is widespread in our society, the law should recognise this. Legal wives are not the only group which are now exposed to the emotional pressure of cohabitation. Therefore if, but only if, the creditor is aware that the surety is cohabiting with the principal debtor, in my judgment the same principles should apply to them as apply to husband and wife.

In addition to the cases of cohabitees, the decision of the Court of Appeal in *Avon Finance Co Ltd v Bridger* [1985] 2 All ER 281 shows (rightly in my view) that other relationships can give rise to a similar result. In that case a son, by means of misrepresentation, persuaded his elderly parents to stand surety for his debts. The surety obligation was held to be unenforceable by the creditor *inter alia* because to the bank's knowledge the parents trusted the son in their financial dealings. In my judgment, that case was rightly decided: in a case where the creditor is aware that the surety reposes trust and confidence in the principal debtor in relation to his financial affairs, the creditor is put on inquiry in just the same way as it is in relation to husband and wife.

Summary

I can therefore summarise my views as follows. Where one cohabitee has entered into an obligation to stand as surety for the debts of the other cohabitee and the creditor is aware that they are cohabitees: (1) the surety obligation will be valid and enforceable by the creditor unless the suretyship was procured by the undue influence, misrepresentation or other legal wrong of the principal debtor; (2) if there has been undue influence, misrepresentation or other legal wrong by the principal debtor, unless the creditor has taken reasonable steps to satisfy himself that the surety entered into the obligation freely and in knowledge of the true facts, the creditor will be unable to enforce the surety obligation because he will be fixed with constructive notice of the surety's right to set aside the transaction; (3) unless there are special exceptional circumstances, a creditor will have taken such reasonable steps to avoid being fixed with constructive notice if the creditor warns the surety (at a meeting not attended by the principal debtor) of the amount of her potential liability and of the risks involved and advises the surety to take independent legal advice.

I should make it clear that in referring to the husband's debts I include the debts of a company in which the husband (but not the wife) has a direct financial interest.

The decision in this case

Applying those principles to this case, to the knowledge of the bank Mr and Mrs O'Brien were man and wife. The bank took a surety obligation from Mrs O'Brien, secured on the matrimonial home, to secure the debts of a company in which Mr O'Brien was interested, but in which Mrs O'Brien had no direct pecuniary interest. The bank should therefore have been put on inquiry as to the circumstances in which Mrs O'Brien had agreed to stand as surety for the debt of her husband. If the Burnham branch had properly carried out the instructions from Mr Tucker of the Woolwich branch, Mrs O'Brien would have been informed that she and the matrimonial home were potentially liable for the debts of a company which had an existing liability of £107,000 and which was to be afforded an overdraft facility of £135,000. If she had been told this, it would have counteracted Mr O'Brien's misrepresentation that the liability was limited to £60,000 and would last for only three weeks. In addition according to the side letter she would have been recommended to take independent legal advice.

Unfortunately, Mr Tucker's instructions were not followed and to the knowledge of the bank (through the clerk at the Burnham branch) Mrs O'Brien signed the documents without any warning of the risks or any recommendation to take legal advice. In the circumstances the bank (having failed to take reasonable steps) is fixed with constructive notice of the wrongful misrepresentation made by Mr O'Brien to Mrs O'Brien. Mrs O'Brien is therefore entitled as against the bank to set aside the legal charge on the matrimonial home securing her husband's liability to the bank.

For these reasons, I would dismiss the appeal with costs.

Rebutting the presumption of undue influence

The presumption of undue influence is rebuttable. If it can be shown that the person alleging undue influence has gone into the transaction with his/her eyes open, it will not be unconscionable to enforce the arrangement he/she has made. The easiest way of establishing that a person has made the contract with a free and independent mind is to show that he/she has received advice from another person. In these circumstances, any influence which might have been presumed will be taken not to have affected the decision to enter into the contract.[54] If the advice given is not independent, for example, where a solicitor acts for both parties to the proceedings, the presumption will not be upset.[55]

---

54 *Inche Noriah v Shaikh Allie Bin Omar* [1929] AC 127, p 135.
55 *Powell v Powell* [1900] 1 Ch 243.

The absence of advice is not necessarily fatal, since the influence of the other party may be weak, or there may be some other reason, independent of the influence, which has persuaded a person to make a contract, but it is by far the most likely way of indicating that the 'influential' party had in fact (despite the influence) acted freely and independently.

Since *Barclays Bank v O'Brien*,[56] the courts have on several occasions been faced with the task of deciding whether independent, informed advice had been received by a female partner so as to discharge the burden on the third party. For example, in *Massey v Midland Bank*,[57] the bank had advised the female partner that she would need to take independent advice from a solicitor before it would agree to proceed. She subsequently saw her partner's solicitor, who explained the nature of a legal charge over property. At both the meeting with the bank and with the solicitor, her partner had been present. Nevertheless, the Court of Appeal held that the bank had discharged its duty, and the charge stood:

Massey v Midland Bank plc [1995] 1 All ER 929, CA, p 934

Steyn LJ: The guidance offered by Lord Browne-Wilkinson in *Barclays Bank plc v O'Brien* postdates the transaction. Lord Browne-Wilkinson made clear in giving the guidance that it was to operate prospectively. On the other hand, since the pre-existing principles offered, if anything, a lesser protection to wives (and others) circumstanced as Miss Massey was, it will be convenient to examine her case in the light of that guidance. I would respectfully put that guidance in context by two observations. First, the guidance was clearly not intended to be exhaustive, as indeed the facts of the present case demonstrate. Secondly, the guidance was intended to strike a fair balance between the need to protect wives (and others in a like position) whose judgmental capacity was impaired and the need to avoid unnecessary impediments to using the matrimonial home as security. The guidance ought therefore not to be mechanically applied. The relief is after all equitable relief. It is the substance that matters. if, as far as the creditor is concerned, the objective of independent advice for the wife (or somebody in a like position) is realised, the fact that there was not an interview between a representative of the creditor and the surety, unattended by the debtor, ought not by itself to be fatal to the creditor's case. In the present case Mr Dixon did not see Miss Massey alone. That was not good practice. But fortunately she did receive independent legal advice. I would therefore hold that in this case the bank complied with the substance of the guidance.

A feature of this case is that Miss Massey was not deceived as to the nature and terms of the charge. She was deceived as to the standing and prospects of Camelot. She was also falsely told that Mr Potts would redeem Lloyds Bank's prior charge over Miss Massey's property. The bank had no actual knowledge of these matters. In a skeleton argument, counsel for the bank submits that if a

---

56 [1994] AC 180.
57 [1995] 1 All ER 929.

bank is to be affected by the debtor's misrepresentation as to a matter other than the meaning or effect of the security, the banker must have either: (i) actual knowledge of the deception; or (ii) wilfully shut his eyes to the obvious. I do not agree that a special rule applies. In my view, the ordinary rules of constructive notice apply. But it is generally sufficient for the bank to avoid a finding of constructive notice if the bank urged the proposed surety to take independent advice from a solicitor. How far a solicitor should go in probing the matter, and in giving advice, is a matter for the solicitor's professional judgment and a matter between him and his client. The bank is not generally involved in the nature and extent of the solicitor's advice. And, in my judgment, there is nothing in the circumstances of the present case which required the bank to do more than urge or insist on independent advice.

But counsel for Miss Massey emphasises what he described as undesirable features of this case. First, he says the crucial point is that Mr Dixon never saw Miss Massey alone. I have already dealt with this point. The short answer to this point is that the solicitors confirmed to the bank that they had given independent advice to Miss Massey. The objective of Lord Browne-Wilkinson's guidance had been achieved: the surety received independent advice.

Secondly, counsel for Miss Massey emphasises that Mr Potts selected the firm of solicitors, he gave the instructions to the solicitors, and he attended the interview with the solicitors. The judge made the following findings of fact:

> Now, it is the case here that the bank left it to Mr Potts to arrange for a solicitor to advise Miss Massey and witness her signature. Mr Potts, however, did do so and a reputable firm, Messrs Walker Morris, was instructed. The charge was sent by the bank directly to that firm, which confirmed that it had accepted instructions to advise Miss Massey. She was so advised by Mr Jones of that firm. The legal charge was witnessed by him and returned by him to the bank. In these circumstances, I do not see how the bank could be said to have left it to Mr Potts to procure the execution of the charge. On the contrary, they left it to a firm of solicitors who, in fact, had accepted instructions to act independently for Miss Massey, and did so act. Whatever the quality of that advice, the bank could not be held responsible for it. Messrs Walker Morris were acting as solicitors to Miss Massey, not to the bank.

The bank did not know what happened between Mr Jones and Miss Massey, or how the interview was conducted. And it was under no duty to inquire. But the bank had every reason to believe (as was the case on the judge's findings) that Miss Massey had received independent advice. Relying on observations of Dillon LJ in *Bank of Baroda v Shah* [1988] 3 All ER 24, p 29, the judge observed that the bank was entitled to assume that the solicitors would act honestly and give proper advice to Miss Massey. I agree. How far the solicitor's advice went was essentially a matter for Miss Massey and Mr Jones. The law does not generally require the creditor to stipulate the nature and extent of the advice. It will be for the solicitor to discuss with the wife (or a surety in an equivalent position) what further advice, if any, she ought to take. In any event, Mr Jones did explain the nature of the charge to Miss Massey and satisfied himself that she entered into it willingly.

More dubiously, in *Banco Exterior Internacional v Mann*,[58] the Court of Appeal held that, even where a bank had not specifically stressed the importance of receiving independent advice, they were protected by the fact that the wife had earlier received advice about the effect of the legal charge from the husband's (company) solicitor. It is seriously open to doubt how far this is in the spirit of *O'Brien*. In *O'Brien*, Lord Browne-Wilkinson (at p 196) emphasises not just the need to obtain independent advice, but for a prior meeting at which the bank (in the absence of the other partner) warns of the risks involved. Implicit in this is surely the need to have brought home to the person concerned how serious the implications are of signing up to the charge, which would then focus his/her concerns in relation to (any) subsequent legal interview. The dissenting judgment of Hobhouse LJ is surely to be preferred:[59]

Banco Exterior Internacional v Mann [1995] 1 All ER 936, p 942

Morritt LJ:

So the question is whether the bank took such steps or made such inquiries as were reasonable to verify whether Mrs Mann was entitled to set aside the declaration vis à vis Mr Mann. As to that, Lord Browne-Wilkinson said ([1993] 4 All ER 417, p 429; [1994] 1 AC 180, p 196):

> Normally, the reasonable steps necessary to avoid being fixed with constructive notice consists of making inquiry of the person who may have the earlier right (that is, the wife) to see ... whether such right is asserted. It is plainly impossible to require of banks and other financial institutions that they should inquire of one spouse whether he or she has been unduly influenced or misled by the other. But, in my judgment, the creditor, in order to avoid being fixed with constructive notice, can reasonably be expected to take steps to bring home to the wife the risk she is running by standing as surety and to advise her to take independent advice.

Lord Browne-Wilkinson recognised that in the case of past transactions, it would depend on the facts of each case whether the steps taken by the creditor satisfied the test. He then indicated for the benefit of those contemplating entering into similar transactions in the future what steps the creditor should take to avoid any subsequent claim that it had constructive notice of the wife's rights, namely:

> ... if [the creditor] insists that the wife attend a private meeting (in the absence of the husband) with a representative of the creditor at which she is told of the extent of her liability as surety, warned of the risk she is running and urged to take independent legal advice. (See [1994] 4 All ER 417, pp 429–30; [1994] 1 AC 180, p 196.)

I do not understand Lord Browne-Wilkinson to be laying down for the future the only steps which will avoid a bank being fixed with constructive notice of

---

58 [1995] 1 All ER 936.
59 For a similar view, see Fehlberg, 1996.

the rights of the wife; rather he is pointing out the procedure which lending institutions may regard as best practice. Nevertheless, it points to the principle to be applied in deciding whether the creditor has done enough to avoid being fixed with constructive notice. The essence of the matter is that the creditor should take reasonable steps to ensure insofar as he can that the undue influence of the husband is counteracted by ensuring that the wife is aware of the consequences to her of entering into the proposed transaction for the benefit of the husband. Thus, in his summary Lord Browne-Wilkinson said:

> ... unless the creditor has taken reasonable steps to satisfy himself that the surety entered into the obligation freely and in knowledge of the true facts, the creditor will be unable to enforce the surety obligation because he will be fixed with constructive notice of the surety's right to set aside the transaction ... [see [1993] 4 All ER 417, p 431; [1994] 1 AC 180, p 198].

In this case, the bank wrote to the company on 31 December 1985, enclosing, amongst other documents, the declaration it would require Mrs Mann and her son to sign. It stipulated that this should be done in the presence of their solicitor 'who will sign to the effect that the contents have been explained'. That requirement is amplified by the form of declaration to be signed by the solicitor that he had 'explained the nature and effect of the above declaration and agreement and of the attached Legal Charge'.

The Judge decided that the bank had not taken such reasonable steps as were necessary to avoid having constructive notice of Mrs Mann's right to have the declaration set aside. He referred to the following elements. First, by asking the company to obtain merely the execution of the declaration, there was nothing in the documents to exclude the possibility that the solicitor would also be the solicitor for the company and Mr Mann as well and would consider that a mere explanation of the document in the presence of the husband was all that was required. Secondly, Mrs Mann did not regard Mr Rochman as independent of her husband. Thirdly, mere understanding was not enough if she thought that she had no choice in the matter. Fourthly, independent advice might have persuaded her that she did have a choice.

Given that the judge found that Mrs Mann's execution of the declaration was the result of the undue influence of Mr Mann and that that finding has not been appealed, it does not appear to me that the second, third and fourth elements are relevant, for the true question is not how Mrs Mann regarded the transaction, but how it appeared to the bank and whether the bank should have taken further or other steps. So regarded, it seems to me that the judgment imposes on the bank an obligation to do much more than is reasonable in all the circumstances.

In *Bank of Baroda v Shah* [1988] 3 All ER 24, this court held that there was no obligation on a creditor to ensure that the surety received entirely independent advice, for it was entitled to assume (in the absence of clear indications to the contrary) that the solicitor who did advise was honest and competent. I do not think that the authority of that decision has been shaken by the decision of the House of Lords in *Barclays Bank v O'Brien*. The proposition was reaffirmed by the decision of this court in *Massey v Midland Bank plc* [1995] 1 All ER 929.

The judge made no reference in his judgment to *Bank of Baroda v Shah*; *Massey v Midland Bank plc* had not been decided.

It is not suggested that the bank did not know that Mr Rochman was a solicitor. Thus it received the warranty of a solicitor that he had explained to Mrs Mann the nature and effect of the declaration. It was a matter for Mr Rochman to consider whether he was able to do so without any conflicting duty or interest. In my view, the bank was entitled to rely on the fact that Mr Rochman undertook the task as showing that he was sufficiently independent for that purpose. The bank was entitled to consider that it would not be possible adequately to explain the effect of the declaration without making it abundantly clear to Mrs Mann the risks she would run if she executed the declaration and the company defaulted. Further, the bank would justifiably assume that the solicitor would appreciate the reason why his advice was being sought and the need for his warranty at the foot of the declaration to be completed. In my judgment, the bank was fully entitled to think that Mr Rochman's explanation would necessarily include some reference to the fact that Mrs Mann was under no obligation to execute the declaration if she did not wish to undertake the risk.

In my judgment, the bank did take such steps as were reasonable to avoid being fixed with constructive notice of the right of Mrs Mann to set aside the declaration as having been executed by her as the result of Mr Mann's undue influence. I think that the judge reached a wrong conclusion because he took account of the position as between Mrs Mann and Mr Rochman, which was irrelevant to this question, and failed to give due weight to the conclusions the bank was entitled to draw from the fact that Mr Rochman had given the warranty the form of declaration required. I would allow this appeal.

Hobhouse LJ (p 948): The present case concerns a transaction which occurred in 1986 and therefore is covered by what Lord Browne-Wilkinson said about 'past transactions'. He identified two things which must be done. The bank must take reasonable steps to bring home to the wife the risk that she is running by signing the document. This was done. They procured that the document should be signed in the presence of another, whom they had reason to believe would be legally qualified, who had 'prior to the execution thereof explained the nature and effect of the above declaration and agreement and of the attached legal charge [to the wife] which she appeared fully to understand'.

But that is not the end of it. The bank must also 'advise her to take independent advice'. In the present case, the bank never communicated with the wife. They never gave her any advice. They did not take any step to see that she was advised by anyone to take independent advice. Indeed, the contrary is the position. The declaration which they required the witness to sign expressly did not cover the giving of any independent advice as to whether the wife should or should not, of her own free will, sign the document. The letter sent by the bank to the husband's company, dated 31 December 1985, simply said that the document should be signed in the presence of her solicitor, who will sign to the effect that the contents have been explained. This approach left open precisely the possibility that materialised. The wife might never receive independent advice. No step might be taken to ensure that the wife was signing the document as a result of the free exercise of her own will and not subject to any undue influence of the husband. The steps taken by the bank simply did not address that aspect at all, which is of the essence of the rebuttal of the presumption of undue influence. The bank did not take any steps, let alone reasonable steps, to advise the wife. It should have been entirely within their contemplation that the wife might well in fact sign the document under the undue influence of her husband which was in fact what occurred.

I do not accept that the requirement that the wife should be separately advised does not visualise that in some circumstances she may be advised not to sign a document. In practical terms, it may be necessary for the independent solicitor to say to the wife:

> I know that you feel that you have no option but to sign, but you are wrong. You do have a choice and I must advise you that it is not in your interest to sign this document. You should feel under no obligation to do so. You are asking for my advice. My advice to you is: do not sign.

It must be remembered that the starting point of this exercise is that the wife's will is being unduly and improperly influenced by the will of her husband. The steps taken have to be directed to freeing her of that influence or, at the least, providing some counterbalance.

For these reasons, I consider that to allow this appeal would fail to recognise the law as is well established and stated by Lord Browne-Wilkinson; in my judgement, the appeal should be dismissed.

Finally, in *Barclays Bank plc v Coleman*,[60] the Court of Appeal confirmed, predictably enough, that a certificate of independent legal advice provided by a legal executive rather than a solicitor is still usually sufficient.

---

60 [2000] 1 All ER 385.

CHAPTER 8

STANDARD FORM CONTRACTS
AND EXEMPTION

The willingness of the courts to intervene and 'police' a bargain, however apparently freely made, was stated in the previous chapter to turn on questions of procedural unfairness, substantive unfairness or (perhaps) both.[1] This section illustrates perhaps better than any other area of the law the tension between traditional notions of contractual freedom, based on the classical model, and the need to ensure that the freedom to contract does not become a licence to exploit superior contractual bargaining strength.[2] At some points, the courts (and, more recently, Parliament) have focused on procedural issues, at others on substantive issues.[3]

In principle, the issues surrounding standard form contracts are general ones, and are not merely concerned with the distinct problems thrown up by exemption clauses. Indeed, later in this chapter, there is some discussion of other difficulties most commonly associated with standard forms, and of the response by the courts or Parliament to them.[4] As will be seen, although standard form contracts may work fairly, particularly where the parties are of approximately equal bargaining strength, and operate in the same area of business,[5] they may also function very unfairly – with effectively non-negotiated small print clauses severely curtailing, or even wholly eliminating the basic contractual rights of one of the parties.[6] Beyond this lies the wider question of how one is to define standard forms. It is easy enough to sketch out typical features; a standardised, printed mode, used for all contracts of the same kind, with relatively little variation in a typical case, and with a general

---

1   See Kessler, 1943, pp 631–32, which finds echoes in a number of English cases, most recently in the judgment of Bingham LJ in *Interfoto Picture Library Ltd v Stiletto Visual Programmes Ltd* [1989] QB 433, referred to in Chapter 2 and below, p 433.

2   See *Schroeder Music Publishing Co Ltd v Macaulay* [1974] 1 WLR 308, *per* Lord Diplock (below) and the Law Commission, *Second Report on Exemption Clauses*, Law Com No 69, 1975, paras 11 and 146 (see below).

3   The provisions in the Consumer Credit Act 1974, s 88, concerning default notices and the general legal controls on relief against forfeiture can be seen as focusing on procedural unfairness, the controls in the Unfair Contract Terms Act (UCTA) 1977 (see below) as being primarily concerned with substantive issues.

4   Eg, the approach in *Interfoto v Stiletto*, various provisions in the Consumer Credit Act, restrictions on the use of penalty clauses, and the provisions in the Unfair Terms in Consumer Contracts Regulations 1999 (see below).

5   Some standard contract terms are settled by trade associations for use by their members. Indeed some are even prescribed by legislation, or are provided under statutory authority (eg, companies' articles of association).

6   See the cases of *L'Estrange v Graucob Ltd* [1934] 2 KB 354 and *Thompson v London, Midland & Scottish Railway* [1930] 1 KB 41, referred to in Chapter 2.

requirement to adhere to the terms, however one-sided, laid down by the stronger party.[7] A general statutory definition is, however, lacking in the UK.[8]

EXEMPTION CLAUSES

Despite the above comments, the main focus of legislative and judicial attention over the years has been on the control of exemption clauses. In many ways, this is unsurprising; clauses which take away, or seriously limit, one party's rights can very clearly illustrate substantive unfairness and their widespread use in consumer transactions often buried in the small print of excessively detailed standard conditions[9] can equally clearly demonstrate procedural unfairness. At its simplest, an exemption (or exclusion) clause is a clause which exempts one party from (or excludes) legal liability to which they would otherwise be subject under the contract, or generally at common law. Equally, the clause (then normally termed a limitation clause) can seek to limit the compensation payable for breach of contract, or to limit the remedies available (for example, by excluding the right to repudiate). At its most general, such a clause may seek to give one party a general discretion over the manner or the substance of their performance.[10] Whatever the form adopted, and there appears to be no magic in the phrase exemption clause *per se*, the problem is the same, namely, is the degree of unfairness (procedural or substantive) sufficient to trigger either judicial or legislative intervention? Legislative intervention has a reasonably long pedigree (dating back to the Canals and Railways Act 1854) but, until relatively recently, such intervention was piecemeal, and the courts were left, largely without legislative assistance, to grapple with the problems thrown up by exemption clauses.

---

7   See Kessler, 1943, for the terminology as well as the arguments.

8   The phrase 'written standard terms of business' is used in the UCTA 1977 (below), but is not defined in the Act, There may, however, be some assistance to be gained from a 'reverse' reading of the Unfair Terms in Consumer Contracts Regulations 1999, reg 5, which does define an 'individually negotiated' term (see below).

9   Which may not have been made directly available to the consumer, but may only have been obliquely alluded to via a ticket or other document. A rather different form of paper-chase!

10 Both UCTA 1977, s 3 and s 13 appear to bring such clauses within the scope of the exemption clauses controlled by the Act. See, also, the wide approach taken by Slade LJ in *Phillips Products Ltd v Hyland* [1987] 1 WLR 659; and *Anglo-Continental Holidays Ltd v Typaldos Lines (London) Ltd* [1967] 2 Lloyd's Rep 61. This concept of an exemption clause is at variance with that adopted by some academics, eg, Coote, 1964, particularly Chapters 1 and 8. Coote treats exemption clauses as affecting the primary obligations under the contract, rather than merely being defensive in character. The weight of judicial opinion, however, supports the above analysis.

JUDICIAL INTERVENTION

Perhaps the earliest, and certainly the most widely used judicial techniques to curb the excesses of the unfettered use of exemption clauses were the rules on incorporation of terms referred to in Chapter 2. Although ostensibly neutral in scope, their use in an exemption clause context was often particularly searching. However, as cases such as *L'Estrange v Graucob*[11] and *Thompson v London Midland & Scottish Railway*[12] illustrate, there were serious limits on how far the courts allowed themselves to go in curbing the use of exemption clauses by scrutinising the forms or procedures of their incorporation.

CONSTRUCTION AND INTERPRETATION

When confronted with a dispute over any term in a contract, the courts will always be engaged in a process of interpretation. However, in the context of exemption clauses judicial liability has manifested itself in a number of distinct rules or approaches. These can be summarised as the *contra proferentem* rule, the negligence rule and the fundamental breach rule. Distinct questions may arise in relation to limitation clauses.

The *contra proferentem* rule

An exemption clause will always be construed strictly against the party seeking to rely on it.

In *Andrews Brothers (Bournemouth) Ltd v Singer & Co Ltd*,[13] the defendants, by a written agreement, appointed the plaintiffs sole dealers within a named area for the sale of 'new Singer cars', and the plaintiffs agreed to purchase from the defendants a certain number of those cars. Clause 5 of the agreement was in these terms: 'All cars sold by the company [the defendants] are subject to the terms of the warranty set out in schedule no 3 of this agreement, and all conditions, warranties and liabilities implied by statute, common law or otherwise are excluded.' By the warranty contained in schedule no 3, which was expressed to be limited to new vehicles manufactured by the defendants and to be 'in lieu of any warranty (or condition) implied by common law, statute, or otherwise', the sole obligation of the defendants was to repair or replace within 12 months of the delivery of the vehicle any fault disclosed where this was due to defective material or workmanship.

---

11 [1934] 2 KB 394. See Chapter 2.
12 [1930] 1 KB 41, CA. See Chapter 2.
13 [1934] 1 KB 17, CA.

The plaintiffs gave an order to the defendants for a new Singer car and a car was delivered to and accepted by the plaintiffs which, by reason of it having already run a considerable mileage, was not a new car within the meaning of the contract. On a claim by the plaintiffs for breach of contract in supplying a car which was not a new car, the defendants relied upon cl 5 of the agreement as exempting them from liability.

The Court of Appeal upheld the judgment of Goddard J, in finding that cl 5, as drafted, did not cover the particular breach which had occurred. On a strict construction, it only applied to the breach of an implied term, and not to the breach of an express term:

Andrews Bros (Bournemouth) Ltd v Singer & Co Ltd [1934] 1 KB 17, CA, p 22

Scrutton LJ: The question therefore is whether the defendants have succeeded in excluding liability in this case – whether they can tender under the contract goods not complying with the description in the contract and say that the plaintiffs, having accepted the car, cannot now sue for breach of contract.

In my opinion, this was a contract for the sale of a new Singer car. The contract continually uses the phrase 'new Singer cars'. At the end of the agreement, I find this: 'In the event of the dealer having purchased from the Company during the period of this agreement 250 new cars of current season's models'; and in the very beginning of the agreement I find this: 'The Company hereby appoint the dealer their sole dealer for the sale of new Singer cars.' The same phrase also occurs in other parts of the agreement, and the subject matter is therefore expressly stated to be 'new Singer cars.' The judge has found, and his view is not now contested, that the car tendered in this case was not a new Singer car. Does then cl 5 prevent the vendors being liable in damages for having tendered and supplied a car which is not within the express terms of the contract? Clause 5 says this: 'All conditions, warranties and liabilities implied by statute, common law or otherwise are excluded.' There are well known obligations in various classes of contracts which are not expressly mentioned, but are implied. During the argument, Greer LJ mentioned an apt illustration, namely, where an agent contracts on behalf of A, he warrants that he has authority to make the contract on behalf of A although no such warranty is expressed in the contract. Mr Pritt relied on s 13 of the Sale of Goods Act 1893, which provides that 'where there is a contract for the sale of goods by description, there is an implied condition that the goods shall correspond with the description ...', and from that, he says it follows that this particular condition comes within the words employed by the section. That, I think, is putting a very strained meaning on the word 'implied' in the section. Where goods are expressly described in the contract and do not comply with that description, it is quite inaccurate to say that there is an implied term; the term is expressed in the contract. Suppose the contract is for the supply of a car of 1932 manufacture, and a car is supplied which is of 1930 manufacture, there has not been a breach of an implied term: there has been a breach of an express term of the contract. It leads to a very startling result if it can be said that cl 5 allows a vendor to supply to a purchaser an article which does not comply with the express description of the article in the contract, and then, though the purchaser did not know of the matter which prevented the article supplied from complying with the express terms of the contract, to say, 'We are under no liability to you because this is a condition implied by statute and we have excluded such liability'.

In my view, there has been, in this case, a breach of an express term of the contract. If a vendor desires to protect himself from liability in such a case, he must do so by much clearer language than this, which, in my opinion, does not exempt the defendants from liability where they have failed to comply with the express term of the contract. For these reasons, I think Goddard J came to a correct conclusion, and this appeal therefore fails.

The inherent limitation in such an approach is that it invites redrafting by the *proferens* (or rather by their lawyer) to take account of the deficiency helpfully identified by the court. Substantive unfairness is not directly confronted. It does invite the most serious speculation as to whether, even if drafted so as to refer to express terms as well as implied terms, any exemption clause could credibly be construed as taking away the core contractual obligation to provide a new car.[14]

The negligence rule

This is perhaps best to be regarded as a particularly severe application of the *contra proferentem* rule. In itself, this rule attaches itself to ambiguity in the exemption clause but, when the clause is used to support an exclusion or limitation of a duty to take care, the courts are likely to require the clearest of language if this object is to be achieved. Statute now imposes particularly severe restrictions on attempts to exclude liability for negligence[15] and, for a long time, the courts have tacitly recognised that there is an inherent improbability in one party wholly absolving the other from all the consequences of their negligence, unless there is the clearest language to this effect.[16] In *White v John Warwick & Co Ltd*,[17] the plaintiff hired a bicycle from the defendants. Clause 11 of the agreement provided that 'Nothing in this agreement shall render the owners liable for any personal injuries ...'. The plaintiff was thrown from the bicycle and injured, when the saddle tilted as he was riding it. The Court of Appeal held that the defendants were liable in negligence. Clause 11 was effective to exclude their strict liability in contract

---

14 A perception which, no doubt, underpins the fundamental breach cases, such as *Karsales (Harrow Ltd) v Wallis* [1956] 1 WLR 936 (see below).

15 See UCTA 1977, s 2(1).

16 See *Gillespie Brothers Ltd v Roy Bowles Transport Ltd* [1973] QB 400, p 419.

17 [1953] 1 WLR 1285 and see Gower, 1954.

(to supply a bicycle in 'hireable' condition), but they were also under a tortious duty to take reasonable care, and cl 11 did not cover that.

Two further questions arise. First, what degree of explicitness will the courts require and, secondly, does this 'clarity' rule apply where the contracting party is only liable in negligence? As regards the former, there is probably no need to specifically mention fault or negligence, but equally general words, such as those used in *White v John Warwick*, will not be sufficient. A common drafting ploy is to use some expression such as 'all loss however arising' or 'all damage or injury howsoever caused'. As regards the latter, it was originally thought that a clause in general terms necessarily did cover negligence since there was nothing else for it to attach to.

In *Alderslade v Hendon Laundry Co Ltd*,[18] the plaintiff left 10 large Irish linen handkerchiefs with the defendants to be cleaned. The defendants lost the handkerchiefs. The plaintiff claimed the cost of replacing the handkerchiefs. In their defence the laundry pleaded a clause in the agreement that 'the maximum amount for lost or damaged articles is 20 times the charge made for laundering' (an amount less that half the plaintiff's claim). The Court of Appeal allowed the defence and overruled the decision at first instance in favour of the plaintiff:

Alderslade v Hendon Laundry Co Ltd [1945] KB 189, CA, p 192

Lord Greene MR: The effect of those authorities can I think be stated as follows: where the head of damage in respect of which limitation of liability is sought to be imposed by such a clause is one which rests on negligence and nothing else, the clause must be construed as extending to that head of damage, because it would otherwise lack subject matter. Where, on the other hand, the head of damage may be based on some other ground than that of negligence, the general principle is that the clause must be confined in its application to loss occurring through that other cause, to the exclusion of loss arising through negligence. The reason is that if a contracting party wishes in such a case to limit his liability in respect of negligence, he must do so in clear terms in the absence of which the clause is construed as relating to a liability not based on negligence. A common illustration of the principle is to be found in the case of common carriers. A common carrier is frequently described, though perhaps not quite accurately, as an insurer, and his liability in respect of articles entrusted to him is not necessarily based on negligence. Accordingly, if a common carrier wishes to limit his liability for lost articles and does not make it quite clear that he is desiring to limit it in respect of his liability for negligence, then the clause will be construed as extending only to his liability on grounds other than negligence. If, on the other hand, a carrier not being a common carrier, makes use of such a clause, then unless it is construed so as to cover the case of negligence there would be no content for it

---

18   [1945] KB 189, CA.

at all seeing that his only obligation is to take reasonable care. That, broadly speaking, is the principle which falls to be applied in this case ...

In the present case, all that we know about the goods is that they are lost. There seems to me to be no case of lost goods, in respect of which, it would be necessary to limit liability, unless it be a case where the goods are lost by negligence. Goods sent to the laundry will not be lost in the act of washing them. On the other hand, they may be lost while they are in the custody of the defendants before washing or after washing has been completed. They may be lost in the process of returning them to the customer after they have been washed, but in each of those two cases, if my view is right, the obligation of the defendants is an obligation to take reasonable care and nothing else. Therefore, the claim of a customer that the defendants are liable to him in respect of articles that have been lost must, I think, depend on the issue of due care on their part. If that be right, to construe this clause, so far as it relates to loss, in such a way as to exclude loss occasioned by lack of proper care, would be to leave the clause so far as loss is concerned – I say nothing about damage – without any content at all. The result is in my opinion is that the clause must be construed as applying to the case of loss through negligence. Therefore this appeal succeeds, and the appropriate reduction in damages must be made in the order.

However, more recently in *Hollier v Rambler Motors (AMC) Ltd*,[19] conventional wisdom on this point was challenged. The facts of the case were outlined in Chapter 2, and, as indicated there, the Court of Appeal held that, in any event, the clause in question had not been validly incorporated. The court's remarks on the construction of the clause were, therefore, *obiter* but, nevertheless, provide a telling contrast with the *Alderslade* approach:

Hollier v Rambler Motors (AMC) Ltd [1972] 2 QB 71, CA, p 78

Salmon LJ (with whom Stamp LJ and Latey J agreed): I think I should deal with the point as to whether or not the words on the bottom of the form, had they been incorporated in the contract, would have excluded the defendants' liability to compensate the plaintiff for damage caused to the plaintiff's car by a fire which in turn had been caused by the defendants' own negligence. It is well settled that a clause excluding liability for negligence should make its meaning plain on its face to any ordinarily literate and sensible person. The easiest way of doing that, of course, is to state expressly that the garage, tradesman or merchant, as the case may be will not be responsible for any damage caused by his own negligence. No doubt, merchants, tradesmen, garage proprietors and the like are a little shy of writing in an exclusion clause quite so bluntly as that. Clearly, it would not tend to attract customers, and might even put many off. I am not saying that an exclusion clause cannot be effective to exclude negligence unless it does so expressly, but in order for the clause to be effective the language should be so plain that it clearly bears that meaning. I do not think that defendants should be allowed to shelter behind

---

19   [1972] 2 QB 71, CA.

language which might lull the customer into a false sense of security by letting him think – unless perhaps he happens to be a lawyer – that he would have redress against the man with whom he was dealing for any damage which he, the customer, might suffer by the negligence of that person.

The principles are stated by Scrutton LJ with his usual clarity in *Rutter v Palmer* [1922] 2 KB 87, p 92: 'For the present purposes, a rougher test will serve. In construing an exemption clause, certain general rules may be applied: First, the defendant is not exempted from liability for the negligence of his servants unless adequate words are used; secondly, the liability of the defendants apart from the exempting words must be ascertained; then the particular clause in question must be considered; and if the only liability of the party pleading the exemption is a liability for negligence, the clause will more readily operate to exempt him.'

Scrutton LJ was far too great a lawyer, and had far too much robust common sense, if I may be permitted to say so, to put it higher than that 'if the only liability of the party pleading the exemption is a liability for negligence, the clause will more readily operate to exempt him'. He does not say that 'if the only liability of the party pleading the exemption is a liability for negligence, the clause will necessarily exempt him'. After all, there are many cases in the books dealing with exemption clauses, and in every case it comes down to a question of construing the alleged exemption clause which is then before the court. It seems to me that in *Rutter v Palmer*, although the word 'negligence' was never used in the exemption clause, the exemption clause would have conveyed to any ordinary, literate and sensible person that the garage in that case was inserting a clause in the contract which excluded their liability for the negligence of their drivers. The clause being considered in that case – and it was without any doubt incorporated in the contract – was: 'Customers' cars are driven by your staff at customers' sole risk.' Any ordinary man knows that, when a car is damaged, it is not infrequently damaged because the driver has driven it negligently. He also knows, I suppose, that if he sends it to a garage and a driver in the employ of the garage takes the car on the road for some purpose in connection with the work which the customer has entrusted the garage to do, the garage could not conceivably be liable for the car being damaged in an accident, unless the driver was at fault. It follows that no sensible man could have thought that the words in that case had any meaning except that the garage would not be liable for the negligence of their own drivers. That is a typical case where, on the construction of the clause in question, the meaning for which the defendant was there contending was the obvious meaning of the clause.

The next case to which I wish to refer is the well known case of *Alderslade v Hendon Laundry Ltd* [1945] 1 KB 189. In that case, articles were sent by the plaintiff to the defendants' laundry to be washed and they were lost. In an action by the plaintiff against the defendants for damages, the defendants relied on the following condition to limit their liability: 'The maximum amount allowed for lost or damaged articles is 20 times the charge made for laundering.' Again, this was a case where negligence was not expressly excluded. The question was: what do the words mean? I have no doubt that they would mean to the ordinary housewife who was sending her washing to the laundry that, if the goods were lost or damaged in the course of being washed through the negligence of the laundry, the laundry would not be liable for more than 20 times the charge made for the laundering. I say that for this reason. It is, I think, obvious that when a laundry loses or damages goods it is almost invariably because there has been some neglect or default on the part of the laundry. It is said that thieves break in and steal, and the goods (in that case handkerchiefs) might have been stolen by thieves. That of course is possible, but I should hardly think that a laundry would be a great allurement to burglars. It is a little far-fetched to think of burglars breaking into a laundry to steal the washing when there are banks, jewellers, post offices, factories, offices and homes likely to contain money and articles far more attractive to burglars. I think that the ordinary sensible housewife, or indeed anyone else who sends washing to the laundry, who saw that clause must have appreciated that almost always goods are lost or damaged because of the laundry's negligence, and therefore this clause could apply only to limit the liability of the laundry, when they were in fault or negligent.

But Mr Tuckey has drawn our attention to the way in which the matter was put by Lord Greene MR in delivering the leading judgment in this court, and he contends that Lord Greene MR was in fact making a considerable extension to the law as laid down by Scrutton LJ in the case to which I have referred. For this proposition, he relies on the following passage in Lord Greene MR's judgment at p 192: 'The effect of those authorities can I think be stated as follows: Where the head of damage in respect of which limitation of liability is sought to be imposed by such a clause is one which rests on negligence and nothing else, the clause must be construed as extending to that head of damage, because it would otherwise lack subject matter.'

If one takes that word 'must' *au pied de la lettre*, that passage does support Mr Tuckey's contention. However, we are not here construing a statute, but a passage in an unreserved judgment of Lord Greene MR, who was clearly intending no more than to re-state the effect of the authorities as they then stood. It is to be observed that MacKinnon LJ, who gave the other judgment in this court, set out the rule or principle which he said was very admirably stated by Scrutton LJ in *Rutter v Palmer* [1922] 2 KB 87. He said at p 195: 'Applying that principle to the facts of the case, I think that the clause in question does avail to protect the proprietors of the laundry in respect of liability for negligence which must be assumed to be the cause of these handkerchiefs having disappeared.'

And clearly it did, for the reasons that I have already given. I do not think that Lord Greene MR was intending to extend the law in the sense for which Mr Tuckey contends. If it were so extended, it would make the law entirely artificial by ignoring that rules of construction are merely our guides and not our masters: in the end you are driven back to construing the clause in question to see what it means. Applying the principles laid down by Scrutton LJ, they lead to the result at which the court arrived in *Alderslade v Hendon Laundry Ltd* [1945] 1 KB 189. In my judgment, these principles lead to a very different result in the present case. The words are: 'The company is not responsible for damage caused by fire to customers' cars on the premises.' What would that mean to any ordinarily literate and sensible car owner? I do not suppose that any such, unless he is a trained lawyer, has an intimate or indeed any knowledge of the liability of bailees in law. If you asked the ordinary man or woman: 'Supposing you send your car to the garage to be repaired and there is a fire, would you suppose that the garage would be liable?' I should be surprised if many of them did not answer, quite wrongly: 'Of course they are liable if there is a fire.' Others might be more cautious and say: 'Well, I had better ask my solicitor,' or, 'I do not know. I suppose they may well be liable.' That is the crucial difference, to my mind, between the present case and *Alderslade v Hendon Laundry Ltd* and *Rutter v Palmer* [1922] 2 KB 87. In those two cases, any ordinary man or woman reading the conditions would have known that all that was being excluded was the negligence of the laundry, in the one case, and the garage, in the other. But here, I think the ordinary man or woman would be equally surprised and horrified to learn that if the garage was so negligent that a fire was caused which damaged their car, they would be without remedy because of the words in the condition. I can quite understand that the ordinary man or woman would consider that, because of these words, the mere fact that there was a fire would not make the garage liable. Fires can occur from a large variety of causes, only one of which is negligence on the part of the occupier of the premises, and that is by no means the most frequent cause. The ordinary man would, I think, say to himself: 'Well, what they are telling me is that if there is a fire due to any cause other than their own negligence they are not responsible for it.' To my mind, if the defendants were seeking to exclude their responsibility for a fire caused by their own negligence, they ought to have done so in far plainer language than the language here used.

There is another case which I think throws some light upon the problem before us, and that is *Olley v Marlborough Court Ltd* [1949] 1 KB 532. In that case, there was a notice in the bedroom of a private residential hotel to this effect: 'Proprietors will not hold themselves responsible for articles lost or stolen, unless handed to manageress for safe custody.' Owing to the negligence of the hotel, a thief managed to get into a room, which had been taken by the plaintiff, and stole a quantity of articles. The plaintiff brought an action against the proprietors of the hotel and succeeded in this court. In that case, there was a question as to whether the notice to which I have referred formed part of the contract between the plaintiff and the hotel proprietors; and there was also some question as to whether the hotel was an inn, in which case they would have been to some extent insurers of the goods, and another question as to whether the hotel was only a private hotel. This court considered the case on the basis that the notice did form part of the contract between the parties, and that the hotel was a private hotel, and came to the conclusion, as I have already indicated, that the plaintiff was entitled to recover. Denning LJ said at p 550: 'Ample content can be given to the notice by construing it as a warning that the hotel company is not liable, in the absence of negligence. As such, it serves a useful purpose. It is a warning to the guest that he must do his part to take care of his things himself, and, if needs be, insure them. It is unnecessary to go further and to construe the notice as a contractual exemption of the hotel company from their common law liability for negligence.'

Similarly, I think, in this case, the words at the bottom of this form can be given ample content by construing them as a warning in the sense that I have already indicated. It seems plain that if the notice in the bedroom of the hotel had read as follows: 'Proprietors will not hold themselves responsible for articles lost or stolen, or for the damage or destruction of articles caused by fire' and then there had been a full stop, and the notice went on to say that to avoid articles being lost or stolen they should be handed to the manageress for safe custody, by a parity of reasoning, the court must have come to the conclusion that the notice would not have excluded the hotel proprietors from liability for the loss of articles by a fire caused by their own negligence.

On the assumption that the reasoning of Salmon LJ would be generally adopted by the courts,[20] it should now be stated that where a contracting party is only liable for negligence an exemption clause in general terms may only be construed as covering negligence[21] but will not necessarily be so construed. Factors to take into account might well be whether the clause seeks to merely limit liability (as in *Alderslade*) or wholly exclude it (as in *Hollier*), and whether the clause is being used in a business or a consumer context.

Fundamental breach

The manifest unfairness of exemption clauses in certain instances and the concomitant judicial hostility to them has already been noted. If concentration is placed on substantive unfairness, then it appears self-evident that the more wide ranging (and potentially unfair) an exemption clause is the harder it will be to justify it. Unsurprisingly, therefore, in a significant number of post-World War II cases, the courts have held that an exemption clause was invalid, because to uphold it would be to undermine the basis of the contract itself.[22] On one analysis, these cases[23] were yet another (particularly strict) manifestation of the *contra proferentem* doctrine – the exemption clause in question not being applicable to very serious (or fundamental) breaches, unless the intention of the parties was clearly that it should apply despite the

---

20 The case was criticised when it was decided (see Barendt, 1972, in particular) and, subsequently, the House of Lords has deplored 'strained' constructions (see Lord Wilberforce in *Ailsa Craig Fishing Co Ltd v Malvern Fishing Co Ltd* [1983] 1 WLR 964).

21 As more recently was held to be the case in *The Raphael* [1982] 2 Lloyd's Rep 42.

22 See, also, UCTA 1977, s 2(1), and *Andrews Bros v Singer & Co Ltd* [1934] 1 KB 17. See, also, *Chanter v Hopkins* (1838) 4 M & W 399, p 404 (a person who had contracted to sell peas instead delivered beans).

23 See *Karsales (Harrow) Ltd v Wallis* [1956] 1 WLR 936; *Smeaton Hanscomb & Co Ltd v Sassoon I Setty & Co Ltd* [1953] 1 WLR 146; *Charterhouse Credit Co Ltd v Tolly* [1963] 2 QB 683; *Harbutt's Plasticine Ltd v Wayne Tank Co Ltd* [1970] 1 QB 477.

seriousness of the breach. On the other analysis, the cases demonstrated a rule of substantive law (not merely a rule of construction) that it was impossible for any clause (however widely drafted) to exclude liability for breaches which were 'fundamental'. Support can be found in the earlier cases for both approaches – with the 'rule of law' approach particularly prominent in the judgments of Lord Denning.

A good example of this was *Karsales (Harrow) Ltd v Wallis*[24] where a secondhand Buick car was delivered to Wallis in an appalling condition (it lacked a cylinder head, valves in the engine had been burned out and two of the pistons had been broken). Indeed, it was incapable of self-propulsion and had been towed to Wallis' premises. In an action by Karsales against Wallis for arrears, they relied on cl 3(9), which stated that 'No condition or warranty that the vehicle is roadworthy or as to its age, condition or fitness for purpose is given by the owner, or implied herein'.[25] The almost astounding decision by the county court judge in favour of Karsales was reversed by the Court of Appeal. In Denning LJ's judgment at least, there is explicit reliance on a rule of law approach.[26]

It should be noted that all these cases predate significant legislative intervention to control the misuse of exemption clauses, and the substantive doctrine was clearly developed as a consumer protection device. However, it was in practice a rather blunt instrument – applying to commercial transactions negotiated at arm's length as much as to consumer cases. In the former cases, it had the potential to operate in arbitrary fashion, upsetting perfectly fair bargains for the reasonable allocation of contractual risks – particularly as the question as to how 'fundamental' a term had to be to trigger the doctrine was itself highly uncertain.[27]

In *Suisse Atlantique Société d'Armement Maritime SA v NV Rotterdamsche Kolen Centrale*,[28] the House of Lords stated unambiguously that fundamental breach was a rule of construction and not a rule of law. In principle, anything could be excluded, so long as the words were clear enough. The notorious reluctance of the Court of Appeal under Lord Denning's tutelage wholly to 'take the point' constrained the House of Lords to reiterate even more clearly:

---

24 [1956] 1 WLR 936.

25 If read literally, this clause would seem to enable the sellers to deliver a car without an engine, or a burned-out wreck.

26 Parker LJ leans, if anything, more towards a construction approach. Birkett LJ can be read either way.

27 Clearly, it had to be more fundamental than a condition which, conventional wisdom dictated, could be excluded. That posed problems, given that a condition had, historically, long been defined as a fundamental term of a contract! Devlin J essayed a definition in *Smeaton Hanscomb v Sassoon I Setty* largely in terms of 'total non-performance ... something which underlies the whole contract so that, if it is not complied with, the performance becomes something totally different from that which the contract contemplates' (p 1470).

28 [1967] 1 AC 361.

Photo Production Ltd v Securicor Transport Ltd [1980] AC 827, HL, p 839

Lord Wilberforce: My Lords, this appeal arises from the destruction by fire of the respondents' factory involving loss and damage agreed to amount to £615,000. The question is whether the appellant is liable to the respondents for this sum.

The appellant is a company which provides security services. In 1968, it entered into a contract with the respondents by which, for a charge of £8 15 s 0d (old currency) per week, it agreed to 'provide their night patrol service, whereby four visits per night shall be made seven nights per week and two visits shall be made during the afternoon of Saturday and four visits shall be made during the day of Sunday'. The contract incorporated printed standard conditions which, in some circumstances, might exclude or limit the appellant's liability. The questions in this appeal are: (i) whether these conditions can be invoked at all in the events which happened; and (ii) if so, whether either the exclusion provision, or a provision limiting liability, can be applied on the facts. The trial judge (MacKenna J) decided these issues in favour of the appellant. The Court of Appeal decided issue (i) in the respondents' favour, invoking the doctrine of fundamental breach. Waller LJ in addition would have decided for the respondents on issue (ii).

What happened was that, on a Sunday night, the duty employee of the appellant was one Musgrove. It was not suggested that he was unsuitable for the job or that the appellant was negligent in employing him. He visited the factory at the correct time, but, when inside, he deliberately started a fire by throwing a match onto some cartons. The fire got out of control and a large part of the premises was burnt down. Though what he did was deliberate, it was not established that he intended to destroy the factory. The judge's finding was in these words: 'Whether Musgrove intended to light only a small fire (which was the very least he meant to do) or whether he intended to cause much more serious damage, and, in either case, what was the reason for his act, are mysteries I am unable to solve.'

This, and it is important to bear it in mind when considering the judgments in the Court of Appeal, falls short of a finding that Musgrove deliberately burnt or intended to burn the respondents' factory.

The condition upon which the appellant relies reads, relevantly, as follows: 'Under no circumstances shall the company [Securicor] be responsible for any injurious act or default by any employee of the company unless such act or default could have been foreseen and avoided by the exercise of due diligence on the part of the company as his employer; nor, in any event, shall the company be held responsible for: (a) any loss suffered by the customer through burglary, theft, fire or any other cause, except insofar as such loss is solely attributable to the negligence of the company's employees acting within the course of their employment ...'

There are further provisions limiting to stated amounts the liability of the appellant upon which it relies in the alternative if held not to be totally exempt.

It is first necessary to decide upon the correct approach to a case such as this where it is sought to invoke an exception or limitation clause in the contract.

The approach of Lord Denning MR in the Court of Appeal was to consider, first, whether the breach was 'fundamental'. If so, he said, the court itself deprives the party of the benefit of an exemption or limitation clause ([1978] 1 WLR 856, p 863). Shaw and Waller LJJ substantially followed him in this argument.

Lord Denning MR in this was following the earlier decision of the Court of Appeal and, in particular, his own judgment in *Harbutt's Plasticine Ltd v Wayne Tank & Pump Co Ltd* [1970] 1 QB 447. In that case, Lord Denning MR distinguished two cases: (a) the case where as the result of a breach of contract the innocent party has, and exercises, the right to bring the contract to an end; (b) the case where the breach automatically brings the contract to an end, without the innocent party having to make an election whether to terminate the contract or to continue it. In the first case, the Master of the Rolls, purportedly applying this House's decision in *Suisse Atlantique Société d'Armement Maritime SA v NV Rotterdamsche Kolen Centrale* [1967] 1 AC 361, but, in effect, two citations from two of their Lordships' speeches extracted a rule of law that the 'termination' of the contract brings it, and with it the exclusion clause, to an end. The *Suisse Atlantique* case, in his view, 'affirms the long line of cases in this court that when one party has been guilty of a fundamental breach of the contract ... and the other side accepts it, so that the contract comes to an end...then the guilty party cannot rely on an exception or limitation clause to escape from his liability for the breach' (*Harbutt's* case [1970] 1 QB 447, p 467).

He then applied the same principle to the second case.

My Lords, whatever the intrinsic merit of this doctrine, as to which I shall have something to say later, it is clear to me that so far from following this House's decision in the *Suisse Atlantique*, it is directly opposed to it and that the whole purpose and tenor of the *Suisse Atlantique* was to repudiate it. The lengthy, and perhaps I may say sometimes indigestible speeches of their Lordships, are correctly summarised in the headnote – holding No 3 [1967] 1 AC 361, p 362 – 'That the question whether an exceptions clause was applicable where there was a fundamental breach of contract was one of the true construction of the contract.' That there was any rule of law by which exceptions clauses are eliminated, or deprived of effect, regardless of their terms, or the view of Viscount Dilhorne, Lord Hodson, or of myself. The passages invoked for the contrary view of a rule of law consist only of short extracts from two of the speeches – on any view a minority. But the case for the doctrine does not even go so far as that. Lord Reid, in my respectful opinion, and I recognise that I may not be the best judge of this matter, in his speech read as a whole, cannot be claimed as a supporter of a rule of law. Indeed, he expressly disagreed with the Master of the Rolls' observations in two previous cases (*Karsales (Harrow) Ltd v Wallis* [1956] 1 WLR 936 and *UGS Finance Ltd v National Mortgage Bank of Greece and National Bank of Greece SA* [1964] 1 Lloyd's Rep 446, in which he had put forward the 'rule of law' doctrine). In order to show how close the disapproved doctrine is to that sought to be revived in *Harbutt's* case, I shall quote one passage from *Karsales* [1956] 1 WLR 936, p 940: 'Notwithstanding earlier cases which might suggest the contrary, it is now settled that exempting clauses of this kind, no matter how widely they are expressed, only avail the party when he is carrying out his contract in its essential respects. He is not allowed to use them as a cover for misconduct or indifference or to enable him to turn a blind eye to his obligations. They do not avail him when he is guilty of a breach which goes to the root of the contract.'

Lord Reid comments at p 401 as to this that he could not deduce from the authorities cited in *Karsales* that the proposition stated in the judgments could be regarded as in any way 'settled law'. His conclusion is stated on p 405: 'In my view, no such rule of law ought to be adopted' – adding that there is room for legislative reform.

My Lords, in the light of this, the passage cited by Lord Denning MR [1970] 1 QB 447, p 465 has to be considered. For convenience, I re-state it: 'If fundamental breach is established, the next question is what effect, if any, that has on the applicability of other terms of the contract. This question has often arisen with regard to clauses excluding liability, in whole or in part, of the party in breach. I do not think that there is generally much difficulty where the innocent party has elected to treat the breach as a repudiation, bring the contract to an end and sue for damages. Then, the whole contract has ceased to exist including the exclusion clause, and I do not see how that clause can then be used to exclude an action for loss which will be suffered by the innocent party after it has ceased to exist, such as loss of the profit which would have accrued if the contract had run its full term.' (*Suisse Atlantique* [1967] 1 AC 361, p 398.)

It is with the utmost reluctance that, not forgetting the 'beams' that may exist elsewhere, I have to detect here a mote of ambiguity or perhaps even of inconsistency. What is referred to is 'loss which will be suffered by the innocent party after [the contract] has ceased to exist' and I venture to think that all that is being said, rather elliptically, relates only to what is to happen in the future, and is not a proposition as to the immediate consequences caused by the breach: if it were that would be inconsistent with the full and reasoned discussion which follows.

It is only because of Lord Reid's great authority in the law that I have found it necessary to embark on what in the end may be superfluous analysis. For I am convinced that, with the possible exception of Lord Upjohn, whose critical passage, when read in full, is somewhat ambiguous, their Lordships, fairly read, can only be taken to have rejected those suggestions for a rule of law which had appeared in the Court of Appeal and to have firmly stated that the question is one of construction, not merely of course of the exclusion clause alone, but of the whole contract.

Much has been written about the *Suisse Atlantique* case. Each speech has been subjected to various degrees of analysis and criticism, much of it constructive. Speaking for myself I am conscious of imperfections of terminology, though sometimes in good company. But I do not think that I should be conducing to the clarity of the law by adding to what was already too ample a discussion a further analysis which in turn would have to be interpreted. I have no second thoughts as to the main proposition that the question whether, and to what extent, an exclusion clause is to be applied to a fundamental breach, or a breach of a fundamental term, or indeed to any breach of contract, is a matter of construction of the contract. Many difficult questions arise and will continue to arise in the infinitely varied situations in which contracts come to be breached – by repudiatory breaches, accepted or not, by anticipatory breaches, by breaches of conditions or of various terms and whether by negligent, or deliberate action or otherwise. But there are ample resources in the normal rules of contract law for dealing with these without the superimposition of a judicially invented rule of law. I am content to leave the matter there with some supplementary observations.

(1) The doctrine of 'fundamental breach', in spite of its imperfections and doubtful parentage, has served a useful purpose. There was a large number of problems, productive of injustice, in which it was worse than unsatisfactory to leave exception clauses to operate. Lord Reid referred to these in the *Suisse Atlantique* case [1967] 1 AC 361, p 406, pointing out at the same time that the doctrine of fundamental breach was a dubious specific. But, since then, Parliament has taken a hand: it has passed the Unfair Contract Terms Act 1977. This Act applies to consumer contracts and those based on standard terms and enables exception clauses to be applied with regard to what is just and reasonable. It is significant that Parliament refrained from legislating over the whole field of contract. After this Act, in commercial matters generally, when the parties are not of unequal bargaining power, and when risks are normally borne by insurance, not only is the case for judicial intervention undemonstrated, but there is everything to be said, and this seems to have been Parliament's intention, for leaving the parties free to apportion the risks as they think fit and for respecting their decisions.

At the stage of negotiation as to the consequences of a breach, there is everything to be said for allowing the parties to estimate their respective claims according to the contractual provisions they have themselves made, rather than for facing them with a legal complex so uncertain as the doctrine of fundamental breach must be. What, for example, would have been the position of the respondents' factory if instead of being destroyed it had been damaged, slightly or moderately or severely? At what point does the doctrine (with what logical justification I have not understood) decide, *ex post facto*, that the breach was (factually) fundamental before going on to ask whether legally it is to be regarded as fundamental? How is the date of 'termination' to be fixed? Is it the date of the incident causing the damage, or the date of the innocent party's election, or some other date? All these difficulties arise from the doctrine and are left unsolved by it.

In *George Mitchell (Chesterhall) Ltd v Finney Lock Seeds Ltd*,[29] Lord Bridge observed that the *Photo Production* case had given 'the final quietus to the doctrine that a "fundamental breach" of contract deprived the party in breach of the benefit of clauses in the contract excluding or limiting his liability'. Particularly given that the main stimulus for the development of the

---

29   [1983] 2 AC 803, p 813.

substantive doctrine, the lack of adequate consumer protection against 'small print' denial of basic rights has now largely been redressed by the Unfair Contract Terms Act 1977, it seems that the substantive doctrine of 'fundamental breach' has 'had its day'. This, of course, still leaves the problem of the status of the earlier (principally Court of Appeal) decisions. In *Photo Production*, the House of Lords did overrule a small number of cases,[30] but the majority remained unscathed. Perhaps it is simplest to say that even on a 'rule of construction' approach, it is hard to see that the majority of decisions could have gone any other way (*Karsales* is a good example of this). A final point is that the practical importance of the cases in this area will now be confined to situations in which the validity of the exemption clause is not affected by the Unfair Contract Terms Act 1977.

Limitation clauses

A consistent theme in recent case law (particularly at House of Lords level) is that limitation clauses (even less than wholesale exclusions of liability) are not to be subjected to 'strained construction', since judicial hostility to them is less.[31] These judicial observations reflect the more limited 'substantive unfairness' which limitation clauses are likely to manifest:

Ailsa Craig Fishing Co Ltd v Malvern Fishing Co Ltd [1983] 1 WLR 964, HL

Lord Wilberforce (p 966): One must not strive to create ambiguities by strained construction, as I think the appellants have striven to do. The relevant words must be given, if possible, their natural, plain meaning. Clauses of limitation are not regarded by the courts with the same hostility as clauses of exclusion; this is because they must be related to other contractual terms, in particular to the risks to which the defending party may be exposed, the remuneration which he receives and possibly also the opportunity of the other party to insure.

Lord Fraser (p 970): In my opinion, these principles are not applicable in their full rigour when considering the effect of clauses merely limiting liability. Such clauses will, of course, be read *contra proferentem* and must be clearly expressed, but there is no reason why they should be judged by the specially exacting standards which we applied to exclusion and indemnity clauses. The reason for imposing such standards on these clauses is the inherent improbability that the other party to a contract including such a clause intended to release the proferens from a liability that would otherwise fall upon him. But there is no such high degree of improbability that he would agree to a limitation of the liability of the *proferens*.

---

30   Eg, *Charterhouse Credit v Tolly* [1963] 2 QB 683 and *Harbutt's Plasticine Ltd v Wayne Tank Co Ltd* [1970] 1 QB 477.

31   A point echoed in UCTA 1977, s 11(4), below.

LEGISLATIVE INTERVENTION

As noted earlier, there is a relatively long history of legislative involvement aimed at curbing the excesses of exemption clauses.[32] However, the first statute of general importance came in 1973 with the Supply of Goods (Implied Terms) Act, which controlled the exclusion or restriction of liability for breach of terms implied under the (then) Sale of Goods Act 1893. The 1973 provisions were the product of the first Law Commission *Report on Exemption Clauses* (Law Com No 24, 1969) and the subsequent (and much more wide ranging) statute, the Unfair Contract Terms Act 1977, again adopted the general approach (and many of the detailed recommendations) of the second Law Commission Report (No 69, 1975) – although, in itself, it was the product of a Private Members' Bill. The Unfair Contract Terms Act 1977 is now the principal mechanism for the control of exemption clauses, but before examining its provisions, it is instructive to examine some of the comments made by the Law Commission in justifying the need for more wide ranging legislative intervention:

Law Commission, *Second Report on Exemption Clauses in Contracts*, Law Com No 69, 1975, London: HMSO

11 The Case for Control

It is clear that exemption clauses are much used both in dealings with private individuals and in purely commercial transactions. We are in no doubt that, in many cases, they operate against the public interest and that the prevailing judicial attitude of suspicion, or indeed of hostility, to such clauses is well founded. All too often, they are introduced in ways which result in the party affected by them remaining ignorant of their presence or import until it is too late. That party, even if he knows of the exemption clause, will often be unable to appreciate what he may lose by accepting it. In any case, he may not have sufficient bargaining strength to refuse to accept it. The result is that the risk of carelessness or of failure to achieve satisfactory standards of performance is thrown on to the party who is not responsible for it or who is unable to guard against it. Moreover, by excluding liability for such carelessness or failure, the economic pressures to maintain high standards of performance are reduced. There is no doubt that the misuse of these clauses is objectionable. Some are unjustified. Others, however, may operate fairly or unfairly, efficiently or inefficiently, depending on the circumstances: for example, the cost and practicability of insurance may be factors in determining how liability should be apportioned between two contracting parties. The problem of devising satisfactory methods of controlling the use of these clauses and, indeed, of identifying some of them has proved both difficult and complicated.

---

32 Certainly as far back as the Canals and Railways Act 1854. Prior to 1973, probably the most significant provisions are to be found in the Road Traffic Act 1960, prohibiting the exclusion of liability for death or personal injury, caused by negligence, of passengers in public service vehicles.

146

... we do not propose to define exemption clauses in general terms; we regard this expression not as a legal term of art, but as a convenient label for a number of provisions which may be mischievous in broadly the same way. Their mischief is that they deprive or may deprive the person against whom they may be invoked either of certain specific rights which social policy requires that he should have (for example the right of a buyer in a consumer sale to be supplied with goods of merchantable quality, or the right of a person to whom a service has been supplied to a reasonable standard of care and skill on the part of the supplier) or of rights which the promisee reasonably believed that the promisor had conferred upon him.

The Unfair Contract Terms Act 1977[33]

The Act, despite its importance and the amount of attention it has received, is not the easiest piece of legislation to come to terms with. This is less to do with the inherent difficulty of the concepts it deploys than with its somewhat incoherent structure (a result perhaps of its 'private member' origins?). The Act begins with what is (in part) a definitions section (s 1(3)). Different types of control seem to appear randomly and a number of key concepts are left (at most) incompletely defined, most noticeably, the concept of 'business'. A section by section commentary of the Act is probably not the easiest way to understand it; instead, a number of the key ideas in the Act are examined first and then attention is given to the main controls which the Act imposes on different sorts of exempting provisions.

What is an exemption clause?

It seems that the drafters of the legislation were astute to the possibility of ingenious drafters seeking to minimise the Act's impact, for example by 'dressing up' an exclusion of liability in some other garb, s 13(1), therefore, seeks to cast the Act's net relatively widely:

Unfair Contract Terms Act 1977

13

(1) To the extent that this Part of this Act prevents the exclusion or restriction of any liability it also prevents:

    (a) making the liability or its enforcement subject to restrictive or onerous conditions;

---

33 Considerable literature has been generated by the Act – the following either comment generally on the Act at its inception (Coote, 1978; Sealy, 1978) or review it generally in the light of case law developments (Adams and Brownsword, 1988b).

(b) excluding or restricting any right or remedy in respect of the liability, or subjecting a person to any prejudice in consequence of his pursing any such right or remedy;

(c) excluding or restricting rules of evidence or procedure,

and (to that extent) ss 2 and 5 to 7 also prevent excluding or restricting liability by reference to terms and notices which exclude or restrict the relevant obligation or duty.

(2) But an agreement in writing to submit present or future differences to arbitration is not to be treated under this Part of this Act as excluding or restricting any liability.

The Act, therefore, appears to cover the majority of clauses which would seek (ostensibly) to curtail the scope of primary contractual duties rather than merely those which are defensive in form.[34]

If there was any doubt that the 'Coote' approach[35] is not to be adopted, it came in *Phillips Products Ltd v Hyland and Hampstead Plant Hire Co Ltd*,[36] where the plaintiff hired JCB excavators from the defendant plant hire company on a number of occasions. On the occasion in question, the JCB driver (Hyland) drove the excavator into one of the plaintiff's buildings, causing considerable damage. Negligence was admitted, the argument at the trial centering on whether condition 8 of Hampstead's standard terms of hire operated as a defence to the plaintiff's claim. As relevant, it stated that drivers such as Hyland:

... shall, for all purposes in connection with their employment in the working of the plant, be regarded as the servants or agents of the hirer, who alone shall be responsible for all claims arising in connection with the operation of the plant by the said drivers and operators.

Amongst the questions which the court had to consider was whether there was 'negligence' within the meaning of s 1(1) of the Unfair Contract Terms Act 1977 and (if so) whether condition 8 was an attempt to 'exclude or restrict' such liability within the meaning of s 2. In many respects, these issues interlock, in that the essence of the defendant's argument was that there had been no 'exclusion' of liability here, merely an allocation of responsibilities between the parties at the outset which had placed responsibility for the driver on the plaintiffs. The Court of Appeal (upholding the judgment of Jones J) robustly rejected the defendant's arguments. First, the court took the view that if a clause (by narrowly confining the primary duty) could preclude the application of the 1977 Act, it would make a nonsense of the primary purpose of Parliament. The court has to leave out of account, at this stage the exemption clause. Secondly (again implicitly rejecting the 'Coote' approach), Slade LJ stated that: (at p 665):

---

34 See *op cit*, fn 10.

35 See *op cit*, fn 10.

36 [1987] 1 WLR 659, considered below in relation to the reasonableness test.

A transfer of liability from A to B necessarily and inevitably involves the exclusion of liability so far as A is concerned.

Later (at p 666):

In applying s 2(2), it is not relevant to consider whether the form of a condition is such that it can aptly be given the label of an 'exclusion' or 'restriction' clause. To decide whether a person 'excludes' liability by reference to a contract term, you look at the effect of the term ... The effect here is beyond doubt.[37]

If any doubt remained on this point, it was removed by the House of Lords in *Smith v Eric S Bush (A Firm)*.[38] In this case, the plaintiff applied to a building society for a mortgage to assist her in purchasing a house. The building society instructed the defendants, a firm of surveyors and valuers, to carry out a visual inspection of the house and to report on its value and any matter likely to affect it value. The defendants' valuer, who carried out the inspection, noticed that two chimney breasts had been removed but he failed to check whether the chimneys had been left adequately supported. His report stated that no essential repairs were necessary. The mortgage application form and the valuation report contained a disclaimer of liability for the accuracy of the report covering both the building society and the valuer. The plaintiff was also informed that the report was not a structural survey and she was advised to obtain independent professional advice. The building society, pursuant to an agreement with the plaintiff who paid an inspection fee, supplied a copy of the report to her, and she relied on it and purchased the house without any further survey. The chimneys were not adequately supported and one of them subsequently collapsed. The plaintiff claimed damages from the defendants in negligence and the defendants relied, *inter alia*, on the disclaimer in the report and the application form as exempting them from liability to the plaintiff. The plaintiff claimed that the defendants were precluded by s 2(2) of the Unfair Contract Terms Act 1977 from so excluding their liability, since the disclaimer did not satisfy the requirement of reasonableness set out in s 11(3) of the Act. The judge gave judgment for the plaintiff. The Court of Appeal dismissed the defendants' appeal.

In rejecting the defendants' further appeal, the House also rejected an argument that a disclaimer by the surveyors could preclude any primary duty of care arising, and so leave the 1977 Act redundant:[39]

---

37 Interestingly, it appears that the same condition can sometimes operate as an exemption clause and sometimes not, depending on the way it functions in the particular circumstances. See (on the same clause as in *Phillips Products Ltd v Hyland*) that of *Thompson v Lohan (Plant Hire) Ltd* [1987] 1 WLR 645 – as to which, see Sealy, 1988 (Adams and Brownsword, 1988a).

38 [1990] 1 AC 831, HL.

39 The case directly concerned a claim in tort for negligence on the part of a surveyor, despite the lack of a direct contractual tie between the surveyor and the prospective purchaser. However, the court's comments on this point at least, appear to be of general application.

Smith v Eric S Bush (A Firm) [1990] 1 AC 831, p 856

Lord Griffiths: In my view, this construction fails to give due weight to the provisions of two further sections of the Act. Section 11(3) provides: 'In relation to a notice (not being a notice having contractual effect), the requirement of reasonableness under this Act is that it should be fair and reasonable to allow reliance on it, having regard to all the circumstances obtaining when the liability arose or (but for the notice) would have arisen.'

And s 13(1): 'To the extent that this Part of this Act prevents the exclusion or restriction of any liability it also prevents: (a) making the liability or its enforcement subject to restrictive or onerous conditions; (b) excluding or restricting any right or remedy in respect of the liability, or subjecting a person to any prejudice in consequence of his pursuing any such right or remedy; (c) excluding or restricting rules of evidence or procedure, and (to that extent) ss 2 and 5 to 7 also prevent excluding or restricting liability by reference to terms and notices which exclude or restrict the relevant obligation or duty.'

I read these provisions as introducing a 'but for' test in relation to the notice excluding liability. They indicate that the existence of the common law duty to take reasonable care, referred to in s 1(1)(b), is to be judged by considering whether it would exist 'but for' the notice excluding liability. The result of taking the notice into account when assessing the existence of a duty of care would result in removing all liability for negligent misstatements from the protection of the Act. It is permissible to have regard to the Second Report of the Law Commission on Exemption Clauses, 1975 (Law Com, No 69), which is the genesis of the Unfair Contract Terms Act 1977 as an aid to the construction of the Act. Paragraph 127 of that Report reads: 'Our recommendations in this part of the report are intended to apply to exclusions of liability for negligence where the liability is incurred in the course of a person's business. We consider that they should apply even in cases where the person seeking to rely on the exemption clause was under no legal obligation (such as a contractual obligation) to carry out the activity. This means that, for example, conditions attached to a licence to enter on to land, and disclaimers of liability made where information or advice is given, should be subject to control ...'

I have no reason to think that Parliament did not intend to follow this advice and the wording of the Act is, in my opinion, apt to give effect to that intention. This view of the construction of the Act is also supported by the judgment of Slade LJ in *Philips Products Ltd v Hyland* (Note) [1987] 1 WLR 659, when he rejected a similar argument in relation to the construction of a contractual term excluding negligence.

Business liability

With limited exceptions, most noticeably s 6(4) and s 8 (amending s 3 of the Misrepresentation Act 1967), s 1(3) provides that the Act only applies to 'business' liability:

Unfair Contract Terms Act 1977

1

(1) For the purposes of this Part of this Act, 'negligence' means the breach:

    (a) of any obligation, arising from the express or implied terms of a contract, to take reasonable care or exercise reasonable skill in the performance of the contract;

    (b) of any common law duty to take reasonable care or exercise reasonable skill (but not any stricter duty);

    (c) of the common duty of care imposed by the Occupiers' Liability Act 1957 or the Occupiers' Liability Act (Northern Ireland) 1957.

(2) This Part of this Act is subject to Pt III; and, in relation to contracts, the operation of ss 2 to 4 and 7 is subject to the exceptions made by Sched 1.

(3) In the case of both contract and tort, ss 2 to 7 apply (except where the contrary is stated in s 6(4)) only to business liability, that is, liability for breach of obligations or duties arising:

    (a) from things done or to be done by a person in the course of a business (whether his own business or another's); or

    (b) from the occupation of premises used for business purposes of the occupier; and references to liability are to be read accordingly but liability of an occupier of premises for breach of an obligation or duty towards a person obtaining access to the premises for recreational or educational purposes, being liability for loss or damage suffered by reason of the dangerous state of the premises, is not a business liability of the occupier unless granting that person such access for the purposes contained falls within the business purposes of the occupier.

(4) In relation to any breach of duty or obligation, it is immaterial for any purpose of this Part of this Act whether the breach was inadvertent or intentional, or whether liability for it arises directly or vicariously.

It might be expected that, given the importance of the concept of 'business' liability to the scope of the Act, it would be closely defined in the Act. Such expectations would be disappointed!

Aside from s 1(3), there is a further (partial) definition in s 14, to the effect that a 'business includes a profession and the activities of any government department or local or public authority.'

This is, of course, far from all inclusive and leaves open what other 'business purposes' the Act envisages. For example, is a 'profit motive' essential? Could analogies be drawn with the case law on business rates, taxation and business premises? Is a charity shop in business? Does a student union operate a business? Does a private club holding a jumble sale to raise revenue act in a business capacity? Questions come more readily to mind than answers. If a 'mischief' or 'purposive' approach were to be adopted in a marginal case, reliance could be placed on the Second Law Commission Report of 1975, which (in para 9) broadly took the view that purely private transactions were not likely to give rise to the same problems concerning the use of exemption clauses as commercial transactions. All areas, then, not clearly private would come within the Act. Certainly, it would be consistent with the policy underlying the 1977 Act to enable it to apply relatively widely.

Dealing as consumer

The scope and consequent definition of 'dealing as a consumer' is too limited to wholly illuminate the 'business' conundrum posed above (although it does shed some light on it). It functions primarily with regard to the differential tests on those in 'business' and 'consumer' as set out in ss 6 and 7, although it also has impact in relation to s 3 (below).[40] A definition of 'dealing as a consumer' can be found in s 12:

Unfair Contract Terms Act 1977

12

(1) A party to a contract 'deals as consumer' in relation to another party if:

    (a) he neither makes the contract in the course of a business nor holds himself out as doing so; and

    (b) the other party does make the contract in the course of a business; and

    (c) in the case of a contract governed by the law of sale of goods or hire-purchase, or by s 7 of this Act, the goods passing under or in pursuance of the contract are of a type ordinarily supplied for private use or consumption.

(2) But on a sale by auction or by competitive tender the buyer is not in any circumstances to be regarded as dealing as consumer.

(3) Subject to this, it is for those claiming that a party does not deal as consumer to show that he does not.

Rather surprisingly in *R & B Customs Brokers Ltd v United Dominions Trust Ltd*,[41] it was held by the Court of Appeal that there may be a consumer sale, even where the buyer operates a business, provided the transaction is only incidental to the business activity, rather than being an integral part of that business. The company here was held to have dealt as a consumer in buying a

---

40 Sections 6 and 7 control attempts to exclude statutory rights under sales, hire purchases and other supplies of goods. Section 3 is something of a catch-all section concerning contractual liability.

41 [1988] 1 WLR 321

car for the use of one of its directors, having only made two or three such purchases in the past.[42, 43]

Dillon LJ (at p 330) said:

> There are some transactions which are clearly integral parts of the business concerned, and these should be held to have been carried out in the course of those businesses ... There are other transactions, however, such as the purchase of the car in the present case, which are at highest only incidental to the carrying on of the relevant business; here a degree of regularity is required before it can be said that they are an integral part of the business carried on, and so entered into in the course of that business.

Other points worth noting are that purporting to be in business may be tantamount to being in business (where does this leave the private user of a trade card?). Further, that there is an additional requirement in supply of goods cases that the goods are of a type 'ordinarily' supplied for private use or consumption (where does this leave the purchaser, say, of a jukebox or a pinball table for her own home?). Finally, in relation to auctions and competitive tenders no one is to be treated as a consumer. Is this in any way realistic given the advantage which skill and knowledge alone can bring to bear at auction?

Controls imposed by the Act

In principle, numerous control mechanisms are open to Parliament when legislating afresh, as was the case when the 1977 Act was passed. The provisions could focus on procedural unfairness by providing for statutory cooling-off periods[44] or for defences based on the unconscionable way in which the contract was brought about.[45] Alternatively, they could focus on substantive unfairness by declaring various provisions to be void or by subjecting them to a reasonableness test. Finally they could quasi-criminalise the law by channelling control through some central regulatory body, such as the Office of Fair Trading.[46] In the event, the primary focus of the 1977 Act

---

42 See Price, 1989. Beale, Bishop and Furmston, 1998, p 706, question whether this is a sensible outcome, since such a purchaser may have considerable bargaining power, to obtain better terms.

43 In *Stevenson v Rogers* [1999] 1 WLR 1064, the Court of Appeal distinguished *R & B Customs Brokers* in holding that, for the purpose of Sale of Goods Act 1979, s 14(2), a wide interpretation was to be given to the phase 'in the course of a business', so that a fisherman engaging in a one-off transaction to sell his fishing boat was still acting 'in the course of business' in doing so. As to whether the cases can be reconciled, see de Lacey, 1999.

44 Eg, Consumer Credit Act 1974, s 67, and the Consumer Protection (Cancellation of Contracts, etc) Regulations 1987 (SI 1987/2117).

45 Eg, as is true (in part) concerning the law on undue influence or on penalty clauses.

46 As is (in part) the case under the Unfair Terms in Consumer Contracts Regulations 1999, regs 10–15 (see below).

was upon substantive unfairness, via the twin controls of voidness and a reasonableness test.

As regards voidness, there is little more that requires stating. Any contractual provision declared to be void within ss 2(1), 5, 6(1) and (2), 7(1), 7(2) and 7(3A) of the Unfair Contract Terms Act 1977 (considered below) is simply of no legal effect and can be disregarded in any dispute concerning the contract in question.

As regards reasonableness, the situation is considerably more complex.

The reasonableness test

Other than the sections mentioned immediately above, the 1977 Act, in line with the Law Commission's thinking in their Second Report, generally adopts controls based on the reasonableness (or otherwise) of the provisions under scrutiny. By this stratagem, it is clearly envisaged that a court will be able to sift all the evidence and determine on the particular facts whether the particular clause is reasonable or not, rather then being constrained by some *a priori* rule.[47] The reasonableness test is set out below:

Unfair Contract Terms Act 1977

11

(1) In relation to a contract term, the requirement of reasonableness for the purposes of this Part of this Act, s 3 of the Misrepresentation Act 1967 and s 3 of the Misrepresentation Act (Northern Ireland) 1967 is that the term shall have been a fair and reasonable one to be included having regard to the circumstances which were, or ought reasonably to have been, known to or in the contemplation of the parties when the contract was made.

(2) In determining for the purposes of s 6 or 7 above whether a contract term satisfies the requirement of reasonableness, regard shall be had in particular to the matters specified in Schedule 2 to this Act; but this sub-section does not prevent the court or arbitrator from holding, in accordance with any rule of law, that a term which purports to exclude or restrict any relevant liability is not a term of the contract.

(3) In relation to a notice (not being a notice having contractual effect), the requirement of reasonableness under this Act is that it should be fair and reasonable to allow reliance on it, having regard to all the circumstances obtaining when the liability arose or (but for the notice) would have arisen.

---

47 This flexibility is easier to understand where the controls may apply to consumers and non-consumers alike (as is true, in general, with the UCTA 1977). By way of contrast, the Unfair Terms in Consumer Contracts Regulations 1999 (below) simply render unfair clauses affected invalid – but equally, they only apply to consumer contracts.

(4) Where, by reference to a contract term or notice a person seeks to restrict liability to a specified sum of money, and the question arises (under this or any other Act) whether the term or notice satisfies the requirement of reasonableness, regard shall be had in particular (but without prejudice to sub-s (2) above in the case of contract terms) to:

(a) the resources which he could expect to be available to him for the purpose of meeting the liability should it arise; and

(b) how far it was open to him to cover himself by insurance.

(5) It is for those claiming that a contract term or notice satisfies the requirement of reasonableness to show that it does.

Schedule 2: 'Guidelines' For Application of Reasonableness Test

Section 11(2) and 24(2)

The matters to which regard is to be had in particular for the purposes of ss 6(3), 7(3) and (4), 20 and 21 are any of the following which appear to be relevant:

(a) the strength of the bargaining positions of the parties to each other, taking into account (among other things) alternative means by which the customer's requirements could have been met;

(b) whether the customer received an inducement to agree to the term, or in accepting it had an opportunity of entering into a similar contract with other persons, but without having to accept a similar term;

(c) whether the customer knew or ought reasonably to have known of the existence and extent of the term (having regard, among other things, to any custom of the trade and any previous course of dealing between the parties);

(d) where the term excludes or restricts any relevant liability if some condition is not complied with, whether it was reasonable at the time of the contract to expect that compliance with that condition would be practicable;

(e) whether the goods were manufactured, processed or adapted to the special order of the customer.

It should be noted that this test could easily (and perhaps more helpfully) be termed a fairness test (see s 11(1)). It has little to do with reasonableness in the sense of adequacy (as in reasonable notice) and everything to do with reasonableness in the sense of fairness.[48] Perhaps the point of most overall importance is that to be found in s 11(1) – that the test to be generally adopted is that of whether the term was a fair and reasonable one to have been

---

48 If it were so framed, it would come (superficially at least) closer to the 'good faith' requirement which is commonly found in civil law codes (eg, BGB (Germany), para 242) and is now central to the Unfair Terms in Consumer Contracts Regulations 1999.

included in the contract in the first place. As regards non-contractual notices, the issue to be decided is one of reasonableness of reliance according to s 11(3). The s 11(1) test differs from the reasonableness of reliance test adopted by the Supply of Goods (Implied Terms) Act 1973 (to which this part of the 1977 Act otherwise bears a reasonably close resemblance) and has generated a fair amount of controversy.[49] Interestingly, the 1977 Act here adopts the proposal of the Scottish Law Commission Report (1975, para 177), the English Commission having proposed a continuation of the existing reliance test (para 183).

The English Law Commission felt that judicial discretion, to take account of all circumstances, pre and post-contract, should not be curtailed. The Scottish Commission reasoned that a reliance test might undermine the planning of relationships and the allocation of risk(s), normally associated with commercial contracts. Whatever else, it seems entirely clear that (unless some form of severance is possible) a clause which, as drafted, is unreasonably wide (on a 'reasonable' construction!) will not be saved merely because it operates fairly in the particular circumstances. This is a clear encouragement for careful and conservative contract planning and drafting.

Secondly, the burden of proof is clearly placed on the person seeking to justify the reasonableness of the clause (s 11(5)). Thirdly, there are distinct 'guidelines' in s 11(4) concerning limitation clauses.[50] Finally, the specific guidelines in Sched 2 are only mandatory in relation to ss 6(3), 7(3) and (4) (in England and Wales), but are likely to be considered by the courts (or at least the same or similar factors) in other cases.[51]

An over-arching question, is whether cases on s 11 and Sched 2 can operate as precedents, or whether the courts are operating a largely unfettered discretion in every case? It seems clear, and has been suggested already,[52] that those who framed the 1977 Act intended judicial discretion to be wide. However, it has also been suggested that one important function of the adoption of a time of incorporation test could be to facilitate judicial consistency – the same types of clauses in the same types of contracts being given broadly the same interpretation.[53] This would suggest a role for appellate courts in helping frame the right questions for trial judges to take

---

49 Adams and Brownsword, 1998b, argue that, if nothing else it is aimed at encouraging judges to infuse some degree of consistency and generality into their rulings and to avoid one-off approaches – particularly to the regulation of commercial standard form exemptions.

50 It might be speculated as to whether they might have had an impact on *George Mitchell (Chesterhall) Ltd v Finney Lock Seeds Ltd* [1983] 2 AC 803 (considered below) had they been in force at that time – particularly s 11(4)(b).

51 An approach explicitly adopted in *Singer (UK) Ltd v Tees & Hartlepool Park Authority* [1988] 2 Lloyd's Rep 164; and *The Flammar Pride* [1990] 1 Lloyd's Rep 434, p 439, and implicitly in *Phillips Products Ltd v Hyland* (see above).

52 See *op cit*, fn 47.

53 See *op cit*, fn 48.

into account (and the wrong ones for them to ignore!). Inevitably, the number of successful appeals is likely to be small, as long as the judge at first instance has not self evidently misdirected him/herself the scope for appellate review is limited. However, in principle, there would seem to be a clear role for appellate courts in helping to shape or channel the application of the reasonableness test. Without this there is the obvious criticism that a judicially administered reasonableness requirement is conducive to considerable uncertainty in the law.[54] Such judicial comment as there has been on this point is a little ambiguous:

George Mitchell (Chesterhall) Ltd v Finney Lock Seeds Ltd [1983] 2 AC 803, HL, p 815

Lord Bridge: ... in having regard to the various matters to which ... s 11 of the Act of 1977 direct(s) attention, the court must entertain a whole range of considerations, put them in the scales on one side or the other, and decide at the end of the day on which side the balance comes down. There will sometimes be room for a legitimate difference of judicial opinion as to what the answer should be, where it will be impossible to say that one view is demonstrably wrong, and the other demonstrably right. It must follow, in my view, that, when asked to review such a decision on appeal, the appellate court should treat the original decision with the utmost respect, and refrain from interference with it unless satisfied that it proceeded upon some erroneous principle or was plainly and obviously wrong.

In *Phillips Products Ltd v Hyland*,[55] Slade LJ (after adopting Lord Bridge's remarks) went on to add that 'our conclusion on the particular facts of this case should not be treated as a binding precedent in other cases where similar clauses fall to be considered, but the evidence of the surrounding circumstances may be very different', This would seem to leave appellate courts with a very limited role in promoting rational and orderly development of the law.

On the other hand, in *George Mitchell (Chesterhall) Ltd v Finney Lock Seeds Ltd*, Lord Bridge, rather confusingly, stated that, concerning decisions on the reasonableness test, 'it would not be accurate to describe such a decision as an exercise of discretion',[56] which suggests, at least, that there are matters here for appellate courts to get their teeth into.[57]

---

54 See Treitel, 1981, pp 13–15. Both Law Commissions in their 1975 reports accepted that this was the case (paras 64–68), but (overall) felt that the advantage of the 'test' (flexibility and selectivity) outweighed the disadvantages (para 170).

55 [1987] 1 WLR 659.

56 [1983] 2 AC 803, p 815, HL.

57 Adams and Brownsword, 1988b, find *George Mitchell* to be a contradictory and even dangerous decision which promotes discretion whilst, *de facto*, undermining it and which is potentially undermining of the *Photo Production* principle of leaving commercial parties free to apportion risks as they choose.

With all the above *'caveats'*, the decisions in *Phillips Products Ltd v Hyland, George Mitchell v Finney Lock Seeds* and *Smith v Bush* can be (at the very least) a useful indication as to how courts are likely to approach the reasonableness test in practice.

The facts of *Phillips* have already been outlined. Despite all the preliminary issues, in the end the validity of condition 8 turned on the application of the reasonableness test. The first instance judge had found the test not to be satisfied and the Court of Appeal dismissed the appeal:

Phillips Products Ltd v Hyland and Others [1987] 1 WLR 659, CA, p 666

Slade LJ: As the judge pointed out, all the relevant circumstances were known to both parties at that time. The task which he therefore set himself was to examine all the relevant circumstances and then ask himself whether, on the balance of probabilities, he was satisfied that cl 8, insofar as it purported to exclude Hamstead's liability for Mr Hyland's negligence, was a fair and reasonable term. As to these matters, his conclusions as set out in his judgment were: 'What then were the relevant circumstances? First, the second defendants carried on the business of hiring out plant and operators. In contrast the first defendants were steel stockholders, and as such had no occasion to hire plant except on the odd occasions when they had building work to be done at their premises. There had been apparently only three such occasions: one in 1979, one in July 1980 when the drainage trench was dug and the final occasion when the damage was done in August 1980.

Secondly, the hire was to be for a very short period. It was arranged at very short notice. There was no occasion for the plaintiffs to address their mind to all the details of the hiring agreement, nor did they do so. The inclusion of condition 8 arose because it appeared in the second defendants' printed conditions. It was not the product of any discussion or agreement between the parties.

Thirdly, there was little if any opportunity for the plaintiffs to arrange insurance cover for risks arising from the first defendant's negligence. In so far as the first defendant was to be regarded as the plaintiffs' servant it might have been an easy matter to ensure that the plaintiffs' insurance policies were extended, if necessary, to cover his activities in relation to third-party claims. Any businessman customarily insures against such claims. He does not usually insure against damage caused to his own property by his own employees' negligence. Thus, to arrange insurance cover for the first defendant would have required time and special and unusual arrangement with the plaintiffs' insurers.

Fourthly, the plaintiffs played no part in the selection of the first defendant as the operator of the JCB. They had to accept whoever the second defendant sent to drive the machine. Further, although they undoubtedly would have had to, and would have had the right to, tell the JCB operator what job he was required to do, from their previous experience they knew they would be unable in any way to control the way in which the first defendant did the job that he was given. They would not have had the knowledge to exercise such control. All the expertise lay with the first defendant. I do not think condition 8 could possibly be construed as giving control of the manner of operation of the JCB to the plaintiffs. Indeed, in the event, the first defendant made it perfectly plain to Mr Pritchard, the plaintiffs' builder, that he would brook no interference in the way he operated his machine.

Those being the surrounding circumstances, was it fair and reasonable that the hire contract should include a condition which relieved the second defendants of all responsibility for damage caused, not to the property of a third party but to the plaintiff's own property, by the negligence of the second defendants' own operators? This was for the plaintiffs in a very real sense a 'take it or leave it' situation. They needed a JCB for a simple job at short notice. In dealing with the second defendants, they had the choice of taking a JCB operator under a contract containing some 43 written conditions or not taking the JCB at all. The question for me is not a general question whether any contract of hire of the JCB could fairly and reasonably exclude such liability, but a much more limited question as to whether this contract of hire entered into in these circumstances fairly and reasonably included such an exemption.

I have come to the conclusion that the second defendants have failed to satisfy me that condition 8 was in this respect a fair and reasonable term ...

In approaching the judge's reasons and conclusions on this issue ... as the judge himself clearly appreciated, the question for the court is not a general question whether or not cl 8 is valid or invalid in the case of any and every contract of hire entered into between a hirer and a plant owner who uses the relevant CPA conditions. The question was and is whether the exclusion of Hamstead's liability for negligence satisfied the requirement of reasonableness imposed by the Act, in relation to this particular contract.

In *George Mitchell (Chesterhall) Ltd v Finney Lock Seeds Ltd*,[58] the plaintiff farmers had contracted with the defendant seed merchants to supply 30 lb of Dutch 'Winter White' cabbage seed. In the event, the crop which emerged was of very inferior quality and clearly was not from the seed specified. In their defence, the seed merchants pleaded a condition in their sales invoice that if the seeds supplied did not comply with the express terms of the contract, the defendants' liability was limited to replacing the seeds or refunding the price. On the facts, this would have amounted to (approximately) £192, whereas the farmer's loss amounted to (approximately) £61,000. Parker J found in favour of the plaintiffs, and this decision was affirmed in both the Court of Appeal[59] and House of Lords:[60]

---

58 [1983] 2 AC 803, HL.

59 The Court of Appeal judgment is also notable as Lord Denning's last case [1983] 1 QB 284, p 294. In his judgment, Lord Denning provides a sweeping and strikingly clear survey of the judicial and legislative approach to exemption clauses over the years.

60 Although the reasons relied upon vary. In particular, the judgments of Parker J in the High Court and Oliver LJ in the Court of Appeal were criticised as (potentially) re-introducing the doctrine of fundamental breach and of utilising strained construction, no longer necessary when statutory controls were to hand.

George Mitchell (Chesterhall) Ltd v Finney Lock Seeds Ltd [1983] 2 AC 803, HL, p 814

Lord Bridge: The statutory issue turns, as already indicated, on the application the provisions of the modified s 55 of the Sale of Goods Act 1979, as set out in para 11 of Sched 1 to the Act. The Act of 1979 is a pure consolidation. The purpose of the modified s 55 is to preserve the law as it stood from 18 May 1973 to 1 February 1978 in relation to contracts made between those two dates. The significance of the dates is that the first was the date when the Supply of Goods (Implied Terms) Act 1973 came into force, containing the provision now re-enacted by the modified s 55; the second was the date when the Unfair Contract Terms Act 1977 came into force and superseded the relevant provisions of the Act of 1973 by more radical and far-reaching provisions in relation to contracts made thereafter...

Turning back to the modified s 55 of the Act of 1979, it is common ground that the onus was on the respondents to show that it would not be fair or reasonable to allow the appellants to rely on the relevant condition as limiting their liability. It was argued for the appellants that the court must have regard to the circumstances as at the date of the contract, not after the breach. The basis of the argument was that this was the effect of s 11 of the Act of 1977 and that it would be wrong to construe the modified s 55 of the Act as having a different effect. Assuming the premise is correct, the conclusion does not follow. The provisions of the Act of 1977 cannot be considered in construing the prior enactment now embodied in the modified s 55 of the Act of 1979. But, in any event, the language of sub-ss (4) and (5) of that section is clear and unambiguous. The question whether it is fair or reasonable to allow reliance on a term excluding or limiting liability for a breach of contract can only arise after the breach. The nature of the breach and the circumstances in which it occurred cannot possibly be excluded from 'all the circumstances of the case' to which regard must be had.

The only other question of construction debated in the course of the argument was the meaning to be attached to the words 'to the extent that' in sub-s (4) and, in particular, whether they permit the court to hold that it would be fair and reasonable to allow partial reliance on a limitation clause and, for example, to decide in the instant case that the respondents should recover, say, half their consequential damage. I incline to the view that, in their context, the words are equivalent to 'insofar as' or 'in circumstances in which' and do not permit the kind of judgment of Solomon illustrated by the example. But, for the purpose of deciding this appeal, I find it unnecessary to express a concluded view on this question.

My Lords, at long last, I turn to the application of the statutory language to the circumstances of the case. Of the particular matters to which attention is directed by paras (a) to (e) of s 55(5), only those in (a) to (c) are relevant. As to para (c), the respondents admittedly knew of the relevant condition (they had dealt with the appellants for many years) and, if they had read it, particularly cl 2, they would, I think, as laymen rather than lawyers, have had no difficulty in understanding what it said. This and the magnitude of the damages claimed in proportion to the price of the seeds sold are factors which weigh in the scales in the appellants' favour.

The question of relative bargaining strength under para (a) and of the opportunity to buy seeds without a limitation of the seedsman's liability under para (b) were interrelated. The evidence was that a similar limitation of liability was universally embodied in the terms of trade between seedsmen and farmers and had been so for very many years. The limitation had never been negotiated between representative bodies but, on the other hand, had not been the subject of any protest by the National Farmers' Union. These factors, if considered in isolation, might have been equivocal. The decisive factor, however, appears from the evidence of four witnesses called for the appellants, two independent seedsmen, the chairman of the appellant company, and a director of a sister company (both being wholly-owned subsidiaries of the same parent). They said that it had always been their practice, unsuccessfully attempted in the instant case, to negotiate settlements of farmers' claims for damages in excess of the price of the seeds, if they thought that the claims were 'genuine' and 'justified'. This evidence indicated a clear recognition by seedsmen in general, and the appellants in particular, that reliance on the limitation of liability imposed by the relevant condition would not be fair or reasonable.

Two further factors, if more were needed, weight the scales in favour of the respondents. The supply of autumn, instead of winter, cabbage seeds was due to the negligence of the appellants' sister company. Irrespective of its quality, the autumn variety supplied could not, according to the appellants' own evidence, be grown commercially in East Lothian. Finally, as the trial judge found, seedsmen could insure against the risk of crop failure caused by supplying the wrong variety of seeds without materially increasing the price of seeds.

Smith v Eric S Bush (A Firm) [1990] 1 AC 831

The surveyor's appeal was dismissed; it was found that the reasonableness test was not satisfied:

Lord Griffiths (p 858): I believe that it is impossible to draw up an exhaustive list of factors that must be taken into account when a judge is faced with this very difficult decision. Nevertheless, the following matters should, in my view, always be considered:

(1) Were the parties of equal bargaining power? If the court is dealing with a one-off situation between parties of equal bargaining power the requirement of reasonableness would be more easily discharged than in a case such as the present where the disclaimer is imposed upon the purchaser who has no effective power to object.

(2) In the case of advice, would it have been reasonably practicable to obtain the advice from an alternative source taking into account considerations of costs and time? In the present case, it is urged on behalf of the surveyor that it would have been easy for the purchaser to have obtained his own report on the condition of the house, to which the purchaser replies, that he would then be required to pay twice for the same advice and that people buying at the bottom end of the market, many of whom will be young first

time buyers, are likely to be under considerable financial pressure without the money to go paying twice for the same service.

(3) How difficult is the task being undertaken for which liability is being excluded? When a very difficult or dangerous undertaking is involved, there may be a high risk of failure which would certainly be a pointer towards the reasonableness of excluding liability as a condition of doing the work. A valuation, on the other hand, should present no difficulty if the work is undertaken with reasonable skill and care. It is only defects which are observable by a careful visual examination that have to be taken into account and I cannot see that it places any unreasonable burden on the valuer to require him to accept responsibility for the fairly elementary degree of skill and care involved in observing, following up and reporting on such defects. Surely, it is work at the lower end of the surveyor's field of professional expertise.

(4) What are the practical consequences of the decision on the question of reasonableness? This must involve the sums of money potentially at stake and the ability of the parties to bear the loss involved, which, in its turn, raises the question of insurance. There was once a time when it was considered improper even to mention the possible existence of insurance cover in a lawsuit. But those days are long past. Everyone knows that all prudent, professional men carry insurance, and the availability and cost of insurance must be a relevant factor when considering which of two parties should be required to bear the risk of a loss. We are dealing in this case with a loss which will be limited to the value of a modest house and against which it can be expected that the surveyor will be insured. Bearing the loss will be unlikely to cause significant hardship if it has to be borne by the surveyor but it is, on the other hand, quite possible that it will be a financial catastrophe for the purchaser who may be left with a valueless house and no money to buy another. If the law in these circumstances denies the surveyor the right to exclude his liability, it may result in a few more claims, but I do not think so poorly of the surveyor's profession as to believe that the floodgates will be opened. There may be some increase in surveyors' insurance premiums which will be passed on to the public, but I cannot think that it will be anything approaching the figures involved in the difference between the Abbey National's offer of a valuation without liability and a valuation with liability discussed in the speech of my noble and learned friend. Lord Templeman. The result of denying a surveyor, in the circumstances of this case, the right to exclude liability, will result in distributing the risk of his negligence among all house purchasers through an increase in his fees to cover insurance, rather than allowing the whole of the risk to fall upon the one unfortunate purchaser.

I would not, however, wish it to be thought that I would consider it unreasonable for professional men in all circumstances to seek to exclude or limit their liability for negligence. Sometimes, breathtaking sums of money may turn on professional advice, against which it would be impossible for the adviser to obtain adequate insurance cover and which would ruin him if he were to be held personally liable. In these circumstances, it may indeed be reasonable to give the advice upon a basis of no liability or possibly of liability limited to the extent of the adviser's insurance cover.

In addition to the foregoing four factors, which will always have to be considered, there is, in this case, the additional feature that the surveyor is only employed in the first place because the purchaser wishes to buy the house and the purchaser in fact provides or contributes to the surveyor's fees. No one has argued that if the purchaser had employed and paid the surveyor himself, it would have been reasonable for the surveyor to exclude liability for negligence, and the present situation is not far removed from that of a direct contract between the surveyor and the purchaser. The evaluation of the foregoing matters leads me to the clear conclusion that it would not be fair and reasonable for the surveyor to be permitted to exclude liability in the circumstances of this case. I would therefore dismiss this appeal.

It must, however, be remembered that this is a decision in respect of a dwelling house of modest value in which it is widely recognised by surveyors that purchasers are in fact relying on their care and skill. It will obviously be of general application in broadly similar circumstances. But I expressly reserve my position in respect of valuations of quite different types of property for mortgage purposes, such as industrial property, large blocks of flats or very expensive houses. In such cases, it may well be that the general expectation of the behaviour of the purchaser is quite different. With very large sums of money at stake, prudence would seem to demand that the purchaser obtain his own structural survey to guide him in his purchase and, in such circumstances, with very much larger sums of money at stake, it may be reasonable for the surveyors valuing on behalf of those who are providing the finance either to exclude or limit their liability to the purchaser.

It is clear that common themes recur: the degree of real notice given, the possibility of genuine negotiation over the clause, the crucial issue of inequality of bargaining power, the question as to who was in the better position to insure and a general reluctance to allow the exclusion of liability for negligence. Judicial discretion (whatever Lord Bridge's views) is clearly wide, but there are clear guidelines (legislative and judicial) as to the likeliest outcome of a case.

Provisions rendering exemption clauses void

Some of the provisions of the 1977 Act have the effect of rendering certain types of exemption clause absolutely void. Section 2(1) declares that any clause which purports to exclude or limit liability for negligently inflicted death or bodily injury will have no effect. By virtue of s 5, exemptions contained in manufacturers' guarantees of consumer goods are void in the circumstances specified in s 5. Furthermore, any purported exclusion or limitation of liability for breach of the implied terms relating to title in s 12 of the Sale of Goods Act 1979 and s 2 of the Supply of Goods and Services Act 1982 is void (ss 6(1) and 7(3A) of the Unfair Contract Terms Act 1977). The attempted exclusion or limitation of liability for breach of the implied terms in supply of goods contracts relating to description, quality, fitness and sales by sample is also rendered void, but only in relation to consumer contracts (ss 6(1), (2) and 7(1), (2) of the Unfair Contract Terms Act 1977):

Unfair Contract Terms Act 1977

2

(1) A person cannot by reference to any contract term or to a notice given to persons generally or to particular persons exclude or restrict his liability for death or personal injury resulting from negligence.

5 'Guarantee' of consumer goods

(1) In the case of goods of a type ordinarily supplied for private use or consumption, where loss or damage:

(a) arises from the goods proving defective while in consumer use; and

(b) results from the negligence of a person concerned in the manufacture or distribution of the goods, liability for the loss or damage cannot be excluded or restricted by reference to any contract term or notice contained in or operating by reference to a guarantee of the goods.

(2) For these purposes:

(a) goods are to be regarded as 'in consumer use' when a person is using them, or has them in his possession for use, otherwise than exclusively for the purposes of a business; and

(b) anything in writing is a guarantee if it contains or purports to contain some promise or assurance (however worded or presented) that defects will be made good by complete or partial replacement, or by repair, monetary compensation or otherwise.

(3) This section does not apply as between the parties to a contract under or in pursuance of which possession or ownership of the goods has passed.

6

(1) Liability for breach of the obligations arising from:

(a) s 12 of the Sale of Goods Act 1979 (seller's implied undertakings as to title, etc);

(b) s 8 of the Supply of Goods (Implied Terms) Act 1973 (the corresponding things in relation to hire-purchase),

cannot be excluded or restricted by reference to any contract term.

(2) As against a person dealing as a consumer, liability for breach of the obligations arising from:

(a) s 13, 14 or 15 of the Sale of Goods Act 1979 (seller's implied undertakings as to conformity with description or sample, or as to their quality or fitness for a particular purpose);

(b) s 9, 10 or 11 of the 1973 Act (the corresponding things in relation to hire purchase),

cannot be restricted by reference to any contract term.

7

(1) Where the possession or ownership of goods passes under or in pursuance of a contract not governed by the law of sale of goods or hire-purchase, sub-ss (2) to (4) below apply as regards the effect (if any) to be given to contract terms excluding or restricting liability for breach of obligation arising by implication of law from the nature of the contract.

(2) As against a person dealing as consumer, liability in respect of the goods' correspondence with description or sample, or their quality or fitness for any particular purpose, cannot be excluded or restricted by reference to any such term.

(3A) Liability for breach of the obligations arising under section 2 of the Supply of Goods and Services Act 1982 (implied terms about title etc in certain contracts for the transfer of property in goods) cannot be excluded or restricted by reference to any such term.

A blanket prohibition on exemptions relating to negligence causing death or injury in any business context is easy enough to comprehend and is in direct line of succession from a number of earlier statutes concerning the carriage of passengers by rail, or by road in a public service vehicle.[61] The prohibition on disclaimers in consumer guarantees reflects the Law Commission recommendation in para 100 of the Second Report on Exemption Clauses (1975, No 69), which stated that 'it is obvious that cases can arise in which [the buyer] will have abandoned rights far more valuable than those he has gained. Such an exemption clause is a potential trap, and we think it should be made void'. The provisions in ss 6 and 7 concerning consumers either re-enact (in s 6) provisions in the Supply of Goods (Implied Terms) Act 1973 or provide for analogous provisions concerning (s 7) the supply of goods under contracts of hire, work and materials (for example, a building contract or a repair contract). The key definition of 'dealing as a consumer' under s 12 was discussed earlier. Again all this reflects Law Commission views (here in the *First Report*, Law Com No 24, 1969). At para 68, the Commission stated that:

.... the Molony Committee [viewed] the practice of contracting out as a general threat to consumer interest [the working party] found an overriding argument in favour of prohibiting 'contracting out'. The mischief was that this practice enabled well organised commerce 'consistently to impose unfair terms on the consumer, and to deny him what the law means him to have ...

This represents a clear substantive unfairness perspective, although it might be argued that the real mischief is the general lack of public awareness of their rights and that procedural matters can hardly be ignored. A well informed consumer in a competitive marketplace might be better able to shop around

---

61   Transport Act 1962, s 43(7) and (now) Public Passenger Vehicles Act 1981, s 29.

(although this, in turn, ignores the likelihood of most – if not all – potential suppliers using the same or similar terms).[62]

Provisions subjecting exemption clauses to the test of reasonableness

Effectively, all the remaining provisions in the Act, plus s 8, which inserts a new s 3 in the Misrepresentation Act 1967, impose a requirement of reasonableness. The main provisions are to be found in s 2(2), s 3 and s 7(3):

2

(2) In the case of other loss or damage, a person cannot so exclude or restrict his liability for negligence except in so far as the term or notice satisfies the requirement of reasonableness.

6

(3) As against a person dealing otherwise than as consumer, the liability specified in sub-s (2) above can be excluded or restricted by reference to a contract term, but only in so far as the term satisfies the requirement of reasonableness.

7

(3) As against a person dealing otherwise than as a consumer, that liability can be excluded or restricted by reference to such a term, but only insofar as the term satisfies the requirement of reasonableness.

Little needs to be said about the provisions extracted above. It is clearly seen as easier to justify excluding liability for property damage or financial loss than for personal injury. Those in business are seen to be more able to look after their own interests than consumers:[63]

3

(1) This section applies as between contracting parties where one of them deals as consumer or on the other's written standard terms of business.

(2) As against that party, the other cannot by reference to any contract term:

(a) when himself in breach of contract, exclude or restrict any liability of his in respect of the breach; or

(b) claim to be entitled:

(i) to render a contractual performance substantially different from that which was reasonably expected of him; or

(ii) in respect of the whole or any party of his contractual obligation, to render no performance at all,

---

62 The Consumer Transactions (Restrictions on Statements) Order 1976 SI 1976/1813 (amended 1978 by SI 1978/127) also makes it a criminal offence to include in a consumer contract of sale an exclusion clause which would be automatically void under UCTA 1977, s 6. See, also, Beale, Bishop and Furmston, 1998, pp 709–11.

63 Although many small businesses may be in a wholly unequal bargaining relationship with a large supplier. The reasonableness test should be able to reflect this.

except so far as (in any of the cases mentioned above in this sub-section) the contract term satisfies the requirement of reasonableness.

It has been observed above[64] that the words 'written standard terms of business' are not defined and it must be open to speculation as to whether a set of terms drafted by a trade association would be included. Interesting comment on the phrase to be found in *St Albans City and District Council v International Computers Ltd*,[65] which concerned the liability of ICL in respect of a failure in software supplied to the council that resulted in an overestimate of the 'chargeable' population and a (consequent) failure to set the charge itself at a sufficiently high level, causing a serious loss of revenue. One issue for the court was the effect of the Unfair Contract Terms Act 1977 on a limitation clause in the contract between ICL and the council. As regards, this, the first question was whether the council contracts on ICL's 'written standard terms of business':

St Albans City and District Council v International Computers Ltd [1996] 4 All ER 481, CA, p 490

Nourse LJ: The first question is whether, as between the plaintiffs and the defendant, the plaintiffs dealt as consumer or on the defendant's written standard terms of business within s 3(1). In the light of s 12(1)(a) and the definition of 'business' in s 14, it is accepted on behalf of the plaintiffs that they did not deal as consumer. So, the question is reduced to this. Did the plaintiff 'deal' on the defendant's written standard terms of business?

Mr Dehn submitted that the question must be answered in the negative, on the ground that you cannot be said to deal on another's standard terms of business if, as was here the case, you negotiate with him over those terms before you enter into the contract. In my view, that is an impossible construction for two reasons first, because as a matter of plain English 'deals' means 'makes a deal', irrespective of any negotiations that may have preceded it; secondly, because s 12(1)(a) equates the expression 'deals as a consumer' with 'makes a contract'. Thus, it is clear that, in order that one of the contracting parties may deal on the other's written standard terms of business within s 3(1), it is only necessary for him to enter into the contract on those terms.

Mr Dehn sought to derive support for his submission from observations of Judge Thayne Forbes QC in *Salvage Association v CAP Financial Services Ltd* [1995] FSR 654, p 671–72. In my view, those observations do not assist the defendant. In that case the judge had to consider, in relation to two contracts, whether certain terms satisfied the description 'written standard terms of business' and also whether there had been a 'dealing' on those terms. In relation to the first contract he said (at p 671):

I am satisfied that the terms in question were ones which had been written and produced in advance by CAP as a suitable set of contract terms for use

---

64 See *op cit*, fn 8.
65 [1996] 4 All ER 481.

in many of its future contracts of which the first contract with [the Salvage Association] happened to be one. It is true that Mr Jones felt free to and did negotiate and agree certain important matters and details relating to the first contract at the meeting of 27 February 1987. However, although he had read and briefly considered CAP's conditions of business, he did not attempt any negotiation with regard to those conditions, nor did he or Mr Ellis consider that it was appropriate or necessary to do so. The CAP standard conditions were terms that he and Mr Ellis willingly accepted as incorporated into the first contract in their predetermined form. In those circumstances, it seems to me that those terms still satisfy the description 'written standard terms of business' and so, so far as concerns the first contract, the actions of Mr Jones and Mr Ellis constituted 'dealing' on the part of [the Salvage Association] with CAP on its written standard terms of business within the meaning of s 3 of the [Unfair Contract Terms Act 1977].

It is true that the judge found that the Salvage Association did not negotiate with CAP over the latter's standard terms and that he held that, in entering into the contract, the Salvage Association dealt with CAP on those terms within s 3. I do not, however, read his observations as indicating a view that the 'dealing' depended on the absence of negotiations. I think that even if there had been negotiations over the standard conditions his view would have been the same.

Scott Baker J dealt with this question as one of fact, finding that the defendant's general conditions remained effectively untouched in the negotiations and that the plaintiffs accordingly dealt on the defendant's written standard terms for the purposes of s 3(1) (see [1995] FSR 686, p 706). I respectfully agree with him. The consequence of that finding is that the defendant cannot rely on cl 9(c) except in so far as it satisfies the requirement of reasonableness. The judge carefully considered that question and held that cl 9(c) did not pass the test (see [1995] FSR 686, p 707-11).

Otherwise, s 3 seems to operate as something of a 'catch-all', sweeping up a wide variety of contractual provisions not dealt with by any other substantive provisions in the 1977 Act. There would appear to be some overlap with s 2(2), in that, if the clause in question (in the consumer or standard form contract) attempts to exclude liability for breach of a duty of take care, it would seem to be covered, in principle, by both s 3(2)(a) and s 2(2).

Section 3(2)(b) is particularly interesting. It is certainly a further indication (in conjunction with s 13) that the 'Coote' approach is not followed by the 1977 Act. If a term operates by narrowly defining the initial obligation, or by allowing for wide alternative or substitute performance methods s 3(2)(b) comes into play.[66] Clear instances where s 3(2)(b)(i) could be triggered would be clauses in package holiday standard conditions allowing for a switch of hotels, or dates or even destinations.[67] In a similar vein, the common practice

---

66 For discussion of this, see Law Commission, No 69, 1975, paras 141 and 143.

67 Compare with the pre-UCTA decision in *Anglo-Continental Holidays Ltd v Typaldos Lines Ltd* [1967] 2 Lloyd's Rep 61: 'Steamers, sailing dates, rates and itineraries are subject to change without notice.' *Typaldos* is discussed by the Law Commission, *ibid*, para 144.

of providing for substitute performers in entertainment contracts could be caught (and subjected to the reasonableness test). One interesting application of s 3(2)(b)(ii) could be to catch the all too common practice in contracts for sporting events of refusing monetary refunds even if there is no play.

General remarks

The Unfair Contract Terms Act 1977 was a major breakthrough in the control of unfairly wide exemption, limitation and disclaimer clauses. However, as already stated, it is neither logical in structure, nor always consistent in approach. Moreover its name is a serious misnomer, being doubly misleading. First, the legislation has a wider sweep than merely the regulation of contractual exemptions. As the discussion of *Smith v Bush* indicates, ss 1(1)(b), (c), (3) and (2) in combination bring the important field of non-contractual disclaimers within the Act. On the other hand, it has little to do with unfair terms as such, but only those terms which are unfair because they exempt too unreasonably or limit liability too severely. The name of the original Bill (the Avoidance of Liability Bill) probably captures the essence of the legislation more accurately. The usual view is that the name was changed as part of the debate (which had already commenced in the mid-1970s) about the harmonisation of laws within the European Community on unfair consumer contracts (see below).

Moreover there are some important limitations on the scope of the Act (see Sched 1) even within the field of exemption clauses. Of most significance is, probably, the exclusion of contracts of insurance in Sched 1, s 1(a). This was criticised at the time the Act was passed, but the new Unfair Terms in Consumer Contracts Regulations 1999 (considered below) may plug this gap.

OTHER REGULATION OF STANDARD FORMS

It was stated at the beginning of this chapter that by far the greatest attention, in our law, has been given to the regulation of clauses, within standard forms, excluding or limiting liability. This is not necessarily true elsewhere, particularly in the civil law jurisdictions and in the US.[68] From time to time in this country, the broader view has been taken, the most famous being Lord Denning's judgment in *Lloyds Bank v Bundy*[69] on the concept of unconscionability and inequality of bargaining power discussed in Chapter 7,

---

68 See, eg the general provisions in the BGB (Germany) concerning good faith (in particular para 242) and the general statute concerning standard form contracts. See, also, Uniform Commercial Code (USA), § 2-302 on unconscionability.

69 [1975] QB 326.

but the following pronouncement on the issue of standard forms *per se* is equally interesting:

Schroeder Music Publishing Co Ltd v Macaulay [1974] 1 WLR 1308, HL, p 1316

> **Lord Diplock**: Standard forms of contracts are of two kinds. The first, of very ancient origin, are those which set out the terms on which mercantile transactions of common occurrence are to be carried out. Examples are bills of lading, charterparties, policies of insurance, contracts of sale in the commodity markets. The standard clauses in these contracts have been settled over the years by negotiation by representatives of the commercial interests involved and have been widely adopted because experience has shown that they facilitate the conduct of trade. Contracts of these kinds affect not only the actual parties to them but also others who may have a commercial interest in the transactions to which they relate, as buyers or sellers, charterers or shipowners, insurers or bankers. If fairness or reasonableness were relevant to their enforceability, the fact that they are widely used by parties whose bargaining power is fairly matched would raise a strong presumption that their terms are fair and reasonable.

> The same presumption, however, does not apply to the other kind of standard form of contract. This is of comparatively modern origin. It is the result of the concentration of particular kinds of business in relatively few hands. The ticket cases in the 19th century provide what are probably the first examples. The terms of this kind of standard form of contract have not been the subject of negotiation between the parties to it, or approved by any organisation representing the interests of the weaker party. They have been dictated by the party whose bargaining power, either exercised alone or in conjunction with others providing similar goods or services, enables him to say: 'If you want these goods or services at all, these are the only terms on which they are obtainable. Take it or leave it.'

> To be in a position to adopt this attitude towards a party desirous of entering into a contract to obtain goods or services provides a classic instance of superior bargaining power.

In general, the common law has been slow to develop these themes, or has been even dismissive of the need to develop them,[70] subject to the rare exception below.

The case of *Interfoto Picture Library Ltd v Stiletto Visual Programmes Ltd*[71] is original enough in its specific context of linking the degree of notice required to the nature of the clause under scrutiny, but, at the beginning of his judgment, Bingham LJ indicates that, in his view, English law is heavily influenced by general notions of contractual unfairness, even if the law does not currently so characterise them:

---

70 See the comments of Lord Scarman in *National Westminster Bank plc v Morgan* [1985] AC 686, p 708, also discussed in Chapter 7.

71 [1989] QB 433, CA. See, further, Chapters 2 and 4.

Interfoto Picture Library Ltd v Stiletto Visual Programmes Ltd [1989] QB 433, CA, p 439

Bingham LJ: In many civil law systems, and perhaps in most legal systems outside the common law world, the law of obligations recognises and enforces an overriding principle that, in making and carrying out contracts, parties should act in good faith. This does not simply mean that they should not deceive each other, a principle which any legal system must recognise; its effect is perhaps most aptly conveyed by such metaphorical colloquialisms as 'playing fair', 'coming clean' or 'putting one's cards face upwards on the table'. It is, in essence, a principle of fair and open dealing.

English law has, characteristically, committed itself to no such overriding principle, but has developed piecemeal solutions in response to demonstrated problems of unfairness. Many examples could be given. Thus, equity has intervened to strike down unconscionable bargains. Parliament has stepped in to regulate the imposition of exemption clauses and the form of certain hire-purchase agreements. The common law also has made its contribution, by holding that certain classes of contract require the utmost good faith, by treating as irrecoverable what purport to be agreed estimates of damage but are in truth a disguised penalty for breach, and in many other ways.

Legislatively there has been more progress in the wider regulation of unfair terms (most typically in standard form contracts) – albeit in rather 'piecemeal' fashion. For example, an elaborate system of legislative control exists in relation to regulated consumer credit agreements under the Consumer Credit Act 1974[72] and associated delegated legislation. Contracts for the provision of financial services are similarly subject to detailed legislative control.[73] There are also the wide regulatory powers of the Director General of Fair Trading under the Fair Trading Act 1973.[74]

However, recent legislative developments provide for a (potentially!) more considered, more general, and more structured approach to the regulation of standard form consumer contracts. It has been observed that a likely reason for the adoption (however misleadingly) of the title Unfair Contract Terms in the 1977 Act was that at the time the bill was first envisaged in 1976, the European Commission was considering harmonisation of laws within the EC concerning unfair contract terms. A number of factors made swift progress difficult, particularly the divergent nature of national contract laws. Moreover, a number of member states enacted legislation on the subject at around the same time, although dealing with it in a variety of ways.[75] However, in 1986, the Commission launched a new initiative on consumer

---

72 Eg, Consumer Credit Act 1974, ss 65(1), 67, 68, 127(3), 127(4), 137, 138 and 139.

73 Financial Services Act 1986, s 48.

74 In particular, the powers in respect of unfair consumer trade practices and the powers to take steps against persistent contract breakers – see ss 13, 14 and 17 and 34, 35 and 37.

75 The German AGB Gesetz of 1976 may indeed provide the blueprint for subsequent Commission initiatives.

policy, which eventually resulted in a draft directive on unfair terms in consumer contracts. This was first published in 1990 and was subsequently amended in 1992.[76] The Directive was finally adopted on 5 April 1993[77] and was expressed as applying from 1 January 1995. In the event, it was directly incorporated into our law (with little significant drafting amendment) by the Unfair Terms in Consumer Contracts Regulations 1994 (SI 1994/3159), although only with effect from 1 July 1995. These regulations have, in turn, been replaced by the Unfair Terms in Consumer Contracts Regulations 1999 (SI 1999/2083), in force 1 October 1999:

Unfair Terms in Consumer Contracts Regulations 1999 (SI 1999/2083)

3 Interpretation

(1) In these Regulations:

'the Community' means the European Community;

'consumer' means any natural person who, in contracts covered by these Regulations, is acting for purposes which are outside his trade, business or profession;

'court' in relation to England and Wales and Northern Ireland means a county court or the High Court, and in relation to Scotland, the Sheriff or the Court of Session;

'Director' means the Director General of Fair Trading;

'EEA Agreement' means the Agreement on the European Economic Area signed at Oporto on 2 May 1992 as adjusted by the protocol signed at Brussels on 17 March 1993;

'Member State' means a State which is a contracting party to the EEA Agreement;

'notified' means notified in writing;

'qualifying body' means a person specified in Sched 1;

'seller or supplier' means any natural or legal person who, in contracts covered by these Regulations, is acting for purposes relating to his trade, business or profession, whether publicly owned or privately owned;

'unfair terms' means the contractual terms referred to in reg 5.

(2) In the application of these Regulations to Scotland for references to an 'injunction' or an 'interim injunction', there shall be substituted references to an 'interdict' or 'interim interdict' respectively.

4 Terms to which these Regulations apply

(1) These Regulations apply in relation to unfair terms in contracts concluded between a seller and a supplier and a consumer.

---

76 COM (90) 322 and COM (92) 66.
77 93/13/EEC OJ 95, 21/4/93, p 29.

(2) These Regulations do not apply to contractual terms which reflect:

    (a) mandatory statutory or regulatory provisions (including such provisions under the law of any Member State or in Community legislation having effect in the UK without further enactment);

    (b) the provisions or principles of international conventions to which the Member States or the Community are party.

5 Unfair Terms

(1) A contractual term which has not been individually negotiated shall be regarded as unfair if, contrary to the requirement of good faith, it causes a significant imbalance in the parties' rights and obligations arising under the contract, to the detriment of the consumer.

(2) A term shall always be regarded as not having been individually negotiated where it has been drafted in advance and the consumer has therefore not been able to influence the substance of the term.

(3) Notwithstanding that a specific term or certain aspect of it in a contract has been individually negotiated, these Regulations shall apply to the rest of a contract if an overall assessment of it indicates that it is a pre-formulated standard contract.

(4) It shall be for any seller or supplier who claims that a term was individually negotiated to show that it was.

(5) Schedule 2 to these Regulations contains an indicative and non-exhaustive list of the terms which may be regarded as unfair.

6 Assessment of unfair terms

(1) Without prejudice to reg 12, the unfairness of a contractual term shall be assessed, taking into account the nature of the goods or services for which the contract was concluded and by referring, at the time of the conclusion of the contract, to all circumstances attending the conclusion of the contract and to all the other terms of the contract or of another contract on which it is dependent.

(2) Insofar as it is in plain intelligible language, the assessment of fairness of a term shall not relate –

    (a) to the definition of the main subject matter of the contract, or

    (b) to the adequacy of the price or remuneration, as against the goods or services supplied in exchange.

7 Written contracts

(1) A seller or supplier shall ensure that any written term of a contract is expressed in plain, intelligible language.

(2) If there is doubt about the meaning of a written term, the interpretation which is most favourable to the consumer shall prevail but this rule shall not apply in proceedings brought under reg 12.

8 Effect of unfair term

(1) An unfair term in a contract concluded with a consumer by a seller or supplier shall not be binding on the consumer.

(2) The contract shall continue to bind the parties if it is capable of continuing in existence without unfair term.

9 Choice of law clauses

These Regulations shall apply notwithstanding any contract term which applies or purports to apply the law of a non-Member State, if the contract has a close connection with the territory of the Member States.

SCHEDULE 2

INDICATIVE AND NON-EXHAUSTIVE LIST OF TERMS WHICH MAY BE REGARDED AS UNFAIR

1 Terms which have the object or effect of:

(a) excluding or limiting the legal liability of a seller or supplier in the event of the death of a consumer or personal injury to the latter resulting from an act or omission of that seller or supplier;

(b) inappropriately excluding or limiting the legal rights of the consumer vis à vis the seller or supplier or another party in the event of total or partial non-performance or inadequate performance by the seller or supplier against any claims which the consumer may have against him;

(c) making an agreement binding on the consumer whereas provision of services by the seller or supplier is subject to a condition whose realisation depends on his own will alone;

(d) permitting the seller or supplier to retain sums paid by the consumer where the latter decides not to conclude or perform the contract, without providing for the consumer to receive compensation of an equivalent amount from the seller or supplier where the latter is the party cancelling the contract;

(e) requiring any consumer who fails to fulfil his obligation to pay a disproportionately high sum in compensation;

(f) authorising the seller or supplier to terminate a contract of indeterminate duration without reasonable notice except where there are serious grounds for doing so;

(h) automatically extending a contract of fixed duration where the consumer does not indicate otherwise, when the deadline fixed for the consumer to express his desire not to extend the contract is unreasonably early;

(i) irrevocably binding the consumer to terms with which he had no real opportunity of becoming acquainted before the conclusion of the contract;

(j) enabling the seller or supplier to alter the terms of the contract unilaterally without a valid reason which is specified in the contract;

(k) enabling the seller or supplier to alter the terms of the contract unilaterally without a valid reason any characteristics of the product or service to be provided;

(l) providing for the price of goods to be determined at the time of delivery or allowing a seller of goods or supplier of services to increase their price without in both cases giving the consumer the corresponding right to cancel the contract if the final price is too high in relation to the price agreed when the contract was concluded;

(m) giving the seller or supplier the right to determine whether the goods or services supplied are in conformity with the contract, or giving him the exclusive right to interpret any term of the contract;

(n) limiting the seller's or supplier's obligation to respect commitments undertaken by his agents or making his commitments subject to compliance with a particular formality;

(o) obliging the consumer to fulfil all his obligations where the seller or supplier does not perform his;

(p) giving the seller or supplier the possibility of transferring his rights and obligations under the contract, where this may serve to reduce the guarantees for the consumer, without the latter's agreement;

(q) excluding or hindering the consumer's right to take legal action or exercise any other legal remedy, particularly by requiring the consumer to take disputes exclusively to arbitration not covered by legal provisions, unduly restricting the evidence available to him or imposing on him a burden of proof which according to the applicable law, should lie with another party to the contract.

2 Scope of paras 1(g), (j) and (l)

(a) Paragraph 1(g) is without hindrance to terms by which a supplier of financial services reserves the right to terminate unilaterally a contract of indeterminate duration without notice where there is a valid reason, provided that the supplier is required to inform the other contracting party or parties thereof immediately.

(b) Paragraph 1(j) is without hindrance to terms under which a supplier of financial services reserves the right to alter the rate of interest payable by the consumer or due to the latter, or the amount of other charges for financial services without notice where there is a valid reason, provided that the supplier is required to inform the other contracting party or parties thereof at the earliest opportunity and that the latter are free to dissolve the contract immediately.

Paragraph 1(j) is also without hindrance to terms under which a seller or supplier reserves the right to alter unilaterally the conditions of a contract of indeterminate duration, provided that he is required to inform the consumer with reasonable notice and that the consumer is free to dissolve the contract.

(c) Paragraphs 1(g), (j) and (l) do not apply to:

- transactions in transferable securities, financial instruments and other products or services where the price is linked to fluctuations in a stock exchange quotation or index or a financial market rate that the seller or supplier does not control;

- contracts for the purchase or sale of foreign currency, traveller's cheques or international money orders denominated in foreign currency.

(d) Paragraph 1(l) is without hindrance to price indexation clauses, where lawful, provided that the method by which prices vary is explicitly described.

These Regulations, and the Directive which bred them, have already been the subject of much academic comment,[78] and there seems little doubt that they have a considerable impact on English consumer protection law. The likely overall impact on the general law of contract is more speculative – particularly the likely impact of the injection of 'good faith' into the law. To date, there is only one reported decision in the English courts and (as a result) a number of interpretative issues concerning the Regulations remain unresolved. One uncertainty however has been eliminated by the 1999 Regulations. As originally drafted the regulations only applied to the sale of goods or the provisions of services, by those in business, to consumers. Some commentators (for example, Treitel, GH, in the 10th edition of his *Law of Contract*, p 246) felt that, as a result, contracts for the sale or disposition of interests in land were implicitly excluded, in that real property could not properly be described as 'goods', given the crucial distinction in English law between real and personal property. Other commentators took the opposite view, pointing out that the original (French) version of the Directive referred (simply) to 'biens' which in French law could encompass land. Certainly the view of the Office of Fair Trading was always that land transactions (including leases) fell within the purview of the Regulations. The 1999 Regulations (reg 4) simply apply to sellers and suppliers, thereby bypassing the above difficulty. Indeed, there are very few consumer contracts to which the Regulations do not (now) apply (for the limited exceptions, see reg 4(2)).

The structure of the regulations is clear enough. Any term in a consumer contract which has not been individually negotiated (reg 5) is not binding on the consumer if it is 'unfair' (reg 8). Such a term will be unfair if:

---

78 Eg, Duffy, 1993; Dean, 1993; Collins, 1994; Brownsword and Howells, 1995; Mortelmans (1988) European Consumer Law Journal 2; Brandt and Ulmer, 1991.

- contrary to the requirement of 'good faith';
- it causes a significant imbalance in the parties' right and obligations;
- to the detriment of the consumer (reg 5(11)).

The issues of *'significant* imbalance' and consumer *'detriment'* seem largely matters of fact to be decided 'case by case', although, significantly, they seem suggestive of substantive unfairness compared to the largely, procedural unfairness perspective of 'good faith' discussed below. *'Consumer'* is defined (reg 3) so as to include only 'natural' persons, thereby immediately ruling out the possibility of an *R & B Customs Brokers* type argument.[79]

The burden of proof (that is, to establish that a term 'challenged' *is fair*) lies on the seller/supplier (reg 5(4)).

Three issues in the regulations seem of particular interest and uncertainty:

(i) *Core terms*

Regulation 6(2) reconfirms that the Regulations will not 'bite' on any term which either: (a) defines the main subject matter of the contract; or (b) relates to the adequacy of the contract price, so long as the term in question is in 'plain intelligible' language. The meaning of (a) is far from clear, as it seems to link back to the 'Coote' perspective on exemption clauses dismissed earlier (see fn 10) and, unless interpreted carefully could lead to a re-emergence of the argument that liability is not being excluded – merely not accepted in the first place. Of course, there must be something at the 'core' of a contract which cannot be challenged as 'unfair' (assuming the consumer entered into the contract freely in the first place) – but this should, surely, be construed narrowly.

(ii) *Good faith*

The remarks of Bingham LJ in *Interfoto v Stiletto* convey lucidly the broad sense of 'good faith', a concept which seems of the essence of the idea of procedural fairness. In many ways, good faith in the codes of countries like Germany seems to play a similar role to that of equity in relation to the common law – giving a 'gloss' of flexibility, humanity and justice to an otherwise rather schematic and technical system. The wording of reg 5(1) suggests that, even if a term shows some evidence of imbalance and detriment, it may be acceptable if the consumer received full and clear information about the implications of the clause and went into it with his/her eyes open.

---

79 See *op cit*, fn 43.

(iii) *Schedule 2*

The significance of Sched 2 is open to debate. Does an illustrative and indicative list mean that, at the very least, any clause falling within one of the Sched 2 examples is, *prima facie,* unfair? What *is* clear is that being in the list does not automatically *make* a term unfair – it is a 'grey' list and not a 'black' list.[80] Moreover, the fact that the clause does not analogise with any of those in Sched 2 equally raises no inference that is 'fair'.

Perhaps of most significance is the fact that enforcement of the Regulations has been largely through the Office of Fair Trading (and the undertakings it has gained from those seen as 'guilty' of unfair terms), rather than through the courts (in the period to 1998, the Office of Fair Trading claims to have 'successfully challenged' more than 1,200 contract terms). The 1999 Regulations (regs 10–13 and Sched 1) grant equivalent powers of intervention to a number of other bodies, including the Consumer Association. There seems to be only one reported higher court decision, *Director General of Fair Trading v First National Bank plc,*[81] which concerned a clause in the defendant bank's standard form loan agreement which provided that if a borrower defaulted, interest on the outstanding principal and accrued unpaid interest existing at the date of judgment would be payable at the contractual rate during the period between judgment, and the discharge of judgment by payment. This would have the effect of leaving a substantial bill for interest remaining to be paid by the borrower after he/she had discharged the instalments. The Office of Fair Trading sought an injunction under the (then) reg 8(2) of the 1994 Regulations, claiming that the terms were unfair. At first instance, Evans-Lombe J held that neither substantive nor procedural unfairness had been demonstrated and refused the injunction. However, very recently, the Court of Appeal has reversed this decision:

Director General of Fair Trading v First National Bank plc [2000] 2 WLR 1353, p 1361

Peter Gibson LJ:

It is not in dispute that the Regulations apply to the bank's consumer credit agreements containing the relevant term and that such agreements are not individually negotiated for the purpose of reg 3(1). It is trite law in England that once a judgment is obtained under a loan agreement for a principal sum and judgment is entered, the contract merges in the judgment and the principal becomes owed under the judgment and not under the contract. If, under the contract, interest on any principal sum is due, absent special provisions the contract is considered ancillary to the covenant to pay the principal, with the result that if judgment is obtained

---

80 The original proposals by the Commission had envisaged a 'black list' along the lines of the German AGB Gesetz.

81 [2000] 1 All ER 240.

for the principal, the covenant to pay interest merges in the judgment. Parties to a contract may agree that a covenant to pay interest will not merge in any judgment for the principal sum due, and in that event interest may be charged under the contract on the principal sum due even after judgment for that sum. This is so notwithstanding that judgment interest prescribed by statute is at a lower rate (see *Economic Life Assurance Society v Usborne* [1902] AC 147, applying *Re Sneyd ex p Fewings* (1883) 25 Ch D 338). (For the sake of completeness, we should record that Lord Goodhart QC for the bank reserved the right to challenge these decisions if this case goes further.) Merger does not apply where there is an independent covenant to pay interest (*Ealing London Borough Council v EI Isaac* [1980] 1 WLR 932, 937). Thus, on the face of the bank's regulated assessments, the effect of the relevant term is to prevent the independent obligation to pay interest merging in the judgment, the provision for interest at the contractual rate continuing to apply after judgment.

It is clear from the decision of this court in *Southern and District Finance plc v Barnes* [1995] CCLR 62 that, where a creditor calls in a loan (such as by bringing a possession action in a case where the loan is secured on property), the outstanding balance of the loan is a sum owed and the court has power to make a time order in respect of future instalments as well as accrued arrears, but when such an order is made the court can, under s 136 of the 1974 Act, amend the regulated agreement by reducing the rate of interest payable under it, if necessary, to nil. But, in practice, in the vast majority of cases in which a regulated agreement is being enforced and an instalment order is made, there is no real hearing by the court, the lender and the borrower usually agreeing on an instalment order and the court making the consent order without more consideration. This occurs even though in some county court claim forms of the bank, which were included in the evidence, attention is drawn by the bank to the fact that the agreement provides for interest to be payable before and after judgment and it is stated that the right to proceed for subsequent interest is reserved. There was no evidence before us as to whether this is now the invariable practice of the bank, nor in any event was the debtor's attention drawn by the bank to the powers of the court under ss 129 and 136.

The Director has received complaints from members of the public about the bank's standard terms. Although many other lenders incorporate in their agreements terms similar to the relevant term, we are told that the Director has not received complaints about those terms from consumers. For present purposes, it is those complaints relating to the impact of the relevant term when judgment has been obtained against borrowers and an order for payment by instalments has been made which raise the relevant issue. Borrowers complained of unfairness in that they found themselves liable to the bank for amounts beyond those provided for in the judgments against them. They, in particular, complained that, when an order for payment by instalments is made, sometimes after offers for repayment by instalments in accordance with what the borrowers could afford have been accepted by the bank, compliance with that order might nevertheless leave the borrowers in debt. The accrual of interest at the contractual rate might mean that the amount of what is owed to the bank substantially increases, even if the debtor duly pays the instalments fixed by the court. Borrowers were not always aware of the effect of the relevant term when they entered the agreements and the attention of the court, when the bank obtained judgment and the court was considering a time order, was not necessarily drawn to the relevant term. That interest at the contractual rate should continue to be payable after judgment is the more striking given that no statutory interest is payable on a county court judgment to recover money due under a regulated agreement or on a judgment debt made payable by instalments when the instalments are duly paid.

There was an exchange of views in correspondence between the Office of Fair Trading and the bank. The Director considered that the relevant term had the potential to put consumers in a significantly worse position than they would be under the legislative regime of the 1974 Act, the 1984 Act and the Order of 1991 and that it was unfair within the meaning of the Regulations. He also regarded the requirement of the relevant term that interest be paid upon interest as falling within para 1(e) of Sched 3 to the Regulations as requiring a consumer to pay a disproportionately high sum in compensation. On 8 March 1999, the Director commenced proceedings against the bank of originating summons, seeking injunctions restraining the bank from including in any agreement with the consumer any contractual term or provision having the object or effect of: (i) making interest payable on the amount of any judgment obtained by the bank for sums owing under a regulated agreement; or (ii) making interest payable upon interest and enforcing any such term already included in any existing agreement. The Director did not pursue the 'interest upon interest' point. The generality of the injunctions sought is to be noted: they are not confined to the particular circumstances giving rise to the complaints made to the Director.

On the hearing of the Originating Summons, the judge considered two issues. One was whether in the light of reg 3(2) of the Regulations the relevant term fell to be assessed for fairness at all. The bank argued that it did not as the provision for the payment of interest consequent on default was a core term falling within reg 3(2). The judge rejected that submission, because he did not think that the average borrower seeking a home improvement loan from the bank would consider default provisions as one of the important terms of the agreement which he would have under consideration in deciding whether or not to accept an offer of an advance. The other issue was whether the relevant term was unfair. The judge's approach was to consider apart from statute or authority whether a potential borrower would have thought the relevant term unfair if its effects were drawn to his attention. The judge said that the borrower would not have considered the term unfair. The judge then considered the requirement of good faith, which, he said, took two forms: substantive unfairness and procedural unfairness. He accepted that if the relevant term deprived a borrower of an advantage which he might reasonably expect to receive or which by statute or as a result of public policy he was entitled to receive there would be substantive unfairness. The judge found that the only substantive advantage of which the borrower was deprived was the exemption from having to pay interest on a judgment obtained against him on his default under the agreement. But he held that there was no statutory or other prohibition against the bank's use of the relevant term. On procedural unfairness, the judge accepted that it would be better practice for the bank to draw the relevant term to the attention of borrowers before entering the agreement. But he held that there was no procedural unfairness. He pointed out that the Director had not sought a mandatory injunction to compel the bank to draw the relevant term to the attention of borrowers. The judge concluded that the Director failed to discharge the onus on him of proving that the relevant term was unfair or operated unfairly. He accordingly refused the relief sought by the Director.

The same two issues arise before this court. The first issue, whether by reason by reg 3(2), the fairness of the relevant term does not fall to be assessed, is raised by way of a respondent's notice by the bank. Lord Goodhart QC argues that the 'core terms' of a consumer credit agreement or any other contract for a loan bearing interest extend beyond the mere rate of interest. He says that the period over which interest is payable (whether payable before or after judgment) and the sum on which it is payable are also core terms falling within para (a) and (b) of reg 3(2) or both, being terms which define the main subject matter of the contract and/or the price or remuneration for the loan. He contends that such status cannot be changed simply because the creditor has entered judgment, because after any judgment the creditor is as much out of his money (till he is paid) as before and the character of the quid pro quo for being out of his money, the interest is exactly the same. He draws our attention to the position in Scotland as established by the decision of the Court of Session in *Bank of Scotland v Davis* 1982 SLT 20. In that case, an appeal was allowed from the order of the sheriff in an undefended action for repayment of a loan, the sheriff having ordered payment of interest from the date of judgment at a rate lower than the contractual rate until payment. The court saw no reason why the contractual rate should not apply after judgment. Lord Goodhart argues that in Scotland the contractual rate of interest is a core term and so the fairness of it cannot be assessed. He submits that the Regulations should be read, if possible, in a way which avoids an anomaly between the position in England and that in Scotland and that the obvious way to do this is to treat the relevant term as conferring a single unbroken right to interest at the contractual rate and so as a core term.

23   Lord Goodhart sought leave to adduce further evidence of the position in three other jurisdiction, Ireland, France and Germany. This was not opposed by the Solicitor-General appearing for the Director and we allowed it. It appears that the position in France is the same as in Scotland. In Ireland and Germany there is a statutory right to interest at a prescribed rate. Lord Goodhart argued that an aim of the Directive was to harmonise the position in Member States of the European Union and he suggested that harmonisation towards the Scottish and French position by

recognising a provision for post-judgment interest as a core term was desirable. We do not know what the laws of other Member States provide. On the material before us, we find it impossible to say that the Directive encourages harmonisation to accord with the Scottish and French model rather than the English or some other model.

The Solicitor-General submits that the relevant term is not a core term for two reasons. First, he says, that condition 8 consists of default provisions dealing with the situation where there is a breach of contract; it is not there that one finds defined the main subject matter of the contract nor does it concern the adequacy of the price or remuneration. Terms concerned with the adequacy of the price or remuneration are, he says, those which define the parties' rights and obligations in the due performance of the contract. Second, he says that the condition defines the circumstances in which interest is and continues to be payable; it is not a provision stipulating the rate at which interest is payable. No point is taken on the requirement of plain and intelligible language.

We agree with the Solicitor-General. The test in respect of the relevant term is not whether it can be called a 'core-term', but whether it falls within one or both of paras (a) and (b) of reg 3(2). Neither paragraph is in our opinion apt to cover the relevant term, which certainly does not define the main subject matter of the contract and which cannot, in our view, realistically be said to concern the adequacy of the remuneration, relating as it does only to a case where the borrower is in default and then merely providing for the continuation of the contractual rate after judgment. As the Solicitor-General pointed out, if the bank was right almost any provision containing any part of the bargain would be capable of falling within the reach of reg 3(2). There is nothing in the Directive to require so wide an interpretation. We would therefore uphold the decision of the judge on the first issue.

We turn to the second issue: is the relevant term unfair? Three elements in the test in the Regulations of unfairness of a contractual term may be noted, viz:

(1) an absence of good faith;

(2) a significant imbalance in the parties' rights and obligations under the contract; and

(3) detriment to the consumer.

'Good faith' has a special meaning in the Regulations, having its conceptual roots in civil law systems. The German Standard Contract Terms Act, providing for the avoidance of a term which is unreasonably disadvantageous to a party 'contrary to the requirements of good faith' (see Markesinis, *The German Law of Obligations*, 1997, Vol 1, p 908), appears to have had a significant influence on the Directive (see *Chitty on Contracts*, 28th edn, 1999, para 15-034). Bingham LJ said in *Interfoto Library Ltd v Stiletto Ltd* [1989] 1 QB 433, 439:

In many civil law systems, and perhaps in most legal systems outside the common law world, the law of obligations recognises and enforces an overriding principle that in making and carrying out contracts parties should act in good faith. This does not simply mean that they should not deceive each other, a principle which any legal system must recognise; its effect is perhaps most aptly conveyed by such metaphorical colloquialisms as 'playing fair', 'coming clean' or 'putting one's cards face upwards on the table'. It is in essence a principle of fair and open dealing'.

Professor Beale, in his chapter 'Legislative control of fairness: the Directive on Unfair Terms in Consumer Contracts', in Beatson and Friedman, *Good Faith and Fault in Contract Law,* 1995, said at p 245:

I suspect that good faith has a double operation. First, it has a procedural aspect. It will require the supplier to consider the consumer's interests.

However, a clause which might be unfair if it came as a surprise may be upheld if the business took steps to bring it to the consumer's attention and to explain it. Secondly, it has a substantive content: some clauses may cause such an imbalance that they should always be treated as unfair.

As is aptly said in *Anson's Law of Contract,* 27th edn, 1999, p 293, the 'good faith' element seeks to promote fair and open dealing, and to prevent unfair surprise and the absence of real choice. A term to which the consumer's attention is not specifically drawn but which may operate in a way which the consumer might reasonably not expect and to his disadvantage may offend the requirement of good faith. Terms must be reasonably transparent and should not operate to defeat the reasonable expectations of the consumer. The consumer, in choosing whether to enter into a contract, should be put in a position where he can make an informed choice.

The element of significant imbalance would appear to overlap substantially with that of the absence of good faith. A term which gives a significant advantage to the seller or supplier without a countervailing benefit to the consumer (such as a price reduction) might fail to satisfy this part of the test of an unfair term.

Finally the element of detriment to the consumer must be present for the term to be found to be unfair.

The Solicitor-General submits that the relevant term is unfair. His complaint is that it operates unfairly in the particular circumstances that: (1) judgment is obtained against a borrower under a regulated agreement; (2) an order is made to pay the debt by instalments, whether under s 71 of the 1984 Act or a time order under s 129 of the 1974 Act; but (3) no order is made under s 136 of the 1974 Act is considered or made to amend the agreement, with the result that interest continues to accrue notwithstanding the due payment of the instalments ordered.

Lord Goodhart submitted that the judge was right for the reasons which he gave. But as we understood him, Lord Goodhart accepted that the relevant term could cause hardship. He expressly accepted that it was 'plainly desirable' that every debtor should have his attention drawn to the availability of time orders and orders under s 136. But he argued that that should be done in a way other than by putting the burden on the bank to amend the agreement. Thus, he said that it could be done by amending the court forms so that when a creditor sues on the default of the borrower attention is drawn to that point. Alternatively, he said, it could be done by amending the Consumer Credit (Enforcement, Default and Termination Notices) Regulations 1983, so that the default notice draws attention to the point. No doubt, the adoption of either of these methods could improve the position. But they do not ensure that the point to which objection is taken and which originates with the relevant term will be met, and we do not see that these palliatives prevent the contractual term from being unfair, if the relevant term can be so categorised.

We are not persuaded that the judge was correct in his approach. The test of unfairness is not to be judged by personal concepts of inherent fairness apart from the requirements of the Directive and Regulations, and we are far from convinced that a borrower would think it fair that when he is taken to court and an order for payment by instalments has been tailored to meet what he could afford and he complied with that order, he should then be told that he has to pay further sums by way of interest. The borrower's attention is not specifically drawn to the point by the bank at or before the conclusion of the contract nor at any later time prior to the making of the order nor in the order itself and the evidence shows that it comes as a disagreeable surprise to the borrower to find that due compliance with the order for payment by instalments, so far from eliminating the debt to the bank, may leave him owing substantial further sums to the bank. It is not enough to say, as the judge did, that if the provisions of ss 129 and 136 of the 1974 Act are correctly used by the courts the inclusion of the relevant term need not operate to impose on a borrower post judgment interest when it would not be appropriate or just to do so. That does not prevent the relevant term operating unfairly in the majority of cases where instalment orders are made without the consideration by the courts of those provisions.

In our judgment, the relevant term is unfair within the meaning of the Regulations to the extent that it enables the bank to obtain judgment against a debtor under a regulated agreement and an instalment order under s 71 of the 1984 Act without the court considering whether to make a time order, or if it does and makes a time order, whether also to make an order under s 136 to reduce the contractual interest rate. The bank, with its strong bargaining position as against the relatively weak position of the consumer, has not adequately considered the consumer's interest in this respect. In our view the relevant term in that respect does create unfair surprise and so does not satisfy the test of good faith, it does cause a significant imbalance in the rights and obligations of the parties by allowing the bank to obtain interest after judgment in circumstances when it would not obtain interest under the 1984 Act and the 1991 Order and no specific benefit to compensate the borrower is provided, and it operates to the detriment of that consumer who has to pay the interest. We would therefore allow the appeal.

The question which then arises is as to the form of the appropriate relief. The effect of holding the relevant term to be unfair, although only in a limited respect, would appear to be that by reg 5(1) it is not binding on the consumer. But the contract continues to bind the parties if it is capable of continuing in existence without the unfair term term (reg 5(2)); plainly the contract is so capable. An injunction against the use of the relevant term in contracts concluded with consumers is at first blush the appropriate form of relief by reason of reg 8(2). But Lord Goodhart complained that the injunction sought by the Director went too wide, going beyond what what needed to meet the Director's objection. In this context it is pertinent to refer to para 6 of the Notice of Appeal:

> The Learned Judge ought to have held that cl 8 was unfair, insofar as it was not limited by a proviso to the effect that the defendant would not seek to rely on it after judgment: (i) in any case where the court made an order for payment of the judgment debt by instalments; or (ii) alternatively, in any such case unless a judge has specifically considered whether to exercise the Court's powers under ss 129 and 136 of the Consumer Credit Act 1974.

The Director thereby appeared to recognise that the unfairness could be cured if an amendment were made to condition 8.

> We have heard no argument on the wording of any such amendment, but if the bank were prepared to draft a suitable amendment to meet the Director's objection and gave an undertaking to incorporate such amendment in its standard terms, we would be minded to accept such undertaking, and the wider or any injunction would be unnecessary. It goes without saying that it would be desirable for the terms of any such amendment to be agreed between the parties.

The Court of Appeal seems to have reversed the High Court principally because it felt that the latter allowed a largely subjective view on 'fairness' to substitute for a close adherence to the wording of the regulations and the Directive. Equally there is no evidence that the High Court failed to take account of the regulations. Is this willingness of the Court of Appeal to reverse a High Court judgment consistent with the approach taken to the Unfair Contract Terms Act 'reasonableness' test?[82]

Relationship between the Regulations and the 1977 Act

Some immediate points strike home. First, the Regulations are both considerably wider than the Unfair Contract Terms Act 1977 'trawling in' a

---

82   See *op cit*, fns 47–48 and 54–56.

very wide range of clauses other than exemption clauses. Scrutiny of Sched 2 indicates control of penalty clauses, forfeiture clauses and a wide range of 'non-negotiated' terms well beyond the exemption clause field (and this is only an indicative and non-exhaustive list!). However, secondly, unlike the 1977 Act, the Regulations only cover consumer contracts. Thirdly, the key test of good faith superficially differs from the reasonableness test in the 1977 Act.[83] Given that the two sets of provisions stand side by side, there is the possibility, at least, of a term being valid under the 1977 Act, but invalid under these Regulations (or vice versa).[84]

In the previous edition of this book, it was stated that:

Finally, and of crucial importance, is the way in which the courts will use their wide new powers. A judge with a 'Denning' or 'Bingham' breadth of perspective will, presumably, feel very comfortable with these provisions, but others may not. Will it be the case that an infinite number of one-off pragmatic decisions are made, as is already the danger with the reasonableness test? Alternatively will appeal courts attempt to give some guidance on phrases such as 'plain, intelligible language', 'significant imbalance' or even good faith? May there even be the admission into our courts of comparative jurisprudence, particularly from the civil law countries where many of these concepts are already part of the legal culture? If so, the comment by Hugh Collins[85] that 'The first whiffs of smoke from the furnaces of European Community Law have now trailed over general contract law' could underestimate the significance of these provisions.

Since then the debate has widened, with some academic opinion very much in support of the idea that the Regulations can act as a catalyst for wider change,[86] whilst other commentators are sceptical.[87] In the Court of Appeal decision in the *First National Bank* case, there is evidence of some 'comparative jurisprudence', although the references to 'good faith' in German law are not particularly illuminating. Perhaps the problem is that only relatively few cases seem likely to 'trouble' the higher courts, with most 'action' taking place a quasi-administrative level. From a practical consumer viewpoint, this may be no bad thing, but, from a theoretical viewpoint, it is a little disappointing that there is no evidence at present that a clear and coherent jurisprudence on the Regulations will be developed through the courts.

---

83 See *op cit*, fn 48.

84 It would arguably have been better in 1994 (or even in 1999) to take the opportunity to rationalise the legislation – perhaps by merging the provisions of Directive 93/13 and the relevant parts of the Act into a consumer 'code', leaving the residue of the UCTA as a business/commercial provision.

85 Collins, 1994.

86 Eg, Weatherill, 1997, p 78.

87 Eg, Teubner, 1998.

PART IV

PERFORMANCE, BREACH AND
REMEDIES FOR BREACH OF CONTRACT

CHAPTER 9

FACTORS GIVING RISE TO A REMEDY

PERFORMANCE OBLIGATIONS
AND BREACH OF CONTRACT

The principal remedies dealt with in later chapters are those of damages, specific performance and injunction. However, there are other remedies, such as an action for an agreed sum, which works in a manner similar to specific performance by requiring a party who has agreed to pay a sum of money for goods, land or services to pay the amount agreed.

Whether or not these remedies are activated will turn on the conduct of the defendant and whether that conduct can be regarded as a breach of contract. However, the mere fact that there has been a breach of contract will not necessarily wholly satisfy the claimant if he finds himself in the position of having to perform his obligations under the contract when the other party is in breach of the contract. If the defendant's breach is sufficiently serious, the claimant may be able to obtain a court order, or act unilaterally, so as to withhold his own performance.

PERFORMANCE

Whether or not an obligation has to be fulfilled may depend upon whether the other party has satisfied the conditions as to liability to perform imposed by the contract. For example, where a sale of goods is effected employing the device of a banker's commercial credit a number of obligations arise. Apart from the obvious duty of the buyer to pay for the goods and the duty of the seller to deliver, the credit device employed to finance the transaction also creates performance obligations. In particular, the duty of the seller to deliver the goods becomes dependent upon the obligation of the buyer to open the credit in the first place.[1]

Order of performance

A contract consists of a number of interrelated promises. At a simple level, in a consumer contract for the sale of goods, the buyer promises to pay the price

---

1   *Trans Trust SPRL v Danubian Trading Co Ltd* [1952] 2 QB 297.

and the seller promises to deliver the goods contracted for. However, the more complex the relationship, the more likely it is that there will be other interrelated promises, some of which may be more important than others. A further problem is to determine the order in which the various promises are to be performed. For example, in the sale of goods case above, does the seller have to deliver before the buyer has to pay or vice versa, or do the two performance obligations coincide?

In determining the order for performance, much will depend on the nature of the conditions of the contract. Lord Mansfield identifies three types of condition, namely, independent, dependent and concurrent conditions:

Kingston v Preston (1773) 99 ER 437

Lord Mansfield: There are three kinds of covenants: (1) Such as are called mutual and independent, where either party may recover damages from the other, for the injury he may have received by a breach of the covenants in his favour, and where it is no excuse for the defendant, to allege a breach of the covenants on the part of the plaintiff. (2) There are covenants which are conditions and dependant, in which the performance of one depends on the prior performance of another and, therefore, till this prior condition is performed, the other party is not liable to an action on his covenant. (3) There is also a third sort of covenant, which are mutual conditions to be performed at the same time; and, in these, if one party is ready, and offered, to perform his part, and the other neglected, or refused, to perform his, he who was ready, and offered, has fulfilled his engagement, and may maintain an action for the default of the other; though it is not certain that either is obliged to do the first act.

It follows from this that independent conditions are those which must be performed despite a breach of contract by the other party. Such conditions are rare, but an example can be found in landlord-tenant relationships under which the tenant must pay rent despite the fact that the landlord has failed to comply with his covenant to repair the property.[2] This also explains why in *Liverpool City Council v Irwin*,[3] the tenant had no right to stage a rent strike when he was dissatisfied with the council's maintenance of common areas such as lifts and staircases.

If a condition is said to be dependent, one party is not obliged to perform until the other has performed. Of necessity, this involves the first performer giving credit to the other party in the sense that there will be a valuable performance on one side before the other has done anything at all. A typical example arises in the field of employment contracts where the employee is expected to work a week or a month in advance, before he receives payment for that work.

---

2 *Taylor v Webb* [1937] 2 KB 283. Although the disrepair is sufficiently serious, it may release the tenant from his/her future contractual obligations.

3 [1977] AC 239, considered in detail in Chapter 5.

A performance condition may be dependent either because the contract so provides[4] or may be implied from the nature of the contract.

In *Trans Trust SPRL v Danubian Trading Co Ltd*,[5] the parties entered a contract for the sale of rolled steel on fob.[6] The terms under which payment was to be made by way of an irrevocable letter of credit, to be opened by the buyer in the seller's favour. The buyers subsequently agreed to sell the steel to American buyers, subject to a requirement that they too should open an irrevocable credit in favour of the first buyers, so as to facilitate the performance of both contracts. The American buyers failed to open a letter of credit. In an action by the sellers against the first buyers, the sellers sought a declaration that they were entitled to be indemnified against any damages payable by them to the American buyers. It was held that the sellers were discharged from further performance of their obligation to deliver when the letter of credit was not opened, since the seller's obligation was dependant on performance of the buyer's obligation to open the credit in the first place:

Trans Trust SPRL v Danubian Trading Co Ltd [1952] 1 All ER 970, CA, p 976

Denning LJ: This is another case concerned with the modern practice whereby a buyer agrees to provide a banker's confirmed credit in favour of the seller. This credit is an irrevocable promise by a banker to pay money to the seller in return for the shipping documents. One reason for this practice is because the seller wishes to be assured in advance, not only that the buyer is in earnest, but also that he, the seller, will get his money when he delivers the goods. Another reason is because the seller often has expenses to pay in connection with the goods and he wishes to use the credit to pay those expenses. He may, for instance, be himself a merchant, who is buying the goods from the growers or the manufacturers and has to pay for them before he can get delivery, and his own bank may only grant him facilities for the purpose if he has the backing of a letter of credit. The ability of the seller to carry out the transaction is, therefore, dependent on the buyer's providing the letter of credit, and for this reason the seller stipulates that the credit should be provided at a specified time well in advance of the time for delivery of the goods.

What is the legal position of such a stipulation? Sometimes, it is a condition precedent to the formation of a contract, that is, it is a condition which must be fulfilled before any contract is concluded at all. In those cases, the stipulation 'subject to the opening of a letter of credit' is rather like a stipulation 'subject to contract.' If no credit is provided, there is no contract between the parties. In other cases, a contract is concluded and the stipulation for a credit is a condition which is an essential term of the contract. In those cases, the

---

4   *Société Générale de Paris v Milders* (1883) 49 LT 55.
5   [1952] 1 All ER 970, CA.
6   'Fob' indicates 'free on board', which means that the seller's obligations in relation to the goods usually come to an end once the cargo has crossed the ship's rail and from that time onwards, the goods and their carriage is the responsibility of the buyer.

provision of the credit is a condition precedent, not to the formation of a contract, but to the obligation of the seller to deliver the goods. If the buyer fails to provide the credit, the seller can treat himself as discharged from any further performance of the contract and can sue the buyer for damages for not providing the credit.

The first question is: what was the nature of the stipulation in this case? When the buyers sent their order, they stated in writing on 25 September 1950, that 'a credit will be opened forthwith'. It was suggested that the buyers were not making any firm promise on their own account, but were only passing on information which had been given to them by their American buyers. The judge did not accept that suggestion and I agree with him. The statement was a firm promise by the buyers by which they gave their personal assurance that a credit would be opened forthwith. At that time, there were some discrepancies about gauges and dates of delivery which had to be cleared up, but these were all resolved at the meetings in Brussels, and there was then, as the judge found, a concluded contract by the sellers to sell, and the buyers to buy, the steel for December/January delivery, and it was a part of that contract that the buyers would be personally responsible for seeing that a credit should be opened forthwith. On those findings, it is clear that the stipulation for a credit was not a condition precedent to the formation of any contract at all. It was a condition which was an essential term of a contract actually made. That condition was not fulfilled. The sellers extended the time for the credit, but it never came, not even after reasonable notice. The sellers were, therefore, discharged from any further performance on their side, and are entitled to claim damages.

The third type of condition identified by Lord Mansfield requires simultaneous performance on both sides. A typical example can be found in sale of goods contracts, under which the seller's obligation to deliver arises simultaneously with the buyer's obligation to pay for the goods.[7] It follows that neither party can sue on the contract until he has performed or is ready to perform his own contractual obligations.

An important feature of the rules on the order of performance is that they can be manipulated so as to protect a weaker party. For example, under a consumer credit agreement, it is possible to protect consumers by making their obligation to pay instalments dependent upon performance by the creditor of his/her statutory obligation to supply relevant information.[8]

Entire and severable obligations

Where there are dependent conditions under which one party must completely perform an obligation before the other party is required to perform his/her side of the contract, it is said that the party who performs

---

7   Sale of Goods Act 1979, s 28.
8   *Bentworth Finance Ltd v Lubert* [1968] 1 QB 680.

first is under an entire performance obligation. An early example of this can be found in the old case of *Cutter v Powell*,[9] under which a seaman agreed to work a ship from its port of embarkation to its destination and back in return for a fixed sum. In the absence of a doctrine of frustration, it was held that, if the round trip was not completed, for whatever reason, the seaman did not become entitled to payment.

In other instances, performance obligations on one side may be subdivided with the result that as each part of the total obligation is completed, the other party comes under an obligation to perform his side of the contract. In these circumstances, the performance obligations are described as severable. Typical examples can be found in construction contracts which provide for payment in stages as the work progresses or instalment contracts for the sale of goods under which the buyer is required to pay separately for each instalment as it is delivered.

The importance of the distinction between entire and severable obligations is that there are different rules as to the order of performance and in respect of the matter of defective performance.

If the seller is under an entire obligation to deliver goods at a particular time, and he fails to do so, the buyer will not be obliged to pay the price. Conversely, if there is a severable instalment contract for the sale of goods and the seller fails to deliver one instalment out of ten, the seller may be able to claim payment for those parts of the work correctly performed.

Generally, sale of goods contracts consist of entire obligations. If the seller delivers less or more than the quantity of goods contracted for, the buyer is entitled to reject the entire consignment, subject to minor deviations in which case the court has a discretion in non-consumer transactions to refuse to allow rejection if this remedy can be regarded as unreasonable:

Sale of Goods Act 1979

30

(1) Where the seller delivers to the buyer a quantity of goods less than he contracted to sell, the buyer may reject them, but if the buyer accepts the goods so delivered, he must pay for them at the contract rate.

(2) Where the seller delivers to the buyer a quantity of goods larger than he contracted to sell, the buyer may accept the goods included in the contract and reject the rest, or he may reject the whole.

(2A) A buyer who does not deal as a consumer may not:

(a) where the seller delivers a quantity of goods less than he contracted to sell, reject the goods under sub-s (1) above; or

(b) where the seller delivers a quantity of goods larger than he contracted to sell, reject the whole under sub-s (2) above,

---

9   (1795) 6 TR 320.

if the shortfall or, as the case may be, excess is so slight that it would be unreasonable for him to do so.

The importance of s 30(2A) is that it represents a clearer and less uncertain statutory variant on the common law rule *de minimis non curat lex*, under which trifling deviations from the terms of the contract as to delivery could be ignored. The problem with the common law rule was that even minuscule deviations of, say, 1%, were probably too great to fall within the *de minimis* rule.[10] Moreover, there were sale of goods cases decided on the basis of the doctrine of strict tender under which a seller was taken to have virtually guaranteed that the goods delivered would comply exactly with the terms of the contract. Thus, in *Re Moore and Landauer's Arbitration*,[11] the seller contracted to deliver 3,000 cans of fruit, to be packed in boxes containing 30 tins each. In fact, the correct number of cans was delivered, but some of the boxes did not contain the prescribed number. Despite the fact that the goods were fit for the buyer's intended use, he was still able to reject.

It seems likely that the result in this case would not survive s 30(2A), although there are problem cases; for example, where the buyer sells on to a third party who has relied upon the description given by the first seller. In these circumstances, it would be wise for the court not to apply s 30(2A) too readily, given the likely reliance by the sub-purchaser on the description applied to the goods and his/her assumption that the description will be complied with exactly.

In a severable contract for the sale of goods, for example, one by instalments, short delivery in one or even a small number of instalments will not necessarily allow a refusal to accept future deliveries:

Sale of Goods Act 1979

31

(1) Unless otherwise agreed, the buyer of goods is not bound to accept delivery of them by instalments.

(2) Where there is a contract for the sale of goods to be delivered by stated instalments, which are to be separately paid for, and the seller makes defective deliveries in respect of one or more instalments, or the buyer neglects or refuses to take delivery of or pay for one or more instalments, it is a question in each case depending on the terms of the contract and the circumstances of the case whether the breach of contract is a repudiation of the whole contract or whether it is a severable breach giving rise to a claim for compensation but not to a right to treat the whole contract as repudiated.

Due to s 31(1), a seller cannot impose on the buyer a delivery by instalments without his consent. Thus, if the seller delivers 500 tons of grain out of a

---

10 See, eg, *Regent OHG Aisenstadt v Francesco of Jermyn Street* [1981] 3 All ER 327.
11 [1921] 2 KB 519

contracted amount of 1,000 tons and seeks to deliver the shortfall two weeks later, the buyer has the right to reject the whole consignment.[12]

The effect of s 31(2) is that, in order to decide whether defective deliveries or refusal to pay or take deliveries is to be regarded as a repudiation giving rise to the right in favour of the innocent party to treat his own performance obligations as being at an end is a question of fact in each case. It has been held that what has to be considered in these circumstances is the 'ratio quantitatively which the breach bears to the contract as a whole' and the likelihood that the breach will or will not be repeated.[13]

Part performance of entire obligations

It has been seen from the earlier discussion of *Cutter v Powell*[14] that a strict application of the rule on performance of entire obligations can have the effect of placing the risk of non-performance on the performer of a contract of personal services.[15] Important considerations in *Cutter v Powell* were that the contract provided for payment only on completion of the voyage from Jamaica to Liverpool and that the sailor was to be paid almost four times the normal rate for the job.

It is not true that English law always adopts a stance requiring absolute performance. Especially where periodic payments are made by way of income, it is possible that the performer can be paid on a day to day basis and be apportioned accordingly:[16]

Apportionment Act 1870

2

> All rents, annuities, dividends and other periodical payments in the nature of income ... shall like interest on money lent, be considered as accruing from day to day, and shall be apportionable in respect of time accordingly.

In the case of construction contracts, if the builder's obligation is regarded as entire, it would seem to follow that partial completion will disentitle the builder to payment, *under the contract*, in respect of his work. However there is still the possibility of a restitutionary remedy based on the reasonable value to the recipient of the benefit of the partial performance.[17]

---

12 *Behrend v Produce Brokers Ltd* [1920] 3 KB 530.
13 *Maple Flock Ltd v Universal Furniture Products Ltd* [1934] 1 KB 148.
14 (1795) 6 TR 320.
15 Albeit subject now to the operation of the doctrine of frustration considered in Chapter 6.
16 See *Taylor v Laird* (1856) 1 H & N 266.
17 *Sumpter v Hedges* [1898] 1 QB 673, CA. For the facts and relevant extracts from this decision, see Chapter 14.

In contrast, the contract may be worded in such a way as to allow payment to be made in stages. A typical example is the use of the phrase 'net cash as the work proceeds and balance on completion'. The effect of this is to render the builder's performance obligation severable rather than entire.

In *Hoenig v Isaacs*,[18] the plaintiff was employed by the defendant to decorate and furnish a flat at a fixed cost of £750. The work was completed, albeit subject to some defects which would cost £55 to rectify. The defendant moved into the flat but refused to pay the balance outstanding under the contract. The contract provided for payment of 'net cash as the work proceeds and balance on completion', so that the defendant had already paid £350 and the plaintiff now sought to recover the remaining £400. The Court of Appeal held that the defendant had not refused to accept the work with the result that he only had an action for damages for the defective work:

Hoenig v Isaacs [1952] 2 All ER 176, CA, p 177

Somervell LJ: Each case turns on the construction of the contract. In *Cutter v Powell*, the condition for the promissory note sued on was that the sailor should proceed to continue and do his duty as second mate in the ship from Jamaica to the port of Liverpool. The sailor died before the ship reached Liverpool and it was held his estate could not recover either on the contract or on a *quantum meruit*. It clearly decided that his continuing as mate during the whole voyage was a condition precedent to payment. It did not decide that if he had completed the main purpose of the contract, namely, serving as mate for the whole voyage, the defendant could have repudiated his liability by establishing that in the course of the voyage the sailor had, possibly through inadvertence, failed on some occasion in his duty as mate whereby some damage had been caused. In these circumstances, the court might have applied the principle applied to ordinary contracts for freight. The shipowner can normally recover nothing unless the goods are carried to their agreed destination. On the other hand, if this is done, his claim is not defeated by the fact that some damage has been done to the goods in transit which has resulted from a breach of the contract ...

The principle that fulfilment of every term is not necessarily a condition precedent in a contract for a lump sum is usually traced back to a short judgment of Lord Mansfield CJ in *Boone v Eyre* – the sale of the plantation with its slaves. Lord Mansfield said (1 Hy Bl 273): '... where mutual covenants go to the whole of the consideration on both sides, they are mutual conditions, the one precedent to the other. But where they go only to a part, where a breach may be paid for in damages, there the defendant has a remedy on his covenant, and shall not plead it as a condition precedent.'

---

18 [1952] 2 All ER 176, CA.

The learned official referee regarded *H Dakin & Co Ltd v Lee* as laying down that the price must be paid subject to set-off or counterclaim if there was a substantial compliance with the contract. I think on the facts of this case where the work was finished in the ordinary sense, though in part defective, this is right. It expresses in a convenient epithet what is put from another angle in the Sale of Goods Act 1893. The buyer cannot reject if he proves only the breach of a term collateral to the main purpose. I have, therefore, come to the conclusion that the first point of counsel for the defendant fails.

The learned official referee found that there was substantial compliance. Bearing in mind that there is no appeal on fact, was there evidence on which he could so find? The learned official referee having, as I hold, properly directed himself, this becomes, I think, a question of fact. The case on this point was, I think, near the border line, and if the finding had been the other way I do not think we could have interfered. Even if I had felt we could interfere, the defendant would be in a further difficulty. The contract included a number of chattels. If the defendant wished to repudiate his liability under the contract he should not, I think, have used those articles, which he could have avoided using. On this view, though it is not necessary to decide it, I think he put himself in the same position as a buyer of goods who by accepting them elects to treat a breach of condition as a breach of warranty.

Denning LJ: This case raises the familiar question: was entire performance a condition precedent to payment? That depends on the true construction of the contract. In this case the contract was made over a period of time and was partly oral and partly in writing, but I agree with the official referee that the essential terms were set down in the letter of 25 April 1950. It describes the work which was to be done and concludes with these words: 'The foregoing, complete, for the sum of £750 net. Terms of payment are net cash, as the work proceeds; and balance on completion.

The question of law that was debated before us was whether the plaintiff was entitled in this action to sue for the £350 balance of the contract price as he had done. The defendant said that he was only entitled to sue on a quantum meruit. The defendant was anxious to insist on a *quantum meruit*, because he said that the contract price was unreasonably high. He wished, therefore, to reject that price altogether and simply to pay a reasonable price for all the work that was done. This would obviously mean an inquiry into the value of every item, including all the many items which were in compliance with the contract as well as the three which fell short of it. That is what the defendant wanted. The plaintiff resisted this course and refused to claim on a *quantum meruit*. He said that he was entitled to the balance of £350 less a deduction for the defects.

In determining this issue, the first question is whether, on the true construction of the contract, entire performance was a condition precedent to payment. It was a lump sum contract, but that does not mean that entire performance was a condition precedent to payment. When a contract provides for a specific sum to be paid on completion of specified work, the courts lean against a construction of the contract which would deprive the contractor of any payment at all simply because there are some defects or omissions. The promise to complete the work is, therefore, construed as a term of the contract, but not as a condition. It is not every breach of that term which absolves the employer from his promise to pay the price, but only a breach which goes to the root of the contract, such as an abandonment of the work when it is only half done. Unless the breach does go to the root of the matter, the employer cannot resist payment of the price. He must pay it and bring a cross-claim for the defects and omissions, or, alternatively, set them up in diminution of the price. The measure is the amount which the work is worth less by reason of the defects and omissions, and is usually calculated by the cost of making them good: see *Mondel v Steel*; *H Dakin & Co Ltd v Lee*, and the notes to *Cutter v Powell* in *Smith's Leading Cases*, 13th edn, Vol 2, pp 19–21. It is, of course, always open to the parties by express words to make entire performance a condition precedent. A familiar instance is when the contract provides for progress payments to be made as the work proceeds, but for retention money to be held until completion. Then entire performance is usually a condition precedent to payment of the retention money, but not, of course, to the progress payments. The contractor is entitled to payment *pro rata* as the work proceeds, less a deduction for retention money. But he is not entitled to the retention money until the work is entirely finished, without defects or omissions. In the present case the contract provided for 'net cash, as the work proceeds; and balance on completion'. If the balance could be regarded as retention money, then it might well be that the contractor ought to have done all the work correctly, without defects or omissions, in order to be entitled to the balance. But I do not think the balance should be regarded as retention money. Retention money is usually only 10%, or 15%, whereas this balance was more than 50%. I think this contract should be regarded as an ordinary lump sum contract. It was substantially performed. The contractor is entitled, therefore, to the contract price, less a deduction for the defects.

Even if entire performance was a condition precedent, nevertheless the result would be the same, because I think the condition was waived. It is always open to a party to waive a condition which is inserted for his benefit. What amounts to a waiver depends on the circumstances. If this was an entire contract, then, when the plaintiff tendered the work to the defendant as being a fulfilment of the contract, the defendant could have refused to accept it until the defects were made good, in which case he would not have been liable for the balance of the price until they were made good. But he did not refuse to accept the work. On the contrary, he entered into possession of the flat and used the furniture as his own, including the defective items. That was a clear waiver of the condition precedent. Just as in a sale of goods the buyer who accepts the goods can no longer treat a breach of condition as giving a right to reject but only a right to damages, so also in a contract for work and labour an employer who takes the benefit of the work can no longer treat entire performance as a condition precedent, but only as a term giving rise to damages.

It is said that the distinction between *Hoenig v Isaacs* and *Sumpter v Hedges* lies in the fact that, in the latter, there was an entire obligation in relation to the quantity of work contracted for, whereas in the former, the defect related to the quality of the work which is only remediable in damages, not giving rise to a right to reject.[19]

The cases considered so far have all involved bilateral contracts in which the parties are normally dependent upon each other for the successful completion of the contract. However, different problems may arise in the case of performance of unilateral contracts, since in this case, the promisee is forced to perform his/her side of the contract before any performance obligation falls upon the promisor.[20]

BREACHES OF CONTRACT GIVING RISE TO THE RIGHT TO WITHHOLD PERFORMANCE

Where there is a breach of contract, there will always be a right in favour of the party not in breach to recover damages. However, monetary compensation may not always be sufficient, if the innocent party's trust in the other party has evaporated and it may be that he wishes to escape from the contract. The types of breach which are sufficiently serious to allow the innocent party to withhold his own performance are said to comprise a repudiatory breach, in the form of a refusal to perform and a breach of condition.

Refusal to perform

Where one party, by his words or conduct, indicates that he will not perform his future contractual obligations, the other party is entitled to treat this as a repudiation of the contract. Assuming the refusal occurs prior to a specified date for performance, it is referred to as an anticipatory repudiation, the effect of which is to give the innocent party the right to treat his own primary performance obligations as being at an end. Such a repudiation may be express or implied. Thus, in *Hochster v De La Tour*,[21] the plaintiff had been engaged by the defendant to act as a courier on a tour commencing on 1 June but, in May, he indicated expressly that he had changed his mind. This action allowed the plaintiff to accept the repudiation immediately and sue for breach of contract without having to wait for the date of intended performance.

Alternatively, the repudiation may be implied.

---

19   See Treitel, 1999.
20   *Carlill v Carbolic Smoke Ball Co Ltd* [1893] 1 QB 256.
21   (1853) 2 E & B 678.

In *Frost v Knight*,[22] the defendant had promised that when the plaintiff's father died, he would marry her. However, during the father's lifetime, the defendant broke off his engagement to the plaintiff. Without waiting for the death of her father, the plaintiff sued immediately for breach of promise of marriage:[23]

Frost v Knight (1872) LR 7 Exch 111, p 112

Cockburn CJ: The law with reference to a contract to be performed at a future time, where the party bound to performance announces prior to the time his intention not to perform it, as established by the cases of *Hochster v De La Tour* and *The Danube and Black Sea Co v Xenos* on the one hand, and *Avery v Bowden*, *Reid v Hoskins* and *Barwick v Buba* on the other, may be thus stated. The promisee, if he pleases, may treat the notice of intention as inoperative, and await the time when the contract is to be executed, and then hold the other party responsible for all the consequences of non-performance: but in that case he keeps the contract alive for the benefit of the other party as well as his own; he remains subject to all his own obligations and liabilities under it, and enables the other party not only to complete the contract, if so advised, notwithstanding his previous repudiation of it, but also to take advantage of any supervening circumstance which would justify him in declining to complete it.

On the other hand, the promisee may, if he thinks proper, treat the repudiation of the other party as a wrongful putting an end to the contract, and may at once bring his action as on a breach of it; and in such action he will be entitled to such damages as would have arisen from the non-performance of the contract at the appointed time, subject, however, to abatement in respect of any circumstances which may have afforded him the means of mitigating his loss.

Considering this to be now settled law, notwithstanding any thing that may have been held or said in the cases of *Phillpotts v Evans* and *Ripley v McClure*, we should have had no difficulty in applying the principle of the decision in *Hochster v De La Tour* to the present case, were it not for the difference which undoubtedly exists between that case and the present, viz, that, whereas there the performance of the contract was to take place at a fixed time, here no time is fixed, but the performance is made to depend on a contingency, namely, the death of the defendant's father during the lifetime of the contracting parties. It is true that in every case of a personal obligation to be fulfilled at a future time, there is involved the possible contingency of the death of the party binding himself, before the time of performance arrives; but here we have a further contingency depending on the life of a third person, during which neither party can claim performance of the promise. This being so, we thought it right to take time to consider whether an action would lie before the death of the defendant's father had placed the plaintiff in a position to claim the fulfilment of the defendant's promise.

---

22 (1872) LR 7 Exch 111.

23 This action has now been abolished by the Law Reform (Miscellaneous Provisions) Act 1970, s 1.

After full consideration, we are of opinion that, notwithstanding the distinguishing circumstance to which I have referred, this case falls within the principle of *Hochster v De La Tour*, and that, consequently, the present action is well brought.

The considerations on which the decision in *Hochster v De La Tour* is founded are that the announcement of the contracting party of his intention not to fulfil the contract amounts to a breach, and that it is for the common benefit of both parties that the contract shall be taken to be broken as to all its incidents, including non-performance at the appointed time; as by an action being brought at once, and the damages consequent on non-performance being assessed at the earliest moment, many of the injurious effects of such non-performance may possibly be averted or mitigated.

It is true, as is pointed out by the Lord Chief Baron in his judgment in this case, that there can be no actual breach of a contract by reason of non-performance, so long as the time for performance has not yet arrived. But, on the other hand, there is – and the decision in *Hochster v De La Tour* proceeds on that assumption – a breach of the contract when the promisor repudiates it and declares he will no longer be bound by it. The promisee has an inchoate right to the performance of the bargain, which becomes complete when the time for performance has arrived. In the mean time he has a right to have the contract kept open as a subsisting and effective contract. Its unimpaired and unimpeached efficacy may be essential to his interests. His rights acquired under it may be dealt with by him in various ways for his benefit and advantage. Of all such advantage the repudiation of the contract by the other party, and the announcement that it never will be fulfilled, must of course deprive him. It is therefore quite right to hold that such an announcement amounts to a violation of the contract in omnibus, and that upon it the promisee, if so minded, may at once treat it as a breach of the entire contract, and bring his action accordingly.

The contract having been thus broken by the promisor, and treated as broken by the promisee, performance at the appointed time becomes excluded, and the breach by reason of the future non-performance becomes virtually involved in the action as one of the consequences of the repudiation of the contract; and the eventual non-performance may therefore, by anticipation be treated as a cause of action, and damages be assessed and recovered in respect of it, though the time for performance may yet be remote.

It is obvious that such a course must lead to the convenience of both parties; and though we should be unwilling to found our opinion on grounds of convenience alone, yet the latter tend strongly to support the view that such an action ought to be admitted and upheld. By acting on such a notice of the intention of the promisor, and taking timely measures, the promisee may in many cases avert, or at all events materially lessen, the injurious effects which would otherwise flow from the non-fulfilment of the contract; and in assessing the damages for breach of performance, a jury will of course take into account whatever the plaintiff has done, or has had the means of doing, and, as a prudent man, ought in reason to have done, whereby his loss has been, or would have been, diminished.

It appears to us that the foregoing considerations apply to the case of a contract the performance of which is made to depend on a contingency, as much as to one in which the performance is to take place at a future time; and we are, therefore, of opinion that the principle of the decision of *Hochster v De La Tour* is equally applicable to such a case as the present.

Whether or not there has been a repudiation is a relatively easy matter to determine when the contractual obligations of the parties are simple, such as will be the case in a non-commercial contract for the sale of goods. However, difficulties may arise in more complex relationships where a party has repudiated one or more of a series of obligations, since it will be necessary to consider whether the innocent party has been substantially deprived of that which he/she contracted for. In these circumstances, the court will have to consider both the overall seriousness of the breach in relation to what was contracted for and the likelihood that the breach will or will not be repeated.

In *Decro-Wall International SA v Practitioners in Marketing Ltd*,[24] the defendants had been appointed as sole concessionaires for UK sales of the plaintiffs' (a French company) product. Because they were short of working capital, the defendants were persistently late in making payments under the contract, but they never failed to pay. The plaintiffs incurred bank interest charges as a result of the defendants' late payments and ultimately responded by appointing someone else as their concessionaire. It was held that the defendants' breach did not justify termination of the contract as the delays in payment were only slight and gave no reason to doubt that payment would be made. Accordingly, an award of damages was seen to be a sufficient remedy:

Decro-Wall International SA v Practitioners in Marketing Ltd [1971] 1 WLR 361 CA , p 379

Buckley LJ: On the first question, it is said on behalf of the plaintiffs that, if one party to a contract manifests an intention not to perform in accordance with the contract some part of his unperformed obligations thereunder throughout the remainder of the subsistence of the contract, the other party is entitled to treat this as a repudiation of the contract. This, it is said, is so however insubstantial the threatened departure from due performance of the contract may be. I cannot accept this contention. Perhaps the nearest statement that can be found in any of the authorities to support it is that of Bingham J in *Millars' Karri and Jarrah Co (1902) v Weddel, Turner & Co*, where the learned judge said: 'It is argued that if [ie the award there under consideration] violates the well known rule of law that where goods are sold to be delivered in different instalments a breach by one party in connection with one instalment does not of itself entitle the other party to rescind the contract as to the other instalments. But I do not agree. The rule, which is a very good one, is, like most rules, subject to qualification. Thus, if the breach is of such a kind, or takes

24   [1971] 1 WLR 361, CA.

place in such circumstances as reasonably to lead to the inference that similar breaches will be committed in relation to subsequent deliveries, the whole contract may there and then be regarded as repudiated, and may be rescinded.

That passage must, in my judgment, be read in relation to the facts of that case, in which, under a contract for the sale of timber by instalments, the vendors had delivered a first instalment which did not accord with the requirements of the contract in circumstances which lead to the conclusion that subsequent instalments would be defective in a similar way. The breach there was, I think, clearly one which went to the root of the contract, for the suppliers were proposing to deliver goods which were not in accordance with the contract. Each party to an agreement is entitled to performance of the contract according to its terms in every particular, and any breach, however slight, which causes damage to the other party will afford a cause of action for damages; but not every breach, even if its continuance is threatened throughout the contract or the remainder of its subsistence, will amount to a repudiation. To constitute repudiation, the threatened breach must be such as to deprive the injured party of a substantial part of the benefit to which he is entitled under the contract. The measure of the necessary degree of substantiality has been expressed in a variety of ways in the cases. It has been said that the breach must be of an essential term, or of a fundamental term of the contract, or that it must go to the root of the contract. Various tests have been suggested: see, for example, *Freeth v Burr, per* Lord Coleridge CJ and Keating J; *Mersey Steel and Iron Co Ltd v Naylor, Benzon & Co, per* the Earl of Selborne LC and Lord Blackburn and *Hong Kong Fir Shipping Co Ltd v Kawasaki Kisen Kaisha Ltd, per* Diplock LJ. I venture to put the test in my own words as follows: will the consequences of the breach be such that it would be unfair to the injured party to hold him to the contract and leave him to the remedy in damages as and when a breach or breaches may occur? If this would be so, then a repudiation has taken place.

The plaintiffs submit that punctual payment on the bills of exchange was of particular importance in the present case. This was not known to the defendants at the date of the agreement, nor were the particular reasons on which the plaintiffs rely for saying that punctual payment was of particular importance then known to the defendants. The plaintiffs showed themselves to be willing on numerous occasions to negotiate extension of bills of exchange and to extend the defendants' credit beyond the 90 days' limit, having regard to the defendants' financial difficulties and to the supervention of devaluation in this country and the imposition of the import quota scheme. The evidence does not establish that the plaintiffs have suffered any grave loss as the result of the defendants' failure to honour the bills punctually, and in many instances the delay in payment was not of long duration. The history of the whole matter indicates that punctual payment was a matter of much less importance to the plaintiffs than other aspects of the contract. The learned judge was, in my judgment, justified in concluding, as he did, that the defendants' conduct did not amount to repudiation. The defendants' failure to honour the bills punctually was not, in my judgment, a breach going to the root of the contract: in other words, it was not a course of conduct calculated to deprive the plaintiffs of the enjoyment of so important a part of the benefits of the contract as to make it unfair to relegate the plaintiffs to recovery of damages for any individual breach of the contract of this kind as and when it occurred.

Mr Ross Munro for the plaintiff company placed considerable reliance on *Withers v Reynolds* (1831) 2 B & Ad 882 In my view, Lord Tenterden CJ in that case proceeded on the basis that by the terms of the agreement there under consideration the plaintiff was to pay for the loads of straw as they were delivered and that this was an essential term of the contract. In the present case, in my judgment, punctual payment of the bills was not, for reasons which I have endeavoured to indicate, an essential term of the contract.

A similar approach is also applied to contracts which create severable obligations, such as instalment contracts for the sale of goods under which each instalment is to be paid for separately.

In *Maple Flock Ltd v Universal Furniture Products (Wembley) Ltd*,[25] the plaintiffs contracted to supply the defendants with 100 tons of rag flock, delivery to be effected at the rate of three weekly instalments of 1.5 tons each, as required. It was a requirement of the contract that the flock should conform to government standards. The first 15 loads delivered were in perfect condition, but the 16th delivery failed to reach government standard. The following four deliveries were again all in conformity with the contract, but the defendant sought to treat the contract as repudiated. The Court of Appeal held that there was no probability of the breach recurring and that in any case, in relation to what was contracted for, the plaintiffs' breach was not sufficiently serious to allow repudiation:

Maple Flock Ltd v Universal Furniture Products (Wembley) Ltd [1934] 1 KB 148, CA, p 154

Lord Hewart CJ: The decision of this case depends on the true construction and application of s 31(2) of the Sale of Goods Act 1893 ...

That sub-section was based on decisions before the Act, and has been the subject of decisions since the Act. A contract for the sale of goods by instalments is a single contract, not a complex of as many contracts as there are instalments under it. The law might have been determined in the sense that any breach of condition in respect of any one or more instalments would entitle the party aggrieved to claim that the contract has been repudiated as a whole; or, on the other hand, the law as established might have been that any breach, however serious, in respect of one or more instalments, should not have consequences extending beyond the particular instalment or instalments or affecting the contract as a whole. The sub-section, however, which deals equally with breaches either by the buyer or by the seller, requires the court to decide on the merits of the particular case what effect (if any) the breach or breaches should have on the contract as a whole. The language of the Act is substantially based on the language used by Lord Selbourne in *Mersey Steel and*

25 [1934] 1 KB 148, CA.

Iron Co Ltd v Naylor, Benzon & Co, where he said (9 App Cas 438): 'I am content to take the rule as stated by Lord Coleridge in *Freeth v Burr* (LR 9 CP 213), which is in substance, as I understand it, that you must look at the actual circumstances of the case in order to see whether the one party to the contract is relieved from its future performance by the conduct of the other; you must examine what that conduct is, so as to see whether it amounts to a renunciation, to an absolute refusal to perform the contract, such as would amount to a rescission if he had the power to rescind, and whether the other party may accept it as a reason for not performing his part.'

The true test will generally be, not the subjective mental state of the defaulting party, but the objective test of the relation in fact of the default to the whole purpose of the contract.

Since the Act, the sub-section has been discussed by a Divisional Court in *Millar's Karri and Jarrah Co (1902) Ltd v Weddel, Turner & Co*, where, the contract being for 1,100 pieces of timber, the first instalment of 750 pieces was rejected by the buyers and an arbitrator awarded 'that the said shipment was, and is, so far from complying with the requirements of the said contract as to entitle the buyers to repudiate and to rescind the whole contract and to refuse to accept the said shipment, and all further shipments under the said contract'.

The court upheld the award. Bingham J thus stated what, in his opinion, was the true test: 'Thus, if a breach is of such a kind as takes place in such circumstances as reasonably to lead to the inference that similar breaches will be committed in relation to subsequent deliveries, the whole contract may there and then be regarded as repudiated and may be rescinded. If, for instance, a buyer fails to pay for one delivery in such circumstances as to lead to the inference that he will not be able to pay for subsequent deliveries; or if a seller delivers goods differing from the requirements of the contract, and does so in such circumstances as to lead to the inference that he cannot, or will not, deliver any other kind of goods in the future, the other contracting party will be under no obligation to wait to see what may happen; he can at once cancel the contract and rid himself of the difficulty.' Walton J concurred.

This ruling was more recently applied in *Robert A Munro & Co Ltd v Meyer*, where, under a contract for the sale of 1,500 tons of bone meal, 611 tons were delivered which were seriously adulterated. The sellers were middlemen, who relied on their suppliers, the manufacturers, for correct delivery; when the buyers discovered that the deliveries did not conform to the contract they claimed that they were entitled to treat the whole contract as repudiated by the sellers. It was held that they were right in so claiming on the ground that, 'in such a case as this, where there is a persistent breach, deliberate so far as the manufacturers are concerned, continuing for nearly one-half of the total contract quantity, the buyer, if he ascertains what the position is, ought to be entitled to say that he will not take the risk of having put upon him further deliveries of this character'.

On the other hand, in *Taylor v Oakes, Roncoroni & Co*, Greer J and the Court of Appeal refused to hold that the buyers were entitled to refuse to go on with the contract, but held that the breach was a severable breach, as it was a case where the instalment delivered failed in a slight, but appreciable degree to come up to the standard required by the contract description.

With the help of these authorities we deduce that the main tests to be considered in applying the sub-section to the present case, are, first, the ratio quantitatively which the breach bears to the contract as a whole and, secondly, the degree of probability or improbability that such a breach will be repeated. On the first point, the delivery complained of amounts to no more than $1^{1/2}$ tons out of a contract for 100 tons. On the second point, our conclusion is that the chance of the breach being repeated is practically negligible. We assume that the sample found defective fairly represents the bulk, but bearing in mind the judge's finding that the breach was extraordinary and that the sellers' business was carefully conducted, bearing in mind also that the sellers were warned, and that the delivery complained of was an isolated instance out of twenty satisfactory deliveries actually made both before and after the instalment objected to, we hold that it cannot reasonably be inferred that similar breaches would occur in regard to subsequent deliveries. Indeed, we do not understand that the learned judge came to any different conclusion. He seems, however, to have decided against the sellers on a third and separate ground – that is, that a delivery not satisfying the government requirements would or might lead to the buyers being prosecuted under the Act. Though we think he exaggerates the likelihood of the buyers in such a case being held responsible, we do not wish to underrate the gravity to the buyers of their being even prosecuted. But we cannot follow the judge's reasoning that the bare possibility, however remote, of this happening would justify the buyers in rescinding in this case. There may, indeed, be such cases, as also cases where the consequences of a single breach of contract may be so serious as to involve a frustration of the contract and justify rescission, or, furthermore, the contract might contain an express condition that a breach would justify rescission, in which case effect would be given to such a condition by the court. But none of these circumstances can be predicated of this case. We think the deciding factor here is the extreme improbability of the breach being repeated, and on that ground, and on the isolated and limited character of the breach complained of, there was, in our judgment, no sufficient justification to entitle the respondents to refuse further deliveries as they did.

The appeal must, accordingly, be allowed and judgment entered for the appellants, with costs here and below, for damages for the respondents' breach of contract in refusing further deliveries.

Further difficulties may arise where the party in breach acts in a manner which he believes to be justified under the terms of the contract, but which is, in fact, not so justified. Whether such action constitutes a repudiation may well depend on the size of the interval between the date of the alleged repudiation and the date for performance of the contract and whether any meaningful relationship between the parties can be salvaged. In *Federal*

Commerce and Navigation Co Ltd v Molena Alpha Inc,[26] the charterers of a ship deducted the amount of a counterclaim against the owners from their periodic payments for hire. In response to this, the owners, after taking legal advice, told the ship's master not to issue freight pre-paid bills of lading. Moreover, they also stipulated that any future bills of lading be endorsed with the terms of the charterparty. The overall effect of these instructions was that the charterers became unable to operate the ship. Accordingly, the charterers sought to treat the contract as repudiated. The House of Lords held that the seriously coercive effect of the owners' actions outweighed the fact that the owners believed they were entitled to take these steps. This decision stood, despite the fact that the owners still wished to continue with the contract, and had attempted to have the deductions dispute resolved by way of arbitration. In contrast, the charterers appeared to have lost all faith in the owners in the light of their coercive behaviour and were not particularly happy at the thought of a continuing relationship with the owners. This contrasts with the case of *Woodar Investment Development Ltd v Wimpey Construction (UK) Ltd.*[27] Under the terms of a contract for the sale of land, the purchasers believed they had an option to withdraw in the event of a statutory authority commencing proceedings for compulsory purchase of the land. In fact, they were not entitled to do so, but it was held by a majority of the House of Lords that the purchaser's conduct did not amount to repudiation. An important factor in the decision appears to have been the fact that there was a considerable period of time to run after the date of the alleged repudiation and the date of performance, which was sufficient to allow the parties to seek a resolution to the dispute:

Woodar Investment Development Ltd v Wimpey Construction (UK) Ltd [1980] 1 WLR 277 HL, p 280

Lord Wilberforce: In considering whether there has been a repudiation by one party, it is necessary to look at his conduct as a whole. Does this indicate an intention to abandon and to refuse performance of the contract? In the present case, without taking the appellant's conduct generally into account, the respondent's contention, that the appellant had repudiated, would be a difficult one. So far from repudiating the contract, the appellants were relying on it and invoking one of its provisions, to which both parties had given their consent. And unless the invocation of that provision were totally abusive, or lacking in good faith, (neither of which is contended for), the fact that it has proved to be wrong in law cannot turn it into a repudiation. At the lowest, the notice of rescission was a neutral document consistent either with an intention to preserve, or with an intention to abandon, the contract, and I will deal with it on this basis, more favourable to the respondents. In order to decide which is correct, the appellant's conduct has to be examined.

---

26   [1979] AC 757.
27   [1980] 1 WLR 277.

One point can, in my opinion, be disposed of at once. The respondents, in March 1974, started proceedings against the appellants: this is one of the actions consolidated in the litigation before us. They claimed a declaration that the appellant's notice of rescission was not valid, and the appellants, by their defence asserted the contrary and they counterclaimed for a declaration to that effect. The respondents now contend that if the original notice did not amount to a repudiation, the defence and counterclaim did. I regard this contention as hopeless. The appellant's pleading carried the matter no further: it simply rested the matter on the contract. It showed no intention to abandon the contract whatever the result of the action might be. If the action were to succeed (ie if the appellants lost) there was no indication that the appellant would not abide by the result and implement the contract.

The facts indicative of the appellant's intention must now be summarised. It is clear in the first place that, subjectively, the appellants in 1974 wanted to get out of the contract. Land prices had fallen, and they thought that if the contract was dissolved, they could probably acquire it at a much lower price. But subjective intention is not decisive: it supplied the motive for serving the notice of rescission; there remains the question whether, objectively regarded, their conduct showed an intention to abandon the contract.

In early 1974, there was a possibility that some planning permission might be granted. If it were, and unless the purchasers could take valid objection to it, completion would (under the conditions) have to follow in two months. Therefore, if a notice of rescission were to be given, it had to be served without delay, that is, before the planning permission arrived. In this situation, the appellant's advisers arranged a meeting with a Mr Cornwell, who was acting for the vendors, or as an intermediary with power to commit the vendors, to discuss the matter. This took place on 7 March 1974 and is recorded as a disclosed *aide memoire* dated the next day. This document was prepared by the appellants, and we have not had the benefit of Mr Cornwell's evidence on it: he died before the trial. But the rest of the correspondence is fully in line with it and I see no reason to doubt its general accuracy. After recording each side's statement of position, the document contained, *inter alia*, these passages: 'He [Mr Cornwell] stated that if we attempted to rescind the contract, then he would take us to court and let the judge decide whether the contract could be rescinded on the point we were making.' This 'point' was undoubtedly that relating to the compulsory purchase of the 2.5 acres. The *aide memoire* continues: 'I told him that our Legal Department would be serving the Notice to Rescind the Contract within a short while – this would ensure that the company was fully protected and was prudent. He assured me that he would accept it on that basis and not regard it as a hostile act.'

The notice was then served on 20 March 1974. On 22 March, the respondent's solicitors wrote that they did not accept its validity. On 30 May 1974, Mr Cornwell wrote a long letter to Sir Godfrey Mitchell, president of Wimpey. I refer to one passage: '... within a few days of the original meeting, a notice of rescission was served upon the vendor company by your organisation that the contract was to be rescinded. Simultaneously with that notice of rescission, proceedings were instituted and there the matter remains so far as the legal situation is concerned and both parties, from the legal point of view, must now await the decision of the court as to the validity of the claim made by Messrs George Wimpey & Co Ltd that they are entitled to rescind this contract upon the grounds which they have so stated.'

On 4 June 1974, Mr Cornwell wrote again: 'All I need say now is that we will retire to our battle stations and it goes without saying I am sure that you will abide by the result as I will.'

My Lords, I cannot find anything which carries the matter one inch beyond, on the appellant's part, an expressed reliance on the contract (in condition E(a)(iii)), on the respondent's side an intention to take the issue of the validity of the notice (nothing else) to the courts, and an assumption, not disputed by the appellant, that both sides would abide by the decision of the court. This is quite insufficient to support the case for repudiation ...

My Lords, in my opinion, it follows, as a clear conclusion of fact, that the appellants manifested no intention to abandon, or to refuse future performance of, or to repudiate the contract. And the issue being one of fact, citation of other decided cases on other facts is hardly necessary. I shall simply state that the proposition that a party who takes action relying simply on the terms of the contract and not manifesting by his conduct an ulterior intention to abandon it is not to be treated as repudiating it, is supported by *James Shaffer Ltd v Findlay Durham & Brodie* and *Sweet & Maxwell Ltd v Universal News Services Ltd*.

In contrast to these is the case in this House of *Federal Commerce and Navigation Co Ltd v Molena Alpha Inc*, which fell on the other side of the line. Of that I said: 'The two cases relied on by the owners (*James Shaffer Ltd v Findley Durham & Brodie* and *Sweet & Maxwell v Universal News Services Ltd*) ... would only be relevant here if the owners' action had been confined to asserting their own view, possibly erroneous, as to the effect of the contract. They went, in fact, far beyond this when they threatened a breach of contract with serious consequences.'

The case of *Spettabile Consorzio Veneziano di Armamento e Navigazione v Northumberland Shipbuilding Co Ltd*, though, in some factual respects, distinguishable from the present, is nevertheless, in my opinion, clear support for the appellants.

In my opinion, therefore, the appellants are entitled to succeed on the repudiation issue, and I would only add that it would be a regrettable development of the law of contract to hold that a party who *bona fide* relies on an express stipulation in a contract in order to rescind or terminate a contract should, by that fact alone, be treated as having repudiated his contractual obligations if he turns out to be mistaken as to his rights. Repudiation is a drastic conclusion which should only be held to arise in clear cases of a refusal, in a matter going to the root of the contract, to perform contractual obligations. To uphold the respondent's contentions in this case would represent an undesirable contention of the doctrine.

Breach of condition

Traditionally, English law distinguishes between conditions and warranties as the two major varieties of contractual term. However, recent years have seen the development of the innominate terms doctrine, under which the courts are prepared to look more closely at the nature and effect of a breach of contract in an *ex post facto* consideration of the seriousness of the breach of contract in the face of the objectives of the parties when the contract was entered into.

Generally, a breach of condition allows the innocent party to treat his/her own primary performance obligations as being at an end, whereas a breach of warranty merely gives rise to an action for damages and is not sufficiently serious to allow termination.

The obvious advantage of a rigid separation between conditions and warranties is that of certainty, which is always an important factor, especially in commercial transactions. The parties have the advantage of being able to label a term, in advance, as a condition or a warranty and both parties then know from the outset what will be the consequence of a breach of that term. Conversely, rigid classification has the drawback of not always being able to achieve the most sensible result where a term is classified as a condition. A typical example of this kind of problem can be found in relation to the implied terms as to quality and fitness in sale of goods contracts. These implied terms are statutorily designated conditions of the contract of sale,[28] with the result that if they apply, it is not open to the court to look at the seriousness of a particular breach of contract under existing common law rules. As a result, even if the goods sold are entirely suited to the buyer's intended use, the common law development of the innominate terms doctrine is inapplicable if the goods proved not to meet the statutory requirement of quality.[29]

As indicated above, a breach of condition, as traditionally understood, is sufficient to allow the innocent party to treat his/her performance obligations as being at an end, no matter how trivial the effect of the breach.

Whether or not the broken contractual term is to be classified as a condition or not will turn on one of a number of different tests. In the first place, if Parliament has designated a term a condition, with no alternative classification, the term must be regarded as one which gives rise to a right in favour of the innocent party to treat his performance obligations as being at an end. Thus, in *Arcos v Ronaasen*,[30] the plaintiffs contracted to supply the defendants with wooden staves for the purpose of manufacturing wooden barrels. The contract specified that the staves should be half an inch thick, but on inspection, it was discovered that a substantial proportion of the delivery

---

28 Sale of Goods Act 1979, s 14(2) and (3).
29 *Cehave NV v Bremer Handelsgesellschaft mbH, The Hansa Nord* [1976] QB 44.
30 [1933] AC 470.

was marginally thicker than half an inch. The defendants sought to reject the whole delivery, despite the fact that the thicker staves were perfectly suited to their requirements. Nonetheless, the House of Lords held that there had been a breach of s 13 of the Sale of Goods Act 1893, which implied a condition that goods supplied were to comply with any description given of them. Accordingly, as there was a breach of condition, the buyers were entitled to reject.

Such an approach would not necessarily succeed today, since there have been amendments to the Sale of Goods Act 1979 which allow the court to disregard the normal consequences of a breach of condition where it would be unreasonable to allow the buyer to activate his right to reject:

Sale of Goods Act 1979

15A

(1) Where in the case of a contract of sale:

    (a) the buyer would, apart from this sub-section, have the right to reject goods by reason of a breach on the part of the seller of a term implied by s 13, 14 or 15 above; but

    (b) the breach is so slight that it would be unreasonable for him to reject them,

    then, if the buyer does not deal as a consumer, the breach is not to be treated as a breach of condition but may be treated as a breach of warranty.

(2) This section applies unless a contrary intention appears in, or is to be implied from, the contract.

(3) It is for the seller to show that the breach fell within sub-s (1)(b) above.

A second factor to consider is that there may be precedents which establish that a term of a particular type is to be regarded as a condition.

In *Maredelanto Compania Naviera SA v Bergbau-Handel GmbH*,[31] a charterparty contract stated that a vessel was 'expected ready to load under this charter at about 1 July 1965'. This was considered to be a condition allowing the innocent party to terminate his performance if it was not complied with:

Maredelanto Cia Naviera SA v Bergbau-Handel GmbH, The Mihalis Angelos [1971] 1 QB 164, CA, p 205

Megaw LJ: I reach that conclusion for four interrelated reasons. First, it tends towards certainty in the law. One of the essential elements of law is some measure of uniformity. One of the important elements of the law is predictability. At any rate, in commercial law, there are obvious and substantial advantages in having, where possible, a firm and definite rule for a

---

31   *The Mihalis Angelos* [1971] 1 QB 164, CA.

particular class of legal relationship, for example, as here, the legal categorisation of a particular definable type of contractual clause in common use. It is surely much better, both for shipowners and charterers (and incidentally, for their advisers) when a contractual obligation of this nature is under consideration, and still more when they are faced with the necessity for an urgent decision as to the effects of a suspected breach of it, be able to say categorically: 'If a breach is proved, then the charterer can put an end to the contract', rather than that they should be left to ponder whether or not the courts would be likely, in the particular case, when the evidence has been heard, to decide that in the particular circumstances the breach was or was not such as to go to the root of the contract. Where justice does not demand greater flexibility, there is everything to be said for, and nothing against, a degree of rigidity in legal principle.

Secondly, it would in my opinion, only be in the rarest case, if ever, that a ship owner could legitimately feel that he had suffered an injustice by reason of the law having given to a charterer the right to put an end to the contract because of the breach of the shipowner of a clause such as this. If a shipowner has chosen to assert contractually, but dishonestly or without reasonable grounds, that he expects his vessel to be ready to load on such and such a date, wherein does the grievance lie? Thirdly, it is, as Mocatta J held, clearly established by authority binding on this court that where a clause 'expected ready to load' is included in a contract for the sale of goods to be carried by sea, that clause is a condition, in the sense that any breach of it enables the buyer to reject the goods without having to show that the dishonest or unreasonable expectation of the seller has in fact been prejudicial to the buyer.

The term which was the centre of the dispute in *The Mihalis Angelos* was an 'expected ready to load' clause, but it also stipulated a time by which the ship was to be ready to load. Time stipulations in contracts have given rise to a certain degree of controversy as to their effect. It is clear that generally, a stipulation in a contract as to the time of payment will not normally be regarded as a condition, unless there is a clear contrary intention expressed by the parties.[32] But time stipulations relating to other types of obligation may be of the essence of the contract and may be treated as conditions as a consequence. According to the House of Lords in *United Scientific Holdings Ltd v Burnley Borough Council*,[33] this will be so in three particular cases. First, a time stipulation will be a condition if this is expressly stated in the contract. Secondly, time will be of the essence where the nature of the subject matter of the contract or its surrounding circumstances demand this.[34] Finally, time is considered to be of the essence of the contract if a party has waived an earlier breach but has subsequently given reasonable notice requiring performance by a new date.[35]

---

32 Sale of Goods Act 1979, s 10(1).

33 [1978] AC 904.

34 Eg, where goods are perishable or the subject matter of the contract is volatile and therefore subject to rapid price fluctuations.

35 *Rickards Ltd v Oppenheim* [1950] 1 KB 616.

In sale of goods contracts where the goods are to be transported by sea, time stipulations relating to the shipment process will often be regarded as conditions.

In *Bunge Corpn New York v Tradax Export SA*,[36] the parties entered into a contract for the sale of 15,000 tons of soya bean meal, 5% more or less, to be shipped from the US. The contract also required the buyers to give 15 consecutive days' notice of probable readiness of the vessels being used to transport the cargo and of the approximate quantity to be carried. Once this was done, it was for the seller to nominate a port of loading. The buyer gave less than 15 days' notice and the seller repudiated the contract at a time when the market price for soya bean meal was falling. The seller's actions were upheld in the Court of Appeal and the House of Lords on the ground that the requirement of 15 days' notice, being a time stipulation, was a condition of the contract rather than an innominate term:

Bunge Corpn New York v Tradax Export SA [1981] 1 WLR 711, HL, p 714

Lord Wilberforce: The main contention of Mr Buckley for the appellant was based on the decision of the Court of Appeal in *Hong Kong Fir Shipping Co Ltd v Kawasaki Kisen Kaisha Ltd* [1962] 2 QB 26, as it might be applied to cl 7. Diplock LJ, in his seminal judgment, illuminated the existence in contracts of terms which were neither, necessarily, conditions nor warranties, but, in terminology which has since been applied to them, intermediate or innominate terms capable of operating, according to the gravity of the breach, as either conditions or warranties. Relying on this, Mr Buckley's submission was that the buyer's obligation under the clause, to 'give at least [15] consecutive days' notice of probable readiness of vessel(s) and of the approximate quantity required to be loaded' is of this character. A breach of it, both generally and in relation to this particular case, might be, to use Mr Buckley's expression, 'inconsequential', that is, not such as to make performance of the seller's obligation impossible. If this were so, it would be wrong to treat it as a breach of condition: *Hong Kong Fir* would require it to be treated as a warranty.

This argument, in my opinion, is based on a dangerous misunderstanding, or misapplication, of what was decided and said in *Hong Kong Fir*. That case was concerned with an obligation of seaworthiness, breaches of which had occurred during the course of the voyage. The decision of the Court of Appeal was that this obligation was not a condition, a breach of which entitled the charterer to repudiate. It was pointed out that, as could be seen in advance, the breaches which might occur of it were various. They might be extremely trivial: the omission of a nail; they might be extremely grave: a serious defect in the hull or in the machinery; they might be of serious but not fatal gravity: incompetence or incapacity of the crew. The decision, and the judgments of the Court of Appeal, drew from these facts the inescapable conclusion that it was impossible to ascribe to the obligation, in advance, the character of a condition.

---

36 [1981] 1 WLR 711, HL.

Diplock LJ then generalised this particular consequence into the analysis which has since become classical. The fundamental fallacy of the appellants' argument lies in attempting to apply this analysis to a time clause such as the present in a mercantile contract, which is totally different in character. As to such a clause, there is only one kind of breach possible, namely to be late, and the questions which have to be asked are: first, what importance have the parties expressly ascribed to this consequence; and, secondly, in the absence of expressed agreement, what consequence ought to be attached to it having regard to the contract as a whole?

The test suggested by the appellants was a different one. One must consider, they said, the breach actually committed and then decide whether that default would deprive the party not in default of substantially the whole benefit of the contract. They even invoked certain passages in the judgment of Diplock LJ in *Hong Kong Fir* to support it. One may observe in the first place that the introduction of a test of this kind would be commercially most undesirable. It would expose the parties, after a breach of one, two, three, seven and other numbers of days, to an argument whether this delay would have left time for the seller to provide the goods. It would make it, at the time, at least difficult, and sometimes impossible, for the supplier to know whether he could do so. It would fatally remove from a vital provision in the contract that certainty which is the most indispensable quality of mercantile contracts, and lead to a large increase in arbitrations. It would confine the seller, perhaps after arbitration and reference through the courts, to a remedy in damages which might be extremely difficult to quantify. These are all serious objections in practice. But I am clear that the submission is unacceptable in law. The judgment of Diplock LJ does not give any support and ought not to give any encouragement to any such proposition; for beyond doubt it recognises that it is open to the parties to agree that, as regards a particular obligation, any breach shall entitle the party not in default to treat the contract as repudiated. Indeed, if he were not doing so he would, in a passage which does not profess to be more than clarificatory, be discrediting a long and uniform series of cases, at least from *Bowes v Shand* (1877) 2 App Cas 455 onwards, which have been referred to by my noble and learned friend Lord Roskill. It remains true, as Roskill LJ has pointed out in *Cehave NV v Bremer Handelsgesellschaft mbH* [1976] QB 44, pp 70–71, that the courts should not be too ready to interpret contractual clauses as conditions. And I have myself commended, and continue to commend, the greater flexibility in the law of contracts to which *Hong Kong Fir* points the way (see *Reardon Smith Line Ltd v Hansen-Tangen*, [1976] 1 WLR 989, p 998). But I do not doubt that, in suitable cases, the courts should not be reluctant, if the intentions of the parties as shown by the contract so indicate, to hold that an obligation has the force of a condition, and that indeed they should usually do so in the case of time clauses in mercantile contracts. To such cases, the 'gravity of the breach' approach of *Hong Kong Fir* would be unsuitable. I need only add on this point that the word 'expressly' used by Diplock LJ in *Hong Kong Fir* [1962] 2 QB 26, p 70 should not be read as requiring the actual use of the word 'condition'; any term or terms of the contract, which, fairly read, have the effect indicated, are sufficient. Lord Diplock himself has given recognition to this in this House (see *Photo Production Ltd v Securicor Transport Ltd* [1980] AC 827, p 849). I therefore reject that part of the appellants' argument which was based on it, and I must disagree with the judgment of the trial judge in so far as he accepted it. I respectfully indorse, on the other hand, the full and learned treatment of this issue in the judgment of Megaw LJ in the Court of Appeal.

I would add that the argument above applies equally to the use which the appellants endeavoured to make of certain observations in *United Scientific Holdings Ltd v Burnley Borough Council* [1978] AC 904, a case on which I do not need to comment on this occasion.

In conclusion, the statement of the law in *Halsbury's Laws,* 4th edn, paras 481–82 (including the footnotes to para 482) (generally approved in the House in the United Scientific Holdings case) appears to me to be correct, in particular, in asserting: (1) that the court will require precise compliance with stipulations as to time wherever the circumstances of the case indicate that this would fulfil the intention of the parties; and (2) that broadly speaking time will be considered of the essence in 'mercantile' contracts, with footnote reference to authorities which I have mentioned.

The relevant clause falls squarely within these principles, and such authority as there is supports its status as a condition (see *Bremer Handelsgesellschaft mbH v JH Rayner & Co Ltd* [1978] 2 Lloyd's Rep 73 and see *Peter Turnbull & Co Pty Ltd v Mundas Trading Co (Australia) Pty Ltd* [1954] 2 Lloyd's Rep 198. In this present context, it is clearly essential that both buyer and seller (who may change roles in the next series of contracts, or even in the same chain of contracts) should know precisely what their obligations are, most especially because the ability of the seller to fulfil his obligation may well be totally dependant on punctual performance by the buyer.

A third test to apply in determining whether a particular term is a condition or not is to look at the parties' intentions as expressed in their contract and its surrounding circumstances, such as the nature and the purpose of the contract made between the parties.

In *Schuler AG v Wickman Machine Tool Sales Ltd,*[37] the contract provided that Wickman would have sole selling rights in respect of presses manufactured by Schuler for a period of four and a half years. One of the provisions of the contract stipulated that it was a condition that Wickman would send representatives to visit the six largest motor vehicle manufacturers in the UK at least once per week in order to solicit orders. This had the effect of imposing on Wickman a duty to make 1,400 visits. The House of Lords held that this could not have been intended as a condition as, if that had been the case, one missed visit out of the vast number expected would have allowed Schuler to treat themselves as discharged from the contract:

---

37   [1974] AC 235. See, also, Chapter 5.

Schuler AG v Wickman Machine Tool Sales Ltd [1974] AC 235, p 247

Lord Reid: Wickman's obligation with regard to the promotion of sales of Schuler products is contained in cll 7 and 12(b), which are in the following terms:

7 Promotion by sales

(a) Subject to cl 17, sales will use its best endeavours to promote and extend the sale of Schuler products in the Territory.

(b) It shall be a condition of this agreement that:

    (i) Sales shall send its representatives to visit the six firms whose names are listed in the Schedule hereto at least once in every week for the purpose of soliciting orders for panel presses;

    (ii) that the same representative shall visit each firm on each occasion, unless there are unavoidable reasons preventing the visit being made by that representative, in which case, the visit shall be made by an alternate representative and Sales will ensure that such a visit is always made by the same alternate representative.

Sales agrees to inform Schuler of the names of the representatives and alternate representatives instructed to make the visits required by this clause...

12

(b) Sales undertakes, at its expense, to look after Schuler's interests carefully and will visit Schuler customers regularly, particularly those customers principally in the motor car and electrical industries whose names are set out on the list attached hereto and initialled by the parties hereto and will give all possible technical advice to customers ...

In order to explain the contention of the parties, I must now set out cl 11 of the agreement.

11 Duration of agreement

(a) This agreement and the rights granted hereunder to Sales shall commence on the first day of May 1963 and shall continue in force (unless previously determined as hereinafter provided) until the 31st day of December 1967 and thereafter, unless and until determined by either party upon giving to the other not less than 12 months' notice in writing to that effect expiring on the said 31st day of December 1967 or any subsequent anniversary thereof PROVIDED that Schuler or Sales may by notice in writing to the other determine this agreement forthwith if:

    (i) the other shall have committed a material breach of its obligations hereunder and shall have failed to remedy the same within 60 days of being required in writing so to do; or

    (ii) the other shall cease to carry on business or shall enter into liquidation (other than a members' voluntary liquidation for the purposes of reconstruction or amalgamation) or shall suffer the appointment of a Receiver of the whole or a material part of its undertaking, and PROVIDED FURTHER that Schuler may by notice determine this agreement forthwith if Sales shall cease to be a wholly owned subsidiary of Wickman Ltd.

(b) The termination of this agreement shall be without prejudice to any rights or liabilities accrued due prior to the date of termination and the terms contained herein as to discount commission or otherwise will apply to any orders placed by Sales with Schuler and accepted by Schuler before such termination.

I think it right first to consider the meaning of cl 11 because, if Wickman's contention with regard to this is right, then cl 7 must be construed in light of the provisions of cl 11. Clause 11 expressly provides that the agreement 'shall continue in force (unless previously determined as hereinafter provided) until' 31 December 1967. That appears to imply the corollary that the agreement shall not be determined before that date in any other way than as provided in cl 11. It is argued for Schuler that those words cannot have been intended to have that implication. In the first place, Schuler say that anticipatory breach cannot be brought within the scope of cl 11 and the parties cannot have intended to exclude any remedy for an anticipatory breach. And, secondly, they say that cl 11 fails to provide any remedy for an irremediable breach however fundamental such breach might be.

There is much force in this criticism. But, on any view, the interrelation and consequences of the various provisions of this agreement are so ill thought out that I am not disposed to discard the natural meaning of the words which I have quoted merely because giving to them their natural meaning implies that the draftsman has forgotten something which a better draftsman would have remembered. If the terms of cl 11 are wide enough to apply to breaches of cl 7, then I am inclined to hold that cl 7 must be read subject to the provisions of cl 11.

It appears to me that cl 11(a)(i) is intended to apply to all material breaches of the agreement which are capable of being remedied. The question, then, is what is meant in this context by the word 'remedy'. It could mean obviate or nullify the effect of a breach so that any damage already done is in some way made good. Or it could mean cure so that matters are put right for the future. I think that the latter is the more natural meaning. The word is commonly used in connection with diseases or ailments and they would normally be said to be remedied if they were cured although no cure can remove the past effect or result of the disease before the cure took place. And, in general, it can only be in a rare case that any remedy of something that has gone wrong in the performance of a continuing positive obligation will, in addition to putting it right for the future, remove or nullify damage already incurred before the remedy was applied. To restrict the meaning of remedy to cases where all damage past and future can be put right would leave hardly any scope at all for this clause. On the other hand, there are cases where it would seem a misuse of language to say that a breach can be remedied. For example, a breach of cl 14 by disclosure of confidential information could not be said to remedied by a promise not to do it again.

So, the question is whether a breach of Wickman's obligation under cl 7(b)(i) is capable of being remedied within the meaning of this agreement. On the one hand, failure to make one particular visit might have irremediable consequences, for example, a valuable order might have been lost when making that visit would have obtained it. But looking at the position broadly, I incline to the view that breaches of this obligation should be held to be capable of remedy within the meaning of cl 11. Each firm had to be visited more than 200 times. If one visit is missed, I think that one would normally say that making arrangements to prevent a recurrence of that breach would remedy the breach. If that is right and if cl 11 is intended to have general application then cl 7 must be read so that a breach of cl 7(b)(i) does not give to Schuler a right to rescind, but only to require the breach to be remedied within 60 days under cl 11(a)(i). I do not feel at all confident that this is the true view but I would adopt it unless the provisions of cl 7 point strongly in the opposite direction; so I turn to cl 7.

Clause 7 begins with the general requirement that Wickman shall 'use its best endeavours' to promote sales of Schuler products. Then there is in cl 7(b)(i) specification of those best endeavours with regard to panel presses, and in cl 12(b) a much more general statement of what Wickman must do with regard to other Schuler products. This intention to impose a stricter obligation with regard to panel presses is borne out by the use of the word 'condition' in cl 7(b). I cannot accept Wickman's argument that condition here merely means term. It must be intended to emphasise the importance of the obligations in sub-cll (b)(i) and (b)(ii). But what is the extent of that emphasis?

Schuler maintain that the word 'condition' has now acquired a precise legal meaning; that, particularly since the enactment of the Sale of Goods Act 1893, its recognised meaning in English law is a term of a contract any breach of which by one party gives to the other party an immediate right to rescind the whole contract. Undoubtedly, the word is frequently used in that sense. There may, indeed, be some presumption that in a formal legal document it has that meaning. But it is frequently used with a less stringent meaning. One is familiar with printed 'conditions of sale' incorporated into a contract and with the words 'for conditions see back' printed on a ticket. There, it simply means that the 'conditions' are terms of the contract.

In the ordinary use of the English language, 'condition' has many meanings, some of which have nothing to do with agreements. In connection with an agreement, it may mean a pre-condition: something which must happen or be done before the agreement can take effect. Or it may mean some state of affairs which must continue to exist if the agreement is to remain in force. The legal meaning on which Schuler rely is, I think, one which would not occur to a layman; a condition in that sense is not something which has an automatic effect. It is a term the breach of which by one party gives to the other an option either to terminate the contract or to let the contract proceed and, if he so desires, sue for damages for the breach.

Sometimes, a breach of a term gives that option to the aggrieved party, because it is of a fundamental character going to the root of the contract, sometimes, it gives that option because the parties have chosen to stipulate that it shall have that effect. Blackburn J said in *Bettini v Gye*: 'Parties may think some matter, apparently of very little importance, essential; and if they sufficiently express an intention to make the literal fulfilment of such a thing a condition precedent, it will be one.'

In the present case, it is not contended that Wickman's failures to make visits amounted in themselves to fundamental breaches. What is contended is that the terms of cl 7 'sufficiently express an intention' to make any breach, however small, of the obligation to make visits a condition so that any such breach shall entitle Schuler to rescind the whole contract if they so desire.

Schuler maintain that the use of the word 'condition' is, in itself, enough to establish this intention. No doubt, some words used by lawyers do have a rigid, inflexible meaning. But we must remember that we are seeking to discover intention as disclosed by the contract as a whole. Use of the word 'condition' is an indication – even a strong indication – of such an intention but it is by no means conclusive. The fact that a particular construction leads to a very unreasonable result must be a relevant consideration. The more unreasonable the result the more unlikely it is that the parties can have intended it, and if they do intend it the more necessary it is that they shall make that intention abundantly clear.

Clause 7(b) requires that, over a long period, each of the six firms shall be visited every week by one or other of two named representatives. It makes no provision for Wickman being entitled to substitute others even on the death or retirement of one of the named representatives. Even if one could imply some right to do this, it makes no provision for both representatives being ill during a particular week. And it makes no provision for the possibility that one or other of the firms may tell Wickman that they cannot receive Wickman's representative during a particular week. So, if the parties gave any thought to the matter at all they must have realised the probability that in a few cases out of the 1,400 required visits a visit as stipulated would be impossible. But if Schuler's contention is right failure to make even one visit entitles them to terminate the contract however blameless Wickman might be. This is so unreasonable that it must make me search for some other possible meaning of the contract. If none can be found then Wickman must suffer the consequences. But only if that is the only possible interpretation.

If I have to construe cl 7 standing by itself, then I do find difficulty in reaching any other interpretation. But if cl 7 must be read with cl 11, the difficulty disappears. The word 'condition' would make any breach of cl 7(b), however excusable, a material breach. That would then entitle Schuler to give notice under cl 11(a)(i), requiring the breach to be remedied. There would be no point in giving such a notice if Wickman were clearly not in fault, but if it were given, Wickman would have no difficulty in shewing that the breach had been remedied. If Wickman were at fault, then, on receiving such a notice, they would have to amend their system so that they could shew that the breach had been remedied. If they did not do that within the period of the notice, then Schuler would be entitled to rescind.

In my view, that is a possible and reasonable construction of the contract and I would therefore adopt it. The contract is so obscure that I can have no confidence that this is its true meaning but for the reasons which I have given I think that it is the preferable construction. It follows that Schuler were not entitled to rescind the contract as they purported to do. So, I would dismiss this appeal.

It is clear from *Schuler v Wickman Machine Tool Sales Ltd* that the courts will not always be prepared to allow the parties to determine for themselves what weight is to be attached to a particular term. Despite the certainty and predictability arguments rehearsed above in *The Mihalis Angelos*, there is now a growing tendency on the part of the courts to look at the effect of the breach, rather than the quality of the term broken, and ask after the event whether the breach of contract is sufficiently serious to justify the consequences which flow from what is traditionally regarded as a breach of condition. One consequence of this approach is that the courts are able to refrain from calling a particular term a condition or a warranty, preferring instead to describe such terms as innominate. The emphasis of the innominate terms approach is to ask whether the effect of the breach is to deprive the party not in breach of substantially the whole benefit which it was intended by the parties that he should obtain.

In *Hong Kong Fir Shipping Co Ltd v Kawasaki Kisen Kaisha Ltd*,[38] under the terms of a time charterparty, the ship *Hong Kong Fir* was hired for a period of 24 months under terms which required the vessel to be 'fitted in every way for ordinary cargo service'. The vessel was made available, but it was discovered that the engine room staff were inefficient and that the engines were old, with the result that the ship was held up for 20 weeks while repairs were carried out in order to make it seaworthy. At that stage, the charterparty still had 20 months to run, but the charterers sought to repudiate the contract on the ground that there had been a breach of condition. The Court of Appeal held that the breach was not sufficiently serious to allow repudiation:

Hong Kong Fir Shipping Co Ltd v Kawasaki Kisen Kaisha Ltd [1962] 2 QB 26, CA, p 65

Diplock LJ: Every synallagmatic contract contains in it the seeds of the problem: in what event will a party be relieved of his undertaking to do that which he has agreed to do but has not yet done? The contract may itself expressly define some of these events, as in the cancellation clause in a charterparty, but, human prescience being limited, it seldom does so exhaustively and often fails to do so at all. In some classes of contracts, such as sale of goods, marine insurance, contracts of affreightment evidenced by bills of lading and those between parties to bills of exchange, Parliament has defined by statute some of the events not provided for expressly in individual contracts of that class; but, where an event occurs the occurrence of which neither the parties nor Parliament have expressly stated will discharge one of

---

38   [1962] 2 QB 26.

the parties from further performance of his undertakings, it is for the court to determine whether the event has this effect or not. The test whether an event has this effect or not has been stated in a number of metaphors all of which I think amount to the same thing: does the occurrence of the event deprive the party who has further undertakings still to perform of substantially the whole benefit which it was the intention of the parties as expressed in the contract that he should obtain as the consideration for performing those undertakings? This test is applicable whether or not the event occurs as a result of the default of one of the parties to the contract, but the consequences of the event are different in the two cases. Where the event occurs as a result of the default of one party, the party in default cannot rely on it as relieving himself of the performance of any further undertakings on his part and the innocent party, although entitled to, need not treat the event as relieving him of the performance of his own undertakings. This is only a specific application of the fundamental legal and moral rule that a man should not be allowed to take advantage of his own wrong. Where the event occurs as a result of the default of neither party, each is relieved of the further performance of his own undertakings, and their rights in respect of undertakings previously performed are now regulated by the Law Reform (Frustrated Contracts) Act 1943.

This branch of the common law has reached its present stage by the normal process of historical growth and the fallacy in Mr Ashton Roskill's contention that a different test is applicable when the event occurs as a result of the default of one party from that applicable in cases of frustration where the event occurs as a result of the default of neither party arises, in my view, from a failure to view the cases in their historical context. The problem (in what event will a party to a contract be relieved of his undertaking to do that which he has agreed to do but has not yet done?) has exercised the English courts for centuries, probably ever since assumpsit emerged as a form of action distinct from covenant and debt, and long before even the earliest cases which we have been invited to examine; but, until the rigour of the rule in *Paradine v Jane* was mitigated in the middle of the last century by the classic judgments of Blackburn J in *Taylor v Caldwell* and Bramwell B in *Jackson v Union Marine Insurance Co*, it was, in general, only events resulting from one party's failure to perform his contractual obligations which were regarded as capable of relieving the other party from continuing to perform that which he had undertaken to do ...

Once it is appreciated that it is the event and not the fact that the event is a result of a breach of contract which relieves the party not in default of further performance of his obligations, two consequences follow: (1) the test whether the event relied on has this consequence is the same whether the event is the result of the other party's breach of contract or not, as Devlin J pointed out in *Universal Cargo Carriers Corpn v Citati*; (2) the question whether an event which is the result of the other party's breach of contract has this consequence cannot be answered by treating all contractual undertakings as falling into one of two separate categories: 'conditions', the breach of which gives rise to an event which relieves the party not in default of further performance of his obligations, and 'warranties', the breach of which does not give rise to such an event. Lawyers tend to speak of this classification as if it were comprehensive, partly for the historical reasons which I have already mentioned, and partly because Parliament itself adopted it in the Sale of Goods Act 1893, as respects a number of implied terms in contracts for the sale of goods and has in that Act used the expressions 'condition' and 'warranty' in that meaning. But it is by no means true of contractual undertakings in general at common law.

No doubt, there are many simple contractual undertakings, sometimes express, but more often because of their very simplicity ('it goes without saying') to be implied, of which it can be predicated that every breach of such an undertaking must give rise to an event which will deprive the party not in default of substantially the whole benefit which it was intended that he should obtain from the contract. And such a stipulation, unless the parties have agreed that breach of it shall not entitle the non-defaulting party to treat the contract as repudiated, is a 'condition'. So, too, there may be other simple contractual undertakings of which it can be predicated that no breach can give rise to an event which will deprive the party not in default of substantially the whole benefit which it was intended that he should obtain from the contract; and such a stipulation, unless the parties have agreed that breach of it shall entitle the non-defaulting party to treat the contract as repudiated, is a 'warranty'.

There are, however, many contractual undertakings of a more complex character which cannot be categorised as being 'conditions' or 'warranties' if the late 19th century meaning adopted in the Sale of Goods Act 1893, and used by Bowen LJ in *Bentsen v Taylor, Sons & Co* be given to those terms. Of such undertakings, all that can be predicated is that some breaches will, and others will not, give rise to an event which will deprive the party not in default of substantially the whole benefit which it was intended that he should obtain from the contract; and the legal consequences of a breach of such an undertaking, unless provided for expressly in the contract, depend on the nature of the event to which the breach gives rise and do not follow automatically from a prior classification of the undertaking as a 'condition' or a 'warranty'. For instance, to take the example of Bramwell B in *Jackson v Union Marine Insurance Co*, by itself, breach of an undertaking by a shipowner to sail with all possible despatch to a named port does not necessarily relieve the charterer of further performance of his obligation under the charterparty, but, if the breach is so prolonged that the contemplated voyage is frustrated, it does have this effect ...

As my brethren have already pointed out, the shipowner's undertaking to tender a seaworthy ship has, as a result of numerous decisions as to what can amount to 'unseaworthiness', become one of the most complex of contractual undertakings. It embraces obligations with respect to every part of the hull and machinery, stores and equipment and the crew itself. It can be broken by the presence of trivial defects easily and rapidly remediable as well as by defects which must inevitably result in a total loss of the vessel. Consequently, the problem in this case is, in my view, neither solved nor soluble by debating whether the owners' express or implied undertaking to tender a seaworthy ship is a 'condition' or a 'warranty'. It is, like so many other contractual terms, an undertaking one breach of which may give rise to an event which relieves the charterer of further performance of his undertakings if he so elects, and another breach of which may not give rise to such an event but entitle him only to monetary compensation in the form of damages. It is, with all deference to counsel for the charterers' skillful argument, by no means surprising that, among the many hundreds of previous cases about the shipowner's undertaking to deliver a seaworthy ship, there is none where it was found profitable to discuss in the judgments the question whether that undertaking is a 'condition' or a 'warranty'; for the true answer, as I have already indicated, is that it is neither, but one of that large class of contractual undertakings, one breach of which may have the same effect as that ascribed to a breach of 'condition' under the Sale of Goods Act 1893, and a different breach of which may have only the same effect as that ascribed to a breach of 'warranty' under that Act ...

What the judge had to do in the present case as in any other case where one party to a contract relies on a breach by the other party as giving him a right to elect to rescind the contract, was to look at the events which had occurred as a result of the breach at the time at which the charterers purported to rescind the charterparty, and to decide whether the occurrence of those events deprived the charterers of substantially the whole benefit which it was the intention of the parties as expressed in the charterparty that the charterers should obtain from the further performance of their own contractual undertakings.

One turns, therefore, to the contract, the Baltime 1939 Charter. Clause 13, the 'due diligence' clause which exempts the shipowners from responsibility for delay or loss or damage to goods on board due to unseaworthiness unless such delay or loss or damage has been caused by want of due diligence of the owners in making the vessel seaworthy and fitted for the voyage, is in itself sufficient to show that the mere occurrence of the events that the vessel was in some respect unseaworthy when tendered or that such unseaworthiness had caused some delay in performance of the charterparty would not deprive the charterer of the whole benefit which it was the intention of the parties he should obtain from the performance of his obligations under the contract – for he undertakes to continue to perform his obligations notwithstanding the occurrence of such events if they fall short of frustration of the contract and even deprives himself of any remedy in damages unless such events are the consequence of want of due diligence on the part of the shipowner.

The question which the judge had to ask himself was, as he rightly decided, whether or not, at the date when the charterers purported to rescind the contract, namely 6 June 1957, or when the owners purported to accept such rescission, namely 8 August 1957, the delay which had already occurred as a result of the incompetence of the engine room staff, and the delay which was likely to occur in repairing the engines of the vessel and the conduct of the owners by that date in taking steps to remedy these two matters, were, when taken together, such as to deprive the charterers of substantially the whole benefit which it was the intention of the parties they should obtain from further use of the vessel under the charterparty. In my view, in his judgment – on which I would not seek to improve – the learned judge took into account and gave due weight to all the relevant considerations and arrived at the right answer for the right reasons.

The effect of refusal to perform and breach of condition

In the event of a breach of contract being sufficiently serious to allow repudiation of the contract, the party not in breach has two options. He can either waive the breach and choose to treat the contract as still remaining in force or he can accept the breach and activate his right to a remedy.

Before the innocent party can be taken to have waived the breach, he must have full knowledge of the facts. Assuming this to be the case, the contract remains in existence, and each party has the right to sue for damages for past and future breaches of contract.

Unfortunately, there are dangers associated with this approach, since other rules relating to the discharge of contractual obligations will continue to apply to the contract while ever it remains in force. Thus, if after the waiver of breach, a supervening event occurs which has the effect of frustrating the common intention of both parties, the contract will be subject to the doctrine of frustration. For example, in *Avery v Bowden*,[39] a ship under charter was required to carry a cargo from Odessa. It became clear from an early stage that no cargo would be available, but the ship's master decided to wait until the date of performance specified in the contract. Before that date arrived, the Crimean War broke out, thereby frustrating the contract with the result that the charterer had lost his chance to activate his remedies in respect of the anticipatory breach of contract.

Similarly, the innocent party may act in such a way that he is in breach of contract to an extent which allows the other party (formerly in breach) to exercise his right to terminate his performance obligations.

In *Fercometal SARL v Mediterranean Shipping Co SA*,[40] the terms of a charterparty stated that if the ship was not ready to load by 9 July, the charterers could cancel the contract. The charterer wrongfully attempted to repudiate the contract before that date, but the owner of the vessel chose to ignore the repudiation, thereby keeping the contract alive. Subsequently, the owners were themselves in breach of contract by not having the ship ready to load on 9 July. Accordingly, the charterers then sought to cancel the contract on the ground of the owners' later breach of contract. The House of Lords held that they were entitled to act in this way:

---

39 (1855) 5 E & B 714.
40 *The Simona* [1989] AC 788.

Fercometal SARL v Mediterranean Shipping Co SA, The Simona [1989] AC 788, p 797

Lord Ackner:

The effect of a repudiation

The earlier authorities, when faced with a wrongful neglect or refusal, were concerned to absolve the 'innocent party' from the need to render useless performance, which the repudiating buyer had indicated he no longer wanted. In *Jones v Barkley* (1781) 2 Doug KB 684, one finds the seeds of the later doctrine of accepted anticipatory breach. Lord Mansfield CJ said: 'One need only state what the agreement, tender and discharge were, as set forth in the declaration. It charges that the plaintiffs offered to assign, and to execute and deliver a general release, and tendered a draft of an assignment and release, and offered to execute and deliver such assignment, but the defendant absolutely discharged them from executing the same, *or any assignment and release whatsoever*. The defendant pleads, that the plaintiff did not actually execute an assignment and release; and the question is, whether there was a sufficient performance. Take it on the reason of the thing. The party must shew he was ready; but, if the other stops him on the ground of an intention not to perform his part, it is not necessary for the first to go farther, and do a nugatory act.'

In *Cort and Gee v Ambergate Nottingham and Boston and Eastern Junction Railway Co* (1851) 17 QB 127, the plaintiffs agreed to manufacture a quantity of iron chairs for the defendant's railway. The defendant, having accepted some of the chairs, informed the plaintiffs that it had as many chairs as it required and that no further chairs would be accepted. The plaintiffs thereupon treated themselves as discharged from all further obligations and commenced proceedings against the defendant for wrongfully refusing to accept the chairs. They pleaded that from the time of making of the contract until the defendant's refusal they were ready and willing to perform their obligations, but that they had been discharged from further performance of the contract by the defendant's repudiation. The defendant denied that an oral renunciation prior to the time for performance excused the plaintiffs from the need to show that they were ready and willing to perform at the time set for performance. Thus, the question was: what sort of *readiness and willingness* (if any) does a plaintiff have to show in order to maintain an action for wrongful repudiation? It was held that the plaintiff's averment was sufficient and Lord Campbell CJ said at p 144: 'In common sense, the meaning of such an averment of readiness and willingness must be that non-completion of the contract was not the fault of the plaintiffs, and that they were disposed and able to complete it if it had not been renounced by the defendants.'

The above case and some of the earlier ones were considered in *Hochster v De La Tour* (1853) 2 E & B 678, where a courier sued his employer who had written in before the time for performance had arrived that his services were no longer required. This was a clear anticipatory breach since, before the time had arrived at which the defendant was bound to perform his contractual obligation, he had evinced an intention no longer to be bound by his contractual obligations. At the conclusion of his judgment Lord Campbell CJ said at pp 693–94: 'If it should be held that, upon a contract to do an act on a future day, a renunciation of the contract by one party dispenses with a condition to be performed in the meantime by the other, there seems no reason for requiring that other to wait till the day arrives before seeking his remedy by action: and the only ground on which the condition can be dispensed with seems to be, that the renunciation may be treated as a breach of the contract.'

Frost v Knight (1872) LR 7 Exch 111 was a case of a breach of promise to marry the plaintiff as soon as his (the defendant's) father should die. During the father's lifetime, the defendant refused absolutely to marry the plaintiff and the plaintiff sued him, his father still being alive. When the case was argued before the Court of Exchequer, Kelly CB concluded that there could be no actual breach of a contract by reason of non-performance so long as the time for the performance had not yet arrived. On appeal to the Exchequer Chamber, Cockburn CJ said: 'The promisee has an inchoate right to the performance of the bargain, which becomes complete when the time for performance has arrived. In the mean time he has the right to have the contract kept open as a subsisting and effective contract. Its unimpaired and unimpeached efficacy may be essential to his interests. His rights acquired under it may be dealt with by him in various ways for his benefit and advantage. Of all such advantage the repudiation of the contract by the other party, and the announcement that it never will be fulfilled, must of course deprive him. It is therefore quite right to hold that such an announcement amounts to a violation of the contract in omnibus, and that upon it the promisee, if so minded, may at once treat it as a breach of the entire contract, and bring his action accordingly.'

The innocent party's option

When one party wrongly refuses to perform obligations, this will not automatically bring the contract to an end. The innocent party has an option. He may either accept the wrongful repudiation as determining the contract and sue for damages or he may ignore or reject the attempt to determine the contract and affirm its continued existence. Cockburn CJ, in *Frost v Knight* (1872) LR 7 Ex Ch 111–13, put the matter thus: 'The law with reference to a contract to be performed at a future time, where the party bound to performance announces prior to the time his intention not to perform it, as established by the cases of *Hochster v De La Tour* (1853) 2 E & B 678, and *The Danube and Black Sea Co v Xenos* (1863) 13 CBNS 825 on the one hand, and *Avery v Bowden* (1855) 5 E & B 714, *Reid v Hoskins* (1856) 6 E & B 953 and *Barwick v Buba* (1857) 2 CBNS 563 on the other, may be thus stated. The promise, if he pleases, may treat the notice of intention as inoperative, and await the time when the contract is to be executed, and then hold the other party responsible for all the consequences of non-performance: but, in that case, he keeps the contract alive for the benefit of the other party as well as his own; he remains subject to all his own obligations and liabilities under it, and enables the other party not only to complete the contract, if so advised, notwithstanding his previous repudiation of it, but also to take advantage of any supervening circumstance which would justify him in declining to complete it. On the other hand, the promise may, if he thinks proper, treat the repudiation of the other party as a wrongful putting an end to the contract, and may at once bring his action as on a breach of it; and in such action he will be entitled to such damages as would have arisen from the non-performance of the contract at the appointed time, subject, however, to abatement in respect of any circumstances which may have afforded him the means of mitigating his loss.'

The way in which a 'supervening circumstance' may turn out to be to the advantage of the party in default, thus relieving him from liability, is illustrated by *Avery v Bowden*, where the outbreak of the Crimean war between England and Russia made performance of the charterparty no longer legally possible. The defendant, who prior to the outbreak of the war had in breach of contract refused to load, was provided with a good defence to an action for breach of contract, since his repudiation had been ignored. As pointed out by Parker LJ in his judgment ([1987] 2 Lloyd's Rep 236, p 240), the law as stated in *Frost v Knight* and *Johnstone v Milling* has been reasserted in many cases since, and in particular in *Heyman v Darwins Ltd* [1942] AC 356, p 361, where Viscount Simon LC said: 'The first head of claim in the writ appears to be advanced on the view that an agreement is automatically terminated if one party "repudiates"it. That is not so. As Scrutton LJ said in *Golding v London & Edinburgh Insurance Co Ltd* ((1932) 43 LlL Rep 487, p 488): "I have never been able to understand what effect the repudiation by one party has unless the other accepts it." If one party so acts or so expresses himself, as to show that he does not mean to accept and discharge the obligations of a contract any further, the other party has an option as to the attitude he may take up. He may, notwithstanding the so called repudiation, insist on holding his co-contractor to the bargain and continue to tender due performance on his part. In that event, the co-contractor *has the opportunity of withdrawing from his false position, and, even if he does not, may escape ultimate liability because of some supervening event not due to his own fault which excuses or puts an end to further performance'* [emphasis added].

If an unaccepted repudiation has no legal effect ('a thing writ in water and of no value to anybody': *per* Asquith LJ in *Howard v Pickford Tool Co Ltd* [1951] 1 KB 417, p 421), how can the unaccepted acts of repudiation by the charterers in this case provide the owners with any cause of action? It was accepted in the Court of Appeal by counsel then appearing for the owners that it was an inevitable inference from the findings made by the arbitrators that the Simona was not ready to load the charterers' steel at any time prior to the charterers' notice of cancellation on 12 July. Counsel who has appeared before your Lordships for the owners has not been able to depart from this concession. Applying the well established principles set out above, the anticipatory breaches by the charterers not having been accepted by the owners as terminating the contract, the charterparty survived intact with the right of cancellation unaffected. The vessel was not ready to load by close of business on the cancelling date, viz 9 July, and the charterers were therefore entitled to and did give what on the face of it was an effective notice of cancellation.

When A wrongfully repudiates his contractual obligations in anticipation of the time for their performance, he presents the innocent party, B, with two choices. He may either affirm the contract by treating it as still in force or he may treat it as finally and conclusively discharged. There is no third choice, as a sort of via media, to affirm the contract and yet be absolved from tendering further performance unless and until A gives reasonable notice that he is once again able and willing to perform. Such a choice would negate the contract being kept alive for the benefit of *both* parties and would deny the party who unsuccessfully sought to rescind the right to take advantage of any supervening circumstance which would justify him in declining to complete.

Towards the conclusion of his able address, counsel for the owners sought to raise what was essentially a new point, argued before neither the arbitrators, Leggatt J nor the Court of Appeal. He submitted that the charterers' conduct had induced or caused the owners to abstain from having the ship ready prior to the cancellation date. Of course, it is always open to A, who has refused to accept B's repudiation of the contract, and thereby kept the contract alive, to contend that, in relation to a particular right or obligation under the contract, B is estopped from contending that he, B, is entitled to exercise that right or that he, A, has remained bound by that obligation. If B represents to A that he no longer intends to exercise that right or requires that obligation to be fulfilled by A and A acts on that representation, then clearly B cannot be heard thereafter to say that he is entitled to exercise that right or that A is in breach of contract by not fulfiling that obligation. If, in relation to this option to cancel, the owners had been able to establish that the charterers had represented that they no longer required the vessel to arrive on time because they had already fixed the *Leo Tornado* and, in reliance on that representation, the owners had given notice of readiness only after the cancellation date, then the charterers would have been estopped from contending they were entitled to cancel the charterparty. There is, however, no finding of any such representation, let alone that the owners were induced thereby not to make the vessel ready to load by 9 July. On the contrary, the owners on 5 July on two occasions asserted that the vessel would start loading on 8 July and on 8 July purported to tender notice of readiness. Indeed, on the following day they instructed their London solicitors to confirm that the vessel was then open in Durban for the charterers' cargo. There is a total lack of any material to show that the owners, because of the charterers' repudiatory conduct, viewed the cancellation clause as other than fully operative and therefore capable of being triggered by the vessel not being ready on time. The non-readiness of the vessel by the cancelling date was in no way induced by the charterers' conduct. It was the result of the owners' decision to load other cargo first.

In short, in affirming the continued existence of the contract, the owners could only avoid the operation of the cancellation clause by tendering the vessel ready to load on time (which they failed to do), or by establishing (which they could not) that their failure was the result of the charterers' conduct in representing that they had given up their option, which representation the owners had acted on by not presenting the vessel on time. I would therefore dismiss the appeal with costs.

Moreover, a refusal by the claimant to accept the defendant's repudiatory behaviour may work in the defendant's favour if the claimant has failed to read the market for possible price fluctuations. For example, in a sale of goods contract, suppose the seller wrongly refuses to deliver, but the buyer does not accept the repudiation, preferring to wait for the date on which performance is due. In these circumstances, there is no breach of contract, with the result that damages cannot be awarded at that stage. If the market price for goods of the kind contracted for is buoyant, the buyer will profit by waiting, but the reverse will be the case in a declining market for the same goods. In this latter event, the buyer would be better off if he were to accept the repudiation and treat the contract as being at an end.

In *Vitol SA v Norelf Ltd*,[41] the House of Lords held that on repudiation of a contract the aggrieved party could elect whether to accept the repudiation or affirm the contract. An 'acceptance' of the repudiation did not require any particular form so long as the aggrieved party clearly and unambiguously demonstrated to the repudiating party that he/she was treating the contract as having been brought to an end by the breach Notification, in any formal sense, was not required where the fact of the 'acceptance' came to the repudiating party's attention.

Moreover, a failure to continue with performance on their part by the innocent party were capable of signifying to the repudiating party that 'acceptance' of repudiation had to take place. In the words of Lord Steyn (at p 811):

> Postulate the case where an employer at the end of a day tells a contractor that he, the employer, is repudiating the contract and that the contract need not return the next day. The contractor does not return the next day or at all. It seems to me that the contractors failure to return may in the absence, of any other explanation, convey a decision to treat the contract as at an end.

Where the innocent party chooses to accept the repudiation or breach of condition, there is some dispute as to the effect of this on the contract. One view is that the contract is rescinded or discharged by the breach.[42] One reason for preferring this view is that an exclusion clause may be disposed of along with the other terms of the contract, if the court so desires. An alternative view is that the contract remains intact, but the innocent party is discharged from further performance.

In *Johnson v Agnew*,[43] the vendors agreed to sell a house and land which were subject to separate mortgages. The purchaser failed to complete on 21 January, the date fixed by a notice making time of the essence of the contract. The vendor obtained an order for specific performance which was not drawn up until 26 November. By that stage, the mortgagees of the house had obtained an order for possession and subsequently in March of the following year, the mortgagees of the land acted likewise. As a result of these

---

41 [1996] AC 800.
42 *Moschi v Lep Air Services Ltd* [1973] AC 331, pp 345–46, *per* Lord Reid.
43 See, also, *Heyman v Darwins Ltd* [1942] AC 356, p 399, *per* Lord Porter; *Moschi v Lep Air Services Ltd* [1973] AC 331, pp 349–50, *per* Lord Diplock, and p 350, *per* Lord Simon.

actions, the vendors were in no position to be able to convey the land so they sought a declaration that the contract was repudiated. The House of Lords held that, in such circumstances, a vendor is entitled to ask for the discharge and termination of the contract, but that the contract is not rescinded *ab initio*, with the result that the contract remains in existence until it is finally terminated. By choosing to ask for specific performance, the vendor had not made a final election, and was able to sue for damages. The vendor, on accepting the purchaser's repudiation, did not end the contract:

Johnson v Agnew [1980] AC 367, p 392

Lord Wilberforce: In this situation it is possible to state at least some uncontroversial propositions of law. First, in a contract for the sale of land, after time has been made, or has become, of the essence of the contract, if the purchaser fails to complete, the vendor can either treat the purchaser as having repudiated the contract, accept the repudiation, and proceed to claim damages for breach of the contract, both parties being discharged from further performance of the contract; or he may seek from the court an order for specific performance with damages for any loss arising from delay in performance. (Similar remedies are of course available to purchasers against vendors.) This is simply the ordinary law of contract applied to contracts capable of specific performance. Secondly, the vendor may proceed by action for the above remedies (viz specific performance or damages) in the alternative. At the trial, he will however have to elect which remedy to pursue. Thirdly, if the vendor treats the purchaser as having repudiated the contract and accepts the repudiation, he cannot thereafter seek specific performance. This follows from the fact that the purchaser, having repudiated the contract and his repudiation having been accepted, both parties are discharged from further performance.

At this point, it is important to dissipate a fertile source of confusion and to make clear that although the vendor is sometimes referred to in the above situation as 'rescinding' the contract, this so called 'rescission' is quite different from rescission *ab initio*, such as may arise for example in cases of mistake, fraud or lack of consent. In those cases, the contract is treated in law as never having come into existence. (Cases of a contractual right to rescind may fall under this principle but are not relevant to the present discussion.) In the case of an accepted repudiatory breach, the contract has come into existence but has been put an end to or discharged. Whatever contrary indications may be disinterred from old authorities, it is now quite clear, under the general law of contract, that acceptance of a repudiatory breach does not bring about 'rescission *ab initio*'. I need only quote one passage to establish these propositions. In *Heyman v Darwins Ltd*, Lord Porter said: 'To say that the contract is rescinded or has come to an end or has ceased to exist may, in individual cases, convey the truth with sufficient accuracy, but the fuller expression that the injured party is thereby absolved from future performance of his obligations under the contract is a more exact description of the position. Strictly speaking, to say that, upon acceptance of the renunciation of a contract, the contract is rescinded is incorrect. In such a case the injured party may accept the renunciation as a breach going to the root of the whole of the consideration. By that acceptance he is discharged from further performance and may bring an action for damages, but the contract itself is not rescinded.'

See, also, *Boston Deep Sea Fishing & Ice Co Ltd v Ansell, per* Bowen LJ, *Mayson v Clouet, per* Lord Dunedin, and *Moschi v Lep Air Services Ltd, per* Lord Reid and Lord Diplock. I can see no reason, and no logical reason has ever been given, why any different result should follow as regards contracts for the sale of land, but a doctrine to this effect has infiltrated into that part of the law with unfortunate results. I shall return to this point when considering *Henty v Schröder* and cases which have followed it down to *Barber v Wolfe* and *Horsler v Zorro*.

Fourthly, if an order for specific performance is sought and is made, the contract remains in effect and is not merged in the judgment for specific performance. This is clear law, best illustrated by the judgment of Greene MR in *Austins of East Ham Ltd v Macey*, in a passage which deals both with this point and with that next following. It repays quotation in full: 'The contract is still there. Until it is got rid of, it remains as a blot on the title, and the position of the vendor, where the purchaser has made default, is that he is entitled, not to annul the contract by aid of the court, but to obtain the normal remedy of a party to a contract which the other party has repudiated. He cannot, in the circumstances, treat it as repudiated except by order of the court and the effect of obtaining such an order is that the contract, which until then existed, is brought to an end. The real position, in my judgment, is that, so far from proceeding to the enforcement of an order for specific performance, the vendor, in such circumstances, is choosing a remedy which is alternative to the remedy of proceeding under the order for specific performance. He could attempt to enforce that order and could levy an execution which might prove completely fruitless. Instead of doing that, he elects to ask the court to put an end to the contract, and that is an alternative to an order for enforcing specific performance.'

Fifthly, if the order for specific performance is not complied with by the purchaser, the vendor may *either* apply to the court for enforcement of the order, or may apply to the court to dissolve the order and ask the court to put an end to the contract. This proposition is as stated in *Austins of East Ham Ltd v Macey* (and see, also, *Sudagar Singh v Nazeer, per* Megarry VC) and is, in my opinion, undoubted law, both on principle and authority. It follows, indeed, automatically from the facts that the contract remains in force after the order for specific performance and that the purchaser has committed a breach of it of a repudiatory character which he has not remedied or, as Megarry VC put it, that he is refusing to complete.

Although the court used the language of rescission in this case, it is important to appreciate that the word rescission is being used in an unusual sense. Normally if a contract is rescinded, in its properly understood sense, no action for damages under the contract will lie. Thus, if a contract is rescinded by reason of a misrepresentation, the only entitlement to damages lies under the Misrepresentation Act 1967. However, in *Johnson v Agnew*, the court 'rescinded' the contract due to the purchaser's breach and allowed the vendor to recover damages. If an action for damages still lies, it follows from this that the contract itself must have survived for some purposes. Accordingly, the better view is that, where there is a repudiatory breach, the innocent party is discharged from performing his obligations under the contract, but the contract itself does not necessarily come to an end.

The phrase 'rescission for breach' is the source of the confusion when it is used to describe discharge from performance. Assuming it is merely the obligation to perform that is discharged by breach, events arising after breach which allow an action for damages do not present a problem. Moreover, terms of the contract which relate to those events are also unaffected by the discharge. Accordingly, it can be said that there are primary and secondary obligations under a contract and the effect of the innocent party seeking discharge for breach is that he is no longer bound to perform his primary obligations, although the contract will survive in order to see off any secondary obligations such as the duty of the party in breach to pay damages in respect of any loss he has caused. Similarly, the likes of exclusion and limitation clauses which generally relate to a secondary obligation may continue to operate, even if this has the effect of reducing the defendant's liability.

In *Photo Production Ltd v Securicor Transport Ltd*,[44] the respondents were a security company employed to guard the appellants' premises. The service provided was one of the cheapest on offer by the respondents and consisted of little more than 'flying' visits to the appellants' premises. During one of these visits one of the respondents' employees negligently set a fire which caused extensive damage to the premises. It was accepted by the House of Lords that there was a serious breach of contract which was sufficient to allow the appellants to treat as being at an end their obligation to continue paying for the security service (primary obligation). However, a clause in the contract which limited the respondents' liability continued to operate as it related to their obligation to pay damages (secondary obligation):

Photo Production Ltd v Securicor Transport Ltd [1980] AC 827, p 848

Lord Diplock: My Lords, it is characteristic of commercial contracts, nearly all of which today are entered into not by natural legal persons, but by fictitious ones, that is, companies, that the parties promise to one another that something will be done, for instance, that property and possession of goods will be transferred, that goods will be carried by ship from one port to another, that a building will be constructed in accordance with agreed plans, that services of a particular kind will be provided. Such a contract is the source of primary legal obligations on each party to it to procure that whatever he has promised will be done is done. (I leave aside arbitration clauses which do not come into operation until a party to the contract claims that a primary obligation has not been observed.)

---

44 [1980] AC 827.

Where what is promised will be done involves the doing to a physical act, performance of the promise necessitates procuring a natural person to do it; but the legal relationship between the promisor and the natural person by whom the act is done, whether it is that of master and servant, or principal and agent or of parties to an independent subcontract, is generally irrelevant. If that person fails to do it in the manner in which the promisor has promised to procure it to be done, as, for instance, with reasonable skill and care, the promisor has failed to fulfil his own primary obligation. This is to be distinguished from 'vicarious liability', a legal concept which does depend on the existence of a particular legal relationship between the natural person by whom a tortious act was done and the person sought to be made vicariously liable for it. In the interests of clarity the expression should, in my view, be confined to liability for tort.

A basic principle of the common law of contract, to which there are no exceptions that are relevant in the instant case, is that parties to a contract are free to determine for themselves what primary obligations they will accept. They may state these in express words in the contract itself and, where they do, the statement is determinative; but in practice a commercial contract never states all the primary obligations of the parties in full; many are left to be incorporated by implication of law from the legal nature of the contract into which the parties are entering. But if the parties wish to reject or modify primary obligations which would otherwise be so incorporated, they are fully at liberty to do so by express words.

Leaving aside those comparatively rare cases in which the court is able to enforce a primary obligation by decreeing specific performance of it, breaches of primary obligations give rise to substituted secondary obligations on the part of the party in default, and, in some cases, may entitle the other party to be relieved from further performance of his own primary obligations. These secondary obligations of the contract breaker and any concomitant relief of the other party from his own primary obligations also arise by implication of law, generally common law, but sometimes statute, as in the case of codifying statutes passed at the turn of the century, notably the Sale of Goods Act 1893. The contract, however, is just as much the source of secondary obligations as it is of primary obligations; and like primary obligations that are implied by law secondary obligations too can be modified by agreement between the parties, although, for reasons to be mentioned later, they cannot, in my view, be totally excluded. In the instant case, the only secondary obligations and concomitant reliefs that are applicable arise by implication of the common law as modified by the express words of the contract.

Every failure to perform a primary obligation is a breach of contract. The secondary obligation on the part of the contract breaker to which it gives rise by implication of the common law is to pay monetary compensation to the other party for the loss sustained by him in consequence of the breach; but, with two exceptions, the primary obligations of both parties so far as they have not yet been fully performed remain unchanged. This secondary obligation to pay compensation (damages) for non-performance of primary obligations I will call the 'general secondary obligation'. It applies in the cases of the two exceptions as well.

The exceptions are: (1) where the event resulting from the failure by one party to perform a primary obligation has the effect of depriving the other party of substantially the whole benefit which it was the intention of the parties that he should obtain from the contract, the party not in default may elect to put an end to all primary obligations of both parties remaining unperformed (if the expression 'fundamental breach' is to be retained, it should, in the interests of clarity, be confined to this exception); (2) where the contracting parties have agreed, whether by express words or by implication of law, that any failure by one party to perform a particular primary obligation ('condition' in the nomenclature of the Sale of Goods Act 1893), irrespective of the gravity of the event that has in fact resulted from the breach, shall entitle the other party to elect to put an end to all primary obligation of both parties remaining unperformed (in the interests of clarity, the nomenclature of the Sale of Goods Act 1893, 'breach of condition', should be reserved for this exception).

Where such an election is made: (a) there is substituted by implication of law for the primary obligations of the party in default which remain unperformed a secondary obligation to pay monetary compensation to the other party for the loss sustained by him in consequence of their non-performance in the future; and (b) the unperformed primary obligations of that other party are discharged. This secondary obligation is additional to the general secondary obligation; I will call it 'the anticipatory secondary obligation'.

In cases falling within the first exception, fundamental breach, the anticipatory secondary obligation arises under contracts of all kinds by implication of the common law, except to the extent that it is excluded or modified by the express words of the contract. In cases falling within the second exception, breach of condition, the anticipatory secondary obligation generally arises under particular kinds of contracts by implication of statute law; though in the case of 'deviation' from the contract voyage under a contract of carriage of goods by sea it arises by implication of the common law. The anticipatory secondary obligation in these cases too can be excluded or modified by express words.

When there has been a fundamental breach or breach of condition, the coming to an end of the primary obligations of both parties to the contract at the election of the party not in default is often referred to as the 'determination' or 'rescission' of the contract or, as in the Sale of Goods Act 1893, 'treating the contract as repudiated'. The first two of these expressions, however, are misleading unless it is borne in mind that for the unperformed primary obligations of the party in default there are substituted by operation of law what I have called the secondary obligations.

The bringing to an end of all primary obligations under the contract may also leave the parties in a relationship, typically that of bailor and bailee, in which they owe to one another by operation of law fresh primary obligations of which the contract is not the source; but no such relationship is involved in the instant case.

I have left out of account in this analysis as irrelevant to the instant case an arbitration or choice of forum clause. This does not come into operation until a party to the contract claims that a primary obligation of the other party has not been performed; and its relationship to other obligations of which the contract is the source was dealt with by this House in *Heyman v Darwins Ltd.*

It has been observed above that if the party not in breach elects to affirm the contract, rather than to accept the repudiation of the other party, the contract remains in force. However, this can have undesirable effects. For example, by affirming the contract, the party not in breach will be able to proceed with his own performance and subsequently claim contractual remuneration from the other party despite the fact that in the case of an anticipatory repudiation all parties concerned are aware that the party in breach is unwilling to go ahead with the contract.[45] In some quarters, this may be regarded as economically wasteful. In any case, it should not be assumed that the innocent party will always be able to adopt this course since the performance of many contractual obligations will be dependant on the co-operation of the other party[46] and, if this is not forthcoming, the ability to hold the other party to his contract becomes a purely academic matter.

---

45 See *White and Carter (Councils) Ltd v McGregor* [1962] AC 413, discussed below, Chapter 11.

46 See, eg, *Hounslow London Borough Council v Twickenham Garden Developments Ltd* [1971] Ch 233.

CHAPTER 10

LONG TERM RELATIONSHIPS

DISCRETE AND RELATIONAL CONTRACTING

A particular difficulty associated with the classical contract rule book is that it is probably better equipped to deal with short term or discrete transactions rather than long term relationships. A discrete transaction is one which can be said to have relatively easily measurable objectives, such as a typical contract for the sale of specific goods. In this type of transaction, the seller performs his contractual obligations by making the goods available for delivery at a time when the buyer is ready and able to take delivery and make payment. Once the primary performance obligations of the two parties have been fulfilled, the buyer and seller may not have anything more to do with each other, as if they were ships which pass in the night.

In contrast, relational contracts, often involving a protracted period of performance, will require a high degree of co-operation, and may involve adjustments being made in mid-course in order to take account of changes in background circumstances affecting performance of the contract in order to achieve the parties' objectives. An example of such a contract can be found in the case of employment relationships under which the terms of a person's employment may have to be adjusted according to changes in economic conditions. Moreover, the parties to negotiations in such cases may not even be the original parties to the contract, especially where the terms of employment of a particular group of employees may be negotiated on a class level by a trade union.

Macneil comments as follows:

Contractual ordering of economic activity takes place along a spectrum of transactional and relational behavior. At one end are discrete transactions. Discrete transactions are contracts of short duration, involving limited personal interactions, and with precise party measurements of easily measured objects of exchange, for example money and grain. They require a minimum of future co-operative behavior between the parties and no sharing of benefits or burdens. They bind the two tightly and precisely. The parties view such transactions as deals free of entangling strings, and they certainly expect no altruism. The parties see virtually everything connected with such transactions as clearly defined and presentiated.[1] If trouble is anticipated at all, it is anticipated only if someone or something turns out unexpectedly badly. The epitome of discrete transactions: at noon two strangers come into town from opposite directions, one walking and one riding a horse. The walker offers to buy the horse, and after brief dickering a deal is struck in which delivery of the horse is to be made at sundown upon the handing over of $10. The two strangers expect to have nothing to do with each other between now and sundown; they expect never to see each other thereafter; and each has as much feeling for the other as has a Viking trading with a Saxon. A modern example with many of these characteristics is a purchase of non-brand name gasoline in a strange town one does not expect to see again.

At the other end of the contract spectrum are ongoing relations. Being more divers than well-honed discrete transactions, they are more difficult to describe concisely, but the following are typical characteristics. The relations are of significant duration (for example franchising). Close whole person relations form an integral part of the relation (employment). The object of exchange typically includes both easily measured quantities (wages) and quantities not easily measured (the projection of personality by an airline stewardess). Many individuals with individual and collective poles of interest are involved in the relation (industrial relations). Future co-operative behavior is anticipated (the players and management of the New York Yankees). The benefits and burdens of the relationship are to be shared rather than entirely divided and allocated (a law partnership). The entangling strings of friendship, reputation, interdependence, morality and altruistic desires are integral parts of the relation (a theatrical agent and his clients, a corporate management team). Trouble is expected as a matter of course (collective bargaining agreement). Finally the participants never intend or expect to see the whole future of the relation as presentiated at any single time, but view the relation as an ongoing integration of behavior to grow and vary with events in a largely unforeseeable future (a marriage; a family business) ...[2]

A feature of relational contracting is that performance of the contract may occupy a considerable period of time. Because of this it may be necessary to adjust or alter the original arrangements in the light of subsequent developments. The original contract may have made provision for alteration, but it is more likely that there is no such provision.

Beale and Dugdale comment as follows:

Contract law may be 'used' in at least two ways. First, use may be made of the remedies which the law provides in the event of something going wrong: for

---

1   Presentiation is the process of making or rendering present in place or time. It is a recognition that the course of the future is bound by present events and that by those events, the future has been brought into the present: Macneil, 1974. Through this process, the classical rules of contract law make a promise relating to the future binding at its inception. It is as if the promise is a matter of existing fact and the remedies for breach treat the promise as binding from the date on which the contract was formed.

2   Macneil, 1978b, pp 12–13.

instance, the victim of a breach of contract may be able to bring the contract to an end or to recover damages. Some of these remedies may be ordered by a court, for instance if damages are awarded, or may form the basis of an out of court settlement. Others, such as termination of the contract, are always exercisable without any court order: the victim simply refuses to go on with the contract. But much more 'use' of contract law is made in a second way. Providing certain criteria are met – normally, the parties must have agreed to a definite arrangement under which each is to contribute something of value, called 'the consideration', in exchange for the other's undertaking – any agreement made by the parties will be 'enforceable', at least to the extent that compensation will be obtainable if loss is caused by a breach of it. The parties may thus 'use' contract law to regulate their relationship, to plan what is to happen in the future. They may plan their primary obligations, for instance in a contract of sale the item, the price and the delivery date, and also mechanisms by which these primary obligations may be adjusted; for instance, what is to happen if the cost of materials increases or an unavoidable delay occurs.

Not every businessman necessarily 'uses' contract law even in the planning sense when making an agreement. So little may be planned that the agreement is unenforceable for uncertainty and, if an enforceable contract is created, the parties may not adhere to it thereafter. If some contingency arises which threatens to disrupt the agreement, the parties may not use the remedies provided by the law or by the agreement itself. If they do appear to adhere to the contract or to use contractual remedies, this may be unconscious. This paper is concerned with the extent to which businessmen consciously use contract law in these two ways and describes the results of some preliminary research. It attempts to suggest why it is that this relatively sophisticated area of law is not always used in practice and what it is that enables businessmen to dispense with contractual planning and contractual remedies.

Professor Stewart Macaulay has published the results of some research into this topic done in Wisconsin, where he interviewed representatives of 48 companies and six law firms. He described contract as involving '… two distinct elements: (a) rational planning of the transaction with careful provision for as many future contingencies as can be foreseen; and (b) the existence or use of actual or potential legal sanctions to induce performance of the exchange or to compensate for non-performance'. He divided the types of issue which might be planned into four – description of the primary obligations, contingencies, defective performances and legal sanctions – and concluded that while many business exchanges will involve a high degree of planning about each category, equally many at least 'reflect no planning, or only a minimal amount of it, especially concerning legal sanctions and the effect of defective performances'. He found little use of 'contractual practices' in the later adjustment of relationships, though there was some evidence of tacit reliance on contractual rights; and very little use of the formal dispute-settlement procedures available through the courts.

The picture which emerges from our research is, as will be seen, broadly similar to that drawn by Macaulay, and many of the general explanations of why contract law may or may not be used are the same as his. We have attempted however to discover more detail than is contained in Macaulay's article about the extent of planning practised on particular issues and on how particular problems might be resolved. Our research was concentrated on formation (as a necessary preliminary) and the four issues of payment and security, cancellation for reasons other than breach, delay and defects. In each area where we found little use of contract planning or of contract remedies, we tried to find out whether this was because of non-legal factors or because of legal devices, which might (like insurance, say) be 'extra-contractual', in the sense of being outside the individual contract concerned or which might be planned as part of the contract.

Before dealing with the particular issues on which we concentrated, it may be useful to indicate some of the more general factors which may influence engineering manufacturers in their decision on whether to plan a contract in detail, whether to adhere to their contractual rights and duties and whether to employ contractual remedies. For instance, the reason why, in most exchanges, the parties agree expressly only on their primary obligations, and not on the effect of, say, late or defective performances may be that on each of the issues studied there appeared to be a certain amount of 'tacit' planning: within the trade certain terms and certain customs or 'unwritten laws' were widely accepted. For instance, it was generally accepted that the seller would not compensate the buyer for certain losses. Thus, although firms would sometimes claim 'unusual' rights the trade custom might provide a basis for settling any dispute. Moreover, most firms traded regularly with the other party, and would know what attitude the other was likely to take. Firms frequently stated that they would take much greater care when contracting with relatively unknown parties, especially those outside the engineering trade.

A second general reason for not planning a transaction in much detail is that such planning is expensive, while the risk of a serious dispute or loss may be low; for instance if orders of low value are sold on credit to a diversity of customers the loss likely to be caused by customers failing to pay may not be great, and may not justify the cost of planning security arrangements. Conversely, a high degree of planning was often explained by a high risk – perhaps a customer who would lose heavily if delivery were late or a machine which might cause great loss of life if it were defective. Even then, there might be reluctance to do any more than was strictly necessary: there seemed to be a feeling that a carefully negotiated contract might be insufficiently flexible to meet even foreseeable events, and too much negotiation might sour a peaceful relationship.

Even if plans had been made to cover possible disruptions, there was usually thought to be no need to fall back on legal rights if the disruption materialised. It was made very clear to us that, besides there being a common acceptance of certain norms within the trade, there was a considerable degree of trust among firms. This was particularly so among smaller firms who obtained most of their orders locally and who frequently placed great trust in the fairness of one or two very large firms. No doubt, belief in mutual fairness was reinforced by the considerable degree of personal contact between officers, usually in the business context but sometimes on social occasions. The firm's general reputation was also at stake. Not only did salesmen stress the need to have a good product and to stand behind it, buyers also emphasised the need to maintain a reputation for the firm as fair and efficient, and both said that any attempt to shelter behind contractual provisions or even frequent citation of contractual terms would destroy the firm's reputation very quickly. But even more important than the general reputation of the firm was the desire to do business again with the other party, or with other firms in the same group of companies. Each side had to be prepared to make concessions and to do so in a spirit of co-operation. The importance of the 'on-going' nature of the relationship will become clear when the individual issues are discussed.

With this need to avoid 'taking sides' and thereby souring the relationship and the time and expense involved in taking legal advice and remedies, it was not surprising to find relatively little use of contractual remedies and almost none of formal dispute-settlement procedures, such as a court hearing or an arbitration. It would be a mistake however to assume that contract law has very little relevance. First, it is always in the background: contract law may not be mentioned but the parties probably know in general what the legal position is and may adjust their attitudes accordingly. As one sales manager put it: 'It is an umbrella under which we operate.' But, secondly, we hope to show that while non-legal factors and extra-contractual devices do commonly reduce the need to use contract law, there are certain problems which, for one reason or another, are not infrequently dealt with by contract planning and sometimes by the use of contractual remedies.[3]

A number of points emerge from this empirical exercise. First, some of the evidence offered by Beale and Dugdale suggests that sometimes businessmen plan a contract in minute detail. This may be for a variety of reasons, for example, the other contracting party may be a relative newcomer to a particular area of business and therefore has no track record of reliability. Alternatively, the authors point to the fact that if an engineering firm contracts with a business which specialises in some other area of manufacture or supply, there may be a need for detailed planning because assumptions in the engineering industry might not be the same as in the other business sector. This would suggest that when a businessman deals with someone who is familiar with the assumptions he is likely to make there is less need to rely on legal remedies since the parties to the relational transaction can generally trust one another.

3 Beale and Dugdale, 1975, pp 45–48.

VARIATION OF THE CONTRACT

A key feature of relational contracting is the need to allow for adjustments as the parties progress towards performance of their respective obligations. A major problem in this regard is that the rules applicable to adjustments in long term relationships are supposed to operate along the same lines as the rules which apply to the formation of discrete contractual relationships. It has been seen already that the rules on contract formation require an agreement, based upon an offer and a corresponding acceptance[4] and an enforceable promise supported by consideration.[5] However, these classical rule book principles may give rise to enormous difficulties in relational transactions. For example, the 'agreement' to vary an existing set of contract terms may be evidenced only by a long period of inactivity, which could fall foul of the classical rule that silence will rarely amount to acceptance of an offer. This may make it difficult for a court, applying classical principles, to conclude that an existing set of terms have been abandoned by mutual consent. Similarly, even where there is an agreement to vary the terms of a long term contract, classical analysis insists that there must be consideration for the promise to vary the terms. This too may give rise to difficulties. Most often the problem is that if one party agrees to pay more than was originally agreed (for example, to take account of currency fluctuations), the consideration provided by the promisee may consist of little more than performing the obligations undertaken by him from the outset. The problem which must be surmounted in these circumstances is that the classical rule book states that the performance of an existing contractual obligation owed to the promisee is not to be regarded as good consideration for the promise of that party.[6] Other difficulties may also be encountered in relational transactions some of which are identified by Macneil:

> *Adjustment and termination of economic relations in a system of discrete transactions* – an economic and legal system dominated by discrete transactions deals with the conflict between various needs for stability and needs for flexibility in ways described below ...

> *Planning flexibility into economic relations* – within itself, a discrete transaction is rigid, there being no intention to achieve internal flexibility. Planning for flexibility must, therefore, be achieved outside the confines of the transaction. Consider, for example, a 19th century manufacturer of stoves who needs iron to be cast into stove parts, but does not know how many stoves he can sell. The required flexibility has to be achieved, in a pattern of discrete transaction, by keeping each iron purchase contract small in amount thereby permitting adjustments of quantity either up or down each time a contract is entered.

---

4   See Chapter 2.
5   See Chapter 3.
6   *Stilk v Myrick* (1809) 3 Camp 317 and see the discussion of this rule in Chapter 3.

Thus, the needed flexibility comes from the opportunity to enter or to refrain from entering the market for iron. This market is external to the transaction rather than within it. The epitome of this kind of flexibility is the purchasing of needs for immediate delivery, rather than using any kind of a forward contract for future delivery. Such flexibility is reduced by use of forward contracts; the larger and longer they are, the greater is the reduction.

Dealing with conflict between specific planning and needs to adapt to change arising thereafter – only rarely in a discrete transaction will the items contracted for become useless before the forward contract is performed or become of such lessened value that the buyer either will not want them or will want them in greatly changed form. To put this another way, only rarely will there be within the transaction a serious conflict between specific planning and changed needs. To return to the stove manufacturer as an example, seldom will the demand for iron stoves drop so much that the manufacturer comes to regret that he contracted for as much iron as he did.

Preserving relations when conflicts arise – where the mode of operation is a series of discrete transactions, no significant relations exist to be preserved when conflicts arise. Inside the discrete transaction, all that remains is a dispute. Outside the discrete transaction, no relation (other than legal rights arising out of the dispute) exists to be preserved. Thus, all that remains is a dispute to be settled or otherwise resolved. The existence of the market that the discrete transactional system presupposes eliminates the necessity for economic relations between the firms to continue in spite of the disputes. That market, rather than continued relations between these particular parties, will supply their future needs ...

Planning flexibility into long term contractual relations and the neo-classical response – two common characteristics of long term contracts are the existence of gaps in their planning and the presence of a range of processes and techniques used by contract planners to create flexibility in lieu of either leaving gaps or trying to plan rigidly. Prior to exploring the legal response to such planning, an examination of the major types of planning for flexibility used in modern American contracts is in order.

Standards – the use of a standard uncontrolled by either of the parties to plan the contractual relation is very common. One important example is the provision in many collective bargaining agreements for adjustment of wages to reflect fluctuations in the Consumer Price Index ...

Direct third party determination of performance – the role of the architect under form construction contracts of the American Institute of Architects provides a good example of direct third party determination of the performance. The architect is responsible for determining many aspects of the performance relation ...

A particularly important and increasingly used technique for third-party determination of performance content is arbitration ...

One party control of terms – rather than use external standards or independent third parties, the contract may provide that one of the parties to the contract will define, directly or indirectly, parts of the relation ...

ment to agree – a flexible technique used more often than one might ılly expect is 'an agreement to agree' ...

Conflict between specific planning and needs for flexibility: the neo-classical response – as a general proposition in American neo-classical contract law, specific planning in contractual relations governs in spite of changes in circumstances making such planning undesirable to one of the parties. The same principle of freedom of contract leading to this result permits the parties, however, to adjust their relations by subsequent agreement. A description of these processes and some of the legal consequences follows.

Adjustments of existing contractual relations occur in numerous ways. Performance itself is a kind of adjustment from original planning. Even meticulous performance of the most explicit planning transforms figments of the imagination, however precise, into a new, and therefore different, reality. A set of blueprints and specifications, however detailed, and a newly built house simply are not the same. Less explicit planning is changed even more by performance. For example, the vaguely articulated duties of a secretary are made concrete by his or her actual performance of a day's work. Perhaps this is merely a way of saying that planning is inherently filled with gaps, and that performance fills the gaps, thereby altering the relations as originally planned.

Events outside the performance of the parties may also *effect* adjustments in contractual relationships. The five dollars per hour promised an employee for his work in 1977 is not the same when it is paid in November 1977 as it was when promised at the beginning of the year; inflation and other economic developments have seen to that. More or less drastic changes in outside circumstances constantly effect contractual adjustments, however firmly the parties may appear to be holding to their original course.

Non-performance by one of the parties without the consent of the other also alters contractual relations, although in a way different from performance. This is true no matter how many powers are available to the other party to redress the situation.

Another kind of adjustment occurring in any contractual relation is that based on either mutual agreement or unilateral concession by one of the parties of a planned right beneficial to him. These alterations, additions, subtractions, terminations and other changes from original planning may take place at any time during any contractual relation. This is vividly illustrated by various processes of collective bargaining, including periodic renegotiation of the 'whole' contract.[7]

Discharge, rescission and variation of the contract

The law must facilitate smooth adjustments in long term relationships while also guarding against the risk of one party exploiting his position so as to

---

7   Macneil, 1978a.

force the other to make an alteration in his favour. In some long term relationships, one of the parties may be in a considerably weaker position compared with the other. For example where the party who has commissioned the construction of a ship which is close to completion urgently requires the vessel to be available for use on the agreed hand-over date, the ship builder could use his knowledge of the urgent requirements of the other party to extort some advantage by threatening not to complete on time. In these circumstances, the court could respond in one of two ways. Either the threat could be regarded as sufficient to amount to actionable economic duress,[8] or any promise by the other party to make additional payments could be regarded as being unsupported by consideration.[9]

It may be questioned whether common law rules do truly facilitate commercial co-operation in long term relational transactions. The classical approach to variation (or 'waiver of breach') is to apply those rules which also apply to contract formation. The parties must reach an agreement either by deed or in accordance with the rules on consideration.

In determining whether there is an agreement to vary an existing set of contractual terms, the courts will apply an objective test. It follows that it will be possible to imply an agreement to vary from the way in which the parties have acted towards each other. However, as a general rule, mere inaction will not be sufficient to allow the courts to infer an agreement.[10] This is particularly important in cases where the contract contains a provision allowing disputes to be referred to arbitration. A problem which may be encountered in these circumstances is that one of the parties may be guilty of excessive delay in appointing an arbitrator, in which case the question will arise whether the parties, by their inaction, have impliedly 'agreed' to abandon the original contract.

In *Paal Wilson & Co A/S v Partenreederei*,[11] the parties entered into a contract for the sale of a ship. Any dispute arising out of the sale was to be settled by arbitration. The buyers complained that the ship's engines were defective, and started proceedings under the arbitration clause in 1972. In 1980, the buyers proposed fixing a date for arbitration, but the sellers argued that the arbitration agreement was discharged on several grounds, including that of rescission. The House of Lords held that the arbitration would be

---

8   See Chapter 7. In particular, examine the discussion of *North Ocean Shipping Co Ltd v Hyundai Construction Co Ltd, The Atlantic Baron* [1979] 1 QB 705 and *Pao On v Lau Yiu Long* [1980] AC 614.

9   See Chapter 3, in particular, the discussion of *Stilk v Myrick* (1809) 3 Camp 317; *Williams v Roffey Bros & Nicholls (Contractors) Ltd* [1991] 1 QB 1; and *Foakes v Beer* (1884) 9 App Cas 605.

10 *Paal Wilson & Co A/S v Partenreederei, The Hannah Blumenthal* [1983] 1 AC 854; *Allied Marine Transport Ltd v Vale do Rio Doce Navegacao, The Leonidas D* [1985] 1 WLR 925

11 *The Hannah Blumenthal* [1983] 1 AC 854.

abandoned if the sellers had acted in reliance on an express or implied representation to this effect given by the buyers. The representation could be inferred from the buyers' conduct, including inactivity. On the facts, it was held that there was no such inference as, by 1980, the sellers' solicitors were still trying to trace witnesses for the arbitration:

Paal Wilson & Co A/S v Partenreederei, The Hannah Blumenthal [1983] 1 AC 854, p 913

Lord Brandon: I pass now to the further question raised by the cross-appeal. That question is, as I indicated earlier, whether, assuming (contrary to the decisions of the courts below) that the agreement to refer in the present case was not frustrated, the conduct of the parties was nevertheless of such a character as to lead to the inference that they impliedly consented with each other to abandon that agreement.

The question whether a contract has been abandoned or not is one of fact. That being so, it would, I think, be sufficient, for the purposes of the present case, to say that there are concurrent findings of fact by both the courts below against the sellers on that question, that it is not the practice of your Lordships' House to interfere with such concurrent findings of fact save in exceptional circumstances which are not here present, and that the cross-appeal fails on that ground alone.

Because the question of the abandonment of a contract is, however, of some general importance, I consider that it may be helpful to examine the matter, as it arises in the present case, somewhat further...

The concept of the implied abandonment of a contract as a result of the conduct of the parties to it is well established in law: see *Chitty on Contracts*, 23rd edn 1968, Vol 1, para 1231 and cases there cited. Where A seeks to prove that he and B have abandoned a contract in this way, there are two ways in which A can put his case. The first way is by showing that the conduct of each party, as evinced to the other party and acted on by him, leads necessarily to the inference of an implied agreement between them to abandon the contract. The second method is by showing that the conduct of B, as evinced towards A, has been such as to lead A reasonably to believe that B has abandoned the contract, even though it has not in fact been B's intention to do so, and that A has significantly altered his position in reliance on that belief. The first method involves actual abandonment by both A and B. The second method involves the creation by B of a situation in which he is estopped from asserting, as against A, that he, B, has not abandoned the contract (see *Pearl Mill Co Ltd v Ivy Tannery Co Ltd* [1919] 1 KB 78).

On whichever of the two bases of abandonment discussed above the sellers seek to reply in the present case, it seems to me that they are bound to fail. As I indicated above, Sinclairs, as the sellers' solicitors, were still, in November 1979, February 1980 and even as late as November 1980, trying to trace, and obtain evidence from, witnesses who might be called at the hearing of the arbitration. Even if it could fairly be said (which I do not think that it can) that the buyers' prolonged delays from 1974 onwards were such as to induce in the minds of the sellers or their solicitors a reasonable belief that the buyers had abandoned the agreement to refer, Sinclairs' continuing conduct with regard to tracing, and obtaining evidence from, witnesses referred to above makes it impossible for the sellers to say that they acted on any such belief, or that they altered their position significantly in reliance on it.

Lord Diplock (p 915): I will deal first with abandonment and in doing so, and later in dealing with the obligations assumed by the parties under an arbitration clause in a commercial contract, I shall use the expressions 'primary and secondary obligations' under a contract in the sense that I used them in *Photo Production Ltd v Securicor Transport Ltd,* [1980] AC 827 and in *Bremer Vulkan* itself. Since I shall be dealing with bipartite synallagmatic contracts only, I will leave the adjectives to be understood whenever I speak of 'contract'.

Abandonment of a contract (the former contract) which is still executory, that is, one in which at least one primary obligation of one or other of the parties remains unperformed, is effected by the parties entering into a new contract (the contract of abandonment) by which each party promises the other to release that other party from further performance of any primary obligations on his part under the former contract then remaining unperformed, without such non-performance giving rise to any substituted secondary obligation under the former contract to pay damages.

It is the latter part of the promise by each party, that is, the release of the other party from all further secondary as well as primary obligations, that distinguishes the legal concept of abandonment of the former contract from the extinction of unperformed primary obligations of both parties under the former contract by fundamental breach of a primary obligation (or breach of condition) by one of them, followed by the election of the party not in breach to put an end to all primary obligations of both parties under the former contract remaining unperformed. Unlike the contract of abandonment, this leaves the secondary obligations under the former contract of the party who committed the breach enforceable against him by the other party.

To the formation of the contract of abandonment, the ordinary principles of the English law of contract apply. To create a contract by exchange of promises between two parties where the promise of each party constitutes the consideration for the promise of the other what is necessary is that the intention of each of mind of the communicator) should coincide. That is what English *as it has been communicated to and understood by the other* (even though that which has been communicated does not represent the actual state lawyers mean when they resort to the latin phrase *consensus ad idem* and the words that I have italicised are essential to the concept of *consensus ad idem*, the lack of which prevents the formation of a binding contract in English law.

Thus if A (the offeror) makes a communication to B (the offeree), whether in writing, orally or by conduct, which, in the circumstances at the time the communication was received: (1) B, if he were a reasonable man, would understand as stating A's intention to act or refrain from acting in some specified manner if B will promise on his part to act or refrain from acting in some manner also specified in the offer; and (2) B does in fact understand A's communication to mean this, and in his turn makes to A a communication conveying his willingness so to act or to refrain from acting which *mutatis mutandis* satisfies the same two conditions as respects A, the *consensus ad idem* essential to the formation of a contract in English law is complete.

The rule that neither party can rely on his own failure to communicate accurately to the other party his own real intention by what he wrote or said or did, as negativing the *consensus ad idem*, is an example of a general principle of English law that injurious reliance on what another person did may be a source of legal rights against him. I use the broader expression 'injurious reliance' in preference to 'estoppel' so as to embrace all circumstances in which A can say to B, 'You led me reasonably to believe that you were assuming particular legally enforceable obligations to me', of which promissory or *High Trees* estoppel (see *Central London Property Trust Ltd v High Trees House Ltd*, [1947] KB 130) affords another example, whereas 'estoppel', in the strict sense of the term, is an exclusionary rule of evidence, though it may operate so as to affect substantive legal rights *inter partes*.

In the instant case, as in most cases where abandonment of a former contract is relied on, the contract of abandonment of the arbitration agreement is said by the sellers to have been created by the conduct of the parties, consisting of their common inaction, after the buyers' letter of 12 December 1979. Where the inference that a reasonable man would draw from the prolonged failure by the claimant in an arbitration procedure is that the claimant is willing to consent to the abandonment of the agreement to submit the dispute to arbitration and the respondent did in fact draw such inference and by his own inaction thereafter indicated his own consent to its abandonment in similar fashion to the claimant and was so understood by the claimant, the court would be right in treating the arbitration agreement as having been terminated by abandonment. In *André & Cie SA v Marine Transocean Ltd, The Splendid Sun*, [1981] 1 QB 694, all three members of the Court of Appeal drew such an inference from the conduct of both parties in the arbitration. That case was, in my view, rightly decided, though not for reasons other than those which were given by Eveleigh and Fox LJJ.

The facts in the instant case, however, are very different from those of *The Splendid Sun*. As my noble and learned friends Lord Brandon and Lord Brightman both point out, they are inconsistent with any actual belief on the part of the sellers that the buyers had agreed to abandon the arbitration before their letter of 30 July 1980, which stated their intention of continuing with it.

Is there any difference in the two approaches above? Does Lord Diplock, bearing in mind his formalist tendencies, require the offeree to understand that an offer is being made to him and to realise that he is accepting that offer? In what ways does Lord Brandon's approach differ in concentrating on the issue of reliance?

If the facts of *The Hannah Blumenthal* were to arise today, an arbitrator would be able to dismiss a claim on the basis that there has been inordinate and inexcusable delay, but only if the contract does not exclude this course of action:

Arbitration Act 1996[12]

41 *Powers of tribunal in case of party's default*

(2) Unless otherwise agreed by the parties, the following provisions apply.

(3) If the tribunal is satisfied that there has been inordinate and inexcusable delay on the part of the claimant in pursuing his claim, and that the delay

(a) gives rise, or is likely to give rise to, a substantial risk that it is not possible to have a fair resolution of the issues in the claim; or

(b) has caused, or is likely to cause, serious prejudice to the respondent,

the tribunal may make an award dismissing the claim.

The other important contract formation issue to arise in the context of variation of long term relationships is that of sufficiency of consideration for the promise to vary. It has been observed already that there is a potential problem in these circumstances based on the possibility that the promisee will have done little more than he is already bound to do under the terms of the existing contract. Moreover, problems may also be encountered as a result of the rule that part-payment is not sufficient to discharge a debt.[13]

One way in which the problems thrown up by the classical rule book in relation to contract formation is to resort to an approach to variation based on the notion of reasonable reliance, and in particular, the development of the rules on promissory estoppel, based on the proposition put forward by Denning J in *Central London Property Trust Ltd v High Trees House Ltd*[14] that where a promise is made:

... which was intended to create legal relations and which to the knowledge of the person making the promise [is] acted on by the person to whom it [is] made, and which [is] in fact so acted on ... the courts have said that the promise must be honoured.

This principle has been developed by subsequent case law, and two main problems have emerged. The first is whether it is necessary for the promisee to have detrimentally relied on the promisor's promise. No clear answer has been given to this question, due partly to the difficulties associated with distinguishing detriment from consideration. It would appear that any change of position on the part of the promisee or a failure by the promisee to take action for his own protection will be sufficient.

In *WJ Alan & Co Ltd v El Nasr Export and Import Co*,[15] the seller entered two contracts for the supply of coffee under terms which required shipment in

---

12   Which replaced the Arbitration Act 1950, s 13A.

13   See Chapter 3, in particular, the discussion of *D & C Builders Ltd v Rees* [1966] 2 QB 617 and *Foakes v Beer* (1884) 9 App Cas 605.

14   [1947] KB 130, p 134. See Chapter 3 for relevant extracts.

15   [1972] 2 QB 189, CA. See Chapter 3 for relevant extracts. See, also, *Brikom Investments Ltd v Carr* [1979] 2 WLR 737.

September/October at a price of 262 Kenyan shillings per hundredweight. The terms of the contracts also required payment in that currency to be confirmed by an irrevocable letter of credit. The letter of credit was opened, but it confirmed payment in pound sterling, which at the time was in parity with the value of the contract prices in Kenyan shillings. Subsequently, the seller drew on the credit in relation to the first of the two contracts. Between that time and performance of the second contract, the pounds sterling was devalued with the result that there was a large discrepancy between payment in pounds sterling and payment, as envisaged by the contract, in Kenyan shillings. The Court of Appeal held that the seller, by acting on the irrevocable letter of credit in the first instance had waived the right to have payment in Kenyan shillings with the result that the seller's appeal was dismissed:

WJ Alan & Co Ltd v El Nasr Export and Import Co [1972] 2 QB 189, CA, p 212

Lord Denning MR:

Variation or waiver

All that I have said so far relates to a 'conforming' letter of credit; that is, one which is in accordance with the stipulations in the contract of sale. But in many cases – and our present case is one – the letter of credit does not conform. Then negotiations may take place as a result of which the letter of credit is modified so as to be satisfactory to the seller. Alternatively, the seller may be content to accept the letter of credit as satisfactory, as it is, without modification. Once this happens, then the letter of credit is to be regarded as if it were a conforming letter of credit. It will rank accordingly as conditional payment.

There are two cases on this subject. One is *Panoutsos v Raymond Hadley Corpn of New York* [1917] 2 KB 473, but the facts are only to be found fully set out in 22 Com Cas 207. The other is *Enrico Furst & Co v WE Fischer Ltd* [1960] 2 Lloyd's Rep 340. In each of those cases, the letter of credit did not conform to the contract of sale. In each case, the non-conformity was in that it was not a confirmed credit. But the sellers took no objection to the letter of credit on that score. On the contrary, they asked for the letter of credit to be extended; and it was extended. In each case, the sellers sought afterwards to cancel the contract on the ground that the letter of credit was not in conformity with the contract. In each case, the court held that they could not do so.

What is the true basis of those decisions? Is it a variation of the original contract or a waiver of the strict rights thereunder or a promissory estoppel precluding the seller from insisting on his strict rights or what else? In *Enrico Furst*, Diplock J said it was a 'classic case of waiver'. I agree with him. It is an instance of the general principle which was first enunciated by Lord Cairns LC in *Hughes v Metropolitan Railway Co* and rescued from oblivion by *Central London Property Trust Ltd v High Trees House Ltd*. The principle is much wider than waiver itself; but waiver is a good instance of its application. The principle of waiver is simply this: if one party, by his conduct, leads another to believe that the strict rights arising under the contract will not be insisted on, intending that the other should act on that belief, and he does act on it, then the first party will not afterwards be allowed to insist on the strict legal rights when it would be inequitable for him to do so: see *Plasticmoda Società per Azioni v Davidsons (Manchester) Ltd* [1952] 1 Lloyd's Rep 527, p 535. There may be no consideration moving from him who benefits by the waiver. There may be no detriment to him by acting on it. There may be nothing in writing. Nevertheless, the one who waives his strict rights cannot afterwards insist on them. His strict rights are at any rate suspended so long as the waiver lasts. He may on occasion be able to revert to his strict legal rights for the future by giving reasonable notice in that behalf, or otherwise making it plain by his conduct that he will thereafter insist on them: see *Tool Metal Manufacturing Co Ltd v Tungsten Electric Co Ltd*. But there are cases where no withdrawal is possible. It may be too late to withdraw; or it cannot be done without injustice to the other party. In that event he is bound by his waiver. He will not be allowed to revert to his strict legal rights. He can only enforce them subject to the waiver he has made.

Instances of these principles are ready to hand in contracts for the sale of goods. A seller may, by his conduct, lead the buyer to believe that he is not insisting on the stipulated time for exercising an option: see *Bruner v Moore* [1940] 1 Ch 305. A buyer may, by requesting delivery, lead the seller to believe that he is not insisting on the contractual time for delivery: see *Charles Rickards Ltd v Oppenheim* [1950] 1 KB 616, p 621. A seller may, by his conduct, lead the buyer to believe that he will not insist on a confirmed letter of credit: see *Plasticmoda*, but will accept an unconfirmed one instead: see *Panoutsos v Raymond Hadley Corpn of New York* and *Enrico Furst v Fischer*. A seller may accept a less sum for his goods than the contracted price, thus inducing him to believe that he will not enforce payment of the balance: see *Central London Property Trust Ltd v High Trees House Ltd* and *D & C Builders Ltd v Rees*. In none of these cases does the party who acts on the belief suffer any detriment. It is not a detriment, but a benefit to him, to have an extension of time or to pay less, or as the case may be. Nevertheless, he has conducted his affairs on the basis that he has that benefit and it would not be equitable now to deprive him of it.

The judge rejected this doctrine because, he said, 'there is no evidence of the [buyers] having acted to their detriment'. I know that it has been suggested in some quarters that there must be detriment. But I can find no support for it in the authorities cited by the judge. The nearest approach to it is the statement of Viscount Simonds in the *Tool Metal* case [1955] 1 WLR 761, p 764 that the other must have been led 'to alter his position', which was adopted by Lord Hodson in E*mmanuel Ayodeji Ajayi v RT Briscoe (Nigeria) Ltd* [1964] 1 WLR 1326, p 1330. But that only means that he must have been led to act differently from what he otherwise would have done. And, if you study the cases in which the doctrine has been applied, you will see that all that is required is that the one should have 'acted on the belief induced by the other party'. That is how Lord Cohen put it in the *Tool Metal* case [1955] 1 WLR 761, p 799 and is how I would put it myself.

Megaw LJ (p 217): The sellers, however, contend that they were, indeed, entitled to make use of the non-conforming letter of credit offered to them, without impairing their rights for the future under the original terms of the contract, if and when they chose to revert. They seek to rely on the analogy of a sale of goods contract where the goods are deliverable by instalments, and one instalment falls short of the prescribed quality. The buyer is not obliged, even if in law he could do so, to treat the contract as repudiated. He is not, it is said, even obliged to complain. But he is in no way precluded from insisting that for future instalments of the goods the seller shall conform with the precise terms of the contract as to quality. That is not, in my opinion, a true analogy. The relevant transaction here is not one of instalments. It is a once-for-all transaction. It is the establishment of a credit which is to cover the whole of the payment for the whole of the contract. Once it has been accepted by the sellers, the bank is committed, and is committed in accordance with its accepted terms, and no other terms. Once the credit is established and accepted, it is unalterable, except with the consent of all the parties concerned, all of whose legal rights and liabilities have necessarily been affected by the establishment of the credit. Hence, the sellers cannot escape from the consequences of the acceptance of the offered credit by any argument that their apparent acceptance involved merely a temporary acquiescence which they could revoke or abandon at will, or on giving notice. It was an acceptance which, once made, related to the totality of the letter of credit transaction; and the letter of credit transaction was, by the contract of sale, the one and only contractual provision for payment. When the letter of credit was accepted as a transaction in sterling as the currency of account, the price under the sale contract could not remain as Kenyan currency.

For the buyers, it was submitted further that, if there were not here a variation of the contract, there was at least a waiver, which was the sellers could not or did not properly revoke. I do not propose to go into that submission at any length. On analysis, it covers much the same field as the question of variation. In my view, if there were no variation, the buyers would still be entitled to succeed on the ground of waiver. The relevant principle is, in my opinion, that which was stated by Lord Cairns LC in *Hughes v Metropolitan Railway Co* [1877] 2 App Cas 439, p 448. The acceptance by the sellers of the sterling credit was, as I have said, a once-for-all acceptance. It was not a concession for a specified period of time or one which the sellers could operate as long as they chose and thereafter unilaterally abrogate; any more than the buyers would have been entitled to alter the terms of the credit or to have demanded a refund from the sellers if, after this credit had been partly used, the relative values of the currencies had changed in the opposite way.

On the simple form of contractual provision for payment in this sale contract with which we are concerned, the sellers, in my view, have no right of requiring payment (I am not, of course, speaking of damages for breach) otherwise than in accordance with, and by means of, a confirmed irrevocable letter of credit: so long, at any rate, as no default is made by the bank in its performance of the letter of credit obligations. There are cases in which a contract on its true construction imposes on the buyer a potential liability to make payment direct to the seller in certain circumstances, outside or in addition to payment by the bank under a duly established letter of credit. An example is to be found in the facts of *Urquhart Lindsay & Co Ltd v Eastern Bank Ltd* [1922] 1 KB 318.. But there is no scope for such an implication in the present contract of sale. Here, the contractual obligation is 'payment by confirmed, irrevocable letter of credit ...'. If such a credit is duly established, and if payment is duly made in accordance with its terms, I see no scope for any liability on the part of the buyers to make, or on the part of the sellers to require, any other or additional payment. Here the credit was, it is true, not duly established. But the non-compliance of the credit with the contract of sale was, in my opinion, unquestionably waived, and irrevocably waived, by the sellers. On the facts of this case, then the credit which was established has to be treated as a conforming credit. On the terms of this contract of sale, there remains no obligation on the buyers to make any payments to the sellers, because they have discharged the whole of their contractual obligation as to payment when a conforming credit has been established and payment has actually been made under that credit, in accordance with its terms, to the full extent that the sellers have properly sought to draw on it. It follows that, even if there were no variation or relevant waiver in respect of the terms of the contract of sale, I should hold that the sellers' claim fails on that quite separate and independent ground.

Megaw LJ (with whom Stephenson LJ agreed) based his decision on the view that there was a binding variation. Is this correct? If so, where was the consideration for the 'promise' to accept payment in pounds sterling?

If the Denning approach based on promissory estoppel is the way to move forward, is this case authority for the proposition that simple reliance without any detriment is sufficient? If so how does this square with the views expressed by the High Court of Australia in *Waltons Stores (Interstate) Ltd v Maher*?[16]

A second area in which the doctrine of promissory estoppel suffers from a lack of clarity arises in relation to the effect of the representation. Different views have been expressed as to whether the representation made by the promisor serves to suspend or to extinguish his rights under the original terms of the contract.

At common law, under the doctrine of waiver of contractual rights, the position appears to be that where a person who validly waives a right and there is consideration to support that waiver, there is an irrevocable effect on the original contractual rights of that party. In contrast, if there is a mere forbearance, not supported by consideration, the forbearance may be retracted if reasonable notice is given.

In *Charles Rickards Ltd v Oppenheim*,[17] in 1947, the defendant ordered a Rolls Royce chassis from the plaintiffs for delivery on a specified date. The

---

16   (1988) 76 ALR 513.
17   [1950] 1 KB 616.

work was not complete by that date, and the defendant agreed to wait another three months, by which time, the chassis was still not complete. The defendant then gave notice that, if the chassis were not complete within four weeks, he would cancel, which he did. It was significant that before this notice was given, the defendant had been assured that the chassis would be available in two weeks. The Court of Appeal held that the defendant had waived his right to insist on delivery by the original contract date, but had made time of the essence of the contract by his notice requiring delivery within four weeks:

Charles Rickards Ltd v Oppenheim [1950] 1 KB 616, CA, p 621

Denning LJ: It is clear on the findings of the trial judge that there was an initial stipulation making time of the essence of the contract between the plaintiffs and the defendant, namely, that it was to be completed 'in six, or, at the most, seven months'. Counsel for the plaintiffs did not seek to disturb that finding – indeed, he could not successfully have done so – but he said that that stipulation was waived. His argument was that, the stipulated time having been waived, the time became at large, and that thereupon the plaintiffs' only obligation was to deliver within a reasonable time. He said that, in accordance with well known authorities, 'a reasonable time' meant a reasonable time in the circumstances as they actually existed, that is, that the plaintiffs would not exceed a reasonable time if they were prevented from delivering by causes outside their control, such as strikes or the impossibility of getting parts, and so forth, and that, on the evidence in this case, it could not be said that a reasonable time was in that sense exceeded. He cited the well known words of Lord Watson ([1893] AC 22, pp 32 and 33) in *Hick v Raymond and Reid* to support the view that in this case, on the evidence, a reasonable time had not been exceeded. If this had been originally a contract without any stipulation in regard to time, and, therefore, with only the implication of reasonable time, it may be that the plaintiffs could have said that they had fulfilled the contract, but, in my opinion, the case is very different when there was an initial contract, making time of the essence, of 'six or, at the most, seven months'. I agree that that initial time was waived by reason of the requests for delivery which the defendant made after March 1948, and that, if delivery had been tendered in compliance with those requests, the defendant could not have refused to accept. Supposing, for instance, delivery had been tendered in April, May, or June 1948, the defendant would have had no answer. It would be true that the plaintiffs could not aver and prove that they were ready and willing to deliver in accordance with the original contract. They would have had, in effect, to rely on the waiver almost as a cause of action. At one time there would have been theoretical difficulties about their doing that. It would be said that there was no consideration, or, if the contract was for the sale of goods, that there was nothing in writing to support the variation. *Plevins v Downing*, coupled with what was said in *Besseler, Waechter Glover & Co v South Derwent Coal Co Ltd* gave rise to a good deal of difficulty on that score, but all those difficulties are swept away now. If the defendant, as he did, led the plaintiffs to believe that he would not insist on the stipulation as to time, and that, if they carried out the work, he would accept it, and they did it, he could not afterwards set up the stipulation in regard to time against them. Whether it be called waiver or forbearance on his part, or an agreed variation or substituted performance, does not matter. It is a kind of estoppel. By his conduct he made a promise not to insist on his strict legal rights. That promise was intended to be binding, intended to be acted on, and was, in fact, acted on. He cannot afterwards go back on it. That, I think, follows from *Panoutsos v Raymond Hadley Corpn of New York,* a decision of this court, and it was also anticipated in *Bruner v Moore.* It is a particular application of the principle which I endeavoured to state in *Central London Property Trust Ltd v High Trees House Ltd.*

So, if the matter stopped there, the plaintiffs could have said that, notwithstanding that more than seven months had elapsed, the defendant was bound to accept, but the matter did not stop there, because delivery was not given in compliance with the requests of the defendant. Time and time again the defendant pressed for delivery, time and time again he was assured that he would have early delivery, but he never got satisfaction, and eventually at the end of June he gave notice saying that, unless the car was delivered by 25 July, he would not accept it. The question thus arises whether he was entitled to give such a notice, making time of the essence, and that is the question which counsel for the plaintiffs has argued before us. He agrees that, if this is a contract for the sale of goods, the defendant could give such a notice. He accepted the statement of McCardie J ([1920] 3 KB 474, pp 494–95) in *Hartley v Hymans,* as accurately stating the law in regard to the sale of goods, but he said that that statement did not apply to contracts for work and labour. He said that no notice making time of the essence could be given in regard to contracts for work and labour. The judge thought that the contract was one for the sale of goods, but, in my view, it is unnecessary to determine whether it was a contract for the sale of goods or a contract for work and labour, because, whichever it was, the defendant was entitled to give a notice bringing the matter to a head. It would be most unreasonable if, having been lenient and having waived the initial expressed time, he should thereby have prevented himself from ever thereafter insisting on reasonably quick delivery. In my judgment, he was entitled to give a reasonable notice making time of the essence of the matter. Adequate protection to the suppliers is given by the requirement that the notice should be reasonable.

The waiver operated to suspend the defendant's right to terminate the contract on the ground of non-delivery by the contract date but, at the same time, it replaced that right with another.

Under the equitable doctrine of promissory estoppel, there are judicial statements which go either way on the issue of the suspensory or extinctive effect of the promise. The clearest statement of opinion seems to be to the effect that the promisor's right to return to the original contract terms will only be extinguished where such a return is no longer possible.

In *EA Ajayi v RT Briscoe (Nigeria) Ltd,*[18] the owners of certain lorries had let the vehicles on hire-purchase to the defendants. The latter experienced

18   [1964] 1 WLR 1326.

difficulty in getting the vehicles serviced, with the result that the owners agreed to instalments under the hire-purchase contract being withheld whenever the vehicles were not in active service. The owners later sought to revert to the original terms, requiring the defendants to pay all instalments due. The Privy Council held that the owners' claim was not defeated by the doctrine of promissory estoppel as there was no proof that the lorries remained unavailable for use:

EA Ajayi v RT Briscoe (Nigeria) Ltd [1964] 1 WLR 1326, PC, p 1329

Lord Hodson: The defendant's final contention was that having altered his position in the manner indicated the owners never gave notice that the period of suspension was at an end before issuing their summons and that accordingly the lorries never having been returned or made available for service he was entitled to rely on the equitable defence as defined by Bowen LJ in the *Birmingham and District Land Co* case. Alternatively he went further and contended on the authority of the cases of *Central London Property Trust Ltd v High Trees House Ltd* and *Combe v Combe* that the promise given by the letter of 22 July was irrevocable, unless the lorries were made available for service and that, since this never happened, the owners cannot enforce their claim.

Their lordships are of opinion that the principle of law as defined by Bowen LJ, has been confirmed by the House of Lords in the case of the *Tool Metal Manufacturing Co Ltd v Tungsten Electric Co Ltd*, where the authorities were reviewed, and no encouragement was given to the view that the principle was capable of extension so as to create rights in the promisee for which he had given no consideration. The principle, which has been described as quasi estoppel and perhaps more aptly as promissory estoppel, is that when one party to a contract in the absence of fresh consideration agrees not to enforce his rights an equity will be raised in favour of the other party. This equity is, however, subject to the qualification: (a) that the other party has altered his position; (b) that the promisor can resile from his promise on giving reasonable notice, which need not be a formal notice, giving the promisee a reasonable opportunity of resuming his position; (c) the promise only becomes final and irrevocable if the promisee cannot resume his position.

The difficulty of this case stems in great part from the fact that the equitable defence was never expressly pleaded and no part of the argument at the trial appears to have been directed thereto. Certainly the trial judge made no reference to it. True it is that the defence contains in para 29 a reference to the letter of 22 July 1957, by which 'the [hire-purchaser] was asked to withhold the instalments due on the Seddon Tippers as long as they are withdrawn from the road'. Again, para 30 reads 'The [hire-purchaser] avers that the fleet of Tippers were not on the road on the receipt of this letter and ever since they have not been on the road (eight are with the [owners] and three lying in the [hire-purchaser's] garage)'...

Their Lordships have referred to these matters of fact not to exclude the raising of the equitable defence but to show that the facts relied on, although covered by the pleaded defence, were not investigated at the trial through no fault of the owners. Battle was joined by the hire-purchaser on the issue of fraud and on that issue the owners succeeded. The defence was first put forward effectively in the Federal Supreme Court and further elaborated before their lordships on inadequate material. It would not be just to the owners to remit the matter either for a new trial or for a decision to be given at this late stage on facts which have not been expressly found. Their lordships agree with the Federal Supreme Court in thinking that an application to that end should be rejected, especially as the defence sought to be raised is of a suspensory or delaying nature and not of itself decisive to defeat the owners' claim for all time.

CHAPTER 11

COMPELLING PERFORMANCE

SPECIFIC PERFORMANCE AND INJUNCTIONS

The principal equitable remedies of specific performance and injunction are both discretionary remedies which serve literally to enforce a contractual obligation. The two differ in that specific performance is used to enforce a positive obligation, such as a promise to sell or purchase land whereas an injunction is used to enforce a negative undertaking such as an agreement not to reveal confidential information to others.

Both remedies are geared towards the protection of the claimant's expectation that the defendant's undertakings will be performed to the letter, but it should be appreciated that literal enforcement is an exceptional remedy because monetary compensation in the form of an award of damages is regarded as the usual remedy. Moreover, a number of bars have been developed which operate to restrict the circumstances in which these equitable remedies may be granted.

Since contract law is supposed to be concerned with the protection of the claimant's expectation interest, it might be supposed that these equitable remedies, being literally concerned with the protection and enforcement of legitimate expectations, might be more frequently granted, but as has been observed already, this is not the case. The reason for this is partly historical. Prior to the Judicature Acts 1873–75, common law and equitable remedies were dispensed in different courts and the common law courts were only able to award damages. In order to avoid a damaging clash between the then separate systems of law, a compromise was reached whereby the courts of equity would only grant a remedy if the common law remedy of damages was inadequate. Since, in a quasi-market economy, monetary compensation will normally suffice, it became unusual for courts literally to enforce a contract except in a limited number of cases. Since that time, courts in this country have continued to pay lip-service to this rule, despite the fact that both common law or equitable remedies may be dispensed by all courts.[1]

There are also economic reasons which operate in favour of an award of damages. In particular, the rules on damages are said to have the advantage of encouraging mitigation by the claimant, whereas specific performance gives

---

1   In the US, the Uniform Commercial Code has extended the remedy of specific performance, making it available either where goods are unique, or '*in other proper circumstances*' (UCC, § 2-716(1)).

no such encouragement, and may lead to a wasteful use of resources by the claimant. Linked to this is the economic notion of an efficient breach of contract which is based on the assumption that if a third party values a commodity more highly than the claimant, the defendant may be justified in selling to the third party instead of to the claimant, thereby producing an efficient breach. To enforce literally the contract between the claimant and the defendant would produce a contract at an undervalue, which would not be economically sensible. In this case, the higher value received from the third party could be used to fund an award of damages paid to the claimant and all parties concerned will be better off in the end.

A further argument is that in the absence of transaction costs, it does not matter what legal rights and remedies are available, because the parties, as rational maximisers of value, will negotiate around them to produce the most efficient result.[2] On this analysis, if a third party values goods more highly than the claimant, the defendant will negotiate with the claimant to be released from his or her obligation to comply with an order for specific performance by offering to pay to the claimant some of the extra profit to be made from selling to the third party. Of course, this approach does not take account of transaction costs such as the time and expenditure involved in these negotiations.

Finally, it is probably understandable that the courts have been reluctant to extend the scope of specific performance too far, given that disobedience of such an order amounts to a contempt of court, which is potentially punishable by imprisonment. There is an element of wishing to avoid the use of a 'sledgehammer to crack a nut'. By way of contrast, German law *starts* with the principle that the 'creditor' is entitled to a judgment compelling performance (BGB, para 241) – an approach no doubt conditioned by the fact that 'execution' is usually against property rather than against the person.

On the other hand, there are arguments in favour of compulsory performance. For example, it may support the morality of promise-keeping. Moreover, by compelling performance, it is possible to protect subjective expectations such as the consumer surplus value placed upon a commodity or a service over and above its market value. Also, where appropriate, specific performance can be used to prevent a person from making profits which might fall foul of the second principle of remoteness in *Hadley v Baxendale*.[3]

Harris, Ogus and Phillips comment as follows in relation to specific performance (for an explanation of what is meant by the consumer surplus, see the extract from this article in Chapter 13):

> An order of specific performance is a judicial order requiring the promisor to do exactly what he promised in the contract. It is obvious that the actual

2   Coase, 1960.
3   (1854) 9 Exch 341, discussed in Chapter 13.

performance of the promise, whether completed voluntarily or in pursuance of an order of specific performance, will give the promisee the benefit of his expected consumer surplus. But in English law, specific performance is treated as an exceptional remedy for breach of contract, to be contrasted with the normal remedy of damages, viz a sum of money designed to compensate for the loss caused by the breach. The courts have not explicitly recognised the consumer surplus aspect of specific performance, but a few judicial dicta indicate some appreciation of the concept, for example, 'damages at law would not give the party the compensation to which he was entitled; that is, would not put him in a situation as beneficial to him as if the agreement were specifically performed; in any event, *quantum* of damages seldom affects the right to specific performance. If X contracts with Y to buy Blackacre or a rare chattel for a fancy price because the property or chattel has caught his fancy, he is entitled to enforce his bargain and it matters not that he could not prove any damage'. (*Beswick v Beswick* [1968] AC 58, p 102, *per* Lord Upjohn.)

As a matter of history, specific performance was an equitable remedy developed by courts of equity to supplement the common law where damages at law would not provide a satisfactory remedy. While within recent years, there is some evidence of a tendency for the principles of equitable intervention to be expressed in general terms (for example, whether specific performance would be 'the more appropriate remedy ... an order which justice requires'), there is still a substantive requirement that the damages remedy should be shown to be inadequate. Clearly, if an award of damages were not to take proper account of the consumer surplus, this might be regarded as a powerful argument for imposing specific performance. There is little overt awareness of this in the reported cases, but the recognition that specific performance is the appropriate remedy in classes of cases where consumer surplus is typically present does suggest that judges have an intuitive sense of the problem. There is, for example, a long tradition that contracts for the purchase of land should normally be specifically enforced. The judges have perceived that land is unique, in that it has a specific location, and that it therefore often has a special value for the purchaser beyond its price in the open market. Sir John Leach said in 1824: 'Thus, a Court of Equity decrees performance of a contract for land, not because of the real nature of the land but because damages at law, which must be calculated upon the general money-value of land, may not be a complete remedy to the purchaser, to whom the land may have a peculiar and special value.' The fact, however, that courts have not been prepared to distinguish cases in which the purchaser intends to live on the land in question from those in which a businessman or corporation intends to use it exclusively to generate profits, suggests that if the concept we label consumer surplus were the original basis of the principle, it has now been lost sight of.

As regards the sale of chattels, the presumption that specific performance will not be available may be supplanted in the case of those which are 'unique', 'when there is, over and above the market value, that which has been called the *pretium affectionis*', and also, 'in the case of chattels which, though not unique, possess a special and peculiar value to the plaintiff'. This latter statement of principle could be interpreted in the light of the consumer surplus concept to mean that whenever, following the seller's failure to deliver a chattel, an award of damages would not enable the buyer to obtain a similar consumer surplus through a substitute purchase, the courts will be willing to grant specific performance. The reported cases show that specific performance has been ordered of contracts to buy a rare jewel, china vases, particular stones from Old Westminster Bridge and an ornamental door designed by the famous architect Adam.

Two further points should be made in relation to the availability of this remedy. First, the broad discretion given to the courts to consider all the circumstances of the case (to determine whether it would be appropriate to make such an order) allows them to have regard to factors which would not be relevant in a common law damages claim. Thus, certain losses which are 'special' to the plaintiff may not be included in the damages award because they are too 'remote'; but the existence of such a loss might be highly influential in the court's decision, in the exercise of its equitable jurisdiction, to order specific performance. Again, the remoteness rules are applied, in assessing damages, to facts known to the parties (or which reasonably ought to have been known to them) at the time of the contract, but to determine whether an award would be inadequate, and therefore whether special performance should be granted, the court may advert to facts as they exist at the time of the hearing. Secondly, as a remedy specific performance has its inherent limitations. Performance may no longer be possible, or it may be useless or extremely difficult to supervise, for example, where personal service is involved. In such circumstances, the court has to devise other methods of providing, or compensating for, the lost consumer surplus.[4]

A further argument in favour of specific performance is that, because of its discretionary basis, a court can take account of the equities of a given relationship in order to achieve what is perceived to be a fair result and to control relationships of dependence. For example, if the defendant stands to make an unjustified gain at the expense of the claimant, a decree of specific performance may be justified, especially if rules on an award of damages would leave the claimant uncompensated.[5] Similarly, the court may be more prepared to make use of the remedy in relationships of dependence. A typical example of such a relationship is a continuing contract, such as a solus agreement under which the tenant of a garage agrees to take supplies of oil from one source only in return for finance in setting up his business. In such cases the tenant is almost wholly reliant upon his supplier, who may be in a position to take advantage.[6]

---

4   Harris, Ogus and Phillips, 1979, pp 586–89.
5   *Beswick v Beswick* [1968] AC 58.
6   See, eg, *Sky Petroleum Ltd v VIP Petroleum Ltd* [1974] 1 WLR 576.

THE BARS TO SPECIFIC PERFORMANCE

A number of bars to the availability of specific performance have been developed. These bars also apply to the award of an injunction where the effect of the remedy is to operate as a form of specific performance.

Adequacy of damages

It is said that specific performance will not be ordered where an award of damages is adequate. As the market places a value on virtually all contractual obligations and the claimant can be compensated for all his foreseeable losses, it might appear that damages will never be an inadequate remedy. However, in some cases, the loss suffered by the claimant may be too remote to be recoverable by way of an award of damages, or the claimant may have placed a subjective value on the thing contracted for which exceeds its market value.

This bar, however, may not be as important as it might have been in the past, and there is some indication that the principles on which the courts now proceed are those of justice and fairness:

Beswick v Beswick [1968] AC 58, p 96

Lord Upjohn: But surely on a number of grounds this is a case for specific performance. First, here is the sale of a business for full consideration wholly executed on A's part who has put C into possession of all the assets. C is repudiating the obligations to be performed by him. To such a case, the words of Kay J in *Hart v Hart* are particularly appropriate: '... when an agreement for valuable consideration between two parties has been partially performed, the court ought to do its utmost to carry out that agreement by a decree for specific performance.'

The fact that A by the agreement was to render such services as consultant as he might find convenient or at his own absolute discretion should decide may be ignored as *de minimis* and the contrary was not argued. In any event, the fact that there is a small element of personal service in a contract of this nature does not destroy that quality of mutuality (otherwise plainly present) want of which may in general terms properly be a ground for refusing a decree of specific performance. See, for example, *Fortescue v Lostwithiel and Fowey Railway Co.*

In the courts below, though not before your Lordships, it was argued that the remedy of specific performance was not available when all that remained was the obligation to make a money payment. Danckwerts LJ, rightly demolished this contention as untenable for the reasons he gives.

But when the money payment is not, however, made once and for all but in the nature of an annuity there is an even greater need for equity to come to the assistance of the common law. It is to do true justice to enforce the true contract that the parties have made and to prevent the trouble and expense of a multiplicity of actions. This has been well settled for over a century: *Swift v*

Swift. In that case, an annuity of £40 per annum was payable to a lady quarterly and Lord Plunket LC enforced specific performance of it. He said: 'It is said she has a complete remedy at law for the breach of this contract and that, therefore, this court should not interfere. Now, the remedy at law could only be obtained in one of two ways, either by at once recovering damages for all the breaches that might occur during the joint lives of herself and the defendant, or by bringing four actions in each year, and recovering in each the amount of a quarterly payment of the annuity. Those are the two modes of redress open to the plaintiff at law. And I am called on to refuse relief here on the ground that such remedies are equally beneficial and effectual for the plaintiff as that which this court could afford. To refuse relief on such a ground would not, in may opinion, be a rational administration of justice. I do not see that there is any authority for refusing relief, and certainly there is no foundation in reason for doing so.'

Then, after referring to the case of *Adderley v Dixon*, he continued: 'Applying this to the present case, leaving the plaintiff to proceed at law and to get damages at once for all the breaches that might occur during the joint lives of her and the defendant, would, in effect, be altering the entire nature of the contract that she entered into: it would be compelling her to accept a certain sum, a sum to be ascertained by the conjecture of a jury as to what was the value of the annuity. This would be most unreasonable and unjust: her contract was for the periodical payment of certain sums during an uncertain period; she was entitled to a certain sum of money, and she agreed to give up that for an annuity for her own and the defendant's lives, and to insist on her now accepting a certain sum of money in the shape of damages for it, would be in effect to make her convert into money, what she, having in money, exchanged for an annuity. As to her resorting four times every year to a court of law for each quarterly payment of this annuity, it a manifest absurdity to call that a beneficial or effectual remedy for the plaintiff; and resting the case on that ground alone, I think I am warranted by the highest authority in granting the relief sought.'

It is in such common sense and practical ways that equity comes to the aid of the common law, and it is sufficiently flexible to meet and satisfy the justice of the case in the many different circumstances that arise from time to time.

To sum up this matter: had C repudiated the contract in the lifetime of A the latter would have had a cast iron case for specific performance. Can it make any difference that by the terms of the agreement C is obliged to pay the annuity no longer to A, but to B? Of course not. On the principle that I have just stated it is clear that there can be nothing to prevent equity making an appropriate decree for specific performance directing payment of the annuity to A but during his life and thereafter to B for her life ...

But when A dies and his rights pass to A1, it is said, however, that the remedy of specific performance is no longer appropriate against C. The argument was first that the estate of A suffered no damage by reason of C's failure to pay B; so A1 is entitled to nominal damages, but as she is not otherwise interested in the agreement as such it would be wrong to grant specific performance; for that remedy is available only where damages be an inadequate remedy. Here, nominal damages are adequate. Further, it was argued, to do so would really be to confer on B a right which she does not have in law or equity to receive the annuity. Then, secondly, it was said that if the remedy of specific performance is granted it might prejudice creditors of A so that the parties ought to be left to their strict rights at law. Thirdly, it is said that there are procedural difficulties in the way of enforcing an order for specific performance in favour of a third party. I will deal with these points, though in reverse order.

As to procedural difficulties, I fear that I do not understand the argument. The point, if valid, applies to an action for specific performance by A just as much as by A1, yet in the authorities which I have quoted no such point was ever taken ...

Then as to the second point. Let me assume (contrary to the fact) that A died with substantial assets but also many creditors. The legal position is that, *prima facie,* the duty of A1 is to carry out her intestate's contracts and compel C to pay B; but the creditors may be pressing and the agreement may be considered onerous; so it may be her duty to try and compromise the agreement with C and save something for the estate even at the expense of B. See *Ahmed Angullia Bin Hadjee Mohamed Salleh Angullia v Estate & Trust Agencies (1927) Ltd,* per Lord Romer. So be it, but how can C conceivably rely on this circumstance as a defence by him to an action for specific performance by A1? Of course not; he, C, has no interest in the estate; he cannot plead a possible *jus tertii* which is no concern of his. It is his duty to fulfil his contract by paying C. A1 alone is concerned with the creditors, beneficiaries or next-of-kin of A, and this point therefore can never be a defence by C if A1 in fact chooses to sue for specific performance rather than to attempt a compromise in the interest of the estate. This point seems to me misconceived. In any event on the facts of this case there is no suggestion that there are any unpaid creditors and B is sole next-of-kin, so the point is academic ...

However, I incline to the view that, on the facts of this case, damages are nominal for it appears that A died without any assets, save and except the agreement which he hoped would keep him and then his widow for their lives. At all events, let me assume that damages are nominal. So it is said nominal damages are adequate and the remedy of specific performance ought not to be granted. That is with all respect wholly to misunderstand that principle. Equity will grant specific performance when damages are inadequate to meet the justice of the case.

But in any event, however, *quantum* of damages seldom affects the right to specific performance. If X contracts with Y to buy Blackacre or a rare chattel for a fancy price because the property or chattel has caught his fancy, he is entitled to enforce his bargain and it matters not that he could not prove any damage.

In this case, the court ought to grant a specific performance order all the more because damages are nominal. C has received all the property; justice demands that he pay the price and this can only be done in the circumstances by equitable relief. It is a fallacy to suppose that B is thereby obtaining additional rights; A1 is entitled to compel C to carry out the terms of the agreement.

The facts and other aspects of this decision are considered in Chapter 15.

Contracts for the sale of land

Specific performance of contracts for the sale of land is regarded as the usual remedy on the ground that each parcel of land is regarded as unique. Accordingly, since a unique parcel cannot be replaced, it has no obvious market value, so that damages could be regarded as an inadequate remedy. Of course, the label of 'uniqueness' is a pure fiction, because the remedy is still available to the purchaser who intends to re-sell immediately and places no subjective value on the land.

In support of the view expressed above, that justice and fairness are more likely to be the reasons for the availability of the remedy, is the rule that specific performance will be refused when it would cause severe hardship.[7]

Contracts for the sale of goods

Under s 52 of the Sale of Goods Act 1979, the court has a discretion to order specific performance of a contract to sell specific or ascertained goods.[8] But this may not be a comprehensive statement of the law on this subject since it appears that a contract for the sale of unascertained goods may also be literally enforced, albeit exceptionally.

In *Sky Petroleum Ltd v VIP Petroleum Ltd*,[9] the plaintiffs were granted an interlocutory injunction to restrain the defendants from withholding supplies of unascertained petroleum products, which they had agreed to sell to the plaintiffs. These events occurred during an oil crisis which had placed the market for such products in an extreme state of uncertainty. In the event, it was very unlikely that the plaintiffs would have been able to obtain supplies elsewhere:

Sky Petroleum Ltd v VIP Petroleum Ltd [1974] 1 WLR 576, p 577

Goulding J: After the making of the agreement, it is common knowledge that the terms of trade in the market for petroleum and its different products changed very considerably, and I have little doubt that the contract is now disadvantageous to the defendant company. After a long correspondence, the defendant company, by telegrams dated 15 and 16 November 1973, has purported to terminate the contract under a clause therein providing for termination by the defendant company if the plaintiff company fails to conform with any of the terms of the bargain. What is alleged is that the plaintiff company has exceeded the credit provisions of the contract and has persistently been, and now is, indebted to the defendant company in larger

---

7   *Denne v Light* (1857) 8 De GM & G 774; *Wroth v Tyler* [1974] Ch 30; *Patel v Ali* [1984] Ch 283.

8   Generally, the court has no power to award specific performance of a contract for the sale of unascertained gods: *Re Wait* [1927] 1 Ch 606.

9   [1974] 1 WLR 576.

amounts than were provided for. So far as that dispute relates, as for the purposes of this motion it must, to the date of the purported termination of the contract, it is impossible for me to decide it on the affidavit evidence. It involves not only a question of construction of the contract, but also certain disputes on subsequent arrangements between the parties and on figures in the accounts. I cannot decide it on motion and the less I say about it, the better.

What I have to decide is whether any injunction should be granted to protect the plaintiff company in the meantime. There is trade evidence that the plaintiff company has no great prospect of finding any alternative source of supply for the filling stations which constitute its business. The defendant company has indicated its willingness to continue to supply the plaintiff company, but only at prices which, according to the plaintiff company's evidence, would not be serious prices from a commercial point of view. There is, in my judgment, so far as I can make out on the evidence before me, a serious danger that, unless the court interferes at this stage, the plaintiff company will be forced out of business. In those circumstances, unless there is some specific reason which debars me from doing so, I should be disposed to grant an injunction to restore the former position under the contract until the rights and wrongs of the parties can be fully tried out.

It is submitted for the defendant company that I ought not to do so for a number of reasons. It is said that, on the facts, the defendant company was entitled to terminate and the plaintiff company was in the wrong. That, of course, is the very question in the action, and I have already expressed my inability to resolve it even provisionally on the evidence now before me. Then it is said that there are questions between the parties as to arrangements subsequent to the making of the contract, in particular regarding the price to be paid, and that they give rise to uncertainties which would make it difficult to enforce any order made by way of interlocutory relief. I do not think I ought to be deterred by that consideration, though I can see it has some force. In fact, during September and October, to go no further back, the defendant company has gone on supplying and the plaintiff company has gone on paying. There has been nothing apparently impracticable in the contract, although the defendant company says, of course, that the plaintiff company has not been paying large enough sums quickly enough.

Now I come to the most serious hurdle in the way of the plaintiff company which is the well known doctrine that the court refuses specific performance of a contract to sell and purchase chattels not specific or ascertained. That is a well established and salutary rule and I am entirely unconvinced by counsel for the plaintiff company when he tells me that an injunction in the form sought by him would not be specific enforcement at all. The matter is one of substance and not of form and it is, in my judgment, quite plain that I am for the time being specifically enforcing the contract if I grant an injunction. However, the ratio behind the rule is, as I believe, that under the ordinary contract for the sale of non-specific goods, damages are a sufficient remedy. That, to my mind, is lacking in the circumstances of the present case. The evidence suggests, and indeed it is common knowledge, that the petroleum market is in an unusual state in which a would-be buyer cannot go out into the market and contract with another seller, possibly at some sacrifice as to price. Here, the defendant company appears for practical purposes to be the plaintiff company's sole means of keeping its business going, and I am prepared so far to depart from the general rule as to try to preserve the position under the contract until a later date. I therefore propose to grant an injunction.

In general, the courts have not interpreted s 52 as affecting the adequacy of damages rule, and have refused specific performance on the ground that an award of damages enables a substitute to be bought in the market. Conversely, if goods are physically unique, the court may be prepared to order specific performance. In *Thorn v Public Works Commissioners*,[10] specific performance was granted on a contract to sell stones from the old, dismantled Westminster Bridge. Similarly, specific performance has been decreed in a contract for the sale of a ship with special characteristics.[11] There are also cases which suggest that English law has recognised the notion of commercial uniqueness, under which, if goods are not delivered there would be serious disruption to the plaintiff's business. In these circumstances, strictly, an award of damages will be adequate, although difficulties of assessment may arise which might justify an order for specific performance. The decision in *Sky Petroleum v VIP Petroleum*[12] is one such example, but, generally, the courts have set themselves against the recognition of commercial uniqueness.

In *Société des Industries Métallurgiques SA v Bronx Engineering Co Ltd*,[13] an interlocutory injunction restraining the sellers from removing machinery from the jurisdiction of the court was refused, as there was no likelihood that the buyers would be granted an order for specific performance at the trial. Evidence was given that the buyers would suffer a nine to 12 month delay in obtaining substitute machinery. The case would appear to reject the notion of commercial uniqueness, even where the goods are specific:

Société des Industries Métallurgiques SA v Bronx Engineering Co Ltd [1975] 1 Lloyd's Rep 465, p 468

Lord Edmund Davies: Mr Tapp has urged (and with great force) that, whereas it should prove a simple matter for the defendants to establish the amount of damages they were entitled to recover pursuant to the plaintiffs' undertaking in the event of the court of trial holding that judgment in the action should be entered for the defendants, it would be a matter of considerable complexity and difficulty for the plaintiffs to establish the measure of their damages should it turn out that, an interlocutory injunction having been refused by this court, the defendants were held to be in the wrong. I dare say that Mr Tapp is right about that, for evidence from Tunis would have to be called and there

---

10 (1863) 32 Beav 490.
11 See *Behnke v Bede Shipping Co Ltd* [1927] 1 KB 649. See, also, *CN Marine Inc v Stena Line A/B, The Stena Nautica (No 2)* [1982] 2 Lloyd's Rep 336.
12 [1974] 1 WLR 576, considered in more detail above.
13 [1975] 1 Lloyd's Rep 465.

might be translation difficulties and other complications, all adding to the cost and duration of the litigation.

But such difficulties frequently and unfortunately arise in litigation and, of themselves, do not justify the granting of such an injunction as is sought in the present case, which is governed by s 52 of the Sale of Goods Act 1893. That section enables the court 'if it thinks fit' to order specific performance of a contract to deliver 'specific or ascertained goods'. For present purposes, I understand the parties to accept that the machinery in question was 'ascertained goods' within the meaning of the section. But it is established law that such an order will not be made if damages would fully compensate the party wronged: *Whiteley Ltd v Hilt* [1918] 2 KB 808, p 819. The crux of the present application accordingly, as I see it, is whether it is proper to draw the conclusion that damages would not or might well not duly compensate the plaintiffs if they establish a contractual breach by the defendants. That the subject matter was not 'an ordinary article of commerce' is not open to doubt. That, if they succeed, the plaintiffs might well recover very substantial damages is certainly on the cards. But the defendants are not the only manufacturers of such machinery and it lacks, in my judgment, the unique quality of such articles as that which was the subject matter of the specific performance decree made in, for example, *Behnke v Bede Shipping Co Ltd* [1927] 1 KB 649; (1927) 27 LlL Rep 24. That case is commonly cited in the textbooks as supporting the proposition that specific performance will be ordered of a contract for the sale of a ship, but merely to say that is to put the matter too broadly. It is of some importance to note that it was not just any ship, for, as Mr Justice Wright said ([1927] 1 KB 661): '... in the present case, there is evidence that the City was of peculiar and practically unique value to the plaintiff. She was a cheap vessel, being old, having been built in 1892, but her engines and boilers were practically new and such as to satisfy the German regulations, and hence the plaintiff could, as a German shipowner, have her at once put on the German register. A very experienced ship valuer has said that he knew of only one other comparable ship, but that could now have been sold. The plaintiff wants the ship for immediate use, and I do not think damages would be an adequate compensation.'

By way of contrast with that case, the real substance of the plaintiffs' claim here is that were they now obliged to go to another manufacturer they would probably have to wait another nine to 12 months before they could get delivery of such new machinery and that, by reason of that delay and other factors, they would stand to lose a substantial sum. There has been no suggestion of financial inability in the defendants to satisfy such a money judgment (whatever its dimensions) as might be awarded against them to cover all such items of damages as the plaintiffs could legitimately rely upon. While sympathising with the dilemma in which the plaintiffs find themselves, I see nothing which removes this case from the ordinary run of cases arising out of commercial contracts where damages are claimed. Of course, if the plaintiffs are right, the delay that has arisen by reason of the assumed breach of the defendants will go to inflate their damages; the greater the delay the plaintiffs experience in getting such new machinery (despite their best efforts), the greater the potential liability of the defendants in the event of the plaintiffs' succeeding. But, for my part, I cannot see that, whatever be the balance of convenience of the parties to which reference has been made, the case is one which, on the authorities, justifies the defendants now being restrained from disposing of the machinery in question as they seek to do and claim they are entitled to do, the plaintiffs, on the other hand, meanwhile seeking to compel the defendants until the trial of the action in what must inevitably be the not very near future to maintain this machinery in store at an expense which runs into several thousand pounds a month. The defendants do undoubtedly run the risk of ultimately being mulcted in what may well be a most substantial sum, but that is a risk which they are seemingly prepared to take and, in my judgment, they must be left free to do so.

Contracts to pay money

As a general rule, where there is an obligation to pay money and the defendant fails to comply, the claimant's only remedy will be in damages. But this will clearly be an inadequate remedy where the plaintiff has suffered no loss and the contract is one to confer a benefit on a third party who would otherwise be defeated by the doctrine of privity.[14]

Performance of contracts which require supervision

An often cited reason for refusing specific performance is that if the contract is to be performed over a protracted period of time, it would be undesirable to order specific performance on the ground that this will require constant supervision by a court officer.

However, a better way of viewing the bar is that the remedy will only be refused if it is unclear what has to be done in order to ensure compliance. In *Ryan v Mutual Tontine Association*,[15] specific performance was refused where it would have required the court to supervise the working habits of a resident porter who was required to be in constant attendance at the claimant's place of residence. However, in contrast, there appears to be no objection to appoint an agent such as a receiver to act on the court's behalf to ensure compliance.[16] Instead, more recent authorities work on the basis that the most important consideration is whether it can be identified what has to be done.

This view is also supported by *Posner v Scott Lewis*,[17] in which (on remarkably similar facts to those in *Ryan v Mutual Tontine Association*) an order for specific performance of a landlord's obligation to employ a caretaker

---

14 See the discussion of *Beswick v Beswick* [1968] AC 58.
15 [1893] 1 Ch 116.
16 *Wolverhampton Corpn v Emmons* [1901] 1 KB 515.
17 [1986] 3 WLR 531.

was granted. The main difference between the two cases is that in *Ryan*, a caretaker had been employed but he had a number of other jobs, to the extent that he was rarely available to carry out his role as a caretaker, whereas, in *Posner*, the landlord had made no appointment at all. In these circumstances it is easy to see what had to be done to ensure compliance in *Posner*. But the same could not be said of *Ryan*, short of attaching a ball and chain to the caretaker's ankle!

In *Tito v Waddell (No 2)*,[18] the defendants were given a right to abstract phosphates from Ocean Island in the Western Pacific on condition that they would replant the island for the benefit of its inhabitants when the abstraction process was complete. They failed to comply with this obligation. However, some of the islanders but not others were joined as parties to the proceedings. On the question whether specific performance was an appropriate remedy, Megarry VC was of the opinion that it was not. One of the reasons given was that the remedy was unsuitable due to the complexity of the obligation to be enforced:

Tito v Waddell (No 2) [1977] 2 WLR 496, p 694

Megarry VC:

Specific performance

I now come to the remedy of specific performance. Is this a case in which an order for specific performance can and should be made? This raised a number of issues:

(a) *Unsuitability* – I will take first a contention by Mr MacCrindle that the obligation to replant is a type of obligation that is unsuitable for a decree of specific performance. He put this on the ground that the work was too complicated and experimental, and that while it was being carried out over the long period that it would take it would repeatedly raise questions of whether the complex operations were being properly carried out. On this, he cited the well known case of *Wolverhampton Corpn v Emmons*. Counsel for the plaintiffs met this in two ways. First, he put forward the draft order that I have already set out, thereby giving a considerable degree of greater certainty to what the court was being asked to order. Secondly, he cited a line of cases, beginning with *Pembroke v Thorpe* and running down to *Jeune v Queen's Cross Properties Ltd*, as tending to show that such a contract was specifically enforceable.

In cases of this kind, it was at one time said that an order for the specific performance of the contract would not be made if there would be difficulty in the court supervising its execution: see, for example, *Ryan v Mutual Tontine Westminster Chambers Association*. Smith MR subsequently found himself unable to see the force of this objection (see *Wolverhampton Corpn v Emmons*); and after it had been discussed and questioned in *CH Giles & Co Ltd v Morris*, the House of Lords disposed of it (I hope finally) in *Shiloh Spinners Ltd v Harding*. The real question is whether there is a sufficient definition to what has to be done in order to comply with the order of the court. That definition may

18 [1977] 2 WLR 496.

be provided by the contract itself, or it may be supplied by the terms of the order, in which case there is the further question whether the court considers that the terms of the contract sufficiently support, by implication or otherwise, the terms of the proposed order.

I have, of course, considered all the cases cited on this point, but I do not think that I need say much about them. In *Storer v Great Western Railway Co*, Knight Bruce VC adopted what I think is the modern approach on difficulties of supervision. He said: 'The court has to order the thing to be done, and then it is a question capable of solution whether the order has been obeyed.' However, what is here of greater importance is the attitude of the courts when specific performance is claimed against defendants who have had some or all of the benefit to which they were entitled under the contract. In such a case, said Wigram VC in *Price v Penzance Corpn*, 'the court will go to any length which it can to compel them to perform the contract in specie'. 'The court', said James VC in *Wilson v Furness Railway Co*, 'would struggle with any amount of difficulties in order to perform the agreement.' In such cases, the court may direct a reference to the master to determine what is necessary and proper to be done, and where and by what means it is to be done: *Sanderson v Cockermouth and Workington Railway Co*; *Lytton v Great Northern Railway Co*.

In this field, however, I must consider the warning to be found in *Wilson v Northampton and Banbury Junction Railway Co*. There, a railway company contracted with a landowner, whose land they were taking, to construct on his land 'a station'. The landowner sued for specific performance, but both Bacon VC and the Court of Appeal in Chancery held that justice required that instead of a decree of specific performance there should be an inquiry as to damages. The basic difficulty lay in the crude simplicity of the words 'a station', with nothing to indicate the nature, materials, style, dimensions or anything else; and it was these difficulties which seemed to have been decisive with Bacon VC.

On appeal, a number of the authorities that I have mentioned on the court struggling with difficulties were duly cited; but, in addition to the indefiniteness of 'a station', the court referred to the further difficulty of there being nothing in the contract which obliged the company to use the station when constructed. The main significance of the decision is, I think, that the court will decree specific performance only if this will do more perfect and complete justice than an award of damages. In assessing damages the court could consider a number of reasonable probabilities, both as to the size and quality of the station and as to its use, whereas a decree for specific performance must either require a thing to be done or else omit it; the order cannot be made on the basis of reasonable probabilities. The decision also seems to me to show that uncertainties which make the court hesitate to order specific performance may well be no bar to an award of damages, especially as damages may be awarded on the footing of resolving uncertainties in favour of the innocent party and against the wrongdoer.

For the reasons that I have given, I think that there is considerably less uncertainty about the meaning of the word 'replant' in the A and C deeds than about the meaning of 'a station' in the *Wilson* case. I certainly do not consider that the case against decreeing specific performance on this score is nearly so strong in the present case as it was in that case; and if in the circumstances it is right to do so, I should certainly seek to struggle with any amount of difficulties to compel the British Phosphate Commissioners to replant in accordance with the A and C deeds under which they have taken the benefit. The complexities of specific performance are weighty and discouraging, but, by themselves, I do not think that they suffice to induce the court to refuse specific performance. At the same time, I can see considerable advantage in making an award of damages instead. In that state of affairs, I think that I must consider the other circumstances of the case before reaching any conclusion on this matter.

Contracts for services and contracts of personal service

As a general rule, any contract involving personal services is not amenable to literal enforcement.[19] This may be because damages is an adequate remedy, but there are other considerations. For example, if there has been a breakdown in a relationship which requires trust and confidence, an order for specific performance would do little to improve that relationship by forcing the parties together. But possibly the most important reason for refusing the remedy is that the order would infringe personal liberty by transforming the contract into one of slavery:[20]

Trade Union and Labour Relations (Consolidation) Act 1992

236 No compulsion to work

No court shall, whether by way of:

(a) an order for specific performance ... of a contract of employment; or

(b) an injunction ... restraining a breach or threatened breach of such a contract,

compel an employee to do any work or attend at any place for the doing of any work.

Exceptionally, where a contract contains an express negative covenant requiring the employee not to work for another person, a prohibitory injunction may be granted to restrain a breach of that covenant. However, no such covenant will be implied from a positive obligation, even where the employee has undertaken to devote the whole of his time to his employer's business.[21]

The effect of an injunction of this kind must not directly compel the employee to work for the employer, but it may have this effect indirectly.

---

19 *Britain v Rossiter* (1879) 11 QB 123.

20 *De Francesco v Barnum* (1890) 45 Ch D 430, p 438, *per* Fry LJ.

21 *Whitewood Chemical Co v Hardman* [1891] 2 Ch 416.

In *Warner Bros Pictures Inc v Nelson*,[22] the actress Bette Davis agreed to work exclusively for the plaintiffs as a film actress and not to work for any other film company during the currency of her employment. She wanted to work for another film producer, but an injunction was granted to prevent her from doing so, even though the practical effect of the order was to compel her to work for the plaintiffs. The court resorted to the fiction that the defendant could take up alternative employment, but it is difficult to imagine Bette Davis in any other role than that of a film star:

Warner Bros Pictures Inc v Nelson [1937] 1 KB 209, p 214

Branson J: I turn then to the consideration of the law applicable to this case on the basis that the contract is a valid and enforceable one. It is conceded that our courts will not enforce a positive covenant of personal service; and specific performance of the positive covenants by the defendant to serve the plaintiffs is not asked in the present case. The practice of the Court of Chancery in relation to the enforcement of negative covenants is stated on the highest authority by Lord Cairns in the House of Lords in *Doherty v Allman*. His Lordship says: 'My Lords, if there had been a negative covenant, I apprehend, according to well settled practice, a Court of Equity would have had no discretion to exercise. If parties, for valuable consideration, with their eyes open, contract that a particular thing shall not be done, all that a Court of Equity has to do is to say, by way of injunction, that which the parties have already said by way of covenant, that the thing shall not be done; and, in such case, the injunction does nothing more than give the sanction of the process of the court to that which already is the contract between the parties. It is not then a question of the balance of convenience or inconvenience, or of the amount of damage or of injury – it is the specific performance, by the court, of that negative bargain which the parties have made, with their eyes open, between themselves.'

That was not a case of a contract of personal service; but the same principle had already been applied to such a contract in *Lumley v Wagner*. The Lord Chancellor used the following language: 'Wherever this court has not proper jurisdiction to enforce specific performance, it operates to bind men's consciences, as far as they can be bound, to a true and literal performance of their agreements; and it will not suffer them to depart from their contracts at their pleasure, leaving the party with whom they have contracted to the mere chance of any damages which a jury may give. The exercise of this jurisdiction has, I believe, had a wholesome tendency towards the maintenance of that good faith which exists in this country to a much greater degree perhaps than in any other; and although the jurisdiction is not to be extended, yet a judge would desert his duty who did not act up to what his predecessors have handed down as the rule for his guidance in the administration of such an equity.' This passage was cited as a correct statement of the law in the opinion of a strong Board of the Privy Council in the case of *Lord Strathcona SS Co v*

---

22   [1937] 1 KB 209.

Dominion Coal Co, and I not only approve it, if I may respectfully say so, but am bound by it.

The defendant, having broken her positive undertakings in the contract without any cause or excuse which she was prepared to support in the witness box, contends that she cannot be enjoined from breaking the negative covenants also. The mere fact that a covenant, which the court would not enforce if expressed in positive form, is expressed in the negative instead, will not induce the court to enforce it. That appears, if authority is needed for such a proposition, from *Davis v Foreman, Kirchner v Gruban*, and *Chapman v Westerby*. The court will attend to the substance and not to the form of the covenant. Nor will the court, true to the principle that specific performance of a contract of personal service will never be ordered, grant an injunction in the case of such a contract to enforce negative covenants if the effect of so doing would be to drive the defendant either to starvation or to specific performance of the positive covenants: see *Whitwood Chemical Co v Hardman* ...

An injunction is a discretionary remedy, and the court in granting it may limit it to what the court considers reasonable in all the circumstances of the case. This appears from the judgment of the Court of Appeal in *William Robinson & Co Ltd v Heuer*. The particular covenant in that case is set out at p 452 and provides that 'Heuer shall not during this engagement, without the previous consent in writing of the said W Robinson & Co Ltd ... carry on or be engaged either directly or indirectly as principal, agent, servant, or otherwise, in any trade, business, or calling, either relating to goods of any description sold or manufactured by the said W Robinson & Co Ltd ... or in any other business whatsoever' ...

Before parting with that case, I should say that the court proceeded to sever the covenants in that case and to grant an injunction, not to restrain the defendant from carrying on any other business whatsoever, but framed so as to give what was felt to be a reasonable protection to the plaintiffs and no more. The plaintiffs waived an option which they possessed to extend the period of service for an extra five years and the injunction then was granted for the remaining period of unextended time.

It is said that this case is no longer the law, but that *Attwood v Lamont* has decided that no such severance is permissible. I do not agree. *Attwood v Lamont* was a case where the covenants were held void as in restraint of trade. There is all the difference in the world between declining to make an illegal covenant good by neglecting that which makes it contrary to law and exercising a discretion as to how far the court will enforce a valid covenant by injunction. The latter was done in the Court of Appeal in *Robinson v Heuer*; the former in *Attwood v Lamont*.

The case before me is therefore one in which it would be proper to grant an injunction, unless to do so would in the circumstances be tantamount to ordering the defendant to perform her contract or remain idle or unless damages would be the more appropriate remedy.

With regard to the first of these considerations, it would, of course, be impossible to grant an injunction covering all the negative covenants in the contract. That would, indeed, force the defendant to perform her contract or remain idle; but this objection is removed by the restricted form in which the injunction is sought. It is confined to forbidding the defendant, without the consent of the plaintiffs, to render any services for or in any motion picture or stage production for anyone other than the plaintiffs.

It was also urged that the difference between what the defendant can earn as a film artiste and what she might expect to earn by any other form of activity is so great that she will in effect be driven to perform her contract. That is not the criterion adopted in any of the decided cases. The defendant is stated to be a person of intelligence, capacity and means, and no evidence was adduced to show that, if enjoined from doing the specified acts otherwise than for the plaintiffs, she will not be able to employ herself both usefully and remuneratively in other spheres of activity, though not as remuneratively as in her special line. She will not be driven, although she may be tempted, to perform the contract, and the fact that she may be so tempted is no objection to the grant of an injunction ...

With regard to the question whether damages is not the more appropriate remedy, I have the uncontradicted evidence of the plaintiffs as to the difficulty of estimating the damages which they may suffer from the breach by the defendant of her contract. I think it is not inappropriate to refer to the fact that, in the contract between the parties, in cl 22, there is a formal admission by the defendant that her services, being 'of a special, unique, extraordinary and intellectual character' gives them a particular value, 'the loss of which cannot be reasonably or adequately compensated in damages' and that a breach may 'cost the producer great and irreparable injury and damage', and the artiste expressly agrees that the producer shall be entitled to the remedy of injunction. Of course, parties cannot contract themselves out of the law; but it assists, at all events, on the question of evidence as to the applicability of an injunction in the present case, to find the parties formally recognising that which is now before the court as a matter of evidence that, in cases of this kind, injunction is a more appropriate remedy than damages.

Furthermore, in the case of *Grimston v Cunningham,* which was also a case in which a theatrical manager was attempting to enforce against an actor a negative stipulation against going elsewhere, Wills J granted an injunction and, on p 130, he used the following language: 'This is an agreement of a kind which is pre-eminently subject to the interference of the court by injunction, for in cases of this nature it very often happens that the injury suffered in consequence of the breach of the agreement would be out of all proportion to any pecuniary damages which could be proved or assessed by a jury. This circumstance affords a strong reason in favour of exercising the discretion of the court by granting an injunction.'

I think that that applies to the present case also and that an injunction should be granted in regard to the specified services.

The more modern approach is illustrated in the case of *Page One Records v Britton*,[23] in which the pop group 'The Troggs' entered a five year management contract with the plaintiff. During the currency of the contract, the group wished to employ another manager and the plaintiff sought an injunction to restrain the threatened breach. This application was refused on the ground that this would have the effect of an order for specific performance of a contract for personal services:

Page One Records Ltd v Britton [1968] 1 WLR 157, p 165

Stamp J: For the purposes of consideration of equitable relief, I must, I think, look at the totality of the arrangements, and the negative stipulations on which the plaintiffs rely, are, in my judgment, no more or less than stipulations designed to tie the parties together in a relationship of mutual confidence, mutual endeavour and reciprocal obligations. These considerations, in the view of Knight Bruce LJ in *Johnson v Shrewsbury and Birmingham Railway Co* and *Pickering v Bishop of Ely*, on which he relied in the former case, distinguish *Lumley v Wagner*. I quote from the judgment of Knight Bruce LJ: 'It is clear in the present case that, had the defendants been minded to compel the plaintiffs to perform their duties against their will, it could not have been done. Mutuality, therefore, is out of the question and, according to the rules generally supposed to exist in courts of equity, that might have been held sufficient to dispose of the matter; cases however have existed where, though the defendant could not have been compelled to do all he had undertaken to do by the contract, yet as he had contracted to abstain from doing a certain thing the court has interfered reasonably enough.

A case, lately much referred to on this point is that of a German singer, who, having found probably that more could be obtained by breaking her promise than by keeping it, determined to obtain the larger sum and accordingly to break her promise. She could not be compelled to sing as she had contracted to do, but as she had contracted not to sing at any other place than the one specified in the agreement, she was (and very properly, in my opinion) restrained from singing at any other place. There all the obligations on the part of the plaintiff could have been satisfied by the payment of money, but not so those of the defendant. Here, the parties are reversed. Here, all the obligations of the defendants can be satisfied by paying money; but not so the obligations of the plaintiffs, who come here for the purpose in effect of compelling the defendants, by a prohibitory or mandatory injunction, to do or abstain from doing certain acts, while the correlative acts are such as the plaintiffs could not be compelled to do.'

Apart altogether, however, from the lack of mutuality of the right of enforcement, this present case, in my judgment, fails on the facts at present before me on a more general principle, the converse of which was conveniently stated in the judgment of Branson J, *Warner Bros Pictures Inc v Nelson*. Branson J stated the converse of the proposition and the proposition, correctly stated, is, I

---

23   [1968] 1 WLR 157.

think, this, that where a contract of personal service contains negative covenants, the enforcement of which will amount either to a degree of specific performance of the positive covenants of the contract or to the giving of a decree under which the defendant must either remain idle or perform those positive covenants, the court will not enforce those negative covenants.

In the *Warner Bros* case, Branson J felt able to find that the injunction sought would not force the defendant to perform her contract or remain idle ...

So, it was said in this case, that if an injunction is granted, The Troggs could, without employing any other manager or agent, continue as a group on their own or seek other employment of a different nature. So far as the former suggestion is concerned, in the first place, I doubt whether consistently with the terms of the agreements which I have read, The Troggs could act as their own managers; and, in the second place, I think that I can and should take judicial notice of the fact that these groups, if they are to have any great success, must have managers. Indeed, it is the plaintiffs' own case that The Troggs are simple persons, of no business experience and could not survive without the services of a manager. As a practical matter on the evidence before me, I entertain no doubt that they would be compelled, if the injunction were granted on the terms that the plaintiffs seek, to continue to employ the first plaintiff as their manager and agent and it is, I think, on this point that this case diverges from the *Lumley v Wagner* case and the cases which have followed it, including the *Warner Bros* case: for it would be a bad thing to put pressure on The Troggs to continue to employ as a manager and agent in a fiduciary capacity one, who, unlike the plaintiff in those cases, who had merely to pay the defendant money, has duties of a personal and fiduciary nature to perform and in whom The Troggs, for reasons good, bad or indifferent, have lost confidence and who may, for all I know, fail in its duty to them.

On the facts before me on this interlocutory motion, I should, if I granted the injunction, be enforcing a contract for personal services in which personal services are to be performed by the first plaintiff. In *Lumley v Wagner*, Lord St Leonards, in his judgment, disclaimed doing indirectly what he could not do directly; and in the present case, by granting an injunction I would, in my judgment, be doing precisely that. I must, therefore, refuse the injunction which the first plaintiff seeks. The claim of the second plaintiff seems to me to be inextricably mixed up with the claim by the first plaintiff and no separate argument has really been addressed to me on the basis that the second plaintiff might succeed although the first plaintiff failed to obtain an injunction at the trial.

So far as the employer is concerned, an employment tribunal may order the reinstatement of an employee who has been unfairly dismissed.[24] However, it would appear that this remedy is rarely used, the courts preferring to order the payment of extra compensation in lieu of reinstatement. In equity, there is also a similar reluctance to compel an employer to reinstate a dismissed

---

24 Employment Rights Act 1996, ss 113–17.

employee.[25] Exceptionally, where an employer fails to comply with accepted dismissal procedures, the court may be prepared to depart from the general rule.

In *Hill v CA Parsons & Co Ltd*,[26] the plaintiff, an engineer, had been employed by the defendants for 35 years and was due to retire in two years' time. For the greater part of his working life, he had not been a trade union member, but the defendants entered into an collective agreement with the trade union DATA that all employees would become union members under a closed shop arrangement. The plaintiff refused to join the union and was dismissed under union pressure. An interlocutory injunction was granted to restrain the employer from wrongfully dismissing an employee. The majority of the Court of Appeal thought that damages were inadequate, and that the granting of an injunction would preserve the contract of employment so that the employee could use the provisions of the Industrial Relations Act 1971, which protected an employee from dismissal if he did not join a trade union. Departure from the general rule was thought to be justified only where damages were inadequate and there was still complete confidence between employer and employee. The order only extended to the payment of wages, and did not allow the employee to attend at his place of work, nor did it compel the employer to provide work for the employee:

Hill v CA Parsons & Co Ltd [1972] 1 Ch 305, CA, p 314

Lord Denning MR: Suppose, however, that the master insists on the employment terminating on the named day? What is the consequence in law? *In the ordinary course of things*, the relationship of master and servant thereupon comes to an end; for it is inconsistent with the confidential nature of the relationship that it should continue contrary to the will of one of the parties thereto.

Accordingly, the servant cannot claim specific performance of the contract of employment. Nor can he claim wages as such after the relationship has determined. He is left to his remedy in damages against the master for breach of the contract to continue the relationship for the contractual period. He gets damages for the time he would have served if he had been given proper notice, less, of course, anything he has, or ought to have earned, in alternative employment. He does not get damages for the loss of expected benefits to which he had no contractual right: see *Lavarack v Woods of Colchester Ltd*.

I would emphasise, however, that that is the consequence in the *ordinary* course of things. The rule is not inflexible. It permits of exceptions. The court can in a proper case grant a declaration that the relationship still subsists and an injunction to stop the master treating it as at an end. That was clearly the

---

25 *Scandinavian Trading Tanker Co AB v Flota Petrolera Ecuatoria, The Scaptrade* [1983] 2 AC 694, p 701.

26 [1972] 1 Ch 305.

view of the Privy Council in the latest case on the subject, *Francis v Municipal Councillors of Kuala Lumpur,* where Lord Morris of Borth-y-Gest said: '... when there has been a purported termination of a contract of service a declaration to the effect that the contract of service still subsists will rarely be made.'

He added that, in 'special circumstances', it may be made. Let me give an example taken from the decided cases. Suppose that a senior servant has a service agreement with a company, under which he is employed for five years certain – and, in return, so long as he is in the service, he is entitled to a free house and coal – and at the end to a pension from a pension fund to which he and his employers have contributed. Now, suppose that, when there is only six months to go, the company, without any justification or excuse, gives him notice to terminate his service at the end of three months. I think it plain that the court would grant an injunction restraining the company from treating the notice as terminating his service. If the company did not want him to come to work, the court would not order the company to give him work. But, so long as he was ready and willing to serve the company, whenever they required his services, the court would order the company to do their part of the agreement, that is, allow him his free house and coal, and enable him to qualify for the pension fund. I take this illustration from *Ball v Coggs; East India Co v Vincent; Cuckson v Stones;* and *Warburton v Co-operative Wholesale Society Ltd.*

It may be said that, by granting an injunction in such a case, the court is indirectly enforcing specifically a contract for personal services. So be it. Lord St Leonards did something like it in *Lumley v Wagner.* And I see no reason why we should not do it here.

It is doubtful whether the *Hill v Parsons* exception can do more than protect employees from abuse of dismissal procedures as, if the correct procedure is followed, there will be no breach of contract on which to base the order.

Other bars

Standard principles of equity will apply to the remedies of specific performance and injunction. Amongst these principles is the rule that a remedy will not be granted if there is a want of mutuality; if the order would cause severe hardship and where the claimant does not have 'clean hands'. Generally, all of these exceptions are geared towards doing justice in the particular circumstances of the case.

Recently, the House of Lords had the opportunity to review the limits of specific performance in an interesting commercial context.[27] Many of the 'bars' and limitations discussed above were considered. In brief, Co-operative Insurance were the developers of a shopping centre in Sheffield. They had secured Argyll (who ran the Safeway supermarket chain) as tenants of one of the major stores in the shopping centre. They viewed this as central to the

---

27 *Co-operative Insurance v Argyll Stores Ltd* [1988] AC 1.

success of the centre, since such stores often persuade smaller shops that customer 'volume' makes it worthwhile to take on a lease. The lease was for 35 years. However, after 15 years, Argyll decided that the supermarket was insufficiently profitable, speedily stripped it out and left. This was, obviously, a serious breach of contract, but the question remained as to how it should be remedied. The Court of Appeal, by a majority, held that an order of specific performance should be granted, primarily because the assessment of damages would be largely a matter of guesswork (in particular as to the projected commercial impact of Argyll's withdrawal). However, the House of Lords unanimously reversed this – the most significant consideration being that to award specific performance would require constant supervision by the courts:

Co-operative Insurance v Argyll Stores Ltd [1998] AC 1, p 9

Lord Hoffman: A decree of specific performance is of course a discretionary remedy and the question for your Lordships is whether the Court of Appeal was entitled to set aside the exercise of the judge's discretion. There are well established principles which govern the exercise of the discretion but these, like all equitable principles, are flexible and adaptable to achieve the ends of equity, which is, as Lord Selborne LC once remarked, to 'do more perfect and complete justice' than would be the result of leaving the parties to their remedies at common law: *Wilson v Northampton and Banbury Junction Railway Co* (1874) LR 9 Ch App 279, p 284. Much therefore depends upon the facts of the particular case ...

Specific performance is traditionally regarded in English law as an exceptional remedy, as opposed to the common law damages to which a successful plaintiff is entitled as of right. There may have been some element of later rationalisation of an untidier history, but, by the 19th century, it was orthodox doctrine that the power to decree specific performance was part of the discretionary jurisdiction of the Court of Chancery to do justice in cases in which the remedies available at common law were inadequate. This is the basis of the general principle that specific performance will not be ordered when damages are an adequate remedy. By contrast, in countries with legal systems based on civil law, such as France, Germany and Scotland, the plaintiff is *prima facie* entitled to specific performance. The cases in which he is confined to a claim for damages are regarded as the exceptions. In practice, however, there is less difference between common law and civilian systems than these general statements might lead one to suppose. The principles upon which English judges exercise the discretion to grant specific performance are reasonably well settled and depend upon a number of considerations, mostly of a practical nature, which are of very general application. I have made no investigation of civilian systems, but *a priori* I would expect that judges take much the same matters into account in deciding whether specific performance would be inappropriate in a particular case.

The practice of not ordering a defendant to carry on a business is not entirely dependent upon damages being an adequate remedy. In *Dowty Boulton Paul Ltd v Wolverhampton Corporation* [1971] 1 WLR 294, Sir John Pennycuick VC refused to order the corporation to maintain an airfield as a going concern because: 'It is very well established that the court will not order specific performance of an obligation to carry on a business.' He added: 'It is unnecessary in the circumstances to discuss whether damages would be an adequate remedy to the company': see p 212. Thus, the reasons which underlie the established practice may justify a refusal of specific performance even when damages are not an adequate remedy.

The most frequent reason given in the cases for declining to order someone to carry on a business is that it would require constant supervision by the court. In *JC Williamson Ltd v Lukey and Mulholland* (1931) 45 CLR 282, pp 297–98, Dixon J said flatly: 'Specific performance is inapplicable when the continued supervision of the court is necessary in order to ensure the fulfilment of the contract.'

There has, I think, been some misunderstanding about what is meant by continued superintendence. It may at first sight suggest that the judge (or some other officer of the court) would literally have to supervise the execution of the order. In *CH Giles & Co Ltd v Morris* [1972] 1 WLR 307, p 318, Megarry J said that 'difficulties of constant superintendence' were a 'narrow consideration' because:

> ... there is normally no question of the court having to send its officers to supervise the performance of the order ... Performance ... is normally secured by the realisation of the person enjoined that he is liable to be punished for contempt if evidence of his disobedience to the order is put before the court; ...

This is, of course, true but does not really meet the point. The judges who have said that the need for constant supervision was an objection to such orders were no doubt well aware that supervision would in practice take the form of rulings by the court, on applications made by the parties, as to whether there had been a breach of the order. It is the possibility of the court having to give an indefinite series of such rulings in order to ensure the execution of the order which has been regarded as undesirable.

Why should this be so? A principal reason is that, as Megarry J pointed out in the passage to which I have referred, the only means available to the court to enforce its order is the quasi-criminal procedure of punishment for contempt. This is a powerful weapon; so powerful, in fact, as often to be unsuitable as an instrument for adjudicating upon the disputes which may arise over whether a business is being run in accordance with the terms of the court's order. The heavy-handed nature of the enforcement mechanism is a consideration which may go to the exercise of the court's discretion in other cases as well, but its use to compel the running of a business is perhaps the paradigm case of its disadvantages and it is in this context that I shall discuss them.

The prospect of committal or even a fine, with the damage to commercial reputation which will be caused by a finding of contempt of court, is likely to have at least two undesirable consequences. First, the defendant, who *ex hypothesi* did not think that it was in his economic interest to run the business at all, now has to make decisions under a sword of Damocles which may descend if the way the business is run does not conform to the terms of the order. This is, as one might say, no way to run a business. In this case, the Court of Appeal made light of the point because it assumed that, once the defendant had been ordered to run the business, self-interest and compliance with the order would thereafter go hand in hand. But, as I shall explain, this is not necessarily true.

Secondly, the seriousness of a finding of contempt for the defendant means that any application to enforce the order is likely to be a heavy and expensive piece of litigation. The possibility of repeated applications over a period of time means that, in comparison with a once and for all inquiry as to damages, the enforcement of the remedy is likely to be expensive in terms of cost to the parties and the resources of the judicial system.

This is a convenient point at which to distinguish between orders which require a defendant to carry on an activity, such as running a business over a more or less extended period of time, and orders which require him to achieve a result. The possibility of repeated applications for rulings on compliance with the order which arises in the former case does not exist to anything like the same extent in the latter. Even if the achievement of the result is a complicated matter which will take some time, the court, if called upon to rule, only has to examine the finished work and say whether it complies with the order. This point was made in the context of relief against forfeiture in *Shiloh Spinners Ltd v Harding* [1973] AC 691. If it is a condition of relief that the tenant should have complied with a repairing covenant, difficulty of supervision need not be an objection. As Lord Wilberforce said, at p 724: '... what the court has to do is to satisfy itself, *ex post facto*, that the covenanted work has been done, and it has ample machinery, through certificates, or by inquiry, to do precisely this.'

This distinction between orders to carry on activities and orders to achieve results explains why the courts have in appropriate circumstances ordered specific performance of building contracts and repairing covenants: see *Wolverhampton Corpn v Emmons* [1901] 1 KB 515 (building contract) and *Jeune v Queens Cross Properties Ltd* [1974] Ch 97 (repairing covenant). It by no means follows, however, that even obligations to achieve a result will always be enforced by specific performance. There may be other objections, to some of which I now turn.

One such objection, which applies to orders to achieve a result and *a fortiori* to orders to carry on an activity, is imprecision in the terms of the order. If the terms of the court's order, reflecting the terms of the obligation, cannot be precisely drawn, the possibility of wasteful litigation over compliance is increased. So is the oppression caused by the defendant having to do things under threat of proceedings for contempt. The less precise the order, the fewer the signposts to the forensic minefield which he has to traverse. The fact that the terms of a contractual obligation are sufficiently definite to escape being void for uncertainty, or to found a claim for damages, or to permit compliance to be made a condition of relief against forfeiture, does not necessarily mean that they will be sufficiently precise to be capable of being specifically enforced. So in *Wolverhampton Corpn v Emmons*, Romer LJ said, at p 525, that the first condition for specific enforcement of a building contract was that:

... the particulars of the work are so far definitely ascertained that the court can sufficiently see what is the exact nature of the work of which it is asked to order the performance.

Similarly, in *Morris v Redland Bricks Ltd* [1970] AC 652, p 666, Lord Upjohn stated the following general principle for the grant of mandatory injunctions to carry out building works:

... the court must be careful to see that the defendant knows exactly in fact what he has to do and this means not as a matter of law but as a matter of fact, so that in carrying out an order he can give his contractors the proper instructions.

Precision is of course a question of degree and the courts have shown themselves willing to cope with a certain degree of imprecision in cases of orders requiring the achievement of a result in which the plaintiffs' merits appeared strong; like all the reasons which I have been discussing, it is, taken alone, merely a discretionary matter to be taken into account: see Spry, *Equitable Remedies,* 4th edn, 1990, p 112. It is, however, a very important one ...

There is a further objection to an order requiring the defendant to carry on a business, which was emphasised by Millett LJ in the Court of Appeal. This is that it may cause injustice by allowing the plaintiff to enrich himself at the defendant's expense. The loss which the defendant may suffer through having to comply with the order (for example, by running a business at a loss for an indefinite period) may be far greater than the plaintiff would suffer from the contract being broken. As Professor R J H Sharpe explains in 'Specific relief for contract Breach' (Chapter 5 of *Studies in Contract Law,* 1980, edited by Reiter and Swan, p129:

In such circumstances, a specific decree in favour of the plaintiff will put him in a bargaining position vis à vis the defendant whereby the measure of what he will receive will be the value to the defendant of being released from performance. If the plaintiff bargains effectively, the amount he will set will exceed the value to him of performance and will approach the cost to the defendant to complete.

This was the reason given by Lord Westbury LC in *Isenberg v East India House Estate Co Ltd* (1863) GJ & S 263, p 273 for refusing a mandatory injunction to compel the defendant to pull down part of a new building which interfered with the plaintiff's light and exercising instead the Court of Chancery's recently-acquired jurisdiction under Lord Cairn's Act 1858 (21 & 22 Vict c 27) to order payment of damages:

... I hold it ... to be the duty of the court in such a case as the present not, by granting a mandatory injunction, to deliver over the defendants to the plaintiff bound hand and foot, in order to be made subject to any extortionate demand that he may by possibility make, but to substitute for such mandatory injunction an inquiry before itself, in order to ascertain the measure of damage that has been actually sustained.

It is true that the defendant has, by his own breach of contract, put himself in such an unfortunate position. But the purpose of the law of contract is not to punish wrongdoing, but to satisfy the expectations of the party entitled to performance. A remedy which enables him to secure, in money terms, more than the performance due to him, is unjust. From a wider perspective, it cannot be in the public interest for the courts to require someone to carry on business at a loss if there is any plausible alternative by which the other party can be given compensation. It is not only a waste of resources but yokes the parties together in a continuing hostile relationship. The order for specific performance prolongs the battle. If the defendant is ordered to run a business, its conduct becomes the subject of a flow of complaints, solicitors' letters and affidavits. This is wasteful for both parties and the legal system. An award of damages, on the other hand, brings the litigation to an end. The defendant pays damages, the forensic link between them is severed, they go their separate ways and the wounds of conflict can heal.

The cumulative effect of these various reasons, none of which would necessarily be sufficient on its own, seems to me to show that the settled practice is based upon sound sense. Of course, the grant or refusal of specific performance remains a matter for the judge's discretion. There are no binding rules, but this does not means that there cannot be settled principles, founded upon practical consideration of the kind which I have discussed, which do not have to be re-examined in every case, but which the courts will apply in all but exceptional circumstances. As Slade J said, in the passage which I have quoted from *Braddon Towers Ltd v International Stores Ltd* [1987] 1 EGLR 209, p 213, lawyers have no doubt for many years advised their clients on this basis. In the present case, Leggatt LJ [1996] Ch 286, p 294 remarked that there was no evidence that such advice had been given. In my view, if the law or practice on a point is settled, it should be assumed that persons entering into legal transactions will have been advised accordingly. I am sure that Leggatt LJ would not wish to encourage litigants to adduce evidence of the particular advice which they received. Indeed, I doubt whether such evidence would be admissible.

The decision of the Court of Appeal

I must now examine the grounds upon which the majority of the Court of Appeal [1996] Ch 286 thought it right to reverse the judge. In the first place, they regarded the practice which he followed as outmoded and treated Lord Wilberforce's remarks about relief against forfeiture in *Shiloh Spinners Ltd v Harding* [1973] AC 691, p 724 as justifying a rejection of the arguments based on the need for constant supervision. Even Millett LJ, who dissented on other grounds, said, at p 303, that such objections had little force today. I do not agree. As I have already said, I think that Lord Wilberforce's remarks do not support this proposition in relation to specific performance of an obligation to carry on an activity and that the arguments based on difficulty of supervision remain powerful.

The Court of Appeal said that it was enough if the contract defined the tenant's obligation with sufficient precision to enable him to know what was necessary to comply with the order. Even assuming this to be right, I do not think that the obligation in cl 4(19) can possibly be regarded as sufficiently precise to be capable of specific performance. It is to 'keep the demised premises open for retail trade'. It says nothing about the level of trade, the area of the premises within which trade is to be conducted, or even the kind of trade, although no doubt the tenant's choice would be restricted by the need to comply with the negative covenant in clause 4(12)(a) not to use the premises 'other than as a retail store for the sale of food groceries provisions and goods normally sold from time to time by a retail grocer food supermarkets and food superstores ...' This language seems to me to provide ample room for argument over whether the tenant is doing enough to comply with the covenant.

The Court of Appeal thought that once Argyll had been ordered to comply with the covenant, it was, as Roch LJ said, at p 298, 'inconceivable that they would not operate the business efficiently'. Leggatt LJ said, at p 292, that the requirement:

> ... was quite intelligible to the defendants, while they were carrying on business there ... If the premises are to be run as a business, it cannot be in the defendants' interest to run it half-heartedly or inefficiently ...

This treats the way the tenant previously conducted business as measuring the extent of his obligation to do so. In my view this is a *non sequitur*: the obligation depends upon the language of the covenant and not upon what the tenant has previously chosen to do. No doubt, it is true that it would not be in the interests of the tenant to run the business inefficiently. But running the business efficiently does not necessarily mean running it in the way it was run before. Argyll had decided that, from its point of view, the most efficient thing to do was to close the business altogether and concentrate its resources on achieving better returns elsewhere. If ordered to keep the business open, it might well decide that the next best strategy was to reduce its costs as far as was consistent with compliance with its obligations, in the expectation that a lower level of return would be more than compensated by higher returns from additional expenditure on more profitable shops. It is in my view wrong for the courts to speculate about whether Argyll might voluntarily carry on business in a way which would relieve the court from having to construe its order. The question of certainty must be decided on the assumption that the court might have to enforce the order according to its terms.

CIS argued that the court should not be concerned about future difficulties which might arise in connection with the enforcement of the order. It should simply make the order and see what happened. In practice, Argyll would be likely to find a suitable assignee (as it, in fact, did) or conduct the business so as to keep well clear of any possible enforcement proceedings or otherwise come to terms with CIS. This may well be true, but the likelihood of Argyll having to perform beyond the requirements of its covenant or buy its way out of its obligation to incur losses seems to me to be in principle an objection to such an order rather than to recommend it. I think that it is normally undesirable for judges to make orders *in terrorem*, carrying a threat of imprisonment, which work only if no one inquires too closely into what they mean.

The likelihood that the order would be effective only for a short time until an assignment is an equivocal argument. It would be burdensome to make Argyll resume business only to stop again after a short while if a short stoppage would not cause any substantial damage to the business of the shopping centre. On the other hand, what would happen if a suitable assignee could not be found? Would Argyll then have to carry on business until 2014? Mr Smith, who appeared for CIS, said that if the order became oppressive (for example, because Argyll were being driven into bankruptcy) or difficult to enforce, they could apply for it to be varied or discharged. But the order would be a final order and there is no case in this jurisdiction in which such an order has been varied or discharged, except when the injuncted activity has been legalised by statute. Even assuming that there was such a jurisdiction if circumstances were radically changed, I find it difficult to see how this could be made to apply. Difficulties of enforcement would not be a change of circumstances. They would have been entirely predictable when the order was made. And so would the fact that Argyll would suffer unquantifiable loss if it was obliged to continue trading. I do not think that such expedients are an answer to the difficulties on which the objections to such orders are based.

Finally, all three judges in the Court of Appeal took a very poor view of Argyll's conduct. Leggatt LJ said [1996] Ch 286, p 295 that they had acted 'with gross commercial cynicism'; Roch LJ began his judgment by saying that they had 'behaved very badly' and Millett LJ said, at p 301, that they had no merits. The principles of equity have always had a strong ethical content and nothing which I say is intended to diminish the influence of moral values in their application. I can envisage cases of gross breach of personal faith, or attempts to use the threat of non-performance as blackmail, in which the needs of justice will override all the considerations which support the settled practice. But although any breach of covenant is regrettable, the exercise of the discretion as to whether or not to grant specific performance starts from the fact that the covenant has been broken. Both landlord and tenant in this case are large, sophisticated commercial organisations and I have no doubt that both were perfectly aware that the remedy for breach of the covenant was likely to be limited to an award of damages. The interests of both were purely financial: there was no element of personal breach of faith, as in the Victorian cases of railway companies which refused to honour obligations to build stations for landowners whose property they had taken: compare *Greene v West Cheshire Railway Co* (1871) LR 13 Eq 44. No doubt, there was an effect on the businesses of other traders in the Centre, but Argyll had made no promises to them and it is not suggested that CIS warranted to other tenants that Argyll would remain. Their departure, with or without the consent of CIS, was a commercial risk which the tenants were able to deploy in negotiations for the next rent review. On the scale of broken promises, I can think of worse cases, but the language of the Court of Appeal left them with few adjectives to spare.

It was, no doubt, discourteous not to have answered Mr Wightman's letter. But to say, as Roch LJ did at p 299 that they had acted 'wantonly and quite unreasonably' by removing their fixtures seems to me an exaggeration. There was no question of stealing a march, or attempting to present CIS with a *fait accompli,* because Argyll had no reason to believe that CIS would have been able to obtain a mandatory injunction whether the fixtures had been removed or not. They had made it perfectly clear that they were closing the shop and given CIS ample time to apply for such an injunction if so advised.

INJUNCTIONS

Injunctions may be *mandatory*, ordering the defendant to do something. This variety of injunction is rarely used because a decree of specific performance will normally fulfil the same function by enforcing positive undertakings. Alternatively, an injunction may be *prohibitory*, ordering the defendant not to do something, such as will be the case where the defendant has entered into an express negative covenant and he proposes to contravene that provision. Such injunctions are likely to be refused if the harm suffered by the claimant is trivial.[28] Finally, pending the outcome of legal proceedings, the court may grant an *interlocutory* injunction, which will last until the matter is finally decided one way or the other.

ACTIONS FOR THE PRICE

If the contract provides for the payment of a specified sum on the fulfilment of a particular performance obligation, the performing party may have an action for that specific sum as opposed to an action for damages for non-payment. The sum in question may be one which is fixed by the contract, but where the contract is silent on the price payable under a contract for the sale of goods or for the supply of services, the court may award a reasonable sum by way of *quantum valebat* or *quantum meruit*.[29]

Since this is an action for a liquidated amount, it is not subject to the same rules which apply to an action for damages. In particular, there is no obligation on the part of the claimant to mitigate his loss and the rules on remoteness of damage and causation do not serve to limit the amount recoverable.

One feature of an action for the price is that a party who is not in breach of contract may wish to continue with the contract after a repudiation on the part of the defendant. It will be, as has been seen already that, in the event of repudiatory conduct, the innocent party has a choice between accepting the repudiation and proceeding to bring an action for breach of contract or he may refuse to accept the repudiation and keep the contract alive.[30] Assuming he adopts the latter course, he can wait for the due date for performance

---

28 *Llandudno Urban District Council v Woods* [1889] 2 Ch 705.
29 Sale of Goods Act 1979, s 8(2); Supply of Goods and Services Act 1982, s 15(1).
30 See Chapter 9.

under the contract and then bring an action for the price, effectively compelling an unwanted performance by the contract breaker.

The problem with allowing the party not in breach to behave in this fashion is that it could easily lead to a wasteful use of resources, particularly where contracts for the sale of goods are concerned, since, if the seller knows that the buyer is unwilling to go through with his contract, he is aware that he is enforcing a sale to someone who places little or no value on the thing contracted for. In order for this possibility to arise, property in the goods contracted for must have passed to the buyer.[31] Accordingly, if the contract provides that property is not to pass until the time of delivery,[32] but before that date, the buyer refuses to accept the goods, the seller's only remedy will be one for damages.[33] Conversely, if property passes at the time of contracting and the buyer declines to take delivery, the seller may sue for the price, provided he has retained possession. If the seller sues for the price, the buyer will be forced to take delivery, which may not necessarily be the most desirable outcome if there is an available market and the seller could easily dispose of the goods to an alternative purchaser. Conversely, the action for the price appears to be a perfectly sensible alternative to an action for damages where there is no available market and the seller would find it difficult to dispose of the goods elsewhere.

Outside of sale of goods cases, limitations have been introduced on a party's right to continue with performance and sue for the agreed price.

In *White and Carter (Councils) Ltd v McGregor*,[34] the appellants were manufacturers of litter bins on which they were able to solicit and display advertisements. The respondents contracted for a three year renewal of their existing contract, advertising their business (the renewal was authorised by the firm's sales manager , unaware that the firm's owner did not wish it to be renewed). Before there had been any action in reliance by the appellants (such as preparing printing plates), the respondents sought to cancel the contract. This action amounted to an anticipatory repudiation. The appellants chose to ignore the repudiation and sought to hold the respondents to their contract. Subsequently, they brought an action for the agreed price. By a bare majority, the House of Lords held that the appellants were justified in what they had done, holding that the party not in breach did have a right to affirm the contract so that the contract remained in force. However, one member of the majority (Lord Reid) imposed restrictions on the circumstances in which this course of action should be permitted and two other members of the court displayed outright dissent:

---

31 Sale of Goods Act 1979, s 49(1).
32 As is usually the case where goods are sold on fob terms.
33 *Colley v Overseas Exporters* [1921] 3 KB 302.
34 [1962] AC 413.

White and Carter (Councils) Ltd v McGregor [1962] AC 413, p 427

Lord Reid: The general rule cannot be in doubt. It was settled in Scotland at least as early as 1848 and it has been authoritatively stated time and again in both Scotland and England. If one party to a contract repudiates it, in the sense of making it clear to the other party that he refuses or will refuse to carry out his part of the contract, the other party, the innocent party, has an option. He may accept that repudiation and sue for damages for breach of contract, whether or not the time for performance has come; or he may if he chooses disregard or refuse to accept it and then the contract remains in full effect ...

I need not refer to the numerous authorities. They are not disputed by the respondent but he points out that in all of them the party who refused to accept the repudiation had no active duties under the contract. The innocent party's option is generally said to be to wait until the date of performance and then to claim damages estimated as at that date. There is no case in which it is said that he may, in face of the repudiation, go on and incur useless expense in performing the contract and then claim the contract price. The option, it is argued, is merely as to the date as at which damages are to be assessed.

Developing this argument, the respondent points out that in most cases the innocent party cannot complete the contract himself without the other party doing, allowing or accepting something, and that it is purely fortuitous that the appellants can do so in this case. In most cases, by refusing co-operation, the party in breach can compel the innocent party to restrict his claim to damages. Then it was said that even where the innocent party can complete the contract without such co-operation, it is against the public interest that he should be allowed to do so. An example was developed in argument. A company might engage an expert to go abroad and prepare an elaborate report and then repudiate the contract before anything was done. To allow such an expert then to waste thousands of pounds in preparing the report cannot be right if a much smaller sum of damages would give him full compensation for his loss. It would merely enable the expert to extort a settlement giving him far more than reasonable compensation.

The respondent founds on the decision of the First Division in *Langford & Co Ltd v Dutch*. There an advertising contractor agreed to exhibit a film for a year. Four days after this agreement was made, the advertiser repudiated it but, as in the present case, the contractor refused to accept the repudiation and proceeded to exhibit the film and sue for the contract price. The sheriff-substitute dismissed the action as irrelevant and his decision was affirmed on appeal. In the course of a short opinion, the Lord President (Lord Cooper) said: 'It appears to me that, apart from wholly exceptional circumstances of which there is no trace in the averments on this record, the law of Scotland does not afford to a person in the position of the pursuers the remedy which is here sought. The pursuers could not force the defender to accept a year's advertisement which she did not want, though they could of course claim damages for her breach of contract. On the averments, the only reasonable and proper course which the pursuers should have adopted would have been to treat the defender as having repudiated the contract and as being on that account, liable in damages, the measure of which we are, of course, not in a position to discuss.'

The Lord President cited no authority and I am in doubt what principle he had in mind ...

We must now decide whether that case was rightly decided. In my judgment, it was not. It could only be supported on one or other of two grounds. It might be said that, because in most cases, the circumstances are such that an innocent party is unable to complete the contract and earn the contract price without the assent or co-operation of the other party, therefore, in cases where he can do so he should not be allowed to do so. I can see no justification for that.

The other ground would be that there is some general equitable principle or element of public policy which requires this limitation of the contractual rights of the innocent party. It may well be that, if it can be shown that a person has no legitimate interest, financial or otherwise, in performing the contract rather than claiming damages, he ought not to be allowed to saddle the other party with an additional burden with no benefit to himself. If a party has no interest to enforce a stipulation, he cannot in general enforce it: so it might be said that if a party has no interest to insist on a particular remedy, he ought not to be allowed to insist on it. And, just as a party is not allowed to enforce a penalty, so he ought not to be allowed to penalise the other party by taking one course when another is equally advantageous to him. If I may revert to the example which I gave of a company engaging an expert to prepare an elaborate report and then repudiating before anything was done, it might be that the company could show that the expert had no substantial or legitimate interest in carrying out the work rather than accepting damages: I would think that the *de minimis* principle would apply in determining whether his interest was substantial and that he might have a legitimate interest other than an immediate financial interest. But if the expert had no such interest, then that might be regarded as a proper case for the exercise of the general equitable jurisdiction of the court. But that is not this case. Here, the respondent did not set out to prove that the appellants had no legitimate interest in completing the contract and claiming the contract price rather than claiming damages, there is nothing in the findings of fact to support such a case, and it seems improbable that any such case could have been proved. It is, in my judgment, impossible to say that the appellants should be deprived of their right to claim the contract price merely because the benefit to them as against claiming damages and reletting their advertising space might be small in comparison with the loss to the respondent: that is the most that could be said in favour of the respondent. Parliament has on many occasions relieved parties from certain kinds of improvident or oppressive contracts, but the common law can only do that in very limited circumstances. Accordingly, I am unable to avoid the conclusion that this appeal must be allowed and the case remitted so that decree can be pronounced as craved in the initial writ.

Lord Morton (dissenting) (p 431): My Lords, I think that this is a case of great importance, although the claim is for a comparatively small sum. If the appellants are right, strange consequences follow in any case in which, under a repudiated contract, services are to be performed by the party who has not repudiated it, so long as he is able to perform these services without the co-operation of the repudiating party. Many examples of such contracts could be given. One, given in the course of the argument and already mentioned by my noble and learned friend, Lord Reid, is the engagement of an expert to go abroad and write a report on some subject for a substantial fee plus his expenses. If the appellants succeed in the present case, it must follow that the expert is entitled to incur the expense of going abroad, to write his unwanted report, and then to recover the fee and expenses, even if the other party has plainly repudiated the contract before any expense has been incurred.

It is well established that repudiation by one party does not put an end to a contract. The other party can say 'I hold you to your contract, which still remains in force'. What, then, is his remedy if the repudiating party persists in his repudiation and refuses to carry out his part of the contract? The contract has been broken. The innocent party is entitled to be compensated by damages for any loss which he has suffered by reason of the breach, and in a limited class of cases the court will decree specific implement. The law of Scotland provides no other remedy for a breach of contract and there is no reported case which decides that the innocent party may act as the appellants have acted. The present case is one in which specific implement could not be decreed, since the only obligation of the respondent under the contract was to pay a sum of money for services to be rendered by the appellants. Yet the appellants are claiming a kind of inverted specific implement of the contract. They first insist on performing their part of the contract, against the will of the other party, and then claim that he must perform his part and pay the contract price for unwanted services. In my opinion, my Lords, the appellants' only remedy was damages, and they were bound to take steps to minimise their loss, according to a well established rule of law. Far from doing this, having incurred no expense at the date of the repudiation, they made no attempt to procure another advertiser, but deliberately went on to incur expense and perform unwanted services with the intention of creating a money debt which did not exist at the date of the repudiation.

The language used by Lord Reid in his judgment has allowed the court in later cases to escape from the less desirable consequences of the majority decision by refusing to sanction a quite wasteful use of resources. In particular, it is still necessary to be able precisely to identify the legitimate interest which the innocent party has in keeping the contract alive.

Later cases have been somewhat hostile towards the decision in *White and Carter*. Moreover, there are serious practical limitations on the extent to which the rule can be applied. In particular, a person can only hold the other party to his contract where to do so does not require his practical co-operation. Thus, in construction contracts, the builder will not be able to complete a building unless he is given access to the site by the building owner.[35]

What is meant by co-operation appears to be a moot point, especially where the decision turns on a desire to distinguish *White and Carter*.

---

35 *Hounslow London Borough Council v Twickenham Garden Developments Ltd* [1971] Ch 233.

In *Clea Shipping Corpn v Bulk Oil International Ltd*,[36] the charterers of a ship repudiated the charterparty. The owners rejected the repudiation and kept the vessel at the disposal of the charterers until the expiry of the period of hire. Although the charterers paid the full cost of hire, they sought to recover it on the ground that the owner should have been restricted to damages and should have accepted the repudiation. It was held that the owners' conduct in refusing to accept the repudiation was wholly unreasonable, and they should be entitled to damages only:

Clea Shipping Corpn v Bulk Oil International Ltd [1984] 1 All ER 129, p 132

Lloyd J: In *White and Carter v McGregor* [1961] 3 All ER 1178; [1962] AC 413, Lord Reid agreed with Lord Hodson and Lord Tucker that, on the facts, the plaintiffs' claim in debt must succeed. But his speech contains two important observations on the law. First, he pointed out that it is only in rare cases that the innocent party will be able to complete performance of his side of the contract without the assent or co-operation of the party in breach. Obviously, if the innocent party cannot complete performance, he is restricted to his claim for damages. A buyer who refuses to accept delivery of the goods, and thereby prevents property passing, cannot, in the ordinary case, be made liable for the price. The peculiarity of *White and Carter v McGregor* [1961] 3 All ER 1178, p 1182; [1962] AC 413, p 429, as Lord Reid pointed out, was that the plaintiffs could completely fulfil their part of the contract without any co-operation from the defendant.

The second observation which Lord Reid made as to the law was that a party might well be unable to enforce his contractual remedy if 'he had no legitimate interest, financial or otherwise, in performing the contract rather than claiming damages'. Lord Reid did not go far in explaining what he meant by legitimate interest except to say that the de minimis principle would apply. Obviously it would not be sufficient to establish that the innocent party was acting unreasonably. Otherwise Lord Reid would not have rejected the formulation of the Lord President (Cooper) in *Langford & Co Ltd v Dutch* (1952) SC 15, p 18 that 'the only reasonable and proper course' was for the pursuers to accept the repudiation.

Nor does Lord Reid go far in explaining the juristic basis on which the court can confine the plaintiff's remedy to a claim for damages. All he says is that, in the absence of legitimate interest, 'that might be regarded as a proper case for the exercise of the general equitable jurisdiction of the court' (see [1961] 3 All ER 1178, p 1183; [1962] AC 413, p 431). This is presumably a reference back to what had been said by Lord Watson in *Graham v Kirkcaldy Magistrates* (1882) 9 R (Ct of Sess) 91, p 92.

It is clear that, on the facts, no attempt had been made by the defendant to establish absence of legitimate interest. Accordingly, counsel for the owners was right when he submitted that the two observations which I have

---

36 [1984] 1 All ER 129.

mentioned were both, strictly speaking, *obiter*. I further accept that the language used by Lord Reid is tentative. But I do not accept counsel's submission that Lord Reid was merely recording the arguments of counsel, a possibility canvassed by Salmon and Buckley LJJ in *Decro-Wall International SA v Practitioners in Marketing Ltd* [1971] 2 All ER 216; [1971] 1 WLR 361.

In addition to arguing that what Lord Reid had said about legitimate interest was only a quotation from counsel, and in any event *obiter*, arguments with which I have already dealt, counsel for the owners submitted that Lord Reid was, quite simply, wrong. It seems to me that it would be difficult for me to take that view in the light of what was said by all three members of the Court of Appeal in *The Puerto Buitrago*. Whether one takes Lord Reid's language, which was adopted by Orr and Browne LJJ in *The Puerto Buitrago*, or Lord Denning MR's language in that case ('in all reason') or Kerr J's language in *The Odenfeld* ('wholly unreasonable ... quite unrealistic, unreasonable and untenable'), there comes a point at which the court will cease, on general equitable principles, to allow the innocent party to enforce his contract according to its strict legal terms. How one defines that point is obviously a matter of some difficulty, for it involves drawing a line between conduct which is merely unreasonable (see *per* Lord Reid in *White and Carter v McGregor* [1961] 3 All ER 1178, p 1182; [1962] AC 473, pp 429–30, criticising the Lord President in *Langford & Co Ltd v Dutch* (1952) SC 15) and conduct which is wholly unreasonable (see *per* Kerr J in *The Odenfeld* [1978] 2 Lloyd's Rep 357, p 374). But however difficult it may be to define the point, that there is such a point seems to me to have been accepted both by the Court of Appeal in *The Puerto Buitrago* and by Kerr J in *The Odenfeld*.

I appreciate that the House of Lords has recently re-emphasised the importance of certainty in commercial contracts, when holding that there is no equitable jurisdiction to relieve against the consequences of the withdrawal clause in a time charter: see *Scandinavian Trading Tanker Co AB v Flota Petrolera Ecuatoriana, The Scaptrade* [1983] 2 All ER 763; [1983] 3 WLR 203. I appreciate, too, that the importance of certainty was one of the main reasons urged by Lord Hodson in *White and Carter v McGregor* in upholding the innocent party's unfettered right to elect. But, for reasons already mentioned, it seems to me that this court is bound to hold that there is some fetter, if only in extreme cases; and, for want of a better way of describing that fetter, it is safest for this court to use the language of Lord Reid, which, as I have already said, was adopted by a majority of the Court of Appeal in *The Puerto Buitrago*.

I turn last to the alternative ground on which the arbitrator based his decision, that this was a contract which called for co-operation between the parties, and therefore fell within Lord Reid's first limitation. Counsel for the charterers argued that a time charter is a contract for services, to be performed by the owners through the master and crew, and through the use of their vessel. As a contract for services, it is, as Lord Diplock pointed out in *The Scaptrade* [1983] 2 All ER 763, p 766; [1983] 3 WLR 203, p 207 – 'the very prototype of a contract of which before the fusion of law and equity a court would never grant specific performance ...'

As in any other contract for services, the owners earn their remuneration by performing the services required. If they are wrongfully prevented from performing any services, then, as in any other contract for services, the only remedy lies in damages. The fact that the owners' remuneration in this case, called hire, is payable in advance makes no difference. Counsel for the owners, on the other hand, argued that the owners earned their hire simply by holding the vessel and the services of their master and crew at the charterers' disposal. He concedes that in the case of master and servant, where the master has wrongfully dismissed the servant, the servant cannot earn remuneration by holding himself at the disposal of his master. He is confined to his remedy in damages. But counsel for the owners submits that a time charter is different. In view of my decision on the legitimate interest point, it is unnecessary for me to decide between these rival arguments, or to explore the nature of a time charter contract any further. All I will say is that, at first blush, there seemed much to be said for the argument of counsel for the charterers. I say no more, because, in *The Odenfeld,* Kerr J found a similar argument unimpressive.

For the reasons I have given, I would dismiss the owners' appeal and uphold the award.

Is there a difference between the wholly unreasonable conduct described by Lloyd J and Lord Reid's interpretation of the phrase 'no legitimate interest' in *White and Carter*? If Lloyd J's interpretation is followed, has the action for the price been brought into line with the restriction on the availability of an action for specific performance to the effect that before the remedy is given, the remedy of damages must be inadequate or inappropriate?

CHAPTER 12

FACTORS LIMITING AN AWARD OF DAMAGES

Once a claimant has established that the defendant is in breach of contract, he will normally seek damages to compensate for the loss flowing from the breach. However, it does not follow that all the loss suffered in consequence of the other party's breach will be recoverable. Three major factors may limit or exclude the claimant's entitlement to damages. First, it must be established that the claimant's loss was caused by the defendant's breach which includes consideration of the issue of contributory fault on the part of the claimant; secondly, the loss suffered must not be too remote; and, thirdly, the claimant must have taken reasonable steps to mitigate that loss.

In addition to these three major limiting factors, it must also be considered whether the minimum contractual obligation of the defendant serves to limit the damages available to the claimant.[1]

An award of damages will not always have the effect of protecting the full expectation interest of the claimant. Very often, the practical effect of an award of damages is to protect only the status quo interest by putting the claimant in the position he was in before the contract was made. For example, if the only obligation broken is a contractual duty to pay money, the sole remedy is to pay the agreed sum, and no additional expectation loss is compensatable by an award of damages.[2]

FACTUAL CAUSATION

General issues

Although it is not frequently an issue, the claimant in an action for breach of contract must be able to establish that the defendant's breach of contract is the cause of the loss complained of. Thus, if a buyer of goods has made a bad bargain and receives from the seller goods which do not conform with the contract, he will recover nothing more than nominal damages if the goods are worth the same as those contracted for.

What is clear is that while the defendant's breach must be a cause of the loss complained of it does not need to be the only cause of that loss.

---

1   *Cockburn v Alexander* (1848) 6 CB 791, p 814, *per* Maule J; *Lavarack v Woods of Colchester Ltd* [1967] 1 QB 278, p 294, *per* Diplock LJ.

2   *London, Chatham and Dover Railway Co v South Eastern Railway Co* [1893] AC 429.

The main causation issue in breach of contract cases tends to arise where some event or the actions of someone other than the defendant intervenes between the time of breach and the time of loss with the result that the defendant's breach cannot be regarded as the cause of the loss suffered by the claimant. For example, where the defendant is required by his contract to make a ship available in July, but is late in doing so, and the vessel is damaged in a typhoon, it would be difficult to say that the breach of contract is the cause of the damage complained of.[3] In these circumstances, there are difficult policy issues for the reason that if an intervening natural event is held to break the chain of causation, unless the claimant is insured against the risk of loss in question, he will have no one else to recover from if the defendant is exonerated.

The intervening event may also be the voluntary act of a third party and provided it is not readily foreseeable,[4] that act may break the chain of causation. Thus, if a contractor is engaged to decorate a house and he leaves the front door unlocked and the house is burgled, the contractor remains liable to the owner because a reasonably foreseeable consequence of his failure to exercise reasonable care is that the house will be broken into.[5]

Although considerations of this kind will normally be found most frequently in relation to negligently inflicted physical harm, there is no reason why they cannot also apply to loss of profit caused by a breach of contract.

In *Beoco Ltd v Alfa Laval Co Ltd*,[6] the first defendant (D1) installed a heat exchanger at the plaintiff's edible oils refinery. Some time after installation, a crack was discovered in the outer casing of the heat exchanger which resulted in a leak. The second defendant (D2) was employed to repair the crack, but their work was only partially successful, since the heat exchanger failed a pressure test. Despite this, the plaintiff put the equipment back into use and two months later it exploded, causing damage to the plaintiff's plant and causing lost production. At first instance, D1 was found guilty of breach of warranty; D2 was found to be in breach of its contract to repair the cracks but in both cases, the cause of the explosion was the plaintiff's recklessness in failing to carry out proper tests.

In the Court of Appeal, it was held that, in a contract action, the plaintiff cannot recover damages in respect of lost profit suffered as a result of the defendants' breach of contract if some supervening event causes even greater damage:

---

3   An illustration given in *Monarch SS Co Ltd v Karlshamns Oljefabriker A/B* [1949] AC 196, p 215.
4   *Weld Blundell v Stephens* [1920] AC 956, p 974.
5   *Stansbie v Troman* [1948] 2 KB 48.
6   [1994] 3 WLR 1179, CA.

Beoco Ltd v Alfa Laval Co Ltd [1994] 3 WLR 1179, CA, p 1188

Stuart-Smith LJ: The second ground of appeal raises an interesting point of law upon which there does not appear to be any authority directly in point. Can the plaintiff recover damages which he would have incurred by way of loss of profit on lost production during the period necessary to repair the defect in goods or materials supplied by the defendant and caused by his breach of contract, where because of some supervening event those repairs are not carried out or are subsumed in other more extensive repairs?

The supervening event in this case was the negligence of the plaintiff's engineers, who when they discovered the hitherto latent defect in the heat exchanger, put it back into service without making proper tests to see that the repair had been correctly carried out, in circumstances where they knew of the risk of explosion if it was not. But the supervening event might equally have been caused by the breach of contract or negligence of the second defendant, if it had been responsible for making all proper tests before the heat exchanger was put back into service; or it may have been some extraneous event, like a fire in the factory for which no one could be held to blame.

It is common ground in this case that the first defendant is liable for the cost of making good the defective casing of the heat exchanger. This is because what was damaged in the explosion was not a sound heat exchanger with 18 years' life in it, but a defective one with much less. The plaintiff's loss *caused by the explosion* was therefore much less than it would otherwise have been. And it could have recovered from its insurers, or the second defendant as the case may be, only the value of the defective heat exchanger.

Mr Knight submits that the same principle should apply to the loss of profit which could have resulted during the time taken to make good the defect. The cause of action for damages for breach of contract arises at the time of the breach, even though this may not be quantifiable until later. On 24 August 1988, therefore, the plaintiff had a claim against the defendant for breach of contract, the measure of which was the cost of repair and the as yet unquantified claim for lost profit. It is immaterial, he submits, that that loss was never in fact incurred or quantified because of the explosion.

Although there do not appear to be any cases in contract, there are a number of authorities in tort which bear upon the point.

In *The Glenfinlas* [1918] P 363, the plaintiff's vessel was damaged in a collision with the defendants' vessel, for which the defendants were solely to blame. Temporary repairs were done; permanent repairs were to be done after the war. However, before they were done the vessel struck a mine and sank. Mr Registrar Roscoe awarded the plaintiff the cost of repairs, but not the £160 a day for 12 days that the permanent repairs would have taken.

This decision was approved by the Court of Appeal in *The Kingsway* [1918] P 344, where the decision in *The Glenfinlas* is reported as a note. In that case, the repairs had not been done at the time of the assessment of damages, but the plaintiff proved that they would be done. The future loss of profit that was likely to be incurred while they were carried out was recoverable ...

Scrutton LJ said at p 362: 'In the courts of common law, two things are perfectly clear. The first thing clear is that when damages which would be otherwise prospective come to be assessed, facts which have actually happened may be taken into account, and when damages are being assessed for a tort which would include some disability of the person or thing injured, it may be taken into account that, before the damages come to be assessed, the person or thing injured has ceased to exist, owing to circumstances not connected with the tort.'

The authority, which in my judgment, is of most assistance, is *Carslogie SS Co Ltd v Royal Norwegian Government, The Carslogie* [1952] AC 292. The plaintiff's vessel, the *Heimgar*, was damaged in a collision with *The Carslogie* for which the defendants, owners of the latter vessel, were to blame. Temporary repairs were carried out to the *Heimgar* to make her seaworthy, but on the way to port where the permanent repairs were to be carried out, she encountered heavy weather and thereby suffered damage which rendered her unseaworthy and requiring immediate repairs. At her destination, both sets of repairs were effected concurrently, the work occupying 30 days. Ten days would have been required to effect the repairs to the damage caused by *The Carslogie* if executed separately. The plaintiffs were held not entitled to loss of profit during the 10 days it would have taken to effect them.

The House of Lords, in so holding, followed an earlier decision of the House in *Vitruvia SS Co Ltd v Ropner Shipping Co Ltd* (1925) SC (HL) 1. Viscount Jowitt said [1952] AC 292, at p 301: 'I am willing to assume without deciding the question that the collision was a cause of her detention. Still, the fact remains that, when she entered the dock at New York she was not a profit earning machine by reason of the heavy weather damage which had rendered her unseaworthy. If there had been no collision, she would have been detained in dock for 30 days to repair this damage. I cannot see that her owners sustained any damage in the nature of demurrage by reason of the fact that for 10 days out of the 30 she was also undergoing repairs in respect of the collision.'

I would allow the first defendant's appeal on this ground; the assessment of damages should be limited to the cost of replacement of the defective casing of the heat exchanger and such losses, if any, which were incurred on and after 24 August 1988 due to loss of production while the repair was being effected.

The alleged intervening event may also be that of the plaintiff himself, but in these circumstances somewhat different considerations may apply. One view is that a voluntary act of the claimant which intervenes between the date of breach and the date of loss is to be regarded as a failure to mitigate the loss resulting from the defendant's breach.[7] Alternatively, if the doctrine of contributory negligence applies to an action for breach of contract,[8] the claimant may be regarded as the author of the harm he suffers with the result that his damages may be reduced to take account of his degree of responsibility. However, a third possibility is that the unreasonableness of the

---

7   See below.
8   See below.

claimant's actions result in his acts being regarded as the cause of the damage complained of. For example, in *Lambert v Lewis*,[9] a retailer sold a defective towing hitch to the plaintiff, a farmer, who continued to use it after becoming aware of its dangerous condition. When the defective hitch was the cause of an accident, it was held that plaintiff's action should fail because his own negligence in continuing to use the towing hitch was sufficient to sever the chain of causation. In contrast, if the action taken by the claimant is regarded as perfectly reasonable in the circumstances, it is unlikely that his act will be regarded as a break in the chain of causation.

In *Compania Naviera Maropan v Bowaters*,[10] the parties entered into a contract to charter a ship for the purposes of a particular voyage. The defendant charterers were in breach of that contract by nominating an unsafe loading place for the ship. The ship's master thought that the point of loading was unsafe, but nonetheless relied on the assurance given by the defendant's experienced pilot that it was safe. Subsequently, the ship was damaged and it arose for decision whether the master's actions broke the chain of causation. The Court of Appeal held that there was no such break as the actions of the master were perfectly reasonable in the circumstances:

Compania Naviera Maropan v Bowaters [1955] 2 QB 68, CA, p 95

Hodson LJ: I come now to the questions of law. The charterers contend that the charterparty contained no warranty of safety, express or implied, and that if the loading place was unsafe the master went there of his own choice, and the shipowners cannot recover for the damage to the ship. Clause 1 of the charterparty provided that the ship should 'proceed to not more than two approved loading places as ordered in Newfoundland on the East coast ... or so near thereunto as she may safely get, and there load, always afloat, or safe aground where customary for vessels of similar size and draft, from the agents of the said charterers, not exceeding what she can reasonably stow and carry over and above her tackle apparel, provisions and furniture, a full and complete cargo of pulpwood maximum four feet lengths (inclusive of a deck load at full freight but at charterers' risk). Charterers have the right to order the ship to load at two safe berths or loading places or one safe berth or loading place combined with one safe anchorage in the same loading place without extra freight' ...

The charterers contend that if they had a right to send the ship only to a safe loading place or berth, nevertheless, if the loading place or berth turns out to be unsafe, this is not a breach of contract, but only the failure of a condition precedent giving the plaintiffs the right to refuse to perform the contract, and has no other consequence. In the alternative, they contend, following the decision of the majority of the High Court of Australia in *Reardon Smith Line Ltd v Australian Wheat Board*, that even if their failure to nominate a safe

---

9   [1982] AC 225.
10 [1955] 2 QB 68, CA.

loading place or berth is a breach of contract, there is no remedy for the shipowner except to refuse to proceed to the loading place or the berth and treat the charterer as in default in providing a cargo in accordance with the conditions of the contract. On this view, if the ship proceeds to the unsafe loading place or berth, there is no breach; the shipowner has waived fulfilment of the condition precedent, that is all, and having chosen to load the cargo, he cannot complain that it was supplied at a place where he need not have taken it. The charterers on this argument drew a distinction between a voyage charter, such as the one now under discussion, and a time charter, where the employment of a ship is placed under the direction of the charterer, and there is usually a provision requiring the latter to indemnify the shipowner for loss or damage occasioned by the master's compliance with the charterer's orders.

I do not propose to attempt the task of reviewing the authorities on these topics. This task has been performed by Devlin J in this case and in a previous decision of his in *GW Grace & Co Ltd v General Steam Navigation Co Ltd*, and by Sir Owen Dixon CJ in the *Reardon Smith* case, in a judgment which I find entirely convincing.

Where there has been a breach of safe port or analogous provisions in a charterparty, whether voyage or time, and damage to the ship flows therefrom, in my judgment, the authorities support the view that the shipowner is entitled to recover, apart altogether from an indemnity clause. I do not think that this right is confined to cases where the master has no opportunity of avoiding the damage (see *Limerick SS Co v WH Stott & Co Ltd*) or where expense is incurred in order to avoid unsafe conditions (see *Hall Bros SS Co Ltd v R & W Paul Ltd*, and *Axel Brostrom & Son v Louis Dreyfus & Co*), as was suggested in argument in the case of *GW Grace & Co Ltd v General Steam Navigation Co Ltd*.

Nor do I think that in construing a charterparty a different construction should be given to the words 'safe port' and the words 'safe berth' on the ground that the finding of a safe berth is a matter of which the charterer is not to be expected to have knowledge and is the special responsibility of the master of the ship; whereas in the case of a safe port the charterer may be expected to have better knowledge than the shipowner. This distinction seems to me to involve a strained and artificial rule of construction. Accordingly, I am unable to accept the *dictum* of Branson J, cited by Sir Owen Dixon CJ, and more fully in the majority judgment of Webb and Taylor JJ in the *Reardon Smith* case which tends to support this distinction. I agree, therefore, with the learned judge that the failure to direct the Stork to a safe berth is a breach of charterparty in the nature of a breach of warranty entitling the plaintiffs to such damages as flow from the breach.

The only remaining question is whether the damages flow from the breach in accordance with the ordinary law of damages for breach of contract. Were they the natural and probable consequences of the breach? If not, they are too remote. No question of the application of the doctrine of *volenti non fit injuria* arises, in my opinion. The question is one of causation. If the master, by acting as he did, either caused the damage by acting unreasonably in the circumstances in which he was placed, or failed to mitigate the damage, the defendants would be relieved, accordingly, from the liability which would otherwise have fallen on them.

The case is put most strongly against the defendants by the master in his letter of 26 October, in which he shows that he recognised the danger of the berth where his ship lay, and is reinforced by the fact that the master had entered Tommy's Arm with his ship on the preceding day and had an opportunity of seeing for himself the area of the anchorage and its condition generally. The master did, however, allow his fears to be overridden and deferred to the advice and assurances of those with local experience, in particular to the pilot who had brought his ship in. He was, I think, in a predicament, having the choice between declining the adventure on the one hand, and possible damage to the ship on the other. In acting as he did, obeying the order of the defendants, he was, in my opinion, acting reasonably in the circumstances and not in such a way as to destroy the chain of causation between the breach of contract committed by the defendants and the damage sustained by his ship.

Generally, the application of causation principles will produce an 'all or nothing' result. Either the claimant's fault is the whole cause of the loss he suffers or the defendant's breach of contract is the operative cause. Thus, it will generally not be possible for a court to apportion damages, as can be done under rules on contributory negligence.[11] However in one notable departure from this rule, it seems that if the claimant and defendant are both in breach of legal duties owed to each other, there can be an apportionment of damages on causal principles,[12] although this view is not without its critics.[13]

Contributory negligence

The defence of contributory negligence is primarily seen as a defence to an action framed in tort. However, since it is now accepted that there may be concurrent contractual and tortious liability, particularly where the defendant is in breach of a contractual duty to take reasonable care and skill,[14] the question has arisen whether a defendant in an action for breach of contract can seek to have the claimant's damages reduced on the grounds of contributory negligence under the provisions of s 1(1) of the Law Reform (Contributory Negligence) Act 1945. If the 1945 Act does not apply to a breach of contract, the claimant may be in a position to avoid a reduction of his damages in the event of any contributory fault on his or her part by choosing to sue for the breach of a contractual duty of care, rather than for the tort:

---

11 See *O'Connor v BD Kirby & Co* [1972] 1 QB 90, p 99.
12 *Tennant Radiant Heat Ltd v Warrington Development Corpn* [1988] 1 EGLR 41 (breach by tenant of a strict covenant to repair and breach by landlord of a duty to take reasonable care to maintain the property).
13 *Bank of Nova Scotia v Hellenic Mutual War Risks Association, The Good Luck* [1990] 1 QB 818, p 904.
14 See *Henderson and Others v Merrett Syndicates Ltd and Others* [1995] 2 AC 1 45; *Spring v Guardian Assurance plc* [1995] 2 AC 296.

Law Reform (Contributory Negligence) Act 1945

1

(1) Where any person suffers damage as the result partly of his own fault and partly of the fault of any other person or persons, a claim in respect of that damage shall not be defeated by reason of the fault of the person suffering the damage, but the damages recoverable in respect thereof shall be reduced to such extent as the court thinks just and equitable having regard to the claimant's share in the responsibility for the damage:

Provided that–

(a) this sub-section shall not operate to defeat any defence arising under a contract ...

4

The following expressions have the meanings hereby respectively assigned to them, that is to say :

... 'fault' means negligence, breach of statutory duty or other act or omission which gives rise to liability in tort or would apart from this Act, give rise to the defence of contributory negligence.

Although s 4 states that damage includes loss of life and personal injury, it is clear that property damage is also damage for the purposes of the defence and to the extent that economic loss is also a recoverable head of damage under the tort of negligence, it would be consistent to assume that this is also relevant damage for the purposes of the 1945 Act.

The principal barrier to the application of the defence of contributory negligence to actions for breach of contract is that under s 1(1) fault on the part of both the claimant and the defendant is a requirement. The definition of fault in s 4 refers to the fault of both parties. The fault of the defendant is covered by the words 'negligence, breach of statutory duty or other act or omission which gives rise to a liability in tort'. The fault of the claimant is adverted to by the closing words of s 4, with the reference to 'an act or omission which would, apart from the Act, give rise to the defence of contributory negligence'.

The cases which have considered the application of the defence of contributory negligence to contract actions have indicated that three types of contractual duty must be distinguished.[15] First, there are strict contractual duties, such as the duty of a seller to supply goods of the desired standard of quality and fitness. Secondly, there are contractual duties of care which are higher than the duty owed in the ordinary law of negligence, such as an express or implied undertaking to exercise care to avoid causing losses which would not be recoverable in a tortious action. Thirdly, there are duties of care which sound concurrently in contract and tort, such as an implied

---

15 The trichotomy is derived from *Forsikringsaktieselskapet Vesta v Butcher* [1986] 2 All ER 488, p 508, *per* Hobhouse J; affd in [1988] 3 WLR 565, CA and on other grounds in [1989] AC 852.

undertaking on the part of an occupier of land to take care in avoiding possible physical injury to a contractual visitor or the duty owed by an employer to an employee to provide a safe system and place of work.

Where there is a breach of a strict contractual duty, the apportionment provisions of the 1945 Act do not apply[16] since the defendant is not guilty of 'fault'.

In *Barclays Bank plc v Fairclough Building Ltd*,[17] the plaintiffs employed the defendants to carry out maintenance work, including the cleaning of roofs made of corrugated asbestos. To do this, the defendants used high pressure water hoses, but this operation required certain precautions to be taken which were not taken. As a result, the plaintiffs' premises became heavily contaminated with asbestos dust, resulting in remedial work having to be carried out at a cost of £4 million. The plaintiffs sued the defendants under the terms of their contract which required the defendants to execute the work in an expeditious, efficient and workmanlike manner and also for breach of the implied term that the work would be executed with reasonable care and skill. The defendants alleged contributory negligence on the part of the plaintiffs' property services division, who, it was alleged, should have ensured that proper safety precautions were taken.

On the question whether the defence of contributory negligence applied in these circumstances, the Court of Appeal gave a negative answer:

Barclays Bank plc v Fairclough Building Ltd [1995] QB 214, CA, p 228

Beldam LJ: Section 4 of the 1945 Act defines 'fault'. It is generally agreed that the first part of the definition relates to the defendant's fault and the second part to the plaintiff's, but debate has focused on the words 'or other act or omission which gives rise to a liability in tort' in the first part and 'other act or omission which ... would, apart from this Act, give rise to the defence of contributory negligence' in the second part. It has been argued that, merely because the plaintiff frames his cause of action as a breach of contract, if the acts or omissions on which he relies could equally well give rise to a liability in tort, the defendant is entitled to rely on the defence of contributory negligence. Examples frequently cited are claims for damages against an employer or by a passenger against a railway or bus company where the plaintiff may frame his action either in tort or in contract and the duty relied on in either case is a duty to take reasonable care for the plaintiff's safety. Contributory negligence has been a defence in such actions for many years. So it is argued that, in all cases in which the contractual duty broken by a defendant is the same as and is co-

---

16   *Forsikringsaktieselskapet Vesta v Butcher* [1986] 2 All ER 488, pp 508–09, *per* Hobhouse J; *Tennant Radiant Heat Ltd v Warrington Development Corpn* [1988] 1 EGLR 41, p 43, *per* Dillon LJ; *Bank of Nova Scotia v Hellenic Mutual War Risks Association (Bermuda) Ltd, The Good Luck* [1990] 1 WB 818, p 904, *per* May LJ (reversed on other grounds in [1991] 3 All ER 1, in which the issue of contributory negligence was not pursued); *Barclays Bank plc v Fairclough Building Ltd* [1995] QB 214, p 228.

17   [1995] QB 214, CA.

extensive with a similar duty in tort, the defendant may now rely upon the defence. An opposing view based upon the second part of the definition is that if the plaintiff framed his action for breach of contract, contributory negligence at common law was never regarded as a defence to his claim and so cannot be relied on under the 1945 Act.

Under the first part of the definition, if the plaintiff claims damages for breach of a contractual term which does not correspond with a duty in tort to take reasonable care, the defendant's acts or omissions would not give rise to a liability in tort and accordingly no question of contributory negligence could arise.

These arguments have led courts to classify contractual duties under three headings:

(1) where a party's liability arises from breach of a contractual provision which does not depend on a failure to take reasonable care;

(2) where the liability arises from an express contractual obligation to take care which does not correspond to any duty which would exist independently of the contract;

(3) where the liability for breach of contract is the same as, and co-extensive with, a liability in tort independently of the existence of a contract.

This analysis was adopted by Hobhouse J in *Forsikringsaktieselskapet Vesta v Butcher* [1986] 2 All ER 488 and by the Court of Appeal in the same case [1989] AC 852. The judgments in the Court of Appeal in that case assert that in category (3) cases, the Court of Appeal is bound by the decision in *Sayers v Harlow Urban District Council* [1958] 1 WLR 623 to admit the availability of the defence.

Since I do not regard the case before the court as being in that category, I am content to accept that decision. To regard the definition of fault in s 4 as extending to cases such as employer's liability places no great strain on the construction of the words used. In 1945, actions brought by an employee, whether framed in contract or tort, were usually regarded as actions in negligence and the defence of contributory negligence was by no means uncommon.

On the other hand, in category (1) cases, there is no decision in which contributory negligence has been held to be a partial defence. There are powerful dicta to the effect that it cannot be (see the judgment of the court in *Tennant Radiant Heat Ltd v Warrington Development Corpn* [1988] 1 EGLR 41; *Bank of Nova Scotia v Hellenic Mutual War Risks Association (Bermuda) Ltd, The Good Luck* [1989] 1 QB 818, p 904; and the observations of Nolan LJ in *Schering Agrochemicals Ltd v Resibel NV SA* [1992] CA Transcript 1298, noted in (1993) 109 LQR 175, p 177).

The contractor's argument that because the bank owed duties to its employees, it was therefore under a duty in its own interest to see that the contractors fulfilled their obligations under the contract is inconsistent with many cases in which it has been held that employers and others liable to third parties for failure of plant or equipment are entitled to rely upon warranties given by their suppliers: see, for example, *Mowbray v Merryweather* [1895] 2 QB 640; *Sims v Foster Wheeler Ltd* [1966] 1 WLR 769, p 777; and *Lambert v Lewis* [1982] AC 225, where, but for the farmer's knowledge that the trailer coupling was no longer in its warranted state, he would have been able to do so. Lord Diplock said [1982] AC 225, p 276: 'Up to that time, the farmer would have had a right to rely on the dealers' warranty as excusing him from making his own examination of the coupling to see if it were safe; but, if the accident had happened before then, the farmer would not have been held to have been guilty of any negligence to the plaintiff.'

If, by relying upon the dealers' warranty, the farmer could not have been held guilty of any negligence to the plaintiff, it is pertinent to ask whether, had he himself suffered injury or loss in the same accident, he could have been held to have been in part responsible for failure to act prudently in his own interest?

That a contracting party is entitled to rely on the other party to a contract to carry out his undertaking and to act carefully in doing so was emphasised by Devlin J in *Cia Naviera Maropan S/A v Bowaters Lloyd Pulp and Paper Mills Ltd* [1955] 2 QB 68, p 77 ...

In my judgment, therefore, in the present state of the law, contributory negligence is not a defence to a claim for damages founded on breach of a strict contractual obligation. I do not believe the wording of the 1945 Act can reasonably sustain an argument to the contrary. Even if it did, in the present case the nature of the contract and the obligation undertaken by the skilled contractor did not impose on the bank any duty in its own interest to prevent the contractor from committing the breaches of contract. To hold otherwise would, I consider, be equivalent to implying into the contract an obligation on the part of the bank inconsistent with the express terms agreed by the parties. The contract clearly laid down the extent of the obligations of the bank as architect and of the contractor. It was the contractor who was to provide appropriate supervision on site, not the architect.

In the case of the second category under which, for example, there is a breach of a purely contractual duty to take care which does not give rise to liability in tort, the presence of the words 'which gives rise to liability in tort' in s 4 would seem to indicate that the defence cannot apply to this particular category. Since the breach of a purely contractual duty to take care gives rise only to liability in contract, it seems to follow that the 1945 Act should not apply in these cases:

Forsikringsaktieselskapet Vesta v Butcher [1988] 3 WLR 565, p 577

O'Connor LJ: I return to *Sayers v Harlow Urban District Council* [1958] 2 All ER 342; [1958] 1 WLR 623. The accident happened in 1956, before the Occupiers' Liability Act 1957. The plaintiff paid to use a public lavatory owned by the defendants; she was therefore a contractual invitee, and the duty of care was owed to her both in contract and tort. The penny in the slot mechanism was defective and she was locked in; attempting to climb out of the cubicle she fell and sustained injury. The judge held that the defendants were in breach of duty, but that the damage suffered was too remote. Lord Evershed MR said at the beginning of his judgment [1958] 1 WLR 623, p 624–25:

... the plaintiff claimed that the damage which she had suffered was due to the fault of the defendants, that fault being in the form of breach of the duty of care owed to her, whether or not arising under the implied contract when she made use of the lavatory. Nothing turns on the foundation of liability, nor, indeed, on the finding of the learned judge that the defendants were negligent; for there has been no appeal on the part of the defendants from that finding. The issue before us has been confined to the second part of the judge's conclusion, namely, that the damage suffered was, in the circumstances, too remote from the negligent act or omission of the defendants and fell outside the famous formula of being the natural and probable consequence of the wrongful act. In those circumstances, he dismissed the plaintiff's claim. The questions, therefore, which have been present on appeal can be stated thus: (i) was the damage suffered by the plaintiff too remote? Put otherwise, was her activity, which I have briefly described, and from which the damage ensued, not a natural and probable consequence of the negligent act of the defendants within the famous formula in *Hadley v Baxendale* ((1854) 9 Exch 341)?; (ii) if the damage was not too remote, then was the plaintiff herself guilty of some degree of fault, of what is called contributory negligence, so as to reduce the total liability of the defendants to her?

It will be seen that Lord Evershed MR was using the language of contract. The argument in the county court and in the Court of Appeal turned on the application of what was said in *Adams v Lancashire and Yorkshire Railway Co* (1869) LR 4 CP 739. The plaintiff, a passenger, tried to shut a defective door in a moving train and fell out. He sued in negligence, but, undoubtedly, the duty was also owed in contract. Two of the judges held that his injury was not caused by the defendants' negligence. Brett J held that his claim failed because of his contributory negligence. In his judgment, Lord Evershed MR referred to the 1945 Act relied on Brett J and apportioned the damages of the plaintiff. Morris and Ormerod LJJ agreed.

In my judgment, *Sayers v Harlow Urban District Council* is a category (3) case and the decision of the Court of Appeal that there is power to apportion was not only right, but is binding on us, just as the judge held it was binding on him.

There are two further possible arguments for saying that there is a power to apportion in a category (3) case, even though the claim is made in contract. I will state them but do not find it necessary to analyse or reach a conclusion on them: (i) contributory negligence was a defence in category (3) cases pleaded in contract before 1945. The argument is supported by railway cases and banking cases; (ii) just as it has been held that a plaintiff cannot escape the Limitation Act 1980 by pleading a negligence case as trespass to the person, so here, the court should hold that a plaintiff cannot escape apportionment by pleading the case in contract. See *Letang v Cooper* [1965] 1 QB 232.

I am satisfied that the judge came to the right conclusion on this topic and, in respect of it, I would dismiss Vesta's appeal.

(The facts of this case are immaterial.)

The third category covers cases in which the defendant is in breach of a contractual duty which is capable of giving rise to liability in the tort of negligence. In these circumstances, it seems to be accepted that the defence is applicable.[18] Thus, where loss is caused by the professional negligence of a solicitor or valuer, but the client is in part to blame for that loss, it will be possible to reduce the claimant's damages, whether the action is framed in contract or in tort.

For the purposes of all of the above categories, there is one overriding difficulty, namely that the definition of the claimant's fault in s 4 requires the defence to have been available at common law before the 1945 Act was passed.[19] However, it remains the case that, at common law, the defence was not available in an action for breach of contract,[20] since one contracting party is not bound to guard against a breach of contract on the part of the other.[21]

LEGAL CAUSATION OR REMOTENESS OF LOSS

Even where the defendant's breach of contract is a factual cause of the claimant's loss, an award of damages may be denied on the ground that the breach was not the legal cause of that loss. Where the claimant complains that he has suffered financial loss, the issue may become clouded by the tort/contract dichotomy and policy issues may play an important part, since economic loss cases are concerned with risk allocation. Where the parties have allocated a risk of loss under the terms of their contract, it seems undesirable that the court should be able to intervene, unless there is a clear imbalance in terms of bargaining power. But if the risk of loss has not been expressly allocated, the court will bear the responsibility of deciding where that risk should lie. Different considerations would appear to apply where the claimant complains that the breach of contract has resulted in physical harm to the person or to property.

---

18   *Sayers v Harlow Urban District Council* [1958] 1 WLR 623, p 624, *per* Lord Evershed MR; *Quinn v Burch Bros Ltd* [1966] 2 QB 370, pp 380–81, *per* Paull J; *Forsikringsaktieselskapet Vesta v Butcher* [1988] 3 WLR 565, p 578, *per* O'Connor LJ; *Youell v Bland Welch & Co Ltd, The 'Superhulls Cover' Case* [1990] 2 Lloyd's Rep 431, *per* Phillips J.

19   As a matter of policy, this approach may be criticised on the basis that 1944 law may not be appropriate to 1990s facts: *Youell v Bland Webb & Co Ltd, The 'Superhulls Cover' Case* [1990] 2 Lloyd's Rep 431, p 460, *per* Phillips J.

20   *Forsikringsaktieselskapet Vesta v Butcher* [1988] 3 WLR 565, p 589, *per* Sir Roger Ormrod; *Tennant Radiant Heat v Warrington Development Corpn* [1988] 1 EGLR 41, p 43, *per* Dillon LJ.

21   For a detailed analysis of the practical workings of the 1945 Act, rejecting any direct linkage of this to factual causation or 'scientific apportionment', see *Platform Home Loans Ltd v Oyston Shipways Ltd.* [1999] 2 WLR 518, HL.

Financial loss cases

Typically, the 19th century contract rule book saw financial loss as an issue for the law of contract. On the issue of remoteness of loss, the leading case is that of *Hadley v Baxendale*,[22] which developed a judicially controlled test based on reasonable foresight of loss. The extent of the confusion created by this test was not immediately apparent until the emerging tort of negligence also adopted a test of reasonable foresight of harm for the purposes of personal injury and property damage cases much later in the 20th century.

In *Hadley v Baxendale*, the plaintiff, a mill owner, required the defendant carriers to transport a broken mill shaft to Greenwich. Due to delay on the part of the carriers, the plaintiff's mill was closed for several days longer than would otherwise have been necessary. The plaintiff sued to recover the profits lost by the delay. The Court of Exchequer found in favour of the defendants on the grounds that the loss suffered could not be fairly and reasonably considered as arising in the usual course of things from the breach of contract, nor could it reasonably be supposed to have been in the contemplation of both parties, at the time they made the contract, as the probable result of the breach of it.

The so called rule in *Hadley v Baxendale* was stated as follows:

> Where two parties have made a contract, which one of them has broken, the damages which the other party ought to receive in respect of such breach of contract should be such as may fairly and reasonably be considered either arising naturally, that is, according to the usual course of things, from such breach of contract itself or such as may reasonably be supposed to have been in the contemplation of both parties, at the time they made the contract, as the probable result of the breach of it – where the plaintiffs, the owners of a flour mill, sent a broken iron shaft to an office of the defendants, who were common carriers, to be conveyed by them, and the defendants' clerk, who attended at the office, was told that the mill was stopped, that the shaft must be delivered immediately, and that a special entry, if necessary, must be made to hasten its delivery; and the delivery of the broken shaft to the consignee, to whom it had been sent by the plaintiffs as a pattern, by which to make a new shaft, was delayed for an unreasonable time; in consequence of which, the plaintiffs did not receive the new shaft for some days after the time they ought to have received it, and they were consequently unable to work their mill from want of the new shaft, and thereby incurred a loss of profits – *held*, that, under the circumstances, such loss could not be recovered in an action against the defendants as common carriers.

Hadley v Baxendale (1854) 9 Ex 341, p 354; (1854) 156 ER 145, p 151

Alderson B: Now we think the proper rule in such a case as the present is this: where two parties have made a contract, which one of them has broken, the

---

22 (1854) 9 Ex 341; (1854) 156 ER 145.

damages which the other party ought to receive in respect of such breach of contract should be such as may fairly and reasonably be considered either arising naturally, that is, according to the usual course of things, from such breach of contract itself, or such as may reasonably be supposed to have been in the contemplation of both parties, at the time they made the contract, as the probable result of the breach of it. Now, if the special circumstances under which the contract was actually made were communicated by the plaintiffs to the defendants, and thus known to both parties the damages resulting from the breach of such a contract, which they would reasonably contemplate, would be the amount of injury which would ordinarily follow from a breach of contract under these special circumstances so known and communicated. But, on the other hand, if these special circumstances were wholly unknown to the party breaking the contract, he, at the most, could only be supposed to have had in his contemplation the amount of injury which would arise generally, and in the great multitude of cases not affected by any special circumstances, from such a breach of contract. For, had the special circumstances been known, the parties might have specially provided for the breach of contract by special terms as to the damages in that case; and of this advantage it would be very unjust to deprive them. Now, the above principles are those by which we think the jury ought to be guided in estimating the damages arising out of any breach of contract. It is said that other cases, such as breaches of contract in the non-payment of money, or in the not making a good title to land, are to be treated as exceptions from this, and as governed by a conventional rule. But as, in such cases, both parties must be supposed to be cognisant of that well known rule, these cases may, we think, be more properly classed under the rule above enunciated as to cases under known special circumstances, because there both parties may reasonably be presumed to contemplate the estimation of the amount of damages according to the conventional rule. Now, in the present case, if we are to apply the principles above laid down, we find that the only circumstances here communicated by the plaintiffs to the defendants at the time the contract was made were that the article to be carried was the broken shaft of a mill and that the plaintiffs were the millers of that mill. But how do these circumstances shew reasonably that the profits of the mill must be stopped by an unreasonable delay in the delivery of the broken shaft by the carrier to the third person? Suppose the plaintiffs had another shaft in their possession put up or putting up at the time, and that they only wished to send back the broken shaft to the engineer who made it; it is clear that this would be quite consistent with the above circumstances, and yet the unreasonable delay in the delivery would have no effect upon the intermediate profits of the mill. Or, again, suppose that, at the time of the delivery to the carrier, the machinery of the mill had been in other respects defective, then, also, the same results would follow. Here it is true that the shaft was actually sent back to serve as a model for a new one, and that the want of a new one was the only cause of the stoppage of the mill, and that the loss of profits really arose from not sending down the new shaft in proper time, and that this arose from the delay in delivering the broken one to serve as a model. But it is obvious that, in the great multitude of cases of millers sending off broken shafts to third persons by a carrier under ordinary circumstances, such consequences would not, in all probability, have occurred; and these special circumstances were here never communicated by the plaintiffs to the defendants. It follows, therefore, that the loss of profits here cannot reasonably be considered such a consequence of the breach of contract as could have been fairly and reasonably contemplated by both the parties when they made this contract. For such loss would neither have flowed naturally from the breach of this contract in the great multitude of such cases occurring under ordinary circumstances, nor were the special circumstances, which, perhaps, would have made it a reasonable and natural consequence of such breach of contract, communicated to or known by the defendants.

This decision had the effect of dividing financial losses into those which could be regarded as 'normal' and therefore recoverable automatically and those which were 'abnormal' and therefore only recoverable if the defendant had been made aware of the special circumstances giving rise to the possibility of such loss at the time the contract was made. It is still not clear whether the defendant should simply know of the special circumstances, or whether he was required to have contracted on the basis that he should bear the loss.[23] Later cases seem to suggest that knowledge alone is sufficient.[24]

The distinction between normal and abnormal losses is illustrated in *Victoria Laundry (Windsor) Ltd v Newman Industries Ltd*.[25] In an attempt to secure lucrative dyeing contracts and as a result of simple business expansion, the plaintiff launderers ordered a boiler from the defendants who delivered late. As a result, the plaintiffs suffered general losses of profit. Moreover, they also lost lucrative dyeing contracts which they might have secured had the boiler been delivered on time. They were held to be entitled to recover only their normal losses of £16 per week. The loss on the dyeing contracts was categorised as an abnormal loss and, since the defendants had no knowledge of the special circumstances giving rise to it, the loss was irrecoverable.

Subsequently, the two rules in *Hadley v Baxendale* were reduced to a single rule, namely that the defendant should be liable for loss which he foresaw, or ought to have foreseen, at the time of contracting:

Victoria Laundry (Windsor) Ltd v Newman Industries Ltd [1949] 2 KB 528, CA, p 536

Asquith LJ: The authorities on recovery of loss of profits as a head of damage are not easy to reconcile. At one end of the scale stand cases where there has been non-delivery or delayed delivery of what is on the face of it obviously a profit earning chattel; for instance, a merchant or passenger ship: see *Fletcher v Tayleur, In re Trent and Humber Co ex p Cambrian Steam Packet Co*; or some essential part of such a ship; for instance, a propeller, in *Wilson v General*

---

23 See *British Columbia Saw Mills Co v Nettleship* (1868) LR 3 CP 499; *Horne v Midland Railway Co* (1873) LR 8 CP 131.

24 *Koufos v Czarnikow, The Heron II* [1969] 1 AC 350, p 422.

25 [1949] 2 KB 528.

Ironscrew Co, or engines, *Saint Line v Richardson*. In such cases, loss of profit has rarely been refused. A second and intermediate class of case in which loss of profit has often been awarded is where ordinary mercantile goods have been sold to a merchant with knowledge by the vendor that the purchaser wanted them for resale; at all events, where there was no market in which the purchaser could buy similar goods against the contract on the seller's default, see, for instance, *Borries v Hutchinson*. At the other end of the scale are cases where the defendant is not a vendor of the goods, but a carrier, see, for instance, *Hadley v Baxendale* and *Gee v Lancashire and Yorkshire Railway*. In such cases, the courts have been slow to allow loss of profit as an item of damage. This was not, it would seem, because a different principle applies in such cases, but because the application of the same principle leads to different results. A carrier commonly knows less than a seller about the purposes for which the buyer or consignee needs the goods, or about other 'special circumstances' which may cause exceptional loss if due delivery is withheld.

Three of the authorities call for more detailed examination. First comes *Hadley v Baxendale* itself. Familiar though it is, we should first recall the memorable sentence in which the main principles laid down in this case are enshrined: 'Where two parties have made a contract which one of them has broken, the damages which the other party ought to receive in respect of such breach of contract should be such as may fairly and reasonably be considered as either arising naturally, that is, *according to the usual course of things, from such breach of contract itself, or such as may reasonably be supposed to have been in the contemplation of both parties, at the time they made the contract, as the probable result of the breach of it.*' The limb of this sentence prefaced by 'either' embodies the so called 'first' rule; that prefaced by 'or' the 'second'. In considering the meaning and application of these rules, it is essential to bear clearly in mind the facts on which *Hadley v Baxendale* proceeded. The headnote is definitely misleading insofar as it says that the defendant's clerk, who attended at the office, was told that the mill was stopped and that the shaft must be delivered immediately. The same allegation figures in the statement of facts which are said on p 344 to have 'appeared' at the trial before Crompton J If the Court of Exchequer had accepted these facts as established, the court must, one would suppose, have decided the case the other way round; must, that is, have held the damage claimed was recoverable under the second rule. But it is reasonably plain from Alderson B's judgment that the court rejected this evidence, for, on p 355, he says: 'We find that the only circumstances here communicated by the plaintiffs to the defendants at the time when the contract was made were that the article to be carried was the broken shaft of a mill and that the plaintiffs were the millers of that mill' and it is on this basis of fact that he proceeds to ask, 'How do these circumstances show reasonably that the profits of the mill must be stopped by an unreasonable delay in the delivery of the broken shaft by the carrier to the third person?'

British Columbia Saw Mills v Nettleship annexes to the principle laid down in *Hadley v Baxendale* a rider to the effect that where knowledge of special circumstances is relied on as enhancing the damage recoverable, that knowledge must have been brought home to the defendant at the time of the contract and in such circumstances that the defendant impliedly undertook to bear any special loss referable to a breach in those special circumstances. The knowledge which was lacking in that case on the part of the defendant was knowledge that the particular box of machinery negligently lost by the defendants was one without which the rest of the machinery could not be put together and would therefore be useless.

Cory v Thames Ironworks Co – a case strongly relied on by the plaintiffs – presented the peculiarity that the parties contemplated respectively different profit making uses of the chattel sold by the defendant to the plaintiff. It was the hull of a boom derrick, and was delivered late. The plaintiffs were coal merchants, and the obvious use, and that to which the defendants believed it was to be put, was that of a coal store. The plaintiffs, on the other hand, the buyers, in fact intended to use it for transhipping coals from colliers to barges, a quite unprecedented use for a chattel of this kind, one quite unsuspected by the sellers and one calculated to yield much higher profits. The case accordingly decides, *inter alia*, what is the measure of damage recoverable when the parties are not *ad idem* in their contemplation of the use for which the article is needed. It was decided that in such a case no loss was recoverable beyond what would have resulted if the intended use had been that reasonably within the contemplation of the defendants, which in that case was the 'obvious' use. This special complicating factor, the divergence between the knowledge and contemplation of the parties respectively, has somewhat obscured the general importance of the decision, which is in effect that the facts of the case brought it within the first rule of *Hadley v Baxendale* and enabled the plaintiff to recover loss of such profits as would have arisen from the normal and obvious use of the article. The 'natural consequence', said Blackburn J, of not delivering the derrick was that £420 representing those normal profits was lost. Cockburn CJ, interposing during the argument, made the significant observation: 'No doubt, in order to recover damage arising from a special purpose, the buyer must have communicated the special purpose to the seller; but there is one thing which must always be in the knowledge of both parties, which is that the thing is bought for the purpose of being in some way or other profitably applied.' This observation is apposite to the present case. These three cases have on many occasions been approved by the House of Lords without any material qualification.

What propositions applicable to the present case emerge from the authorities as a whole, including those analysed above? We think they include the following:

(1) It is well settled that the governing purpose of damages is to put the party whose rights have been violated in the same position, so far as money can do so, as if his rights had been observed: *Sally Wertheim v Chicoutimi Pulp Co*. This purpose, if relentlessly pursued, would provide him with a complete indemnity for all loss *de facto* resulting from a particular breach, however improbable, however unpredictable. This, in contract at least, is recognised as too harsh a rule. Hence,

(2) In cases of breach of contract, the aggrieved party is only entitled to recover such part of the loss actually resulting as was at the time of the contract reasonably foreseeable as liable to result from the breach.

(3) What was at that time reasonably so foreseeable depends on the knowledge then possessed by the parties or, at all events, by the party who later commits the breach.

(4) For this purpose, knowledge 'possessed' is of two kinds; one imputed, the other actual. Everyone, as a reasonable person, is taken to know the 'ordinary course of things' and consequently what loss is liable to result from a breach of contract in that ordinary course. This is the subject matter of the 'first rule' in *Hadley v Baxendale*. But to this knowledge, which a contract-breaker is assumed to possess, whether he actually possesses it or not, there may have to be added in a particular case knowledge which he actually possesses, of special circumstances outside the 'ordinary course of things', of such a kind that a breach in those special circumstances would be liable to cause more loss. Such a case attracts the operation of the 'second rule', so as to make additional loss also recoverable.

(5) In order to make the contract-breaker liable under either rule, it is not necessary that he should actually have asked himself what loss is liable to result from a breach. As has often been pointed out, parties at the time of contracting contemplate not the breach of the contract, but its performance. It suffices that, if he had considered the question, he would as a reasonable man have concluded that the loss in question was liable to result (see certain observations of Lord du Parcq in the recent case of *A/B Karlshamns Oljefabriker v Monarch SS Co Ltd*).

(6) Nor, finally, to make a particular loss recoverable, need it be proved that upon a given state of knowledge the defendant could, as a reasonable man, foresee that a breach must necessarily result in that loss. It is enough if he could foresee it was likely so to result. It is indeed enough, to borrow from the language of Lord du Parcq in the same case, at p 158, if the loss (or some factor without which it would not have occurred) is a 'serious possibility' or a 'real danger'. For short, we have used the word 'liable' to result. Possibly, the colloquialism 'on the cards' indicates the shade of meaning with some approach to accuracy.

If these, indeed, are the principles applicable, what is the effect of their application to the facts of this case? We have, at the beginning of this judgment, summarised the main relevant facts. The defendants were an engineering company supplying a boiler to a laundry. We reject the submission for the defendants that an engineering company knows no more than the plain man about boilers or the purposes to which they are commonly put by different classes of purchasers, including laundries. The defendant company were not, it is true, manufacturers of this boiler or dealers in boilers, but they gave a highly technical and comprehensive description of this boiler to the plaintiffs by letter of 19 January 1946, and offered both to dismantle the boiler at Harpenden and to re-erect it on the plaintiffs' premises. Of the uses or purposes to which boilers are put, they would clearly know more than the uninstructed layman. Again, they knew they were supplying the boiler to a company carrying on the business of laundrymen and dyers, for use in that business. The obvious use of a boiler, in such a business, is surely to boil water for the purpose of washing or dyeing. A laundry might conceivably buy a boiler for some other purpose; for instance, to work radiators or warm bath water for the comfort of its employees or directors, or to use for research, or to exhibit in a museum. All these purposes are possible, but the first is the obvious purpose which, in the case of a laundry, leaps to the average eye. If the purpose, then, be to wash or dye, why does the company want to wash or dye, unless for purposes of business advantage, in which term we, for the purposes of the rest of this judgment, include maintenance or increase of profit, or reduction of loss? (We shall speak henceforward not of loss of profit, but of 'loss of business'.)

No commercial concern commonly purchases for the purposes of its business a very large and expensive structure like this – a boiler 19 feet high and costing over £2,000 – with any other motive, and no supplier, let alone an engineering company which has promised delivery of such an article by a particular date, with knowledge that it was to be put into use immediately on delivery, can reasonably contend that it could not foresee that loss of business (in the sense indicated above) would be liable to result to the purchaser from a long delay in the delivery thereof. The suggestion that, for all the supplier knew, the boiler might have been needed simply as a 'stand-by', to be used in a possibly distant future, is gratuitous and was plainly negatived by the terms of the letter of 26 April 1946.

We would wish to add: First, that the learned judge appears to infer that because certain 'special circumstances' were, in his view, not 'drawn to the notice of' the defendants and therefore, in his view, the operation of the 'second rule' was excluded, ergo nothing in respect of loss of business can be recovered under the 'first rule'. This inference is, in our view, no more justified in the present case than it was in the case of *Cory v Thames Ironworks Co*. Secondly, that while it is not wholly clear what were the 'special circumstances' on the non-communication of which the learned judge relied, it would seem that they were, or included, the following: (a) the 'circumstance' that delay in delivering the boiler was going to lead 'necessarily' to loss of profits. But the true criterion is surely not what was bound 'necessarily' to result, but what was likely or liable to do so, and we think that it was amply conveyed to the defendants by what was communicated to them (plus what was patent without express communication) that delay in delivery was likely to lead to 'loss of business'; (b) the 'circumstance' that the plaintiffs needed the boiler 'to extend their business'. It was surely not necessary for the defendants to be specifically informed of this, as a pre-condition of being liable for loss of business. Reasonable persons in the shoes of the defendants must be taken to foresee without any express intimation, that a laundry which, at a time when there was a famine of laundry facilities, was paying £2,000 odd for plant and intended at such a time to put such plant 'into use' immediately, would be likely to suffer in pocket from five months' delay in delivery of the plant in question, whether they intended by means of it to extend their business, or merely to maintain it, or to reduce a loss; (c) the 'circumstance' that the plaintiffs had the assured expectation of special contracts, which they could only fulfil by securing punctual delivery of the boiler. Here, no doubt, the learned judge had in mind the particularly lucrative dyeing contracts to which the plaintiffs looked forward and which they mention in para 10 of the statement of claim. We agree that, in order that the plaintiffs should recover specifically and as such the profits expected on these contracts, the defendants would have had to know, at the time of their agreement with the plaintiffs, of the prospect and terms of such contracts. We also agree that they did not in fact know these things. It does not, however, follow that the plaintiffs are precluded from recovering some general (and perhaps conjectural) sum for loss of business in respect of dyeing contracts to be reasonably expected, any more than in respect of laundering contracts to be reasonably expected.

Thirdly, the other point on which Streatfield J largely based his judgment was that there is a critical difference between the measure of damages applicable when the defendant defaults in supplying a self-contained profit-earning whole and when he defaults in supplying a part of that whole. In our view, there is no intrinsic magic, in this connexion, in the whole as against a part. The fact that a part only is involved is only significant in so far as it bears on the capacity of the supplier to foresee the consequences of non-delivery.

The difficulty with a test of reasonable foreseeability is to determine what must be reasonably foreseeable. It cannot be the breach of contract, since the parties contemplate performance of the contract rather than breach of it. Thus, what the foresight test has to determine is the kind of loss the parties would have contemplated in the event of a breach.

Hadley v Baxendale and *Victoria Laundry v Newman* indicate that normal losses are foreseeable but that abnormal losses are not, unless the defendant had knowledge of the special circumstances.

A more difficult issue is to determine the degree to which the defendant has to foresee damage, whether normal or abnormal.

In *Koufos v Czarnikow*,[26] a chartered ship deviated, in breach of contract, with the result that it reached its destination nine days later than would otherwise have been the case. The market value of its cargo of sugar had fallen in the meantime. The defendant shipowners were held liable for this loss, which arose in the usual course of things:

Koufos v C Czarnikow Ltd, The Heron II [1969] 1 AC 350, pp 382–85, 388

Lord Reid: McNair J, following the decision in *The Parana*, decided this question in favour of the appellant. He said: 'In those circumstances, it seems to me almost impossible to say that the shipowner must have known that the delay in prosecuting the voyage would probably result, or be likely to result, in this kind of loss.'

The Court of Appeal by a majority (Diplock and Salmon LJJ, Sellers LJ dissenting) reversed the decision of the trial judge. The majority held that *The Parana* laid down no general rule and, applying the rule (or rules) in *Hadley v Baxendale*, as explained in *Victoria Laundry (Windsor) Ltd v Newman Industries Ltd*, they held that the loss due to fall in market price was not too remote to be recoverable as damages.

---

26 *The Heron II* (1969) 1 AC 350.

It may be well first to set out the knowledge and intention of the parties at the time of making the contract so far as relevant or argued to be relevant. The charterers intended to sell the sugar in the market at Basrah on arrival of the vessel. They could have changed their mind and exercised their option to have the sugar delivered at Jeddah, but they did not do so. There is no finding that they had in mind any particular date as the likely date of arrival at Basrah or that they had any knowledge or expectation that in late November or December, there would be a rising or a falling market. The shipowner was given no information about these matters by the charterers. He did not know what the charterers intended to do with the sugar. But he knew there was a market in sugar at Basrah, and it appears to me that, if he had thought about the matter, he must have realised that at least it was not unlikely that the sugar would be sold in the market at market price on arrival. He must also be held to have known that in any ordinary market prices are apt to fluctuate from day to day: but he had no reason to suppose it more probable that during the relevant period such fluctuation would be downwards rather than upwards – it was an even chance that the fluctuation would be downwards.

So, the question for decision is whether a plaintiff can recover as damages for breach of contract a loss of a kind which the defendant, when he made the contract, ought to have realised was not unlikely to result from a breach of contract causing delay in delivery. I use the words 'not unlikely' as denoting a degree of probability considerably less than an even chance but nevertheless not very unusual and easily foreseeable.

For over a century, everyone has agreed that remoteness of damage in contract must be determined by applying the rule (or rules) laid down by a court including Parke, Martin and Alderson BB in *Hadley v Baxendale*; but many different interpretations of that rule have been adopted by judges at different times. So, I think that one ought first to see just what was decided in that case, because it would seem wrong to attribute to that rule a meaning which, if it had been adopted in that case, would have resulted in a contrary decision of that case.

In *Hadley v Baxendale*, the owners of a flour mill at Gloucester, which was driven by a steam engine, delivered to common carriers, Pickford & Co, a broken crank shaft to be sent to engineers in Greenwich. A delay of five days in delivery there was held to be in breach of contract, and the question at issue was the proper measure of damages. In fact, the shaft was sent as a pattern for a new shaft and, until it arrived, the mill could not operate. So, the owners claimed £300 as loss of profit for the five days by which resumption of work was delayed by this breach of contract; but the carriers did not know that delay would cause loss of this kind. Alderson B, delivering the judgment of the court, said: '... we find that the only circumstances here communicated by the plaintiffs to the defendants at the time the contract was made were that the article to be carried was the broken shaft of a mill and that the plaintiffs were the millers of that mill. But how do these circumstances show reasonably that the profits of the mill must be stopped by an unreasonable delay in the delivery of the broken shaft by the carrier to the third person? Suppose the plaintiffs had another shaft in their possession put up or putting up at the time, and that they only wished to send back the broken shaft to the engineer who made it; it is clear that this would be quite consistent with the above circumstances, and yet the unreasonable delay in the delivery would have no effect upon the intermediate profits of the mill. Or, again, suppose that at the time of the delivery to the carrier the machinery of the mill had been in other respects defective, then, also the same results would follow.'

Then, having said that in fact the loss of profit was caused by the delay, he continued: 'But it is obvious that, in the great multitude of cases of millers sending off broken shafts to third persons by a carrier under ordinary circumstances, such consequences would not, in all probability, have occurred ...'

Alderson B clearly did not and could not mean that it was not reasonably foreseeable that delay might stop the resumption of work in the mill. He merely said that in the great multitude – which I take to mean the great majority – of cases this would not happen. He was not distinguishing between results which were foreseeable or unforeseeable, but between results which were likely because they would happen in the great majority of cases, and results which were unlikely because they would only happen in a small minority of cases. He continued: 'It follows, therefore, that the loss of profits here cannot reasonably be considered such a consequence of the breach of contract as could have been fairly and reasonably contemplated by both the parties when they made this contract.'

He clearly meant that a result which will happen in the great majority of cases should fairly and reasonably be regarded as having been in the contemplation of the parties, but that a result which, though foreseeable as a substantial possibility, would happen only in a small minority of cases should not be regarded as having been in their contemplation. He was referring to such a result when he continued: 'For such loss would neither have flowed naturally from the breach of this contract in the great multitude of such cases occurring under ordinary circumstances, nor were the special circumstances, which perhaps, would have made it a reasonable and natural consequence of such breach of contract, communicated to or known by the defendants.'

I have dealt with the latter part of the judgment before coming to the well known rule, because the court were there applying the rule and the language which was used in the latter part appears to me to throw considerable light on the meaning which they must have attached to the rather vague expressions used in the rule itself. The rule is that the damages: '... should be such as may fairly and reasonably be considered either arising naturally, that is, according to the usual course of things, from such breach of contract itself, or such as may reasonably be supposed to have been in the contemplation of both parties at the time they made the contract as the probable result of the breach of it.'

I do not think that it was intended that there were to be two rules or that two different standards or tests were to be applied. The last two passages which I quoted from the end of the judgment applied to the facts before the court, which did not include any special circumstances communicated to the defendants; and the line of reasoning there is that because, in the great majority of cases, loss of profit would not in all probability have occurred, it followed that this could not reasonably be considered as having been fairly and reasonably contemplated by both the parties, for it would not have flowed naturally from the breach in the great majority of cases.

I am satisfied that the court did not intend that every type of damage which was reasonably foreseeable by the parties when the contract was made should either be considered as arising naturally, that is, in the usual course of things, or be supposed to have been in the contemplation of the parties. Indeed the decision makes it clear that a type of damage which was plainly foreseeable as a real possibility but which would only occur in a small minority of cases cannot be regarded as arising in the usual course of things or be supposed to have been in the contemplation of the parties: the parties are not supposed to contemplate as grounds for the recovery of damage any type of loss or damage which, on the knowledge available to the defendant, would appear to him as only likely to occur in a small minority of cases ...

It may be that there was nothing very new in this, but I think that *Hall's* case must be taken to have established that damages are not to be regarded as too remote merely because, on the knowledge available to the defendant when the contract was made, the chance of the occurrence of the event which caused the damage would have appeared to him to be rather less than an even chance. I would agree with Lord Shaw; it is generally sufficient that that event would have appeared to the defendant as not unlikely to occur. It is hardly ever possible in this matter to assess probabilities with any degree of mathematical accuracy. But I do not find in that case, or in cases which preceded it, any warrant for regarding as within the contemplation of the parties any event which would not have appeared to the defendant, had he thought about it, to have a very substantial degree of probability.

But then it has been said that the liability of defendants has been further extended by *Victoria Laundry (Windsor) Ltd v Newman Industries Ltd.* I do not think so. A large part of the profits claimed would have resulted from some specially lucrative contracts which the plaintiffs could have completed if they had had the boiler: that was rightly disallowed because the defendants had no knowledge of these contracts. But Asquith LJ then said: 'It does not, however, follow that the plaintiffs are precluded from recovering some general (and perhaps conjectural) sum for loss of business in respect of dyeing contracts to be reasonably expected, any more than in respect of laundering contracts to be reasonably expected.'

It appears to me that this was well justified on the earlier authorities. It was certainly not unlikely on the information which the defendants had when making the contract that delay in delivering the boiler would result in loss of business: indeed it would seem that that was more than an even chance. And there was nothing new in holding that damages should be estimated on a conjectural basis. This House had approved of that as early as 1813 in *Hall v Ross.*

But what is said to create a 'landmark', is the statement of principles by Asquith LJ. This does to some extent to beyond the older authorities and in so far as it does so, I do not agree with it. In para (2), it is said that the plaintiff is entitled to recover 'such part of the loss actually resulting as was at the time of the contract reasonably foreseeable as liable to result from the breach'. To bring in reasonable foreseeability appears to me to be confusing measure of damages in contract with measure of damages in tort. A great many extremely unlikely results are reasonably foreseeable: it is true that Asquith LJ, may have meant foreseeable as a likely result and, if that is all he meant, I would not object farther than to say that I think that the phrase is liable to be misunderstood. For the same reason I would take exception to the phrase 'liable to result' in para (5). Liable is a very vague word, but I think that one would usually say that when a person foresees a very improbable result he foresees that it is liable to happen.

I agree with the first half of para (6). For the best part of a century, it has not been required that the defendant could have foreseen that a breach of contract must necessarily result in the loss which has occurred; but I cannot agree with the second half of para (6). It has never been held to be sufficient in contract that the loss was foreseeable as 'a serious possibility' or 'a real danger' or as being 'on the cards'. It is on the cards that one can win £100,000 or more for a stake of a few pence – several people have done that; and anyone who backs a 100 to one chance regards a win as a serious possibility – many people have won on such a chance. Moreover, *The Wagon Mound (No 2) Overseas Tankship (UK) Ltd v Miller SS Co Pty Ltd* could not have been decided, as it was unless the extremely unlikely fire should have been foreseen by the ship's officer as a real danger. It appears to me that, in the ordinary use of language, there is a wide gulf between saying that some event is not unlikely or quite likely to happen and saying merely that it is a serious possibility, a real danger, or on the cards. Suppose one takes a well shuffled pack of cards; it is quite likely or not unlikely that the top card will prove to be a diamond – the odds are only three to one against – but most people would not say that it is quite likely to be the nine of diamonds, for the odds are then 51 to one against. On the other hand, I think that most people would say that there is a serious possibility or a real danger of its being turned up first and, of course, it is on the cards. If the tests of 'real danger' or 'serious possibility' are in future to be authoritative, then the *Victoria Laundry* case would indeed be a landmark, because it would mean that *Hadley v Baxendale* would be differently decided today. I certainly could not understand any court deciding that, on the information available to the carrier in that case, the stoppage of the mill was neither a serious possibility nor a real danger. If those tests are to prevail in future, then let us cease to pay lip service to the rule in *Hadley v Baxendale*. But, in my judgment, to adopt these tests would extend liability for breach of contract beyond what is reasonable or desirable. From the limited knowledge which I have of commercial affairs, I would not expect such an extension to be welcomed by the business community and, from the legal point of view, I can find little or nothing to recommend it.

Lord Asquith took the phrases 'real danger' and 'serious possibility' from the speech of Lord du Parcq in *Monarch SS Co Ltd v AB Karlshamns Oljefabriker*.

It appears to me that, without relying in any way on the *Victoria Laundry* case, and taking the principle that had already been established, the loss of profit claimed in this case was not too remote to be recoverable as damages. So, it remains to consider whether the decision in *The Parana* established a rule which, though now anomalous, should nevertheless still be followed. In that case, owing to the defective state of the ship's engines, a voyage which ought to have taken 65 to 70 days took 127 days and, as a result, a cargo of hemp fetched a much smaller price than it would have done if there had been no breach of contract. The Court of Appeal held, however, that the plaintiffs could not recover this loss as damages. The vital part of their judgment was as follows: 'In order that damages may be recovered, we must come to two conclusions – first, that it was reasonably certain that the goods would not be sold until they did arrive; and, secondly, that it was reasonably certain that they would be sold immediately after they arrived, and that that was known to the carrier at the time when the bills of lading were signed.'

If that was the right test then the decision was right, and I think that that test was in line with a number of cases decided before or about that time (1877); but, as I have already said, so strict a test has long been obsolete; and, if one substitutes for 'reasonably certain' the words 'not unlikely' or some similar words denoting a much smaller degree of probability, then the whole argument in the judgment collapses.

One issue confronted for the first time was the nature of the conflict between the reasonable foresight test adopted in negligence cases[27] and the test based on apparently similar language adopted in *Victoria Laundries Ltd v Newman Industries*.

What the House of Lords concluded was that reasonable foreseeability, in the sense of the low degree of probability required in a tort action, was inappropriate in cases involving economic loss suffered as a result of a breach of contract. However, it should not be concluded from this that the high degree of foreseeability required in *The Heron II* is necessarily the most appropriate test to apply in relation to types of damage other than economic loss, such as loss of profit.

The rationale for the rule in *Hadley v Baxendale* may be described as being based on fairness and economic efficiency.[28] It is fair, in that it prevents a party who is in breach of contract from being responsible for unexpected amounts. The rule also facilitates negotiation between parties who are known to each other and allows a contracting party to raise his price to take account of a known or foreseeable risk, or limit his liability in respect of that risk. Conversely, to hold a contracting party liable for unlikely losses would not make economic sense, unless the party who is likely to suffer such loss has disclosed relevant information. Once that information has been disclosed, the other party can then safeguard his position through the use of permitted exclusions of liability or he may insure against the possibility of loss.

---

27 Considered below in relation to physical damage cases.
28 See Beale, 1980, p 180; and Posner, 1977, pp 94–95.

Physical damage cases

The expression 'physical damage' covers personal injuries, damage to property and consequential expenses. This form of loss is recoverable in both contract and tort cases, but the majority of such actions arise in the law of tort.

For the purposes of the tort of negligence in particular, the relevant test of remoteness of damage or legal causation is relatively favourable to the claimant for reasons considered below. The test applied, following the Privy Council decision in the *Wagon Mound (No 1)*,[29] is that damage of the kind suffered by the claimant must be a reasonably foreseeable consequence of the defendant's breach of duty. However, it does not matter if the damage complained of came about in an unforeseeable way. Accordingly, recoverable loss may, on occasions, appear to be a relatively distant possibility, but nonetheless recoverable if the general kind of damage could have been foreseen in little more than the most general of senses. This stance is readily understandable when the distinction between paradigm contract and tort claimants is considered. The typical tort claimant is a complete stranger to the defendant – for example, the victim of a road traffic accident – with the result that there is no opportunity for the parties to communicate with each other over potential losses flowing from the defendant's actions. In contrast, the claimant in a contract action will have had the opportunity to negotiate with the defendant and any worries about possible losses may have been raised in the course of those negotiations:

Koufos v Czarnikow, The Heron II [1969] AC 350, p 385

Lord Reid: In cases like *Hadley v Baxendale* or the present case, it is not enough that, in fact, the plaintiff's loss was directly caused by the defendant's breach of contract. It clearly was so caused in both. The crucial question is whether, on the information available to the defendant when the contract was made, he should, or the reasonable man in his position would, have realised that such loss was sufficiently likely to result from the breach of contract to make it proper to hold that the loss flowed naturally from the breach or that loss of that kind should have been within his contemplation.

The modern rule in tort is quite different and it imposes a much wider liability. The defendant will be liable for any type of damage which is reasonably foreseeable as liable to happen even in the most unusual case, unless the risk is so small that a reasonable man would in the whole circumstances feel justified in neglecting it; and there is good reason for the difference. In contract, if one party wishes to protect himself against a risk which to the other party would appear unusual, he can direct the other party's attention to it before the contract is made, and I need not stop to consider in what circumstances the other party will then be held to have accepted responsibility in that event. In tort, however, there is no opportunity for the injured party to protect himself in

---

29 [1961] AC 388.

that way, and the tortfeasor cannot reasonably complain if he has to pay for some very unusual but nevertheless foreseeable damage which results from his wrongdoing. I have no doubt that, today, a tortfeasor would be held liable for a type of damage as unlikely as was the stoppage of Hadley's Mill for lack of a crank shaft: to anyone with the knowledge, the carrier had that may have seemed unlikely, but the chance of it happening would have been seen to be far from negligible. But it does not at all follow that *Hadley v Baxendale* would today be differently decided.

As long ago as 1872, Willes J said in *Horne v Midland Railway Co*: 'The cases as to the measure of damages for a tort do not apply to a case of contract. That was suggested in a case in Bulstrode, but the notion was corrected in *Hadley v Baxendale*. The damages are to be limited to those that are the natural and ordinary consequences which may be supposed to have been in the contemplation of the parties at the time of making the contract.'

It is true that, in some later cases, opinions were expressed that the measure of damages is the same in tort as it is in contract, but those were generally cases where it was sought to limit damages due for a tort and not cases where it was sought to extend damages due for breach of contract, and I do not recollect any case in which such opinions were based on a full consideration of the matter. In my view these opinions must now be regarded as erroneous.

The issue of information transfer is generally irrelevant in physical damage cases, except in so far as it relates to the initial question of liability. For this reason, it is submitted that there is no valid reason for applying a different test of remoteness of damage to actions brought for breach of contract from that which applies to an action for a breach of a tortious duty.

In physical damage cases, the claimant is at an advantage. Once liability has been established, the defendant effectively becomes an insurer. All the claimant must show is that the damage suffered is of a kind likely to result from the defendant's breach of duty. The difficulty is to determine what is meant by such a kind of damage.

Provided the kind of damage is foreseeable, it does not matter that it is more extensive than could have been foreseen. In *Vacwell Engineering Co Ltd v BDH Chemicals Ltd*,[30] the defendants sold quantities of a chemical, but negligently failed to warn that it was liable to explode in contact with water. A scientist working for the claimants placed the chemical in water, thereby causing a violent explosion which resulted in extensive damage. The defendants were held liable for their negligence, even though the extent of the damage was unforeseeable. Moreover, it seemed to make little difference to the outcome of the case that it was also pleaded on the basis of a breach of the implied contractual terms in sale of goods contracts relating to quality and fitness.

---

30 [1971] 1 QB 88.

As the rules on remoteness of damage are presently set out, there appears to be a distinction between contract actions and those framed in tort. However, it should be appreciated that the major cases on remoteness in actions for breach of contract all concern economic loss. Accordingly, the question arises whether there should be a different test of remoteness where the damage complained of as a result of the defendant's breach of contract comprises physical harm to the person or to property.

It is possible that a defendant may find him/herself liable to one person for a breach of contract giving rise to physical harm and to another person due to a breach of tortious duty. For example, the manufacturer of a defective product, the occupier of premises or a doctor may all find themselves in this position. The defendant may also be concurrently liable for physical damage to a claimant in both contract and tort.

It has been seen that there is no liability for abnormal financial losses, unless the defendant has been informed of special circumstances likely to give rise to those losses. However, there would appear to be no reason for this rule to apply to cases of physical damage. While a party to a contract might think of possible financial losses before making the contract, he is much less likely to contemplate the possibility of physical harm. The typical view is that, in tort cases, there is no opportunity for the injured party to protect himself.[31] However, this is not strictly true as, in many tort cases, the parties are known to each other and may even be in a contractual relationship. A better view is probably that physical harm is not something which any contracting party is likely to contemplate, and that losses of this sort should be recoverable, so long as the harm suffered is not too remote. It would seem to follow that there is little justification for applying separate tests of remoteness in tortious and contractual actions for physical damage.

In *Parsons (Livestock) Ltd v Uttley Ingham & Co Ltd*,[32] the plaintiffs were pig farmers who contracted with the defendants for the supply and installation of a food storage hopper. The defendants negligently failed to unseal a ventilator in the hopper, with the result that pignuts stored therein became mouldy. As a result of this, the plaintiff's pigs died of a rare intestinal disease. It was held that the defendants' breach of contract was the cause of the pigs' death and, according to the majority, the loss was not too remote even within the strict test laid down in *The Heron II*. Lord Denning MR differed in his approach, preferring to distinguish between the kind of damage caused, rather than between causes of action. His preferred view was that the *Wagon Mound* test should be applied to all physical damage cases, regardless of whether the action was framed in contract or in tort.[33] Under this test, the defendants

---

31 *Koufos v Czarnikow, The Heron II* [1969] 1 AC 350, pp 385–86, *per* Lord Reid.
32 [1978] QB 791, CA.
33 *Parsons (Livestock) Ltd v Uttley Ingham & Co Ltd* [1978] QB 791 at p 804.

would be liable for the death of the pigs if death could have been reasonably foreseen as a possible consequence, even if it was only a slight possibility. In contrast, the majority considered that the type, rather than the extent of damage was what mattered and that the type of harm suffered was foreseeable at the time of contracting:

Parsons (Livestock) Ltd v Uttley Ingham & Co Ltd [1978] QB 791, CA, p 801

Lord Denning MR:

The law as to remoteness

Remoteness of damage is beyond doubt a question of law. In *The Heron II, Koufos v C Czarnikow Ltd*, the House of Lords said that, in remoteness of damage, there is a difference between contract and tort. In the case of a *breach of contract*, the court has to consider whether the consequences were of such a kind that a reasonable man, at the time of making the contract, would contemplate them as being of a very substantial degree of probability. (In the House of Lords, various expressions were used to describe this degree of probability, such as: not merely 'on the cards' because that may be too low, but as being 'not unlikely to occur'; or 'likely to result or at least not unlikely to result'; or 'liable to result'; or that there was a 'real danger' or 'serious possibility' of them occurring.)

In the case of a *tort*, the court has to consider whether the consequences were of such a kind that a reasonable man, at the time of the tort committed, would foresee them as being of a much lower degree of probability. (In the House of Lords, various expressions were used to describe this, such as: it is sufficient if the consequences are 'liable to happen in the most unusual case'; or in a 'very improbable' case; or that 'they may happen as a result of the breach however unlikely it may be, unless it can be brushed aside as far fetched'.)

I find it difficult to apply those principles universally to all cases of contract or to all cases of tort, and to draw a distinction between what a man 'contemplates' and what he 'foresees'. I soon begin to get out of my depth. I cannot swim in this sea of semantic exercises – to say nothing of the different degrees of probability – especially when the cause of action can be laid either in contract or in tort. I am swept under by the conflicting currents. I go back with relief to the distinction drawn in legal theory by Professors Hart and Honoré in their book *Causation in the Law*. They distinguish between those cases in contract in which a man has suffered no damage to person or property, but only *economic loss,* such as loss of profit or loss of opportunities for gain in some future transaction: and those in which he claims damages for an *injury actually done* to his person or *damage actually done* to his property (including his livestock) or for ensuing expense (*damnum emergens*) to which he has actually been put. In the law of tort, there is emerging a distinction between economic loss and physical damage: see *Spartan Steel & Alloys Ltd v Martin & Co (Contractors) Ltd*. It underlies the words of Lord Wilberforce in *Anns v London Borough of Merton* recently, where he classified the recoverable damage as 'material, physical damage'. It has been much considered by the Supreme Court of Canada in *Rivtow Marine Ltd v Washington Iron Works* and by the High Court in Australia in *Caltex Oil (Australia) Pty Ltd v The Dredge Willemstad*.

It seems to me that, in the law of contract too, a similar distinction is emerging. It is between loss of profit consequent on a breach of contract and physical damage consequent on it.

Loss of profit cases

I would suggest as a solution that, in the former class of case, loss of profit cases, the defaulting party is only liable for the consequences if they are such as, at the time of the contract, he ought reasonably to have contemplated as a *serious* possibility or real danger. You must assume that, at the time of the contract, he had the very kind of breach in mind, such a breach as afterwards happened, as for instance, delay in transit, and then you must ask: ought he reasonably to have contemplated that there was a serious possibility that such a breach would involve the plaintiff in loss of profit? If Yes, the contractor is liable for the loss unless he has taken care to exempt himself from it by a condition in the contract as, of course, he is able to do if it was the sort of thing which he could reasonably contemplate. The law on this class of case is now covered by the three leading cases of *Hadley v Baxendale, Victoria Laundry (Windsor) Ltd v Newman Industries Ltd* and *Koufos v C Czarnikow Ltd, The Heron II*. These were all 'loss of profit' cases and the test of 'reasonable contemplation' and 'serious possibility' should, I suggest, be kept to that type of loss or, at any rate, to economic loss.

Physical damage cases

In the second class of case, the physical injury or expense case, the defaulting party is liable for any loss or expense which he ought reasonably to have foreseen at the time of the breach as a possible consequence, even if it was only a *slight* possibility. You must assume that he was aware of his breach, and then you must ask: ought he reasonably to have foreseen, at the time of the breach, that something of this kind might happen in consequence of it? This is the test which has been applied in cases of tort, ever since *The Wagon Mound* cases. But there is a long line of cases which support a like test in cases of contract. One class of case which is particularly apposite here concerns latent defects in goods. In modern words: 'product liability'. In many of these cases, the manufacturer is liable in contract to the immediate party for a breach of his duty to use reasonable care, and is liable in tort to the ultimate consumer for the same want of reasonable care. The ultimate consumer can either sue the retailer in contract and pass the liability up the chain to the manufacturer, or he can sue the manufacturer in tort and thus bypass the chain. The liability of the manufacturer ought to be the same in either case. In nearly all these cases the defects were outside the range of anything that was in fact contemplated, or could reasonably have been contemplated by the manufacturer or by anyone down the chain to the retailers. Yet the manufacturer and others in the chain have been held liable for the damage done to the ultimate user, as for instance the death of the young pheasants in *Henry Kendall & Sons (A Firm) v William Lillico & Sons Ltd* and of the mink in *Ashington Piggeries Ltd v Christopher Hill Ltd*. Likewise, the manufacturers and retailers were held liable for the dermatitis caused to the wearer in the woollen underwear case of *Grant v Australian Knitting Mills Ltd*, even though they had not the faintest suspicion of any trouble. So were the manufacturers down the chain to the subcontractors for the disintegrating roofing tiles in *Young & Marten Ltd v McManus Childs Ltd*.

Another familiar class of case is where the occupier of premises is under the common duty of care, both in pursuance of a contract with a visitor or under the Occupiers Liability Act 1957. If he fails in that duty and a visitor is injured, the test of remoteness must be the same no matter whether the injured person enters by virtue of a contract or as a visitor by permission without a contract. No matter whether in contract or tort, the damages must be the same. Likewise, when a contractor is doing work on premises for a tenant, and either the tenant or a visitor is injured, the test of remoteness is the same no matter whether the person injured is a tenant under the contract or a visitor without a contract: see *AC Billings & Sons Ltd v Riden*.

Yet another class of case is where a hospital authority renders medical services in contract to a paying patient and gratuitously to another patient without any contract. The paying patient can sue in contract for negligence. The poor patient can sue in tort: see *Cassidy v Ministry of Health*. The test of remoteness should be the same whether the hospital authorities are sued in contract or in tort: see *Esso Petroleum Co Ltd v Mardon*.

Instances could be multiplied of injuries to persons or damage to property where the defendant is liable for his negligence to one man in contract and to another in tort. Each suffers like damage. The test of remoteness is, and should be, the same in both.

Coming to the present case, we were told that in some cases the makers of these hoppers supply them direct to the pig farmer under contract with him, but in other cases they supply them through an intermediate dealer who buys from the manufacturer and resells to the pig farmer on the self-same terms, in which the manufacturer delivers direct to the pig farmer. In the one case, the pig farmer can sue the manufacturer in contract. In the other, in tort. The test of remoteness should be the same. It should be the test in tort.

Conclusion

The present case falls within the class of case where the breach of contract causes physical damage. The test of remoteness in such cases is similar to that in tort. The contractor is liable for all such loss or expense as could reasonably have been foreseen, at the time of the breach, as a possible consequence of it. Applied to this case, it means that the makers of the hopper are liable for the death of the pigs. They ought reasonably to have foreseen that, if the mouldy pig nuts were fed to the pigs, there was a possibility that they might become ill. Not a serious possibility. Nor a real danger. But still a slight possibility. On that basis, the makers were liable for the illness suffered by the pigs. They suffered from diarrhoea at the beginning. This 'triggered off' the deadly E coli. That was a far worse illness than could then be foreseen. But that does not lessen this liability. The type or kind of damage was foreseeable even though the extent of it was not: see *Hughes v Lord Advocate*. The makers are liable for the loss of the pigs that died and of the expenses of the vet, and such like. But not for loss of profit on future sales or future opportunities of gain; see *Simon v Pawson & Leafs Ltd*.

So, I reach the same result as Swanwick J, but by a different route. I would dismiss the appeal.

Scarman LJ (pp 806 and 811): My conclusion in the present case is the same as that of Lord Denning MR, but I reach it by a different route. I would dismiss the appeal. I agree with him in thinking it absurd that the test for remoteness of damage should, in principle, differ according to the legal classification of the cause of action, though one must recognise that parties to a contract have the right to agree on a measure of damages which may be greater or less than the law would offer in the absence of agreement. I also agree with him in thinking that, notwithstanding the interpretation put on some *dicta* in *Koufos v C Czarnikow Ltd, The Heron II*, the law is not so absurd as to differentiate between contract and tort save in situations where the agreement, or the factual relationship, of the parties with each other requires it in the interests of justice. I differ from him only to this extent: the cases do not, in my judgment, support a distinction in law between loss of profit and physical damage. Neither do I think it necessary to develop the law judicially by drawing such a distinction. Of course (and this is a reason for refusing to draw the distinction in law), the type of consequence, loss of profit or market or physical injury, will always be an important matter of fact in determining whether in all the circumstances the loss or injury was of a type which the parties could reasonably be supposed to have in contemplation ...

The judge's other findings of fact may be summarised as follows. He found that there was a warranty, its existence is not disputed by the defendants, to the effect that the hopper should be reasonably fit for the purpose of storing pig nuts in a condition suitable for feeding to the plaintiffs' pigs. He found that the hopper, being unventilated, was not so fit; that this defect was a breach of the warranty, and that the pig nuts were unfit by reason of the breach. He found that the plaintiffs' loss was caused by the breach of warranty. On the basis of these findings, the judge held that, since the first question is whether 'the damage' claimed arises in the ordinary course of things from the breach, 'there is no need to have recourse to the question of the presumed contemplation'. He then considered the meaning of the implied term 'pleaded and admitted' that the hopper should be reasonably fit for the purpose of storing pig nuts to be fed to the plaintiffs' pigs and reached the conclusion, which I respectfully think was inevitable, that it meant that, insofar as proper storage could achieve it, the hopper would keep the pig nuts in a condition such as not to make the plaintiffs' pigs ill. He stressed the importance to be attached to the particular nature of this herd of pigs, a very different set of animals from the ordinary farmyard pig, and to the intensive nature of the plaintiffs' farming operation, all of which matters were made known to the defendants before contract. He stated his conclusion in these words: 'On this interpretation the inevitable conclusion from the findings I have already made would be that this hopper was not reasonably fit for that purpose and that this caused the nuts to become toxic and that the illness of the pigs was a direct and natural consequence of such breach and toxicity, and that the plaintiffs do not have to prove that the toxicity or its results were foreseeable to either party. To put it another way, once the question of foreseeability of the breach is eliminated, as it is by the absolute warranty, the consequences of the breach flow naturally from it.'

Mr Drake criticises strongly this part of the judgment. He says it is based on a misunderstanding of *Hadley v Baxendale*; and he referred us to the well known passage in Lord Reid's speech in *Koufos v C Czarnikow Ltd, The Heron II*, where he said that it is not enough that, in fact, the plaintiff's loss was directly caused by the defendant's breach of contract. Lord Reid said: 'The crucial question is whether, on the information available to the defendant when the contract was made, he should, or the reasonable man in his position would, have realised that such loss was sufficiently likely to result from the breach of contract to make it proper to hold that the loss flowed naturally from the breach or that loss of that kind should have been within his contemplation.'

Notwithstanding his choice of language, I think the judge was making the approach which, according to Lord Reid, is the correct one. He was saying, in effect, that the parties to this contract must have appreciated that, if, as happened in the event, the hopper, unventilated, proved not to be suitable for the storage of pig nuts to be fed to the plaintiffs' pigs, it was not unlikely, there was a serious possibility, that the pigs would become ill. The judge put it in this way: 'The *natural* result of feeding toxic food to animals is damage to their health and maybe death, which is what occurred, albeit from a hitherto unknown disease and to particularly susceptible animals. There was therefore no need to invoke the question of *reasonable* contemplation in order to make the defendants liable.' (My underlining.)

The judge in this critical passage of his judgment is contrasting a natural result, that is, one which people placed as these parties were would consider as a serious possibility, with a special, specific result, that is, *E coli* disease, which, as he later found, the parties could not at the time of contract reasonably have contemplated as a consequence. He distinguishes between 'presumed contemplation' based on a special knowledge from ordinary understanding based on general knowledge and concludes that the case falls within the latter category. He does so because he has held that the assumption or hypothesis to be made is that the parties had in mind at the time of contract not a breach of warranty limited to the delivery of mouldy nuts, but a warranty as to the fitness of the hopper for its purpose. The assumption is of the parties asking themselves not what is likely to happen if the nuts are mouldy, but what is likely to happen to the pigs if the hopper is unfit for storing nuts suitable to be fed to them. While, on his finding, nobody at the time of contract could have expected E coli to ensue from eating mouldy nuts, he is clearly, and, as a matter of common sense, rightly, saying that people would contemplate, on the second assumption, the serious possibility of injury and even death among the pigs.

And so, the question becomes: was he right to make the assumption he did? In my judgment, he was (see *Grant v Australian Knitting Mills Ltd* [1936] AC 85) and, particularly, the well known passage in the speech of Lord Wright at pp 97–100.

I would agree with McGregor, 13th edn, 1972, pp 131–32 on damages that: 'in contract, as in tort, it should suffice that, if physical injury or damage is within the contemplation of the parties, recovery is not to be limited because the degree of physical injury or damage could not have been anticipated.'

This is so, in my judgment, not because there is, or ought to been, a specific rule of law governing cases of physical injury, but because it would be absurd to regulate damages in such cases on the necessity of supposing the parties had a prophetic foresight as to the exact nature of the injury that does in fact arise. It is enough if on the hypothesis predicated physical injury must have been a serious possibility. Though, in loss of market or loss of profit cases, the factual analysis will be very different from cases of physical injury, the same principles, in my judgment, apply. Given the situation of the parties at the time of contract, was the loss of profit or market a serious possibility, something that would have been in their minds had they contemplated breach?

It does not matter, in my judgment, if they thought that the chance of physical injury, loss of profit, loss of market, or other loss as the case may be, was slight or that the odds were against it, provided they contemplated as a serious possibility the type of consequence, not necessarily the specific consequence, that ensued on breach. Making the assumption as to breach that the judge did, no more than common sense was needed for them to appreciate that food affected by bad storage conditions might well cause illness in the pigs fed on it.

Suppose the farmer had been asked at the time of contracting 'would you buy this equipment if there was a serious possibility of your pigs dying or becoming seriously ill?'. Would he have purchased the hopper? It is submitted that Lord Denning's approach is preferable on the grounds that the courts are generally more willing to protect a claimant against physical damage than loss of profit, and it is unlikely that a contracting party will inform the other of the risk of abnormal physical losses.[34]

MITIGATION OF LOSS

Once the defendant's breach of contract has been established, it is often said that the claimant comes under a duty to mitigate his loss. Strictly, it is wrong to regard this as a duty, since this suggests breach of some legally imposed obligation in the event of a failure to mitigate. Instead, the consequence of the failure to mitigate is that that part of the loss suffered by the claimant which is attributable to the unreasonable action or inaction of the claimant becomes irrecoverable.

The so called duty to mitigate loss comprises two separate functions. First, the claimant must not take any step which unreasonably increases the loss

---

34   See *Kemp v Intersun Holidays Ltd* [1987] 2 Trading LR 234.

suffered in consequence of the defendant's breach of contract. This rule only applies to expenses incurred after breach. Other unreasonable acts will be treated as an intervening cause of the harm suffered. Secondly, the claimant must take such reasonable, positive steps as are necessary to minimise the loss he or she suffers. For example, a wrongfully dismissed employee must attempt to find a comparable job, and where a seller fails to deliver goods, the buyer must go into the market to obtain substitute goods.

The rules on mitigation also significantly reduce the likelihood that the claimant will be able to recover in full any expectations of full performance on the part of the defendant which he may have harboured. He/she cannot sit back, do nothing and sue for damages in respect of all the loss he claims to have suffered in consequence of the defendant's defective performance. Instead, he must take positive steps to reduce his losses by going into the market and seeking a replacement performance, where this is possible.

In determining the rules on mitigation, the courts are faced with a conflict between not depriving a party of a legal remedy and not encouraging a wasteful use of resources, taking account, especially, of the fact that it is the defendant's breach of contract which has placed the claimant on the horns of a dilemma. The innocent party is entitled to reject an offer which requires him/her to surrender his/her right to damages, with the effect that he/she will not be in as good a position as if the contract had been performed.[35] However, he must not act unreasonably in refusing an offer if to accept it would have reduced his/her losses.

In *Payzu Ltd v Saunders*,[36] an instalment contract for the sale of silk provided for payment within one month of each delivery. The sellers insisted on cash on delivery, thereby committing a breach of contract. The buyers refused to proceed with the contract on that basis and sued for the difference between the market price and the contract price on the date they accepted the repudiation. It was held that the buyers should have mitigated their loss by accepting the offer of cash on delivery terms:

Payzu Ltd v Saunders [1919] 2 KB 581, CA, p 587

Bankes LJ: At the trial of this action, the defendant, then present respondent, raised two points: first, that she had committed no breach of the contract of sale, and secondly that, if there was a breach, but had offered and was always ready and willing to supply the pieces of silk, the subject of the contract, at the contract price for cash; that it was unreasonable on the part of the plaintiffs to refuse to accept that offer, and that therefore they cannot claim damages beyond what they would have lost by paying cash with each order instead of having a month's credit and a discount of 21/2%. We must take it that this was the offer made by the respondent. The case was fought and the learned judge

---

35 *Shindler v Northern Raincoat Co Ltd* [1960] 2 All ER 239.
36 [1919] 2 KB 581, CA.

has given judgment upon that footing. It is true that the correspondence suggests that the defendant was at one time claiming an increased price. But in this court we must take it that the offer was to supply the contract goods at the contract price except that payment was to be made by cash instead of being on credit. In these circumstances the only question which arises is whether the plaintiffs can establish that as matter of law they were not bound to consider any offer made by the defendant because of the attitude she had taken up. Upon this point McCardie J, referred to *British Westinghouse Electric and Manufacturing Co v Underground Electric Railways Co of London Ltd*, where Lord Haldane LC said: 'The fundamental basis is thus compensation for pecuniary loss naturally flowing from the breach; but this first principle is qualified by a second, which imposes on a plaintiff the duty of taking all reasonable steps to mitigate the loss consequent on the breach, and debars him from claiming any part of the damage which is due to his neglect to take such steps. In the words of James LJ in *Dunkirk Colliery Co v Lever*: "The person who has broken the contract is not to be exposed to additional cost by reason of the plaintiffs not doing what they ought to have done as reasonable men, and the plaintiffs not being under any obligation to do anything otherwise than in the ordinary course of business."'

It is plain that the question what is reasonable for a person to do in mitigation of his damages cannot be a question of law, but must be one of fact in the circumstances of each particular case. There may be cases where, as matter of fact, it would be unreasonable to expect a plaintiff in view of the treatment he has received from the defendant to consider an offer made. If he had been rendering personal services and had been dismissed after being accused in presence of others of being a thief, and if after that his employer had offered to take him back into his service, most persons would think he would be justified in refusing the offer, and that it would be unreasonable to ask him in this way to mitigate the damages in an action of wrongful dismissal. But that is not to state a principle of law, but a conclusion of fact to be arrived at on a consideration of all the circumstances of the case. Mr Matthews complained that the defendant had treated his clients so badly that it would be unreasonable to expect them to listen to any proposition that she might make. I do not agree. In my opinion each party to the contract was ready to accuse the other of conduct unworthy of a high commercial reputation, and there was nothing to justify the appellants in refusing to consider the respondent's offer. I think the learned judge came to a right conclusion on the facts, and that the appeal must be dismissed.

Scrutton LJ (p 589): I am of the same opinion. Whether it be more correct to say that a plaintiff must minimise his damages, or to say that he can recover no more than he would have suffered if he had acted reasonably, because any further damages do not reasonably follow from the defendant's breach, the result is the same. The plaintiff must take 'all reasonable steps to mitigate the loss consequent on the breach' and this principle 'debars him from claiming any part of the damage which is due to his neglect to take such steps': *British Westinghouse Electric and Manufacturing Co v Underground Electric Railways Co of London Ltd*, per Lord Haldane LC. Counsel for the plaintiffs has contended that, in considering what steps should be taken to mitigate the damage, all contractual relations with the party in default must be excluded. That is contrary to my experience. In certain cases of personal service, it may be unreasonable to expect a plaintiff to consider an offer from the other party who has grossly injured him; but in commercial contracts it is generally reasonable to accept an offer from the party in default. However, it is always a question of fact. About the law, there is no difficulty.

How important was it in this case that silk was not a readily available commodity? What effect would this have had on the plaintiff's claim for damages?

What would have been the position had silk been a readily available commodity so that there was a reasonable market price?

Reasonable steps to minimise loss

What is reasonable is a question of fact in each case, but there are some general indications as to what steps the party not in breach should take in order to minimise the loss flowing from the defendant's breach. For example, where the party in breach offers a defective performance or, after the breach, offers to cure the defect, it may be reasonable for the innocent party to accept the defective performance or the cure.

If a seller offers sub-standard goods at a reduced price, which the court considers the buyer should accept, the buyer is deprived of his right of rejection.[37] Despite this acceptance of a defective performance, subject to appropriate adjustments, is often seen as the desired course as is illustrated in *Payzu v Saunders,* above.

Subjective factors are particularly important in commercial contracts where business reputation is concerned. For example, the innocent party will not be compelled to take steps which would ruin his reputation. Thus, a building society will not be required to enforce a covenant to repair against a borrower in order to mitigate the loss caused by a surveyor's negligent failure to take account of property defects when preparing a valuation.[38] Where an employee has been dismissed, it may be that he/she is subsequently offered renewed employment, but whether he/she is required to accept or not will depend on matters such as the nature of the post offered compared with the old post, and whether the personal relationship between employer and employee has been destroyed.[39]

---

37 *Heaven and Kesterton v Etablissement Francois Albiac & Cie* [1956] 2 Lloyd's Rep 316.

38 *London and South of England Building Society v Stone* [1983] 1 WLR 1242.

39 *Yetton v Eastwoods Froy Ltd* [1967] 1 WLR 104.

A further subjective factor affecting the ability to mitigate will be the financial position of the innocent party. For example, a consumer of goods or services may be required to acquire a replacement where the defendant fails to deliver the promised goods or services. However, impecuniosity may prevent the claimant from purchasing a replacement outright, with the result that it is not necessarily a failure to mitigate if an alternative, but more expensive, replacement is hired.[40]

The court will have regard to the fact that it is the defendant's breach which has placed the claimant in the position whereby he must mitigate his loss. This often justifies the refusal of a court to insist on complex or difficult steps being taken by the claimant.

In *Pilkington v Wood*,[41] title to property was found to be defective when the plaintiff came to sell his house. The plaintiff sued his solicitor and it was held that he was not obliged to mitigate his loss by bringing an action against the vendor of the property for conveying a defective title. This step would have involved a complex process of litigation unwarranted in the circumstances and with no obviously successful outcome:

Pilkington v Wood [1953] Ch 770, p 775

Harman J: It was admitted before me that the class of persons claiming under the will of which the vendor Wilks was a trustee was not closed, and might embrace infants or persons unborn, and that, for a number of years at any rate, it would be impossible to say with certainty that no claim could arise to upset the transaction, although hitherto in fact no claim has been made. This is clearly a serious blot on the title, and not one that can be described with any propriety as a technical defect. There is a real danger that anyone acquiring this property with notice may be dispossessed of it hereafter. A beneficiary claiming to have the property restored to the trust must agree that the original purchase money paid by Colonel Wilks and, in addition, money spent in improvements shall be repaid. That sum was assumed here to amount to £2,500. I ought to say that the defect in title does not extend to the further plot purchased by the plaintiff in 1951, but that plot by itself is of no greater value than the amount that the plaintiff paid for it.

It would appear then at first sight that the measure of the defendant's liability is the diminution in value of the property; that is to say, the difference between the value in 1950, the date of the plaintiff's purchase of the property with a good title and with the title which it in fact had.

The defendant, however, argues that it is the duty of the plaintiff before suing him in damages to seek to recover damages against his vendor Colonel Wilks under the covenant for title implied by reason of the conveyance as beneficial owner. It is said that this duty arises because of the obligation which rests on a

---

40   *Robbins of Putney Ltd v Meek* [1971] RTR 345.
41   [1953] Ch 770.

person injured by a breach of contract to mitigate the damages. This suggestion seems to me to carry the doctrine of mitigation a stage further than it has been carried in any case to which I have been referred. The classic statement of the doctrine is that of Lord Haldane in *British Westinghouse Electric and Manufacturing Co Ltd v Underground Electric Railways Co of London Ltd.*

Ought then the plaintiff as a reasonable man to enter on the litigation suggested? It was agreed that the defendant must offer him an indemnity against the costs, and it was suggested on the defendant's behalf that if an adequate indemnity were offered, if, secondly, the proposed defendant appeared to be solvent, and if, thirdly, there were a good *prima facie* right of action against that person, it was the duty of the injured party to embark on litigation in order to mitigate the damage suffered. This is a proposition which, in such general terms, I am not prepared to accept, nor do I think I ought to entertain it here, because I am by no means certain that the foundations for it exist.

It may be conceded that the indemnity offered would be adequate and that Colonel Wilks is a man of substance. It was clear, however, that he would resist any claim and would in his turn claim over against his solicitors, for that was his attitude in the witness box.

I do not propose to attempt to decide whether an action against Colonel Wilks would lie or be fruitful. I can see it would be one attended with no little difficulty. I am of opinion that the so called duty to mitigate does not go so far as to oblige the injured party, even under an indemnity, to embark on a complicated and difficult piece of litigation against a third party. The damage to the plaintiff was done once and for all directly the voidable conveyance to him was executed. This was the direct result of the negligent advice tendered by his solicitor, the defendant, that a good title had been shown; and, in my judgment, it is no part of the plaintiff's duty to embark on the proposed litigation in order to protect his solicitor from the consequences of his own carelessness.

Not increasing loss

The claimant must not take any unreasonable steps which have the effect of increasing the loss as a result of the defendant's breach of contract. Similar factors to those outlined in the previous section are also considered here.

Generally, reasonable costs may be incurred in order to offset the effect of the breach of duty. For example, interest payable as a result of having to borrow money in order to purchase a replacement will be recoverable, so long as the additional amounts paid are not unreasonable.

In *Compania Financiera Soleada SA v Hamoor Tanker Corpn Inc,*[42] the parties entered into a contract for the management of a ship. The owners of the ship agreed to reimburse the managers in respect of any expenses incurred. In

---

42 *The Borag* [1981] 1 WLR 274.

1971, the managers incurred very heavy expenditure on repairs. When the owners failed to make prompt payment, the managers caused the ship to be arrested at Cape Town. These actions amounted to a breach of contract on the part of the managers.

In order to free the ship from arrest, the owners had to borrow substantial amounts of money which resulted in them having to pay compound interest of £95,000, which amount they sought to recover in an action for damages.

The Court of Appeal held that the expense incurred by the owners was wholly unreasonable and was not recoverable either because of the rule on mitigation or because the loss suffered was too remote:

Compania Financiera Soleada SA v Hamoor Tanker Corpn Inc, The Borag [1981] 1 WLR 274, CA, p 283

Templeman LJ: Approaching the consequences of that breach of contract with the spectacles adopted by the managers, it was reasonably foreseeable that the owners would seek to procure the release of their vessel arrested in breach of contract and, for this purpose, they might obtain a guarantee for payment of their debt, and they would incur expense in obtaining a guarantee. That expense, if reasonable, would be recoverable as foreseeable damages.

Approaching the case with the slightly different coloured spectacles put on by the owners, the obtaining of a guarantee was a reasonable form of mitigation. The reasonable expenses of obtaining a guarantee must be recoverable whichever pair of spectacles is adopted, either as being foreseeable damages or as being expenses of mitigation.

The owners paid a commission and bank charges to obtain a guarantee from their bankers. The umpire held that the commission and the bank charges were recoverable from the managers. Subsequently to the grant of the guarantee, the bankers debited an overdraft account of the owners with interest, compounded by quarterly rests, on the maximum sum secured by the guarantee. The owners submitted to and accepted liability for these interest charges were not recoverable from the managers.

The owners had ample opportunity in the course of the arbitration to explain and justify their submission to interest charges in respect of money which they had never borrowed. Paragraphs 79 to 87 of the findings of fact requested by the owners were designed to establish that it was reasonable and necessary for the owners to incur and pay the interest charges. Conversely, the managers had ample opportunity in the course of the arbitration to establish that the interest charges were wholly unreasonable or, alternatively, partly unreasonable. Paragraphs 56 to 82 of the findings of fact requested by the managers were designed to establish that it was unreasonable for the owners to incur and pay the interest charges.

It is inconceivable that the umpire overlooked the necessity of making up his mind on these problems and overlooked the necessity of deciding in brief whether it was reasonable or unreasonable for the owners to incur these interest charges.

It was thus the task of the umpire to determine whether or not the interest charges were reasonable. This was not a difficult path for an umpire to follow. Unfortunately, the umpire was plunged into a murky pool and was urged to distinguish between the shallow end of mitigation of damages, the middle depths of causation of damages, and the deep end of remoteness of damages. It is not surprising that the umpire reported the results of his journey, and short-circuited the requests for detailed findings of fact, and avoided the legal arguments to which he had been subjected, and avoided everything except the ultimate answer, namely that the interest charges were not reasonably foreseeable damages suffered by the owners as a result of the manager's breach of contract ...

The umpire found that the owners submitted to the interest charges because, as Lord Denning MR has quoted, they 'operated on the basis of a very substantial bank overdraft (finding this method of conducting their business convenient ...)', and he held that 'the interest charges ... are not recoverable as damages naturally and foreseeably flowing from the wrongful arrest'. To reach this conclusion, he must have determined that the interest charges were unreasonable and unnecessary; and, although as between the owners and their bank it may have suited the owners in their business interests and having regard to their relationship with their bankers to suffer this interest, nevertheless as between the owners and the managers the interest charges were wholly unreasonable and should not have been incurred.

Whatever principle is invoked, whether it be the principle of causation or mitigation, the acid test in the present circumstances must have been reasonableness; and, if the interest charges were unreasonable, they were not damages for which the managers are liable. I agree with counsel for the owners that, in some circumstances, different principles may require different tests and produce different results, but, in the present case, if the interest charges were unreasonable, they were too remote; they were not caused by the breach; they were not part of a reasonable form of mitigation; all these matters hang together. In view of the fact that the umpire found that the interest charges were not recoverable and were not damages which were foreseeable, I have no doubt that he concluded that the interest charges were wholly unreasonable for the purpose of any and every principle which had been canvassed before him. As I said, he avoided all the detailed questions he was asked to find on and all the theoretical aspects of the matter and simply ruled that the interest charges were not recoverable.

I too would restore the umpire's award.

The courts will also take account of the claimant's business reputation in deciding what is reasonable.

In *Banco de Portugal v Waterlow & Sons Ltd*,[43] the defendants, in breach of contract, delivered a large number of bank notes to a criminal, who put them into circulation. The plaintiff bank had ordered the notes, and undertook to exchange them. This was held to be reasonable, bearing in mind the bank's

---

43 [1932] AC 452.

commercial obligations to the public. The defendants were held liable for the full face value of the notes, rather than for the cost of printing alone:

Banco de Portugal v Waterlow & Sons Ltd [1932] AC 452, p 468

Viscount Sankey LC: The main questions in the appeal are briefly: (a) Whether the bank, issuing an inconvertible currency, that is, having the right to issue notes, but no obligation to honour them otherwise than by giving in exchange other notes, until some future return to convertibility at a date so remote and unlikely to occur that it could not be taken practically into account, suffered any other than a merely nominal loss (apart from the cost of printing) when they called in bad notes put into circulation by forgers and gave good notes in exchange for them; (b) whether in the circumstances of this case the bank, when they gave in exchange for a forged note of the face value of 500 escudos a good note of that face value, could properly be said to have suffered a loss of 500 escudos, with the result that Waterlows, who are liable by reason of a breach of contract which enabled the forged notes to be put into circulation, are bound to pay to the bank 500 escudos converted into sterling at the rate current at the date of the loss; (c) whether the bank gave evidence of, or proved, any loss at all; (d) whether, if the bank proved any loss, such loss was not caused in whole or in part by the voluntary action of the bank themselves or was not in whole or in part such a loss could not fairly and reasonably be considered as arising naturally from the breach of contract or such a loss as could not be reasonably supposed to have been in contemplation by both parties at the time of making the contract as the probable result of the breach, or whether the loss was not aggravated by the failure of the bank to take reasonable steps to limit the loss. Messrs Waterlow, on appeal, did not dispute the proposition that they were guilty of a breach of absolute duty under an implied term of the contract.

In England, the law is that a person is not obliged to minimise damages on behalf of another who has broken a contract if by doing so he would have injured his commercial reputation by getting a bad name in the trade: *James Finlay & Co Ltd v NV Kwik Hoo Tong, Handel Maatschappij*. The evidence is that the bank – remembering always that they were the issuing bank of the paper currency – had to protect before anything else the confidence which such currency inspired in the Portuguese public. 'What confidence', they asked, 'would all the other notes of the Bank of Portugal merit if the bank did not adopt such a policy?' 'It is one', they say, 'always adopted and similar to that adopted as a rule by banks of issue, even when they can allege the forgery is manifest and that the public has not taken the precautions necessary in receiving false notes.' I have come to the conclusion that the bank would have been failing in their duty to their shareholders, their customers and their country if they had not taken the step they did.

In my opinion, these findings are correct, and the bank had no alternative on 7 December, but to do what they, in fact, did. They were in a position of extreme difficulty and extreme danger, caused, as I think, by the unfortunate and unwitting breach of contract on the part of Messrs Waterlow. As the bank urge, for a country to find that what it believed to be a substantial portion of its legal wealth was nothing more than worthless pieces of paper instead of genuine notes of the bank would have created an economic panic and confusion which would have caused the gravest damage to the credit of the bank and might even have shaken the whole economic and commercial life of the country.

ANTICIPATORY BREACH OF CONTRACT

Where the defendant is in breach of contract and the claimant seeks damages in respect of that breach, the claimant comes under an obligation to mitigate his/her loss. However, the position is potentially different in the case of an anticipatory breach of contract, namely where the defendant conducts him/herself in such a way as to lead the claimant to believe, prior to the due date for performance, that no performance will be forthcoming.

Where there is an anticipatory repudiation of the contract, the innocent party is traditionally thought to be under a duty to mitigate his loss only if he accepts the repudiation and pursues his normal remedies for breach of contract.

In *Melachrino v Nicholl and Knight & Co Ltd*,[44] the seller of goods repudiated the contract of sale in advance of the date for performance at a time when the market price was in excess of the contract price. However, by the time the date of performance had arrived, the market price had fallen to a level below the contract price. The buyers went to arbitration on 14 December and claimed damages based on the difference between the contract price and the market price at the time of repudiation. However, the court was only prepared to award nominal damages:

Melachrino v Nicholl and Knight & Co Ltd [1920] 1 KB 693, p 697

Bailhache J: Anticipatory breach occurs when the seller refuses to deliver before the contractual time for delivery and the buyer accepts his refusal as a breach of contract.

In that case, the following rules are well established, subject, of course, to any express provisions to the contrary in any particular contract.

Immediately upon the anticipatory breach, the buyer may bring his action whether he buys against the seller or not.

It is the duty of the buyer to go into the market and buy against the defaulting seller if a reasonable opportunity offers. This is expressed in the phrase 'It is the buyer's duty to mitigate damages'. In that event, the damages are assessed with reference to the market price on the date of the repurchase. If the buyer does not perform his duty in this respect, the seller is none the less entitled to have damages assessed at the date when a fresh contract might and ought to have been made.

---

44 [1920] 1 KB 693.

As a corollary to this rule, the buyer may if he pleases go into the market and buy against the seller: as he is bound to do so to mitigate damages, so he is entitled to do so to cover himself against his commitments or to secure the goods. In that case again, the damages are assessed with reference to the market price at the date of repurchase.

It is also settled law that when default is made by the seller by refusal to deliver within the contract time the buyer is under no duty to accept the repudiation and buy against him but may claim the difference between the contract price and the market price at the date when under the contract the goods should have been delivered.

It looks, therefore, at first sight as though the date at which the difference between the contract price and the market price ought to be taken for assessment of damages when the buyer does not buy against the seller should follow by analogy the rule adopted where the buyer goes into the market and buys, or where the breach is failure to deliver at the due date and should be at or about the date when the buyer intimates his acceptance of the repudiation though he does not actually go into the market against the seller. If so, in this case, the date would be about 14 December, when the buyer claimed arbitration ... Against this line of reasoning, it must be remembered that the object of damages is to place a person whose contract is broken in as nearly as possible the same position as if it had been performed. This result is secured by measuring damages either at the date of the repurchase, in the case of repurchase on an anticipatory breach, or at the date when the goods ought to have been delivered when there is no anticipatory breach whether there is a repurchase or not. In these cases, the buyer gets a new contract and the defaulting seller pays the extra expense incurred by the buyer in restoring his position.

Where however there is an anticipatory breach but no buying against the defaulting seller, and the price falls below the contract price between the date of the anticipatory breach and the date when the goods ought to have been delivered, the adoption of the date of the anticipatory breach as the date when the market price ought to be taken would put the buyer in a better position than if his contract had been duly performed. He would if that date were adopted be given a profit and retain his money wherewith to to buy the goods if so minded on the fall of the market. It would be in effect, to use a homely phrase, to allow him to have his cake and eat it ... In my opinion, the true rule is that where there is an anticipatory breach by a seller to deliver goods for which there is a market at a fixed date the buyer without buying against the seller may bring his action at once, but that if he does so his damages must be assessed with reference to the market price of the goods at the time when they ought to have been delivered under the contract ... The result in this case is that the damages are nominal.

However, if the party not in breach rejects the repudiation and keeps the contract in existence, no duty to mitigate will arise.[45] Where a party is found to have acted wholly unreasonably in refusing to accept a repudiation, he will be limited to an action for damages, which will require the innocent party to mitigate his loss.[46]

---

45   *Tredegar Iron and Coal Co Ltd v Hawthorn* (1902) 18 TLR 716; *White and Carter (Councils) Ltd v McGregor* [1962] AC 413. Contrast the seemingly more sensible approach in the US (*Restatement, Contracts* (2nd), para 388), under which the party not in breach cannot enhance his/her damages by unreasonably omitting to act in a way which would prevent harm. To a limited extent, English law appears to be moving in this direction following the decision in *Clea Shipping Corpn v Bulk Oil International Ltd, The Alaskan Trader* [1984] 1 All ER 129.

46   *Clea Shipping Corpn v Bulk Oil International Ltd, The Alaskan Trader* [1984] 1 All ER 129, p 137, *per* Lloyd J.

CHAPTER 13

QUANTIFICATION OF DAMAGES

TYPES OF DAMAGE

Losses suffered as a result of a breach of contract are of three possible varieties, namely personal injury, property damage and economic loss. Since contracts are essentially concerned with the exchange of economic resources between the parties, it is more likely than not that the most frequently encountered loss resulting from a breach of contract will be of the economic variety. However, it should not be forgotten that a breach of contract might also result in physical harm to the person or to property. For example, defective food sold by a retailer is more likely to result in a complaint by the consumer that he/she has suffered some illness than a complaint to the effect that the food is not worth the amount paid for it at the checkout. Similarly, while a defective motor supplied for use by a lobster farmer may well cause economic loss in the form of lost profit if the motor malfunctions, but it is also just as likely to result in the death of the lobsters, thereby occasioning property damage as well.[1]

PERSONAL INJURIES INCLUDING MENTAL DISTRESS

Personal injury is normally seen as the province of the law of tort, in particular the tort of negligence, to which important policy considerations apply. Where a person suffers personal injuries as a result of the wrongful conduct of another, the objective of an award of damages is to compensate him for his loss. This is achieved, so far as is possible, by means of a monetary payment, by placing him in the position he would have occupied had the wrong not been committed. The majority of claims for personal injuries are based in the law of tort, but the same principle applies to actions for breach of contract, subject to the apparently different rules on causation and remoteness of damage.[2] Accordingly, if a buyer purchases a defective plastic catapult which breaks in use with the result that the user suffers injury to the eye and endures pain and suffering, these losses are recoverable in an action for damages for breach of contract as items of consequential loss.[3]

---

1 See, eg, *Muirhead v Industrial Tank Specialities Ltd* [1986] 1 QB 507; and also note *Parsons v Uttley Ingham* [1978] QB 791 – see Chapter 12.

2 See Chapter 12.

3 *Godley v Perry* [1960] 1 WLR 9.

The reason for treating personal injury claims separately is that they raise problems not encountered in actions for other types of loss. In an action for financial loss, monetary compensation is adequate. Similarly, physical damage to property can be compensated by a monetary payment equivalent to the market value of the property damaged. But, where a person loses a leg or suffers pain, money is the only compensation available, but the market value of a leg or pain is impossible to ascertain. The concentration of English law on property rights appears to be to blame for this. As far as possible, the courts have treated personal injuries as depriving a person of a property right, but this approach is difficult to justify in relation to subjective losses, such as pain, suffering and mental distress.

A particular variety of loss which creates difficulty of assessment of damage is that of mental distress. Such distress can be caused in one of two ways. In the first place, it may be distress consequent on physical injury and, secondly, it may result from some cause quite separate from any form of physical harm. The first of these two is readily dealt with as a variety of consequential loss, and provided it is not too remote it should be recoverable. The second variety is more problematic, but it should not be believed that English law gives no remedy for mental distress. In the first place, just as in the law of tort, an action for damages for breach of contract will be allowed where it is foreseeable at the time of contracting that the claimant might suffer psychiatric harm. For example, in *Cook v Swinfen*,[4] the respondent solicitors negligently handled a divorce action with the result that the appellant, their client, suffered from an anxiety neurosis. In the event, it was held, on the facts, that a breakdown in health was not a foreseeable consequence of the failed litigation, but the court, nonetheless accepted that had it been a foreseeable loss, it would have been actionable.[5]

The expression mental distress covers not just psychiatric harm, but also grief, disappointment, fear or worry suffered as a result of the defendant's wrong. These lesser forms of distress are treated differently and are not to be treated as types of personal injury in the normal sense.

In the sense that an award of damages for distress compensates the claimant for harm caused by the defendant's breach of contract, the award appears to protect the claimant's status quo interest. However, in many of the cases which an award of damages is given for mental distress, it is because the contract entered into by the parties was designed to alleviate distress in the first place. In this sense, the claimant would have had an expectation that he would not suffer the distress or inconvenience which results from the defendant's breach of contract. An unfortunate aspect of the cases concerned

---

4   [1967] 1 WLR 457.
5   *Ibid*, p 460, *per* Lord Denning MR.

with mental distress is that there is a piecemeal approach to the question, under which sometimes the award is disguised as aggravated damages.

The traditional rule is that damages are not recoverable for mental distress caused by a breach of contract.

In *Addis v Gramophone Co Ltd*,[6] the plaintiff was employed by the defendant on a salary of £15 per week plus commission under terms which allowed him to be dismissed by six months' notice. He was given six months' notice but, at the same time, the defendants also immediately appointed a successor, with the result that the plaintiff was unable to earn any commission and was unable to work as a manager. At first instance, he was awarded only his lost commission and damages for wrongful dismissal. On appeal, the question arose whether he was entitled to damages in respect of his injured feelings resulting from the demeaning way in which he had been dismissed. The House of Lords held that such an award could not be made and that the plaintiff was entitled to recover his lost commission and lost salary:

Addis v Gramophone Co Ltd [1909] AC 488, p 493

Lord Atkinson: The rights of the plaintiff are ... in my opinion, clear. He had been illegally dismissed from his employment. He could have been legally dismissed by the six months' notice which he in fact received, but the defendants did not wait for the expiration of that period. The damages which he sustained by this illegal dismissal were: (i) the wages for the six months during which his former notice would have been current; (ii) the profits or commission which would, in all reasonable probability, have been earned by him during the six months, had he continued in the employment; and, possibly (iii) damages in respect of the time which might reasonably elapse before he could obtain other employment. He has been awarded a sum of some hundreds of pounds, not in respect of any of these heads of damage, but in respect of the harsh and humiliating way in which he was dismissed, including, presumably, the pain which he experienced, as is alleged, by reason of the imputation upon him conveyed by the manner of his dismissal. This is the only circumstance which makes the case of general importance, and this is the only point with which I think it necessary to deal.

I have been unable to find any case decided in this country in which any countenance is given to the notion that a dismissed employee can recover, in the shape of exemplary damages for illegal dismissal, in effect, damages for defamation except the case of *Maw v Jones*.

I have always understood that damages for breach of contract were in the nature of compensation, not punishment, and that the general rule of law applicable to such cases was in effect that stated by Cockburn CJ in *Engell v Fitch* in these words: 'By the law, as a general rule, a vendor who from whatever cause fails to perform his contract is bound, as was said by Lord Wensleydale in a case which has been referred to, to place the purchaser, so far

---

6   [1909] AC 488.

as money will do it, in the position in which he would have been if the contract had been performed. If a man sells a cargo of goods not yet come to hand, which he believes to have been consigned to him from abroad, and the goods fail to arrive, it will be no answer to the intending purchaser to say that a third party, who had engaged to consign the goods to seller, had deceived or disappointed him. The purchaser will be entitled to the difference between the contract price and the market price.'

In *Sikes v Wild*, Blackburn J says: 'I do not know how misconduct can alter the rule of law by which damages for breach of contract are to be assessed. It may render the contract voidable on the ground of fraud, or give a cause of action for deceit, but surely it cannot alter the effect of the contract itself.'

There are three well known exceptions to the general rule applicable to the measure of damages for breach of contract, namely, actions against a banker for refusing to pay a customer's cheque when he has in his hands funds of the customer's to meet it; actions for breach of promise to marry; and actions like that in *Flureau v Thornhill*, where the vendor of real estate, without any fault on his part, fails to make a title. I know of none other. The peculiar nature of the first two of these exceptions justifies their existence. Ancient practice upholds the last, though it has often been adversely criticised, as in *Bain v Fothergill*. If there be a tendency to create a fourth exception, it ought, in my view, to be checked rather than stimulated, in as much as to apply in their entirety the principles on which damages are measured in tort to cases of damages for breaches of contract would lead to uncertainty and confusion in commercial affairs, while to apply them only in part and, in particular cases, would create anomalies, lead occasionally to injustice, and make the law a still more lawless science that it is said to be. For instance, in actions of tort, motive, if it may be taken into account to aggravate damages, as undoubtedly it may be, may also be taken into account to mitigate them, as may also the conduct of the plaintiff himself who seeks redress. Is this rule to be applied to actions for breach of contract? There are few breaches of contract more frequent than those which arise where men omit or refuse to repay what they have borrowed, or to pay for what they have bought. Is the creditor or vendor who sues for one of such breaches to have the sum which he recovers lessened if he should be shown to be harsh, grasping, or pitiless, or even insulting in enforcing his demand or lessened because the debtor has struggled to pay, has failed because of misfortune, and has been suave, gracious, and apologetic in his refusal? On the other hand, is that sum to be increased if it should be shown that the debtor could have paid readily without any embarrassment, but refused with expressions of contempt and contumely from a malicious desire to injure his creditor? Few parties to contracts have more often to complain of ingratitude and baseness than sureties. Are they, because of this, to be entitled to recover from the principal, often a trusted friend who has deceived and betrayed them, more than they paid on that principal's behalf? If circumstances of aggravation are rightly to be taken into account in actions of contract at all, why should they not be taken into account in the case of the surety, and the rules and principles applicable to cases of tort applied to the full extent?

In many other cases of breach of contract, there may be circumstances of malice, fraud, defamation, or violence, which would sustain an action of tort as an alternative remedy to an action for breach of contract. If one should select the former mode of redress he may, no doubt, recover exemplary damages, or what are sometimes styled 'vindictive' damages; but if he should choose to seek redress in the form of an action for breach of contract, he lets in all the consequences of that form of action: *Thorpe v Thorpe*. One of the consequences, is, I think, that he is to be paid adequate compensation in money for the loss of that which he would have received had his contract been kept, and no more. I can conceive nothing more objectionable and embarrassing in litigation than trying in effect an action of libel or slander as a matter of aggravation in an action for illegal dismissal, the defendant being permitted, as he must in justice be permitted, to traverse the defamatory sense, rely on privilege, and raise every point which he could raise in an independent action brought for the alleged libel or slander itself.

Moreover, it is especially clear that, in contracts of a purely commercial nature, it is unlikely in the extreme that a court will award damages for distress, inconvenience or disappointment. It would appear that only consumers can suffer these varieties of harm.

In *Hayes v James & Charles Dodd (A Firm)*,[7] the plaintiffs operated a motor vehicle repair business which they wished to expand by purchasing larger premises. They entered into negotiations to purchase the lease on a workshop. The defendants, a firm of solicitors, who were acting for the plaintiffs, informed their clients that there was access to the workshop via land at the rear of the premises when, in fact, there was no such access. The existence of a right of access was crucial so as to allow the free movement of vehicles to and from the premises. Having purchased the premises, including an attached, freehold maisonette, for £65,000 with the assistance of a bank loan of £55,000, the plaintiffs discovered that the owner of the land to the rear had blocked off the only means of access, with the result that they were unable to run their business. Subsequently, the plaintiffs closed their business and were forced to sell part of the property at a loss. They were awarded damages representing both the capital expenditure incurred in the purchase of the premises and damages for anguish and vexation. In the Court of Appeal, it was held that damages in this last respect were not recoverable as a result of the breach of a purely commercial contract:

Hayes v James & Charles Dodd (A Firm) [1990] 2 All ER 815, CA, p 818

Staughton LJ:

Basis of assessment

The first question in this appeal relates to the basis on which damages should be assessed. Like Hurst J I start with the principle stated by Lord Blackburn in

---

7   [1990] 2 All ER 815, CA.

Livingstone v Rawyards Coal Co (1880) 5 App Cas 25, p 39: '... you should as nearly as possible get at that sum of money which will put the party who has been injured, or who has suffered, in the same position as he would have been in if he had not sustained the wrong for which he is now getting his compensation or reparation.'

One must therefore ascertain the actual situation of the plaintiffs and compare it with their situation if the breach of contract had not occurred.

What, then, was the breach of contract? It was not the breach of any warranty that there was a right of way: the defendant solicitors gave no such warranty. This is an important point: see *Perry v Sidney Phillips & Son (A Firm)* [1982] 3 All ER 705; [1982] 1 WLR 1297. The breach was of the solicitors' promise to use reasonable skill and care in advising their clients. If they had done that, they would have told the plaintiffs that there was no right of way; and it is clear that, on the receipt of such advice, the plaintiffs would have decided not to enter into the transaction at all. They would have bought no property, spent no money and borrowed none from the bank.

That at first sight is the situation which one should compare with the actual financial state of the plaintiffs. I will call this the 'no-transaction method'. There are, however, authorities which show that, instead, one takes for the first element in the comparison the situation which the plaintiff would have been in if the transaction had gone through in accordance with his legitimate expectations. This I call the 'successful-transaction method'. Thus, in *Perry's* case, the plaintiff recovered from negligent surveyors the difference between the value of the house at the date when he bought it if it had not been defective and its actual value at that date. However, it appears to have been found, or assumed, in that case that the plaintiff would still have bought the house if he had been given correct advice as to its condition, albeit at a lower price. It was not a case where he would never have entered into the transaction at all ...

The difference between the two methods is unlikely to be of importance in a case which concerns some commodity that is readily saleable, such as peas or beans, and if there is no difficulty or delay in ascertaining that a breach has occurred. A plaintiff who has agreed to buy beans at the current market price and has received a quantity which is defective can sell them forthwith and realise their actual value. If he intended to perform a profitable subcontract, he can buy other beans in the market for that purpose. In such a case it makes no difference whether damages are assessed on the no-transaction method, so that he recovers the price paid less the sum realised on disposition of the defective beans, or on the successful-transaction method, which gives him the difference between the value of sound beans and the value of defective beans.

However, this case is not concerned with a readily saleable commodity: it took the plaintiffs nearly five years from the date of their purchase to dispose of the maisonette, and another year expired before they were free from the obligations imposed by the lease of the workshop and yard. During all that period, they were incurring expenses, such as rent and other items, together with interest on the money which they had borrowed from the bank. Furthermore, they did not receive, until the first year had almost expired, any acknowledgment by the defendants that there was, in fact, no right of way;

that only happened on 6 July 1983, whereas they had completed their purchase on 28 July 1982, and the right of way had first been challenged two days later.

I am quite satisfied that Hirst J was entitled to award damages in this case on the no transaction basis, and that he was right to do so. Indeed, it may well be that the plaintiffs were, as he held, entitled to elect between that method and the successful-transaction method; but I need not express any concluded view on that. So, they should recover all the money which they spent, less anything which they subsequently recovered, provided always that they acted reasonably in mitigating their loss. But they were quite properly denied any sum for the profit which they would have made if they had operated their business successfully ...

Mental distress

Hirst J awarded £1,500 to each of the plaintiffs under this head. There can be no doubt, and it was accepted in this court, that each of them suffered vexation and anguish over the years to a serious extent, for which the sum awarded was but modest compensation. There is, however, an important question of principle involved.

For my part, I would have wished for a rather more elaborate argument than we received on this point, before deciding it, since the law seems to be in some doubt. But I would be most reluctant to impose on the plaintiffs, on top of their other misfortunes, two or three days of scholarly argument whether and in what circumstances damages can be awarded for mental distress consequent on breach of contract in a business transaction, possibly at their expense, when the sum involved is only £3,000 or roughly 3% of their total claim. The difficulty is that almost any other case where a plaintiff claims to have suffered mental distress would present a similar problem, that the individual plaintiff ought not to be expected to be a the burden and perhaps also the cost of an elaborate argument. If, as I think, the law needs clarification, it is to be hoped that a case can be found where that will be provided by the House of Lords. Or it may be that the Law Commission can supply it.

Like the judge, I consider that the English courts should be wary or adopting what he called 'the United States' practice of huge awards'. Damages awarded for negligence or want of skill, whether against professional men or anyone else, must provide fair compensation, but no more than that. And I would not view with enthusiasm the prospect that every shipowner in the Commercial Court, having successfully claimed for unpaid freight or demurrage, would be able to add a claim for mental distress suffered while he was waiting for his money.

In a sense, the wrong done to the plaintiffs in this action, for which they seek compensation under this head, lay in the defendants' failure to admit liability at an early stage. On 6 July 1983, the defendants acknowledged that there was no right of way, but denied negligence. Had they on that very day admitted liability and tendered a sum on account of damages, or offered interim reparation in some other form, the anxiety of the plaintiffs, and their financial problems, could have been very largely relieved. But liability was not admitted until January 1987. I believe that in one or more American states, damages are awarded for wrongfully defending an action. But there is no such remedy in this country, so far as I am aware.

In *Perry v Sidney Phillips & Son (A Firm)* [1982] 3 All ER 705; [1982] 1 WLR 1297, damages were awarded for the distress, worry, inconvenience and trouble which the plaintiff had suffered while living in the house he bought, owing to the defects which his surveyor had overlooked. Lord Denning MR considered that these consequences were reasonably foreseeable (see [1982] 3 All ER 705, p 709; [1982] 1 WLR 1297, p 1302). Kerr LJ stated a narrower test ([1982] 3 All ER 705, p 712; [1982] 1 WLR 1297, p 1307): 'So far as the question of damages for vexation and inconvenience is concerned, it should be noted that the deputy judge awarded these not for the tension or frustration of a person who is involved in a legal dispute in which the other party refuses to meet its liabilities. If he had done so, it would have been wrong, because such aggravation is experienced by almost all litigants. He awarded these damages because of the physical consequences of the breach, which were all foreseeable at the time. The fact that in such cases damages under this head may be recoverable, if they have been suffered but not otherwise, is supported by the decision of this court in *Hutchinson v Harris* (1978) 10 Build LR 19.'

I would emphasise the reference to physical consequences of the breach.

I am not convinced that it is enough to ask whether mental distress was reasonably foreseeable as a consequence, or even whether it should reasonably have been contemplated as not unlikely to result from a breach of contract. It seems to me that damages for mental distress in contract are, as a matter of policy, limited to certain classes of case. I would broadly follow the classification provided by Dillon LJ in *Bliss v South East Thames Regional Health Authority* [1987] ICR 700, p 718: '... where the contract which has been broken was itself a contract to provide peace of mind or freedom from distress ...'

It may be that the class is somewhat wider than that. But it should not, in my judgment, include any case where the object of the contract was not comfort or pleasure, or the relief or discomfort, but simply carrying on a commercial activity with a view to profit. So, I would disallow the item of damages for anguish and vexation.

However, a number of important exceptions to the *Addis* principle have been developed. For example, where the objective of the contract is to confer either enjoyment, such as where a holiday is ruined,[8] relief from distress[9] or where the distress is consequent on physical inconvenience caused by the breach of contract:[10]

---

8   *Jarvis v Swans Tours* [1973] QB 233. See, also, *Diesen v Samson* 1971 SLT 49 (wedding photographs lost by photographer).

9   *Heywood v Wellers* [1976] QB 446 (solicitor employed to obtain non-molestation order).

10 *Perry v Sidney Phillips & Son (A Firm)* [1982] 1 WLR 1297 (distress caused by professional surveyor who had been engaged to provide peace of mind); *Bailey v Bullock* [1950] 2 All ER 1167 (inconvenience caused to client in having to live with his parents-in-law when solicitor failed to take proceedings for the recovery of the client's house). In *Farley v Skinner* (2000) *The Times*, 14 April, the Court of Appeal refused (by a majority) to accept that disturbance by aircraft noise amounted to physical inconvenience and discomfort.

Jarvis v Swan's Tours Ltd [1973] QB 233, CA, p 235

Lord Denning MR: Mr Jarvis is a solicitor, employed by a local authority at Barking. In 1969, he was minded to go for Christmas to Switzerland. He was looking forward to a skiing holiday. It is his one fortnight's holiday in the year. He prefers it in the winter rather than in the summer.

Mr Jarvis read a brochure issued by Swans Tours Ltd. He was much attracted by the description of Mörlialp, Giswil, Central Switzerland. I will not read the whole of it, but just pick out some of the principal attractions:

> House Party Centre with special resident host ...

> Mörlialp is a most wonderful little resort on a sunny plateau ... Up there, you will find yourself in the midst of beautiful alpine scenery, which in winter becomes a wonderland of sun, snow and ice, with a wide variety of fine ski-runs, a skating rink and exhilarating toboggan run ... Why did we choose the Hotel Krone ... mainly and most of all because of the 'Gemütlichkeit' and friendly welcome you will receive from Herr and Frau Weibel ... The Hotel Krone has its own Alphütte Bar which will be open several evenings a week ... No doubt, you will be in for a great time, when you book this house party holiday ... Mr Weibel, the charming owner, speaks English.

On the same page, in a special yellow box, it was said:

> Swans House Party in Mörlialp. All these House Party arrangements are included in the price of your holiday. Welcome party on arrival. Afternoon tea and cake for 7 days. Swiss dinner by candlelight. Fondue party. Yodler evening. Chali farewell party in the 'Alphütte Bar'. Service of representative.

Alongside on the same page, there was a special note about ski-packs – 'Hire of Skis, Sticks and Boots ... Ski Tuition ... 12 days £11.10'.

In August 1969, on the faith of that brochure, Mr Jarvis booked a 15 day holiday, with ski-pack. The total charge was £63.45, including Christmas supplement. He was to fly from Gatwick to Zurich on 20 December 1969 and return on 3 January, 1970.

The plaintiff went on the holiday, but he was very disappointed. He was a man of about 35 and he expected to be one of a house party of some 30 or so people. Instead, he found there were only 13 during the first week. In the second week, there was no house party at all. He was the only person there. Mr Weibel could not speak English. So there was Mr Jarvis, in the second week, in this hotel with no house party at all, and no one could speak English except himself. He was very disappointed, too, with the skiing. It was some distance away at Giswil. There were no ordinary length skis. There were only mini-skis, about three feet long. So, he did not get his skiing as he wanted to. In the second week, he did get some longer skis for a couple of days, but then, because of the boots, his feet got rubbed and he could not continue even with the long skis. So his skiing holiday, from his point of view, was pretty well ruined.

There were many other matters, too. They appear trivial when they are set down in writing, but I have no doubt they loomed large in Mr Jarvis's mind when coupled with the other disappointments. He did not have the nice Swiss cakes which he was hoping for. The only cakes for tea were potato crisps and little dry nut cakes. The yodler evening consisted of one man from the locality who came in his working clothes for a little while, and sang four or five songs very quickly. The 'Alphütte Bar' was an unoccupied annexe which was only open one evening. There was a representative, Mrs Storr, there during the first week, but she was not there during the second week.

The matter was summed up by the judge:

> During the first week, he got a holiday in Switzerland which was, to some extent, inferior ... and, as to the second week, he got a holiday which was very largely inferior to what he was led to expect.

What is the legal position? I think that the statements in the brochure were representations or warranties. The breaches of them give Mr Jarvis a right to damages. It is not necessary to decide whether they were representations or warranties: because, since the Misrepresentation Act 1967, there is a remedy in damages for misrepresentation as well as for breach of warranty.

The one question in the case is: what is the amount of damages? The judge seems to have taken the difference in value between what he paid for and what he got. He said that he intended to give 'the difference between the two values and no other damages' under any other head. He thought that Mr Jarvis had got half of what he paid for. So, the judge gave him half the amount which he had paid, namely, £31.72. Mr Jarvis appeals to this court. He says that the damages ought to have been much more.

There is one point I must mention first. Consel together made a very good note of the judge's judgment. They agreed it. It is very clear and intelligible. It shows plainly enough the ground of the judge's decision: but, by an oversight, it was not submitted to the judge, as it should have been: see *Bruen v Bruce (Practice Note)* [1959] 1 WLR 684. In some circumstances, we should send it back to the judge for his comments. But I do not think we need to do so here. The judge received the notice of appeal and made notes for our consideration. I do not think he would have wished to add to them. We will, therefore, decide the case on the material before us.

What is the right way of assessing damages? It has often been said that, on a breach of contract, damages cannot be given for mental distress. Thus, in *Hamlin v Great Northern Railway Co* (1856) 1 H & N 408, p 411, Pollock CB said that damages cannot be given 'for the disappointment of mind occasioned by the breach of contract'. And, in *Hobbs v London & South Western Railway Co* (1875) LR 10 QB 111, p 122, Mellor J said that:

> ... for the mere inconvenience, such as annoyance and loss of temper, or vexation, or for being disappointed in a particular thing which you have set your mind upon, without real physical inconvenience resulting, you cannot recover damages.

The courts in those days only allowed the plaintiff to recover damages if he suffered physical inconvenience, such as having to walk five miles home, as in *Hobbs'* case; or to live in an overcrowded house: *Bailey v Bullock* [1950] 2 All ER 1167.

I think that those limitations are out of date. In a proper case damages for mental distress can be recovered in contract, just as damages for shock can be recovered in tort. One such case is a contract for a holiday, or any other contract to provide entertainment and enjoyment. If the contracting party breaks his contract, damages can be given for the disappointment, the distress, the upset and frustration caused by the breach. I know that it is difficult to assess in terms of money, but it is no more difficult than the assessment which the courts have to make every day in personal injury cases for loss of amenities. Take the present case. Mr Jarvis has only a fortnight's holiday in the year. He books it far ahead, and looks forward to it all that time. He ought to be compensated for the loss of it.

A good illustration was given by Edmund Davies LJ in the course of the argument. He put the case of a man who has taken a ticket for Glyndbourne. It is the only night on which he can get there. He hires a car to take him. The car does not turn up. His damages are not limited to the mere cost of the ticket. He is entitled to general damages for the disappointment he has suffered and the loss of the entertainment which he should have had. Here, Mr Jarvis's fortnight's winter holiday has been a grave disappointment. It is true that he was conveyed to Switzerland and back and had meals and bed in the hotel. But that is not what he went for. He went to enjoy himself with all the facilities which the defendants said he would have. He is entitled to damages for the lack of those facilities, and for his loss of enjoyment.

A similar case occurred in 1951. It was *Stedman v Swan's Tours* (1951) 95 SJ 727. A holidaymaker was awarded damages because he did not get the bedroom and the accommodation which he was promised. The county court judge awarded him £13.15. This court increased it to £50.

I think the judge was in error in taking the sum paid for the holiday, £63.45, and halving it. The right measure of damages is to compensate him for the loss of entertainment and enjoyment which he was promised, and which he did not get.

Looking at the matter quite broadly, I think the damages in this case should be the sum of £125. I would allow the appeal, accordingly.

An apparent justification for these cases is that the consumer has placed a value on the service provided by the other party which exceeds its market value. Accordingly, what is protected is the consumer's expectation interest and what is compensated is the value placed upon the service by the consumer which is over and above its market value.

Harris, Ogus and Philips[11] comment on this as follows:

This is an example of what economists refer to as 'consumer surplus', the excess utility or subjective value obtained from a 'good' over and above the utility associated with its market price. (As explained below, the consumer surplus expected by a person who intends to use a good is an equivalent to the

---

11   Harris, Ogus and Philips, 1979, pp 582–83, 595–97.

profit which a businessman expects to make from a contract.) The concept of consumer surplus is important in any attempt to measure consumer losses because, unlike firms, consumers make purchases for the pleasure or utility they confer; this utility has no necessary relationship with the price paid, and is of quite a different order from market prices or business profits. It is, of course, difficult to measure utility, but generally economists avoid the conceptual problem by measuring utility in terms of the maximum amount a consumer would pay for a particular purchase. For instance, if a purchaser can buy a plot of land for £1,000, when he would be prepared to pay up to £1,500 for it, the extra £500 represents his 'consumer surplus'. Without using this term, an intending bidder at an auction thinks in this way when he decides beforehand what is the maximum bid, he is prepared to make: the difference between any lower price he pays and the higher price he is prepared to pay measures the consumer surplus expected at that time. Therefore, willingness to pay, rather than market price, is the appropriate measure for estimating the value of a purchase, and the consumer surplus is the difference between this value and the market price.

Consumer surplus may arise from services as well as from the possession of land or goods. Thus, a holiday is generally worth more to the tourist than the price he has to pay for it, and the value to the family of wedding photographs exceeds their price. These illustrations show how individuals value performance of non-commercial contracts.

Damages for non-pecuniary loss

Clearly, one method of recognising a promisee's personal and special interest in the fulfilment of a contractual obligation is to award him a sum on breach which is not referable to any financial criterion. The civil law systems have shown much greater readiness to award 'non-material' or 'non-pecuniary' damages for some breaches of contract. Of particular interest is a provision under the Louisiana Civil Code (itself derived from civilian as opposed to common law influences): 'Where the contract has for its object the gratification of some intellectual enjoyment, whether in religion, morality or taste, or some convenience or other legal gratification, although these are not appreciated in money by the parties, yet damages are due for their breach ...'

The common law systems have traditionally been hesitant to award non-pecuniary damages for breach of contract. This may again be attributed to the failure to distinguish between commercial and consumer contracts and to recognise that almost by definition the latter are concerned with the transfer to the promisee of a benefit to be enjoyed rather than a marketable good. But the absence of the award from the reported cases may also be explained by the fact that in most situations it is assumed that the promisee can avoid the loss by obtaining equivalent satisfaction from a substitute. In other words, the problem would arise only where such substitution was not available. This emerges clearly from a new trend in contract damages which occurred in the 1970s, first in Scotland and then in England. In *Diesen v Samson,* the defendant employed to take photographs at the plaintiff's wedding failed to appear. The Sheriff-Substitute recognised that the photographs would have been of interest to no one except the family and friends of the bridal couple, and therefore had no market value. He nevertheless awarded a sum of £30 for being permanently denied the pleasure in the years ahead from the recollection of a happy occasion. In *Jarvis v Swans Tours Ltd,* the plaintiff's holiday, arranged under a contract with the defendant travel agency, was disappointing in several significant respects compared with what had been promised. The Court of Appeal rejected the argument that the plaintiff should be limited in damages to the difference between the market value of the holiday as promised and that in fact experienced. It awarded a sum for the loss of entertainment and enjoyment, presumably intended to represent the difference between the entertainment and enjoyment reasonably expected and that (positive or negative) actually provided.

While, within the context of contractual remedies, these decisions may be viewed as a new and important development, they nevertheless are consistent with principles long established within the law of tort (ie where the liability arises from a duty imposed by the law itself, independently of an agreement) which may be interpreted as recognising an interest analogous to the consumer surplus: the award of damages for 'loss of amenities' or 'pain and suffering' in an action for personal injuries provides the most frequently encountered example. Here, the sum awarded may be characterised as intended to provide the plaintiff with some alternative pleasure to that lost as a result of the injury, thus recognising that a sound body was worth more to him than its market value (viz its profit earning potential). So, also, where a plaintiff is able to claim damages for the infringement of an interest in property. The invasion of a man's land by a nauseous smell entitled him to substantial damages even though he could not show that the market value of the property had been affected. Finally, in actions based on the destruction of property, there is some authority for assessing damages above the market value to represent sentimental attachment. The notion involved must be that of consumer surplus which arises through association with a particular asset over time and which cannot therefore be obtained from a substitute.[12]

In consumer cases, the limits of the situations in which distress and disappointment' damages can be awarded are not mathematically precise. *Ruxley* (see fn 12) demonstrates that the categories are not closed. *Hayes v Dodd* (above) broadly determines that, in purely commercial cases, such awards are inappropriate. A contract of employment had elements of both the consumer and the commercial (if ultimately *qui generis*). However, *Addis* has traditionally been thought to rule out awards in a typical case of wrongful dismissal, no matter how forcedly accompanied by intense personal distress, perhaps exacerbated by the manner of the dismissal. The conventional 'reading' of *Addis* here, however, has recently been challenged by the House of Lords in *Mahmud and Malik v Bank of Credit and Commerce International SA.*[13]

---

12 An excellent example of a 'consumer surplus' based award is the House of Lords decision in *Ruxley Electronics and Construction Ltd v Forsyth* [1996] 1 AC 344, discussed in the next section. In particular, see Lord Mustull, at p 360.

13 [1998] AC 20.

In *Malik,* the two appellants were (respectively) a branch manager and a senior accounts executive of BCCI before the bank suffered a catastrophic (and notorious) collapse in the summer of 1991. The House of Lords allowed their appeal from a dismissal of their claim for substantial damages because of the way in which the nature of their (ex) employers breach of the implied term of trust and confidence had 'blighted' their future employment prospects. Once made redundant from BCCI, they would be seriously 'tarred with the brush' of the fraud linked to BCCI's collapse. This was, perhaps, less to do with an award for 'distress' *per se* than for the loss to their reputation which the circumstances attending their loss of employment would produce:

Mahmud and Malik v BCCI [1998] AC 20, pp 33–34, 36

Lord Nicholls of Birkenhead: In the Court of Appeal and in your Lordships' House, the parties were agreed that the contracts of employment of these two former employees each contained an implied term to the effect that the bank would not, without reasonable and proper cause, conduct itself in a manner likely to destroy or seriously damage the relationship of confidence and trust between employer and employee. Argument proceeded on this footing and ranged round the type of conduct and other circumstances which could or could not constitute a breach of this implied term. The submissions embraced questions such as the following: whether the trust-destroying conduct must be directed at the employee, either individually or as part of a group; whether an employee must know of the employer's trust-destroying conduct while still employed; and whether the employee's trust must actually be undermined. Furthermore, and at the heart of this case, the submissions raised an important question on the damages recoverable for breach of the implied term, with particular reference to the decisions in *Addis v Gramophone Co Ltd* [1909] AC 488 and *Withers v General Theatre Corporation Ltd* [1933] KB 536.

...

Remedies: (2) damages

Can an employee recover damages for breach of the trust and confidence term when he first learns of the breach after he has left the employment? The answer to this question is inextricably bound up with the further question of what damages are recoverable for a breach of this term. In turn, the answer to this further question is inextricably linked with one aspect of the decision in *Addis v Gramophone Co Ltd* [1909] AC 488.

At first sight, it seems almost a contradiction in terms that an employee can suffer recoverable loss if he first learns of the trust-destroying conduct after the employment contract has already ended for other reasons. But of the many forms which trust-destroying conduct may take, some may have continuing adverse financial effects on an employee, even after his employment has ceased. In such a case the fact that the employee only learned of the employer's conduct after the employment had ended ought not, in principle, to be a bar to recovery. If it were otherwise, an employer who conceals a breach would be better placed than an employer who does not.

Premature termination losses

This proposition calls for elaboration. The starting point is to note that the purpose of the trust and confidence implied term is to facilitate the proper functioning of the contract. If the employer commits a breach of the term and, in consequence, the contract comes to an end prematurely, the employee loses the benefits he should have received had the contract run its course until it expired or was duly terminated. In addition to financial benefits such as salary and commission and pension rights, the losses caused by the premature termination of the contract ('the premature termination losses') may include other promised benefits, for instance a course of training, or publicity for an actor or pop star. *Prima facie*, and subject always to established principles of mitigation and so forth, the dismissed employee can recover damages to compensate him for these promised benefits lost to him in consequence of the premature termination of the contract.

It follows that premature termination losses cannot be attributable to a breach of the trust and confidence term if the contract is terminated for other reasons, for instance, for redundancy or if the employee leaves of his own volition. Since the trust-destroying conduct did not bring about the premature termination of the contract, *ex hypothesi*, the employee did not sustain any loss of pay and so forth by reason of the breach of the trust and confidence term. That is the position in the present case.

Addis v Gramophone Co Ltd

Against this background, I turn to the much discussed case of *Addis v Gramophone Co Ltd* [1909] AC 488. Mr Addis, it will be recalled, was wrongfully and contumeliously dismissed from his post as the defendant's manager in Calcutta. At trial, he was awarded damages exceeding the amount of his salary for the period of notice to which he was entitled. The case is generally regarded as having decided, echoing the words of Lord Loreburn LC, at p 491, that an employee cannot recover damages for the manner in which the wrongful dismissal took place, for injured feelings or for any loss he may sustain from the fact that his having been dismissed of itself makes it more difficult for him to obtain fresh employment. In particular, *Addis*'s case is generally understood to have decided that any loss suffered by the adverse impact on the employee's chances of obtaining alternative employment is to be excluded from an assessment of damages for wrongful dismissal – see, for instance: *O'Laoire v Jackel International Ltd (No 2)* [1991] ICR 718, pp 730–31, following earlier authorities; in Canada, the decision of the Supreme Court in *Vorvis v Insurance Corporation of British Columbia* (1989) 58 DLR (4th) 193, p 205; and, in New Zealand, *Vivian v Coca-Cola Export Corporation* [1984] 2 NZLR 289, p 292; *Whelan v Waitaki Meats Ltd* [1991] 2 NZLR 74, where Gallen J disagreed with the decision in *Addis*'s case, and *Brandt v Nixdorf Computer Ltd* 3 NZLR 750.

For present purposes, I am not concerned with the exclusion of damages for injured feelings. The present case is concerned only with financial loss. The report of the facts in *Addis*'s case is sketchy. Whether Mr Addis sought to prove that the manner of his dismissal caused him financial loss over and above his premature termination losses is not clear beyond a peradventure. If he did, it is surprising that their Lordships did not address this important feature more specifically. Instead, there are references to injured feelings, the fact of dismissal of itself, aggravated damages, exemplary damages amounting to damages for defamation, damages being compensatory and not punitive, and the irrelevance of motive. The dissenting speech of Lord Collins was based on competence to award exemplary or vindictive damages.

However, Lord Loreburn LC's observations were framed in quite general terms, and he expressly disagreed with the suggestion of Lord Coleridge CJ in *Maw v Jones* (1890) 25 QBD 107, p 108, to the effect that an assessment of damages might take into account the greater difficulty which an apprentice dismissed with a slur on his character might have in obtaining other employment. Similarly general observations were made by Lord James of Hereford, Lord Atkinson, Lord Gorell and Lord Shaw of Dunfermline.

In my view, these observations cannot be read as precluding the recovery of damages where the manner of dismissal involved a breach of the trust and confidence term and this caused financial loss. *Addis v Gramophone Co Ltd* was decided in the days before this implied term was adumbrated. Now that this term exists and is normally implied in every contract of employment, damages for its breach should be assessed in accordance with ordinary contractual principles. This is as much true if the breach occurs before or in connection with dismissal as at any other time.

This approach would accord, in its result, with the approach adopted by courts and tribunals in unfair dismissal cases when exercising the statutory jurisdiction, currently limited to a maximum of £11,300, to award an amount of compensation which the court or tribunal considers 'just and reasonable' in all the circumstances. Writing on a clean slate, the courts have interpreted this as enabling awards to include compensation in respect of the manner and circumstances of dismissal if these would give rise to a risk of financial loss by, for instance, making the employee less acceptable to potential employers: see ss 123 and 124 of the Employment Rights Act 1996 and *Norton Tool Co Ltd v Tewson* [1973] 1 WLR 45.

I do not believe this approach gives rise to artificiality. On the contrary, the trust and confidence term is a useful tool, well established now in employment law. At common law, damages are awarded to compensate for *wrongful* dismissal. Thus, loss which can employee would have suffered even if the dismissal had been after due notice is irrecoverable, because such loss does not derive from the wrongful element in the dismissal. Further, it is difficult to see how the mere fact of wrongful dismissal, rather than dismissal after due notice, could of itself handicap an employee in the labour market. All this is in line with *Addis*. But the manner and circumstances of the dismissal, as measured by the standards of conduct now identified in the implied trust and confidence term, may give rise to such a handicap. The law would be blemished if this were not recognised today. There now exists the separate cause of action whose absence Lord Shaw of Dunfermline noted with 'a certain regret': see *Addis v Gramophone Co Ltd* [1909] AC 488, p 504. The trust and confidence term has removed the cause for his regret.

Continuing financial losses

Exceptionally, however, the losses suffered by an employee as a result of a breach of the trust and confidence term may not consist of, or be confined to, loss of pay and other premature termination losses. Leaving aside injured feelings and anxiety, which are not the basis of the claim in the present case, an employee may find himself worse off financially than when he entered into the contract. The most obvious example is conduct, in breach of the trust and confidence term, which prejudicially affects an employee's future employment prospects. The conduct may diminish the employee's attractiveness to future employers.

The loss in the present case is of this character. BCCI promised, in an implied term, not to conduct a dishonest or corrupt business. The promised benefit was employment by an honest employer. This benefit did not materialise. Proof that Mr Mahmud and Mr Malik were handicapped in the labour market in consequence of BCCI's corruption may not be easy, but that is an assumed fact for the purpose of this preliminary issue.

There is here an important point of principle. Are financial losses of this character, which I shall call 'continuing financial losses', recoverable for breach of the trust and confidence term? This is the crucial point in the present appeals. In my view, if it was reasonably foreseeable that a particular type of loss of this character was a serious possibility, and loss of this type is sustained in consequence of a breach, then, in principle, damages in respect of the loss should be recoverable.

In the present case, the agreed facts make no assumption, either way, about whether the applicants' handicap in the labour market was reasonably foreseeable by the bank. On this, there must be scope for argument. I would not regard the absence of this necessary ingredient from the assumed facts as a sufficient reason for refusing to permit the former employees' claims to proceed further.

The contrary argument of principle is that, since the purpose of the trust and confidence term is to preserve the employment relationship and to enable that relationship to prosper and continue, the losses recoverable for breach should be confined to those flowing from the premature termination of the relationship. Thus, a breach of the term should not be regarded as giving rise to recoverable losses beyond those I have described as premature termination losses. In this way, the measure of damages would be commensurate with, and not go beyond, the scope of the protection the trust and confidence term is intended to provide for the employee.

This is an unacceptably narrow evaluation of the trust and confidence term. Employers may be under no common law obligation, through the medium of an implied contractual term of general application, to take steps to improve their employees' future job prospects. But failure to improve is one thing, positively to damage is another. Employment, and job prospects, are matters of vital concern to most people. Jobs of all descriptions are less secure than formerly, people change jobs more frequently, and the job market is not always buoyant. Everyone knows this. An employment contract creates a close personal relationship, where there is often a disparity of power between the parties. Frequently the employee is vulnerable. Although the underlying purpose of the trust and confidence term is to protect the employment relationship, there can be nothing unfairly onerous or unreasonable in requiring an employer who breaches the trust and confidence term to be liable if he thereby causes continuing financial loss of a nature that was reasonable foreseeable.

Employers must take care not to damage their employees' future employment prospects, by harsh and oppressive behaviour or by any other form of conduct which is unacceptable today as falling below the standards set by the implied trust and confidence term.

This approach brings one face to face with the decision in the wrongful dismissal case of *Addis v Gramophone Co Ltd* [1909] AC 488. It does so because the measure of damages recoverable for breach of the trust and confidence term cannot be decided without having some regard to a comparable question which arises regarding the measure of damages recoverable for wrongful dismissal. An employee may elect to treat a sufficiently serious breach of the trust and confidence term as discharging him from the contract and, hence, as a constructive dismissal. The damages in such a case ought, in principle, to be the same as they would be if the employer had expressly dismissed the employee. The employee should be no better off, or worse off, in the two situations. In principle, so far as the recoverability of continuing financial losses are concerned, there is no basis for distinguishing: (a) wrongful dismissal following a breach of the trust and confidence term; (b) constructive dismissal following a breach of the trust and confidence term; and (c) a breach of the trust and confidence term which only becomes known after the contract has ended for other reasons. The present case in the last category, but a principled answer cannot be given for cases in this category without considering the other two categories from which it is indistinguishable.

DAMAGE TO PROPERTY

The defendant's breach of contract may result in the destruction of, or damage to, the claimant's property. Alternatively, it may result in the claimant being deprived of the use of his property. Although the conventional measure of damages in cases of breach of contract is the amount required to put the claimant into the position he would have occupied had there been no breach of contract[14] and the conventional tort measure involves putting the claimant

---

14 *Robinson v Harman* (1848) 1 Ex 850, p 855, *per* Parke B.

in the position he was in before the defendant committed his tort,[15] in the case of property damage, there is, very often, little difference between the two measures of damage.

Where the claimant's property is destroyed or damaged, the basic principle is *restitutio in integrum*, that is, the claimant must be put into as good a position as if his property had not been damaged.[16] For these purposes, there are two alternative methods of compensation. First, the claimant may be given an amount representing the reduction in value of the property, alternatively, he may receive the cost of curing the defect. In addition, the claimant may also recover losses consequential on the damage.

Where the defendant's breach results in damage to land, there are two possible bases for assessment of damages. Either the claimant may recover the difference between capital value of the property in an undamaged state and to compare it with its value in a damaged state or the cost of repair or reinstatement.[17] In deciding which measure should apply, various considerations may be taken into account. In particular, it is relevant to consider the claimant's intended use of the land. For example, a claimant who intends to continue in occupation, either in a residential or a business capacity, is more likely to be able to recover the cost of reinstatement than is a claimant who has acquired the land as an investment and is therefore only interested in its capital value.

The reason for the distinction lies in the duty of the claimant to mitigate his loss.

In *Harbutt's Plasticine Ltd v Wayne Tank and Pump Co Ltd*,[18] the plaintiffs' factory was burned down as a result of the defendant's breach of contract in installing an unsuitable heating system insulated with unsafe material. By the time of trial, the plaintiffs had already had the factory rebuilt, and were awarded £146,581 as the cost of rebuilding rather than £116,785 as the reduction in value. The fact that the plaintiffs had acquired a more modern factory did not require any deduction from their damages:

Harbutt's Plasticine Ltd v Wayne Tank and Pump Co Ltd [1970] 1 QB 447, CA, p 472

Widgery LJ: I must now turn to the issues raised as to the measure of damage. The distinction between those cases in which the measure of damage is the cost of repair of the damaged article, and those in which it is the diminution in value of the article, is not clearly defined. In my opinion, each case depends on its own facts, it being remembered, first, that the purpose of the award of

---

15   *Livingstone v Rawyards Coal Co* (1880) 5 App Cas 25, p 35, *per* Lord Blackburn.

16   *The Liesbosch Dredger* [1933] AC 449, p 459, *per* Lord Wright.

17   *Dodd Properties (Kent) Ltd v Canterbury City Council* [1980] 1 WLR 433, pp 438 and 456, *per* Donaldson LJ.

18   [1970] 1 QB 447, CA.

damages is to restore the plaintiff to his position before the loss occurred and, secondly, that the plaintiff must act reasonably to mitigate his loss. If the article damaged is a motor car of popular make, the plaintiff cannot charge the defendant with the cost of repair when it is cheaper to buy a similar car on the market. On the other hand, if no substitute for the damaged article is available and no reasonable alternative can be provided, the plaintiff should be entitled to the cost of repair. It was clear in the present case that it was reasonable for the plaintiffs to rebuild their factory, because there was no other way in which they could carry on their business and retain their labour force. The plaintiffs, rebuilt their factory to a substantially different design, and if this had involved expenditure beyond the cost of replacing the old, the difference might not have been recoverable, but there is no suggestion of this here. Nor do I accept that the plaintiffs must give credit under the heading of 'betterment' for the fact that their new factory is modern in design and materials. To do so would be the equivalent of forcing the plaintiffs to invest their money in the modernising of their plant which might be highly inconvenient for them. Accordingly, I agree with the sum allowed by the trial judge as the cost of replacement.

Lord Denning MR (p 467):

Replacement or indemnity

A question was raised on the measure of damages. The plaintiffs were not allowed to rebuild the old mill (which was five storeys high) for use as a factory. They had to put up a new factory of two storeys. But it had no more accommodation. Are they entitled to the actual cost of replacement or are they limited to the difference in value of the old mill before and after the fire? ...

The defendants said that it should be the difference in value before and after the fire, relying on *Philips v Ward*. The plaintiffs said that it should be the cost of replacement, relying on *Hollebone v Midhurst & Fernhurst Builders*.

The destruction of a building is different from the destruction of a chattel. If a secondhand car is destroyed, the owner only gets its value; because he can go into the market and get another secondhand car to replace it. He cannot charge the other party with the cost of replacing it with a new car. But, when this mill was destroyed, the plaintiffs had no choice. They were bound to replace it as soon as they could, not only to keep their business going, but also to mitigate the loss of profit (for which they would be able to charge the defendants). They replaced it in the only possible way, without adding any extras. I think they should be allowed the cost of replacement. True, it is they got new for old, but I do not think the wrongdoer can diminish the claim on that account. If they had added extra accommodation or made extra improvements, they would have to give credit. But that is not this case.

I think the judge was right on this point.

A similar principle also applies where the claimant uses the premises as his residence and has already had them repaired.[19] Alternatively, if the claimant

---

19 *Hollebone v Midhurst and Fernhurst Builders Ltd* [1970] 1 QB 447. This is known as the betterment principle, whereby the court will not make deductions, since the claimant would not be over-compensated unless he were to sell the property.

gives an undertaking that he will have the necessary repairs carried out, he may be able to recover the cost of reinstatement as opposed to the simple reduction or diminution in value of the property concerned.[20] Generally, there are two alternative bases for the assessment of damages in these circumstances, namely, the diminution in capital value or the cost of reinstatement. Usually, the latter will apply especially where this amount is less than the diminution in capital value. However, there may be circumstances in which it would be wholly unreasonable to award the cost of reinstatement even where the diminution in value is negligible or nothing at all. In these circumstances, the claimant may be limited to general damage for loss of amenity (in consumer cases bolstered by perhaps a need to take account of the 'consumer surplus').

In *Ruxley Electronics and Construction Ltd v Forsyth*,[21] the plaintiff contracted to construct a swimming pool for the defendant under terms which required the pool to be built to a depth of 7 ft 6 in at its deepest point. In fact the pool constructed, at its deepest point was only 6 ft deep. The defendant (Forsyth) had paid certain sums on account but refused to pay the outstanding balance of £39,000. He had given an undertaking that he would have the remedial work done to increase the depth of the pool which would cost of £21,560. The Court of Appeal [1994] 1 WLR 650 held that, normally, the difference in value method of assessing damages would be appropriate in a case where the thing contracted for failed to live up to its contract specification, since it would normally be possible for the party not in breach to purchase a replacement on the market. However, if, as in this case, the thing contracted for had some special or unique quality, the alternative measure of damages based on the reinstatement cost could be applied. Moreover, the majority of the Court of Appeal (Mann and Stroughton LJJ) appeared to think that there were only two possible bases for assessing damages in such a case; either the cost of 'curing' the defect, or the depreciation in the value of the property. In a case such as this one where there was little or no consequent depreciation ex hypothesi the 'cost of cure' had to be awarded.

In the House of Lords, the trial judge's decision to give only general damages of 2,500 representing 'loss of amenity' was restored:

Ruxley Electronics and Construction Ltd v Forsyth [1996] AC 344, p 366

Lord Lloyd:

Reasonableness

In building cases, the pecuniary loss is almost always measured in one of two ways; either the difference in value of the work done or the cost of reinstatement. Where the cost of reinstatement is less than the difference in

---

20 *Radford v De Froberville* [1977] 1 WLR 1262.
21 [1996] AC 344.

value, the measure of damages will invariably be the cost of reinstatement. By claiming the difference in value the plaintiff would be failing to take reasonable steps to mitigate his loss. In many ordinary cases, too, where reinstatement presents no special problem, the cost of reinstatement will be the obvious measure of damages, even where there is little or no difference in value, or where the difference in value is hard to assess. This is why it is often said that the cost of reinstatement is the ordinary measure of damages for defective performance under a building contract.

But it is not the only measure of damages. Sometimes it is the other way round. This was first made clear in the celebrated judgment of Cardozo J giving the majority opinion in the Court of Appeal of New York in *Jacob & Youngs v Kent* (1921) 129 NE 889 ... Cardozo J's judgment is important, because it establishes two principles, which I believe to be correct, and which are directly relevant to the present case: first, the cost of reinstatement is not the appropriate measure of damages if the expenditure would be out of all proportion to the good to be obtained, and, secondly, the appropriate measure of damages in such a case is the difference in value, even though it would result in a nominal award ...

If the court takes the view that it would be unreasonable for the plaintiff to insist on reinstatement, as where, for example, the expense of the work involved would be out of all proportion to the benefit to be obtained, then the plaintiff will be confined to the difference in value. If the judge had assessed the difference in value in the present case at, say, £5,000, I have little doubt that the Court of Appeal would have taken that figure rather than £21,560. The difficulty arises because the judge has, in the light of the expert evidence, assessed the difference in value as nil. But that cannot make reasonable what he has found to be unreasonable.

So, I cannot accept that reasonableness is confined to the doctrine of mitigation. It has a wider impact ... Mr Jacob argues that this was not an ordinary commercial contract but a contract for a personal preference ... I am far from saying that personal preferences are irrelevant when choosing the appropriate measure of damages ('predilections' was the word used by Ackner LJ in *GW Atkins Ltd v Scott* (1980) 7 Const LJ 215, adopting the language of Oliver J in *Radford v De Froberville* [1977] 1 WLR 1262. But such cases should not be elevated into a separate category with special rules ... The eccentric landowner is entitled to his whim, provided the cost of reinstatement is not unreasonable. But the difficulty of that line of argument in the present case is that the judge, as is clear from his judgment, took Mr Forsyth's personal preferences and predilections into account. Nevertheless, he found as a fact that the cost of reinstatement was unreasonable in the circumstances. The Court of Appeal ought not to have disturbed that finding ... I have confined my citation of authority to building cases, since that is the subject matter of the present dispute. But the principle that a plaintiff cannot always insist on being placed in the same physical position as if the contract had been performed, where to do so would be unreasonable, is not confined to building cases ...

The House of Lords' decision was unanimous, but there are differences of emphasis in the judgements. In particular, Lord Mustill was acutely aware of the dangers of sending the wrong signal to the deliberate contract breaker (albeit on the facts of this case, Ruxley had behaved perfectly properly, with Forsyth being the intransigent party) and of the need for an award to properly take account of legitimate consumer expectations:

Lord Mustill (p 359): My Lords, I agree that this appeal should be allowed for the reasons stated by my noble and learned friends, Lord Jauncey of Tullichettle and Lord Lloyd of Berwick. I add some observations of my own on the award by the trial judge of damages in a sum intermediate between, on the one hand, the full cost of reinstatement and, on the other, the amount by which the malperformance has diminished the market value of the property on which the work was done: in this particular case, nil. This is a question of everyday practical importance to householders who have engaged contractors to carry out small building works, and then find (as often happens) that performance has fallen short of what was promised. I think it proper to enter on the question here, although there is no appeal against the award, because the possibility of such a recovery in a suitable case sheds light on the employer's claim that reinstatement is the only proper measure of damage.

The proposition that these two measures of damage represent the only permissible bases of recovery lie at the heart of the employer's case. From this, he reasons that there is a presumption in favour of the cost of restitution, since this is the only way in which he can be given what the contractor had promised to provide. Finally, he contends that there is nothing in the facts of the present case to rebut this presumption.

The attraction of this argument is its avoidance of the conclusion that, in a case such as the present, unless the employer can prove that the defects have depreciated the market value of the property the householder can recover nothing at all. This conclusion would be unacceptable to the average householder, and it is unacceptable to me. It is a common feature of small building works performed on residential property that the cost of the work is not fully reflected by an increase in the market value of the house, and that comparatively minor deviations from specification or sound workmanship may have no direct financial effect at all. Yet the householder must surely be entitled to say that he chose to obtain from the builder a promise to produce a particular result because he wanted to make his house more comfortable, more convenient and more conformable to his own particular tastes; not because he had in mind that the work might increase the amount which he would receive if, contrary to expectation, he thought it expedient in the future to exchange his home for cash. To say that in order to escape unscathed the builder has only to show that to the mind of the average onlooker, or the average potential buyer, the results which he has produced seem just as good as those which he had promised would make a part of the promise illusory, and unbalance the bargain. In the valuable analysis contained in *Radford v De Froberville* [1977] 1 WLR 1262, Oliver J emphasised, at p 1270, that it was for the plaintiff to judge what performance he required in exchange for the price. The court should honour that choice. *Pacta sunt servanda*. If the appellant's argument leads to the conclusion that, in all cases like the present, the employer is entitled to no more than nominal damages, the average householder would say that there must be something wrong with the law.

In my opinion, there would indeed be something wrong if, on the hypothesis that cost of reinstatement and the depreciation in value were the only available measures of recovery, the rejection of the former necessarily entailed the adoption of the latter; and the court might be driven to opt for the cost of reinstatement, absurd as the consequence might often be, simply to escape from the conclusion that the promisor can please himself whether or not to comply with the wishes of the promise which, as embodied in the contract, formed part of the consideration for the price. Having taken on the job the contractor is morally, as well as legally, obliged to give the employer what he stipulated to obtain, and this obligation ought not to be devalued. In my opinion however the hypothesis is not correct. There are not two alternative measures of damage, at opposite poles, but only one; namely, the loss truly suffered by the promisee. In some cases, the loss cannot be fairly measured except by reference to the full cost of repairing the deficiency in performance. In others, and in particular those where the contract is designed to fulfil a purely commercial purpose, the loss will very often consist only of the monetary detriment brought about by the breach of contract. But these remedies are not exhaustive, for the law must cater for those occasions where the value of the promise to the promisee exceeds the financial enhancement of his position which full performance will secure. This excess, often referred to in the literature as the 'consumer surplus' (see, for example, the valuable discussion by Harris, Ogus and Philips (1979) 95 LQR 581) is usually incapable of precise valuation in terms of money, exactly because it represents a personal, subjective and non-monetary gain. Nevertheless, where it exists, the law should recognise it and compensate the promisee if the misperformance takes it away. The lurid bathroom tiles or the grotesque folly instanced in argument by my noble and learned friend, Lord Keith of Kinkel, may be so discordant with general taste that, in purely economic terms, the builder may be said to do the employer a favour by failing to install them. But this is too narrow and materialistic a view of the transaction. Neither the contractor nor the court has the right to substitute for the employer's individual expectation of performance a criterion derived from what ordinary people would regard as sensible. As my Lords have shown, the test of reasonableness plays a central part in determining the basis of recovery, and will indeed be decisive in a case such as the present when the cost of reinstatement would be wholly disproportionate to the non-monetary loss suffered by the employer. But it would be equally unreasonable to deny all recovery for such a loss. The amount may be small, and since it cannot be quantified directly there may be room for difference of opinion about what it should be. But, in several fields, the judges are well accustomed to putting figures to intangibles, and I see no reason why the imprecision of the exercise should be a barrier, if that is what fairness demands.

My Lords, once this is recognised the puzzling and paradoxical feature of this case, that it seems to involve a contest of absurdities, simply falls away. There is no need to remedy the injustice of awarding too little, by unjustly awarding far too much. The judgment of the trial judge acknowledges that the employer has suffered a true loss and expresses it in terms of money. Since there is no longer any issue about the amount of the award, as distinct from the principle, I would simply restore his judgment by allowing the appeal.

What interest is protected by the award of damages for loss of 'amenity' in this case? If the diminution in value is nil, presumably the award for loss of amenity represents compensation for harm to the consumer surplus? In many respects, is it, at root, an equivalent to damages for 'distress and disappointment' (see Lord Lloyd, p 373).

Is the effect of *Ruxley* that a builder can prepare a low tender in order to win a contract, then deliberately cut corners by not producing the requested end product? If so, does it amount to a 'cowboy's charter'?[22]

If all the claimant loses is the value of the land as an economic asset, he will receive no more than the reduction in the selling price.

In *Taylor (Wholesale) Ltd v Hepworths Ltd*,[23] the plaintiff's billiard hall, the site of which was intended to be resold for development purposes, was destroyed by a fire which resulted from the defendant's negligence. Damages for reinstatement were refused, as the £2,500 reduction in value of the site was offset by saving the expense of clearing the site:

Taylor (Wholesale) Ltd v Hepworths Ltd [1977] 1 WLR 659, p 666

May J: Finally, in *McGregor on Damages*, there are these passages: 'It was for long said that the normal measure of damages was the amount of the diminution of the value of the land, a proposition based on what was generally considered to be the leading, but somewhat ancient, case of *Jones v Gooday*, where the alternative measure of cost of replacement or repair, that is, the sum which it would take to restore the land to its original state, was rejected ... However, as was pointed out in the 12th edition of this work, not only is *Jones v Gooday* the sole case where a plaintiff in possession and with full ownership was refused the cost to him of replacement or repair of the damage done, but Alderson B's remark there suggests that the cost of replacement or repair may be an inappropriate measure only because it is out of all proportion to the injury to the plaintiff. That this is the true reason of the result in *Jones v Gooday* is now supported by *Hollebone v Midhurst and Fernhurst Builders*, a decision which has been adopted by the Court of Appeal, in the context of a claim for breach of contract, in *Harbutt's Plasticine v Wayne Tank and Pump Co* ... The difficulty in deciding between diminution in value and cost of reinstatement arises from the fact that the plaintiff may want his property in the same state as before the commission of the tort but the amount required to effect this may be substantially greater than the amount by which the value of the property has been diminished. The test which appears to be the appropriate one is the reasonableness of the plaintiff's desire to reinstate the property; this will be

---

22 See Poole, J (1996) 59 MLR 272.
23 [1977] 1 WLR 659.

judged in part by the advantages to him of reinstatement in relation to the extra cost to the defendant in having to pay damages for reinstatement rather than damages calculated by the diminution in the value of the land.'

I think that these passages which I have just read from *McGregor on Damages* correctly reflect the state of the law. The various decided cases on each side of the line to which my attention has been drawn, and to some of which, I have referred in this judgment, reflect in my opinion merely the application in them of two basic principles of law to the facts of those various cases. These two basic principles are, first, that whenever damages are to be awarded against a tortfeasor or against a man who has broken a contract, then those damages shall be such as will, so far as money can, put the plaintiff in the same position as he would have been had the tort or breach of contract not occurred. But, secondly, the damages to be awarded are to be reasonable, reasonable that is as between the plaintiff on the one hand and the defendant on the other. That these are the underlying principles is, I think, quite clear, for instance, from the judgments in *Jones v Gooday* and, in particular, in the judgment of Alderson B. In *Moss v Christchurch Rural District Council,* the plaintiff was the reversioner and could reasonably be and was put into the same position so far as money was concerned, as he would have been had the relevant tort not occurred by the award to him of the diminution in value of his property caused by the fire which was the subject matter of that case. That all these cases do really only reflect the application of the two basic principles to which I have referred to their special facts can, if I may say so, be demonstrated by adopting the judgment of O'Connor LJ in the Irish case of *Hepenstall v Wicklow County Council*. Again, in *Hole & Son (Sayers Common) Ltd v Harrisons of Thurnscoe Ltd,* the facts were that before the relevant accident the plaintiffs had intended to demolish the cottages which were extensively damaged by the lorry which ran into them. At no time had they intended to repair them, but so soon as the statutory tenancy in one of the cottages had been determined, it had been their intention to redevelop the site by building new and different premises on it in place of the cottages. On the facts of that case, clearly, the damage suffered by the plaintiffs was only the cost of temporary repairs and any proved loss of rent. To have awarded them the cost of reinstating the promises would have put them in a better position than they would have been from a monetary point of view had the collision by the lorry never occurred and would, in any event, clearly have been unreasonable as between the plaintiffs and the defendants.

On the other hand, in *Hollebone v Midhurst and Fernhurst Builders Ltd,* the plaintiff was the freehold owner of the damaged premises actually in occupation of them as his dwelling house, and that house was itself unique. The learned judge found as a fact that the diminution in value due to the relevant fire was just under £15,000. Nevertheless, in order to repair the premises and so allow the plaintiff and his family to continue to occupy their own home would have cost nearly £19,000. On these facts, the learned judge came to the conclusion that the proper application of the relevant principles to which I have referred required him to award the larger of the two sums. On the facts of that case, such a sum was required to put that particular plaintiff in the same position, so far as money could, as he would have been had the tort not occurred and the award of that amount was not unreasonable in all the circumstances as between the two parties. The learned judge referred to the words of Viscount Dunedin in *The Susquehanna*, namely that no rigid rule or rules that apply in all cases can be laid down, but that one must consider all the relevant circumstances. He referred also to the proposition of Lord Sumner in *Admiralty Comrs v SS Checkiang*: 'The measure of damages ought never to be governed by mere rules of practice, nor can such rules override the principles of the law on this subject.'

Similarly, in *Harbutt*'s case, merely to have awarded the plaintiffs the diminution in value of their factory premises caused by the fire would not have been reasonable so far as they were concerned. Theirs were factory premises, they were in production and it was only reasonable that they should get back into production and into full production as soon as they could. It was found as a fact that they had acted reasonably in rebuilding the premises as they did; they sought to obtain nothing effectively better or more valuable than they had had before the fire. In these circumstances, the court held that in order to put the plaintiffs into the same position as they would have been had the fire not occurred, it was, in truth, necessary to award them the cost of rebuilding the damaged part of their factory, although this was rebuilt differently from what had been there before, and that such an award of damages was on the facts of that case reasonable as between plaintiff and defendant ...

What then is the result of applying the basic principles to the facts of the present case as I have found them, bearing in mind of course the assistance that I can and do obtain from the earlier cases, but remembering that they were decisions on their own particular facts?

First, it is irrelevant for my decision that the plaintiffs have been paid over £28,000 by their own insurers as the theoretical cost of reinstating their premises after the fire on 26 October 1970. They were no doubt entitled to this pursuant to the contract which they had made with their insurers. That they had made that contract and that it had that result is of no relevance so far as the present claim is concerned. There is no doubt that, in the present case, at the time of the fire, the plaintiffs were the freeholders in possession of their premises, with the minor exception of shop 19, which cannot affect the overall position. I have found as a fact that the plaintiffs' premises immediately before the fire occurred wore not worth something of the order of £58,000 as deposed to by Mr Dudley. As I have indicated, I think that the value of the plaintiffs' premises at that time was £42,500. After the fire, I think that the value of the premises was £40,000 and that, accordingly, the diminution in value caused by the fire was £2,500. Are the plaintiffs only entitled to this figure or are they entitled to the notional cost of restoring the billiard hall to its pre-fire condition? I think that they are merely entitled to the former. To award the plaintiffs the cost of reinstatement, theoretical or not, if it is intended thereby to put them in the same position as they would have been had the fire not occurred, so far as money can, and also be reasonable as between themselves and the defendants, one must at least be able to contemplate the possibility, if not probability that the plaintiffs were indeed minded to rebuild their billiard hall and shops. For the reasons which I have indicated, had the defendants gone to the plaintiffs the day after the fire and offered to reinstate the premises themselves at their own cost for the plaintiffs, the latter would, I think, have immediately told them to do no such thing. They would have said that it would only be a waste of money because not only had the premises not been occupied for some years before but also they had no intention of occupying themselves or letting them for occupation to others: they were merely holding on to the premises in only one particular sense as an investment, that is to say, an investment which might over the years show capital appreciation by way of increase in development value. That development value lay in the site itself, not in the building whole or destroyed which had previously been erected on it. In these circumstances, it would in my opinion not only be totally unrealistic, but also unreasonable as between the plaintiffs and the defendants, to award the former the notional cost of reinstating the premises. To do so would be to put them in a far better position, from the point of view of money, than they were immediately before the fire occurred. Whereas, in another case in the same field of law, it might be irrelevant to consider any special purpose to which an owner of premises had intended to put them immediately prior to a fire which gutted them, nevertheless, as between the owners of the premises and the persons responsible for the fire, it is both relevant and reasonable to consider of what nature were the premises alleged to have been damaged. The premises in the present case comprised a site the building on which it was intended in the fullness of time would be razed to the ground by developers' bulldozers for the purposes of redevelopment without any investment letting, in Mr Dudley's meaning of that phrase, in the meantime.

Prima facie, therefore, the plaintiffs would have been entitled to the sum of £2,500 as the diminution in value of their property as damages for the injury to those premises by the fire. However, as I have already indicated, the evidence clearly is that it would have cost the plaintiffs at least this amount to clear the site for development purposes to the extent that it was cleared by the fire. In respect of this head of damage, therefore, I do not think that the plaintiffs are entitled to recover anything from the defendants. They are, however, entitled to recover the cost of the immediately necessary remedial and safety work, namely £2,643.63. In addition, they are entitled to the agreed figure of £74 for damage to trade fixtures and fittings and to the further agreed sum of £650 in respect of the cost of the removal of debris.

Where a chattel has been destroyed,[24] there is no difference between its reduction in value and the cost of repair. The court must apply the principle of *restitutio in integrum,* in which case, the claimant will recover the replacement value of the destroyed chattel so as to put him in the position he was in before the loss was caused.[25]

---

24 Destruction includes constructive total loss whereby damage is so great that it would not be economic to effect a repair.

25 *The Liesbosch Dredger* [1933] AC 449, p 459, *per* Lord Wright.

If the claimant suffers consequential loss as a result of the property damage, such as expense incurred or profits lost as a result of the destruction of a ship subject to a charterparty, that loss is recoverable, except where it amounts to loss of general future profit.[26] The claimant may also recover for the cost of hiring a substitute until the replacement is available.[27]

Where loss suffered by the claimant constitutes simple damage to personal property, the claimant is entitled to recover either the cost of repair or the replacement value of the damaged goods.

FINANCIAL LOSS

The claimant is entitled to recover in respect of both losses caused and gains prevented by the breach of contract. This necessitates making a deduction where the claimant has saved money or has made a gain as a result of the breach.

In *British Westinghouse Co Ltd v Underground Electric Railways Ltd*,[28] the defendants contracted to supply turbines which proved to be defective. The plaintiff purchased replacement turbines, manufactured by Parsons, which were more efficient and more profitable. The gain made on the new turbines exceeded the loss suffered as a result of those supplied by the defendants. Accordingly, the plaintiff was only entitled to nominal damages:

British Westinghouse Co Ltd v Underground Electric Railways Ltd [1912] AC 673, p 688

Viscount Haldane: The arbitrator appears to me to have found clearly that the effect of the superiority of the Parsons' machines and efficiency in reducing working expenses was, in point of fact, such that all loss was extinguished and that actually the respondents made a profit by the course which they took. They were doubtless not bound to purchase machines of a greater kilowatt power than those originally contracted for, but they, in fact, took the wise course in the circumstances of doing so, with pecuniary advantage to themselves. They had, moreover, used the appellants' machines for several years and had recovered compensation for the loss incurred by reason of these machines not being during these years up to the standard required by the contract. After that period, the arbitrator found that it was reasonable and prudent to take the course which they actually did in purchasing the more powerful machines, and that all the remaining loss and damages was thereby wiped out.

---

26   *The Racine* [1906] P 273; *The City of Rome* (1887) 8 Asp 17 MLC 542.
27   *Moore v DER Ltd* [1971] 1 WLR 1476 (concerning the hiring of a car after the plaintiff's car was destroyed in an accident caused by one of the defendant's drivers and before delivery of a new car to the plaintiff).
28   [1912] AC 673

In order to come to a conclusion on the question as to damages thus raised, it is essential to bear in mind certain propositions which I think are well established. In some of the cases, there are expressions as to the principles governing the measure of general damages which at first sight seem difficult to harmonise. The apparent discrepancies are, however, mainly due to the varying nature of the particular questions submitted for decision. The quantum of damage is a question of fact, and the only guidance which the law can give is to lay down general principles which afford, at times, but scanty assistance in dealing with particular cases. The judges who give guidance to juries in these cases have necessarily to look at their special character and to mould for the purposes of different kinds of claim the expression of the general principles which apply to them, and this is apt to give rise to an appearance of ambiguity. Subject to these observations, I think that there are certain broad principles, which are quite well settled. The first is that, as far as possible, he who has proved a breach of a bargain to supply what he contracted to get is to be placed, as far as money can do it, in as good a situation as if the contract had been performed. The fundamental basis is thus compensation for pecuniary loss naturally flowing from the breach; but this first principle is qualified by a second, which imposes on a plaintiff the duty of taking all reasonable steps to mitigate the loss consequent on the breach, and debars him from claiming in respect of any part of the damage which is due to his neglect to take such steps ...

But when, in the course of his business, he has taken action arising out of the transaction, which action has diminished his loss, the effect in actual diminution of the loss which he has suffered may be taken into account, even though there was no duty on him to act.

Staniforth v Lyall illustrates this rule. In that case the defendants had chartered a ship to New Zealand, where they were to load her or by an agent there to give the plaintiff, the owner, notice that they abandoned the adventure, in which case they were to pay £500. The ship went to New Zealand, but found neither agent nor cargo there, and the captain chose to make a circuitous voyage home by way of Batavia. This voyage, after making every allowance for increased expense and loss of time, was more profitable than the original venture to New Zealand would have been. The Court of Common Pleas decided that the action was to be viewed as one for a breach of contract to put the cargo on board the plaintiff's vessel for which the plaintiff was entitled to recover all the damages which he had incurred, but that he was bound to bring into account, in ascertaining the damages arising from the breach, the advantages which had accrued to him because of the course which he had chosen to adopt. I think that this decision illustrates a principle which has been recognised in other cases that, provided the course taken to protect himself, by the plaintiff, in such an action was one which a reasonable and prudent person might in the ordinary conduct of business properly have taken, and in fact did take whether bound to or not, a jury or an arbitrator may properly look at the facts and ascertain the result in estimating the quantum of damage.

...

I think that the principle which applies here is that which makes it right for the jury or arbitrator to look at what actually happened, and to balance loss and gain. The transaction was not *res inter alios acta*, but one in which the person whose contract was broken took a reasonable and prudent course arising quite naturally out of the circumstances in which he was placed by the breach. Apart from the breach of contract, the lapse of time had rendered the appellants' machines obsolete and men of business would be doing the only thing which they could properly do in replacing them with new and up to date machines. The arbitrator does not in his finding of fact lay any stress in the increase in kilowatt power of the new machines and I think that the proper inference is that such increases was regarded by him as a natural and prudent course followed by those whose object was to avoid further loss, and that it formed part of a continuous dealing with the situation in which they found themselves, and was not an independent or disconnected transaction. For the reasons which I have given, I think that the questions of law stated by the arbitrator in the Special Case have been wrongly answered by the courts below. The result is that the award cannot stand and must be sent back to the arbitrator, with a declaration that the contention of the appellants on the first question so far, but only so far as they contended that the several facts relied upon by them were relevant matter to be considered by the arbitrator in assessing the damages was right, and that of the respondents on the second question was wrong. The appellants are entitled to their costs, here, and in the Court of Appeal, and of the proceedings in the Divisional Court on the motion to set aside the award.

Three interests are protected at common law, namely, the expectation interest, the status quo (or reliance) interest, and the restitution interest. Traditional analysis insists that the expectation interest is only protected in contract law, and that a tort action will only protect the status quo interest, but this has long ceased to be inflexibly the case since a tort action may, in limited circumstances, protect a claimant's expectations of gain.[29]

The traditional objective of an award of damages for breach of contract is said to be the protection of the claimant's reasonable expectations. This is done by putting him in the position he or she would have been in if the contract had been performed.[30] The basic premise underlying this measure of damages is that there has been a bargain promise by the defendant which has engendered in the claimant a reasonable expectation of gain. If there was such a thing as a perfect market, the claimant would be able to find a replacement contract elsewhere at the same cost to him as the lost contract with the defendant. In such perfect conditions, the claimant's expectation loss would be the same as his status quo loss.[31] However, it has to be recognised that market conditions are frequently imperfect so that losses of profit may occur

---

29 See *Ross v Caunters* [1980] Ch 297; *White v Jones* [1995] 2 AC 207.
30 *Robinson v Harman* (1848) 1 Ex 850, p 855, *per* Parke B.
31 Fuller and Perdue, 1936/37, p 62.

due to market fluctuations. Accordingly, in contracts for the sale of goods, the damages awarded to the buyer where the seller fails to deliver or to the seller where the buyer wrongly refuses to take delivery may have to take into account the difference between the contract price and the market price for the goods in question, provided there is an available market:

Sale of Goods Act 1979

50 Damages for non-acceptance

(1) Where the buyer wrongfully neglects or refuses to accept and pay for the goods, the seller may maintain an action against him for damages for non-acceptance.

(2) The measure of damages is the estimated loss directly and naturally resulting, in the ordinary course of events, from the buyer's breach of contract.

(3) Where there is an available market for the goods in question the measure of damages is *prima facie* to be ascertained by the difference between the contract price and the market or current price at the time or times when the goods ought to have been accepted or (if no time was fixed for acceptance) at the time of the refusal to accept.

51 Damages for non-delivery

(1) Where the seller wrongfully neglects or refuses to deliver the goods to the buyer, the buyer may maintain an action against the seller for damages for non-delivery.

(2) The measure of damages is the estimated loss directly and naturally resulting, in the ordinary course of events, from the seller's breach of contract.

(3) Where there is an available market for the goods in question the measure of damages is *prima facie* to be ascertained by the difference between the contract price and the market or current price at the time or times when the goods ought to have been delivered or (if no time was fixed) at the time of the refusal to deliver.

These provisions raise the question, what is an available market? If there is no such market, the loss suffered by the innocent party must be assessed on the basis of that which directly and naturally results from the breach of contract, in the ordinary course of events.

In *Thompson (WL) v Robinson (Gunmakers) Ltd*,[32] the parties entered into a contract for the sale of a new Standard Vanguard motor vehicle. After conclusion of the contract, the buyers indicated that they would not accept the vehicle. The plaintiffs were able to return the car to the manufacturer under the terms of a resale price maintenance agreement and the manufacturer did not claim compensation from the plaintiffs. The plaintiffs had, nonetheless,

---

32 [1955] 1 Ch 177.

lost a sale which would have given them a profit of £61, which amount the plaintiffs sought to recover from the defendants. At the time of the contract, there was no demand for Standard Vanguard vehicles; accordingly, the plaintiff was entitled to substantial damages under s 50(2) of the Sale of Goods Act 1893 (now 1979):

Thompson (WL) Ltd v Robinson (Gunmakers) Ltd [1955] 1 Ch 177, p 182

Upjohn J: The law is not really in doubt. It is set out in s 50 of the Sale of Goods Act 1893.

That section was declaratory of the existing law and the general principle which has been observed in all cases I take conveniently from the speech of Viscount Haldane LC in *British Westinghouse Electric & Manufacturing Co Ltd v Underground Electric Railways Co of London Ltd*. Viscount Haldane LC said ([1912] AC at p 689): 'Subject to these observations, I think that there are certain broad principles which are quite well settled. The first is that, as far as possible, he who has proved a breach of a bargain to supply what he contracted to get is to be placed, as far as money can do it, in as good a situation as if the contract had been performed.'

That is the general rule.

Apart altogether from authority and statute, it would seem to me on the facts to be quite plain that the plaintiffs' loss in this case is the loss of their bargain. They have sold one Vanguard less than they otherwise would. The plaintiffs, as the defendants must have known, are in business as dealers in motor cars and make their profit in buying and selling motor cars, and what they have lost is their profit on the sale of this Vanguard. There is no authority exactly in point in this country, although it seems to me that the principle to be applied is a clear one. It is to be found in *Re Vic Mill Ltd*, in which the supplier was to supply certain machines which he had to make and they were to be made to the particular specification of the purchaser, although they were of a type generally in common use. It was not, as the present case is, a sale by a motor dealer of a standardised product. The purchaser repudiated his order, and with a view to mitigating damages the supplier, on getting another order for somewhat similar machinery, very sensibly made such alterations as were necessary to the machinery that he had made for the original purchaser and sold the machinery so altered to the second purchaser. His costs of doing that were comparatively trivial. It was said by the supplier that the measure of his damages was the loss of his bargain; by the purchaser that the measure of damages was merely the cost of the conversion of the machinery for the second purchaser and his slight loss on the re-sale.

Buckley LJ put the matter succinctly in this way: 'As regards No 1, where the goods were manufactured, the respondents are, I think, entitled to both profits, because they were not bound to give the appellants the benefit of another order that the respondents had received. The respondents were left with these goods on their hands. They altered them and sold them to another buyer, but they could have made, and would otherwise, I suppose, have made other goods for that buyer, and not employed these goods for that purpose. If they had done so, they would have made both profits.'

It seems to me that, in principle, that covers this case. True, the motor car in question was not sold to another purchaser, but the plaintiffs did what was reasonable, they got out of their bargain with George Thompson Ltd, but they sold one less Vanguard, and lost their profit on that transaction ...

The main case, however, put by the defendants is this: they submit that s 50(3) of the Sale of Goods Act 1893 applies, because they say there is an available market for the goods in question and, in that available market, we know that the price of the Vanguard is fixed. It is fixed by the manufacturers. Therefore, they say the measure of damages must necessarily be little more than nominal. Had the plaintiffs kept the car and sold it to another at a later stage, no doubt, they would have been entitled to the costs of storage in the meantime, possibly interest on their money laid out, and so on, but, as they, in fact, mitigated damages by getting out of the contract, damages are nil.

Mr Platts-Mills said that the market now must not be treated as a market or fair in a limited or technical sense. It is curious that there is a comparative absence of authority on the meaning of the phrase 'available market', because one would have thought there would have been many cases, but the researches of counsel have only disclosed one authority on s 50(3). It is *Dunkirk Colliery Co v Lever*, a decision of the Court of Appeal. The facts were far removed from the facts before me and I need not recite them. It will be sufficient if I read an extract from the judgment of James LJ He said: 'Under those circumstances, the only thing that we can do is to send it back to the referee with an intimation that we are of opinion upon the facts (agreeing with the Master of the Rolls in that respect) that the facts do not warrant the application of the principle mentioned in the award, namely, that there was what may be properly called a market. What I understand by a market in such a case as this is, that when the defendant refused to take the 300 tons the first week or the first month, the plaintiffs might have sent it in waggons somewhere else, where they could sell it, just as they sell corn on the Exchange, or cotton at Liverpool: that is to say, that there was a fair market where they could have found a purchaser either by themselves or through some agent at some particular place. That is my notion of the meaning of a market under those circumstances.'

If that be the right principle to apply, it was proved that there is nothing in the nature of a market like a Cotton Exchange or Baltic or Stock Exchange, or anything of the sort, for the sale of new motor cars. But Mr Platts-Mills submits that the word 'market' is of no fixed legal significance.

I think that in that state of affairs the decision of the Court of Appeal in *Dunkirk Colliery Co v Lever* is binding on me, and, therefore, unless one finds something in the nature of a market in the sense used by James LJ, s 50(3) has no further application. However, the point seems to me of somewhat academic interest in this case, because, if one gives to the word 'market' an extended meaning, in my view, on the facts which I have to consider, a precisely similar result is reached.

Had the matter been *res integra*, I think I should have found that an 'available market' merely means that the situation in the particular trade in the particular area was such that the particular goods could freely be sold, and that there was a demand sufficient to absorb readily all the goods that were thrust on it, so that if a purchaser defaulted the goods in question could readily be disposed of. Indeed, such was the situation in the motor trade until very recently. It was, of course, notorious that dealers all over the country had long waiting lists for new motor cars. People put their names down and had to wait five or six years, and whenever a car was spared by the manufacturer from export, it was snatched at. If any purchaser fell out, there were many waiting to take his place, and it was conceded that if those circumstances were still applicable to the Vanguard motor car, the claim for damages must necessarily have been purely nominal. But, on the assumed facts, circumstances had changed in relation to Vanguard motor cars and, in March 1954, there was not a demand in the East Riding which could readily absorb all the Vanguard motor cars available for sale. If a purchaser defaulted, that sale was lost and there was no means of readily disposing of the Vanguard contracted to be sold, so that there was not, even on the extended definition, an available market. But there is this further consideration: even if I accepted Mr Platts-Mills' broad argument that one must now look at the market as being the whole conspectus of trade, organisation and marketing, I have to remember that s 50(3) provides only a *prima facie* rule and if, on investigation of the facts, one finds that it is unjust to apply that rule, in the light of the general principles mentioned above, it is not to be applied. In this case, as I said in the earlier part of my judgment, it seems to me plain almost beyond argument that, in fact, the loss to the plaintiffs is £61. Accordingly, however one interprets s 50(3), it seems to me on the facts that I have to consider one reaches the same result.

In contrast, if the seller can dispose of all the cars he is able to get hold of, the claimant is likely to be able to recover nominal damages only since there will be no loss 'directly and naturally resulting from the defendant's breach of contract'.[33]

However, there are instances in which it is not practicable for the claimant to seek damages in respect of his/her expectation interest. In such a case, the claimant may have the alternative of an action for his status quo loss, where, for example, he/she has incurred expense. Since the claimant seeking to recover loss of profit must prove that he would have made a profit had the contract been performed, there may be circumstances in which that proof is not easy to find. This is particularly the case where the claimant is deprived of a chance of future gain, in which case, the court is faced with the difficult task of assessing the value of the lost chance. The mere fact that such an assessment is difficult is not, however, to be treated as an excuse for not awarding damages.

In *Chaplin v Hicks*,[34] the defendant, in breach of contract, failed to give the plaintiff the opportunity to attend an audition, where 12 people out of 50 auditioned were to be given a theatrical engagement (the shortlist of 50 had been drawn up on the basis of 'votes' by readers of a newspaper after the

---

33   *Charter v Sullivan* [1957] 2 QB 117.
34   [1911] 2 KB 786, CA.

publication of relevant photographs in the newspaper). The plaintiff could recover no damages for loss of a theatrical engagement, as she could not prove she would have been one of the 12, but recovered £100 for loss of the chance:

Chaplin v Hicks [1911] 2 KB 786, CA, p 795

Fletcher Moulton LJ: The very object and scope of the contract, was that the plaintiff should have the chance of being selected by the defendant for one of the theatrical engagements he offered, and his refusal to fulfil his part of the contract is the breach complained of. Damages are, therefore, a fair compensation to the plaintiff for being excluded from the limited class of candidates. It seems to me that nothing more direct or more intimately connected with the contract could be found.

Then the learned counsel takes up a more hopeful position. He says that the damages are difficult to assess because it is impossible to say that the plaintiff would have obtained any prize. This is the only point of importance left for our consideration. Is expulsion from a limited class of competitors an injury? To my mind, there can be only one answer to that question; it is an injury and may be a very substantial one. Therefore, the plaintiff starts with an unchallengeable case of injury and the damages given in respect of it should be equivalent to the loss. But it is said that the damages cannot be arrived at because it is impossible to estimate the *quantum* of the reasonable probability of the plaintiff's being a prize-winner. I think that, where it is clear that there has been actual loss resulting from the breach of contract, which it is difficult to estimate in money, it is for the jury to do their best to estimate; it is not necessary that there should be an absolute measure of damages in each case. There are no doubt well settled rules as to the measure of damages in certain cases, but such accepted rules are only applicable where the breach is one that frequently occurs. In such cases, the Court weighs the pros and cons and gives advice, and I may almost say directions, to the jury as regards the measure of damages. This is especially the case in actions relating to the sale of goods of a class for which there is an active and ready market. But, in most cases, it may be said that there is no recognised measure of damages and that the jury must give what they think to be an adequate solatium under all the circumstances of the case. Is there any such rule as that, where the result of a contract depends on the volition of an independent party, the law shuts its eyes to the wrong and says that there are no damages? Such a rule, if it existed, would work great wrong. Let us take the case of a man under a contract of service to serve as a second class clerk for five years at a salary of 200l a year, which expressly provides that, at the end of that period, out of every five second class clerks two first class clerks will be chosen at a salary of 500l a year. If such a clause is embodied in the contract, it is clear that a person thinking of applying for the position would reckon that he would have the advantage of being one of five persons from whom the two first class clerks must be chosen, and that that might be a very substantial portion of the consideration for his appointment. If, after he has taken the post and worked under the contract of service, the employers repudiate the obligation, is he to have no remedy? He has sustained a very real loss and there can be no possible reason why the law should have leave it to the jury to estimate the value of that of which he has been deprived. Where, by contract, a man has a right to belong to a limited class of competitors, he is possessed of something of value, and it is the duty of the jury to estimate the pecuniary value of that advantage if it is taken from him. The present case is a typical one. From a body of 6,000 who sent in their photographs, a smaller body of 50 was formed, of which the plaintiff was one and, among that smaller body, 12 prizes were allotted for distribution; by reason of the defendant's breach of contract, she has lost all the advantage of being in the limited competition and she is entitled to have her loss estimated. I cannot lay down any rule as to the measure of damages in such a case; this must be left to the good sense of the jury. They must, of course, give effect to the consideration that the plaintiff's chance is only one out of four and that they cannot tell whether she would have ultimately proved to be the winner. But, having considered all this, they may well think that it is of considerable pecuniary value to have got into so small a class and they must assess the damages accordingly.

This consideration decides the case, but I wish to refer to the decision of Jelf J in *Sapwell v Bass*. That decision was, in my opinion, right on the facts of the particular case. The plaintiff had acquired by contract a right to send a mare during the following year to a renowned stallion belonging to the defendant, and the defendant broke his contract. The right to send the mare was coupled with the payment of a fee of 800 guineas. Jelf J held that, for the breach of contract, the plaintiff was only entitled to nominal damages. The ground of the decision was that there was no evidence to show that the right was worth more to the plaintiff than the 300 guineas which he would have had to pay for the services of the stallion and that there was therefore no evidence that the damages were more than nominal. If, however, the learned judge meant to hold that there were no damages for breach of an undertaking to serve the mare, there is, in my opinion, no justification for such a view. The contract gave the plaintiff a right of considerable value, one for which many people would give money; therefore, to hold that the plaintiff was entitled to no damages for being deprived of such a right because the final result depended on a contingency or chance would have been a misdirection. This appeal must be dismissed.

If the claimant cannot prove that he/she would have made a profit had the contract not been broken, difficulties may arise. However, the court may have the alternative of protecting the claimant's status quo interest instead of his/her expectation interest. Where this is done, the emphasis of any award of damages will be upon the expenditure incurred by the claimant in reliance upon the defendant's promise of performance.

In *CCC Films (London) Ltd v Impact Quadrant Films Ltd*,[35] the plaintiffs were granted a licence to exploit and distribute three motion pictures in various countries. The defendants failed to deliver these films, but the plaintiffs were

---

35 [1984] 3 WLR 245. See, also, *McRae v Commonwealth Disposals Commission* (1950) 84 CLR 377.

unable to produce any evidence of loss of profit. Instead, they elected to recover the expenditure incurred by them in acquiring these rights contracted for ($12,000). This was held to be an appropriate measure of damages and the onus fell on the defendants to prove that the plaintiffs would not have recouped their initial expenditure:

CCC Films (London) Ltd v Impact Quadrant Films Ltd [1984] 3 WLR 245, p 254

Hutchison J: [In *Anglia Television Ltd v Reed*, Lord Denning said:] 'Anglia Television then sued Mr Reed for damages. He did not dispute his liability, but a question arose as to the damages. Anglia Television do not claim their profit. They cannot say what their profit would have been on this contract if Mr Reed had come here and performed it. So, instead of a claim for loss of profits, they claim for the wasted expenditure. They had incurred the director's fees, the designer's fees, the stage manager's and assistant manager's fees, and so on. It comes in all to £2,750. Anglia Television say that all that money was wasted because Mr Reed did not perform his contract ... It seems to me that a plaintiff in such a case as this has an election: he can either claim for loss of profits or for his wasted expenditure. But he must elect between them. He cannot claim both. If he has not suffered any loss of profits – or if he cannot prove what his profits would have been – he can claim in the alternative the expenditure which has been thrown away, that is, wasted, by, reason of the breach. That is shown by *Cullinane v British 'Rema' Manufacturing Co Ltd* [1954] 1 QB 292, pp 303 and 308. If the plaintiff claims the wasted expenditure, he is not limited to the expenditure incurred after the contract was concluded. He can claim also the expenditure incurred before the contract, provided that it was such as would reasonably be in the contemplation of the parties as likely to be wasted if the contract was broken. Applying that principle here, it is plain that, when Mr Reed entered into this contract, he must have known perfectly well that much expenditure had already been incurred on director's fees and the like. He must have contemplated – or, at any rate, it is reasonably to be imputed to him – that if he broke his contract, all that expenditure would be wasted, whether or not it was incurred before or after the contract. He must pay damages for all the expenditure so wasted and thrown away.'

He went on to cite in support of his decision the decision of Brightman J in *Lloyd v Stanbury* [1971] 1 WLR 535.

In *Cullinane v British 'Rema' Manufacturing Co Ltd* [1954] 1 QB 292, the issue was whether the plaintiffs could claim both diminution in value occasioned by breach of warranty and loss of profits or must elect between them; and the majority of the Court of Appeal held that he must elect. Sir Raymond Evershed MR, said, at p 303: 'As a matter of principle also, it seems to me that a person who has obtained a machine, such as the plaintiff obtained, being a machine which was mechanically in exact accordance with the order given but which was unable to perform a particular function which it was warranted to perform, may adopt one of two courses. He may say, when he discovers its incapacity, that it was not what he wanted, that it is quite useless to him, and he may claim to recover the capital cost he has incurred, deducting anything he can obtain by disposing of the material that he got. A claim of that kind puts the plaintiff in the same position as though he had never made the contract at all. In other words, he is back where he started; and, if it were shown that the profit earning capacity was in fact very small, the plaintiff would probably elect so to base his claim. But, alternatively, where the warranty in question relates to performance, he may, in my judgment, make his claim on the basis of the profit which he has lost because the machine as delivered fell short in its performance of that which it was warranted to do. If he chooses to base his claim on that footing, it seems to me that depreciation has nothing whatever to do with it.'

I interpret the passage I have just read and that cited from Lord Denning MR's judgment in *Anglia Television Ltd v Reed* [1972] 1 QB 60, p 63 as indicating that in these cases the plaintiff has an unfettered choice. He is not permitted to frame his claim as one for wasted expenditure only in those cases where he establishes by evidence that he cannot prove loss of profit or that such loss of profits as he can prove is small. I consider that when Lord Denning MR says: 'If he has not suffered any loss of profits – or if he cannot prove what his profits would have been – he can claim in the alternative the expenditure which has been thrown away ...' and when Sir Raymond Evershed MR says in *Cullinane v British 'Rema' Manufacturing Co Ltd* [1954] 1 QB 292, p 303, 'if it were shown that the profit earning capacity was, in fact, very small, the plaintiff would probably elect so to base his claim', each is describing factors which would be likely to motivate the plaintiff to elect to claim on the lost expenditure basis rather than laying down what must be proved before such a claim can be entertained. In other words, I consider that those cases are authority for the proposition that a plaintiff may always frame his claim in the alternative way if he chooses. I reach this conclusion all the more readily when I reflect that to hold that there had to be evidence of the impossibility of making profits might, in many cases, saddle the plaintiff with just the sort of difficulties of proof that this alternative measure is designed to avoid.

It is, I think, important in this context to distinguish between the term 'loss of profit' and the term 'recovery of expenditure'. When Lord Denning MR speaks in *Anglia Television* of the plaintiffs not having suffered loss of profits or of its being impossible for them to prove what their profits would have been, he is referring, I believe, to profits after recoupment of expenditure – net profits. The plaintiffs in *Anglia Television* were by the defendant's breach deprived of putting to the test whether and to what extent they would have: (a) recouped their expenditure; and (b) gone on to make a net profit and of how much. It may well be that they could have led some evidence as to the probabilities in relation at least to the first of these matters. They had a script and no doubt they had budget and profit forecasts which could have been reinforced by evidence as to their experience with other similar projects. It seems that they did not adduce any such evidence any more than did the plaintiffs in the present case, though Mr Brauner, with his vast experience in the film industry and the advantage of having viewed these films, could, no doubt, have given some general evidence as to his expectations. Nevertheless, the difficulties of proof would clearly be enormous and it is hard to envisage how the plaintiffs could, in the present case, in practice have proved a claim based on loss of profits.

It is, however, common ground that a claim for wasted expenditure cannot succeed in a case where, even had the contract not been broken by the defendant, the returns earned by the plaintiff's exploitation of the chattel or the rights the subject matter of the contract would not have been sufficient to recoup that expenditure ...

In my judgment, *Anglia Television Ltd* was a case in which it must be taken to have been assumed that the plaintiffs would, had they made the film, at least have recouped their expenditure. For the reasons I have endeavoured to indicate, it is a decision inconsistent with, in the sense of being more favourable to plaintiffs than, *McRae*'s case. Though it does not decide that, in such cases, the onus is on the defendant to show that the expenditure would not have been recouped, it is a decision consistent with such a rule. It is also, in my judgment, a case which in many ways, though by no means all, is similar to the present case; and, of course, to the extent that it is inconsistent with *McRae*'s case, it is a case by which I am bound and which I should follow.

On this crucial question of where the onus of proof lies in relation to whether or not the exploitation of the subject matter of the contract would or would not have recouped the expenditure, there are, however, a number of cases which are more directly relevant. Mr Willer, on behalf of the plaintiffs, submits that *C & P Haulage v Middleton* [1983] 1 WLR 1461 is binding English authority for the view that the onus is on the defendant. I have already pointed out that in that case no question arose as to where the onus lay ...

I turn, therefore, to the Canadian and American cases. In the *Bowlay Logging* case [1978] 4 WWR 105, Berger J held that the onus of showing that the exploitation of the contract would have lost money lay on the defendant. In doing so, he based himself on the American cases *L Albert & Son v Armstrong Rubber Co* (1949) 178 F 2d 182 and *Dade County v Palmer & Baker Engineers Inc* (1965) 339 F 2d 208, so it is those cases that I must consider.

In the former case, where a claim for damages for breach of contract in relation to the sale of some machines designed to recondition old rubber was advanced on the wasted expenditure rather than the loss of profit basis, Learned Hand CJ held that the onus was on the defendants ...

The judgment in the *Dade County* case (1965) 339 F 2d 208, while again being direct authority on the point, again favourable to Mr Willer, is very brief and contains the bare statement: 'The burden is on the defendant to prove that full performance would have resulted in a net loss.'

I am, of course, not bound by any of these cases, but, plainly, they are of great persuasive authority. I am impressed by, and respectfully adopt, the reasoning of Learned Hand CJ in *L Albert & Son v Armstrong Rubber Co* (1949) 178 F 2d 182 and I do so the more readily because, as I have already mentioned, that case and *Bowlay Logging Ltd v Domtar Ltd* [1978] 4 WWR 105 were relied upon by Ackner LJ in *C & P Haulage v Middleton* [1983] 1 WLR 1461 in a different context without eliciting from Ackner LJ any adverse comment on this point.

Even without the assistance of such authorities, I should have held on principle that the onus was on the defendant. It seems to me that, at least in those cases where the plaintiff's decision to base his claim on abortive expenditure was dictated by the practical impossibility of proving loss of profit, rather than by unfettered choice, any other rule would largely, if not entirely, defeat the object of allowing this alternative method of formulating the claim. This is because, notwithstanding the distinction to which I have drawn attention between proving a loss of net profit and proving, in general terms, the probability of sufficient returns to cover expenditure, in the majority of contested cases, impossibility of proof of the first would probably involve like impossibility in the case of the second. It appears to me to be eminently fair that in such cases where the plaintiff has by the defendant's breach been prevented from exploiting the chattel or the right contracted for and, therefore, putting to the test the question of whether he would have recouped his expenditure, the general rule as to the onus of proof of damage should be modified in this manner.

It follows that, the onus being on the defendants to prove that the expenditure incurred by the plaintiffs is irrecoverable because they would not have recouped their expenditure (and that onus admittedly not having been discharged), the plaintiffs are entitled to recover such expenditure as was wasted as a result of such breach or breaches of contract as they have proved.

In *Anglia Television Ltd v Reed*,[36] the plaintiffs had decided to make a television film and secured the services of the defendant, an American actor, to play the leading role. At a very late stage, the defendant repudiated the contract and the question arose whether the plaintiffs were entitled to damages for this breach of contract. The difficulty with this type of case is that until the film is completed and available for general viewing, it is highly unlikely that any precise figure can be placed on the plaintiffs' expectations of gain. However, in this case, the court was prepared to assess the plaintiffs' loss on the basis of their wasted expenditure, both before and after the contract with Reed was entered into. A difficulty presented by the *Anglia Television* case is that if the purpose of status quo damages is to put the claimant in the position he *would have been in if no contract had been made*, should the claimant have been able to recover pre-contractual expenditure? In the US, such damages are not recoverable according to the decision in *Chicago Coliseum Club v Dempsey* (1932) 256 Ill App 542.

Where the claimant has relied, to his/her detriment, on the defendant's promise, he or she should be compensated for that detrimental reliance. An award of status quo damages puts the claimant in the position he or she would have been in had he not entered the contract in the first place. Such an award equates with the compensatory objective of tortious damages in seeking to put the claimant in the position he/she would have been in had the wrong not been committed.

---

36 [1972] 1 QB 60.

Status quo damages may be awarded in an action for breach of contract, both as an alternative to and as a complement to expectation damages. In the latter case, it is important that the same losses are not recovered twice over under the two bases of assessment. Conversely, the court should not make the mistake of insisting that the two measures are mutually exclusive of one another. Provided it is appreciated that expenditure has to be incurred (status quo loss) and taken into account in seeking to make a profit (expectation loss), there should be no objection to recovery under both heads.

In *Cullinane v British 'Rema' Manufacturing Co,*[37] the defendant sold the plaintiff a clay pulverising machine for £6,578 with a warranty that the machine could process six tons of clay per hour. In fact, it produced only two tons of clay powder per hour and was, therefore, commercially useless. The plaintiff claimed damages in respect of: (1) the difference between the total of the contract price and the cost of buildings to house the machine and their estimated break up value (capital loss); (2) interest on gross capital expenditure; and (3) loss of profit for a period of three years.

The Court of Appeal (Morris LJ dissenting) held that the plaintiff could recover capital losses or he could recover loss of profit, but not both. Accordingly, he was allowed to recover (2) and (3) above, amounting to £10,521:

Cullinane v British 'Rema' Manufacturing Co [1954] 1 QB 292, CA, p 299

Lord Evershed MR: This appeal relates only to the proper measure of the damages which flow from what has been found to be a breach of warranty in regard to certain plant manufactured by the defendants and supplied to the plaintiff. It is, in my judgment, important to have clearly in mind the nature of the contract and, particularly, of the warranty. The plant, as I understand, was built according to a detailed specification and there is no doubt that as supplied it strictly conformed with the specification. Unfortunately, however, as the official referee found, it did not satisfy the warranty, because the machine, although capable of handling the plaintiff's clay and of cutting, drying and grinding it so as to produce a dry clay powder, was not capable of producing it at the rate of six tons per hour, and the difference in rate, commercially speaking, was the difference between a profitable and an unprofitable commercial venture.

His Lordship referred to the particulars of damage and continued:

It is, I think, obvious that damages of approximately £37,000 was a very large sum to claim for plant for which the purchase price was about £6,000, and which was to be used in an enterprise ... of a somewhat speculative character. The total amount awarded was considerably less, namely, £16,813 odd. That reduction is attributable almost entirely to a reduction of the sum awarded for loss of profit.

---

37 (1954) 1 QB 292, CA.

The argument of the defendants in this court has been that the award involves giving damages twice over to the plaintiff. The machine was made precisely according to the specification. It was delivered and is now in the plaintiff's possession and is, in fact, I understand, working, though it does not perform its productive function in the way that was warranted. The principle on which damages for breach of contract are awarded has been many times stated and was carefully considered by Asquith LJ, in delivering the judgment of this court in *Victoria Laundry (Windsor) Ltd v Newman Industries Ltd*. The passages from that judgment which we have read are expository of the original principle laid down in *Hadley v Baxendale* as follows (9 Exch 354): 'Where two parties have made a contract which one of them has broken, the damages which the other party ought to receive in respect of such breach of contract should be such as may fairly and reasonably be considered either arising naturally, that is, according to the usual course of things, from such breach of contract itself, or such as may reasonably be supposed to have been in the contemplation of both parties, at the time they made the contract, as the probable result of the breach of it.'

It seems to me, as a matter of principle, that the full claim for damages, in the form in which it is pleaded, was not sustainable, insofar as the plaintiff sought to recover both the whole of his original capital loss and also the whole of the profit which he would have made. That, I think, as a proposition is self-evident, because a claim for loss of profits could only be founded on the footing that the capital expenditure had been incurred. As I have said, however, there was a deduction in respect of depreciation at 10%, and, if the life of the plant is taken at 10 years, it follows that, during the period of 10 years in which profits must be assumed to have been earned, the whole of the capital cost would have been written off. In other words, if the estimation of damages under head E. had been carried on for the whole period of 10 years, the effect of these considerable calculations would have been that A plus B plus C, having been elaborately set out, would have all been deducted again in the course of calculating E.

As a matter of principle also, it seems to me that a person who has obtained a machine such as the plaintiff here obtained, which was mechanically in exact accordance with the order given, but was unable to perform a particular function which it was warranted to perform, may adopt one of two courses. He may, when he discovers its incapacity and that it is not what he wanted and is useless to him, claim to recover the capital cost he has incurred less anything he can obtain by disposing of the material that he got. A claim of that kind puts the plaintiff in the same position as though he had never made the contract at all. He is, in other words, back where he started, and, if it were shown that the profit earning capacity was, in fact, very small, the plaintiff would probably elect so to base his claim. Alternatively, he may, where the warranty in question relates to performance, make his claim on the basis of the profit he has lost, because the machine as delivered fell short in its performance of that which it was warranted to do. If he chooses to base his claim on that footing, depreciation has nothing whatever to do with it ...

But, whatever be the answer to these problems, I come back to the point, which I left a little time ago. I think, that the plaintiff could choose either to claim on the basis that he had wasted capital and that he ought to be put in the position he would have been in if he had never bought this machine, or 'I have got the machine. What I am claiming is the loss I have suffered because its performance falls short of that which was warranted, and, therefore, I have not made the profitable sales which I would have made, and I claim, accordingly, the loss of resultant profits'. The second alternative being the larger, he is entitled to choose that, but, in my judgment, he should be limited to it. He is not, in my judgment, by stating that his claim for lost profit is limited to three years, able to claim (as he admittedly could not claim if he had not placed the limitation on the profit) both for loss of capital and for loss of profit. It is said that he may do so provided that in the computation of profits he makes due allowance for depreciation, but, in my judgment (as I have already stated), depreciation has nothing to do with the profit lost as a consequence of the breach of warranty, and the effect of so reducing the profit would appear to be that the plaintiff first recovers for loss of capital and then has to bring into account against the profit, part of what he has recovered for loss of capital.

Morris LJ (dissenting) (p 315): It seems to me that the basis on which the pleader for the plaintiff pleaded the damage in this case was permissible and logical ... Supposing that a machine cost £10,000 and had a life of 10 years, and supposing it were found that there would be net profits of £2,000 a year. At the end of 10 years with fulfilment of the warranty, the purchaser would have received £20,000, and allowing for the £10,000 he had spent in buying the machine he would be £10,000 for it and supposing it is found to be entirely valueless, the purchaser might say 'Well, I am claiming simply my profits, £20,000'. But it seems to me that he could alternatively say this: 'Out of £2,000 received by me each year I would have allocated £1,000 each year over the 10 years to pay for the plant, and so my net profit would be £1,000 a year. Instead of claiming £20,000, I claim back the £10,000 I have paid for the plant, which is valueless, and I claim the profits that I would have made, £1,000 a year over 10 years, £10,000.' In either way of statement, the amount of the claim is the same. It seems to me that what was done in the statement of claim here was to put the matter in that latter way. It was pleaded on behalf of the plaintiff that, by reason of the breach of warranty, the plaintiff was out of pocket. He had spent sums for the plant and for accessory plant and for buildings. He says 'I want those sums back, less, of course, the present scrap value of what I have got and, in addition, I want the profits that I would have made, namely, my net profits, out of the profits that I would have received each year. I make an allocation of one-tenth and making that allowance I arrive at my net profits'. It seems to me that that is permissible and logical to formulate the claim in that way.

Under the heading E, 'loss of profit' in the particulars of damage in the present case there was a subtraction of depreciation at 10% per annum. There came the time when the plaintiff, being asked for particulars, limited his claim. It was, in the first place, a claim for what he had spent less the scrap value of what he still had, together with net profits for the whole period which was covered by the words 'and continuing'. Being asked for particulars, he limited his claim as regards the item of profits to the period of almost precisely three years from the date of the delivery of the plant. The claim being so limited, it seems to me that when computing profits, if they are being given in addition to what the plaintiff has lost, it would be right to follow the pattern of the statement of claim and make a deduction each year (the life of the plant being 10 years) of 10% from the net profits, as was originally done in the statement of claim. Mr Wilson has submitted, as being his minimum submission, that in any event there should be such a deduction from the damages as awarded. To that extent, I, for my part, would accede to his submission. I would say that the damages as awarded should be reduced by three times £1,448 which I think makes a deduction of £4,344. But if such a reduction is made, then, in my judgment, the result is logical and the resultant figure correct. As it seems to me, it was reasonable for the plaintiff to have limited his claim as regards profits in the way he did. There would have come a time when it would have had to be recognised as a matter of reality that the plant was no good and that the whole project with that plant was a fiasco. Time had passed which was unproductive and that time was irretrievably lost. That being so, I should have thought it was rational for the plaintiff to say 'Well, then I limit my claim for loss of profit'. He would have to do his best to mitigate his loss. The defendants themselves said that the plaintiff had not done enough to mitigate his loss. The plaintiff would have to see what alternative steps he could take to make such profit in business as he had hoped to make as a result of a satisfaction by the defendants of the warranty that they gave in regard to the machine that they had sold. Hence, I think that it was reasonable to limit the claim.

Which view is correct? Is Lord Evershed wrong in his view that an award of damages comprising both expenditure loss and loss of profit will inevitably involve over compensation? Morris LJ in his dissenting judgment emphasises the difference between net profit and gross profit. How does this serve to cut out any element of over-compensation?

DAMAGES FOR MISREPRESENTATION AND FRAUD

Where the claimant has been induced to enter a contract in reliance on the defendant's misrepresentation or has incurred detrimental reliance loss as a result of a misstatement or deceit, the measure of damages is assessed by restoring the status quo. It should not be forgotten that although a misrepresentation induces a contractual relationship, the action for damages is one which effectively sounds in tort – the tort being either that of deceit if the misrepresentation is fraudulent or the statutory tort created by the Misrepresentation Act 1967.

For these purposes, a fraudulent misrepresentation is one made knowingly, or without belief in its truth or recklessly careless whether it be true or false.[38] The award of damages is designed to place the claimant in the

---

38   *Derry v Peek* (1889) 14 App Cas 337.

same position he/she would have been in if the statement had not been made rather than to put him into the position he/she would have been in had it been true.

In cases of fraudulent misrepresentation, the defendant is also liable for all the damage to the claimant which flows directly from the fraudulent statement.

In *Doyle v Olby (Ironmongers) Ltd,*[39] the defendant advertised his business for sale, claiming that it had an annual turnover of £27,000. The plaintiff, who was interested in purchasing the business, was shown copies of the accounts and was informed that trade entailed 'Two-thirds retail, one-third wholesale – all over the counter', which indicated that the purchaser would have no need to employ a commercial traveller to canvass for orders. In fact, turnover was less than had been represented and half the trade was wholesale, requiring a traveller to canvass for orders. However, the plaintiff could not afford to employ a traveller, with the result that all that trade was lost. It was accepted that the relevant misrepresentations were fraudulent and the plaintiff sued for damages.

The Court of Appeal held that, for the purposes of a fraud action, the plaintiff could recover in respect of all the damage which flows from the fraudulent statement:

Doyle v Olby (Ironmongers) Ltd [1969] 2 QB 158, CA, p 166

Lord Denning MR: It appears, therefore, that counsel for the plaintiff submitted, and the judge accepted, that the proper measure of damages was the 'cost of making good the representation', or what came to the same thing, 'the reduction in value of the goodwill' due to the misrepresentation. In so doing, he treated the representation as if it were a contractual promise, that is, as if there were a contractual term to the effect 'The trade is all over the counter. There is no need to employ a traveller'. I think it was the wrong measure. Damages for fraud and conspiracy are assessed differently from damages for breach of contract.

It was submitted by counsel for the defendants that we could not or, at any rate, ought not, to correct this error. I do not agree. We never allow a client to suffer for the mistake of his counsel if we can possibly help it. We will always seek to rectify it as far as we can. We will correct it whenever we are able to do so without injustice to the other side. Sometimes, the error has seriously affected the course of the evidence, in which case, we can at best order a new trial. But there is nothing of that kind here. The error was made at the end of the case. All the evidence had been taken on the footing that the damages were at large. It was only in the final submission that the error was made. Such an error we can, and will, correct.

---

39 [1969] 2 QB 158, CA.

The second question is what is the proper measure of damages for fraud, as distinct from damages for breach of contract. It was discussed during the argument in *Hadley v Baxendale*, and finds a place in the notes to *Smith's Leading Cases*, 13th edn, p 563, where it is suggested there is no difference. But, in *McConnel v Wright*, Sir Richard Henn Collins MR pointed out the difference. It was an action for fraudulent statements in a prospectus whereby a man was induced to take up shares. He said of the action for fraud: 'It is not an action for breach of contract and, therefore, no damages in respect of prospective gains which the person contracting was entitled by his contract to expect come in, but it is an action of tort – it is an action for a wrong done whereby the plaintiff was tricked out of certain money in his pocket; and, therefore, *prima facie*, the highest limit of his damages is the whole extent of his loss, and that loss is measured by the money which was in his pocket and is now in the pocket of the company.'

But that statement was the subject of comment by Lord Atkin in *Clark v Urquhart, Stracey v Urquhart*. He said: 'I find it difficult to suppose that there is any difference in the measure of damages in an action of deceit depending upon the nature of the transaction into which the plaintiff is fraudulently induced to enter. Whether he buys shares or buys sugar, whether he subscribes for shares, or agrees to enter into a partnership or in any other way alters his position to his detriment, in principle, the measure of damages should be the same, and whether estimated by a jury or a judge. I should have thought it would be based on the actual damage directly flowing from the fraudulent inducement. The formula in *McConnel v Wright* may be correct or it may be expressed in too rigid terms.'

I think that Lord Collins did express himself in too rigid terms. He seems to have overlooked consequential damages. On principle the distinction seems to be this: in contract, the defendant has made a promise and broken it. The object of damages is to put the plaintiff in as good a position, as far as money can do it, as if the promise had been performed. In fraud, the defendant has been guilty of a deliberate wrong by inducing the plaintiff to act to his detriment. The object of damages is to compensate the plaintiff for all the loss he has suffered, so far, again, as money can do it. In contract, the damages are limited to what may reasonably be supposed to have been in the contemplation of the parties. In fraud, they are not so limited. The defendant is bound to make reparation for all the actual damage directly flowing from the fraudulent inducement. The person who has been defrauded is entitled to say 'I would not have entered into this bargain at all but for your representation. Owing to your fraud, I have not only lost all the money I paid you, but, what is more, I have been put to a large amount of extra expense as well and suffered this or that extra damages'. All such damages can be recovered and it does not lie in the mouth of the fraudulent person to say that they could not reasonably have been foreseen. For instance, in this very case, the plaintiff has not only lost the money which he paid for the business, which he would never have done if there had been no fraud – he put all that money in and lost it – but, also, he has been put to expense and loss in trying to run a business which has turned out to be a disaster for him. He is entitled to damages for all his loss, subject, of course, to giving credit for any benefit that he has received. There is nothing to be taken off in mitigation: for there is nothing more that he could have done to reduce his loss. He did all that he could reasonably be expected to do.

An action for damages for fraud, being tortious in nature, will not allow the recovery of expectation losses. But, it appears, this need not necessarily mean that an award cannot be made for loss of profit (although, of course, that will be the usual consequence). It appears that, in appropriate circumstances, status quo damages may include not just losses caused, but also an element in respect of gains prevented. However, it is nonetheless important for the court to ensure that it does not end up placing the claimant in precisely the same position he would have been in had the defendant's statement been true, as this would have the effect of satisfying the claimant's expectations of performance and would convert the defendant's statement from a mere inducement into a contractual promise.

In *East v Maurer*,[40] the defendant owned two hairdressing businesses in the same area. The plaintiffs sought to purchase one of these. An important influencing factor in the plaintiffs' decision to purchase was a statement by the defendant to the effect that he would not work at the other hairdressing salon owned by him, except in cases of emergency and that he intended to work abroad. This statement was of some significance, since the defendant was a specialist with a considerable local reputation. In fact, the defendant continued to work at the other salon after the plaintiffs purchased his business for £20,000. Subsequently, the plaintiffs were forced to sell the business, but only obtained £7,500, because it never took off, due to the defendant's continued presence in the area.

At first instance, the plaintiffs were awarded £33,328 damages, comprising the diminished value of the business and £15,000 for loss of profit, on the assumption that these were the profits which would have been made by the defendant had he not sold the business, discounted to allow for the plaintiffs' lack of experience.

The Court of Appeal reduced the latter element of the award to £10,000 on the basis that an award of £15,000 amounted to compensating the plaintiffs for their full expectation loss, whereas since this was an action for fraud, damages for breach of warranty were not recoverable:

East v Maurer [1991] 1 WLR 461, CA, p 464

Beldam LJ: That the measure of damages for the tort of deceit and for breach of contract are different no longer needs support from authority. Damages for deceit are not awarded on the basis that the plaintiff is to be put in as good a position as if the statement had been true; they are to be assessed on a basis which would compensate the plaintiff for all the loss he has suffered, so far as money can do it.

---

40 [1991] 1 WLR 461, CA.

This was confirmed in *Doyle v Olby (Ironmongers) Ltd* [1969] 2 All ER 119 ...

In the present case, it seems to me that the difference can be put in this way. The first defendant did not warrant to the plaintiffs that all the customers with whom he had a professional rapport would remain customers of the salon at Exeter Road. He represented that he would not be continuing to practise as a stylist in the immediate area ...

Mr Shawcross has pointed out that in *Doyle v Olby* ... none of the judgments referred to loss of profit as a recoverable head of damage; it may well be that the facts of each of those cases and the period involved before the claims were made may not have made loss of profit a considerable head of damage. But, as to the statements of principle to which I have referred, it seems to me clear that there is no basis upon which one could say that loss of profits incurred whilst waiting for an opportunity to realise to its best advantage a business which has been purchased are irrecoverable. It is conceded that losses made in the course of running the business of a company are recoverable. If, in fact, the plaintiffs lost the profit which they could reasonably have expected from running a business in the area of a kind similar to the business, in this case, I can see no reason why those do not fall within the words of Lord Atkin in *Clark v Urquhart, Stracey v Urquhart* [1930] AC 28, p 68: '... actual damage directly flowing from the fraudulent inducement.'

So, I consider that, on the facts found by the judge in the present case, the plaintiffs did establish that they had suffered a loss due to the defendant's misrepresentation which arose from their inability to earn the profits in the business which they hoped to buy in the Bournemouth area.

I would therefore reject the submission of Mr Shawcross that loss of profits is not a recoverable head of damage in cases of this kind.

However, I am not satisfied that, in arriving at the figure of £15,000, the judge approached the quantification of those damages on the correct basis. It seems to me that he was inclined to base his award on an assessment of the profits which the business actually bought by the plaintiffs might have made if the statement made by the first defendant had amounted to a warranty that customers would continue to patronise the salon in Exeter Road; further, that he left out of account a number of significant factors. What he did was to found his award on an evaluation which he made of the profits of the business at Exeter Road made by the first defendant in the year preceding the purchase of the business by the plaintiffs. Basing himself on figures which had been given to him by an accountant, and making an allowance for inflation he arrived at a figure for the profits which might have been made if the first defendant had continued to run the business at Exeter Road during the three and a quarter years. He then made an allowance only for the fact that the second plaintiff's experience in hair styling and hairdressing was not as extensive or as cosmopolitan as that of the first defendant. Thus, he based his award on an assessment of what the profits would have been, less a deduction of 25% for the second plaintiff's lack of experience.

It seems to me that he should have begun by considering the kind of profit which the second plaintiff might have made if the representation which induced her to buy the business at Exeter Road had not been made, and that involved considering the kind of profits which she might have expected to make in another hairdressing business bought for a similar sum. Mr Nicholson has argued that on the evidence of Mr Knowles, an experienced accountant, the learned judge could have arrived at the same or an equivalent figure on that basis. I do not agree. The judge left out of account the fact that the second plaintiff was moving into an entirely different area and one in which she was, comparatively speaking, a stranger, secondly, that she was going to deal with a different clientele and, thirdly, that there were almost certainly in that area of Bournemouth other smart hairdressing salons which represented competition and which, in any event, if the first defendant had, as he had represented, gone to open a salon on the continent, could have attracted the custom of his former clients.

The judge, as Mr Nicholson has pointed out, had two clear starting points: first, that any person investing £20,000 in a business would expect a greater return than if the sum was left safely in the bank or in a building society earning interest, and a reasonable figure for that at the rates then prevailing would have been at least £6,000; secondly, that the salary of a hairdresser's assistant in the usual kind of establishment was at this time £40 per week and that the assistant could expect tips in addition. That would produce a figure of over £2,000, but the proprietor of a salon would clearly expect to earn more, having risked his money in the business. It seems to me that those are valid points from which to start to consider what would be a reasonable sum to award for loss of profits of a business of this kind. As was pointed out by Winn LJ in *Doyle v Olby*, this is not a question which can be considered on a mathematical basis. It has to be considered essentially in the round, making what he described as a 'jury assessment' ([1969] 2 QB 158, p 169).

Taking all the factors into account, I think that the learned judge's figure was too high; for my part, I would have awarded a figure of £10,000 for that head of damage and, to this extent, I would allow the appeal.

The award made in *East v Maurer* is unusual and the mechanism by which such notional lost profits (based on some hypothetical alternative business) is not clear. Nevertheless, it has more recently received House of Lords support. In *Smith New Court Securities Ltd Citibank NA*,[41] Lord Steyn commented 'Counsels for Citibank argued that in the case of a fraudulently induced sale of a business loss of profits is only recoverable on the basis of the contractual measure, and never on the basis of the tort measure applicable to fraud. This is an over-simplification. The plaintiff is not entitled to demand that the defendant must pay to him the profits of the business as represented. On the other hand, *East v Maurer* shows that an award based on the hypothetical profitable business in which the plaintiff would have engaged but for deceit is permissible: it is classic consequential loss'.

Until 1967, if the misrepresentation was not made fraudulently, there was no obvious basis for an award of damages, unless the statement fell within the

---

41 [1997] AC 254, p 282.

common law rule in *Hedley Byrne & Co v Heller & Partners Ltd*[42] relating to tortious liability for negligent misstatement or if the court was able to treat the statement as forming the basis of a collateral contract.[43] However, since the enactment of s 2(1) of the Misrepresentation Act 1967, there is now an available action for damages for a negligent misrepresentation which has the added advantage of placing on the misrepresentor the duty of disproving negligence, while, at the same time, conferring on the claimant the advantages of the rules on remoteness and assessment of damages for the tort of deceit:

Misrepresentation Act 1967

2

(1) Where a person has entered into a contract after a misrepresentation has been made to him by another party thereto and, as a result thereof, he has suffered loss, then, if the person making the misrepresentation would be liable to damages in respect thereof had the misrepresentation been made fraudulently, that person shall be so liable, notwithstanding that the misrepresentation was not made fraudulently, unless he proves that he had reasonable ground to believe and did believe up to the time the contract was made that the facts represented were true.

The measure of damages under s 2(1) is designed to put the claimant in the position he would have been in if the statement had not been made.[44] As such, this clearly involves the application of tortious principles of assessment and remoteness of loss. Moreover, the following extract also shows that the relevant tort rules to apply are not those employed in relation to a negligence action, but instead, those applicable to fraud actions.

In *Royscot Trust Ltd v Rogerson*,[45, 46] a customer agreed to buy a car from a dealer for £7,600. Hire-purchase was arranged with the plaintiffs, but the dealer falsified the figures on the hire-purchase proposal, stating that the customer had paid a deposit of £1,600 representing 20% of the purchase price of £8,000. In fact, D1 paid a deposit of £1,200, representing less than 20% of the actual price of £7,600. The end result was that the plaintiff's finance company still advanced £6,400 in respect of the intended purchase.

Subsequently, the customer paid instalments amounting to £2,774, but then dishonestly sold the car to a third party who acquired a good title. In an

42 [1964] AC 465.

43 See materials on collateral contracts in Chapter 5, especially the discussion of *Evans J & Son (Portsmouth) Ltd v Merzario (Andrea)* [1976] 1 WLR 1078 and *Esso Petroleum Ltd v Mardon* [1978] 1 QB 801.

44 *André et Cie SA v Ets Michel Blanc & Fils* [1977] 2 Lloyd's Rep 166; *Royscot Trust Ltd v Rogerson* [1991] 2 QB 297.

45 The reason for the deception was that the finance company had a policy of not considering hire-purchase applications, unless the deposit payable was, at least, 20% of the total cash price.

46 [1991] 2 QB 297, CA.

action for damages, the plaintiffs were awarded £1,600 against the dealer representing the extra amount they had been induced to pay on the basis that if the actual deposit of £1,200 had been stated, the sale price should have been only £6,000 rather than £7,600, with the result that the plaintiffs would have advanced only £4,800, rather than £6,400.

The dealer appealed against this decision and the plaintiffs cross-appealed, contending that its actual loss was £3,625 representing the difference between the amount advanced and the outstanding balance owed to them by D1 under the hire-purchase agreement.

The Court of Appeal held that the appropriate measure of damages to apply was that applicable to fraud actions in tort, so that the plaintiff was entitled to recover all the loss which flowed directly from the misrepresentation, even if not foreseeable. On this basis, the plaintiff was entitled to the £3,625 under the counterclaim, subject to allowance being made in respect of payments already made:

Royscot Trust Ltd v Rogerson [1991] 2 QB 297, CA, p 303

Balcombe LJ: Before us neither side sought to uphold the judge's assessment of damages. It assumed a hypothetical sale of the car with a deposit of £1,200 and a balance of £4,800 payable by the finance company to the dealer, and there was no evidence that such a sale would ever have taken place ...

So, I turn to the issue on this appeal which the dealer submits raises a pure point of law: where: (a) a motor dealer innocently misrepresents to a finance company the amount of the sale price of, and the deposit paid by the intended purchaser of, the car; and (b) the finance company is thereby induced to enter into a hire-purchase agreement with the purchaser which it would not have done if it had known the true facts; and (c) the purchaser thereafter dishonestly disposes of the car and defaults on the hire-purchase agreement from the motor dealer?

The finance company's cause of action against the dealer is based on s 2(1) of the Misrepresentation Act 1967 ...

As a result of some *dicta* by Lord Denning MR in two cases in the Court of Appeal – *Gosling v Anderson* [1972] EGD 709 and *Jarvis v Swans Tours Ltd* [1973] QB 233, p 237 – and the decision at first instance in *Watts v Spence* [1976] Ch 165, there was some doubt whether the measure of damages of an innocent misrepresentation giving rise to a cause of action under the 1967 Act was the tortious measure, so as to put the representee in the position in which he would have been if he had never entered into the contract, or the contractual measure, so as to put the representee in the position in which he would have been if the misrepresentation had been true, and thus in some cases give rise to a claim for damages for loss of bargain ...

In view of the wording of the sub-section, it is difficult to see how the measure of damages under it could be other than the tortious measure and, despite the initial aberrations referred to above, that is now generally accepted. Indeed, counsel before us did not seek to argue the contrary.

The first main issue before us was: accepting that the tortious measure is the right measure, is it the measure where the tort is that of fraudulent misrepresentation, or is it the measure where the tort is negligence at common law? The difference is that, in cases of fraud, a plaintiff is entitled to any loss which flowed from the defendant's fraud, even if the loss could not have been foreseen: see *Doyle v Olby (Ironmongers) Ltd* [1969] 2 QB 158. In my judgment, the wording of the sub-section is clear: the person making the innocent misrepresentation shall be 'so liable', that is, liable to damages as if the representation had been made fraudulently ...

By 'so liable', I take it to mean liable as he would be if the misrepresentation had been made fraudulently.

This was also the original view of the academic writers. In Atiyah and Treitel, 'Misrepresentation Act 1967' (1967) 30 MLR 369, pp 373–74, it says: 'The measure of damages in the statutory action will apparently be that in an action of deceit ... But, more probably, the damages recoverable in the new action are the same as those recoverable in an action of deceit ...'

It seems to me ... that we must follow the literal wording of s 2(1), even though that has the effect of treating, so far as the measure of damages is concerned, an innocent person as if he were fraudulent. *Chitty on Contracts*, 26th edn, 1989, para 439 says: '... it is doubtful whether the rule that the plaintiff may recover even unforeseeable losses suffered as the result of fraud would be applied; it is an exceptional rule which is probably justified only in cases of actual fraud.'

With all respect to the various learned authors whose works I have cited above, it seems to me that to suggest that a different measure of damage applies to an action for innocent misrepresentation under the section than that which applies to an action for fraudulent misrepresentation (deceit) at common law is to ignore the plain words of the sub-section and is inconsistent with the cases to which I have referred. In my judgment, therefore, the finance company is entitled to recover from the dealer all the losses which it suffered as a result of its entering into the agreements with the dealer and the customer, even if those losses were unforeseeable, provided that they were not otherwise too remote.

If the question of foreseeability had been the only issue in this appeal, the judgment so far would have rendered it unnecessary to decide whether, in the circumstances of the present case, the wrongful sale of the car by the customer was reasonably foreseeable by the dealer. Since the judge did not expressly deal with this point in his judgment, it might have been preferable that we should not do so. Nevertheless, there is a separate issue of whether the wrongful sale of the car was *novus actus interveniens* and thus broke the chain of causation, and the reasonable foreseeability of the event in question is a factor to be taken into account on that issue. Accordingly, it is necessary to deal with this matter. Mr Kennedy, for the dealer, submitted that, while a motor car dealer might be expected to foresee that a customer who buys a car on hire-purchase may default in payment of his instalments, he cannot be expected to foresee that he will wrongfully dispose of the car. He went on to submit that, in the particular circumstances of this case, where the customer was apparently reputable, being a young married man in employment, it was even less likely that the dealer could have foreseen what might happen. There appears to have been no oral evidence directed to this particular point.

In my judgment, this is to ignore both the reality of the transaction and general experience. While, in legal theory, the car remains the property of the finance company until the last hire-purchase instalment is paid, in practice the purchaser is placed in effective control of the car and treats it as his own. Further, there have been so many cases, both civil and criminal, where persons buying a car on hire-purchase have wrongfully disposed of the car that we can take judicial notice that this is an all too frequent occurrence. Accordingly, I am satisfied that, at the time when the finance company entered into the agreements with the dealer and the customer, it was reasonably foreseeable that the customer might wrongfully sell the car ...

I doubt whether further citation of authority will be helpful: in this field, authority is almost too plentiful. For the reasons I have already given, in my judgment, the dealer should reasonably have foreseen the possibility that the customer might wrongfully sell the car. In my judgment, therefore, the sale was not *novus actus interveniens* and did not break the chain of causation.

Mr Kennedy's final submission was that the normal rule is that the plaintiff's loss must be assessed as at the date of his reliance upon the misrepresentation: since the finance company paid £6,400 to the dealer and, in return, acquired title to a car which was worth at least that sum, its loss assessed at that date was nil. This submission again falls into the error of treating the transaction according to its technicalities: that the finance company was interested in purchasing the car. That was not the reality: the finance company was interested in receiving the totality of the instalments from the customer. Once the transaction is looked at in this way, the authorities on which Mr Kennedy relied to support·this submission, being all concerned with misrepresentations leading to the acquisition of chattels, can be seen to be of little assistance. But even in such a case, the rule is not a hard and fast one – see the recent case of *Naughton v O'Callaghan* [1990] 3 All ER 191. So, I reject this submission also.

Accordingly, I would dismiss the dealer's appeal. I would allow the finance company's cross-appeal, set aside the judgment of 22 February 1990 and direct that, in its place, judgment be entered for the finance company against the dealer in the sum of £3,625.24, together with interest. The finance company accepts that it will have to give credit for any sums that it may receive from its judgment against the customer.

There are many criticisms which can be made of this decision, firstly, is this decision strictly in line with *Doyle v Olby*? If the claimant can recover that loss which flows *directly* from the misrepresentation, does that include losses resulting from the breach of an associated transaction, or is such loss the *indirect* consequence of the misrepresentation? Secondly, the construction placed upon s 2(1) – and the adoption of the (so called) 'fiction of fraud' represents a highly literal 'reading' of the section when alternative constructions were available, which would have produced a more sensible result, and which would have been more in line with the weight of academic opinion. It surely makes more sense to construe the words 'so liable' in s 2(1) as merely referring to the general existence of damages under s 2(1), which had formerly only existed in respect of fraudulent misrepresentation rather than as importing all the rules of fraud into what is, at root, a negligence action. In *Smith New Court Ltd v Citibank NA*,[47] Lord Steyn at the very least raised a critical eyebrow. 'The question is whether the rather loose wording of [s 2(1)] compels the court to treat a person who was morally innocent as if he was guilty of fraud when it comes to the measure of damages. There has been trenchant academic criticism of the *Royscott* case: see *Richard Hooley* ... (1991) 107 LQR 547. Since this point does not directly arise in the present case, I express no concluded view on the correctness of the decision in *Royscott*'.

Of course, fact that fraud rules on damages and remoteness of loss apply to an action under s 2(1) does not mean that all the rules applicable to actions for deceit are also applicable. For example, there may be different rules for the purposes of limitation of actions.

Much of the law in relation to damages for fraudulent and negligent misrepresentations have been reviewed recently by the House of Lords in *Smith New Court Securities Ltd v Citibank NA* (originally *Scrimgeour Vickers Ltd and Another*).[48] The case concerned the losses caused by the dramatic fall in the shares of Ferranti caused by the discovery of serious fraud which had inflated the company share price. In total, the plaintiffs suffered losses of around £11 m. The plaintiffs had been induced to buy the shares in the first place, at a higher price than they would otherwise have done, by fraudulent misrepresentation that they were competing with two other bidders (this amounted to an 'over' payment of some 4 p per share). What was the correct method of assessing damages; to compensate the plaintiff for the difference between the price they had paid for the shares and the market price at the time (approximately £1.2 m) or the difference between the price they had paid and the true value of the shares (approx £11 m)? The Court of Appeal thought the former, but the House of Lords felt the latter and reversed the decision. As a general rule, the value of any 'property' was to be taken as at the time of its acquisition, but this general rule would not apply where the innocent party was 'locked into' the property (as here):

---

47 [1997] AC 254, p 283.
48 *Ibid,* p 254.

Smith New Court Securities Ltd v Citibank NA [1997] AC 254, p 278

Lord Steyn:

Damages

The issue

Given the fact that the subsequent dramatic fall in the value of Ferranti shares was caused by the disclosure of an earlier fraud practised on Ferranti by a third party the question is whether Smith is entitled to recover against Citibank the entire loss arising from the fraudulently induced transaction. Smith submits that the Court of Appeal adopted the wrong measure. Smith seeks to recover damages calculated on the basis of the price paid less the aggregate of subsequent realisations. Citibank contends that the loss attributable to the subsequent disclosure of the fraud by a third party is a misfortune risk and is irrecoverable. Citibank argues that the Court of Appeal adopted the correct measure.

Horses and shares

The fraud perpetrated by Mr Roberts on Smith related to shares quoted on the Stock Exchange. Undoubtedly, the legal measure of damages in an action in deceit when applied to transactions in shares may throw up special problems. It is not simply a matter of the perception of the market as to the value of the shares. If loss is to be determined by way of the price paid less a valuation of the shares at a given date, the determination of the real or true value of the shares, absent the deceit forming the basis of the claim, may give rise to difficult hypothetical problems. Even more difficult problems arise if it is alleged that for extrinsic reasons there has been a false market, for example, because investors have been misled by widespread false statements about the value of the stock of the company. None of these practical considerations justify the adoption of a special rule in respect of share transactions. The same legal principle must govern sales of shares, goods, a business or land. It is therefore possible to simplify the problem. The example given by Cockburn CJ in *Twycross v Grant* (1877) 2 CPD 469 is instructive. He said, at pp 544–45:

> If a man buys a horse as a racehorse, on the false representation that it has won some great race, while, in reality, it is a horse of very inferior speed, and he pays 10 or 20 times as much as the horse is worth, and after the buyer has got the animal home, it dies of some latent disease inherent in its system at the time he bought it, he may claim the entire price he gave; the horse was, by reason of the latent mischief, worthless when he bought; but if it catches some disease and dies, the buyer cannot claim the entire value of the horse, which he is no longer in a condition to restore, but only the difference between the price he gave and the real value at the time he bought.

Counsel for Citibank argued that Cockburn CJ erred in saying that if the horse had some latent disease at the time of the transaction the buyer may claim the entire price he paid. He argued that, in such a case, there was no sufficient causal link between the latent disease and the eventual death of the horse.

Counsel for Smith argued that the transaction, which was induced by deceit, directly led to the loss of the entire value of the horse. On any view it is clear that, if Cockburn CJ is right, the law imposes liability in an action for deceit for some consequences that were unforeseen and unforeseeable when the tortfeasor committed the wrong. And, if that is right, it may tell us something about the correct disposal of the present case.

The justification for distinguishing between deceit and negligence.

That brings me to the question of policy whether there is a justification for differentiating between the extent of liability for civil wrongs depending on where in the sliding scale from strict liability to intentional wrongdoing the particular civil wrong fits in. It may be said that logical symmetry and a policy of not punishing intentional wrongdoers by civil remedies favour a uniform rule. On the other hand, it is a rational and defensible strategy to impose wider liability on an intentional wrongdoer. As *Hart and Honoré, Causation in the Law*, 2nd edn, 1985, p 304 observed, an innocent plaintiff may, not without reason, call on a morally reprehensible defendant to pay the whole of the loss he caused. The exclusion of heads of loss in the law of negligence, which reflects considerations of legal policy, does not necessarily avail the intentional wrongdoer. Such a policy of imposing more stringent remedies on an intentional wrongdoer serves two purposes. First, it serves a deterrent purpose in discouraging fraud.

...

And, in the battle against fraud, civil remedies can play a useful and beneficial role. Secondly, as between the fraudster and the innocent party, moral considerations militate in favour of requiring the fraudster to bear the risk of misfortunes directly caused by his fraud. I make no apology for referring to moral considerations. The law and morality are inextricably interwoven. To a large extent the law is simply formulated and declared morality. And, as *Oliver Wendell Holmes, The Common Law* (Howe, M De W, p 106, observed, the very notion of deceit with its overtones of wickedness is drawn from the moral world.

...

Doyle v Olby (Ironmongers) Ltd

Eventually, the idea took root that an intentional wrongdoer is not entitled to the benefit of the reasonable foreseeability test of remoteness. He is to be held liable in respect of 'the actual damage directly flowing from the fraudulent inducement': see the *obiter dictum* of Lord Atkin in *Clark v Urquhart* [1930] AC 28, p 68, and compare *dicta* of Dixon J in *Potts v Miller* (1940) 64 CLR 282, pp 298–99 and in *Toteff v Antonas* (1952) 87 CLR 647, p 650. It was, however, not until the decision of the Court of Appeal in *Doyle v Olby (Ironmongers) Ltd* [1969] 2 QB 158 that the governing principles were clearly laid down. By fraudulent misrepresentation, the defendant induced the plaintiff to buy a business. The trial judge awarded damages to the plaintiff on the basis of a contractual measure of damages, that is, the cost of making good the representations. The Court of Appeal ruled that this was an error and substituted a higher figure assessed on the basis of the tort measure, that is, restoration of the status quo ante. Lord Denning MR explained, at p 167:

In contract, the damages are limited to what may reasonably be supposed to have been in the contemplation of the parties. In fraud, they are not so limited. The defendant is bound to make reparation for all the actual damages directly flowing from the fraudulent inducement. The person who has been defrauded is entitled to say: 'I would not have entered into this bargain at all but for your representation. Owing to your fraud, I have not only lost all the money I paid you, but, what is more, I have been put to a large amount of extra expense as well and suffered this or that extra damages.' All such damages can be recovered and it does not lie in the mouth of the fraudulent person to say that they could not reasonably have been foreseen.

Winn and Sachs LJJ expressed themselves in similar terms.

The logic of the decision in *Doyle v Olby (Ironmongers) Ltd* justifies the following propositions: (1) the plaintiff in an action for deceit is not entitled to be compensated in accordance with the contractual measure of damage, ie the benefit of the bargain measure. He is not entitled to be protected in respect of his positive interest in the bargain; (2) the plaintiff in an action for deceit is, however, entitled to be compensated in respect of his negative interest. The aim is to put the plaintiff into the position he would have been in if no false representation had been made; (3) the practical difference between the two measures was lucidly explained in a contemporary case note on *Doyle v Olby (Ironmongers) Ltd*: Treitel, GH, 'Damages for deceit' (1969) 32 MLR 556, pp 558–59. The author said:

> If the plaintiff's bargain would have been a bad one, even on the assumption that the representation was true, he will do best under the tortious measure. If, on the assumption that the representation was true, his bargain would have been a good one, he will do best under the first contractual measure (under which he may recover something even if the actual value of what he has recovered is greater than the price);

(4) concentrating on the tort measure, the remoteness test whether the loss was reasonably foreseeable had been authoritatively laid down in *The Wagon Mound* in respect of the tort of negligence a few years before *Doyle v Olby (Ironmongers) Ltd* was decided – *Overseas Tankship (UK) Ltd v Morts Dock & Engineering Co Ltd (The Wagon Mound)* [1961] AC 388. *Doyle v Oldby (Ironmongers) Ltd* settled that a wider test applies in an action for deceit; (5) the *dicta* in all three judgments, as well as the actual calculation of damages in *Doyle v Olby (Ironmongers) Ltd* make clear that the victim of the fraud is entitled to compensation for all the actual loss directly flowing from the transaction induced by the wrongdoer. That includes heads of consequential loss; (6) Significantly, in the present context, the rule in the previous paragraph is not tied to any process of valuation at the date of the transaction. It is squarely based on the overriding compensatory principle, widened in view of the fraud to cover all direct consequences. The legal measure is to compare the position of the plaintiff as it was before the fraudulent statement was made to him with his position as it became as a result of his reliance on the fraudulent statement.

The date of transaction rule

That brings me to the perceived difficulty caused by the date of transaction rule. The Court of Appeal [1994] 1 WLR 1271, p 1283G, referred to the rigidity of 'the rule in *Waddell v Blockey* (1879) 4 QB 678, which requires the damages to be calculated as at the date of sale'. No doubt, this view was influenced by the shape of arguments before the Court of Appeal which treated the central issue as being in reality a valuation exercise. It is right that the normal method of calculating the loss caused by the deceit is the price paid less the real value of the subject matter of the sale. To the extent that this method is adopted, the selection of a date of valuation is necessary. And, generally, the date of the transaction would be a practical and just date to adopt. But it is not always so. It is only *prima facie* the right date. It may be appropriate to select a later date. That follows from the fact that the valuation method is only a means of trying to give effect to the overriding compensatory rule: *Potts v Miller*, 64 CLR 282, p 299, *per* Dixon J; and *County Personnel (Employment Agency) Ltd v Alan R Pulver & Co* [1987] 1 WLR 916, pp 925–26, *per* Bingham LJ. Moreover, and more importantly, the date of transaction rule is imply a second order rule applicable only where the valuation method is employed. If that method is inappropriate, the court is entitled simply to assess the loss flowing directly from the transaction without any reference to the date of transaction or indeed any particular date. Such a course will be appropriate whenever the overriding compensatory rule requires it. An example of such a case is to be found in *Cemp Properties (UK) Ltd v Dentsply Research & Development Corporation* [1991] 2 EGLR 197, p 201, *per* Bingham LJ. There is in truth only one legal measure of assessing damages in an action for deceit: the plaintiff is entitled to recover as damages a sum representing the financial loss flowing directly from his alteration of position under the inducement of the fraudulent representations of the defendants. The analogy of the assessment of damages in a contractual claim on the basis of cost of cure or difference in value springs to mind. In *Ruxley Electronics and Construction Ltd v Forsyth* [1996] AC 344, p 360G, Lord Mustill said: 'There are not two alternative measures of damages, as opposite poles, but only one; namely, the loss truly suffered by the promisee.' In an action for deceit, the price paid less the valuation at the transaction date is simply a method of measuring loss, which will satisfactorily solve many cases. It is not a substitute for the single legal measure: it is an application of it.

Where a misrepresentation is made neither fraudulently nor negligently, there is no automatic right to recover damages, but the court has a discretion under s 2(2) of the Misrepresentation Act 1967 to award damages in lieu of rescission:

Misrepresentation Act 1967

2

(2) Where a person has entered into a contract after a misrepresentation has been made to him otherwise than fraudulently, and he would be entitled, by reason of the misrepresentation, to rescind the contract, then, if it is claimed in any proceedings arising out of the contract that the contract ought to be or has been rescinded, the court or arbitrator may declare the contract subsisting and award damages in lieu of rescission, if of the

opinion that it would be equitable to do so, having regard to the nature of the misrepresentation and the loss which would be caused by it if the contract were upheld, as well as to the loss that rescission would cause to the other party.

As is the case with s 2(1), s 2(2) is silent on the appropriate rules for assessment of damages. Moreover, unlike s 2(1), there is no authoritative judicial statement on the matter. However, since s 2(2) is concerned with merely innocent misrepresentations, it seems highly unlikely that the rules appropriate to a fraud action would apply. Also, since for the purposes of a negligent misrepresentation, the court will not apply the contractual measure of damages for a lost bargain, this would seem to suggest the application of the rules which apply to a negligent misstatement, namely that the tortious status quo loss principle should apply and that the appropriate rule on remoteness should require the loss to be a reasonably foreseeable consequence of the defendant's misrepresentation.

In *Thomas Witter Ltd v TBP Industries Ltd*,[49] Jacob J discussed a number of the uncertainties surrounding the scope of s 2(2). The defendants here argued that they had a defence of innocence both in relation to pattern book expenditure and in relation to the Allied problem, and so escaped s 2(1). I reject that on the facts (see below). But even if the 'innocence defence' applies, then s 2(2) comes into play. Mr Kaye argued that it could not do so because rescission is no longer available. He argued that the discretion under s 2(2) to award damages crucially depends upon the rescission remedy remaining extant at the time the court comes to consider the question. Whether that argument is right has been a moot point since the Act was passed. The leading article of the time, Atiyah and Treitel, 'Misrepresentation Act 1967' [1967] MLR 369, noticed the point at once. I found the argument unattractive: rescission might or might not be available at the time of trial depending on a host of factors which have nothing to do with behaviour of either party. I was not surprised to find that the authors of *Chitty on Contracts*, 27th edn, 1994, para 6-058, p 372 found the suggested construction 'strange', even though Mustill J had apparently accepted it *obiter* in *Atlantic Lines and Navigation Co Inc v Hallam Ltd, The Lucy* [1983] 1 Lloyd's Rep 188 and one of the plaintiffs conceded it in *Alman v Associated Newspapers Ltd* (20 June 1980, unreported).

The argument assumes that the Act is referring to the remedy of 'rescission', though this is not clear. If it were only the remedy referred to then it is difficult to understand the reference to 'has been rescinded' in the section. It seemed to me that the reference might well be to a claim by the representee that he was entitled to rescission, in which case it would be enough for the court to find that the agreement was 'rescissionable' at least by the date when the representee first claimed rescission or at any time. There was enough ambiguity here to look to see what was said in Parliament at the time of the passing of the Act, pursuant to the limited new-found freedom given by *Pepper (Inspector of Taxes) v Hart* [1993] 1 All ER 42; [1993] AC 593. Mr Foxton found

---

49 [1996] 2 All ER 573.

what the Solicitor General of the time said in the House of Commons. Even though it was against his and Mr Kaye's case, in the usual fine tradition of the Bar, he drew it to my attention. The Solicitor General said (741 HC Official Report (5th series) cols 1388–89, 20 February 1967):

> ... the Hon Gentleman put to me the case of the sale of a house. He asked me to suppose that there had been the sale of a house, some defect was discovered afterwards, it might be that a third party had come into the matter, and it might be entirely unjust or inequitable to insist on rescission in such a case. I suggest that, in such a case, as the Lord Chancellor said, the conveyance is unlikely to be rescinded because of the impossibility of restitution. My answer is that a case of that sort would be covered by cl 2(2), which says [here the material words of the present section were read]. That is the option which is given to the court, and in the sort of case which has been put to me ... it would follow that the court or arbitrator would almost certainly award damages in lieu of rescission. Therefore, that matter is really fully covered'.

So, the Solicitor General told the House of Commons that it was his view that damages could be awarded under s 2(2) when there was an impossibility of restitution. Accordingly, I hold that the power to award damages under s 2(2) does not depend upon an extant right to rescission – it only depends upon a right having existed in the past. Whether it depends upon such a right existing at any time, or depends upon such a right subsisting at the time when the representee first claims rescission, I do not have to decide. It was here first claimed by letter of 25 April 1990, which is only some four months from the contract date. In principle, however, I would have thought that it is enough that at any time a right to rescind subsisted. It is damages in lieu of that right (even if barred by later events or lapse of time) which can be awarded.

Given that construction of s 2(2), it may be asked: what is the difference between s 2(2) and s 2(1)? In particular, since s 2(1) has a defence of 'innocence', is that in practical terms useless, because damages can be had under s 2(2)? There is, of course, overlap between the two sub-sections on any construction, and s 2(3) explicitly recognises this. But if my construction covered all the cases covered by s 2(1), then the latter would be pointless and my construction would probably be wrong. However, I do not think there is complete overlap. First, under s 2(1) damages can be awarded in addition to rescission. So if there is 'innocence' the representor cannot have both remedies and never could, whatever the date of the decision. Secondly, the question of an award of damages under s 2(2) is discretionary and the court must take into account the matters referred to in the concluding words of the sub-section. Thirdly, the measure of damages under the two sub-sections may be different – s 2(3) certainly contemplates that this may be so and moreover contemplates that s 2(1) damages may be more than s 2(2) damages and not the other way round. It is fair to say, as *Chitty*, para 6-059, p 373 observes, that 'the Act gives little clue as to how damages are to be assessed under this sub-section if they are not to be assessed in the same way as under sub-s (1)'. However both *Chitty* and Treitel, *Law of Contract*, 8th edn, 1991, p 326 (see, also, Atiyah and Treitel [1967] MLR 369, p 376) suggest that damages under s 2(2) may be limited to the loss in value of what is bought under the contract, whereas s 2(1) damages may also include consequential loss.

I reach my conclusions under s 2(2) without misgivings: as between the person making the innocent misrepresentation and his misrepresentee, the 'merits' favour the latter. The constant and justified academic criticism of the Act indicates a subject well worth the attention of the Law Commission. Fortunately, so far as I am concerned, in the circumstances of this case, there can be no difference between the two sub-sections, for no consequential loss is claimed.

CHAPTER 14

RESTITUTIONARY REMEDIES

Restitutionary remedies are based on the reversal of an unjust enrichment by the defendant at the expense of the claimant. Since the law of restitution is quite distinct from the law of contract,[1] the availability of a restitutionary remedy does not depend upon a breach of contract, but there is an overlap between the two branches of the law of obligations where a breach of contract does result in an unjust enrichment.

In many respects, restitutionary remedies represent a separate branch of obligations law, epitomised by the recognition of the notion of autonomous unjust enrichment, under which the gain to the defendant is a mirror image of the loss suffered by the claimant. Typically, such a situation may arise where there has been an induced mistake of fact caused by, for example, a deliberate misrepresentation which results in a transfer of wealth by the claimant to the misrepresentor.

For present purposes, the principal restitutionary remedies are those of account of profits, an action for moneys had and received and restitutionary damages.

ENRICHMENT

Enrichment may consist of either making a profit or by saving on expenditure which might otherwise have been incurred, although in both cases, the breach of contract must have been the factual cause of the enrichment. Identification of an enrichment is relatively easy when it is in monetary form, as the defendant's gain will normally mirror the claimant's loss. Where the enrichment is in the form of a benefit conferred on the defendant, the tests of free acceptance, incontrovertible benefit or objective valuation may be employed.

The test of free acceptance is not universally regarded as an adequate basis for explaining when a restitutionary remedy may become available.[2] But those who do defend the notion of free acceptance explain its operation by asking whether the defendant, as a reasonable man, should have known that a person in the position of the claimant would expect to be paid for a benefit which has been freely accepted by the defendant in circumstances in which

---

1   *Lipkin Gorman v Karpnale* [1991] 2 AC 548.
2   See, eg, Burrows, 1993, pp 11–14.

665

the defendant has declined to take a reasonable opportunity to reject the benefit.[3] This principle will be especially relevant where there has been a request from the defendant that the benefit be conferred, such as is common where work is commenced on the basis of a letter of intent where the parties subsequently intend to enter into a contract but the contract fails to materialise due to an inability to agree on fundamental terms.[4]

The test of incontrovertible benefit justifies a restitutionary remedy if no reasonable man could say that the defendant was not enriched. Such will be the case where the work done by the claimant would have had to be paid for by the defendant had it been carried out by someone else.[5]

The test of objective valuation requires the court to consider what value would have been placed on the benefit conferred by a reasonable man. This particular test of enrichment is most likely to apply in cases where it is difficult to say whether the work performed has any particular value at the time when the remedy is sought. For example, if an author is commissioned to write a book but is prevented from completing the work by an anticipatory repudiation, it would be difficult to say that the part written book had any subjective value at all. Nonetheless, the court will be able to place an objective value on the work done in a *quantum meruit* claim.[6] However, to say that the defendant has been enriched through the receipt of an unfinished book might be going too far and it may be better to regard this type of case as turning on the notion of reasonable reliance.[7]

UNJUST FACTORS

Whether the enrichment is unjust can be judged by the tests of non-voluntary transfer, free acceptance[8] or by reference to policy considerations.[9] The test of non-voluntary transfer requires the court to consider the reasons why an enrichment has been conferred on the defendant by the claimant. In the context of restitution within contract the main reasons why an enrichment

---

3 Jones, 'The law of restitution: the past and the future', in Burrows (ed), 1991, p 4.

4 See, eg, *British Steel Corpn v Cleveland Bridge & Engineering Co Ltd* [1984] 1 All ER 504; *Peter Lind & Co Ltd v Mersey Docks & Harbour Board* [1972] 2 Lloyd's Rep 234.

5 See, eg, *Craven-Ellis v Cannons Ltd* [1936] 2 KB 403.

6 See, eg, *Planché v Colburn* (1831) 8 Bing 14.

7 See Goff and Jones, 1993, p 53.

8 It is arguable that this does not reveal an unjust factor at all, since the fact that the defendant has freely received a benefit from the plaintiff does not in itself make that receipt unjust. Instead, it can be argued that the unjust factor in this type of case will be the fact that nothing has been given for the benefit and that there is a total failure of consideration: Burrows, 1988, p 577. Now updated in Burrows, 1998.

9 This will most usually be the case in instances of rescue or salvage at sea so as to encourage acts of rescue.

may be regarded as unjust are that the benefit has been conferred by mistake[10] or due to a misrepresentation,[11] by compulsion.[12] Moreover, subsequent events may unfold in such a way that a benefit is conferred in circumstances which suggest that to allow it to be retained would create injustice.

Mistake

Before the relationship of mistake and restitutionary principles is considered, it is important to distinguish a mistake from a mere misprediction. The latter does not give rise to a remedy and is something the claimant must live with. Thus, if one of two joint owners of a house decorates it in the hope that the other owner will contribute to the cost, but later chooses not to, there will be no remedy.[13]

Where there is an operative mistake of fact, a remedy available to the mistaken party is that of rescission of the contract. This remedy cuts across both the law of contract and the law of restitution. In the case of contract law, the effect of rescission is to invalidate the contract, but it also serves to reverse an enrichment made by the defendant at the claimant's expense.

It has been seen already that at common law, the effect of a common mistake is to render a contract void.[14] In terms of restitution, this is not the end of the tale, since a consequence of the mistake may have been a payment by the claimant to the defendant. If losses were left to lie where they fall, the consequence would be an unjust enrichment of the defendant. However, an order for return of any moneys paid will serve to reverse the defendant's enrichment. Thus, if the parties enter into a contract of insurance which fails because at the time of contracting neither party was aware that the subject matter of the contract was non-existent, the insured will be able to recover back any premium he has paid under the mistaken belief that the contract was valid, on the basis that either the consideration has wholly failed[15] or that money has been paid and received under a mistake of fact.[16] In terms of restitutionary principles, both of these alternative approaches can be justified since an operative mistake renders the contract void in which case a payment by the claimant to the defendant needs to be disgorged and a total failure of consideration means that there is no value given in return for a payment made

10 For the general rules on what constitutes an operative mistake at common law and in equity, see Chapters 2 and 6.

11 For the general rules on the requirements for a misrepresentation, see Chapter 4.

12 For the common law and equitable rules on duress and undue influence, see Chapter 7.

13 *Re McArdle* [1951] Ch 669.

14 See Chapter 6.

15 *Strickland v Turner* (1852) 7 Exch 208.

16 *Pritchard v Merchant's & Tradesman's Mutual Life Assurance Society* (1858) 3 CBNS 622.

by the claimant. In either case, the claimant should get back what he has paid otherwise the defendant would be unjustly enriched.

In equity, there is a wider jurisdiction in respect of mistakes made in the process of contracting, coupled with a more mellow array of remedies. Although the rule at common law and in equity is that the mistake must be fundamental before the court will intervene, what appears to be fundamental in equity seems to differ from the very narrow range of mistakes recognised at common law. An important feature of the equitable remedies for mistake is that the court may rescind the contract but at the same time may impose terms upon the order for rescission, thereby recognising the restitutionary and counter-restitutionary claims of both parties. For example, in *Cooper v Phibbs*,[17] a mistake as to the ownership of certain fishery rights rendered a contract for the sale of those rights invalid. The court ordered rescission, but because the party in occupation had improved the fishery during his period of occupation, the order was tempered by a requirement that those improvements should be paid for by allowing a lien to be exercised over the fishery by way of security.

Misrepresentation

It has been seen already that a misrepresentation can cause a person to enter into a contract he would not otherwise have made. Apart from the remedy of damages considered elsewhere,[18] the standard remedy for misrepresentation is that of rescission of the contract, at the instance of the party misled, so as to restore the parties to the positions they occupied before the misrepresentation was made. This restoration differs according to the subject matter of the contract. Where the benefit conferred by the representee is in monetary form, the claimant's restitution measure is the value received. The claimant need not identify the money held by the defendant in order to obtain restitution. Where the subject matter of the contract is not money, the effect of rescission is to ignore the contract and leave a right *in rem* in favour of the property transferred.

However, there are also cases in which an indemnity may be allowed, so as to restore to the claimant particular losses which flow from entering into the contract induced by the misrepresentation. In form, both of these remedies are restitutionary; and should be clearly distinguished from compensatory damages which (even if – in part – based on restitutionary principles, rather than focusing on loss of the bargain) encompasses a wider range of potential liability.[19]

---

17 (1867) LR 2 HL 149. For similar conditions requiring a new contract to be entered into, see *Solle v Butcher* [1950] 1 KB 671 and *Grist v Bailey* [1967] Ch 532.

18 See Chapter 13.

19 See Chapter 13 and *Whittington v Seale Hayne* (1900) WN 31.

In *Redgrave v Hurd*,[20] the plaintiff contracted to purchase a house attached to a solicitor's business in reliance upon a non-fraudulent misrepresentation as to its profitability. Although, today, it would be difficult to argue that there was any form of reasonable reliance upon the misrepresentation sufficient to give rise to an action in tort, it remains the case that it was the defendant's mis-statement which led the plaintiff to believe that he was buying a more profitable business than in fact was the case. In these circumstances, to allow the defendant to keep the purchase price might be seen to involve an unjust enrichment, which was reversed by an order for rescission of the contract, which included the return of a £100 deposit:

Redgrave v Hurd (1881) 20 Ch D 1, CA, p 12

Jessel MR: As regards the rescission of a contract, there was no doubt a difference between the rules of courts of equity and the rules of courts of common law – a difference which of course has now disappeared by the operation of the Judicature Act, which makes the rules of equity prevail. According to the decisions of courts of equity it was not necessary, in order to set aside a contract obtained by material false representation, to prove that the party who obtained it knew at the time when the representation was made that it was false. It was put in two ways, either of which was sufficient. One way of putting the case was, 'A man is not to be allowed to get a benefit from a statement which he now admits to be false. He is not to be allowed to say, for the purpose of civil jurisdiction, that when he made it he did not know it to be false; he ought to have found that out before he made it'. The other way of putting it was this: 'Even assuming that moral fraud must be shewn in order to set aside a contract, you have it where a man, having obtained a beneficial contract by a statement which he now knows to be false, insists upon keeping that contract. To do so is a moral delinquency: no man ought to seek to take advantage of his own false statements.' The rule in equity was settled and it does not matter on which of the two grounds it was rested. As regards the rule of common law, there is no doubt it was not quite so wide. There were, indeed, cases in which, even at common law, a contract could be rescinded for misrepresentation, although it could not be shewn that the person making it knew the representation to be false. They are variously stated, but I think, according to the later decisions, the statement must have been made recklessly and without care, whether it was true or false, and not with the belief that it was true. But, as I have said, the doctrine in equity was settled beyond controversy, and it is enough to refer to the judgment of Lord Cairns in the *Reese River Silver Mining Co v Smith*, in which he lays it down in the way which I have stated.

There is another proposition of law of very great importance which I think it is necessary for me to state, because, with great deference to the very learned judge from whom this appeal comes, I think it is not quite accurately stated in his judgment. If a man is induced to enter into a contract by a false

---

20   (1881) 20 Ch D 1, CA.

representation, it is not a sufficient answer to him to say, 'If you had used due diligence, you would have found out that the statement was untrue. You had the means afforded you of discovering its falsity, and did not choose to avail yourself of them.' I take it to be a settled doctrine of equity, not only as regards specific performance, but also as regards rescission, that this is not an answer, unless there is such delay as constitutes a defence under the Statute of Limitations. That, of course, is quite a different thing. Under the statute, delay deprives a man of his right to rescind on the ground of fraud, and the only question to be considered is from what time the delay is to be reckoned. It had been decided, and the rule was adopted by the statute, that the delay counts from the time when by due diligence the fraud might have been discovered. Nothing can be plainer, I take it, on the authorities in equity than that the effect of false representation is not got rid of on the ground that the person to whom it was made has been guilty of negligence. One of the most familiar instances in modern times is where men issue a prospectus in which they make false statements of the contracts made before the formation of a company, and then say that the contracts themselves may be inspected at the offices of the solicitors. It has always been held that those who accepted those false statements as true were not deprived of their remedy merely because they neglected to go and look at the contracts. Another instance with which we are familiar is where a vendor makes a false statement as to the contents of a lease, as, for instance, that it contains no covenant preventing the carrying on of the trade which the purchaser is known by the vendor to be desirous of carrying on upon the property. Although the lease itself might be produced at the sale, or might have been open to the inspection of the purchaser long previously to the sale, it has been repeatedly held that the vendor cannot be allowed to say, 'You were not entitled to give credit to my statement'. It is not sufficient, therefore, to say that the purchaser had the opportunity of investigating the real state of the case, but did not avail himself of that opportunity. It has been apparently supposed by the learned judge in the court below that the case of *Attwood v Small* conflicts with that proposition. He says this: 'He inquired into it to a certain extent, and if he did that carelessly and inefficiently it is his own fault. As in *Attwood v Small,* those directors and agents of the company who made ineffectual inquiry into the business which was to be sold to the company were nevertheless held by their investigation to have bound the company, so here, I think, the defendant who made a cursory investigation into the position of things on 17 February must be taken to have accepted the statements which were in those papers.' I think that those remarks are inaccurate in law, and are not borne out by the case to which the learned judge referred ...

Such being the facts, even if no observation arose as to the delay, as to the adoption and affirmance of the contract, purging it of all objections which might be made, and supposing that they had come in time, instead of delaying so many months; then I ask myself this question. In these circumstances, have these parties a right to be released from their contract by the interposition of a court of equity, according to those principles which I have stated? When I ask myself that question, upon which alone my judgment must turn, I am bound to say no. So that the two grounds taken by Lord Brougham are that there was no misrepresentation, and that the purchasers did not rely on the representations. He agreed in one with Lord Cottenham and in the other with Lord Devon. The three grounds taken by the three noble lords, one of which grounds was taken by one only of the lords, and each of the others by two, were that there was no fraud – that there was actual knowledge of the facts before the contract, and that no reliance was placed upon the representation. In no way, as it appears to me, does the decision, or any of the grounds of decision, in *Attwood v Small*, support the proposition that it is a good defence to an action for rescission of a contract on the ground of fraud that the man who comes to set aside the contract inquired to a certain extent, but did it carelessly and inefficiently and would, if he had used reasonable diligence, have discovered the fraud ...

The learned judge came to the conclusion either that the defendant did not rely on the statement, or that if he did rely upon it he had shown such negligence as to deprive him of his title to relief from this court. As I have already said, the latter proposition is in my opinion not founded in law, and the former part is not founded in fact; I think also it is not founded in law, for when a person makes a material representation to another to induce him to enter into a contract, and the other enters into that contract, it is not sufficient to say that the party to whom the representation is made does not prove that he entered into the contract, relying upon the representation. If it is a material representation calculated to induce him to enter into the contract, *it is an inference of law* that he was induced by the representation to enter into it, and in order to take away his title to be relieved from the contract on the ground that the representation was untrue, it must be shown either that he had knowledge of the facts contrary to the representation, or that he stated in terms, or showed clearly by his conduct, that he did not rely on the representation. If you tell a man, 'You may enter into partnership with me, my business is bringing in between £300 and £400 a year', the man who makes that representation must know that it is a material inducement to the other to enter into the partnership, and you cannot investigate as to whether it was more or less probable that the inducement would operate on the mind of the party to whom the representation was made. Where you have neither evidence that he knew facts to show that the statement was untrue, or that he said or did anything to shew that he did not actually rely upon the statement, the inference remains that he did so rely, and the statement being a material statement, its being untrue is a sufficient ground for rescinding the contract. For these reasons, I am of opinion that the judgment of the learned judge must be reversed and the appeal allowed.

As regards the form of the judgment, as the appellant succeeds on the counterclaim, I think it would be safer to make an order both in the action and the counterclaim, rescinding the contract and ordering the deposit to be returned. As I have already said, it is not a case in which damages should be given.

Where the claimant seeks the remedy of rescission, the circumstances must be such that none of the bars to rescission applies. These bars include affirmation, lapse of time, the existence of third party rights and that *restitutio in integrum* is not possible.

Affirmation means that the party seeking relief is aware of the facts which give rise to the right to rescind and that, by words or conduct, he has decided not to exercise that right. Typical examples of affirmation include the situation in which the buyer of goods, after becoming aware of the falsity of a misrepresentation, continues to use them. Similarly lapse of time may be taken as evidence of affirmation as may an agreement to accept a cure of defects in the subject matter of the contract.

In *Leaf v International Galleries*,[21] the plaintiff purchased from the defendant a painting entitled 'Salisbury Cathedral' for £85. The defendant had innocently, but falsely, represented that the painting was by John Constable, but, five years after the purchase, it was discovered that this was not the case. The plaintiff sought to return the picture to the defendants and to recover the price he had paid. The Court of Appeal refused to grant rescission of the contract on the ground that the buyer, due to the lapse of time, must be taken to have accepted the goods sold under the contract:

Leaf v International Galleries [1950] 2 KB 86, CA, p 89

Denning LJ: The question is whether the buyer is entitled to rescind the contract on that account. I emphasise that this is a claim to rescind only. There is no claim in this action for damages for breach of condition or breach of warranty. The claim is simply one for rescission. At a very late stage before the country court judge, counsel for the buyer did ask for leave to amend by claiming damages for breach of warranty, but it was not allowed. So, no claim for damages is before us. The only question is whether the buyer is entitled to rescind.

The way in which the case is put by Mr Weitzmann is this. He says this was an innocent misrepresentation and that in equity he is entitled to claim rescission even of an executed contract of sale on that account. He points out that the judge has found that it is quite possible to restore the parties to their original position. It can be done by simply handing back the picture to the defendants.

In my opinion, this case is to be decided according to the well known principles applicable to the sale of goods. This was a contract for the sale of goods. There was a mistake about the quality of the subject matter, because both parties believed the picture to be a Constable, and that mistake was in one sense essential or fundamental. Such a mistake, however, does not avoid the contract. There was no mistake about the subject matter of the sale. It was a specific picture of 'Salisbury Cathedral'. The parties were agreed in the same terms on the same subject matter, and that is sufficient to make a contract: see *Solle v Butcher*.

There was a term in the contract as to the quality of the subject matter, namely, as to the person by whom the picture was painted – that it was by Constable. That term of the contract was either a condition or a warranty. If it was a condition, the buyer could reject the picture for breach of the condition at any

---

21 [1950] 2 KB 86, CA.

time before he accepted it or was to be deemed to have accepted it, whereas, if it was only a warranty, he could not reject it but was confined to a claim for damages.

I think it right to assume in the buyer's favour that this term was a condition, and that, if he had come in proper time, he could have rejected the picture, but the right to reject for breach of condition has always been limited by the rule that once the buyer has accepted, or is deemed to have accepted, the goods in performance of the contract, he cannot thereafter reject, but is relegated to his claim for damages: see s 11(1)(c) of the Sale of Goods Act 1893 and *Wallis, Son and Wells v Pratt and Haynes*.

The circumstances in which a buyer is deemed to have accepted goods in performance of the contract are set out in s 35 of the Act which provides that the buyer is deemed to have accepted this goods, among other things, 'when after the lapse of a reasonable time, he retains the goods without intimating to the seller that he has rejected them'. In this case, this buyer took the picture into his house, and five years passed before he intimated any rejection. That, I need hardly say, is much more than a reasonable time. It is far too late for him at the end of five years to reject this picture for breach of any condition. His remedy after that length of time is for damages only, a claim which he has not brought before the court.

Is it to be said that the buyer is in any better position by relying on the representation, not as a condition, but as an innocent misrepresentation? I agree that on a contract for the sale of goods an innocent material misrepresentation may in a proper case be a ground for rescission even after the contract has been executed. The observations of Joyce J in *Seddon v North Eastern Salt Co* are, in my opinion, too widely stated. Many judges have treated it as plain that an executed contract of sale may, in a proper case, be rescinded for innocent misrepresentation: see, for instance, Warrington LJ and Scrutton LJ in *Harrison v Knowles* ([1918] 1 KB 609, p 610); Lord Atkin in *Bell v Lever Bros Ltd* ([1932] AC 224); Scrutton LJ and Maugham LJ in *L'Estrange v F Graucob Ltd* ([1934] 2 KB 400, p 405).

Apart from that, there is now the decision of the majority of this court in *Solle v Butcher* which overrules the first ground of decision in *Angel v Jay*. It is unnecessary, however, to pronounce finally on these matters because, although rescission may in some cases be a proper remedy, nevertheless it is to be remembered that an innocent misrepresentation is much less potent than a breach of condition. A condition is a term of the contract of a most material character, and, if a claim to reject for breach of condition is barred, it seems to me *a fortiori* that a claim to rescission on the ground of innocent misrepresentation is also barred.

So, assuming that a contract for the sale of goods may be rescinded in a proper case for innocent misrepresentation, nevertheless, once the buyer has accepted, or is deemed to have accepted, the goods, the claim is barred. In this case, the buyer must clearly be deemed to have accepted the picture. He had ample opportunity to examine it in the first few days after he bought it. Then was the time to see if the condition or representation was fulfilled, yet he has kept it all this time. Five years have elapsed without any notice of rejection. In my judgment, he cannot now claim to rescind, and the appeal should be dismissed.

The traditional approach to the bar of affirmation does not appear to be universally accepted, especially in relation to the issue of rescission for breach of contract. It should be noted that, in *Leaf v International Galleries*, Denning LJ took the view that the misrepresentee could not be in a better position than that of a party who complains of a breach of contract. However, in relation to rescission for breach of contract, it was held in *Peyman v Lanjani*[22] that affirmation requires knowledge of the legal right to rescind. In that case, the plaintiff's legal adviser, who also acted for the defendant, urged him to perform a contract after he became aware of the fact that the defendant was guilty of impersonation amounting to fraud. Continuing with the contract was held not to amount to affirmation since the plaintiff was taken not to be aware of his legal right to rescind the contract:

Peyman v Lanjani [1985] Ch 457, CA, p 500

Slade LJ: One significant point, in my opinion, clearly emerges from the passages which I have cited from the four last mentioned decisions. Where the other stated conditions for the operation of the common law doctrine of 'election' are present, a person may be held to his election even though the other party has not in any way acted to his detriment in reliance on the relevant communication; the mere facts of the unequivocal act or statement, coupled with the communication thereof to the other party, suffice to bring the doctrine into play. For this reason, if no other, as appears from the judgments of Lord Diplock and Lord Scarman, a clear distinction has to be drawn between election on the one hand and estoppel or waiver by conduct on the other hand.

The relevant argument in the present case has primarily been directed to election. Before us it has been common ground that the injured party to a contract who has a right of rescission cannot be said to have elected to affirm it at a time before he became aware of the facts which gave rise to this right. However, as Stephenson LJ has demonstrated, statements of the highest authority seem at first sight to give conflicting answers to the question whether knowledge of the existence of the legal right to rescind is also a condition precedent to an effective election.

Lord Blackburn in *Kendall v Hamilton* 4 App Cas 504, p 542, said, 'there cannot be election until there is knowledge of the right to elect'. For the reasons given by Stephenson and May LJJ, I am of the opinion that this statement, which was cited by Lord Porter in *Young v Bristol Aeroplane Co Ltd* [1946] AC 163, p 186, as being the foundation of the principle of election, still correctly represents the law. With Stephenson and May LJJ, I do not think that a person (such as the plaintiff in the present case) can be held to have made the irrevocable choice

---

22 [1985] Ch 457, CA.

between rescission and affirmation which election involves unless he had knowledge of his legal right to choose and actually chose with that knowledge.

I would like to make a few observations as to the practical consequences of this court's decision on this point, as I see them. If A wishes to allege that B, having had a right of rescission, has elected to affirm a contract, he should in his pleadings, so it seems to me, expressly allege B's knowledge of the relevant right to rescind, since such knowledge will be an essential fact upon which he relies. The court may, and no doubt often will, be asked to order A to give further and better particulars of the allegation: see RSC Ord 18, r 12(4). In many cases, the best particulars that A will be able to give will be to invite the court to infer knowledge from all the circumstances. However strong that *prima facie* inference may be, it will still be open to the court at the trial, after hearing evidence as to B's true state of mind, to hold on the balance of probabilities that he did not in fact have the requisite knowledge. In the latter event A's plea that B has elected will fail. Yet it should not be thought that injustice to A will necessarily follow. For if A has acted to his detriment in reliance of an apparent election by B, he will in most cases be able to plead and rely on an estoppel by conduct, in the alternative. If, on the other hand, A has not acted to his detriment in reliance on any such apparent election, justice would not seem to preclude B from sheltering behind his ignorance of his legal rights. These brief observations may perhaps serve to highlight the distinction between election and estoppel.

Since the plaintiff had no knowledge of his legal right to rescind the restaurant agreement, until he consulted new solicitors, his conduct in entering into possession of the restaurant and paying £10,000 to the first defendant, for this reason if no other, cannot in my opinion have amounted to an election to affirm the contract; the only remaining question can be whether the plaintiff by that conduct has estopped himself from relying on his right to rescind.

However, even if I am wrong in thinking that knowledge of the relevant legal right is a pre-condition to an effective election, the result on the facts of the present case is, in my opinion, still the same for these reasons. Whatever knowledge may be requisite, the passages which I have cited above from the judgments in *Clough v London and North Western Railway Co* (1871) LR 7 Ex 26, p 34; *Scarf v Jardine* (1882) 7 App Cas 345, pp 360–61; and *China National Foreign Trade Transportation Corpn v Evlogia Shipping Co SA of Panama* [1979] 1 WLR 1018, pp 1024, 1034–35, in my opinion make it quite clear that a person who has the right to rescind a contract cannot be treated as having elected to affirm it unless and until he has done an unequivocal act, or made an unequivocal statement, which demonstrates to the other party to the contract that he still intends to proceed with it, notwithstanding the relevant breach. An unequivocal act or unequivocal statement on the part of the plaintiff is no less necessary if the first defendant is to rely on an estoppel by conduct.

The judge considered that the arrangements by which the plaintiff took possession of the restaurant and paid the first defendant £10,000 of the purchase price did amount to 'an unequivocal affirmation of the contract'. He thought that the first defendant acted on this affirmation by giving up possession of the restaurant and going away to Iran. The plaintiff, he considered, by these arrangements, 'accepted the title through his solicitors and that as between him and the first defendant is that'.

This conduct of the plaintiff on 22 February 1979 undeniably indicated that, at least for the time being, he intended to proceed with the restaurant agreement. In my opinion, however, this does not by itself suffice to indicate any relevant final choice on his part. The question is whether his conduct on 22 February 1979 would have led the first defendant and his legal advisers reasonably to infer that he did not intend to object to the particular defect in title which had arisen through the first impersonation.

For my part, I do not think that the first defendant or his legal advisers could reasonably have drawn any such inference for the following reasons, among others: (1) neither the first defendant nor anyone acting on his behalf had informed the plaintiff (as the first defendant should have done) of the first impersonation which had been perpetrated by his agent, Mr Moustashari, nor of the consequent defect in his title to the lease of 26 James Street. This defect was a latent one. So far as the evidence shows, it was not even mentioned in discussion or correspondence between the plaintiff and the first defendant or their respective solicitors until the plaintiff consulted new solicitors, Fremont & Co. Until this happened, the first defendant and his solicitors had no reasonable grounds for assuming that the plaintiff was even aware of the facts which gave rise to the defect.

If the approach in *Peyman v Lanjani* is correct, how does this square with the rule that a mistake of law is not recognised?[23]

The second of the bars to rescission is concerned with the issue of third party rights. If a contract is made as a result of a misrepresentation, the contract is voidable rather than void and the party misled can only seek rescission of the contract if this does not infringe a vested right in favour of a third party. Thus, in the case of a contract for the sale of goods it is possible for a rogue to obtain possession of goods under a voidable title[24] and sell those goods to a third party. If the third party buys in good faith and without notice of any defect in title before the claimant has communicated his intention to rescind[25] the contract with the rogue, it will then be too late to allow rescission.[26]

The remaining bar to rescission is that the remedy will not be granted where *restitutio in integrum* is no longer possible. From the point of view of restitutionary principles, if the parties are to be restored to the positions they were in before the commission of the wrong which gives rise to the remedy of

---

23 However see, now, *Kleinwort Benson Ltd v Lincoln City Council* [1998] 4 All ER 513, in which the House of Lords has abrogated the mistake of law bar, for the purposes of restitutionary remedies.

24 Sale of Goods Act 1979, s 23.

25 Or has done the next best thing where the rogue has put it out of the claimant's power to communicate: *Car & Universal Finance Co Ltd v Caldwell* [1965] 1 QB 525.

26 *Lewis v Averay* [1972] 1 QB 198.

rescission, the claimant must be able to give back to the defendant any benefits conferred on him under the contract. Without this return to the pre-contract position, the claimant himself would be unjustly enriched by granting rescission of the contract.

The most likely event preventing *restitutio in integrum* involves consumption or disposal of the subject matter of the contract. Thus, if the thing which the claimant seeks to restore is radically different from the thing contracted, rescission will not be allowed.

In *Clarke v Dickson*,[27] the plaintiff purchased shares in a company from the defendants. Subsequently, with the consent of the plaintiff, the company was reorganised as one with limited liability. When that limited liability company was wound up, the plaintiff discovered that the defendants had been guilty of a misrepresentation and he sought to rescind his contract with the defendants in order to recover the purchase price. However, what he proposed to return to the defendants would have been different in kind to that which was contracted for. Accordingly, rescission was not granted:

Clarke v Dickson (1858) EB & E 148, p 154; 120 ER 463

Crompton J: When once it is settled that a contract induced by fraud is not void, but voidable at the option of the party defrauded, it seems to me to follow that, when that party exercises his option to rescind the contract, he must be in a state to rescind; that is, he must be in such a situation as to be able to put the parties into their original state before the contract. Now here I will assume, what is not clear to me, that the plaintiff bought his shares from the defendants and not from the company, and that he might at one time have had a right to restore the shares to the defendants if he could, and demand the price from them. But then what did he buy? Shares in a partnership with others. He cannot return those; he has become bound to those others. Still stronger, he has changed their nature: what he now has and offers to restore are shares in a quasi-corporation now in process of being wound up. That is quite enough to decide this case. The plaintiff must rescind *in toto* or not at all; he cannot both keep the shares and recover the whole price. That is founded on the plainest principles of justice. If he cannot return the article he must keep it, and sue for his real damage in an action on the deceit. Take the case I put in the argument, of a butcher buying live cattle, killing them, and even selling the meat to his customers. If the rule of law were as the plaintiff contends, that butcher might, upon discovering a fraud on the part of the grazier who sold him the cattle, rescind the contract and get back the whole price: but how could that be consistently with justice? The true doctrine is, that a party can never repudiate a contract after, by his own act, it has become out of his power to restore the parties to their original condition.

Lord Campbell CJ (p 155): I will only say that I remain of the opinion which I expressed at the trial. The plaintiff, on his own shewing, cannot rescind the

---

27 (1858) EB & E 148; (1858) 120 ER 463.

contract and sue for money had and received, but must seek his remedy by a special action for deceit. In that action, if he proves what he states, he will recover, not the original price, but whatever is the real damage sustained.

Strict application of this particular bar to rescission is not always insisted upon since in some cases it is possible to put a value to a non-monetary benefit and thereby allow rescission, subject to an offset, so as to cover the benefit conferred on the claimant by the defendant.

In *Erlanger v New Sombrero Phosphate Co*,[28] the plaintiffs purchased a phosphate mine which they worked for some time. Subsequently, they discovered an actionable non-disclosure on the part of the defendants which was sufficient to allow them to rescind the contract. However, precise restitution was not possible due to the fact that the mine had been worked, but this problem was circumvented by an order for account of profits whereby the plaintiff was required to pay for the benefit derived by him:

Emile Erlanger v The New Sombrero Phosphate Co (1878) 3 App Cas 1218, p 1278

Lord Blackburn: It is, I think, clear on principles of general justice, that as a condition to a rescission there must be a *restitutio in integrum*. The parties must be put in statu quo. See *per* Lord Cranworth in *Addie v The Western Bank*. It is a doctrine which has often been acted upon both at law and in equity. But there is a considerable difference in the mode in which it is applied in courts of law and equity, owing, as I think, to the difference of the machinery which the courts have at command. I speak of these courts as they were at the time when this suit commenced, without inquiring whether the Judicature Acts make any, or if any, what difference.

It would be obviously unjust that a person who has been in possession of property under the contract which he seeks to repudiate should be allowed to throw that back on the other party's hands without accounting for any benefit he may have derived from the use of the property, or if the property, though not destroyed, has been in the interval deteriorated, without making compensation for that deterioration. But as a court of law has no machinery at its command for taking an account of such matters, the defrauded party, if he sought his remedy at law, must in such cases keep the property and sue in an action for deceit, in which the jury, if properly directed, can do complete justice by giving as damages a full indemnity for all that the party has lost: see *Clarke v Dixon* and the cases there cited.

But a court of equity could not give damages, and, unless it can rescind the contract, can give no relief. And, on the other hand, it can take accounts of profits, and make allowance for deterioration. And I think the practice has always been for a court of equity to give this relief whenever, by the exercise of its powers, it can do what is practically just, though it cannot restore the parties precisely to the state they were in before the contract. And a court of equity

28 (1878) 3 App Cas 1218, HL.

requires that those who come to it to ask its active interposition to give them relief, should use due diligence, after there has been such notice or knowledge as to make it inequitable to lie by. And any change which occurs in the position of the parties or the state of the property after such notice or knowledge should tell much more against the party *in morá*, than a similar change before he was *in morá* should do.

In *Lindsay Petroleum Co v Hurd*, it is said: 'The doctrine of laches in courts of equity is not an arbitrary or a technical doctrine. Where it would be *practically unjust* to give a remedy, either because the party has, by his conduct, done that which might fairly be regarded as equivalent to a waiver of it, or where, by his conduct and neglect he has, though perhaps not waiving that remedy, yet put the other party in a situation in which it would not be reasonable to place him if the remedy were afterwards to be asserted, in either of these cases, lapse of time and delay are most material. But, in every case, if an argument against relief, which otherwise would be just, is founded upon mere delay, that delay of course not amounting to a bar by any statute of limitations, the validity of that defence must be tried upon principles substantially equitable. Two circumstances always important in such cases are the length of the delay and the nature of the acts done during the interval, which might affect either party and cause a balance of justice or injustice in taking the one course or the other, so far as relates to the remedy.' I have looked in vain for any authority which gives a more distinct and definite rule than this; and I think, from the nature of the inquiry, it must always be a question of more or less, depending on the degree of diligence which might reasonably be required, and the degree of change which has occurred, whether the balance of justice or injustice is in favour of granting the remedy or withholding it. The determination of such a question must largely depend on the turn of mind of those who have to decide, and must therefore be subject to uncertainty; but that, I think, is inherent in the nature of the inquiry.

The remedy of indemnity is equally concerned with the giving back to the claimant of that amount which constitutes an advantage to or enrichment of the defendant. It is this feature which distinguishes this remedy from that of discretionary damages for innocent misrepresentation under s 2(2) of the Misrepresentation Act 1967. It is clear that all the claimant is entitled to recover is the amount paid over to the defendant as a result of entering into the contract induced by the misrepresentation. Accordingly, there is no room for damages for consequential losses since these are a matter of compensation which must fit within existing rules of contract or tort, as the case might be.

In *Newbigging v Adam*,[29] the plaintiff was induced to enter into a partnership agreement under which he had paid £9,700 to buy into the business and had paid £324 in discharge of certain existing debts. On the credit side, he had received payments from the partnership amounting to £745, which had to be deducted from any indemnity granted to him.

---

29 (1887) 34 Ch D 582, CA.

Moreover, the plaintiff was also entitled to be indemnified against all outstanding debts and liabilities of the partnership that he was or would become liable to pay as a partner. Had this not been the case, the defendants would have derived some advantage at the expense of the plaintiff which could reasonably be regarded as unjust:

Newbigging v Adam (1887) 34 Ch D 582, CA, p 592

Bowen LJ: If we turn to the question of misrepresentation, damages cannot be obtained at law for misrepresentation which is not fraudulent, and you cannot, as it seems to me, give in equity any indemnity which corresponds with damages. If the mass of authority there is upon the subject were gone through I think it would be found that there is not so much difference as is generally supposed between the view taken at common law and the view taken in equity as to misrepresentation. At common law it has always been considered that misrepresentations which strike at the root of the contract are sufficient to avoid the contract on the ground explained in *Kennedy v Panama, New Zealand, and Australian Royal Mail Co*; but when you come to consider what is the exact relief to which a person is entitled in a case of misrepresentation it seems to me to be this, and nothing more, that he is entitled to have the contract rescinded, and is entitled accordingly to all the incidents and consequences of such rescission. It is said that the injured party is entitled to be replaced *in statu quo*. It seems to me that when you are dealing with innocent misrepresentation you must understand that proposition that he is to be replaced *in statu quo* with this limitation – that he is not to be replaced in exactly the same position in all respects, otherwise he would be entitled to recover damages, but is to be replaced in his position so far as regards the rights and obligations which have been created by the contract into which he has been induced to enter. That seems to me to be the true doctrine, and I think it is put in the neatest way in *Redgrave v Hurd*. In that case there was a misrepresentation, but, though there was a suggestion of fraud in the pleadings, the Court of Appeal thought that fraud was not so expressly pleaded as to enable the court to treat the case as one of fraud, and that the relief given must depend on misrepresentation alone. The Master of the Rolls, so treating it, says:

> Before going into the details of the case I wish to say something about my view of the law applicable to it, because in the text-books, and even in some observations of noble Lords in the House of Lords, there are remarks which I think, according to the course of modern decisions, are not well founded, and do not accurately state the law. As regards the rescission of a contract, there was no doubt a difference between the rules of courts of equity and the rules of courts of common law – a difference which of course has now disappeared by the operation of the Judicature Act, which makes the rules of equity prevail. According to the decisions of courts of equity, it was not necessary, in order to set aside a contract obtained by material false representation, to prove that the party who obtained it knew at the time when the representation was made that it was false. It was put in two ways, either of which was sufficient. One way of putting the case was, 'A man is not to be allowed to get a benefit from a statement which he

now admits to be false. He is not to be allowed to say, for the purpose of civil jurisdiction, that when he made it he did not know it to be false; he ought to have found that out before he made it'. The other way of putting it was this, 'Even assuming that moral fraud must be shewn in order to set aside a contract, you have it where a man, having obtained a beneficial contract by a statement which he now knows to be false, insists upon keeping that contract. To do so is a moral delinquency: no man ought to seek to take advantage of his own false statements'. The rule in equity was settled, and it does not matter on which of the two grounds it was rested. As regards the rule of common law there is no doubt it was not quite so wide. There were, indeed, cases in which, even at common law, a contract could be rescinded for misrepresentation, although it could not be shewn that the person making it knew the representation to be false. They are variously stated, but I think, according to the later decisions, the statement must have been made recklessly, and without care whether it was true or false, and not with the belief that it was true.

With great respect for the shadow and memory of that great name, I cannot help saying that this is not a perfect exposition of what the common law was, but, so far as the rule of equity goes, I must assume that the Master of the Rolls spoke with full knowledge of the equity authorities, and he treats the relief as being the giving back by the party who made the misrepresentation of the advantages he obtained by the contract. Now those advantages may be of two kinds. He may get an advantage in the shape of an actual benefit, as when he receives money; he may also get an advantage if the party with whom he contracts assumes some burden in consideration of the contract. In such a case it seems to me that complete rescission would not be effected unless the misrepresenting party not only hands back the benefits which he has himself received – but also re-assumes the burden which under the contract the injured person has taken upon himself. Speaking only for myself, I should not like to lay down the proposition that a person is to be restored to the position which he held before the misrepresentation was made, nor that the person injured must be indemnified against loss which arises out of the contract, unless you place upon the words 'out of the contract' the limited and special meaning which I have endeavoured to shadow forth. Loss arising out of the contract is a term which would be too wide. It would embrace damages at common law, because damages at common law are only given upon the supposition that they are damages which would naturally and reasonably follow from the injury done. I think *Redgrave v Hurd* shews that it would be too wide, because in that case the court excluded from the relief which was given the damages which had been sustained by the plaintiff in removing his business, and other similar items. There ought, as it appears to me, to be a giving back and a taking back on both sides, including the giving back and taking back of the obligations which the contract has created, as well as the giving back and the taking back of the advantages. There is nothing in the case of *Rawlins v Wickham* which carries the doctrine beyond that. In that case, one of three partners having retired, the remaining partners introduced the plaintiff into the firm, and he, under his contract with them, took upon himself to share with them the liabilities which otherwise they would have borne in their entirety.

That was a burthen which he took under the contract and in virtue of the contract. It seems to me, therefore, that upon this principle indemnity was rightly decreed as regards the liabilities of the new firm. I have not found any case which carries the doctrine further, and it is not necessary to carry it further in order to support the order now appealed from. A part of the contract between the plaintiff and Adam & Co was that the plaintiff should become and continue for five years partner in a new firm and bring in £10,000. By this very contract, he was to pledge his credit with his partners in the new firm for the business transactions of the new firm. It was a burthen or liability imposed on him by the very contract. It seems to me that the £9,000 odd, and, indeed, all the moneys brought in by him or expended by him for the new firm up to the £10,000, were part of the actual moneys which he undertook by the true contract with Adam & Co to pay. Of course, he ought to be indemnified as regards that. I think, also, applying the same doctrine, he ought to be indemnified against all the liabilities of the firm, because they were liabilities which under the contract he was bound to take upon himself. It seems to me upon those grounds that the decision of the Vice-Chancellor ought to be supported.

Compulsion

Where a transfer of wealth occurs as a result of duress, the innocent party may have the right to rescind the contract, although this is subject to the normal bars to rescission of the contract considered in relation to misrepresentation above. What constitutes actionable duress at common law has been considered already.[30] In terms of restitutionary principles, clearly, it would be unjust to allow a person to take the benefit of an illegitimate threat. Moreover, it has also been seen already that there is an equitable jurisdiction in relation to undue influence which allows the court to rescind a contract in cases where the relationship of the parties is such that pressure or influence can be presumed.

Qualification by later events

The principal subsequent events which are likely to give rise to restitutionary problems are, first, a breach of contract which gives rise to a total failure of consideration; secondly, a contract may fail for example where it is void for uncertainty or where some element essential to its validity is absent and thirdly there may be an event external to the contract which serves to frustrate the contract. The issue of frustration and the remedies arising out of the provisions of the Law Reform (Frustrated Contracts) Act 1943 has already been dealt with elsewhere.[31]

---

30 See Chapter 7.
31 See Chapter 6.

Restitution for breach of contract

Generally, where there is a breach of a valid contract, the appropriate monetary remedy is an award of damages to protect the claimant's expectation or status quo interest. However, the claimant may find himself in the position whereby he may terminate his performance obligations due to a breach of the contract by the other party. In these circumstances, the claimant may seek to recover any payment he has made on the ground that there has been a total failure of consideration. Alternatively, he may seek to recover the value of his own partial performance prior to termination on a *quantum meruit* basis. Both of these remedies are restitutionary in nature since in either event the contract has come to an end, in which case the remedy provided cannot be regarded as contractual in the sense that the claimant's expectation interest is being protected.

Conversely, there are remedies which might appear to be restitutionary in nature which flow from a breach of contract, but which should not be regarded as such. For example, in *Teacher v Calder*,[32] the defendant agreed to invest £15,000 in the plaintiff's business, but failed to fulfil his promise, choosing instead to invest the same amount in another business. By doing this the defendant managed to make a much greater profit on his investment than he would have done had he invested in the plaintiff's business. Had the court been concerned with the unjust enrichment of the defendant resulting from his breach of contract, the measure of damages would have represented the profit he made from being in breach of his contract with the plaintiff. However, the court made it clear that they were concerned with the defendant's breach of contract, damages for which were directed towards compensating the plaintiff for the loss suffered by his business, which was a lesser amount than the restitution measure.

Similar principles also apply to a saving of expenditure as a result of breaking the contract with the claimant. Thus, in *Tito v Waddell (No 2)*,[33] the defendants entered into a contract whereby they were entitled to prospect on Ocean Island for a stated period of time. One of the obligations undertaken by the defendants was that they would replant the island when they finished operations. The defendants failed to honour this obligation with the result that they saved themselves considerable expense. However, this was seen to be an action for damages for breach of contract, with the result that the measure of damages stipulated by the court was concerned with the loss to the plaintiff rather than the gain or saving to the defendant.

The relevant principles in this area have been recently restated in *Surrey County Council v Bredero Homes Ltd*,[34] where the plaintiffs sold two adjoining

32 [1899] AC 451.
33 [1977] Ch 106.
34 [1993] 1 WLR 1361.

plots of land to the defendants for the purposes of house construction. It was a term of the contract that the development would proceed along the lines set out in the plaintiffs' development scheme. However, the defendants built more houses than was permitted by the development scheme, with the result that they made a substantial profit from their breach of contract. The plaintiffs were aware of the breach from an early stage but did not seek an injunction. Instead they waited until the development was complete and then sought restitutionary damages based on the profit made by the defendant. The court awarded only nominal damages on the ground that the plaintiff had suffered no loss as a result of the breach of contract:

Surrey County Council v Bredero Homes Ltd [1993] 1 WLR 1361, CA, p 1369

Steyn LJ: Dillon LJ has reviewed the relevant case law. It would not be a useful exercise for me to try to navigate through those much traveled waters again. Instead, it seems to me that it may possibly be useful to consider the question from the point of view of the application at first principles. An award of compensation for breach of contract serves to protect three separate interests. The starting principle is that the aggrieved party ought to be compensated for loss of his positive or expectation interests. In other words, the object is to put the aggrieved party in the same financial position as if the contract had been fully performed. But the law also protects the negative interest of the aggrieved party. If the aggrieved party is unable to establish the value of a loss of bargain he may seek compensation in respect of his reliance losses. The object of such an award is to compensate the aggrieved party for expenses incurred and losses suffered in reliance of the contract. These two complementary principles share one feature. Both are pure compensatory principles. If the aggrieved party has suffered no loss, he is not entitled to be compensated by invoking these principles. The application of these principles to the present case would result in an award of nominal damages only.

There is, however, a third principle which protects the aggrieved party's restitutionary interest. The object of such an award is not to compensate the plaintiff for a loss, but to deprive the defendant of the benefit he gained by the breach of contract. The classic illustration is a claim for the return of goods sold and delivered where the buyer has repudiated his obligation to pay the price. It is not traditional to describe a claim for restitution following a breach of contract as damages. What matters is that a coherent law of obligations must inevitably extend its protection to cover certain restitutionary interests. How far that protection should extend is the essence of the problem before us. In my view, *Wrotham Park Estate Co v Parkside Homes Ltd* [1974] 1 WLR 798 is only defensible on the basis of the third or restitutionary principle (see *McGregor on Damages*, 15th edn, 1988, para 18 and Professor PBH Birks' *Civil Wrongs: A New World*, [1990–91] Butterworths Lectures 55, p 71). The appellants' argument that the *Wrotham Park* case can be justified on the basis of a loss of bargaining opportunity is a fiction. The object of the award in the *Wrotham Park* case was not to compensate the plaintiff for financial injury, but to deprive the defendants of an unjustly acquired gain. Whilst it must be acknowledged that

Wrotham Park represented a new development, it seems to me that it is based on a principle of legal theory, justice and sound policy. In the respondent's skeleton argument, some doubt was cast, by way of alternative submission, on the correctness of the award of damages for breach of covenant in the *Wrotham Park* case. In my respectful view, it was rightly decided and represents a useful development in our law. In *Tito v Waddell (No 2)* [1977] Ch 106 at pp 335c–36c, Megarry VC interpreted the *Wrotham Park* case and the decision in *Bracewell v Appleby* [1975] Ch 408, which followed *Wrotham Park*, as cases of the invasion of property rights. I respectfully agree. *Wrotham Park* is analogous to cases where a defendant has made use of the aggrieved party's property and thereby saved expenses: see *Penarth Dock Engineering Co Ltd v Pounds* [1963] 1 Lloyd's Rep 359. I readily accept that the word 'property' in this context must be interpreted in a wide sense. I would also not suggest that there is no scope for further development in this branch of the law.

But, in the present case, we are asked to extend the availability of restitutionary remedies for breach of contract considerably. I question the desirability of any such development. The acceptance of the appellants' primary or alternative submissions, as outlined by Dillon LJ, will have a wide ranging impact on our commercial law. Even the alternative and narrower submission will, for example, cover charterparties and contracts of affreightment where the remedy of a negative injunction may be available. Moreover, so far as the narrower submission restricts the principle to cases where the remedies of specific performance and injunction would have been available, I must confess that that seems to me a bromide formula without any rationale in logic or common sense. Given a breach of contract, why should the availability of a restitutionary remedy, as a matter of legal entitlement, be dependant on the availability of the wholly different and discretionary remedies of injunctions specific to performance? If there is merit in the argument I cannot see any sense in restricting a compensatory remedy which serves to protect the restitutionary interests to cases where there would be separate remedies of specific performance or injunction, designed directly and indirectly to enforce payment.

For my part, I would hold that if Sir William's wider proposition fails, the narrower one must equally fail. Both submissions hinge on the defendant's breach being deliberate. Sir William invoked the principle that a party is not entitled to take advantage of his own wrongdoing. Despite Sir William's disclaimer, it seems to me that the acceptance of the propositions formulated by him will inevitably mean that the focus will be on the motive of the party who committed the breach of contract. That is contrary to the general approach of our law of contract and, in particular, to rules governing the assessment of damages. In my view, there are also other policy reasons which militate against adopting either Sir William's primary or narrower submission. The introduction of restitutionary remedies to deprive cynical contract breakers of the fruits of their breaches of contract will lead to greater uncertainty in the assessment of damages in commercial and consumer disputes. It is of paramount importance that the way in which disputes are likely to be resolved by the courts must be readily predictable. Given the premise that the aggrieved party has suffered no loss, is such a dramatic extension of restitutionary remedies justified in order to confer a windfall in each case on the aggrieved party? I think not. In any event, such a widespread availability of restitutionary remedies will have a tendency to discourage economic activity in relevant situations. In a range of cases, such liability would fall on underwriters who have insured relevant liability risks. Inevitably, underwriters would have to be compensated for the new species of potential claims. Insurance premiums would have to go up. That, too, is a consequence which militates against the proposed extension. The recognition of the proposed extension will in my view not serve the public interest. It is sound policy to guard against extending the protection of the law of obligations too widely. For these substantive and policy reasons, I regard it as undesirable that the range of restitutionary remedies should be extended in the way in which we have been invited to do so.

The present case does not involve any invasion of the plaintiff property interests even in the broadest sense of that word, nor is it closely analogous to the *Wrotham Park* position. I would therefore rule that no restitutionary remedy is available and there is certainly no other remedy available.

I would dismiss the appeal.

Does it seem unjust that a defendant can cynically break a contract, make a substantial profit and get away with it? Should this be an area where the law should allow a successful claim for damages on the part of the claimant, but would allowing such a claim also enrich the claimant if he has suffered no loss as a result of the breach of contract?

To the general rule stated above, there is an exception, although it has been given a narrow interpretation in *Surrey County Council v Bredero Homes*. In *Wrotham Park Estate Co Ltd v Parkside Homes Ltd*,[35] the defendants built houses in such a way that there was an infringement of a restrictive covenant intended to benefit the plaintiffs' land. An application for an injunction requesting the demolition of the houses was refused, and damages were awarded instead. The amount awarded represented the sum which the owner of the benefited land might have accepted for relaxing the covenant. In assessing this figure, the court took into account the profit made by the defendants from the houses. As the plaintiffs would not have relaxed the covenant, it is unlikely that damages were compensatory and can be regarded as restitutionary.

Breach of condition and anticipatory repudiation

Where the claimant has transferred wealth and a condition precedent to liability to pay has failed, there is a total failure of consideration. Such a failure most commonly arises where the defendant is in breach of his primary contractual obligations, thereby allowing the claimant to treat his own

---

35   [1974] 1 WLR 798.

performance obligations as being at an end. In such cases, an action will lie for damages or for restitution.

The main obstacle to a restitutionary award is the insistence that the claimant must have received nothing under the contract. Accordingly, a mere partial failure of consideration does not give rise to a restitutionary remedy,[36] unless the contract is severable or easily apportionable. Thus, in *Ebrahim Dawood Ltd v Heath (Est 1927) Ltd*,[37] a buyer was held to have justifiably rejected part of a consignment of steel sheets for which he had paid in advance. The court allowed him to recover a proportionate part of the price on the basis that he had received and accepted those consignments which were in accordance with the contract, but could reject those which did not conform, provided, as in this case, it was possible to sever the non-conforming goods from the remainder of the goods contracted for.[38]

Where the claimant has performed work for the defendant, he may claim in respect of the reasonable value of the work he has done on the basis of a *quantum meruit*. In *Planché v Colburn*,[39] the plaintiff contracted to write a book for the defendant. Prior to the date of submission of the manuscript, the defendant suspended the series in which the book was to appear at a time when the plaintiff had carried out some research and had started to write the book. The plaintiff was awarded a sum as a *quantum meruit* for the work done, although the defendant had obtained no benefit. The problem with this case is whether it may properly be regarded as applying restitutionary principles. Undoubtedly, the plaintiff could be said to have an action for breach of contract, but it was impossible to ascertain what expectation of gain he might have had.[40] Equally, it is arguable that the remedy given could not be truly restitutionary, since it would be difficult to say that a part-written book is of any benefit to the defendant. Moreover, quantifying that gain or benefit appears to be unimaginably difficult. Possibly the best approach is to treat this case as one which turns on reliance loss – the plaintiff reasonably relied on the defendant to see the series of books through to publication with the result that the plaintiff was entitled to reasonable remuneration in respect of the work he had put in prior to the anticipatory repudiation on the part of the defendant. But to say that this disgorges from the defendant the benefit he has derived from the plaintiff's performance seems to take to the limits the meaning of the word 'benefit'.

---

36   *Whincup v Hughes* (1871) LR 6 CP 78.

37   [1961] 2 Lloyd's Rep 512.

38   See, also, Sale of Goods Act 1979, s 35A, now allowing a right of partial rejection in all contracts for the sale of goods.

39   (1831) 8 Bing 14.

40   This problem is considered in more detail in Chapter 13, with particular reference to the decisions in *Anglia Television Ltd v Reed* [1971] 3 All ER 690 and *CCC Films (London) Ltd v Impact Quadrant Films Ltd* [1985] QB 16.

Where the claimant has entered into a bad bargain, it will be to his advantage to claim on a *quantum meruit* if the defendant is in breach. In *Boomer v Muir*,[41] the plaintiff terminated a contract to build a dam, following a serious breach of contract on the part of the defendant which justified that act of termination. The court awarded the plaintiff $258,000, representing the value of his work in part-building it, despite the fact that this amount represented more than the amount he would have received under the contract itself. There is no direct English authority which has decided whether a claimant can recover more on a *quantum meruit* than he could had he brought an action in contract. Possibly, the answer to this lies in the fact that if the remedy provided is purely restitutionary, the fact that the defendant has abandoned the contract and that the claimant has accepted that abandonment, what would have happened if the contract had been performed becomes entirely irrelevant.[42] But a counter-argument here is that restitutionary remedies serve to subvert contracts which have been freely entered into.[43] Conversely, it should be observed that by the time the remedy is granted, there are no continuing primary contractual obligations to be performed by the parties.

Where the party seeking restitution is in breach of the contract, normally, but not always, no action will lie.

In *Sumpter v Hedges*,[44] a builder who abandoned a contract for the construction of a house because he became insolvent was unable to claim for the work he had performed, as there was no free acceptance, although he was permitted to recover in respect of the materials he had supplied:

Sumpter v Hedges [1898] 1 QB 673, CA, p 676

Collins LJ: I think the case is really concluded by the finding of the learned judge to the effect that the plaintiff had abandoned the contract. If the plaintiff had merely broken his contract in some way so as not to give the defendant the right to treat him as having abandoned the contract, and the defendant had then proceeded to finish the work himself, the plaintiff might perhaps have been entitled to sue on a *quantum meruit* on the ground that the defendant had taken the benefit of the work done. But that is not the present case. There are cases in which, though the plaintiff has abandoned the performance of a contract, it is possible for him to raise the inference of a new contract to pay for the work done on a *quantum meruit* from the defendant's having taken the benefit of that work, but, in order that that may be done, the circumstances must be such as to give an option to the defendant to take or not to take the

---

41 (1933) 24 P 2d 570 (California).

42 *Lodder v Slowey* (1901) 20 NZLR 321, p 358, *per* Williams J.

43 See Goff and Jones, 1993, pp 467–68.

44 [1988] 1 QB 673, CA. See, also, *Bolton v Mahadeva* [1972] 1 WLR 1009 and *Boston Deep Sea Fishing & Ice Co Ltd v Ansell* (1888) 39 Ch D 339.

benefit of the work done. It is only where the circumstances are such as to give that option that there is any evidence on which to ground the inference of a new contract. Where, as in the case of work done on land, the circumstances are such as to give the defendant no option whether he will take the benefit of the work or not, then one must look to other facts than the mere taking the benefit of the work in order to ground the inference of a new contract. In this case, I see no other facts on which such an inference can be founded. The mere fact that a defendant is in possession of what he cannot help keeping, or even has done work upon it, affords no ground for such an inference. He is not bound to keep unfinished a building which in an incomplete state would be a nuisance on his land. I am therefore of opinion that the plaintiff was not entitled to recover for the work which he had done. I feel clear that the case of *Whitaker v Dunn*, to which reference has been made, was the case which as counsel I argued in the Court of Appeal, and in which the court dismissed the appeal on the ground that the case was concluded by *Munro v Butt*.

Does it remain the case that the claimant in this type of case gets something for nothing? If so, does this, in itself, amount to an unjust enrichment of the claimant? Alternatively, since there is a rule which prevents a party from alleging that a contract is frustrated due to a self-induced event, is *Sumpter v Hedges* in line with this rule by preventing the defendant from benefiting from his own breach of contract? Alternatively, in *Sumpter v Hedges*, since the plaintiff had the building work completed and went on to occupy the premises, it is surely reasonable to assume that he has derived some benefit from the work performed by the defendant, in which case there is an argument to the effect that restitution should have been denied.

Despite the implication in *Sumpter v Hedges*, there is no rule that a party in breach of contract cannot claim a restitutionary remedy.[45]

---

45   *Dies v British and International Mining and Finance Corpn Ltd* [1939] 1 KB 724.

CHAPTER 15

PRIVITY OF CONTRACT – THE RANGE OF LIABILITY FOR BREACH OF CONTRACT

INTRODUCTION

In an action for breach of contract, the doctrine of privity of contract provides that only the parties to the contract can sue or be sued on it. The difficulty is to determine who is a party to the contract. A strict application of the doctrine ignores the economic problem of externalities, namely that the economic relations of the parties to a contract can adversely affect a third party. This is especially so in cases where a contract between A and B is specifically intended to benefit a third party, C.

Moreover, the doctrine, having been developed in the 19th century is heavily influenced by market-individualist theory, assuming that contracts are essentially bilateral arrangements. But this tends to ignore the value of co-operation, which engenders a greater respect for the interests of others, including third parties. For this reason, various methods have been adopted to circumvent the unfortunate effects of a strict application of the doctrine.

THE GENERAL RULE

The general rule of privity stipulates that a person who is not a contracting party can neither derive a benefit from the contract nor be subject to any burden imposed by it. Although the doctrine has as its object the definition of the range of contractual liability, because of its origins, it has become closely related to the doctrine of consideration. The rule as stated in *Price v Easton*[1] was couched in terms of two principles, namely that there is no privity between a contracting party and a third party,[2] and that the third party does not give any consideration for the promise.[3] It is objectionable that the doctrines of privity and consideration should be confused in this way since the rules on consideration serve the separate purpose of identifying those promises which the law will enforce whereas the privity rule is concerned with the issue of who is entitled to a remedy.

For good reasons, the privity rule has been subject to much hostile criticism, but it was confirmed as a rule of English law by the House of Lords

---

1   (1833) 4 B & Ad 433. See, also, *Tweddle v Atkinson* (1861) 1 B & S 393.
2   *Ibid*, p 434, *per* Littledale J.
3   *Ibid*, *per* Lord Denman CJ.

in *Dunlop Pneumatic Tyre Co Ltd v Selfridge & Co Ltd*,[4] in which it was held that English law knows nothing of a *jus quaesitum tertio* arising by way of contract.[5] According to this general rule, contractual provisions cannot be enforced for the benefit of a third party, even if it is abundantly clear, as in *Dunlop*, that the contract is entered into for the benefit of the third party. It should be noted, however, that what was said in *Dunlop* about privity of contract is strictly *obiter*, as the ratio of the decision is based on the rule that consideration must move from the promisee.

A strict application of the doctrine of privity ignores the economic problem of externalities, namely that an arrangement between two people can affect a third party. Moreover, the doctrine, having been developed in the 19th century, is heavily influenced by market individualist theory, assuming that contracts are essentially bilateral arrangements. But this tends to ignore the value of co-operation that engenders a greater respect for the interests of others, including third parties. For this reason, various methods have been adopted to circumvent the unfortunate effects of a strict application of the doctrine and in other quarters the doctrine has been attacked on the basis that there is no doctrinal, logical or other policy reason to justify its existence.[6] To say that a person cannot sue on a contract because he could not be sued is also misleading, since this is precisely the result achieved in cases involving unilateral contracts.

In other parts of the common law world, the need to reflect the value of co-operation in commercial dealings has also led to a number of head-on conflicts with the basic rule of privity. This has been the case in relation to insurance arrangements made by, for example, a main building contractor wishing to extend the benefit of an insurance policy to his subcontractors[7] and cases in which it is intended that nominated third parties should be protected by an exemption clause in a contract between two other related parties, such as is often the case where goods subject to a contract of sale are stored in a warehouse[8] or are transported to their ultimate destination by a carrier.[9] In each of these cases, the contractual dealings of a third party may be based on the assumption that there is a provision in a contract between two other parties which is intended to protect him or provide him with some benefit. As a result of this, the third party may be able to adjust his own contractual dealings, for example, by reducing the price he charges for his services, on the assumption that he is to be benefited in some other way by co-operation with

---

4   [1915] AC 847. See, also, *Beswick v Beswick* [1968] AC 58.
5   *Dunlop Pneumatic Tyre Co Ltd v Selfridge & Co Ltd* [1915] AC 847, p 853, *per* Lord Haldane.
6   *Darlington Borough Council v Wiltshier Northern Ltd* [1995] 1 WLR 68, p 76, *per* Steyn LJ.
7   See *Trident General Insurance Co Ltd v McNiece Bros Pty Ltd* (1988) 165 CLR 107.
8   See *London Drugs Ltd v Kuehne & Nagel International Ltd* [1993] 1 WWR 1.
9   See *New Zealand Shipping Co Ltd v AM Satterthwaite & Co Ltd, The Eurymedon* [1975] AC 154.

the other parties to a related contract. As will be seen below, some of these relationships, although not all, will be covered by the provisions of the Contracts (Rights of Third Parties) Act 1999 and may, more easily be regarded as giving rise to enforceable contractual rights in favour of a third party.

In *Dunlop Pneumatic Tyre Co Ltd v Selfridge & Co Ltd*,[10] Dew & Co, a firm of motor factors agreed to distribute Dunlop tyres. Part of the agreement was that Dew would adhere to a price maintenance structure set out by Dunlop and that Dew would require any subsequent purchaser from them of Dunlop tyres also to adhere to that price maintenance structure. Dew sold Dunlop tyres to Selfridge, who then proposed to sell those tyres at a price lower than had been stipulated by Dunlop. The contract between Dew and Selfridge provided that Selfridge would adhere to Dunlop's minimum prices and the question arose whether Dunlop could enforce the relevant term in their favour, despite the fact that they were not parties to the contract which contained the relevant term.

The House of Lords held that as no consideration moved from Dunlop to Selfridge, the contract was unenforceable by Dunlop against Selfridge:

Dunlop Pneumatic Tyre Co Ltd v Selfridge & Co Ltd [1915] AC 847, HL, p 853

Viscount Haldane: My Lords, in the law of England, certain principles are fundamental. One is that only a person who is a party to a contract can sue on it. Our law knows nothing of a *jus quaesitum tertio* arising by way of contract. Such a right may be conferred by way of property, as, for example, under a trust, but it cannot be conferred on a stranger to a contract as a right to enforce the contract *in personam*. A second principle is that if a person with whom a contract not under seal has been made is to be able to enforce it consideration must have been given by him to the promisor or to some other person at the promisor's request. These two principles are not recognised in the same fashion by the jurisprudence of certain continental countries or of Scotland, but here they are well established. A third proposition is that a principal not named in the contract may sue upon it if the promisee really contracted as his agent. But, again, in order to entitle him so to sue, he must have given consideration either personally or through the promisee, acting as his agent in giving it.

My Lords, in the case before us, I am of opinion that the consideration, the allowance of what was in reality part of the discount to which Messrs Dew, the promisees, were entitled as between themselves and the appellants, was to be given by Messrs Dew on their own account, and was not in substance, any more than in form, an allowance made by the appellants. The case for the appellants is that they permitted and enabled Messrs Dew, with the knowledge and by the desire of the respondents, to sell to the latter on the terms of the contract of 2 January 1912. But it appears to me that even if this is

---

10 [1915] AC 847, HL.

so, the answer is conclusive. Messrs Dew sold to the respondents goods which they had a title to obtain from the appellants independently of this contract. The consideration by way of discount under the contract of 2 January was to come wholly out of Messrs Dew's pocket, and neither directly nor indirectly out of that of the appellants. If the appellants enabled them to sell to the respondents on the terms they did, this was not done as any part of the terms of the contract sued on.

No doubt, it was provided as part of these terms that the appellants should acquire certain rights, but these rights appear on the face of the contract as *jura quaesita tertio*, which the appellants could not enforce. Moreover, even if this difficulty can be got over by regarding the appellants as the principals of Messrs Dew in stipulating for the rights in question, the only consideration disclosed by the contract is one given by Messrs Dew, not as their agents, but as principals acting on their own account.

The conclusion to which I have come on the point as to consideration renders it unnecessary to decide the further question as to whether the appellants can claim that a bargain was made in this contract by Messrs Dew as their agents; a bargain which, apart from the point as to consideration, they could therefore enforce. If it were necessary to express an opinion on this further question, a difficulty as to the position of Messrs Dew would have to be considered. Two contracts – one by a man on his own account as principal, and another by the same man as agent – may be validly comprised in the same piece of paper. But they must be two contracts, and not one as here. I do not think that a man can treat one and the same contract as made by him in two capacities. He cannot be regarded as contracting for himself and for another *uno flatu*.

My Lords, the form of the contract which we have to interpret leaves the appellants in this dilemma, that, if they say that Messrs Dew contracted on their behalf, they gave no consideration, and if they say they gave consideration in the shape of a permission to the respondents to buy, they must set up further stipulations, which are neither to be found in the contract sued upon nor are germane to it, but are really inconsistent with its structure. That contract has been reduced to writing, and it is in the writing that we must look for the whole of the terms made between the parties. These terms cannot, in my opinion consistently with the settled principles of English law, be construed as giving to the appellants any enforceable rights as against the respondents.

Dismissed with costs.

Lord Dunedin: My Lords, I confess that this case is to my mind apt to nip any budding affection which one might have had for the doctrine of consideration. For the effect of that doctrine in the present case is to make it possible for a person to snap his fingers at a bargain deliberately made, a bargain not in itself unfair, and which the person seeking to enforce it has a legitimate interest to enforce. Notwithstanding these considerations, I cannot say that I have ever had any doubt that the judgment of the Court of Appeal was right.

My Lords, I am content to adopt from a work of Sir Frederick Pollock, to which I have often been under obligation, the following words as to consideration: 'An act or forbearance of one party, or the promise thereof, is the price for which the promise of the other is bought, and the promise thus given for value is enforceable.' (*Pollock on Contracts*, 8th edn, p 175.)

Now the agreement sued on is an agreement which on the face of it is an agreement between Dew and Selfridge. But speaking for myself, I should have no difficulty in the circumstances of this case in holding it proved that the agreement was truly made by Dew as agent for Dunlop, or in other words that Dunlop was the undisclosed principal, and as such can sue on the agreement. Nonetheless, in order to enforce it, he must show consideration, as above defined, moving from Dunlop to Selfridge.

In the circumstances, how can he do so? The agreement in question is not an agreement for sale. It is only collateral to an agreement for sale; but that agreement for sale is an agreement entirely between Dew and Selfridge. The tyres, the property in which upon the bargain is transferred to Selfridge, were the property of Dew, not of Dunlop, for Dew under his agreement with Dunlop held these tyres as proprietor, and not as agent. What, then, did Dunlop do, or forbear to do, in a question with Selfridge? The answer must be, nothing.

To my mind, this ends the case. That there are methods of framing a contract which will cause persons in the position of Selfridge to become bound, I do not doubt. But that has not been done in this instance; and as Dunlop's advisers must have known of the law of consideration, it is their affair that they have not so drawn the contract.

I think the appeal should be dismissed.

The parties to the agreement

The classical rules of contract law generally envisage only the two parties to a bilateral arrangement whose communications with each other form the basis of the contract. If a third party were allowed to sue on the contract, this would serve to fetter the contracting parties' ability to vary or rescind an agreement.[11] However, many modern transactions are more complex involving a network of related contractual arrangements involving more than two parties.[12] In these circumstances, the need for co-operation between the various parties and regard for the interests of others is much greater and it becomes more difficult to justify the strict privity approach.

The strict effects of the privity doctrine can be avoided through the use of the collateral contract device. For example, if a manufacturer expressly warrants the suitability of a product which a consumer later purchases from a retail supplier, the consumer may have recourse to the manufacturer should the product prove to be qualitatively defective.[13]

---

11 *Re Schebsman* [1944] Ch 83.
12 See Adams and Brownsword, 1990.
13 *Shanklin Pier Ltd v Detel Products Ltd* [1951] 2 KB 854; *Wells (Merstham) Ltd v Buckland Sand and Silica Ltd* [1965] 2 QB 170.

A number of these collateral contract cases may well be covered by the provisions of the Contracts (Rights of Third Parties) Act 1999,[11] since in many such cases there will be an express or implied intention to confer a contractual right on a third party. For example, in *Charnock v Liverpool Corpn*,[12] the defendants agreed to repair the plaintiff's car under an arrangement with the plaintiff's insurers, but took an excessive time to complete the work, thereby occasioning the plaintiff additional loss. It is relatively easy to see that the contractual arrangements between the insurance company and the garage effecting repairs on the plaintiff's car were intended to confer a right on the plaintiff as owner of the car.

In certain cases, it is possible that a contracting party is considered to contract on behalf of others, for example, where one member of a family books a ferry crossing on behalf of himself and his family, all members of the family are contracting parties.[13] Likewise, a meal booked at a restaurant by one person for a large group is said to create a contract between the restaurateur and each member of the group.[14]

The parties to the consideration

As the doctrine of privity of contract and the rule that consideration should move from the promisee appear to achieve the same result, it has been argued that they amount to the same rule[15] since if a contract involves a bargain, a person who is not a party to the bargain is not a party to the contract. This presents two reasons for denying the third party action. First, there is a lack of reciprocity and secondly the third party might receive something for nothing and should be treated as if he were a gratuitous beneficiary. The argument against this is that if there is a bargained for exchange under which the contracting parties intend to benefit the third party, there may be an act of reasonable reliance on the part of the third party.[16]

Nevertheless, there are close affinities between the two doctrines, since in classical terms, if no consideration has moved from the promisee, it is difficult to say that he is a party to the alleged bargain. However, the fact that there is such a close relationship between the doctrine of privity and the rule that consideration should move from the promisee could give rise to difficulty. It will be seen below that the Contracts (Rights of Third Parties) Act 1999 creates

---

11 Contracts (Rights of Third Parties) Act 1999, s 1(1)(b).
12 [1968] 3 All ER 473.
13 *Daly v General Steam Navigation Co Ltd, The Dragon* [1980] 2 Lloyd's Rep 145.
14 *Lockett v A M Charles Ltd* [1938] 4 All ER 170.
15 See Furmston, 1960, pp 382–84. See, also, *Tweddle v Atkinson* (1861) 1 B & S 393, p 398, *per* Crompton J.
16 See *Shadwell v Shadwell* (1860) 9 CBNS 159, p 174, *per* Erle CJ.

an exception whereby a third party may be given the right to enforce a term of a contract between two other parties where that term expressly or by implication is intended to benefit the third party. But, on the face of it, this merely relaxes the rules on privity of contract and not those relating to consideration. The answer to this problem seems to turn on the reasoning employed by the Law Commission,[17] on whose report the provisions of the 1999 Act are based. The Law Commission expressed the view that the consideration question related only to the relationship between the original parties to the contract and should not apply also to the third party, since this would only raise questions of enforceability and would have no bearing on whether or not there was a bargain. Had the reasoning in the report stopped there, there would have been little difficulty. However, in a later section of the report, there are further views that the 1999 Act may have the effect of relaxing rules on consideration in certain respects.[18] In particular, this view was arrived at on the ground that the effect of the 1999 Act will be to treat a third party more favourably than the way in which the law has hitherto treated a gratuitous promisee. Neither of these provides consideration, yet the former may be able to enforce the terms of a contract made for his benefit, but the latter will not be in a position to enforce a promise made to him due to want of consideration. This prompted the Law Commission to the view that rules on consideration might have become relaxed. However, this ignores the earlier reasoning of the Law Commission that rules on privity are not concerned with the question whether there is an enforceable bargain. In the case of a gratuitous promisee, there is no bargain, whereas in the case of a third party, there will be an enforceable bargain between the two contracting parties and all the 1999 Act will do is to give the third party a right to enforce those terms expressed to be for his benefit.

A perceived effect of the privity doctrine, then, is to allow a person to snap his fingers at a bargain deliberately made which is not unfair and in which the third party has a legitimate interest.[19] Since the promisor has broken his promise to the promisee, it is arguable that he should pay for the damaged expectations of the third party, assuming those expectations were in contemplation. If, in this type of case, the third party cannot enforce a promise made for his own benefit, you end up with the equally monstrous result that the only person with a valid claim has suffered no loss and the person who has suffered loss has no valid claim.[20]

---

17   Law Commission, Law Com No 242, 1996.

18   *Ibid*, para 6.13.

19   *Dunlop Pneumatic Tyre Co Ltd v Selfridge & Co Ltd* [1915] AC 847, p 855, *per* Lord Dunedin.

20   *Ross v Caunters* [1979] 3 All ER 580, p 583, *per* Megarry VC.

An illustration that the doctrines of consideration and privity are separate can be found in cases in which a person is a contracting party, but has provided no consideration. This may be the case where consideration is provided by one person on his own and a third party's behalf.[21]

The operation of the doctrine of privity

The general effect of the doctrine is that a third party acquires neither the benefit nor is subject to the burden of a contract to which he is not a party even if it is made for his benefit. But this does not affect the position of the promisor and the promisee. Some of the promisee's remedies may serve to assist the third party for whose benefit the contract is made. This means that the relationship between the third party and the promisee is crucial, since the third party may want the promisee to take action on his behalf.

The promisee's action to compel performance

If the promisee can obtain an order for specific performance[22] of the promisor's undertakings, there would be undoubted benefit to the third party.

In cases where a contract is for the benefit a third party, an award of damages to the promisee would usually be nominal only, since the actual loss to the promisee is likely to be negligible.[23] However, there may be circumstances in which the loss to the promisee could be substantial, such as where he is required to make good the failure of the promisor to fulfil his promise.[24] In other cases, a refusal to hold the promisor liable on his promise could result in an unjust enrichment if the agreed benefit were not to be conferred on the third party.[25] The practical effect of an order for specific performance would be to reverse the enrichment and enforce the promise in favour of the third party.

In *Beswick v Beswick*,[26] the appellant agreed to buy a business from his uncle on terms that the the appellant would pay an annuity to his aunt and uncle during their joint lives. After the uncle died, the appellant refused to make further payments to the aunt. The House of Lords held that, while the aunt could not enforce payment in her personal capacity, she could enforce the promise in her capacity as the administratrix of her deceased husband's estate. Accordingly, a decree of specific performance was ordered:

21 *Coulls v Bagot's Executor and Trustee Co* (1967) 119 CLR 460.
22 The same result could also be achieved where a negative stipulation is enforced by means of an injunction or where the promisee brings an action for an agreed sum.
23 *Beswick v Beswick* [1968] AC 58, p 102, *per* Lord Upjohn.
24 *Ibid*, p 88, *per* Lord Pearce.
25 *Trident General Insurance Co Ltd v McNiece Bros Pty Ltd* (1988) 165 CLR 107, pp 175–76, *per* Gaudron J.
26 [1967] 2 All ER 1197, HL.

Beswick v Beswick [1967] 2 All ER 1197, HL, p 1212

Lord Pearce: My Lords, if the annuity had been payable to a third party in the lifetime of Beswick, senior, and there had been default, he could have sued in respect of the breach. His administratrix is now entitled to stand in his shoes and to sue in respect of the breach which has occurred since his death. It is argued that the estate can recover only nominal damages and that no other remedy is open, either to the estate or to the personal plaintiff. Such a result would be wholly repugnant to justice and common sense. And if the argument were right it would show a very serious defect in the law. In the first place, I do not accept the view that damages must be nominal. Lush LJ, in *Lloyd's v Harper* said: 'Then the next question which, no doubt, is a very important and substantial one, is, that Lloyds, having sustained no damage themselves, could not recover for the losses sustained by third parties by reason of the default of Robert Henry Harper as an underwriter. That, to my mind, is a startling and alarming doctrine, and a novelty, because I consider it to be an established rule of law that where a contract is made with A for the benefit of B, A can sue on the contract for the benefit of B, and recover all that B could have recovered if the contract had been made with B himself.'

I agree with the comment of Windeyer J in *Bagot's Executor and Trustee Co Ltd v Coulls* in the High Court of Australia that the words of Lush LJ cannot be accepted without qualification and regardless of context, and also with his statement: 'I can see no reason why in such cases the damages which A would suffer upon B's breach of his contract to pay C $500 would be merely nominal: I think that in accordance with the ordinary rules for the assessment of damages for breach of contract they would be substantial. They would not necessarily be $500; they could I think be less or more.'

In the present case, I think that the damages, if assessed, must be substantial. It is not necessary, however, to consider the amount of damages more closely, since this is a case in which, as the Court of Appeal rightly decided, the more appropriate remedy is that of specific performance.

The administratrix is entitled, if she so prefers, to enforce the agreement rather than accept its repudiation, and specific performance is more convenient than an action for arrears of payment followed by separate actions as each sum falls due. Moreover, damages for breach would be a less appropriate remedy since the parties to the agreement were intending an annuity for a widow; and a lump sum of damages does not accord with this: and if (contrary to my view) the argument that a derisory sum of damages is all that can be obtained be right, the remedy of damages in this case is manifestly useless. The present case presents all the features which led the equity courts to apply their remedy of specific performance. The contract was for the sale of a business. The appellant could on his part clearly have obtained specific performance of it if Beswick senior or his administratrix had defaulted. Mutuality is a ground in favour of specific performance. Moreover, the appellant on his side has received the whole benefit of the contract and it is a matter of conscience for the court to see that he now performs his part of it. Kay J said in *Hart v Hart*: '... when an agreement for valuable consideration ... has been partially performed, the court ought to do its utmost to carry out that agreement by a decree for specific performance.'

What, then, if the obstacle to granting specific performance? It is argued that, since the respondent personally had no rights which she personally could enforce, the court will not make an order which will have the effect of enforcing those rights.

I can find no principle to this effect. The condition as to payment of an annuity to the widow personally was valid. The estate (though not the widow personally) can enforce it. Why should the estate be barred from exercising its full contractual rights merely because in doing so it secures justice for the widow who, by a mechanical defect of our law, is unable to assert her own rights? Such a principle would be repugnant to justice and fulfil no other object than that of aiding the wrongdoer. I can find no ground on which such a principle should exist.

In *Hohler v Aston*, Sargant J enforced a contract relating to the purchase of a house for the benefit of third parties. The third parties were joined as plaintiffs, but the relief was given to the plaintiff who had made the contract for their benefit: 'The third parties, of course, cannot themselves enforce a contract made for their benefit, but the person with whom the contract is made is entitled to enforce the contract.'

Recently, in *Bagot's* case, the chief justice of Australia, Garfield Barwick CJ, in commenting on the report of the Court of Appeal's decision in the present case, said: 'I would myself, with great respect, agree with the conclusion that where A promises B for a consideration supplied by B to pay C that B may obtain specific performance of A's promise, at least where the nature of the consideration given would have allowed the debtor to have obtained specific performance. I can see no reason whatever why A in those circumstances should not be bound to perform his promise. That C provided no part of the consideration seems to me irrelevant.'

Windeyer J, in that case said: 'It seems to me that contracts to pay money or transfer property to a third person are always, or at all events very often, contracts for breach of which damages would be an inadequate remedy – all the more so if it be right (I do not think it is) that damages recoverable by the promisee are only nominal. Nominal or substantial, the question seems to be the same, for when specific relief is given in lieu of damages it is because the remedy, damages, cannot satisfy the demands of justice. 'The court', said Lord Selborne LC, 'gives specific performance instead of damages only when it can by that means do more perfect and complete justice': *Wilson v Northampton and Banbury Junction Railway Co*. Lord Erskine LC, in *Alley v Deschamps,* said of the doctrine of specific performance: 'This court assumed the jurisdiction upon this simple principle; that the party had a legal right to the performance of the contract; to which right the courts of law, whose jurisdiction did not extend beyond damages, had not the means of giving effect.' Complete and perfect justice to a promisee may well require that a promisor perform his promise to pay money or transfer property to a third party. I see no reason why specific performance should not be had in such cases – but, of course, not where the promise was to render some personal service. There is no reason today for limiting by particular categories, rather than by general principle, the cases in which orders for specific performance will be made. The days are long past when the common law courts looked with jealousy upon what they thought was a usurpation by the chancery court of their jurisdiction.'

He continued later: 'It is, I think, a faulty analysis of legal obligations to say that the law treats the promisor as having a right to elect either to perform his promise or to pay damages. Rather, using one sentence from the passage from Lord Erskine's judgment which I have quoted above the promisee has 'a legal right to the performance of the contract'. Moreover, we are concerned with what Fullagar J, once called 'a system which has never regarded strict logic as its sole inspiration, *Tatham v Huxtable*.'

I respectfully agree with these observations.

It is argued that the court should be deterred from making the order, because there will be technical difficulties in enforcing it. In my opinion, the court should not lightly be deterred by such a consideration from making an order which justice requires, but I do not find this difficulty. RSC Ord 45 r 9 provides under the heading 'Execution by or against a person not being a party': '9(1) Any person, not being a party to a cause or matter, who obtains any order or in whose favour any order is made, shall be entitled to enforce obedience to the order by the same process as if he were a party.'

This would appear by its wide terms to enable the widow for whose benefit the annuity is ordered to enforce its payment by the appointment of a receiver, by writ of *fi fa*, or even by judgment summons. I see no reason to limit the apparent meaning of the words of the rule, which would appear to achieve a sensible purpose. Moreover, I see no objection in principle to the estate enforcing the judgment, receiving the fruits on behalf of the widow and paying them over to the widow, just as a bailee of goods does when he recovers damages which should properly belong to the true owner of the goods.

It is contended that the order of the Court of Appeal is wrong and there should be no specific performance because the condition that the appellant should pay off two named creditors has been omitted, and there can be no enforcement of part of the contract; but the assumption, since we have no evidence on the matter, is that the creditors have both already been paid off. Even if they have not, a party is entitled to waive a condition which is wholly in his favour; and its omission cannot be used by the appellant as a ground for not performing his other parts of the contract. It is unnecessary, therefore, to consider in what circumstances a contract may be enforced in part. In my opinion, the respondent as administratrix is entitled to a decree of specific performance.

Where the promisor is in breach of a negative stipulation, such as an undertaking not to compete in business with the third party, the court may be able to grant an injunction to enforce the promise in favour of the third party.

The same also appears to hold good where there has been a promise to the promisee that a third party will not be subject to liability in specified circumstances. This is especially the case where the result of a breach of contract by the promisor is that the promisee is exposed to liability to the third party. It is said that in order for the promisee to be able to sue in such cases, he must have a sufficient interest in the outcome of the proceedings;[27] however, this may not always be the case.

In *Snelling v John G Snelling & Co Ltd*,[28] the plaintiff was one of three brothers who were directors of a family business. All three brothers had lent money to the company on condition that should any of them resign his directorship, he would forfeit his right to recover the loan from the company. When the plaintiff resigned, he sought to recover the amount of his loan. The other brothers were joined as defendants and were able to obtain a stay of proceedings. The plaintiff's action was dismissed, despite the fact that the defendant brothers appeared not to be under any legal liability to the company if the money lent by the plaintiff were to be recovered:

Snelling v John G Snelling & Co Ltd [1972] 1 All ER 79, p 86

Ormrod J: I now turn to the position of the defendant company. Counsel for the plaintiff contends that it has no defence to this claim and relies on the well-known case, *Scruttons Ltd v Midland Silicones Ltd*, in which the House of Lords reaffirmed unequivocally the common law doctrine that in the absence of a trust or agency, a person cannot rely on a term in a contract to which he is not a party even if he is the person whom the contract is intended to benefit. Counsel contends, therefore, that the company cannot rely on the agreement between the brothers and claim that in the events which have happened the plaintiff's loan account has been forfeited, and consequently is no longer payable to him. There can be no doubt that this proposition is supported by the speeches in the *Midland Silicones* case. Counsel for the defendants, however, submits that some of the broad statements of principle in that case went too far and relies on the later case of *Beswick v Beswick*.

The critical difference between *Beswick v Beswick* and these other cases is that in all of them a person who was not a party to the contract from which the obligation in question arose, was attempting to enforce the contract. In *Beswick*, the widow in her capacity as the personal representative of her deceased husband's estate, was the promisee under the contract out of which the son's obligation to pay the annuity of £5 per week arose. She was therefore entitled to enforce the obligation. The fact that in her personal capacity she was the beneficiary of it was clearly irrelevant.

Counsel for the plaintiff has called my attention to *Gore v Van der Lann (Liverpool Corpn Intervening)* in the Court of Appeal and I must now deal with it. In that case, the Liverpool corporation applied to the court under s 41 to stay an action which was proceeding between the plaintiff and a conductor of one of their buses for damages for negligent management of a bus. The plaintiff, as an old-age pensioner, had been given a permit by the corporation entitling her to travel at reduced rates or free on their buses. The permit contained a provision exempting the corporation and their servants, including the defendant conductor, from liability for negligence to persons travelling under

27 *Gore v Van Der Lann* [1967] 1 All ER 360.
28 [1972] 1 All ER 79.

it. The corporation sought to protect their conductor, who had been sued personally, by alleging that the plaintiff's claim was a fraud on the corporation, but they failed. The primary ground of the decision of the Court of Appeal was that the permit was a contract (not a licence as the corporation contended) and as such was caught by s 151 of the Road Traffic Act 1960, which rendered any such exemption clause illegal. But, in the alternative, the Court of Appeal held that the exemption clause was not sufficiently precise in its terms to justify the granting of a stay of the plaintiff's action against the conductor. So, in the present case, counsel for the plaintiff says that there was no specific promise by the plaintiff not to sue the defendant company and consequently the court should refuse to stay the plaintiff's action. I do not think that the Court of Appeal can have intended to lay down a general proposition of law that the court will not stay proceedings in such circumstances unless the plaintiff has expressly undertaken not to sue. I do not think that the Court of Appeal intended to go further than to say that the promise which is to be enforced by the granting of a stay must be clear and unambiguous. In this connection, an observation by Kelly CB in *Slater v Jones* is of assistance. In that case, which concerned the effect of a resolution of creditors to accept a composition, he said: '... I think that a person who is bound by such a resolution is also bound, by necessary implication, not to sue the debtor before the time for payment comes, and until default is made.'

So here, it is a necessary implication of cl 4 of the agreement of 22 March 1968 that the plaintiff will not sue the company.

In my judgment, therefore, the second and third defendants have made out an unambiguous case and have shown that the interests of justice require that the plaintiff be not permitted to recover against the defendant company. It follows that this is a proper case in which to grant a stay of all further proceedings in the plaintiff's action against the company.

Counsel for the defendants, however, has submitted that he is entitled to go further and ask for the plaintiff's claim against the company to be dismissed. He relies on three cases: *West Yorkshire Darracq Agency Ltd v Coleridge; Hirachand Punamchand v Temple;* and *Re William Porter & Co Ltd*. In the *West Yorkshire* case, all the directors of a company in liquidation agreed to forgo their respective claims to outstanding directors' fees. The liquidator was a party to an oral agreement to this effect. Horridge J held that the company was entitled to rely on the agreement as a good defence to a subsequent claim by one of the directors for his fees. The basis of the judgment was that the company, through the liquidator, was a party to the agreement, although no consideration moved from it to the plaintiff. In *Re William Porter & Co Ltd,* the opposite situation arose. Following a resolution passed by the directors of a company that no directors' fees be paid until a further resolution was passed, the trustee in bankruptcy of the governing director submitted a proof in the liquidation of the company for subsequent fees due to the director. The liquidator rejected the proof. Simonds J held that the company was not a party to any agreement with the directors and that the *West Yorkshire* case did not apply. He went on to hold, however, that the directors, by assenting to the postponement or abrogation of their rights, had induced the company to a course of conduct from which it could have abstained. He, therefore, upheld the rejection of the proof by the liquidator.

In the present case the defendant company was not specifically mentioned as a party to the agreement of 22 March 1968 which, in form at any rate, was an agreement between the three directors concerned. On the other hand, the minutes of the defendant company contain references to it and it was an important item on the agenda at two meetings of the board of directors. There being no liquidator, there was no physical person other than the directors who could have been a party to it on behalf of the defendant company, and they themselves never applied their minds to the question whether the company was to be a party to it or not. They regarded the business, the company and its associated companies, and themselves as an amalgam for most purposes, and their intention was to act for the benefit of the amalgam. However, it is not possible to distinguish this case on its facts from *Re William Porter & Co Ltd* in this respect. I must, therefore, hold that the defendant company was not a party to the agreement. I have no evidence that the defendant company took any action in reliance on the agreement which it would not otherwise have done so that Simonds J's decision cannot be relied on to support the view that the company is entitled to have this action dismissed.

Does the reasoning in this case accord with the sentiment implied in *Beswick v Beswick* that, where a promisee seeks to enforce a contract on behalf of a third party, the court will grant whatever remedy is most appropriate and just in the circumstances?

A third method of compelling the promisor's performance is an action for an agreed sum. The major difficulty here is that, since the action is brought by the promisee and the contractual obligation is to pay the third party, it could be seen to be wrong to pay the sum to the promisee.[29]

The promisee's action for damages

The normal rule is that an award of damages should compensate the claimant in respect of *his own* losses, not those of a third party. Accordingly, where a contract is made solely for the benefit of a third party, it is difficult to see how the promisee can argue that he has suffered a compensatable loss in his own right, in which case, the promisee should recover no more than nominal damages. Generally, where the promisee does suffer loss as well, he can recover damages, but only in respect of his own loss.

In some exceptional cases, it seems that recovery on behalf of a third party may be permitted. For example, a consignor of goods can recover damages in respect of the loss suffered by a person to whom the goods have been sold by suing the shipper, in circumstances where the buyer has not acquired the right to sue.[30]

---

29 See *Coulls v Bagot's Executor and Trustee Co Ltd* (1967) 119 CLR 460.
30 *Dunlop v Lambert* (1839) 2 Cl & F 626.

Occasionally, the loss suffered by the third party can be treated as the loss of the promisee, although this does appear to be exceptional.

In *Jackson v Horizon Holidays Ltd*,[31] the plaintiff sued for damages on his own behalf and on behalf of other members of his family following the severe disappointment suffered by all concerned as a result of a ruined holiday. It was assumed that the plaintiff's wife and children were not parties to the contract,[32] but damages were awarded on the basis that the distress suffered by the plaintiff was exacerbated by witnessing the distress of his wife and children or because the plaintiff had contracted for the benefit of the entire family:

Jackson v Horizon Holidays Ltd [1975] 3 All ER 92, CA, p 96

James LJ: In this case, Mr Jackson, as found by the judge on the evidence, was in need of a holiday at the end of 1970. He was able to afford a holiday for himself and his family. According to the form which he completed, which was the form of Horizon Holidays Ltd, he booked what was a family holiday. The wording of that form might, in certain circumstances, give rise to a contract in which the person signing the form is acting as his own principal and as agent for others. In the circumstances of this case, as indicated by Lord Denning MR, it would be wholly unrealistic to regard this contract as other than one made by Mr Jackson for a family holiday. The judge found that he did not get a family holiday.

Lord Denning MR (p 94): In *Jarvis v Swans Tours Ltd*, it was held by this court that damages for the loss of a holiday may include not only the difference in value between what was promised and what was obtained, but also damages for mental distress, inconvenience, upset, disappointment and frustration caused by the loss of the holiday. The judge directed himself in accordance with the judgments in that case. He eventually awarded a sum of £1,100.

The judge took the cost of the holidays at £1,200. The family only had about half the value of it. Divide it by two and you get £600. Then add £500 for the mental distress.

On this question, a point of law arises. The judge said that he could only consider the mental distress to Mr Jackson himself, and that he could not consider the distress to his wife and children. He said: '... the damages are the plaintiff's; that I can consider the effect upon his mind of his wife's discomfort, vexation and the like, although I cannot award a sum which represents her vexation.'

Counsel for Mr Jackson disputes that proposition. He submits that damages can be given not only for the leader of the party, in this case, Mr Jackson's own distress, discomfort and vexation, but also for that of the rest of the party.

---

31 [1975] 3 All ER 92, CA.
32 See *Daly v General Steam Navigation Co Ltd, The Dragon* [1980] 2 Lloyd's Rep 145.

We have had an interesting discussion as to the legal position when one person makes a contract for the benefit of a party. In this case, it was a husband making a contract for the benefit of himself, his wife and children. Other cases readily come to mind. A host makes a contract with a restaurant for a dinner for himself and his friends. The vicar makes a contract for a coach trip for the choir. In all these cases there is only one person who makes the contract. It is the husband, the host or the vicar, as the case may be. Sometimes, he pays the whole price himself. Occasionally, he may get a contribution from the others. But, in any case, it is he who makes the contract. It would be a fiction to say that the contract was made by all the family, or all the guests, or all the choir, and that he was only an agent for them. Take this very case. It would be absurd to say that the twins of three years old were parties to the contract or that the father was making the contract on their behalf as if they were principals. It would equally be a mistake to say that, in any of these instances, there was a trust. The transaction bears no resemblance to a trust. There was no trust fund and no trust property. No, the real truth is that, in each instance, the father, the host or the vicar was making a contract himself for the benefit of the whole party. In short, a contract by one for the benefit of third persons.

What is the position when such a contract is broken? At present, the law says that the only one who can sue is the one who made the contract. None of the rest of the party can sue, even though the contract was made for their benefit. But when that one does sue, what damages can he recover? Is he limited to his own loss? Or can he recover for the others? Suppose the holiday firm puts the family into a hotel which is only half-built and the visitors have to sleep on the floor? Or suppose the restaurant is fully booked and the guests have to go away, hungry and angry, having spent so much on fares to get there? Or suppose the coach leaves the choir stranded half-way and they have to hire cars to get home? None of them individually can sue. Only the father, the host or the vicar can sue. He can, of course, recover his own damages. But can he not recover for the others? I think he can. The case comes within the principle stated by Lush LJ in *Lloyd's v Harper*: '... I consider it to be an established rule of law that where a contract is made with A for the benefit of B, A can sue on the contract for the benefit of B, and recover all that B could have recovered if the contract had been made with B himself.'

It has been suggested that Lush LJ was thinking of a contract in which A was trustee for B. But I do not think so. He was a common lawyer speaking of the common law. His words were quoted with considerable approval by Lord Pearce in *Beswick v Beswick*. I have myself often quoted them. I think they should be accepted as correct, at any rate so long as the law forbids the third persons themselves to sue for damages. It is the only way in which a just result can be achieved. Take the instance I have put. The guests ought to recover from the restaurant their wasted fares. The choir ought to recover the cost of hiring the taxis home. There is no one to recover for them except the one who made the contract for their benefit. He should be able to recover the expense to which they have been put, and pay it over to them. Once recovered, it will be money had and received to their use. (They might even, if desired, be joined as plaintiffs.) If he can recover for the expense, he should also be able to recover for the discomfort, vexation and upset which the whole party have suffered by reason of the breach of contract, recompensing them accordingly out of what he recovers.

Applying the principles to this case, I think that the figure of £1,100 was about right. It would, I think, have been excessive if it had been awarded only for the damage suffered by Mr Jackson himself. But when extended to his wife and children, I do not think it is excessive.

The views expressed by Lord Denning have subsequently been held, *obiter*, to be incorrect. What mistake did he make in relying upon the *dictum* of Lush J in *Lloyd's v Harper*?[33] Why does the approach of James LJ do less damage to the doctrine of privity?

Woodar Investment Development Ltd v Wimpey Construction (UK) Ltd [1980] 1 All ER 571, HL, p 576

Lord Wilberforce: The second issue in this appeal is one of damages. Both courts below have allowed Woodar to recover substantial damages in respect of condition I under which £150,000 was payable by Wimpey to Transworld Trade Ltd on completion. On the view which I take of the repudiation issue, this question does not require decision, but in view of the unsatisfactory state in which the law would be if the Court of Appeal's decision were to stand I must add three observations:

(1) The majority of the Court of Appeal followed, in the case of Goff LJ with expressed reluctance, its previous decision in *Jackson v Horizon Holidays Ltd*. I am not prepared to dissent from the actual decision in that case. It may be supported either as a broad decision on the measure of damages (*per* James LJ) or possibly as an example of a type of contract, examples of which are persons contracting for family holidays, ordering meals in restaurants for a party, hiring a taxi for a group, calling for special treatment. As I suggested in *New Zealand Shipping Co Ltd v AM Satterthwaite & Co Ltd*, there are many situations of daily life which do not fit neatly into conceptual analysis, but which require some flexibility in the law of contract. *Jackson's* case may well be one.

I cannot agree with the basis on which Lord Denning MR put his decision in that case. The extract on which he relied from the judgment of Lush LJ in *Lloyd's v Harper* was part of a passage in which Lush LJ was stating as an 'established rule of law that an agent (sc an insurance broker) may sue on a contract made by him on behalf of the principal (sc the assured) if the contract gives him such a right, and is no authority for the proposition required in *Jackson's* case, still less for the proposition, required here, that, if Woodar made a contract for a sum of money to be paid to Transworld, Woodar can, without showing that it has itself suffered loss or that Woodar was agent or trustee for Transworld, sue for damages for non-payment of that sum. That would certainly not be an established rule of law, nor was it quoted as such authority by Lord Pearce in *Beswick v Beswick'*.

The facts of this case are irrelevant for present purposes.

---

33 (1880) 16 Ch D 290, p 301.

More recently, the list of exceptions to the rule appears to have been extended. In *Linden Gardens Trust v Lenesta Sludge Disposals Ltd,*[34] a building contract entered into between parties who described themselves as employer and contractor required the contractor to develop a site of shops, offices and flats. Later, the site, but not the benefit of the contract, was transferred by the employer to a third party, who discovered that the work done by the contractor was defective and required a considerable amount of remedial work. Some of these defects also came into existence after transfer of the site. The employer sued the contractor, but the latter argued that, since only the third party had suffered loss, the employer was not entitled to substantial damages. Lord Griffiths considered that the employer had suffered loss since he was required to spend money in order to obtain the benefit he had expected to receive from the contractor.[35] Although he added, as a rider, that the court will want to be satisfied that the repairs in respect of which substantial damages are given have been or are likely to be carried out. The majority in *Lenesta* based their reasoning on a slightly narrower ground, namely that the loss was suffered by the third party rather than the employer. On this basis, it became necessary to ask whether property and risk had passed to the third party purchaser and it was essential that the third party had acquired no independent contractual rights of his own. In these circumstances, it is reasonable to assume that the parties to the initial contract of carriage have made that contract with the intention of benefiting all third parties who might be expected to acquire an interest in the goods. Similarly, in *Lenesta*, it is reasonable to assume that both the employer and the contractor had intended that the site be sold off to third parties when it was ready to be occupied.

Since *Lenesta*, there have been further decisions which appear to take the exception still further. In *Darlington Borough Council v Wiltshier Northern Ltd,*[36] a local authority intended to develop land which it already owned, but was not in a position to borrow money due to government restrictions on local authority spending. As a result of this, the council entered into two parallel agreements, namely, a building contract under which a bank prepared to lend the required money was the employer and the defendants were the building contractors. Alongside this, there was a second contract under which the bank agreed to procure the building, to pay all amounts due under the building contract and to assign to the council the benefit of any rights they had against the defendant. This contract also provided that the bank would not be liable to the council for any incompleteness in the building work. Since this second contract operated by way of an assignment, the clause relating to

---

34   [1994] 1 AC 85.

35   *Ibid*, p 97.

36   [1995] 1 WLR 68. Cf *Alfred McAlpine Construction Ltd v Panatown Ltd* (2000) *The Times*, 26 August, HL.

incompleteness of the building work gave rise to difficulties. Normally, the rule is that an assignee will not be allowed to recover any more than the assignor could have done. As a result, it was argued on behalf of the builders that the council could not sue in respect of incompleteness since the bank was not liable for any incompleteness. The Court of Appeal, however, rejected this argument holding that the bank could have recovered substantial damages from the defendants, apparently on the basis that this case was covered by the principle established in *Lenesta*. However, it would appear that there are differences between *Darlington Borough Council v Wiltshier and Lenesta* since, in the earlier case, it was assumed to be a requirement that the original contracting parties always envisaged a transfer of property in the thing which was the main subject matter of the contract. In contrast, in the *Darlington* case, ownership of the land remained with the council throughout. Steyn LJ's reasoning in this case seems to be based more on pragmatic grounds than on a strict application of legal principle, since he makes the point that, but for an application of the principle in *Lenesta*, an otherwise meritorious claim would have disappeared down a legal black hole, but this was a black hole created by the parties themselves due to the clause relieving the bank of any liability for incompleteness. In any case, it has been established by the House of Lords in *Alfred McAlpine Construction Ltd v Panatown Ltd* that if a party has a valid claim under some other rule of law, the *Lenesta* exception will not apply.

The relations between third party and promisee

It is clear that the promisee may be able to enforce the contract on behalf of the third party or possibly recover damages in respect of the third party's loss. Accordingly, the relations between the two are important. No problem arose in *Beswick v Beswick*, since the promisee and the third party were the same person. However, the issue may arise whether the third party can require the promisee to seek an order for specific performance or an injunction, or whether he can require the promisee to hand over the damages he has been awarded. In the Court of Appeal in *Beswick v Beswick*,[37] Lord Denning MR suggested that it might be possible for the third party to sue the promisor and join the promisee as co-defendant,[38] in which case, the promisee will hold any payment as moneys had and received.[39] However, this view was not shared by the majority in the same case.

---

37 [1966] Ch 538.
38 *Ibid*, p 557.
39 *Jackson v Horizon Holidays Ltd* [1975] 1 WLR 1468, p 1473, *per* Lord Denning MR.

CIRCUMVENTING THE DOCTRINE OF PRIVITY

The doctrine of privity merely indicates that someone who is not a contracting party is unable to enforce the benefits created by or be subject to the burdens imposed under a contract made between two other people. Accordingly, rights may be conferred on a third party, and to a lesser extent, burdens may be imposed otherwise than under a contract. For example, such rights and burdens may arise by way of tort, trust, agency or assignment.

Two main questions need to be considered in deciding whether a third party (T) can claim the benefit of rights created under a contract between A and B. These questions are:

- can T enforce the terms of a contract between A and B which is expressed to be for the benefit of T?;

- can T claim to set up a defence contained in a contract between A and B in an action brought against him by A or B?

The tort of negligence

Where A and B enter a contract, for example, for the supply of a service, the promisor may have agreed to take care in relation to a third party. It follows that a contract between a main building contractor and a subcontractor may require the subcontractor to exercise reasonable care in relation to the main contractor's client.[40] The difficulty with duties of care of this kind is that they are usually concerned with the issue of economic loss, in the form of diminution in the value of a defective building which is said to be rarely recoverable in a tortious action.[41] Moreover, even where the third party suffers physical harm to his property, he might not be able to maintain a negligence action against the promisor where the third party is not the legal owner or a person with possessory title to the goods damaged.[42]

While it is clear that recent decisions concerning the recovery of economic loss in the tort of negligence have restricted the extent to which T can enforce the terms of a contract between A and B, even where it is expressed to be for his benefit, there are cases where recovery will be allowed. In such cases, there are three essential requirements. First, there must be a close relationship of proximity between T and A. Secondly, it must not be unjust or inequitable for a duty of care to be imposed on A. Thirdly, the harm suffered by T generally

---

40 See, eg, *Junior Books Ltd v Veitchi Co Ltd* [1983] 1 AC 520.
41 See *Murphy v Brentwood DC* [1990] 2 All ER 908; *D and F Estates Ltd v Church Comrs for England* [1988] 2 All ER 992.
42 *Leigh and Sillivan Ltd v Aliakmon Shipping Co Ltd* [1986] 2 All ER 145. But see Carriage of Goods by Sea Act 1992, s 2(4).

must be classified as physical harm to property or to the person, although, in some cases, particularly involving negligent mis-statements or negligent advice, claims for pure economic loss will be allowed.

In the area of negligent advice, it is well established that a duty of care may be owed by the giver of the advice under the principles set out in *Hedley Byrne Co Ltd v Heller & Partners Ltd*,[43] as qualified by a number of later decisions of the House of Lords. The basis of the tortious liability imposed in such cases is largely that the claimant has reasonably relied upon the advice given by the defendant. That defendant has knowledge that the advice will be relied upon and that there is a sufficiently close relationship of proximity between the parties, that it is just and reasonable to impose a duty of care and, in appropriate circumstances, there may be an additional requirement that the defendant should have voluntarily assumed responsibility for the accuracy of his statement by freely entering into the relationship with the claimant. Thus, in *White v Jones*,[44] a solicitor undertook to advise his client on the preparation of an effective will which was intended to confer a benefit on the plaintiff, with whom the solicitor had no contractual relationship. Because of this state of affairs, it was clear that there was no privity of contract between the solicitor and the intended beneficiaries. Because the solicitor had voluntarily entered into a relationship with the client, he had undertaken obligations to the intended beneficiaries which lay in the tort of negligence. The justification for this was that the plaintiffs had reasonably relied on the solicitor to advise properly and that the solicitor could be taken to be aware of that reliance, that they might foreseeably suffer loss if he were not to give advice as would be expected of a reasonable solicitor and that it was just and reasonable to impose liability in the circumstances. Earlier case law[45] had raised the question whether voluntary assumption of responsibility was a proper issue to raise in the context of tortious duties of care, since the accepted view is that tortious duties are imposed by law rather than by virtue of any voluntary acceptance of responsibility towards the claimant. However, this was answered in *White v Jones* by holding that the defendant did not voluntarily assume the duty of care, since this was imposed by law, but he did voluntarily enter into a relationship with his client. This relationship led to the acceptance of a responsibility towards persons who might be foreseeably affected by his actions or omissions. What can be seen from this is that, in appropriate circumstances, a person who gives advice may owe a duty of care to a third party, despite the fact that there is no contractual connection with that person, but it is important to emphasise that the duty lies in tort rather than in contract. Moreover, even following the introduction of new means of side-stepping the doctrine of privity in the Contracts (Rights of Third Parties) Act

---

43 [1964] AC 465.
44 [1995] 1 All ER 691. See, also, *Carr-Glynn v Frearsons* [1998] 4 All ER 225.
45 See *Smith v Eric S Bush (A Firm)* [1990] 1 AC 831.

1999, cases such as *White v Jones* will not come to be regarded as actions in contract, since it must be the contract between the relevant contracting parties which expressly or impliedly confers a benefit on the third party and, in *White v Jones*, it was the will, rather than the contract which conferred the relevant benefit.

The second question above asks if T can seek to rely on a defence contained in the contract between A and B in an action brought against him by A or B. Typically, such cases will involve the question of whether T is entitled to the protection of an exemption clause.

Many commercial transactions involve many parties. Typical examples include international trade dealings under which there is a complex of relations between the buyer, seller, carrier and other parties involved in the process of shipment of a cargo. Similarly, many contracts entered into for the purposes of the construction of a building or a ship may involve a number of subcontractors as well as the party commissioning the work and the main contractor. These multipartite relationships are often difficult to explain in terms of traditional rules of the law of contract which appear to treat the two-party contract as the norm. Where exemption clauses are concerned, a simple application of the doctrine of privity of contract would suggest that a third party cannot claim the benefit of such a provision if it is part of a contract between two other parties.

If a firm of stevedores, employed by a carrier to unload a cargo, negligently damages goods carried under the terms of a contract of carriage made between the consignor of goods and the carrier, the question may arise whether the stevedore, in an action brought by the purchaser of the cargo, can claim the benefit of an exclusion clause in the contract between the consignor and the carrier which purports to protect both the carrier and the stevedore. Commercial reality suggests that if the risk of loss or damage to a cargo has already passed to the buyer then he should be insured against that risk. Accordingly, since there is likely to be a valid insurance policy covering the risk of damage in the course of unloading, it makes commercial sense for the stevedores to be able to claim the protection of the exemption clause. However, a rigid application of the doctrine of privity of contract in this type of case would mean that the stevedores could be sued for the damage to the cargo despite the fact that the buyer was insured against that risk.

The commercial reality approach suggests that there should be a doctrine of vicarious immunity under which the third party may rely upon an exemption clause in a contract to which he is not a party, provided it is the intention of all concerned that the benefit should be extended to such a person. However, the doctrine of vicarious immunity was later rejected by the House of Lords in *Scruttons Ltd v Midland Silicones Ltd*,[46] where the

---

46 [1962] AC 446.

defendants, a firm of stevedores, negligently damaged a drum of chemicals and sought the immunity offered by a limitation clause contained in the bill of lading which governed the relationship between the plaintiffs and the carrier. The relevant clause provided that the 'carrier' included any person bound by the bill of lading, whether acting as carrier or bailee. The House of Lords held that, since the stevedores were not parties to the contract of carriage, they could not rely on the limitation clause, especially since the limitation clause did not mention the stevedores by name.

One consequence of this decision was to restrict the effectiveness of exemption clauses, which, at the time, was a prime concern of the courts. However, desirable though it was seen to be to operate in this way, particularly in consumer contracts, the same result could have undesirable consequences in business dealings, as was demonstrated in *Scruttons* itself, by allowing a successful action against a third party in circumstances in which he could legitimately believe that the risk of loss had been allocated in a different direction. Since the decision in *Scruttons*, the Unfair Contract Terms Act 1977 has made it less important for the courts to manipulate common law rules in order to minimise the effect of exemption clauses,[47] in which case, the courts should now be able to take a more realistic view of agreed allocations of risk, especially in consumer contracts.

Because of the undesirable effects of the decision in *Scruttons*, methods have been employed to circumvent it. For example, it may be possible to treat one of the parties to the contract as the agent of the third party, but this requires a contractual provision worded in such a way as to include the third party within the range of people protected by the limitation. Moreover, the provision will also have to stipulate that a carrier, for example, contracts on his own behalf and as agent for the stevedore, and that the carrier has authority from the stevedore to contract in this way.

In *New Zealand Shipping Co Ltd v AM Satterthwaite & Co Ltd*,[48] machinery belonging to the consignees was damaged by the defendant stevedores in the course of unloading a ship. The defendants sought the protection of a limitation clause contained in the bill of lading which formed the basis of a contract between the carriers and the consignors. Accordingly, the dispute arose between two litigants, neither of whom was a party to the contract of carriage. The relevant clause provided that no servant or agent, including an independent contractor of the carrier was to be liable for any act or default while acting in the course of his employment. Furthermore, the clause provided that every limitation available to the carrier should also be available to specified third parties; that the carrier should be deemed to act as agent and

---

47   See *Adler v Dickson* [1955] 1 QB 158; *Genys v Matthews* [1965] 3 All ER 24; *Gore v Van der Lann* [1967] 2 QB 31.

48   [1975] AC 154.

trustee for such persons, and that such persons should be deemed to be parties to the contract. The Privy Council unanimously agreed that an appropriately worded clause could protect a third party and a majority held that this clause did serve to protect the stevedores. The court was prepared to treat the presentation of the bill of lading by the consignee as a unilateral offer of exemption which was capable of creating mutual obligations when the stevedores performed services for the benefit of the consignee by discharging the goods:

New Zealand Shipping Co Ltd v AM Satterthwaite & Co Ltd [1975] AC 154, p 166[49]

Lord Wilberforce: The question in the appeal is whether the stevedore can take the benefit of the time limitation provision. The starting point, in discussion of this question, is provided by the House of Lords decision in *Midland Silicones Ltd v Scruttons Ltd* [1962] AC 446. There is no need to question or even to qualify that case in so far as it affirms the general proposition that a contract between two parties cannot be sued on by a third person, even though the contract is expressed to be for his benefit. Nor is it necessary to disagree with anything which was said to the same effect in the Australian case of *Wilson v Darling Island Stevedoring and Lighterage Co Ltd* (1956) 95 CLR 43. Each of these cases was dealing with a simple case of a contract the benefit of which was sought to be taken by a third person not a party to it, and the emphatic pronouncements in the speeches and judgments were directed to this situation. But *Midland Silicones* left open the case where one of the parties contracts as agent for the third person: in particular, Lord Reid's speech spelt out, in four propositions, the pre-requisites for the validity of such an agency contract. There is, of course, nothing unique to this case in the conception of agency contracts: well known and common instances exist in the field of hire purchase, of bankers' commercial credits and other transactions. Lord Reid said, at p 474: 'I can see a possibility of success of the agency argument if (first) the bill of lading makes it clear that the stevedore is intended to be protected by the provisions in it which limit liability, (secondly) the bill of lading makes it clear that the carrier, in addition to contracting for these provisions on his own behalf, is also contracting as agent for the stevedore that these provisions should apply to the stevedore, (thirdly) the carrier has authority from the stevedore to do that, or perhaps later ratification by the stevedore would suffice, and (fourthly) that any difficulties about consideration moving from the stevedore were overcome. And then to affect the consignee it would be necessary to show that the provisions of the Bills of Lading Act 1855 apply.'

The question in this appeal is whether the contract satisfies these propositions.

Clause 1 of the bill of lading, whatever the defects in its drafting, is clear in its relevant terms. The carrier, on his own account, stipulates for certain exemptions and immunities: among these is that conferred by Art III, r 6 of the Hague Rules, which discharges the carrier from all liability for loss or damage

---

49   See, also, *Elder Dempster & Co v Paterson, Zochonis & Co Ltd* [1924] AC 522.

unless suit is brought within one year after delivery. In addition to these stipulations on his own account, the carrier as agent for, *inter alios*, independent contractors stipulates for the same exemptions.

Much was made of the fact that the carrier also contracts as agent for numerous other persons; the relevance of this argument is not apparent. It cannot be disputed that among such independent contractors, for whom, as agent, the carrier contracted, is the appellant company which habitually acts as stevedore in New Zealand by arrangement with the carrier and which is, moreover, the parent company of the carrier. The carrier was, indisputably, authorised by the appellant to contract as its agent for the purposes of cl 1. All of this is quite straightforward and was accepted by all the judges in New Zealand. The only question was, and is, the fourth question presented by Lord Reid, namely that of consideration.

It was on this point that the Court of Appeal differed from Beattie J, holding that it had not been shown that any consideration for the shipper's promise as to exemption moved from the promisee, that is, the appellant company.

The conception of a 'unilateral' contract was recognised in *Great Northern Railway Co v Witham* (1873) LR 9 CP 16 and is well established. This way of regarding the matter is very close to if not identical to that accepted by Beattie J in the Supreme Court: he analysed the transaction as one of an offer open to acceptance by action such as was found in *Carlill v Carbolic Smoke Ball Co* [1893] 1 QB 256. But whether one describes the shipper's promise to exempt as an offer to be accepted by performance or as a promise in exchange for an act seems in the present context to be a matter of semantics. The words of Bowen LJ in *Carlill v Carbolic Smoke Ball Co* [1893] 1 QB 256, p 268: '... why should not an offer be made to all the world which is to ripen into a contract with anybody who comes forward and performs the condition?' seem to bridge both conceptions: he certainly seems to draw no distinction between an offer which matures into a contract when accepted and a promise which matures into a contract after performance, and, though in some special contexts (such as in connection with the right to withdraw) some further refinement may be needed, either analysis may be equally valid. On the main point in the appeal, their Lordships are in substantial agreement with Beattie J.

The following points require mention:

(1) In their Lordships' opinion, consideration may quite well be provided by the appellant, as suggested, even though (or if) it was already under an obligation to discharge to the carrier. (There is no direct evidence of the existence or nature of this obligation, but their Lordships are prepared to assume it.) An agreement to do an act which the promisor is under an existing obligation to a third party to do, may quite well amount to valid consideration and does so in the present case: the promisee obtains the benefit of a direct obligation which he can enforce. This proposition is illustrated and supported by *Scotson v Pegg* (1861) 6 H & N 295, which their Lordships consider to be good law.

(2) The consignee is entitled to the benefit of, and is bound by, the stipulations in the bill of lading by his acceptance of it and request for delivery of the goods thereunder. This is shown by *Brandt v Liverpool, Brazil and River Plate*

Steam Navigation Co Ltd [1924] 1 KB 575 and a line of earlier cases. Section 1 of the Bills of Lading Act 1855 (in s 13 of the New Zealand the Mercantile Law Act 1908) gives partial statutory recognition to this rule, but, where the statute does not apply, as it may well not do in this case, the previously established law remains effective.

(3) The appellant submitted, in the alternative, an argument that, quite apart from contract, exemptions from, or limitation of, liability in tort may be conferred by mere consent on the part of the party who may be injured. As their Lordships consider that the appellant ought to succeed in contract, they prefer to express no opinion upon this argument: to evaluate it requires elaborate discussion.

(4) A clause very similar to the present was given effect by a US District Court in *Carle & Montanari Inc v American Export Isbrandtsen Lines Inc* [1968] 1 Lloyd's Rep 260. The carrier in that case contracted, in an exemption clause, as agent, for, *inter alios*, all stevedores and other independent contractors, and although it is no doubt true that the law in the United States is more liberal than ours as regards third party contracts, their Lordships see no reason why the law of the Commonwealth should be more restrictive and technical as regards agency contracts. Commercial considerations should have the same force on both sides of the Pacific.

In the opinion of their Lordships, to give the appellant the benefit of the exemptions and limitations contained in the bill of lading is to give effect to the clear intentions of a commercial document, and can be given within existing principles. They see no reason to strain the law or the facts in order to defeat these intentions. It should not be overlooked that the effect of denying validity to the clause would be to encourage actions against servants, agents and independent contractors in order to get round exemptions (which are almost invariable and often compulsory) accepted by shippers against carriers, the existence, and presumed efficacy, of which is reflected in the rates of freight. They see no attraction in this consequence.

Contrast the dissenting view of Lord Simon of Glaisdale:

Lord Simon of Glaisdale (p 182):

The stevedore's fourth proposition

It is really sufficient to dispose of this proposition in the circumstances of the instant case to say that, were it correct, all five of Lord Reid's conditions, which were common ground between the parties, would be entirely irrelevant: *Midland Silicones Ltd v Scrutons Ltd* [1962] AC 446 should have been decided the other way.

Furthermore, in my opinion, the stevedore's fourth proposition is inconsistent with both the reasoning and the actual decision in *Cosgrove v Horsfall* (1945) 175 LT 334. It was argued for the stevedore in *Midland Silicones* [1962] AC 446, p 465, that *Cosgrove's* case was wrongly decided; but the decision in *Midland Silicones* was inconsistent with that contention (*cf* Lord Denning, dissenting, at p 489). In *Cosgrove's* case (1945) 175 LT 334, the plaintiff, an employee of a transport company, was travelling in one of their omnibuses on a free pass, when a collision occurred with another of the company's omnibuses, causing the plaintiff injuries. One of the conditions to which the grant of the free pass was subject was that neither the company nor their servants were to be liable to the holder of the pass for personal injury however caused. The plaintiff sued the driver of his omnibus and recovered damages. The defendant's appeal to the Court of Appeal was dismissed on the ground that the defendant was not a party to the contract between the plaintiff and the company, the condition of exemption from liability not having been imposed by the company as agent for the defendant. On the stevedore's fourth proposition (unlike the first three), agency is quite irrelevant; moreover, the stevedore's fourth proposition, if valid, merely needs rephrasing to fit the facts of *Cosgrove v Horsfall*, so that the defendant should have succeeded.

Counsel relied for the stevedore's fourth proposition on the cases where a licence is coupled with a disclaimer of liability and on *Hedley Byrne & Co Ltd v Heller & Partners Ltd* [1964] AC 465. In all these cases, however, the right or service extended was gratuitous; and, obviously, any person making a gift can delimit its extent. The cases give no ground, in my opinion, for any such general principle of law as is implicit in the stevedore's fourth proposition, which, if valid, would seem to provide a revolutionary short cut to a *jus quaesitum tertio*.

Since I cannot accept the stevedore's fourth proposition, it is unnecessary to discuss the fine and difficult distinctions which counsel sought to draw between this proposition and the doctrine of *volenti non fit injuria*.

The decision in *Satterthwaite* represents the triumph of commercial reality over the formal rules of contract formation by recognising that those engaged in the carriage business are aware that agents and subcontractors are used, and that such persons are likely to operate on the basis that their liability is limited.

The assumption in *Satterthwaite* was that the stevedores were liable in tort to the consignee. However if the court wishes to avoid the possibility of finding the third party liable for breach of a tortious obligation, this may be done on the basis that the terms of the various contracts entered into between the parties are inconsistent with the existence of or serve to limit the extent of a duty of care on the part of the third party.

In *Southern Water Authority v Carey*,[50] because there was no previous connection between the subcontractor and the main contractor, the agency argument employed in *Satterthwaite* was inapplicable. However, the terms of the building contract between the main contractor and the owner were held sufficient to negate the duty of care which would otherwise have been owed by the subcontractor.

In *Norwich City Council v Harvey*,[51] a contract between the plaintiff council and a firm of main building contractors envisaged that work on a sports centre would be carried out by subcontractors engaged by the main

---

50   [1985] 2 All ER 1077.
51   [1989] 1 All ER 1180, CA.

contractors. The main contract indicated that the council was expected to have the premises insured against accidental damage, including damage by fire. An assumption upon which the Court of Appeal proceeded was that subcontractors could be taken to have assumed that the council would comply with the insurance requirement of the main contract. Accordingly, the terms of that contract were taken to be inconsistent with the finding of a duty to take reasonable care on the part of the subcontractor:

Norwich City Council v Harvey [1989] 1 All ER 1180, CA, p 1183

May LJ: Clearly, therefore, as between the employer and the main contractor, the former was solely liable in respect of any loss or damage to his premises caused by, *inter alia*, fire.

Insofar as the second defendants, as subcontractors, were concerned, they were invited to tender by the main contractor. The document doing so identified the form of the main contract and in attached extracts from the relevant bill of quantities the main contractor expressly stated that cl 20[C] (employer's risk) would apply. In their own additional conditions, they also provided, *inter alia*: 'The work is to be carried out in accordance with the contract which exists between Bush Builders (Norwich) Ltd (hereinafter called the Main Contractor) and the Employer, and the acceptance of this order binds the subcontractors and Suppliers to the same terms and conditions as those of the Main Contract. It is not, however, the intention of the Main Contractor to issue formal Sub-Contract Documents unless specifically required.'

I trust I do no injustice to the plaintiffs argument in this appeal if I put it shortly in this way. There is no dispute between the employer and the main contractor that the former accepted the risk of fire damage: see *James Archdale & Co Ltd v Comservices Ltd* [1954] 1 All ER 210; [1954] 1 WR 459 and *Scottish Special Housing Association v Wimpey Construction UK Ltd* [1986] 2 All ER 957; [1986] 1 WLR 995. However, cl 20[C] does not give rise to any obligation on the employer to indemnify the subcontractor. That clause is primarily concerned to see that the works were completed. It was intended to operate only for the mutual benefit of the employer and the main contractor. If the judge and the subcontractors are right, the latter obtain protection which the rules of privity do not provide. Undoubtedly, the subcontractors owed duties of care in respect of damage by fire to other persons and in respect of other property (for instance the lawful visitor, employees of the employer or other buildings outside the site); in those circumstances, it is impracticable juridically to draw a sensible line between the plaintiffs on the one hand and others on the other to whom a duty of care was owed. The employer had no effective control over the terms on which the relevant subcontract was let and no direct contractual control over either the subcontractors or any employee of theirs.

In addition, the plaintiffs pointed to the position of the first defendant, the subcontractors' employee. *Ex hypothesi*, he was careless and, even if his employers are held to have owed no duty to the building employers, on what grounds can it be said that the employee himself owed no such duty? In my opinion, however, this particular point does not take the matter very much further. If, in principle, the subcontractors owed no specific duty to the building owners in respect of damage by fire, then neither, in my opinion, can any of their employees have done so.

In reply, the defendants contend that the judge was right to hold that, in all the circumstances, there was no duty of care on the subcontractors in this case. Alternatively, they submit that the employers' insurers have no right of subrogation to entitle them to maintain this litigation against the subcontractors.

In the instant case, it is clear that, as between the employer and the main contractor, the former accepted the risk of damage by fire to its premises arising out of and in the course of the building works. Further, although there was no privity between the employer and the subcontractor, it is equally clear from the documents passing between the main contractors and the subcontractors to which I have already referred that the subcontractors and contracted on a like basis. In *Scottish Special Housing Association v Wimpey Construction UK Ltd* [1986] 2 All ER 957; [1986] 1 WLR 995, the House of Lords had to consider whether, as between the employer and main contractors under a contract in precisely the same terms as those of the instant case, it was in truth intended that the employer should bear the whole risk of damage by fire, even fire caused by the contractor's negligence. The position of subcontractors was not strictly in issue in the *Scottish Housing* case, which I cannot think the House did not appreciate, but having considered the terms of cll 18, 19 and 20[C] of the same standard form as was used in the instant case. Lord Keith, in a speech with which the remainder of their Lordships agreed, said ([1986] 2 All ER 957, p 959; [1986] 1 WLR 995, p 999): 'I have found it impossible to resist the conclusion that it is intended that the employer shall bear the whole risk of damage by fire, including fire caused by the negligence of the contractor or that of subcontractors.'

As Lord Keith went on to point out, a similar conclusion was arrived at by the Court of Appeal in England in *James Archdale & Co Ltd v Comservices Ltd* [1954] 1 All ER 210; [1954] 1 WLR 459 on the construction of similarly, but not identically worded corresponding clauses in a predecessor of the standard form used in the *Scottish Housing* and instant cases. Again, the issue only arose in the earlier case as between employer and main contractor, but, approaching the question on the basis of what is just and reasonable, I do not think that the mere fact that there is no strict privity between the employer and the subcontractor should prevent the latter from relying on the clear basis on which all the parties contracted in relation to damage to the employer's building caused by fire, even when due to the negligence of the contractors or subcontractors.

The cases considered so far all raise the question whether a person is entitled to claim the benefit of a provision contained in a contract between two other related parties and it should not be assumed that the reasoning in these cases will extend to instances in which it is sought to subject a third party to the burden of a contract made between others. The general rule is that the burden of an exclusion clause in a contract between the seller of goods and a shipper does not bind a third party, such as the buyer of goods under shipment.[52] However, there are some exceptions. In *Pyrene Co Ltd v Scindia Steam Navigation Co Ltd*,[53] a contract for the sale of goods provided that the buyer should arrange shipment. Arrangements were made and the contract between the buyer and carrier contained terms which excluded the carrier's liability. While the goods were still at the seller's risk, they were damaged due to the carrier's negligence. It was held that the seller was bound by the exclusion on the ground that the buyer was the seller's agent.[54] A second exception arises in cases of bailment, where a sub-bailee's terms may sometimes bind the customer who has contracted with the principal bailee.[55] For example, where a bailor knows that his property will be passed to a sub-bailee, for example, for the purposes of repair or storage, the terms of the contract between the bailee and the sub-bailee may bind the bailor.

Assignment of contractual rights

A person who owns a contractual right, such as a debt, can assign that right to a third party, subject to certain conditions. As a consequence, the person to whom the right has been assigned may then sue the debtor. At common law, assignments were generally not recognised, unless there was a novation under which the debtor agreed to the assignment. In these circumstances, the right of the assignee is said to be based on an agreement with the debtor.[56]

In equity, there is a wider jurisdiction in relation to assignments of property rights. For example, under s 136(1) of the Law of Property Act 1925, a debt or other legal chose in action can be assigned in writing. The assignment must be absolute, therefore, assignment of part of a debt,[57] as opposed to the balance of a debt[58] is not assignable. An unwritten assignment can be enforced in equity, but, to be effective, it must be communicated to the assignee by the assignor, and the debtor must be aware of the assignment.

---

52 *Leigh & Sillivan Ltd v Aliakmon Shipping Co Ltd, The Aliakmon* [1986] AC 785.
53 [1954] 2 QB 402.
54 *Ibid*, pp 423–25.
55 See *Johnson Matthey Ltd v Constantine Terminals Ltd* [1976] 2 Lloyd's Rep 215. See, also, *Morris v CW Martin & Sons Ltd* [1966] 1 QB 716.
56 *Rasbora Ltd v JCL Marine Ltd* [1977] 1 Lloyd's Rep 645. Alternatively, a debtor can create third party rights by way of an acknowledgment that a debt has been transferred: *Shamia v Joory* [1958] 1 QB 448.
57 *Forster v Baker* [1910] 2 KB 636.
58 *Durham Bros v Robertson* [1898] 1 QB 765.

Negotiability

A negotiable instrument such as a bill of exchange, a cheque or a promissory note may be negotiated to another person. The holder of the bill of exchange is treated as a holder for value if consideration for the bill has, at any time, been given. Accordingly, the holder can enforce the bill against the person responsible to make payment.

Agency

An agency relationship usually arises where a principal authorises a willing agent to act on his behalf in the making of contracts and the transfer of property. The effect of an agency relationship is that the third party with whom the agent deals may acquire rights and be subject to obligations. While agency is not an exception to the doctrine of privity, it is a useful means of avoiding the harsher effects of that doctrine, where one person is deemed to be the agent of another.

Although agency is generally regarded as arising by way of consent, there are circumstances in which a principal is liable for the acts of a person to whom he has not actually given authority. This will usually be the case where the principal has led a third party to believe that a particular person has authority to act, in which case, the principal will be estopped from denying the authority of the agent. The necessary ingredients of an estoppel are that there has been a representation by the principal to the third party, that the agent has authority to act, that the third party has relied on the representation and that the reliance has resulted in an alteration in the position of the third party.[59] The traditional requirement of representation appears to be in the process of being watered down in the light of cases, which suggest that ostensible or apparent authority is moving closer to something which resembles vicarious liability for the torts of an employee. Accordingly, there can be an ostensible authority where the agent acts in a manner which is consistent with the type of work he is employed to do and the agent is considered authorised to indicate to a third party that his principal has approved the actions he has taken.[60]

In some instances, an agent may perform an unauthorised act which finds favour with the principal. The principal can ratify the agent's act, so that binding obligations arise between the principal and the third party.

Where a contract of agency exists, the agent can make contracts on the principal's behalf which are binding on the principal and the third party. This is also the case, subject to exceptions, where the principal is undisclosed, that

---

59 *Rama Corpn v Proved Tin and General Investments Ltd* [1952] 2 QB 147, p 149, *per* Slade J.
60 *First Energy (UK) Ltd v Hungarian International Bank Ltd* [1993] 2 Lloyd's Rep 194.

is, where the third party is unaware of the fact that the agent is a representative at all. The right of the undisclosed principal to sue is independent of the right of the agent to sue. The principal is also liable on a contract made by his agent, except where circumstances show that the agent has accepted personal responsibility.[61]

Trusts

A trust is an equitable device which allows a person to pass property to a trustee subject to a requirement that he should hold that property for the benefit of a third person, the beneficiary. The beneficiary is able to enforce the terms of the trust for his benefit, provided that it can be shown that there was an intention on the part of the donor to create a trust.

For the purposes of the law of contract and the doctrine of privity of contract in particular, the most important development is that of the trust of contractual rights. It has been held that one party to a contract may be declared to be a trustee of the promise of performance given by the other party, for the benefit of a third party. While the trust concept is concerned with property interests, it has been possible in equity to regard a promise to pay money as a property interest.[62]

In *Les Affréteurs Réunis SA v Leopold Walford (London) Ltd*,[63] a clause in a charterparty provided for payment of a 3% commission by the shipowner to a broker (a third party), in respect of the estimated gross amount of hire. In fact, no hire was earned under the charterparty. The charterer, to whom the promise was made, was regarded as a trustee for the promise, which allowed the broker, as beneficiary, to enforce the promise against the shipowner:

Les Affréteurs Réunis SA v Leopold Walford (London) Ltd [1919] AC 801, HL, p 806

Lord Birkenhead LC: My Lords, so far as I am aware, that case has not before engaged the attention of this House, and I think it right to say plainly that I agree with that decision and I agree with the reasoning, shortly as it is expressed, upon which the decision was founded. In this connection, I would refer to the well known case of *In Re Empress Engineering Co*. In the judgment of Sir George Jessel MR, the principle is examined which, in my view, underlies and is the explanation of the decision in *Robertson v Wait*. The Master of the Rolls uses this language: 'So, again, it is quite possible that one of the parties to the agreement may be the nominee or trustee of the third person. As Lord Justice James suggested to me in the course of the argument, a married woman may nominate somebody to contract on her behalf, but then the person makes

---

61 *Basma v Weeks* [1950] AC 441.
62 *Tomlinson v Gill* (1756) Amb 330.
63 [1919] AC 801, HL.

the contract really as trustee for somebody else, and it is because he contracts in that character that the *cestui que* trust can take the benefit of the contract.'

It appears to me plain that for convenience, and under long established practice, the broker in such cases, in effect, nominates the charterer to contract on his behalf, influenced probably by the circumstances that there is always a contract between charterer and owner in which this stipulation, which is to ensure to the benefit of the broker, may very conveniently be inserted. In these cases the broker, on ultimate analysis, appoints the charterer to contract on his behalf. I agree therefore with the conclusion arrived at by all the learned judges in *Robertson v Wait* that, in such cases, charterers can sue as trustees on behalf of the broker.

Subsequent developments show that there are limitations upon the use of the trust concept. The first essential requirement is that there should be an intention to create a trust on the part of the promisee, for example, where the words trust or trustee are used. Decisions since *Walford*'s case show that there is a general reluctance to make use of the trust concept, since it has the effect of preventing the parties to the contract from varying or rescinding it, by creating a property interest in favour of a third party.[64]

A further limitation on the use of the trust concept is that there must be an intention to benefit the third party. Thus, if there is evidence that the promisee intends to take the benefit of the promised performance himself, the third party is unlikely to succeed.

Even if there is an intention to create a trust for the benefit of the third party, reliance on the trust concept will still be precluded if the intention to benefit the third party is not irrevocable. For example, if the benefit of the promise is capable of being diverted for the benefit of the promisee, no trust will arise.

In *Re Schebsman, ex p The Official Receiver*,[65] Schebsman, was employed for a number of years by a Swiss company and its English subsidiary. That employment came to an end in 1940, but by an agreement between Schebsman and the two companies, he would be paid £2,000 immediately and a further £5,500 by instalments over a period of six years. It was further agreed that should Schebsman die, certain sums would be paid to his widow. Schebsman was adjudicated bankrupt in 1942 and subsequently died. The trustee in bankruptcy claimed the sums due under the agreement as part of the bankrupt's estate. An argument relied on in this regard was that, since Schebsman always had the right to intercept the sums agreed upon, this right was now vested in the trustee in bankruptcy. Uthwatt J had held, *inter alia*, that Schebsman was neither a trustee nor an agent of those entitled to receive payment:

---

64 *Re Schebsman* [1944] Ch 83.
65 [1943] 2 All ER 768, CA.

Re Schebsman ex p The Official Receiver [1943] 2 All ER 768, CA, p 777

Du Parcq LJ: It is, in my opinion, convenient to approach the problems raised in this appeal by first considering the position of the parties at common law. It is clear that Mrs Schebsman, who was not a party to the agreement of 20 September 1940, acquired no rights under it and has never been in a position to maintain an action upon it. It is common ground, also, that the personal representatives of Schebsman (whom I will call the debtor) could not have recovered any sums which had been paid to Mrs Schebsman under the agreement as money had and received or by any process known to the common law. It is not disputed that the English company, which, under the agreement was liable to make the payments, properly performed that agreement by paying into the hands of Mrs Schebsman those sums which it had bound itself to pay to Mrs Schebsman, and, at common law, could not be called upon to pay them to the personal representatives of the debtor. Nor, I think, is it disputed, and it may be said to be self-evident, that the English company's agreement to pay these moneys into the hands of Mrs Schebsman was a valid agreement, a breach of which would be regarded by the courts as an 'unlawful act' and a 'legal wrong'. I borrow those expressions from a well known passage in the speech of Lord Lindley in *South Wales Miners' Federation v Glamorgan Coal Co.*

The rules according to which damages for breach of contract are assessed sometimes allow a person guilty of the legal wrong constituted by the breach to escape very lightly, but that fact does not affect the illegality of his act.

So far, there is general agreement. I may now express my own agreement with a proposition submitted by counsel for the appellant. He said that the duty to pay into the hands of a nominated person is discharged when the money has been paid to that person, and that the party bound to make an payment has no control over its destination. As a general proposition, that is true and can hardly be questioned. In the case before us Mrs Schebsman, being no party to the contract, is clearly under no obligation to the English company to apply the money in any particular way, nor is the English company concerned with any agreement she may choose to make with third parties binding herself to apply it in a particular manner. But the proposition, accurate as it is, may be misleading unless it is considered together with another proposition which I take to be equally unexceptionable and which I will now state.

It is open to parties to agree that, for a consideration supplied by one of them, the other will make payments to a third person for the use and benefit of that third person, and not for the use and benefit of the contracting party who provides the consideration. Whether or not such an agreement has been made in a given case is clearly a question of construction, but assuming that the parties have manifested their intention so to agree, it cannot, I think, be doubted that the common law would regard such an agreement as valid and as enforceable (in the sense of giving a cause of action for damages for its breach to the other party of the contract) and would regard the breach of it as an unlawful act. If the party from whom the consideration moved somehow succeeded in intercepting a payment intended for the named payee, he would be guilty of a tort, and, in certain circumstances, of a crime, and he would also be breaking his contract, since it would be implicit in his agreement with the other party that he would do nothing to prevent the money paid from reaching the payee. If he sought to argue that, because he himself provided the consideration, he alone was interested in the destination of the money, the answer would be that the other contracting party had not agreed (and perhaps might never have thought of agreeing) to make a payment either to him or for his benefit. If he can persuade the payee to hand the money over to him by lawful means, he is, of course, at liberty to do so, and there may be circumstances *dehors* the contract which would give him rights against the payee. Subject to that qualification, he can never, in the case of such a contract as I have supposed, lawfully claim payment of the money for himself while the contract remains unaltered. That the common law allows it to be varied nobody doubts. At any time the parties may agree that payment shall in future be made not to the payee named in the contract, but to the party from whom the consideration moved, or, for that matter, to any other person. But in the case of such a contract there cannot be a variation at the will of one of the parties, any more than a condition introduced into a contract for the benefit of both parties can be waived by only one of them.

I have said that the question whether a contract imposes a liability on one of the parties to confer a benefit on a third party, not privy to the contract, is always one of construction.

From the point of view of the common law, with which alone I am now dealing, I have no doubt that the general rule of construction laid down by Blackburn J in *Burges v Wickham* must be applied. According to the general law of England, the written record of a contract must not be varied or added to by verbal evidence of what was the intention of the parties.

I now turn to the agreement in the present case, in order to seek in the document itself the answer to the question whether the parties intended that, after the debtor's death, the company should be under an obligation to make payments to Mrs Schebsman for her own benefit, and the debtor's personal representatives under a corresponding obligation to accept payment to Mrs Schebsman for her own benefit as a fulfilment of the contract. It seems to me to be plain upon the face of the contract that this was the intention of the parties. In this connection, the most striking feature of the agreement, in my opinion, is that, after the deaths of Mrs and Miss Schebsman (assuming that the debtor were to pre-decease them, as in fact he did), all payments were to cease, even though a large part of the amount payable by the company might remain unpaid. This provision points clearly, as it seems to me, to the conclusion that both parties were concerned with benefiting Mrs Schebsman and the daughter, and that the company did not intend to bind itself to pay a penny for the benefit of the debtor's estate after the death of these ladies. It is impossible, in my judgment, to regard this as in effect an aleatory contract, under which the amount of payments intended to accrue for the benefit of the debtor's estate was to be dependant on events so uncertain as the duration of the two lives. Further, it is, I think, proper to have regard to the fact that, in the circumstances disclosed by the agreement itself, both parties might be expected to wish to confer a benefit on the debtor's dependants. Lastly, I attach some importance to the language of cl 6 which speaks of payments 'due to' Mrs and Miss Schebsman.

I may now summarise the position at common law as follows: (i) it is the right, as well as the duty, of the company to make the prescribed payments to Mrs Schebsman and to no other person; (ii) Mrs Schebsman may dispose of the sums so received as she pleases, and is not accountable for them to the personal representatives of the debtor, or to anyone claiming to stand in the shoes of the debtor; (iii) if anyone standing in the shoes of the debtor were to intercept the sums payable to Mrs Schebsman and refuse to account to her for them, he would be guilty of a breach of the debtor's contract with the company; (iv) the obligation undertaken by the company cannot be varied at the will of the other party to the contract, but may be varied consensually at any time although the debtor is no longer living, as it could have been in his lifetime.

It now remains to consider the question whether and, if so, to what extent, the principles of equity affect the position of the parties.

It was argued by counsel for the appellant that one effect of the agreement of 20 September 1940 was that a trust was thereby created, and that the debtor constituted himself trustee for Mrs Schebsman of the benefit of the covenant under which payments were to be made to her. Uthwatt J rejected this contention and the argument has not satisfied me that he was wrong. It is true that, by the use possibly of unguarded language, a person may create a trust, as Monsieur Jourdain talked prose, without knowing it, but unless an intention to create a trust is clearly to be collected from the language used and the circumstances of the case, I think that the court ought not to be astute to discover indications of such an intention. I have little doubt that, in the present case, both parties (and certainly the debtor) intended to keep alive their common law right to vary consensually the terms of the obligation undertaken by the company, and, if circumstances had changed in the debtor's lifetime, injustice might have been done by holding that a trust had been created and that those terms were accordingly unalterable. On this point, therefore, I agree with Uthwatt J.

Where a trust in favour of a third party does arise, its effect is to allow the third party to sue the promisor and keep the money payable. However, the promisee should be joined as a party to the action unless the promisor waives this requirement, as in *Walford*'s case. If the promisee is unwilling to enforce the promise, the third party can commence proceedings in his own name and subsequently join the promisee as a party to the action.[66]

---

[66] *Vandepitte v Preferred Accident Insurance Corpn of New York* [1933] AC 70.

EXCEPTIONS TO THE DOCTRINE OF PRIVITY

Property interests

The vendor of land may subject the land he sells to restrictive conditions as to future use. The effect of these restrictive covenants, according to the rule in *Tulk v Moxhay*,[67] passes with the land so that a subsequent purchaser of the protected property is entitled to the benefit of the covenant and the purchaser of the land subject to that covenant takes the burden. At one stage, a similar principle was applied to movable property such as ships subject to a charterparty[68] provided the subsequent purchaser of the chartered vessel had notice of charterer's interest. However, later authority goes against this approach.

In *Port Line Ltd v Ben Line Steamers Ltd*,[69] the plaintiffs entered into a time charter in 1954 for a period of 30 months under terms which allowed the owner to remain in possession. Fifteen months later, the owner sold the ship, with the plaintiffs' consent, to the defendants. The defendants immediately chartered the ship back to the original owners with the result that the ship never left the owners' possession. The plaintiffs raised no objection because under the terms of their charterparty, the ship was to remain available to them. However, the charter entered into between the defendants and the original owners provided that should the vessel be requisitioned, the charter would cease to continue. Subsequently, the ship was requisitioned in 1956, the defendants being paid compensation. The plaintiffs now sued to recover this compensation payment.

Diplock J gave judgment for the defendants on the ground that they did not have actual notice of the plaintiffs' interest in the ship:

Port Line Ltd v Ben Line Steamers Ltd [1958] 1 All ER 787, p 793

Diplock J: The plaintiffs contend: (1) that, throughout the relevant period, they had a valid and subsisting contract with Silver Line Ltd; (2) that, by virtue of that contract, they were entitled, as against the defendants, on the principle laid down in *Lord Strathcona SS Co v Dominion Coal Co* ([1926] AC 108) to have the vessel used for the carriage of their goods; (3) that they are entitled to recover from the defendants: (a) under the Compensation (Defence) Act 1939, if it applies, the whole compensation, or alternatively the bareboat element of the compensation received by the defendants in respect of the requisition; or (b) if the Compensation (Defence) Act does not apply, a portion of the compensation, such portion being ascertained in accordance with the principles laid down by Lord Parker of Waddington in *FA Tamplin SS Co Ltd v*

---

67 (1848) 2 Ph 774.
68 *Lord Strathcona SS Co v Dominion Coal Co* [1926] AC 108.
69 [1958] 1 All ER 787.

Anglo-Mexican Petroleum Products Co Ltd ([1916] 2 AC 397) and applied in *Chinese Mining & Engineering Co Ltd v Sale & Co* ([1917] 2 KB 599) and other cases; or (c), as an alternative to (a) and (b), the profits made by the defendants out of the requisition of the vessel.

The defendants challenge these contentions to the polls and to the array. The plaintiffs' contract with Silver Line Ltd, they say, was frustrated by the requisition; the *Strathcona* case was wrongly decided; even if rightly decided, it applies only where the subsequent purchaser has express notice of the terms of a subsisting charterparty; in any event, it lays down no principle which entitles the plaintiffs to have the vessel used for the carriage of their goods, and it imposes no obligation on the defendants to account as constructive trustees; the Compensation (Defence) Act 1939, applies, but gives no rights to the plaintiffs. The *Tamplin* case apportionment is excluded by the Compensation (Defence) Act 1939 and, in any event, does not apply. It is conceded that if the defendants are right as to the plaintiffs' gross time charter being frustrated by the requisition, the plaintiffs' claim must fail.

It is contended that the plaintiffs' rights against the defendants stem from the principle laid down by Knight Bruce LJ in *De Mattos v Gibson* ((1858) 4 De G & J 276, p 282), as approved by the Privy Council in the *Strathcona* case. The principle laid down by Knight Bruce LJ in *De Mattos v Gibson* in granting on appeal an interlocutory injunction to restrain a mortgagee of a ship who had acquired his mortgage with knowledge of the plaintiffs' subsisting charterparty from interfering with the performance of a subsisting voyage-charter was in the following oft-quoted terms (p 282): 'Reason and justice seem to prescribe that, at least as a general rule, where a man, by gift or purchase, acquires property from another, with knowledge of a previous contract, lawfully and for valuable consideration made by him with a third person, to use and employ the property for a particular purpose in a specified manner, the acquirer shall not to the material damage of the third person, in opposition to the contract and inconsistently with it, use and employ the property in a manner not allowable to the giver or seller.'

It may be relevant to note that, in the *Strathcona* case, the buyers of the vessel subject to the time charter in favour of the plaintiffs had express notice of the terms of the charter, and had covenanted with the sellers to perform and accept all responsibilities under it. It was, as the Board said ([1926] AC 108 at p 116), not a mere case of notice of the existence of a covenant affecting the use of the property sold, but a case of acceptance of the property expressly subconditioned. The initial emphasis on this, and the reference at a later stage to the possibility that a shipowner might declare himself a trustee of his obligations under a charterparty so as to bind his assignee might suggest as a possible *ratio decidendi* that the *Strathcona* case was one where either the purchaser used expressions which amounted to a declaration of trust in favour of the charterers, or the vendor himself accepted the benefit of the covenant as trustee for the charterers. But an examination of Lord Shaw's opinion as a whole seems to indicate that the Board accepted the full doctrine of Knight Bruce LJ, as respects chattels, namely, that mere notice does give rise to the equity, the only qualification that the Board imposed (p 122) being that 'an interest must remain [sc in the person seeking the remedy] in the subject matter of the covenant before a right can be conceded to an injunction against the violation by another of the covenant in question'.

The only remedy which the Board in terms recognised is a remedy by injunction against the use of the ship by the purchaser inconsistent with the charterparty, but they said (p 125) – a passage on which counsel for the plaintiffs strongly relies – that the purchaser 'appears to be plainly in the position of a constructive trustee with obligations which a court of equity will not permit him to violate'.

These passages pose several problems. (1) If, as the Board state ([1926] AC 108 at p 123), the ship is the 'subject matter' of the covenant of which the violation by another is to be restrained, it is difficult to see in what sense a charterer under a gross time charter has an interest in that subject matter except in the broad sense that it is to his commercial advantage that his covenantor should continue to use the ship to perform the services which he has covenanted to perform. But the time charter is a contract for services. The time charterer has no proprietary or possessory rights in the ship, and if the covenantee's commercial advantage in the observance of the covenant is sufficient to constitute an 'interest' in the chattel to which the covenant relates, it is difficult to see why the principle does not apply to price-fixing cases such as *Dunlop Pneumatic Tyre Co Ltd v Selfridge & Co Ltd* ([1915] AC 847). The Board ([1926] AC 108 at p 121) explain *Dunlop Pneumatic Tyre Co Ltd v Selfridge & Co Ltd* which had been cited to them, as a case where the plaintiff had no interest in the subject matter of the covenant. They say ([1926] AC 108 at p 123) that the charterer has and will have during the continuance of the charterparty a plain interest (in the ship) 'so long as she is fit to go to sea'.

Plain though it may be, if the expression 'interest' is used colloquially, the Board nowhere explain what the legal nature of that interest is. (2) Whether the reference to the subsequent purchaser with notice as being, also 'plainly', in the position of a constructive trustee imports that equity provides other remedies against him by his *cestui que* trust, such as the right to an account, the making of a vesting order or the appointment of a new trustee is nowhere discussed in the *Strathcona* case; but the whole trend of the opinion, the actual order made and the observation of Lord Shaw (p 125), 'It is incredible that the owners will lay up the vessel rather than permit its use under the contract', all strongly suggest that the only remedy in the view of the Board that the charterer acquired against the subsequent purchaser was the purely negative remedy, namely, to restrain a user of the vessel inconsistent with the terms of his charter with the former owner, and the obligations of the purchaser which a court of equity will not allow him to violate are the negative obligation not to make such inconsistent user of the vessel. As a 'constructive trustee', the subsequent purchaser seems to be one *sui generis*, and I should hesitate as a common lawyer to seek to devise other remedies against him which did not apparently occur to the Board. (3) The Board in the *Strathcona* case, beyond saying that that case was not one of 'mere notice', did not discuss what kind of notice to the purchaser of the charterer's rights gives rise to the equity, for example, whether at the time of his acquisition of his interest in the vessel he must have actual knowledge of the charterer's rights against the seller, the violation of which it is sought to restrain, or whether 'constructive notice' will suffice. 'Reason and justice' – the sole though weighty grounds on which Knight Bruce LJ based the equity – do not seem to me to prescribe the introduction into commercial matters, such as the sale of a ship, of the doctrine of constructive notice. Furthermore, as between vendor and purchaser of real property, where the doctrine has been developed, constructive notice – like estoppel in less esoteric matters – is a shield not a weapon of offence. It protects an already existing equitable interest from being defeated by a purchaser for value without notice. It is not itself the source of an equitable interest.

The *Strathcona* case, although decided over 30 years ago, has never been followed in the English courts, and has never come up for direct consideration.

It seems, therefore, that it is in this case for the first time after more than 30 years that an English court has to grapple with the problem of what principle was really laid down in the *Strathcona* case, and whether that case was rightly decided. The difficulty that I have found in ascertaining its *ratio decidendi*, the impossibility which I find of reconciling the actual decision with well-established principles of law, the unsolved and to me insoluble problems which that decision raises combine to satisfy me that it was wrongly decided. I do not propose to follow it. I naturally express this opinion with great diffidence, but having reached a clear conclusion it is my duty to express it.

If I am wrong in my view that the case was wrongly decided, I am certainly averse from extending one iota beyond that which, as I understand it, it purported to decide. In particular I do not think that it purported to decide: (1) that anything short of actual knowledge by the subsequent purchaser at the time of the purchase of the charterer's rights, the violation of which it is sought to restrain, is sufficient to give rise to the equity; (2) that the charterer has any remedy against the subsequent purchaser with notice except a right to restrain the use of the vessel by such purchaser in a manner inconsistent with the terms of the charter; (3) that the charterer has any positive right against the subsequent purchaser to have the vessel used in accordance with the terms of his charter. The third proposition follows from the second; *ubi jus, ibi remedium*. For failure by the subsequent purchaser to use the vessel in accordance with the terms of the charter entered into by his seller, there is no remedy by specific performance as was held in the *Strathcona* case itself. There is equally no remedy in damages, a consideration which distinguishes the *Strathcona* case from such cases as *Lumley v Wagner* (1852) I De GM & G 604) and *Lumley v Gye*. The charterer's only right is co-terminous with his remedy, namely, not to have the ship used by the purchaser in violation of his charter.

An important statutory provision which affects property interests is the following:

Law of Property Act 1925

56

(1) A person may take an immediate or other interest in land or other property, or the benefit of any condition, right of entry, covenant or

agreement over or respecting land or other property, although he may not be named as a party to the conveyance or other instrument.

One view of this provision is that it constitutes a statutory repeal of the doctrine of privity of contract in most respects, since the words 'or other property', on a wide interpretation, may be taken to cover both real and personal property, including things in action.[70] The Court of Appeal in *Beswick v Beswick*[71] held that this allowed a third party to acquire an interest in any property conferred by a contract made between others. Accordingly, in that case, the widow was considered to have a personal right to sue for the annuity promised by her nephew. However, this interpretation of s 56 was rejected in the House of Lords[72] where the section was confined to dispositions of land, and that it was not intended to displace the doctrine of privity of contract.

On the interpretation of s 56(1) of the Law of Property Act 1925, the following comments were made in the case of *Beswick v Beswick* (for the facts of which, see above):

Beswick v Beswick [1967] 2 All ER 1197, HL, p 1202

Lord Reid: The respondent's first answer is that the common law has been radically altered by s 56(1) of the Law of Property Act 1925, and that that section entitles her to sue in her personal capacity and to recover the benefit provided for her in the agreement although she was not a party to it. Extensive alterations of the law were made at that time, but it is necessary to examine with some care the way in which this was done.

In constructing any Act of Parliament, we are seeking the intention of Parliament, and it is quite true that we must deduce that intention from the words of the Act. If the words of the Act are only capable of one meaning we must give them that meaning no matter how they got there. If, however, they are capable of having more than one meaning we are, in my view, well entitled to see how they got there.

In *Re Miller's Agreement, Uniake v AG*, two partners covenanted with a retiring partner that on his death they would pay certain annuities to his daughters. The revenue's claim for estate duty was rejected. The decision was clearly right. The daughters, not being parties to the agreement, had no right to sue for their annuities. Whether they received them or not depended on whether the other partners were willing to pay or, if they did not pay, whether the deceased partner's executor was willing to enforce the contract. After citing the earlier cases Wynn-Parry J, said: 'I think it emerges from these cases that the section has the effect, not of creating rights, but only of assisting the protection of rights shown to exist.'

---

70 Law of Property Act 1925, s 205(1)(xx).
71 [1966] Ch 538.
72 *Beswick v Beswick* [1968] AC 58.

In *Smith v River Douglas Catchment Board*, Denning LJ, after stating his view that a third person can sue on a contract to which he is not a party, referred to s 56 as a clear statutory recognition of this principle, with the consequence that *Miller's* case was wrongly decided. I cannot agree with that. In *Drive Yourself Hire Co (London) Ltd v Strutt*, Denning LJ again expressed similar views about s 56.

I can now return to consider the meaning and scope of s 56. It refers to any 'agreement over or respecting land or other property'. If 'land or other property' means the same thing as 'tenements or hereditaments' in the Act of 1845, then this section simply continues the law as it was before the Act of 1925 was passed, for I do not think that the other differences in phraseology can be regarded as making any substantial change. So, any obscurities in s 56 are obscurities which originated in 1845; but if its scope is wider, then two points must be considered. The section refers to agreements 'over or respecting land or other property'. The land is something which existed before and independently of the agreement and the same must apply to the other property. So, an agreement between A and B that A will use certain personal property for the benefit of X would be within the scope of the section, but an agreement that if A performs certain services for B, B will pay a sum to X would not be within the scope of the section. Such a capricious distinction would alone throw doubt on this interpretation.

Perhaps more important is the fact that the section does not say that a person may take the benefit of an agreement, although he was not a party to it: it says that he may do so although he was not named as a party in the instrument which embodied in the agreement. It is true that s 56 says 'although he may not be named'; but s 5 of the Act of 1845 says 'although [he] be not named a party'. Such a change of phraseology in a consolidation Act cannot involve a change of meaning. I do not profess to have a full understanding of the old English law regarding deeds; but it appears from what Simonds J said in *White's* case and from what Vaisey J said in *Chelsea and Walham Green Building Society v Armstrong* that being in fact a party to an agreement might not be enough; the person claiming a benefit had to be named a party in the indenture. I have read the explanation of the old law given by my noble and learned friend Lord Upjohn. I would not venture to criticise it, but I do not think it necessary for me to consider it if it leads to the conclusion that s 56 taken by itself would not assist the present respondent.

It may be, however, that additional difficulties would arise from the application to s 56 of the definition of property in the definition section. If so, it becomes necessary to consider whether that definition can be applied to s 56. By express provision in the definition section, a definition contained in it is not to be applied to the word defined if, in the particular case, the context otherwise requires. If application of that definition would result in giving to s 56 a meaning going beyond that of the old section, then in my opinion the context does require that the definition of 'property' shall not be applied to that word in s 56. The context in which this section occurs is a consolidation Act. If the definition is not applied the section is a proper one to appear in such an Act, because it can properly be regarded as not substantially altering the pre-existing law; but if the definition is applied the result is to make s 56 go far beyond the pre-existing law. Holding that the section has such an effect would involve holding that the invariable practice of Parliament has been departed from *per incuriam*, so that something has got into this consolidation Act which neither the draftsman nor Parliament can have intended to be there. I am reinforced in this view by two facts. The language of s 56 is not at all what one would have expected if the intention had been to bring in all that the application of the definition would bring in. Second, s 56 is one of 25 sections which appear in the Act of 1925 under the cross-heading 'Conveyances and other Instruments'. The other 24 sections come appropriately under that heading and so does s 56 if it has a limited meaning: but, if its scope is extended by the definition of property, it would be quite inappropriately placed in this part of the Act of 1925. For these reasons, I am of opinion that s 56 has no application to the present case.

Insurance

If the doctrine of privity were to apply, in all cases, to insurance policies, this would create immense inconvenience, since life policies and third party motor vehicle cover, in particular, are taken out for the benefit of third parties. The effects of the doctrine of privity have been minimised through an application of rules on agency and trusts. Moreover, a number of statutory exceptions to the rule allow third parties to recover directly against the insurer:

Married Women's Property Act 1882

11 Moneys payable under policy of assurance not to form part of estate of the insured

A married woman may ... effect a policy upon her own life or the life of her husband for her [own benefit]; and the same and all benefit thereof shall enure accordingly.

A policy of assurance effected by any man on his own life, and expressed to be for the benefit of his wife, or of his children, or of his wife and children, or any of them, or by any woman on her own life, and expressed to be for the benefit of her husband, or of her children, or of her husband and children, or any of them, shall create a trust in favour of the objects therein named, and the moneys payable under any such policy shall not, so long as any object of the trust remains unperformed, form part of the estate of the insured, or be subject to his or her debts: Provided, that if it shall be proved that the policy was effected and the premiums paid with intent to defraud the creditors of the insured, they shall be entitled to receive, out of the moneys payable under the policy, a sum equal to the premiums so paid. The insured may by the policy, or by any memorandum under his or her hand, appoint a trustee or trustees of the moneys payable under the policy and, from time to time, appoint a new trustee or new trustees thereof, and may make provision for the appointment of a new trustee or new trustees thereof, and for the investment of the moneys payable under any such policy. In default of any such appointment of a trustee such policy, immediately on its being effected, shall vest in the insured and his or her legal personal representatives, in trust for the purposes aforesaid ... The receipt of a trustee or trustees duly appointed, or in default of any such appointment, or in default of notice to the insurance office, the receipt of the legal personal representatives of the insured shall be a discharge to the office for the sum secured by the policy, or for the value thereof, in whole or in part.

Road Traffic Act 1988

148

(7) Notwithstanding anything in any enactment, a person issuing a policy of insurance under s 145 of this Act shall be liable to indemnify the person or classes of persons specified in the policy in respect of any liability which the policy purports to cover in the case of those persons or classes of persons.

Third Parties (Rights Against Insurers) Act 1930

1 Rights of third parties against insurers on bankruptcy, etc, of the insured

(1) Where under any contract of insurance a person (hereinafter referred to as the insured) is insured against liabilities to third parties which he may incur, then:

(a) in the event of the insured becoming bankrupt or making a composition or arrangement with his creditors; or

(b) in the case of the insured being a company, in the event of a winding-up order [or an administration order] being made, or a resolution for a voluntary winding-up being passed, with respect to the company, or of a receiver or manager of the company's business or undertaking being duly appointed, or of possession being taken, by or on behalf of the holders of any debentures secured by a floating charge, of any property comprised in or subject to that charge [or of a voluntary arrangement proposed for the purposes of Part I of the Insolvency Act 1986 being approved under that Part]; if, either before or after that event, any such liability as aforesaid is incurred by the insured, his rights against the insurer under the contract in respect of the liability shall, notwithstanding anything in any Act or rule of law to the contrary, be transferred to and vest in the third party to whom the liability was so incurred.

(2) Where [the estate of any person falls to be administered in accordance with an order under s 421 of the Insolvency Act 1986], then, if any debt provable in bankruptcy is owing by the deceased in respect of a liability against which he was insured under a contract of insurance as being a liability to a third party, the deceased debtor's rights against the insurer under the contract in respect of that liability shall, notwithstanding anything in [any such order], be transferred to and vest in the person to whom the debt is owing.

(3) Insofar as any contract of insurance made after the commencement of this Act in respect of any liability of the insured to third parties purports,

whether directly or indirectly, to avoid the contract or to alter the rights of the parties thereunder upon the happening to the insured of the events specified in para (a) or para (b) of sub-s (1) of this section or upon the [estate of any person falling to be administered in accordance with an order under s 421 of the Insolvency Act 1986], the contract shall be of no effect.

(4) Upon a transfer under sub-s (1) or sub-s (2) of this section, the insurer shall, subject to the provisions of s three of this Act, be under the same liability to the third party as he would have been under to the insured, but:

   (a) if the liability of the insurer to the insured exceeds the liability of the insured to the third party, nothing in this Act shall affect the rights of the insured against the insurer in respect of the excess; and

   (b) if the liability of the insurer to the insured is less than the liability of the insured to the third party, nothing in this Act shall affect the rights of the third party against the insured in respect of the balance.

(5) For the purposes of this Act, the expression 'liabilities to third parties', in relation to a person insured under any contract of insurance, shall not include any liability of that person in the capacity of insurer under some other contract of insurance.

(6) This Act shall not apply:

   (a) where a company is wound up voluntarily merely for the purposes of reconstruction or of amalgamation with another company; or

   (b) to any case to which sub-ss (1) and (2) of s 7 of the Workmen's Compensation Act 1925 applies.

The Contracts (Rights of Third Parties) Act 1999

In the light of continued criticism of the effects of the doctrine of privity of contract, the matter of reform of the doctrine was referred to the Law Commission[73] who concluded that, in certain circumstances, a third party should be given the right to enforce terms of a contract to which he is not a party, provided those terms are expressed to be for the benefit of the third party. Accordingly, the extent of the reform is such that it will apply only to benefits and will not relax the current rules applicable to burdens under a contract and their effect on third parties. The difficulty with this approach is that, in some instances, it may be difficult to properly distinguish between benefits and burdens. The question whether a third party can enforce a term of a contract expressed to be for his benefit and the question whether a third party can rely on an exemption clause in a contract entered into by two others both raise issues of benefit. Conversely, the question whether A can enforce

---

73   Law Commission, No 242, 1996.

the terms of his contract with B against T clearly raises the issue of burden. However, there are other cases in which A seeks to set up a defence based on the terms of his contract with B in order to defeat a claim made against him by T.[74] The view expressed by the Law Commission initially seems to suggest that this last group of cases raises the issue of burden,[75] but there may be instances in which the contract between A and B confers a benefit on T, subject to a condition. The Law Commission give the example of a contract between A and B which confers on T a right of way, subject to a condition that T should keep it in a good state of repair.[76] Similar problems might also arise where a benefit is conferred on T, but is subject to an exemption clause which limits T's ability to sue A in respect of the benefit conferred. On this matter the Law Commission state that T's right to enforce the benefit must be read subject to the exemption clause.[77] If the 1999 Act is to apply in such a case, it would appear that the burden element will have to be conflated with the related benefit conferred by A and B on T.

The general effect of the 1999 Act is to make the right of a third party (T) to enforce a term intended to benefit him subject to the intentions of the main contracting parties (A and B). Under s 1(1), T may enforce such a term in his own right if: (a) the contract expressly provides that he may; or (b) the relevant term purports to confer a benefit on him. However, in this last case, the right of T is subject to the proviso in s 1(2) that if, on a proper construction of the contract, it appears that the parties to the contract did not intend the term to be enforceable by the third party, T will have no right of enforcement:

The Contracts (Rights of Third Parties) Act 1999

1

(1) Subject to the provisions of this Act, a person who is not a party to a contract ('a third party') may in his own right enforce a term of the contract if:

(a) the contract expressly provides that he may; or

(b) subject to sub-s (2), the term purports to confer a benefit on him.

(2) Sub-section (1)(b) does not apply if, on a proper construction of the contract, it appears that the parties did not intend the term to be enforceable by the third party.

(3) The third party must be expressly identified in the contract by name, as a member of a class or as answering a particular description but need not be in existence when the contract is entered into.

(4) This section does not confer a right on a third party to enforce a term of a contract otherwise than subject to and in accordance with any other relevant terms of the contract.

---

74 See *Scruttons Ltd v Midland Silicones Ltd* [1962] AC 446.
75 Law Commission, Law Com No 242, 1996, para 2.1.
76 *Ibid*, para 10.26–10.27.
77 *Ibid*, para 10.30.

(5) For the purpose of exercising his right to enforce a term of the contract, there shall be available to the third party any remedy that would have been available to him in an action for breach of contract if he had been a party to the contract (and the rules relating to damages, injunctions, specific performance and other relief shall apply accordingly).

(6) Where a term of the contract excludes or limits liability in relation to any matter references in this Act to the third party enforcing the term shall be construed as references to his availing himself of the exclusion or limitation.

(7) In this Act, in relation to a term of a contract which is enforceable by a third party:

'the promisor' means the party to the contract against whom the term is enforceable by the third party; and

'the promisee' means the party to the contract by whom the term is enforceable against the promisor.

2

(1) Subject to the provisions of this section, where a third party has a right under s 1 to enforce a term of the contract, the parties to the contract may not, by agreement, rescind the contract, or vary it in such a way as to extinguish or alter his entitlement under that right, without his consent if:

(a) the third party has communicated his assent to the term to the promisor;

(b) the promisor is aware that the third party has relied on the term; or

(c) the promisor can reasonably be expected to have foreseen that the third party has in fact relied on it.

(2) The assent referred to in sub-s (1)(a):

(a) may be by words or conduct; and

(b) if sent to the promisor by post or other means, shall not be regarded as communicated to the promisor until received by him.

(3) Sub-section (1) is subject to any express term of the contract under which:

(a) the parties to the contract may by agreement rescind or vary the contract without the consent of the third party; or

(b) the consent of the third party is required in circumstances specified in the contract instead of those set out in sub-s (1)(a) to (c).

(4) Where the consent of a third party is required under sub-s (1) or (3), the court or tribunal may, on the application of the parties to the contract, dispense with his consent if satisfied:

(a) that his consent cannot be obtained because his whereabouts cannot reasonably be ascertained; or

(b) that he is mentally incapable of giving his consent.

(5) The court or arbitral tribunal may, on the application of the parties to a contract, dispense with any consent that may be required under sub-s (1)(c) if satisfied that it cannot reasonably be ascertained whether or not the third party has, in fact, relied on the term.

(6) If the court or arbitral tribunal dispenses with a third party's consent, it may impose such conditions as it thinks fit, including a condition requiring the payment of compensation to the third party.

3

(1) Sub-sections (1) to (5) apply where, in reliance on s 1, proceedings for enforcement of a term of a contract are brought by a third party.

(2) The promisor shall have available to him by way of defence or set-off any matter that:

    (a) arises from or in connection with the contract and is relevant to the term; and

    (b) would have been available to him by way of defence or set-off if the proceedings had been brought by the promisee.

(3) The promisor shall also have available to him by way of defence or set-off any matter if:

    (a) an express term of the contract provides for it to be available to him in proceedings brought by the third party; and

    (b) it would have been available to him by way of defence or set-off if the proceedings had been brought by the promisee.

(4) The promisor shall also have available to him:

    (a) by way of defence or set-off any matter; and

    (c) by way of counterclaim any matter not arising from the contract,

that would have been available to him by way of defence or set-off or, as the case may be, by way of counter-claim against the third party if the third party had been a party to the contract.

(5) Sub-sections (2) and (4) are subject to any express term of the contract as to the matters that are not to be available to the promisor by way of defence, set-off or counter-claim.

(6) Where, in any proceedings brought against him, a third party seeks in reliance on s 1 to enforce a term of a contract (including, in particular, a term purporting to exclude or limit liability), he may not do so if he could not have done so (whether by reason of any particular circumstances relating to him or otherwise) had he been a party to the contract.

4   Section 1 does not affect any right of the promisee to enforce any term of the contract.

5   Where, under s 1, a term of a contract is enforceable by a third party, and the promisee has recovered from the promisor a sum in respect of:

    (a) the third party's loss in respect of the term; or

    (b) the expense to the promisor of making good to the third party the default of the promisor,

then, in any proceedings brought in reliance on that section by the third party, the court or arbitral tribunal shall reduce any award to the third party to such extent as it thinks appropriate to take account of the sum recovered by the promisee.

6

(1) Section 1 confers no rights on a third party in the case of a contract on a bill of exchange, promissory note or other negotiable instrument.

(2) Section 1 confers no rights on a third party in the case of any contract binding on a company and its members under s 14 of the Companies Act 1985.

(3) Section 1 confers no right on a third party to enforce:

(a) a term of any contract of employment against an employee;

(b) any term of a worker's contract against a worker (including a home worker); or

(c) any term of a relevant contract against an agency worker ...

(5) Section 1 confers no right on a third party in the case of:

(a) a contract for the carriage of goods by sea; or

(b) a contract for the carriage of goods by rail or road, or for the carriage of cargo by air, which is subject to rules of the appropriate international transport convention,

except that a third party may in reliance on that section avail himself of an exclusion or limitation of liability in such a contract.

Under s 1(1)(a), a third party may enforce a term of a contract between A and B if the parties to that contract have expressly provided for this. Thus, a case such as *Tweddle v Atkinson*,[78] in which two relatives of a couple intending to get married entered into an agreement to pay a specified sum of money each to the third party on the occasion of his marriage, would now give the third party a right to enforce the respective promises of the two relatives, since it was their joint intention to benefit the third party. Similarly, s 1(1)(a) would also appear to apply to cases in which a third party seeks to rely on an exemption clause contained in a bill of lading forming the basis of a contract between a consignor and a shipper. In these cases, discussed above, it is a requirement that the protected third party be named, in which case there will be an express intention to confer a benefit on the third party. This view follows from the provisions of s 1(6) which defines the word 'enforcing' as including 'availing himself of the exclusion or limitation'.

Unlike the position before the 1999 Act, there will be no need to employ devices to allow the third party to sue such as creating a trust of the promises of the contracting parties or by making the third party a joint promisee. Furthermore, since the third party has a direct right to enforce the promise(s), he will not need to join the promisee as a party to his action.

Under s 1(1)(b), the third party may enforce a term of a contract entered into between A and B if the term purports to confer a benefit on him.

---

78 (1861) 1 B & S 393.

However, this is subject to the proviso that there will be no such right of enforceability if, on a proper construction of the contract, it was not the intention of A and B to confer such a right. It would appear that cases such as *Beswick v Beswick*[79] would fall within this provision. In that case, there was no express provision in the contract between the uncle and his nephew that the uncle's spouse had a right to enforce the contract. Nevertheless, it was clear on the facts of the case that the contract did purport to confer a right to an annuity on Mrs Beswick. Likewise, in the holiday cases, such as *Jackson v Horizon Holidays Ltd*,[80] it is likely that provided the person ordering the holiday names the other members of the party when making the booking that those third parties will be considered to have a right of enforcement. In contrast, if a person were to rent a holiday cottage from an owner who advertises the availability of the property in a national newspaper, without specifying the names of the members of his family who are to accompany him, there would appear to be little basis on which a joint intention to benefit those others could be inferred.

It is also important to emphasise that, under s 1(1)(b), it must be the contractual term that purports to confer the right of enforceability. Thus, in cases such as *White v Jones*,[81] in which a client asked his solicitor to assist in the preparation of a will intended to benefit the claimant, it was the will which purported to confer the benefit on the third party, rather than the contract between the client and his solicitor. Moreover, in other tort cases such as *Junior Books Ltd v Veitchi Co Ltd*[82] it is likely that the 1999 Act will have no effect, since even if the subcontract named T (the owner) as an intended beneficiary of the subcontractor's expected performance, a probable interpretation of the contract between the main contractor and the subcontractor is that it was intended to regulate the relationship between the principal contracting parties rather than to confer a benefit on the owner of the building. Moreover, it is common to find that, in cases of construction contracts, there may be an express provision that one of the parties has an alternative contractual right of enforceability other than against the party he is seeking to render liable. In these circumstances, there ought to be a strong presumption against enforceability of a contract other than the one under which he has been given specific rights.[83]

The proviso in s 1(2) is likely to give rise to substantial litigation, since it will be crucial to ascertain what were the true intentions of the parties to the contract in determining whether the third party has a direct right of enforceability. It might be argued that if there is no specific provision in the contract conferring such a right on a third party, then the parties did not

79 [1968] AC 58.
80 [1975] 3 All ER 92.
81 [1995] 2 AC 207.
82 [1983] 1 AC 520.
83 See *Alfred McAlpine Construction Ltd v Panatown Ltd* (2000) *The Times*, 26 August, HL.

intend the third party to have such a right. For these purposes, it seems that there is a rebuttable presumption of enforceability and it will be up to the party contesting liability to prove that there was no intention to confer a benefit on the third party.[84] In seeking to rebut this presumption, it is important to emphasise that what s 1(2) provides is that it must be demonstrated that the parties to the contract did not intend to confer a benefit on T. Thus, it will be insufficient for a contracting party to show that he, personally, did not intend to confer a benefit on T. Instead, it must be established that A *and* B did not intend to confer that benefit.

For the purposes of s 1(2), it is important to emphasise that the relevant term must purport to confer a benefit on the third party. Thus, it will not be sufficient for the third party to demonstrate simply that the relevant term does, in fact, confer a benefit on him. For example, if A employs B to 'cut the hedge adjoining T's land', T would undoubtedly benefit from B's performance, but there is nothing in the relevant contractual term which purports to confer a benefit on T.[85] A more difficult case, however, might arise where A contracted with B to perform some service specifically referable to T's property, since, in such a case, there might be a strong presumption that the contract was intended to benefit T, even though there was no specific right of enforceability conferred on T. Thus, in cases like *Linden Gardens Trust v Lenesta Sludge Developments Ltd*,[86] there is clear evidence that the work to be done would ultimately benefit the owner of the land, when property was eventually transferred. However, it would be difficult to argue that the relevant term of the contract was intended to confer a benefit on the ultimate owner, which he was entitled to enforce. One way in which A and B can make their position clear would be by way of some specific provision in their contract to the effect that either T has or does not have a right to enforce the term of the contract which purports to benefit him. Difficulties will arise, however, in cases in which A and B do not make it clear what their intentions are.

Under s 1(3) of the Contracts (Rights of Third Parties) Act 1999, it is provided that the third party must be expressly identified by name, as a member of a class or as answering to a particular description. However, there is no need for that person to be in existence at the time the contract between A and B is entered into. Thus, T will have no right of enforceability simply on the basis that he, or the class to which he belongs, is intended to be benefited by implication. On the other hand, a contract between A and B which makes specific reference to the children of a specified third party will be enforceable

---

84 See Law Commission, Law Com No 242, 1996, para 7.46, dealing with the facts of *Beswick v Beswick*. Their conclusion was that the nephew would not have been able to rebut the presumption.

85 See Treitel, 1999, p 601.

86 [1994] 1 AC 85.

by those children, even if they were not born at the time the contract between A and B was entered into. A similar approach will also be taken in relation to future spouses or limited companies that have not yet been formed.

In cases where there is no express identification of the third party, the 1999 Act will be of no assistance. Thus, in *Scruttons Ltd v Midland Silicones Ltd*,[87] the fact that the third party was not specifically referred to in the bill of lading would prove to be crucial under the 1999 Act. In contrast, in those cases such as *New Zealand Shipping Co v Satterthwaite*,[88] a different result would be likely to obtain because of the specific identification of employees, agents and subcontractors as intended beneficiaries of the exemption clause.

Under the provisions of s 1(5), it is specified that T will have a direct right of enforcement. This avoids the problem of T having to rely on the right of enforcement being transferred to him via either A or B. However, in doing this, s 1(5) does employ the fiction of transfer of rights, since it is specified that T will have such rights as would have been available to him had he been a party to the contract between A and B. It follows from this that T will be able to pursue all remedies which would have been available to B, such as seeking an order for injunction, specific performance or expectation damages, despite the fact that he was not a party to the bargain. But since general principles of contract law will apply, presumably, T's remedies will also be limited by rules on remoteness of loss, mitigation of damage and the general restrictions on the availability of specific relief. The difficulty with this is that since, by definition, T is not a party to the bargain, he may not have had the opportunity to state his concerns over the appropriate allocation of particular losses, in which case under rules on remoteness of loss, he may find himself in a position whereby the requirements of *Hadley v Baxendale*[89] are not satisfied.

The Contracts (Rights of Third Parties) Act 1999 also deals specifically with the issue of rescission or variation of the main contract. It should be observed that one of the common law objections to third party rights has been that to create such a right would interfere with the right of the principal contracting parties to vary the terms of their contract. Section 2(1) of the 1999 Act provides, generally, that if T has acquired the right to enforce a term of a contract made between A and B under s 1, then it follows that A and B cannot vary the terms of their contract so as to extinguish or alter T's entitlement without T's consent, provided the requirements of s 2 are satisfied. Clearly, to extinguish T's rights would be wrong, but it should be noted that an 'alteration' may be either beneficial or prejudicial to T, but the Act appears to make no distinction between the two forms of alteration. Clearly, in the case of beneficial alterations, it is likely that T will immediately consent. For example,

---

87   [1962] AC 446.

88   [1975] AC 154.

89   (1854) 9 Exch 341.

if an alteration were to increase payments otherwise payable to T, it is unlikely that he would object.

Where T has communicated his assent, by words or conduct,[90] to the term in the contract between A and B which confers a benefit upon him, it will not be possible for the terms of the original contract to be varied. But it is important that T's assent is communicated to the promisor rather than the promisee.[91] For these purposes, the 'postal rule' applicable to communication of acceptance of an offer does not apply with the result that the assent has to be received by the promisor.[92] Difficulties may arise, in this context, where T has 'sent' notification of his assent in the form of a letter by post or where he has sent a message by facsimile or email and the message has arrived, but has not been read by the addressee. Logic would seem to suggest that in such circumstances, the courts are likely to apply a fault principle similar to that used in relation to rules on offer and acceptance. Thus, if the message is sent at a time when it would be expected that no one would be present to receive it, the communication would not become effective until the promisor's business has been open and operative for a reasonable time.[93]

The right of the promisor (A) to rescind or vary his contract with the promisee (B) is also lost where A is aware that T has relied upon the term of the contract or where A could reasonably have been aware of such reliance which has actually occurred.[94] For these purposes, given the provisions in s 1(5) regarding remedies, it would appear to be the case that T will have a right to ask for promised performance and to recover damages in respect of any loss suffered in reliance upon that promise, subject to the avoidance of possible double recovery.

There may be circumstances in which the parties to the main contract rescind or vary that contract without the consent of T. The way in which the provisions of the 1999 Act are worded, T may choose to ignore the purported rescission or variation and seek to treat it as being ineffective.[95] However, there may be circumstances in which this is not an option, since the effect of the rescission may be that further performance of the contract for the benefit of T becomes impossible. In this instance, it would seem to be appropriate to allow T to maintain an action for damages in respect of quantifiable loss he has suffered.

Since the basis of the provisions of the 1999 Act is the intention of the parties to the main contract, there are provisions in s 2(3)(a) to the effect that

---

90 Contracts (Rights of Third Parties) Act 1999, s 2(2)(a)
91 *Ibid*, s 2(1)(a).
92 *Ibid*, s 2(2)(b).
93 See, eg, *The Brimnes* [1975] QB 929.
94 Contracts (Rights of Third Parties) Act 1999, s 2(1)(b) and (c) respectively.
95 *Ibid*, s 2(1).

the main contract may still be cancelled or varied without the consent of T, if the contract expressly so provides. In these circumstances, if the contract makes such express provision, it will make no difference whether T consents to the variation or cancellation and it will be irrelevant that T has in fact relied on the promise to confer a benefit upon him. Moreover, by virtue of s 2(3)(b), an express term of the main contract may also require the consent of T in any circumstance other than those specified in s 2(1). For example, it would be open to the contracting parties to specify the form in which the consent is to be given, in which case, T's consent would be ineffective unless given in the form specified by A and B.

In certain circumstances, the court has a discretion to dispense with the requirement of consent. Under s 2(4), the court may, on an application by A and B, order that T's consent is not necessary. The first of these is where T cannot be found and the second where T is mentally incapable of giving consent. Likewise, under s 2(5), the requirement of T's consent may be waived where it cannot reasonably be ascertained whether T has, in fact, relied on the terms in the contract between A and B. In these circumstances, the court has a power to award compensation to T.

The 1999 Act provides for a number of defences to an action brought by a third party. Under s 3(2), where T seeks to enforce a term expressed to be for his benefit against the promisor (A), A may rely, by way of defence or set off, on 'any matter that arises from or in connection with the contract and is relevant to the term'. For these purposes, the relevant defence must be one which would have been available to A in proceedings brought by the promisee (B).[96] Thus, A would be able to rely on any exemption clause in the main contract or would be able to pursue relief in respect of an actionable mistake or misrepresentation. The general rule established by s 3(2) can be displaced by an express provision in the contract between A and B. Thus, it would be open to the parties to the main contract to narrow or widen the defences or set offs available to A or to exclude the availability of such defences altogether.[97] The Act also envisages the possibility that there may be defences which can be pleaded against T which would not have been available in an action between A and B. For example, there may be circumstances in which T owes obligations to A under another contract. In these circumstances, it is provided that A may rely on these defences as if T had been a party to the contract.[98]

Section 6 of the 1999 Act provides for a number of exceptional cases in which s 1 of the Act will not apply. These include contracts on negotiable instruments, contracts for the carriage of goods by sea and the contract which

---

96 Contracts (Rights of Third Parties) Act 1999, s 3(2)(b).
97 *Ibid,* s 3(3) and 3(5).
98 *Ibid,* s 3(4).

binds a company and its members under the terms of the memorandum and articles of association. In each case, there is separate provision for these varieties of contract under other legislation.

Apart from the provisions of the 1999 Act, the third party's rights arising under some other rule of law will remain unaffected.[99] Thus, if an existing common law or equitable exception to the doctrine of privity of contract applies in favour of T, he may rely on that instead of invoking the provisions of the 1999 Act. This will be particularly important in cases in which T is unable to prove that he has relied on the term in the contract between A and B or in any other case in which the restrictive provisions of s 1 and s 2 might work against T. Thus, if T can establish the existence of a trust of the promise made in his favour or if he has an action in the tort of negligence or if some other statutory exception applies in his favour, T will still be able to avail himself of that alternative route. Although s 7(1) only refers to T's right under s 1, it must follow that the provisions of ss 2 and 3 are also inapplicable, since both of these provisions expressly state that they apply where T has relied on s 1.

It has been seen above that at common law there is nothing to prevent the promisee from enforcing a term expressed to be for the benefit of the third party, if he wishes to do so. This position is preserved under s 4 of the 1999 Act.

---

99 Contracts (Rights of Third Parties) Act 1999, s 7(1).

BIBLIOGRAPHY

Adams, J, 'The battle of the forms' (1979) 95 LQR 481.

Adams, J, 'The battle of the forms' [1983] JBL 297.

Adams, J and Brownsword, R, 'Double indemnity: contractual indemnity clauses revisited' (1988a) [1988] JBL 146.

Adams, J and Brownsword, R, 'The Unfair Contract Terms Act: a decade of discretion' (1988b) (1988) 104 LQR 94.

Adams, J and Brownsword, R, 'Privity and the concept of a network contract' (1990) 10 Legal Studies 12.

Adams, J and Brownsword, R, *Key Issues in Contract*, 1995, London: Butterworths.

Adams, J and Brownsword, R, *Understanding Contract Law*, 3rd edn, 2000, London: Fontana/HarperCollins.

American Law Institute, *Restatement, Contracts* (2d), 1981, St Paul, Minn: American Law Institute.

Atiyah, PS, 'Contracts, promises and the law of obligations' (1978) 94 LQR 193.

Atiyah, PS, *The Rise and Fall of Freedom of Contract*, 1979, Oxford: OUP.

Atiyah, PS, *Promises, Morals and the Law*, 1981, Oxford: OUP.

Atiyah, PS, *Consideration in Contracts*, 1986, Oxford: OUP.

Atiyah, PS, *Essays on Contract*, 1986 (reprinted 1990), Oxford: OUP.

Atiyah, PS, '*The Hannah Blumenthal* and classic contract law' (1986) 102 LQR 363.

Barendt, E, '*Hollier v Rambler Motors (AMC) Ltd*' (1972) 35 MLR 644.

Beale, H, *Remedies for Breach of Contract*, 1980, London: Sweet & Maxwell.

Beale, H, Bishop, W and Furmston, M, *Contract: Cases and Materials*, 4th edn, 1998, London: Butterworths.

Beale, H and Dugdale, A, 'Contracts between businessmen: planning and the use of contractual remedies' (1975) 2 British Journal of Law and Society 45.

Beatson, J, 'Abandoning the contract of abandonment' (1986) 102 LQR 19.

Beatson, J and Friedman, D (eds), *Good Faith and Fault in Contract Law*, 1995, Oxford: Clarendon.

Brandt and Ulmer, 'The Community Directive on Unfair Terms in Consumer Contracts' (1991) 28 CML Rev 647.

Brownsword, R and Howells, G, 'The implementation of the EC Directive on Unfair Terms in Consumer Contracts – some unresolved questions' [1995] JBL 243.

Brownsword, R, Howells, G and Wilhelmsson, T (eds), *Welfarism in Contract*, 1994, Aldershot: Dartmouth.

Burrows, A, (ed), *Essays on the Law of Restitution*, 1991, Oxford: Clarendon.

Burrows, A, *The Law of Restitution*, 1993, London: Butterworths.

Burrows, A, *Understanding the Law of Obligations*, 1998, Oxford: Hart.

Burrows, A, 'Free acceptance and the law of restitution' (1988) 104 LQR 576.

Carr, C, 'Lloyd's Bank Ltd v Bundy' (1975) 38 MLR 463.

Cheshire, G, Fifoot, C and Furmston, M, *Law of Contract*, 13th edn, 1996, London: Butterworths/Tolley.

Chitty (Guest, AG (ed)), *Contracts: General Principles*, 27th edn, 1994, London: Sweet & Maxwell.

Coase, R, 'The problem of social cost' (1960) 3 Journal of Law and Economics 1.

Collins, H, *Law of Contract*, 3rd edn, 1997, London: Butterworths.

Collins, H, 'Good faith in European contract law' (1994) OJLS 229.

Cooke, PJ and Oughton, DW, *The Common Law of Obligations*, 3rd edn, 2000, London: Butterworths.

Coote, B, *Exception Clauses*, 1964, London: Sweet & Maxwell.

Coote, B, 'The Unfair Contract Terms Act 1977' (1978) 41 MLR 312.

De Lacey, J, 'Selling in the course of a business under the Sale of Goods Act 1979' (1999) 62 MLR 776.

Dean, M, 'Unfair contract terms – the European approach' (1993) 56 MLR 581.

Duffy, P, 'Unfair terms and the draft EC Directive' (1993) JBL 67.

Evans, A, 'The Anglo-American mailing rule' (1966) 15 ICLQ 553.

Fehlberg, B, 'The husband, the bank, the wife and her signature – the sequel' (1996) 59 MLR 675.

Fried, C, *Contract as Promise*, 1981, Cambridge, Mass: Harvard UP.

Fuller, L, 'Consideration and form' (1941) 41 Columbia LR 799.

Fuller, L and Perdue, W, 'The reliance interest in contract damages' (1936–37) 46 Yale LJ 52.

Furmston, M, 'Return to *Dunlop v Selfridge*?' (1960) 23 MLR 373.

Gardner, S, 'Trashing with Trollope: a deconstruction of postal rules in contract' (1992) 2 OJLS 170.

Goff, R, and Jones, G, *The Law of Restitution*, 4th edn, 1993, London: Sweet & Maxwell.

Gower, L, 'Exemption clauses – contractual and tortious liability' (1954) 17 MLR 155.

Hamson, C, 'The reform of consideration' (1938) 54 LQR 233.

Harris, D, Ogus, A and Phillips, J, 'Contact remedies and the consumer surplus' (1979) 95 LQR 581.

Harrison, *Good Faith in Sales*, 1997, London: Sweet & Maxwell.

Howarth, W, 'The meaning of objectivity in contract' (1984) 100 LQR 265.

Jacobs, J, 'The battle of the forms: standard term contracts in comparative perspective' (1985) 34 ICLQ 297.

Kessler, 'Contracts of adhesion: some thoughts about freedom of contract' (1943) Columbia LR 629.

Law Commission, *First Report on Exemption Clauses in Contracts*, Law Com No 24, 1969, London: HMSO.

Law Commission, *Firm Offers*, 1975, Working Paper No 60, London: HMSO.

Law Commission, *Second Report on Exemption Clauses in Contracts*, Law Com No 69, 1975, London: HMSO.

Law Commission, *Law of Contract: The Parol Evidence Rule*, Law Com No 154, Cmnd 9700, 1986, London: HMSO.

Law Commission, *Privity of Contract: Contracts For The Benefit of Third Parties*, Law Com No 242, Cm 3329, 1996, London: HMSO.

Macneil, IR, 'Restatement (second) of contracts and presentation' (1974) 60 Virginia LR 589.

Macneil, IR, 'Contracts adjustment of long term economic relations under classical, neo-classical and relational contract law' (1978a) 72 Northwestern University LR 854.

Macneil, IR, *Contract: Exchange Transactions and Relations*, 2nd edn, 1978b, Playa Vista, California: Foundation.

McKendrick, E, 'The battle of the forms and the law of restitution' (1988) 8 OJLS 197.

Phang, A, 'Implied terms revisited' (1990) JBL 394.

Phang, A, 'Implied terms in English law – some recent developments' (1993) JBL 242.

Pollock, G, *Principles of Contract*, 13th edn, 1950, London: Sweet & Maxwell.

Poole, J, 'Damages for breach of contract – compensation and "personal preferences"' (1996) 59 MLR 272.

Posner, RA, *Economic Analysis of Law*, 4th edn, 1992, Boston: Little, Brown.

Price, D, 'When is a consumer not a consumer?' (1989) 52 MLR 245.

Sealy, L, 'The Unfair Contract Terms Act 1977' [1978] CLJ 15.

Sealy, L, 'Thompson v Lohan (Plant Hire) Ltd' [1988] CLJ 6.

Simpson, A, *A History of the Common Law of Contract*, 1975, Oxford: OUP.

Simpson, A, 'Innovation in 19th century contract law' (1975) 91 LQR 247.

Spencer, JR, 'Signature, consent and the rule in *L'Estrange v Graucob*' [1973] CLJ 104.

Teubner, G, 'Legal irritants: good faith in British law' (1998) 61 MLR 11.

Thompson, MP, 'Representation to expectation: estoppel as a cause of action' [1983] CLJ 257.

Treitel, GH, *Doctrine and Discretion in the Law of Contract*, 1981, Oxford: Clarendon.

Treitel, GH, 'Mistake in contract' (1989) 104 LQR 501.

Treitel, GH, *Frustration and* Force Majeure, 1994, London, Sweet & Maxwell.

Treitel, GH, *The Law of Contract*, 10th edn, 1999, London: Sweet & Maxwell.

Unger, J, 'Self-service stores and the law of contract' (1953) 16 MLR 369.

Vorster, 'A comment on the meaning of objectivity in contract' (1987) 103 LQR 274.

Waddams, S, '*Lloyds Bank Ltd v Bundy*' (1976) 39 MLR 369.

Weatherill, S, *EC Consumer Law and Policy*, 1997, London: Longman.

Winfield, P, 'Some aspects of offer and acceptance' (1939) 55 LQR 499.

INDEX